Lecture Notes in Computer Science　　10860

Commenced Publication in 1973
Founding and Former Series Editors:
Gerhard Goos, Juris Hartmanis, and Jan van Leeuwen

More information about this series at http://www.springer.com/series/7407

Yong Shi · Haohuan Fu
Yingjie Tian · Valeria V. Krzhizhanovskaya
Michael Harold Lees · Jack Dongarra
Peter M. A. Sloot (Eds.)

Computational Science – ICCS 2018

18th International Conference
Wuxi, China, June 11–13, 2018
Proceedings, Part I

 Springer

Editors
Yong Shi
Chinese Academy of Sciences
Beijing
China

Michael Harold Lees
University of Amsterdam
Amsterdam
The Netherlands

Haohuan Fu
National Supercomputing Center in Wuxi
Wuxi
China

Jack Dongarra
University of Tennessee
Knoxville, TN
USA

Yingjie Tian
Chinese Academy of Sciences
Beijing
China

Peter M. A. Sloot ⓘ
University of Amsterdam
Amsterdam
The Netherlands

Valeria V. Krzhizhanovskaya ⓘ
University of Amsterdam
Amsterdam
The Netherlands

ISSN 0302-9743   ISSN 1611-3349   (electronic)
Lecture Notes in Computer Science
ISBN 978-3-319-93697-0   ISBN 978-3-319-93698-7   (eBook)
https://doi.org/10.1007/978-3-319-93698-7

Library of Congress Control Number: 2018947305

LNCS Sublibrary: SL1 – Theoretical Computer Science and General Issues

Printed on acid-free paper

This Springer imprint is published by the registered company Springer International Publishing AG
part of Springer Nature
The registered company address is: Gewerbestrasse 11, 6330 Cham, Switzerland

Preface

Welcome to the proceedings of the 18th Annual International Conference on Computational Science (ICCS: https://www.iccs-meeting.org/iccs2018/), held during June 11–13, 2018, in Wuxi, China. Located in the Jiangsu province, Wuxi is bordered by Changzhou to the west and Suzhou to the east. The city meets the Yangtze River in the north and is bathed by Lake Tai to the south. Wuxi is home to many parks, gardens, temples, and the fastest supercomputer in the world, the Sunway TaihuLight. ICCS 2018 was jointly organized by the University of Chinese Academy of Sciences, the National Supercomputing Center in Wuxi, the University of Amsterdam, NTU Singapore, and the University of Tennessee.

The International Conference on Computational Science is an annual conference that brings together researchers and scientists from mathematics and computer science as basic computing disciplines, researchers from various application areas who are pioneering computational methods in sciences such as physics, chemistry, life sciences, and engineering, as well as in arts and humanitarian fields, to discuss problems and solutions in the area, to identify new issues, and to shape future directions for research.

Since its inception in 2001, ICCS has attracted increasingly higher quality and numbers of attendees and papers, and this year was no an exception, with over 350 expected participants. The proceedings series have become a major intellectual resource for computational science researchers, defining and advancing the state of the art in this field.

ICCS 2018 in Wuxi, China, was the 18th in this series of highly successful conferences. For the previous 17 meetings, see: http://www.iccs-meeting.org/iccs2018/previous-iccs/.

The theme for ICCS 2018 was "Science at the Intersection of Data, Modelling and Computation," to highlight the role of computation as a fundamental method of scientific inquiry and technological discovery tackling problems across scientific domains and creating synergies between disciplines. This conference was a unique event focusing on recent developments in: scalable scientific algorithms; advanced software tools; computational grids; advanced numerical methods; and novel application areas. These innovative novel models, algorithms, and tools drive new science through efficient application in areas such as physical systems, computational and systems biology, environmental systems, finance, and others.

ICCS is well known for its excellent line up of keynote speakers. The keynotes for 2018 were:

- Charlie Catlett, Argonne National Laboratory|University of Chicago, USA
- Xiaofei Chen, Southern University of Science and Technology, China
- Liesbet Geris, University of Liège|KU Leuven, Belgium
- Sarika Jalan, Indian Institute of Technology Indore, India
- Petros Koumoutsakos, ETH Zürich, Switzerland
- Xuejun Yang, National University of Defense Technology, China

This year we had 405 submissions (180 submissions to the main track and 225 to the workshops). In the main track, 51 full papers were accepted (28%). In the workshops, 97 full papers (43%). A high acceptance rate in the workshops is explained by the nature of these thematic sessions, where many experts in a particular field are personally invited by workshop organizers to participate in their sessions.

ICCS relies strongly on the vital contributions of our workshop organizers to attract high-quality papers in many subject areas. We would like to thank all committee members for the main track and workshops for their contribution toward ensuring a high standard for the accepted papers. We would also like to thank Springer, Elsevier, Intellegibilis, Beijing Vastitude Technology Co., Ltd. and Inspur for their support. Finally, we very much appreciate all the local Organizing Committee members for their hard work to prepare this conference.

We are proud to note that ICCS is an ERA 2010 A-ranked conference series.

June 2018

Yong Shi
Haohuan Fu
Yingjie Tian
Valeria V. Krzhizhanovskaya
Michael Lees
Jack Dongarra
Peter M. A. Sloot
The ICCS 2018 Organizers

Organization

Local Organizing Committee

Co-chairs

Yingjie Tian	University of Chinese Academy of Sciences, China
Lin Gan	National Supercomputing Center in Wuxi, China

Members

Jiming Wu	National Supercomputing Center in Wuxi, China
Lingying Wu	National Supercomputing Center in Wuxi, China
Jinzhe Yang	National Supercomputing Center in Wuxi, China
Bingwei Chen	National Supercomputing Center in Wuxi, China
Yuanchun Zheng	University of Chinese Academy of Sciences, China
Minglong Lei	University of Chinese Academy of Sciences, China
Jia Wu	Macquarie University, Australia
Zhengsong Chen	University of Chinese Academy of Sciences, China
Limeng Cui	University of Chinese Academy of Sciences, China
Jiabin Liu	University of Chinese Academy of Sciences, China
Biao Li	University of Chinese Academy of Sciences, China
Yunlong Mi	University of Chinese Academy of Sciences, China
Wei Dai	University of Chinese Academy of Sciences, China

Workshops and Organizers

Advances in High-Performance Computational Earth Sciences: Applications and Frameworks – IHPCES 2018
Xing Cai, Kohei Fujita, Takashi Shimokawabe

Agent-Based Simulations, Adaptive Algorithms, and Solvers – ABS-AAS 2018
Robert Schaefer, Maciej Paszynski, Victor Calo, David Pardo

Applications of Matrix Methods in Artificial Intelligence and Machine Learning – AMAIML 2018
Kourosh Modarresi

Architecture, Languages, Compilation, and Hardware Support for Emerging Manycore Systems – ALCHEMY 2018
Loïc Cudennec, Stéphane Louise

Biomedical and Bioinformatics Challenges for Computer Science – BBC 2018
Giuseppe Agapito, Mario Cannataro, Mauro Castelli, Riccardo Dondi, Rodrigo Weber dos Santos, Italo Zoppis

Computational Finance and Business Intelligence – CFBI 2018
Shouyang Wang, Yong Shi, Yingjie Tian

Computational Optimization, Modelling, and Simulation – COMS 2018
Xin-She Yang, Slawomir Koziel, Leifur Leifsson, T. O. Ting

Data-Driven Computational Sciences – DDCS 2018
Craig Douglas, Abani Patra, Ana Cortés, Robert Lodder

Data, Modeling, and Computation in IoT and Smart Systems – DMC-IoT 2018
Julien Bourgeois, Vaidy Sunderam, Hicham Lakhlef

Mathematical Methods and Algorithms for Extreme Scale – MATH-EX 2018
Vassil Alexandrov

Multiscale Modelling and Simulation – MMS 2018
Derek Groen, Lin Gan, Valeria Krzhizhanovskaya, Alfons Hoekstra

Simulations of Flow and Transport: Modeling, Algorithms, and Computation – SOFTMAC 2018
Shuyu Sun, Jianguo (James) Liu, Jingfa Li

Solving Problems with Uncertainties – SPU 2018
Vassil Alexandrov

Teaching Computational Science – WTCS 2018
Angela B. Shiflet, Alfredo Tirado-Ramos, Nia Alexandrov

Tools for Program Development and Analysis in Computational Science – TOOLS 2018
Karl Fürlinger, Arndt Bode, Andreas Knüpfer, Dieter Kranzlmüller, Jens Volkert, Roland Wismüller

Urgent Computing – UC 2018
Marian Bubak, Alexander Boukhanovsky

Program Committee

Ahmad Abdelfattah
David Abramson
Giuseppe Agapito
Ram Akella
Elisabete Alberdi
Marco Aldinucci
Nia Alexandrov
Vassil Alexandrov
Saad Alowayyed
Ilkay Altintas
Stanislaw
  Ambroszkiewicz

Ioannis Anagnostou
Michael Antolovich
Hartwig Anzt
Hideo Aochi
Tomasz Arodz
Tomàs Artés Vivancos
Victor Azizi Tarksalooyeh
Ebrahim Bagheri
Bartosz Balis
Krzysztof Banas
Jörn Behrens
Adrian Bekasiewicz

Adam Belloum
Abdelhak Bentaleb
Stefano Beretta
Daniel Berrar
Sanjukta Bhowmick
Anna Bilyatdinova
Guillaume Blin
Nasri Bo
Marcel Boersma
Bartosz Bosak
Kris Bubendorfer
Jérémy Buisson

Aleksander Byrski
Wentong Cai
Xing Cai
Mario Cannataro
Yongcan Cao
Pedro Cardoso
Mauro Castelli
Eduardo Cesar
Imen Chakroun
Huangxin Chen
Mingyang Chen
Zhensong Chen
Siew Ann Cheong
Lock-Yue Chew
Ana Cortes
Enrique
    Costa-Montenegro
Carlos Cotta
Jean-Francois Couchot
Helene Coullon
Attila Csikász-Nagy
Loïc Cudennec
Javier Cuenca
Yifeng Cui
Ben Czaja
Pawel Czarnul
Wei Dai
Lisandro Dalcin
Bhaskar Dasgupta
Susumu Date
Quanling Deng
Xiaolong Deng
Minh Ngoc Dinh
Riccardo Dondi
Tingxing Dong
Ruggero Donida Labati
Craig C. Douglas
Rafal Drezewski
Jian Du
Vitor Duarte
Witold Dzwinel
Nahid Emad
Christian Engelmann
Daniel Etiemble

Christos
    Filelis-Papadopoulos
Karl Frinkle
Haohuan Fu
Karl Fuerlinger
Kohei Fujita
Wlodzimierz Funika
Takashi Furumura
David Gal
Lin Gan
Robin Gandhi
Frédéric Gava
Alex Gerbessiotis
Carlos Gershenson
Domingo Gimenez
Frank Giraldo
Ivo Gonçalves
Yuriy Gorbachev
Pawel Gorecki
George Gravvanis
Derek Groen
Lutz Gross
Kun Guo
Xiaohu Guo
Piotr Gurgul
Panagiotis Hadjidoukas
Azzam Haidar
Dongxu Han
Raheel Hassan
Jurjen Rienk Helmus
Bogumila Hnatkowska
Alfons Hoekstra
Paul Hofmann
Sergey Ivanov
Hideya Iwasaki
Takeshi Iwashita
Jiří Jaroš
Marco Javarone
Chao Jin
Hai Jin
Zhong Jin
Jingheng
David Johnson
Anshul Joshi

Jaap Kaandorp
Viacheslav Kalashnikov
George Kampis
Drona Kandhai
Aneta Karaivanova
Vlad Karbovskii
Andrey Karsakov
Takahiro Katagiri
Wayne Kelly
Deepak Khazanchi
Alexandra Klimova
Ivan Kondov
Vladimir Korkhov
Jari Kortelainen
Ilias Kotsireas
Jisheng Kou
Sergey Kovalchuk
Slawomir Koziel
Valeria Krzhizhanovskaya
Massimo La Rosa
Hicham Lakhlef
Roberto Lam
Anna-Lena Lamprecht
Rubin Landau
Johannes Langguth
Vianney Lapotre
Jysoo Lee
Michael Lees
Minglong Lei
Leifur Leifsson
Roy Lettieri
Andrew Lewis
Biao Li
Dewei Li
Jingfa Li
Kai Li
Peijia Li
Wei Li
I-Jong Lin
Hong Liu
Hui Liu
James Liu
Jiabin Liu
Piyang Liu

Weifeng Liu
Weiguo Liu
Marcelo Lobosco
Robert Lodder
Wen Long
Stephane Louise
Frederic Loulergue
Paul Lu
Sheraton M. V.
Scott MacLachlan
Maciej Malawski
Michalska Malgorzatka
Vania
   Marangozova-Martin
Tomas Margalef
Tiziana Margaria
Svetozar Margenov
Osni Marques
Pawel Matuszyk
Valerie Maxville
Rahul Mazumder
Valentin Melnikov
Ivan Merelli
Doudou Messoud
Yunlong Mi
Jianyu Miao
John Michopoulos
Sergey Mityagin
K. Modarresi
Kourosh Modarresi
Jânio Monteiro
Paulo Moura Oliveira
Ignacio Muga
Hiromichi Nagao
Kengo Nakajima
Denis Nasonov
Philippe Navaux
Hoang Nguyen
Mai Nguyen
Anna Nikishova
Lingfeng Niu
Mawloud Omar
Kenji Ono
Raymond Padmos

Marcin Paprzycki
David Pardo
Anna Paszynska
Maciej Paszynski
Abani Patra
Dana Petcu
Eric Petit
Serge Petiton
Gauthier Picard
Daniela Piccioni
Yuri Pirola
Antoniu Pop
Ela Pustulka-Hunt
Vladimir Puzyrev
Alexander Pyayt
Pei Quan
Rick Quax
Waldemar Rachowicz
Lukasz Rauch
Alistair Rendell
Sophie Robert
J. M. F Rodrigues
Daniel Rodriguez
Albert Romkes
James A. Ross
Debraj Roy
Philip Rutten
Katarzyna Rycerz
Alberto Sanchez
Rodrigo Santos
Hitoshi Sato
Robert Schaefer
Olaf Schenk
Ulf D. Schiller
Bertil Schmidt
Hichem Sedjelmaci
Martha Johanna
   Sepulveda
Yong Shi
Angela Shiflet
Takashi Shimokawabe
Tan Singyee
Robert Sinkovits
Vishnu Sivadasan

Peter Sloot
Renata Slota
Grażyna Ślusarczyk
Sucha Smanchat
Maciej Smołka
Bartlomiej Sniezynski
Sumit Sourabh
Achim Streit
Barbara Strug
Bongwon Suh
Shuyu Sun
Martin Swain
Ryszard Tadeusiewicz
Daisuke Takahashi
Jingjing Tang
Osamu Tatebe
Andrei Tchernykh
Cedric Tedeschi
Joao Teixeira
Yonatan Afework
   Tesfahunegn
Andrew Thelen
Xin Tian
Yingjie Tian
T. O. Ting
Alfredo Tirado-Ramos
Stanimire Tomov
Ka Wai Tsang
Britt van Rooij
Raja Velu
Antonio M. Vidal
David Walker
Jianwu Wang
Peng Wang
Yi Wang
Josef Weinbub
Mei Wen
Mark Wijzenbroek
Maciej Woźniak
Guoqiang Wu
Jia Wu
Qing Wu
Huilin Xing
Wei Xue

Contents – Part I

Contents – Part II

**Track of Architecture, Languages, Compilation and Hardware
Support for Emerging ManYcore Systems**

**Track of Biomedical and Bioinformatics Challenges
for Computer Science**

Track of Computational Finance and Business Intelligence

Track of Computational Optimization, Modelling and Simulation

Track of Data, Modeling, and Computation in IoT and Smart Systems

Track of Data-Driven Computational Sciences

Track of Mathematical-Methods-and-Algorithms for Extreme Scale

Track of Multiscale Modelling and Simulation

Contents – Part III

Track of Solving Problems with Uncertainties

Track of Teaching Computational Science

Poster Papers

ICCS Main Track

Optimizing the Efficiency, Vulnerability and Robustness of Road-Based Para-Transit Networks Using Genetic Algorithm

Briane Paul V. Samson[1,2]([⊠]) [iD], Gio Anton T. Velez[1], Joseph Ryan Nobleza[1], David Sanchez[1], and Jan Tristan Milan[1]

[1] De La Salle University, Manila, Philippines
{gio_velez,joseph_ryan_nobleza,david_sanchez,jan_milan}@dlsu.edu.ph
[2] Future University Hakodate, Hakodate, Hokkaido, Japan
b-samson@sumilab.org

Abstract. In the developing world, majority of people usually take para-transit services for their everyday commutes. However, their informal and demand-driven operation, like making arbitrary stops to pick up and drop off passengers, has been inefficient and poses challenges to efforts in integrating such services to more organized train and bus networks. In this study, we devised a methodology to design and optimize a road-based para-transit network using a genetic algorithm to optimize efficiency, robustness, and invulnerability. We first generated stops following certain geospatial distributions and connected them to build networks of routes. From them, we selected an initial population to be optimized and applied the genetic algorithm. Overall, our modified genetic algorithm with 20 evolutions optimized the 20% worst performing networks by 84% on average. For one network, we were able to significantly increase its fitness score by 223%. The highest fitness score the algorithm was able to produce through optimization was 0.532 from a score of 0.303.

Keywords: Complex networks · Network optimization
Genetic algorithm

1 Introduction

As cities grow with the influx of urban migration, the capacity and efficiency of their transportation systems have consistently been challenged with the consequential boost in travel demands [3]. And before our transportation systems reach their limits, governments must focus more on improving transportation capabilities instead of focusing on adding more infrastructure (Braess's Paradox [5,6]).

© Springer International Publishing AG, part of Springer Nature 2018
Y. Shi et al. (Eds.): ICCS 2018, LNCS 10860, pp. 3–14, 2018.
https://doi.org/10.1007/978-3-319-93698-7_1

Dense urban areas like Metro Manila, Philippines have had little success addressing transportation capabilities. Due to the limited operations of high-capacity transport systems, passengers have mostly preferred road-based para-transit services like jeepneys[1], express shuttles, tricycles[2], and pedicabs[3] [2]. This is also the case in other developing world cities, with diverse vehicle categories (i.e. tuk-tuk, minivans, etc.), because they can pass through smaller roads, and are more demand-responsive and affordable [13]. However, such transportation services do not have formal stops and were arbitrarily planned to serve the entrepreneurial interests of its private operators. In particular, they have been observed to stop anywhere to pick up a hailing passenger and to drop them off. As a response, local governments have attempted to regulate, integrate and rationalize their services [3] by re-assessing and formalizing the route network, and consolidating operators.

Inasmuch as we want to improve the efficiency of public transportation networks, some topological and geospatial optimizations bear negative consequences to their operations [12]. One can reduce the spacing between designated stops, which can result to an increased number of stops available in an area. With more stops, public utility vehicles will stop more often, resulting to longer waiting times in subsequent stops. Thus, there has to be a balance between accessibility and efficiency by assessing how the geospatial layout and spacing between designated stops could affect the overall performance of a road-based transportation network. In addition, since road networks in the developing world are more prone to disruptions (i.e. flooding, poor road conditions, etc.) [7], we also have to consider the robustness and vulnerability of any mode of transportation that will use them.

This study aims to use network centrality measures and genetic algorithm to optimally design efficient, robust and invulnerable para-transit networks, that governments can use in planning the integration of para-transit services to higher-capacity transportation networks. As a case study, we applied this methodology to four (4) cities in Metro Manila and generated intra-city jeepney networks.

The next section discusses some significant related works in designing transportation networks. Section 3 discusses our methodology for network generation and optimization. In Sect. 4, we share our results and analysis on the performance of our methodology. Lastly, we provide our conclusion and plans for future work in Sect. 5.

2   Related Works

Planning transportation systems require stakeholders to look at different aspects like travel demand, land use and urban form, and transportation coordination and scheduling, among others. Focused on minimizing the number of transfers,

---

[1] A popular public utility vehicle with a capacity of 20–22 passengers.

[2] An auto rickshaw consisting of a motorbike and a sidecar.

[3] A cycle rickshaw consisting of a bicycle and a sidecar.

[8] developed an optimization model using an operations research approach. However, its mixed integer programming implementation can be limiting given the large search space and multiple conflicting constraints involved.

In a survey of works from 1998 to 2012 on designing transport networks by [9], they concluded that genetic algorithms are more suited to handle the complex and non-linear nature of this problem. And in almost all works surveyed, they optimized irregular grid network structures to have the least cost for passengers and operators. In addition, [14] considered the location of school dormitories to optimize the location of bus stops to be installed. The resulting bus network design reduced the number of bus stops, total route length, and travel distance between dormitories. On the other hand, [11] focused on maximizing the number of satisfied passengers while minimizing transfers and travel time. Taking a different direction, [12] designed transport networks based on a city's geospatial distribution and used genetic algorithm to generate bus routes with the least travel time for passengers. After which, they assessed how each type of geospatial distribution affected the robustness of the network. However, the networks were not recreated to address negative effects on their robustness.

In relation to para-transit operations, [1] minimized the operation costs of a jeepney route in Taft Avenue, Manila by considering the waiting time before operation, length of the time when ignoring stops, the number of passengers and amount of time to board the jeepney, waiting cost of commuters for the jeepneys to arrive, length of travel time, length of time to accelerate and decelerate, and length of time a jeepney dwells in a particular stop. In China, [10] optimized the networks of customized buses in terms of maximum passengers served, passenger travel time and arrival delays, and line revenues.

While many have considered operational factors in optimizing transportation networks, which represent regular occurrences, very few have regarded unprecedented scenarios and anticipated interruptions in planning their networks. Thus, we intend to simulate random failures and targeted attacks on the designed transport network and iterate using genetic algorithm to minimize their effects.

3   Methodology

This section discusses our methodology which starts with the collection and preprocessing of road network data, followed by the generation of an initial set of candidate stops. Then, the stops are connected to form routes. Finally, the generated networks are optimized for its efficiency, robustness and invulnerability.

3.1   Data

We collected the road networks and boundaries of four (4) Metro Manila cities, namely, Manila, Makati, Paranaque, and Quezon City using OSMnx [4]. To avoid redundancies, we used a network that only contains nodes for road intersections and joints.

3.2   Stop Generation

First, we generated stops by following the lattice, random and N-hub geospatial layouts [12]. In a lattice layout, stops are generated equidistant from each other, while in a random layout, the location coordinates were uniformly distributed within the city boundaries. Lastly, the stop locations in an N-hub layout is generated by first defining the location of the N hubs representing areas of high trip generation, such as central business districts. We used a covariance coefficient of 65 to provide an ideal shape of a circle revolving around the specified hub. The stops were generated by getting random samples from a multivariate normal distribution. After generating the stops, some were positioned in unusual and unrealistic locations, like in the middle of parks. Thus for poorly placed stops, we adjusted their locations to nearest road segments (Fig. 1).

Fig. 1. Two stops (red circles) were initially generated far from intersections of major roads. The yellow circles indicate where their new locations are. (Color figure online)

3.3   Route Network Generation

In connecting the stops, we used a maximum allowable walking distance (d_{max}) value as a threshold for choosing candidate stops to connect to. This is based on a person's tolerance of how far they can walk from a stop to their destination.

In creating a route R_0, a starting stop $S_{(0,0)}$ is chosen in random. Then, we used d_{max} as a discriminating factor for nearby stops, so they cannot be selected anymore until the creation of another route. The stops beyond d_{max} are now candidates and are assigned exponentially decreasing probabilities based on their Euclidean distance from the stop to connect to:

$$p(n_d) = \frac{e^{-d(n_s, n_d)}}{\lambda} \tag{1}$$

where n_s is the starting stop and n_d is the destination stop, d is the Euclidean distance function and λ is a normalization constant. From these candidates, we select $S_{(0,1)}$ and connect it to $S_{(0,0)}$. We repeated the same steps until there are no more stops to discriminate or to connect to. With this algorithm, we made sure that there are no cycles, but there will be instances wherein not all stops will be part of the network. In such cases, they will be removed. In this study, we created 25 routes to build the networks.

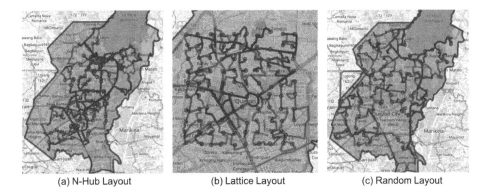

| (a) N-Hub Layout | (b) Lattice Layout | (c) Random Layout |

Fig. 2. Generated route networks for Quezon City with 100 stops following the (a) N-Hub, (b) Lattice, and (c) Random geospatial layouts.

Generated Route Networks. We generated 960 undirected route networks using a combination of layout and maximum allowable walking distance values to observe the consistency of our algorithms. For each of the four (4) cities in our scope, we used the lattice, random, and 1-hub and 2-hub layouts (Fig. 2). For each of these layouts, we generated route networks using 300 m, 550 m, and 800 m as d_{max} values. Each edge has a corresponding weight representing distances in meters.

3.4   Network Optimization

After initially generating route networks, we optimized them in terms of efficiency, robustness, and vulnerability using a genetic algorithm.

Network Metrics. In optimizing the generated route networks, we used the following network metrics in evaluating their fitness scores. First, we computed for the efficiency of a route network that gives us an idea of how straightforward a simulated trip is from a source to a destination. For each network, we randomly selected 1,000 source and destination stop pairs and computed their weighted radius of gyration by (a) creating an adjacency matrix, (b) computing for the shortest path using Dijkstra's algorithm, and (c) incorporating a penalty for possible transfers between routes. The weighted adjacency matrix for all selected pairs (i,j) in the network is represented by:

$$A_{i*j} \begin{cases} d(n_i, n_j), & \text{if a route directly connects from } n_i \text{ to } n_j \\ w * d(n_i, n_j), & \text{if there is more than 1 transfer from } n_i \text{ to } n_j \\ 0, & \text{if } i = j. \end{cases}$$

It has all the edges in the graph, including the walking edges between stops connecting different routes. We assigned a weight of 10 to these edges because walking is roughly 10 times slower than riding a jeepney. Lastly, we normalized the efficiency scores by getting the ratio of its score to the number of randomly selected source-destination pairs (Eq. 2).

$$E = \frac{\sum_{i=1}^{1000} \frac{d_p}{\sum_{p \in \text{Paths}} w_i d_p + 20T}}{1000} \tag{2}$$

Next, we assessed their robustness by randomly removing stops from the network until there's nothing to remove. This simulates the possibility of stops suddenly becoming inaccessible because of unexpected closures, floods, and congestion. Aside from network robustness, we also measured how vulnerable the network is to targeted attacks by removing stops in order of their degrees, starting from the highest degree until nothing is left. As we removed stops from the network for both robustness and vulnerability simulations, we computed for the average path length and network diameter. The average path length is the mean of the lengths of all shortest paths. This factor tells us the average number of stops needed to traverse the network from any stop. The network diameter is the longest shortest path of a network which gives us an idea of the maximum number of stops needed to traverse without repetition or cycles.

Using these simulations and metrics, we computed for the ratio of the average path length over the network diameter at every 5% interval, which indicates how close the network is to being destroyed. For this ratio, higher values indicate low robustness and high vulnerability.

After running these metrics for all 960 generated route networks, we observed that most route networks got disconnected or have reached their peak at 15% and 30% node removals, after simulating vulnerability and robustness, respectively. Thus for computational efficiency, we used the ratio of the average path length over the network diameter at those thresholds for the fitness function.

Fitness Function. Considering the efficiency, robustness, and vulnerability scores, we derived the fitness function as:

$$F(G) = \frac{\alpha E - \beta R - \delta V}{\alpha + \beta + \delta} \tag{3}$$

where E is the efficiency score, R is the robustness score, and V is the vulnerability score, with α, β, and δ as they respective weights. A higher weight of

80% significance (α) was used for efficiency since the straightforwardness from source to destination affects daily operations. Straightforwardness aside, it was also observed that a minimum of 70% is required to produce positive fitness scores for better optimized networks. On the other hand, robustness and vulnerability were given the weights of 10% each (β and δ) since they simulate seasonal events.

Higher scores are better for efficiency while lower scores are better for robustness and vulnerability. Thus, we subtracted the vulnerability and robustness scores from the efficiency of the network. Lastly, everything is then divided by the sum of the weights for normalization.

Genetic Algorithm. In this study, we optimized the 20% worst performing networks from the pool of 960 generated networks. We ranked them based on their current fitness scores. For each network to be optimized, N_A, we randomly selected a network with a good fitness score from the 20% best performing networks as its pair, N_O.

At the beginning of each evolution, we randomly selected the number of routes to be mutated: $M \in \{0, ..., 3\}$ where $P(M = 0) = 0.7$, $P(M = 1) = 0.2$ and $P(M = 2, 3) = 0.05$. To produce a child network, we randomly selected route IDs from both parents and replaced the routes from N_A with the routes of the same route IDs from N_O. In each evolution, we produced a generation of 10 child networks, ranked by their fitness scores. If the highest ranked child network had a higher fitness score than one of the parents, then that child is selected as a parent in the next evolution, replacing the current parent with the lower fitness score. If no child had a higher fitness score than both parents, the current parents are selected again for generating children in the next evolution. We stopped the genetic algorithm at the 20th evolution because it was observed to have reached a plateau.

4   Results and Analysis

In evaluating the generated route networks, we first looked into the effects of an initial stop layout and different values for the maximum allowable walking distance on the efficiency, robustness, and vulnerability of route networks. After optimizing the worst performing networks, we looked at how much the networks improve in terms of efficiency, robustness, and vulnerability.

Effects of Layout and Maximum Allowable Walking Distance. For each city, we generated 20 networks per combination of geospatial layouts (Lattice, Random, 1 Hub, 2 Hubs) and d_{max} (300 m, 550 m, 800 m). Each network had 100 stops and 25 routes. We had a total of 960 generated routes. We first analyzed how our defined network characteristics correlate with our metrics from the fitness score.

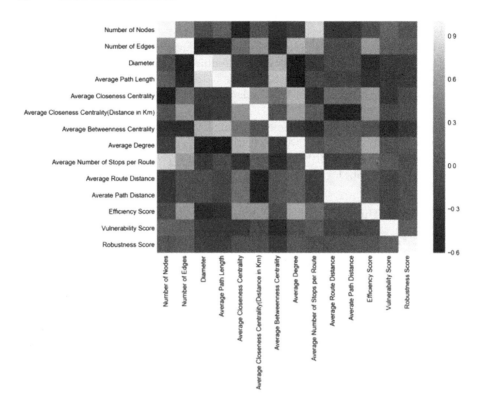

Fig. 3. Correlation matrix of all network characteristics with the derived fitness function metrics.

In Fig. 3, we focused on the correlation of the network characteristics towards our fitness function. Based on the matrix, we observed that among the three fitness function metrics, the efficiency of a network had strong positive correlation to five (5) route network characteristics.

First, a high number of edges meant that there will be more possible paths from source to destination. It lessens the possibility of selecting paths that use routes that are either not directly connected at a stop or have many route transfers. Second, as more stops become close to each other in terms of number of hops in between, the straightforwardness of the route network becomes better. This reduces the need to transfer between routes even in longer distances but this would also mean that distances between stops are much greater.

Aside from closeness in terms of the number of stops in between, the efficiency scores also showed a strong positive correlation with the closeness centrality using spatial distance. This time, as the spatial distance of a path (in km) becomes shorter for most source-destination pairs, the faster it is to travel because of shorter trips. At the same time, as more stops get used by multiple routes and become hubs, it allows shorter commutes between stops. A passenger could reach different destinations provided from a stop with a high degree.

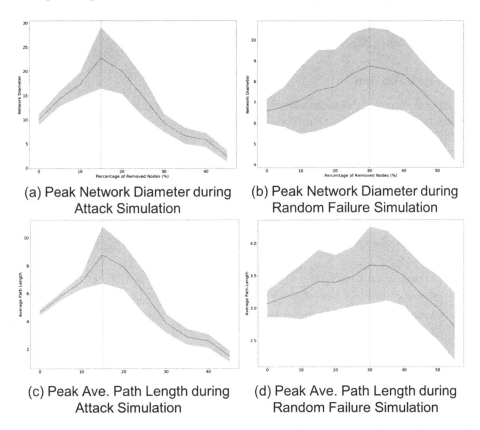

(a) Peak Network Diameter during
Attack Simulation

(b) Peak Network Diameter during
Random Failure Simulation

(c) Peak Ave. Path Length during
Attack Simulation

(d) Peak Ave. Path Length during
Random Failure Simulation

Fig. 4. Network diameters and average path lengths during the simulation of targeted attacks and random failures after every removal of additional 5% stops from the network for Manila having a Lattice Layout with a d_{max} of 300 m.

Lastly, a high average number of stops per route means that there are many stops which can be connected to connect shorter paths with other straightforward routes. Having more available paths will contribute to the lessening of transfers between routes, thus, improving the efficiency score of a network.

Threshold of Robustness and Vulnerability. After simulating random failures and targeted attacks, we then observed at which point a route network's diameter and average path length reached their peaks. The peak indicates the destruction or disconnection of network. We got the average network diameter and average path length at every 5% stop removals among the 20 route networks for each configuration. Once this has been achieved, we recorded the stop removal with the highest average value. Finally, we got the most frequent occurring percentage removal among all the configurations.

After simulating targeted attacks to the networks, we observed that 44% of them started to disconnect after removing at least 15% of the stops (Fig. 4a and c). At the same time, 31% of the networks had their longest diameters after removing at least 30% stops (Fig. 4b and d).

4.1 Optimization

We then compared the network metrics of the 20% worst performing networks before and after optimization. Having a positive difference for efficiency means that the efficiency score improved. Having a negative difference for the robustness and vulnerability means that the robustness and vulnerability scores improved.

Table 1. Average network characteristics of the 20% worst performing route networks

Metric	Unoptimized	Optimized
Number of edges	162.037	166.22
Diameter	8.667	10.185
Average path length	3.814	4.017
Average closeness centrality	0.238	0.259
Average closeness centrality (distance in Km)	0.0001	0.0001
Average betweenness centrality	0.03	0.034
Average degree	3.638	3.741
Average number of stops per route	76.951	73.412
Average route distance	14.855	24.846
Average path distance	2.277	2.213
Efficiency score	0.33	0.552
Vulnerability score	0.42	0.415
Robustness score	0.42	0.423

Table 1 shows the average network characteristics of 27 route networks sampled from the 20% worst performing networks, before and after their optimization. It can be observed that the number of edges, network diameter, average path length, and average route distance increased as the efficiency score increased for the optimized network as compared to the unoptimized network scores. This is because having longer routes in the network means that more stops are reachable in one route and if more stops are reachable in one route, it reduces the possibility of more transfers, making a network more straightforward and efficient. It can also be observed that the vulnerability score decreased a little while the robustness score almost maintained its score. A decrease in the vulnerability and robustness scores means that the scores got better, even by a little margin. It makes sense that there is little improvement for the scores since they have lower weights as compared to the weight of the total efficiency or total weighted radius of gyration. However, the average scores for the characteristics tell us that the efficiency, vulnerability, and robustness scores improved in general for the optimized versions.

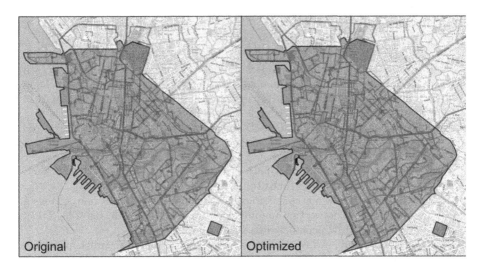

Fig. 5. A sample optimized network for Manila with a random layout and a d_{max} of 300 m.

As an example, Fig. 5 shows an original and optimized network for Manila. Though the changes are not so visually apparent, it has gained a lot in terms of number of edges (from 175 to 228) and average distance per route (from 14 km to 30 km). At the same time, we were able to decrease its diameter (from 9 to 6) and average path length (from 4 to 3).

Overall after the optimization, 18 out 27 networks improved its efficiency, 13 out of 27 networks improved its robustness, and 9 out of 27 networks improved in terms of vulnerability. In terms of the overall fitness scores, the optimized route networks showed an 84% improvement over the unoptimized networks on average. However, there are 2 instances, among the 27 networks, that had lower optimized scores.

5   Conclusion and Future Work

In this study, we devised a methodology to design transportation networks for para-transit services. In generating the networks, we initially followed a geospatial layout for distributing stops and used a maximum allowable walking distance to connect the routes. We then optimized the networks in terms of efficiency, robustness and invulnerability. To test our methodology, we generated 960 routes for four (4) Metro Manila cities. Our genetic algorithm was able to improve the network metrics of the worst performing networks.

There are still some aspects of the research that we were not able to consider. For example, instead of following a geospatial layout, a database of amenities or travel demand data could improve the positioning of the stops. Another recommendation is considering the width of a road in deciding how many routes can use it.

References

1. Abad, R.P.B., Fillone, A.M., Dadios, E.P., Roquel, K.I.Z.: An application of genetic algorithm in optimizing Jeepney operations along Taft Avenue, Manila. In: 8th International Conference on Humanoid, Nanotechnology, Information Technology, Communication and Control, Environment and Management, HNICEM 2015 (2016). https://doi.org/10.1109/HNICEM.2015.7393243
2. Asian Development Bank: Philippines: Transport Sector Assessment, Strategy, and Road Map, p. 18 (2012)
3. Attard, M., Haklay, M., Capineri, C.: The potential of volunteered geographic information (VGI) in future transport systems. Urban Plan. **1**(4), 6–19 (2016). https://doi.org/10.17645/up.v1i4.612
4. Boeing, G.: OSMnx: new methods for acquiring, constructing, analyzing, and visualizing complex street networks. Comput. Environ. Urban Syst. **65**, 126–139 (2017). https://doi.org/10.1016/j.compenvurbsys.2017.05.004
5. Braess, D., Nagurney, A., Wakolbinger, T.: On a paradox of traffic planning. Transp. Sci. Unternehm. **39**(12), 446–450 (2005). https://doi.org/10.1287/trsc.1050.0127
6. Di, X., He, X., Guo, X., Liu, H.X.: Braess paradox under the boundedly rational user equilibria. Transp. Res. Part B: Methodol. **67**, 86–108 (2014). https://doi.org/10.1016/j.trb.2014.04.005
7. Jain, V., Sharma, A., Subramanian, L.: Road traffic congestion in the developing world. In: Proceedings of the 2nd ACM Symposium on Computing for Development, pp. 1–10. ACM, New York (2012)
8. Jaramillo-Alvarez, P., González-Calderón, C., González-Calderón, G.: Route optimization of urban public transportation. Dyna **80**(180), 41–49 (2013). http://www.scielo.org.co/pdf/dyna/v80n180/v80n180a06.pdf
9. Johar, A., Jain, S.S., Garg, P.K.: Transit network design and scheduling using genetic algorithm - a review. Int. J. Optim. Control: Theor. Appl. (IJOCTA) **6**(1), 9–22 (2016). https://doi.org/10.11121/ijocta.01.2016.00258. http://ijocta.balikesir.edu.tr/index.php/files/article/view/258
10. Ma, J., Zhao, Y., Yang, Y., Liu, T., Guan, W., Wang, J., Song, C.: A model for the stop planning and timetables of customized buses. PLoS ONE **12**(1), 1–28 (2017). https://doi.org/10.1371/journal.pone.0168762
11. Nayeem, M.A., Rahman, M.K., Rahman, M.S.: Transit network design by genetic algorithm with elitism. Transp. Res. Part C: Emerg. Technol. **46**, 30–45 (2014). https://doi.org/10.1016/j.trc.2014.05.002
12. Pang, J.Z.F., Bin Othman, N., Ng, K.M., Monterola, C.: Efficiency and robustness of different bus network designs. Int. J. Mod. Phys. C **26**(03), 1–15 (2015). https://doi.org/10.1142/S0129183115500242
13. Schalekamp, H., Behrens, R.: An international review of paratransit regulation and integration experiences: lessons for public transport system rationalisation and improvement in South African cities. In: Proceedings of the 28th Southern African Transport Conference, Pretoria, South Africa, pp. 442–450 (2009)
14. Takakura, M., Furuta, T., Tanaka, M.S.: Urban bus network design using genetic algorithm and map information. In: Proceedings of the Eastern Asia Society for Transportation Studies 2015, pp. 1–13 (2015)

On the Configuration of Robust Static Parallel Portfolios for Efficient Plan Generation

Mauro Vallati[1(✉)], Lukáš Chrpa[2,3], and Diane Kitchin[1]

[1] School of Computing and Engineering, University of Huddersfield, Huddersfield, UK
{m.vallati,d.kitchin}@hud.ac.uk
[2] Faculty of Mathematics and Physics, Charles University in Prague,
Prague, Czech Republic
[3] Artificial Intelligence Center, Czech Technical University in Prague,
Prague, Czech Republic
chrpaluk@fel.cvut.cz

Abstract. Automated Planning has achieved a significant step forward in the last decade, and many advanced planning engines have been introduced. Nowadays, increases in computational power are mostly achieved through hardware parallelisation. In view of the increasing availability of multicore machines and of the intrinsic complexity of designing parallel algorithms, a natural exploitation of parallelism is to combine existing sequential planning engines into parallel portfolios.

In this work, we introduce three techniques for an automatic configuration of static parallel portfolios of planning engines. The aim of generated portfolios is to provide a good tradeoff performance between coverage and runtime, on previously unseen problems. Our empirical results demonstrate that our techniques for configuring parallel portfolios combine strengths of planning engines, and fully exploit multicore machines.

Keywords: Automated planning · Parallel portfolio
Portfolio configuration

1 Introduction

Automated planning is one of the most prominent Artificial Intelligence (AI) challenges; it has been studied extensively for several decades and has led to a large number of real-world applications. AI planning deals with finding a partially or totally ordered sequence of actions to transform the environment from an initial state to a desired goal state [6]. In recent years, also fostered by International Planning Competitions (IPCs) there has been considerable progress in developing powerful domain-independent planning engines. However, as in many different areas of AI, none of these systems clearly dominates all others in terms

© Springer International Publishing AG, part of Springer Nature 2018
Y. Shi et al. (Eds.): ICCS 2018, LNCS 10860, pp. 15–27, 2018.
https://doi.org/10.1007/978-3-319-93698-7_2

of performance over a broad range of planning domains. This observation motivates the design and exploitation of portfolio approaches in planning. In particular, much work has been done in the area of *sequential* portfolios, where selected planning engines are executed sequentially on a single CPU. Well-known examples include approaches such as PbP [5], Cedalion [18], and MIPlan [14], which are able to configure *static* sequential portfolios, and systems like IBaCoP [2], which instead aim at configuring *instance-specific* portfolios. Static approaches configure portfolios once, and then re-use the same configuration for any testing instance. Instead, instance-specific approaches can configure a different portfolio for each testing instance, according to some information extracted from the instance to be solved.

Nowadays, increases in computational power are mostly achieved through hardware parallelisation; as a result, multicore machines are cheap and widely available. Consequently, parallel solvers are gaining more and more importance, also because they can tackle more computationally demanding problems. However, the manual construction of parallel planning engines is a challenging task, and it often requires a fundamental redesign of existing sequential approaches in order to fully exploit the computational power given by the parallel hardware [7]. In fact, results from IPC 2014 [19] confirm that state-of-the-art parallel planners are not able to outperform standard sequential planning engines. This is also due to the intrinsic complexity of designing parallel algorithms. One promising approach for exploiting the computational power provided by multicore machines is the design of parallel portfolios of engines, i.e. a set of sequential planning engines that run in parallel for solving a given planning problem. Notably, parallel portfolios have been recently introduced in other areas of AI, such as SAT and ASP [12].

In this work, we consider an automatic construction of static domain-independent parallel portfolios. In particular, we introduce three new methodologies: one approach that schedules a single planning engine per available core, and two approaches that are able to allocate a sequence of different engines per each core. Portfolios are configured in order to be *robust*, i.e., they aim at providing good tradeoff performance between runtime and coverage. The designed techniques are able to configure parallel portfolios for any given number of processing units –here we focus on 2 and 4 cores, which correspond to widely available machines currently on the market– and for different cutoff times. Our extensive empirical analysis demonstrates the usefulness and robustness of generated parallel portfolios.

2   Configuration of Robust Parallel Portfolios

Automated Planning is about finding a sequence of actions, a plan, that transforms the environment from a given initial state to some goal state [6]. An action is specified via a precondition, i.e., what must hold prior its application, and effects, i.e., how the environment is transformed after its application. A planning engine accepts a planning problem description on the input and returns a plan (if it exists) on the output. In our case, we consider planning engines as "back-boxes", i.e., we do not investigate the techniques they exploit, but we consider their performance, i.e., whether they solve the problem and how fast.

Every approach requires as an input: (i) a set of homogeneous CPU cores U, where $|U| = k$, (ii) the maximum available runtime for the configured portfolio T, (iii) a set of planners P, (iv) a set of training planning problem instances Π, and (v) measures of performance of planners on the training instances $per : P \times \Pi \rightarrow \mathbb{R}^+$. Planners' performance are measured in terms of Penalised Average Runtime (PAR10) score. PAR10 is a metric usually exploited in machine learning and algorithm configuration techniques. This metric trades off coverage and runtime for solved problems: if a planner p solves a training instance π in time $t \leq T$, then $per(p, \pi) = t$, otherwise $per(p, \pi) = 10T$.

Portfolios are configured for minimising the overall PAR10 score, and are defined by: (i) the selected planning engines; (ii) the core on which each planner will be run, and (iii) the time interval allocated to each planning engine. More formally, we define a *parallel portfolio of planning engines* C as a set of tuples in the form of $\langle p, u, t_s, t_e \rangle$, where p is an engine, u is a core, t_s and t_e, where $t_s < t_e$ and $t_e \leq T$, determine the time interval of p's execution on u. Moreover, for each u, there are no tuples $\langle p, u, t_s, t_e \rangle$ and $\langle p', u, t'_s, t'_e \rangle$ such that $t_s \leq t'_s < t_e$ or $t_s < t'_e \leq t_e$ – in other words, intervals in which planners run on particular cores do not overlap. We say that a parallel portfolio is *complete* if and only if for each $p \in P$, $u \in U$ and $t \in [0; T]$ there exists $\langle p, u, t_s, t_e \rangle \in C$ such that $t_s \leq t \leq t_e$. Otherwise the portfolio is *incomplete*, i.e, some cores might be unallocated for some time intervals. Moreover, we assume that a planning engine can be used at most once, i.e., for each p there exists at most one tuple $\langle p, u, t_s, t_e \rangle \in C$.

The first approach, called *Overall*, selects a single planning engine per available core. It iteratively allocates engines in order to maximise the improvement of the PAR10 score of the portfolio. In an x-th step (from $x = 1$ to $x = k$, where k is the number of cores), where $C' = \{\langle p_1, u_1, 0, T \rangle, \ldots, \langle p_{x-1}, u_{x-1}, 0, T \rangle\}$ is an incomplete parallel portfolio and P' is a set of unallocated engines, we select $p_x \in P'$ such that for each $p' \in P'$ it is the case that
$$\sum_{\pi \in \Pi} \min(per(p_1, \pi), \ldots, per(p_{x-1}, \pi), per(p_x, \pi))$$
$$\leq \sum_{\pi \in \Pi} \min(per(p_1, \pi), \ldots, per(p_{x-1}, \pi), per(p', \pi)).$$
Then we update $C' = C' \cup \{\langle p_x, u_x, 0, T \rangle\}$ and $P' = P' \setminus \{p_x\}$. If it is not possible to further improve the PAR10 score of C', the portfolio is completed by allocating planning engines with the best PAR10 score that are not yet members of the portfolio to remaining available cores. Ties are broken by considering problem coverage (i.e., the number of solved problem instances), and then randomly.

Our next two approaches, called *Iterative-Single* and *Iterative-All*, are inspired by the hill-climbing method introduced in Fast Downward Stone Soup [9]. Notably, Stone Soup focused on combining planning techniques into a sequential portfolio that maximises the quality of generated solutions. It is well-known that for portfolios aiming at maximising the quality of solutions, the order in which planning engines are executed is irrelevant, however, engines' order is of pivotal importance when runtime is considered in the optimisation metric [20]. In our case, the portfolio has to execute engines that are more likely to quickly find solutions earlier.

Algorithm 1. The Iterative-Single algorithm. Iterative-All can be obtained by swapping the For loops (Lines 2 and 3) and by replacing C^{u_i} for C in Lines 7, 11 and 13.

Input: P,k,q,τ,per
Output: C
1: $C = \langle \rangle$; $P' = P$
2: **for** $i = 1$ to k **do**   ▷ Allocating cores
3:     **for** $j = 0$ to $q - 1$ **do**   ▷ Allocating time slots
4:         $C_{ext} = \emptyset$
5:         **for all** $\langle p, u_i, t_s, t_e \rangle \in C^{u_i}$ **do**   ▷ Extending the execution time of p on u_i
6:             $C'_{ext} = (C \setminus \{\langle p', u_i, t'_s, t'_e \rangle \mid \langle p', u_i, t'_s, t'_e \rangle \in C \wedge t'_s \geq t_s\}) \cup \{\langle p, u_i, t_s, t_e + \tau \rangle\} \cup$
               $\{\langle p', u_i, t'_s + \tau, t'_e + \tau \rangle \mid \langle p', u_i, t'_s, t'_e \rangle \in C \wedge t'_s > t_s\}$
7:             **if** $\sum_{\pi \in \Pi} per(C'^{u_i}_{ext}, \pi) < \sum_{\pi \in \Pi} per(C^{u_i}_{ext}, \pi)$
8:                 $C_{ext} = C'_{ext}$
9:             **end if**
10:         **end for**
11:         $p' = \arg\min_{p' \in P'} \sum_{\pi \in \Pi} per(C^{u_i} \cup \{\langle p', u_i, j * \tau, (j + 1) * \tau \rangle\}, \pi)$
12:         $C_{new} = C \cup \{\langle p', u_i, j * \tau, (j + 1) * \tau \rangle\}$ ▷ Allocating a new engine on u_i
13:         **if** $\sum_{\pi \in \Pi} per(C^{u_i}_{new}, \pi) < \sum_{\pi \in \Pi} per(C^{u_i}_{ext}, \pi)$
14:             $P' = P' \setminus \{p'\}$ ▷ Removing the recently allocated engine from the available engines
    set
15:             $C = C_{new}$
16:         **else**
17:             $C = C_{ext}$
18:         **end if**
19:     **end for**
20: **end for**

To introduce Iterative-Single and Iterative-All we extend our terminology as follows. The time interval $[0; T]$ is evenly split into $q \in \mathbb{N}$ subintervals of length τ (i.e, $T = q * \tau$). Let $C^u = \{\langle p, u, t_s, t_e \rangle \mid u \in U, \langle p, u, t_s, t_e \rangle \in C\}$ be a sequential portfolio of planning engines on a core u. We extend the *per* function for tuples representing the elements of parallel portfolios in such a way that $per(\langle p, u, t_s, t_e \rangle, \pi) = t_s + t$ if p solves π in time $t \leq t_e - t_s$, otherwise $per(\langle p, u, t_s, t_e \rangle, \pi) = 10T$. Then, we extend *per* for a parallel portfolio C such that $per(C, \pi) = \min_{\langle p, u, t_s, t_e \rangle \in C} per(\langle p, u, t_s, t_e \rangle, \pi)$.

The Iterative-Single and Iterative-All algorithms are described in Algorithm 1. The difference between Iterative-Single and Iterative-All is that the former allocates engines core by core while the latter time slot by time slot. In an intermediate step, i.e., considering i-th core and $(j+1)$-st time slot, we either extend the time interval of the planning engine allocated on the i-th core by τ, or allocate a new engine on the i-th core and $(j+1)$-st time slot depending what reduces the *per* value for the current (incomplete) portfolio the most (only the current core is considered for Iterative-Single). As formally described in Line 6, extending the time interval of $\langle p, u_i, t_s, t_e \rangle$ by τ is done by unallocating all planning engines p' allocated to u_i with start time greater or equal t_s (i.e., including p), then by extending the time interval of p, i.e., allocating $\langle p, u_i, t_s, t_e + \tau \rangle$, and then, finally, re-inserting the rest of the engines (p') on timeslots shifted by τ. It should be noted that in an intermediate step of the j for loop (Lines 3–19), planning engines can be allocated only on first $j+1$ slots, i.e., $t_e \leq (j+1) * \tau$ for any tuple $\langle p, u_i, t_s, t_e \rangle \in C$ (for the core u_i in the Iterative-Single algorithm, or any core for the Iterative-All algorithm). Consequently, there is no engine such that its $t_e > q * \tau$ (i.e., no planner is scheduled "outside" the given time interval) after Algorithm 1 terminates. In a nutshell, the Iterative-Single approach configures a different portfolio for each core, without considering other available cores; Iterative-All instead is able to reason upon all the available cores. Therefore, in Iterative-Single, the portfolio configured for a given core does not exploit any information about the portfolios running on the other processing units, or the number of available cores. This has been done for fostering the inclusion of (potentially many) different planners, hence maximising diversity of portfolios. On the contrary, Iterative-All has a complete overview of the performance of the portfolio across all the available cores.

Table 1. PAR10, coverage, and IPC score achieved by the generated portfolios and considered planning engines running on the 140 testing benchmark instances for 300 wallclock-time seconds (left) and 300 CPU-time seconds (right). VBS stands for the Virtual Best Solver, and grey rows indicate portfolio-based planners. Systems are listed in the order of increasing PAR10. 2 and 4 indicate the number of cores exploited by the portfolio.

Wallclock Time				CPU-time			
Planner	PAR10	Cov.	IPC	Planner	PAR10	Cov.	IPC
VBS	554.9	82.1	115.0	VBS	554.9	82.1	115.0
Iterative-All-4	678.2	79.3	90.9	Iterative-All-4	1358.7	55.0	66.1
Iterative-Single-4	725.5	77.1	84.6	Iterative-Single-4	1421.5	52.9	59.4
Overall-4	1115.9	63.6	80.4	Iterative-All-2	1426.8	52.9	62.5
Iterative-Single-2	1194.4	61.4	61.3	Iterative-Single-2	1491.2	50.7	52.0
Iterative-All-2	1228.4	60.0	68.0	Super-Naive-4	1677.4	44.3	60.0
Super-Naive-4	1431.0	52.9	60.4	Overall-4	1677.4	44.3	60.0
Overall-2	1569.7	48.6	41.8	Mpc	1797.7	40.7	40.4
Mpc	1797.7	40.7	40.4	Jasper	1871.0	38.6	24.8
Super-Naive-2	1837.3	39.3	42.2	Overall-2	1917.0	36.4	41.2
Jasper	1871.0	38.6	24.8	Mercury	1957.2	35.7	22.5
Mercury	1957.2	35.7	22.5	Freelunch	2007.4	33.6	34.3
Freelunch	2007.4	33.6	34.3	Probe	2029.7	32.9	30.6
Probe	2029.7	32.9	30.6	Bfs	2172.2	27.9	22.9
Bfs	2172.2	27.9	22.9	Lama	2107.8	30.7	18.4
Lama	2107.8	30.7	18.4	Yahsp3	2277.2	24.3	33.3
Yahsp3	2277.2	24.3	33.3	Super-Naive-2	2297.5	23.6	32.8
LPG	2343.4	22.1	23.8	LPG	2343.4	22.1	23.8
FF	2682.7	10.7	9.7	FF	2682.7	10.7	9.7

3   Experimental Analysis

We selected 10 planning engines, based on their performance in the Agile track of IPC 2014 and in previous IPCs, that accommodate very different planning techniques: Lama [16], LPG [4], FF [10], Bfs [21], Freelunch [21], Jasper [21], Madagascar-C (Mpc) [21], Mercury [21], Probe [21], and Yahsp3 [21].

Table 2. Planning engines included in the portfolios configured by the proposed techniques. ■ indicates that the engine is running on a core for the maximum available time, otherwise allocated CPU-time seconds are shown. SN, O, IS, and IA stand respectively for Super-Naive, Overall, Iterative-Single, and Iterative-All. 2 and 4 indicates the number of cores on which the portfolio runs.

	SN2	SN4	O2	O4	IS2	IS4	IA2	IA4
Bfs					150	150	200	200
FF						150		
Freelunch						150		100
Jasper		■				150		250
Lama						150	50	100
LPG			■	■	150	150	100	150
Mercury	■	■	■	■	50	50	50	50
Mpc				■	50	50	50	50
Probe		■			150	150	100	250
Yahsp3	■	■		■	50	50	50	50

Experiments were performed on a quad-core 3.0 Ghz CPU, with 4GB of RAM available for each core. We especially considered 2 and 4 cores to emphasise the ability of our approaches to configure portfolios on limited resources. In order to account for randomised algorithms and noise, results provided are averaged across three runs. Where possible, seeds of planning engines have been fixed. Planning engines (and configured portfolios) are stopped after the first solution is found. Unless differently specified, as in the Agile track of IPC 2014, the cutoff time (T) for each instance was 300 wallclock-time seconds. Minimum time slot (τ) was set to 50 s according to the results of our preliminary experiments.

As training instances, we included all the problems used in the deterministic and learning tracks (testing problems) of IPC 2008 and IPC 2011. Repeated problems were removed. In the case of repeated domains, only the most recent benchmarks were considered for training. In total, more than 600 instances are included in the training set.

For testing purposes we considered instances from the domains used in the Agile track of IPC 2014, that were not included in the training set. This was done for assessing the robustness of generated portfolios, i.e. their ability in generalising on different domains and problems. In total, 7 domains where used for testing: Cave Diving, Child-Snack, CityCar, GED, Hiking, Maintenance, and Tetris.

Performance is measured in terms of IPC score, PAR10 and coverage. We defined IPC score as in the Agile track of IPC 2014: for a planning engine $\mathcal{C}$ and a problem p, $Score(\mathcal{C}, p)$ is 0 if p is unsolved, and $1/(1 + \log_{10}(T_p(\mathcal{C})/T_p^*))$ otherwise (where T_p^* is the minimum time required by compared systems to solve the problem). The IPC score on a set of problems is given by the sum of the scores achieved on each considered instance.

As a baseline for evaluating the performance of introduced parallel portfolios, we consider a technique that allocates a single planning engine to each available core. Engines are selected merely according to PAR10 on training instances. This approach is called –pragmatically– *Super-Naive*.

Table 1 shows the PAR10, coverage and IPC scores of all the portfolios, planning engines, and the Virtual Best Solver (VBS) on the 140 testing instances when run for 300 wallclock-time seconds (left) and 300 CPU-time seconds (right). The VBS shows the performance of a (virtual) oracle which always selects the best (fastest) engine for the given problem. This provides the upper bound of performance achievable by combining considered solvers. By taking into account the performance gap between the VBS and the basic planners, it becomes apparent that if considered planning engines are substantially complementary, then configuring portfolios can be a fruitful way for improving overall performance.

In terms of performance boost given by exploiting parallel portfolios on 2 or 4 cores, results shown in Table 1 clearly indicate that most of the proposed configuration approaches outperform the best planning engine. Interestingly, even exploiting the Iterative approach for configuring a sequential portfolio running on a single core (notice that Iterative-Single and Iterative-All configure the same portfolio) results in better performance than Super-Naive and Overall on 2 cores. Remarkably, coverage and PAR10 performance achieved by the Iterative-All portfolio configured for exploiting 4 cores, are close to those achieved by the VBS. This confirms that the proposed configuration technique is able to effectively combine engines into high-performance portfolios. It comes as no surprise that the only portfolio that shows performance worse than the best single solver is the Super-Naive. In order to investigate cases in which the number of cores is similar to the number of available planning engines, we configured parallel portfolios to be run on 8 cores. Under such circumstances, Overall and Iterative-All approaches –but even a random selection– tend to perform close to VBS. Such a result is, however, not surprising because only a few engines, which had the worst performance on training instances, were not included in the portfolio.

In order to shed some light on the actual portfolios configuration, Table 2 shows the CPU-time allocated to each planner by the proposed configuration techniques. As expected, Iterative-All and Iterative-Single portfolios include a large number of solvers (sometimes all those made available). They mainly differ in terms of CPU-time allocated to each planning engine, and in the order in which engines are executed (not shown). We observed that Iterative-All and Iterative-Single approaches tend to schedule "highly promising" engines with shorter timeslots first. Longer timeslots are allocated later to slower but still promising solvers. Overall and Super-Naive approaches always include Mercury, as it is the planning engine that achieves the best PAR10 score on the training set. The remaining selected engines are slightly different and, according to delivered performance, the focus on complementarity of planning engines allows the Overall approach to configure a more robust portfolio.

3.1   From Wallclock to CPU Time

Results shown in the left side of Table 1 refer to portfolios run using a 300 wallclock time seconds limit. Evidently, this means that the actual CPU-time given to portfolios is twice (in case of 2 cores) or four times (4 cores) larger than the CPU-time available for basic planners. To investigate this aspect, we re-configured our portfolios for running 75 wallclock seconds when 4 cores are available, and 150 wallclock seconds when 2 cores are made available. For these shorter time horizons, the granularity value of iterative-based approaches has been reduced to 25 s. The performance of the configured portfolios, along those of the best and worst planning engines, are shown in the right side of Table 1. All the configured portfolios that outperform the best engine, achieved statistically significant better performance (according to the Wilcoxon test) than Mpc (the best performing basic solver). Only the performance achieved by the Overall and Super-Naive portfolios, configured for running on 2 cores, are worse than Mpc when wallclock time was considered (Table 1 left), and even worse when CPU was considered (Table 1 right). These approaches are strongly penalised when short wallclock time is made available, also in the light of the fact that training and testing instances are very different: this is because they tend to prefer planners that solve "easy" problems very quickly, that provide immediate PAR10 reward. Also, as they can select only 2 planners, mistakes come with a high price.

Results in Table 1 indicate that best PAR10 and coverage performance are achieved when portfolios can run on four cores, despite the fact that less "sequential" CPU-time is available. When configuring for four cores, our approaches tend to include in the portfolios short runs of many different planning engines: this strategy provides better performance and guarantees a high level of robustness. This behaviour of our portfolio configuration techniques is supported by the results discussed in [11] stating that an engine is likely to solve a problem either fast or not at all.

3.2   Domain-by-Domain Analysis

Table 3 presents the domain-by-domain performance of the configured parallel portfolios, exploiting 2 or 4 cores. It also gives details on the performance of the best basic planner (Mpc), and the VBS. It is worth reminding that portfolios have been configured for minimising the PAR10 score on the training problems. Interestingly, the portfolios configured by the Iterative-All approach –which delivered the best total PAR10 performance– do not excel in most of the domains. They rarely obtain the best performance on a domain, but the achieved PAR10 score is usually very close to the best one, and significantly better than the worst observed performance. Although Super-Naive and Overall approaches can achieve the best performance on some domains they can be dramatically weak in many others. Remarkably, Super-Naive and Overall run on 2 cores achieved worse performance than Iterative-Single/All run on a single core. With a relatively small number of cores (with respect to the number of basic

Table 3. PAR10, coverage, and IPC score achieved by the generated portfolios and the considered planners running on the 140 testing benchmark instances. VBS stands for the Virtual Best Solver. Bold (underline) indicates best performance achieved when using 2 (4) cores. Due to rounding, some totals may not correspond with the sum of the separate values.

PAR10

Domain	Super-Naive		Overall		Iterative-Single		Iterative-All		Mpc	VBS
	2	4	2	4	2	4	2	4		
CaveDiving	2573.1	1951.9	2573.1	2128.0	1995.6	1995.6	**1965.2**	<u>1950.2</u>	2418.5	1950.2
ChildSnack	2286.4	2286.4	**20.0**	<u>19.1</u>	135.6	135.6	257.2	44.9	1951.7	19.1
CityCar	2702.8	1655.7	2702.8	1657.5	**1363.1**	<u>1363.1</u>	1369.6	1364.2	1657.5	1357.7
GED	**18.3**	<u>18.3</u>	99.2	<u>18.3</u>	457.2	457.2	457.2	40.8	1383.7	18.3
Hiking	1063.9	<u>488.7</u>	1376.2	**919.8**	920.9	920.9	1079.0	930.7	1961.1	488.5
Maintenance	1506.9	906.4	1506.9	1055.8	630.9	<u>176.2</u>	**615.5**	194.5	1055.8	20.0
Tetris	**2709.8**	2709.8	**2709.8**	2012.7	2857.4	<u>30.2</u>	2854.9	222.2	2155.9	30.2
Total	1837.3	1431.0	1569.7	1115.9	1194.4	725.5	1228.4	678.2	1797.7	554.9

IPC score

Domain	Super-Naive		Overall		Iterative-Single		Iterative-All		Mpc	VBS
	2	4	2	4	2	4	2	4		
CaveDiving	0.9	3.7	0.9	2.6	2.3	2.3	**3.1**	<u>7.0</u>	1.9	7.0
ChildSnack	1.3	1.3	**17.3**	<u>20.0</u>	8.9	8.9	12.5	15.5	6.5	20.0
CityCar	0.7	7.4	0.7	7.4	**8.6**	8.6	**8.6**	<u>8.8</u>	7.4	11.0
GED	**20.0**	<u>20.0</u>	9.8	<u>20.0</u>	17.0	17.0	17.0	19.0	4.9	20.0
Hiking	12.7	<u>16.8</u>	6.4	13.8	**13.8**	13.8	12.0	13.1	3.8	17.0
Maintenance	5.4	9.5	5.4	12.3	9.5	13.3	**13.7**	<u>16.1</u>	12.3	20.0
Tetris	**1.0**	1.0	**1.0**	3.5	0.4	<u>20.0</u>	0.5	10.6	3.0	20.0
Total	42.2	60.4	41.8	80.4	61.3	84.6	68.0	90.9	40.4	115.0

Coverage

Domain	Super-Naive		Overall		Iterative-Single		Iterative-All		Mpc	VBS
	2	4	2	4	2	4	2	4		
CaveDiving	15.0	<u>35.0</u>	15.0	30.0	**35.0**	<u>35.0</u>	**35.0**	<u>35.0</u>	20.0	35.0
ChildSnack	25.0	25.0	**100.0**	<u>100.0</u>	**100.0**	<u>100.0</u>	95.0	<u>100.0</u>	35.0	100.0
CityCar	10.0	45.0	10.0	45.0	**55.0**	<u>55.0</u>	**55.0**	<u>55.0</u>	45.0	55.0
GED	**100.0**	<u>100.0</u>	**100.0**	<u>100.0</u>	85.0	85.0	85.0	<u>100.0</u>	55.0	100.0
Hiking	65.0	<u>85.0</u>	55.0	70.0	**70.0**	70.0	65.0	70.0	35.0	85.0
Maintenance	50.0	70.0	50.0	65.0	**80.0**	<u>95.0</u>	**80.0**	<u>95.0</u>	65.0	100.0
Tetris	**10.0**	10.0	**10.0**	35.0	5.0	<u>100.0</u>	5.0	<u>100.0</u>	30.0	100.0
Total	39.3	52.9	48.6	63.6	61.4	77.1	60.0	79.3	40.7	82.1

planners), the Iterative approaches are able to effectively combine planners into parallel portfolios, as can be seen from the results presented in Table 1 when using 2 or 4 cores. From this perspective, it is safe to claim that the Iterative-All approach is able to configure robust portfolios regardless of the cores/basic planners ratio. Robustness of the portfolios is also confirmed by their high coverage. On the contrary, Super-Naive and Overall approaches can be extremely performant on specific domains, but they dramatically fail to generalise in many others. This is possibly because selected planners are not very complementary, and they tend to perform well on the same set of testing problems. Interestingly, Iterative-All is the approach that maximises the PAR10 improvement given by 2 additional cores. In the light of the already high coverage delivered by Iterative-All running on 2 cores, such a result highlights the ability of this approach in selecting and combining planners that can quickly solve challenging planning instances.

3.3   Comparison Against the State of the Art

For better contextualising the performance achieved by the configured portfolios, we compared them with the winner of the Multicore track of IPC 2014: ArvandHerd [21]. When run on 4 cores, with a 300 wallclock seconds timeout, ArvandHerd was able to solve 60.7% of the testing problems, and achieved a PAR10 score of 1229.4 and an IPC score of 48.7. According to the results shown in Table 1, coverage and PAR10 are similar to those achieved by Iterative-All running on 2 cores. Remarkably, Iterative-All-2 shows significantly better performance in terms of IPC score (+19.3), indicating that despite the smaller number of cores, Iterative-All-2 is faster in providing solutions. Furthermore, we extended the wallclock time available to ArvandHerd to 1800 s, as in the Multicore track of IPC 2014. With this extended timeout, ArvandHerd is able to solve 78.0% of the testing problems. This is in line with the coverage result of our Iterative-Single portfolio, and worse than the coverage of the Iterative-All portfolio, both running on 4 cores but with a 300 s timeout. Such results support the hypothesis that combining planners in parallel portfolios is, at the state of the art, the most fruitful way for exploiting multicore machines.

Table 4. PAR10, coverage, and IPC score achieved by the generated portfolios, ArvandHerd, running on the 140 testing benchmark instances for 300 wallclock-time seconds. Systems are listed in the order of increasing PAR10. 2 and 4 indicate the number of cores exploited by the portfolio.

Planner	PAR10	Cov.	IPC
Iterative-All-4	678.2	79.3	90.9
Iterative-Single-4	725.5	77.1	84.6
Overall-4	1115.9	63.6	80.4
Iterative-Single-2	1194.4	61.4	61.3
Iterative-All-2	1228.4	60.0	68.0
ArvandHerd	1229.4	60.7	48.7
Super-Naive-4	1431.0	52.9	60.4
Overall-2	1569.7	48.6	41.8
PbP-like	1837.3	39.3	42.2
Super-Naive-2	1837.3	39.3	42.2

In order to compare the proposed approaches with the state of the art of static portfolio generation, here we consider PbP [5], which won the Learning track of IPC 2008 and IPC 2011. To the best of our knowledge, PbP is the only portfolio-based approach for planning that is able to configure static portfolios of different planning engines, optimised for minimising the CPU-time needed to find a solution to a given planning instance.

The PbP configuration approach relies on a statistical analysis of the performance of the planners in order to configure a portfolio. Since the performance of a portfolio is highly affected by the pool of basic planners which are made available, we run the PbP portfolio configuration technique using exactly the same training instances and the same basic planners which are exploited by our methods. Therefore, PbP has been used for configuring a single domain-independent portfolio. For this reason, it does not include any macro-action or any domain-specific configuration of the considered basic planners. It is worth remembering that PbP has been designed for configuring sequential portfolios: planners that are included in the portfolio are scheduled using a round-robin strategy. In our experiments, we used PbP for configuring a sequential portfolio with 1,200 CPU-time seconds allocated (300 seconds × 4 cores). Then, for parallelising the execution of the configured portfolio, each included planner has been run on an available core. Table 4 shows the performance achieved by a parallel portfolio configured using the PbP technique. It should be noted that it includes two planners: Mercury and Yahsp3, which are also the planners selected by the Super-Naive-2 technique. Such results provide evidence indicating that the configuration of parallel approaches requires some specifically designed techniques, as it is intrinsically different from the configuration of sequential portfolios.

4   Related Work

Parallel portfolio techniques have been recently introduced and investigated in several areas of AI, such as SAT and ASP [1,13].

Focusing on automated planning systems that took part in IPC 2014, IBaCoP [2] is an approach that configures instance-specific portfolios by extracting and assessing instance features –numerical values summarising properties of a given instance–, and empirical predictive models of the performance of considered planners. Planners can be combined with the aim of maximising the quality of generated plans, or to minimise the runtime. IBaCoP took part in IPC 2014, and has been used also to configure parallel portfolios –it was the runner-up of the multicore track– optimising the quality of plans. Unlike static portfolios, instance-specific portfolios require additional knowledge to be extracted by both training and testing instances, under the form of instance features. MIPlan [14,15] exploits a Mixed-Integer Programming approach for combining planners into static portfolios, either sequential or parallel. Portfolios are optimised to maximise the probability of providing the best available quality plans at any point in time. Cedalion [18] is an approach able to configure sequential portfolios by automatically generating different configurations of a given planner.

Starting with an empty portfolio, it adds the most improving configuration to the existing portfolio in each iteration, according to a given metric. In order to maximise the complementarity of configurations, they are generated using different training sets.

Other well-known approaches include PbP and Fast Downward StoneSoup [17]. The former has been discussed in the previous section. The latter combines different heuristic of Fast Downward [8] into a sequential portfolio, optimised for maximising the quality of generated plans.

5 Conclusion

According to the recent trend of increasing parallelism of hardware, in this work we considered the problem of configuring robust domain-independent parallel portfolios of planners. We introduced four new methods: two approaches assign each available core to a single planner, while the other two techniques can allocate more than one planner per core. We tested our approaches on benchmarks from the last IPC, and considered 10 state-of-the-art sequential planners for the configuration of the portfolios.

Our extensive experimental analysis showed that: (i) selected planners at the state of the art have a high level of complementarity and are therefore suitable to be combined in portfolios; (ii) iterative-based approaches are more robust, and perform consistently better than approaches that assign one single planner per core; (iii) parallel portfolios outperform state-of-the-art parallel planning engine ArvandHerd, thus are a fruitful way for exploiting the availability of multicore machines; (iv) parallel portfolios are able to outperform sequential planners also when run for the same CPU-time; and (v) the proposed approaches outperform the (parallelised) portfolio designed by the state-of-the-art configuration technique.

Future work includes the configuration of portfolios of planners for maximising plans' quality, and the extension of the proposed approaches to cope with other planning areas, such as optimal planning. Finally, we see promise in techniques, based on planning features [3], for configuring instance-specific parallel portfolios, and in the exploitation of different sequential portfolios, generated using diverse techniques and basic planners, on available CPUs.

Acknowledgements. Research was partially funded by the Czech Science Foundation (project no. 17-17125Y).

References

1. Balyo, T., Sanders, P., Sinz, C.: HordeSat: a massively parallel portfolio SAT solver. In: Heule, M., Weaver, S. (eds.) SAT 2015. LNCS, vol. 9340, pp. 156–172. Springer, Cham (2015). https://doi.org/10.1007/978-3-319-24318-4_12
2. Cenamor, I., de la Rosa, T., Fernández, F.: The ibacop planning system: instance-based configured portfolios. J. Artif. Intell. Res. **56**, 657–691 (2016)

3. Fawcett, C., Vallati, M., Hutter, F., Hoffmann, J., Hoos, H., Leyton-Brown, K.: Improved features for runtime prediction of domain-independent planners. In: Proceedings of ICAPS (2014)
4. Gerevini, A., Saetti, A., Serina, I.: Planning through stochastic local search and temporal action graphs. J. Artif. Intell. Res. (JAIR) **20**, 239–290 (2003)
5. Gerevini, A., Saetti, A., Vallati, M.: Planning through automatic portfolio configuration: the PbP approach. J. Artif. Intell. Res. (JAIR) **50**, 639–696 (2014)
6. Ghallab, M., Nau, D., Traverso, P.: Automated Planning, Theory and Practice. Morgan Kaufmann, Burlington (2004)
7. Hamadi, Y., Wintersteiger, C.: Seven challenges in parallel SAT solving. AI Mag. **34**(2), 99–106 (2013)
8. Helmert, M.: The fast downward planning system. J. Artif. Intell. Res. **26**, 191–246 (2006)
9. Helmert, M., Röger, G., Karpas, E.: Fast downward stone soup: a baseline for building planner portfolios. In: Proceedings of the PAL Workshop (2011)
10. Hoffmann, J.: The metric-ff planning system: translating "ignoring delete lists" to numeric state variables. J. Artif. Intell. Res. **20**, 291–341 (2003)
11. Howe, A.E., Dahlman, E.: A critical assessment of benchmark comparison in planning. J. Artif. Intell. Res. (JAIR) **17**, 1–33 (2002)
12. Kotthoff, L.: Algorithm selection for combinatorial search problems: a survey. CoRR abs/1210.7959 (2012). http://arxiv.org/abs/1210.7959
13. Lindauer, M., Hoos, H., Hutter, F.: From sequential algorithm selection to parallel portfolio selection. In: Dhaenens, C., Jourdan, L., Marmion, M.-E. (eds.) LION 2015. LNCS, vol. 8994, pp. 1–16. Springer, Cham (2015). https://doi.org/10.1007/978-3-319-19084-6_1
14. Núñez, S., Borrajo, D., Linares López, C.: Automatic construction of optimal static sequential portfolios for AI planning and beyond. Artif. Intell. **226**, 75–101 (2015)
15. Núñez, S., Borrajo, D., Linares López, C.: Sorting sequential portfolios in automated planning. In: Proceedings of IJCAI, pp. 1638–1644 (2015)
16. Richter, S., Westphal, M.: The lama planner: guiding cost-based anytime planning with landmarks. J. Artif. Intell. Res. **39**, 127–177 (2010)
17. Seipp, J., Braun, M., Garimort, J., Helmert, M.: Learning portfolios of automatically tuned planners. In: Proceedings of ICAPS, pp. 369–372 (2012)
18. Seipp, J., Sievers, S., Helmert, M., Hutter, F.: Automatic configuration of sequential planning portfolios. In: Proceedings of AAAI, pp. 3364–3370 (2015)
19. Vallati, M., Chrpa, L., Grzes, M., McCluskey, T., Roberts, M., Sanner, S.: The 2014 international planning competition: progress and trends. AI Mag. **36**(3), 90–98 (2015)
20. Vallati, M., Chrpa, L., Kitchin, D.: Portfolio-based planning: state of the art, common practice and open challenges. AI Commun. **28**(4), 717–733 (2015)
21. Vallati, M., Chrpa, L., McCluskey, T.: Description of participating planners. In: Proceedings of the 8th International Planning Competition (IPC-2014) (2014)

SDF-Net: Real-Time Rigid Object Tracking Using a Deep Signed Distance Network

Prayook Jatesiktat[(⊠)], Ming Jeat Foo, Guan Ming Lim, and Wei Tech Ang

School of Mechanical and Aerospace Engineering, Nanyang Technological University,
50 Nanyang Avenue, Singapore 639798, Singapore
{prayook001,foom0009,guanming001}@e.ntu.edu.sg, wtang@ntu.edu.sg

Abstract. In this paper, a deep neural network is used to model the signed distance function (SDF) of a rigid object for real-time tracking using a single depth camera. By leveraging the generalization capability of the neural network, we could better represent the model of the object implicitly. With the training stage done off-line, our proposed methods are capable of real-time performance and running as fast as 1.29 ms per frame on one CPU core, which is suitable for applications with limited hardware capabilities. Furthermore, the memory footprint of our trained SDF-Net for an object is less than 10 kilobytes. A quantitative comparison using public dataset is being carried out and our approach is comparable with the state-of-the-arts. The methods are also tested on actual depth records to evaluate their performance in real-life scenarios.

Keywords: Deep neural network · Signed distance
Object representation · Object tracking · Depth image

1 Introduction

The tracking of a rigid object in 3D can be characterized as a problem of estimating the six degrees of freedom (6-DOF) trajectory of an object as it moves around a scene. Rigid object tracking is a useful tool in various applications such as augmented reality in which a user interacts with an object, or industrial automation in which a robot manipulates an assembly part. There are multiple approaches to achieve 3D tracking such as the use of inertial sensors or fiducial markers attached to the object. However, the readings of inertial sensors may drift with time and the marker-based approach can be intrusive. To overcome those limitations, vision-based tracking offers solutions that are non-invasive, practical, and cheap [15].

Since the introduction of commodity depth cameras, the availability of depth data extends RGB tracking methods by utilizing depth information in particle

Supported by Rehabilitation Research Institute of Singapore (Ref. No. RRG2/16001).

© Springer International Publishing AG, part of Springer Nature 2018
Y. Shi et al. (Eds.): ICCS 2018, LNCS 10860, pp. 28–42, 2018.
https://doi.org/10.1007/978-3-319-93698-7_3

filter algorithm [5,14], Gaussian filter algorithm [8], and also the well-established Iterative Closest Point (ICP) algorithm [3,30]. The ICP aims to find the best pose estimate to minimize the distance between two sets of depth data and while there are several variants of ICP with more efficient and robust solutions [23], the main process of searching for point correspondences can be computationally expensive and error-prone.

Thus, to avoid the time-consuming point-to-point correspondence search, depth data could be modelled implicitly to allow point-to-model distance minimization [21]. For example, a minimal set of primitive shapes is used to model a simple industrial part [26], but for a more complex model, implicit functions such as implicit B-Spline can be employed to provide a richer data representation for a better registration [22]. The signed distance function (SDF) is another representation that implicitly encodes 3D surfaces and can be used directly to define a cost function for accurate registration [4]. As such, SDF has been applied in recent works on scene reconstruction [12,25] and rigid object tracking [19]. The SDF of basic geometric shapes such as spheres, cubes, and ellipsoids can be represented implicitly. For example, the SDF of a sphere of radius r centred at the origin can be written using the implicit expression $\sqrt{x^2 + y^2 + z^2} - r$.

However, the SDF of more complex shapes are much more difficult to define and are thus often represented as sampled volumes [6]. To obtain a continuous representation of a complex object surface, there are a few works that incorporate machine learning techniques. For instance, Radial Basis Function (RBF) neural network can be used to classify a 3D point into three classes, namely internal, on-surface, and external [17]. To date, the use of a multi-layer neural network to model the SDF of an object has only been done for brain structures segmentation [9]. To the best of our knowledge, our work is the first to model the SDF of an object using a deep neural network for object tracking purpose.

Recently, learning-based methods have revolutionized many areas of computer vision including object tracking. Since Tan and Ilic [27] have proposed a random-forest-based method to regress the movement of the object from the change in the observed point cloud, several improvements [1,28,29] have been made to advance the state-of-the-arts in temporal 3D object tracking without GPU. On the other hand, Garon and Lalonde [7] claimed to develop the first end-to-end deep learning for temporal object tracking. However, it needs GPU for real-time tracking due to the large network size.

The contribution of this paper is the adoption of a learning-based method to train a deep neural network, which we term as SDF-Net, to approximate the SDF of an object. In addition, we also propose two methods to utilise the trained SDF-Net for rigid object tracking. Furthermore, a quantitative comparison on a public dataset is carried out to compare our approach against the state-of-the-arts. Our methods are also tested with real depth data from two different commodity depth cameras to demonstrate the real-time object tracking capability in different scenarios.

This paper is organized as follows. Section 2 details the methodology to train a deep neural network that models the SDF of an object and the two different ways to use the network for object tracking. Section 3 outlines the evaluation methods and Sect. 4 discusses the results. Finally, Sect. 5 presents the conclusion, as well as the limitation and future work.

2   Method

Our goal is to estimate the current 6-DOF pose θ_t, which contains an orientation R_t and a translation t_t, of the given object in the camera reference frame $\{C\}$.

A depth camera is used to provide a sequence of depth images. For each depth frame, the following inputs are used in our method:

1. The depth image of the current frame t and the previous frame $t - 1$.
2. Pose estimation results from the previous frames $(\theta_{t-h}, ..., \theta_{t-1})$ where $h > 1$

Also, the method has access to the camera intrinsic parameters and the triangular mesh model of the target object in the object reference frame $\{H\}$.

2.1   Method Overview

The SDF of an object is simply a function that takes a 3D point p and returns a signed Euclidean distance to the closest point on the object surface. In this paper, the signed distance is defined to be negative when p is inside the object, and positive when p is outside the object. The intuition behind our fitting approaches is to use SDF in a form of trained neural network to guide the pose update in moving sampled points from the observation towards zero signed distance value.

Our method can be divided into two stages. The first stage is to prepare an approximation of the SDF of the object by training a neural network, while the second stage utilizes the network for pixel sampling and pose tracking. Two different methods of pose tracking are proposed. The first method is based on the conventional ICP approach with an adaptation at the correspondence search. The second method is based on an optimization approach. Both methods share the same sparse sampling mechanism which is designed to increase the robustness of tracking when there is an occlusion. Nonetheless, both methods depend heavily on the quality of learned SDF-Net.

2.2   Building a Signed Distance Network

Training Data Preparation. The 3D model of the object to be tracked is translated to make its centroid stays at the origin. To facilitate the learning process, the model is scaled with a scaling factor $s = 1/d$, where d is the maximum diameter of the object; one unit in this scaled world $\{S\}$ is equivalent to d.

Three sets of 100,000 points, namely A_I, A_S and A_O, are sampled from the region inside the object, on the surface, and outside the object respectively. The points in A_O are only sampled from the space outside object up to 1.5 units from the surface. The space is divided equally into 100 sections with a thickness of 0.015 units each. One thousand points are then randomly sampled from each section to ensure that the training data obtained in A_O are evenly distributed.

Let $K : \mathbb{R}^3 \mapsto \mathbb{R}^3$ maps a 3D position to the closest point on the object surface and $\varPhi' : \mathbb{R}^3 \mapsto \mathbb{R}^3$ be the expected gradient that returns a unit direction, which points towards the closest point on the surface when the input lies inside the object. In contrast, the direction will point away from the closest point on the surface if the input falls outside the object. All the associated expected gradients and closest surface mapping at all points in A_I and A_O are pre-calculated.

Network Structure. Our neural network has three input nodes for a 3D position and one output node for the signed distance. The hidden layers are fully-connected. All the hidden nodes use tanh activation function, except for the output node which uses linear activation function.

In this study, two different diamond-shaped networks are tested. Network $\mathcal{A}$ is a smaller network with 10 hidden layers, while network $\mathcal{B}$ is a bigger network with 12 hidden layers. The number of nodes in all layers are 3-6-9-12-15-18-15-12-9-6-3-1 for network $\mathcal{A}$ and 3-6-9-12-15-18-21-18-15-12-9-6-3-1 for network $\mathcal{B}$, with total tunable parameters of 1,369 and 2,162 respectively. The diamond structure allows a gradual projection of the 3D data to a higher dimensional space before being slowly reduced to one dimension. Given the same number of tunable parameters, shallower networks with equal numbers of hidden nodes for all layers seems to be less effective in learning.

Cost Function. Let $\varTheta$ represent all weights and biases of a target network. Function $N_\varTheta : \mathbb{R}^3 \mapsto \mathbb{R}$ does a feed-forwarding that maps a 3D position (input layer) to a single number at the output node. Function $N_\varTheta' : \mathbb{R}^3 \mapsto \mathbb{R}^3$ maps a 3D position to the gradient of $N_\varTheta$ at that spot. The cost function is defined as:

$$
Cost(\varTheta) = \left(\frac{1000}{s^2|A_S|} \sum_{\boldsymbol{p}_i \in A_S} N_\varTheta(\boldsymbol{p}_i)^2 \right)
$$
$$
+ \left(\frac{1000}{s|A_O|} \sum_{\boldsymbol{p}_i \in A_O} \max(0, -N_\varTheta(\boldsymbol{p}_i)) \right) + \left(\frac{1000}{s|A_I|} \sum_{\boldsymbol{p}_i \in A_I} \max(0, N_\varTheta(\boldsymbol{p}_i)) \right)
$$
$$
+ \left(\frac{1}{|A_I| + |A_O|} \sum_{\boldsymbol{p}_i \in A_I \cup A_O} \|N_\varTheta'(\boldsymbol{p}_i) - \varPhi'(\boldsymbol{p}_i)\| + \|N_\varTheta'(K(\boldsymbol{p}_i)) - \varPhi'(\boldsymbol{p}_i)\| \right)
$$
$$
(1)
$$

The first (*SurfaceDistancePenalty*) term penalizes the network when some outputs at surface points deviate from zero. The second term penalizes the network when some outputs at outsider points are negative. The third term penalizes the network when some outputs at insider points are positive. Since the gradient is applied directly in our tracking methods, it is also considered in the training. Thus, the last (*GradientPenalty*) term is introduced to penalize the deviation of gradient from the expectation. This term also applies gradient constraints on the object surface using the same expected gradient from its correspondence.

All the weights and biases (Θ) are trained to minimize the cost function in Eq. 1. The training is done on TensorFlow using ADAM optimizer [13] with a learning rate of 0.001 for 100,000 iterations.

Notation. After the training, the network is ready to be used in the scaled reference frame $\{S\}$. To make the notation more compact, the network is augmented so that it can work in the object reference frame $\{H\}$ and output the signed distance that relates to the real world scale. We define our learned signed distance function $D : \mathbb{R}^3 \mapsto \mathbb{R}$ and its gradient function $G : \mathbb{R}^3 \mapsto \mathbb{R}^3$ as

$$D(_H\boldsymbol{p}) = N_\Theta(s \cdot {}_H\boldsymbol{p})/s \quad \text{and} \quad G(_H\boldsymbol{p}) = N'_\Theta(s \cdot {}_H\boldsymbol{p}) \tag{2}$$

given that $_H\boldsymbol{p}$ is the input position in the object reference frame $\{H\}$. The function D and G are implemented in a closed-form using the standard feed-forwarding and back-propagation algorithm. This technique allows the computation to be vectorised and to run efficiently on a CPU with SIMD capability.

The state of orientation R_t and translation $\boldsymbol{t}_t$ represents the transformation of the object with respect to the camera reference frame at time t:

$$_C\boldsymbol{p} = R_t {}_H\boldsymbol{p} + \boldsymbol{t}_t \tag{3}$$

2.3   Current Frame Pose Prediction

At the current frame t, when the θ_t is not yet calculated, the predicted pose $\hat{\theta}_t$ will be calculated using a short series of pose estimation results from the previous frames ($\theta_{t-h}, ..., \theta_{t-1}$). The predicted translation $\hat{\boldsymbol{t}}_t$ and the predicted orientation $\hat{R}_t$ are calculated independently. For translation, a weighted linear regression is used to extrapolate $\hat{\boldsymbol{t}}_t$ with weights $v_1, ..., v_h$. For orientation, all the past orientations are expressed in quaternions. Then, we predict the current orientation $\hat{q}_t$ with the following equation:

$$\hat{q}_t = \vartheta\left(\sum_{i=1}^{h-1} w_i \cdot (q_{t-1} \times (\sigma_{t-2}(t-1-i, t-1))^{-1} \times q_{t-1}) \right) \tag{4}$$

given that $\sigma_c(a, b)$ is a quaternion spherical linear interpolation (Slerp) between q_a and q_b at frame c. The function $\vartheta(\cdot)$ represents quaternion normalization. The weights $v_1, ..., v_h$ and $w_1, ..., w_{h-1}$ allow the adjustment of the responsiveness of the prediction. An incremental geometric series 2^{i-1}, with $i = 1, 2, \ldots, h$, is used for both weight series.

2.4   Object Pixel Sampling

Among all the depth pixels in the current frame, a number of pixels will be sampled and used in object tracking. If a few non-object pixels are sampled to fit with the object, it could reduce the tracking accuracy and lead to a loss of tracking eventually. Therefore, it is important to ensure that all the pixels used are sampled from the object surface.

As the pose estimation from the previous frame ($\theta_{t-1} = [R_{t-1}, t_{t-1}]$) is known, we can transform the 3D associated position of every pixel (from the previous frame) into the object reference frame and use the learned SDF to classify whether the pixel belongs to the tracked object. If $D(R_{t-1}^T(_C p_i - t_{t-1}))$ is less than a small positive value (e.g. 0.004 m), the pixel i of previous frame will be classified as object surface. Otherwise, it will be classified as non-object.

To accelerate this process, we introduce a classification interval k. Then, we only consider pixels every k-th row and k-th column with distance from t_{t-1} less than the maximum object radius r_o. All the classified object and non-object points are kept in the object reference frame as $_H p_i = R_{t-1}^T(_C p_i - t_{t-1})$.

In the current frame t, the collected non-object points $_H p_i$ from the previous frame will be transformed by the previous pose θ_{t-1} and the predicted pose $\hat{\theta}_t$ separately to represent both non-object points from the previous frame and predicted non-object points in the current frame. The transformed points are then projected onto the image plane. When a transformed non-object point is projected to a pixel, that pixel and its neighbor within Chebyshev distance of k will record the shallowest depth from all non-object projections. All these records can be considered as potential occluders, meaning that any point in the volume behind them should not be sampled.

Then, the collected object points from the previous frame will be transformed by θ_{t-1} and $\hat{\theta}_t$ and then projected to the depth image. If the projected depth is at least 10 cm shallower than the occluder at that pixel and if the current observed depth is within 5 cm from the projected depth, we consider that pixel to be safe to sample. Among those survivals, m pixels will be sampled randomly.

The rationale of this method is to cover both static occlusions and those which move together with the object such as hand and fingers. Therefore, θ_{t-1} and $\hat{\theta}_t$ are used to represent the two kinds of occlusions. Moreover, the expansion of the occlusions after projection will give some margins for the error in pose prediction and unpredicted movements of those occlusions.

2.5   ICP-Based Fitting Approach

This approach is similar to the well-established ICP except for the correspondence searching step. Instead of finding the exact closest point on the object surface, the trained SDF is used to infer the correspondence. The latest state of the pose $\tilde{\theta} = [\tilde{R}, \tilde{t}]$, initialized as $\tilde{\theta} := [R_{t-1}, \hat{t}_t]$, will be updated iteratively until a stopping condition is met.

Pseudo-Correspondence Inference.   Given $_H p_i = \tilde{R}^T(_C p_i - \tilde{t})$, with $i = 1, 2, \ldots, m$, as the transformed sampled 3D points from Sect. 2.4 using the latest state of the pose $\tilde{\theta}$, their correspondences will be

$$_H e_i = {_H p_i} - D(_H p_i) \cdot \mathcal{N}(G(_H p_i)) \tag{5}$$

where $\mathcal{N}(\cdot)$ is the vector normalization.

Pose Update. Let $_H c_p$ be the centroid location calculated from all $_H p_i$ and $_H c_e$ be the centroid location calculated from all $_H e_i$. The optimal orientation ΔR can be found by minimizing the sum of pair-wise distances:

$$E(\Delta R) = \sum_{i=1}^{m} \| (_H c_e + \Delta R(_H p_i - {}_H c_p)) - {}_H e_i \|^2. \tag{6}$$

Let P be a matrix whose i-th column is a vector $_H p_i - {}_H c_p$ and Q be a matrix whose i-th column is a vector $_H e_i - {}_H c_e$. E is minimized by performing a singular value decomposition (SVD) to the cross-covariance matrix $M = PQ^\top$ which results in $M = UWV^\top$. The rotation matrix is obtained from $\Delta R = VU^\top$. As a consequence, the optimal translation will be $\Delta t = {}_H c_e - \Delta R {}_H c_p$.

While ΔR and Δt moves the sampled observation points to fit with the signed distance field in the object reference frame, the state $\tilde{R}$ and $\tilde{t}$ perform the opposite. Therefore, an inversion will be applied to update the parameters in the following order:

$$\tilde{t} := \tilde{t} - \tilde{R}\Delta t \qquad \text{then} \qquad \tilde{R} := \tilde{R}(\Delta R)^T \tag{7}$$

Stopping Condition. The iteration will stop when the number of iterations has reached n_{max} or the update is small. For the latter criterion, we set the condition to be $(3 - \text{Trace}(\Delta R))/3 < 10^{-6}$ and $\Delta t < 10^{-5}$. Then, the latest state will be assigned to the final pose estimation $\theta_t := \tilde{\theta}$.

2.6   Optimization-Based Fitting Approach

Cost Function. This approach makes use of an optimization algorithm to perform the fitting for current frame t. In our application, the Levenberg-Marquardt algorithm (LM) is used to minimize a cost function defined as

$$F(\Delta R, \Delta t) = \sum_{i=1}^{m} D\Big(\Delta R\tilde{R}^\top \big[{}_C p_i - (\tilde{t} + \Delta t)\big]\Big)^2 \tag{8}$$

where ΔR and Δt are the changes of orientation and translation respectively, and m is the number of sampled points used in the optimization.

In contrast to Sect. 2.5, the current state $\tilde{\theta} = [\tilde{R}, \tilde{t}]$ is initialized as $\tilde{\theta} := [R_{t-1}, t_{t-1}]$, while ΔR and Δt are initialized to be the identity rotation and the zero vector respectively.

Formulation of Jacobian. For the cost function in Eq. 8, the rotation ΔR is represented using a quaternion $q = w + x\hat{i} + y\hat{j} + z\hat{k}$.

Given that $\omega = [x \ y \ z]^\top$, a point p rotated by the quaternion q is

$$p_{rotated} = p + 2w(\omega \times p) + 2[\omega \times (\omega \times p)] \tag{9}$$

For each point $_C\boldsymbol{p}_i$, we define $\boldsymbol{p}'_i = \tilde{R}^{\top}\big[{}_C\boldsymbol{p}_i - (\tilde{\boldsymbol{t}} + \Delta\boldsymbol{t})\big]$, $D_i = D(\Delta R\boldsymbol{p}'_i)$ and $\boldsymbol{G}_i = \boldsymbol{G}(\Delta R\boldsymbol{p}'_i)$. The Jacobian J can be derived as follow:

$$\left(\frac{\partial F}{\partial \Delta t}\right)_i = -\boldsymbol{G}_i^{\top}(\Delta R\tilde{R}^{\top}) \tag{10}$$

$$\left(\frac{\partial F}{\partial w}\right)_i = 2\,\boldsymbol{G}_i^{\top}\left([\boldsymbol{\omega}]_{\times}\boldsymbol{p}'_i\right) \tag{11}$$

$$\left(\frac{\partial F}{\partial v}\right)_i = 2\,\boldsymbol{G}_i^{\top}\Big[\big(w[\boldsymbol{e}_v]_{\times} + [\boldsymbol{e}_v]_{\times}[\boldsymbol{\omega}]_{\times} + [\boldsymbol{\omega}]_{\times}[\boldsymbol{e}_v]_{\times}\big)\boldsymbol{p}'_i\Big] \tag{12}$$

where $v \in \{x, y, z\}$, $\boldsymbol{e}_v$ are the respective standard basis vectors, and $[\cdot]_{\times}$ represents the skew symmetric matrix.

When ΔR and $\Delta\boldsymbol{t}$ are the identity rotation and the zero vector respectively, we have $\boldsymbol{p}'_i = \tilde{R}({}_C\boldsymbol{p}_i - \tilde{\boldsymbol{t}})$ and the Jacobian calculations are simplified to

$$\left(\frac{\partial F}{\partial \Delta t}\right)_i = -\boldsymbol{G}_i^{\top}\tilde{R}^{\top}, \qquad \left(\frac{\partial F}{\partial w}\right)_i = 0, \qquad \left(\frac{\partial F}{\partial v}\right)_i = 2\,\boldsymbol{G}_i^{\top}\left([\boldsymbol{e}_v]_{\times}\boldsymbol{p}'_i\right) \tag{13}$$

Pose Update. The change in pose parameters $\boldsymbol{\delta}$ is computed from

$$\left[J^{\top}J + \lambda K\right]\boldsymbol{\delta} = J^{\top}\boldsymbol{r} \tag{14}$$

where $\boldsymbol{r} = -[D_1\, D_2\, \ldots\, D_m]^{\top}$, λ is the damping factor of the optimization. K can be chosen as the identity matrix or diag $(J^{\top}J)$.

Adding the respective components of $\boldsymbol{\delta}$ to the zero translation and the identity quaternion, we have $\Delta\boldsymbol{t} = [\Delta t_x\, \Delta t_y\, \Delta t_z]^{\top}$ and $\Delta q = 1 + \Delta x\hat{i} + \Delta y\hat{j} + \Delta z\hat{k}$, where the latter is normalizedbefore being converted to the rotation matrix ΔR.

The current pose $\tilde{R}$ and $\tilde{\boldsymbol{t}}$ are updated with $\tilde{R} := \tilde{R}(\Delta R)^{\top}$ and $\tilde{\boldsymbol{t}} := \tilde{\boldsymbol{t}} + \Delta\boldsymbol{t}$. The terms ΔR and $\Delta\boldsymbol{t}$ are always reset to the identity rotation and the zero vector for the next iteration.

The optimization process is iterated until the cost function (Eq. 8), its change, or the magnitude of $\boldsymbol{\delta}$ falls below their respective thresholds, or the number of iterations has reached n_{max}.

3 Evaluation

3.1 Quantitative Evaluation

Our proposed method is evaluated using synthetic dataset from Choi and Christensen [5] which consists of four RGB-D sequences with ground truth object trajectories. The parameters used in the ICP-based method are $m = 50$, $k = 5$, and $n_{max} = 20$. The parameters used in the LM-based method are $m = 30$, $k = 11$, $\lambda_{init} = 0.1$, $\lambda_{scaling} = 2$, $n_{max} = 20$, and $K = I$. The pose is initialized using the ground truth in the first frame for each sequence. The algorithms are run on a single CPU thread on Intel Core i7-4770 @ 3.4 GHz.

3.2   Qualitative Evaluation

The tracking methods are tested on two different real objects, namely the Stanford Bunny and a detergent bottle. The bunny is 3D-printed using the mesh model obtained from the Stanford 3D Scanning Repository [16]. Meanwhile, the detergent bottle is scanned using Microsoft Kinect V2 and *3D Scan* software. In the evaluation, we demonstrate our dynamic tracking with occlusions by nearby objects and by the hand holding the object. We have also tested the algorithms on two types of depth cameras: Intel RealSense SR300 that uses a structured-light sensor and Microsoft Kinect V2 that uses a time-of-flight (ToF) sensor.

4   Results and Discussion

4.1   The Trained Networks

Multiple Stages in the Training. All the networks, despite the randomized weight initializations, have evolved automatically through a few stages in a surprisingly systematic way. During the initial few thousands of iterations, the network would flatten the value of the output node to a very small value as it tries to satisfy the *SurfaceDistancePenalty* term in Eq. 1. As a side effect, all the gradient magnitudes in the whole volume would be almost close to zero. Most of the gradient errors in the *GradientPenalty* term will stay slightly below one as we expect all the gradients to have a magnitude of one. Next, the network will slowly shape the terrain to satisfy the *GradientPenalty* term while the surface points are already loosely nailed at the near zero output value.

Single Point Convergence. To verify that the SDF-Net and its gradient can be used to guide any point in the surrounding region towards the object surface, we try to reconstruct the surface using random points sampled from the region. Each point will get updated by $p := p - 0.01\,G(p) \cdot \text{sign}(D(p))$ iteratively until $D(p)$ passes a zero-crossing point. Then, the zero-crossing position is linearly interpolated from the two latest positions. The estimated zero-crossing points are collectively shown in Fig. 1. All the random points are able to converge on the surface in a virtually straight trajectory without being trapped in any local minimum. Refer to the interactive results in the supplementary materials [10].

Surface Smoothing Error. One inherent nature of the neural network is to smooth out noises in its training data. Thus, some small regions on the object surface may not be modelled accurately, especially protruding volumes such as the corner of a box or a deep concave surface that is too small. As they are small relative to the whole surface area, it should not largely affect the tracking.

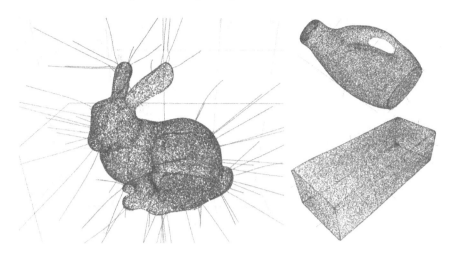

Fig. 1. Convergence of random points. Grey cloud: points on the actual model surface. Red cloud: points converged from random positions. Green lines: some examples of point travelling paths from a random position to the surface. 3D interactive interface of all trained network can be found in the supplementary repository [10]. (Color figure online)

4.2 Object Tracking

Quantitative Results. For the ICP-based method, we obtain the best average accuracy with a 0.85 mm translation error and a 0.27° orientation error with an average processing time of 5.11 ms. The accuracy is better than the LM-based method, which has average accuracies of 0.93 mm and 0.48° for translation and rotation errors respectively. However, the LM-based method runs at a faster rate of 1.29 ms. In terms of memory usage, our method requires the least memory footprint among the state-of-the-arts at 9 kB or lower if a smaller network is used.

Among the methods that can run at sub-degree accuracy with a real-time speed on CPU, most of them [1,28,29] are developed on a decision-forest-based regression method [27]. Some methods are learning-free [11,20] but developed on a well-established PWP3D method [18] which relies heavily on the colour data. Our new branch of methods has reached the similar level of accuracy and calculation time on one CPU core without relying on any decision forest or colour-based method. Refer to Table 1 for detailed results.

According to Table 1, the translation errors perpendicular to the optical axis (t_x and t_y) are 2–3 times larger than the translation errors along the depth axis (t_z) in our methods and in Tan et al.'s method [29]. However, the drifts (t_x and t_y) are minimized in Tan et al.'s later method [28] as they utilise colour to extract edge points, which constrain the whole model from sliding along the plane perpendicular to the optical axis; hence, the overall error is reduced significantly.

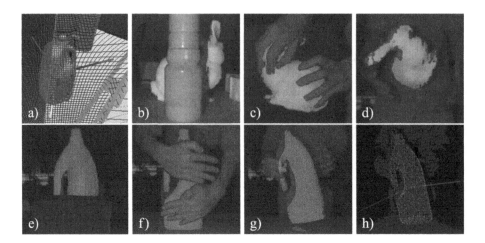

Fig. 2. (a) An example of fitting results from the dataset [5] with partial occlusion. (b–g) Examples of post-fitting segmentation of objects with occlusions; green and red regions represent pixels classified as object and non-object points respectively. (g–h) When the object is lifted abruptly, the tracking fails as the predicted pose $\hat{\theta}$ lags behind the actual observation, causing the failure in sampling some key features, e.g. the handle of the detergent, that are critical in determining the object pose. (Color figure online)

The comparison between the ICP-based and the LM-based methods is presented in Table 2. The LM-based method is found to take much lesser time when compared with the ICP-method. This is because of the fast convergence rate due to the low damping factor λ, which results in lower iteration count. In addition, a sparser classification interval k and a lower number of sampled points m are used. This configuration greatly reduces the computational time without compromising much accuracy.

Table 2 also compares the result from the small and the large neural network. As expected, network $\mathcal{B}$ with more memory capacity has a better overall accuracy but requires additional 20% of calculation time when compared with network $\mathcal{A}$.

In terms of memory footprint, our representation is the most compact, with 6 kB and 9 kB for the network $\mathcal{A}$ and $\mathcal{B}$ respectively. With this size, a discrete representation of SDF can only represent a crude model of the surface.

Qualitative Results. The results show that the object remains tracked even when more than half of it is occluded (Fig. 2b, f). Also, our methods are able to track the object when it is toppled and thrown (Fig. 2d). Videos of our tracking results can be found in the supplementary repository [10].

When the object is static, the fitted model generally shows slight jitter when the ICP-based method is used; this is less likely to be seen for the LM-based method. This is because the LM algorithm always verifies if a particular update

Table 1. Benchmark comparison of the RMS errors in translation (mm), orientation (degree) and the runtime (ms) on a synthetic dataset [5]. The required memory footprints used to store pre-calculated content are approximated. The results from our two methods, ICP-based and LM-based, are from the bigger network $\mathcal{B}$.

	Errors	PCL [24]	C&C [5]	Krull [14]	Tan'15 [29]	Kehl [11]	S.A [2]	Tan'17 [28]	Ours ICP	LM
Kinect box	t_x	43.99	1.84	0.83	1.54	0.76	0.30	0.15	1.27	1.12
	t_y	42.51	2.23	1.67	1.90	1.09	0.49	0.19	1.22	1.81
	t_z	55.89	1.36	0.79	0.34	0.38	0.31	0.09	0.50	0.56
	Roll	7.62	6.41	1.11	0.42	0.17	0.21	0.09	0.16	0.16
	Pitch	1.87	0.76	0.55	0.22	0.18	0.27	0.06	0.17	0.30
	Yaw	8.31	6.32	1.04	0.68	0.20	0.23	0.04	0.10	0.17
	Time	4539	166	143	1.5	8.10	1.71	2.2	5.62	1.37
Milk	t_x	13.38	0.93	0.51	1.23	0.64	0.63	0.09	0.98	1.01
	t_y	31.45	1.94	1.27	0.74	0.59	1.19	0.11	0.80	0.76
	t_z	26.09	1.09	0.62	0.24	0.24	0.48	0.08	0.32	0.36
	Roll	59.37	3.83	2.19	0.50	0.41	0.19	0.07	0.20	0.34
	Pitch	19.58	1.41	1.44	0.28	0.29	0.28	0.09	0.27	0.76
	Yaw	75.03	3.26	1.90	0.46	0.42	0.27	0.06	0.15	0.22
	Time	2205	134	135	1.5	8.54	1.70	2.1	4.99	1.26
Orange juice	t_x	2.53	0.96	0.52	1.10	0.50	0.39	0.11	1.12	1.15
	t_y	2.20	1.44	0.74	0.94	0.69	0.37	0.09	0.88	0.96
	t_z	1.91	1.17	0.63	0.18	0.17	0.37	0.09	0.67	0.67
	Roll	85.81	1.32	1.28	0.35	0.12	0.12	0.08	0.41	0.44
	Pitch	42.12	0.75	1.08	0.24	0.20	0.17	0.08	0.25	0.65
	Yaw	46.37	1.39	1.20	0.37	0.19	0.15	0.08	0.39	0.65
	Time	1637	117	129	1.5	8.79	1.69	2.2	4.79	1.25
Tide	t_x	1.46	0.83	0.69	0.73	0.34	0.42	0.08	0.99	1.01
	t_y	2.25	1.37	0.81	0.56	0.49	0.51	0.09	1.03	1.05
	t_z	0.92	1.20	0.81	0.24	0.18	0.64	0.07	0.28	0.30
	Roll	5.15	1.78	2.10	0.31	0.15	0.22	0.05	0.09	0.24
	Pitch	2.13	1.09	1.38	0.25	0.39	0.29	0.12	0.54	1.03
	Yaw	2.98	1.13	1.27	0.34	0.37	0.30	0.05	0.13	0.34
	Time	2762	111	116	1.5	9.42	1.70	2.2	5.04	1.30
Mean	Transl	18.72	1.36	0.82	0.81	0.51	0.50	0.10	0.85	0.93
	Rot.	29.70	2.45	1.38	0.37	0.26	0.22	0.07	0.27	0.48
	Time	2786	132	131	1.5	8.71	1.7	2.2	5.11	1.29
Requires	Memory	-	-	-	7.4 MB	10 MB	123 kB	13 MB	9 kB	
	GPU	-	✓	✓	-	-	-	-	-	
	Colour	✓	✓	✓	-	✓	-	✓	-	
	Depth	✓	✓	✓	✓	✓	✓	✓	✓	

Table 2. Comparison of our methods using two different networks on the synthetic dataset [5]. Note that the translation and orientation errors in this table are different from those in Table 1; we use the Euclidean distance and the angle difference between the estimated and the ground truth orientation to compute the errors as these measures are invariant under coordinate transformation.

Network	ICP-based method		LM-based method	
	$\mathcal{A}$ (smaller)	$\mathcal{B}$ (bigger)	$\mathcal{A}$ (smaller)	$\mathcal{B}$ (bigger)
Average translation error (mm)	1.62	1.49	1.70	1.55
Maximum translation error (mm)	15.75	4.82	10.02	8.27
Average orientation error (deg)	0.43	0.33	0.77	0.74
Maximum orientation error (deg)	3.59	3.06	6.80	4.30
Average number of iterations	13.84	12.89	2.32	2.05
Calculation time per frame (ms)	4.03	5.11	1.11	1.29

will lower the cost function (Eq. 8), making it tend to stay at its pose from the previous frame; this feature is not present in the ICP-based method.

The comparison between the tracking results on both short-ranged and long-ranged cameras shows that the latter generally yields sub-par performance. This is mainly due to a larger depth error at far distance together with the *multi-path effect* which only occurs in ToF camera.

After the fitting process is done in each frame, as a by-product, SDF-Net can be used to differentiate object and non-object pixels without the use of colour. Hands and fingers on the object are also segmented out (Fig. 2c, f). This feature could be useful in hand tracking applications with object interaction.

5   Conclusion and Future Work

We have shown that a deep neural network trained with our proposed method could be used to learn an approximation of an object SDF which is accurate enough for object tracking purpose. Our results have been shown to reach up to sub-millimeter and sub-degree accuracy when evaluated on a public dataset. The real-time capability of our rigid object tracking method has been demonstrated using depth data from commodity depth cameras and the algorithm could run on a single CPU thread.

As the proposed tracking method works by finding the transformation parameters between consecutive frames, the initial pose of the object must be provided. Also, in case of tracking loss, the object pose has to be reinitialized manually. Hence, initialization and detection of the object in real-time are to be investigated in the future.

References

1. Akkaladevi, S., Ankerl, M., Heindl, C., Pichler, A.: Tracking multiple rigid symmetric and non-symmetric objects in real-time using depth data. In: IEEE International Conference on Robotics and Automation, pp. 5644–5649 (2016). https://doi.org/10.1109/ICRA.2016.7487784
2. Akkaladevi, S.C., Ankerl, M., Fritz, G., Pichler, A.: Real-time tracking of rigid objects using depth data. In: Proceedings of OAGM&ARW Joint Workshop (2016). https://doi.org/10.3217/978-3-85125-528-7-14
3. Besl, P.J., McKay, N.D.: A method for registration of 3-D shapes. IEEE Trans. Pattern Anal. Mach. Intell. **14**(2), 239–256 (1992). https://doi.org/10.1109/34.121791
4. Canelhas, D.R., Stoyanov, T., Lilienthal, A.J.: SDF tracker: a parallel algorithm for on-line pose estimation and scene reconstruction from depth images. In: IEEE/RSJ International Conference on Intelligent Robots and Systems, pp. 3671–3676 (2013). https://doi.org/10.1109/IROS.2013.6696880
5. Choi, C., Christensen, H.I.: RGB-D object tracking: a particle filter approach on GPU. In: IEEE/RSJ International Conference on Intelligent Robots and Systems (2013). https://doi.org/10.1109/IROS.2013.6696485
6. Frisken, S.F.: Designing with distance fields. In: International Conference on Shape Modeling and Applications, pp. 58–59 (2005). https://doi.org/10.1109/SMI.2005.16
7. Garon, M., Lalonde, J.F.: Deep 6-DOF tracking. IEEE Trans. Vis. Comput. Graph. **23**(11), 2410–2418 (2017). https://doi.org/10.1109/TVCG.2017.2734599
8. Issac, J., Wthrich, M., Cifuentes, C.G., Bohg, J., Trimpe, S., Schaal, S.: Depth-based object tracking using a robust Gaussian filter. In: 2016 IEEE International Conference on Robotics and Automation (2016). https://doi.org/10.1109/ICRA.2016.7487184
9. Jabarouti Moghaddam, M., Soltanian-Zadeh, H.: Automatic segmentation of brain structures using geometric moment invariants and artificial neural networks. In: Prince, J.L., Pham, D.L., Myers, K.J. (eds.) IPMI 2009. LNCS, vol. 5636, pp. 326–337. Springer, Heidelberg (2009). https://doi.org/10.1007/978-3-642-02498-6_27
10. Jatesiktat, P., Foo, M.J., Lim, G.M.: SDF-Net: Supplementary materials repository. https://koonyook.github.io/SDF-Net-materials/
11. Kehl, W., Tombari, F., Ilic, S., Navab, N.: Real-time 3D model tracking in color and depth on a single CPU core. In: IEEE Conference on Computer Vision and Pattern Recognition, pp. 465–473 (2017). https://doi.org/10.1109/CVPR.2017.57
12. Kehl, W., Navab, N., Ilic, S.: Coloured signed distance fields for full 3D object reconstruction. In: Proceedings of the British Machine Vision Conference (2014). https://doi.org/10.5244/C.28.41
13. Kingma, D.P., Ba, J.: Adam: a method for stochastic optimization. Computing Research Repository abs/1412.6980 (2014). http://arxiv.org/abs/1412.6980
14. Krull, A., Michel, F., Brachmann, E., Gumhold, S., Ihrke, S., Rother, C.: 6-DOF model based tracking via object coordinate regression. In: Cremers, D., Reid, I., Saito, H., Yang, M.-H. (eds.) ACCV 2014. LNCS, vol. 9006, pp. 384–399. Springer, Cham (2015). https://doi.org/10.1007/978-3-319-16817-3_25
15. Lepetit, V., Fua, P.: Monocular model-based 3D tracking of rigid objects. Found. Trends. Comput. Graph. Vis. **1**(1), 1–89 (2005). https://doi.org/10.1561/0600000001

16. Levoy, M.: The Stanford 3D scanning repository. http://graphics.stanford.edu/data/3Dscanrep/
17. Lu, G., Ren, L., Kolagunda, A., Wang, X., Turkbey, I.B., Choyke, P.L., Kambhamettu, C.: Representing 3D shapes based on implicit surface functions learned from RBF neural networks. J. Vis. Commun. Image Represent. **40**, 852–860 (2016). https://doi.org/10.1016/j.jvcir.2016.08.014
18. Prisacariu, V., Reid, I.: PWP3D: real-time segmentation and tracking of 3D objects. Int. J. of Comput. Vis. **98**, 1–20 (2012). https://doi.org/10.1007/s11263-011-0514-3
19. Ren, C.Y., Prisacariu, V., Murray, D., Reid, I.: STAR3D: simultaneous tracking and reconstruction of 3D objects using RGB-D data. In: IEEE International Conference on Computer Vision, pp. 1561–1568 (2013). https://doi.org/10.1109/ICCV.2013.197
20. Ren, C.Y., Prisacariu, V.A., Kähler, O., Reid, I.D., Murray, D.W.: Real-time tracking of single and multiple objects from depth-colour imagery using 3D signed distance functions. Int. J. Comput. Vis. **124**(1), 80–95 (2017). https://doi.org/10.1007/s11263-016-0978-2
21. Rouhani, M., Sappa, A.D.: Correspondence free registration through a point-to-model distance minimization. In: International Conference on Computer Vision, pp. 2150–2157 (2011). https://doi.org/10.1109/ICCV.2011.6126491
22. Rouhani, M., Sappa, A.D.: The richer representation the better registration. IEEE Trans. Image Process. **22**(12), 5036–5049 (2013). https://doi.org/10.1109/TIP.2013.2281427
23. Rusinkiewicz, S., Levoy, M.: Efficient variants of the ICP algorithm. In: Proceedings of the Third International Conference on 3-D Digital Imaging and Modeling, pp. 145–152 (2001). https://doi.org/10.1109/IM.2001.924423
24. Rusu, R.B., Cousins, S.: 3D is here: point cloud library (PCL). In: IEEE International Conference on Robotics and Automation, pp. 1–4 (2011). https://doi.org/10.1109/ICRA.2011.5980567
25. Slavcheva, M., Kehl, W., Navab, N., Ilic, S.: SDF-2-SDF: highly accurate 3D object reconstruction. In: Leibe, B., Matas, J., Sebe, N., Welling, M. (eds.) ECCV 2016. LNCS, vol. 9905, pp. 680–696. Springer, Cham (2016). https://doi.org/10.1007/978-3-319-46448-0_41
26. Somani, N., Cai, C., Perzylo, A., Rickert, M., Knoll, A.: Object recognition using constraints from primitive shape matching. In: Bebis, G., et al. (eds.) ISVC 2014. LNCS, vol. 8887, pp. 783–792. Springer, Cham (2014). https://doi.org/10.1007/978-3-319-14249-4_75
27. Tan, D.J., Ilic, S.: Multi-forest tracker: a chameleon in tracking. In: IEEE Conference on Computer Vision and Pattern Recognition, pp. 1202–1209 (2014). https://doi.org/10.1109/CVPR.2014.157
28. Tan, D.J., Navab, N., Tombari, F.: Looking beyond the simple scenarios: combining learners and optimizers in 3D temporal tracking. IEEE Trans. Vis. Comput. Graph. **23**(11), 2399–2409 (2017). https://doi.org/10.1109/TVCG.2017.2734539
29. Tan, D.J., Tombari, F., Ilic, S., Navab, N.: A versatile learning-based 3D temporal tracker: scalable, robust, online. In: IEEE International Conference on Computer Vision (2015). https://doi.org/10.1109/ICCV.2015.86
30. Zhang, Z.: On local matching of free-form curves. In: Hogg, D., Boyle, R. (eds.) BMVC 1992, pp. 347–356. Springer, London (1992). https://doi.org/10.1007/978-1-4471-3201-1_36

Insider Threat Detection with Deep Neural Network

Fangfang Yuan[1,2,3], Yanan Cao[1,3], Yanmin Shang[1,3],
Yanbing Liu[1,3(✉)], Jianlong Tan[1,3], and Binxing Fang[4]

[1] Institute of Information Engineering,
Chinese Academy of Sciences, Beijing, China
{yuanfangfang, caoyanan, shangyanmin,
liuyanbing, tanjianlong}@iie.ac.cn
[2] School of Cyber Security, University of Chinese Academy of Sciences,
Beijing, China
[3] National Engineering Laboratory for Information Security Technologies,
Beijing, China
[4] Institute of Electronic and Information Engineering of UESTC in Guangdong,
Dongguan, Guangdong, China
fangbx@cae.cn

Abstract. Insider threat detection has attracted a considerable attention from the researchers and industries. Existing work mainly focused on applying machine-learning techniques to detecting insider threat. However, this work requires "feature engineering" which is difficult and time-consuming. As we know, the deep learning technique can automatically learn powerful features. In this paper, we present a novel insider threat detection method with Deep Neural Network (DNN) based on user behavior. Specifically, we use the LSTM-CNN framework to find user's anomalous behavior. First, similar to natural language modeling, we use the Long Short Term Memory (LSTM) to learn the language of user behavior through user actions and extract abstracted temporal features. Second, the extracted features are converted to the fixed-size feature matrices and the Convolutional Neural Network (CNN) use these fixed-size feature matrices to detect insider threat. We conduct experiments on a public dataset of insider threats. Experimental results show that our method can successfully detect insider threat and we obtained AUC = 0.9449 in best case.

Keywords: Insider threat · Anomaly detection · Deep learning
Network security

1 Introduction

Insider threat is becoming a serious security challenge for many organizations. It is generally defined as malicious actions performed by an insider in a secure environment, often causing system sabotage, electronic fraud and information theft. Hence, it is potentially harmful to individuals, organizations and state security. Recently, insider threat detection has attracted considerable attention in both academic and industrial community.

© Springer International Publishing AG, part of Springer Nature 2018
Y. Shi et al. (Eds.): ICCS 2018, LNCS 10860, pp. 43–54, 2018.
https://doi.org/10.1007/978-3-319-93698-7_4

Insider threat detection becomes an extremely complex and challenging task. The reasons are as follows. First, insiders do unauthorized things by the use of their trusted access. Hence, external network security devices (intrusion detection, firewalls, and anti-virus) cannot detect them. Second, insider attack manifests in various forms, such as a disgruntled employee planting a logic bomb to disrupt systems, stealing intellectual property for personal gain, etc. The diversity of insider attack increases the complexity of insider threat detection. The last but not the least, insider threat often performed by insiders during working hours, causing insider's anomalous behaviors scattered in large amounts of normal working behaviors. Therefore, it increases the difficulty of insider threat detection.

The key of insider threat detection is to model a user's normal behavior to detect anomalous behavior. Much work has been proposed to address the issue [1, 2]. They aggregate all the actions of a user in one day to represent the user's behavior in the same day. However, the anomalous behavior happening within one day may be missed. For example, a user logs on to his assigned computer after hours and uploads data to wikileaks.org. We argue that using user action sequences for each user is very important in detecting insider threat.

To address this problem, we propose a novel insider threat detection method to detect whether user behavior is normal or anomalous. Specifically, it is not efficient that we directly use the LSTM to classify the user action sequence, because the output of the LSTM only contains a single bit of information for every sequence. Instead, we use the trained LSTM to predict next user action, and use a series of hidden states of the LSTM model to generate a fixed-size feature matrix that is given to the CNN classifier. The LSTM can better capture the long term temporal dependencies on user action sequence, because hidden units of the LSTM potentially record temporal behavior patterns.

To summarize, in this paper, we make the following contributions:

(1) We present a novel insider threat detection method with LSTM and CNN based on user behavior.
(2) We use the LSTM to learn the language of user behavior through user actions and extract abstracted temporal features which are the input of the CNN classifier.
(3) Experimental results on a public dataset of insider threats show that our proposal can successfully detect insider threat and we obtained AUC = 0.9449 in best case.

The rest of this paper is organized as follows. We summarize the related work in Sect. 2, and give a detailed description of our insider threat detection method in Sect. 3. Implementation details and experimental results for this work are shown in Sect. 4. Finally, we conclude the paper's work in Sect. 5.

2 Related Work

Related work falls into two main categories, insider threat detection and deep neural network.

Insider Threat Detection: The problem of insider threat detection is usually framed as an anomaly detection task. A comprehensive and structured overview of anomaly detection techniques was provided by Chandola et al. [3]. They defined that the purpose of anomaly detection is finding patterns in data which did not conform to the expected behavior. The key problem of anomaly detection is how to model a user's normal behavior profile. A lot of research work has been proposed to develop anomaly detection, especially machine learning.

Early work on anomaly detection based on user command proposed by Davison and Hirsh [4] and Lane and Brodley [5]. They examine user command sequences and compute the match degree of a current command pattern with the historical command pattern to classify user behavior as normal or anomalous.

After that, anomaly detection begins to take advantage of machine learning techniques, such as Naive Bayes [6], Eigen Co-occurrence Matrix (ECM) [7], One-Class Support Vector Machine (OC-SVM) [8] and Hidden Markov [9]. Schonlau et al. compared the performance of six masquerade-detection algorithms on the data set of "truncated" UNIX shell commands for 70 users and experimental results revealed that no single method completely dominated any other. Maxion and Townsend [6] applied the Naive Bayes classifier to the same data set [17], inspired by Naive Bayes text classification. They also provided a thorough and detailed investigation of classification errors of the classifier in [18]. Oka et al. [7] argued that the causal relationship embedded in sequences of events should be considered when modeling a user's profile. They developed the layered networks approach based on the Eigen Co-occurrence Matrix (ECM) and extracted the causal relationships embedded in sequences of commands to supplement user behavior model. Salem et al. [19] evaluated the accuracy performance of the nine methods mentioned above using the Schonlau dataset, but the results revealed that their detection rates were not high. Szymanski and Zhang [8] used an OC-SVM classifier for insider threat detection. However, the approach needed mixing user data and it was hard to implement in a real-world setting. Rashid et al. [9] proposed an approach to insider threat detection by the use of Hidden Markov. They used Hidden Markov to model user's normal behavior via user actions and regarded deviations from the normal behavior as anomalous behavior. The effectiveness of the method is highly impacted by the number of the states. However, the computational cost of the Hidden Markov model increases as the number of states increases.

The works mentioned above make use of machine learning techniques to build a classifier. On one hand, machine learning requires "feature engineering" which is time-consuming and difficult. On the other hand, the classifier is too simple, resulting in a low detection rate.

Deep Neural Network: Recently, deep neural network that can automatically learn powerful features has led to new ideas for anomaly detection. Tang et al. [10] applied the deep learning methodology to build up an anomaly detection system, but the experimental results in the testing phase were not good enough. Veeramachananeni et al. [11] used a neural network auto-encoder to detect insider threat. They aggregated a number of numeric features over a time window and fed these features to an ensemble of anomaly detection methods: Principal Component Analysis, neural networks, and a probabilistic model. However, individual user activity was not explicitly modeled over time. Tuor et al. [2] proposed a deep learning approach to detect anomalous network activity from system logs. They trained Recurrent Neural Networks (RNNs) to recognize characteristic of each user on a network and concurrently assessed whether user behavior is normal or anomalous. While this method aggregates features over one day for individual users, it is possible to miss anomalous behavior happening within one day. Instead, our model is trained using user action sequences with DNN. The actions that a user takes over a period of time on a system can be modeled as a sequence. The action sequences of user's normal behavior are seen often or on a usual basis. Observed action sequences deviated from those normal action sequences are regarded as anomalous behavior. Therefore, our model can detect anomalous behavior through user actions and even can detect anomalous behavior happening within one day.

3   Proposed Method

In this section, we introduce the details of our insider threat detection method. The proposal applies DNN in two stages. The first stage extracts the abstracted temporal features of user behavior by the LSTM and outputs feature vectors. Then the feature vectors are transformed into fixed-size feature matrices. In the second stage, these fixed-size feature matrices are fed to the CNN to classify them as normal or anomaly.

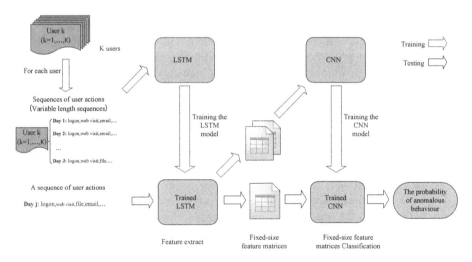

Fig. 1. Overview of proposed method

3.1   Overview

The overview of our insider threat detection method is shown in Fig. 1. The individual action (e.g., logging onto an assigned computer afterhours) represents the operation of a user; actions taken by a user in one day represent user behavior. Similar to natural language modeling, an action is corresponding to a word and an action sequence is corresponding to a sentence. For that reason, we attempt to learn the language of user behavior as a new method for detecting insider threat. The LSTM is used to extract the features of user behavior. The CNN uses these features to find anomalous behavior.

Let $U = \{u_1, u_2, \cdots, u_K\}$ be the set of K users. For a user $u_k (1 \leq k \leq K)$, we can obtain his action sequences over J days, $\mathbf{S} = \left[\mathbf{s}_{u_{k,1}}, \mathbf{s}_{u_{k,2}}, \cdots, \mathbf{s}_{u_{k,J}}\right]$, where $\mathbf{s}_{u_{k,j}} (1 \leq j \leq J)$ is a vector which denotes the action sequence on the day indexed by j. In the training phase, we first obtain an action sequence $\mathbf{s}_{u_{k,j}}$ that user u_k has performed within the day indexed by j. Second, the action sequence $\mathbf{s}_{u_{k,j}}$ is then fed into the LSTM and the LSTM is trained to construct a feature extractor to obtain the abstracted feature vectors in the deep layer. Third, the feature vectors are transformed into a fixed-size matrix $\mathbf{M}^{u_{k,j}}$. The fixed-size feature matrix potentially contains various abstracted temporal features that represent user behavior. Finally, we use these fixed-size matrices annotated with normal or anomalous to train the CNN. In the testing phase, we evaluate the approach with the trained LSTM and the trained CNN. The detail of each step is described in the following subsections.

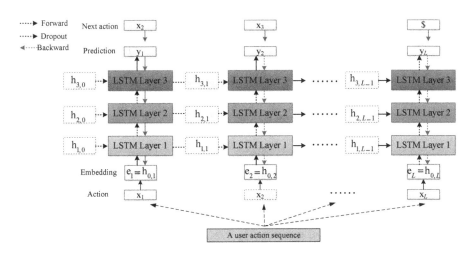

Fig. 2. Flow of LSTM training

3.2 Training LSTM for Feature Extraction

Based on the user action sequences, we construct a feature extractor which can automatically extract abstracted temporal features from each input action sequence. The LSTM consists of an input layer, an embedding layer, three LSTM layers, and an output layer. The flow of the LSTM is shown in Fig. 2.

For user u_k on the day indexed by j, let T be the length of the action sequence, $\mathbf{s}_{u_{k,j}} = \left[\mathbf{x}_1^{u_{k,j}}, \mathbf{x}_2^{u_{k,j}}, \cdots, \mathbf{x}_T^{u_{k,j}}\right]$. $\mathbf{x}_t^{u_{k,j}} (1 \leq t \leq T)$ represents an individual action at time instance t. $\mathbf{h}_{l,t}^{u_{k,j}} (0 \leq l \leq 3, 1 \leq t \leq T)$ denotes the hidden state of hidden layer l at time instance t. $\mathbf{y}_t^{u_{k,j}} (1 \leq t \leq T)$ denotes the output at time instance t. Here we use one-hot encoding to embed the input $\mathbf{x}_t^{u_{k,j}}$ as a vector $\mathbf{e}_t^{u_{k,j}}(1 \leq t \leq T)$. The one-hot encoding is performed as follows:

1. Creating a dictionary in which IDs and actions are associated with each other, such as logging on an assigned PC after hours is denoted as 1, logging off an assigned PC after hours is denoted as 2, etc.
2. Converting actions to one-hot vectors, which is 1 at the action ID position, and 0 elsewhere.

The LSTM with three hidden layers ($l = 1, 2, 3$) is described by the following equations:

$$\mathbf{i}_{l,t}^{u_{k,j}} = \sigma\left(\mathbf{W}_l^{(i,x)}\mathbf{h}_{l-1,t}^{u_{k,j}} + \mathbf{W}_l^{(i,h)}\mathbf{h}_{l,t-1}^{u_{k,j}} + \mathbf{b}_l^i\right) \tag{1}$$

$$\mathbf{f}_{l,t}^{u_{k,j}} = \sigma\left(\mathbf{W}_l^{(f,x)}\mathbf{h}_{l-1,t}^{u_{k,j}} + \mathbf{W}_l^{(f,h)}\mathbf{h}_{l,t-1}^{u_{k,j}} + \mathbf{b}_l^f\right) \tag{2}$$

$$\mathbf{o}_{l,t}^{u_{k,j}} = \sigma\left(\mathbf{W}_l^{(o,x)}\mathbf{h}_{l-1,t}^{u_{k,j}} + \mathbf{W}_l^{(o,h)}\mathbf{h}_{l,t-1}^{u_{k,j}} + \mathbf{b}_l^o\right) \tag{3}$$

$$\mathbf{g}_{l,t}^{u_{k,j}} = \tanh\left(\mathbf{W}_l^{(g,x)}\mathbf{h}_{l-1,t}^{u_{k,j}} + \mathbf{W}_l^{(g,h)}\mathbf{h}_{l,t-1}^{u_{k,j}} + \mathbf{b}_l^g\right) \tag{4}$$

$$\mathbf{c}_{l,t}^{u_{k,j}} = \mathbf{f}_{l,t}^{u_{k,j}} \odot \mathbf{c}_{l,t-1}^{u_{k,j}} + \mathbf{i}_{l,t}^{u_{k,j}} \odot \mathbf{g}_{l,t}^{u_{k,j}} \tag{5}$$

$$\mathbf{h}_{l,t}^{u_{k,j}} = \mathbf{o}_{l,t}^{u_{k,j}} \odot \tanh\left(\mathbf{c}_{l,t}^{u_{k,j}}\right) \tag{6}$$

Where $\mathbf{h}_{0,t}^{u_{k,j}} = \mathbf{e}_t^{u_{k,j}}$, and $\mathbf{c}_{l,0}^{u_{k,j}}$, $\mathbf{h}_{l,0}^{u_{k,j}}$ are set to zero vector for all $1 \leq l \leq 3$. $\sigma(\cdot)$ is the sigmoid function and $\odot$ denotes element-wise multiplication. Vector $\mathbf{g}_{l,t}^{u_{k,j}}$ is a hidden representation, vector $\mathbf{i}_{l,t}^{u_{k,j}}$ decides which values to update, vector $\mathbf{f}_{l,t}^{u_{k,j}}$ decides which things to forget, vector $\mathbf{o}_{l,t}^{u_{k,j}}$ decides what to be outputted. 24 weight matrices ($\mathbf{W}$) and 12 bias vectors ($\mathbf{b}$) are learned parameters.

The LSTM is repeatedly trained using user action sequences. First, we take an input series of user u_k as a vector $\mathbf{A}^{u_{k,j}} = \left[\mathbf{x}_1^{u_{k,j}}, \mathbf{x}_2^{u_{k,j}}, \cdots, \mathbf{x}_T^{u_{k,j}}\right]$. Second, the embedding layer converts the series of actions $\mathbf{A}^{u_{k,j}}$ to one-hot vectors $\mathbf{E}^{u_{k,j}} = \left[\mathbf{e}_1^{u_{k,j}}, \mathbf{e}_2^{u_{k,j}}, \cdots, \mathbf{e}_T^{u_{k,j}}\right]$. Third, we sequentially input each one-hot vector $\mathbf{e}_t^{u_{k,j}}$ to the LSTM and the LSTM outputs prediction $\mathbf{y}_t^{u_{k,j}}$. Finally, we calculate the cross-entropy loss function by comparing prediction $\mathbf{y}_t^{u_{k,j}}$ with answer $\mathbf{x}_{t+1}^{u_{k,j}}$.

In training phase, we apply Dropout [12] to the LSTM in a way that can reduce overfitting. The dropout operator is only applied to the non-recurrent connections. One epoch means that all training user action sequences are inputted to the LSTM. The order of user action sequences is randomized in every epoch. The LSTM training is executed for multiple epochs. After training, we obtain the trained feature extractor. Then we extract the hidden state of the last hidden layer (the third layer in Fig. 2) for every input and obtain a series of feature vectors $\mathbf{H}^{u_{k,j}} = \left[\mathbf{h}_{3,1}^{u_{k,j}}, \mathbf{h}_{3,2}^{u_{k,j}}, \cdots, \mathbf{h}_{3,T}^{u_{k,j}}\right]$.

3.3 Fixed-Size Feature Representations

As the designed classifier accepts fixed-size representations and the number of actions differs between user action sequences, we need to construct a fixed-size feature matrix for the series of feature vectors which is provided as input of the CNN.

To deal with this, we decided on a maximal length N^{u_k} and a minimal length n^{u_k} for any action sequence for user u_k. We ignore all sequences whose length are shorter than n^{u_k}. For all sequences with more than N^{u_k} steps, we keep only the first N^{u_k} actions. For all sequences whose length T is between n^{u_k} and N^{u_k}, we pad them with zeros until their lengths reach N^{u_k}. By this way, we can convert the series of feature vectors $\mathbf{H}^{u_{k,j}} = \left[\mathbf{h}_{3,1}^{u_{k,j}}, \mathbf{h}_{3,2}^{u_{k,j}}, \cdots, \mathbf{h}_{3,T}^{u_{k,j}}\right]$ into a fixed-size feature matrix $\mathbf{M}^{u_{k,j}}$ of dimensions $N^{u_k} \times V^{u_k}$, where V^{u_k} is the dimension of the last hidden layer. We map each element of $\mathbf{M}^{u_{k,j}}$ to the [0,1] space by sigmoid function. Finally, we obtain the fixed-size feature matrix $\mathbf{M}^{u_{k,j}}$ of dimensions $N^{u_k} \times V^{u_k}$.

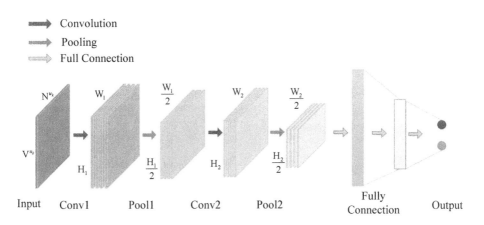

Fig. 3. Structure of the CNN

3.4 Training CNN for Detecting Insider Threat

The final component of our approach is the classification stage. We use the CNN to classify the fixed-size feature matrices of user behavior into normal behavior and anomalous behavior. The CNN consists of an input layer, two convolution-pooling layers, a fully-connected layer, and an output layer. For user u_k, the dimension of the input layer is $N^{u_k} \times V^{u_k}$ and the dimension of the output layer is two. Figure 3 shows the structure of the CNN.

We first train the CNN by using fixed-size feature matrices annotated with normal or anomaly. Also the softmax function is applied to the output of the CNN. After training, we use the trained CNN to calculate anomalous probability of a user action sequence.

Table 1. Enumeration of user actions

Time	Computer	Activities	ID	Action	Description
In hour Action (8am and 5pm) or After hour Action (5pm and 8am)	On an assigned PC or an unassigned PC	Logon/Logoff activity	1	Logon	User logged on a computer
			2	Logoff	User logged on a computer
		File activity	3	Copy exe file	A exe file copy to a removable media device
			4	Copy doc file	A doc file copy to a removable media device
			5	Copy pdf file	A pdf file copy to a removable media device
			6	Copy txt file	A txt file copy to a removable media device
			7	Copy jpg file	A jpg file copy to a removable media device
			8	Copy zip file	A zip file copy to a removable media device
		HTTP activity	9	Neutral website	User visited a neutral website
			10	Hacktivist website	User visited a hacktivist website
			11	CloudStorage website	User visited a cloudstorage website
			12	JobHunting website	User visited a jobhunting website
		Email activity	13	Internal email	All recipients are company email addresses
			14	External email	There is an external address
		Device activity	15	Connect	User inserted a removable media device
			16	Disconnect	User removed a removable media device

4 Experiments

This section reports the experimental validation of the proposed method. We apply our method to the CMU-CERT insider threat dataset [13], which provides a synthetic dataset describing a user's computer based activity. The dataset consists of information on several different activities over a period of 17 months. Next, we first describe details of the dataset and evaluation method. Then we present the experimental results of our approach.

4.1 Dataset

We perform experiments on the CERT insider threat dataset V4.2, because it contains more instances of insider threats compared to the other version of datasets. The dataset captures the 17 months of activity logs of the 1000 users (with 70 insiders) in an organization, which consists of five different types of activities: logon/logoff, email, device, file and http. Each log line is parsed to obtain details like a timestamp, user ID, PC ID, action details etc. We choose a comprehensive set of 64 actions over the five types of activities and build 1000 user specific profiles based on user action sequences. An example of a user action is visiting a job-hunting website between the hours of 8:00 am and 5:00 pm on an assigned computer. The enumeration of user actions is listed in Table 1.

Over the course of 17 months, 1000 users generate 32,770,227 log lines. Among these are 7323 anomalous activity instances manually injected by domain expert, representing three insider threat scenarios taking place.

We split the dataset into two subsets: training and testing. The former subset ($\sim 70\%$ of the data) is used for model selection and hyper-parameter tuning. The latter subset ($\sim 30\%$ of the data) is used for evaluating the performance of the model. Our classifications are made at the granularity of user-day. One note is that we removed the weekends of the data when we classify at the granularity of user-day, because the user behavior is qualitatively different for weekdays and weekends.

Table 2. Parameters of the LSTM

Model	Dimension of three hidden layers	Mini-batch size	Epoch num
LSTM1	60	20	10
LSTM2	40	20	10
LSTM3	20	20	10

Table 3. Parameters of the CNN

Model	Conv1	Conv2	Activate function	Mini-batch size	Epoch num
CNN1	32(4)	64(4)	tanh	20	500
CNN2	32(5)	64(5)	tanh	20	500
CNN3	32(6)	64(6)	tanh	20	500
CNN4	32(4)	64(4)	relu	20	500

4.2 Evaluation Method

The dataset used for experiment is unbalanced, so we choose the Receiver Operating Characteristics Curves (ROC) and Area-Under-Curve (AUC) measure for evaluating the proposed method. On one hand, we can visualize the relation between TPR and FPR of a classifier. On the other hand, the accuracy with two or more classifiers can be compared.

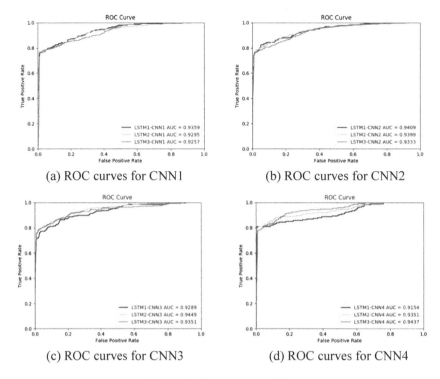

(a) ROC curves for CNN1   (b) ROC curves for CNN2

(c) ROC curves for CNN3   (d) ROC curves for CNN4

Fig. 4. ROC curves for CNNs

4.3   Results

To compare the performance of the model with different parameters, we train our model with several parameters. When setting the parameters of the LSTM, we refer the setting of [14] which uses the LSTM in language modeling. In addition, the LSTM is trained using the ADAM [15] variant of gradient descent. The parameter settings of the LSTM are shown in Table 2.

The parameters of the CNN were set by referring the setting of LeNet [16], which is used for recognizing hand written digit. Let a(b) denotes the number of filters (the shape of each filter) per convolutional layer. Max-pooling reduces the size of the input into 1/2 with stride of 2. The parameter settings of the CNN are shown in Table 3.

We evaluated the ROC curves for each of these CNNs, and later we compare the best performing CNN against the logistic regression classifier-based architectures (see Fig. 5). Figure 4(a), (b), (c) and (d) show the ROC curves when CNN1, CNN2, CNN3 and CNN4, respectively, are used for classification. We can see that the different parameter settings differ only slightly. The performance of relu activation function is similar to the tanh activation function, using the same parameter settings. The LSTM2 with CNN3 provides better result than the other CNNs and gets the best result AUC = 0.9449.

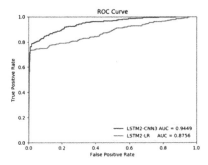

Fig. 5. ROC curves for CNN3 and logistic regression

Figure 5 compares the ROC curves of the best performing CNN3 plus the logistic regression classifier-based architectures. The ROC results for the CNN classifier based architectures are better than the Logistic Regression version with the same language model (LSTM2).

5   Conclusion

In this paper, we proposed the insider threat detection method with deep neural network. Because insider threat manifest in various forms, it is not practical to explicitly model it. We frame insider threat detection as an anomaly detection task and use anomalous behavior of a user as indicative of insider threat. The LSTM extracts user behavior features from sequences of user actions and generates fixed-size feature matrices. The CNN classifies fixed-size feature matrices as normal or anomaly. We evaluated the proposed method using the CERT Insider Threat dataset V4.2. Experimental results show that our method can successfully detect insider threat and we obtained AUC = 0.9449 in best case.

Acknowledgement. This work was partly supported by the National Key R&D Program of China under Grant No. 2016YFB0800300, Xinjiang Uygur Autonomous Region Science and Technology Project under Grant No. 2016A030007-4, the National Natural Science Foundation of China under grant No. 61602466.

References

1. Gavai, G., Sricharan, K., Gunning, D., Hanley, J., Singhal, M., Rolleston, R.: Supervised and unsupervised methods to detect insider threat from enterprise social and online activity data. JoWUA 6(4), 47–63 (2015)
2. Tuor, A., Kaplan, S., Hutchinson, B., Nichols, N., Robinson, S.: Deep learning for unsupervised insider threat detection in structured cybersecurity data streams. arXiv preprint arXiv:1710.00811(2017)
3. Chandola, V., Banerjee, A., Kumar, V.: Anomaly detection: a survey. ACM Comput. Surv. (CSUR) 41(3), 1–58 (2009)

4. Davison, B.D., Hirsh, H.: Predicting sequences of user actions. In: AAAI/ICML 1998 Workshop on Predicting the Future: AI Approaches to Time-Series Analysis, pp. 5–12 (1998)

5. Lane, T., Brodley, C.E.: Sequence matching and learning in anomaly detection for computer security. In: AAAI Workshop: AI Approaches to Fraud Detection and Risk Management, pp. 43–49 (1997)

6. Maxion, R.A., Townsend,T.N.: Masquerade detection using truncated command lines. In: DSN 2002 Proceedings of the 2002 International Conference on Dependable Systems and Networks, pp. 219–228 (2002)

7. Oka, M., Oyama, Y., Kato, K.: Eigen co-occurrence matrix method for masquerade detection. Publications of the Japan Society for Software Science and Technology(2004)

8. Szymanski, B.K., Zhang, Y.: Recursive data mining for masquerade detection and author identification. In: Information Assurance Workshop, pp. 424–431 (2004)

9. Rashid, T., Agrafiotis, I., Nurse, J.R.: A new take on detecting insider threats: exploring the use of hidden markov models. In: Proceedings of the 2016 International Workshop on Managing Insider Security Threats, pp. 47–56 (2016)

10. Tang, T.A., Mhamdi, L., McLernon, D., Zaidi, S.A.R., Ghogho, M.: Deep learning approach for network intrusion detection in software defined networking. In: Wireless Networks and Mobile Communications (WINCOM), pp. 258–263 (2016)

11. Veeramachaneni, K., Arnaldo, I., Korrapati, V., Bassias, C., Li, K.: AI2: training a big data machine to defend. In: IEEE International Conference on Big Data Security on Cloud HPSC, and IEEE International Conference on IDS, pp. 49–54 (2016)

12. Hinton, G.E., Srivastava, N., Krizhevsky, A., Sutskever, I., Salakhutdinov, R.R.: Improving neural networks by preventing co-adaptation of feature detectors. arXiv preprint arXiv:1207. 0580 (2012)

13. Glasser, J., Lindauer, B.: Bridging the gap: a pragmatic approach to generating insider threat data. In: Security and Privacy Workshops (SPW), pp. 98–104 (2013)

14. Zaremba, W., Sutskever, I., Vinyals, O.: Recurrent neural network regularization. arXiv preprint arXiv:1409.2329 (2014)

15. Kingma, D., Ba, J.: Adam: a method for stochastic optimization. arXiv preprint arXiv:1412. 6980 (2014)

16. Theano Development Team, "Convolutional Neural Networks (LeNet)". http://deeplearning. net/tutorial/lenet.html

17. Maxion, R.A., Townsend, T.N.: Masquerade detection using truncated command lines. In: International Conference on Dependable Systems and Networks, pp. 219–228 (2002)

18. Maxion, R.A., Townsend, T.N.: Masquerade detection augmented with error analysis. IEEE Trans. Reliab. **53**(1), 124–147 (2004)

19. Salem, M.B., Hershkop, S., Stolfo, S.J.: A survey of insider attack detection research. In: Insider Attack and Cyber Security, pp. 69–90 (2008)

Pheromone Model Based Visualization of Malware Distribution Networks

Yang Cai[✉], Jose Andre Morales, Sihan Wang, Pedro Pimentel, William Casey, and Aaron Volkmann

Carnegie Mellon University, 5000 Forbes Ave., Pittsburgh, PA 15213, USA
ycai@cmu.edu

Abstract. We present a novel computational pheromone model for describing dynamic network behaviors in terms of transition, persistency, and hosting. The model consists of a three-dimensional force-directed graph with bi-directional pheromone deposit and decay paths. A data compression algorithm is developed to optimize computational performance. We applied the model for visual analysis of a Malware Distribution Network (MDN), a connected set of maliciously compromised domains used to disseminate malicious software to victimize computers and users. The MDN graphs are extracted from datasets from Google Safe Browsing (GSB) reports with malware attributions from VirusTotal. Our research shows that this novel approach reveals patterns of topological changes of the network over time, including the existence of persistent sub-networks and individual top-level domains critical to the successful operation of MDNs, as well as the dynamics of the topological changes on a daily basis. From the visualization, we observed notable clustering effects, and also noticed life span patterns for high-edge-count malware distribution clusters.

Keywords: Pheromone · Visualization
Malware · Malware distribution network · Force-directed graph
Biologically-inspired computing · Security · Dynamics · 3D graph · Graph

1 Introduction

Pheromones in nature are chemical messages that act within a species. They are used widely by insects for communication within a community and within the body by means of hormones. This usage led to these substances also being referred to as "social hormones" [16]. Pheromones are external memories that are physically projected onto the ground or into the air, and are shared within a group. The dynamics of depositing and vaporizing pheromones are very sophisticated processes. These chemical messages have diverse biological effects and differ widely in their modes of action. In practice, the term "pheromone" proves useful in describing behaviors such as trail formation, defensive secretions, and social coherence. For the past several decades, several computational pheromone models have been proposed such as the classic ant colony optimization model [18] and a contemporary online shopping cart product recommendation model patented by Amazon [20]. Pheromone models have been used in visualization of

© Springer International Publishing AG, part of Springer Nature 2018
Y. Shi et al. (Eds.): ICCS 2018, LNCS 10860, pp. 55–68, 2018.
https://doi.org/10.1007/978-3-319-93698-7_5

human activities in CCTV footages, social media, and digital forensics [17, 19]. Digital pheromone models not only represent simultaneous localization, navigation, and optimization, but also provide perceptual motion intelligence simulations such as low-pass filters and visual episodic memory. Consequently, digital pheromone models bridge collective intelligence and primitive intuition, enabling dynamic data modeling and motion pattern recognition for humans and machines.

In this study, we explore a novel pheromone model for visualization of topological changes of a large dynamic network. Similar to virus distribution networks in nature, a cyber malware distribution network (MDN) is a connected set of maliciously compromised top-level domains (TLDs) used to facilitate the dissemination of malicious software attempting to victimize computers. It acts like a platform for spreading malwares to other nodes in the network. The challenge here is that MDNs are normally hidden and constantly change over time. The topological structures, such as domains hosting and malware and acting as intermediaries assisting in distribution are not revealed until the network traffic data is collected, attributed from multiple data sources, and systematically plotted.

MDNs have been used in botnets [1, 2], spam campaigns [3] and distributed denial of service attacks (DDoS) [4]. In general, MDNs are the essential back end distribution highway fueling underground economies in monetized schemes generating large revenues for malicious actors [3]. In this study, we provide a biologically-inspired approach for the construction and visualization of an MDN's topological structure. We collect and visualize an MDN data over a period of 9 month in order to gain insight on its structure, persistence, and evolution over time. Our MDN graphs were based on the Google Safe Browsing (GSB) transparency report [5] and malware attribution from the VirusTotal website. Our research shows the novel approach of leveraging GSB and VirusTotal reports to graph MDNs reveals deep insight into structural changes over time. The main contributions of this paper include the novel pheromone-based visualization model that reveals the existence of persistent sub-networks and individual TLDs critical to the successful operation of MDNs and use of crowdsourcing data from Google Safe Browsing and VirusTotal for constructing MDN networks.

2   Related Work

A corpus of research [6, 7] has proposed various approaches to identify malicious URLs. Research such as [8, 9] describe and analyze the use of MDNs and their various components in monetized schemes such as botnets, pay-per-install affiliate programs and traffic direction systems. In the study [10], Behfarshad describes MDNs as a set of landing pages, redirectors, and malware repositories. The authors suggest detecting the presence of an MDN by identifying drive by download attempts via two methods: top-down and bottom-up. The research of Provos, et al. [11, 12] is part of the early work describing web based malware and the existence and identification of MDNs. Their research provided insight on identifying malicious URLs and explains the critical role of *iframes*, which are a simple and widely accepted mechanism for redirection in http traffic, as the fundamental link binding multiple URLs together in an MDN. The culmination of their work is the Google Safe Browsing service that is the key data source for our research. We enhance the current literature by defining an MDN and visualizing a graphical topological structure including vertex role based node types indicative of a TLD's role in malware distribution. The authors of this paper developed an early version of a 3D interactive visualization system that revealed basic distribution patterns from the GSB data collected in 2014 [21]. In this study, we want to advance visual analytics with a pheromone simulation model to explore the attributed malware distribution network data collected in 2017, in order to gain insight on network structure, evolution, and persistence over time.

3   Malware Distribution Network as a Graph

An MDN is a dynamic structure topologically consisting of interconnected TLDs. An MDN changes over time that is captured with topological structure visualization at different points in time. We formally define a graph capturing the temporal topological structure of an MDN. A representation of an MDN at a given point in time is defined as a directed graph $M(t) = \{V(t), E(t)\}$ such that $V(t)$ is a set of vertices at time t, $E(t)$ is a set of directed edges: $\{v_i(t), v_j(t)\} \in V(t)$ at time t. In a given graph $M(t)$, a vertex $v \in V(t)$ represents an MDN node in one or more modes. The full range of a node's modality in the MDN is unknown. We suggest, based on GSB reports, three possible roles: in an MDN, a node may act as an intermediary (MI) by facilitating malicious traffic, a malicious host (MH) or root malicious host (RMH) if malware files were hosted from that domain. In our visualizations, MI and MH nodes have incoming edges, but RMH nodes do not. This implies malware in RMH nodes came from some source other than those represented by a node in the MDN. Figure 1 illustrates an MDN structure.

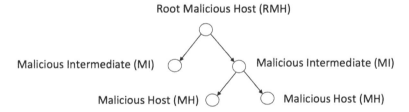

Fig. 1. Definition of a malware distribution network

4   Pheromone Model

We first build a dynamic graph of the malware distribution network. Graphs are represented by an augmented adjacency list data structure that is designed to capture both the dependencies of graph links and the mode of linkage type – MI or MH. We describe this data structure as a list of key – value pairs, whose keys are the top level domain of a website, denoted as a source and key values are a pair <mode, destination> where by destination is top-level domain which is reported as being affected by the source. To place all the top-level domains on the visualization, we used a Dynamic Behavioral Graph [22] to incorporate event frequencies, protocol types, packet contents and data flow information into one graph. In contrast to a typical Force-Directed Graph such as D3 [16], our model goes beyond the aesthetic layout of a graph to reveal the dynamic sequential patterns in a three-dimensional virtual space. In the model, the attraction force between a pair of nodes is calculated using formula:

$$f_a = \frac{\left\| x_j - x_i \right\|^2}{\alpha \cdot T} \tag{1}$$

$$f_r = \frac{\beta}{\left\| x_j - x_i \right\|^2} \tag{2}$$

where: i and j are distinct nodes, α is the value of elasticity where a greater value increases the length of the edge. β is the coefficient for repulsion force. T is equal to the average time between each nodes' timestamps and $\left\| x_i - x_j \right\|$ is the distance between two nodes.

We use a gradient arc for displaying the direction of edges. The decrease of alpha value indicates the direction, with 1 at the source and 0 at the end. This novel visual representation also enables us to add the attributes to the edges. See Fig. 2.

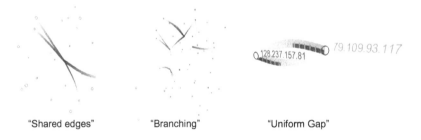

"Shared edges"   "Branching"   "Uniform Gap"

Fig. 2. Examples of the dynamic behavior graph of an MDN

Simple pheromone-based movement can produce sophisticated dynamic patterns. Conventional Ant Colony Optimization (ACO) models assume that insects walk along paths that connect various nodes. Pheromones can be overlaid in multiple layers. Furthermore, pheromones decay at a certain rate. If they did not decay, ants would risk repeating the same route and not respond to a rapidly changing environment. Here, we generalize pheromone deposit and decay on paths of a network. The amount of pheromones at a pixel position at time t is:

$$\text{Deposit:} \quad D(t) = min \left(\sum_{i=0}^{N} u_i(t), M \right) \tag{3}$$

$$\text{Decay:} \quad D(t) = max \left(u_i(t) - r \cdot t, L \right) \tag{4}$$

where, $D(t)$ is the current pheromone level at a particular path i between two nodes. M and L are the upper and lower bound limits to it. $u_i(t)$ is an individual pheromone deposit at time t and N is the total number of deposits on that particular edge. 'r' is the linear decay rate. See Fig. 3.

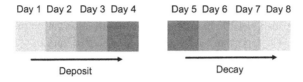

Fig. 3. Pheromone deposit and decay model for representing the persistency of the malware distribution channels (connected edges in the graph).

5   Graph Display Optimization

Whenever there is a new node entering the visualization space, the algorithm has to measure the distance between the new node and all the rest of the nodes nearby to ensure that they won't collide to each other, which is computationally expensive. In order to speed up the process, we optimize the repulsion calculation along the Z-axis. Here is the pseudo code of the method:

```
1.   Calculate repulsive forces
2.   Propagate backwards
3.   Calculate repulsion displacement from search_node to current_node
4.   Propagate forwards
5.   Calculate repulsion displacement from search_node to current_node
```

This enables to speed-up in orders of magnitude and to handle more nodes in the model. For example, before the optimization, it took 30 min to process 2,000 nodes. After the optimization, it takes less than 5 min to process the same amount of the nodes. See Fig. 4.

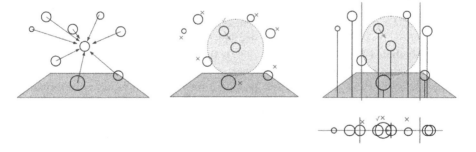

Fig. 4. A compression mapping along Z-axis in order to filter out the nodes that are further than a threshold.

6 Data Collection

We have collected the data for creating MDN graphs for a 9-month period from 19 January 2017 to 25 September 2017. We used the Google Safe Browsing (GSB) Transparency Report as our main source of data. We seeded the process by requesting a GSB report for the known websites such as notorious *vk.net* once every 24 h. The site *vk.net* was selected as the seed website based on a four month observation of the site reliably appearing on GSB. The report, in JSON format, consisted of various statistics as shown in Appendix A. The statistics of interest to us were labeled: *name, sendsToAttackSites, receivesTrafficFrom, sendsToIntermediary-Sites, lastVisitDate,* and *lastMaliciousDate.* If the returned report listed domains for labels 2, 3, or 4, those domains were added to the queue to be requested to GSB. This was an exhaustive recursive process that continued until a report with no more domains listed for these labels was received from GSB. We labeled nodes for domains listed with nonempty statistic 2 and 4 as an Intermediate Site (MI), and domains with empty statistic 3 as a Malicious Host (MH) or Root Malicious Host (RMH). The data provided in the GSB report only allowed us to create outgoing edges form the node for the current domain under analysis. All nodes are initially labeled as a Malicious Node (MN) and could be relabeled to MH or MI if the GSB report for a domain listed in 3 contained the current domain name in 2 or 4. If this was the case, an incoming edge can be created from the domain listed in 3 to the current domain under analysis. An MN with no incoming edges for the current collection was relabeled to a Root Malicious Node (RMN). This node is unique to our MDN graphs as it cannot be determined from the GSB reports alone. Our collection process occurred daily starting at 9:00 am EST and required from 4 to 11 h to complete, thus starting and finishing within the same calendar date. We decided on collecting just once a day after extensive manual analysis of the GSB report's value for label 6 over several weeks revealed GSB tended to perform diurnal updates of their report details.

7 Malware Attribution

We constructed a filtered data set because we want to retain significant patterns for effective visualizing and the design of such a filter must prevent over-trivializing the data. We therefore used VirusTotal scans sites that perform malware distribution on submitted URLs and files logs a report for each query. When given the list of malicious domains, VirusTotal gives the set of reports which list malware linked to the sites. Our malware-attributed data set is the set of TLDs that appear in at least one report of a known malware from VirusTotal. However, as reports are generated only when a malware scan query is sent to VirusTotal, there may not be a report corresponding precisely to the last malicious time reported by Google Safe Browsing. Therefore, the filtered dataset is the set of TLDs that have a report that marks the site as containing malware within 10 days of when Google Safe Browsing determined the site to be malicious. The visualization images provided are based upon this malware-attributed set. More specifically, the visualized dataset is the set of edges that either receive or send traffic from a site that has a properly timed report denoting it as malicious. See Appendix

B and C for a sample of the VirusTotal report and the statistical summary of the collected data from GSB and VirusTotal. See Fig. 5.

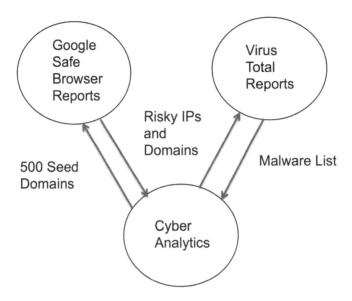

Fig. 5. The malware distribution data collection and attribution process

8   Visualization Results

The data we visualized are the malware-attributed data as described in the prior section, containing all edges that have at least one endpoint being a malware attributed site. Each edge is label with corresponding capture date time stamps, and rendered in chronological order, spanning across the entire 9 months of data. The rendering process iteratively adds each edge supplied to the graph, depending on whether both endpoints of the edge already exists in the graph, the visualization process will add nodes to the graph and then render a cold colored edge. Each day, the color of the existing edge becomes warmer until it reaches red, reflecting the age of each malicious link. If an existing edge is present in a later collection, the edge will be reassigned a cold color. When an edge is red, it will disappear when the visualization reaches the next day if the edge is not present in the data set for the next day. Given that each edge is directed, opaqueness of the edge demonstrates which node is sending traffic and which node is receiving traffic in the link. Figure 6 through Fig. 8 show the clusters of MDN evolved on January 19th, 20th, and 21st of 2017. Figure 9 shows a close-up of the MDN on September 25th of 2017 (Fig. 7).

From our visualization of the malware-attributed dataset, we can observe five key dynamic phenomena: First, having a clear distinction between days, we can observe the clustering effect of the malware nodes. Large clusters do not form rapidly. Instead, a cluster of significant size in general requires one to two weeks to form. It is rare for edges to be continuously added to a singular node in succession to form a super node, instead, smaller chains will first form over time before multiple chains gather together to form a large cluster. In particular, for the months of January, March, and June, we are able to observe a large centralized cluster of similar websites. This highlights potential large-scale malware attacks that may be occurring during those particular periods and the similarities in the distribution network used for those attacks.

Second, the visualization process highlights the quantitative differences in number of malicious nodes that exist for any particular month visually. By examining the time stamps presented and the quantity of edges present on screen we can visually determine the change in quantity of data over time. For example, we can observe that the quantity of malicious nodes peaks in our dataset during February. We can also visually compare the outbound and inbound edge frequencies across different time periods as well as examine whether high-edge-count sites are scattered or closely interconnected.

Third, the visualization is the ease of determining and examining the site with traits of particular interest. For example, root malicious nodes (RMN) are easily identified visually as each edge has a gradient effect where the opaque end marks the source and the transparent end marks the destination, so a node with only outgoing edges can be identified as a root malicious host (RMH) while examining the visualization. Furthermore, because the visualization allows us to traverse the graph in 3D as well as zoom in and out, we can examine the changes in the nodes, such as a malicious root node (RMN), is connected to, as well as observe the chains that the root malicious nodes (RMN) are part of as they dissipated and form. For example, in Fig. 9, we can zoom in to a specific node to see the node's address as well as the address of the adjacent nodes in the visualization.

Fourth, given that the data visualized is labeled with time stamps, we can observe changes per specific quantity of time. As mentioned the prior section, the data is filtered to those with a malware-attributed date within 10 days of the capture date. With this time frame in mind, when combined with the timestamps displayed in the visualization, we can view specific changes in whether a link is malicious or not and the time frame which it is malicious. Using this we can view whether past links are deprecated as new links are established and have approximations for overlapping active times in a malware distribution chain.

Finally, the timestamps are further supplemented by the pheromone effect. As describe at the beginning of this section, edges decay over time, with colors representing the age of the edge. The key benefit of this method is the ability to observe the frequency a link is used in malware distribution, at each time in a new collection, when an existing edge is mentioned again, it will be restored to the color that represents very recent. Therefore, in the duration which an edge remains in existence, the frequency of being reset to the coldest color will approximate the frequency the link was malicious. This pheromone method also highlights the order of deprecation in malware distribution chains by showing which links first becomes unused. By decaying edges gradually, we can more easily see changes in chains as malware distribution links shift over time. Overall, the pheromone effect in the visualization give visual feedback on such pattern in a visually identifiable manner.

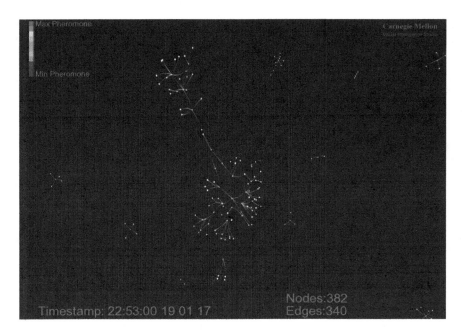

Fig. 6. A cluster of malware distribution network on January 19, 2017. (Color figure online)

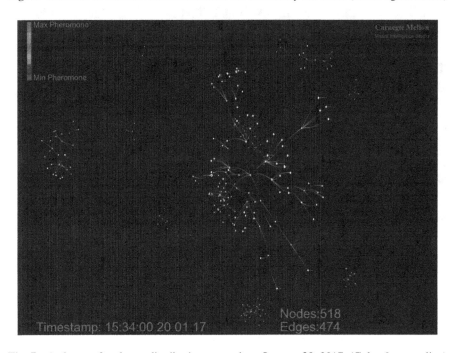

Fig. 7. A cluster of malware distribution network on January 20, 2017. (Color figure online)

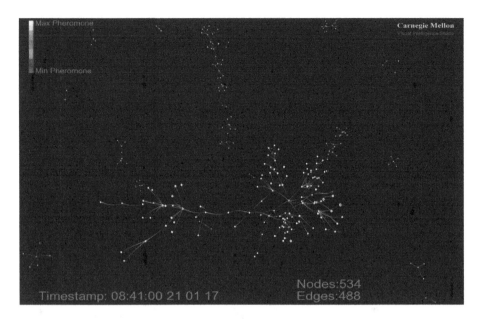

Fig. 8. A cluster of malware distribution network on January 21, 2017. (Color figure online)

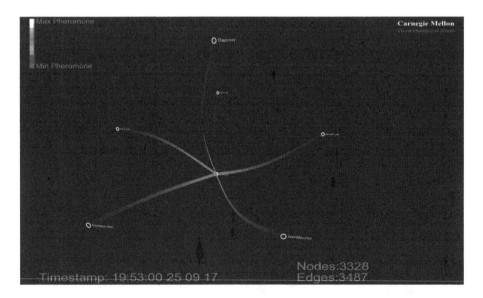

Fig. 9. A close-up of the cluster of malware distribution on September 25, 2017. (Color figure online)

9   Conclusions

In this study, we provide a biologically-inspired approach for the construction and visualizing an MDN's topological structure. We collect and visualize an MDN data over a period of 9-month in order to gain insight on its structure, persistence, and evolution over time. Our MDN graphs were based on Google Safe Browsing (GSB) reports and malware attribution from VirusTotal. Our research shows the novel approach of leveraging GSB and VirusTotal reports to graph MDNs reveals deep insight into structural changes over time. We found that the pheromone-based visualization model reveals the existence of persistent subnet works and individual TLDs' critical to the successful operation of MDNs.

The pheromone model shows the evolving MDN dynamics on daily basis, which enables analysts to zoom in and out, pause, replay, and fast-forward the animation interactively. Furthermore, we found use of crowdsourcing data from Google Safe Browsing and VirusTotal are critical for constructing MDN networks. We need to explore the open source space for better availability of data and more accuracy of the attribution of malware types, names, and contents.

From the visualization, we are able to notice significant malware distribution clusters. Specifically we found large malware distribution clusters in the months of January, March, and June. The visualization also highlighted how large distribution clusters require approximately two weeks to form and also an approximate life span of two weeks.

Acknowledgement. The authors would like to thank VIS research assistants Sebastian Peryt for initial 3D model prototyping and data processing. This project is in part funded by Cyber-Security University Consortium of Northrop Grumman Corporation. The authors are grateful to the discussions with Drs. Neta Ezer, Robert Pike, Paul Conoval, and Donald Steiner. This material is based upon work funded and supported by the Department of Defense under Contract No. FA8721-05-C-0003 with Carnegie Mellon University for the operation of the Software Engineering Institute, a federally funded research and development center. References herein to any specific commercial product, process, or service by trade name, trademark, manufacturer, or otherwise, does not necessarily constitute or imply its endorsement, recommendation, or favoring by Carnegie Mellon University or its Software Engineering Institute. [Distribution Statement A] This material has been approved for public release and unlimited distribution. Please see Copyright notice for non-US Government use and distribution. Carnegie Mellon® is registered in the U.S. Patent and Trademark Office by Carnegie Mellon University DM-0004676.

Appendix A: Sample GSB Data in JSON Format

```
{"date": 1484884380.0, "website": {"name": "nowcheck247freshandforfree. online/",
"partialUnknownDowHosts": [], "partialMalwareDowHosts": [], "malwareSite":
{"sendsToAttackSites": ["milleniumforum.info/"], "receivesTrafficFrom":
["veryhotmom.com/"], "type": 8, "sendsToIntermediarySites": []},
"uwsDownloadListStatus": "unlisted", "partialUwsDowHosts": [], "uwsListStatus":
"unlisted", "unknownDownloadListStatus": "unlisted", "partialUwsHosts": [],
"malwareDownloadListStatus": "unlisted", "partialSocialEngHosts": [],
"malwareListStatus": "unlisted", "numAses": 1, "asList": ["AS12876 (AS12876)"],
"numListedTimes": 0, "partialMalwareHosts": [], "socialListStatus": "listed"},
"lastVisitDate": 1482084799, "numTested": 7, "as": {}, "dataUpdatedDate":
1484871006, "lastMaliciousDate": 0}
```

Appendix B: Sample VirusTotal Data in CSV Format

```
ameritag.com,1493672220.0
Trojan.Script.682678,JS.Dropper.JU,JS.Trojan.Iframe.nm,Trojan.Gen.7,
JS/Iframe.MO,JS:Iframe-EPR [Trj], HEUR:Trojan.Script.Generic,
Trojan.Script.682678, Trojan.Script.Iframe.ecnmvw, Troj.Script.Generic!c,
Trojan.Script.682678, Trojan.Script.682678(B), TrojWare.JS.Iframe.MO,
Trojan.Script.682678,SCRIPT.Virus, JS_AXPERGLE.SM, HTML/ExpKit.Gen2,
VirTool:JS/Obfuscator, JS.Z.Agent.4728.I[h],
HEUR:Trojan.Script.Generic,Script.Trojan.IFrame.AL,
Trojan.Script.682678,Win32.Script.Agent.Pgwl, Trojan.HTML.Framer,
JS/Moat.6D1444D0!tr, HTML/Framer,virus.js.qexvmc.1
```

Appendix C: Statistics of the 9-Month Dataset

Months	Nodes	Inbound edges	Outbound edges	Attributed nodes
January*	14810	19199	36655	156
February	18660	24830	46896	222
March	15664	20229	36084	173
April	15880	21251	36719	188
May	14620	19953	34129	125
June**	12352	17055	30204	178
July	12057	18111	33202	136
August	8813	12272	22350	88
September***	7731	10699	21122	45

*Started on January 19, 2017
**There were 5 days down time
***The ending date was September 25, 2017

References

1. Gu, G., Perdisci, R., Zhang, J., Lee, W.: BotMiner: clustering analysis of network traffic for protocol- and structure-independent botnet detection. In: Proceedings of the 17th USENIX Security Symposium Security 2008 (2008)
2. Gu, G., Zhang, J., Lee, W.: BotSniffer: Detecting botnet command and control channels in network traffic. In: Proceedings of the 15th Annual Network and Distributed System Security Symposium (NDSS 2008), February 2008
3. McCoy, D., Pitsillidis, A., Jordan, G., Weaver, N., Kreibich, C., Krebs, B., Voelker, G.M., Savage, S., Levchenko, K.: PharmaLeaks: understanding the business of online pharmaceutical affiliate programs. In: Proceedings of the 21st USENIX Conference on Security Symposium, Series Security 2012, Berkeley, CA, USA. USENIX Association, pp. 1 (2012)
4. Karami, M., Damon, M.: Understanding the emerging threat of DDOS-as-a-Service. In: Proceedings of the USENIX Workshop on Large-Scale Exploits and Emergent Threats (2013)
5. Google safe browsing. https://developers.google.com/safe-browsing/
6. Zhang, J., Seifert, C., Stokes, J.W., Lee, W.: Arrow: generating signatures to detect drive-by downloads. In: Srinivasan, S., Ramamritham, K., Kumar, A., Ravindra, M.P., Bertino, E., Kumar, R. (eds.) Proceedings of the 20th International Conference on World Wide Web, WWW 2011, Hyderabad, India, 28 March–1 April 2011. ACM (2011)
7. Rossow, C., Dietrich, C., Bos, H.: Large-scale analysis of malware downloaders. In: Flegel, U., Markatos, E., Robertson, W. (eds.) DIMVA 2012. LNCS, vol. 7591, pp. 42–61. Springer, Heidelberg (2013). https://doi.org/10.1007/978-3-642-37300-8_3
8. Caballero, J., Grier, C., Kreibich, C., Paxson, V.: Measuring pay-per-install: the commoditization of malware distribution. In: Proceedings of the 20th USENIX Conference on Security, Series SEC 2011, Berkeley, CA, USA. USENIX Association (2011)
9. Goncharov, M.: Traffic direction systems as malware distribution tool. Trend Micro, Technical report (2011)
10. Behfarshad, Z.: Survey of malware distribution networks, Electrical and Computer Engineering, University of British Columbia, Technical report (2012)
11. Provos, N., McNamee, D., Mavrommatis, P., Wang, K., Modadugu, N.: The ghost in the browser analysis of web-based malware. In: Proceedings of the First Conference on First Workshop on Hot Topics in Understanding Botnets, Series HotBots 2007, Berkeley, CA, USA. USENIX Association (2007)
12. Provos, N., Mavrommatis, P., Rajab, M.A., Monrose, F.: All your iframes point to us. In: Proceedings of the 17th conference on Security symposium, Series SS 2008, Berkeley, CA, USA. USENIX Association (2008)
13. http://www.stachliu.com/2012/08/search-diggity-install/
14. Bing linkfromdomain search operator. http://www.bing.com/blogs/site_blogs/b/search/archive/2006/10/16/search-macros-linkfromdomain.aspx
15. http://www.d3.org
16. Wigglesworth, V.B.: Insect Hormones, pp. 134–141. W.H. Freeman and Company, Stuttgart (1970)
17. Cai, Y.: Instinctive Computing. Springer, London (2016). https://doi.org/10.1007/978-1-4471-7278-9
18. Bonabeau, E., Dorigo, M., Theraulaz, G.: Sawrm Intelligence: From Nature to Artificial Systems. Oxford University Press, Oxford (1999)
19. Cai, Y.: Ambient Diagnostics. CRC Press, Boca Raton (2014)

20. Jacobi, J.A., Benson, E.A., Linden, G.D.: Personalized recommendations of items represented within a database. US Patent. US 7113917 B2
21. Peryt, S., Morales, J.A., Casey, W., Volkmann, A., Cai, Y.: Visualizing malware distribution network. In: IEEE Conference on Visualization for Security, Baltimore, October 2016
22. Rossi, R.A., Gallagher, B., Neville, J., Henderson, K.: Modeling dynamic behavior in large evolving graphs. In: Proceedings of the Sixth ACM International Conference on Web Search and Data Mining (WSDM 2013), pp. 667–676. ACM, New York. http://dx.doi.org/10.1145/2433396.2433479

Detecting Wildlife in Unmanned Aerial Systems Imagery Using Convolutional Neural Networks Trained with an Automated Feedback Loop

Connor Bowley[1], Marshall Mattingly[1], Andrew Barnas[2], Susan Ellis-Felege[2], and Travis Desell[1(✉)]

[1] Department of Computer Science, University of North Dakota, Grand Forks, ND, USA
{connor.bowley,marshall.mattingly,travis.desell}@und.edu
[2] Department of Biology, University of North Dakota, Grand Forks, ND, USA
{andrew.barnas,susan.felege}@und.edu

Abstract. Using automated processes to detect wildlife in uncontrolled outdoor imagery in the field of wildlife ecology is a challenging task. This is especially true in imagery provided by an Unmanned Aerial System (UAS), where the relative size of wildlife is small and visually similar to its background. This work presents an automated feedback loop which can be used to train convolutional neural networks with extremely unbalanced class sizes, which alleviates some of these challenges. This work utilizes UAS imagery collected by the Wildlife@Home project, which has employed citizen scientists and trained experts to go through collected UAS imagery and classify it. Classified data is used as inputs to convolutional neural networks (CNNs) which seek to automatically mark which areas of the imagery contain wildlife. The output of the CNN is then passed to a blob counter which returns a population estimate for the image. The feedback loop was developed to help train the CNNs to better differentiate between the wildlife and the visually similar background and deal with the disparate amount of wildlife training images versus background training images. Utilizing the feedback loop dramatically reduced population count error rates from previously published work, from +150% to −3.93% on citizen scientist data and +88% to +5.24% on expert data.

1 Introduction

Image classification is an important problem for wildlife ecology. Many of today's ecological projects use video or imagery for monitoring and tracking species [1–7]. Learning ecological patterns becomes a problem of annotating images and classifying the wildlife they contain. Due to the ease of obtaining video and imagery and the large geographic areas to cover, the amount of data collected can quickly become too large for ecological researchers to go through manually.

© Springer International Publishing AG, part of Springer Nature 2018
Y. Shi et al. (Eds.): ICCS 2018, LNCS 10860, pp. 69–82, 2018.
https://doi.org/10.1007/978-3-319-93698-7_6

To overcome this problem, some projects [1–4] have turned to citizen scientists to create a larger workforce that can more quickly examine the data, provided enough ordinary people volunteer to examine sometimes monotonous video and imagery. However, manual examination is prone to human errors, such as fatigue, eye strain, or lack of domain knowledge. To deal with these problems, computer vision techniques can be used to automate classification of the data.

Wildlife@Home is a ecological project with over 100,000 h of collected video, over 65,000 images from unmanned aerial systems (UAS), and over 1.8 million images from trail cameras. An end goal of the project is to create an automated system that can classify the video and imagery and differentiate among different species. To obtain labeled data for training computer vision techniques and testing their efficacy, Wildlife@Home also employs citizen scientists using a webpage that they can visit to record observations.

A major goal for this UAS imagery is to perform population counts of lesser snow geese (*Anser caerulescens caerulescens*), which take up a tiny fraction of each image and are visually similar to the background. In this imagery, a typical snow goose takes up an area less than 18×18 pixels in UAS mosaic images (generated from mosaicing images collected over a region) that range from 844×755 to over 2000×3000 pixels. It is also common for multiple or no geese to be in each image. For these images, the information needed is not only if they contain snow geese, but also how many. The difference in the proportion of imagery containing snow geese relative to the background is great, making the UAS dataset extremely unbalanced. These features, and the fact that the background can vary heavily in color and appearance, begin to detail some of the challenges of image classification on this dataset.

Convolutional Neural Networks (CNNs) have seen a surge in popularity due to advances in deep learning techniques and their ability to be applied generically to problems based on labeled training data. Many CNNs have achieved great accuracy on benchmark datasets such as the MNIST handwritten digit dataset [8], ImageNet [9], and the CIFAR 10 and CIFAR 100 datasets [10]. However, most datasets used with CNNs have fixed size images where the object of interest fills a large area in the image. The labeled training data also tends to be fairly uniform in the number of training examples for each class, as unbalanced datasets lead to bias in the training process. For example, if a two-class dataset is unbalanced 99 to 1, if the CNN simply predicts everything as the first class it's accuracy will be 99%. This is a significant problem in this data set, where the wildlife takes up significantly less that 0.1% of the imagery.

Previous work on Wildlife@Home's UAS imagery [11] sought to calculate the population of the white phase lesser snow geese that were contained in the imagery. This work trained CNNs on a dataset labeled separately by experts and citizen scientists, which allowed for the comparison of data provided by citizen scientists vs. experts for training CNNs. While improving over state of the art results in optical (red, green, blue) imagery, there was still an 88% and 150% overestimate when using expert and matched citizen scientist [12] labels, respectively.

This work presents an automated feedback loop, which updates training data during backpropagation to account for the false positives that cause overestimation, allowing the CNNs learn from that information and allowing the class sizes to remain more balanced. This approach resulted in significant improvements in accuracy, with an average error of +5.24% achieved when using the expert provided data and an average error of −3.93% error using the matched citizen scientist provided data – results comparable or improving on manual population counts. Further, this work is generic and can be applied to any significantly unbalanced data sets.

2   Related Work

There are a number of projects in many disciplines that have used citizen scientists to examine data and generate results. PlanetHunters [13] used citizen scientists to inspect the NASA Kepler public data release using the Zooniverse tool set [14] and identified two new planet candidates. GalaxyZoo [15], had more than 100,000 citizen scientists classify galaxies in images from the Sloan Digital Sky Survey [16]. Snapshot Serengeti [1] employs the use of citizen scientists to aid ecological research by having them classify wildlife in data from camera traps in Serengeti National Park. Like PlanetHunters, Snapshot Serengeti also uses Zooniverse. Cornell has also produced multiple projects that employed citizen scientists, such as NestWatch [2,3] and FeederWatch [2], both of which used citizen scientists to help answer questions about avian species and their population sizes. CamClickr is another citizen scientist project that is used to record nesting behavior and was used in a university biology class to teach identification of objects to students [17].

Computer vision has also been used to aid ecological research. Xu and Zhu [5] worked on automatically finding and identifying seabirds with complex and uncontrolled backgrounds using a method called Grabcut [18] to find and segment the seabirds. After segmentation, features were extracted and run through three models (k-Nearest Neighbor [19], Logistic Boost [20,21], and Random Forest [22]) which voted on the final classification. When their system was run over 900 samples of 6 species of seabirds, their recognition accuracy was 88.1%. Villa et al. [23] used the data gathered from the Snapshot Serengeti project and trained CNNs over that data. Their best results had 88.9% Top-1 accuracy.

Abd-Elrahman et al. [6] used feature-based analysis (with color and shape as the features) to detect birds in UAS video. They manually selected the input objects needed for feature-testing. In the end, their system had false-negative and false-positives rates of under 20% each. Another project by Chrétien et al. [7] used RGB and thermal infrared (TIR) UAS images of white-tailed deer. They were unsuccessful in using supervised and unsupervised pixel-based detection methods to accurately find the deer, but they were able to use object-based image analysis (OBIA) on the RGB and TIR data to achieve 50% detection results with no false positives matching manned aerial surveys. However, when using only RGB imagery which contained 4 deer, OBIA detected 1,946 deer.

3   Wildlife@Home Dataset

3.1   Gathering the Data

The UAS imagery used in this project was collected using a Trimble UX5[1] fixed wing UAS. The images were collected in Wapusk National Park in Manitoba, Canada in 2015 and 2016. Flights were flown at altitudes of 75 m, 100 m, and 120 m above ground level. A 16 megapixel Sony camera placed in the nadir position recorded the images with an 80% overlap between consecutive images. Over 65,000 images were taken in total, which reached over 3TB in size.

The images taken were then used to create mosaics for each flight. The Trimble Business Center[2] (version 3.51) was used for the 2015 data and Pix4D[3] (version 3.2.23) was used for the 2016 data. In total, 36 distinct mosaics were created that were over 50 GB in size. Each mosaic was then split down into mosaic split images (MSIs) that could be shown to experts and citizen scientists through a web portal. From the 36 mosaics, 8,759 MSIs were created.

3.2   Labeling of the Data

Wildlife@Home uses a web portal (Fig. 1), to allow experts and citizen scientists (collectively known as users) to go through collected imagery and make observations. Users are shown an image and instructed to draw a box around each observed wildlife in such a way as to completely envelop the wildlife while minimizing the amount of negative space (background) in the box. The users then label the box according to the species and coloration they believe the wildlife to be. Documentation is available for them to compare against. Should they find no wildlife in an image, they can mark "nothing here".

Fig. 1. The graphical user interface (GUI) of the web portal for identifying objects in ecological imagery for the Wildlife@Home projects. This screenshot shows a UAS image with two white snow geese identified by the user.

The boxes and labels marked by the users are recorded in a database for further usage.

The data generated through the web portal is given one of two designations, expert or unmatched. Unmatched observations are the raw observations from the citizen scientists, which were matched against each other to increase the accuracy of the data using the 10 pixel corner point and intersection methods found in [12]. This brings the number of designations to three:

---

[1] http://uas.trimble.com/ux5.

[2] http://www.trimble.com/Survey/trimble-business-center.aspx.

[3] https://pix4d.com/.

1. Expert - if the recording user is a trained expert. This data is considered to be true without fault (although in reality there are errors) and is considered the baseline by which all others (citizen scientists and CNN predictions) are judged against.
2. Unmatched - if the recording user is a citizen scientist with no training by the project leaders.
3. Matched - if two or more citizen scientist observations are matched, the intersection of their bounding boxes is a matched observation [12].

For this project, only expert and matched data were considered, as Mattingly et al. [12] determined that matched data greatly improves on unmatched data.

3.3   Technical Issues and Corrections

In 2015, there was a mechanical error in the RGB camera used that resulted in the images having a strong blue tint. To fix this, the 2015 images were compared and normalized against the 2016 images. Each of the red, green, and blue channels were multiplied by 233.0/150.0, 255.0/189.0, and 236.0/190.0, respectively, floored, and then capped at 255. These numbers were chosen by sampling several images from both 2015 and 2016 data and comparing the RGB values of white phase snow geese in both datasets.

4   Methodology

Previous work on the Wildlife@Home dataset in [11] has promising results. CNNs were trained that produced a number of false positives, ending with an 88% overestimation of the population due to certain areas of background, mainly rocks with similar features to the geese, being misclassified (Fig. 2). One possible reason for this has to do with the nature of the data. The UAS dataset is extremely unbalanced, and while the unbalanced datasets problem is well defined with many solutions, it is also important to note that the per pixel percentage of background with similar features to the snow geese is quite small compared to the rest of a back-

(a) Part of an image containing white phase snow geese

(b) A CNN prediction over the image

Fig. 2. An example of an image and CNN prediction from previous work [11]. Note that it correctly identifies the white phase snow geese, but misclassifies background with similar features to the geese. The boxes in the prediction are at the actual locations of the geese.

ground class that varies vastly in color and features. As it happens, a small subset of this background class looks more like a snow goose (a different class) than it looks like the rest of background (the same class). The small subset of background data, thus, is of primary interest.

Let us define two subclasses of the background class: "hard" background is similar to the foreground, and "easy" background is everything else. Let us also define "background similar to foreground" as "background data that might be marked as a false positive by an arbitrary, trained CNN". If the majority class is undersampled (to deal with the unbalanced dataset) and images are taken from the background class randomly, few hard background images would ever be trained against.

In a sense, the Wildlife@Home dataset has an unbalanced dataset inside another unbalanced dataset. Background is a strong majority over foreground, and easy background is a strong majority over hard background. One solution, and the one explored in this work, would be to present more hard background images to the CNN, *i.e.*, undersample the easy background and/or oversample the hard background.

One way to do this is to split the background into two separately labeled classes, hard and easy, and have the CNN consider them separately. The largest inhibitor to this method, however, is labeling of the hard and easy background, which would be infeasible to do manually, especially with such an open-ended definition. A similar method is ensuring that hard background is shown to the CNN at higher rates than found in the dataset (oversample the minority sub-class, or undersample the majority sub-class). This runs into the same problem of trying to identify hard and easy background as the previous method. As strict truth labels are not needed, an automated feedback loop approach can be used.

4.1   Feedback Loop

Let us change the definition of "background similar to the foreground" to "background data that might be marked as a false positive by a *particular*, trained CNN". With this definition, when a CNN is run over the dataset, one can define the false positives as hard and the remaining background as easy (Fig. 3).

In the feedback loop, a CNN is given feedback by identifying hard background and retraining the CNN over the same overall dataset, but with more sampling of hard background. Ideally, after retraining, the CNN should have less false positives. Multiple iterations of retraining should benefit this even more. To retrain a CNN at iteration t of the feedback loop, the starting weights will be the weights from iteration $t - 1$.

This approach provides a benefit where in each training iteration, only a small subsample of the entire background set needs to be used for train-

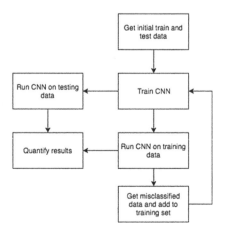

Fig. 3. Basic flowchart for feedback loop.

ing. However, it does need to run over the background data after each training iteration to determine false positives. However, If the network correctly predicted an image at iteration t of the feedback loop, it will *probably* predict that same image correctly at iteration $t+1$. In order to mitigate this cost, if the CNN at iteration t misclassifies an example, then the retrained CNN at iteration $t+1$ will run over that example to see if the retraining corrected it. If the example was correctly classified or not run over that iteration, then the CNN at iteration $t+1$ has some probability of running over that example. This handles the case where the retraining caused a previously correct classification to become incorrect.

4.2 Counting Objects

The process of training and running the CNNs in such a way that the detected objects can be counted was the same as in [11,24]. CNNs were trained on fixed size images which had relatively small dimensions. The fixed size images were comprised of sub-images of larger images (the MSIs). Experts and citizen scientists placed bounding boxes around snow geese in the imagery, and those bounding boxes were used to label the sub-images.

Fig. 4. Example of striding a CNN across an image. When the CNN reaches the right edge, it will move down and start again at the left edge.

Once a CNN was trained (or retrained) on these sub-images, it was run over full size images. To run the CNN over the full size images, the CNN was first run over its sub-image of appropriate size in the top left-hand corner of the image, then it was strided across the image, generating predictions on the sub-images as it goes (Fig. 4).

The outputs from each sub-image were reconstructed into a prediction for the whole image. When an image is run through a CNN using a softmax classifier, a probability between 0 and 1 is returned for each class. Each pixel in the prediction image also has probabilities that it is of each class. The formula for calculating this vector is $C_0(p_j) = \sum_{s \in S(p_j)} CNN(s)$ where p_j is the jth pixel in the image, $C_0(p_j)$ is a function returning a vector of confidences that pixel j is of each class, $S(p_j)$ is the set of all sub-images containing pixel j, and $CNN(s)$ is the output from running the CNN on sub-image s. The sums may total to greater than one for a particular class, so they are normalized using the square of the value over the sum of squares for all values in the vector. The equation for the probability of each class, c in the set of all classes C, for pixel j is: $P(p_{jc}) = \frac{p_{jc}^2}{\sum_{i \in C} p_{ji}^2}$. Each class is assigned a color, and by counting blobs of the color assigned to snow geese, population can be predicted.

5   Implementation

5.1   Data

One goal of this project was to compare expert data and citizen scientist data for training CNNs. So, only MSIs that had both expert observations and matched observations were used to facilitate direct comparison. There are far more MSIs that have no observed wildlife than MSIs that do (2803 vs. 1351), so 20% of the MSIs with observations in them (262 MSIs) and 20% of the MSIs that did not have observations in them (558 MSIs) were set aside for testing. The total dataset had 3334 training MSIs and 820 test MSIs.

The observations from the users are contained in bounding boxes of various sizes, and the MSIs themselves are not of a consistent size. However, CNNs need labeled fixed size input for training and running. To deal with this, sub-images from the MSIs were put into IDX files (same format used for MNIST). A fixed image size was chosen as the input size of the CNN. The images of snow geese (foreground) were obtained separately for each user designation, while the background images were shared amongst the different designations. For each designation the initial training IDXs were created by combining the unique foreground set with the shared background set.

To obtain foreground data on wildlife observations of a different size than the needed input, the center of the observation became the center of a new bounding box of the input size, which was then extracted and added to the IDX data[4]. There were 2054 and 6560 foreground observations for the expert and matched data, respectively. The difference between the classes is because more citizen scientists looked at the data than experts. Increasing the number of citizen scientists looking at an MSI causes an increase in 2-way matched observations that is greater than linear (n citizen scientists cause $nC2$ matched observations). Experts are unmatched so the number of observations is linear in the number of experts. Eight input sized background sub-images were taken from each training MSI for a total of 26,672 background examples. The locations within the MSIs were chosen at random while ensuring that they did not overlap with an observation from *any* user designation.

5.2   CNN and Feedback Loop

The CNN was implemented using C++ and OpenCL. Each type of layer had their feed forward and backpropagation functions computed using OpenCL, while the C++ code preprocessed the data and made the appropriate OpenCL calls. OpenCV was used for reading and writing images. All code is available at https://github.com/Connor-Bowley/neuralNetwork. The feedback loop was implemented using C++ and Qt. It comprised of a simple interface to get the needed inputs and call the C++ programs for training and running the CNNs.

---

[4] Care was taken to ensure the new box did not run off any of the edges of the image. In this case, the new box was shifted the appropriate direction to ensure that it was entirely on the image.

Because the CNNs are trained on IDX files and tested against PNG images, the feedback loop searched the PNGs for false positives[5] and extracted those areas into IDX files. Areas close to a bounding box were exempt from being extracted because the area predicted to be a snow goose was often larger than the goose itself. The definition of "close" was set to be: any sub-image with a pixel contained in a box that extends from a user supplied bounding box by N pixels in each direction is exempt from being marked as misclassified where N is the CNN input size. All misclassified sub-images were appended onto the previous iteration's training IDXs.

5.3   CNN Architecture and Settings

The size of the training sub-images in the IDXs was set to 18×18 pixels, as most of the bounding boxes around the snow geese were within this size. Given the 18×18 input, the CNN architecture was created (Fig. 5), which is the same as used in [11]. After each convolutional layer, a batch normalization layer [25] and an activation layer (Leaky ReLU [26] bounded to $[-5000.0, 5000.0]$) was placed, in that order. For batch normalization, γs were initialized to 1 and βs to 0.

Weights for the neurons in the convolutional and fully connected layers were initialized using $N(\mu, \sigma)$, $\mu = 0$, $\sigma = \sqrt{2/n}$ where n is the number of inputs to the neuron. After each weight update, the value was bounded such that $|w| \leq 50.0$ for each weight w. The bound here and for Leaky ReLU were to prevent outputs from reaching NaN or $\pm\infty$.

Prior to training or prediction, all data was normalized. When training, the normalization used was to subtract each pixel by the mean and divide by the standard deviation with respect to all pixels from all training images. The mean and standard deviation calculated during training was then used for preprocessing at run time. For instances of retraining, the mean and standard deviation was from all images ever trained on, including images from previous iterations.

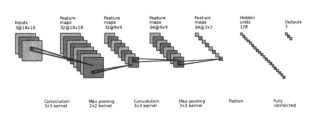

Minibatch gradient descent was used, with minibatch size of 64. The learning rate started at 1×10^{-3} and was multiplied by 0.75 each epoch. L2 Regularization [27] was used with a λ of 0.05. Training was done for 30 epochs, and the

Fig. 5. Architecture of the CNNs used in this work

epoch whose weights had the best accuracy on the training data was chosen as the final output. Nesterov Momentum [28] was used with a momentum constant of 0.9.

---

[5] False negatives were included in early trials, but due mislabeled data by users, most of the CNNs' false negatives were actually *true* negatives.

For the feedback loop, each dataset and sampling rate pair had 3 separate trials run. Each trial had 5 iterations, consisting of 1 base training and 4 retraining iterations. Each retraining iteration had its initial weights, γs, and βs set to the result of the previous iteration's training. Other parameters, such as number of epochs, were the same.

For predictions over the training and test MSIs, the stride used for striding the CNN across the MSIs was 9 pixels in each direction.

Four different ratios of background to foreground were used, 1:1, 3:1, 5:1, and 7:1. In general an N:M ratio would say that the CNN trained on N background examples for every M foreground examples it trained on. Because the amount of background to foreground is greater than even 7:1, the subset of background used each epoch was chosen at random from the background in the IDXs and differed each epoch.

The CNNs were trained and run on a Mac Pro using a 3.5 GHz 6-Core Intel Xeon E5 processor.

6 Results

Three runs were conducted for each configuration of training set and background to foreground sampling ratio. The results of the blob counter over the prediction images were averaged (Table 1). CNNs trained on the expert dataset and the CNNs trained on the matched dataset both had low error. Interestingly, the CNNs trained on the matched data performed better under higher background to foreground ratios than the ones trained with expert data. One possible reason for this is that the citizen scientist data is matched while the expert data is not. There was not enough expert data to do matching over it, and there are confirmed cases of expert misclassification.

CNNs that went through the feedback loop even one iteration had significantly less error than their baselines (Table 2). This decrease was larger than the decrease in error that happened when the sampling rates were changed. While increasing sampling of background did reduce error in the baseline, it usually increased the error

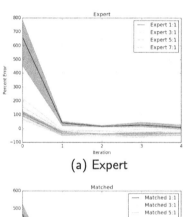

(a) Expert

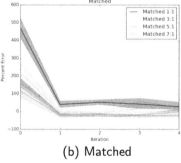

(b) Matched

Fig. 6. Average error based on iteration for each dataset and BG:FG sampling ratio. Line is average; filled in portion shows max and min values at each iteration.

when using the feedback loop. The exception to this was going from a 1:1 to a 3:1 with the matched data. This suggests that the bias introduced from the large

Table 1. Blob counter results

Data set	BG:FG	Predict	Actual	Error	|%Error|
Expert	**1:1**	**348.33**	**331**	**17.33**	**5.24**
Expert	3:1	288.67	331	−42.33	12.79
Expert	5:1	255.00	331	−76.00	22.96
Expert	7:1	218.00	331	−113.00	34.14
Matched	1:1	398.67	331	67.67	20.44
Matched	*3:1*	*318.00*	*331*	*−13.00*	*3.93*
Matched	5:1	301.33	331	−29.67	8.96
Matched	7:1	271.33	331	−59.67	18.03

CNNs were trained using given data set and the background to foreground sampling ratio, BG:FG. Predict is predicted population on test set. Actual is actual count over test set by experts. The numbers are average of best iteration results of 3 runs. Bold face rows are best for their training set. Italicized row is best overall.

Table 2. Comparison of feedback loop to baseline.

Training set	BG:FG	Iteration	Predict	Actual	|%Error|
Expert	1:1	0	2518.33	331	660.83
Expert	1:1	1	468.67	331	41.59
Expert	1:1	Best (3.67)	348.33	331	5.24
Expert	3:1	0	850.00	331	156.80
Expert	3:1	1	279.00	331	15.71
Expert	3:1	Best (3.00)	288.67	331	12.79
Expert	5:1	0	699.00	331	111.18
Expert	5:1	1	224.00	331	32.33
Expert	5:1	Best (1.67)	288.67	331	22.96
Expert	7:1	0	626.33	331	89.22
Expert	7:1	1	203.33	331	38.57
Expert	7:1	Best (1.33)	218.00	331	34.14
Matched	1:1	0	1878.33	331	467.47
Matched	1:1	1	461.67	331	39.48
Matched	1:1	Best (3.67)	398.67	331	20.44
Matched	3:1	0	1054.33	331	218.53
Matched	3:1	1	330.00	331	0.30*
Matched	3:1	Best (2.67)	318.00	331	3.93
Matched	5:1	0	856.00	331	151.61
Matched	5:1	1	272.33	331	17.72
Matched	5:1	Best (2.67)	301.33	331	8.96
Matched	7:1	0	708.00	331	113.90
Matched	7:1	1	251.00	331	24.17
Matched	7:1	Best (2.67)	271.33	331	18.03

*While these numbers averaged to a very low amount of error from the actual, the individual numbers themselves were not the best in their respective runs.

At iteration 0, the feedback loop has not yet been employed, which makes it an effective baseline. It can be seen that even one iteration of retraining drastically cuts the error. The best iteration varied between trials. The average best iteration for each CNN is given in parentheses.

ratios caused too many false negatives in the retraining. Note the population predictions after the feedback loop are low for all ratios other than 1:1.

The estimates generated by the CNNs for each configuration of training set and background to foreground ratio were graphically represented at each iteration. The worst error obtained by any CNN that had been through the feedback loop at all, did better than the very best baseline (Fig. 6; a 215 goose under-estimate for the worst feedback CNN over expert 7:1 compared to 273 over-estimate for the best baseline run over matched 7:1).

7   Conclusion

This paper used data gathered from citizen scientists and experts to train convolutional neural networks. These networks were able to provide estimates of the population of white phase snow geese collected from from UAS imagery. While previous work yielded a large number of false positives [11], the addition of a feedback loop in this work drastically reduced the error and yielded runs whose population estimates were not always overestimates.

The feedback loop introduced is simple, yet effective, way to increase accuracy on massively unbalanced datasets. It provided an automated approach to choosing which examples from the majority class were most important to include in training. As the focus of the feedback loop was more the data itself than the CNNs, any new improvements in CNN training techniques could be easily applied to system. In fact, any image classification method that uses supervised training could most likely be used with the feedback loop.

The best results for CNNs trained on the data provided by the citizen scientists had an average error of only 3.93% for their population estimates, down from 150% in previous work. Similarly, CNNs trained on expert provided data had an average error of 5.24% down from 88% in previous work. The low error for both datasets shows both the viability of using citizen scientists to produce training data for CNNs and the viability of using CNNs in ecological research.

References

1. Lion Research Center, University of Minnesota. http://www.snapshotserengeti.org/. Accessed 2012
2. Bonney, R., Cooper, C.B., Dickinson, J., Kelling, S., Phillips, T., Rosenberg, K.V., Shirk, J.: Citizen science: a developing tool for expanding science knowledge and scientific literacy. BioScience **59**(11), 977–984 (2009)
3. Phillips, T., Dickinson, J.: Tracking the nesting success of north America's breeding birds through public participation in NestWatch (2008)
4. Wood, C., Sullivan, B., Iliff, M., Fink, D., Kelling, S.: eBird: engaging birders in science and conservation. PLoS Biol. **9**(12), e1001220 (2011)
5. Xu, S., Zhu, Q.: Seabird image identification in natural scenes using grabcut and combined features. Ecol. Inf. **33**, 24–31 (2016)
6. Abd-Elrahman, A., Pearlstine, L., Percival, F.: Development of pattern recognition algorithm for automatic bird detection from unmanned aerial vehicle imagery. Surv. Land Inf. Sci. **65**(1), 37 (2005)

7. Chrétien, L.-P., Théau, J., Ménard, P.: Visible and thermal infrared remote sensing for the detection of white-tailed deer using an unmanned aerial system. Wildl. Soc. Bull. **40**(1), 181–191 (2016)
8. LeCun, Y., Cortes, C.: MNIST handwritten digit database. AT&T Labs (2010). http://yann.lecun.com/exdb/mnist
9. Russakovsky, O., Deng, J., Su, H., Krause, J., Satheesh, S., Ma, S., Huang, Z., Karpathy, A., Khosla, A., Bernstein, M., Berg, A.C., Fei-Fei, L.: ImageNet large scale visual recognition challenge. Int. J. Comput. Vis. (IJCV) **115**(3), 211–252 (2015)
10. Krizhevsky, A., Hinton, G.: Learning multiple layers of features from tiny images (2009)
11. Bowley, C., Mattingly, M., Ellis-Felege, S., Desell, T.: Toward using citizen scientists to drive automated ecological object detection in aerial imagery. In: 2017 IEEE 12th International Conference on e-Science (e-Science). IEEE (2017)
12. Mattingly, M., Barnas, A., Ellis-Felege, S., Newman, R., Iles, D., Desell, T.: Developing a citizen science web portal for manual and automated ecological image detection. In: 2016 IEEE 12th International Conference on e-Science (e-Science), pp. 223–232. IEEE (2016)
13. Fischer, D.A., Schwamb, M.E., Schawinski, K., Lintott, C., Brewer, J., Giguere, M., Lynn, S., Parrish, M., Sartori, T., Simpson, R., Smith, A., Spronck, J., Batalha, N., Rowe, J., Jenkins, J., Bryson, S., Prsa, A., Tenenbaum, P., Crepp, J., Morton, T., Howard, A., Beleu, M., Kaplan, Z., vanNispen, N., Sharzer, C., DeFouw, J., Hajduk, A., Neal, J.P., Nemec, A., Schuepbach, N., Zimmermann, V.: Planet hunters: the first two planet candidates identified by the public using the kepler public archive data. Mon. Not. R. Astron. Soc. **419**(4), 2900–2911 (2012)
14. Simpson, R., Page, K.R., De Roure, D.: Zooniverse: observing the world's largest citizen science platform. In: Proceedings of the 23rd International Conference on World Wide Web, pp. 1049–1054. ACM (2014)
15. Lintott, C.J., Schawinski, K., Slosar, A., Land, K., Bamford, S., Thomas, D., Raddick, M.J., Nichol, R.C., Szalay, A., Andreescu, D., Murray, P., Vandenberg, J.: Galaxy zoo: morphologies derived from visual inspection of galaxies from the sloan digital sky survey. Mon. Not. R. Astron. Soc. **389**(3), 1179–1189 (2008)
16. York, D.G., Adelman, J., Anderson Jr., J.E., Anderson, S.F., Annis, J., Bahcall, N.A., Bakken, J., Barkhouser, R., Bastian, S., Berman, E., et al.: The sloan digital sky survey: technical summary. Astron. J. **120**(3), 1579 (2000)
17. Voss, M.A., Cooper, C.B.: Using a free online citizen-science project to teach observation & quantification of animal behavior. Am. Biol. Teach. **72**(7), 437–443 (2010)
18. Rother, C., Kolmogorov, V., Blake, A.: GrabCut: interactive foreground extraction using iterated graph cuts. In: ACM Transactions on Graphics (TOG), vol. 23, no. 3. pp. 309–314. ACM (2004)
19. Cover, T., Hart, P.: Nearest neighbor pattern classification. IEEE Trans. Inf. Theory **13**(1), 21–27 (1967)
20. Freund, Y., Schapire, R.E., et al.: Experiments with a new boosting algorithm. In: ICML, vol. 96, pp. 148–156 (1996)
21. Friedman, J.H.: Additive logistic regression: a statistical view of boosting. Ann. Statist. **28**, 337–407 (2000)
22. Breiman, L.: Random forests. Mach. Learn. **45**(1), 5–32 (2001)
23. Gomez, A., Salazar, A., Vargas, F.: Towards automatic wild animal monitoring: identification of animal species in camera-trap images using very deep convolutional neural networks, arXiv preprint arXiv:1603.06169 (2016)

24. Bowley, C., Andes, A., Ellis-Felege, S., Desell, T.: Detecting wildlife in uncontrolled outdoor video using convolutional neural networks. In: 2016 IEEE 12th International Conference on e-Science (e-Science), pp. 251–259. IEEE (2016)

25. Ioffe, S., Szegedy, C.: Batch normalization: accelerating deep network training by reducing internal covariate shift. In: International Conference on Machine Learning, pp. 448–456 (2015)

26. Maas, A.L., Hannun, A.Y., Ng, A.Y.: Rectifier nonlinearities improve neural network acoustic models. In: Proceedings of the ICML, vol. 30, p. 1 (2013)

27. Ng, A.Y.: Feature selection, L1 vs. L2 regularization, and rotational invariance. In: Proceedings of the Twenty-first International Conference on Machine Learning, p. 78. ACM (2004)

28. Nesterov, Y.: A method of solving a convex programming problem with convergence rate O (1/k2). In: Soviet Mathematics Doklady, vol. 27, no. 2, pp. 372–376 (1983)

Incentive Mechanism for Cooperative Intrusion Detection: An Evolutionary Game Approach

Yunchuan Guo[1], Han Zhang[1,2], Lingcui Zhang[1], Liang Fang[1],
and Fenghua Li[1,2(✉)]

[1] State Key Laboratory of Information Security,
Institute of Information Engineering, Chinese Academy of Sciences, Beijing, China
`lifenghua@iie.ac.cn`
[2] School of Cyber Security, University of Chinese Academy of Sciences,
Beijing, China

Abstract. In Mobile Ad-Hoc Networks, cooperative intrusion detection is efficient and scalable to massively parallel attacks. However, due to concerns of privacy leak-age and resource costs, if without enough incentives, most mobile nodes are often selfish and disinterested in helping others to detect an intrusion event, thus an ef-ficient incentive mechanism is required. In this paper, we formulate the incentive mechanism for cooperative intrusion detection as an evolutionary game and achieve an optimal solution to help nodes decide whether to participate in detection or not. Our proposed mechanism can deal with the problems that cooperative nodes do not own complete knowledge about other nodes. We develop a game algorithm to maximize nodes utility. Simulations demonstrate that our strategy can efficiently incentivize potential nodes to cooperate.

Keywords: Mobile Ad-Hoc Networks
Cooperative intrusion detection · Privacy · Evolutionary game

1 Introduction

The Mobile Ad-Hoc Networks (MANETs), equipped with wireless transceivers that can communicate with one another without the aid of any centralized infrastructure, are complex networks and widely used in various applications, *e.g.*, military surveillance, commercial sector and personal area networks [1]. However, due to the limitation of resources and openness nature, MANETs are suffering from an increasing number of security intrusions e.g., DDoS, wormhole and sybil attack [2]. To prevent and mitigate these intrusions, one important thing that should be done is to design intrusion detection systems (IDS) to identify intruders, intrusion time/location and intrusion activity. The existing IDSs are roughly divided into two categories: non-cooperative IDS (NCIDS), and cooperative IDS (CIDS) [3]. Because no interaction between multiple NCIDSs takes

© Springer International Publishing AG, part of Springer Nature 2018
Y. Shi et al. (Eds.): ICCS 2018, LNCS 10860, pp. 83–97, 2018.
https://doi.org/10.1007/978-3-319-93698-7_7

place, NCIDSs cannot detect sophisticated and distributed attacks. To address this problem, CIDS has been proposed. In CIDS, if an IDS node detects an intrusion with weak or inconclusive evidence, then it initiates a global detection procedure and invites other nodes that run IDS agents to cooperatively participate in the detection. Compared with NCIDSs, CIDSs with high accuracy, high scalability and low computation overhead have been widely used.

Motivation: In spite of the above advantages, the existing CIDS scheme cannot efficiently work in MANETs, because most nodes in MANETs are selfish and disinterested in helping others to detect an intrusion event for the following reasons: (1) *Resource limitation.* Most nodes in MANETs own the limited resources (including computation resources and communication resources); they have to save these resources for their own communications. (2) *Privacy issues.* Most nodes depend on open wireless channels to communicate. As a result, an attacker easily detects other nodes presence, recognizes their identifications and tracks their locations by periodically monitoring data traffic. Thus, without enough incentives a selfish node cannot cooperate timely and the number of cooperators drastically decreases, thus intrusion detection rate is greatly reduced. Therefore, we should design an incentive mechanism to incentivize nodes to cooperate timely and ensure that, once a detection task is released, potential cooperators will immediately participate in task.

From the aspect of *methodology* being used to incentive participation, the existing work can be roughly divided into two categories [4]: *game-theoretical* approaches and *non-game-theoretical* approaches. In most of *non-game-theoretical* approaches, a center platform is often designed to allocate incentive resources (*e.g.*, digital cash) to cooperators and maximize its utility. However, these approaches often ignore the optimal utility of cooperators. To address this problem, the *game-theoretical* approaches are proposed. In these approaches, each potential cooperator is usually assumed to be rational. That is, individual users make their strategic choice on a wholly rationally determined evaluation of probable outcomes to maximize their utility. However, this assumption is not reasonable enough for MANETs, because MANETs have a large number of mobile nodes and their network topology frequently changes. As a result, most nodes do not know the global topology completely in practice. Namely, compared with the adequate rationality assumption in traditional game theory, it is more realistic to consider the nodes in MANETs to be with bounded rationality.

Contribution: In this paper, we assume that nodes in MANETs are not adequate rationality but bounded rationality, and the game aspects of CIDSs are investigated. Our main contributions are as follows.

(1) Considering bounded rationality of users and dynamics of cooperative intrusion detection, we formulate the incentive mechanism for cooperative detection as an evolutionary game.

(2) We design a budget-assignment mechanism to encourage nodes to timely cooperate and achieve the Evolutionary Stable Strategy (ESS) in our evolutionary game.
(3) We design an ESS-based algorithm and carry out the simulation. The results show that our proposed strategy can efficiently incentivize nodes to participate in cooperation.

The rest of this paper is organized as follows. In Sect. 2, we discuss the related work. In Sect. 3, we introduce our system model. Section 4 formulates the incentive scheme as an evolutionary game and analyzes the factors that affect nodes benefit. We conduct game analysis in Sect. 5. Simulations and their analysis are given in Sect. 6. We draw a conclusion in Sect. 7.

2   Related Work

2.1   Cooperative IDS

In our paper, selfishness of nodes in MANETs is assumed to be caused by the privacy issues and concerns of resource overhead; thus, in this subsection, we discuss the related work from the aspects of privacy protection and resource overhead.

Privacy Protection. A large number of techniques (*e.g.* Bloom filter [5], multi-party computation [6,7] and different privacy [8]) have been proposed to address the privacy requirements in intrusion detection. For example, Shu *et al.* [5] designed a privacy protection scheme by combining Bloom filters along with a trusted list of participant peers. In *GrIDS* [3], a cooperator can only observe intrusion activity restricted within its boundaries to protect privacy. Using additive homomorphic encryption, Do and Ng [7] designed a privacy-preserving scheme for sharing and processing intrusion alert data. Jin *et al.* [9] formulated privacy protection in cooperative IDS as a Stackelberg game and obtained Stackelberg-Nash equilibrium. Although these approaches try their best to protect privacy, privacy information might be still leaked in practice [10]. Thus, a selfish node might be disinterested in helping others to detect abnormal behaviors.

Resource Overhead. In CIDSs, a cooperative node has to exchange its local observations with others, thus, incurring high resource overhead. To reduce overhead, several solutions have been proposed. For instance, Hassanzadeh and Stoleru [11] formulated optimal monitoring in CIDS as a multi-objective optimization problem and developed a genetic algorithm to decrease computation complexity. Gil Perez *et al.* [12] introduced the notion of trust diversity among to increase both in detection quality and reduce communication overhead. Subba et al. [13] used a packet header anomaly detector to analyze the data packets header and minimize the computational overhead. Undoubtedly, if a node cooperates, its consumed resources could not be ignored. Thus, a selfish node does not cooperate still.

2.2   Incentive Mechanism

Although a large number of efforts have been spent on incentivizing selfish nodes to cooperate, little work focuses on the incentives in IDS. Thus, in this subsection, incentive mechanisms, designed for participatory sensing (which can be potentially used in CIDS) are overviewed. From the aspect of *methodology*, the existing incentive mechanism can be roughly divided into the two categories [4]: *non-game-theoretical* approaches and *game-theoretical* approaches.

The *non-game-theoretical* approaches, designed for specific or general applications can be divided into three categories: QoI (quality of information)-aware mechanisms [14,15], resource-aware mechanisms [4,16] and privacy-aware mechanisms [17]. Guo et al. [14] designed an incentive mechanism for IoT searches to collect real-time data. Considering data quality, Peng et al. [15] paid the participants as how well they do, to motivate the rational participants to efficiently perform tasks. Zheng et al. [16] studied on the coverage problem for incentive-compatible mobile crowd-sensing and proposed a budget feasible and strategy-proof incentive mechanism for weighted coverage maximization. Ma et al. [17] leveraged a conditional random field to model the spatio-temporal correlations among the contexts, and proposed a speed-up algorithm to preserve privacy while maximizing the amount of data collection. Although these approaches efficiently maximize the data quality at acceptable costs, they do not maximize the participant utility.

To address this problem, the *game-theoretical* approaches are proposed. In these approaches, each player is assumed to be rational and selfish and interested in maximizing its own utility. Yang et al. [18] used a Stackelberg game to design an incentive mechanism and show how to compute the unique Equilibrium. Guo et al. [19] and Lv et al. [18] used coalitional game theories to evaluate cooperation in MANETs and VANETs, respectively. Mukhopadhyay et al. [20] proposed a truthful quality adaptive participatory sensing in an online double auction environment. However, these efforts focus on the short-term utility of cooperators and ignore the long-term benefit. To address this problem, the repeated game for MONs is proposed [21]. Yin et al. [21] use the "dissemination interesting" to motivate nodes to forward advertisement. Obviously, notation "dissemination interesting" is not suitable for intrusion detection.

In these approaches, players are assumed to be completely rational. These assumptions are not reasonable enough for MANETs, because nodes in MANETs moves over time and network topology frequently changes. As a result, the global topology is unknown by most nodes in practice. This means that nodes in MANETs are not adequate rationality but bounded rationality. Additionally, in these approaches, the *real-time* requirement is not considered. Obviously, this requirement is critical for intrusion detection and if, without timely detection, cooperative detection will not come to fruition.

3   Basic Idea and System Model

In CIDSs for MANETs, a potential cooperator that runs an IDS agent participates in the global intrusion detection, as follows. If a node (named initiator, $e.g.$, n_0) detects an intrusion even with weak or inconclusive evidence, then it initiates a global detection procedure and sends a detection request (or detection task) to potential cooperators $\mathcal{N} = \{n_1, \ldots, n_N\}$, where N is the number of potential cooperators. Once receiving this request, cooperators start local detections and report the detected abnormal behaviors to the initiator. After receiving r detection reports, the initiator clusters, merges and correlates these abnormal behaviors. If the initiator confirms an intrusion with sufficient evidence, then it alerts the whole networks regarding an attack. Generally, the more nodes participate in the detection, the higher is the intrusion detection rate. Without loss of generality, we assume that detection rate for each node is ρ. If r nodes participate in cooperating, then the overall detection rate odr is

$$odr(r, \rho) = 1 - (1 - \rho)^r \tag{1}$$

As shown in Sect. 1, if a node participates in detecting an intrusion, its privacy might be exposed and its resource might be consumed. Thus, selfish nodes are typically disinterested in helping others. To encourage nodes to timely cooperate, an auction approach is used in this paper. In detail, we regard the detection service as goods, each potential cooperator that detects an intrusion event acts as an offer, sells its service and wins virtual credits, and the initiator n_0 acts as a bidder and pays for the service to cooperators.

More specially, for each potential intrusion event to be detected, node n_0 divides the whole detection time into slices with the same length, indexed by natural numbers. In a time slice, a sub-auction is performed. In each sub-auction, the detection service that a potential cooperator provides is called a sub-service. Before each sub-auction ($i.e.$, at the first time-slice) starts, the initiator n_0 constructs a sub-auction pool. Before the sub-auction ends, each potential cooperator can enter the pool. When the auction starts, the initiator n_0 broadcasts the total of budget $\gamma \in R$ that n_0 will pay for the total detection service. A potential cooperator n_i ($1 \leq i \leq N$) calculates its cost for the service and evaluates its possible benefit. Based on the cost and the benefit, cooperator n_i decides whether to make an offer or not. When a time-slice ends ($i.e.$, this sub-auction ends), the winning neighboring nodes provide the sub-services. After completing the service, the potential cooperator obtains the rewards from initiator n_0 and the next sub-auction starts. Note: the intrusion event to be detected in the next sub-auction is the same with the intrusion of the previous sub-auction. The whole auction ends if all time-slices are exhausted or odr is greater than the threshold value given by initiator n_0.

4   Budget and Cost

In this section, we discuss the budget of the initiator and the cost of potential cooperators in cooperative detection.

4.1   Total Budget

In our work, we use virtual credits to motivate nodes to cooperate. That is, virtual credits are paid to cooperators after a detection task is completed. The total reward for the whole detection relies on budget. Because the main goal of an initiator is to improve the intrusion detection rate, a higher detection rate required means a more budget that initiator n_0 should pay to cooperators. In our work, for an intrusion event to be detected, we use γ to denote the budget that n_0 is willing to pay for the detection. Let odr' be the actual detection rate provided by the neighboring nodes after the total auction ends. The total reward paid to all cooperators for the whole detection is $odr' \times \gamma$. Note: the total reward depends on the budget γ and the actual odr', and the entire budget does not have to be used up. This approach is rational. For example, assume that initiator n_0 offers the higher budget to encourage more cooperators, but only one node cooperates. Obviously, in this case, it would be inappropriate for n_0 to assign the total budget to the only cooperator.

4.2   Budget Assignment

It is of importance to design an appropriate mechanism to assign the budget to the cooperators. In cooperative detection, one of important concerns is the real-time. That is, an assignment mechanism should ensure that, once initiator n_0 requests its potential cooperators to help it detect its data, these cooperators will immediately participate in detection and no one will be in a "wait and see" state. If a node is in this state, data provided by this node are the old ones. To address this problem, the designed budget-assignment scheme should guarantee that, a cooperator who timely participates in detection receives more rewards than a procrastinator. That is, the earlier a node participates in a cooperation, the more its reward is.

Let r_i denote the number of nodes who cooperatively complete the detection at the end of sub-auction i. Thus, the number r_i^{co} of cooperators in sub-auction i is $r_i^{co} = r_i - r_{i-1}$. The reward $reward(i)$, paid to a cooperative node in sub-auction i, is defined as follows.

$$reward\,(i) = \gamma \times \frac{odr(r_i, \rho) - odr(r_{i-1}, \rho)}{r_i^{co}} \tag{2}$$

Proposition 1. If $0 \le \rho < 1$ and the arriving rate is the same, the $reward(i)$ paid to the cooperator of sub-auction i is always greater than $reward(i+j)$ paid to the node of sub-auction $i + j(i, j > 0)$.

Proof. According to Formula (2), the second derivative of $odr(x, \rho)$ with respect to variable x is

$$\frac{\partial^2 odr(x, \rho)}{\partial x^2} = -\gamma \left((1 - \rho)^x (\ln(1 - \rho))^2 \right) \tag{3}$$

Due to $0 \leq \rho < 1$ and $\gamma > 0$, $\frac{\partial^2 odr(x,\rho)}{\partial x^2} < 0$ holds. This means that $odr(x,\rho)$ is convex regarding variable x. Because $odr(r,\rho)$ is the discrete version of $odr(x,\rho)$, $reward(i) > reward(i+j)$ holds. We can reach this proposition.

Note: This budget-assignment scheme guarantees that, the benefit of an early cooperator is greater than or equals the benefit of the later one, but not "strictly greater than" (because all cooperators in a sub-auction averagely share the rewards paid for this sub-auction). If there is only one cooperator in each sub-auction, the benefit of an early cooperator is strictly greater than the benefit of the later one. We do not adopt this scheme because of privacy protection, discussed in the next subsection.

4.3 Privacy Cost

As shown in Sect. 1, privacy is a key element that affects a potential coopera-tor whether to participate in cooperation. To mitigate privacy leakage, several techniques (e.g., pseudonyms and different privacy [8]) have been designed. In our work, pseudonyms technique is used to protect privacy: in a sub-auction, cooperators simultaneously and silently change their pseudonym. We use *uncer-tainty*, describing a situation involving ambiguous and/or unknown information, to measure a privacy level [22], as follows.

Assume that r_i^{co} cooperators simultaneously and silently change their pseudonym while detecting an intrusion. Then the privacy level of each cooper-ator is defined as $\log_2(1 + r_i^{co})$. When $r_i^{co} = 1$ (that is, only one node changes its pseudonym), the privacy level reaches minimum and equals 1. In this case, an adversary can accurately relate the new pseudonym with the old one, thus, privacy cost reaches the highest. In our model, privacy cost $pc(i)$ of a cooperator in sub-auction i inversely proportional to its current privacy level, defined as follows.

$$pc(i) = \begin{cases} \frac{\lambda}{\log_2(1+r_i^{co})} & if\ r_i^{co} > 0 \\ 0 & otherwise \end{cases} \tag{4}$$

where $\lambda > 0$ is the cost of a pseudonym. From Formula (4), we can see that, privacy cost equals λ, if there is only one cooperator.

5 Evolutionary Cooperation Game and Its Analysis

We model cooperative detection in an inadequate rational environment as an evolutionary game. We refer to this model as *Evolutionary Cooperation game*. The key aspect of the game-theoretic analysis is to consider benefit and cost of a potential cooperator. For a potential cooperator, if its benefit is greater than its cost, it will cooperate. Next we define our game.

5.1   Evolutionary Cooperation Game

Evolutionary Cooperation game is defined as a triplet $G = (\{n_0\} \cup \mathcal{N}, \mathcal{S}, \mathcal{U})$, where $\mathcal{N} = \{n_1, \ldots, n_N\}$ is the set of a potential cooperators, $\mathcal{S} = \{S_j\}_{j=1}^{N}$ is the set of strategies of nodes, where $S_j = \{C, D\}$ denotes the strategy chosen by $n_j (1 \leq j \leq N)$, C and D stand for *Cooperation* and *Defect*, respectively. For simplicity, the strategy chosen by node j is denoted by s_j and strategies of all nodes but j are denoted by set $\mathbf{s_{-j}}$. $\mathcal{U} = \{u_{i,1}(s_1, \mathbf{s_{-1}}), \ldots, \mathbf{u_{i,N}(s_N, s_{-N})}\}$ is the set of payoff functions of nodes at sub-auction i, where the payoff $u_{i,j}(s_j, \mathbf{s_{-j}})$ of node j in sub-auction i is the difference between its gain and its cost, defined as follows.

- If there are $r_i^{co} > 0$ cooperators in sub auction i, then the payoff $u_{i,j}(s_j, \mathbf{s_{-j}})$ for cooperator j is $u_{i,j}(s_j, \mathbf{s_{-j}}) = reward(i) - pc(i)$

$$= \gamma \times \frac{(1-\rho)^{r_i-1}\left(1-(1-\rho)^{r_i^{co}}\right)}{r_i^{co}} - \frac{\lambda}{log_2(1+r_i^{co})} \tag{5}$$

- Otherwise, the payoff $u_{i,j}(s_j, \mathbf{s_{-j}})$ for defector j equals 0.

In Formula (5), a potential cooperator easily obtain parameters γ, ρ, λ and r_{i-1}. If a node knows the number r_i^{co} of cooperators in Formula (5) in advance, then it can easily make an optimal decision. Namely, for node j, if $u_{i,j}(s_j, \mathbf{s_{-j}})$ ¿0, then its optimal section is to participate in cooperation; otherwise it will reject cooperation. However, in practice, no node apart from the initiator knows r_i^{co} because r_i^{co} is the private information of the initiator. To address this problem, we formulate the game as evolutionary game. Namely, a potential cooperator plays game repeatedly and its behavior evolves over time. At time t, a potential cooperator chooses strategy s ($s \in \{C, D\}$) with probability X ($X \in [0, 1]$); at time $(t+1)$, it adjusts the probability with the growth rate $X\frac{dX}{dt}$, where is proportional to the difference between its current payoff $u(s)$ that adopts strategy s and the current average payoff $\overline{u(s)}$ of all nodes. Given parameters γ, ρ, λ and r_{i-1}, if probability X converges to evolutionary stable strategy (ESS) x regardless the initial value of X, then the optimal decision for the potential cooperator is to cooperate with probability x. To calculate the ESS, we define replicator dynamics as follows.

5.2   Replicator Dynamics

To specify replicator dynamics, we first define the notations as shown in Table 1, where $u(C) = \gamma\frac{odr(r_{i-1}+XN,\rho)-odr(r_{i-1},\rho)}{XN} - \frac{\lambda}{log_2(1+XN)}$ and $\overline{u(C)} = Xu(C)$. Replicator dynamic express which describes how X change with time t, can be defined as follows.

$$\frac{\mathrm{d}X}{\mathrm{d}t} = X(u(C) - \overline{u(C)})$$

$$= X(1-X)\left(\frac{\gamma(1-\rho)^{r_i-1}\left(1-(1-\rho)^{XN}\right)}{XN} - \frac{\lambda}{\log_2(1+XN)}\right) \tag{6}$$

Table 1. Notations in replicator dynamics.

X	Probability with which nodes use the *cooperation* strategy
N	Number of potential cooperators
$u(C)$	Benefit of a cooperator
$\overline{u(C)}$	Average benefit of cooperators

5.3 Replicator Dynamics

An evolutionary stable strategy (ESS) is a strategy which if adopted by a population cannot be invaded by any competing alternative strategy[1]. Namely, strategy X is an ESS if the following two conditions are satisfied [23]: (1) an individual adopting strategy X must do better against another individual adopting strategy X than any other strategy; and (2) should a new strategy evolve (X') that does equally well against strategy X for X to be an ESS, an individual employing strategy X must do better than an individual employing strategy X'. Formally, let $u(s,t)$ represent the utility for playing strategy s against strategy t, the strategy pair (s,s) is an ESS in a two player game if and only if one of the following conditions is true for both players and for all $t \neq s$:

1. $u(s,s) > u(t,s)$, or
2. $u(s,s) = u(t,s)$ and $u(s,t) > u(t,t)$

Next, we conduct an ESS analysis.

Let $f(X) = \frac{\mathrm{d}X}{\mathrm{d}t} = 0$. We have $X = 0, 1$ or X which satisfy the following equation:

$$\frac{\gamma(1-\rho)^{r_i-1}\left(1-(1-\rho)^{XN}\right)}{XN} = \frac{\lambda}{\log_2(1+XN)} \tag{7}$$

The derived function of $f(X)$ is

$$f'(X) = (1-2X)\left(\frac{\gamma(1-\rho)^{r_i-1}(1-(1-\rho)^{XN})}{XN}\right) + X(1-X)g(X), \text{ where}$$

$$g(X) = \frac{\lambda N \frac{\log_2 e}{1+XN}}{(\log_2(1+XN))^2} + \frac{\gamma(1-\rho)^{r_i-1}((1-\rho)^{XN}(-NX\ln(1-\rho)+1)-1)}{X^2N}$$

---

[1] https://en.wikipedia.org/wiki/Evolutionarily_stable_strategy.

- Consider $X = 1$. If $f'(1) = -\left(\frac{\gamma(1-\rho)^{r_{i-1}}\left(1-(1-\rho)^N\right)}{N} - \frac{\lambda}{\log_2(1+N)}\right) < 0$, then $X = 1$ can be ESS. That is, if $\frac{\gamma}{\lambda} > \frac{N}{\log_2(1+N)(1-\rho)^{r_{i-1}}(1-(1-\rho)^N)}$, then $X = 1$ is ESS.
- Consider $X = 0$. Because the derived function of $f(X)$ is not well-defined at 0, we consider the limit of derived function at 0.
$\lim\limits_{X\to 0^+} f'(X) = Z_1 + Z_2 + Z_3$, where

$$Z_1 = \lim_{X\to 0^+}(1-2X)\left(\frac{\gamma(1-\rho)^{r_{i-1}}\left(1-(1-\rho)^{XN}\right)}{XN} - \frac{\lambda}{\log_2(1+XN)}\right)$$

$$= -\gamma(1-\rho)^{r_{i-1}}\ln(1-\rho) - \lim_{X\to 0^+}\frac{\lambda(1-2X)}{\log_2(1+XN)}$$

$$Z_2 = \lim_{X\to 0^+}X(1-X)\frac{\lambda N\frac{\log_2 e}{1+XN}}{(\log_2(1+XN))^2}$$

$$Z_3 = \lim_{X\to 0^+}X(1-X)\frac{\gamma(1-\rho)^{r_{i-1}}((1-\rho)^{XN}(-NX\ln(1-\rho)+1)-1)}{X^2 N} = 0$$

So, $\lim\limits_{X\to 0^+}f'(X) = Z_1 + Z_2$

$$= -\gamma(1-\rho)^{r_{i-1}}\ln(1-\rho) - \lim_{X\to 0^+}\frac{\lambda(1-2X)}{\log_2(1+XN)} + \lim_{X\to 0^+}X(1-X)\frac{\lambda N\frac{\log_2 e}{1+XN}}{(\log_2(1+XN))^2}$$

Due to $\lim\limits_{X\to 0^+}X(1-X)\frac{\lambda N\frac{\log_2 e}{1+XN}}{(\log_2(1+XN))^2} - \lim\limits_{X\to 0^+}\frac{\lambda(1-2X)}{\log_2(1+XN)} = \frac{-\lambda(N-2)}{2N}\ln 2$, we have the following results.

$$\lim_{X\to 0^+}f'(X) = -\gamma(1-\rho)^{r_{i-1}}\ln(1-\rho) + \frac{-\lambda(N-2)}{2N}\ln 2$$

Namely, when $\gamma(1-\rho)^{r_{i-1}}\ln(1-\rho) > \frac{\lambda(N-2)}{2N}\ln 2$ holds, $X = 0$ is ESS.
- Given ρ, λ, γ, N and r_{i-1}, if the solution of equation exists (let it be X') and $f'(X) < 0$, then $X = X'$ is an ESS.

Given ρ, λ, γ, N and r_{i-1}, we can easily obtain its solutions of Formula (7) using either bisection or Newton's method [24]. Based on the ESS, we can design algorithms (as shown in Algorithms 1 and 2) to incentivize inadequately rational nodes to maximize their benefit.

Algorithm 1. Game for Initiator

Initiating phase: given a potential intrusion event to be detected, n_0 selects a budget γ, the round rd of the allowed sub-auctions, the allowed auction period apd for each sub-auction and the expected overall detection rate $\overline{odr}$; n_0 sets the initial number of cooperators $r_0 = 0$, the initial overall detection rate $odr = 0$ and the current auction round $i = 1$;

Auction phase:

while $i \leq$ rd *and odr* $< \overline{odr}$ **do**

    n_0 broadcasts i, γ and $r_i - 1$ to its all potential cooperators;

    $i = i + 1$;

    for *(;;)* **do**

        n_0 records the number r_i^{co} of bidders;

        if *the sub-auction period* $>$ apd **then**

            break;

        end

    end

    $r_i = r_{i-1} + r_i^{co}$;

    Computing $odr = odr(r_i, \rho)$ according to Formula (1);

end

Pay-off phase: After completing detection, n_0 allocates *rewards* to each bidder according to Formula (3).

6 Experiment Evaluation

In the simulation, without the special statement, we set the default value of the parameters to $\rho = 0.5$, $\lambda = 1$, $\gamma = 100$, and $N = 15$.

Evolution Process. We fixed parameters ρ, λ, and N, and then picked different γ and initial cooperation probability x of a neighboring node in order to check how the evaluation process is conducted. The evolution was updated in the following manner: $x = x + \frac{\mathrm{d}x}{\mathrm{d}t} \times t$, where t $= 0.001$ is a step size. From Fig. 1, we can see that for a given total budget γ, the replication dynamics always converges to the ESS x^* regardless the initial probability x.

Cost v.s. Cooperation Probability. Figure 2 presents the change of cooperation probability over pseudonyms cost. From Fig. 2, we can see that, given the number of potential cooperators N, the cooperation probability x decreases as the pseudonyms cost λ increases, and increases as budget γ increases. This phenomenon is reasonable: if privacy cost increases or budget decreases, then the benefit of a node in each cooperation decreases, thus, it is disinterested in cooperation.

Algorithm 2. Game for Potential Cooperator

Initiating phase: Each potential cooperator first sets ρ, λ and observes the number N of potential cooperators;

Auction phase:

The potential cooperator receives i, γ and r_{i-1} from the initiator;

if $\frac{\gamma}{\lambda} > \frac{N}{\log_2(1+N)(1-\rho)^{r_i-1}(1-(1-\rho)^N)}$ **then**
| the potential cooperator participates in detecting the intrusion event;
end

else if $-\gamma(1-\rho)^{r_i-1}\ln(1-\rho) < \frac{\lambda(N-2)}{2N}\ln 2$ *holds* **then**
| the potential cooperator refuses to cooperate;
end

else
   Calculate the probability X by solving Formula (7)
   if $f'(X) < 0$ *holds* **then**
   | the potential cooperator participates in detecting the intrusion
   | event with probability X;
   end
   else
   | the potential cooperator refuses to cooperate.
   end
end

Pay-off Phase: If the potential cooperator bids, then it participates in detection. After detecting the intrusion, it gets rewards from the initiator.

Number of Completed Tasks . In the experiment, we adopted a city scenario including 17937 GPS records of 1792 taxis in three representative areas of Beijing C the Guangqumen area, covering $1.885\,\mathrm{km} \times 1.752\,\mathrm{km}$, the Shijingshan area, covering $1.078\,\mathrm{km} \times 2.532\,\mathrm{km}$, and the Changping area, covering $3.144\,\mathrm{km} \times 5.701\,\mathrm{km}$. These records were gathered from 8:00:00 a.m. to 8:59:59 a.m. on August 13, 2015. During this period, the densities of vehicles in the Guangqumen, Shijingshan and Changping areas were high, middle and low, respectively (namely a dense scenario, a medium scenario, and a sparse scenario, respectively). The numbers N of potential coopera-tors of the three areas (which denote the numbers of taxis of the three areas) are 824, 526 and 442, respectively. We assume that: (1) each passenger in a taxi own a smartphone to collect data, (2) budget $\gamma = 50$, detection rate $\rho = 0.65$, pseudonyms cost $\lambda = 0.2$, the *odr* required by node n_0 is greater than 0.98, then according to Formula (1), at least 5 neighboring nodes cooperatively detect the data collected by n_0. Assume that Next, we discuss 5 strategies: 'selflessness' strategy (i.e., all nodes are selfless), '70%-selflessness' strategy (i.e., 70% of nodes are selfless), '30%-selflessness' strategy (i.e., 30% of nodes are selfless), 'selfishness' strategy (i.e., all nodes are selfish) and our strategy.

As shown in Fig. 3, the number of tasks completed in our approach is always greater than the number in the other approaches. For instance, when the number

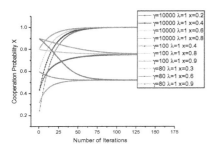

Fig. 1. Evolution process

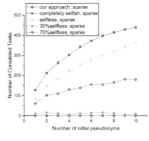

Fig. 2. Cost *v.s.* cooperation probability

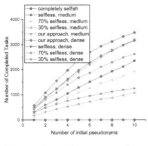

(a) Dense / medium scenario   (b) Sparse scenario

Fig. 3. Number of initial pseudonyms *v.s.* number of completed tasks.

of initial pseudonyms is 10, we can see that: (1) In the dense scenario, 2622 tasks were completed if the *70%-selfless* approach was used, 3158 tasks were completed if the selfless approach was used, and 3478 tasks were completed if our approach was used. (2) In the sparse scenario, the number of tasks completed in our approach was 54 times greater than the number of tasks completed in the *30%-selfless* approach. The reason is as follows: if without incentive, once pseudonyms of a node are exhausted, it does not detect messages any more. In our approach, even if pseudonyms of a node are exhausted, it can use the obtained reward enough to purchase new pseudonyms. Therefore, our approach has overwhelming advantages over the other approaches.

7   Conclusion

We have considered the incentive mechanism for cooperative detection to motivate nodes to participate in cooperation. In detail, a game-theoretic approach is proposed to guarantee that mobile nodes participating in detection maximize their utility while reducing resource consumption. To address the problem that nodes are inadequately rational, we have established evolutionary games. We also have developed algorithms for evolutionary game to encourage nodes to participate in cooperation. The simulation demonstrates the efficiency of our approach.

Acknowledgement. This work is supported by the National Key Research and Development Program of China (No. 2016YFB0801001) and the National Natural Science Foundation of China (No. 61672515).

References

1. Loo, J., Mauri, J.L., Ortiz, J.H.: Mobile Ad-Hoc Networks: Current Status and Future Trends. CRC Press, Boca Raton (2016)
2. Nadeem, A., Howarth, M.P.: An intrusion detection & adaptive response mechanism for MANETs. Ad Hoc Netw. **13**, 368–380 (2014)
3. Vasilomanolakis, E., Karuppayah, S., Muhlhauser, M., Fischer, M.: Taxonomy and survey of collaborative intrusion detection. ACM Comput. Surv. **47**, 1–33 (2015)
4. Restuccia, F., Das, S.K., Payton, J.: Incentive mechanisms for participatory sensing: survey and research challenges. ACM Trans. Sens. Netw. **12**, 1–40 (2016)
5. Shu, X., Yao, D., Bertino, E.: Privacy-preserving detection of sensitive data exposure. IEEE Trans. Inf. Forensics Secur. **10**, 1092–1103 (2015)
6. Niksefat, S., Sadeghiyan, B., Mohassel, P., Sadeghian, S.: ZIDS: a privacy-preserving intrusion detection system using secure two-party computation protocols. Comput. J. **57**, 494–509 (2014)
7. Do, H.G., Ng, W.K.: Privacy-preserving approach for sharing and processing intrusion alert data. In: Proceedings of IEEE Tenth International Conference on Intelligent Sensors, Sensor Networks and Information Processing (ISSNIP), pp. 7–9 (2015)
8. Reed, J., Aviv, A.J., Wagner, D., Haeberlen, A., Pierce, B.C., Smith, J.M.: Differential privacy for collaborative security. In: Proceedings of the Third European Workshop on System Security, pp. 1–7 (2010)
9. Jin, R., He, X., Dai, H.: On the tradeoff between privacy and utility in collaborative intrusion detection systems - a game theoretical approach. In: Proceedings of the Hot Topics in Science of Security: Symposium and Bootcamp (HotSoS), pp. 45–51 (2017)
10. Niksefat, S., Kaghazgaran, P., Sadeghiyan, B.: Privacy issues in intrusion detection systems: a taxonomy, survey and future directions. Comput. Sci. Rev. **25**, 69–78 (2017)
11. Hassanzadeh, A., Stoleru, R.: Towards optimal monitoring in cooperative IDS for resource constrained wireless networks. In: Proceedings of IEEE ICCCN, pp. 1–8 (2011)
12. Gil Perez, M., Tapiador, J.E., Clark, J.A., Martnez Perez, G., Skarmeta Gomez, A.F.: Trustworthy placements: improving quality and resilience in collaborative attack detection. Comput. Netw. **58**, 70–86 (2014)
13. Subba, B., Biswas, S., Karmakar, S.: Enhancing effectiveness of intrusion detection systems: a hybrid approach. In: Proceedings of IEEE International Conference on Advanced Networks and Telecommunications Systems, pp. 1–6 (2016)
14. Guo, Y., Fang, L., Geng, K., Yin, L., Li, F., Chen, L.: Real-time data incentives for IoT searches. In: IEEE International Conference on Communications (2018)
15. Peng, D., Wu, F., Chen, G.: Data quality guided incentive mechanism design for crowdsensing. IEEE Trans. Mob. Comput. **17**, 307–319 (2018)

16. Zheng, Z., Wu, F., Tang, S.: A budget feasible incentive mechanism for weighted coverage maximization in mobile crowdsensing. IEEE Trans. Mob. Comput. **16**, 2392–2407 (2017)

17. Ma, Q., Zhang, S., Zhu, T., Liu, K., Zhang, L., He, W., Liu, Y.: PLP: protecting location privacy against correlation analyze attack in crowdsensing. IEEE Trans. Mob. Comput. **16**, 2588–2598 (2017)

18. Yang, D., Xue, G., Fang, X., Tang, J.: Crowdsourcing to smartphones: incentive mechanism design for mobile phone sensing. In: Proceedings of IEEE MOBILCOM, pp. 173–184 (2012)

19. Guo, Y., Yin, L., Liu, L., Fang, B.: Utility-based cooperative decision in cooperative authentication. In: Proceedings of IEEE INFOCOM, pp. 1006–1014 (2014)

20. Mukhopadhyay, J., Pal, A., Mukhopadhyay, S., Singh, V.K.: Quality adaptive online double auction in participatory sensing. J. Inform. Math. Sci. **9**, 571–593 (2017)

21. Yin, L., Guo, Y., Li, F., Sun, Y., Qian, J., Vasilakos, A.: A game-theoretic approach to advertisement dissemination in ephemeral networks. World Wide Web J. **21**, 241–260 (2018)

22. Yu, R., Kang, J., Huang, X., Xie, S., Zhang, Y., Gjessing, S.: MixGroup: accumulative pseudonym exchanging for location privacy enhancement in vehicular social networks. IEEE Trans. Dependable Secur. Comput. **13**, 93–105 (2016)

23. Cowden, C.C.: Game theory, evolutionary stable strategies and the evolution of biological interactions. Nat. Educ. Knowl. **3**, paper 6 (2012)

24. Boyd, S.P., Vandenberghe, L.: Convex Optimization. Cambridge University Press, Cambridge (2004)

Hybrid Genetic Algorithm
for an On-Demand First Mile Transit
System Using Electric Vehicles

Thilina Perera[✉], Alok Prakash, Chathura Nagoda Gamage,
and Thambipillai Srikanthan

Nanyang Technological University, 50 Nanyang Avenue, Singapore 639798, Singapore
pere0004@e.ntu.edu.sg, {alok,astsrikan}@ntu.edu.sg, chathuratng@gmail.com

Abstract. First/Last mile gaps are a significant hurdle in large scale adoption of public transit systems. Recently, demand responsive transit systems have emerged as a preferable solution to first/last mile problem. However, existing work requires significant computation time or advance bookings. Hence, we propose a public transit system linking the neighborhoods to a rapid transit node using a fleet of demand responsive electric vehicles, which reacts to passenger demand in real-time. Initially, the system is modeled using an optimal mathematical formulation. Owing to the complexity of the model, we then propose a hybrid genetic algorithm that computes results in real-time with an average accuracy of 98%. Further, results show that the proposed system saves travel time up to 19% compared to the existing transit services.

Keywords: Demand responsive transit · Genetic algorithm
First/last mile problem · Electric vehicles

1 Introduction

Public transit systems around the world are constantly challenged to meet the diversified needs of passengers. Not only are these systems expected to provide high quality of service (in terms of reliability and efficiency) but also ensure a high degree of penetration. Furthermore, higher ridership in public transit systems can also lead to easing traffic congestion and pollution in addition to economic gains. Consequently, in the United States, growth of public transit trips outplay both population growth and vehicle miles traveled (VMT) [3].

A public transit journey typically consists of multiple legs and is served by different modalities of transit, such as buses, trains, subways, etc. Thus, in the

This research project is partially funded by the National Research Foundation Singapore under its Campus for Research Excellence and Technological Enterprise (CREATE) programme with the Technical University of Munich at TUMCREATE.
Nagoda Gamage contributed to this research while he was an intern at Nanyang Technological University, Singapore.

© Springer International Publishing AG, part of Springer Nature 2018
Y. Shi et al. (Eds.): ICCS 2018, LNCS 10860, pp. 98–113, 2018.
https://doi.org/10.1007/978-3-319-93698-7_8

first leg of a multi-modal public transit journey, a passenger travels to the nearest public transit node, typically a bus stop, to board a bus, which brings him/her to a major transit node. The last leg of the journey is also completed in a similar fashion. However, in a significant number of cases, the nearest public transit node is located outside a comfortable walking distance, typically accepted as 400 m [18]. As a result, passengers sometimes have to walk 10–15 min to and from the nearest bus stop, mass rapid transit (MRT) or light rail transit (LRT) station in the first and last legs of the journey respectively, which is a significant bottleneck [12]. Thus, the first and last legs are the most troublesome parts of a public transit journey, termed as the first/last mile (FM/LM) problem.

It has been shown in existing work [18,25] that the root causes of the FM/LM problem are the fixed routes and designated stops of transit buses serving the FM/LM. Further, the problem of excessive walking distance is exacerbated with the addition of waiting times at the bus stops, especially during off-peak hours owing to low frequency fixed schedules of the existing transit buses. At the same time, under-utilization of buses is a significant issue in terms of economic viability for the transit service operator. Thus, it is evident that addressing the FM/LM problem has benefits for both passengers and operators.

Mobility solutions that attempt to tackle the FM/LM problem, strive to extend the penetration of public transit systems by linking FM/LM connections [23]. These solutions are categorized as conventional or innovative mobility solutions. Conventional mobility solutions, also termed as transit oriented development, specifically focus on the creation of compact, walkable, pedestrian oriented, mixed-use communities centered around high quality transit systems [22]. On the contrary, private vehicles and taxis, collectively known as single occupancy vehicles (SOV) are also used to bridge the FM/LM. However, due to the negative impact on traffic congestion and environment, SOVs are highly discouraged in urban cities. On the other hand, technological advancements have led to economical, greener and easier innovative mobility solutions such as bike-sharing [15], casual car-pooling [22], personal mobility devices [30] and ride-sharing [23] being proposed. However, due to the added comfort of using motor vehicles (mini buses, vans) and viability to satisfy diversified user groups, ride-sharing is the preferred solution to the FM/LM problem.

Ride-sharing, also known as dial-a-ride, is a mode of demand responsive transit (DRT) system in which drivers traveling towards a single destination, pick-up and drop-off other passengers traveling towards the same destination or traveling along the same route [26]. Static ride-sharing, where all ride requests are known a-priori has been studied for many years [28]. Traditionally, static DRT, also known as para-transit services, have been used for door-to-door transportation services for the elderly and disabled. It has also been deployed in rural areas and areas of low passenger demand, where operating a fixed-route service is not economically viable. On the other hand, dynamic ride-sharing has gained traction only in recent years due to technological advancements in GPS based tracking, smart phones and wireless communications [5]. Thus, dynamic DRT is arguably one of the most popular and fast evolving new mobility options on the market that can be used to conveniently bridge FM/LM inefficiencies for users by providing quick and easy connections to/from public transit nodes [23].

However, existing work on DRT based public transit systems is limited to one or two ride matches [23]. On the contrary, systems which match multiple passengers to a single vehicle require advanced reservations to account for the significantly high computation time of the algorithms [7,32]. In a public transit system, however, the ride-matches should occur instantaneously and also, the outcome needs to be communicated to both the passenger and the driver at once. Hence, *there is a need for rapid and scalable solutions for DRT in order for it to be useful in public transit systems for FM/LM problem.*

To this end, we propose a DRT solution consisting of a **homogeneous** fleet of **electric** vehicles with fixed capacity and range (in terms of maximum number of passengers and VMT per vehicle) dispersed in a neighborhood, which responds in **real-time**, to the demand of passengers by picking them from their origin and dropping them off at a predetermined nearest rapid transit node. Moreover, the objective of the proposed solution is to **minimize the total passenger travel time** (waiting time + riding time). In addition, each passenger is guaranteed that the maximum travel time is less than a predetermined value. Also, we consider large instances of passenger requests in real-time. Hence, the proposed solutions require scalable, real-time computation of routes and schedules, which, as discussed in Sect. 2, cannot be obtained from the existing state-of-the-art techniques. Thus, the **contributions** of this work are: (1) an optimal mixed-integer quadratically constrained programming (MIQCP) model, (2) owing to the complexity of the MIQCP model, we then propose a scalable hybrid genetic algorithm which computes near-optimal results in real-time.

The rest of the paper is organized as follows. In Sect. 2, we discuss the existing state-of-the-art work on the DRT problem and highlight the limitations. Next, in Sect. 3, we present the proposed methodology. The results and conclusions of the study are discussed in Sects. 4 and 5 respectively.

2   Related Work

DRT services are classified as static and dynamic based on the mode of operation. In the static mode all requests are known beforehand, while in the dynamic mode requests are received in real-time. However, it should be noted that dynamic DRTs rarely exist in pure form since a number of requests are often known prior to the planning cycle [4]. Similarly, based on the objective, DRTs are classified as problems which (1) minimize costs subject to full demand satisfaction and side constraints, (2) maximize satisfied demand subject to vehicle availability and side constraints [10]. Irrespective of the classification, the basic DRT problem consists of finding routes and schedules for a fleet of m homogeneous vehicles originating at a single depot, serving the requests of n passengers. However, in literature, many variants of the DRT problem are considered with different features such as heterogeneous vehicles, multiple depots, pickup and delivery etc. Further, it should be noted that literature on DRT problems also consider delivery of goods. However, since the focus of this work is on public transit, our discussion is limited to works that consider DRT for passenger transit.

One of the pioneering work of solving the single vehicle DRT problem was presented in [27]. The author presents a dynamic programming based solution to the capacity constrained single vehicle, many-to-many, immediate-request, static and dynamic DRT problems. Later, the work has been extended by introducing new constraints and solution methods. However, owing to an exact approach, the usefulness of this work is limited to instances of low passenger requests (demand). Heuristic approaches such as parallel tabu-search [16] and neighborhood search [17] focus on instances of high demand. However, in reality DRT problems mostly occur for a fleet of vehicles. Thus, the applicability of the heuristic approaches are limited to specific scenarios.

Similarly, there are many exact and heuristic formulations for the multi-vehicle DRT problem such as column generation [13], branch-and-cut [9], tabu-search [11], sequential insertion heuristic [20], parallel insertion heuristic [14] and genetic algorithms [6,21,29]. Even though these methods solve instances with relatively high passenger requests to near-optimality, most of the works consider only the traditional use of DRT services. Thus, either the impact of execution time is minimal or the systems require advanced reservations. As reported in [36], solving the DRT for instances with high passenger requests take about 10 h. Similarly, the work in [7] requires passengers to book seats 4 h in advance.

On the contrary, we find limited work that focus specifically on DRT based solutions for the FM/LM problem. Perera et al. propose a scalable local-search heuristic for the FM transit problem [26]. Here, the use of time-window constraints limit the optimization capability which in turn facilitates the local-search. Further, the authors do not consider vehicle range and maximum traveling time constraints. Uchimura et al. propose a 3-tier public transit system connecting neighborhoods with major transit nodes using a DRT system [33]. Here, the authors use a genetic algorithm to solve the DRT problem. They present results for instances with 10 passenger requests (demand) computed within 40 s. However, such a system is expected to be used by a large number of passengers and hence, the system needs to be tested with instances of high demand to validate the scalability of the algorithm.

Tsubouchi et al. propose a DRT bus system that responds to real-time transit requests of passengers by computing routes and schedules using a cloud computing platform [32]. The authors claim an algorithm with linear time complexity compared to exponential complexity of the state-of-the-art work. However, they test the algorithm with only 5 vehicles and also the shared ride-ratio is significantly low. A similar effort to bridge the FM/LM gap using DRT is proposed in [34] and further improved in [35]. In this work, authors propose to connect people living in sub-urban areas, through a DRT service to a major urban transit node. Here, they use an insertion heuristic for path planning. However, the system requires advanced (one day prior to departure) passenger reservations.

MIT real-time ride-share research [24] highlights the importance of focusing on large employers and personal choice in clustering passengers. The benefit of focusing on large employers is attributed to the increased match rates that contribute to the economic viability. On the other hand, in the case of "Kutsuplus" in Helsinki, Finland [31], low ridership resulted in the seizure of operations. As stated in [31], the main reason for the empty Kutsuplus buses was the difficulty in matching passengers who are going in the same direction around the same time. Further, Kutsuplus was not designed to serve only the FM/LM connections. As such, our study is focused on providing a DRT based FM/LM solution to localities with low penetration of public transit and high population density.

3   Methodology

3.1   System Overview

The proposed system comprises of a homogeneous fleet of electric vehicles (supply) dispersed in a neighborhood. The system responds to passenger requests (demand) in real-time by picking them from their origins and dropping them off at a predetermined nearest rapid transit node. We assume that (1) all vehicles have a fixed capacity and range, (2) passengers request the service using a mobile application. All requests, origins and the real-time traffic data are logged using Google Maps APIs [1]. The proposed algorithm is executed periodically to find an optimum schedule for passengers and the fleet of vehicles. However, using a substantially small periodic value, not only are we able to provide real-time service to the passengers but also reduce the overhead incurred by re-optimizing the routes each time a request is logged. Thus, we model the dynamic DRT problem as a set of periodic static DRT problems. The objective of the problem is to devise a set of routes and schedules in real-time to minimize the total travel time of passengers while satisfying the full demand within the constraints, which include vehicle capacity, range and the maximum travel time per passenger. In this paper, we focus on the case where all vehicles are homogeneous.

3.2   Model Formulation

The problem is modeled using the graph-based structure as proposed in [26], which uses a directed acyclic graph. Here, we summarize the model for clarity. We assume that there are m vehicles and n passengers. Further, irrespective of the number of passengers at the same origin, each passenger is modeled using a node in the graph. Table 1 defines the nodes represented in the graph. Table 2 presents the decision variables in the mathematical formulation, x and s. Finally, Table 3 defines the terms used in the mathematical formulation. The decision variable x_{ijk} is defined for each edge (i, j) and each vehicle V_k, where $i \neq j$, $i \neq m + n + 1$ & $j \neq 1, 2, 3, \cdots, m$ and s_{ik} is defined for each node i and each vehicle V_k, where $i \neq 1, 2, 3, \cdots, m$. They are defined in Eqs. 1 and 2 respectively. Also, it should be noted that l, r, u and t_{ij} are positive integers and d_{ij} is a non-negative integer. The constraints involved in the model are (1) each passenger is serviced by exactly one vehicle; (2) vehicles with assigned passengers start service from origin of the vehicle and end service at the transit node (node ϑ); (3) number of passengers in each vehicle does not exceed the maximum capacity l; (4) vehicle miles traveled (VMT) of each vehicle does not exceed the range r; and (5) maximum travel time of a passenger is bounded by u.

Table 1. Terminology of nodes in the graph

Term	Description	Nodes represented in graph
Φ	Set of all nodes	$1, 2, 3, \cdots, m+n+1$
ν	Subset of vehicles	$1, 2, 3, \cdots, m$
ρ	Subset of passengers	$m+1, m+2, m+3, \cdots, m+n$
ϑ	Transit node	$m+n+1$

Table 2. Decision variables in the mathematical formulation

Decision variable	Type	Description
x_{ijk}	Binary	Vehicle V_k travels along the edge (i,j) from i to j
s_{ik}	Integer	Time vehicle V_k reaches node i

Table 3. Terminology of the mathematical formulation

Term	Description
V_v	v^{th} vehicle in the fleet of v vehicles
P_p	p^{th} passenger in the set of p passengers
$P_{i[a]}$	Request time of ith passenger
d_{ij}	Travel distance from node i to j
t_{ij}	Travel time from node i to j
m	Number of vehicles
n	Number of passengers
l	Maximum capacity of a vehicle
r	Maximum range of a vehicle
u	Maximum travel time of a passenger

$$x_{ijk} = \begin{cases} 1, & \text{vehicle } V_k \text{ travels from node } i \text{ to node } j, \\ 0, & \text{otherwise.} \end{cases} \tag{1}$$

$$s_{ik} = \begin{cases} f, & \text{vehicle } V_k \text{ services node } i, \quad f \epsilon z^+, \\ 0, & \text{otherwise.} \end{cases} \tag{2}$$

3.3   Optimal Mathematical Formulation

Based on the model in Sect. 3.2, we present an optimal mixed-integer quadratically constrained programing (MIQCP) mathematical formulation. Equation 3 shows the objective function of the mathematical formulation, which minimizes the total travel time of all passengers. All constraints in the model given in Eqs. 5–18 are classified into routing, timing, side and subtour elimination, which are explained in detail subsequently.

Objective function:

$$minimize \sum_{i \in \rho} \sum_{j \in \Phi} \sum_{k \in \nu} (x_{ijk} * s_{\vartheta k} - P_{i[a]}); \tag{3}$$

Subject to:
∗ *Routing Constraints*

$$\sum_{j \in \rho} x_{kjs} = 0 \quad \forall k \in \nu, \quad \forall s \in \nu; \quad where \quad k \neq s; \tag{4}$$

$$\sum_{j \in \rho} x_{kjk} \leq 1 \quad \forall k \in \nu; \tag{5}$$

$$x_{\vartheta jk} = 0 \quad \forall j \in \Phi, \quad \forall k \in \nu; \tag{6}$$

$$x_{ikk} = 0 \quad \forall i \in \rho, \quad \forall k \in \nu; \tag{7}$$

$$\sum_{i \in \Phi} x_{ibk} - \sum_{j \in \Phi} x_{bjk} = 0 \quad \forall k \in \nu, \forall b \in \rho; \tag{8}$$

$$\sum_{i \in \rho} x_{i \vartheta k} \leq 1 \quad \forall k \in \nu; \tag{9}$$

$$\sum_{i \in \rho} \sum_{k \in \nu} x_{i \vartheta k} \geq 1 \quad \forall k \in \nu; \tag{10}$$

∗ *Timing Constraints*

$$s_{kk} = 0 \quad \forall k \in \nu; \tag{11}$$

$$x_{ijk}(s_{ik} + t_{ij} - s_{jk}) \leq 0 \quad \forall i \in (\Phi \backslash \vartheta), \forall j \in \Phi, \forall k \in \nu; \tag{12}$$

∗ *Side Constraints*

$$\sum_{i \in \rho} \sum_{j \in \Phi} x_{ijk} \leq l \quad \forall k \in \nu; \tag{13}$$

$$\sum_{i \in \Phi} \sum_{j \in \Phi} x_{ijk} * d_{ij} \leq r \quad \forall k \in \nu; \tag{14}$$

$$s_{\vartheta k} \leq u_l \quad \forall k \in \nu; \quad u_l = min(l_{m+1}, l_{m+2}, \cdots, l_{m+n}); \tag{15}$$

∗ Subtour Elimination Constraints

$$x_{k\vartheta s} = 0 \quad \forall k \in \nu, \quad \forall s \in \nu; \tag{16}$$

$$x_{iik} = 0 \quad \forall i \in \rho, \quad \forall k \in \nu; \tag{17}$$

$$\sum_{j \in \Phi} \sum_{k \in \nu} x_{ijk} = 1 \quad \forall i \in \rho; \tag{18}$$

The first routing constraint in Eq. 4 sets the origin of the routes to each vehicle location. Equation 5 ensures that at least one vehicle moves from its' origin to serve passenger requests. Equations 6 and 7 prevents routes from originating at the transit node and finishing at vehicle nodes respectively. Equation 8 ensures that a route does not end at a passenger node. The final two routing constraints deal with the completion of the route. Equation 9 ensures that a vehicle will reach the transit node only through a passenger node. Similarly, Eq. 10 enforces that at least one vehicle reaches the transit node. Thus, in the best case one vehicle serves the passenger requests and reaches the transit node.

Timing constraints in Eqs. 11 and 12 initializes the service time of each vehicle and models the travel time between nodes respectively. Side constraints, namely vehicle capacity, range and maximum travel time of passengers are modeled in Eqs. 13, 14 and 15 respectively. Also, it should be noted that, we assume the range of the vehicle is directly comparable to the VMT. Thus, in Eq. 14 the summation of the VMT is compared with the maximum allowable range. In Eq. 15 we assume that the upper bound of the maximum riding time for each vehicle is equal to the minimum value among all passengers, irrespective of the assigned passengers. This assumption is realistic since the minute periodicity of the algorithm prevents significant deviations in the travel time among the passengers. Subtour elimination constraints further tighten the model and prevents any loops or subtours. Equation 16 prevents the vehicles traveling directly from origin to the transit node. Equation 17 prevents loops in the route. Finally, Eq. 18 ensures that there is only one outgoing edge at a passenger node.

The solution from the above formulation provides an optimal set of routes and schedules for the fleet of vehicles. However, due to the complexity of the model (NP-hard) [14], execution time grows exponentially with the size of the problem. Thus, we are motivated to develop a scalable approach that can solve the problem in real-time with significant accuracy for large instances.

3.4   Hybrid Genetic Algorithm

Genetic algorithms (GA) use principles of natural evolution to model real-world problems. Generally, they produce high quality results for complex combinatorial optimization problems [19]. In the past, GAs have been successfully used in various VRPs [6,21,29]. GAs can be easily adapted and improved for different problems using knowledge local to the problem. Further, they can be easily controlled to complete within a predefined number of iterations which favors real-time computations. Thus, we propose a hybrid meta-heuristic combining a modified GA with local-search and savings heuristic [8]. The pseudo-code of the proposed hybrid genetic algorithm (HGA) is given in Algorithm 1.

Algorithm 1. Pseudo Code of the Hybrid Genetic Algorithm

Input: passenger requests (P), fleet of vehicles (V)
Output: route & schedule of the fleet of vehicles
 1: **INITIALIZE** population
 2: **FITNESS EVALUATION** of each candidate
 3:
 4: **repeat**(
 5:     i: **PARENT SELECTION**;
 6:     ii: **MUTATION**;
 7:     exchange mutation
 8:     insertion mutation
 9:     iii: **PARENT SELECTION**;
10:     iv: **CROSSOVER**;
11:     modified heuristic crossover
12:     re-insertion crossover
13:     )
14: **until** TERMINATION CONDITION is satisfied

Genetic Encoding and Fitness Calculation: We use **path based representation**, to depict a single chromosome. Each chromosome consists of $m * l$ genes, where m and l are defined in Table 3. Thus, we effectively eliminate infeasible solutions in terms of capacity. Further, we use **integer encoding** to represent each passenger. The same objective function given in Eq. 3 is used as the fitness function. Thus, for each vehicle the fitness function evaluates total travel time of all passengers in a vehicle.

Initial Population Construction: The intuitive method of selecting the initial populations in GA is random selection. However, good initial populations can significantly improve the execution time of the algorithm [36]. Thus, we propose to use the method given in [26], which uses a **local-search heuristic** to generate initial solutions. Further, we modify the method in [26] and generate multiple chromosomes along with several random chromosomes.

Parent Selection: Based on the encoding scheme, fitness value of each gene is directly proportional to the fitness value of the chromosome. Thus, we use the **roulette wheel selection** procedure for parent selection. However, as the objective of the work is minimization of total travel time, chromosomes with higher fitness values (weak parents) are considered as candidates for reproduction. Further, in order to maintain strong parents across generations, the two most **elite** parents are directly included in the next generation.

Mutation: Mutation is performed on a single individual and it helps to explore new states and avoid local optima. In our algorithm, we use two mutation operators, namely **exchange** and **insertion** mutation. In the exchange mutation operator, a selected sub-tour is swapped across a randomly selected point. However, in the proposed HGA a **local optimization** is used to find a suitable point. In the insertion mutation, a gene is removed from the tour and inserted back into a different position in the tour. However, when inserting we use the **savings heuristic**.

Crossover: Crossover operator improves the average quality of the population by simulating the reproduction between two individuals. As in mutation, we propose two crossover operators. The first crossover operator is a **modified heuristic crossover**, where genes with the highest fitness value of the selected parents are swapped to produce two new individuals. In the next crossover operator the gene with the highest fitness value is removed from the selected parent and inserted into the path of another randomly selected parent. The re-insertion is done based on the **savings heuristic**. Thus, the fitness value of the parent with the removed gene improves in contrast to the other parent. However, as the goal is collectively reducing the fitness value this approach may yield better results at the expense of one parent.

4   Results

In this section, we present the results of the computational experiments to verify the proposed HGA. *IBM ILOG CPLEX OPTIMIZATION STUDIO 12.7.1* [2] is used to implement the mathematical model in Sect. 3.3 and the in-built constraint programming solver is used to solve the formulation to optimality. The HGA proposed in Sect. 3.4 is implemented in C++. Runtime measurement is done on a PC with 32 GB RAM, running Windows 10 on an Intel Xeon E5-1630V3 CPU at 3.70 GHz.

4.1   Experimental Setup

The motivation of our study is to devise an algorithm capable of handling large instances of passenger requests in real-time. This is a common scenario within the premises of any university, thus we select a university for our experimental setup shown in Fig. 1. Here, demand in terms of passenger requests can originate from any location within the given zone. However, for clarity we limit the origins of demand to a set of fixed locations (bus stops), indicated in Fig. 1. In contrast, vehicles (supply) are considered to be dispersed in the zone. Also, it is noteworthy that there may be multiple passengers in a single origin for a given problem.

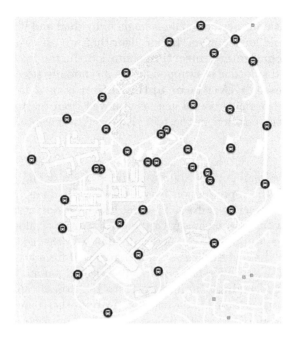

Fig. 1. Sample bus stop distribution

4.2   Experiments

Given the complexity of the optimal mathematical formulation and hence, the exponential increase in time required to obtain results, we have divided our experiments into two categories. First, we study 10 small-sized problems, where we compare the accuracy of the proposed Hybrid Genetic Algorithm (HGA) with the optimal results. The next set of experiments comprise of 30 medium-large problems. However, in this case we compare the results of the proposed HGA with two realistic upper and lower bounds obtained from Google Maps APIs [1]. Also, each problem is repeated 5 times and for each instance the origins of demand and supply are selected randomly. Further, in each instance passengers are distributed randomly among the origins. In both experiments, the maximum capacity and driving range of a vehicle are set to constant values of 8 and 30 km respectively. Also, we ensure that the supply (available seats) is equal to or greater than the demand (number of passengers).

4.3   Evaluation

Evaluation of the algorithm is performed under three criteria. Criteria 1: Scalability of the proposed HGA, Criteria 2: Comparison of the proposed HGA to the optimal results and bounds obtained through *CPLEX* and Google Maps respectively, and Criteria 3: Analysis of the travel time saving with vehicle utilization.

Scalability: As mentioned in Sect. 3.3, the time complexity of the optimal mathematical formulation is NP-hard. However, the proposed HGA computes the routes and schedules in a significantly low time. The average execution time of the 5 instances of all the 40 problems are shown Fig. 2. Here, the horizontal and vertical axes represent the number of nodes $(m+n+1)$ and the average execution time of the algorithm in seconds respectively. Here, we observe the significantly low increase of average execution time with the problem size.

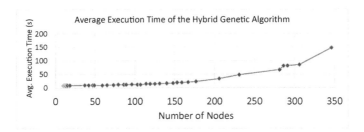

Fig. 2. Scalability of the Hybrid Genetic Algorithm

Performance: Performance of the proposed HGA, in terms of accuracy of results compared to the optimal values (experiment 1) and bounds (experiment 2) are analyzed. In experiment 1, we compare the results of *CPLEX* and the proposed HGA. However, for experiment 2 we define two bounds obtained from Google Maps for each problem. For the **lower bound (LB)**, we assume that all passengers use their own vehicles to travel to the transit node (SOV time). In contrast, for the **upper bound (UB)** we obtain the time taken for the journey using public transit (Transit time). However, when calculating the UB, we assume that buses have sufficient capacity to cater the demand and also use schedules of off-peak day time. Results and the corresponding parameters for the two experiments are given in Tables 4 and 5 respectively. In both tables, we present the average total travel time for the passengers in minutes. In experiment 1, the average deviation of results from the optimal values is **1.72%**. In experiment 2, 28 problems are within the bounds. However, in problem 13 and 19 the HGA result is marginally higher than the UB. The reasons for the deviation is analyzed in the subsequent section. Further, due to the randomness of passenger and vehicle allocation we observe an outlier in problem 3.

Variation of Travel Time Savings: Travel time saving against the vehicle utilization is shown in Fig. 3. Here, the horizontal and vertical axes represent vehicle utilization and travel time saving percentage respectively. Also, the corresponding problem number is marked in the graph. Travel time saving implies

Table 4. Results for experiment 1

Problem No	Vehicles	Parameters Passengers	Bus Stops	No of Nodes	HGA (min)	CPLEX (min)	Deviation (%)
1	4	5	5	10	72.2	71.6	0.83
2	4	6	6	11	95.6	93.6	2.17
3	4	7	7	12	106.4	104.4	1.99
4	4	8	8	13	131	126.2	3.73
5	5	6	6	12	84.8	84.4	0.47
6	5	7	7	13	102	101	0.98
7	5	8	8	14	117.4	115.2	1.95
8	6	7	7	14	95.8	95.8	0.00
9	6	8	8	15	117	114.6	2.10
10	7	10	10	18	143.8	139.6	3.00

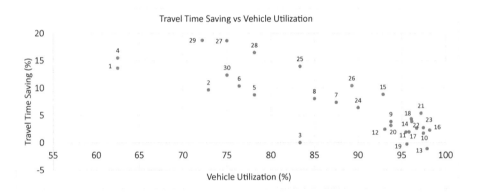

Fig. 3. Travel time saving of the proposed DRT system

the benefit passengers' gain in terms of travel time by using the proposed DRT system with respect to public transit. In general, when the vehicle utilization is moderate, the proposed system outperforms the transit system with savings of up to **19%**. However, when vehicle utilization is significantly high ($\geq 95\%$) the benefit obtained from the proposed system is marginal. These points lie on the bottom right of the graph. Hence, problems 13 and 19 with vehicle utilization of 98% and 97% respectively under-perform compared to the transit system.

Table 5. Results for experiment 2

Problem No	Vehicles	Parameters Passengers	Bus Stops	No of Nodes	HGA (min)	LB (min)	UB (min)
1	6	30	30	37	652.4	325.6	755.2
2	6	35	35	42	804.2	382.6	890
3	6	40	40	47	1014.2	435	1014
4	8	40	25	49	848.8	438.6	1004.2
5	8	50	30	59	1152.4	539.2	1262.6
6	9	55	32	65	1236.8	606.6	1379.8
7	9	63	34	73	1487.8	682.4	1606
8	10	68	25	79	1576	738.6	1713.8
9	10	75	30	86	1825.2	810.8	1897.8
10	10	78	18	89	1952.8	841	1987.2
11	11	84	27	96	2062	900.6	2102.4
12	12	90	30	103	2183.2	986	2253.4
13	12	94	21	107	2386	1024	2359.8
14	13	100	22	114	2393.4	1078.2	2489.2
15	14	104	25	119	2476.6	1110	2716.2
16	14	110	40	125	2764	1188.6	2828.4
17	15	115	35	131	2831.8	1258.6	2887.8
18	16	123	19	140	2965.2	1341.2	3099.4
19	17	130	28	148	3187	1383.6	3178.8
20	18	134	37	153	3241.4	1464	3322.4
21	18	140	26	159	3431.4	1492.6	3626.2
22	19	147	17	167	3568.6	1599.8	3664.8
23	20	156	23	177	3816.8	1700.2	3923.4
24	25	180	27	206	4207.8	1962	4494
25	30	200	32	231	4448.6	2172.8	5168.4
26	35	250	16	286	5694.2	2703.8	6355.2
27	40	240	26	281	5081.4	2591.8	6243.4
28	40	250	25	291	5267.8	2678.8	6304.8
29	45	260	37	306	5422.6	2805	6668.8
30	45	300	25	346	6617.2	3214.6	7548.8

5 Conclusion

This paper proposes a scalable hybrid genetic algorithm (HGA) for an on-demand first mile transit system using electric vehicles. The problem is first modeled using an optimal mathematical formulation and solved for small instances.

Next, we propose a HGA, which computes near-optimal results in real-time. Further, the proposed system achieves considerable travel time savings with respect to public transit services. In future, we plan to extend the work for heterogeneous vehicles (in terms of capacity and range) and for last mile transit.

References

1. Google Maps APIs: Build the next generation of location experiences. https://developers.google.com/maps/
2. IBM ILOG CPLEX Optimization Studio. https://ibm.co/2vXgzRC
3. American Public Transportation Association: Public Transportation Benefits (2017). http://www.apta.com/mediacenter/ptbenefits/Pages/default.aspx
4. Borndörfer, R., et al.: Telebus Berlin: vehicle scheduling in a dial-a-ride system (1999)
5. Cao, B., et al.: SHAREK: a scalable dynamic ride sharing system. In: MDM (2015)
6. Carballedo, R., et al.: A new evolutionary hybrid algorithm to solve demand responsive transportation problems. In: Abraham, A., Corchado, J.M., González, S.R., De Paz Santana, J.F. (eds) International Symposium on Distributed Computing and Artificial Intelligence. AINSC, vol. 91, pp. 233–240. Springer, Heidelberg (2011). https://doi.org/10.1007/978-3-642-19934-9_29
7. Chevrier, R., et al.: Comparison of three algorithms for solving the convergent demand responsive transportation problem. In: ITSC (2006)
8. Clarke, G., Wright, J.W.: Scheduling of vehicles from a central depot to a number of delivery points. Oper. Res. 12(4), 568–581 (1964)
9. Cordeau, J.F.: A branch-and-cut algorithm for the dial-a-ride problem. Oper. Res. 54(3), 573–586 (2006)
10. Cordeau, J.F., Laporte, G.: The Dial-A-Ride Problem (DARP): variants, modeling issues and algorithms. Q. J. Belg. Fr. Ital. Oper. Res. Soc. 1(2), 89–101 (2003)
11. Cordeau, J., Laporte, G.: A tabu search heuristic for the static multi-vehicle dial-a-ride problem. Transp. Res. Part B: Methodol. 37(6), 579–594 (2003)
12. TUM CREATE: The last mile problem (2012). http://bit.ly/2qKpCaY
13. Desrosiers, J., et al.: A dynamic programming solution of the large-scale single-vehicle dial-a-ride problem with time windows. Am. J. Math. Manag. Sci. 6(3–4), 301–325 (1986)
14. Diana, M., Dessouky, M.M.: A new regret insertion heuristic for solving large-scale dial-a-ride problems with time windows. Transp. Res. Part B: Methodol. 38(6), 539–557 (2004)
15. Elliot, F.: Bikeshare: a review of recent literature. Transp. Rev. 36(1), 92–113 (2016)
16. Gendreau, M., et al.: A dynamic model and parallel tabu search heuristic for real-time ambulance relocation. Parallel Comput. 27, 1641–1653 (2001)
17. Gendreau, M., et al.: Neighborhood search heuristics for a dynamic vehicle dispatching problem with pick-ups and deliveries. Transp. Res. Part C Emerg. Technol. 14(3), 157–174 (2006)
18. Gibson, A.: Eliminating Public Transit's First-Mile/Last-Mile Problem (2016). http://bit.ly/2mgw6sm
19. Gonzlez, M., et al.: Using genetic algorithms for maximizing technical efficiency in data envelopment analysis. Procedia Comput. Sci. 51(C), 374–383 (2015)

20. Jaw, J.J., et al.: A heuristic algorithm for the multi-vehicle advance request dial-a-ride problem with time windows. Transp. Res. Part B: Methodol. **20**(3), 243–257 (1986)
21. Jorgensen, R.M., et al.: Solving the dial-a-ride problem using genetic algorithms. J. Oper. Res. Soc. **58**(10), 1321–1331 (2007)
22. Lesh, M.C.: Innovative concepts in first-last mile connections to public transportation. In: International Conference on Urban Public Transportation Systems (2013)
23. Logan, S., et al.: First and Last Mile Connections: New Mobility (2016). http://on.nrdc.org/2utPxUd
24. MIT: Welcome to MIT Real-Time Rideshare Research (2010). http://ridesharechoices.scripts.mit.edu/home/
25. Osaba, E., et al.: An asymmetric multiple traveling salesman problem with backhauls to solve a dial-a-ride problem. In: SAMI (2015)
26. Perera, T., et al.: A scalable heuristic algorithm for demand responsive transportation for first mile transit. In: INES (2017)
27. Psaraftis, H.N.: A dynamic programming solution to the single vehicle many-to-many immediate request dial-a-ride problem. Transp. Sci. **14**(2), 130–154 (1980)
28. Psaraftis, H.N., et al.: Dynamic vehicle routing problems: three decades and counting. Networks **67**(1), 3–31 (2016)
29. Rekiek, B., et al.: Handicapped person transportation: an application of the grouping genetic algorithm. Eng. Appl. Artif. Intell. **19**(5), 511–520 (2006)
30. Robyn, D., et al.: Use of personal mobility devices for first-and-last mile travel: the Macquarie Ryde trial. In: ARSC (2015)
31. Sulopuiso, O.: Why Helsinki's innovative on-demand bus service failed (2016). http://bit.ly/2mkeUDg
32. Tsubouchi, K., et al.: Innovative on-demand bus system in Japan. IET Intell. Transp. Syst. **4**(4), 270–279 (2010)
33. Uchimura, K., et al.: Demand responsive services in hierarchical public transportation system. IEEE Trans. Veh. Technol. **51**(4), 760–766 (2002)
34. Uehara, K., et al.: A proposal of a transport system connecting demand responsive bus with mass transit. In: ICCE (2014)
35. Uehara, K., et al.: Evaluation of a hierarchical cooperative transport system using demand responsive bus on a dynamic simulation. IEICE Trans. Fundam. Electron. Commun. Comput. Sci. **E99.A**(1), 310–318 (2016)
36. Xiang, Z., et al.: A fast heuristic for solving a large-scale static dial-a-ride problem under complex constraints. Eur. J. Oper. Res. **174**(2), 1117–1139 (2006)

Comprehensive Learning Gene Expression Programming for Automatic Implicit Equation Discovery

Yongliang Chen[1], Jinghui Zhong[1(✉)], and Mingkui Tan[2]

[1] School of Computer Science and Engineering,
South China University of Technology, Guangzhou, China
`jinghuizhong@gmail.com`
[2] School of Software Engineering, South China University of Technology,
Guangzhou, China

Abstract. Implicit equation is loose in form, which makes it more powerful than explicit equation for data regression. The mainstream method for automatic implicit equation discovery is based on calculating derivatives. However, this derivative-based mechanism requires high time consumption and it is difficult to solve problems with sparse data. To solve these deficiencies, this paper proposes a new mechanism named Comprehensive Learning Fitness Evaluation Mechanism (CL-FEM). The mechanism learns knowledge from *disturbed* information collected from several previously generated stochastic datasets, to check the validity of the equation model. Only the valid equations can be candidates of selection, which is a process to pick out the equation with the smallest output. We integrate the proposed mechanism with the simplified Self-Learning Gene Expression Programming (SL-GEP) and propose the Comprehensive Learning Gene Expression Programming (CL-GEP). The experiment results have demonstrated that CL-GEP can offer very promising performance.

Keywords: Implicit equation · Symbolic regression
Gene expression programming (GEP) · *disturbed* knowledge learning

1 Introduction

Genetic programming (GP) is a powerful evolutionary computing technique that has been used to solve complicated optimization problems [3,5]. Due to its high efficacy, GP has aroused people's attention these years, and many enhanced variants of GP [1,6,7] have been developed, such as Gene Expression Programming (GEP) [2,12] and Self-Learning Gene Expression Programming (SL-GEP) [14]. Thus far, GEP has been applied to a number of science and engineering fields [4,8,11,13].

One of the most common applications of GP is symbolic regression, which requires finding proper mathematic equations to fit the given observed data.

© Springer International Publishing AG, part of Springer Nature 2018
Y. Shi et al. (Eds.): ICCS 2018, LNCS 10860, pp. 114–128, 2018.
https://doi.org/10.1007/978-3-319-93698-7_9

Symbolic regression problem has profound influence on our life, for finding proper equations to express data can help people predict future incidents or even excavate unknown laws of nature. The existing GPs, however, are mostly focused on finding explicit equation. An explicit equation in an D-dimension space can be described as $y = f(\boldsymbol{x_{D-1}})$, where $\boldsymbol{x_{D-1}}$ is a $(D-1)$-dimension variable vector, the dependent variable y is separated and is expressed by an explicit formula. As y is separated and the form is fixed, it somehow sacrifices the expression capability of y, therefore, implicit equation is proposed. The form of an implicit equation in an D-dimension space can be $f(\boldsymbol{x_{D-1}}, y) = 0$, putting y in the function $f(...)$ can make the equation more expressive.

To find an approximate implicit model seems very direct and concise, however, there exists many perennial and fundamental problems. The most attractive problem is how to guarantee the feasibility of a model. The aim of symbolic regression problems for implicit equation is to find out a mathematical rule $f(...)$ consisting of $x_1, x_2, ..., x_D$, which can fit the target dataset best to make $f(x_1, x_2, ..., x_D) = 0$. Some direct methods which only focus on reducing $f(...)$ to zero will always converge very fast to some meaningless functions, like $x - x$ and $sin^2(x) + cos^2(x) - 1$, which are equivalent to zero. Therefore, how to avoid models converging to these misleading equations is the key to handle implicit symbolic regression problems.

The mainstream method to avoid finding infeasible models is to minimize the differences of gradients between the model and the dataset [9]. The core idea is assigning fitness value by calculating the differences between the partial derivatives of each dimension of the target point and the derivatives calculated using the neighboring point of the target one. This technique has proved to be useful because it considers the shape of the model rather than only concentrating on the output of the function.

We have practiced solving implicit equation tasks with this method, however, we found some weakness of the derivative-based fitness evaluation mechanism (DB-FEM). On the one hand, a large training dataset is needed. Once the data points are not continuous enough, partial derivatives will be lacking in reliability and accuracy. On the other hand, calculating derivatives is time-consuming and inconvenient. When the set is large (contrast to the previous point) and the model is in high dimension space, using this method seems impractical.

To solve these problems, we propose a new mechanism to evaluate symbolic regression problems for implicit equations, named Comprehensive Learning Fitness Evaluation Mechanism (CL-FEM). Traditional GPs only learn from positive training data (i.e., those need to fit), using these data to guide the search process. While in our method, we learn from not only positive training data, but also negative training data, so we call it Comprehensive Learning. Rather than calculating derivatives, we test the model function not only by using the target dataset, but also by using several randomly generated, stochastic datasets produced in advance. Each dataset focuses on one dimension of the equation, and the equation model makes sense only if every dimension makes contribution to solving the problem. Otherwise, the model will be regarded as a failure.

To test this mechanism, we combine it with a simplified Self-Learning Gene Expression Programming (SL-GEP), and propose a new algorithm for automatic implicit equation discovery, named Comprehensive Learning Gene Expression Programming (CL-GEP). We implement CL-GEP to some typical implicit function models to test the new mechanism. We not only pay attention to the success rate of finding accurate functions, but also the time consumption. Also, we use sparse datasets to test the proposed CL-FEM. To demonstrate the superiority, we make comparisons with the DB-FEM. Results have shown that CL-FEM is promising.

2   Preliminaries

To ensure that readers can have a better understanding of the paper, this section will present some preliminary knowledge about the implicit equation, and the derivative-based fitness evaluation mechanism (DB-FEM).

2.1   Implicit Equation Problem

An implicit equation is a function adopting x_D as input and the output is equivalent to zero, which is expressed as $f(x_D) = 0$.

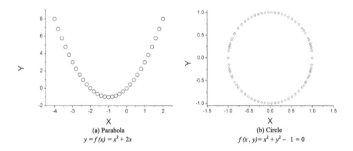

Fig. 1. Examples for explicit equation (parabola) and implicit equation (circle).

The need for implicit equation models arises when there is no independent variable in a dataset, or at least we do not know which variable can be the independent variable. To try to find an independent variable or make assumption is impractical, therefore, implicit equation is the best choice. Transferring an explicit equation to an implicit equation is very easy. For example, $y = f(x) = x^2 + 2x$ (Fig. 1a) can be translated into an implicit form $g(x, y) = f(x) - y = x^2 + 2x - y = 0$ very easily. On the contrary, if you want to transfer an implicit equation, like $x^2 + y^2 = 1$ (Fig. 1b), to an explicit equation, it is a piecewise function $y = \pm\sqrt{1 - x^2}$, which is very inconvenient. Therefore, implicit equations are loose in form and are more powerful than explicit equations in expressing data to some extent.

As the advantages of implicit equation are realized, several trials for implicit equation discovery have been made previously. The main challenge is that there are infinite implicit equations that are valid for any dataset, which proves finding $f(\boldsymbol{x}_D) = 0$ directly infeasible, as mentioned above. To make symbolic regression more comprehensive, the need for effective implicit equation evaluation mechanism is highly emergent.

2.2 Derivative-Based Fitness Evaluation Mechanism

The mostly used method today to solve implicit equation regression problems is using partial derivatives. Using this mechanism not only can ensure that the target point fits the data, but also can predict the indirect relationships between variables of the system.

For an implicit equation $f(x, y) = 0$, abandon the $= 0$ symbol, we can calculate the partial derivatives $\delta f/\delta x$, $\delta f/\delta y$. Then, from derivative rules, we have

$$\frac{\delta y}{\delta x} = -\frac{\delta f/\delta x}{\delta f/\delta y} \qquad (1)$$

where $\frac{\delta y}{\delta x}$ is the implicit derivative which can express the gradient of the implicit equation. When it comes to three or more dimension equations, more derivative values like $\frac{\delta z}{\delta x}$, $\frac{\delta z}{\delta y}$ should be used to describe the information of the equations. Then, we estimate the implicit derivatives $\triangle y/\triangle x$ from the dataset, where $\triangle x = x_a - x_{a+1}$ and $\triangle y = y_a - y_{a+1}$, a is the index of the target point in the dataset, the data need to be in *order* when calculating derivatives. To evaluate an implicit equation model, differences between the model and the dataset are expressed as

$$\frac{1}{N} \sum_{n=1}^{N} log(1 + |\frac{\triangle y}{\triangle x} - \frac{\delta y}{\delta x}|) \qquad (2)$$

where N is the size of the dataset. When the number of dimensions is more than two, the estimation of $f(x_1, x_2, ..., x_D)$ becomes

$$\frac{1}{N} \sum_{n=1}^{N} log(1 + |\frac{\triangle x_2}{\triangle x_1} - \frac{\delta x_2}{\delta x_1}| + |\frac{\triangle x_3}{\triangle x_1} - \frac{\delta x_3}{\delta x_1}| + ... + |\frac{\triangle x_D}{\triangle x_{D-1}} - \frac{\delta x_D}{\delta x_{D-1}}|) \qquad (3)$$

From Eq. 3, we can easily find that the examination cost of DB-FEM in computational time is $O(ND^2)$, where D is the number of dimensions. The $O(ND^2)$ time consumption is high when the estimated mechanism should be repeated thousands of times during GP. Besides, finding the nearest point of the target point in the dataset is another time consuming task. What's more, using derivatives as criterion to evaluate a model requires the dataset to be large and crowded enough, otherwise, derivatives may convey wrong information (see Fig. 2).

Fig. 2. Example for a dataset with few data points. The red curve represents the target equation, while the DB-FEM tends to find the equation represented by the blue curve, for it is smoother and fits the derivatives better. (Color figure online)

3   The Proposed Mechanism and Algorithm

This section will first describe the proposed CL-FEM, which is a new direction to evaluate an implicit function model. Then the proposed CL-GEP will be introduced.

3.1   Comprehensive Learning Fitness Evaluation Mechanism

In contrast to the existing mechanism like calculating derivatives, the application of CL-FEM is more direct and concise. As mentioned in previous sections, the main difficulty of finding proper implicit equation model is how to avoid being trapped in equations which are equivalent to zero. Instead of concentrating on partial constitution, we focus on the output of $f(\boldsymbol{x_D})$, but selectively.

The CL-FEM regards a model meaningful under a premise that each dimension of $\boldsymbol{x_D}$ contributes to solving the problem. To be more specific, the model is illegal when some dimensions are missed, like $f(x, y) = x^3 + x$, or some dimensions are useless, like $f(x, y) = y + x^2 - y$. We estimate outputs of the functions by implementing data and computing the mean square error (MSE) of the results with zero, which is defined as

$$MSE = \frac{1}{N} \sum_{j=1}^{N} s_j^2 \qquad (4)$$

Most of all, we need to ensure that a model is not misleading. To justify the validity of a model, CL-FEM uses the *disturbed* data.

Step 1-Form stochastic datasets

For each dimension of the variable vector $\boldsymbol{x_D}$, we generate a stochastic dataset. Data in the stochastic datasets are generated at the beginning of GP, the dataset for the kth dimension is produced following the rule of

$$x_{ij} = \begin{cases} randval(L_k, U_k) & j = k \\ t_{ij} & otherwise \end{cases} \quad i = 1, 2, ..., N \quad j = 1, 2, ..., D \qquad (5)$$

where N is the volume of the dataset, D is the dimension number for each point, $randval(a, b)$ returns a random value in the range of (a, b), L_k and U_k are the upper bound and the lower bound of the kth dimension, and t_{ij} is variable from the target dataset. Points are distributed randomly in one dimension, which can be a tool for us to judge whether every dimension is meaningful.

Step 2-Estimate target models

We use the datasets generated in *Step 1* to estimate whether every dimension contributes to the target model.

First, calculate the results using the target dataset and all stochastic datasets, forming a set consisting $(D + 1)$ result vectors $\{S, S^1, S^2, ..., S^D\}$. S is the result vector gained from the target dataset, and the others are result vectors gained from the D stochastic datasets. Then, we estimate the model by calculating MSE between S and S^is

$$m_i = \frac{1}{N} \sum_{j=1}^{N} (s_j - s_j^i)^2, s_j^i \in S^i, \quad i = 1, 2, ..., D \tag{6}$$

It is easy to justify that if the i-dimension makes sense in the model, there must be $m_i > 0$. We set $1E - 4$ to be the *tolerance degree*, and set the fitness value V of the obtained model by

$$V = \begin{cases} MSE & (m_1 > 1E - 4) \wedge (m_2 > 1E - 4) \wedge ... \wedge (m_D > 1E - 4) = TRUE \\ 1E10 & otherwise \end{cases} \tag{7}$$

where $1E10$ is a huge constant which means the model is obsolete. Like the direct methods, a smaller V is preferred during the evolution. When there is a D-dimension equation model, the examination time consumption of CL-FEM is $O(ND)$, and the calculation processes are convenient and practical.

3.2   The Comprehensive Learning Gene Expression Programming Algorithm

The CL-GEP adopts a simplified SL-GEP [14], using a novel representation in chromosomes. What's more, we make some fine-tunings for the convenience of use.

Fig. 3. The chromosome representation of an individual.

Chromosome Representation. The proposed CL-GEP removes the mechanism of using subfunctions, for we want to get more concise and readable results, however, it keeps the basic chromosome representation of SL-GEP. In CL-GEP, each chromosome consists of a *Head* and a *Tail*. The *Head* and the *Tail* are stored in a chromosome continuously. The *Head* can contain both functions (e.g., + or -) and terminals (e.g., x, y, or 1), while the *Tail* can only store terminals. Suppose that the length of the *Head* is H, then the length of the *Tail* should be $H + 1$, to ensure that the chromosome can be decoded successfully even if the *Head* only contains functions.

The form of the chromosome is presented in Fig. 3 and an example of decoding an implicit equation is presented in Fig. 4. Notice that, as the length of a chromosome is fixed, some information in the chromosome may not be used, however, as the length of the used chromosome is flexible, it can improve the diversity of population to some extent.

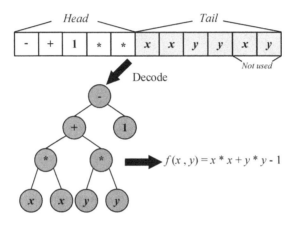

Fig. 4. Decode a chromosome to an implicit equation.

Function Set and Terminal Set. We make some fine-tunings of the terminal set and function set of SL-GEP to construct CL-GEP's. The function set of CL-GEP is much simpler

$$\Psi = \{+, -, *\} \tag{8}$$

We abandon the function / in CL-GEP, for implicit equations are equivalent to zero, which is only affected by numerator in a fraction. Therefore, adding / to the function set is unnecessary, and it will make the output more difficult to comprehend.

As for the terminal set, we add constant 1 to be a terminal, and the set can be expressed as

$$\Gamma = \{x_1, x_2, ..., x_D, 1\} \tag{9}$$

Because we remove / from the function set, constant 1 or other constant can not be decoded as x/x in CL-GEP. In order to improve the capability of precise expression, we make 1 a terminal choice. It is proved to be necessary, for 1 is always an important component of an implicit equation.

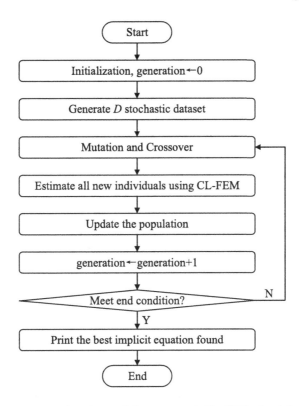

Fig. 5. The flowchart of the proposed CL-GEP algorithm.

Mutation and Crossover. Mutation and Crossover in CL-GEP are the same as SL-GEP. The mutation process is a variant of the mutation in traditional Differential Evolution (DE) [10], making three main improvements, *Distance measuring*, *Distance adding* and *Distance scaling*, to ensure that it is feasible in the unique chromosome representation. Crossover is performed after mutation to make offsprings vary in diversity.

Selection. In this step, good offsprings are selected to replace their parents to become new individuals in the new population. The result of selection is based on CL-FEM.

The flowchart of the algorithm is shown in Fig. 5. We set limits to the number of generations as the terminal condition. At last, the best-so-far implicit equation model, which has the smallest fitness value V, will be regarded as the final solution to the problem.

4   Experiments

This section investigates the performance of the proposed CL-GEP algorithm. First, the experimental settings are presented. We also implement the DB-FEM to the simplified SL-GEP and generate a testing algorithm named DB-GEP, whose fitness value V is calculated by

$$V = MSE + diff \tag{10}$$

where $diff$ is calculated by Eq. 3.

The settings for the two algorithms are the same and they are competed with each other. Then, we will present the experiment results and have some discussions.

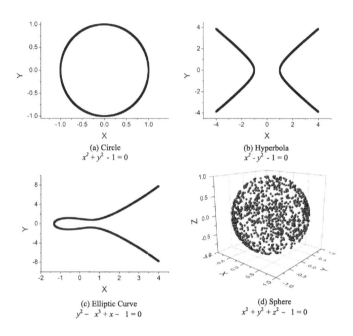

Fig. 6. Data sampled from the four target implicit equation systems.

4.1   Experimental Settings

We experiment with four typical implicit equation problems with varying difficulty (Fig. 6). The first two equations, *Circle* and *Hyperbola*, are the simplest implicit equations, for the feature of the two curves are easy to capture and the combining rule for x and y is concise. The third equation is *Elliptic Curve*, which is more complex in form and harder to predict. For these three equations, we take 500 sample points randomly from each system. The forth one is a 3-dimension equation *Sphere*, which is the most difficult one in the four tasks. For this equation, We sample 1000 points from the space.

The four equations are estimated by the two algorithms, CL-GEP and DB-GEP. For each equation, we run 30 times, 20,000 generations in each time, then calculate the success times during the 30 runs and the average time consumption

Table 1. Parameter settings.

Parameter	Value	Summary
H	15	The length of Heads
F	$rand(0, 1)$	Scaling factor of mutation
CR	$rand(0, 1)$	Crossover rate
$MAXGENS$	20,000	Maximum generations
$POPSIZE$	200	Size of the population

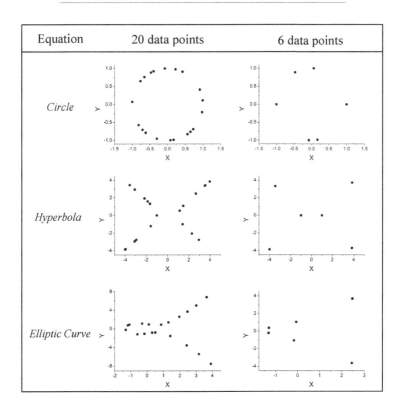

Fig. 7. Sparse datasets of *Circle*, *Hyperbola* and *Elliptic Curve*.

for one run. Programs are run on a computer with INTEL I7-6500U CPU. The detailed parameter settings for the algorithms are listed in Table 1.

To test the algorithms' practicability when faced with datasets of different densities, experiments are implemented for sparse data on the first three equations, *Circle*, *Hyperbola* and *Elliptic Curve*. Each equation is run for 30 times, 20,000 generations in each time. We calculate the success times when there are respectively 500, 100, 20 and 6 data in the set, and make comparisons between the two algorithms.

To show the sparse datasets more intuitively, we mark the points in the space for sets containing 20 and 6 data points, which are shown in Fig. 7. It can be observed that when the datasets contain 20 data points, we can still recognize the general features of the curves. When it comes to datasets containing 6 data points, however, it is almost impossible to tell out what they refer to. If the algorithm is able to help find out the relationships between variables from these sparse datasets, it will be of great significance.

4.2   Experimental Results and Discussion

We conduct experiments from two directions. The first one focuses on the capability of the algorithms to find the right equation models, where data are crowded enough in the datasets. The second one aims to test how the two algorithms perform when the datasets are sparse.

Experiments on the Four Equations. Table 2 shows the results of the first experiment, the success times and average time consumption to find a successful equation are presented.

Table 2. Results on running four implicit equations.

Problem	CL-GEP		DB-GEP	
	Suc	*Time* (s)	*Suc*	*Time* (s)
Circle	30	231.57	30	371.13
Hyperbola	30	91.62	30	405.03
Elliptic curve	29	148.78	20	467.59
Sphere	0	\	0	\

The results have shown that the proposed CL-GEP algorithm has gained promising performance against DB-GEP. It can be observed that both of the algorithms can perfectly solve the first two problems, which are concise in forms. When it comes to *Elliptic Curve*, however, the superiority of CL-GEP reveals distinctly, with the DB-GEP only getting the success rate of 66.7%, while the CL-GEP only fails in one run, holding the success rate of 96.7%.

Consider the DB-GEP, concentrating on the partial feature of the model can guarantee the validity of the model to some extent, and it is certainly an effective angle of solving symbolic regression problems, however, it may give little attention to the original definition of an implicit equation, which is $f(\boldsymbol{x_D}) = 0$. On the contrary, CL-GEP focuses only on the output of $f(\boldsymbol{x_D})$. It can adopt the output as fitness value because it can ensure that all equations are valid and meaningful. Previous works have doubts on the reliability and feasibility of the output, experiments have proved that it works in CL-GEP.

As for another index of the experiment, CL-GEP has gained outstanding performance in time consumption. The gap of time consumption between the two algorithms is apparently huge. In equation *Circle*, the time cost by DB-GEP is 150% of CL-GEP. What's more, the differences of *Elliptic Curve* and *Hyperbola* between the two algorithms are triple and quadruple. Regarding the time consumption cost of the fitness evaluation mechanisms, DB-FEM mostly spends time in calculating partial derivatives, the quotients of derivatives and finding the nearest points, while CL-FEM spends time only when calculating the output of $D+1$ datasets. The results prove effectively that the CL-FEM has evident advantages.

Nevertheless, problems arise when solving the 3-dimension equation *Sphere*. To our surprise, neither of the algorithms can find out the right equation. As for DB-GEP, the DB-FEM performs weakly when handling complex and high-dimension datasets. It is easy to be trapped in local optima, and the low converging speed can be another factor that accounts for the results. We analyse the outputs of CL-GEP, and the outputs are in high similarity. We take one of them for an example

$$f(x,y,z) = (((z*x)*(((z*z)-y)*(y*(x+x)))) * ((x*(x*x))*(x*y))) \quad (11)$$

It can be observed from function (11) that the outputs of CL-GEP are in the multiple multiplication. The sampled data for *Sphere* are ranged in $[-1, +1]$, which determines that the multiple multiplication function can finally produce very small outputs. As all variables are contributing to the problem based on CL-FEM, these wrong functions are regarded as favorable by mistakes.

Experiments on Sparse Datasets. The results of the experiments on sparse datasets are shown in Table 3, the numbers are success times in 30 runs. To provide a more direct view, the variational curves are presented in Fig. 8.

Table 3. Results of experiments on sparse datasets.

	CL-GEP				DB-GEP			
Problem	Data quantity				Data quantity			
	500	**100**	**20**	**6**	**500**	**100**	**20**	**6**
Circle	30	30	30	30	30	30	22	0
Hyperbola	30	30	30	30	30	30	29	0
Elliptic curve	29	28	29	26	20	20	12	0

From the results, we can find that DB-GEP performs weakly in handling implicit symbolic regression problems with sparse datasets. For datasets containing 500, 100 and 20 data, the relationships between different points are still able to be recognized, therefore, it is still possible for it to find out the right solution. When the quantity of data is reduced to 6, however, it fails in all the 90 runs.

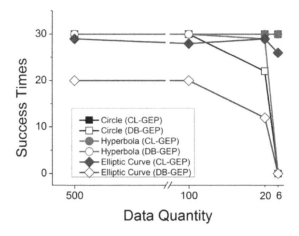

Fig. 8. The curves of the results on sparse datasets.

From our perspective, the feature of sparse data accounts for the results. On the one hand, if the sparse data are crowded in one specific region, they somehow will be related, however, they can not represent the whole equation model in the space. On the other hand, if the sparse data are separated randomly in the space, the neighboring points can not provide useful information to construct the model, it may sometimes even bring out misleading information (Fig. 2). These two factors seriously restrict the performance of DB-FEM, which makes it incapable of solving sparse data problems.

Take a look at the results provided by CL-GEP, the performance is stable and outstanding. For the two simple equations *Circle* and *Hyperbola*, the success times are all 30 regardless of different datasets. When it comes to the *Elliptic Curve*, the failure times when solving the 6-data set are only 4, the reducing trend is weak.

Compared with the DB-FEM, CL-GEP wins the comparison because it only concentrates on the target data. The information conveyed by a certain point is only the position represented by coordinates, which is precise and authentic. Information collected from the neighboring points may be disturbances when solving sparse data problems, therefore, the CL-FEM has the superiority over the DB-FEM.

5   Conclusions

In this paper, we have proposed a new evaluation mechanism for implicit equation model estimation, named CL-FEM. The proposed CL-FEM improves the previously arisen direct methods of subtracting the function output to zero, by embedding a new mechanism of learning knowledge from *disturbed* data. The core idea of the mechanism is to compare the outputs calculated from stochastic datasets with outputs from the target set. If there are no differences between the two sets of outputs, then the equation will be regarded as invalid. This mechanism can effectively avoid the evolution being trapped in misleading equations, which is the main trouble of solving implicit symbolic regression problems.

We use a simplified SL-GEP to generate a new algorithm with CL-FEM named CL-GEP. To demonstrate the superiority of CL-GEP, we make comparisons with the algorithm named DB-GEP, which embeds the mainstream fitness evaluation mechanism DB-FEM. The proposed CL-GEP not only is more convenient and practical, but also gets more promising results. When solving equations with complex features, the CL-GEP can get a higher success rate. What's more, the $O(ND)$ examination time consumption makes the proposed CL-FEM much faster than the DB-FEM. Most significantly, the proposed algorithm can handle problems with sparse datasets, which can not be tackled by the DB-FEM.

Nevertheless, there exists some weaknesses of the proposed CL-GEP, one of which is the deficient capability of solving problems with datasets consisting of small value data, which means avoiding being trapped in local optima caused by multiple multiplication. There are also some other interesting research directions. One direction is to enhance the capability of finding proper constant by combining other evolutionary algorithms. Another direction is to reduce the complexity of the output to make it more readable and comprehensible. We can consider incorporating the multiobjective optimization or other techniques to make it more practical in applications.

Acknowledgment. This work was supported in part by the National Natural Science Foundation of China (Grant No. 61602181), and by the Fundamental Research Funds for the Central Universities (Grant No. 2017ZD053).

References

1. Brameier, M.F., Banzhaf, W.: Linear Genetic Programming. Springer, Heidelberg (2007). https://doi.org/10.1007/978-0-387-31030-5
2. Ferreira, C.: Gene expression programming in problem solving. In: Roy, R., Köppen, M., Ovaska, S., Furuhashi, T., Hoffmann, F. (eds.) Soft Computing and Industry, pp. 635–653. Springer, Heidelberg (2002). https://doi.org/10.1007/978-1-4471-0123-9_54
3. Koza, J.R.: Genetic Programming: on the Programming of Computers by Means of Natural Selection, vol. 1. MIT Press, Cambridge (1992)
4. Lee, Y.S., Tong, L.I.: Forecasting time series using a methodology based on autoregressive integrated moving average and genetic programming. Knowl.-Based Syst. **24**(1), 66–72 (2011)
5. McPhee, N.F., Poli, R., Langdon, W.B.: Field Guide to Genetic Programming. Lulu Enterprises, UK Ltd (2008)
6. Miller, J.F., Thomson, P.: Cartesian genetic programming. In: Poli, R., Banzhaf, W., Langdon, W.B., Miller, J., Nordin, P., Fogarty, T.C. (eds.) EuroGP 2000. LNCS, vol. 1802, pp. 121–132. Springer, Heidelberg (2000). https://doi.org/10.1007/978-3-540-46239-2_9
7. O'Neil, M., Ryan, C.: Grammatical evolution. In: Grammatical Evolution, pp. 33–47. Springer, Heidelberg (2003). https://doi.org/10.1007/978-1-4615-0447-4_4

8. Sabar, N.R., Ayob, M., Kendall, G., Qu, R.: Automatic design of a hyper-heuristic framework with gene expression programming for combinatorial optimization problems. IEEE Trans. Evol. Comput. **19**(3), 309–325 (2015)
9. Schmidt, M., Lipson, H.: Symbolic regression of implicit equations. In: Riolo, R., O'Reilly, U.M., McConaghy, T. (eds.) Genetic Programming Theory and Practice VII, pp. 73–85. Springer, Heidelberg (2010). https://doi.org/10.1007/978-1-4419-1626-6_5
10. Storn, R., Price, K.: Differential evolution-a simple and efficient heuristic for global optimization over continuous spaces. J. Global Optim. **11**(4), 341–359 (1997)
11. Zhong, J., Cai, W., Lees, M., Luo, L.: Automatic model construction for the behavior of human crowds. Appl. Soft Comput. **56**, 368–378 (2017)
12. Zhong, J., Feng, L., Ong, Y.S.: Gene expression programming: a survey. IEEE Comput. Intell. Mag. **12**(3), 54–72 (2017)
13. Zhong, J., Luo, L., Cai, W., Lees, M.: Automatic rule identification for agent-based crowd models through gene expression programming. In: Proceedings of the 2014 International Conference on Autonomous Agents and Multi-agent Systems, pp. 1125–1132. International Foundation for Autonomous Agents and Multiagent Systems (2014)
14. Zhong, J., Ong, Y.S., Cai, W.: Self-learning gene expression programming. IEEE Trans. Evol. Comput. **20**(1), 65–80 (2016)

Multi-population Genetic Algorithm for Cardinality Constrained Portfolio Selection Problems

Nasser R. Sabar[1](✉) , Ayad Turky[2], Mark Leenders[2], and Andy Song[2]

[1] La Trobe University, Melbourne, VIC 3083, Australia
n.sabar@latrobe.edu.au
[2] RMIT University, Melbourne, VIC 3000, Australia
{ayad.turky,mark.leenders,andy.song}@rmit.edu.au

Abstract. Portfolio Selection (PS) is recognized as one of the most important and challenging problems in financial engineering. The aim of PS is to distribute a given amount of investment fund across a set of assets in such a way that the return is maximised and the risk is minimised. To solve PS more effectively and more efficiently, this paper introduces a Multi-population Genetic Algorithm (MPGA) methodology. The proposed MPGA decomposes a large population into multiple populations to explore and exploit the search space simultaneously. These populations evolve independently during the evolutionary learning process. Yet different populations periodically exchange their individuals so promising genetic materials could be shared between different populations. The proposed MPGA method was evaluated on the standard PS benchmark instances. The experimental results show that MPGA can find better investment strategies in comparison with state-of-the-art portfolio selection methods. In addition, the search process of MPGA is more efficient than these existing methods requiring significantly less amount of computation.

Keywords: Optimisation · Portfolio selection problems
Genetic algorithms · Multi-population GA

1 Introduction

Investment is one of the most essential activities in the finance industry, and a key mean of stimulating economic growth. A good investment strategy is obviously to achieve maximum return back to the investors while the risk of investment loss should be minimal [1–3]. In reality high investment profit often associates with high risk. Therefore, professional investors and brokers often maintain a portfolio of investment consisting of a collection of relative small assets instead of a single or a small set of large assets. So the risk can be mitigated if one or two investments went wrong. Setting the optimal portfolio is a key part of daily tasks of portfolio managers. The challenge here is not only finding an optimal

© Springer International Publishing AG, part of Springer Nature 2018
Y. Shi et al. (Eds.): ICCS 2018, LNCS 10860, pp. 129–140, 2018.
https://doi.org/10.1007/978-3-319-93698-7_10

or near optimal portfolio investment, but also to find a good solution efficiently so the professionals can react to events such as market changes quickly.

The above problem is known as the Portfolio Selection (PS) problem, which is also a challenge for computer scientists and optimisation practitioners. PS is one of the key roles of portfolio mangers whose goal is obviously needed to maximise customer satisfaction. The selection process can be done manually by a manager. However, that is only suitable when this manager is very experienced and the choice is rather limited. In many circumstances formulating the best portfolio strategy by hand is not feasible as the problem is combinatorial in nature, with high computational complexity. For circumstances where the market changes fast or the asset structure is complicated, the complexity of PS can go higher and become difficult to solve even for computing methods. Establishing a fast and effective portfolio selection algorithm remains as a challenge. The PS problem has some notable extensions. The most studied is probably a variation with the addition of cardinality and boundary constraints [3]. Cardinality constraint means the total number of assets to be included in the solution portfolio can not go beyond a certain threshold. Boundary constraint specifies the lower and upper limits of investment that can go to each asset in the formed portfolio. The task is known as cardinality constrained portfolio selection problem.

It is known that finding the optimal portfolio is an NP-hard problem. One of the widely used methods in PS is the Markowitz mean-variance model, which forms a single portfolio. This model captures the expected return and the risk of the portfolio [1,4]. This model is and still remains as the core of existing PS methodology. However, the practicality of this model in real world scenarios has been criticized because the assumptions of the model are not very realistic. For example, it assumes the returns are in normal distributions. It also assumes that correlations between assets are fixed and never change. Utilizing the Markowitz mean-variance PS model, a PS task can be formulated as a quadratic programming problem [3]. This is an exact method which can find the actual optimal solution. However, that is only feasible when the number of variables in the model is small. When the number of variables is large, exact methods become impractical, if not impossible, to find the optimal solution within an acceptable amount of time.

In contrast to exact methods, heuristic and meta-heuristic approaches search for near-best solutions. It is well known that meta-heuristic algorithms can find good quality solutions within a reasonable period of time [5]. This approach has indeed been introduced to Portfolio Selection problems. That includes the use of Genetic Algorithm [3], Tabu Search [3], Simulated Annealing [3], Particle Swarm Optimisation [6], Harmony Search [7] and hybrid algorithms [8,9].

To further improve the PS solving mechanism, we thereby propose a new approach based on Genetic Algorithm (GA). Also we address the extended version of PS which has cardinality and boundary constraints embedded as these constraints are more realistic but add many more difficulties in finding a good solution. GA is a well-known population based meta-heuristic search method which simulates the survival of the fittest principle for problem solving [5,10]. In the past GA has demonstrated its effectiveness in solving optimisation problems from a wide range of fields that include many difficult real-world applications. However, classical GA does have certain drawbacks. For example the convergence of the GA evolution process can be slow hence affecting the time required for finding a satisfactory solution. In constrained optimisation problems in particular the PS problem in this study, slow convergence may jeopardise GA as the chosen method due to the efficiency issue. One of the causes of this phenomenon is the use of a single population in classical GA, as the exploitation in the search space may not unfold well because the coverage in the search space of only one population may not be sufficient even if the population size is big [11].

To address the aforementioned issues in classical GA, we propose a variation of GA which allows multiple populations co-exist during one GA evolution process. We denote that method as MPGA which is designed for the constrained PS. By MPGA one or more populations will explore the search space of a problem, whilst other populations can perform exploitation in the same space. With the combination of both exploration and exploitation the convergence of a GA search process is expected to be quicker. In addition, MPGA allows good individuals to be passed across different populations. So good genetic materials can be shared periodically to help different populations find better solutions more effectively. The well known PS benchmark dataset [3] is used for performance evaluation in this study. This benchmark has been widely used in the PS literature. On this benchmark MPGA is compared against state of the art portfolio selection algorithms that are widely used by PS researchers, developers and managers.

The rest of the paper is organised as such. Section 2 describes the portfolio selection problem in detail. Section 3 discusses the main components of the proposed method. Section 5 shows the experimental results with the comparison with existing methods. The conclusion of this study is presented at Sect. 6.

2   Problem Descriptions

This paper focuses on the cardinality constrained portfolio selection problem which has two constraints added, the cardinality constraint and boundary constraint. These constraints are to reduce the transaction cost and avoid investment assets that are too small or too large. Cardinality constraint limits the number of assets to be included in the formed portfolio. Boundary constraint set a lower bound and upper bound for each asset of the formed portfolio. The formulation of the PS model is proposed by [3,12]:

$$
min \ \lambda \left[\sum_{i=1}^{n} \sum_{j=1}^{n} w_i w_j \alpha_{ij} \right] + (1 - \lambda) \left[- \sum_{i=1}^{n} w_i \mu_i \right] \tag{1}
$$

Subject to

$$
\sum_{i=1}^{n} w_i = 1 \tag{2}
$$

$$\sum_{i=1}^{n} s_i = K \tag{3}$$

$$\varepsilon_i s_i \leq w_i \leq \delta_i s_i, i = 1, ..., n \tag{4}$$

$$s_i \in \{0, 1\}, i = 1, ..., n \tag{5}$$

where n is the total number of assets, w_i is the proportion of the budget invested in the i-th asset, α_{ij} is the covariance between i-th and j-th assets, λ is the risk aversion, λ in $[0, 1]$, μ_i is the expected return of the i-th asset, K is the number of assets to be invested in assets in a portfolio, s_i is a decision variable represents whether the i-th asset has been selected or not, and ε_i and δ_i respectively are the upper and lower bounds. The cardinality constrained PS model involves two sub-problems: (1) the selection problem that seeks to select a subset of assets and (2) the allocating problem which aims at determining the proportion for each of the selected asset. In the literature, PS formulations are treated as a mixed integer programming [3].

3   Methodology

The classical GA has shown slow convergence and difficulties in handling constrained optimisation problems [11]. While Memetic Algorithms (MAs), which combine GA with local search algorithms, have been proposed to improve the convergence process of GA [11,13–16]. A local search algorithm is called at every generation to further improve the generated solutions and exploitation process [17]. Nevertheless, calling the local search algorithm at every generation would be time consuming and may lead to premature convergence. Our proposed multi-population GA (MPGA) is a remedy of this issue of memetic algorithms while still addressing the slow convergence problem [18].

Figure 1 shows the flowchart of the proposed MPGA. It starts from generating a population of random solutions. Then MPGA decomposes the whole population into multiple subpopulations from *Subpopulation* 1 to *Subpopulation* n. The subpopulations are scattered over the search space. This is to encourage exploration. While the search of each sub population acts like exploitation in nearby space similar to that in local search. These subpopulations evolve independently during the search process. From Fig. 1 we can see that the process of each subpopulation is identical, all following selection, which is to pick good solutions to produce the next generation; crossover and mutation, which are to produce offspring solutions based on the picked solutions. When better solutions are found, the subpopulation will be updated as shown in the figure.

However at each generation, if the update criterion is met but the stopping criterion is not met, these subpopulations will be combined into a large population for the next generation, which will start from splitting the large population into multiple subpopulations again. So the exploration and exploitation will start over again. The update criterion is that the best solution has not been improved for a certain steps. The stopping criterion is that the maximum number of generation has been reached. We can see from the algorithm that the search progress

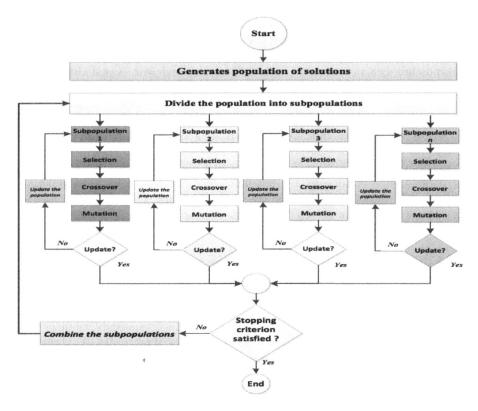

Fig. 1. Visual representations of the proposed multi-population genetic algorithm (MPGA)

may progress further if it is trapped in a local optima because it can be detected and dealt with by the combining and dividing of populations.

Asset Index	1	2	3	4	5	6	...	n
Selection	1	1	0	0	0	1	...	1
Boundary Value	0.1	0.5	0	0	0	0.2	...	0.1

Fig. 2. An example of solution representation

In terms of problem representation, each individual of GA is a solution for PS. A solution is represented by a two-dimensional array where the array size is equal to the total number of assets n, as shown in Fig. 2. The first row represents the selection. The value of each cell is either 0 or 1, while 1 indicates the corresponding asset is selected and 0 is not. The second row represents the boundary value of the chosen asset which takes a real value within the given lower and upper boundary constraint.

Each cell of the first row is randomly assigned either 0 or 1 while makes sure that the total number of 1s satisfies the cardinality constraint, the max number of assets in the portfolio. Next, for each column with a 1 at the first row, the corresponding cell in the second row will be assigned with a real value. That value has to be in between the predefined upper and lower bounds to satisfy the constraint. In addition, the sum of these values in the second row has to be 1 indicating 100% allocation of the investment fund.

Once solutions in the initial populations are generated, they will be assigned with fitness values before the standard GA selection process. The calculation of the fitness value is based on Eq. (1) described above. The decomposition into n subpopulations is done in a random manner. That is, each subpopulation contains a set of solutions randomly selected from the whole populations. No duplicates will occur in the selections so there is no overlaps between these subpopulations.

All subpopulations use roulette wheel as the selection mechanism. They all use one point crossover operator, one point mutation operator and steady state updating rule. The crossover operator, which exchanges parts between two selected solutions, runs with a low probability and only generates one offspring by picking the best one generated by the parents. This is to increase the efficiency of the search. The mutation operator, which randomly modifies the selected solution, can be viewed as a local search algorithm in MPGA. Mutation has relatively high probability in order to give better chances to perturb cell values to exploit surround areas in the search space. Only those changes that lead to an improvement in the fitness values are accepted in the offspring. If the best solution in all subpopulations cannot be improved for a consecutive number of generations, all subpopulations are merged into one population to combine their genetic materials for the next round of decomposition. By this approach, solutions will be regrouped for the new episode of search. The regrouping will stimulate the search in new areas while still maintain the best solution obtained so far. Hence it has a better chance to overcome local optima. As mentioned early and shown in Fig. 1, the entire process repeats until the maximum number of generations is reached.

4   Experiment Settings

This section first discusses the characteristics of instances from the PS benchmark which is used to evaluate the performance of the proposed MPGA. Then the MPGA parameter settings is presented in detail.

4.1   Benchmark Instances

The PS benchmark instances from the OR–library are used to evaluate the effectiveness of the proposed MPGA. This benchmark is commonly used in the literature of Portfolio Selection studies [19]. It comprises five different sets each representing the weekly share prices at the stock market of a country [19]. The main characteristics of these five instances are listed in Table 1. In this table, n represents total number of the assets, k represents the maximum number of assets in a formed portfolio (cardinality constraint), ε_i $(i = 1,...,n)$ is the lower bound of the asset and δ_i $(i = 1,...,n)$ is the upper bound of the asset.

Table 1. Portfolio selection benchmark datasets

#	Data set	Country	n	k	ε	δ
1	Hang Seng	Hong Kong	31	10	0.01	1
2	DAX 100	Germany	85	10	0.01	1
3	FTSM 100	UK	89	10	0.01	1
4	S&P 100	USA	98	10	0.01	1
5	Nikkei	Japan	255	10	0.01	1

4.2 Parameter Settings

The proposed MPGA involves six parameters that need to be set in advance. To calibrate MPGA parameters, we randomly selected two data sets for parameter tuning purpose. The selected sets are: DAX 100 and Nikkei. Next, we conducted a preliminary experiment to set the parameters value of MPGA. For each parameter, we have tested a range of values within the predefined range and the value that leads to good results are used. Also the trade-off between the solution quality and the computational time is considered. Based on this empirical study, parameters are settled with the suggested values which are shown in Table 2. The λ value of Eq. (1) was tested using 51 different values and each value is tested for $1000 \times n$ times of evaluations. That is the same as the experiments in [3, 6].

Table 2. MPGA parameter setting

Parameters	Tested range	Suggested values	
		Exploration	Exploitation
Crossover rate	0.01–0.99	0.8	0.2
Mutation rate	0.01–0.99	0.3	0.85
Population size	10–500	300	
Number of sub-populations N	2–10	6	
Number of consecutive non-improvement generations	5–100	Every 50 fitness evaluations	
Maximum number of generations $MaxG$	$1000 \times n$		

5   Results and Comparisons

To evaluate the effectiveness of the proposed MPGA, two sets of experiments were conducted. In the first set of experiments, we evaluated the benefit of using multi-population by comparing the results of GA with multi-population (MPGA) and the results of classical single population GA. In addition, we also investigated the impact of the number of subpopulations in MPGA. In the second set of experiments, MPGA was compared with the existing state of the art methods. To make a fair and consistent comparison, our MPGA used the same PS benchmark and applied the same stopping condition as reported in these studies, the maximum number of evaluations.

5.1   Effectiveness Evaluation

To ensure a fair comparison, both MPGA and GA have been tested on same population of solutions, stopping condition and computer resources. All the experiments of both MPGA and GA are conducted for 51 independent runs with different random seeds. All five datasets from the benchmark were used in this comparison.

The results from both MPGA and GA are statistically compared using the Wilcoxon test with a confidence level of 0.05. MPGA consistently outperformed classical GA. The actual results are shown in Table 3 which combines a few other comparison results. Here we only show the p-value of MPGA against GA in Table 3. In this table, a p-value <0.05 means that the MPGA is statistically better than GA (shown in bold). A p-value >0.05 means that the difference between these two algorithms are not significant.

Table 3. The p-value of comparing MPGA with GA

	Data set	p-value
1	Hang Seng	0.059
2	DAX 100	**0.023**
3	FTSM 100	**0.016**
4	S&P 100	**0.037**
5	Nikkei	**0.011**

The p-values tabulated in Table 3 show that MPGA is statistically better than GA on four out of five data sets. From this experiment, we observe that the multi-population approach has a positive impact on the performance GA.

Now we show the studies on the impact of n, the number of subpopulations, to see how this influences the performance of MPGA in term of solution quality as well as the computational cost. MPGA was evaluated on two data sets, DAX 100 and Nikkei. The n value tested from $n = 2$ to $n = 10$ are presented in

Table 4. The impact of n: the number of subpopulations, on solution quality and computational cost

	$n = 2$	$n = 4$	$n = 6$	$n = 8$	$n = 10$
λ (DAX 100)	2.8324	2.7461	2.3116	2.3027	2.2875
s (DAX 100)	16.21	17.11	18.21	26.33	28.14
λ (Nikkei)	0.7643	0.7275	0.6328	0.6279	0.6248
s (Nikkei)	56.18	67.26	73.14	105.16	115.71

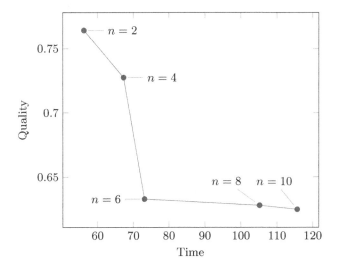

Fig. 3. Runtime and solution quality under different n for Nikkei

Table 4. For each dataset, the solution quality λ and runtime in seconds s are recorded in two rows of the table. It can be seen that with the increased n value, the quality improves as the goal of PS is to minimise the λ value. As expected the computational cost climbs quite quickly with the size n as well.

The relationships between solution quality and run time are also shown in Figs. 3 and 4 which are for Nikkei and DAX 100 dataset respectively. From the obtained results, we can see that the best trade-off is when $n = 6$. Although $n = 8$ and $n = 10$ are slightly better, their computational cost are higher that than $n = 6$ and they do not add much extra value to the solution.

5.2 Comparisons with State of the Art Methods

In this section, the proposed MPGA is compared with the state of the art methods. The methods included in the comparison are the following four:

- Tabu search algorithm (TS) [3]
- Simulated annealing (SA) [3]

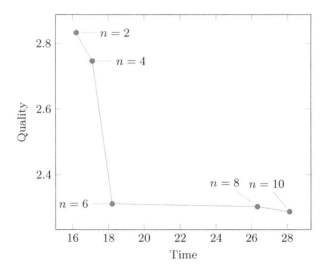

Fig. 4. Runtime and solution quality under different n for DAX 100

– Genetic algorithm (GA) [3]
– Particle swarm optimisation (PSO) [6]

The comparison includes the solutions found by MPGA against those from TS, SA, GA and PSO. The minimum mean percentage error over 51 independent runs was used. Table 5 shows the results from MPGA and the results from the aforementioned four existing PS methods. These results of the compared methods are taken form the corresponding publication. In the table, the best results are shown in bold. Table 5 shows that, on all five tested data sets, the proposed MPGA obtained better results compared to the state of the art methods. When considering the overall average result, which is shown in the last row of Table 5, MPGA is also achieved better solution than other algorithms.

To compare above methods in term of efficiency, we measured the computational runtime of these methods on the five datasets. Table 6 presents the time of MPGA, GA, SA, TS and PSO in seconds. In the table, the best computa-

Table 5. MPGA comparing with existing state-of-the-art methods

#	Data Set	MPGA	GA	SA	TS	PSO
1	Hang Seng	**1.0952**	1.0974	1.0957	1.1217	1.0953
2	DAX 100	**2.3116**	2.5424	2.9297	3.3049	2.5417
3	FTSM 100	**1.0543**	1.1076	1.4623	1.6080	1.0628
4	S&P 100	**1.6482**	1.9328	3.0696	3.3092	1.6890
5	Nikkei	**0.6328**	0.7961	0.6732	0.8975	0.6870
	Average overall	**1.34842**	1.49526	1.8461	2.04826	1.41516

Table 6. Computation cost of MPGA and existing state-of-the-art methods (in seconds)

#	Data set	MPGA	GA	SA	TS	PSO
1	Hang Seng	**1.3**	172	79	74	4.8
2	DAX 100	**18.21**	544	210	199	26.8
3	FTSM 100	**28.34**	573	215	246	31.4
4	S&P 100	**30.44**	638	242	225	36.6
5	Nikkei	**73.14**	1964	553	545	75.8

tional time are also highlighted in bold. As can be seen, the computational time of MPGA is considerably lower than that of compared methods on all tested instances. Note that MPGA and all the methods in this comparison use the number of fitness evaluation as the main stopping condition. That is fixed and identical for all runs regardless of the method. Hence the advantage of MPGA is valid.

6   Conclusion

In this work, a multi-population genetic algorithm is presented for solving the cardinality constrained portfolio selection problem. The proposed MPGA can improve the convergence of the search process. The combining and splitting of subpopulations has the effect of hybridising exploration and exploitation in the search space. The sharing of genetic materials during the evolution process encourages the search to step out local optima more effectively. The performance of the proposed MPGA was evaluated on the benchmark datasets of cardinality constrained portfolio selection problem. The experiments showed the effectiveness of MPGA by comparing it with GA as well as the current state-of-the-art methods. In addition, the computational cost of MPGA is much lower than that of these state-of-the-art methods. Thus, we conclude that MPGA, multiple population of GA, is an effective and efficient method for the cardinality constrained portfolio selection problems.

This study of PS is still at its early stage. A few extensions will be investigated in the near future, for example improving the sharing and collaboration between multi-populations and introducing MPGA into other similar domains. In addition we will study the impact of the solution distribution of multiple population.

References

1. Markowitz, H.: Portfolio selection*. J. Finan. **7**(1), 77–91 (1952)
2. Varian, H.: A portfolio of nobel laureates: Markowitz, Miller and Sharpe. J. Econ. Perspect. 159–169 (1993)

3. Chang, T.-J., Meade, N., Beasley, J.E., Sharaiha, Y.M.: Heuristics for cardinality constrained portfolio optimisation. Comput. Oper. Res. **27**(13), 1271–1302 (2000)
4. Markowitz, H.M.: Portfolio selection: efficient diversification of investments, vol. 16. Yale University Press, New Haven (1968)
5. Gendreau, M., Potvin, J.-Y.: Handbook of Metaheuristics, vol. 2. Springer, Heidelberg (2010)
6. Deng, G.-F., Lin, W.-T., Lo, C.-C.: Markowitz-based portfolio selection with cardinality constraints using improved particle swarm optimization. Expert Syst. Appl. **39**(4), 4558–4566 (2012)
7. Sabar, N.R., Kendall, G.: Using harmony search with multiple pitch adjustment operators for the portfolio selection problem. In: 2014 IEEE Congress on Evolutionary Computation (CEC), pp. 499–503. IEEE (2014)
8. Kendall, G., Yan, S.: Imperfect evolutionary systems. IEEE Trans. Evol. Comput. **11**(3), 294–307 (2007)
9. Fernández, A., Gómez, S.: Portfolio selection using neural networks. Comput. Oper. Res. **34**(4), 1177–1191 (2007)
10. Holland, J.H.: Adaptation in Natural and Artificial Systems: An Introductory Analysis with Applications to Biology, Control, and Artificial Intelligence. U Michigan Press, Oxford (1975)
11. Neri, F., Cotta, C.: Memetic algorithms and memetic computing optimization: a literature review. Swarm Evol. Comput. **2**, 1–14 (2012)
12. Moral-Escudero, R., Ruiz-Torrubiano, R., Suárez, A.: Selection of optimal investment portfolios with cardinality constraints. In: IEEE Congress on Evolutionary Computation, CEC 2006, pp. 2382–2388. IEEE (2006)
13. Sabar, N.R., Aleti, A.: An adaptive memetic algorithm for the architecture optimisation problem. In: Wagner, M., Li, X., Hendtlass, T. (eds.) ACALCI 2017. LNCS (LNAI), vol. 10142, pp. 254–265. Springer, Cham (2017). https://doi.org/10.1007/978-3-319-51691-2_22
14. Sabar, N.R., Song, A., Zhang, M.: A variable local search based memetic algorithm for the load balancing problem in cloud computing. In: Squillero, G., Burelli, P. (eds.) EvoApplications 2016. LNCS, vol. 9597, pp. 267–282. Springer, Cham (2016). https://doi.org/10.1007/978-3-319-31204-0_18
15. Sabar, N.R., Abawajy, J., Yearwood, J.: Heterogeneous cooperative co-evolution memetic differential evolution algorithm for big data optimization problems. IEEE Trans. Evol. Comput. **21**(2), 315–327 (2017)
16. Sabar, N.R., Chung, E., Tsubota, T., Maciel de Almeida, P.E., et al.: A memetic algorithm for real world multi-intersection traffic signal optimisation problems. Eng. Appl. Artif. Intell. **63**, 45–53 (2017)
17. Abuhamdah, A., Ayob, M., Kendall, G., Sabar, N.R.: Population based local search for university course timetabling problems. Appl. Intell. **40**(1), 44–53 (2014)
18. Sabar, N.R., Song, A.: Dual population genetic algorithm for the cardinality constrained portfolio selection problem. In: Dick, G., et al. (eds.) SEAL 2014. LNCS, vol. 8886, pp. 703–712. Springer, Cham (2014). https://doi.org/10.1007/978-3-319-13563-2_59
19. Beasley, J.E.: Or-library: distributing test problems by electronic mail. J. Oper. Res. Soc. 1069–1072 (1990)

Recognition and Classification of Rotorcraft by Micro-Doppler Signatures Using Deep Learning

Ying Liu[1,2(✉)] and Jinyi Liu[1] (iD)

[1] School of Computer and Control, University of Chinese Academy of Sciences,
Beijing 100190, China
yingliu@ucas.ac.cn
[2] Key Lab of Big Data Mining and Knowledge Management,
Chinese Academy of Sciences, Beijing 100190, China

Abstract. Detection and classification of rotorcraft targets are of great significance not only in civil fields but also in defense. However, up to now, it is still difficult for the traditional radar signal processing methods to detect and distinguish rotorcraft targets from various types of moving objects. Moreover, it is even more challenging to classify different types of helicopters. As the development of high-precision radar, classification of moving targets by micro-Doppler features has become a promising research topic in the modern signal processing field. In this paper, we propose to use the deep convolutional neural networks (DCNNs) in rotorcraft detection and helicopter classification based on Doppler radar signals. We apply DCNN directly to raw micro-Doppler spectrograms for rotorcraft detection and classification. The proposed DCNNs can learn the features automatically from the micro-Doppler signals without introducing any domain background knowledge. Simulated data are used in the experiments. The experimental results show that the proposed DCNNs achieve superior accuracy in rotorcraft detection and superior accuracy in helicopter classification, outperforming the traditional radar signal processing methods.

Keywords: Convolutional neural network · Deep learning · Target detection
Classification · Micro-Doppler

1 Introduction

As the carrier of air transport and reconnaissance, rotorcraft plays a significant role in military and civil fields. However, it is difficult to distinguish a rotorcraft from ground targets by the conventional pulsed-Doppler radar when the rotorcraft is flying or hovering with a low speed at a low altitude. For example, the traditional radar signal processing algorithm can neither distinguish a helicopter from the armored vehicles in battlefields, nor distinguish the unmanned aerial vehicles from the pedestrians in urban environments, etc. Moreover, it is even more challenging to classify different types of rotorcrafts. Thus, an automatic rotorcraft detection technique is in real demand [1, 2].

The concepts of Micro-motion and Micro-Doppler were introduced by Chen et al. [3]. In many cases, an object or any structural component of an object may have

© Springer International Publishing AG, part of Springer Nature 2018
Y. Shi et al. (Eds.): ICCS 2018, LNCS 10860, pp. 141–152, 2018.
https://doi.org/10.1007/978-3-319-93698-7_11

oscillatory motion, called micro motion [3]. The source of micro motion may be a rotating propeller of a fixed-wing aircraft, the rotating rotor blades of a helicopter, a rotating antenna, the flapping wings of birds, or a walking person with swinging arms and legs, etc. The Doppler shift caused by micro motion is called micro-Doppler. Target recognition based on micro-Doppler features can extract motion signatures of target from the radar returns, which opens up a probe to new ways of target recognition.

Rotorcraft blade is usually made of metal or composite material, which produces a strong radar reflex. As the speed of the rotor tip is faster than that of the fuselage or the fretting of other ground targets, rotor rotation caused by Doppler shift occupy a unique position. Micro-Doppler is therefore very suitable for rotorcraft target recognition and classification. However, most of the existing recognition or classification algorithms devise discriminative features on the post-processed signals rather on the raw micro-Doppler signals. Such dependence on the domain knowledge of micro-Doppler signals limits the scalability of those algorithms.

Deep learning algorithms have revolutionized several applications such as image classification, speech recognition, etc. in recent years. Comparing with the previous state-of-the-art algorithms that principally rely on domain knowledge-based features, the classification accuracy of deep learning-based algorithms has been improved significantly. Therefore, in this paper, we consider an alternative deep learning approach to overcome such limitations. To the best of our knowledge, deep learning approach has not been widely used in the radar community, particularly for rotorcraft recognition with Doppler signatures.

In this paper, we propose to use deep convolutional neural networks (DCNNs) to recognize micro-Doppler signatures in spectrograms and then classify and recognize the rotorcraft targets. By training the convolutional neural network on micro-Doppler spectrograms, the model can learn the inner features automatically so that it can recognize the rotorcraft targets and distinguish various rotorcrafts. In the experiments, we train the proposed DCNN on simulated micro-Doppler spectrograms and then apply the model to rotorcraft detection and helicopter classification. High recognition rate is observed in the experiments.

The remainder of this paper is organized as follows. Section 2 introduces the related work. Section 3 presents our rotorcraft recognition method in detail. Section 4 presents the rotorcrafts classification. Finally, we conclude our work in Sect. 5.

2 Related Work

In recent year, most of the existing research in micro-Doppler target recognition follows the following prototype: firstly, explicitly extract some unique features from micro-Doppler signals that are able to distinguish different targets; then, apply such features in target classification [4]. Molchanov *et al.* extracts different types of targets from micro-Doppler signals and then classifies the ground moving targets [5, 6]. Molchanov *et al.* also classifies helicopters and fixed-wing aircraft based on their difference in Doppler energy distribution [7]. Thayaparan *et al.* decomposes micro-Doppler signals by wavelet decomposition and then extracts the micro-Doppler features by time-frequency analysis. Cai *et al.* extracts the micro-Doppler signals by

Hilbert-Huang transformation [9]. Since such approaches explicitly extract features, the algorithms rely on prior knowledge and expert empirical experience seriously.

In recent years, with the development of high-performance processors, such as Graphic Processing Unit (GPUs) and FPGAs, CNN has achieved excellent empirical performance in a number of applications, such as speech recognition, image recognition, and natural language processing [10, 11]. CNN employ a deep neural network structure which stacks multiple layers of simple neural network, through a supervised back propagation algorithm.CNN extracts hierarchical abstractions from the training data. Comparing with the traditional image recognition algorithm, CNN is not necessary to extract empirical features. In the ImageNet LSVRC-2010 competition, 17% in top-5 error rate was obtained when classifying 1.2 million HD images of 1000 different classes [12], meanwhile the top-5 error rate using the traditional algorithm was up to 25.7% [13]. In 2014, a face recognition method based on CNN are presented and achieved an accuracy of 99.15% [14, 15]

3   Rotorcraft Recognition Through Micro-Doppler Signatures Using CNN

The main purpose of rotorcraft recognition is to find the signals from rotorcraft targets in various echo signals received by radar. In addition to find the rotating rotor, we simulate the radar echo of oscillating pendulums, spinning tops, walking people and flying birds at the same time. The emulated radar echo are processed with the short-time Fourier transform so we can obtain the micro-Doppler spectrograms. During the observation window, 100 radar micro-Doppler spectrograms are simulated for each class of the targets. The corresponding sample spectrograms are shown in Fig. 1.

(a) Emulation of the radar backscattering from the rotating rotor blades is shown as follows: the radar is located at $(X = 10$ m, $Y = 0$ m, $Z = 20$ m) with a wavelength of 0.06 m at the C-band, the rotor center is located at $(X = 0$ m, $Y = 0$ m, $Z = 0$ m), the length of the blade is $L = 6$ m, the width of the blade is $W = 1$ m, and the rotation rate is Ω from 2 rev/s to 6 rev/s following the normal distribution, the observation window is 1 s and the number of blades is $N = 3$.

(b) When emulating the radar backscattering from an oscillating pendulum, given the location of the radar at $(X = 10$ m, $Y = 0$ m, $Z = 20$ m), the pivot point of the pendulum is assumed at $(X = 0$ m, $Y = 0$ m, $Z = 2$ m). The string length L falls in 0.3 m to 2 m and the mass of the small bob is from 10 g to 80 g. In cases of damping and driving, let the damping constant be $\gamma = 0.07$ and the driving amplitude be $A = 15$, and the normalized driving frequency be $f = 0.2$. The radar wavelength is 0.03 m at the X-band, the observation time is $T = 10$ s.

(c) Emulation of the radar backscattering from a precession top. During the radar observation time interval, the simulated spinning and precession top is $m = 25$ kg, located at $(X = 0$ m, $Y = 0$ m, $Z = 2$ m). The distance between the center of mass and the fixed tip point is $L = 0.563$ m, the moments of inertia $I_1 = I_2 = 0.117 \, \text{kg} \cdot \text{m}^2$, $I_3 = 8.5 \, \text{kg} \cdot \text{m}^2$, and the initial nutation angle $\theta_0 = 20°$. The radar wavelength is 0.03 m at the X-band radar located at $(X = 10$ m, $Y = 0$ m, $Z = 20$ m). The observation time is $T = 8$ s.

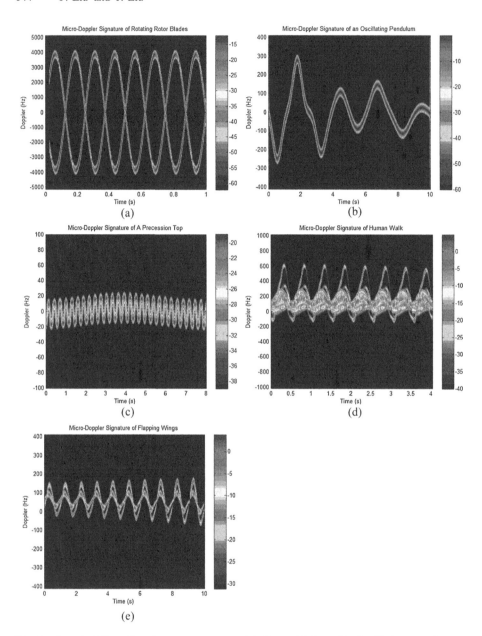

Fig. 1. Sample Micro-Doppler spectrograms. (a) Rotor blades. (b) Oscillating pendulums. (c) Spinning and precession top. (d) Walking humans. (e) Wing-flapping birds.

(d) Emulation of the radar backscattering from walking humans using the human walking model in [16]. Assume that the relative velocity of the walking person range from 0.2 m/s to 3 m/s following the normal distribution, the height of the person be $H = 1.8$ **m**, where the radar is located at $(X = 10$ m, $Y = 0$ m, $Z = 20$ m$)$ with a wavelength of 0.02 m. The starting point of the human base is located at $(X = 0$ m, $Y = 0$ m, $Z = 0$ m), and the observation window is 4 s.

(e) Emulation of the radar backscattering from the flapping wings of birds. The mean of the flapping frequency is set at 0.1 Hz with variance 0.1, the mean of the arm length is 0.5 cm with variance 0.1, and the birds is flying with a velocity from 0.7 m/s to 1.3 m/s, where all the parameters above follow the normal distribution. Meanwhile, the X-band radar is located at $(X = 20$ m, $Y = 0$ m, $Z = -10$ m) and the observation window is 10 s.

We simulated 100 spectrograms for each target, and get 500 spectrograms in total. In this paper, we employ spectrogram itself as the input to the CNN. In other words, we regard the spectrogram classification problem as an image recognition problem. The observation window is set long enough to capture the periodic micro-Doppler signatures. The size of the input spectrogram is normalized to 218×127 pixels. Among the 500 data, 80% are used as the training dataset, and the rest are used as the testing dataset.

As the number of the training samples is relatively small, we designed a small-scaled CNN for the purpose of rotorcraft recognition. The proposed CNN consists of six layers, three convolution layers followed by three fully-connected layers. As show in Fig. 2, the first convolution layer filters the 218×127 input image with 128 kernels of size 5×5 with a stride of 3 pixels (this is the distance between the receptive field centers of neighboring neurons in a kernel map). The second convolutional layer takes as input the (response-normalized and pooled) output of the first convolutional layer and filters it with 256 kernels of size 3×3 and 3 pixels per stride. The last convolutional layer had 256 convolution filters of size 3×3. For max pooling, we used 3×3 max pooling with 3 pixels per stride for the first layer, 2×2 max pooling with 3 pixels per stride for the second layer and the 3×3 max pooling with 2 pixels per stride for the third layer. Furthermore, three full-connected layers are directly connected to the output of the third pooling layer and the target classes and each layer had 256 neurons.

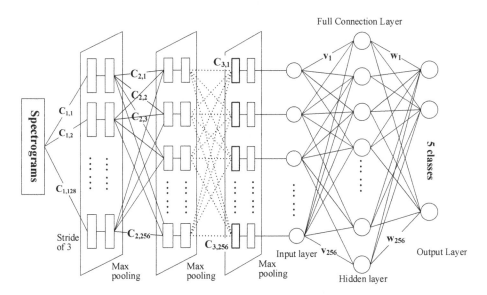

Fig. 2. CNN for rotorcraft recognition

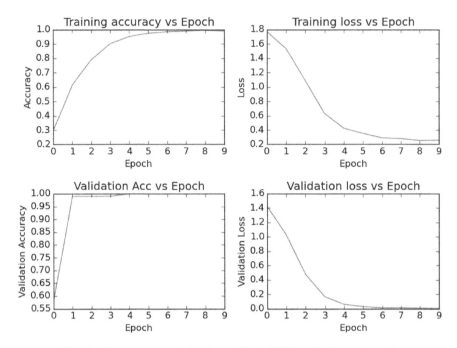

Fig. 3. The accuracy and the loss of the DCNN model in each epoch.

Figure 3 presents the how the accuracy improves as the training goes on. It is easy to observe that the accuracy of the model reached 99% after the 4th epoch. The training time of each epoch is less than 1 s., that is, the total training time of the deep neural network is less than 10 s.

Figure 4 visualizes the feature representations extracted by the DCNN model at different levels. It is evident that the feature maps at each layer are more abstract than those at its previous layer. The feature maps at the very first layer contain more edges and structures, while the feature maps at subsequent layers contain more implicit understandings of the spectrogram.

In order to test the robustness of the proposed DCNN model, we reduced the resolution of the spectrogram to 109 × 86 and 55 × 43, and conducted the same experiments on the two sets of data separately. The experimental results are presented in Table 1. It is evident that when the resolution is 109 × 87, the recognition accuracy of 99% can be achieved at the 2nd epoch, when the resolution reduced to 55 × 43, 99% accuracy can also be achieved but at the 10th epoch. It is indicating that our proposed DCNN model is robust because it is able to maintain a high recognition accuracy when the resolution of the input is reduced.

Input data

Output of the first convolution layer

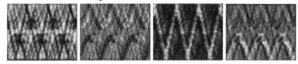

Output of the first max pooling layer

Output of the second convolution layer

Fig. 4. Visualization of part of the features extracted in different layers in the DCNN model.

Table 1. The accuracy of the DCNN model on the testing datasets with different resolution.

Number of epoch	Accuracy (109 × 86)	Accuracy (55 × 43)
1/10	0.58	0.32
2/10	0.9	0.32
3/10	0.99	0.46
4/10	0.99	0.69
5/10	1.00	0.70
6/10	1.00	0.71
7/10	1.00	0.72
8/10	1.00	0.72
9/10	1.00	0.97
10/10	1.00	0.99

4 Rotorcraft Classification Through Micro-Doppler Signatures Using CNN

The classification of the rotorcraft is to further classify the rotorcraft after the rotor is recognized. Table 2 lists a few features of different helicopters. These estimated feature parameters are important for classifying the type of an unknown helicopter. In this emulation, radar is located at (X = 500 m, Y = 0 m, Z = 20 m) with a wavelength of

0.06 m at the C-band, observation window is 1 s, range resolution is 0.5 m, number of pulses is 10240. The rotor center is located at (X = 0 m, Y = 0 m, Z = 0 m), other features are show in Table 2. In each type of rotorcraft, variance of blade length and rotation rate is 0.1, and showed a normal distribution, for each helicopter, we simulated 500 spectrograms.

Table 2. Main rotor features of typical helicopters

Typical helicopter	Number of blades	Diameter (m)	Rotation rate (r/s)	Tip velocity (m/s)
A	2	14.63	4.9	227
B	3	14.63	4.8	221
C	3	16.36	4.3	221
D	7	24.08	2.9	223
E	5	8.05	8.2	207
F	4	11.0	6.4	222
G	4	15.6	4.4	217

During the observation time of 0.2 s, 500 radar backscattering is simulated for each class of targets and their sample spectrograms are shown in Fig. 5, the size of the extracted spectrogram was 218 × 172.

Because the data and type we employed are significantly larger than those of the first experiment. In this study, the CNN had eight layers, the first five layers are convolution layers, and the other three layers are full connected layers. The first convolution layer filters the 218 × 127 input image with 128 kernels of size 7 × 7 with a stride of 3 pixels. The second had 256 kernels of size 3 × 3 and 2 pixels per stride. For max pooling, we used the 3 × 3 max pooling with 3 pixels per stride for the first layer, the 2 × 2 max pooling with 3 pixels per stride for the second layer. The third and fourth convolutional layer had 256 convolution filters of size of 3 × 3. The last convolutional layer is max pooling layer with 256 max pooling filters of 5 × 5 and 5 pixels per stride. Furthermore, we had three full-connected layers that directly connects the output of the last pooling and seven target classes and each layer had 256 neurons (see Fig. 6).

We used a fourfold cross validation to evaluate the classification performance in this study. The training and test sets in each fold contained 2800 and 500 samples respectively. For learning, we used the mini-batch SGD with a learning rate of 0.001 and a batch size of 10 and dropout was applied for the final fully connected layer with a probability of 0.5.

In this paper, we used the open-source toolkit Keras, which uses the NVIDIA GPU and CUDA library (e.g., cuDNN [17]) to speed up the computation. We used the NVIDIA GeForce GTX Titan X edition GPU (with a 12-GB memory) and Intel(R) Xeon(R) CPU(4 cores) with a 8-GB memory in our experiments. The resulting classification accuracy was 100%, as listed in Fig. 7.

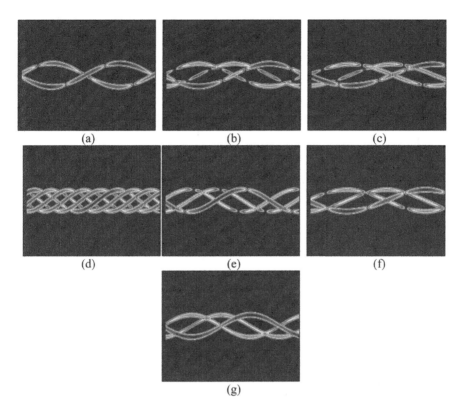

Fig. 5. Sample spectrograms of helicopter. (a) A-Helicopter. (b) B-Helicopter. (c) C-Helicopter. (d) D-Helicopter. (e) E-Helicopter. (f) F-Helicopter. (g) G-Helicopter.

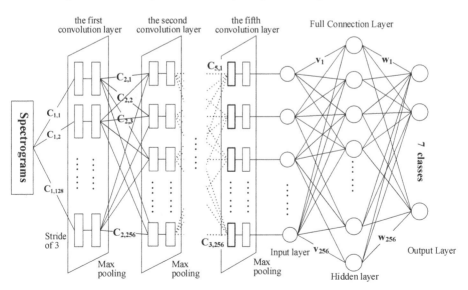

Fig. 6. CNN for rotorcraft classification

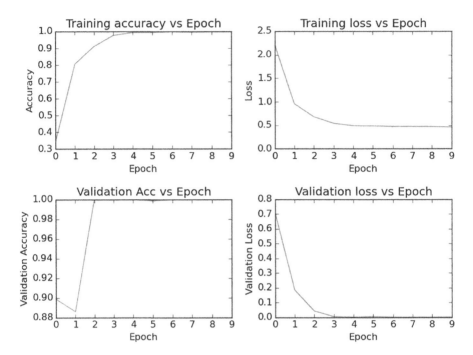

Fig. 7. Accuracy and loss of DCNN for each epoch in rotorcraft classification

Table 3. Training time of DCNN

Number of spectrum	Time
3500	40 s
4000	2 s
2000	<1 s

In addition, we also tested the recognition speed of the trained convolutional neural network and the results is show in Table 3. The testing time for each fold with 4000 spectrograms was about 2 s on average, meet the real-time requirements. Table 4 show the accuracy from other machine learning algorithm, it can be seen that only DCNN achieve great accuracy in this term.

Table 4. The classification accuracy for different classifiers

	KNN	SVM	DCNN
Accuracy	81.53%	82.46%	100%

5 Conclusion

In this paper, a deep learning-based moving target recognition method is proposed for rotorcraft recognition and classification. We propose to use DCNN models to recognize rotorcrafts from the ground moving targets on raw micro-Doppler spectrums. Comparing with the traditional radar signal processing techniques, DCNN-based models automatically extract features from the micro-Doppler spectrograms rather than introducing any explicit domain knowledge. Simulated data are used in the experiments. The proposed DCNN model successfully detected the rotorcraft from five types of moving objects with 100% accuracy. Similarly, he proposed DCNN classified seven types of helicopters with 100% accuracy. In addition to the superior accuracy, the performance is very high, 2 s for 4000 spectrums on average, which satisfied the requirement of real time prediction in real applications. In the future, we will focus on optimizing the proposed models on real radar micro-Doppler data.

Acknowledgement. This project was partially supported by Grants from Natural Science Foundation of China #71671178/#91546201/#61202321, and the open project of the Key Lab of Big Data Mining and Knowledge Management. It was also supported by Hainan Provincial Department of Science and Technology under Grant No. ZDKJ2016021, and by Guangdong Provincial Science and Technology Project 2016B010127004.

References

1. Tahmoush, D., Silvious, J.: Radar micro-Doppler for long range front-view gait recognition. In: Proceedings of IEEE 3rd International Conference on Biometrics, Theory, Applications and Systems, 28–30 September, Washington, DC, USA, pp. 1–6 (2009)
2. van Dorp, P., Groen, F.C.A.: Human walking estimation with radar. In: Proceedings of Institution of Electrical Engineers—Radar, Sonar Navigation, vol. 150, no. 5, pp. 356–365, October 2003
3. Chen, V.C., Li, F., Ho, S.-S., Wechsler, H.: Micro-Doppler effect in radar: phenomenon, model, and simulation study. IEEE Trans. Aerosp. Electron. Syst. **42**(1), 2–21 (2006)
4. Stove, A.G., Sykes, S.R.: Doppler-based automatic target classifier for a battlefield surveillance radar. In: Proceedings of IEEE International Radar Conference, 15–17 October, Edinburgh, U.K., pp. 419–423 (2002)
5. Molchanov, P., Astola, J., Egiazarian, K., et al.: Classification of ground moving radar targets by using joint time-frequency analysis. In: Radar Conference (RADAR), pp. 0366–0371 (2012)
6. Molchanov, P., Astola, J., Egiazarian, K., et al.: Ground moving target classification by using DCT coefficients extracted from micro-Doppler radar signatures and artificial neuron network. In: Microwaves, Radar and Remote Sensing Symposium (MRRS), pp. 173–176 (2011)
7. Molchanov, P., Harmanny, R.I.A., de Wit, J.J.M., et al.: Classification of small UAVs and birds by micro-Doppler signatures. Int. J. Microw. Wirel. Technol. **6**(3–4), 435–444 (2014)
8. Thayaparan, T., Abrol, S., Riseborough, E.: Micro-Doppler radar signatures for intelligent target recognition. Defence Research and Development Canadaottawa (Ontario) (2004)

9. Cai, C., Liu, W., Fu, J.S., et al.: Radar micro-Doppler signature analysis with HHT. IEEE Trans. Aerosp. Electron. Syst. **46**(2), 929–938 (2010)

10. Hinton, G., Deng, L., Yu, D., et al.: Deep neural networks for acoustic modeling in speech recognition: the shared views of four research groups. IEEE Sig. Process. Mag. **29**(6), 82–97 (2012)

11. Mikolov, T., Deoras, A., Povey, D., et al.: Strategies for training large scale neural network language models. In: 2011 IEEE Workshop on Automatic Speech Recognition and Understanding (ASRU), pp. 196–201. IEEE (2011)

12. Krizhevsky, A., Sutskever, I., Hinton, G.E.: Imagenet classification with deep convolutional neural networks. In: Advances in Neural Information Processing Systems, pp. 1097–1105 (2012)

13. Sánchez, J., Perronnin, F.: High-dimensional signature compression for large-scale image classification. In: 2011 IEEE Conference on Computer Vision and Pattern Recognition (CVPR), pp. 1665–1672. IEEE (2011)

14. Sun, Y., Chen, Y., Wang, X., et al.: Deep learning face representation by joint identification-verification. In: Advances in Neural Information Processing Systems, pp. 1988–1996 (2014)

15. Sun, Y., Wang, X., Tang, X.: Deep learning face representation from predicting 10,000 classes. In: Proceedings of the IEEE Conference on Computer Vision and Pattern Recognition, pp. 1891–1898 (2014)

16. Boulic, R., Thalmann, N.M., Thalmann, D.: A global human walking model with real-time kinematic personification. The Vis. Comput. **6**(6), 344–358 (1990)

17. Chetlur, S., Woolley, C, Vandermersch P, et al.: cuDNN: Efficient primitives for deep learning. arXiv preprint arXiv:1410.0759 (2014)

Data Allocation Based on Evolutionary Data Popularity Clustering

Ralf Vamosi[1]([✉]), Mario Lassnig[1], and Erich Schikuta[2]

[1] CERN, Geneva, Switzerland
`ralf.vamosi@cern.ch`
[2] Faculty of Computer Science, University of Vienna, Vienna, Austria

Abstract. This study is motivated by the high-energy physics experiment ATLAS, one of the four major experiments at the Large Hadron Collider at CERN. ATLAS comprises 130 data centers worldwide with datasets in the Petabyte range. In the processing of data across the grid, transfer delays and subsequent performance loss emerged as an issue. The two major costs are the waiting time until input data is ready and the job computation time. In the ATLAS workflows, the input to computational jobs is based on grouped datasets. The waiting time stems mainly from WAN transfers between data centers when job properties require execution at one data center but the dataset is distributed among multiple data centers. The proposed novel data allocation algorithm redistributes the constituent files of datasets such that the job efficiency is increased in terms of a cost metric. An evolutionary algorithm is proposed that addresses the data allocation problem in a network based on data popularity and clustering. The number of expected job's file transfers is used as the target metric and it is shown that job waiting times can be decreased by faster input data readiness.

Keywords: Grid computing · Data layout
Distributed data management · Data allocation · Data placement
Popularity · Data clustering

1 Introduction

Grid computing aggregates distributed computing, storage, and network resources to support unified, secure, and coordinated high-level access to the combined capabilities [9].

The ATLAS experiment at CERN acquires, stores, and processes data for detector operation and physics analysis. For these purposes, it utilizes part of the worldwide Large Hadron Collider (LHC) Computing Grid (WLCG), which is here referred to as the *grid*.

The data acquisition process deals with huge quantities of information. After passing a hardware trigger, event data from the experiment is immediately stored in form of files at the local CERN data center. Experimental data is usually

© Springer International Publishing AG, part of Springer Nature 2018
Y. Shi et al. (Eds.): ICCS 2018, LNCS 10860, pp. 153–166, 2018.
https://doi.org/10.1007/978-3-319-93698-7_12

packed into files in the GB range, which are subsequently transferred to other data centers. Computational jobs, which are referred to as *jobs*, read sets of files which contain different numbers of files. Those file collections are referred to as *datasets*. Each job is assigned to a data center in order to minimize the expected total waiting time. A job must wait for a free job slot, i.e. until the computation can commence on a worker node of the data center. After a data center is chosen, the job has to wait for the input data, i.e. its input dataset.

2   Motivation

In the LHC Computing Grid, physicists from institutions all over the world submit tasks to process stored data on the grid. To perform analysis, users prepare tasks on specific sets of data, which are then executed in form of jobs at the shared resources of the grid.

In such data-intensive workflow, the network represents a bottleneck for data transfer due to the high amount of file transfers triggered by jobs: Every time the corresponding computation takes place at a node, missing input data must be shipped over the network to the target node. The posed network load resulting in transfer delays represent a time-consuming part of any data-intensive job in the grid. This is especially problematic due to the fact that computational job properties, e.g., memory requirements, do not conform to the amount of available storage. There can be data centers with large storage systems but few processing capabilities, and vice versa.

The current operating standard procedure for storing data across storage resources is to distribute data *uniformly* in free storage resources. To cope with this situation, users interact with the grid storage system, cleaning and moving data with the aim to keep work-in-progress data sets on available data centers and to remove obsolete data sets to free storage.

The following simplified example provides an incentive for the optimization process. Three data centers supplying computing and storage resource are assumed. Without loss of generality, each up- and downlink shall be symmetrical. The time period in which a job waits for its input dataset is referred to as *'waiting time'* T_{wait}. In this scenario, the average T_{wait} between data center 1 and 2 is 2 h, between data center 2 and 3 is 0.5 h, and between data center 1 and 3 is 1 h yielding approximated T_{wait} coefficients of

$$\overline{T}_{wait} = \begin{bmatrix} 0 & 2 & 1 \\ 2 & 0 & 0.5 \\ 1 & 0.5 & 0 \end{bmatrix} h$$

where we assume that data center internal LAN links do not pose delays. The first data center has a large storage capacity, whereas the others don't. In general, statistics must be gathered about the usage of the network, i.e. jobs, and their access patterns in order to compute expectation values:

– Datasets and their files are associated with access likelihoods
– For a job, likelihoods emerge for running on data centers

Table 1. File allocation and the effect of optimization in two use cases.

State	Data center 1	Data center 2	Data center 3	T_{wait}
Scenario 1				
Uniform	33% files	33% files	33% files	2 h
Optimized	50% files		50% files	1 h
Best	100% files			0 h
Scenario 2				
Uniform	33% files	33% files	33% files	1.66 h
Optimized	50% files		50% files	1.33 h
Best			100% files	0.5 h

Now estimations for the waiting time for two different scenarios are given. The first scenario covers jobs with high memory requirements running at data center 1. Only data center 1 is capable of running this job type. Different possibilities of data allocation for these jobs and respective waiting times are illustrated in Table 1.

Scenario 2 considers jobs that are being balanced out across the computing resources. In this case, 33% at each of the three data centers. Data allocation and observed values are depicted in Table 1.

In *scenario 1*, data center 1 is able to accommodate the set of jobs, thus the best outcome can be achieved through placing all possible input files to the corresponding storage node. Upon assignment of these jobs, the job broker places them at data center 1. The job execution can launch promptly since the input files are available at this site. T_{wait} vanishes. Even in the *scenario 2*, where the considered jobs are being mapped equally likely across all data centers, the best optimization results in a reduction of waiting time from 1.66 h to 0.5 h. This example illustrates the basic idea although the network load was assumed constant with fixed delay times over network links. The considered jobs represent a small amount of the total quota.

3   State of the Art

In the context of data sharing, there are two shortcomings that have been studied and trialed extensively: *Data allocation* and *duplication of data*. Data allocation should reduce default communication cost. Replication results in multiple data source nodes to enable routing from these sources to the target node. Replication is not addressed in this work.

File allocation problem and data allocation problem is here used interchangeable, even though this may not be true from a strict semantic point of view and both generally differ from each other. In the data allocation process, the objects dealt with are not necessarily fixed, or unknown a priori. The relationship between these objects can be complex and access to some of the data may demand several transmissions across involved data.

The data allocation problem has been analyzed in the past when distributed databases were studied and parallelization had to be utilized. In [8], a linear model for file allocation with storage and transmission costs is elaborated, and the simulation covers five files and three computers.

In [11], a store-and-forward computer network is investigated. Network constraints are considered to be availability and delay, which is demonstrated in a model with a total of 10 files.

Data placement is modeled on different abstract levels in [3] and it is proven that the data placement problem is extremely difficult to solve. It is shown that data placement problem is NP-Complete.

The file allocation problem is discussed under concurrency constraints to build a model with storage cost and communication cost in [14]. Constraints of the model are the multiplicity of databases, variable routing of data, and available capacity of the network nodes.

Attempting to cluster datasets according to their interdependency and subsequently to store the clusters on separate machines have been investigated [9].

The problem has been coined as solving a multi-constraint hypergraph partitioning problem for task and data assignment [6].

A further clustering algorithm is described in [19] that uses k-means algorithm for finding locations for the clustered data, resulting in task allocation to the data centers with most of the input dataset. This is comparable to the ATLAS workflow.

Evolutionary algorithms were also applied to this kind of problem. In [10], data allocation strategies have been investigated to reduce transaction costs. A genetic algorithm was used here, with the goal of limiting communication effort between data centers by balancing the load.

Replication and placement of files across different nodes can lead to improvements in job execution, makespan, and bandwidth [7]. However, caution is advised since a priori movement of data to improve the access to data can lead to a bottleneck in network performance between data centers. To avoid drops in performance, data replication is used in the ATLAS grid very rarely and selectively [12].

Further efforts have been undertaken in previous studies for database optimizations. The authors of [18] discuss database allocation optimization and propose a mathematical model concerning average waiting time. Other database approaches attempt to arrange data effectively over the network nodes, such as in [1,2,4]. However, these studies investigate idealized database cases. For example, they focus on a single query type or do not consider any constraints on communication characteristics. Room for improvement would comprise user behavior and workflow characteristics. Analysis of access patterns can be beneficial for network utilization.

A well-known approach is ranking data according to the number of accesses per time unit. This characteristic is referred to as data *popularity* [5]. In [5], a successful popularity model is established which uses different structured and unstructured sources for collecting historical data. A popularity model is implemented as an autonomous service for finding obsolete data and used in the cleaning process [13,17].

Summing up, the actual research on data partitioning and allocation techniques is specific or limited. Due to complexity and variety, simplified models and local optimizations were studied and applied. A thorough analysis of data usage and data optimization point of view for data grids is necessary. Storage resources and the use of data has to be appropriately treated in the process of file placement [15,16]. The lack of information has prompted this work, where grid computational application uses data in big quantities. Research on data management will have a strong impact on usability, performance, cost and the acceptance of worldwide spanning grids on a large scale.

4   An Evolutionary Data Allocation Approach

4.1   Idea

For data-intensive workflows, an evolutionary data cluster and allocation algorithm is proposed to minimize the overall network load and thereby reducing average waiting times across the network.

The approach is based on an evolutionary algorithm generating solutions to the allocation problem built upon two heuristics to improve the decision-making process. Thus, the data allocation approach rests on two solid pillars which are combined in a novel way:

The algorithm's *first pillar* is calculating the data dependency and thus possibly clustering the dataset on correlated features. These features are subject to big data studies. Today, machine learning algorithms classify and assess the multidimensional datasets of ATLAS already. Filters and clustering can be applied to extract parameters and collect statistics.

The *second pillar* of the proposed algorithm is the popularity of datasets that stipulates how likely the dataset will be accessed in the near future. The best practice would be to allocate more popular files to more efficient, higher performing data centers.

4.2   Data Dependency

Data dependency is used for estimating the likelihood of files being in the same input dataset essential to perform a job. Files within datasets with high dependency provide more similar features, e.g. type of contained data, naming etc., and are more likely to be part of a new common dataset processed together by a job.

In this context, a simple idea relates to clustering highly dependent datasets together such that new datasets for upcoming jobs are more likely to find the majority of those files at a single node. Thus, fewer files have to be transferred to complete the datasets at the target node. The fewer WAN transfers per job, the more LAN transfers per job occur. In general, these data center internal transfers occurring between the storage node and the worker node at the same site are, however, not the focus of attention, since they are sufficiently and quickly executed, thus they may be ignored in terms of performance. The use of internal LAN transfers rather than WAN transfers reduces the bottleneck effect on the global WAN network.

In the implemented simulation, dataset dependency (DSD) values are mapped to pairs of datasets, i.e., $DSD : \{DS\} \times \{DS\} \rightarrow [0, 1], (DS_n, DS_k) \mapsto DSD_{n,k}$. The mapping can be normalized to 1 for each sample set.

This is represented as a symmetrical matrix with 1s in the main diagonal and values <1 otherwise.

4.3   Data Popularity

Data popularity describes the usage importance of files by the number of occurred accesses to them. The chosen time window and the weighting for counting are not subject here. It is used as a measure for how likely a data element, here files in datasets, will be accessed in the near future. More often accessed datasets will be more likely to be accessed in the near future. In the simulation, normalized data popularity values are assigned to all datasets, i.e., $Pop : \{DS\} \rightarrow [0, 1], DS_n \mapsto Pop_n$.

Figure 1 depicts popularity values of datasets in the test cases with 20% respectively 35% access rate to popular data. The leftmost bin comprises 80% respectively 65% accesses to data with popularity value 0, i.e., the portion of data for which no conclusion about popularity could have been drawn. It can be seen that very popular data is used more often than less popular data.

4.4   Data Arrangement S

The solution of the allocation problem is denoted as a *storage matrix* of a set of possible storage matrices, $S \in \mathcal{S}$ by clustering and storage allocation. The storage matrix S is a *permutation matrix* specifying the mapping of files to storage nodes. The set $\mathcal{S}$ contains the matrices which obey the storage constraints in the inequality 1. Jobs read file collections expressed by so-called file datasets. Files of those datasets are arranged across storage nodes as defined by the output of the algorithm, S.

4.5   Algorithm

Every file in the grid is assigned to a respective dataset. Overlaps are omitted. However, if original datasets have overlaps, these can be eliminated before applying test jobs: Intersections become new sub-datasets with, for example, composed values for popularity and dependencies. For test job samples, datasets are generated out of existing ones based on popularity, so that more popular files are more likely moved into new datasets. In this analysis, approximately a half of the files have a popularity value of 0 which means there is no corresponding

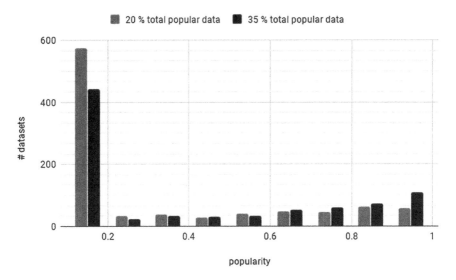

Fig. 1. Access frequencies of datasets with and without popularity. Datasets with popularity are accessed with a rate of 20%, and 35%. The leftmost bin implies the majority with 0 popularity.

information on these files. So far, these files would be considered unclassifiable if, for instance, they were of a type never seen before.

The chosen data centers provide all storage capacities and computing power, i.e. they are represented as computing and storage nodes in the simulation. The simulation can be parametrized with special cases: For example, if a data center represents a data warehouse or cloud storage, the workload manager could be set to omit this node and no WAN transmission would occur to this node in Eq. 1.

The proposed algorithm generates a file arrangement S with the goal to minimize the expected number of WAN transfers per job. After each evolutionary iteration, which produces a version of S, the target metric is evaluated again and the evolution takes place as described in details below. Given a test job sample, the problem can be formalized with S as a parameter and the expected cost functional $\#tx_{WAN}$ as a target metric. $\#tx_{WAN}$ can be decomposed into single $\#tx_{WAN}(i)$ giving the triggered WAN transfers for job i:

$$\underset{S}{argmin} \ \mathbb{E}[\#tx_{WAN}] \approx \underset{S}{argmin} \sum_{j \in \{jobs\}} \#tx_{WAN}(j) \tag{1}$$

$$such \ that \tag{2}$$

$$\boldsymbol{S}^T \times \mathbf{w}_{file} \leq \mathbf{w}_{storage} \tag{3}$$

where $\mathbf{w}_{file}$ is a column vector which represents the file sizes for $file_1, \ldots, file_M$ and $\mathbf{w}_{storage}$ is a column vector which represents the storage capacities of data centers 1, 2, ..., N. The expectation value is denoted as $\mathbb{E}$. A normalization is not needed for *argmin* seeking a minimum of the expression.

The Algorithm 1 illustrates the working principle of the approach. **Step 1**, building the DSD matrix for the given datasets, must be performed only once.

Step 2.1 covers the evolutionary part of the file partitioning. A clustering algorithm of the algorithm evaluates the file affinity to the constructed partitions $S_1, ..., S_N$ by the dataset dependency matrix. Datasets with higher DSD belong together and their files should be placed in one common partition if possible. The coarseness on the dataset level rather than file level is beneficial for a quicker evaluation. Datasets are logical clusters themselves, whose properties allow comparison to each other. In each solution, i.e., an entity in the population, a random number of partitions prefer high popularity data, whereas the rest of the partitions do not. Files are collected in a random trajectory which determines the aimed solution in the solution space.

Step 2.2, after constructing the partitions $S_1, ..., S_N$, they are logically mapped to the data center storages in terms of minimization of the target metric in Eq. 1. If a partition does not fit into a data center, the drop-out files will be mapped to other free gaps of storages not yet completely filled under the application of the target metric as well.

Step 2.1 rapidly results in generations with a fixed number of partitions. The storage constraint holds in *step 2.2* if a total set of files is picked such that there is sufficient total storage capacity under the considered circumstances. Should the capacity constraint not be obeyed, only a subset may be allocated in place of the optimized storage nodes, and the complementary subset, which must be discarded, are allocated to storage nodes outside of the optimized storage nodes. The complementary subset consists of the files less worthy according to the heuristics.

A less strict optimization goal could be addressed by dealing with a subset of the total files, but a deeper analysis would exceed the scope of this work.

Each entity in the population is evaluated by its achieved performance in terms of the metric in Eq. 1. It is evaluated by simulating a job sample set and summing up incurred WAN data transfer values for each computing job. Over several iterations, evolution continues until no further improvements can be achieved. The process comprises selection, mutation, and crossover steps which are iteratively applied in-between:

- Mutation partially alters clustering of files and mapping those partitions to the storages as described above. The prior outcome S transforms into another $\tilde{S}$.
- Crossover merges the initial clustering and mapping of two entities into the common offspring. If both entities share overlapping files mapped to different storages, not yet assigned files of those overlaps are assigned uniquely for a single target storage. This avoids illegal double use since files can only be selected once in the allocation.
- Selection keeps the best entities. If the population starves, then new entities are added to enrich the pool of solutions.

```
   // Generate dataset dependency values (DSD) , i.e. pairwise
      correlation values (interdependencies) (step 1)
```
1   $DSD_{n,k} \leftarrow cor(n,k)$ $\forall n, k \in \{datasets\}$
2   $N \leftarrow number\ of\ data\ centers$
```
   // Generate population (step 2)
```
3   **while** $\{termination\ condition\ not\ met\}$ **do**
4   **while** $\{population\ starved\}$ **do**
```
         // Add one entity S ∈ S with N random dataset clusters Sₙ ∈ S
```
5       $k \leftarrow random[1, N]$
6       $S \leftarrow (S_1 = \{\}, S_2 = \{\}, ..., S_N = \{\})$
7       $datasets \leftarrow available\ datasets\ on\ storage_{1,..,N}$
8   **while** $\{datasets.nonempty()\}$ **do**
9   **foreach** $\{S_{n=1,...,k}\}$ **do**
10           $S_n.add(datasets.get(S_n.dependency(high), popularity(high))$
11   **end**
12   **foreach** $\{S_{n=k+1,...,N}\}$ **do**
13           $S_n.add(datasets.get(S_n.dependency(high), popularity(low))$
14   **end**
15   **end**
16       $population.add(S)$
17   **end**
```
      // Make compatible partitions allocated to network storages for
         each entity
```
18   **foreach** $\{S \leftarrow population.next()\}$ **do**
19       $(S_1, ..., S_N) \leftarrow (S.S_1, ..., S.S_N)$
20   **foreach** $\{S_n\}$ **do**
21   **foreach** $\{storage_{\{1,...,N\}}\}$ **do**
22           $storage_k.add(S_n.top(popular))$ // add datasets
23           $S_n.remove(storage_k)$ // remove allocated datasets
24   **end**
25   **end**
26   **foreach** $\{S_n.nonempty().top(size)\}$ **do**
```
            // not allocated
```
27   **foreach** $\{storage_k.nonfull().top(size)\}$ **do**
```
               // not yet completed storage, biggest first
```
28           $storage_k.add(S_n.top(popular))$ // add datasets
29           $S_n.remove(storage_k)$ // remove allocated datasets
30   **if** $\{S_n = \{\}\}$ **then**
31   break // inner loop
32   **end**
33   **end**
34   **end**
35   **end**
36   population.apply(\{selection, mutation, crossover\})
37 **end**
38 return population.best();

Algorithm 1: Popularity-based data allocation algorithm

5 Evaluation

This section shows the efficiency of the algorithm on the basis of the simulated network of data centers. The data centers should represent the most important ones of the grid in reality, i.e., they provide most of the total capacity. This set of data centers can be extended. However, from the perspective of data management, the rest of the grid holds less significance, since the situation would considerably improve through better management just in these data centers. Datasets are present with the following characteristics:

– Datasets comprise 10 to 40 files to reflect dynamic dataset sizes.
– A popularity value is assigned to each dataset.
– A dataset dependency value (DSD) is assigned to each pair of datasets.

A job sample is generated in the following way:

– Each new job is assigned to a newly generated dataset derived from the pre-defined datasets covering all files. Thereby random files are selected from the pre-defined datasets.
– The workload manager, i.e., job broker, is set to aim at WAN transfer minimization.

Each of the data centers can hold between 200 and 2000 files for the sake of run time of the simulation on a single personal computer. Capacities are chosen randomly at the start of the simulation. This adds up to approximately 20 k files and 1 k datasets. The simulation initiates multiple runs in different configurations. Jobs access different shares of the popular datasets in each configuration. A configuration with 20% popularity use significance that jobs have an expected 20% access rate to datasets with some popularity and 80% to purely random datasets, including the majority, i.e. datasets with popularity $= 0$. Highly popular datasets are accessed more likely than others, as seen in Fig. 1. Figures 2 and 3 present the results of the optimized file allocations for different configurations:

– The *random case* shows the initial random dataset spread across available network storages.
– The *optimized case* gives the achieved outcomes from the optimization algorithm in the experiment.

It is evident that the utility of popularity declines as the number of data storages in the network increases. This could contribute to a weakness of the algorithm's evolution process in varying the target popularity of the different partitions. In addition, the number of WAN transfers per job increase by the number of possible network nodes. Input data is spread across more network nodes. Furthermore, there are more network nodes where a job can execute, increasing the uncertainty for target nodes where the input files are requested and transmitted to.

A better outcome can be achieved in networks with a smaller number of data storages. The complexity of the optimization problem grows due to bigger

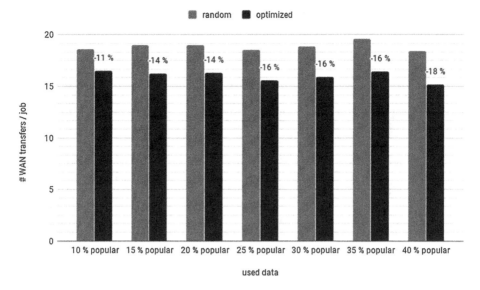

Fig. 2. Runs with 10 data centers comprising different job configurations in terms of used data popularity

networks and so the rise in the number of possibilities in the solution space worsens the convergence rate. The descent of the cost function towards higher total popularity rate is explained by more predictability on some part of the file population. In any case, a strong deviation from this pattern can be observed by the randomness of the load and the data access in the experiment. Random effects in choosing worker nodes and associated data may lead to distorted results.

The workload manager plays a central role in the technique proposed in this work. A network metric, such as average network load, depends directly on the task of the workload manager. The job has to be placed most likely to the node with the majority of input files. In the hypothetical worst case, jobs would run just remotely from the input data. This situation would bear the maximum load on the network due to the fact that all the input files have to be transferred.

This goes in hand with the described data management which is rooted in the described DSD clustering. The used clustering adjusts to the stochastic usage of global data. Hashing algorithms take the reverse way which provides data arrangements with efficient parallelism to maximize throughput. However, in this consideration, since all network nodes provide some portions of data, parallelization occurs through the workload manager combined with the data management of interest.

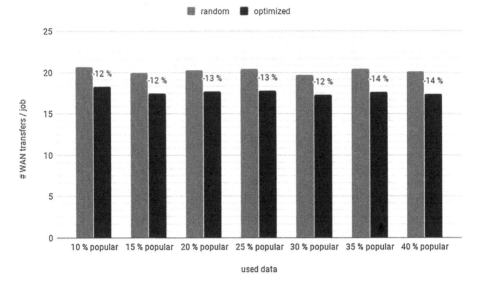

Fig. 3. Runs with 20 data centers comprising different job configurations in terms of used data popularity

6   Conclusion

The proposed algorithm clusters and allocates grid data in a more sophisticated way by focusing on the importance of data and minimizing the effort by changing the solution slightly. More popular data should be held together at better performing data centers. With this form of data allocation policy, less overall network load and shorter network waiting times occur, which reduces the cost of computational jobs in terms of expected WAN transfer time. The adaptable model uses a rapid popularity-based partitioning for optimized clustering that in general can be applied to other workflow environments and used for various control and optimization tasks in dynamic systems.

However, so far, the proposed model represents an idealized toy model which was optimized in terms of the overall inter-data center communication on a basis of transparent data in a uniform grid. Further constraints must be imposed in order for the model to cope with a real case. Real data may not necessarily be transparent in the first step. The evaluation of access patterns could be extended over time which would yield more information. Also, the effects of replication of files and dataset overlaps were not investigated in this work. Equal copies of files should be declustered in the network. This means, different storage nodes with sufficient distance between one another are selected for storing equal copies of files. Furthermore, data sets placed by the user should not be moved to another storage location. This would restrict the total optimization. However, optimization on the enabled subsets can be carried out by the proposed algorithm. Fixed subsets can be flagged accordingly and must not be moved automatically. User interactability can be incorporated into a grid service of the proposed algorithm to enable or disable datasets. Users could identify interesting datasets that would be the focus of computation, or alternatively single out the uninteresting datasets that should no longer be in use. So far, ATLAS users and users of other research collaborations move datasets with rigid policies or by hand on a dataset basis. The implementation of this feature into a service could replace the manual way by an at least semi-automatic mechanism of rebalancing data. *Future research* will focus on:

- The algorithm will be refined in terms of flexibility for use in various environments with even more input parameters. One additional feature will be enabling/disabling datasets, allowing the user to control whether a dataset is able to move or not. This makes the algorithm more efficient and reliable.
- The algorithm is highly parallelizable. Hence, runtime improvements are expected to be achieved in order to apply it to more complex use cases. The current code base represents a first version which proves the concept. It runs on a single standard personal computer.
- Further constraints should be refined in the model. On the network side, I/O bandwidth between data centers can be defined into the cost metric. Various job classes can be considered, an issue that has not yet been covered in this work.

References

1. Abdel-Ghaffar, K.A.S., Abbadi, A.E.: Optimal allocation of two-dimensional data (extended abstract). In: Afrati, F., Kolaitis, P. (eds.) ICDT 1997. LNCS, vol. 1186, pp. 409–418. Springer, Heidelberg (1997). https://doi.org/10.1007/3-540-62222-5_60
2. Atallah, M.J., Prabhakar, S.: (Almost) optimal parallel block access to range queries. In: Proceedings of the Nineteenth ACM SIGMOD-SIGACT-SIGART Symposium on Principles of Database Systems, pp. 205–215. ACM (2000)
3. Bell, D.A.: Difficult data placement problems. Comput. J. **27**(4), 315–320 (1984)
4. Berchtold, S., Böhm, C., Braunmüller, B., Keim, D.A., Kriegel, H.P.: Fast parallel similarity search in multimedia databases. In: Proceedings of the 1997 ACM SIGMOD International Conference on Management of Data, SIGMOD 1997, pp. 1–12. ACM, New York (1997). https://doi.org/10.1145/253260.253263
5. Bonacorsi, D., Boccali, T., Giordano, D., Girone, M., Neri, M., Magini, N., Kuznetsov, V., Wildish, T.: Exploiting CMS data popularity to model the evolution of data management for run-2 and beyond. J. Phys.: Conf. Ser. **664**, 032003 (2015). IOP Publishing
6. Campello, R.J.G.B., Hruschka, E.R.: On comparing two sequences of numbers and its applications to clustering analysis. Inf. Sci. **179**(8), 1025–1039 (2009)
7. Chang, R.S., Chang, H.P.: A dynamic data replication strategy using access-weights in data grids. J. Supercomput. **45**(3), 277–295 (2008)
8. Chu, W.W.: Optimal file allocation in a multiple computer system. IEEE Trans. Comput. **100**(10), 885–889 (1969)
9. Foster, I., Kesselman, C., Tuecke, S.: The anatomy of the grid: enabling scalable virtual organizations. Int. J. High Perform. Comput. Appl. **15**(3), 200–222 (2001)

10. Guo, W., Wang, X.: A data placement strategy based on genetic algorithm in cloud computing platform. In: 2013 10th Web Information System and Application Conference (WISA), pp. 369–372. IEEE (2013)
11. Laning, L.J., Leonard, M.S.: File allocation in a distributed computer communication network. IEEE Trans. Comput. 3, 232–244 (1983)
12. Lassnig, M., Garonne, V., Branco, M., Molfetas, A.: Dynamic and adaptive data-management in atlas. J. Phys.: Conf. Ser. 219, 062054 (2010). IOP Publishing
13. Megino, F.B., Cinquilli, M., Giordano, D., Karavakis, E., Girone, M., Magini, N., Mancinelli, V., Spiga, D.: Implementing data placement strategies for the CMS experiment based on a popularity model. J. Phys.: Conf. Ser. 396, 032047 (2012). IOP Publishing
14. Ram, S., Marsten, R.E.: A model for database allocation incorporating a concurrency control mechanism. IEEE Trans. Knowl. Data Eng. 3(3), 389–395 (1991)
15. Sato, H., Matsuoka, S., Endo, T.: File clustering based replication algorithm in a grid environment. In: Proceedings of the 2009 9th IEEE/ACM International Symposium on Cluster Computing and the Grid, pp. 204–211. IEEE Computer Society (2009)
16. Sato, H., Matsuoka, S., Endo, T., Maruyama, N.: Access-pattern and bandwidth aware file replication algorithm in a grid environment. In: Proceedings of the 2008 9th IEEE/ACM International Conference on Grid Computing, pp. 250–257. IEEE Computer Society (2008)
17. Spiga, D., Giordano, D., Barreiro Megino, F.H.: Optimizing the usage of multi-Petabyte storage resources for LHC experiments. In: Proceedings of the EGI Community Forum 2012/EMI Second Technical Conference (EGICF12-EMITC2), 26–30 March 2012, Munich, Germany (2012). https://pos.sissa.it/162/107/
18. Wang, J.Y., Jea, K.F.: A near-optimal database allocation for reducing the average waiting time in the grid computing environment. Inf. Sci. 179(21), 3772–3790 (2009)
19. Yuan, D., Yang, Y., Liu, X., Chen, J.: A data placement strategy in scientific cloud workflows. Future Gen. Comput. Syst. 26(8), 1200–1214 (2010)

Hyper-heuristic Online Learning
for Self-assembling Swarm Robots

Shuang Yu[1]([✉]) [iD], Aldeida Aleti[1] [iD], Jan Carlo Barca[1] [iD], and Andy Song[2] [iD]

[1] Monash University, Clayton 3168, Australia
shuang.yu@monash.edu
[2] RMIT University, Melbourne 3000, Australia

Abstract. A robot swarm is a solution for difficult and large scale tasks. However, controlling and coordinating a swarm of robots is challenging, because of the complexity and uncertainty of the environment where manual programming of robot behaviours is often impractical. In this study we propose a hyper-heuristic methodology for swarm robots. It allows robots to create suitable actions based on a set of low-level heuristics, where each heuristic is a behavioural element. With online learning, the robot behaviours can be improved during execution by autonomous heuristic adjustment. The proposed hyper-heuristic framework is applied to surface cleaning tasks on buildings where multiple separate surfaces exist and complete surface information is difficult to obtain. Under this scenario, the robot swarm not only needs to clean the surfaces efficiently by distributing the robots, but also to move across surfaces by self-assembling into a bridge structure. Experimental results showed the effectiveness of the hyper-heuristic framework; the same group of robots was able to autonomously deal with multiple surfaces of different layouts. Their behaviours can improve over time because of the online learning mechanism.

Keywords: Hyper-heuristics · Online learning · Swarm robots
Robotic behaviors · Self-assembling robots · Robotic surface cleaner

1 Introduction

Robotics is a fast growing area due to the explosive development in Artificial Intelligence. Robots can automate many tasks that are considered risky and undesirable for humans. In addition they may accomplish tasks that are considered difficult for humans. One example is swarm robots where many robots, typically small droids, can collaborate and behave cohesively in one accord to achieve tasks that are difficult or expensive such as surveying, rescue and patrol.

A reliable and capable robot swarm can gain significant advantage in various domains such as mining, agriculture, smart cities and even military applications. However, coordinating a collection of robots is not a trivial task. All robots need to operate collaboratively to achieve a common goal. Manually developing behavioral strategies for each robot using a collaboration strategy to coordinate them can be difficult and ineffective, especially when the environment is dynamic.

© Springer International Publishing AG, part of Springer Nature 2018
Y. Shi et al. (Eds.): ICCS 2018, LNCS 10860, pp. 167–180, 2018.
https://doi.org/10.1007/978-3-319-93698-7_13

Instead we propose a learning based hyper-heuristic approach for swarm robots. With the hyper-heuristic approach, we only supply low level operators instead of a full control strategy. These operators are elements for constructing instructions for various tasks and environments. More importantly, the instructions can be adjusted over time because of the learning mechanism. Therefore it is not necessary to manually define the robot behaviors beforehand as the performance of these robots can improve during execution.

As a case study, we apply the proposed hyper heuristic framework to a surface cleaning problem, where multiple building surfaces need to be cleaned. Basic moves and operators are supplied for the hyper-heuristic engine to build cleaning strategies. The robots are required to clean varied surface layouts using different swarm behaviours. Moreover the robots should be capable of self-assembly in order to cross gaps in the surfaces and travel from surface to surface. Through a range of test scenarios, we demonstrate the effectiveness of the proposed hyper heuristic approach. Analysis on the learning behaviors is also present to give insight into this method.

The rest of the paper is organised as follows: Sect. 2 reviews the related work, Sect. 3 describes the proposed hyper-heuristic methodology. A case study on self-assembly swarm robot behaviours demonstrates an implementation of the methodology, and is given in Sect. 4; this also includes the implementation of the heuristic repository. Section 5 shows simulations of the system used in the real-world application of cleaning multiple surfaces.

2   Related Work

Hyper-heuristics have been used in various complex problems, such as bin-packing, timetabling and vehicle routing. The aim of hyper-heuristic approaches is to design a generic method that can automatically generate algorithms from a repository of low-level heuristics or operators to solve a given problem [2]. It searches for solvers instead of solutions. To give a brief background of hyper-heuristic methods, a tabu search hyper-heuristic is applied on nurse timetabling and scheduling [4], [16] used a choice function to rank heuristics for selection, and [3] explored the use of Genetic Programming as a hyper-heuristic, and demonstrated it on Boolean Satisfiability problem and online bin-packing. Combined with online learning, which continuously learns the knowledge while performing actions, hyper-heuristics solve problems with dynamic environments. For example, [20] performs online learning to assist hybridising Estimation Distribution Algorithms with hyper-heuristics in dynamic environments. In [8], to determine shipper sizes for storage and transportation, reinforcement learning with tabu search is used to modify the performance score for each low-level heuristic at every decision point.

Regarding heuristic learning, there are enormous amount of existing studies in robotics. However, most of them concern single robots, hence are not included in our review. In robot swarms, the local control laws executed by every robot give rise to overall system dynamics, which is defined as a swarm behaviour [14].

Rule-based algorithms allow complex and collective behaviours to emerge from local behavioural rules, such as collective building construction [21]. Heuristic learning techniques have been widely used in robot swarms to guide navigation (search and path planning), task scheduling, motion control, etc., but they are all tailored to their intended applications, and are not re-usable for other purposes, such as sequencing swarm behaviours. [14] defined the problem of swarm behaviour composition, and proposed an off-line learning method to generate behaviour sequences for a human operator to execute in a known and static environment. This lacks the ability to cope with dynamic environments. Moreover, the existing methods require manual algorithm re-design from task to task, while hyper-heuristics, on the other hand, are often used to automatically generate algorithms for a new problem.

The feasibility of this will be demonstrated through a case study on self-assembling robot behaviours. Self-assembling robots can physically join and form larger structures, as seen for example in Swarmanoid [6] and REPLICATOR projects [9]. They have demonstrated great mobility in complex environments by crossing gaps and moving across surfaces that could not have been traversed by a single robot. The Swarm-bot project [7] demonstrates the hardware implementation of completing tasks, such as retrieving heavy objects and passing over holes in a collective manner.

All these systems require manual input, such as a human operator or a control station, to determine and inform the robots when to start assembling/disassembling and what behaviour to perform for different problems and scenarios.

3   Methodology of the Hyper-heuristics Framework

We first introduce the hyper-heuristic methodology that is proposed to guide the self-assembling in a robot swarm.

Hyper-heuristics are built on heuristics. They treat heuristics as general purpose building blocks to be simultaneously and iteratively applied to a problem [18]. More importantly, hyper-heuristics are problem-independent, and the same repository of heuristics can be used to solve new problems.

3.1   Multi-robot Hyper-heuristic Structure

An overview of the proposed hyper-heuristics framework structure for swarm robots is given in Fig. 1. Each robot is **initialised** with a starting heuristic, then takes **action** corresponding to that heuristic. If the **termination criteria** is satisfied, meaning the objective is accomplished, then the process stops. Otherwise the robot behaviours are **evaluated** against the objective(s). Based on the evaluation result, heuristics then are selected from the pre-defined **heuristic repository** to construct new ones. All the robots will **update** their heuristics, take actions then enter the next iteration of the process unless a termination criterion is met.

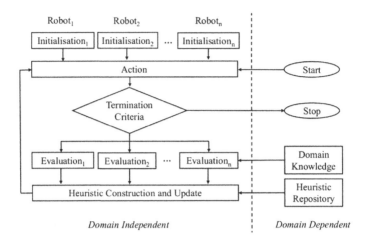

Fig. 1. Overview of the methodology.

In terms of evaluation of the objective, domain knowledge is required. In robotics, domain knowledge is usually dependent on the available sensors and robot communication mechanisms. Performance evaluation represents some "benefits" from the environment and can be translated and stored as performance scores within each robot. These scores are used to influence the heuristic selection. The heuristic repository is also domain relevant, and contains a variety of low-level heuristics.

3.2   Heuristic Construction

Our proposed hyper-heuristic structure allows the actions for a given problem to be automatically constructed and updated at each time interval. The performance of a heuristic measured in the environment is stored in each robot as heuristic scores. Through online learning, the robots can gradually learn to select better heuristics.

Heuristic Scores. If there is no prior knowledge, heuristic scores are initialised with the same value. The initial score can be obtained from prior learning. The heuristic scoring method is inspired by Choice Function (CF) and Multi-armed Bandit (MAB), as described in [5,16] respectively. Each robot calculates the score of the last action locally for each heuristic based on the objective function.

$$h_t^i = \sum (\alpha f_t + \beta f_t^{ij} + \gamma M_t^i), \tag{1}$$

where

- f_t is the objective function value evaluated at time step t,
- f_t^{ij} is the objective function value of heuristic i given the previous heuristic j at time step t, and

- M_t^i is the MAB term for heuristic i at time step t.

α, β and γ are parameters that control the weight of each term on the overall score of a heuristic. The performance of the heuristic and the joint performance of pairs of heuristics are measured using the objective function. For instance, in the case of cleaning tasks, f_t would be the cleaning efficiency measured from robot dirt sensors. The MAB term M_t^i is introduced as in Eq. 2 to compensate for heuristics that are unexplored [5].

$$M_t^i = \sqrt{\frac{2 \log \sum_{j=1}^{k} n_j}{n_i}} \tag{2}$$

where k is the total number of heuristics and i represents the index of the current heuristic. The MAB term is inversely proportional to how many times the current heuristic has been used n_i, and directly proportional to the total number of times the other heuristics have been used $\sum_{j=1}^{k} n_j$. This ensures that unexplored heuristics are given more weight than the ones that have been used often, which prevents the algorithm from becoming trapped in a local optima.

Learning the Heuristic Scores. The scores $\hat{H}_t = \{\hat{h}_t^1, \hat{h}_t^2 \ldots, \hat{h}_t^k\}$ are updated at the end of each iteration according to previous experience and current performance, as shown in Eq. 3.

$$\hat{h}_t^i = \theta h_t^i + (1 - \theta)\hat{h}_{t-1}^i \tag{3}$$

where $\hat{h}_{t-1}^i$ is the previous score of heuristic i, and θ is the learning rate. Higher θ values favour recent knowledge over the accumulated knowledge.

Heuristic Selection. The heuristic scores learned in the previous t iterations affect the heuristic to be selected in the next iteration $t + 1$. There are different strategies that could be used to select the appropriate heuristic from a heuristic repository. One of them is Greedy selection, always selecting the heuristic with the highest score. Relatively worse heuristics would not be re-used even if it may lead to better solutions when the environment changes. The second method is Roulette Wheel selection (RW) [10]. A good heuristic has greater chance to participate, while "bad" ones also have the chance to be selected. This method is quick to explore heuristics. This is further discussed through simulations in Sect. 5.

Group Acceptance and Update. The robots can communicate to reach an agreement on which heuristic to execute next. In software optimisation problems, after a selected heuristic is applied to the problem, hyper-heuristics use a move acceptance method to determine if the heuristic, or the "move" should be accepted or rejected [1]. In a robotic system, the move acceptance strategy is "always accept", because rejecting a heuristic means going back to the robot's original state (position), which in the real-world is impractical and consumes energy. In addition, we use a **decentralised group acceptance strategy** which only accepts heuristics that benefit the whole group.

For swarm robotics, decentralised systems are more robust, scalable and flexible. No single robot possesses the entire swarm's knowledge of the environment. Every robot can evaluate a heuristic based on its local knowledge, and communicate the result to its neighbours.

The decentralised strategies are similar to that in [15]. A heuristic is accepted if $\sum_{n=1}^{N} d_n \geq \delta$, where d_n is the robot decision on acceptance, N is the number of robot decisions received, with "accept the heuristic" as $d_n = 1$, and reject as $d_n = 0$. δ is the acceptance threshold.

After the new heuristic is selected and accepted by the swarm, all the robots will update their own heuristics to be the new heuristic, and take another action.

4   Case Study on Self-assembling Multi-robot Systems

To show the feasibility and effectiveness of the proposed hyper-heuristics methodology, we present a case study using self-assembling robots.

4.1   Problem Description

In self-assembling robots, swarm behaviours emerge from the physical connections and interactions between robots. A robot can be seen as a module and an emergent behaviour can result from the interaction between these modules.

For example, robots can connect to cross gaps, scatter to cover surfaces, or flock to stay close but separated. A repository of such basic behaviours $B = \{b^1, b^2 \ldots b^k\}$, defines the set of robot control laws that read sensor data, and execute actions accordingly. The task is then, *given a set of self-assembling robot behaviours, and an objective function, construct a sequence of such behaviours autonomously to maximize the objective value $f(t)$ in unknown environments.*

4.2   Implementation

To solve this problem, we consider a type of swarm robot behaviour as a *heuristic*, which is defined by the control rules that take in environmental input and control actions periodically.

Robots start with an initial heuristic, and the same score $\hat{h}_0^i$ for each heuristic in the repository. This is based on the assumption that the environment is unknown, which means there is no knowledge of which heuristic is better. The robots perform actions for a period of time guided by the initial heuristic, and learn heuristic scores online according to the method described in Sect. 3.2.

Any robot can propose a candidate heuristic for the next time interval to the group, and in order to physically achieve the group decision process described in Sect. 3.2, the robots send communication messages to each other following the diagrams in Fig. 2. A robot sends a candidate heuristic to neighbouring robots.

The neighbouring robots then run RW selections according to their locally kept heuristic scores and compare their selections with others. If they match, the neighbour will inform the proposing robot of its acceptance.

If the number of robots accepting passes the acceptance threshold d_n, then the group has collectively decided to accept the candidate heuristic and will apply that heuristic for the next iteration. If the candidate heuristic is rejected, another proposal will be made, and the process repeats until a candidate is accepted by the group.

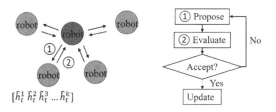

Fig. 2. Implementation of evaluation and group acceptance.

There are three benefits in this approach. Firstly, the robots do not require a human operator or centralised control, making the group scalable and robust against single-point failure. Secondly, it allows robots to collectively adapt to unknown or dynamic environments. Lastly, the behaviour construction is not problem-specific. New tasks only require the change of an objective function, not any re-design of the hyper-heuristic. For instance, for surface cleaning tasks, the area cleaned is used to evaluate the performance; for multi-robot rendezvous, the distance to the meeting point would be the objective function.

4.3   Heuristic Repository

The heuristic repository for this cleaning task comprises: sweeping, bridging, exploring, circling and flocking, as described below:

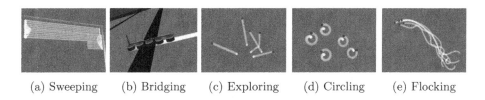

(a) Sweeping   (b) Bridging   (c) Exploring   (d) Circling   (e) Flocking

Fig. 3. Heuristic repository

Sweeping. As shown in Fig. 3(a), the sweeping behaviour allows robots to physically connect to form a vertical line, and perform horizontal back-and-forth movements.

Bridging. Bridging behaviour enables the swarm to connect and form a bridge structure, as demonstrated in Fig. 3(b). It allows a group of robots to cross gaps and small obstacles, as a connection is formed between robots to keep them from falling when they lose contact with the surface.

Exploring. Exploring is a behaviour that allows the robots to scatter in random directions (which change at random time intervals) on the surface, as indicated in Fig. 3(c). To prevent any robot from moving outside other robots' communication range, each robot keeps estimating its distance to the furthest robot in range, and if the distance is outside a threshold, the robot moves towards its furthest neighbour, until it is within the threshold again.

Circling. Circling performs a spiral motion, following with straight lines in random directions, as shown in Fig. 3(d). This is a cleaning pattern widely used by floor cleaning robots.

Flocking. This local controller enables robots to follow a flocking behaviour [17], as illustrated in Fig. 3(e). This heuristic allows robots to stay relatively close to each other, making it easier for the swarm to assemble when needed, while preserving some degree of random exploration. Assume the position of the robot $P_0 = (x_0, z_0)$. $\overline{P}(\overline{x}, \overline{z})$ is the average position of neighbours, and $\overline{O}$ is the average orientation of neighbours within the sensing range. A repulsion vector $R(x_R, z_R)$ prevents robots from being too close to each other, and $R = -P_{min}$, where P_{min} is the relative position of the nearest neighbour. The alignment vector for each robot $P'(x', z')$ is calculated as:

$$x' = \overline{x} + S_x \cdot \cos \overline{O} + x_R$$
$$z' = \overline{z} + S_z \cdot \sin \overline{O} + z_R$$

where S_x and S_z are scaling factors, which can be determined empirically.

The Obstacle and Gap Avoidance Mechanism. This is implemented for all heuristics. In a complex environment, there could be obstacles which the robots need to avoid and go around, and gaps that the robots cannot cross on their own. In this case study, we use potential field based obstacle avoidance [19], which applies a multiplier v_{multi} to linear velocity, and another multiplier ω_{multi} to the robot's angular velocity. The multipliers are calculated as follows:

$$v_{multi} = 1 - e^{-\frac{K_{rise} d_{obs}}{R_{avoid}}}$$

$$\omega_{multi} = \begin{cases} K_\omega(\pi/2 - \theta_{obs}), & \text{if } \pi > \theta_{obs} > 0 \\ K_\omega(-\pi/2 - \theta_{obs}), & \text{otherwise} \end{cases}$$

where K_{rise} and K_ω are control parameters to be tuned empirically, d_{obs} is the distance between obstacle and robot, and θ_{obs} is the angle between robot orientation and the obstacle. If a gap is detected, the robot will rotate in a random direction until it orients away from the gap, and continue to move.

5   Experiments and Results

The specific task in our experiment is building facade cleaning where multiple surfaces exist. To move from surface to surface, robots need to physically connect to move each other across surfaces. To clean the surface efficiently, robots need to scatter on the surface according to the environmental layout. This means that no single behaviour is able to clean multiple surfaces, and the problem requires combinations of heuristics.

In the real-world, the outer surfaces of a building are often complex and large. It is costly to build a map of each building for robot cleaners. Even if a map is built, during the cleaning process, the changes caused by window opening/closing or decorations will make the map inaccurate. In such a dynamic environment, swarm behaviours should be adaptive and decentralised.

5.1   Experimental Setups

The experiments are simulated in Webots Simulator with emulated real-world physics [13]. The robot model is based on the non-holonomic robots in [22], as shown in Fig. 4. Each robot is equipped with differential wheels, a dirt sensor, obstacle sensors, wireless communication, suction cups, cleaning wipes and a gripper arm to connect to a neighbouring robot. The robots are simulated to clean at the maximum speed of $2.98\,\mathrm{m}^2$ per time interval of $40\,\mathrm{s}$, which for simplicity, we define as one unit area. The table in Fig. 4 contains the configuration of the simulated robots. To model cleaning in the real world, robots collect 14.9% of the available dirt each time when travelling at the maximum speed of $0.5\,\mathrm{m/s}$. Every robot is controlled by the hyper-heuristic controller as described in Sect. 3.

The objective function $f(t)$ indicates robot cleaning efficiency, which is given by: $f(t) = \frac{\sum(L_t D_t)}{T}$ where L_t is the distance travelled since the last measure, D_t is the dirtiness reading from the dirt sensor at iteration t, and T is the amount of time the current heuristic is applied. The termination criteria is set to be terminating after 50 iterations.

Radius	0.3m
Maximum Cleaning Speed	$0.0745m^2/s$
Maximum Linear Velocity	$0.5m/s$
Maximum Angular Velocity	$0.66rad/s$
IR Sensing Range	$0.53m$
Wireless Communication Range	$200m$

Fig. 4. LEFT: robots forming a larger structure. The lighter areas have been cleaned by robots. RIGHT: robot configurations of the simulation

Parameter tuning for the system involves two independent stages. The heuristic parameters are tuned individually as separate control algorithm units, in order to achieve better performance by themselves. The hyper-parameters are tuned with the whole system integrated. In this application, Iterated Racing (*irace*) tuning method [11] is used because it is effective and prunes the space of parameter value combinations that have to be checked. The tuning results are shown in Table 1, and are the parameters used in all experiments.

Table 1. Tuned values of hyper-parameters and controller parameters.

Heuristic Parameters

flocking: S_x	0.5
flocking: S_z	0.5
K_{rise}	1.0
K_ω	10.0
R_{avoid}	$0.46m$

Hyper-parameters

Learning rate θ	0.29
Choice Function α	0.99
Choice Function β	0.01
Choice Function γ	0.9
Group acceptance δ	0.5
Time interval length T	$40s$

5.2   Robustness in Different Environments

Four different layouts of facade surfaces are used in the experiments as shown in Fig. 5. Environment (a) is a flat surface that is 8 m × 8 m, bounded by four barriers; environment (b) is the same size, with 50 obstacles; (c) has four gaps on the surface, which single robots cannot cross; (d) has four gaps and 30 obstacles.

The positions of obstacles and gaps are randomly generated, thus different in each experimental run. Robots have no prior knowledge about the surfaces.

Figure 5 shows the cleaning progress of the robots using the hyper-heuristics at 5, 25 and 50 iterations. Since the purpose of the experiments is not to show the completeness of cleaning, but the effectiveness of behaviour sequence construction, 50 iterations are adequate to show the characteristics of the performance curve, as detailed in the resulting plots. It can be seen that the robots are able to perform the cleaning task continuously and robustly for 50 iterations, as the area cleaned over the four environments is continuously increasing. In environments (c) and (d), robots are able to automatically assemble to move across surfaces, and disassemble on new surfaces. This shows the feasibility of the proposed hyper-heuristic methodology on self-assembling robots, and that it can be applied in real-world applications.

We further investigate the performance in each environment in Fig. 6. For comparison, a hyper-heuristic with no learning is implemented, where heuristics are randomly sampled from the repository at each decision point. To reach all surfaces, and move effectively in environments with many obstacles, the swarm needs to learn the heuristics that perform better in these scenarios. Comparison results with the baseline method shows that the online learning hyper-heuristic is successful in finding sequences that perform better, based on the improvement of 28.86%, 37.34%, 21.51% and 18.86% in each environment, and overall improvement of 27.52%.

	(a)	(b)	(c)	(d)

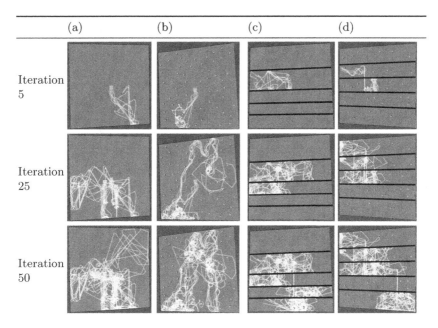

Fig. 5. Cleaning progress of the swarm at 5, 25 and 50 iterations in four types of environmental layouts: (a) flat empty surface, (b) surface with obstacles (indicated by red blobs), (c) five surfaces separated by gaps (black stripes), and (d) five separated surfaces with obstacles. (Color figure online)

We also plot the efficiency improved by learning in each iteration:

$$e(t) = \frac{\sum_{i=1}^{t}(f_i^L - f_i^{NL})}{\sum_{i=1}^{t} f_i^{NL}},$$

where f_i^L and f_i^{NL} are the areas cleaned (objective values) at iteration t by the swarms with and without learning respectively. It can be observed from the results shown in Fig. 7 that in the majority of the cases, the behaviour construction with learning is superior (95% of the points are above 0). Also the method gets better with time, as shown by the blue solid line representing the trend, indicating that our method continuously improves at learning the best behavior.

This proves that without knowing each particular layout, the robots are able to learn the suitable heuristics and autonomously clean multiple surfaces. This offers the advantage of performing tasks without prior knowledge of the environment, and without human supervision. It means that human workers will only need to transport the robot cleaners from building to building and install them on the starting surface, without providing prior knowledge of the building facade layout. Very little or no re-programming of the robots is required between tasks, and no human intervention is needed during the cleaning process.

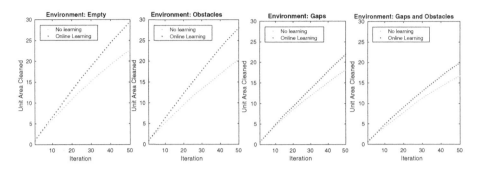

Fig. 6. Comparing mean performance of online learning and no learning over 50 experimental runs

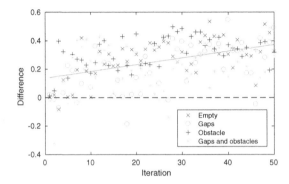

Fig. 7. Performance difference for every iteration between online learning hyperheuristics and no learning.

5.3   Comparison of Heuristic Selection Methods

In this part we compare three different heuristic selection methods as discussed in Sect. 3.2: Roulette Wheel selection, Greedy selection and Simple Random selection, which randomly samples heuristics from the repository. Each group performs cleaning tasks for 200 runs across the four types of layouts (Fig. 5). Figure 8 plots the performance distribution grouped by environment types.

Through Mann-Whitney U tests [12], it can be confirmed that both RW and Greedy methods have statistically better performance than Simple Random. Greedy has the best performance in empty and obstacles environments, while RW outperforms Greedy in environments that have gaps. RW also gives 48.19% less variance in performance over the four environments. This is because RW selection hyper-heuristic is quick to explore the heuristics that have not performed the best, but could lead to better performance later, therefore is more adaptive in complex environments. Greedy hyper-heuristic is very effective in simple environments, such as the empty surface, but if the user requires robustness in different environment types, RW is a better option.

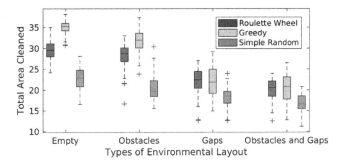

Fig. 8. Comparing three hyper-heuristic selection methods: Roulette Wheel, Greedy and Simple Random over four types of environments.

6 Conclusions

This study proposed a novel hyper-heuristics methodology combined with online learning to coordinate swarm robots, in particular, self-assembling robots. Building surface cleaning is used as a case study to evaluate the framework. The task was carried out on a real-physics robot simulator, and a range of surface types were used as test scenarios. The experiments verify that the robot swarm can adapt in different environmental layouts and automatically find appropriate actions to fulfill the given task without manual programming and centralised control. The study also shows that the performance of the robot swarm can be improved through online learning of heuristic scores.

Hence we conclude that hyper-heuristics are effective and advantageous in coordinating swarm robots in complex tasks. With the proposed approach, robots can construct and adjust behaviours based on a repository of heuristics. Combined with online learning, robots can adapt to different environments and different types of tasks. This feature is particularly beneficial for dynamic environments and complex tasks where prior programming is often difficult.

References

1. Burke, E., Kendall, G., Newall, J., Hart, E., Ross, P., Schulenburg, S.: Hyper-heuristics: an emerging direction in modern search technology. In: Glover, F., Kochenberger, G.A. (eds.) Handbook of Metaheuristics, pp. 457–474. Springer, Boston (2003). https://doi.org/10.1007/0-306-48056-5_16
2. Burke, E.K., Gendreau, M., Hyde, M., Kendall, G., Ochoa, G., Özcan, E., Qu, R.: Hyper-heuristics: a survey of the state of the art. J. Oper. Res. Soc. **64**(12), 1695–1724 (2013)
3. Burke, E.K., Hyde, M.R., Kendall, G., Ochoa, G., Ozcan, E., Woodward, J.R.: Exploring hyper-heuristic methodologies with genetic programming. In: Mumford, C.L., Jain, L.C. (eds.) Computational Intelligence, vol. 1, pp. 177–201. Springer, Heidelberg (2009). https://doi.org/10.1007/978-3-642-01799-5_6
4. Burke, E.K., Kendall, G., Soubeiga, E.: A Tabu-search hyperheuristic for timetabling and rostering. J. Heurist. **9**(6), 451–470 (2003)

5. DaCosta, L., Fialho, A., Schoenauer, M., Sebag, M.: Adaptive operator selection with dynamic multi-armed bandits. In: Proceedings of the 10th Annual Conference on Genetic and Evolutionary Computation, pp. 913–920. ACM (2008)
6. Dorigo, M., Floreano, D., Gambardella, L.M., Mondada, F., Nolfi, S., Baaboura, T., Birattari, M., Bonani, M., Brambilla, M., Brutschy, A., et al.: Swarmanoid: a novel concept for the study of heterogeneous robotic swarms. IEEE Robot. Autom. Mag. **20**(4), 60–71 (2013)
7. Dorigo, M., et al.: The SWARM-BOTS project. In: Şahin, E., Spears, W.M. (eds.) SR 2004. LNCS, vol. 3342, pp. 31–44. Springer, Heidelberg (2005). https://doi.org/10.1007/978-3-540-30552-1_4
8. Dowsland, K.A., Soubeiga, E., Burke, E.: A simulated annealing based hyperheuristic for determining shipper sizes for storage and transportation. Eur. J. Oper. Res. **179**(3), 759–774 (2007)
9. Levi, P., Meister, E., Van R, A., Krajnik, T., Vonasek, V., Stepan, P., Liu, W., Caparrelli, F.: A cognitive architecture for modular and self-reconfigurable robots. In: Systems Conference, pp. 465–472. IEEE (2014)
10. Lipowski, A., Lipowska, D.: Roulette-wheel selection via stochastic acceptance. Phys. A **391**(6), 2193–2196 (2012)
11. López-Ibáñez, M., Dubois-Lacoste, J., Cáceres, L.P., Birattari, M., Stützle, T.: The irace package: iterated racing for automatic algorithm configuration. Oper. Res. Perspect. **3**, 43–58 (2016)
12. McKnight, P.E., Najab, J.: Mann-Whitney U test. In: Corsini Encyclopedia of Psychology (2010)
13. Michel, O.: Webots: symbiosis between virtual and real mobile robots. In: Heudin, J.-C. (ed.) VW 1998. LNCS (LNAI), vol. 1434, pp. 254–263. Springer, Heidelberg (1998). https://doi.org/10.1007/3-540-68686-X_24
14. Nagavalli, S., Chakraborty, N., Sycara, K.: Automated sequencing of swarm behaviors for supervisory control of robotic swarms. In: IEEE International Conference on Robotics and Automation, pp. 2674–2681. IEEE (2017)
15. Özcan, E., Mısır, M., Kheiri, A.: Group decision making hyper-heuristics for function optimisation. In: UK Workshop on Computational Intelligence, pp. 327–333. IEEE (2013)
16. Rattadilok, P., Gaw, A., Kwan, R.S.K.: Distributed choice function hyper-heuristics for timetabling and scheduling. In: Burke, E., Trick, M. (eds.) PATAT 2004. LNCS, vol. 3616, pp. 51–67. Springer, Heidelberg (2005). https://doi.org/10.1007/11593577_4
17. Reynolds, C.W.: Flocks, herds and schools: a distributed behavioral model. ACM SIGGRAPH Comput. Graph. **21**(4), 25–34 (1987)
18. Sabar, N.R., Ayob, M., Kendall, G., Qu, R.: A dynamic multiarmed bandit-gene expression programming hyper-heuristic for combinatorial optimization problems. IEEE Trans. Cybern. **45**(2), 217–228 (2015)
19. Seng, W.L., Barca, J.C., Sekercioglu, Y.A.: Distributed formation control in cluttered environments. In: IEEE/ASME International Conference on Advanced Intelligent Mechatronics, pp. 1387–1392. IEEE (2013)
20. Uludag, G., Kiraz, B., Uyar, A.E., Özcan, E.: Heuristic selection in a multi-phase hybrid approach for dynamic environments. In: 2012 12th UK Workshop on Computational Intelligence (UKCI), pp. 1–8. IEEE (2012)
21. Werfel, J., Petersen, K., Nagpal, R.: Designing collective behavior in a termite-inspired robot construction team. Science **343**(6172), 754–758 (2014)
22. Yu, S., Barca, J.C.: Autonomous formation selection for ground moving multi-robot systems. In: IEEE International Conference on Advanced Intelligent Mechatronics, pp. 54–59. IEEE (2015)

An Innovative Heuristic
for Planning-Based Urban Traffic Control

Santiago Franco[✉], Alan Lindsay, Mauro Vallati, and Thomas Lee McCluskey

School of Computing and Engineering, University of Huddersfield, Huddersfield, UK
{s.franco,a.lindsay,m.vallati,t.l.mccluskey}@hud.ac.uk

Abstract. The global growth in urbanisation increases the demand for services including road transport infrastructure, presenting challenges in terms of mobility. In this scenario, optimising the exploitation of urban road network is a pivotal challenge, particularly in the case of unexpected situations. In order to tackle this challenge, approaches based on mixed discrete-continuous planning have been recently proposed and although their feasibility has been demonstrated, there is a lack of informative heuristics for this class of applications. Therefore, existing approaches tend to provide low-quality solutions, leading to a limited impact of generated plans on the actual urban infrastructure.

In this work, we introduce the Time-Based heuristic: a highly informative heuristic for PDDL+ planning-based urban traffic control. The heuristic, which has an admissible and an inadmissible variant, has been evaluated considering scenarios that use real-world data.

Keywords: Urban traffic control · Automated planning
Heuristic for planning

1 Introduction

It is expected that, during the 21st century, there will be a huge growth in urbanisation. In 2014, 54% of the global population were living in urban areas, and this is projected to rise to 66% by 2050. This increase in urbanisation, coupled with the socio-economic motivation for increasing mobility, is going to push the transport infrastructure well beyond its current capacity. In response, more stringent and intelligent control mechanisms are required to better monitor, exploit, and react to unforeseen conditions.

Urban Traffic Control (UTC) is normally the responsibility of local authorities whose aims include reducing congestion, improving journey times, increasing the reliability of the road network, safety regulation compliance and traffic pollution limitation. Conventional UTC techniques are widely deployed in urban areas, and help to minimise delay within day to day traffic flows, by providing strategies for traffic light phases. This is the case of traffic-responsive systems like SCOOT [8] and SCATS [1], fixed time light strategies optimised using historical data, or model-based predictive controllers [5]. These approaches work

© Springer International Publishing AG, part of Springer Nature 2018
Y. Shi et al. (Eds.): ICCS 2018, LNCS 10860, pp. 181–193, 2018.
https://doi.org/10.1007/978-3-319-93698-7_14

reasonably well in normal or expected conditions, but are not designed to work adequately in the face of unexpected or unplanned events. In these cases Transport Operators may struggle to find a strategy tailored to solve the unexpected situation. Creating such strategies is a manual task that may take several days or weeks, and is therefore infeasible to be done in real-time.

Recently, in order to overcome the aforementioned issues of conventional UTC techniques, the application of AI Planning to help in the management of road traffic has been investigated. Works like [4,9] have shown the feasibility of applying planning to deal with unexpected circumstances in urban traffic control, by optimising the length of traffic signal phases in the controlled region in order to achieve some specified high level goals. These works also highlighted that the representation of vehicles through the urban network needs to be performed at a macroscopic level – i.e., no explicit representation of each single vehicle – to cope with large volumes of traffic. The main choice is then between using PDDL and discretising the traffic density (using a sequence of density descriptors) on road sections, as done in [4], or use a numeric representation of traffic density and explicit continuous flow processes by encoding using the PDDL+ [3] language, as done in [9] and, more recently, in [6]. An advantage in using PDDL+ resides in its accuracy, i.e. the representation contains exact counts of vehicles, and models continuous change of vehicle numbers on road sections according to traffic light phases. A very significant drawback is that the few available domain-independent heuristics fail because of the high complexity of mixed discrete/continuous planning, and the size of region-wide urban networks.

In this paper, we introduce the innovative Time-Based heuristic, a domain-specific heuristic designed for improving the performance of a PDDL+ planning-based urban traffic solution. The Time-Based heuristic considers each road section which is present in the planning task goal in isolation, and performs an analysis of the expected input/output traffic flows in order to estimate the distance from a goal state. During the design, emphasis has been given to reducing the computational complexity by pre-calculating –in a pre-processing phase– most of the information needed. The Time-Based heuristic has two variants: an admissible one, which can be fruitfully exploited also by optimal PDDL+ planning engines, and an inadmissible version, which instead focuses on maximising the informativeness of the heuristic value at the cost of the general admissibility. The experimental analysis, that considers a region of the Manchester (UK) city centre and different challenging scenarios using real-world data, demonstrates the beneficial impact of the Time-Based heuristic on the performance of the state-of-the-art PDDL+ planning engine UPMurphi [2], and shows that the Time-Based heuristic outperforms the state of the art of domain-specific heuristics in terms of quality of generated plans.

2   PDDL+ Model for Region-Wide Traffic Control

PDDL+ [3] is an extension of the standard planning domain modelling language, PDDL, to model mixed discrete-continuous domains. In addition to instantaneous and durative actions, PDDL+ introduces *continuous processes* and *exogenous events*, that are triggered by changes in the environment. In 2016, Vallati et al. [9] proposed the first PDDL+ model for region-wide traffic control. The model was subsequently re-engineered by McCluskey and Vallati [6], in order to improve scalability and to provide a more accurate representation of the involved constraints. In the remainder of this paper, we will refer to the 2017 model.

A region of the urban *road network* is represented by a directed graph, where edges stand for *road sections* and vertices stand for *intersections*. One vertex is used for representing the *outside* of the modelled region. Intuitively, vehicles enter (leave) the network from road sections connected with the outside. Each road section has a given maximum *occupancy*, i.e. the maximum number of vehicles that can be, at the same time, in the road, and the current number of vehicles of a road section, which is denoted as the current occupancy.

Traffic in intersections is distributed by *flow rates* that are defined between each pair of road links. Given two road sections r_x, r_y, an intersection i, and a traffic signal phase p such that r_x is an incoming road section to the intersection i, r_y is an outgoing road section from i, and the flow is active (i.e., has green light) during phase p. Flow rates stand for the number of vehicles – expressed in terms of *Passenger Car Unit* (PCU) – that can leave r_x, pass through i and enter r_y per time unit.

A road section connected with the outside area can either have incoming or outgoing flows of vehicles. In the first case, vehicles from the outside region are entering the modelled area through the section, otherwise the road section is used by vehicles that are leaving the modelled area. Each road section connected with the outside has a corresponding *entering* (*leaving*) rate, that indicates the maximum flows of vehicles, in either direction, that can be served by the section.

Intersections are described in terms of a sequence of traffic signal phases. Specifically, intersections *contain* signal phases, which are connected using a *next* predicate. According to the active traffic light phase, one (or more) flow rates are activated, corresponding to the traffic lights that are turned green. For each phase, the *minimum* and *maximum* phase length is specified. Within this range, the planner can decide whether to stop the phase currently active, or not. Between two subsequent signal phases, an *intergreen* interval is specified. Intergreens are (usually) short periods of time designed to allow vehicles that are stacked in the middle of the junction to leave, and pedestrian crossing time, before the next phase is started. Intergreens have a fixed length, which cannot be modified by the planner (or by traffic controllers).

Processes are used for modelling the continuous flow of vehicles through a junction, and for measuring the time phases and intergreens are kept on. Limits and boundaries are controlled by specifically designed PDDL+ events. The planner can influence the behaviour of the network, and actually perform traffic control, by using the *switchPhase(p, i)* action, shown in Fig. 1. This action can be used for stopping the currently active phase p in intersection i, if the intersection i is controllable, and minimum phase time of p (increased by the corresponding process) has been reached.

```
(:action switchPhase
    :parameters (?p - phase ?i - intersection)
    :precondition (and
        (controllable ?i)
        (activePhase ?p)
        (contains ?i ?p)
        (> (phaseTime ?i) (minPhaseTime ?p) ))
    :effect (and
        (trigger ?i) ))
```

Fig. 1. The PDDL+ model of the only action under the control of the planning engine: *switchPhase*, used for stopping the currently active phase ?p in intersection ?i.

Given a traffic planning problem, traffic operators are concerned about the degree of saturation of road sections –in other words, the closeness of the current number of vehicles travelling along a section to its capacity. The degree of saturation determines, for example, whether or not traffic can flow at the maximum allowed speed limit –if it is too high, this results in "stop-start" conditions. Hence, the goal of operator interventions during an exceptional or emergency event would be to de-saturate the surrounding roads in an efficient manner. This immediately translates to goals specified in terms of required occupancy of road sections (since capacities are well known), e.g., road section, r_x, should have an occupancy of less than 50 PCU.

2.1   Existing Heuristics for Planning-Based UTC

A domain-specific heuristic for discrete-continuous planning-based UTC, the queue-based heuristic, was introduced in [9]. Such a heuristic is based on relaxing the constraints that vehicles can leave a road only when the corresponding traffic signal is green. More formally:

$$h(s) = \sum_{r_i \in G} (O_c(r_i)/leave(r_i))$$

where $r_i \in G$ are the road sections specified in the planning task goal, $O_c(r_x)$ is the current occupancy of road section r_x, and $leave(r_x)$ represents the total flow of vehicles that can leave road section r_x, obtained by summing all the outgoing flows over all the traffic signal phases (abstracting from the status of the traffic signals).

The queue-based heuristic is obtained by summing the heuristic value of each road section in the goal. It is not admissible because it does not consider the possibility that two (or more) road sections can have outgoing flows of vehicles active at the same time.

3   The Time-Based Heuristic

The proposed heuristic is designed to be used by a forward search planning engine, that deals with continuous processes via discretisation.

The Time-Based heuristic considers each road section r_i specified in the planning task goal in isolation. For each r_i, the Algorithm 1 is invoked for assessing the heuristic distance h_{r_i}, expressed in terms of number of discretised time steps, from a state in which the goal is satisfied. Computed heuristic values are then combined as follows:

$$h(s) = \max_{r_i \in G} (h_{r_i})$$

where $r_i \in G$ are the road sections specified in the planning task goal, and h_{r_x} is the heuristic distance from a goal state for the r_x road section, computed in isolation.

In order to compute the heuristic value of a goal road section r_i efficiently, a pre-processing step is needed. In the pre-processing step, the sequence of phases for maximising the outgoing traffic flows from r_i, called P^o, is calculated as follows. We consider the sequence $P = \langle p1, \ldots, pm \rangle$ of traffic signal phases of the intersection x, that receives the outgoing traffic flows of road section r_i. Each phase pn carries information about the minimum and maximum green time, and the maximum outflow traffic that the phase enables from r_i. The initial P^o is the sequence where all the traffic signal phases of the intersection are set to the minimum green time length. Then, the length of the phase(s) with the highest outgoing traffic flow from the road section in object r_i is maximised, according to the maximum allowed value specified in the model. After that, iteratively:

- (i) calculate the average outgoing flow from r_i, called a_{ri}, of P^o.
- (ii) considering the phases that are not already maximised $pl, \ldots, py$: the phase pn with the highest outgoing flow from r_i is selected;
- (iii) the green time length of pn is maximised if its outgoing flow from r_i, per time-step, is higher than the average a_{ri}.

The cycle terminates when the length of all the traffic light phases have been maximised in P^o, or there is no phase within P^o with an outgoing flow higher than the current a_{ri}. This leaves us with the final value of P^o.

In a nutshell, the underlying idea is to optimise the sequence of phases following a "common sense" solution that would have been applied by human controllers. This is done by applying the described hill-climbing approach, that divides phases into "good" and "bad". Good phases get the maximum possible green time, as they provide a significant outgoing flow from the road section in consideration; bad phases instead are minimised, in order to reduce the time spent between good phases.

Intergreen intervals are taken into account in P^o and considered during the computation of the heuristic value, in Algorithm 1. They were not mentioned in the explanation above, for the sake of readability. Although the average outgoing flow is maximal for the considered road section, r_i, the pre-computation step can overestimate the time needed for reaching the goal for r_i. This can be corrected by considering alternatives to P^o in the final sequence of phases, which we will describe below.

Algorithm 1 shows how the heuristic value of a road section of the planning task goal r_i is computed. The core of the procedure is the while loop (lines 3–16)

Algorithm 1. The procedure for assessing the admissible version of the Time-Based Heuristic for a road section r_i which is listed in the planning task goal. Input of the procedure are: p_c^o, current active traffic light phase for the outgoing flow from r_i; O_c, current occupancy of the road section; O_g goal required occupancy for the road section; P^o, optimised sequence of phases for maximising the outgoing flows; and Δ, the discretisation step.

Input: $p_c^o, O_c, O_g, P^o, \Delta$
Output: h
1: $h = 0$
2: $j = \text{position}(p_c^o, P^o)$ ▷ Initial phase set for Outgoing flows
3: **while** $O_c > O_g$ **do**
4:     **if** phase_at(j) not maximised in P^o
5:         $f = \text{potential\_flow\_before\_maximised}(\text{phase\_at}(j), P^o)$
6:         **if** $(O_c - O_g) \le f$
7:             $\langle h', O_c' \rangle = \text{try\_optimise}(P^o, O_c, O_g, h, j)$
8:             **if** $O_c' == O_g$
9:                 **return** h'
10:            **end if**
11:        **end if**
12:    **end if**
13:    $O_c = O_c - \text{flow}(P^o, j, \Delta)$
14:    $j = j + \Delta$
15:    $h = h + \Delta$
16: **end while**
17: **return** h

---

where, considering the optimised sequence of phases P^o, the occupancy of the section r_i is updated for each discretisation step. The general case is described in lines 13–15. Lines 4–12 are designed to tackle the last steps of the heuristic evaluation, where the use of the optimised sequence of phases may not lead to the best possible solution, thus making the heuristic value inadmissible.

Let us use an example for explaining under which circumstances this may happen. We assume that the considered intersection, from which vehicles can leave the road section r_i, has four traffic signal phases: $\langle p1, p2, p3, p4 \rangle$. In this example we ignore intergreens for readability, but the same reasoning would have applied in the presence of intergreens. $p1$ has an outgoing flow from r_i of 5 PCUs per time step, $p2$ has an outgoing flow of 1 PCU per time step, while no vehicles can leave r_i when phases $p3$ or $p4$ are active. For the sake of simplicity, we can assume that each phase has a minimum length of 1 time step and a maximum length of 5 time steps. The optimised sequence of phases calculated during pre-processing would be $P^o = \langle p1(0\text{–}4), p2(5), p3(6), p4(7) \rangle$: $p1$ is active for 5 time steps (0–4) and each of the other phases is active for one time step. This cycle then repeats. Let us now assume that, during the heuristic evaluation, the current occupancy O_c of the considered road section is of 2 PCUs, the goal is to have the road section completely empty, and phase $p1$ has just terminated. By using the optimised sequence of phases, the goal would be 4 time steps away:

one PCU leaves the road section during $p2$, then $p3$ and $p4$ are active for one time step each (but no vehicles leave r_s), and finally the remaining PCU leaves the road section in the first time step of $p1$. However, by extending the length of $p2$, the goal could have been reached in 2 time steps, instead of 4.

Generalising from the described example, the use of P^o may prevent the shortest heuristic distance from the goal being found in the cases in which there is a sequence of bad phases, and the remaining number of PCUs in the road section can be cleared by extending the length of one (or more) of them, before the start of the subsequent good phase(s). Lines 4–12 of Algorithm 1 are dedicated to handle these cases.

3.1 Admissibility

In order to demonstrate the admissibility of the Time-Based heuristic, we have to focus on the three aspects which are involved in the computation of the heuristic distance from the goal of a given r_i: current occupancy, outflows, and inflows. Each of them must not lead to an overestimation of the distance from the closest state in which the goal is satisfied. The admissibility of the Time-Based heuristic is always guaranteed because:

- the current occupancy is provided as input to Algorithm 1, and is then updated according to the outflows and inflows as follows;
- inflows are relaxed: it is assumed that no incoming flows of vehicles are activated for the considered road section r_i;
- vehicles can always leave r_i if an appropriate traffic light phase is active, regardless of the congestion of the subsequent road sections;
- the use of the optimised phase sequence P^o, in conjunction with the control previously described, can provide an accurate estimation of the distance from the goal, but it does not overestimate the distance.

Finally, the heuristic evaluation of a state is done by considering only the maximum heuristic value among the heuristic values of road sections included in the planning task goal. In this way, any possible overestimation due to the combination of heuristic values is avoided.

3.2 An Inadmissible Variant of the Time-Based Heuristic

Relaxing the problem by assuming incoming flows to the road section r_i are zero is important in guaranteeing the admissibility of the heuristic. As the road section is considered in isolation r_i, with no information about the surrounding network, it may be the case that some expected traffic flows are not "available", for instance because a road section is empty. However, assuming incoming traffic flows always exist can usually lead to a more accurate evaluation of the distance from the goal compared to ignoring them completely. For this reason, we devised an inadmissible version of the Time-Based heuristic, that is presented in Algorithm 2. Beside P^o, in the pre-processing step of the inadmissible heuristic it is

Algorithm 2. The procedure for calculating the inadmissible version of the Time-Based Heuristic for a road section r_i which is listed in the planning task goal. Input of the procedure are: p_c^o, current active traffic light phase for the outgoing flow from r_i; p_c^i, current active traffic light phase for the upstream intersection; O_c, current occupancy of the road section; O_g goal required occupancy for the road section; P^o, optimised sequence of phases for maximising the outgoing flows; P^i, optimised sequence of phases for minimising the incoming flows to r_i; S, is the list of road sections receiving traffic flows from r_i, and their current occupancies; and Δ, the discretisation step.

Input: $p_c^o, p_c^i, O_c, O_g, P^o, P^i, S^o, \Delta$
Output: h
 1: $h = 0$
 2: $i = \text{position}(p_c^i, P^i)$ ▷ Initial phase set for Incoming flows
 3: $j = \text{position}(p_c^o, P^o)$ ▷ Initial phase set for Outgoing flows
 4: **while** $O_c > O_g$ **do**
 5:     $O_c = O_c - \text{flow}(P^o, j, \Delta) + \text{flow}(P^i, i, \Delta)$
 6:     $h = h + \Delta + \text{potential\_delay}(S)$
 7:     $i = i + \Delta$
 8:     $j = j + \Delta$
 9: **end while**
10: **return** h

---

also required to compute P^i, which is an optimised sequence of phases for the intersection that has incoming flows to r_i. As the goal is to de-congest as soon as possible r_i, P^i is optimised in order to *minimise* the incoming flow to r_i, following the dual approach of the one previously described. Phases reducing the average incoming traffic flow are given the maximum green time, while others are given the minimum green time. This optimisation encodes the domain knowledge of a human expert that, for reducing the congestion on a given road section, minimises the incoming traffic to that section by reducing the corresponding green times.

The core of the procedure for computing the inadmissible heuristic resides in lines 5 and 6, where the occupancy of road section r_i is updated according to the expected incoming and outgoing flows in the considered time step, and the heuristic distance from the goal is updated. The calculation in line 5 of Algorithm 2 is reminiscent of the kind of conservation equation that a model predictive control approach would entail, en route to deriving the solution for a matrix of intersections for the region [5]. The *potential_delay* method deals with a very important aspect of traffic flows. Outgoing vehicles from r_i are either leaving the controlled region, or entering subsequent road sections. If the receiving sections are full or heavily congested, then some delay in the flow of vehicles has to be taken into account. In our implementation, the potential delay is assessed by computing the queue-based heuristic of each road section r_j that receives traffic flows from r_i. The queue-based heuristic is then multiplied by the ratio of traffic of r_i that r_j receives over a cycle of the optimised P^o

traffic signal phases. For each iteration of the loop (lines 4–9 of Algorithm 2), the current occupancy of receiving road sections is updated by considering the outflows from r_i. Taking into account the potential delay can greatly improve the accuracy of the heuristic evaluation but has two main drawbacks: since it relies on the queue-based heuristic, the admissibility can not be guaranteed, and –due to the additional calculations– the complexity is increased.

In Algorithm 1, lines 4–12 a forward search was made in attempt to find alternatives to P^o. This can allow the goal to be discovered early and is therefore necessary for admissibility. However, as admissibility cannot be guaranteed in Algorithm 2, this part has been omitted in the interest of performance.

4   Experimental Evaluation

In this section we evaluate the performance of the introduced heuristics. For our experimental evaluation, we consider the urban network presented in [6]. The modelled region is shown in Fig. 2, and represents an area of the Manchester (UK) urban network. This urban network allows to design scenarios which are the most challenging currently available for PDDL+-based urban traffic control, and that are based on real data. The region is considered already congested with the typical morning peak hour traffic, that is derived from historical data. The region includes 15 junctions and 34 road links: 7 junctions are controllable junctions (in red) and the 8 outer junctions are not modelled as controllable, but act as a boundary to the region. Each controllable junction has between 2 and 7 traffic light phases. For this experimental analysis we considered three scenarios, which have been crafted by traffic experts from Manchester; they provided the required data and validated the strategies generated by the planning approach. **Scenario A** simulates an extreme vehicle build upon a road section entering into the controlled region. The scenario focuses on clearing the road section as soon as possible. It is formalised by assuming the road section connecting intersection 1202 (Fig. 2) and the southernmost entry point of the region contains at the initial state an unexpectedly large number of vehicles (in this case, 300), and the goal state is to reduce the number to less than 10. The focus of **Scenario B** is to clear congestion from 3 road links leading into the junctions 1867, 1349 and 1202 shown in Fig. 2, where an extra 600 vehicles are entering as a result of a disturbance in another region. Finally, **Scenario C** simulates cases where a large number of vehicles have to leave a specific area of the controlled region in a short time horizon, like in the case of sport or cultural events where vehicles are rapidly emerging from car parks. For this scenario we considered an extra 200 vehicles on the road section heading from intersection 1349 to intersection 1867. In our models, one time step corresponds to approximately five real-world seconds.

All results were achieved by running the considered systems on a machine equipped with i7-4750HQ CPU, 16 GBs of memory, running Ubuntu 16.10 OS. A 10 CPU-time minutes cut-off time limit was enforced.

The proposed heuristics have been plugged in the UPMurphi [2] planning framework, compiled with g++ version 4.9. for a 32 bit architecture. Hereinafter,

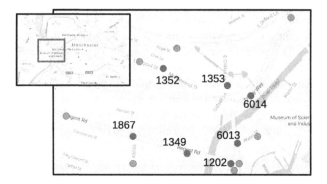

Fig. 2. The Modelled Area (large picture) and the position of the modelled area with regards to the city centre of Manchester, UK (small picture, red-limited area). Blue points indicate the sources (destinations) of incoming (outgoing) vehicles. (Color figure online)

we will use *Ad-Tb* for referring to UPMurphi enhanced with the admissible version of the Time-Based heuristic, and *In-Tb* for referring to the inadmissible version of the proposed heuristic. UPMurphi has been selected due to its ability to handle PDDL+ features, and because it has been used in previous works involving PDDL+ for controlling urban traffic control, as well as other real-world applications. We compare Ad-Tb and In-Tb with UPMurphi extended using the previously introduced *queue-based* heuristic. For the sake of completeness, we also considered UPMurphi with no heuristic and DiNo [7] in this experimental analysis. The former could provide some insights into the performance of non-heuristically guided search, while the latter is a state-of-the-art PDDL+ planner, guided by a domain-independent heuristic. Unfortunately, they did not solve any of the considered benchmarks, and are therefore excluded from the rest of this empirical evaluation.

4.1   Results

The results of the full range of experiments are shown in Table 1. The three scenarios have been tested by considering different initial states in which different traffic light phases are active for the road sections which are in the planning task goal. As a first remark, we observed that the Queue heuristic is very sensitive to this aspect. Specifically, if vehicles can not leave the road section(s) from the initial state, because all possible traffic flows are on red signal, then the queue heuristic is not informative, and UPMurphi is not able to find a solution within the 10 min CPU-time limit. This condition has been named as Queue-R in Table 1. Queue-G shows the performance delivered when traffic lights are initially on green for the considered road section(s). The results indicate that, as expected, the Time-Based heuristic is robust with regards to the traffic light phase that is initially active.

Table 1. Average performance, in terms of plan quality (time needed to reach a goal state), number of visited states during search, and CPU-time, delivered by UPMurphi using the admissible Time-Based heuristic (Ad-Tb), the inadmissible version (In-Tb), and the Queue heuristic. Queue heuristic shows very different performance when the traffic light on the goal road sections is on green (Queue-G) or on red (Queue-R). ATPVS stands for Average Time per Visited State.

	Plan quality	Visited states	Runtime	ATPVS
Scenario A				
Queue-G	350	492	0.5	$10.16 * 10^{-3}$
Queue-R	–	–	–	–
Ad-Tb	350	497	0.5	$10.06 * 10^{-3}$
In-Tb	350	497	0.5	$10.06 * 10^{-3}$
Scenario B				
Queue-G	1710	2343	10.0	$4.27 * 10^{-3}$
Queue-R	–	–	–	–
Ad-Tb	1805	6270	314.1	$50.09 * 10^{-3}$
In-Tb	1360	4687	180.0	$38.40 * 10^{-3}$
Scenario C				
Queue-G	280	1814	5.5	$3.03 * 10^{-3}$
Queue-R	–	–	–	–
Ad-Tb	420	2743	10.5	$3.83 * 10^{-3}$
In-Tb	185	1435	3.3	$2.99 * 10^{-3}$

In Scenario A, Queue-G, Ad-Tb, and In-Tb allow UPMurphi to deliver very similar performance, this is mainly because the goal includes a single road section that is on the border of the controlled region, so the incoming flow of traffic is modelled as continuous in the PDDL+ model and is not explicitly considered by any of the heuristics. Scenarios B and C allows to shed some light into the usefulness and informativeness of the different heuristics. Ad-Tb is usually the slowest, and the quality of provided plans tends to be lower than those of plans found using different heuristics. This is mainly due to the fact that, for the sake of admissibility, useful sources of information can not be considered by the heuristic. In Scenario B, the number of states expanded by In-Tb and Ad-Tb is significantly higher than for Queue-G. Our analysis indicates that the focus on the maximum heuristic value, among values calculated for road sections in the planning task goal, can lead to a jeopardised exploration of the search space, by focusing on the road section that is more distant from its goal. Nevertheless, the In-Tb heuristic outperforms the Queue heuristic in terms of quality of the generated plans. The delivered plan allows to de-congest the road sections 20% faster than when using the plan generated by the Queue-G heuristic.

Regarding scenario C, the In-Tb heuristic finds very quickly a significantly better quality plan than the Queue heuristic (34% better). This is because In-

Tb takes fully into account the dynamics of both the inflows and outflows to the goal's road section. On the other hand, Ad-Tb not only takes significantly longer to find a solution than the queue heuristic, but it is also significantly worse. According to our analysis, this is because its time prediction is over-optimistic, as it does not consider at all the very relevant input flows. Under such conditions, the queue heuristic is then more accurate than the Ad-Tb, as it can find a monotonic path towards a solution.

One would expect the queue heuristic to be faster to compute on average than the Time-Based. The ATPVS data shows the combined average expansion, generation and heuristic evaluation times per visited state. In some cases the Time-Based heuristic can significantly increase the average cost per visited state. Interestingly, the inadmissible version is generally cheaper than its counterpart, this is to be expected as the admissible version requires some search, based on the current active phase.

It should be noted that the better quality of generated plans is an extremely important aspect for the UTC application domain. In the real-world application, this would have an impact on the air quality of the area, due to a noticeable emission reduction, and to a reduced level of stress for drivers in the network.

5   Conclusion

In this paper, we proposed a domain-specific heuristic designed for improving the performance of PDDL+ planning-based urban traffic control, called Time-Based. We introduced two variants of the Time-Based heuristic: an admissible version, that can be exploited for optimal planning, and an inadmissible one, which instead focuses on maximising the informativeness. The performed experimental analysis, conducted using historical data describing the traffic in the region of a large European city, indicates that: (i) existing domain-independent heuristics are not able to cope effectively with mixed discrete-continuous planning-based UTC; (ii) the Time-Based heuristic –particularly the inadmissible variant– outperforms the state-of-the-art queue-based heuristic in terms of quality of the generated plans; and (iii) the Time-Based heuristic is robust with regards to the initial conditions of the network.

For the future, we propose to extensively test the proposed heuristic on significantly different urban networks, and using different domain-independent PDDL+ planning engines. We are also interested in extending the heuristic, and the PDDL+ model, for handling more traffic control actions, such as variable-message signs for route guidance or variable speed limits.

References

1. Chong-White, C., Millar, G., Shaw, S.: SCATS and the environment study: definitive results. In: Proceedings of the 19th World Congress on Intelligent Transportation Systems (ITS) (2012)
2. Della Penna, G., Magazzeni, D., Mercorio, F., Intrigila, B.: UPMurphi: a tool for universal planning on PDDL+ problems. In: Proceedings of the 19th International Conference on Automated Planning and Scheduling (ICAPS) (2009)
3. Fox, M., Long, D.: Modelling mixed discrete-continuous domains for planning. J. Artif. Intell. Res. **27**, 235–297 (2006)
4. Gulić, M., Olivares, R., Borrajo, D.: Using automated planning for traffic signals control. PROMET-Traffic Transp. **28**(4), 383–391 (2016)
5. Lin, S.: Efficient Model Predictive Control for Large-Scale Urban Traffic Networks. TU Delft, Delft University of Technology, Delft (2011)
6. McCluskey, T.L., Vallati, M.: Embedding automated planning within urban traffic management operations. In: 27th International Conference on Automated Planning and Scheduling (ICAPS) (2017)
7. Piotrowski, W.M., Fox, M., Long, D., Magazzeni, D., Mercorio, F.: Heuristic planning for PDDL+ domains. In: Proceedings of the Twenty-Fifth International Joint Conference on Artificial Intelligence, IJCAI, pp. 3213–3219 (2016)
8. Taale, H., Fransen, W., Dibbits, J.: The second assessment of the SCOOT system in Nijmegen. In: IEEE Road Transport Information and Control, no. 21–23, April 1998
9. Vallati, M., Magazzeni, D., De Schutter, B., Chrpa, L., McCluskey, T.L.: Efficient macroscopic urban traffic models for reducing congestion: a PDDL+ planning approach. In: Thirtieth AAAI Conference on Artificial Intelligence (AAAI), pp. 3188–3194 (2016)

Automatic Web News Extraction Based on DS Theory Considering Content Topics

Kaihang Zhang[1,2], Chuang Zhang[1(✉)], Xiaojun Chen[1], and Jianlong Tan[1]

[1] Institute of Information Engineering, Chinese Academy of Sciences, Beijing, China
craigzkh@163.com, zhangchuang@iie.ac.cn
[2] School of Cyber Security, University of Chinese Academy of Sciences,
Beijing, China

Abstract. In addition to the news content, most news web pages also contain various noises, such as advertisements, recommendations, and navigation panels. These noises may hamper the studies and applications which require pre-processing to extract the news content accurately. Existing methods of news content extraction mostly rely on non-content features, such as tag path, text layout, and DOM structure. However, without considering topics of the news content, these methods are difficult to recognize noises whose external characteristics are similar to those of the news content. In this paper, we propose a method that combines non-content features and a topic feature based on Dempster-Shafer (DS) theory to increase the recognition accuracy. We use maximal compatibility blocks to generate topics from text nodes and then obtain feature values of topics. Each feature is converted into evidence for the DS theory which can be utilized in the uncertain information fusion. Experimental results on English and Chinese web pages show that combining the topic feature by DS theory can improve the extraction performance obviously.

Keywords: Content extraction · Dempster-Shafer theory
Maximal compatibility blocks · Information fusion

1 Introduction

The Internet has become one of the main accesses to news information, and therefore news websites produce a great number of news contents for users' daily demands. With the fast development of front-end techniques, programmers can use Cascading Style Sheets (CSS) and JavaScript to develop more and more complicated web pages, therefore we will face increasing challenges to extract the main contents from highly heterogeneous web pages. In addition to the news

---

Supported by the National Natural Science Foundation of China (No. 61602474) and Xinjiang Uygur Autonomous Region Science and Technology Project (No. 2016A03007-4).

Y. Shi et al. (Eds.): ICCS 2018, LNCS 10860, pp. 194–207, 2018.
https://doi.org/10.1007/978-3-319-93698-7_15

content, a news web page commonly contains lots of irrelevant texts which are known as noises, such as advertisements, navigation panels, comments, etc. The studies and applications, such as news topic detection and tracking, require the news contents which have been processed and stored. Extracting the news content automatically is important for massive news information management, retrieval, analysis, and integration.

There are some online content extraction methods that provide theoretical supports for this paper, such as CEPR [1], CETR [2], and CETD [3]. These methods are efficient and concise, which do not need training and pre-processing. Non-content features (e.g. tag path, text layout, DOM structure, hyperlink) used by these methods are easy to be obtained from an HTML page. However, online extraction methods mentioned above do not pay much attention to topics of news content and only rely on the non-content features. These methods are difficult to recognize the noise whose external characteristics are similar to those of the news content.

In this paper, we present Content Extraction based on DS Theory (CEDST) which is an efficient and accurate news content extraction method. CEDST combines the topic feature and non-content features to improve the extraction performance. The contributions of this method are as follows: (1) Improving the recognition accuracy of news content extraction by introducing the topic feature. (2) Maximal compatibility blocks are used to generate topics from text nodes without linguistic analysis, therefore our method can be easily applied at websites in different languages by replacing a word segmentation method. (3) DS theory has the ability to represent and quantify uncertainties, which combine features in a reasonable way.

2   Related Work

Web pages are very heterogeneous and there are no rigid guidelines on how to build HTML pages and how to declare the implicit structure [4]. HTML tags without semantic information bring a lot of difficulties in the content extraction. If we want to develop a precise extraction method which is fully automated, the method should be restricted to a specific domain, such as news extraction [1,4], data records extraction [5,6], e-commerce information extraction [7,8], title extraction [9]. In this paper, we aim at extracting entire news articles from HTML pages automatically and efficiently.

Content extraction for HTML pages has been researched more than a decade. Most of the early studies on the content extraction are rule-based methods. Users write extraction rules with a specific language on the extraction system which assists in generating wrappers quickly, such as TSIMMIS [10] and W4F [11]. In order to reduce manual steps, some semi-automatic methods [12,13] had been developed. Semi-automatic methods need users to identify regions of interest on web pages, and then use inductive or heuristic algorithms to generate extraction rules. Although rule-based methods extract content accurately, users have to do much hard work manually.

Numerous methods for automatic content extraction have been presented, but each method has its drawbacks. The template-based [4,6] methods assume that web pages in the same cluster share the same template. These methods can filter out noises from web pages automatically, but any change of websites may lead to templates' failure, therefore the templates need to be trained again. Deng et al. [14] proposed a classical vision-based method named VIPS, which segments a web page into visually grouped blocks based on the DOM tree. Song et al. [15] proposed a method to rank blocks based on VIPS. The biggest disadvantage of the vision-based methods is high consumption of computer resources and time, because these methods need to render the HTML page and retrieve all the CSS files which relate to the page. Gali et al. [9] proposed a linguistics-based method which can extract titles from web pages, but this method cannot be put into general use, because it requires manual effort and domain knowledge to build the part-of-speech (POS) pattern trees. CEPR [1], CETR [2], and CETD [3] are the online Web content extraction methods without training and preprocessing, inspired by these methods, we propose a novel method named CEDST for news content extraction.

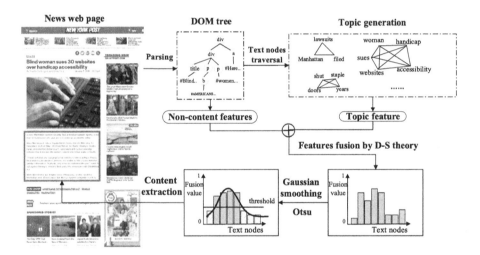

Fig. 1. Process of extracting the news content in the red solid frame. (Color figure online)

3   News Content Extraction Method

The HTML page can be parsed into a Document Object Model (DOM) tree. We define the leaf node that contains text as a text node. The process of our news content extraction method is shown in Fig. 1, which consists of following steps: (1) **Parsing the HTML page into a DOM tree**: computing values of non-content features for each text node of DOM tree. (2) **Text nodes traversal**: traversing text nodes of DOM tree in a pre-order manner. (3) **Topic generation**:

using maximal compatibility blocks to generate topics from text nodes, and then computing the topic feature of each text node. (4) **Features fusion by DS theory**: combining non-content features and a topic feature by DS theory for obtaining the fusion value of each text node. (5) **Content extraction**: after smoothing the fusion values, we compute a threshold to distinguish the news content from noises by using Otsu algorithm.

3.1   Features Fusion by DS Theory

DS theory [16] is a method for uncertainty. The ability to represent and quantify uncertainties is a key advantage of DS theory. We use DS theory to combine features of a text node to calculate the probability that the text node belongs to news content. We convert features into pieces of evidence by basic mass assignment (BMA) [17]. In the news extraction domain, the frame of discernment for a text node is $\Theta = \{news, \sim news\}$. The BMA function is m:$2^{\Theta} \to [0, 1]$, where 2^{Θ} is the power set which can be denoted as $2^{\Theta} = \{\emptyset, \{news\}, \{\sim news\}, \Theta\}$. The BMA function should satisfy two conditions: $m(\emptyset) = 0$ and $\sum_{U \subseteq 2^{\Theta}}(U) = 1$. We use the labels "*news*" and "$\sim news$" to denote positive and negative status respectively. If the feature f_i is positive, which supports the text node belonging to the news content, the feature can only assign the probability to label "*news*". The BMA formula is as follows:

$$\left.\begin{array}{l} m_{f_i}(\{news\}) = \alpha_{f_i} \times h_{f_i} \\ m_{f_i}(\{\sim news\}) = 0 \\ m_{f_i}(\Theta) = 1 - m_{f_i}(news) \end{array}\right\} \tag{1}$$

Otherwise, the feature is negative, which can only assign the probability to the label "$\sim news$". The BMA formula is as follows:

$$\left.\begin{array}{l} m_{f_i}(\{news\}) = 0 \\ m_{f_i}(\{\sim news\}) = \beta_{f_i} \times h_{f_i} \\ m_{f_i}(\Theta) = 1 - m_{f_i}(\sim news) \end{array}\right\} \tag{2}$$

h_{f_i} is the feature value normalized between 0 and 1. α_{f_i} and β_{f_i} are the weights assigned between 0 and 1 for features, but we set the feature weights near to 1 in order to avoid the normalizing parameter K of Eq. (5) appearing zero. All the features obtained from BMA can be combined together by using Eq. (3). Given BMA functions $m_{f_1}, m_{f_2} \dots m_{f_n}$ which are reasoned by features of a text node, the fusion function which is denoted as $\oplus$ in Fig. 1 as follows:

$$(m_{f_1} \oplus m_{f_2} \cdots \oplus m_{f_n})(A) = \frac{1}{K} \sum_{\cap_{i=1}^{n} A_i = A} \prod_{j=1}^{n} m_{f_j}(A_j) \qquad when\ A \neq \emptyset \tag{3}$$

$$(m_1 \oplus m_2 \cdots \oplus m_n)(\emptyset) = 0 \tag{4}$$

$$Where: \quad K = 1 - \sum_{\bigcap_{i=1}^{n} A_i = \emptyset} \prod_{j=1}^{n} m_{f_j}(A_j) \tag{5}$$

$(m_{f_1} \oplus m_{f_2} \cdots \oplus m_{f_n})(\{news\})$ is the fusion value which captures the probability that a text node belongs to news content. All the features f_i need to be converted into pieces of evidence which assign the probability to $\{\{news\}, \{\sim news\}, \Theta\}$ in the BMA formula m_{f_i}. Note that the positive and negative features assign the BMA in different manners.

3.2   Topic Generation

Figure 2 shows the process of topics generation. Firstly, each text node is transformed into a set of keywords, the steps are as follows: word segmentation, deleting stop words and keywords generation by textRank [18]. Maximal compatibility blocks are utilized to generate topics from keywords sets. Compatibility relation is a binary relation which satisfies reflexive and symmetry, so the relation can be denoted as a lower triangular matrix in Fig. 3. Compatibility relation R on keywords is a pair-wise relation between any two words which occur more than γ times in the same text nodes. We set $\gamma = 2$ which will be discussed in Sect. 4.3.

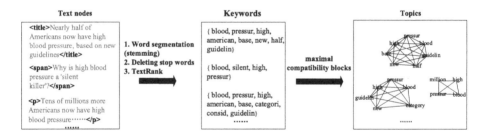

Fig. 2. Process of topic generation

Definition 1 *(maximal compatibility block). Let U be the set of all the keywords, if $W \subseteq U$, where any $x, y \in W$ has the relation xRy, W is a compatibility block. If there doesn't exist $k \in U - W$ which can be added to the compatibility block W, the W is a maximal compatibility block.*

The process of solving maximum compatibility blocks is shown in Fig. 3. Each node represents a keyword and the line between two nodes represents the compatibility relation R. The numbers assigned to the lower triangular matrix are co-occurrence frequencies for any two words which occur more than γ times in the same text nodes. Topics are the maximum compatibility blocks generated from left to right on the lower triangular matrix. As shown in the dotted box below the matrix in Fig. 3, the node n has the relation R with nodes $x, y, z, k,$

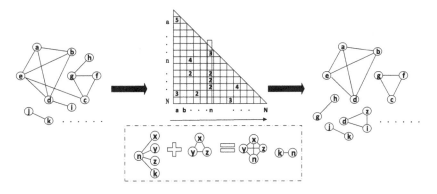

Fig. 3. Process of solving maximum compatibility blocks

and nodes x, y, z belong to an existing compatibility block, so node n and x, y, z can be combined into a bigger compatibility block. After scanning all the nodes on the triangular matrix, all the compatibility blocks that seem like complete polygons can be found out. After removing the compatibility blocks which can be covered by a bigger compatibility block, the rest are the maximal compatibility blocks. The time complexity of topic generation is $O(N * E * R)$, where N, E and R are the number of all the key words, existing compatibility blocks and related text nodes respectively. The compatibility relation matrix in Fig. 3 is a sparse matrix, so the maximum compatibility blocks can be generated quickly.

Topics may belong to news content, advertisement, recommendation, etc. A text node has topics with higher weights, which is more likely to belong to news content. The topic weight formula is as follows:

$$tw(topic) = \sum\nolimits_{n \in \{relate(x,y)|x,y \in \ topic\}} n \tag{6}$$

where $relate(x, y)$ is the co-occurrence frequency of words x, y recorded on the lower triangular matrix in Fig. 3. The value of topic feature is as follows:

$$h_{topic}(text) = \frac{max(\{tw(m)|m \in \ topic(text)\})}{max(\{tw(n)|n \in \ topics\})} \tag{7}$$

where $topic(text)$ is a set of topics generated from the *text*, *topics* is a set of all the topics generated from the web page. The greater the h_{topic}, the more possible the *text* belongs to news content. The feature value h_{topic} is positive, which can be put into Eq. (1) for obtaining the mass function m_{topic}.

3.3 Non-content Features

Non-content features focus on external characteristics of text nodes. For example, the news content commonly contains long texts with a simple format. After observing lots of news websites and considering the features mentioned by [1] and [3], we design the following features to evaluate the probability of a text node belonging to news content.

Text Cluster Feature. In general, news content consists of continuous text nodes which are commonly appended to several parent nodes. More nodes with long text are appended to the same parent node, these text nodes are more likely to belong to news content, the feature value is as follows:

$$h_{cluster}(text) = \frac{\sum_{t \in sb(text)} size(t)}{max(\{\sum_{w \in sb(n)} size(w) | n \in TextNodes\})} \tag{8}$$

where $TextNodes$ denotes a set of all the text nodes in a web page, $sb(text)$ is the set of $text$ and its sibling text nodes. Function $size(\cdot)$ counts the total number of words in a text node. The text cluster feature is positive, so the feature value $h_{cluster}$ should be put into the Eq. (1) for obtaining $m_{cluster}$.

Text Variance Feature. Paragraphs of news content are commonly written with various lengths. But the noise contains brief and neat sentences in general. If the variance of text lengths of a text node and its sibling text nodes is high, the text node is more likely to belong to news content. The feature value is as follows:

$$h_{var}(text) = \frac{var(sb(text))}{max(\{var(sb(n)) | n \in TextNodes\})} \tag{9}$$

where $var(sb(text))$ is the variance of text lengths of the $text$ and its siblings. The variance feature h_{var} is positive, which can be put into Eq. (1) for obtaining m_{var}.

Hyperlink Feature. The noises, such as advertisements and navigation panels, commonly have a high ratio of words nested in hyperlink anchors. Because these noises aim at leading users to other web pages. The feature value is as follows:

$$h_{href}(text) = \frac{size(href(text))}{size(text)} \tag{10}$$

where $href(text)$ is the words nested in hyperlink of the $text$. The more words of a text are nested in hyperlink anchors, the less likely the text belongs to news content. h_{href} is negative, which should be put into Eq. (3) for obtaining m_{href}.

   After transforming all the values of features into the evidence construction by using BMA, these features can be combined by using the DS fusion method (Eq. (3)). The fusion value is denoted as $m_{topic} \oplus m_{cluster} \oplus m_{var} \oplus m_{href}(\{news\})$, which is the probability of the text node belonging to news content.

3.4   Content Extraction

Gaussian Smoothing. After combining all the features by DS theory, we obtain the fusion values of all the text nodes on a web page. The preliminary fusion values might not recognize some special texts of news content, such as short texts without news topics. Although these short texts belong to the news content, their fusion values are low. These texts of news content may be lost without smoothing. We use the one-dimensional Gaussian smoothing mentioned by [1,2] to solve this problem. Figure 4 shows the fusion values of a news web page of CNN, where the histograms present the fusion values of text nodes before and after smoothing on the web page. The numbers below the abscissa axis represent text nodes traversed in a pre-order manner. Text nodes of news content with low fusion values can be smoothed to higher values. We see that between text nodes 310 and 345, most of the text nodes with high fusion values are identified as news content.

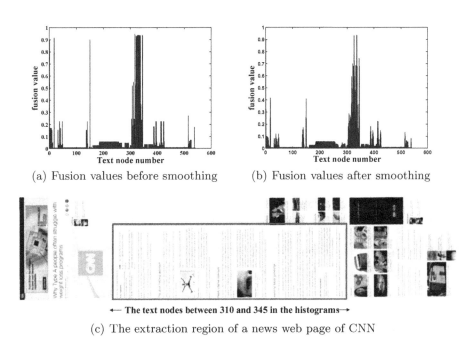

(a) Fusion values before smoothing   (b) Fusion values after smoothing

← The text nodes between 310 and 345 in the histograms →

(c) The extraction region of a news web page of CNN

Fig. 4. Fusion values before and after Gaussian smoothing in a news web page of CNN

Threshold Segmentation. Based on the fusion values of the histogram after smoothing, we use the Otsu algorithm to compute a threshold which divides the text nodes into two categories. The category with higher fusion values belongs to the news content. Given a threshold t, w_0 and w_1 are the proportions of the two categories separated by the threshold t, u_0 and u_1 are the average fusion values of these two categories.

$$g = w_0(u_0 - \mu)^2 + w_1(u_1 - \mu)^2 \tag{11}$$

$$Where: \quad \mu = w_0 \times u_0 + w_1 \times u_1 \tag{12}$$

μ is the global average and g is the objective function. We calculate the objective function g by using t from 0 to 1 with the step size 0.1. The Otsu algorithm aims to find the threshold t to maximize the objective function g. We use Otsu algorithm to work out that the threshold of Fig. 4(b) is 0.3.

4   Experimental Result

4.1   Performance Metrics

In this paper, precision, recall and F_1-score are used to evaluate and compare the performance of different content extraction methods. N_e represents the text nodes extracted from a web page and N_l represents the text nodes that are manual labeled results. (Note that in CETR [2], N_e and N_l represent the lines are extracted and hand-labeled respectively). Precision(P), Recall(R) and F_1-score(F_1) are as follows:

$$P = \frac{\sum_{t \in N_e \cap N_l} size(t)}{\sum_{w \in N_e} size(w)}, \ R = \frac{\sum_{t \in N_e \cap N_l} size(t)}{\sum_{w \in N_l} size(w)}, \ F_1 = \frac{2PR}{P + R} \qquad (13)$$

4.2   Method Evaluation

The experimental data contains two kinds of data sets. (1) **News:** This data set contains news web pages from four Chinese and five English news websites: Xinhuanet, Phoenix News Media (Ifeng), 163 News, People, Freep, CNN, NY Post, Yahoo! News, BBC. Each website contains 100 news web pages which are chosen randomly. (2) **CleanEval:** This corpus contains Chinese and English data sets (ClenaEval-zh and CleanEval-en) from the CleanEval competition mentioned by CEPR [1] and CETR [2]. The CleanEval contains various kinds of web pages, but our goal is to extract entire articles of news web pages, hence we choose the web pages whose structures are similar to news web pages to join the experiment, such as forums and blogs. The manual labeled result of each web page should be restricted to the entire article.

Tables 1 and 2 show the news extraction results of our method and comparison methods on different data sets. CEDST is the method proposed by this paper. CEDST-NC uses the fusion value $m_{cluster} \oplus m_{var} \oplus m_{href}(\{news\})$ to denote that combining all the non-content features mentioned in this paper. CEDST-TF only uses the topic feature $m_{topic}(\{news\})$ to recognize the news content. CEPR and CETR are the content extraction methods which have similar ideas to our method. CETR is a classical online content extraction method which offers the framework to extract content without training and preprocessing. CEPR is an excellence method which aims at extracting news content automatically and accurately.

Table 1 shows that CEDST is 1.19% higher than CEPR and 7.15% higher than CETR on average F_1-score. It represents that our method outperforms the comparison methods in most cases. CETR performs best on average recall, but

Table 1. Recall(R), Precision(P), F_1-score(F_1) of each method on different news websites, the highest values are in bold.

	Methods	Datasets				
		CEDST	CEDST-NC	CEDST-TF	CEPR [1]	CETR [2]
R(%)	Xinhua net	96.73	98.23	80.62	94.31	**99.42**
	Ifeng	97.72	97.25	88.21	98.22	**99.37**
	163 News	89.62	96.54	86.54	**97.69**	92.00
	People	**94.42**	93.91	83.42	93.33	93.62
	Freep	92.73	**93.55**	76.43	81.23	92.55
	CNN	**97.74**	97.55	89.23	96.28	97.42
	NY post	89.27	83.23	60.72	90.45	**92.32**
	Yahoo! News	94.32	93.24	82.52	92.42	**96.48**
	BBC	96.52	95.11	82.32	96.34	**98.07**
	Average	94.34	94.29	81.11	93.36	**95.69**
P(%)	Xinhua net	**94.41**	76.40	86.26	87.23	71.32
	Ifeng	**96.96**	87.52	95.27	90.75	76.75
	163 News	85.34	94.73	82.96	**95.84**	78.63
	People	90.32	88.32	**91.03**	89.54	78.58
	Freep	82.36	80.33	**91.72**	72.47	62.25
	CNN	**96.14**	87.21	87.55	92.39	73.32
	NY post	71.42	73.54	64.22	**80.23**	79.56
	Yahoo! News	91.65	86.73	**93.21**	92.24	83.25
	BBC	**94.68**	92.51	94.35	90.22	78.42
	Average	**89.25**	85.25	87.40	87.88	75.79
F_1(%)	Xinhua net	**95.56**	85.95	83.34	90.63	83.06
	Ifeng	**97.34**	92.13	91.60	94.34	86.61
	163 News	87.43	95.63	84.71	**96.76**	84.79
	People	**92.32**	91.03	87.06	91.40	85.44
	Freep	**87.24**	86.44	83.38	76.60	74.43
	CNN	**96.93**	92.09	88.38	94.29	83.67
	NY post	79.35	78.09	62.42	85.03	**85.47**
	Yahoo! News	**92.97**	89.87	87.54	92.33	89.38
	BBC	**95.59**	93.79	87.93	93.18	87.15
	Average	**91.73**	89.54	84.14	90.54	84.58

it performs worst on average precision. Taking the web page of Xinhuanet news website as an example, it has long abstracts of recommended articles under the news content. CETR can not distinguish these long text noises from news content, because it relies on the tag ratios which focus on the text length and the number of tags. CEPR is a brief and efficient method, which performs stably on all websites. Although CEPR makes full use of non-content features, CEDST outperforms CEPR on the precision with considering topics of news content. Especially on Xinhuanet, People and Freep, CEDST distinguishes the long text noise with the topic feature, while CEPR depends on fusion values after smoothing. Without relating to the main topics of news content, some long text noises are easy to be identified as news content by these comparison methods. CEDST outperforms the CEDST-NC, which means that introducing topic feature can improve the precision obviously, because the non-content features are weak in describing the noise formatted like the news content. Although CEDST-TM performs high precision, the recall is low, because this method only extracts key paragraphs of news content and losses some paragraphs without the main topics. Therefore, CEDST balance the non-content features and the topic feature, which performs best on extraction performance.

Table 2 shows the extraction result on CleanEval. Our method is 2.95% higher than CEPR and 4.74% higher than CETR on average F_1-score, which represents that our method is more suitable to extract entire articles from web pages. CEDST achieves great progress in extracting Chinese web page, because the news topics in Chinese web pages are easier to be captured. Beside the news web page, CleanEval contains many different types of web pages, such as blogs and forums. The result indicates that our method is robust and can be widely used in various web pages with main articles.

Table 2. Recall(R), Precision(P), F_1-score(F_1) of each method on CleanEval, the highest values are in bold.

	Methods	Datasets		
		CleanEval-en	ClenaEval-zh	Average
R(%)	CEDST	86.62	**90.73**	88.68
	CEPR [1]	87.42	85.68	86.55
	CETR [2]	**91.33**	89.42	**90.38**
P(%)	CEDST	**90.41**	**92.87**	**91.64**
	CEPR [1]	89.32	86.34	87.83
	CETR [2]	83.25	78.64	80.95
F_1(%)	CEDST	**88.47**	**91.79**	**90.13**
	CEPR [1]	88.36	86.01	87.18
	CETR [2]	87.10	83.68	85.39

Despite many advantages of our algorithm, there are some weaknesses in dealing with extreme circumstances. For example, CEDST performs worst in NY post obviously, because a recommendation may appear many times with identical texts in a web page of NY post. The topic generation method may assign high weights to topics of such recommendations, therefore the noises of these recommendations may be identified as news contents with high values of topic feature.

Table 3 shows that our method is slower than CEPR and CETR on execution time, because the time complexity of topic generation is approximately $O(n^3)$, which is the most time-consuming portion of our method. Although we need more time to construct the topic feature for extracting content from a news web page, our method is the most accurate method. CETR extracts content slower than CEPR, because CETR uses the K-means clustering to distinguish the news content from the noises, while CEPR calculates a simple threshold to segment news content with time complexity $O(1)$. CEPR compresses execution time of processes of content extraction, but sacricing accuracy for speed and simplicity. For example, CEPR calculates fusion values of text nodes with the same tag path simultaneously, but losing accuracy when the tag path of noise is the same as news content.

Table 3. Average execution time for each method to extract a news web page

	CEDST	CEPR [1]	CETR [2]
Average execution time	5.39 s	1.21 s	4.07 s

4.3 Parameter Setting

The threshold γ mentioned in Sect. 3.2 is used to adjust compatibility relation among keywords. If the co-occurrence frequency of two keywords is higher than threshold γ, the relation can be recorded in the lower triangle matrix shown in Fig. 3. Threshold γ determines the generation of maximal compatibility blocks, which greatly impacts performance of CEDST. The Fig. 5 shows the tradeoff between recall and precision. Observing trends with the threshold increasing,

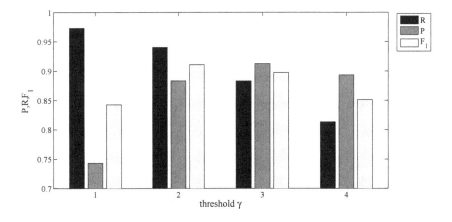

Fig. 5. The extraction performance of CEDST with different γ thresholds

when $\gamma < 2$, the recall is high, but the precision is low. When $\gamma > 2$, we can see that with the γ increasing, the recall decreases. When $\gamma > 3$, the precision decreases too. $\gamma = 2$ is the best selection for news content extraction, which achieves the highest F_1.

5   Conclusion

In this paper, we have proposed a method named CEDST for extracting news contents from news web pages based on DS theory. Considering most of existing online extraction methods that only use the non-content features to recognize the news content, we combine the topic feature and non-content features to achieve the best performance among comparison methods. The proposed method uses maximal compatibility blocks to generate topics from text nodes without complicated linguistics analysis, therefore our method can be applied at websites in different languages easily. DS theory is a method for uncertainty, with the BMA framework, we combine all features to obtain fusion values which are the probabilities of text nodes belonging to new content. The experimental result shows that CEDST outperforms other methods in most cases and performs robustly on various news websites in different languages. CEDST is a concise and efficient method which can extract news content automatically and accurately.

References

1. Wu, G., Li, L., Hu, X., Wu, X.: Web news extraction via path ratios. In: Proceedings of the 22nd ACM international conference on Information & Knowledge Management. pp. 2059–2068. ACM (2013)
2. Weninger, T., Hsu, W.H., Han, J.: Cetr: content extraction via tag ratios. In: Proceedings of the 19th international conference on World wide web. pp. 971–980. ACM (2010)
3. Sun, F., Song, D., Liao, L.: Dom based content extraction via text density. In: Proceedings of the 34th international ACM SIGIR conference on Research and development in Information Retrieval. pp. 245–254. ACM (2011)
4. Reis, D.d.C., Golgher, P.B., Silva, A.S., Laender, A.: Automatic web news extraction using tree edit distance. In: Proceedings of the 13th international conference on World Wide Web. pp. 502–511. ACM (2004)
5. Fang, Y., Xie, X., Zhang, X., Cheng, R., Zhang, Z.: Stem: a suffix tree-based method for web data records extraction. Knowledge and Information Systems pp. 1–27 (2017)
6. Gulhane, P., Madaan, A., Mehta, R., Ramamirtham, J., Rastogi, R., Satpal, S., Sengamedu, S.H., Tengli, A., Tiwari, C.: Web-scale information extraction with vertex. In: Proceedings of the 27th International Conference on Data Engineering (ICDE). pp. 1209–1220. IEEE (2011)
7. Bing, L., Wong, T.L., Lam, W.: Unsupervised extraction of popular product attributes from e-commerce web sites by considering customer reviews. ACM Transactions on Internet Technology (TOIT) 16(2), 1–17 (2016)
8. Charron, B., Hirate, Y., Purcell, D., Rezk, M.: Extracting semantic information for e-commerce. In: Proceedings of the International Semantic Web Conference. pp. 273–290. Springer (2016)

9. Gali, N., Mariescu-Istodor, R., Fränti, P.: Using linguistic features to automatically extract web page title. Expert Systems with Applications **79**, 296–312 (2017)
10. Hammer, J., McHugh, J., Garcia-Molina, H.: Semistructured data: the TSIM-MIS experience. In: Proceedings of the East-European Conference on Advances in Databases and Information Systems pp. 1–8 (1997)
11. Sahuguet, A., Azavant, F.: Building intelligent web applications using lightweight wrappers. Data & Knowledge Engineering **36**(3), 283–316 (2001)
12. Ashish, N., Knoblock, C.A.: Semi-automatic wrapper generation for internet information sources. In: Proceedings of the Ifcis International Conference on Cooperative Information Systems. pp. 160–169. IEEE (1997)
13. Liu, L., Pu, C., Han, W.: Xwrap: An xml-enabled wrapper construction system for web information sources. In: Proceedings of the 16th International Conference on Data Engineering. pp. 611–621. IEEE (2000)
14. Deng, C., Shipeng, Y., Jirong, W., Wei-Ying, M.: Vips: a vision-based page segmentation algorithm. Technical Report MSR-TR-2003-79 (2003)
15. Song, R., Liu, H., Wen, J.R., Ma, W.Y.: Learning block importance models for web pages. In: Proceedings of the 13th international conference on World Wide Web. pp. 203–211. ACM (2004)
16. Sentz, K., Ferson, S., et al.: Combination of evidence in Dempster-Shafer theory, vol. 4015. Citeseer (2002)
17. Dong, F., Shatz, S.M., Xu, H.: Reasoning under uncertainty for shill detection in online auctions using dempster-shafer theory. International Journal of Software Engineering and Knowledge Engineering **20**(07), 943–973 (2010)
18. Mihalcea, R., Tarau, P.: Textrank: Bringing order into text. In: Proceedings of the 2004 conference on empirical methods in natural language processing pp. 404–411 (2004)

DomainObserver: A Lightweight Solution for Detecting Malicious Domains Based on Dynamic Time Warping

Guolin Tan[1,2], Peng Zhang[2(✉)], Qingyun Liu[2], Xinran Liu[3], and Chunge Zhu[3]

[1] Institute of Information Engineering, Chinese Academy of Sciences, Beijing, China
tanguolin@iie.ac.cn
[2] School of Cyber Security, University of Chinese Academy of Sciences, Beijing, China
pengzhang@iie.ac.cn
[3] National Computer Network Emergency Response and Coordination Center, Beijing, China

Abstract. People use the Internet to shop, access information and enjoy entertainment by browsing web sites. At the same time, cyber-criminals operate malicious domains to spread illegal content, which poses a great risk to the security of cyberspace. Therefore, it is of great importance to detect malicious domains in the field of cyberspace security. Typically, there are broad research focusing on detecting malicious domains either by blacklist or learning the features. However, the former is infeasible due to its unpredictability of unknown malicious domains, and the later requires complex feature engineering. Different from most of previous methods, in this paper, we propose a novel lightweight solution named DomainObserver to detect malicious domains. Our technique of Domain-Observer is based on dynamic time warping that is used to better align the time series. To the best of our knowledge, it is a new trial to apply passive traffic measurements and time series data mining to malicious domain detection. Extensive experiments on real datasets are performed to demonstrate the effectiveness of our proposed method.

Keywords: Malicious domain · Detection · Passive traffic
Time series · Dynamic time warping

1 Introduction

The domain plays an important role in the operation of the Internet by providing convenience to identify Internet resources, such as computers, networks, and services. At the same time, cyber-criminals operate malicious domains to spread illegal information (phishing, malware, fraud and adult content, etc.). It is noted that close to one-third of all websites are potentially malicious in nature [16]. To make things worse, new malicious domains emerge on the Internet in endlessly.

© Springer International Publishing AG, part of Springer Nature 2018
Y. Shi et al. (Eds.): ICCS 2018, LNCS 10860, pp. 208–220, 2018.
https://doi.org/10.1007/978-3-319-93698-7_16

To provide a safe Internet environment for the vast number of Internet users, there are extensive research focusing on detecting malicious domains. Although a variety of methods have been applied to the problem of malicious domain detection with some successes, it is still very challenging for the reason that the patterns of malicious domains can be evolved by the adversaries to avoid being detected. Therefore, it is of great importance to discover the inherent patterns of malicious domains from the perspective of passive traffic measurements.

The passive traffic measurement is the process of measuring the amount and type of traffic on a particular network, which can help network operators better understand the properties of traffic. By using the passive measurement techniques, we can observe and reveal the inherent access patterns of domains. Moreover, this passive observation has the advantage that the cyber-criminals have no means to hide or change the access patterns of domains.

In this paper, we propose a novel lightweight solution, i.e., DomainObserver, to detect malicious domains. The highlight of our solution is that DomainObserver is based on dynamic time warping that is used to better align the time series. As far as we know, it is a new trial to apply passive traffic measurements and time series data mining to detect malicious domains.

To that end, the primary contributions of this paper are as follows:

1. First, we carefully observe and study the access patterns between Internet users and domains based on passive traffic measurements. This observation has the advantage that the cyber-criminals have no means to hide or change the patterns that we find in passive traffic measurements.
2. Based on the above analysis, we propose a novel lightweight method, i.e., DomainObserver, to detect malicious domains, which does not require constant crowd updates or complex feature engineering. To the best of our knowledge, no prior work in the literature applies this method to detect malicious domains.
3. Third, we evaluate our solution on real datasets collected from backbone networks. Experiment results show that DomainObserver is effective by achieving 83.14% accuracy and 87.11% F_1 score in the detection of malicious domains.

The rest of the paper is organized as follows. In the next section, we review the related work. In Sect. 3, we describes the time series datasets collected by using passive traffic measurements. Section 4 introduces the classification model based on time series data mining. We evaluate our approach on real world datasets in Sect. 5. Finally we conclude our work in Sect. 6.

2   Related Work

In the past few decades, the problem of malicious domain detection has been extensively studied. Much of these techniques can be broadly divided into two categories: (1) based on crowd-generated blacklists [2,11,20], (2) based on machine learning [5,10,13,17,19].

Generally, the typical methods based on blacklist are simple and efficient. However, the number of malicious domains drastically increased over time, which requires constant updates generated by crowd. Moreover, it is almost impossible to maintain an exhaustive blacklist of malicious domains [16]. That is to say, these methods cannot predict newly registered malicious domains. In order to overcome these shortcomings, researchers proposed methods based on machine learning to detect malicious domains, which requires complex feature engineering to obtain discriminative features.

In [10], the authors proposes a method for identifying the C&C domains by using supervised machine learning and the feature points obtained from WHOIS and the DNS. To ensure the effectiveness of a URL blacklist, the authors of [17] proposes a framework called automatic blacklist generator (AutoBLG) that automatically expands the blacklist using passive DNS database and web crawler. [13] employs visible attributes collected from social networks to classify malicious short URLs on Twitter. The work of [19] presents a new deep learning framework (SdA) for detection of malicious JavaScript codes. In this method, 480 features are extracted from the JavaScript code. In a nutshell, all of these machine learning methods either need to extract complex features or require preconditions and specific data input.

The benefit from using our solution (DomainObserver) as opposed to existing methods is the fact that, our solution is not only more comprehensive in detecting a variety of malicious domains, but also more lightweight that does not require specific data input or complex feature engineering. The comparison is as shown in Table 1

Table 1. Qualitative comparison of existing work and our solutions.

	Types of malicious	Feature engineering	Data collection
AutoBLG	Unlimited	Yes	Active and passive
SdA	JavaScript	Yes	active
DomainObserver	Unlimited	No	Passive

3   Passive Traffic Measurements

To discover the different access patterns between benign and malicious domains, we tracked and studied the passive network traffic of thousands of the most popular domains. In this section, we first introduce the domain dataset that we collect from multiple reliable sources. Then we describe the time series data collected from backbone networks based on passive traffic measurements. Finally, we demonstrate how they can be used to detect interesting, anomalous domain access patterns.

3.1   Domain Dataset

As a starting point for our times series data collection we first construct domain dataset from multiple reliable sources. We used the Alexa top 20,000 global sites [1] as the whitelist. For malicious domains we extensively investigated many blacklists of various malicious domains, such as malwaredomains.com [11], Antivirus [2] and Phishtank [14], etc. It is worth mentioning that we are conservative when constructing the domain dataset, since the ground truth has a great impact on the performance of the classifier. In order to determine whether the domain we collected is really malicious, for each domain, we validate it multiple times using different third-party platforms, such as 360 Fraud Reporting [15], Baidu Website Security Center [3]. Table 2 shows the verification results using [3]. Finally, we identified 1402 malicious domains and 1813 benign domains as the seed dataset.

Table 2. Verification results of Alexa top 20,000 domains using Baidu Website Security Center only.

Type	# of domains	Results
1	84	Fraud
2	5	Malware
3	196	Adult
4	23	Gambling
5	9509	Benign
6	10183	Unknown

3.2 Time Series Data

A time series is a series of data points indexed in time order. In the last decade, data mining of time series has attracted significant interest, due to the fact that time series data are present in a wide range of real-life fields [9]. In this paper, we combined passive traffic measurements and time series data mining to detect malicious domains. We categorize the collected time series data as three types: *access*, *users* and *entropy*, which will be explained later. According to our experimental evaluation, these data with high discriminative ability are sufficient to achieve a highly accurate classifier for malicious domain detection.

Passive traffic measurements play a crucial role in understanding the complex temporal properties of traffic [7]. In our passive traffic measurements, we count and aggregate the traffic traversing each Point of Presence (PoP) in the backbone networks to obtain time series data. We formalize the notion employed in time series data collection as follows:

Definition 1: *Traffic Measurement.* A traffic measurement M is a tuple (*timestamp, sip, domain*), representing a web request to the *domain*. Specifically, *timestamp* is the current time when a user start to access a website (represented by a URL), *sip* is the source IP address of the user, and *domain* is the second level domain name extracted from the URL.

Definition 2: *Time Window.* A time window W is a time bin (e.g., 1 h). When collecting time series data, we aggregate the traffic measurements by each time window.

Definition 3: *Time Series.* A time series $T = t_1, t_2, \ldots, t_n$ is a time-ordered set of n real-valued variables, where n is length of time series T. In our application, t_i is the aggregated number of traffic measurements in each time window.

Definition 4: *Time Series Dataset.* A time series dataset $D = T_1, T_2, \ldots, T_m$ is a collection of m such time series.

Definition 5: *Time Series Distance.* The distance d between two time series T and S is a function $dist(T,S)$ that measures the similarity between T and S. Since time series distance plays a crucial role in time series data mining, we will introduce it in detail in the next section.

In order to collect time series datasets, we monitor web requests of each domain in the domain dataset (Sect. 3.1) on the backbone networks. Using passive traffic measurements, finally, we collect three types of time series data.

Access. The time series $Access = t_1, t_2, \ldots, t_n$, where t_i is the number of traffic measurements in a time window W.

User. The time series $User = t_1, t_2, \ldots, t_n$, where t_i is the number of distinct sip in a time window W.

Entropy. The time series $Entropy = t_1, t_2, \ldots, t_n$, where t_i is entropy of sip in a time window that is defined as follows.

$$E(sip) = -\sum_{i=1}^{I} \frac{n_i}{N} \log(\frac{n_i}{N}) \tag{1}$$

I is the number of distinct sip, n_i is the number of a sip and N is the total number of all sip.

It is important to note that in our passive traffic measurements, not all domains in domain dataset are observed, simply because some of the domains have never been accessed by users during passive measurement. Table 3 shows some basic information of our collected time series datasets over 94 h.

Table 3. Time series datasets.

Type	# of domains in dataset	# of observed domains	Start time	End time
Malicious	1402	1296	2017/11/22 11:45	2017/11/26 10:20
Benign	1813	373	2017/11/22 11:45	2017/11/26 10:20

For different types of websites, we find that the access patterns appearing in time series are different. For example, for pornographic websites, users are more likely to access these websites at night. Figure 1 shows the different domain access patterns. We can see that the number of users accessing malicious domains usually reaches a significant peak around midnight, while there is no such phenomenon of benign domains. These potential domain access patterns are very easy to find when using passive traffic measurements. In the next section, we will introduce how we detect malicious domains using time series data mining.

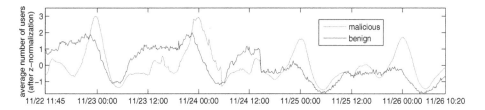

Fig. 1. The different access patterns of malicious and benign domains.

4   Time Series Classification

As mentioned in the previous section, time series distance plays a crucial role in time series data mining. Before we introduce how to detect malicious domains, we will first describe the time series distance used in our classification algorithm.

4.1   Dynamic Time Warping

There are plenty of distance measures used for evaluating similarity of time series, such as Euclidean distance (ED) [8], Dynamic Time Warping (DTW) [4]. Although it is simple and efficient, Euclidean distance is very sensitive to even slight misalignments. Inspired by the need to handle time warping in similarity computation, Dynamic Time Warping was proposed in order to allow a time series to be "stretched" or "compressed" to provide a better match with another time series [18]. That is to say, by warping a little to match the nearest neighbor, DTW can better measure the similarity of time series. The dynamic programming formulation of DTW is defined as follows.

$$D(i,j) = d(i,j) + min[D(i-1,j), D(i-1,j-1), D(i,j-1)] \qquad (2)$$

That is, the DTW distance is the sum of the distance between current points and the minimum of the DTW distances of the neighboring points. In our work, we use DTW as the measure of distance because we found that there may be an advance or delay of the patterns. Figure 2 illustrates this temporal shifting of malicious domain access patterns.

   In order to improve the computation efficiency, it is important to restrict the space of possible warping paths. Therefore, there is a variant of the DTW algorithm by adding a temporal constraint ω on the warping window size of

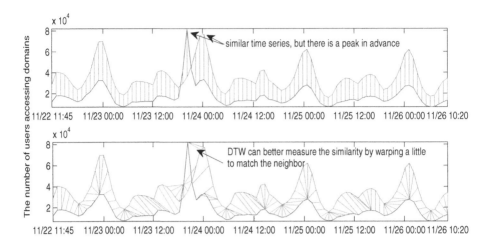

Fig. 2. A larger similarity distance measured by the Euclidean distance (top). Compared with ED, DTW can better measure the similarity by warping a little to match the nearest neighbor (bottom). Similarity is proportional to the sum of the pairwise distances (indicated by gray lines).

DTW, which is called constrained DTW. The details of the constrained DTW that is used in our paper are described in Algorithm 1 based on the dynamic programming approach.

Given two time series t and s, and time warping window ω, we initialize a two-dimensional DTW matrix whose value represents the DTW distance of the corresponding points within time series t and s (lines 2–10). Then we traverse the DTW matrix to calculate the DTW distances (lines 11–19). According to the time warping window ω, we determine the range of the DTW matrix that needs to be traversed (lines 12–13). The DTW distance is calculated according to Eq. 2 (lines 15–17). In order to allow meaningful comparisons between DTW distances of different DTW path lengths, length normalization must be used. The subroutine DTWPathLen (shown in Algorithm 2) returns the length of the DTW path (line 20). We calculate the final DTW distance using length normalization (line 21).

As we show in Algorithm 1, the function DTWPathLen is called to calculate the length-normalized DTW (NDTW for short) distance. For concreteness, we briefly discuss the DTWPathLen function in Algorithm 2 below.

Given the DTW matrix, the DTW path can be found by tracing backward in the matrix by choosing the previous points with the lowest DTW distance [4]. In line 5, we calculate the position of the neighboring points with the minimum DTW distance. From lines 7 to 14, we move the DTW path from the current position to the neighboring position with the minimum DTW distance until the start position. And the length of DTW path increases by one for each move in line 15.

Algorithm 1. Dynamic Time Warping

Input: time series t, s; warping window ω;
Output: DTW distance $dist$;
 1: **function** DTWDISTANCE(t, s, ω)
 2:　　$m \leftarrow size(t)$
 3:　　$n \leftarrow size(s)$
 4:　　$DTW \leftarrow zeros(m + 1, n + 1)$
 5:　　**for** $i = 1 \rightarrow m + 1$ **do**
 6:　　　　**for** $j = 1 \rightarrow n + 1$ **do**
 7:　　　　　　$DTW(i, j) \leftarrow Inf$
 8:　　　　**end for**
 9:　　**end for**
10:　　$DTW(1, 1) \leftarrow 0$
11:　　**for** $i = 2 \rightarrow m + 1$ **do**
12:　　　　$lowerBound \leftarrow max(2, i - \omega)$
13:　　　　$upperBound \leftarrow min(n + 1, i + \omega)$
14:　　　　**for** $j = lowerBound \rightarrow upperBound$ **do**
15:　　　　　　$currentDist \leftarrow (t(i - 1) - s(j - 1))^2$
16:　　　　　　$minDist \leftarrow min(DTW(i - 1, j), DTW(i, j - 1), DTW(i - 1, j - 1))$
17:　　　　　　$DTW(i, j) \leftarrow currentDist + minDist$
18:　　　　**end for**
19:　　**end for**
20:　　$pathLen \leftarrow$ DTWPATHLEN(DTW);
21:　　$dist \leftarrow sqrt(DTW(m + 1, n + 1)/pathLen)$;
22:　　**return** $dist$
23: **end function**

Algorithm 2. DTW Path Length

Input: DTW distance matrix DTW;
Output: DTW path length $pathLen$;
 1: **function** DTWPATHLEN(DTW)
 2:　　$i \leftarrow row(DTW)$
 3:　　$j \leftarrow col(DTW)$
 4:　　$pathLen \leftarrow 0$
 5:　　**while** $i \neq 2$ **or** $j \neq 2$ **do**
 6:　　　　$[\sim, minIndex] \leftarrow min(DTW(i - 1, j), DTW(i, j - 1), DTW(i - 1, j - 1))$
 7:　　　　**if** $minIndex \equiv 1$ **then**
 8:　　　　　　$i \leftarrow i - 1$
 9:　　　　**else if** $minIndex \equiv 2$ **then**
10:　　　　　　$j \leftarrow j - 1$
11:　　　　**else**
12:　　　　　　$i \leftarrow i - 1$
13:　　　　　　$j \leftarrow j - 1$
14:　　　　**end if**
15:　　　　$pathLen \leftarrow pathLen + 1$
16:　　**end while**
17:　　**return** $pathLen$
18: **end function**

4.2 KNN Classification

We are now in a position to explain how to detect malicious domains. We consider the most common classification algorithms K-Nearest Neighbor (KNN) [6] in the time series mining community. In this method, for a new test instance, the nearest k neighbors are derived from the training dataset using similarity distance, and then it defines the class of the instance according to the class of the majority of its k nearest neighbors.

5 Evaluation

In order to examine the feasibility of our solution for detecting malicious domains, a series of experiments are carried out using the datasets introduced in Sect. 3.2. In our default experimental evaluation, we use the time series data of 70% domains as the training data while the remaining 30% as the testing data. Unless otherwise stated, we use KNN as the underlying classifying algorithm, and the final values are the averages of ten random runs.

5.1 Evaluation Metrics

In order to evaluate our method comprehensively, we utilize the well-known precision (P), recall (R), accuracy (A) and F_1 score to evaluate the performance of malicious domain detection. These evaluation metrics are functions of the confusion matrix as shown in Table 4.

Table 4. The confusion matrix of binary classification tasks.

	Predicted positive	Predicted negative
Actual positive	True Positive (TP)	False Negative (FN)
Actual negative	False Positive (FP)	True Negative (TN)

$$P = \frac{TP}{TP + FP} \tag{3}$$

$$R = \frac{TP}{TP + FN} \tag{4}$$

$$F_1 = \frac{2 * P * R}{P + R} \tag{5}$$

$$A = \frac{TP + TN}{TP + FP + TN + FN} \tag{6}$$

5.2   Results and Analysis

Varying Distance Measures: The first experiment is to evaluate the performance of different distance measures on three time series datasets. Table 5 shows the experimental results, from which several observations can be drawn. First of all, experiments on real datasets demonstrate that our solution based on dynamic time warping is effective in detecting malicious domains with 86.43% F_1 score and 81.58% accuracy. We thus believe the proposed method is suitable for malicious domain detection. Secondly, among these distance measures, the NDTW is better than the other two. This is because it is not sensitive to noise and misalignments in time, and able to handle local time shifting, i.e., similar segments that are out of phase (Fig. 2). As for the time performance, the ED distance is more efficient, because this distance measure is simpler than DTW and NDTW, which sacrifices the accuracy. Finally, we observe that there is no significant difference between datasets *Access*, *User*, and *Entropy*. For the sake of simplicity, in the following experiments, we use *User* as the default dataset and NDTW as the default distance measure.

Table 5. Performance comparison between different distance measures

Dataset	Distance	P(%)	R(%)	A(%)	F_1(%)	Avg time (s)
Access	ED	82.84	87.97	73.78	85.31	0.0001
	DTW	83.20	88.97	79.80	85.98	0.3428
	NDTW	83.77	89.41	**80.40**	**86.49**	0.6584
User	ED	87.20	85.02	79.30	86.09	0.0001
	DTW	84.86	87.92	80.32	86.35	0.5335
	NDTW	85.55	87.35	**81.58**	**86.43**	0.6512
Entropy	ED	87.70	82.48	79.00	84.89	0.0001
	DTW	88.11	84.89	80.26	85.45	0.5493
	NDTW	85.74	85.90	**80.72**	**85.70**	0.6722

Varying Warping Windows: The most important parameter of DTW is the warping window ω (see Algorithm 1), which enforces a temporal constraint on the warping range and has great influence on the experiment results. We will test it in the following experiments. The results of malicious domain detection are presented in Fig. 3(a). It can be clearly seen that the performance of malicious domain detection does not increase as the warping window ω increases. And when $\omega = 4$, it achieves the best F_1 score of 87.21%. This is because too wide warping window may introduce pathological matching between two time series and distort the true similarity [18]. Therefore, we set $\omega = 4$ in the following experiments.

Varying Time Windows: Another important parameter is the time window of time series (see Definition 2). As shown in Fig. 3(b), the smaller size of time window has a higher accuracy. This may be because the finer grained time series can better reflect the domain access patterns. While the F_1 score is not sensitive to the size of time window, which varies only in a narrow range from 85.71% to 87.32%.

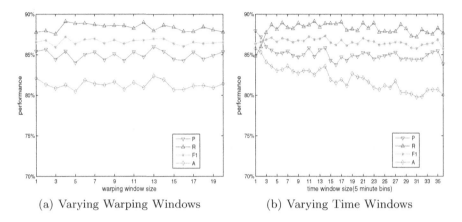

(a) Varying Warping Windows   (b) Varying Time Windows

Fig. 3. (a) Impact of warping window ω to the performance of malicious domain detection. (b) Impact of time window w to the performance of malicious domain detection.

Varying K-Nearest Neighbor: Finally, we conduct a set of experiments to evaluate the performance of our solution with different numbers of nearest neighbors. We perform experiments on two time window sizes, 14 and 24 respectively. Experimental results show that the KNN classifier gives the best F_1 score and accuracy for the value K = 10 over both two time window sizes, which we report in Table 6.

5.3   Discussion

In a sense, the approach taken here may appear surprising. Most malicious domain name detection methods are very complicated and heavy-weight, such as [5,10,12,13,17,19,20]. These methods require complex feature engineering and specific data input and even constant update of models. So we propose a lightweight solution that requires very few preconditions can be easily deployed, although it will slightly deteriorate the performance at an acceptable level.

Table 6. Performance comparison between different numbers of nearest neighbors.

K	Time window size $w = 24$					Time window size $w = 14$				
	P(%)	R(%)	F_1(%)	A(%)	Time(s)	P(%)	R(%)	F_1(%)	A(%)	Time (s)
1	84.90	83.95	84.41	75.70	319.15	85.68	86.79	86.22	80.12	542.03
2	87.88	79.57	83.50	71.90	312.72	87.53	81.65	84.47	76.26	571.93
3	84.37	86.62	85.46	79.02	315.55	85.52	87.37	86.43	82.18	576.50
4	86.35	84.20	85.25	78.02	313.30	86.34	85.58	85.95	80.44	584.49
5	83.70	88.29	85.92	80.24	312.91	85.07	88.96	86.97	82.64	585.85
6	85.50	87.12	86.28	79.92	310.79	86.32	86.76	86.53	82.76	584.55
7	84.40	89.45	86.84	81.14	310.01	83.93	90.14	86.91	82.12	582.32
8	85.15	87.71	86.39	80.48	309.86	84.59	88.35	86.41	81.50	584.57
9	83.57	89.66	86.49	80.80	310.32	84.01	89.57	86.69	82.20	575.36
10	85.43	89.33	**87.33**	**81.58**	310.28	85.12	89.23	**87.11**	**83.14**	572.11
11	83.41	90.16	86.65	81.10	323.93	83.30	91.13	87.03	82.06	574.61
12	83.89	89.53	86.61	80.56	312.64	84.14	89.78	86.86	82.26	572.83
13	83.37	90.85	86.94	80.64	322.02	82.80	90.79	86.60	81.54	569.33
14	84.25	90.12	87.08	81.16	337.83	83.83	89.94	86.76	82.24	571.26
15	82.54	90.27	86.22	80.68	333.79	82.89	91.43	86.93	81.44	572.30

6 Conclusion

In this paper, we have described a novel lightweight solution named DomainObserver for malicious domain detection, which does not require constant crowd updates or complex feature engineering. By using time series data mining, we apply DomainObserver to three different time series data collected in the actual network. Extensive experiments show that our method can effectively detect malicious domains by achieving 83.14% accuracy and 87.11% F_1 score.

Future work includes: (1) investigate how to improve the efficiency. This is especially needed for online deployment on real-time ISP networks. (2) study the misclassified samples to further improve the detection performance.

Acknowledgment. The author gratefully acknowledges support from National Key R&D Program 2016 (Grant No. 2016YFB0801300), National Natural Science Foundation of China (No. 61402464), and Youth Innovation Promotion Association CAS. And we also want to thank the anonymous reviewers for the valuable comments.

References

1. Alexa: Alexa top 1m. http://s3.amazonaws.com/alexa-static/top-1m.csv.zip. Accessed 7 Nov 2017
2. Antivirus: Network Security Threat Information Sharing Platform. https://share.anva.org.cn/en/index

3. Baidu: Baidu Website Security Detection Platform. http://bsb.baidu.com/
4. Berndt, D.J., Clifford, J.: Using dynamic time warping to find patterns in time series. In: KDD Workshop, Seattle, WA, vol. 10, pp. 359–370 (1994)
5. Bilge, L., Sen, S., Balzarotti, D., Kirda, E., Kruegel, C.: Exposure: a passive DNS analysis service to detect and report malicious domains. ACM Trans. Inf. Syst. Secur. (TISSEC) **16**(4), 14 (2014)
6. Cover, T., Hart, P.: Nearest neighbor pattern classification. IEEE Trans. Inf. Theory **13**(1), 21–27 (1967)
7. Duffield, N.: Sampling for passive internet measurement: a review. Stat. Sci. 472–498 (2004)
8. Faloutsos, C., Ranganathan, M., Manolopoulos, Y.: Fast subsequence matching in time-series databases. In: SIGMOD 1994. Citeseer (1994)
9. Grabocka, J., Schilling, N., Wistuba, M., Schmidt-Thieme, L.: Learning time-series shapelets. In: Proceedings of the 20th ACM SIGKDD International Conference on Knowledge Discovery and Data Mining, pp. 392–401. ACM (2014)
10. Kuyama, M., Kakizaki, Y., Sasaki, R.: Method for detecting a malicious domain by using WHOIS and DNS features. In: Third International Conference on Digital Security and Forensics (DigitalSec2016), p. 74 (2016)
11. Malware: Malware Domain Block List. http://www.malwaredomains.com/
12. Manadhata, P.K., Yadav, S., Rao, P., Horne, W.: Detecting malicious domains via graph inference. In: Kutyłowski, M., Vaidya, J. (eds.) ESORICS 2014. LNCS, vol. 8712, pp. 1–18. Springer, Cham (2014). https://doi.org/10.1007/978-3-319-11203-9_1
13. Nepali, R.K., Wang, Y.: You look suspicious!!: leveraging visible attributes to classify malicious short URLs on Twitter. In: 2016 49th Hawaii International Conference on System Sciences (HICSS), pp. 2648–2655. IEEE (2016)
14. OpenDNS: Phishtank. http://www.phishtank.com/
15. Qihu 360: 360 Fraud Reporting Center. https://110.360.cn/
16. Sahoo, D., Liu, C., Hoi, S.C.: Malicious URL detection using machine learning: a survey. arXiv preprint arXiv:1701.07179 (2017)
17. Sun, B., Akiyama, M., Yagi, T., Hatada, M., Mori, T.: Autoblg: automatic URL blacklist generator using search space expansion and filters. In: 2015 IEEE Symposium on Computers and Communication (ISCC), pp. 625–631. IEEE (2015)
18. Wang, X., Mueen, A., Ding, H., Trajcevski, G., Scheuermann, P., Keogh, E.: Experimental comparison of representation methods and distance measures for time series data. Data Min. Knowl. Discov. **26**, 1–35 (2013)
19. Wang, Y.: Cai, W.d., Wei, P.c.: A deep learning approach for detecting malicious Javascript code. Secur. Commun. Netw. **9**(11), 1520–1534 (2016)
20. Zhang, J., Porras, P.A., Ullrich, J.: Highly predictive blacklisting. In: USENIX Security Symposium, pp. 107–122 (2008)

You Have More Abbreviations Than You Know: A Study of AbbrevSquatting Abuse

Pin Lv[1,2], Jing Ya[1,2(✉)], Tingwen Liu[1,2], Jinqiao Shi[1,2], Binxing Fang[1,2], and Zhaojun Gu[3]

[1] Institute of Information Engineering, Chinese Academy of Sciences, Beijing, China
[2] School of Cyber Security, University of Chinese Academy of Sciences, Beijing, China
[3] Information Security Evaluation Center of Civil Aviation, Civil Aviation University of China, Tianjin, China
{lvpin,yajing,liutingwen,shijinqiao,fangbx}@iie.ac.cn,
15620968007@163.com

Abstract. Domain squatting is a speculative behavior involving the registration of domain names that are trademarks belonging to popular companies, important organizations or other individuals, before the latters have a chance to register. This paper presents a specific and unconcerned type of domain squatting called "AbbrevSquatting", the phenomena that mainly happens on institutional websites. As institutional domain names are usually named with abbreviations (*i.e.*, short forms) of the full names or official titles of institutes, attackers can mine abbreviation patterns from existed pairs of abbreviations and full names, and register forged domain names with unofficial but meaningful abbreviations for a given institute. To measure the abuse of AbbrevSquatting, we first mine the common abbreviation patterns used in institutional domain names, and generate potential AbbrevSquatting domain names with a data set of authoritative domains. Then, we check the maliciousness of generated domains with a public API and seven different blacklists, and group the domains into several categories with crawled data. Through a series of manual and automated experiments, we discover that attackers have already been aware of the principles of AbbrevSquatting and are monetizing them in various unethical and illegal ways. Our results suggest that AbbrevSquatting is a real problem that requires more attentions from security communities and institutions' registrars.

Keywords: Domain squatting · AbbrevSquatting
Institutional domain names · Abbreviations

1 Introduction

The Domain Name System (DNS) plays a critical role in supporting the Internet infrastructure by providing a distributed and fairly robust mechanism that

© Springer International Publishing AG, part of Springer Nature 2018
Y. Shi et al. (Eds.): ICCS 2018, LNCS 10860, pp. 221–233, 2018.
https://doi.org/10.1007/978-3-319-93698-7_17

resolves Internet host names into IP addresses. The reliability and agility that DNS offers has been fundamental to the effort for institutions, companies and organizations to scale information, business and service across the Internet. However, because of this, many attackers heavily rely on DNS to implement and scale their malicious operations.

In fact, domain squatting is a very common tactic used to facilitate DNS abuse by registering domains that are confusingly similar [1] to those belonging to popular companies, important organizations or other individuals. Domain squatting is hard to be eliminated. Because it involves the education of users' DNS interaction, rather than the technical correction of a protocol shortcoming, or a software vulnerability. There are several types of domain squatting techniques proposed in past researches. Typosquatting takes advantage of typographical errors [2–4]. Bit squatting utilizes accidental bit flips [5,6]. Homograph-based squatting domains abuse the visual similarity of different characters [7,8]. Homophone-based squatting domains abuse the pronunciation similarity of different words [9]. And, combosquatting combines a recognizable brand name with other common keywords [10].

In this paper, we present a specific and unconcerned type of domain squatting called "AbbrevSquatting", the phenomena that mainly happens on institutional websites. Institutional websites are created by associations, organizations or public institutes which aim to release official information and provide online services. In order to make users memorize them easily, such websites usually are bound to domains of abbreviated names that correspond to their full names or official titles (*i.e.*, using abbreviations of the names or titles). For example, the domain name 'cocc[.]net.cn' is named after its official title 'China Ocean and Climate Change Information Network'. And, the 'cocc' in the domain name is the combination of the first letter of 'China Ocean and Climate Change', which is part of the official title. While, we can also name it with 'coaccin', which is the combination of the first letter of the official title. Obviously, there are other patterns of abbreviation. AbbrevSquatting takes advantage of the variety of abbreviations for a full name or official title and the users' confusion of which abbreviation represents the institute. They mine abbreviation patterns from existed pairs of abbreviations and full names, and register forged domain names with unofficial but meaningful abbreviations for a given institute. AbbrevSquatting is quite different from known domain squatting techniques. First, for a given institute, the Abbrevsquatting domain names are generated with its full name or official title, but not its official domain names. Second, the AbbrevSquatting domain names are generated with different types of abbreviation patterns but not slight changes on the input domain names.

To measure AbbrevSquatting abuse, we first analyse common abbreviation patterns used in institutional websites with a data set of one hundred thousands of institutional domains, and eight abbreviation patterns are minded. We generate 6,219,924 potential AbbrevSquatting domains with three popular abbreviation patterns, and find 1,370,014 (22.03%) of which are already registered. Then, we check the maliciousness of registered AbbrevSquatting domains with

VirusTotal API and seven different blacklists, and group the domains into several categories with crawled webpages and final links. Through a series of manual and automated experiments, we find that attackers have already been aware of the principles of AbbrevSquatting and are monetizing them in various unethical and illegal ways. AbbrevSquatting abuse is a real problem that security communities and institutions' registrars should pay more attentions to.

Our main contributions in this paper are:

- In this paper, we present a specific and unconcerned type of domain squatting called "AbbrevSquatting". It mainly happens on institutional websites. Attackers mine the abbreviation patterns from existed pairs of abbreviations and full names, and register forged domain names with unofficial but meaningful abbreviations for a given institute.
- We analyze a data set of one hundred thousands of institutional domains, and mine eight abbreviation patterns (can cover up 89.27% of data set). We generate 6,219,924 potential AbbrevSquatting domains with three popular abbreviation patterns, and find 1,370,014 (22.03%) of which are already registered.
- Through a series of manual and automated experiments, we find that attackers have already been aware of the principles of AbbrevSquatting. Most of the generated domains are used to be parked, and some are listed in public blacklists. Our findings show that AbbrevSquatting is a real problem that requires more attentions from security communities and institutions' registrars.

The rest of this paper is structured as follows. In Sect. 2, we provide background information on institutional domain names and definition of AbbrevSquatting in general. Section 3 describes the analysis of our dataset and the way we generate potential AbbrevSquatting domains. We measure the abuse of AbbrevSquatting domain names in Sect. 4. Section 5 summarizes the related work. Finally, Sect. 6 concludes the paper's work.

2   Background

2.1   Institutional Domain Names

A domain name is a unique and easy-to-remember name that identifies and links to the address of a website on the internet. Domain names can generally be divided into two parts: second level domain and top level domain. Second level domain is the customisable part of the domain name that individuals, organisations or companies register to represent them on the internet. Top-level domains (also known as TLDs) are the next level of organisation on the internet. There are typically two kinds of TLDs, including Generic TLDs (gTLDs, *e.g.* '.com', '.net', '.org', '.edu', '.gov', *etc.*) and Country-code TLDs (ccTLDs, *e.g.* '.uk', '.cn', '.com.cn', '.net.cn', '.org.cn', '.edu.cn', '.gov.cn', *etc.*).

Institutional domain names are created and registered by associations, organizations or public institutes to release official information and provide online services. They provide varieties of comprehensive and convenient platforms for institution administrators and Internet users to deal with public affairs online. In order to make Internet users remember them easily, the customisable parts (*i.e.*, second level domains) of such domain names are usually created and registered which correspond to their full names or official titles (*i.e.*, using abbreviations of the corresponding names).

For instance, the domain name 'cocc[.]net.cn' links to the institutional website with official title of 'China Ocean and Climate Change Information Network'. And, the second level domain 'cocc' of the domain name is named with the combination of the first letter of 'China Ocean and Climate Change', which is part of the official title.

2.2 AbbrevSquatting

For a given institute, we can create multiple abbreviations with its full name or official title. As for 'China Ocean and Climate Change Information Network', the official domain name is 'cocc[.]net.cn'. We can replace the 'cocc' in the domain name with 'coaccin', which is the first letter of all the words in the corresponding name. AbbrevSquatting takes advantage of the variety of abbreviation patterns for an institutional name and the users' confusion of which abbreviation represents the official website. The attack is based on abbreviations of domain names, *i.e.*, sets of abbreviations that are all coming from the same institute, but are named in different patterns.

AbbrevSquatting is quite different from other kinds of known domain squatting techniques mainly in two aspects. Firstly, for a given institute, the Abbrevsquatting domain names are generated with its full name or official title, but not its official domain names. Secondly, the AbbrevSquatting domain names are generated with different types of abbreviation patterns but not slight changes on the input domain names. Theoretically, AbbrevSquatting is much more difficult for Internet users to distinguish.

3 Measurement Methodology

Given the definition of AbbrevSquatting in Sect. 2.2, we provide a methodical way to measure AbbrevSquatting abuse using a dataset of one hundred thousands of institutional domains as the authoritative domains. First, we give a description of our data set, and mine the common abbreviation patterns they usually use. Then, we generate potential AbbrevSquatting domain names with three popular abbreviation patterns which are different from the official domains.

3.1 Data Set

The discovery of domain squatting activity requires a set of authoritative domains as targets. We obtain 134,806 Chinese institutional domain names from our cooperative partner as the authoritative domains. In our dataset, each

Table 1. An example of data, 'CP' means 'Chinese Pinyin', 'EN' is 'English Words'.

Domain name	`cocc[.]net.cn`
Full Name_CP	Guo Jia Hai Yang Xin Xi Zhong Xin
Full Name_EN	National Marine Information Center
OfficialTitle_CP	Zhong Guo Hai Yang Yu Qi Hou Bian Hua Xin Xi Wang
OfficialTitle_EN	China Ocean and Climate Change Information Network

Table 2. Percentages of TLDs used in authoritative domain list

TLD	Percent (%)	TLD	Percent (%)	TLD	Percent (%)
gov.cn	36.44	net	4.24	edu.cn	0.57
com	34.69	org	2.81	ac.cn	0.28
cn	12.50	org.cn	2.44	sh.cn	0.21
com.cn	4.48	net.cn	0.69	others	0.66

domain name has a full name and an official title both in Chinese language. The full name is the name of a association, organization or institute, and the official title is the title of its institutional website. The two names may be the same. We use a Python package named Pinyin[1] and Baidu translation API[2] to extract the Chinese Pinyin and English words of each name or title. Table 1 shows an example item of our dataset used in this paper.

We further analyse the Top-Level Domains (TLDs) used in our dataset, as shown in Table 2. From Table 2, we can observe that TLDs used by institutional domain names are various and the common ones are '.gov.cn', '.com', '.cn', '.com.cn', '.net', '.org' and '.org.cn', which are more than one percent of all the domains. In the later generation process, we choose the seven most commonly used TLDs as the suffix of domain names.

3.2 Abbreviation Patterns Mining

To generate the potential AbbrevSquatting domain names, we also need a list of rules and models in addition to the authoritative domains. In this section, we mine the common abbreviation patterns used in the institutional domains.

Specifically, we mine the association relationships between the second level domains and full names (including four phrases as shown in Table 1) with strong rules. We finally extract eight rules (*i.e.*, abbreviation patterns) in the institutional domain names of our data set. The eight abbreviation patterns can cover up 89.27% of all the domains. The distribution of each pattern is shown in Table 3. We also give a manual analysis for the remained 10.73% domain names

---

[1] https://pypi.python.org/pypi/pinyin.
[2] http://fanyi-api.baidu.com/api/trans/product/index.

Table 3. Abbreviation patterns used in the 134,786 Chinese institutional domain names

Pattern	Comment	Count	Percent
AFL	The first letter of all the words in a name	9366	6.95
PFL	The first letter of parts of the words in a name	56470	41.89
FLS	First Letters of several words in a name	15838	11.75
PWS	Parts of the words in a name	6378	4.73
CEC	Combination of English and Chinese Pinyin	8295	6.15
CSL	Contain sign '-' in the domain name	2612	1.94
CIR	Contain integers in the domain name	6045	4.48
SDN	Sub domains of the superior websites	15343	11.38
UNK	Unknown patterns	14459	10.73

Table 4. Common abbreviations of English words used in our dataset

Word	Abbreviate	Count	Word	Abbreviate	Count
Education	edu	408	Technology	te	65
School	sc	220	Science	sc	63
Chinese	chin	176	Information	info	56
Library	lib	170	Agriculture	agri	48
Small	sm	167	Statistical	stat	47
Agricultural	agri	126	Taxatio	tax	46
Tourism	tour	113	Technology	tech	39
Network	ne	109	Network	net	30
Center	ce	106	Commerce	com	30
Investment	invest	97	Photography	photo	18
Statistics	stat	86	Company	co	15
Cooperative	coop	68	Geological	geo	14
Institute	in	65	Standardization	standard	9

with unknown pattern, and find that they are not related to the corresponding full names or official titles at all.

The eight abbreviation patterns are defined as follows:

AFL Pattern. In this pattern, a domain name is named with the first letter of all the words in a full name or official title. For example, 'tpeh' in 'tpeh[.]net' is named after the full name 'Tianjin Planning Exhibition Hall'.

PFL Pattern. In this pattern, a domain name is named with the first letter of part of the words in a name. For example, 'cocc' in 'cocc[.]net' is named after the official title 'China Ocean and Climate Change Information Network'.

FLS Pattern. In this pattern, a domain name uses first letters of several words in a full name or official title. For example, 'tianjinswim' in 'tianjinswim [.]com' is named after the full name 'Tianjin Swimming Center'.

We further analyse the FLS abbreviation pattern in depth, and find that the condition that first few letters of a word used in Chinaes Pinyin usually happens in initial consonants, *i.e.*, 'zh', 'sh', 'ch'. As for the English words, we analyse some abbreviations for English words. The most commonly used abbreviations are as shown in Table 4.

PWS Pattern. In this pattern, a domain name is named with parts of the words in a full name or official title. For example, 'hanbofood[.]com' is named after the full name 'Taiyuan Hanbo Food Industry Co Ltd'.

CEC Pattern. In this pattern, a domain name is named with the combination of English words and Chinese Pinyin. For example, 'nxzwnews' in domain name 'nxzwnews[.]net' is named after the Chinese name 'Ning Xia Zhong Wei Xin Xi Wang' and English name 'Zhongwei News Network'.

CSL Pattern and **CIR Pattern.** The two patterns contain sign '-' or integers in domain names. The details of the two patterns are complex. We will discuss them in our future work.

SDN Pattern. In this pattern, an institute uses a sub domain of its superior institute, such as 'czj.xlgl.gov.cn', 'tjj.xlgl.gov.cn'. As sub domain names are administrated by the main registered domains (*i.e.*, second level domains), we consider that AbbrevSquatting only exists in the second level domains.

3.3 Generating Domains

As we discuss in Sect. 2.1, a registered domain name includes two parts, *i.e.*, second level domain and top level domain. The top level domains we use in this paper are '.gov.cn', '.com', '.cn', '.com.cn', '.net', '.org' and '.org.cn', which are most commonly used in the institutional domain names of our data set. The second level domains are customisable, and generated by the abbreviation patterns of the full names or official titles.

In order to generate a controlled number of domain names and simultaneously measure AbbrevSquatting abuse effectively, we implement three generation methods with the most popular abbreviation patterns. The three methods are used to generate the customisable parts of the domains (*i.e.*, second level domains). And, the generation process is based on the four phrases of each institute as shown in Table 1.

Next, we give a detailed description of each generation method with the data in Table 1 as an example. From Table 1, we can observe that 'cocc' in the domain name 'cocc[.]net.cn' is named after the English official title 'China Ocean and Climate Change Information Network' with the PFL pattern.

The first method is called "**ComAllMethod**". In this method, we generate the customisable parts of the potential AbbrevSquatting domains with a combination of the first letter of all the words in a phrase. For 'cocc' in 'cocc[.]net.cn', we can also name it with 'gjhyxxzx', 'nmic', 'zghyyqhbhxxw', and 'coaccin'.

The second method is called "**ComTopMethod**". In this method, we generate the customisable parts of the potential AbbrevSquatting domains with a combination of the first letter of the top n (*e.g.*, $n = 4, 5, 6$) words in each phrase. The length of the second level domain is limited between 4 and 6. The range is decided from the statistics of our data set. If the length of a phrase is less than 4, we handle it with the first method. For 'cocc' in 'cocc[.]net.cn', we can also name it with 'gjgy', 'gjhyx', and 'gjhyxx' after the Chinese full name with this method.

The third method is called "**ComSegMethod**". The customisable parts of the potential AbbrevSquatting domains are generated based on word segmentation. For the two Chinese phrases, we use a Python package named Jieba[3] to segment each phrase. For the two English phrases, we use the prepositions (*e.g.*, 'in', 'on', 'of', 'at' *etc.*) as delimiters to segment each phrase. For instance, the official title 'China Ocean and Climate Change Information Network' can be segmented into 'China Ocean', 'Climate Change Information Network'. So, we can name it with 'co', 'ccin' and 'coccin'. We set the length of the second level domain is less than 7 according to statistics.

We generate the customisable parts of domains with the above three methods. A potential AbbrevSquatting domain name is the combination of the customisable part and a suffix (*i.e.*, top level domain).

The profiles of our generated domain names are shown in Table 5. We totally generate 6,219,924 potential AbbrevSquatting domain names, targeting the 134,806 Chinese institutional domains in our data set.

Table 5. Profiles of the generated domain names

Method	Generated	Registered	Percent (%)	HTMLs	Percent (%)
ComAll	1,858,230	179,591	9.66	96,135	53.53
ComTop	1,725,810	570,892	33.08	339,527	59.47
ComSeg	2,635,884	619,531	23.50	376,074	60.70
Total	**6,219,924**	**1,370,014**	**22.03**	**811,736**	**59.25**

---

[3] https://pypi.python.org/pypi/jieba/.

In order to identify registered domain names, we perform a `whois` lookup for each domains. Then, we implement a crawler to visit the websites of the registered domain names to extract those provide web services. We also record the HTMLs and final URLs for further analysis. As shown in Table 5, we finally identify 1,370,014 domain names (22.03% of all the generated domain names) are already registered, and extract 811,736 (59.25% of all the registered domains) HTMLs. This paper focuses on the analysis of the domains which are registered and provide web services.

4   Measuring Results

In this section, we measure the AbbrevSquatting abuse through a series of automated and manual experiments. First, we check the maliciousness of the registered potential AbbrevSquatting domains with a public scanning API and seven different domain name blacklists. Second, we group the domain names into several categories according to the HTMLs and final URLs we crawled in Sect. 3.3.

4.1   Checking Maliciousness

To shed light on the malicious use of the registered potential AbbrevSquatting domain names, we check the generated domain names with a public scanning API and seven different domain name blacklists.

Firstly, we check the domains with a public API provided by VirusTotal [11]. VirusTotal is a website which aggregates many antivirus products and online scan engines, in addition to a myriad of tools to extract malicious signals from the input domains/urls/files. VirusTotal provides a public API that allows for automation of some of its online features. We get the scanned results of each domain through the public API. And, 2769 domains are found to be involved with virus or malicious activities.

Secondly, we check the generated domain names against seven different domain name blacklists [12–18]. The seven domain name blacklists come from malwaredomainlist.com, Ransomware Tracker, urlvir.com, abuse.ch's list of Zeus Tracker, nothink.org, joewein.de LLC, and malware domain blocklist by RiskAnalytics. The check is performed on the second level domains, as AbbrevSquatting domains may choose different top level parts. We find that 2087 domain names have been public in the seven blacklists.

4.2   Categorization Results

With crawled data, we group the generated domain names into several categories. The crawled data includes a HTML and a final URLs for each domain. The final URL is used to detect redirection from the visited domain name to another different domain name. The HTML is a web page and contains the content of the website. We categorize each domain according to a full text analysis.

Specially, we follow a semi-automatic approach to implement the categorization. Firstly, we manually skim over the contents of a few pages and group together pages that with similar contents. The majority of these are parked pages, *i.e.*, pages that show ads, somewhat relevant to the domain name and usually also advertise that the domain may be for sale. Other groups are pages with little content, stating that the site is 'under construction', placeholder pages by popular registrars informing their clients how to setup a website on their registered domain, and pages containing generic errors, such as '404 Forbidden'. There are also websites with some normal content.

Table 6. Descriptions of categories

Category	Description
Redirection	Pages redirecting to another link
Parked/For Sale	Pages that have no content other than being advertised as for sale
Entertainment	Pages showing entertainment/gambling/lottery content
Server Error	Pages displaying an error, which caused by a server-side problem
Adult Content	Pages showing adult/pornographic content
No Content	Pages that have no content (*e.g.*, blank pages)
Containing	Pages containing legitimate content that happen to reside on a squatting variant of an authoritative domain
Other	Unclassified pages that do not fall into any of the above categories

We summarize seven main categories according to the content of the websites. The descriptions of all the categories are shown in Table 6.

Next, we create generic content-signatures that could automatically categorize the remaining pages into each category. With this method, we can eventually automatically classify 85.98% of all the crawled webpages. The remaining unclassified domains are classified manually by a random sampling analysis.

Table 7. Results of the categorization

Generated domains			Redirection domains		
Category	Count	Percent	Category	Count	Percent
Redirection	203751	**25.10%**	Parked	106479	52.26%
Parked	472163	58.17%	AdultContent	3617	1.78%
Entertainment	42995	5.30%	Entertainment	15572	7.64%
ServerError	114725	14.13%	ServerError	29382	14.42%
AdultContent	19427	2.39%	Others	48701	23.90%

By combining the results of the automatic classification and those of our manual investigation, we categorize all the potential AbbrevSquatting domains. The results of the categorization are shown in Table 7.

Parked/For Sale Domains : Parked domains are the preferred monetizing way for domain squatters [19–21]. As we mentioned earlier, these domains contain no real content, except ads which are constructed on demand, usually by a domain-parking agency, based on the words included in a domain name and preferences by the owner of the domain. In total, parked/for sale domains represent the largest chunk of existing potential AbbrevSquatting domain names, with 471,526 cases (58.17% of all the webpages).

Redirection Domains : While examining the AbbrevSquatting domains that redirect users to other different domains, we find that most of them are redirected to parked domains. We totally detect 203,751 redirection domains by checking the final URLs of each domain. While, 106,479 (52.26% of all the redirection domains) cases are parked domains. These domains are mainly redirected to large parked service agency websites, e.g., sedoparking.com, www.buydomains. com, cashparking.com and so on. Redirection domains are also used in other categories, such as **Entertainment**, **Server Error**, **Adult Content**, and the distributions of each category are shown in Table 7. The left column shows the categories distribution for all the webpages. The right column shows the distribution of each category for all the redirection domain names.

We also find 152 websites with blank pages, which have no content. For the remaining unclassified pages, we randomly select 100 samples to analyze manually. We find that most of them contain legitimate content that happen to reside on a squatting variant of an authoritative domain.

5 Related Work

Domain squatting is a type of cybersquatting involving the registration of domain names that are trademarks belonging to other companies, institutions or individuals, before the latter have a chance to register [22,23]. Several studies have been proposed and focused on domain squatting abuse in general.

Wang et al. [19] proposed models for the generation of typosquatting domains from authoritative ones. Janos et al. [2,4] proposed techniques for identifying typosquatting. Agten et al. [3] studied typosquatting using crawled data over a period of seven months and found out that few trademark owners protect themselves by defensively registering typosquatting domains. Apart from typosquatting, Nikiforakis et al. [6] quantified the extent to which attackers are leveraging bitsquatting, where random bit-errors occurring in the memory of commodity hardware can redirect Internet traffic to attacker-controlled domains. Their experiments show that new bitsquatting domains are registered daily and monetized through ads, affiliate programs and even malware installations. They later performed a measurement of another type of domain squatting called 'sound-squatting', where attackers abuse homophones to attract users and confuse text-to-speech systems [9].

As for AbbrevSquatting, the Chinese website '`xinhuanet.com`' ever reported some similar illegal behaviors [24]. But, to the best of our knowledge, this paper is the first one which deeply analyze the principles and measure the abuse of AbbrevSquatting. We mine abbreviation patterns from a data set of author-itative domains, and generate a large number of potential AbbrevSquatting domains. We measure the AbbrevSquatting abuse through a series of experi-ments.

6   Conclusion and Future Work

In this paper, we present a specific and unconcerned type of domain squatting technique, which is called "AbbrevSquatting". It mainly happens on institutional websites. Attackers mine the abbreviation patterns from existed pairs of abbre-viations and full names, and register forged domain names with unofficial but meaningful abbreviations for a given institute. We analyze a data set of institu-tional domains, and mine eight abbreviation patterns (can cover up 89.27% of data set). We generate 6,219,924 potential AbbrevSquatting domains with three popular abbreviation patterns, and find 1,370,014 (22.03%) of which are already registered. Through a series of manual and automated experiments, we find that attackers have already been aware of the principles of AbbrevSquatting. Most of the generated domains are used to be parked domains, and some are listed in public blacklists. Our findings show that AbbrevSquatting is a real problem that requires more attentions from security communities and institutions' registrars.

We measure the abuse of the registered potential AbbrevSquatting domains which provide web services in this paper. In our future work, we would like to analyze the abuse of the potential AbbrevSquatting domains which do not provide web services. And, we also will analyze the changes of AbbrevSquatting domains with time.

Acknowledgement. This work was supported in part by the National Key Research and Development Program of China under Grant No. 2016YFB0801003 and the Open Project Foundation of Information Security Evaluation Center of Civil Aviation, Civil Aviation University of China No. CAAC-ISECCA-201801.

References

1. Anticybersquatting Consumer Protection Act - Wikipedia. https://en.wikipedia. org/wiki/Anticybersquatting_Consumer_Protection_Act
2. Janos, S., Balazs, K., Gabor, C., Jonathan, S., Mark, F., Chris, K.: The long "Taile" of typosquatting domain names. In: Proceedings of USENIX Security Symposium (USENIXSecurity), pp. 191–206 (2014)

3. Agten, P., Joosen, W., Piessens, F., Nikiforakis, N.: Seven months' worth of mistakes: a longitudinal study of typosquatting abuse. In: Proceedings of Network and Distributed System, Security Symposium (NDSS) (2015)
4. Mohammad, T.K., Huo, X., Li, Z., Kanich, C.: Every second counts: quantifying the negative externalities of cybercrime via typosquatting. In: Proceedings of IEEE Symposium on Security and Privacy (2015)
5. Dinaburg, A.: Bitsquatting: DNS hijacking without exploitation. In: Proceedings of BlackHat Security (2011)
6. Nikiforakis, N., Van Acker, S., Meert, W., Desmet, L., Piessens, F., Joosen, W.: Bitsquatting: exploiting bit-flips for fun, or profit? In: Proceedings of International Conference on World Wide Web, pp. 989–998 (2013)
7. Evgeniy, G., Alex, G.: The homograph attack. Commun. ACM **45**(2), 128 (2002)
8. Holgers, T., Watson, D.E., Gribble, S.D.: Cutting through the confusion: a measurement study of homograph attacks. In: Proceedings of USENIX Annual Technical Conference, pp. 261–266 (2006)
9. Nikiforakis, N., Balduzzi, M., Desmet, L., Piessens, F., Joosen, W.: Soundsquatting: uncovering the use of homophones in domain squatting. In: Chow, S.S.M., Camenisch, J., Hui, L.C.K., Yiu, S.M. (eds.) ISC 2014. LNCS, vol. 8783, pp. 291–308. Springer, Cham (2014). https://doi.org/10.1007/978-3-319-13257-0_17
10. Panagiotis, K., Najmeh, M., Charles, L., Chen, Y., et al.: Hiding in plain sight: a longitudinal study of combosquatting abuse. In: Proceedings of CCS, pp. 569–586 (2017)
11. VirusTotal. https://www.virustotal.com
12. Malware Domain List. https://www.malwaredomainlist.com
13. Ransomware Domain Blocklist. https://ransomwaretracker.abuse.ch
14. Monitor Malicious Executable Urls. http://www.urlvir.com/export-hosts/
15. ZeuS Tracker: ZeuS Blocklist. https://zeustracker.abuse.ch/blocklist.php?download=domainblocklist
16. NoThink! http://www.nothink.org/blacklist/blacklist_malware_dns.txt
17. joewein.de LLC. http://www.joewein.net/dl/bl/dom-bl.txt
18. DNS-BH. http://www.malwaredomains.com
19. Wang, Y.-M., Beck, D., Wang, J., Verbowski, C., Daniels, B.: Strider typo-patrol: discovery and analysis of systematic typo-squatting. In: Proceedings of SRUTI, pp. 31–36 (2006)
20. Moore, T., Edelman, B.: Measuring the perpetrators and funders of typosquatting. In: Sion, R. (ed.) FC 2010. LNCS, vol. 6052, pp. 175–191. Springer, Heidelberg (2010). https://doi.org/10.1007/978-3-642-14577-3_15
21. Vissers, T., Joosen, W., Nikiforakis, N.: Parking sensors: analyzing and detecting parked domains. In: Proceedings of NDSS (2015)
22. Edelman, B.: Large-scale registration of domains with typographical errors (2003). http://cyber.harvard.edu/archived_content/people/edelman/typo-domains/
23. Coull, S.E., White, A.M., Yen, T.-F., Monrose, F., Reiter, M.K.: Understanding domain registration abuses. In: Rannenberg, K., Varadharajan, V., Weber, C. (eds.) SEC 2010. IAICT, vol. 330, pp. 68–79. Springer, Heidelberg (2010). https://doi.org/10.1007/978-3-642-15257-3_7
24. Report. http://news.xinhuanet.com/politics/2015-07/23/c_1116010850.htm

Large Scale Retrieval of Social Network Pages by Interests of Their Followers

Elena Mikhalkova[✉][ID], Yuri Karyakin[ID], and Igor Glukhikh[ID]

Tyumen State University, Tyumen, Russia
{e.v.mikhalkova,y.e.karyakin,i.n.glukhikh}@utmn.ru

Abstract. Social networks provide an opportunity to form communities of people that share their interests on a regular basis (circles of fans of different music, books, kinds of sports, etc.). Every community manifests these interests creating lots of linguistic data to attract new followers to certain pages and support existing clusters of users. In the present article, we suggest a model of retrieving such pages that attract users with similar interests, from a large collection of pages. We test our model on three types of pages manually retrieved from the social network Vkontakte and classified as interesting for a. football fans, b. vegetarians, c. historical reenactors. We use such machine learning classifiers as Naive Bayes, SVM, Logistic Regression, Decision Trees to compare their performance with the performance of our system. It appears that the mentioned classifiers can hardly retrieve (i.e. single out) pages with a particular interest that form a small collection of 30 samples from a collection as large as 4,090 samples. In particular, our system exceeds their best result (F1-score = 0.65) and achieves F1-score of 0.72.

Keywords: Interest discovery · Social group · Major interest
Social network · Supervised machine learning

1 Introduction and Related Work

Classifying a page as interesting or not for a user who is scrolling through a social network is not a challenge. The main issue is rather the overload of pages they have to look through before they find what they want. Hence, advancement of recommender systems that help users find communities of interest is an ongoing process characterized by a variety of approaches. The focus of these approaches is usually the user. As [13] puts it, user-modelling that generally deals with behavior and actions of a user in a computer system includes inferring interests from them (interest discovery[1]). From this perspective, one user can exhibit a variety of interests, and the task of modelling is to infer them. In this paradigm, the main marker of interests is linguistic data (user-generated content). Hence, interests are mined as tags [11,18,32,36], keywords [4,35,37],

---

[1] The field is called so by [18,39] and some other.

© Springer International Publishing AG, part of Springer Nature 2018
Y. Shi et al. (Eds.): ICCS 2018, LNCS 10860, pp. 234–246, 2018.
https://doi.org/10.1007/978-3-319-93698-7_18

named entities [3,28,33], user classified interests from profiles [17,24], topics [2,19,20,39] in microblogs [3,29,38], most commonly derived with the help of LDA and LSA algorithm [7,34][2]. Other approaches, e.g. the social network analysis, employ such non-linguistic information as friends, followers [12], contacts [31], clicks [1,4], likes [8] and reposts, retweets, social recommendations [9,10,16]. Some projects unite users into clusters that can be represented with a graph-model [23,40]. In all approaches, the main target is to facilitate the search functions of social networks by a more effective recommendation.

As for the algorithms of interest classification, their choice depends on the model. Where machine classification is possible, according to [25], traditionally the following classifiers are used: Decision Trees, Nearest Neighbors, Naive Bayes, linear algorithms separating hyperplanes (variations of commonly known Support Vector Machines, or SVM). [6] use Nearest Neighbors and Naive Bayes to suggest NLP-based recommendation of "news of interest". However, none of the works we know focus on community pages that attract users with similar interests. As we demostrate below, such pages provide valuable information on existing user clusters and user interests.

In the present research, we would like to shift the focus from modelling a single user's list of interests to modelling a social network community that a user might like, and we will do it based on a linguistic model. We assume (and discuss further) that one main interest is what attracts a user to a page if they start to follow it[3].

Our solution presumes we already know a page that a user likes, or we have a set of pages that a user's friends like - we will call such pages *model*. A recommender system can find more pages that are similar to the *model* ones with the help of text similarity algorithms[4]. We can also view this task as a text classification problem usually solved with such algorithms as Decision Trees, k-Nearest Neighbors, Naive Bayes, etc. Additionally, classification presupposes that pages followed by users with a common interest belong to a certain *class*, especially from the sociological and linguistic point of view.

2   Interest Classification from the Sociological Perspective

Although interests are personal, in communities they have to be shared (sociologists call this phenomenon "contagion" [30]). In social networks, interest sharing produces linguistic content that makes online communities a valuable object of research.

Although there is no universal definition of social groups, many authors among whom are [5,14,21], etc. agree that a social group is a collection of individuals interacting in a certain way on the basis of shared expectations of each member of the group in relation to others. A social group can be viewed as an

---

[2] [27] evaluate importance of these types of linguistic content in user-modelling.

[3] Unless they already know the page owner and follow them to confirm the previously established contact.

[4] A good account of such algorithms is given by [15].

abstract whole that has certain features distinguishing it from others. For example, football fans as a social group are known around the world for their typical behavior: attending football matches, collecting sports memorablia, and quite often for violation of public conduct. Accordingly, adherence of an individual to the social group shows in speech. An individual who claims to belong to a social group calls himself or herself by a special name (a football fan of some team, a hoolie), mentions attributes of the group (a team's name and players, leagues, places, sports memorabilia), performs activities typical of all members of the group and reports about it (attending matches, play-offs). When in social networks representatives of a social group interact, linguistic data serve as a means of identification and role assignment. Hence, network pages of social groups *can* be viewed as representatives of a class. And we can use such linguistic data as keywords, topics, named entities, terminology for automatic differentiation of these groups.

At the same time, what hinders classification is that groups can have points of intersection (for example, both football and hockey *matches* happen at *stadiums*, *teams* participate in *leagues*, etc.). Even names of teams and players can be the same. In such cases, fans often invent nicknames (using flag colors or mascots) to differentiate between them. Hence, linguistic content marks difference between unrelated social groups and simultaneously shows relation between allied groups.

Previously, we stated that there is one main interest that attracts users to a page. We will call it the Major Interest (MaI). The MaI is bound to the social group that joins for interaction on a social network page. If the people interacting do not belong to the same social group, they express different interests, and the MaI becomes unclear.

To study the phenomenon of MaI, we conducted a survey of the Russian social network Vkontakte (vk.com). We had to work with the Russian language as we were able to only find enough Russian-speaking experts. Vkontakte was created by Pavel Durov, who currently develops Telegram, in 2006. The network was chosen as one of the largest sources of linguistic content in Russian. In the experiment described in [22], we asked ten experts (certified and currently employed as linguists, sociologists, marketing specialists) to give their opinion on what social group manifests itself in a dialogue taken from a social network page. We instructed experts to define if authors in the sample dialogue belong to the same social group and, if yes, explain why they think so. The experts were not prompted by multiple choice answers. Three dialogues were marked correctly and unanimously as belonging to football fans, historical reenactors, and vegetarians. Two dialogues (fans of rock music and "bros") got a 50% agreement. And the control sample where people did not express adherence to one social group[5] got a 90% agreement that there is no social group and that these people do not share any interests.

---

[5] The sample was taken from a page where people discussed a concert of Madonna that they attended or read about. Some of them expressed discontent with her religious and political views, some *vice versa* expressed admiration. [14] calls such accidental interactions "quasi-groups".

After the experiment we conducted automatic classification of social network pages by the three MaIs (football, rock music, vegetarianism) across networks and languages. For each MaI in the three sets (English Twitter, Russian Twitter, Russian Vkontakte), we prepared 30 text samples downloaded from social network pages. We used several classifiers (SVM, Neural Networks, Naive Bayes, Logistic Regression, Decision Trees, and k-Nearest Neighbors) to predict the three MaIs in each set. Logistic Regression proved to be the best performing algorithm when operating on vector representations of 1,000 most frequent words (0 denoting presence and 1 - absence of a word in a text). Table 1 illustrates the result of classification; the score given is the average F1-score of five tests performed with Monte-Carlo cross-validation.

Table 1. Interclass classification of pages with supervised machine learning classifiers: F1-score. F - football, R - rock music, V - vegetarianism, T - Twitter, Vk - Vkontakte, En - English, Ru - Russian.

	Vk Ru			T Ru			T En		
	F	R	V	F	R	V	F	R	V
Logistic regression	1.000	1.000	1.000	1.000	1.000	1.000	1.000	0.988	0.988

Generally, in this experiment we faced the efficiency of Bernoulli model of feature representation, i.e. word frequencies are not as important as their absence or presence. We also found out that human expertise is not a guarantee that a MaI will be difficult for classification. For example, Rock music and Vegetarianism were classified similarly well.

We tend to think that MaIs are more like umbrella terms to a variety of topics discussed by communities (for example, the MaI "football" encompasses matches, players, stadiums, events, ticket sales, memorablia). On the one hand, MaIs can be generalized into *types* of social groups: football fans are a type of sports fans, rock music fans are a type of music fans. Within the type, the variety of topics is quite similar (as in the case of hockey and football fans). On the other hand, MaIs can break into specific representatives, for example, rock music fans can be Metallica fans, Slipknot fans, etc.; football fans can be fans of Manchester United, Spartak, etc. The type determines the stable part of the user-generated content that relates some social groups, and representatives of a MaI are in charge of the entropy content that differentiates them from other representatives.[6]

---

[6] Therefore, it is important to understand what kind of content a user would like to get if they are looking for pages of interest. E.g. if a football fan is looking for other fans, do they need fans of a particular team? Which is usually the case of football fans. However, with the music or anime, they might be looking for more diverse communities - fans of different music bands, cartoons.

3   Retrieving Texts with a Certain MaI from a Large Collection

In the present research, we will describe an algorithm that is quite efficient when searching for pages with the same MaI in a collection much larger than the number of pages to be retrieved. We designed it on the grounds of interviews with the experts evaluating the texts in the experiment described above.

Every text T_i in the test set is weighed on the basis of one or two model texts united into one T_m in the training set to state its similarity to the model in every given class C_j (each class corresponds to one MaI). The weights are evaluated by the Relevance Function. The result is a list of texts that are considered to represent the same MaI. The classes are three MaIs from the experiment: football, vegetarianism, and historical reenactment.

A Model Text T_m is a text, chosen as a standard representative of a class. Ideally, it contains as many characteristic features of the class as possible[7]. The Relevance Function extracts these features for every class. Then, in every class, the Distribution function weighs all the texts in the test set and rates them choosing the top ranked as representatives of the class. Thus, every text can occur in more than one class.

3.1   Data Selection

We conducted our retrieval experiment on a corpus of texts downloaded from Vkontakte. For the present analysis, we automatically searched through 20,000 VKontakte open access pages using Vkontakte API. 4,460 pages turned out to contain user-generated content of size from 1 to 100,523 words. We asked a panel of three experts (certified linguists and sociologists) to manually search through them to find texts of football fans, historical reenactors, and vegetarians. In the final set of texts, the three MaIs were represented by a different number of items. Next, we asked experts to find more pages (using recommended links, user reposts and Vkontakte search) to create a set of 30 texts in each class. We also removed all texts belonging to the three MaIs and texts with the lowest number of words from the initial corpus. All in all, our corpus contains 4,000 unclassified items ("Miscellaneous") and 30 texts belonging to each of the three MaIs (90 texts, in total). We consider the ratio between the class "Miscellaneous" and each of the other classes to be large-scale because the joint probability to retrieve a succession of 30 items of one class from 4,030 is very low: $\frac{30}{4030} \times \frac{29}{4029} \cdots \times \frac{1}{4001} = 6.82936273447e-78$.

---

[7] Model Texts are characterised by intense communication of multiple representatives of a social group and are often quite large. But if the text is too large, it becomes noisy. Empirically we found out that selection of approximately 1,000 features is most effective. However, this observation requires more research. Also, we observed that some Model Texts provide better results than other; often using two texts instead of one is more effective. However, unlike common supervised learning algorithms, with the increase in the number of Model Texts (even up to 10–15) our algorithm becomes less efficient.

Every text in the corpus of 4,090 was preprocessed to extract the following four parameter features:

1. *Key-words.* Key-words are selected from the normalized list of words of T_m based on differences in their frequency. In a list of words, ranked by their frequency, a key-word is a word with a frequency that differs by more than one from the word with the next lower rank (e.g. 4, 7, 11 is a good list of frequencies with large enough steps; 1, 2, 3 is not). This method excludes all n legomena (hapax, dis, tris, etc.) to single out the most characteristic set of keywords. The normalized list of keywords has stop-words excluded. For short texts the result is a list of 1–2 words, and up to 20–30 for long texts.

2. *Stems.* Stems are selected from the vocabulary after stemming words with the Porter stemmer. Interestingly, when we preprocessed the vocabulary with a morphological analyser, it lowered down the performance. Therefore, no preprocessing except stemming was employed. In the resulting list of stemmed words, if each stem is found more than three times, it is added to the list of stems. This procedure is based on the expert opinion that social groups not only use some words frequently, but develop a whole vocabulary with derivatives of these words: vegetables - vegan, vegetarian, vegetarianism, lacto-vegetarian, ovo-vegetarian, etc.

3. *Uniques.* Lists of stemmed words, that were collected in the stemming procedure (without frequencies), are compared to each other in all pairs of classes, and stems that are found only within one class are added to the list of uniques. These words are a kind of terminological dictionary that describes a group's uniqueness. In the interviews, the experts also stated that groups use unique words that are understandable only by the representatives of this group or have a special value within this group. But tests showed that these lists are formed not only from some inner vocabulary, but also from common-knowledge words describing group activities.

4. *Named entities.* Named entities are a natural part of a social group vocabulary, as the group shares its impression of people, places, etc. Also, names of a group's leaders unite it. To extract named entities from social network posts and comments, we wrote a simple heuristic NER-parser. We take only named entities with frequency more than three.

3.2 Relevance Function

The Relevance Function creates a list of features for each class. The number of types of features can vary in optimization. For the further analysis frequencies are not needed. In the tested version, we cut down Model Texts so that they would produce about 1,000 features in sum. Empirically, this method showed to be the most effective.

The four lengths of feature arrays form a vector (v_1, v_2, v_3, v_4) in the 4-dimensional space, which serves as the basis for a right rectangular prism (a hyperrectangle, or a box). The volume of the box P_m (Model Box) is a model volume and can neither be superseded or be equal to 0. To avoid it, Laplace smoothing $\alpha = 1$ is applied to every vector:

$$\Theta_i = v_i + \alpha \tag{1}$$

Once the classifier parameters are found, the system proceeds to the analysis of the test set. Every text T_i in a test set is analyzed in the same way as the Model Text except *uniques*. Instead of them, a list of stems is used. Within each class, the algorithm searches for every element of the train text arrays among the elements of T_i and adds smoothing:

$$f(x_k, T_i) = \{1(true), \text{ if } x_k \in T_i, 0(false), \text{ if } x_k \notin T_i\} + \alpha \tag{2}$$

The result of evaluation is a set of vectors Θ_{li} for each text. Now we compare volumes of "boxes" made with these vectors, the volume being considered as the main definitive factor in similarity analysis:

$$V_{P_i} = \prod_{l=1}^{4} \Theta_{li} \tag{3}$$

For each text in the test set, as many box volumes are calculated as there are classes. After that within each class, the texts are sorted in the decreasing order by these volumes. The bigger the volume is, the more likely it is that the text belongs to this class. Hence, the texts at the beginnig of the list are supposedly relevant. However, we would want to establish a borderline after which we are not likely to meet relevant texts anymore.

3.3 Distribution Function

The Distribution Function states which texts are relevant for the query based on their weight distribution. Note that attribution of a text to more than one class is possible.

Let us first consider weighting a list of texts based on two model texts from the class "football fans" with the help of the Relevance Function. Figure 1 demonstrates a list of 4,030 text weights ("box volumes") sorted in the decreasing order.

It forms an exponent-like curve. The few texts in the left part of it have very high results (these are mainly texts of football communities) compared to the long "tail" on the right. The tail commences after a very steep passage between relevant and non-relevant texts. Hence, the point that separates relevant texts from irrelevant (the break point) should be somewhere at this steep part of the curve. To calculate it, we will analyze difference between weights by the slope of a characteristic line connecting each point $(x_i; y_i)$ and the X-axis at $(x_i + 1; 0)$.

To compare slopes of BC and DE, let us rearrange the diagram so that every segment starts at the point $(x_0; y_0)$ and goes to $(x_n; y_j)$. See Fig. 2, on the left.

The slope $a \in [0; +\infty]$ is calculated at the point $(x_1; y_1)$, where $y_i = a \cdot x_1 + b$. As the segment begins at 0, $b = 0$. We calculate x as an arithmetic mean of the text weights:

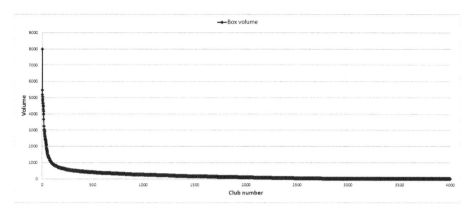

Fig. 1. Box volumes of 4,030 texts evaluated for the MaI "football".

$$x_1 = \frac{\sum V_{P_i}}{N} \tag{4}$$

So:

$$y_i = a_i \cdot x_1 \implies a_i = \frac{y_i N}{V_{P_i}} \tag{5}$$

Empirically, we found out that the best results have $a > 7.01$. Table 2 demonstrates relevant results of the mentioned calculations for the class "football fans".

3.4 Tests

To test the efficiency of our algorithm, we tried several existing implementations of supervised learning algorithms from the "Scikit-learn" package [26] with different optimization parameters: SVM, Neural Networks, Naive Bayes, Logistic Regression, Decision Trees, and k-Nearest Neighbors. The training set included two Model Texts in each of the three classes; the training set for the "Miscellaneous" class was formed with the four Model Texts, belonging to two other classes. For example, for the class of "football fans", two Model Texts go to the training set as class representatives, and the four Model Texts of historical reenactors and vegetarians form the training set for the class "Miscellaneous"[8]. The test set contained 30 texts of the studied class (e.g. football fans), 30 texts of the two other classes from the training set (e.g. historical reenactors and vegetarians) and 4,000 texts of the class "Miscellaneous" (i.e. not belonging to any of the three). The only algorithm providing a comparable result in such conditions was SVM (with the linear kernel, $C = 5$). Table 3 demonstrates it.

It is of interest that in all the three classes the F-score of our algorithm was very close in value. "Vegetarianism" appears to be the most well-balanced class by the three measures varying within the scale of 0.02. The results would

---

[8] These are conditions similar to what our algorithm requires. To extract features, it needs one or two Model Texts and a couple of non-class texts to extract *uniques*.

Table 2. Results of the distribution function in the class of football fans.

Text rating	Class	Box volume	Slope
1	Football	8000	38.92
2	Football	5460	26.56
3	Football	5187	25.23
4	Football	5054	24.59
5	Football	4921	23.94
6	Football	4921	23.94
7	Football	4800	23.35
8	Football	4680	22.77
9	Football	4662	22.68
10	Football	4662	22.68
11	Football	4536	22.07
12	Football	4446	21.63
13	Misc	4284	20.84
14	Football	4165	20.26
15	Football	4000	19.46
16	Football	3996	19.44
17	Football	3675	17.88
18	Football	3240	15.76
19	Football	3240	15.76
20	Misc	3240	15.76
21	Football	3060	14.89
22	Football	3038	14.78
23	Football	2964	14.42
24	Misc	2940	14.30
25	Misc	2890	14.06
26	Football	2805	13.65
27	Misc	2720	13.23
28	Misc	2640	12.84
29	Misc	2625	12.77
30	Misc	2592	12.61
31	Misc	2520	12.26
32	Football	2448	11.91
33	Misc	2448	11.91
34	Misc	2436	11.85
35	Misc	2400	11.68
36	Football	2380	11.58
37	Misc	2325	11.31
38	Misc	2325	11.31
39	Misc	2240	10.90
40	Misc	2176	10.59

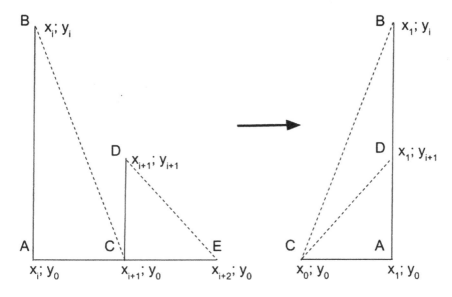

Fig. 2. The slope of the characteristic line.

Table 3. Retrieval of the three MaIs from a collection of 4,090 texts.

MaI	Measure	Own algorithm	SVM (linear)
Vegetarianism	Precision	0.73	0.62
	Recall	0.71	0.50
	F1-score	0.72	0.56
Historical reenactment	Precision	0.53	0.18
	Recall	1.00	0.30
	F1-score	0.70	0.23
Football	Precision	0.97	0.52
	Recall	0.52	0.87
	F1-score	0.67	0.65

be better if the value of the slope at the break point were optimized for every particular class. But that is the drawback of having just one Model Text without a large set of labeled data. How the break point moves in different classes and with sets of different size is yet an issue to be studied.

4   Conclusion

In the present article, we attempted to describe a new approach to classification of social network pages by interests of users. We suggested that retrieval of pages of interest should be based on one or two Model Texts rather than on a large collection. Even such a classifier as SVM that is typically used with large datasets gives a reasonably good (beyond the chance) classification result with only six texts in the training set and 4,090 texts in the test set. However, we suggested our own supervised learning algorithm that outperforms SVM in the same conditions. The algorithm can be applied in a recommender system for recommendation of pages of interest based on a page that a user already follows.

In a way, our algorithm can be viewed as a simplified and more intuitive and expertise-based version of SVM, designed for a particular task. It also separates vectors in a hyperspace but in a "fuzzy" way so that one text can be attributed to several classes. However, with the lack of a large set of labeled data for training we cannot be sure that the break point is always the same. In a real life situation, a user can be offered the whole rated list of pages starting with the top results until they stop scrolling for further pages.

As for the further research, we are planning to modify our algorithm for tasks like learning individual user interests and their specification, i.e. when a major interest can be specified into smaller ones which attract subgroups of users. For example, vegetarians call themselves "vegans", "rawatarians", "fruitarians"; football fans support one particular football team; historical reenactors deal with particular periods of time and certain cultures. Finally, we think that detecting a social group automatically when nothing is known about it yet (unsupervised learning of interests) is the most challenging task.

References

1. Agichtein, E., Brill, E., Dumais, S., Ragno, R.: Learning user interaction models for predicting web search result preferences. In: Proceedings of the 29th Annual International ACM SIGIR Conference on Research and Development in Information Retrieval, pp. 3–10. ACM (2006)
2. Ahmed, A., Low, Y., Aly, M., Josifovski, V., Smola, A.J.: Scalable distributed inference of dynamic user interests for behavioral targeting. In: KDD (2011)
3. Al-Kouz, A., Albayrak, S.: An interests discovery approach in social networks based on semantically enriched graphs. In: 2012 IEEE/ACM International Conference on Advances in Social Networks Analysis and Mining (ASONAM), pp. 1272–1277. IEEE (2012)
4. Bakalov, F., König-Ries, B., Nauerz, A., Welsch, M.: A hybrid approach to identifying user interests in web portals. In: IICS, pp. 123–134 (2009)
5. Bentley, A.F.: The Process of Government. Ripol Klassik, Moskva (1955)
6. Billsus, D., Pazzani, M.J.: A hybrid user model for news story classification. In: Kay, J. (ed.) UM99 User Modeling. CICMS, vol. 407, pp. 99–108. Springer, Vienna (1999). https://doi.org/10.1007/978-3-7091-2490-1_10
7. Blei, D.M., Ng, A.Y., Jordan, M.I.: Latent Dirichlet allocation. J. Mach. Learn. Res. **3**(January), 993–1022 (2003)
8. Bonhard, P., Sasse, M.A.: 'Knowing me, knowing you' - using profiles and social networking to improve recommender systems. BT Technol. J. **24**(3), 84–98 (2006)
9. Brown, J., Broderick, A.J., Lee, N.: Word of mouth communication within online communities: conceptualizing the online social network. J. Interact. Mark. **21**(3), 2–20 (2007)

10. Dugan, C., Muller, M., Millen, D.R., Geyer, W., Brownholtz, B., Moore, M.: The Dogear game: a social bookmark recommender system. In: Proceedings of the 2007 International ACM Conference on Supporting Group Work, pp. 387–390. ACM (2007)
11. Firan, C.S., Nejdl, W., Paiu, R.: The benefit of using tag-based profiles. In: Web Conference, LA-WEB 2007. Latin American, pp. 32–41. IEEE (2007)
12. Fire, M., Puzis, R.: Organization mining using online social networks. Netw. Spat. Econ. **16**(2), 545–578 (2016)
13. Fischer, G.: User modeling in human-computer interaction. User Model. User-Adap. Inter. **11**(1), 65–86 (2001)
14. Frolov, S.: Sociology: personality and society. The main factors of personality development (1994)
15. Gomaa, W.H., Fahmy, A.A.: A survey of text similarity approaches. Int. J. Comput. Appl. **68**(13) (2013)
16. Groh, G., Ehmig, C.: Recommendations in taste related domains: collaborative filtering vs. social filtering. In: Proceedings of the 2007 International ACM Conference on Supporting Group Work, pp. 127–136. ACM (2007)
17. Guy, I., Zwerdling, N., Carmel, D., Ronen, I., Uziel, E., Yogev, S., Ofek-Koifman, S.: Personalized recommendation of social software items based on social relations. In: Proceedings of the Third ACM Conference on Recommender Systems, pp. 53–60. ACM (2009)
18. Li, X., Guo, L., Zhao, Y.E.: Tag-based social interest discovery. In: Proceedings of the 17th International Conference on World Wide Web, pp. 675–684. ACM (2008)
19. Li, Y., Dong, M., Huang, R.: Special interest groups discovery and semantic navigation support within online discussion forums. In: IEEE International Joint Conference on Neural Networks, IJCNN 2008. (IEEE World Congress on Computational Intelligence), pp. 3904–3911. IEEE (2008)
20. McCallum, A., Corrada-Emmanuel, A., Wang, X.: Topic and role discovery in social networks. In: IJCAI, vol. 5, pp. 786–791. Citeseer (2005)
21. Merton, R.K.: Social structure and anomie. Am. Sociol. Rev. **3**(5), 672–682 (1938)
22. Mikhalkova, E., Karyakin, Y., Ganzherli, N.: A comparative analysis of social network pages by interests of their followers. arXiv preprint arXiv:1707.05481v2 (2017)
23. Newman, M.E., Girvan, M.: Finding and evaluating community structure in networks. Phys. Rev. E **69**(2), 026113 (2004)
24. Pazzani, M.J.: A framework for collaborative, content-based and demographic filtering. Artif. Intell. Rev. **13**(5–6), 393–408 (1999)
25. Pazzani, M.J., Billsus, D.: Content-based recommendation systems. In: Brusilovsky, P., Kobsa, A., Nejdl, W. (eds.) The Adaptive Web. LNCS, vol. 4321, pp. 325–341. Springer, Heidelberg (2007). https://doi.org/10.1007/978-3-540-72079-9_10
26. Pedregosa, F., Varoquaux, G., Gramfort, A., Michel, V., Thirion, B., Grisel, O., Blondel, M., Prettenhofer, P., Weiss, R., Dubourg, V., Vanderplas, J., Passos, A., Cournapeau, D., Brucher, M., Perrot, M., Duchesnay, E.: Scikit-learn: machine learning in Python. J. Mach. Learn. Res. **12**, 2825–2830 (2011)
27. Piao, G., Breslin, J.G.: Interest representation, enrichment, dynamics, and propagation: a study of the synergetic effect of different user modeling dimensions for personalized recommendations on Twitter. In: Blomqvist, E., Ciancarini, P., Poggi, F., Vitali, F. (eds.) EKAW 2016. LNCS (LNAI), vol. 10024, pp. 496–510. Springer, Cham (2016). https://doi.org/10.1007/978-3-319-49004-5_32

28. Piao, S., Whittle, J.: A feasibility study on extracting Twitter users' interests using NLP tools for serendipitous connections. In: 2011 IEEE Third International Conference on Privacy, Security, Risk and Trust (PASSAT) and 2011 IEEE Third International Conference on Social Computing (SocialCom), pp. 910–915. IEEE (2011)

29. Ramage, D., Dumais, S.T., Liebling, D.J.: Characterizing microblogs with topic models. ICWSM **10**(1), 16 (2010)

30. Reicher, S.: The determination of collective behaviour. Soc. Ident. Intergroup Relat., pp. 41–83 (1982)

31. Scott, J.: Social Network Analysis. SAGE Publications, Thousand Oaks (2017)

32. Sen, S., Vig, J., Riedl, J.: Tagommenders: connecting users to items through tags. In: Proceedings of the 18th International Conference on World Wide Web, pp. 671–680. ACM (2009)

33. Shen, W., Wang, J., Luo, P., Wang, M.: Linking named entities in tweets with knowledge base via user interest modeling. In: Proceedings of the 19th ACM SIGKDD International Conference on Knowledge Discovery and Data Mining, pp. 68–76. ACM (2013)

34. Shi, L.L., Liu, L., Wu, Y., Jiang, L., Hardy, J.: Event detection and user interest discovering in social media data streams. IEEE Access **5**, 20953–20964 (2017)

35. Stefani, A., Strapparava, C.: Exploiting NLP techniques to build user model for web sites: the use of WordNet in SiteIF project. In: Proceedings of the 2nd Workshop on Adaptive Systems and User Modeling on the WWW (1999)

36. Szomszor, M., Alani, H., Cantador, I., O'Hara, K., Shadbolt, N.: Semantic modelling of user interests based on cross-folksonomy analysis. In: Sheth, A., Staab, S., Dean, M., Paolucci, M., Maynard, D., Finin, T., Thirunarayan, K. (eds.) ISWC 2008. LNCS, vol. 5318, pp. 632–648. Springer, Heidelberg (2008). https://doi.org/10.1007/978-3-540-88564-1_40

37. Volkova, S., Coppersmith, G., Van Durme, B.: Inferring user political preferences from streaming communications. In: Proceedings of the 52nd Annual Meeting of the Association for Computational Linguistics (Long Papers), vol. 1, pp. 186–196 (2014)

38. Wang, Q., Xu, J., Li, H.: User message model: a new approach to scalable user modeling on microblog. In: Jaafar, A., Mohamad Ali, N., Mohd Noah, S.A., Smeaton, A.F., Bruza, P., Bakar, Z.A., Jamil, N., Sembok, T.M.T. (eds.) AIRS 2014. LNCS, vol. 8870, pp. 209–220. Springer, Cham (2014). https://doi.org/10.1007/978-3-319-12844-3_18

39. Xu, S., Shi, Q., Qiao, X., Zhu, L., Zhang, H., Jung, H., Lee, S., Choi, S.P.: A dynamic users' interest discovery model with distributed inference algorithm. Int. J. Distrib. Sens. Netw. **10**(4), Article ID 280892 (2014)

40. Yang, J., Leskovec, J.: Defining and evaluating network communities based on ground-truth. Knowl. Inf. Syst. **42**(1), 181–213 (2015)

Parallel Data-Driven Modeling of Information Spread in Social Networks

Oksana Severiukhina$^{(\boxtimes)}$, Klavdiya Bochenina, Sergey Kesarev,
and Alexander Boukhanovsky

ITMO University, Saint Petersburg, Russia
oseveryukhina@gmail.com, k.bochenina@gmail.com,
kesarevs@gmail.com, avb_mail@mail.ru

Abstract. Models of information spread in social networks are widely used to explore the drivers of content contagion and to predict the effect of new information messages. Most of the existing models (aggregated as SIR-like or network-based as independent cascades) use the assumption of homogeneity of an audience. However, to make a model plausible for a description of real-world processes and to measure the accumulated impact of information on individuals, one needs to personalize the characteristics of users as well as sources of information. In this paper, we propose an approach to data-driven simulation of information spread in social networks which combines a set of different models in a unified framework. It includes a model of a user (including sub-models of reaction and daily activity), a model of message generation by information source and a model of message transfer within a user network. The parameters of models (e.g. for different types of agents) are identified by data from the largest Russian social network vk.com. For this study, we collected the network of users associated with charity community (~ 33.7 million nodes). To tackle with huge size of networks, we implemented parallel version of modeling framework and tested it on the Lomonosov supercomputer. We identify key parameters of models that may be tuned to reproduce observable behavior and show that our approach allows to simulate aggregated dynamics of reactions to a series of posts as a combination of individual responses.

Keywords: Multi-agent modeling · Information spreading · Parallel computing
Social networks · Complex networks · Data-driven model

1 Introduction

At present, social networks are widely spread. This type of communication allows you to quickly disseminate information through personal messages, posts on the wall in the profile and group, etc. For example, the popular Russian social network VK has an audience of more than 97 million people every month, users send about 5 billion messages every day [1]. The structure of cyberspace like a social network can be represented by a complex network, whose nodes are entities represented as users and/or communities. The relationship between individual entities reflects the interests of a user and can be represented as permanent and temporal links of type "user-user" or "user-community".

© Springer International Publishing AG, part of Springer Nature 2018
Y. Shi et al. (Eds.): ICCS 2018, LNCS 10860, pp. 247–259, 2018.
https://doi.org/10.1007/978-3-319-93698-7_19

Existing models of information spread in networks are oriented to the reproduction and forecasting of aggregated dynamics of reactions and patterns of spread (e.g. cascade structures) and do not take into account the information-psychological influence on specific users. Nevertheless, the reaction of each user is unique and is determined by the conditions of access to information, the content of the information message, the internal state of the user, the history of his or her interaction with the source of information, and so on.

On the other hand, a completely individualized approach is impossible because of the rarity of the observed reactions (social networks contain a large amount of information about the population, but a small amount for specific users), and the impossibility to distinguish and to identify all factors that determine user reaction.

The solution in this situation can be the use of surrogate models that can be identified by data for different types of social network entities, different roles relative to the source of information, different profile parameters, different levels of involvement, etc. The combination of these models allows to provide a sufficient level of personalization and adjustment for the specific context of the social network where the process is modelled (in this study, the context is a community dedicated to charity) and to reproduce the aggregated dynamics in a proper way.

In this paper, we present a general approach to creating and combining different types of data-driven models (message generation, daily activity, response to messages, message transmission) and demonstrate their applicability by simulating reaction dynamics for a large charity community in a social network. To make our framework suitable for handling social networks of enormous size (e.g. a single video blogger may have millions of subscribers), we also provide a parallel implementation of the simulation algorithm.

The rest of the paper is organized as follows. Some background information and related works are given in Sect. 2. Section 3 presents simulation framework, description of different models and details of parallel implementation. In Sect. 4, we describe the dataset consisting information about charity community in vk.com, discuss the identification of model parameters and demonstrate the results of the simulation. Section 5 presents conclusions and a discussion of further research.

2   Related Works

Models of information spreading in cyberspace can be classified according to several distinctive features: (i) way of describing the process of information spread (network, multi-agent, parametric models), (ii) way of presenting an entity (e.g. binary opinion, states in SIR model, profile in a social network), (iii) way of presenting an information message (IM), (iv) the goal – explanatory or predictive model, (v) observables – parameters of cascade, number of reactions of different types or distribution of nodes in different states. The extensive review of the research methods and techniques on information diffusion can be found in [2].

Models of opinion dynamics are aimed to study the evolution of groups of nodes with different inner states (representing the opinion of a given topic) in a networked virtual society. For example, [3] describes the emergence of consensus and polarization as a result of evolution of opinions, [4] describes polarization of coalitions in an agent-based model of political discourse. Typically, these models use synthetic networks (Barabasi-Albert, Watts-Strogatz) to define connections between nodes. A state of a node is updated with simple rules accounting states of neighbors (e.g. majority rule [5]). Recent studies in this field investigate coevolution of opinions and network structure. The example of such approach is given in [6] where agents with a similar opinion may create community and may tend to remove connection with an agent having a significantly different opinion.

A vast amount of works is devoted to the study of the dynamics of reposts and their cascades in social networks. In [7], authors propose RepostsTree model to represent temporal dynamics of reposts in a hierarchical fashion for microblogging service Sina Weibo. Another article [8] is devoted to the Random Recursive Tree (RRT) for modeling the cascade tree topologies. Authors studied key features of a cascade tree like the average path length and degree variance in relation to a size of the tree.

Another strand of literature uses multi-agent approach where explicit rules for processing information by agents and interaction of agents are given. As an agent, different entities of cyberspace may be considered. In the first approach, messages appear to be the agents [9]. Each agent is characterized by an energy that changes during the life cycle, the energy increases in case of the repost of the message and decreases every iteration until it becomes equal to 0. In the second approach, users are selected as the agents. Authors of [10] propose Hashkat – agent-based software package for simulation of large-scale social networks. Each agent has some internal characteristics like language, region, ideology, creation time and following and follower set. The Hashkat's aim is to study the growth of social networks and information flows in them. However, it does not have a performance sufficient for real-time predictive modeling on large real-world networks. In [11], authors combine multi-agent and network-based approaches and identify internal models by real data thus implementing emerging complex agent networks approach. The authors of [12] consider a bottom-up approach for what-if analysis, where agents (micro level) define the emergent behavior in a network (macro level). They used an egocentric network and various daily activities for the reproduction of post's publications in microblogging-based Online Social Network.

Continuing the review of agent models, it is possible to single out other studies that differ in the features of the representation of agents and their characteristics. For example, some of the psychological characteristics of individuals, such as the curiosity, may improve the diffusion of information in traditional spreading models [13]. Thus, authors try to relate the characteristics of the dissemination of information to the personal properties of the agent. Sayin [14] singled out a list of the main points that must be taken into account for a realistic presentation of the information dissemination process like popularity of the source, strength of relations among users, content of the information and so on. She also highlights the presence of different internal user states like ignorant, aware or other. However, in this model there is no connection with the data of real social networks. The model presented in [15] takes into account heterogeneity of stateful agents. However, this research was conducted only on artificial networks, such as the small-world or the scale-free networks. In addition, the conductivity of links between users may differ thus influencing information spreading [16].

The idea is that users who have more common friends will be identified in the same group and have a greater weight for the dissemination of information. There are examples of studies where the characteristics of the agent are diverse, nevertheless the majority of existing algorithms use fixed probabilities of information transfer (i.e. agents are interchangeable).

From the review of the existing literature in the field, we may conclude that classical models of opinion dynamics do not use realistic network structures and properties of nodes while most of the cascade models use the assumption of homogeneity of nodes. Some studies that implement an agent approach investigate the issue of the interrelation between personal properties of an agent and characteristics of information process. However, there is clear lack of research combining: (i) a network approach with realistic heterogeneity of nodes and edges, (ii) support for different drivers and restrictions of information spread (message characteristics, internal state and user parameters, history of interaction with information sources, daily rhythm and so on) by combining models for different types of social network entities, (iii) identification of models from the data of large-scale social networks.

In this article, we propose data-driven approach for parallel modeling of information spread in social networks based on the composition of models. The model is identified using the data collected by Internet crawling; parallel version of modeling framework can handle millions of agents.

3   Method

This section contains the description of the approaches used in the study. In the first part, we describe main components of the model. The second part is dedicated to description of the parallel algorithm.

3.1   Description of Models

Proposed model of information spreading is discrete; each iteration corresponds to a daily time interval. We include in the model three main entities: IMs, communities and users. The last two are the vertices in the network. IM is a unit of information which can be transferred between vertices. The edges in the network are represented by the following links: a subscription (community – user), a friend (user – user). IM represents the post and may have such characteristics as topic, publication time, virality coefficient, number of likes, reposts, comments. Relationships between the main components of the model is presented in Fig. 1.

In the model, there are three main internal models characterizing the processes of information dissemination and defining the behavior of entities: model of IM's generation, model of activity and model of reaction. Model of IM's generation is responsible for the appearance of new messages, it determines the time of creation of messages and their content. The message generator can be either a society (external environment) or an individual user. Model of activity sets the status of each agent: e.g. active or inactive. If the result of the agent activity model is a transition to active status, an agent reads messages in a newsfeed (a set of awaiting messages from communities

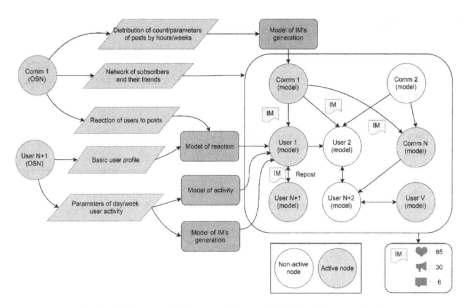

Fig. 1. Structural diagram of the model (Color figure online)

or users, provided with information on the current number of responses). This operation can be implemented based on requests from agents to communities, and it is possible to translate new information into agent pools. After that, the model of the reaction to IM determines the result of the user's interaction with the messages available: inaction, approval (like), the generation of a text message (comment), participation in the dissemination of information (repost). If the user reposts the IM, it will appear in the newsfeed of his subscribers.

Implementations of internal models can be tailored to the peculiarities of considered social network and information process to be modelled. Thus, proposed framework can be used to implement various existing models. For example, independent cascade model [17] can be represented as a combination of: (i) simplified activity model (users always have an active status), (ii) user profile with three parameters: current state (involved, not involved) and two flags (isSeedNode, isNewNode), (iii) generation model which is turned on for seed users, (iv) reaction model which uses fixed probability p of message transmission. To make a model more specific, it is possible to combine a generation model based on an impulse random process, the reaction model based on decision theory [18], an activity model based on hidden Markov models [19] and so on.

Parameters of different models from Fig. 1 are tuned according to the data collected from a social network (types of data are represented in Fig. 1 by green blocks). Public data contains a large amount of information about behavior of users and communities: basic profiles, distribution of count/parameters of posts by hours/weeks, parameters of day/week user activity. In general, the relationship of users and the community forms a network where the edges represent a friendship and subscription relationships.

3.2   Parallel Implementation

To be able to finish simulation of the information spread for large social networks (up to several millions of nodes) in a reasonable time, it is necessary to use a parallel calculation scheme. It can be of great importance for the scenarios when one is trying to predict the coverage of a given information message using preliminary tuned models and real-time data assimilation.

Algorithm 1. Parallel simulation scheme for the information spreading process (for a worker w)

Input: Gm – generative model, Am – activity model, Rm – reaction model, N – news feed in the chronological order, T – a number of iterations, M – master node for worker w

---

1: **for** t = 1,...,T:	15: **while** s<-nextSpreader(n):
2: sync_news(M)	16: **for each** e in s.edges:
3: **for each** n in N:	17: **if** dest(e) != w:
4: **while** p <- nextPotentialViewer(n):	18: add (n, e) to send_pools[dest(e)]
5: **if** !Am.isActive(p, t):	19: **else**:
6: continue	20: **if** !isViewed(n, e):
7: **if** Rm.isLike(n, p, t):	21: addPotentialViewer(n, e)
8: addLike(n, p, t)	22: deleteAllSpreaders(n)
9: **if** Rm.isRepost(n, p, t):	23:
10: addSpreader(n, p, t)	24: send_pools()
11: **if** Rm.isComment(n, p, t):	25: **for each** (n, e) in recv_pools():
12: addComment(n, p, t)	26: **if** !isViewed(n, e):
13: deletePotentialViewer(n, p)	27: addPotentialViewer(n, e)
14: addViewer(n, p)	

Algorithm 1 presents a scheme of the simulation of the information spreading process in a social network (for a single worker with index w). The simulation is discrete and operates according to models described in Sect. 3.1: generative model G_m, activity model A_m and reaction model R_m. This scheme was then implemented on a C++ language with MPI standard for message interchange.

This algorithm is an extension of the previously published Master-Slave algorithm from [20]. In this setting, Master nodes forward data between subnetworks and generate news, Slave (worker processes) store a subnetwork and perform local computations. The function dest(v) returns the index of worker hosting vertex v.

The model assumes that each information message (publication) in the social network stores three vectors that describe the state of each user with respect to this publication. More specifically, the publication stores:

- viewers – users who have already seen this publication;
- potential viewers – users who have not yet seen this publication, but have it included in their news feeds;
- spreaders – users who decided to share this publication to all their subscribers (i.e. post it on their own personal page).

For the sake of memory optimization, these data are stored as bitsets, which represent a subset of the social network hosted on the current Slave. This scheme allows to reduce the overhead associated with storing and synchronizing information about IMs.

On each iteration, Slave process receives the list of generated news from the Master node (step 2). The main cycle loops through the common news feed of this Slave, starting from the most recent news to the very first publication that was generated in the system. For each publication, each user in the list of potential viewers of this publication is examined. If the user is not active, the cycle proceeds to the next user (steps 5–6). If this user is active, the system models his interaction with the publication according to the R_m. R_m determines how the user p at the moment t reacts to the publication n (steps 7–12). Depending on the type of reaction, statistics for the publication on this Slave is updated respectively. If the user wants to repost this publication, he is added to the list of spreaders of this publication. After simulation of user reaction, the user is moved from the list of potential viewers to the list of viewers of this publication (steps 13–14). Now the system has to process the list of spreaders. The publication will be offered to each subscriber of each of the spreaders (steps 15–21). These suggestions for subscribers from other subnetworks should be sent to corresponding workers. We aggregate suggestions to be sent to other workers in a set of pools *send_pools* (steps 17–18) and send them after spreaders are processed (step 24). Subscribers from the current subnetwork are added to the list of potential viewers if they have never seen this publication before (steps 20–21). Since after this processing the publication is offered to all subscribers, the list can now be cleaned up (step 22). When all local processing is done, Slave node receives all messages from other Slaves (step 25). Users from these messages are added to the lists of the potential viewers of respective news if they have never seen these publications before (steps 26–27). After data synchronization, the clock ticks and the cycle starts over from the step 2.

4 Experimental Study

4.1 Dataset Description

The research of information dissemination processes among users of social networks was held on the example of users of vk.com. The network was formed on the basis of a public community dedicated to charity[1], its subscribers and subscribers' friends. To conduct the study, a full-size sample of the network consisting of one community, 294,345 subscribers and 33,478,369 subscriber friends was obtained via Internet

---

[1] https://vk.com/public27655043.

crawling. The network contains 80,629,758 edges, which form links between 33,768,037 nodes of the network.

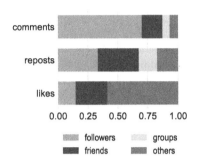

Fig. 2. Distribution of reaction to IMs

The dataset includes information about 805 IMs, including such characteristics as creation time, number of likes, reposts and comments, times of reposting and commenting and the user's id for each activity.

According to the distribution of the characteristics of IMs, depending on the types of users (Fig. 2), it can be concluded that most of the responses characterizing the distribution and discussion of messages belong to the followers and their friends.

Figure 3 shows the distribution of activity during the day for each type of weekdays and weekends. To determine the parameters of the model, data on the activity of users on public walls (reposts, comments) were used, to calculate statistics, the data of users who committed 5 or more activities during the considered interval were used.

Based on data of the user's reactions number, several groups of users with different probability of activity and distribution of users of these groups was obtained.

The collected data allow to simulate reactions on posts in the community on the subscribers' network and their friends taking into account the characteristics of the aggregated agent profile, the daily and weekly rhythm of use of online contexts by agents, and the generation of new information messages by the community.

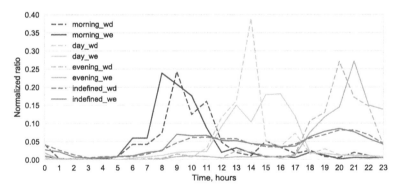

Fig. 3. Dynamics of daily activity for different groups of subscribers of the community, "wd" and "we" in legend denote weekdays and weekends, respectively

4.2 Simulation Scenario and Implementation of Internal Models

To investigate our approach, we apply our scheme to study the response of users (described in Sect. 4.1) to community's posts taking into account the characteristics of the users and the community. Below is a description of the three internal models that were used in our scheme. In Sect. 3.1, it was described that the presented scheme allows to change these models according to the considered problem.

Community behavior in the network is presented in the IM generation model and is characterized by the frequency of generation of messages on the wall, depending on the time of day and day of the week. To restore the dynamics of message generation, the distribution of the number of publications on the community wall can be used, depending on the day of the week and the time of day. Each message has a parameter of virality, which is determined by the distribution of responses to messages in the dataset. This parameter is characterized by the Gamma distribution.

The activity model determines a current context of a user within a given time frame. At each moment a user has one of the following states: active (online), inactive (offline). The state is affected by type of daily activity, weekday/weekend schedule for types of daily activity and the parameter for determining the frequency to be online. The status is determined depending on the type of daily activity of the user (morning, day, night, uncertain). An undefined type refers to users who commit activities at different intervals of the day.

To determine if the user is actively working with information from his or her newsfeed (denoted as probability p_{nf}), we use the probability of active processing of information by a given type of agent, time interval and day of week $p_{nf}(i, t, d)$ which is estimated by observed traces of activity on his or her wall. To account for the fact that: (i) a user may not use a social network each consequent day, (ii) only small part of the processed messages are shared by the user, and (iii) newsfeed of an agent contains information from several communities, we add a modifier γ. So, the resulting expression is given as:

$$p_{nf} = p_{nf}(i, t, d) \cdot \gamma, \tag{1}$$

where i is a type of agent according to Fig. 3, t is a current model time, and d is a current day.

To determine the dynamics of information spread, a reaction model is used. The reaction to the post in the community can be neglecting (no observable trace), approval (like), sharing (repost) and discussing (comment). Depending on the frequency of activity, several types of users' reaction are distinguished, which determines the likelihood of doing possible actions:

$$p_r(j) = p_r(j, u) \cdot v_{IM}, \tag{2}$$

where $p_r(j, u)$ determines the probability of reaction of j-th type for user u, depending on the type of reaction (like, repost or comment), v_{IM} – the virality of the messages. This parameter is set based on the gamma distribution of the number of responses per message, normalized, so that the average value is 1.

4.3   Simulation Results

The experiments were carried out using the resources of the supercomputer Lomonosov [21]. The modeling cycle consists of sequential iterations; the iteration duration is 10 min of model time. The program was run on 8 processes (one master and 7 slaves). The computation time of one run for modeling the activity in the network for 3 months is about 3 h.

Figure 4a shows a comparison of the number of posts for several days of the week, the MAE (mean absolute error) is 0.099. A comparison of the probability of posts is shown in Fig. 4b. MAE is 0.007. The unevenness of publications throughout the day is related to the peculiarities of a work of the administrator of considered community.

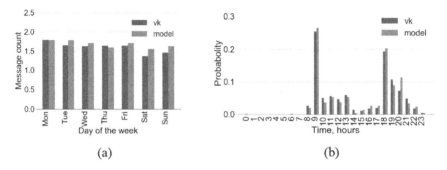

(a)   (b)

Fig. 4. Comparison of publication time and result of generative model

The dynamics of responses for several messages from the moment of publication is presented in Fig. 5. In our model, each IM has individual dynamics and the number of reactions associated with its characteristics, for example, publication time that affects the response in the first hours after publication or the virality factor that influences the opinion of users.

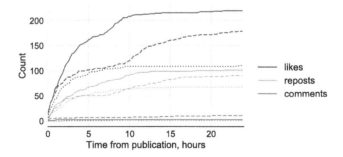

Fig. 5. Example of IMs' life during simulation, types of lines denote different IM

Figure 6 depicts the dynamics of the reaction to the messages in the first 24 h from the time of publication. In our model, there are 4 basic types of agent activity (Fig. 3)

and their distribution. Therefore, the publication time affects the response to the message. So, the number of responses at night is less than in the daytime. For example, the number of reactions to a message published in the evening is less within 5 to 10 h from the time of publication. Curve for morning reports increases faster because all users have opportunity to read the message during the day.

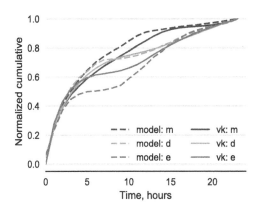

Fig. 6. Curves of repost reaction in first 24 h; m, d, e denotes morning, day and evening

The saturation time and the shape of the curves make it possible to reproduce the dynamics of the number of reposts, but no less important characteristic in the reproduction of dynamics is the finite number of reactions to information messages. In our model, there were three possible reactions to the message: like, repost and comment. Figure 7 shows the distribution of these characteristics for the real and model community. Model results are quite similar to the reaction from the real social network. Tails in a distribution based on real data are associated with the emissions that are present in the response to messages.

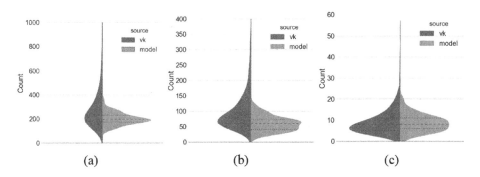

Fig. 7. Comparison of reactions to posts in the community and in the model, where the vertical axis represents the distribution of the number of reactions: (a) likes; (b) reposts; (c) comments

5 Conclusion and Future Works

In this paper, we describe the first results of parallel modeling of information spread based on the composition of models. This composition is presented by three internal models representing different drivers of information process and defining the behavior of entities: model of IM's generation, model of activity and model of reaction. Each of the models is independent and can be tailored to the simulation problem under consideration. Further, we developed the parallel version of modeling framework, which can handle millions of agents. This part of the work is necessary for sufficiently fast processing of all entities, because social networks contain millions of users with different connections and characteristics.

Parameters of models are trained using the data collected from a Russian social network vk.com, which allows us to validate the proposed model. We compare several aggregated characteristics provided by model with the real data: number of IMs' publications depending on the time of day and day of the week, the dynamics of response to a single message and accumulated reactions of subscribers to a series of IMs. The "violin plot" graphs demonstrate that the model allows to reproduce the aggregated response to messages reliably. Thus, modeling the behavior of individual users on the network, we were able to reproduce the reaction of the whole community to IMs (like a bottom-up approach from micro to macro level).

Future work includes automatic training of parameters of the models using meta-algorithm and investigation of importance of different drivers of information spread within proposed framework. A separate line of research will be devoted to modeling the longitudinal evolution of user states in terms of their level of involvement in interaction with the community. In addition, the important task is to improve the scalability of the framework, which will reduce the computation time for a large number of model entities.

This research was supported by The Russian Scientific Foundation, Agreement #14–21–00137–П (02.05.2017).

References

1. VK. https://vk.com/page-47200925_44240810
2. Li, M., Wang, X., Gao, K., Zhang, S.: A survey on information diffusion in online social networks: models and methods. Information **8**, 118 (2017). https://doi.org/10.3390/info8040118
3. Hegselmann, R., Krause, U.: Opinion dynamics and bounded confidence: models, analysis and simulation. J. Artif. Soc. Soc. Simul. (JASSS) **5**(3), (2002)
4. Leifeld, P.: Polarization of coalitions in an agent-based model of political discourse. Leifeld Comput. Soc. Netw. **1**, 1–22 (2014)
5. Lambiotte, R., Ausloos, M., Hołyst, J.A.: Majority model on a network with communities. Phys. Rev. E **75**, 30101 (2007). https://doi.org/10.1103/PhysRevE.75.030101
6. Yu, Y., Xiao, G., Li, G., Tay, W.P., Teoh, H.F.: Opinion diversity and community formation in adaptive networks. Chaos: Interdisc. J. Nonlinear Sci. **27**, 103115 (2017). https://doi.org/10.1063/1.4989668

7. Lu, X., Yu, Z., Guo, B., Zhou, X.: Modeling and predicting the re-post behavior in Sina Weibo. In: Proceedings - 2013 IEEE International Conference on Green Computing and Communications and IEEE Internet of Things and IEEE Cyber, Physical and Social Computing, GreenCom-iThings-CPSCom 2013, pp. 962–969 (2013)
8. Liu, L., Qu, B., Chen, B., Hanjalic, A., Wang, H.: Modeling of information diffusion on social networks with applications to WeChat, 1–17 (2017). https://doi.org/10.1016/j.physa.2017.12.026
9. Lande, D.V, Hraivoronska, A.M., Berezin, B.O.: Agent-based model of information spread in social networks, 7 p. (2016)
10. Ryczko, K., Domurad, A., Buhagiar, N., Tamblyn, I.: Hashkat: large-scale simulations of online social networks. Soc. Netw. Anal. Min. **7**, 4 (2017). https://doi.org/10.1007/s13278-017-0424-7
11. Mei, S., Zarrabi, N., Lees, M., Sloot, P.M.A.: Complex agent networks: an emerging approach for modeling complex systems. Appl. Soft Comput. J. **37**, 311–321 (2015). https://doi.org/10.1016/j.asoc.2015.08.010
12. Gatti, M., Cavalin, P., Neto, S.B., Pinhanez, C., dos Santos, C., Gribel, D., Appel, A.P.: Large-scale multi-agent-based modeling and simulation of microblogging-based online social network. In: Alam, S.J., Van Dyke Parunak, H. (eds.) MABS 2013. LNCS (LNAI), vol. 8235, pp. 17–33. Springer, Heidelberg (2014). https://doi.org/10.1007/978-3-642-54783-6_2
13. Vega-Oliveros, D.A., Berton, L., Vazquez, F., Rodrigues, F.A.: The impact of social curiosity on information spreading on networks (2017). https://doi.org/10.1145/3110025.3110039
14. Sayin, B., Şahin, S.: A novel approach to information spreading models for social networks. In: Sixth International Conference on Data Analytics III, DATA Analytics 2017 (2017)
15. Zhu, Z.Q., Liu, C.J., Wu, J.L., Xu, J., Liu, B.: The influence of human heterogeneity to information spreading. J. Stat. Phys. **154**, 1569–1577 (2014). https://doi.org/10.1007/s10955-014-0924-z
16. Ou, C., Jin, X., Wang, Y., Cheng, X.: Modelling heterogeneous information spreading abilities of social network ties. Simul. Model. Pract. Theory **75**, 67–76 (2017). https://doi.org/10.1016/j.simpat.2017.03.007
17. Shakarian, P., Bhatnagar, A., Aleali, A., Shaabani, E., Guo, R.: The independent cascade and linear threshold models. Diffusion in Social Networks. SCS, pp. 35–48. Springer, Cham (2015). https://doi.org/10.1007/978-3-319-23105-1_4
18. van Maanen, P.P., van der Vecht, B.: An agent-based approach to modeling online social influence. In: Proceedings of the 2013 IEEE/ACM International Conference on Advances in Social Networks Analysis and Mining (2013). https://doi.org/10.1145/2492517.2492564
19. Raghavan, V., Ver Steeg, G., Galstyan, A., Tartakovsky, A.G.: Coupled hidden markov models for user activity in social networks. In: 2013 IEEE International Conference on Multimedia Expo Work (ICMEW), pp. 1–6 (2013). https://doi.org/10.1109/icmew.2013.6618397
20. Bochenina, K., Kesarev, S., Boukhanovsky, A.: Scalable parallel simulation of dynamical processes on large stochastic Kronecker graphs. Future Gener. Comput. Syst. **78**, 502–515 (2017). https://doi.org/10.1016/j.future.2017.07.021
21. Sadovnichy, V., Tikhonravov, A., Voevodin, V., Opanasenko, V.: "Lomonosov": supercomputing at Moscow State University. In: Contemporary High Performance Computing: From Petascale Toward Exascale (Chapman & Hall/CRC Computational Science). CRC Press, Boca Raton, pp. 283–307 (2013)

Topology of Thematic Communities in Online Social Networks: A Comparative Study

Valentina Guleva$^{(\boxtimes)}$, Danila Vaganov, Daniil Voloshin, and Klavdia Bochenina

ITMO University, Saint Petersburg, Russia
{guleva,vaganov}@corp.ifmo.ru, achoched@gmail.com, k.bochenina@gmail.com

Abstract. The network structure of communities in social media significantly affects diffusion processes which implement positive or negative information influence on social media users. Some of the thematic communities in online social networks may provide illegal services or information in them may cause undesired psychological effects; moreover, the topology of such communities and behavior of their members are influenced by a thematic. Nevertheless, recent research does not contain enough detail about the particularities of thematic communities formation, or about the topological properties of underlying friendship networks. To address this gap, in this study we analyze structure of communities of different types, namely, carders, commercial sex workers, substance sellers and users, people with radical political views, and compare them to the 'normal' communities (without a single narrow focus). We discovered that in contrast to ordinary communities which have positive assortativity (as expected for social networks), specific thematical communities are significantly disassortative. Types of anomalous communities also differ not only in content but in structure. The most specific are the communities of radicalized individuals: it was shown that they have the highest connectivity and the larger part of nodes within a friendship graph.

Keywords: Network topology · Data analysis · Online social media
Normal communities · Anomalous communities
Subscribers friendship networks

1 Introduction and Motivation

Online social media play an important role in our daily life, providing official news, presenting a ground for sharing our activities and opinions, and helping in the realization of our personal interests. In this way, one can easily see an enormous informational impact provided by the combination of news sources on each individual, and the contribution of each individual to this flow propagation and its correction, in turn. Consequently, friendship networks reflect the most probable paths of information transmission and their topological properties allows for the estimation of information diffusion effectiveness.

© Springer International Publishing AG, part of Springer Nature 2018
Y. Shi et al. (Eds.): ICCS 2018, LNCS 10860, pp. 260–273, 2018.
https://doi.org/10.1007/978-3-319-93698-7_20

Nevertheless, some kinds of informational influence may be undesired or even disruptive providing messages of illegal content, propaganda, or cyberbullying. Since undesired content is often provided by corresponding communities, the problem of their detection is of great interest.

The existing methods of anomaly detection in online social networks do not discover the laws of network formation process, the reasons of the emergence of differences between types of social communities, and topological properties common to them. The study presented contributes to this gap by presenting the analysis of topological differences in various types of communities and thus forms the basis for novel methods of identifying anomalous communities.

A structure of online social networks (OSNs) reflects real-world interactions, on the one hand, and on the other, facilitates the emergence of new virtual links. Formation of a structure is also influenced by the interface and the functionality of particular OSN. The third factor affecting the topology of friendship networks is a thematic of the community as it may cause specific behavioral and friending patterns of the individuals. Depending on these factors, resulting network topologies can vary. For example, Hu and Wang [1] show that assortativity coefficient can be positive or negative depending on the online social network. They show MySpace, Flickr and LiveJournal have positive assortativity, while YouTube, Gnunella, and pussokram have the negative one. At the same time, real social networks were shown to have positive assortativity coefficient.

In this way, one can see social media crucially affects the formation of observed patterns. Twitter and Youtube restrict subscribers in the spectrum of possible interactions via limited functionality, and, consequently, an underlying network does not reflect real-world patterns well. Nevertheless, all of the online social media allows for discovering information flows and studying their informational effects. The most interpretable and comprehensive opportunities are presented by general-purpose online social networks, like Facebook and the largest Russian social network vk.com (VK), which support multilayer interactions between entities of different types.

Due to the prevalence of online social networks and the relative simplicity of OSN data collection via open APIs, nowadays they are widely studied by researchers from different fields. One of them is the analysis and detection of illegal activity, like terrorist communities and dark nets [2,3]. At the same time, there are techniques for identification of statistical anomalies, which do not correspond to any certain topic and are presented as outliers in the general distribution of a set of systemic characteristic [4]. Online anomalous behavior can be also distinguished between temporal anomalies, local topological outliers, overall outliers or outliers in communities [5]. The vast majority of existing anomaly detection methods are aimed at discovering the suspicious activities of special types mainly based on probabilistic and linguistic methods (especially for anomalies, related to some special topics), or topological differences. Thus, actual structures and formation mechanisms of anomalous communities remain poorly studied.

This paper contributes to the topological analysis of user communities in online social media. We consider a friendship graph of community subscribers, which (in some sense) represents the 'backbone' of a given community and determines the aggregated characteristics of information spread. To justify the differences between normal and anomalous communities, and between anomalous communities of different types, we perform the analysis for a wide range of VK communities, from hundreds to several dozens of thousands of subscribers, and compare average characteristics for varying number of users.

The rest of the paper includes a review of literature related to influence maximization and anomaly detection in online social media (see Sect. 2), the description of data used for analysis (Sect. 3), the results of a comparative study (Sect. 4), discussion and conclusion (Sect. 5).

2   Related Studies

One of the goals of abnormal communities may be an intensive informational-psychological influence on their users. In this way, the important role belongs to the influence maximization and to the formation of propagation-efficient network structures. A local topology of super-spreaders is thought to be related to degree properties, sums of neighboring node degrees, or is conditional on belonging to k-core [6]. In particular, Quax et al. [7] questions an influence of high-degree nodes, which is based on information theory approach along with Markov random fields. Pei et al. [8] note the degree distribution and PageRank do not characterize information spread enough, and these are k-core and sums of neighbors degrees to play an important role. Elsharkawy et al. [6] provide a dynamic simulation of information spreading with the evolution of a k-core, and suggest to consider k-core descendants to estimate a potential effect. They also show an influence of the relation between k-core and cascade size. In addition, a message content affects its contagiosity [9].[1]

Existing methods for detecting the suspicious communities do not discover the principles of network organization or the particularities of the patterns observed. The vast majority of them use machine learning techniques without identifying the factors playing a predominant role. Ratkiewicz et al. present a classification method for political astroturfing detection based on topological features, nevertheless, they do not disclose topological particularities of political communities aimed at informational influence [10]. Varol et al. [11] also build a classifier, based on network and diffusion features, user-based, timing, sentiment, content and language features (total of 487 features). Since they are correlated, authors also accompany the classification process with feature selection procedure.

The description of abnormal communities is met in Bindu research [12] suggesting spammer communities discovering algorithm. Firstly, they suppose spammers to have high local clustering coefficient with other spammers. Then, they

---

[1] Authors of [9] provide a classification method for rumor detection. In our case, this corresponds to relations between subscribers interests and message content.

present an algorithm of spammer clusters detection, showing the clusters discovered have high clustering coefficient (0.15 for the network of 4000 nodes) and diameter of 9. Nevertheless, spammer communities are out of interest in current research since their behavior seems to be artificial and aimed at information spreading.

3   Data

Friendship graphs for different types of communities were analyzed. We have chosen certain thematical communities in social media vk.com (VK), collected their subscribers and then built a friendship graph for the subscribers (Fig. 1). Two types of networks were considered: (i) a network of a single community, (ii) a network joining all subscribers for a single category (type) of communities (e.g., a network of all carders).

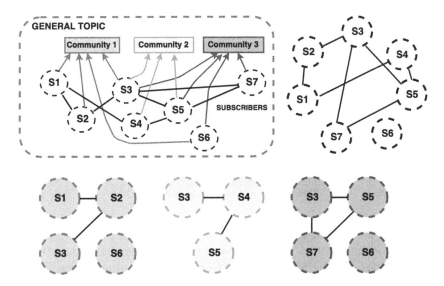

Fig. 1. Subscribers network in social media and resulting friendship networks, based on individual communities and general groups of communities

A set of normal communities ("Work in Saint-Petersburg", "Movie", "Humor", "Ideas for Handicraft and Gifts", etc.) contained about 630 units with maximum subscribers count of 62,949. Also, 630 anomalous communities were collected with maximal subscribers count of 176,527. The anomalous communities contained five following themes, which were marked manually during the stage of data collection: carders — 48 communities, substance users — 9 communities, substance sellers — 75 communities, people with radical political views — 43 communities, commercial sex workers — 210 communities.

4   Results

4.1   Network Topology of Normal and Anomalous Communities

After data collection, we divide whole range of subscribers count into bins (Table 1). As different bins contain the different number of normal and anomalous communities, for the analysis presented further we sampled the equal number of each community type from each bin (maximum possible, e.g. 66 for the third bin) to compare average characteristics for a bin. Sampling procedure for each bin was repeated 100 times to get more consistent results.

Table 1. Distribution of a number of normal and anomalous communities by the number of subscribers

Subscribers count	#Normal	#Anomalous
(0, 1000]	227	368
(1000, 2500]	118	91
(2500, 5000]	83	66
(5000, 10000]	84	52
(10000, 15000]	64	26
(15000, 20000]	24	9
(20000, 30000]	18	8
(30000, 40000]	7	3
(40000, 50000]	2	1
(50000, 60000]	1	1
(60000, 200000]	1	4

The analysis of different bins shows that density tends to decrease with increase in community size. Figure 2 demonstrates that small communities density is ten times greater than the density of the rest of communities. The reason of that may be that the formation of small communities is based on the existing networks of real or virtual friends; also, small communities present an opportunity of more intensive interactions between the participants due to their restricted number. Density in normal communities of medium and large is quite higher than in the anomalous communities and does not change significantly.

The comparison of other topological characteristics also shows significant differences (Fig. 2). Anomalous communities have a lower number of links between their participants, which demonstrates a dive with the increase in community size. Clustering coefficient and average degree are also much greater in normal communities. These differences may be related to the fact that the audience of anomalous communities is often composed of strangers with specific interests while normal communities tend to unite people who are familiar with each other. In other words, people in anomalous communities often become friends

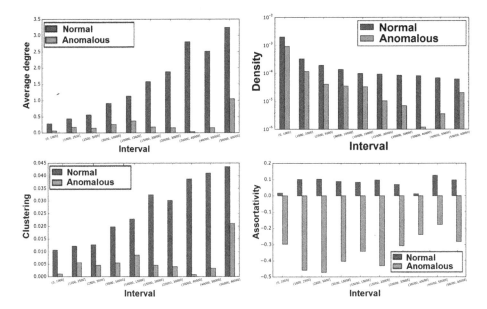

Fig. 2. Comparison of average topological properties for normal and anomalous communities

because of their shared membership while networks of normal communities are mostly formed by previously existing friendship links. The clear illustration of the difference in the mechanism of topology formation is represented in the plot with degree assortativity coefficients. This plot shows that normal communities are characterized by positive assortativity (as expected for ordinary OSN). In contrast, anomalous communities indicate strong disassortativity. This means that the subscribers with high degree (hubs) are more likely to be connected with low-degree subscribers.

Summarizing, one can see that normal and anomalous communities have drastically different topology. Figure 3 demonstrates the slow transition from high to low node degrees in normal communities, which corresponds to positive assortativity coefficient. This is associated with the necessity of communication prevailing in normal societies. For this case, the community is the space for sharing common interests, and this type of structure exists without special organization, without presenting any special services; therefore activities are mostly provided from bottom to top. The main intention of subscribers, in this case, is to communicate with other similar users. In contrast, anomalous communities often present some special services or content, which determines a specific structure of a network and roles of nodes. The existence of roles, which are impossible for being acted by an arbitrary subscriber, provides a strong distinction between participants, resulting in disassortativity.

Current analysis demonstrates a clear distinction between normal and anomalous communities, which is mostly explained by the degree assortativity

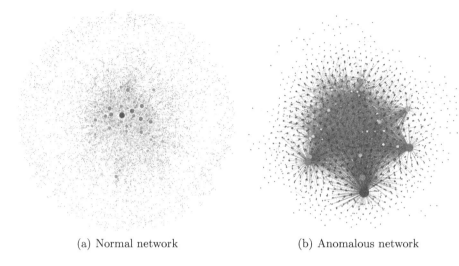

(a) Normal network   (b) Anomalous network

Fig. 3. Normal and anomalous networks

characteristic. These observed patterns allow for wondering how the goals of networks functionality are reflected in observed topological patterns. For this reason, the rest of the section is aimed at comparison of different types of anomalous communities.

4.2 Anomalous Communities of Different Types

Since abnormal communities are aimed at providing different services, we suppose them to be formed by different mechanisms, and, consequently, their structural properties probably demonstrate systematic dependencies on the themes. To check this hypothesis we compare anomalous communities of different types. They are carders, in the context of credit card fraud, people with radical political views, commercial sex workers, substance users, and substance sellers. Figure 4 visualizes corresponding joint networks (connecting the users of all communities from a category) and demonstrates the following particularities:

- Carders friendship networks (Fig. 4(a)) are extremely connected, with visually higher density than in communities of other types. One can see two strongly connected modules, corresponding to the union of high-degree nodes and to the union with lower degree nodes. In this way, a k-core, where all hubs (providing informational influence) are located, can be distinguished. Assortativity patterns are visualized similar to the anomalous community in Fig. 3(b).
- Radicalized users demonstrate strong connections between different communities of this type. The majority of the hubs are concentrated inside the k-core, nevertheless, there are hubs attracting low-degree nodes to the periphery. A network contains many hubs connecting isolated nodes of degree 1, which results in the negative assortativity.

- Commercial sex workers communities demonstrate more isolated structure (Fig. 4(c)). There are many connected components and many separable modules inside the largest connected component. Hubs do not have so many neighbors as in communities of other types, which is reflected by the size and color intensity of green nodes. Modules in the largest connected component are not so interconnected as in radical users communities.
- Substance users network (Fig. 4(d)) demonstrates quite high density and connectivity, and bigger hubs than in commercial sex networks. Number of hubs is much less than that in carder and political networks, and they are not concentrated in a core. On the opposite, the network looks more homogeneous. Nevertheless, there are segments weakly connected to giant component and containing own hubs. These modules correspond to separate communities. In this way, one can conclude, that substance users, as well as commercial sex workers, do not demonstrate strong interconnections between communities.
- Substance sellers network is similar to substance users one, for this reason, we do not present them both in Fig. 4.

To disclose differences more accurately, the communities have been separated into several bins similarly with Sect. 4.1. After that, we obtained the distribution demonstrating which sizes of communities are prevailing in different thematic groups (Fig. 5). In this way, one can see commercial sex workers group is described by the most representative data, and the community size of [0; 1000] is the most frequent. On the other hand, several community themes tend to be more concentrated in other bins. For example, considered radical politician communities are more common for [1000; 5000] subscribers; at the same time, for the range [10,000; 25,000] substance users are more prevalent.

It should be emphasized, that patterns in community size distribution demonstrated above are not correlated with other topological patterns described below, that means, further results are not reasoned by the imperfection of data used for analysis.

Topological analysis of all groups demonstrates quick dive in density with increase in community size, which is accompanied by a gradual increase in the average shortest path and gradual decrease in assortativity coefficient. One can notice, all types of communities demonstrate similar dynamics reflected by density, average path, and assortativity coefficients since the dynamics is mainly caused by general dependencies between network properties and its size. Clustering coefficient presents no strong dependencies between an increase in community size and network characterization.

Figure 6 shows that community of users with radical political views has four times higher clustering than others communities of more than 10,000 nodes. Their superiority is observed also for communities of 1,000–5,000 nodes. For other community sizes, substance sellers and users have the leadership. The smallest clustering is exhibited by commercial sex workers and carders, which can be due to the undesirability of identity broadcasting.

Density tends to decrease with the increase of community size for all types of abnormal communities. Commercial sex worker communities demonstrate values

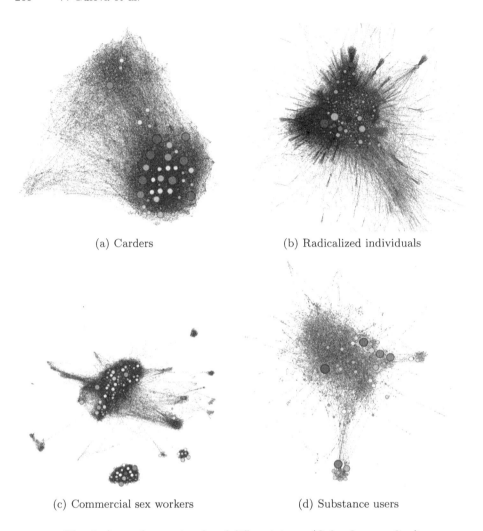

(a) Carders   (b) Radicalized individuals

(c) Commercial sex workers   (d) Substance users

Fig. 4. Anomalous networks of different types (Color figure online)

superiority for communities of 2,500–25,000 subscribers. Their density is several times greater. At the same time, smaller communities do not follow the same pattern. Shortest path naturally increases with the size of societies.

The example of small carders community of 500 nodes (Fig. 7) demonstrates the particularities of its organization, which are potentially inefficient for information spreading, but can be quite enough for reaching their local goals.

The vast majority of hubs' friends are of degree 1. Several friends are connected with other hubs. In this way, disassortative mixing arises, since hubs are not connected directly, but they are connected via nodes with lowest degrees. The network contains several connected components. Components without hubs also have the nodes with maximal degrees connected via nodes with minimal

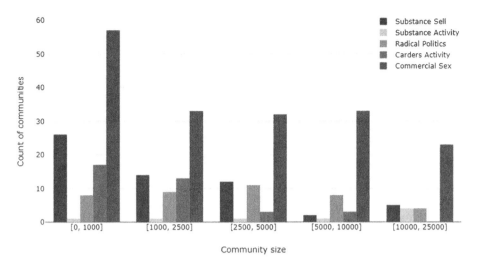

Fig. 5. The distribution of community sizes for different themes

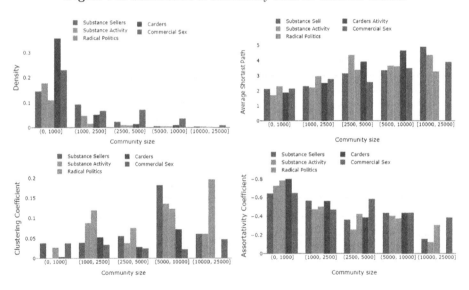

Fig. 6. Comparison of average topological properties for anomalous communities

degrees. This results in low clustering coefficient and high density as was presented in Fig. 6.

A plot with degree distribution (Fig. 8) demonstrates all types of communities, normal and anomalous, follow a power law with different exponents. Heavy tails demonstrate different behavior due to networks size as well due to their organization. Users with radical political views have higher degrees and more

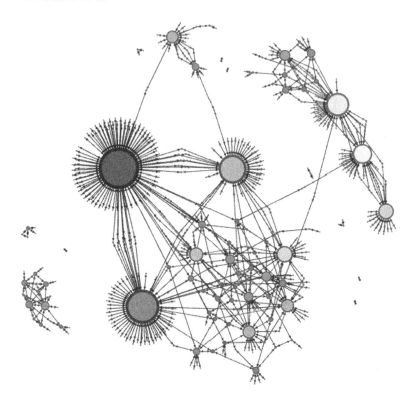

Fig. 7. Carder community of 500 nodes

heavy-tailed distribution, which differs with power-law exponent from other types of communities. Normal communities show shorter tails.

The main difference in the degree distributions is in their left part. Here we see straight lines for anomalous communities and rounded line for normal one. That means that normal communities have usually fewer nodes of degree 1, while they have more nodes with degrees 3–10. The relatively small number of users with a medium number of friends within the community and the predominance of hubs and nodes with a single link thus may be considered as distinctive features of anomalous thematic communities.

To liquidate the effect of network size we also analyzed a distribution of the proportion of connected nodes to all subscribers (Fig. 9). Firstly, we consider a part of nodes in a friendship network for different size categories. People with radical views are the most "friendly" since the majority of subscribers are in a friendship network. Nevertheless, as it was shown in the previous section, this is due to hubs activity and their interaction with low-degree nodes. Substance users, carders, and commercial sex workers demonstrate less share of nodes in a friendship network. Secondly, we analyzed a cumulative distribution with probability of an arbitrary size network to have a certain part of nodes within a friendship network. One can see the similarity of all community types and sharp

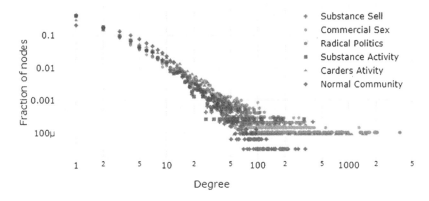

Fig. 8. Degree distribution for biggest connected component

difference of political community. Figure 9(b) reflects the fact that users with radical political views have the significant share of nodes in a friendship graph of the thematic community more probably.

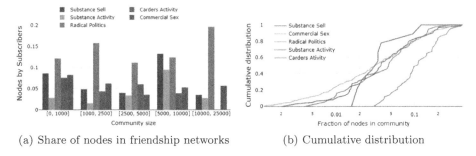

(a) Share of nodes in friendship networks   (b) Cumulative distribution

Fig. 9. Relation between the communities size and the corresponding friendship networks

Summarizing, the analysis of different types of anomalous communities shows the significant difference of political communities since they have more friends in the subscribers' network, which is associated with lower assortativity coefficient, higher clustering, and strong interconnections between different communities inside the type.

5 Conclusion

Structure of social networks reflects particularities of agents interactions and allows for detection of the "goals" of a system functionality. In particular, it reflects systemic activity and "openness" of considered communities. In this study, we analyzed an extensive dataset from a largest Russian social network vk.com consisting of ordinary communities (having publicly acceptable thematic) and abnormal (anomalous) communities of different types.

The comparison showed that normal communities demonstrate positive assortativity coefficient, while negative assortativity is pertinent to abnormal communities. Analysis of different anomalous communities showed the division based on the involvement of subscribers to friendship networks. All considered groups were concentrated around the similar cumulative functions, while users with radical political views showed the highest percentage of users involved in the friendship network. At the same time, political communities demonstrated highest clustering values for groups of 1,000–5,000 and 10,000–25,000. The densest communities were demonstrated by carders (less than 1,000 subscribers) and commercial sex workers (more than 5,000 subscribers). However, for commercial sex workers communities, it was shown that subscribers are not involved in active interaction inside them.

A hypothesis explaining this behavior supposes that groups, providing a kind of services inside social networks, do not require any special broadcast and/or organization. At the same time, radicalized users are aimed at dissemination of their ideas, which implies more publicity. Consequently, their structure is more connected and clustered, and contain more subscribers and users in a friendship network, which should provide a sufficient opportunity for information propagation.

In this study, we showed that the thematic significantly influences the structure. It is even able to emerge opposite patterns of topology formation, as it was demonstrated by degree assortativity. The most interesting part here is that the resulting topology reflects the predominant "use cases" of community and roles of its subscribers within a given context. Uncovering of such hidden roles (as political opinion leaders and their devotees) is a next planned step of our research as well as studying the interplay between user similarity, their context-dependent roles, and characteristics of information spread.

Acknowledgements. This research was financially supported by Ministry of Education and Science of the Russian Federation, Agreement #14.578.21.0196 (03.10.2016). Unique Identification RFMEFI57816X0196.

References

1. Hu, H.B., Wang, X.F.: Disassortative mixing in online social networks. EPL (Europhys. Lett.) **86**(1) (2009). Article no. 18003
2. Rowe, M., Saif, H.: Mining pro-ISIS radicalisation signals from social media users. In: ICWSM, pp. 329–338 (2016)
3. Lau, R.Y., Xia, Y., Ye, Y.: A probabilistic generative model for mining cybercriminal networks from online social media. IEEE Comput. Intell. Mag. **9**(1), 31–43 (2014)
4. Akoglu, L., Tong, H., Koutra, D.: Graph based anomaly detection and description: a survey. Data Min. Knowl. Discov. **29**(3), 626–688 (2015)

5. Savage, D., Zhang, X., Yu, X., Chou, P., Wang, Q.: Anomaly detection in online social networks. Soc. Netw. **39**, 62–70 (2014)
6. Elsharkawy, S., Hassan, G., Nabhan, T., Roushdy, M.: Effectiveness of the k- core nodes as seeds for influence maximisation in dynamic cascades. Int. J. Comput. **2** (2017)
7. Quax, R., Apolloni, A., Sloot, P.M.: The diminishing role of hubs in dynamical processes on complex networks. J. R. Soc. Interface **10**(88) (2013). Article no. 20130568
8. Pei, S., Muchnik, L., Andrade Jr., J.S., Zheng, Z., Makse, H.A.: Searching for super-spreaders of information in real-world social media. Sci. Rep. **4**, (2014). Article no. 5547
9. Liu, Y., Jin, X., Shen, H., Cheng, X.: Do rumors diffuse differently from non-rumors? A systematically empirical analysis in sina weibo for rumor identification. In: Kim, J., Shim, K., Cao, L., Lee, J.-G., Lin, X., Moon, Y.-S. (eds.) PAKDD 2017. LNCS (LNAI), vol. 10234, pp. 407–420. Springer, Cham (2017). https://doi.org/10.1007/978-3-319-57454-7_32
10. Ratkiewicz, J., Conover, M., Meiss, M.R., Gonçalves, B., Flammini, A., Menczer, F.: Detecting and tracking political abuse in social media. ICWSM **11**, 297–304 (2011)
11. Varol, O., Ferrara, E., Menczer, F., Flammini, A.: Early detection of promoted campaigns on social media. EPJ Data Sci. **6**(1), 13 (2017)
12. Bindu, P., Mishra, R., Thilagam, P.S.: Discovering spammer communities in twitter. J. Intell. Inf. Syst. 1–25 (2018)

Topological Street-Network Characterization Through Feature-Vector and Cluster Analysis

Gabriel Spadon$^{(\boxtimes)}$[iD], Gabriel Gimenes, and Jose F. Rodrigues Jr.[iD]

University of Sao Paulo, Sao Carlos, SP, Brazil
spadon@usp.br, {ggimenes,junio}@icmc.usp.br

Abstract. Complex networks provide a means to describe cities through their street mesh, expressing characteristics that refer to the structure and organization of an urban zone. Although other studies have used complex networks to model street meshes, we observed a lack of methods to characterize the relationship between cities by using their topological features. Accordingly, this paper aims to describe interactions between cities by using vectors of topological features extracted from their street meshes represented as complex networks. The methodology of this study is based on the use of digital maps. Over the computational representation of such maps, we extract global complex-network features that embody the characteristics of the cities. These vectors allow for the use of multidimensional projection and clustering techniques, enabling a similarity-based comparison of the street meshes. We experiment with 645 cities from the Brazilian state of Sao Paulo. Our results show how the joint of global features describes urban indicators that are deep-rooted in the network's topology and how they reveal characteristics and similarities among sets of cities that are separated from each other.

Keywords: Network topology · Feature vector · Cluster analysis

1 Introduction and Related Works

Complex networks are used to shape real-world systems, *e.g.* networks of protein interaction, street meshes, and subway lines. These networks, as mathematical models, stand out due to their algebraic properties and computing potential, with analytical applicability to support cognitive processes of decision-making [1]. Through metrics and methods based on topology and/or geometry, it is possible to identify characteristics of interest that are not obvious for human inspections based on reading; this is because the networks may be wide (high number of vertices), intricate (high number of edges), or may hold non-trivial patterns and attributes whose observation depends on the application of algorithms.

In the specific case of the representation of street networks, complex networks describe factors related to the displacement of individuals, allocation of services,

© Springer International Publishing AG, part of Springer Nature 2018
Y. Shi et al. (Eds.): ICCS 2018, LNCS 10860, pp. 274–287, 2018.
https://doi.org/10.1007/978-3-319-93698-7_21

the improvement of tasks related to transport, and even to the study of factors from collective behavior, when the network is weighted by the associated data. In this regard, we observed a lack of methods to characterize groups of cities by means of the features that can be extracted from their topology, which is the aim of this research. This methodology has potential to enhance the understanding of an urban space and to explain the reason why cities share properties of interest.

To this end, we developed a methodology composed of *Data Acquisition and Preparation, Feature Extraction and Selection*, and *Feature Vector Analysis*. We analyzed 645 cities from the state of Sao Paulo, aiming to provide comprehension of peculiarities from different cities by interpreting global network-characteristics. These cities are representations of street meshes that were extracted from digital maps, such that they were gathered and analyzed by using machine-learning methods of feature extraction, multidimensional projection, and cluster analysis. In order to demonstrate our methodology, we investigate the following hypotheses: (**A**) *the network topology is a tool-set that can reveal groups of cities with similar characteristics, potentially revealing disparities*; (**B**) *although cities may share administrative boundaries with others, they cluster with cities with no apparent geographical similarity*; and, (**C**) *there might be interesting correlations between urban and/or territorial indicators and the features extracted from the street-network topology of a given set of cities*. The answering of such assumptions allows us to render better analysis of urban agglomerations by helping in the understanding of cities by comprehending how they are arranged within the geographical extent of their territorial boundaries.

Aiming to solve questions related to the urban scenario, a vast number of studies have been conducted to explain cities considering their intense flow of vehicles [2] and collective behaviors [3], while others analyzed the accidents density in street networks [4] and the discrepancies between cities driven by their urban indicators [5]. Furthermore, some authors investigated metrical and analytical methods applied to cities [6,7], others approached the assistance to the urban planning and design [8–10], and there are those who advanced with facility-location analysis and planning in street meshes [11]. However, although cluster analysis has been less focused [12,13], it is still an important toolset [14].

Two state-of-the-art works used clustering techniques to analyze groups of cities, but both of them left open questions to be explored. The first one had the intention to measure the similarity among ten European cities [12], while the second one performed an eye-based cluster evaluation considering the proximity and overlap of 1,150 cities, mainly from the Anglo-Saxon America [13]. Their lack of proficiency is mainly because they do not employ clustering algorithms in the same fashion that we do, including validation metrics and analytical indicators.

In this paper, we contribute with a methodology that advances the analysis of cities modeled as complex networks. To present our contributions, this paper is organized as follows: Sect. 2 displays our methodology while explaining the validation of its results; Sect. 3 discusses the results about the applicability of the proposed methods; and, Sect. 4 presents the conclusions and final remarks.

2   Methodology

Our methodology is based on the intersection of methods of data **A**cquisition, **M**odeling, and **C**omputation, and it follows a process flow depicted in Fig. 1.

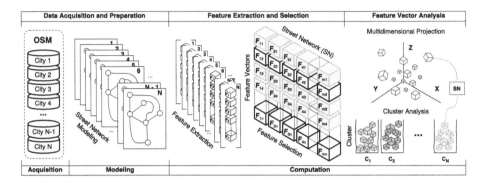

Fig. 1. Methodology for street-network characterization through feature-vector and cluster analysis based on data **A**cquisition, **M**odeling, and **C**omputation. The methodology starts by acquiring digital maps of cities from the OpenStreetMap (OSM), such maps are used for the modeling of complex networks. The resulting networks are used in the processes of extraction and selection of topological-features. These features are analyzed according to data-mining methods of multidimensional projection and cluster detection.

2.1   Preliminaries

Hereinafter, we represent complex networks as distance-weighted directed graphs. Notice that, despite different, complex networks and graphs are considered to be equivalent. A graph $\mathbf{G} = \{V, E\}$ is composed of a set of $|V|$ nodes and a set of $|E|$ edges. Furthermore, each edge $e \in E$ is known to be an ordered pair $\langle o, d \rangle$, in which $o \in V$ is named *origin* and $d \in V$ is named *destination*, $o \neq d$. We provided to the edges a double-precision floating-point weight d_{od}, which refers to the *great-circle distance* between node o and node d. The *great-circle distance* refers to the Euclidean distance between two points on the surface of a sphere; which in our case, the sphere is a projection of the Earth.

2.2   Data Acquisition and Preparation

For each one of the 645 cities from the Brazilian state of Sao Paulo, we got their administrative boundaries and indicators related to territorial extension and demography from the Brazilian Institute of Geography and Statistics (IBGE)[1]. The boundaries served as shapefiles to crop data obtained from OpenStreetMap (OSM)[2], which is an open data repository and a social network of collaborative

---

[1] www.ibge.gov.br.
[2] www.openstreetmap.org.

street mapping. The OSM's data describe real-world abstractions represented by georeferenced objects. These objects are described by means of its relations, which, in turn, refer to the streets (edges) and crossings (nodes) of a city, which were turned into complex networks where the edges intersect only at the nodes.

2.3   Feature Extraction and Selection

Metrics of graphs, referred to as *features*, can be divided into local and global [15]; local metrics describe properties of individual elements that form the network,

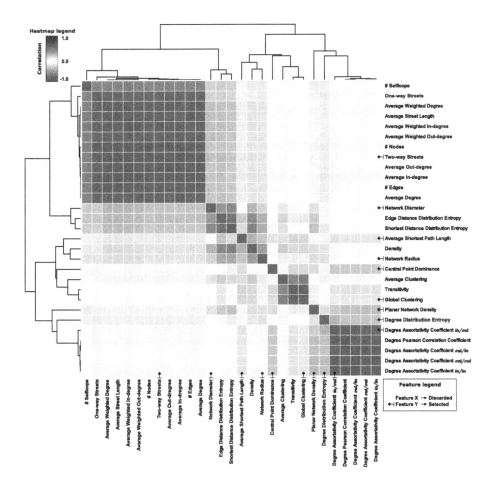

Fig. 2. A visualization of the mutual-correlation matrix of all the metrics we considered. The color describes the correlation between pairs of features. The metrics were hierarchically grouped through a dendrogram by means of the correlation of their values. Consequently, correlated metrics tend to stay in the same group; non-correlated metrics tend to be in separated groups. Additionally, the metrics we selected are colored in black and highlighted by a diamond marker. (Color figure online)

while global metrics characterize the whole network by a single value that is computed considering all of their elements. We rather use global metrics than local ones because they allow straightforward comparison between cities.

In order to gather these metrics, we designed a feature extractor to calculate a feature vector from any complex network given as input. First, we selected various metrics as candidates to render characteristics about cities, from which 29 metrics were chosen by their potential in providing insights about a given street network (see Fig. 2 for details). Such metrics were selected because they are linked to the network topology, which describes the streets of the cities.

After collecting all the metrics, we removed the non-relevant ones based on their mutual correlation. We computed the Pearson correlation coefficient [16] for each pair of metrics; such coefficient is defined in the interval $[-1.0, 1.0]$ where the extreme values indicate, respectively, the maximum negative and positive correlation, while 0.0 indicates no linear correlation at all. Following, we removed all the metrics with strong mutual correlation as indicated by the Pearson correlation in the interval $[-0.5, 0.5]$. In cases where any two metrics are outside this interval, one of the metrics was randomly discarded. Such process of metrics selection ensures that just metrics that are unique and non-related with the others will be used to describe the cities. Other processes of feature selection can be used in this step; even the multidimensional projection by itself can provide reasonable results. Notice that, the reduction of the dimensionality of the data was not our main priority, but rather to find the most complete set of metrics, that is the one that better characterizes the networks, without including redundant information; and, to this end, features correlation plays an import role. All metrics are depicted in Fig. 2; the ones that remained, 9 out of 29, were highlighted and are defined according to Costa *et al.* [17], as follows:

Degree Distribution Entropy $(\mathcal{H})$. The degree distribution of a network describes the probability of finding a vertex with a given degree. Whereas, the entropy represents the amount of uncertainty and randomness in a certain piece of information. By using the entropy in a city degree distribution, we can measure the uncertainty between street connections. Equation 1 describes such metric, where P_k represents the ratio of nodes with degree k.

Average Shortest Path $(\mathcal{L})$. It quantifies the average of all shortest paths (d_{ij}^S) that link all the pairs of nodes in a complex network (Eq. 2), it is used to quantify the capacity of locomotion through the shortest paths of a city.

$$\mathcal{H} = -\sum_{k=0}^{\infty} P_k \times \log(P_k) \quad (1) \qquad \mathcal{L} = \frac{\sum_{i=1}^{|V|} \sum_{j=1}^{|V|} d_{ij}^S}{|V|(|V|-1)} \quad (2)$$

Degree Assortativity Coefficient $(\mathcal{R})$. It refers to the *in and/or out* degree correlation between pairs of nodes. That is, positive values indicate that nodes with similar degrees tend to connect to each other, while negative values indicate the same, but regarding nodes with different degrees. It can be understood as the probability of moving from an unimportant street to an important one based only on the number of adjacent streets to both of them. Equation 3 uses e_{xy} to refer to the fraction of edges that join together vertices with degree x and y, a_x and b_y to the fractions of edges that start and end at vertices with degree x and y; and, σ_a and σ_b to the standard deviations of the distributions a_x and b_y.

Eccentricity ($\mathcal{E}$). This metric is a local one, measuring for a vertex the longest shortest distance between all the other vertices of a given graph [18] (see Eq. 4). In a global perspective, the greatest eccentricity from a graph is known to be the *network diameter*, while the smallest one is regarded as the *network radius*. They can reveal cities that may suffer from access issues by being sparse if the radius of a network is too small when compared to its diameter.

$$R = \frac{\sum_{xy} xy(e_{xy} - a_x b_y)}{\sigma_a \sigma_b} \quad (3) \qquad \mathcal{E}_i = \frac{1}{max\{d_{ij}^S | \forall j \in V\}} \quad (4)$$

Planar Network Density ($\mathcal{D}$). The density of a planar graph is defined as the ratio between the number of edges E and the number of all possible edges in a network with N nodes with no intersecting edges. It can be used to describe how dense is the street mesh of a city or a neighborhood. The metric is unique to each network, once the position of the nodes interferes in the number of edges. It is an algorithmic adaptation of the graph density [19], described in Eq. 5.

Central Point Dominance (C_D^P). This metric assesses the global centrality of a whole network by means of its network's betweenness deviation, which is a distance-based centrality metric. Values close to 0 indicate plenty of distance-efficient routes similar to the shortest one; whereas, values close to 1 indicate that the network might become vulnerable without its central node because the node might be used to connect different components, serving as an access point (*e.g.* bridges and tunnels). In Eq. 6, $\bar{v}$ is the node with the highest betweenness and $\mathcal{B}(v)$ is the normalized betweenness of the node v that lies in the range $[0, 1]$.

$$\mathcal{D} = \frac{|E|}{|N|(|N| - 1)} \quad (5) \qquad C_D^P = \frac{\sum_v^{|V|} \mathcal{B}_{\bar{v}} - \mathcal{B}_v}{|V|(|V| - 1)} \quad (6)$$

Two-way Streets ($\mathcal{T}_w$). It refers to the number of double edges in a network, which are edges that provide two-way routes between the same pair of nodes. This metric follows Eq. 8, in which f_{ij} is a clause-based auxiliary function.

Global Clustering ($\mathcal{G}_c$). The metric, which is described by Eq. 8, consists of the *fraction* of the number of triangles $\mathbb{N}_\triangle$ and triples $\mathbb{N}_3$ of the network. It refers to how the streets tend to cluster in the crossings of a given city, such that the greater the value the more possibilities of locomotion in fewer steps.

$$\mathcal{T}_w = \frac{\sum_{\langle i,j \rangle}^E f_{ij}}{2}, \quad f_{ij} = \begin{cases} 1, & \langle j, i \rangle \in E \\ 0, & otherwise \end{cases} \quad (7) \qquad \mathcal{G}_c = \frac{(3 \times \mathbb{N}_\triangle)}{\mathbb{N}_3} \quad (8)$$

2.4   Feature Vector Analysis

In this step, we focused on two methods from the data mining literature, the first one of multidimensional projection and the second one of clustering detection. Multidimensional projection allows the visualization of data by reducing its dimensional space, revealing particularities and behaviors to be explored through cluster-based analysis. Cluster analysis, in turn, focuses on the study of data interactions, inferring that two elements are similar because they are in the same cluster or dissimilar because they are in different ones. Consequently, the combination of these two methods contributes to the assessment of cities by their potential to reveal patterns that are not evident through an eye-based analysis.

Regarding multidimensional projection, our methodology consists of using two techniques [20]; the first one is named Isomap and the second one is known as Principal Components Analysis (PCA). Isomap is a nonlinear dimensionality reduction technique, which provides an embedding in a lower dimension while maintaining the geodesic distance between the data elements. Contrarily, PCA is a linear technique, which uses orthogonal conversions to turn a set of variables into linearly uncorrelated values with the largest possible variance. To choose both techniques, we used knowledge about the domain; we have kept track of some already-known dissimilar cities, seeking for approaches to distinguish them.

In the cluster analysis part, we used the technique KMeans [21], which splits the data into groups of equal variance, minimizing the sum-of-squares distance within clusters. The KMeans algorithm assumes that (i) the distribution of features within each cluster resembles spheres, which means that all features have equal variance and they are independent of each other; (ii) regarding the cluster size, the dataset is balanced; and, (iii) the density of the clusters is similar. The dataset we used consists of uncorrelated values and balanced instances of feature vectors, all of which have quasi-equal variance, meeting the algorithm requirements. In addition, KMeans is widely used in the related literature due to its robustness, versatility, and scalability. To validate our results we considered cluster quality metrics [22]. Their focus is to analyze the similarity between elements that have been assigned to the same cluster. We used a combination of the Silhouette score [23] and the Dunn index [24]; both of which are known to be internal-quality metrics, not requiring a pre-labeled dataset. The Silhouette is defined between $[-1, 1]$ for each cluster, the closer to 1 the better; it measures the cohesion and separation of clusters by evaluating how similar an element is in its own cluster when contrasted to other clusters. To further enhance the reliability of our analysis, we applied the Dunn index, which is a cluster distance-based quality metric that measures the separation among clusters, whose values are in between of $[0, \infty]$. In cases when the Dunn's index distance is greater than one, there is little or none cluster overlapping. Using both together, we have a double validation of quality by means of cohesion and separation of our set of clusters.

3   Results

3.1   Relationship of Population Size and Topological Features

With regard to the population density — see Fig. 3 for details —, the majority of the cities in our dataset is of tiny or small size, but the dataset has a substantial number of medium-sized cities and a small number of large-sized ones, including Sao Paulo — the biggest Brazilian city. Prior analyses can be done by observing Fig. 4, where cities (depicted as points) were sized by their number of nodes.

A first evidence that the topological features we selected can describe relevant knowledge about cities is the fact that Sao Paulo is isolated from the other ones in the PCA projection. A similar fact can be observed on a small scale considering the large-sized city of Campinas and the medium-sized cities of Marilia and Piracicaba, which are apart from the main group of cities located on the left part of the image. We believe that such behavior is connected to the demographics of the cities.

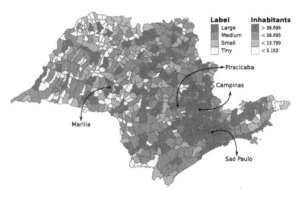

Fig. 3. Urban indicator related to the population density of the cities of the state of Sao Paulo. The cities were divided into four classes that describe the number of inhabitants of each one of them.

On a large scale, topological features can predict demographic characteristics of a city, whereas, on a small scale, they can reflect the neighborhoods that are densely or sparsely populated. For a less unbalanced view, we removed Sao Paulo from the dataset, depicting in Fig. 5 the normalized values of the feature vectors of the cities that remained using both PCA and Isomap techniques.

The two techniques show us that the majority of the data is concentrated in a small region, while the rest of it is sparse and distributed along the axes. The main difference between both of them is that Isomap implies multiple areas with considerable density, while PCA has a single dense area and many sparse data. This is evidence that tiny and small-sized cities tend to cluster isolating medium and large-sized cities that are too different from them. Despite the fact that such cities tend to cluster, Isomap shows that they have particularities that make them split into smaller clusters inside a bigger one. Also, it is safe to infer that by being scattered, medium-sized and large-sized cities have no clear pattern, but still, they may share common characteristics to be further explored with clustering algorithms. Even so, we can show, by using correlation, that the network's demography can be inferred from the city's topology – see Fig. 6.

To prove that the network's demography can be inferred from the city's topology, we measured the relationship between the topological features and the

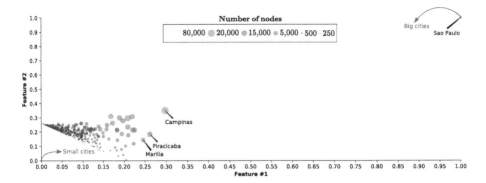

Fig. 4. Projection of feature vectors in two dimensions by using PCA; the size of the points refers to the number of nodes (intersections) in the cities' complex-network. The projected features reveal that the city of Sao Paulo (on the right-hand side) is an outlier when compared to the others (on the left-hand side).

demography by means of correlation. To this end, we reduced the dimensionality of the feature vectors of each city to one, using both techniques, PCA and Isomap, resulting in one single value for each one of the 645 cities. Next, we correlated such values with the size of their population. As a result, we got 0.803 and 0.799 of correlation for PCA and Isomap, respectively. Both values indicate that the data has a strong correlation, allowing us to state that in the case of the Brazilian state of Sao Paulo, topological features and demographics are strongly correlated. Such pattern opens doors for new investigations, as the ones placed by the dynamics of the social behavior; as in the case of criminality and mobility.

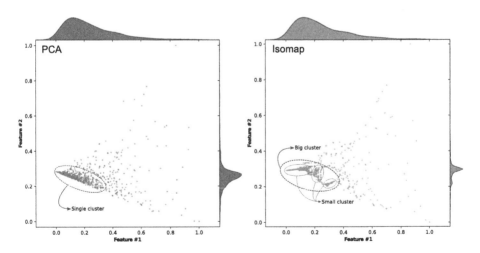

Fig. 5. Projection of the features, excluding Sao Paulo, using PCA and Isomap. PCA shows a single dense area with many sparse data, while Isomap shows multiple dense areas together with several sparse data. As a consequence, PCA implies a single cluster while Isomap points to an inherent hierarchy of clusters.

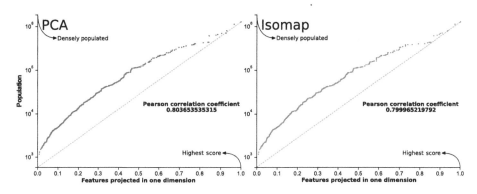

Fig. 6. Correlation test between the population density and a one-dimension projection of the cities' topological-features regarding both PCA and Isomap. Both images show a strong correlation, revealing that, on a large scale, the topological features of the cities can indicate, or even predict, their demography.

3.2 Relationship of Cluster Assignment and Territorial Extension

The cluster analysis aimed at the identification of the best number of clusters to describe our dataset. Consequently, we exhaustively tested the KMeans' cluster-quantity parameter from 2 to 644 clusters — the total number of cities without considering Sao Paulo. During the test, *we were seeking for the greatest average Silhouette score (AVG) only when the Dunn index (DNN) was larger than one.*

The previous experiment suggests that the best way to split our data is into two clusters. Such configuration has an AVG of 0.59 and a DNN of 1.10 (see Fig. 7). When dividing the data into two, the clusters are better balanced rather than when considering Sao Paulo — a big outlier — as part of the dataset.

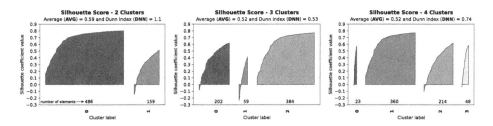

Fig. 7. Silhouette analysis of the subset of our data without Sao Paulo, in which clusters are represented as color-coded polygons. In each scenario that we have tested, the results were validated according to the Dunn index together with the Silhouette score. Although we have depicted the first three tested scenarios, which are also the best ones, the experiment considers a total of 643 scenarios. (Color figure online)

Subsequently, we investigated the reason why the cities were better arranged into only two clusters. By analyzing indicators related to population and territory extension, we found that 61.20% of the state's population is in the first cluster and 38.80% is in the second one (see Fig. 8a), and that the first cluster is mainly populated with cities that are considered to be of tiny or small territorial extension (see Fig. 8b), while the second cluster has the opposite behavior. Bearing in mind that our dataset does not imply any relationship between indicators of territorial extension and population density, we concluded that the relation that favored two clusters, as the arrangement with best values of Silhouette and Dunn index, was the territorial extension of the cities. Hence, we found evidence that there is a significant relationship between topological features, territorial extension, and demographics of the cities of Sao Paulo state.

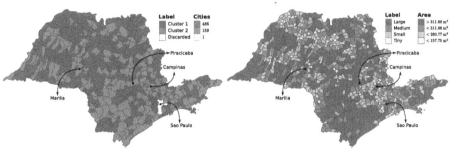

(a) Clustering Sao Paulo's cities.   (b) Sao Paulo's territorial extension.

Fig. 8. Investigating cities through clustering techniques; Fig. 8a shows the results of the clustering of topological features when removing the Sao Paulo city from the dataset; this layout has an average Silhouette of 0.59 and Dunn Index of 1.1. Figure 8b describe the area within the cities' administrative boundaries.

The relationship between the cluster arrangement and territorial extension can be understood as the way cities organize within their available space. In fact, regarding the territorial extension, 30.51% of the cities from the first cluster are tiny-sized, 31.13% are small-sized, 25.78% are medium-sized, and 12.58% are large-sized; whereas, 7.59% of the ones from the second cluster are tiny-sized, 6.32% are small-sized, 22.78% are medium-sized, and 63.29% are large-sized. Therefore, cities in the first cluster can be considered smaller and heavily populated, while the ones in the second cluster are larger and less populated.

3.3   Discussions on Results Generalization

We have chosen to present a joint of direct findings and analytical conclusions in our results section. This was done so that one can follow the practical application of the proposed methodology in a way that can be adapted and generalized for different domains and scenarios. Our methodology can also be used in non-urban applications, such as in the characterization of the topology in any group of complex networks, however, depending on the specificities of the domain, it may be necessary to use different network metrics and features to be more effective.

Additionally, while our findings cannot be generalized for any set of cities, we believe that the proposed methodology can be used to find non-trivial properties in different urban scenarios and not only to the cities that shape the state of Sao Paulo. Comprising a straightforward framework of analysis that can be useful to the academic community and cities' governing body, *e.g.* planners and designers.

Finally, our proposal has intricacies that can be explored in further studies: **(1)** using hierarchical clustering to reveal additional knowledge, which may also demand prior expertise about the cities (*e.g.* history and geography); and, **(2)** using more complex feature selection techniques such as fractal-dimension based methods or by applying ones related to mutual information. Notice that, this refinement might reveal other patterns of the data, but will not change the ones we discussed; and, **(3)** including non-topological features to capture different characteristics of cities, enhancing our methods capabilities and its versatility.

4   Conclusion

In this paper we proposed a three-folded method encompassing the data **A**cquisition, **M**odeling, and **C**omputation. Furthermore, our methodology comprises the following phases: *Data Acquisition and Preparation*, *Feature Extraction and Selection*, and *Feature Vector Analysis*; culminating in the use of multidimensional projection and cluster analysis algorithms to assess feature vectors of complex-network metrics. To validate our proposal, we investigated the following hypotheses: **(A)** *the network topology is a tool-set that can reveal groups of cities with similar characteristics, potentially revealing disparities*; **(B)** *although cities may share administrative boundaries with others, they cluster with cities with no apparent geographical similarity*; and, **(C)** *there might be interesting correlations between urban and/or territorial indicators and the features extracted from the street-network topology of a given set of cities.* Such hypotheses were investigated by analyzing relations between 645 cities that constitute the Brazilian state of Sao Paulo. Our main findings confirm the hypotheses of our work, allowing us to state that, on a large scale, the topological features of the cities can indicate, or even predict, their demography and that cities group themselves by means of their territorial extension, which describes the way that cities organize within their available space. Therefore, our main contributions are: **(i)** *the description of how the network topology is capable of revealing groups of cities with similar characteristics*; **(ii)** *the correlation analysis between the demography of the cities and their features*; and, **(iii)** *the discussion of why cities cluster with other cities distant apart instead of with those that they share boundaries with.* As a future work, we will measure the similarity between cities by means of non-topological features, looking for discrepancies in the collective behavior that emerges from this same set of cities.

Acknowledgment. We are thankful to CNPq (grant 167967/2017-7), FAPESP (grants 2014/25337-0, 2016/17078-0 and 2017/08376-0) and CAPES that supported this research.

References

1. Boccaletti, S., Latora, V., Moreno, Y., Chavez, M., Hwang, D.: Complex networks: structure and dynamics. Phys. Rep. **424**(4–5), 175–308 (2006)
2. Masucci, A.P., Stanilov, K., Batty, M.: Limited urban growth: London's street network dynamics since the 18th century. PLoS ONE **8**(8), 1–10 (2013)
3. Blumer, H.: Social problems as collective behavior. Soc. Probl. **18**(3), 298–306 (1971)
4. Anderson, T.K.: Kernel density estimation and K-means clustering to profile road accident hotspots. Accid. Anal. Prev. **41**(3), 359–364 (2009)
5. Grauwin, S., Sobolevsky, S., Moritz, S., Gódor, I., Ratti, C.: Towards a comparative science of cities: using mobile traffic records in New York, London, and Hong Kong. In: Helbich, M., Jokar Arsanjani, J., Leitner, M. (eds.) Computational Approaches for Urban Environments. GE, vol. 13, pp. 363–387. Springer, Cham (2015). https://doi.org/10.1007/978-3-319-11469-9_15
6. Crucitti, P., Latora, V., Porta, S.: Centrality measures in spatial networks of urban streets. Phys. Rev. E: Stat. Nonlinear Soft Matter Phys. **73**(3), 1–6 (2006)
7. Costa, L.F., Travençolo, B.A.N., Viana, M.P., Strano, E.: On the efficiency of transportation systems in large cities. EPL (Europhys. Lett.) **91**(1), 1–10 (2010)
8. Porta, S., Latora, V., Wang, F., Strano, E., Cardillo, A., Scellato, S., Iacoviello, V., Messora, R.: Street centrality and densities of retail and services in Bologna, Italy. Environ. Plan. B: Plan. Des. **36**(3), 450–465 (2009)
9. Strano, E., Nicosia, V., Latora, V., Porta, S., Barthélemy, M.: Elementary processes governing the evolution of road networks. Sci. Rep. **2**, 1–8 (2012)
10. Spadon, G., Gimenes, G., Rodrigues-Jr., J.F.: Identifying urban inconsistencies via street networks. In: International Conference on Computational Science, ICCS 2017, 12–14 June 2017, Zurich, Switzerland, vol. 108, pp. 18–27. Elsevier (2017)
11. Li, X., Parrott, L.: An improved genetic algorithm for spatial optimization of multi-objective and multi-site land use allocation. Comput. Environ. Urban Syst. **59**, 184–194 (2016)
12. Strano, E., Viana, M., Costa, L.F., Cardillo, A., Porta, S., Latora, V.: Urban street networks, a comparative analysis of ten European cities. Environ. Plan. B: Plan. Des. **40**(6), 1071–1086 (2013)
13. Domingues, G.S., Silva, F.N., Comin, C.H., Costa, L.F.: Topological characterization of world cities. arXiv preprint arXiv:1709.08244 (2017)
14. Pan, G., Qi, G., Zhang, W., Li, S., Wu, Z., Yang, L.T.: Trace analysis and mining for smart cities: issues, methods, and applications. IEEE Commun. Mag. **51**(6), 120–126 (2013)
15. Scripps, J., Nussbaum, R., Tan, P.N., Esfahanian, A.H.: Link-based network mining. In: Dehmer, M. (ed.) Structural Analysis of Complex Networks, pp. 403–419. Springer, Heidelberg (2011). https://doi.org/10.1007/978-0-8176-4789-6_16
16. Chiang, C.: Statistical Methods of Analysis. World Scientific, Singapore (2003)
17. Costa, L.F., Rodrigues, F.A., Travieso, G., Boas, P.R.V.: Characterization of complex networks: a survey of measurements. Adv. Phys. **56**(1), 167–242 (2007)
18. Hage, P., Harary, F.: Eccentricity and centrality in networks. Soc. Netw. **17**(1), 57–63 (1995)
19. Brath, R., Jonker, D.: Graph Analysis and Visualization: Discovering Business Opportunity in Linked Data. Wiley, Hoboken (2015)
20. Spiwok, V., Oborský, P., Pazúriková, J., Kenek, A., Králová, B.: Nonlinear vs. linear biasing in trp-cage folding simulations. J. Chem. Phys. **142**(11), 1–8 (2015)

21. MacQueen, J., et al.: Some methods for classification and analysis of multivariate observations. In: Proceedings of the Fifth Berkeley Symposium on Mathematical Statistics and Probability, vol. 1, pp. 281–297 (1967)

22. Kremer, H., Kranen, P., Jansen, T., Seidl, T., Bifet, A., Holmes, G., Pfahringer, B.: An effective evaluation measure for clustering on evolving data streams. In: Proceedings of the 17th ACM SIGKDD International Conference on Knowledge Discovery and Data Mining, KDD 2011, pp. 868–876. ACM, New York (2011)

23. Rousseeuw, P.J.: Silhouettes: a graphical aid to the interpretation and validation of cluster analysis. J. Comput. Appl. Math. **20**(1), 53–65 (1987)

24. Dunn, J.C.: Well-separated clusters and optimal fuzzy partitions. J. Cybern. **142**(1), 95–104 (1974)

A Distance-Based Tool-Set to Track Inconsistent Urban Structures Through Complex-Networks

Gabriel Spadon[1]([✉]) [ID], Bruno B. Machado[2] [ID], Danilo M. Eler[3] [ID], and Jose F. Rodrigues Jr.[1] [ID]

[1] University of Sao Paulo, Sao Carlos, SP, Brazil
`spadon@usp.br, junio@icmc.usp.br`
[2] Federal University of Mato Grosso do Sul, Ponta Pora, MS, Brazil
`bruno.brandoli@ufms.br`
[3] Sao Paulo State University, Presidente Prudente, SP, Brazil
`daniloeler@fct.unesp.br`

Abstract. Complex networks can be used for modeling street meshes and urban agglomerates. With such a model, many aspects of a city can be investigated to promote a better quality of life to its citizens. Along these lines, this paper proposes a set of distance-based pattern-discovery algorithmic instruments to improve urban structures modeled as complex networks, detecting nodes that lack access *from/to* points of interest in a given city. Furthermore, we introduce a greedy algorithm that is able to recommend improvements to the structure of a city by suggesting where points of interest are to be placed. We contribute to a thorough process to deal with complex networks, including mathematical modeling and algorithmic innovation. The set of our contributions introduces a systematic manner to treat a recurrent problem of broad interest in cities.

Keywords: Complex network · Network analysis · Urban structure

1 Introduction and Related Works

The synergy of real-world systems can be described as complex networks that exchange information through their entities' relationships. Such networks can model complex systems from neuronal networks to subway systems [1] and also, they can shape cities when linking the network topology with georeferenced data.

By analyzing the complex network of a city, it is possible to extract features that can describe urban problems, which are meaningful indicators for city planners [2]. Such features can reveal, for instance, sites where social activities are more intense, regions where facilities should be placed, and neighborhoods that lack street access. Particularly, these networks can expose distance-based inconsistencies, which is how we refer to nodes that lack efficient street access *from/to* others in the same network, possibly resulting in structural bottlenecks.

© Springer International Publishing AG, part of Springer Nature 2018
Y. Shi et al. (Eds.): ICCS 2018, LNCS 10860, pp. 288–301, 2018.
https://doi.org/10.1007/978-3-319-93698-7_22

Along these lines, we identified a lack of methods to analyze and improve the structure, mobility, and street access of cities. Consequently, in this paper, we contribute with a mathematical tool-set and algorithms to track distance-based inconsistencies by analyzing the complex-network topology of a city. Our results have implications for the street access, supporting a finer street planning by enhancing mobility indicators and providing better city's structural assessment.

The core assumption of this study is that the network is supposed to provide streets that render the shortest distance between places. In this regard, our tool-set uses two distance-functions to track nodes that do not provide shortest distance routes between them and other nodes that are of some interest. Nodes that fail in providing minimum-length routes are considered to be inconsistent nodes, which are evidence of problems in the city structure. Accordingly, in the face of an inconsistency, we raise two hypotheses: **(A)** the network lacks a more appropriate mesh; or, instead, **(B)** the city lacks its points of interest placed in better locations. The first one indicates the need for new points of interest to distribute their load. Contrarily, the second one indicates the need for relocating points of interest because the topology of the terrain cannot afford new streets.

A vast number of studies have been conducted to analyze inherent properties and behaviors found in cities. For instance, multiple metrics have been adopted to explain their structural conditions [3], their intense traffic of vehicles [4], and the emergence of collective behavior [5]. In other studies, the authors centered on the geometrical perspective of the network [6], and on the elements positioning [7,8]. Furthermore, there are those who reviewed the role of the city elements [9,10], that addressed the support to the urban planning and design [11,12], and that improved the facility-location analysis and planning of street meshes [13]. In addition to the ones that inspected the effectiveness of the underground systems [10] and the improvement of long-range connections [14], besides those who defined the concept of accessibility through complex networks and cities [15] and that tested the centrality of cities considering their space syntax [16–18].

In this paper, we contribute with a tool-set that improve the analysis of cities by tracking inconsistent urban structures through complex networks. This proposal follows by showing that the distance between two nodes can reveal ill-located points of interest and that such information can be used to make a city better distance-efficiently to their citizens. To present our contributions, this paper is organized as follows: Sect. 2 discusses our mathematical formulation and related algorithms; Sect. 3 discusses the results about the applicability of the proposed tool-set; and, Sect. 4 presents the conclusions and final remarks.

2 Mathematical Formulation and Algorithms

2.1 Preliminaries

Along the text, we refer to a complex network as a distance-weighted directed graph $G = \{V, E\}$, which is composed by a set V of $|V|$ nodes and a set E of $|E|$

edges. To model a city as a complex network, we considered streets as the edges and their crossings as the nodes, aiming to preserve their element's geometry. An edge $e \in E$ is an ordered pair $\langle i, j \rangle$, in which $i \in V$ is named *source* and $j \in V$ is named *target*, $i \neq j$. Each node $i \in V$ has two properties $\{\mathcal{L}_{at}^i, \mathcal{L}_{on}^i\}$ that correspond to their coordinates—$\mathcal{L}_{at}^i$ is the latitude and $\mathcal{L}_{on}^i$ the longitude. Based on such coordinates, we conferred to the edges in E a floating-point weight that refers to the great-circle (or *inline*) distance between their *source* and *target*.

Our mathematical tool-set tracks inconsistencies identified through distance functions to detect which element does not follow a pattern. The pattern that we consider refers to the real-world distance between the nodes of the network, which in turn can provide insights about the locomotion through the city streets. In this regard, we begin by tracking a set $P \subset V$ of points of interest; the idea, then, is to determine two sets of nodes that surrounds a point of interest $p \in P$, which can reveal the city's inconsistencies through applying algebraic operations. We introduce these two sets as the *perimeter set of p* and the *network set of p*.

2.2   Grouping Nodes in the Surroundings of Points of Interest

The first set matches the closest nodes to a point of interest p according to the great-circle (or *inline*) distance, which is referred as the *perimeter set of p*:

$$V_p^E = \{v \in V | d_{vp}^E < d_{v\bar{p}}^E, \forall p \in P, \forall \bar{p} \in P, p \neq \bar{p}\} \qquad (1)$$

where d_{ij}^E is the great-circle distance between i and j in the surface of Earth:

$$d_{ij}^E = \mathcal{R} \times \arccos\left(\sin(\mathcal{L}_{at}^i)\sin(\mathcal{L}_{at}^j) + \cos(\mathcal{L}_{at}^i)\cos(\mathcal{L}_{at}^j)\cos(\triangle_{\mathcal{L}_{on}^{ij}})\right) \qquad (2)$$

where $\mathcal{L}_{at}^i$ and $\mathcal{L}_{at}^j$ are the latitudes, $\triangle_{\mathcal{L}_{on}^{ij}}$ is the difference between the longitudes $\mathcal{L}_{on}^i$ and $\mathcal{L}_{on}^j$, both of nodes i and j. Also, $\mathcal{R}$ is the radius of Earth (6,378 km), and all values are represented in radians. Given a graph $G = \{V, E\}$ and a set of points of interest P, a node $v \in V$ pertains to the perimeter set of only one $p \in P$.

$$\therefore V_p^E \text{ and } V_{\bar{p}}^E \text{ — } \forall p \in P, \forall \bar{p} \in P, p \neq \bar{p} \text{ — are mutually disjoint.}$$

The second set corresponds to the *network set of p*, which is made of nodes closest to a point of interest p according to the length of their shortest paths:

$$V_p^N = \{v \in V | d_{vp}^N < d_{v\bar{p}}^N, \forall p \in P, \forall \bar{p} \in P, p \neq \bar{p}\} \qquad (3)$$

where d_{ij}^N is the length of the shortest directed path ($\texttt{spath}_{ij}$) between i and j—*i.e.* the sum of weights of all the edges in a minimum-length path, as follows:

$$\texttt{minimum\_length}(\texttt{spath}_{ij}) = \sum_{e \in \texttt{spath}_{ij}} \texttt{weight}(e) \qquad (4)$$

Recall that, the edge weight is given by the straight-line distance between their nodes using the great-circle distance (see Eq. 2). We refer to the shortest path length as *network distance*, in the sense that one must necessarily (in the best case) move across this path to go from the source node to the target node. Notice that any node $v \in V$ is network-closest to one and only one $p \in P$.

$$\therefore V_p^N \text{ and } V_{\bar{p}}^N - \forall p \in P, \forall \bar{p} \in P, p \neq \bar{p} - \text{ are mutually disjoint.}$$

In cases where the complex network is directed, the *network-distance TO a point of interest* is not necessarily the same as the *network-distance FROM a point of interest*, which may result in different network sets for the same p. This detail is addressed in the following section, where we define the network set from a point of interest to the nodes in V by mean of the *reversed network-set of p*:

$$\bar{V}_p^N = \{v \in V | d_{pv}^N < d_{\bar{p}v}^N, \forall p \in P, \forall \bar{p} \in P, p \neq \bar{p}\} \qquad (5)$$

2.3 Compartmentalizing Inconsistencies for Directed Networks

Consider different public services of a city as points of interest; such services may have different ways to assist the population, but all of them must require locomotion as a condition for assistance. For example, in the case of doctors' clinics, it is desired that patients get there efficiently. In turn, police stations require that their police officers efficiently reach the house of the citizens. In the case of schools, the daily routine demands an efficient back-and-forth transit to students. Along with other services that can be fitted with this assumption. Notice that, we are referring to efficient paths as the ones with minimum length.

In the first example, there is an implicit displacement from a node v to a node p; in the second one, the displacement is from the node p to the node v; and, in the third case, there is a bi-directional displacement between v and p, in which v is an ordinary node and p is a specific point-of-interest. Based on the network direction, those three cases led to the following definitions:

1. **Inward Inconsistency:** nodes that are inline-closest to a point of interest, but network-closest (from v to p, as given by Eq. 3) to a different one:

$$\Psi_p^I = V_p^E - V_p^N \qquad (6)$$

2. **Outward Inconsistency:** the same as the previous category, but in the opposite direction (from p to v, as given by Eq. 5), resulting in the set:

$$\Psi_p^O = V_p^E - \bar{V}_p^N \qquad (7)$$

3. **Absolute Inconsistency:** nodes that are, simultaneously, considered to be inward and outward inconsistencies—*i.e.* nodes in the sets' intersection:

$$\Psi_p^A = \Psi_p^I \cap \Psi_p^O \qquad (8)$$

As mentioned, these categories rely on the direction of the network. In cases where there is no direction, there will be no minimum-length divergence between paths of a round trip, but yet the inconsistencies can be tracked by calculating the difference between the perimeter set V_p^E and the network set V_p^N of p. To provide further discussion, hereinafter we are considering just directed networks.

2.4   Tracking Distance-Based Inconsistencies

In this section, we discuss Algorithm 1 that joins the concepts that we previously introduced. The aim of such algorithm is to track distance-based inconsistencies in distance-weighted directed networks by using a set P of $|P|$ of points of interest. Notice that, despite the definition of inconsistency is segmented into three types (see Sect. 2.3), the algorithm considers a single inconsistency type at a time.

The algorithm starts by filling a set of empty sets, each one reserved to store the inconsistencies of a single point of interest (see lines 1 to 2). Subsequently, we use p^E and p^N to store, respectively, the inline-closest and network-closest points of interest to a node $v \in V$ (see lines 5 and 6). We used the external functions `inline_closest` and `network_closest` (see lines 8 and 9) to extract the closest point of interest to the node v; they implement, respectively, Eq. 2 and 4. Following, we perform a test to check whether a node is an inconsistency or not; thus, if the inline-closest point p^E and the network-closest point p^N are not the same (see line 11) then v is an inconsistency of p^E (see line 12). Finally, a set of the inconsistencies of $|P|$ points of interest is returned as the result (see line 13).

Data: $G = \{V, E\}$, $P \subset V$, and $c \in \{I, O, A\}$ — c is used to indicate the direction
Result: $\{\Psi_p^c, \forall p \in P\}$ — a set of inconsistencies for all points of interest $p \in P$

1 $\Psi^c \leftarrow \emptyset$
2 **for each** $p \in P$ **do**
3 $\quad$ $\Psi_p^c \leftarrow \emptyset$ // notice that $\Psi_p^c \subset \Psi^c, \forall p \in P$, therefore $|\Psi^c| = |P|$
4 **for each** $v \in V$ **do**
5 $\quad$ $p^E \leftarrow \emptyset$
6 $\quad$ $p^N \leftarrow \emptyset$
7 $\quad$ **for each** $\bar{p} \in P$ **do**
8 $\quad\quad$ $p^E \leftarrow$ `inline_closest`$(v, \langle p^E, \bar{p} \rangle)$
9 $\quad\quad$ $p^N \leftarrow$ `network_closest`$(v, \langle p^N, \bar{p} \rangle, c)$
10 $\quad$ **if** $p^E \neq \emptyset$ **and** $p^N \neq \emptyset$ **then**
11 $\quad\quad$ **if** $\{p^E\} - \{p^N\} \neq \emptyset$ **then**
12 $\quad\quad\quad$ $\Psi_{p^E}^c \leftarrow \Psi_{p^E}^c \cup \{v\}$ // v should be closer to p^E than to p^N

13 **return** Ψ^c

Algorithm 1: An algorithm to track distance-based inconsistencies in cities modeled as networks. We use p^E and p^N to refer to the closest points of interest to a node v considering, respectively, the inline and the network distances; other methods are related to the ones of Sect. 2.2.

Given a graph $G = \{V, E\}$, a set P of $|P|$ points of interest, and an inconsistent node i; such node is known to be an inconsistency to one and only one $p \in P$.

$\therefore \Psi_p^c$ and $\Psi_{\bar{p}}^c$ — $\forall p \in P, \forall \bar{p} \in P, p \neq \bar{p}, c \in \{I, O, A\}$ — are mutually disjoint.

Consequently, it is possible to derive two other sets from a point of interest p: (i) the inconsistency set Ψ_p^c; and (ii) the set of consistent nodes $\bar{\Psi}_p^c = V_p^E - \Psi_p^c$, such that $\bar{\Psi}_p^c \cap \Psi_p^c = \emptyset$. The consistent nodes are fundamental to the process of suggesting locations to points of interest because they provide a smaller average distance to the nodes in their perimeter, different than an inconsistent node.

2.5 Reducing Distance-Based Inconsistencies

In this section, we introduce Algorithm 2, which was designed to suggest changes in the location of points of interest to improve their access through the streets of a city. The task of finding a perfect location for a point of interest might demand the test of all possibilities through an exhaustive search. Consequently, our algorithm has a greedy approach that uses information about centrality metrics to guide the placement of a point of interest. Centrality is not only an adequate technique to quantify the importance of a node but also it is capable to indicate central locations that are equally accessible to all nodes of a network.

Along these lines, we decided to adopt **Straightness Centrality** [9] as the centrality metric of Algorithm 2 because it analyzes the nodes of a network by joining both inline and network distances. It is noteworthy that any distance-based centrality metric could be employed, as well as multiple metrics together; however, different metrics tend to provide dubious or bad choices for a relocation.

Our algorithm starts by initializing auxiliary variables (see line 1) and by tracking the inconsistent nodes in the original version of the network (see line 2). In line 4, it starts looping until all points of interest have been replaced or until there are no more inconsistencies to be reduced from the original network. After that, it tries to change one point of interest at a time (see line 7). The candidates to host a point of interest pertains to the induced subgraph G_p^E of consistent nodes (see line 8). By using the induced subgraph the algorithm searches for the node that has the highest centrality value among all the other ones (see line 9).

The algorithm continues by testing the highest central node as the new location to the point of interest; such that, it temporally replaces the node (see line 10) and then it collects information about the inconsistencies of this network configuration (see line 11). Following, it tests whether the new configuration causes fewer inconsistencies then the previous one (see line 12) before marking the node for relocation (see lines 13 to 15). In a greedy fashion, it first selects the point of interest that by being replaced will lead to the highest elimination of inconsistencies. After choosing the one to be replaced, we perform integrity tests, we mark the node as relocated, and then we remove it (see lines 16 to 19).

The algorithm ends when there are no more profitable changes (see line 21). It is noteworthy to mention that each point of interest can be moved only once; this is due to the greedy nature of the algorithm. Otherwise, it would run until there are no more inconsistencies in the network at a prohibitive computational cost. The output of the algorithm is a set R of new locations (see line 22); each element $r \in R$ is an ordered pair $r = \langle old_p, new_p \rangle$ that denotes the current (old_p) node where a point of interest is and a better node (new_p) for placing it.

Algorithm 2 runs in $O(|V||P|^3)$ in the average case, where $|P|$ is the number of points of interest and $|V|$ is the number of nodes, $|P| \ll |V|$. Besides that, the algorithm was designed to be straightly parallelized; and, moreover, in our tests, it took less than a minute to compute a whole city with 200,000 inhabitants.

Correctness of the algorithm formulation

In this section, we demonstrate that Algorithm 2 is finite and it never increases the number of inconsistencies of a city, as required by the problem formulation.

Theorem 1. *We hypothesize that Algorithm 2 provides a set of central and consistent nodes that can replace specific points of interest in a city because replacing them will **never increase the total number of inconsistencies**.*

Proof. Hereinafter, aiming to prove Theorem 1 by reduction to absurdity, we are supposing that the use of Algorithm 2 can increase the number of inconsistencies.

Data: $G = \{V, E\}$, $P \subset V$, and $c \in \{I, O, A\}$ — c is used to indicate the direction
Result: R — set of suggested positions for points of interest
1 $R \leftarrow \emptyset$ $\bar{P} \leftarrow \emptyset$ $\tilde{P} \leftarrow \emptyset$
2 $\Psi^c \leftarrow$ algorithm_1(G, P, c)
3 $\Phi^c \leftarrow \Psi^c$ // copy of the original set
4 **while** $|P| - |\bar{P}| > 0$ **and** $\left(\sum_{i=1}^{|P|} |\Psi_i^c| \geq \sum_{i=1}^{|P|} |\Phi_i^c| \right)$ **do**
5 | $\text{old}_p \leftarrow \emptyset$
6 | $\text{new}_p \leftarrow \emptyset$
7 | **for each** $p \in (P - \bar{P})$ **do**
8 | | $G_p^E \leftarrow G\left(V_p^E - \Psi_p^c \right)$ // induced subgraph of consistent nodes
9 | | $\bar{p} \leftarrow$ extract_central(G_p^E)
10 | | $\mathbb{P} \leftarrow \left(((P - \bar{P}) \cup \tilde{P}) - \{p\} \right) \cup \{\bar{p}\}$
11 | | $\Omega^c \leftarrow$ algorithm_1$(G, \mathbb{P}, c)$
12 | | **if** $\left(\sum_{i=1}^{|P|} |\Phi_i^c| > \sum_{i=1}^{|P|} |\Omega_i^c| \right)$ **then**
13 | | | $\Phi^c \leftarrow \Omega^c$ // new lowest number of inconsistencies
14 | | | $\text{old}_p \leftarrow p$
15 | | | $\text{new}_p \leftarrow \bar{p}$
16 | **if** $\text{old}_p \neq \emptyset$ **and** $\text{new}_p \neq \emptyset$ **then**
17 | | $R \leftarrow R \cup \{\text{old}_p, \text{new}_p\}$ // old_p was moved to new_p
18 | | $\bar{P} \leftarrow \bar{P} \cup \{\text{old}_p\}$ // old location
19 | | $\tilde{P} \leftarrow \tilde{P} \cup \{\text{new}_p\}$ // new location
20 | **else**
21 | | break // there are no more enhancements to be made
22 **return** R

Algorithm 2: An algorithm that uses the contributions of Algorithm 1 to reduce distance-based inconsistencies of cities shaped as networks.

Bearing in mind that the type of the inconsistency has no effect on such proof, we will follow by proving the algorithm using Inward Inconsistency (see Sect. 2.3).

Consider the existence of a city mapped as a complex network $G = \{V, E\}$ and a set P of $|P|$ points of interest located in this same city. We start by finding the *perimeter set of p* (V_p^E) for each $p \in P$, which is given by Eq. 1. Subsequently, we proceed with gathering the *network set of p* (V_p^N) that is defined by Eq. 3.

Following, we detect a consistent node $\bar{p}$ that is the most central by an arbitrary centrality metric. The most central node is the one that has the highest centrality when compared to the other nodes, potentially being a better place for positioning a point of interest in a city. We follow by replacing p by the most central node $\bar{p}$ in its perimeter. Then, we calculate the updated perimeter $(V_{\bar{p}}^E)$ and network $(V_{\bar{p}}^N)$ sets, both of $\bar{p}$. Notice that $p \neq \bar{p}$, thus $V_p^E \neq V_{\bar{p}}^E$ and $V_p^N \neq V_{\bar{p}}^N$.

At this point, there are two pairs of answers, one pair for p and the other one for $\bar{p}$, as follows: $\langle V_p^E, V_p^N \rangle$ and $\langle V_{\bar{p}}^E, V_{\bar{p}}^N \rangle$. The algorithm we proposed will replace p by $\bar{p}$ following Eq. 9, which corresponds to a clause saying that the sets computed from $\bar{p}$ will be used just if they provide fewer inconsistencies than the original set; otherwise, it will keep the original one without making any changes.

$$\Psi_p^I = \begin{cases} V_p^E - V_p^N, & |V_p^E - V_p^N| \leq |V_{\bar{p}}^E - V_{\bar{p}}^N| \\ V_{\bar{p}}^E - V_{\bar{p}}^N, & \text{otherwise} \end{cases} \tag{9}$$

The algorithm ceases when all the points of interest are changed at least once or when no change will result in inconsistency elimination (see Sect. 2.5); as such, the algorithm is guaranteed to be finite. Therefore, by reduction to absurdity, it is an *absurdum* to suppose that the number of inconsistencies increases due to the use of Algorithm 2 because the algorithm provides a set with less or equal inconsistencies than the original set—as defined by Eq. 10.

$$\therefore |\Psi_p^I| \leq |V_p^E - V_p^N| \tag{10}$$

3   Results and Discussions

The tool-set we proposed was validated over the Brazilian city of Sao Carlos. Such city was instantiated as a complex network through a digital map from *OpenStreetMap*[1]. We considered streets as edges and their crossings as nodes; this way, we preserved the georeferenced attributes of the city that are necessary to the distance computation of our tool-set. The resulting network is planar and it can be represented in two dimensions, in which edges intersect only at nodes.

3.1   Assessing Inconsistency Recovery

In this section, we analyze the inconsistent nodes found in the city of Sao Carlos regarding the location of hospitals, police stations, and public schools, which are our points of interest; such public services are known to be affected respectively

---

[1] www.openstreetmap.org.

by inward, outward, and absolute inconsistencies as described in Sect. 2.3. It is noteworthy that each set of points of interest are independent, as such, the inconsistencies of one set of points have no relationship with the ones of others.

The inconsistent nodes we tracked are in Table 1, which suggest that their occurrence is connected to the number of points of interest. In fact, they appear whenever different perimeters meet; as a consequence, there is no way to eradicate them without altering the network topology by changing the streets' direction or creating new streets. In addition, more points of interest mean more boundaries, what tends to increase their number. Hence, the challenge is to find locations to points of interest that reduce, rather than eradicate, inconsistencies.

We used Algorithm 2 so to reduce the inconsistencies from Sao Carlos (see Table 1). The algorithm suggested relocating 6 hospitals, 2 police stations, and 9 public schools; such configuration, was able to reduce 160 inconsistencies from the hospitals (from 559 to 399), 123 inconsistencies from the police stations (from 342 to 219), and 179 inconsistencies from the public schools (from 663 to 484). Notice that the inconsistencies of some points of interest raised in number from the original to the enhanced city, which is a setback of our approach. However, as we have already proved, the total number of inconsistencies is always smaller.

Table 1. Analysis of the inconsistencies of the city of Sao Carlos, in which we considered police stations, hospitals, and public schools as points of interest; we use # to refer to the total number of inconsistencies and % to their percentage.

n^{th} POI	Original City						Enhanced City						n^{th} POI
	Hospitals		Police Stations		Schools		Hospitals		Police Stations		Schools		
	#	%	#	%	#	%	#	%	#	%	#	%	
01	013	02.3%	032	09.3%	015	02.2%	14	03.5%	30	13.7%	19	03.9%	01
02	002	00.3%	004	01.1%	077	11.6%	02	00.5%	48	21.9%	13	02.6%	02
03	012	02.1%	086	25.1%	043	06.4%	18	04.5%	96	43.8%	37	07.6%	03
04	019	03.4%	029	08.4%	071	10.7%	04	01.0%	32	14.6%	58	11.9%	04
05	030	05.3%	191	55.8%	114	17.1%	87	21.8%	13	05.9%	57	11.7%	05
06	049	08.7%	—	—	003	00.4%	51	12.7%	—	—	01	00.2%	06
07	145	25.9%	—	—	008	01.2%	26	06.5%	—	—	01	00.2%	07
08	039	06.9%	—	—	015	02.2%	22	05.5%	—	—	18	03.7%	08
09	012	02.1%	—	—	078	11.7%	31	07.7%	—	—	77	15.9%	09
10	043	07.6%	—	—	051	07.6%	63	15.7%	—	—	48	09.9%	10
11	072	12.8%	—	—	038	05.7%	45	11.2%	—	—	41	08.4%	11
12	095	16.9%	—	—	015	02.2%	17	04.2%	—	—	11	02.2%	12
13	028	05.0%	—	—	056	08.4%	19	04.7%	—	—	10	02.0%	13
14	—	—	—	—	008	01.2%	—	—	—	—	16	03.3%	14
15	—	—	—	—	060	09.0%	—	—	—	—	51	10.5%	15
16	—	—	—	—	011	01.6%	—	—	—	—	26	05.3%	16
Total	559	100%	342	100%	663	100%	399	100%	219	100%	484	100%	Total

3.2   Supporting the Designing of Urban Structures

Our tool-set is not only to be used in the automatic recovery of inconsistencies, but also to assist human-made urban-planning decisions. This is the case, for instance, when a specialist designs a city by having knowledge of the citizens' needs. In this case, Algorithms 1 and 2 can aid the process by analyzing and recommending distance-efficiently locations that are feasible to points of interest.

This section introduces two hypothetical case studies that depict our tool-set in practice. Both of them were conducted considering a subset of hospitals and public schools of the city of Sao Carlos (see Sect. 3.1). Nonetheless, our tool-set is extendable to any point of interest since it is equivalent to all of them.

Both case studies follow as in Fig. 1, in which we start by finding a point of interest, next we try to solve the problem by ourselves, and then we use the algorithms to improve our results; all steps are guided under the light of the nodes' *straightness centrality*. Furthermore, all case studies are represented by the induced subgraph of the point of interest being analyzed and, although we have illustrated the inconsistencies in Fig. 1, in the case studies they are not visible because they do not provide visual information to the other images.

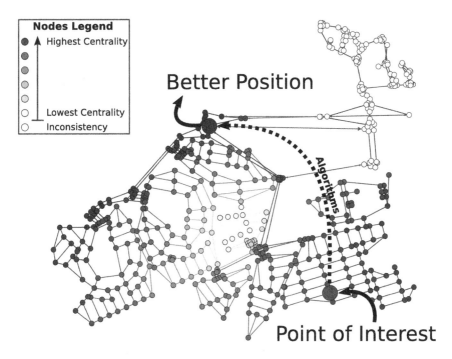

Fig. 1. Illustration of the process of designing urban structures under the light of centrality metrics. This process starts by identifying nodes that are of interest, then it follows by tracking their inconsistencies, and it ends by suggesting new locations—that reduce the number of inconsistencies—to place these nodes.

Case Study 1: Creating a new hospital to reduce demand

From the set of hospitals of the city of Sao Carlos, we identified one that, when compared to another hospital in the city, has excessive nodes in its perimeter (see Fig. 2a). There is no specific explanation of the hospital's location and, for instance, we can think that the city may have grown after the hospital has been built or the planners did not take the surroundings of the hospital into account. One thing is for sure, an extensive area with an ill-positioned point of interest will deprive the street access of the nodes; in this case, when points of interest are healthcare facilities, time-critical activities, as the transportation of patients in a critical state, can be jeopardized by lack of street access. Hence, the problem becomes where to build a hospital and how to avoid inconsistencies.

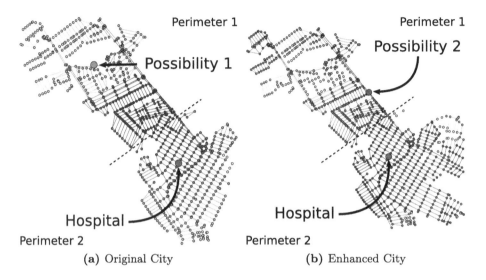

(a) Original City   (b) Enhanced City

Fig. 2. Illustration of the assisted urban planning task from the first case study, in which the point of interest is a hospital and the color of the nodes denotes their centrality—the darker, the higher. Figure 2a shows a hospital's perimeter that is too large causing lack of access. We placed a new hospital in an eye-based central location in that same area to solve this issue. Afterwards, we used the algorithm to reduce inconsistencies, which suggested relocating the new hospital to a more central location that reduces the hospital's inconsistencies; as in Fig. 2b.

First, we tried to solve the problem manually by an eye-based analysis of a location that could provide equal nodes to the perimeters of both hospitals. Figure 2a shows a possible place to the new hospital as well as the resulting perimeter of both of them, which are defined by a line that cuts the image in half. After that, we inserted the proposed location in the set of hospitals and we used Algorithm 1 to track the inconsistencies of the resulting configuration. Such configuration lead us to 615 inconsistencies, which is a bigger value than the original city. Thus, we succeeded in building a hospital that splits the perimeter into two, but we failed in providing efficient access to both old and new hospital.

In a second approach, we analyzed the nodes' centrality together with a supporting visualization. We colored the nodes by their centrality, what allowed us to notice that the selected location for the new hospital is a node with low centrality. Then, we used Algorithm 2 to suggest a better place for the new hospital while keeping the location of the old one. Doing so, the city inconsistencies were reduced from 615 to 352 (see Fig. 2b), which positively reflected in the mobility of this area by distributing the demand between both hospitals. Thus, creating a new hospital in a specific location was able to reduce almost half of the inconsistencies of the city without relocating the existing ones.

Case Study 2: Merging schools to centralize public resources

In a similar fashion, we identified two public schools that are adjacent and support a short set of nodes. In this case, the proximity of the schools (see Fig. 3a) is a problem since none of them is used up to its capacity implying a waste of public resources. In a first approach, by using Algorithm 2 to relocate them, the number of inconsistencies was reduced from 663 to 635.

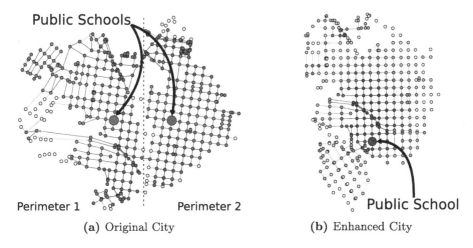

(a) Original City   (b) Enhanced City

Fig. 3. Illustration of the assisted urban planning task from the second case study, in which the points of interest are public schools and the color of the nodes denotes their centrality—the darker, the higher. In this case study, we treated a problem related to the waste of resources that was caused by having two schools near each other; Fig. 3a shows the problematic area, which is small, increasing the drawbacks related to access. By replacing both schools with a single one we achieved a better coverage of nodes, as depicted in Fig. 3b.

Considering the size of the perimeter of both schools, we decided to remove one school to improve the utility of the one that remained. By centralizing the schools in a single node, we can reduce inconsistencies because there will be fewer perimeters bordering each other; hence, the inconsistencies, located whenever two of them meet, will be naturally decreased. To further enhance this process, we used the color-coded centrality metric to choose a candidate to be the new sole school. Afterward, we used Algorithm 2 to provide a better location (see Fig. 3b), which reduced the total number of inconsistencies from 635 to 445.

3.3 Discussions on Results Generalization

For a concise results presentation, we have assumed: **(i)** that any displacement is through cities' streets; and, **(ii)** a city with a uniform population distribution. However, our tool-set holds for scenarios where these assumptions are not true.

We can use weights in accordance with the type of the displacement rather than using streets distance. This is because our tool-set uses a general concept of weight and when providing additional information such weight can assume any quantitative value—*i.e.* travel time, edge capacity, route cost, and so on.

About the population distribution, it is possible, for instance, to use a normal distribution peaked at the center of the city, multimodal distributions, or census data. This information can aid in the analysis of urban agglomerations if it is used to assign values to sets of nodes corresponding to the population density of the area that they belong to. Nevertheless, the set of inconsistencies would depend on the analysis of a specialist rather than being a self-explanatory result.

Also, despite being central to our problem formulation, the viability of redesigning a city is not suited for most cases. Furthermore, changing the topology of the network will alter the centrality of its elements, which will modify regions that attract vehicles and people. Our tool-set is not only to be used in redesigning a city but also on the initial design when all possibilities are open.

Finally, our proposal has open problems that support further studies: **(1)** the tool-set to track inconsistencies is categorical, then further algebra can aid in identifying the severity of a network inconsistency in a continuous, rather than binary, manner; **(2)** for simplicity's sake, we assumed the origin and destination of all paths as nodes of the network; such nodes are street intersections, which might not be real-world points of interest, requiring the addition of new nodes.

4 Conclusion

This paper was instantiated as a set of mathematical formalisms and algorithms to track and reduce distance-based inconsistencies improving access *to/from* points of interest in a city. Beyond the mathematical formulation, we provided a proof of concept and case studies, all of which indicate that our tool-set is able to suggest better placements for points of interest at the same time that it improves the access to the majority of the nodes of a city by reducing its inconsistencies.

More specifically, our contributions are in the definition of a concept based on intrinsic problems to urban structures that are caused by the misallocation of points of interest in cities; also, in two algorithms that were devised to track and reduce inconsistent nodes in complex networks; and, finally, in a case study, in which we show how our tool-set and algorithms can aid planners and designers.

In summary, our methods were proved empirically and formally, granting potential for prompt contribution and for opening new research questions. In addition, as a future work, we shall embrace link prediction methods for suggesting relocations in the network topology, *i.e.* proposing variations in the flow's direction, in the task of looking for a better topological setting for a city.

Acknowledgment. We would like to thank the Brazilian agencies CNPq (167967/2017-7), FAPESP (2016/17078-0 and 2017/08376-0) and CAPES that fully supported this research.

References

1. Boccaletti, S., Latora, V., Moreno, Y., Chavez, M., Hwang, D.: Complex networks: structure and dynamics. Phys. Rep. **424**(4–5), 175–308 (2006)
2. Porta, S., Latora, V., Wang, F., Strano, E., Cardillo, A., Scellato, S., Iacoviello, V., Messora, R.: Street centrality and densities of retail and services in Bologna, Italy. Environ. Plan. B: Plan. Des. **36**(3), 450–465 (2009)
3. Masucci, A.P., Stanilov, K., Batty, M.: Limited urban growth: London's street network dynamics since the 18th century. PLoS One **8**(8), e69469 (2013)
4. Kaczynski, A.T., Koohsari, M.J., Stanis, S.A.W., Bergstrom, R., Sugiyama, T.: Association of street connectivity and road traffic speed with park usage and park-based physical activity. Am. J. Health Promot. **28**(3), 197–203 (2014)
5. Sopan, A., Rey, P.J., Shneiderman, B.: The dynamics of web-based community safety groups: lessons learned from the nation of neighbors. IEEE Sig. Process. Mag. **30**(6), 157–162 (2013)
6. Corcoran, P., Jilani, M., Mooney, P., Bertolotto, M: Inferring semantics from geometry. In: Proceedings of the 23rd SIGSPATIAL International Conference on Advances in Geographic Information Systems, GIS 2015. ACM (2015)
7. Barthélemy, M., Flammini, A.: Modeling urban street patterns. Phys. Rev. Lett. **100**(13), 138702 (2008)
8. Zhong, C., Arisona, S.M., Huang, X., Batty, M., Schmitt, G.: Detecting the dynamics of urban structure through spatial network analysis. Int. J. Geogr. Inf. Sci. **28**(11), 2178–2199 (2014)
9. Crucitti, P., Latora, V., Porta, S.: Centrality measures in spatial networks of urban streets. Phys. Rev. E **73**(3), 036125 (2006)
10. Costa, L.F., Travençolo, B.A.N., Viana, M.P., Strano, E.: On the efficiency of transportation systems in large cities. EPL (Europhys. Lett.) **91**(1), 18003 (2010)
11. Strano, E., Nicosia, V., Latora, V., Porta, S., Barthélemy, M.: Elementary processes governing the evolution of road networks. Sci. Rep. **2**, 296 (2012)
12. Spadon, G., Gimenes, G., Rodrigues Jr, J.F.: Identifying urban inconsistencies via street networks. In: International Conference on Computational Science, ICCS 2017, 12–14 June 2017, Zurich, Switzerland, vol. 108, pp. 18–27. Elsevier BV (2017)
13. Li, X., Parrott, L.: An improved genetic algorithm for spatial optimization of multi-objective and multi-site land use allocation. Comput. Environ. Urban Syst. **59**, 184–194 (2016)
14. Viana, M.P., Costa, L.F.: Fast long-range connections in transportation networks. Phys. Lett. A **375**(15), 1626–1629 (2011)
15. Travençolo, B., Costa, L.F.: Accessibility in complex networks. Phys. Lett. Sect. A: General, Atomic Solid State Phys. **373**(1), 89–95 (2008)
16. Crucitti, P., Latora, V., Porta, S.: Centrality in networks of urban streets. Chaos: an interdisciplinary. J. Nonlinear Sci. **16**(1), 015113 (2006)
17. Porta, S., Crucitti, P., Latora, V.: The network analysis of urban streets: a dual approach. Phys. A **369**(2), 853–866 (2006)
18. Cardillo, A., Scellato, S., Latora, V., Porta, S.: Structural properties of planar graphs of urban street patterns. Phys. Rev. E **73**(6), 066107 (2006)

A Conceptual Framework for Social Movements Analytics for National Security

Pedro Cárdenas[1(✉)], Georgios Theodoropoulos[2], Boguslaw Obara[1], and Ibad Kureshi[3]

[1] Durham University, Durham, UK
{pedro.cardenas-canto,boguslaw.obara}@durham.ac.uk
[2] Southern University of Science and Technology, Shenzhen, China
theogeorgios@gmail.com
[3] Inlecom Systems, Brussels, Belgium
ibad.kureshi@inlecomsystems.com

Abstract. Social media tools have changed our world due to the way they convey information between individuals; this has led to many social movements either starting on social media or being organised and managed through this medium. At times however, certain human-induced events can trigger *Human Security Threats* such as Personal Security, Health Security, Economic Security or Political Security. The aim of this paper is to propose a holistic Data Analysis Framework for examining Social Movements and detecting pernicious threats to National Security interests. As a result of this, the proposed framework focuses on three main stages of an event (Detonating Event, Warning Period and Crisis Interpretation) to provide timely additional insights, enabling policy makers, first responders, and authorities to determine the best course of action. The paper also outlines the possible computational techniques utilised to achieve in depth analysis at each stage. The robustness and effectiveness of the framework are demonstrated by dissecting Warning Period scenarios, from real-world events, where the increase of Human Security aspects were key to identifying likely threats to National Security.

Keywords: National Security · Natural language processing
Social movements · Cyberactivism

1 Introduction

Massive social gatherings and social networks under-pinned by technology are two concepts that walk on the same path, especially when the basic structures or essential norms and values of a social system have been disrupted [14]. As a result of a set of social instability issues, a crisis may be triggered and affect the "homeostasis" or internal balance among those elements that maintain the

Y. Shi et al. (Eds.): ICCS 2018, LNCS 10860, pp. 302–315, 2018.
https://doi.org/10.1007/978-3-319-93698-7_23

stability of a state such as the economy, public order, health, environment or even life. Social movements are a clear example of these disruptive events because people's behaviour change according to the situation they face and a violent crowd reaction may lead to an instability scenario.

Microblogging websites and services have served as platforms to express ideas as well as to organise and coordinate crowds during a crisis event. Twitter, with over 800 million registered users [24], has seen itself at the centre of several large-scale Social Movements, with individuals conveying their ideas and frustrations within 140 any now 280 characters. Hence, understanding the way Social Movements use microblogs such as Twitter to organise, disseminate ideas, collaborate, coordinate and connect groups or cells of people linked to similar beliefs is, therefore, an essential task to appreciate the evolution of these social events.

There are models that describe how online social movements evolve [16], which parameters describe National Security considerations [21,25], what computational techniques help to get the private state of individuals, and how to find topics within a data corpus. However, no attention has been paid to create a holistic data analysis framework that links all the above elements and processes it in a timely fashion, to anticipate and detect the core stages of a Social Movement and when the crisis event can affect one or more National Security variables.

The present paper introduces a holistic framework for analysing Social Movements which use Twitter as their primary mean of communication. Our aim is to leverage the capabilities of different computational techniques and aggregating them to understand how these social events evolve and describe a system that can detect whether a social disruption can become a pernicious threat to National Security interests.

The rest of the paper is organised into five sections. Section 2 defines National Security threats, focusing on people as the primary element, and provides a short discussion on the link between social movements and social media. Section 3 offers a high-level description of the proposed framework. Section 4 presents a detailed description of each framework component. Section 5 illustrates the operationalisation of the framework using tweets from the Libyan uprising in 2011, focusing on the earlier stages of the event (referred to as the Warning Period). Section 6 concludes the paper outlining challenges and future work required to realise the proposed framework.

2   National Security in the Social Media Era

Security is a complex concept that has different facets depending on the person or entity in question. At times the different types of *security* can be at odds with each other. National Security is one of these challenging dimensions. It can be qualified by two main concepts: ensuring the security of the state security; and ensuring the security of its people (Human Security) [21]. [21,25] make arguments for how Human Security and State Security are mutually supportive.

Human Security, being people-centred, can be broken down using the United Nations Development Programme [25] into: Economic Security, Food Security,

Health Security, Environmental Security, Personal Security, Communal Security and Political Security.

In the digital era, social media tools have been valuable to spread messages related to those major disasters that have struck a society. Hence, social media platforms can help to identify those human security vulnerabilities that have snowballed into a challenge and required immediate attention.

In the light of the Arab Spring revolutions, the Internet in general and social media networks in particular have gained attention as essential instruments for organising people and communicating ideas and plans. This make social media the catalyst that enables movements to mobilise hundreds of thousands of individuals in a few hours [16,22]. Social media facilitates the link between social movements and collective action theory, where individuals share common interests or objectives, and they work as a single unit to accomplish their expectations [13].

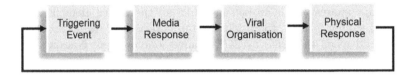

Fig. 1. Model for social media movements. Adapted from [16]

One of the ways to analyse the evolution of Social Movements which use virtual platforms is described in a circular flow model proposed by Sandoval-Almazan and Gil-Garcia [16]. Figure 1 demonstrates the links between the four stages of this model, outlined below.

1. **Triggering Event:** This conceives an opportunity in which individuals tend to become active, as a result of a disruptive incident;
2. **Media Response:** This stage considers that the detonating event brings about an instant response supported by a social media platform which allows people and activists to convey ideas, but at the same time works as a natural channel to uncover important events and show them to a domestic or international audience;
3. **Viral Organisation:** Once a detonating event opens a window for individuals to express their political views using a citizen to citizen channel [5], they create online communities where collective ideas of co-production and collaboration are exchanged to reinforce the community engagement;
4. **Physical Response:** The final stage reflects the power of the massive reaction, where protesters tend to organise resistance using different disruptive actions.

3   Conceptual Framework

Figure 2 outlines an iterative cycle that comprises three main stages, forming the core of our proposed model. These steps allow the dissection of the crisis event into core elements that interpret the possible evolution of a National Security instability scenario, and at the end, the results can be used to create a fine-grained strategy (Crisis Scorecard) to deal with the event and determine the best course of action.

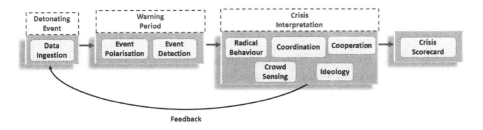

Fig. 2. Conceptual model

This framework takes its root and can be better understood by looking at the medical domain. Within a human health context, diagnosis, detection and interventions are planned using an illness-treatment schema (see Fig. 3). In line with this idea, the process begins with the patient assessment, and in a National Security environment, the state plays the patient role. Therefore the illness can be seen as the crisis event that triggered a crowd reaction (Detonating Event). The Diagnosis involves a twofold process; the first step (Warning Period) detects the "symptoms" such as changes in sentiments or opinions overtime. When applying this model to Social media, these symptoms activate a computational analysis to identify which National Security variables were affected (Economic Security, Food Security, Health Security, Environmental Security, Personal Security, Communal Security and Political Security).

Once the former analysis reaches a threshold based on domestic National Security Policies, it starts a second step (Crisis Interpretation) which is focused on recognising and analysing other societal characteristics such as violence; coordination and cooperation for radical events; emotions and opinions spilled over virtual communities (crowd sensing), and a holistic view of those individuals who are playing a main role in the event (ideology).

These sets of results can avoid "collateral damages" when they are organised in a "Crisis Scorecard" that works as a cluster of support decision indicators that decide the treatment (course of action) that the specialist (decision makers) will prescribe.

When a disruptive event triggers an online crowd reaction, analysing data from virtual platforms provides a rich source of information for understanding its

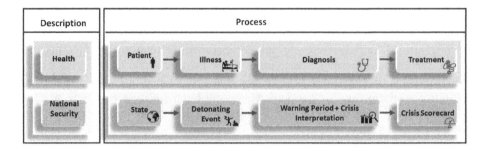

Fig. 3. Diagnostic schema example

genesis and likely evolution. Hence, examining the steps involved using a holistic approach is an essential point for examining Social Movements and detecting Human Security issues.

4   Framework Component Analysis

4.1   Detonating Event

As described in [16], once a political opportunity has triggered a radical societal behaviour, digital information becomes the core asset to identify potential problems.

The preliminary task is to collect those messages or tweets related to the disruptive event; however, as suggested by [16] information flows in four ways: from citizen to citizen, citizen to organisations, organisations to citizens and organisations to organisations. Consequently, selecting the volume of messages that epitomises the disrupting event is the crux of the process.

To tackle this multi-party information exchange process, *retweets* provide a critical conversational infrastructure as they knit all those voices that need to be heard, and those posts are an adopted practice for those users that want to share and spread thoughts, feelings and ideas to new audiences, as well as trying to engage in conversations [3].

4.2   Warning Period

A central step that needs to be taken relies on detecting the probable danger that follows the detonating incident. As proposed by [20] a disaster can be distinguished according to functional time phases. One of these stages is the Warning Period which refers to the length of time where information reveals a likely menace; however, the detection has to be done just before the aftermath of the crisis becomes perceivable.

In a decision-making scenario, the Warning Period represents a core stage due to the outcome that a correct diagnosis may yield, and can contribute to outlining the "course of action" that has to be followed.

National Security theory comprises a set of complex societal terms, and computational techniques are a valuable tool to solve a high range of problems. Thus in an attempt to couple both concepts to detect potential significant incidents, a two-pronged strategy can be evolved, namely, Event Polarisation and Event Detection.

Event Polarisation. As Social Media facilitates the interaction and communication with others [26], people tend to be a primary source of crisis information during a mass emergency event [23], because they use this social software infrastructure to inform their friends, family and acquaintances about their private states (attitudes).

As a result of these set of messages, a significant challenge is to analyse the subjective information to extract and categorise mass opinions that convey a radical idea or oppression feelings [16] and would become the raw material in decision-making.

A computational technique that may be used to detect and analyse Event Polarisation is Sentiment Analysis. This machine learning technique can be used to classify sentiments into three categories: positive, negative and neutral.

The aim to include this process is not limited to detect opinion polarisations, as sentiment fluctuations symbolise the occurrence of sub-events [17], and it can answer questions that surround a collective negative feeling in a selected geographical region.

Event Detection. A mass emergency event has a large number of individuals and stakeholders sharing information which is why the volume of messages related to a specific topic increases. However, all these disruptive events are not isolated because they include subevents [5] that can represent a significant milestone for an effective intervention.

Upon the Event Polarisation process, the system takes each sentiment stream separately (positive, negative and neutral) and extract the topics related to them. A potential clustering method is Latent Dirichlet Allocation (LDA) as it is one of the most popular techniques for this task and has been used to extract topics in major disasters [9].

The next step relies on creating a specialised dictionary that handles words related to human security and is enriched with synonyms to get a reliable wordlist (e.g. ammunition, ammo or munitions).

The fourth step deals with a semantic matching process, where the topics of each cluster is semantically analysed with the wordlist previously created.

Finally, to identify the nature of the event, this component employs the percentage of topics that are related to each Human Security aspect (economic security, food security, health security, environmental security, personal security, communal security and political security).

A core aspect is that National Security policies are the main reference to evaluate which set of human security components describe a local instability scenario.

4.3   Crisis Interpretation

A common problem that comes after detecting Human Security issues is to create a "big picture" of the disruptive situation. Figure 2 shows in the Crisis Interpretation stage five components that help to interpret radical behavioural elements as well as the way individuals offer or ask for supplies (e.g. money, medicines or weapons) that can be used to help or damage other groups of people.

These components are: Radical Behaviour, Coordination and Cooperation, Communication channels and the Ideology behind opinion leaders.

Radical Behaviour. Violence is a radical expression that can be encouraged using social media tools, and during a massive crisis, radical groups tend to distribute their ideology through Twitter users [1].

In accordance with [6], two behavioural markers that describe the way a risk has been increased are: *Leakage* and *Fixation*. The former expresses an intent to harm a specific target (facility, person or any other critical objective).

The second one refers to the tendency to mention with a higher frequency a critical objective; for this paper, Fixation will consider as critical entities: people, facilities, locations and organisations.

Detecting these radical markers is a computational challenge. In our framework, it can be used a natural language processing tool like Named Entity Recognition (NER) to extract the required entities.

Entities are linked to knowledge which is why dissecting the information behind them is a significant aspect. Regarding people, organisations and facilities, fixation can be detected according to the frequency found on tweets.

By contrast, intentions, as explained by [4], are extracted using intention verbs which are associated with an intention action (e.g. "I plan to stay at the Theater"); whereas radical intentions comprise a combination of verbs that keep specific semantic properties. In line with this idea, Levin's analysis of verbs [12] provide a strong background to create a radical intention structure which is shown in Table 1.

Table 1. Proposed radical intention structure

Radical intention structure	Example
[Levin Verb (Desire)] + [Levin Verb (Killing)] + [Entity]	"I want to eliminate wild animals"
[Levin Verb (Desire)] + [Levin Verb (Destroy)] + [Entity]	"I desire to burn the Police Station"

As suggested by Levin, verbs of **desire** are: want, crave, desire and need; while verbs of **killing** are: assassinate, eliminate, execute, immolate, kill, liquidate, murder and slaughter and **destroy** verbs are: demolish, destroy, devastate, exterminate and ruin.

Coordination and Cooperation. Microblogging sites offer a broad channel to enhance mass communication during a disruptive event and can be used to express and spread ideas or even radical ideologies and propaganda. However, to achieve shared goals within these virtual communities, collaboration plays a key factor and can be seen as an amalgamation of three main features: communication, coordination and cooperation [7]. Hence, coordination and cooperation create a cooperative system that can monitor the conduct of individuals who interact.

This cooperative system can be divided into two groups: Seekers and Suppliers; both stakeholders are equally important as they can help to detect whether an entity (person or organisation) is reporting their needs or is offering help (e.g. food, medical supplies, water, vehicles, guns, ammunition or money). Natural Language processing and intent mining can deal with both sides of the story as lexical pattern-based structures have been used to solve this issue [15].

Crowd Sensing. When mining tweets, people post URL references related to the event they live, and the frequency of these messages suggest the importance of the content. Therefore crawling the information within those websites may discover relevant data (e.g. http://www.libyafeb17.com/?p=916).

The proposed framework requires an iterative loop because the content of these websites needs a complete analysis (Detonating Event, Warning Period and Crisis Interpretation) to identify radical ideology and uncover new events (see Fig. 2).

Ideology. Tweets allow individuals and organisations to share not only opinions but pictures, videos, links and email addresses. The later ones represent a source of information to identify likely radical activists. An email address has the following structure: a username and a hostname or domain e.g. username@domain.com (see Table 2).

Table 2. Email dissection

Email	Hostname	DBpedia abstract
abc@bbc.co.uk	bbc.co.uk	"BBC Online, formerly known as BBCi, is the BBC's online service"

The username is the crucial element that matches a person against a unique social profile. Twitter and Linkedin are social platforms that have key attributes such as first name, last name, username or date of birth [19]. Assuming that a person X has both online social accounts, a pattern matching process will verify whether these attributes are the same.

Regarding the hostname or domain, it can be matched against large-scale knowledge base such as DBpedia, Wikidata or Freebase to get a "holistic profile" of the person.

Once the profile has been flagged, its content needs a complete analysis (Warning Period and Crisis Interpretation) in order to detect radical behaviour traits and to understand what kind of coordination and cooperation activity is reigning.

5   Appying Framework on the Libyan Warning Period

Twitter has been a valuable tool used by activists to "overthrow" established governments. Libya made history when Gaddafi's regime was removed in 2011, and this microblogging service was used to broadcast pictures, telephone numbers, websites and opinions that allowed the escalation of the Libyan uprising.

As a demonstration, this section demonstrates the computational techniques and their results at each sub-stage of the of the Warning Period: Event Polarisation and the Event Detection (see Fig. 2) using as input a set of tweets, related to the Libyan conflict using the hashtag #libya, dated from Feb. 1st to Feb. 28th 2011.

As described in Sect. 5.1 only retweets were considered, and from a language analysis standpoint, messages written in English were selected. Consequently, the data corpus were reduced from 28,524 to 20,149 tweets.

5.1   Event Polarisation

Before analysing sentiments, the data was cleansed by following three preprocessing steps: 1. URLs, RT and Mention terms were removed; 2. contractions and abbreviations were replaced, and 3. informal ways to convey information (short words) such as: "plz", "pls", "ppl", "peeps", "pleasert" or "prt" were replaced by its word of origin (e.g. "plz" → please or "ppl" → people).

To begin with the Sentiment Analysis process, we used the Stanford CoreNLP library with the Recursive Neural Tensor Network model [18] as our baseline to compute sentiments measures (positive, negative and neutral).

Fig. 4. Sentiment orientation

Our data shows that 73% of the analysed messages have a negative polarization (Fig. 4), which is why these double figures suggest a clear negative orientation.

Once the polarisation has been detected, the next step focuses on identifying sentiment fluctuations; as described by [17] we calculated the correlation among the percentage of positive and the percentage of negative messages, and a correlation of −0.29 showed that both sentiments were moving towards opposite paths. As can be seen in the Fig. 5(a), the ThemeRiver visualization [10] shows that the volume of polarised messages (negative, positive and neutral) increased from February 18th to February 25th, and this gives the chance to identify three visible sentiment shifts (A, B and C) and two essential time frames (Feb. 18th to Feb. 21st and Feb. 21st to Feb. 25th).

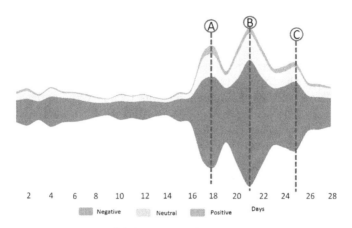

(a) Sentiment changes

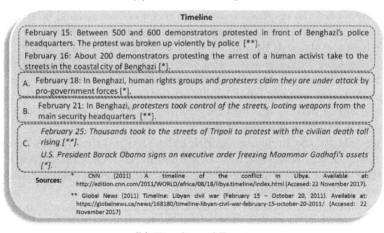

(b) Timeline of Events

Fig. 5. Sentiment fluctuations and timeline

Figure 5(b) shows a timeline of the Libyan conflict, outlining the critical events where the sentiment explosions appeared.

5.2   Event Detection

After identifying the sentiment bursts and considering those points as critical subevents, two questions that come to mind are: (1) What topics were conveyed over those time frames? Moreover, (2) are those topics related to National Security?

The first question was tackled by using a topic modelling technique known as LDA which was developed by [2]. However, one of the leading issues lies in determining the number of topics. For this purpose Perplexity analysis was used to evaluate the optimum number of topics, whereas the cross-validation methodology proposed by [8] was used to assess the performance of the topic extraction model.

The second question requires a semantic component to associate those topics that were found in the topic extraction phase, to a Human Security dictionary. One way to deal with this semantic issue was to query the Integrated Public Sector Vocabulary [11], which is a public wordlist that contains a set of terms related to a variety of categories, and some of them are linked to Human Security aspects (Economic Security, Food Security, Health Security, Environmental Security, Personal Security, Communal Security and Political Security). However, to get an enriched dictionary, synonyms were added by using the Wordnet lexical database.

As negative sentiments had a predominant role, the topics extracted from this set of tweets were semantically matched to the expanded dictionary; however, as the volume of tweets had different growth rates and the number of topics was dissimilar overtime, the resulting matched topics were normalised by calculating the percentage of each Human Security aspect per day (see Fig. 6).

To understand the way Human Security variables behaved overtime, a Normalised Cross-Correlation analysis was calculated between all of them; but not only in those time frames where the sentiments burst, but a "step before" because it is essential to understand what happened in those previous days. Hence, the Breakout anomaly detection algorithm released by Twitter was used to identify those previous variation points suitably.

As Fig. 7 shows, the Breakout algorithm detected two time frames before the changes in sentiment; however, the area shaded in red (AA) and the one shaded in blue (BB and CC) were analysed to understand what happened before and during the sentiment fluctuations appearance.

Table 3 illustrates the cross-correlation results between some of the Human Security aspects such as Public Order, People and Information, and it outlines the following relationships: Public Order – Defence, Public Order – Life, Public Order – Information, People – Defence, People – Health, People – Life, Information – Government and Information – Defence.

According to the Table 3 two scenarios can be identified. The first one (AA to BB) shows that only four out of eight variables had positive increments. On the other hand, the second scenario (BB to CC) shows in as many as seven out of eight analysed variables had positive increases. Hence, the latest scheme suggests that people were strongly engaged in topics related to Public Order and

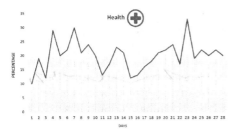

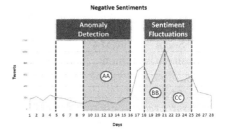

Fig. 6. Health security percentages overtime

Fig. 7. Sentiment fluctuations and breakout detection (Color figure online)

Table 3. Correlation of human security parameters

Topics	Correlations				
	Anomaly Detection	Sentiment Fluctuations		Percentage Difference (%)	
	Feb. 9 - Feb. 16	Feb. 18 -Feb. 21	Feb. 21 - Feb. 25		
	(AA)	(BB)	(CC)	(AA) to (BB)	(BB) to (CC)
Public Order -Defence	0.2132	0.3133	0.503	**46.95%**	**60.55%**
Public Order -Life	0.3109	-0.3919	0.4897	**-226.05%**	**224.96%**
Public Order - Information	-0.53079	0.08	0.2473	**115.07%**	**209.13%**
People - Defence	-0.6181	0.7065	-0.5028	**214.30%**	**-171.17%**
People - Health	-0.3129	-0.7065	0.6383	**-125.79%**	**190.35%**
People - Life	-0.1256	-0.2175	0.8116	**-73.16%**	**473.15%**
Information - Government	0.525	0.3002	0.7492	**-42.82%**	**149.57%**
Information - Defence	-0.3551	-0.3248	0.8323	**8.53%**	**356.25%**

Life (224.96%), Public Order and Information (209.13%) and People and Life (473.15%).

As a result, the more positive increments that have been found over a time frame, the more attention that has to be paid to them. This is a key feature that triggers the next stage (Crisis Interpretation). However, the nature of the event and National Security policies will decide which set of Human Security aspects have to be considered to create the Crisis Scorecard and the suitable percentages that have to be reached to activate the next phase.

6   Conclusion and Future Work

This paper has proposed a holistic conceptual framework that utilises computational techniques for examining Social Movements and detecting threats to Human Security.

To demonstrate the feasibility of the framework, the paper has presented a preliminary analysis of tweets related to the Libyan events focussing in particular on the Warning Period. This analysis has helped to identify two essential frames where critical events occurred. Another core result was the detection of those Human Security variables that had positive variations. This suggests that the more positive increments, the more attention that has to be paid to them because these set of changes showed which aspects epitomised the social disruption.

This preliminary experimental phase has already pointed to some challenges with regard to the components involved in the Warning Period phase. First, slang expressions are still a great challenge because the language has semantic variations from country to country. Hence, creating a robust dictionary may improve radical behaviour detection. Second, spelling mistakes correction is an important issue that NLP has to deal with because it can improve the Event Detection Phase. Third, microblogging platforms tend to spread opinions, but anonymity within this virtual communities is hard to probe.

Going forward, we envisage a robust real-time platform constantly monitoring social media and social behaviour, attempting to identify and predict threats to Human Security. A particular challenge in this endeavour will be the ability to deal with false positives. The next steps are to use different computational techniques and data sets to create and validate an efficient end-to-end monitoring, analysis, predictive and prescriptive responsive platform based on Fig. 2. The working system is expected to enable timely and effective responses to possible crises.

References

1. Ashcroft, M., Fisher, A., Kaati, L., Omer, E., Prucha, N.: Detecting jihadist messages on Twitter. In: European Intelligence and Security Informatics Conference, pp. 161–164 (2015)
2. Blei, D.M., Ng, A.Y., Jordan, M.I.: Latent Dirichlet allocation. J. Mach. Learn. Res. **3**, 993–1022 (2003)
3. Boyd, D., Golder, S., Lotan, G.: Tweet, tweet, retweet: conversational aspects of retweeting on Twitter. In: Hawaii International Conference on System Sciences, pp. 1–10 (2010)
4. Castellanos, M., Hsu, M., Dayal, U., Ghosh, R., Dekhil, M., Ceja, C., Puchi, M., Ruiz, P.: Intention insider: discovering people's intentions in the social channel. In: International Conference on Extending Database Technology, pp. 614–617. ACM (2012)
5. Castillo, C.: Big Crisis Data: Social Media in Disasters and Time-Critical Situations. Cambridge University Press, Cambridge (2016)
6. Cohen, K., Johansson, F., Kaati, L., Mork, J.C.: Detecting linguistic markers for radical violence in social media. Terror. Polit. Violence **26**, 246–256 (2014)
7. Ferreira, D.E., Barbosa, C.E., Oliveira, J., de Souza, J.M.: Analyzing the collaborative aspects of the future-oriented technology analysis. In: IEEE International Conference on Computer Supported Cooperative Work in Design, pp. 139–144 (2016)
8. Grun, B., Hornik, K.: Topic models-an R package for fitting topic models. J. Stat. Softw. **40**, 1–30 (2011)

9. Hashimoto, T., Kuboyama, T., Chakraborty, B.: Topic extraction from millions of tweets using singular value decomposition and feature selection. In: Asia-Pacific Signal and Information Processing Association Annual Summit and Conference, pp. 1145–1150 (2015)
10. Havre, S., Hetzler, B., Nowell, L.: ThemeRiver: visualizing theme changes over time. In: 2000 IEEE Symposium on Information Visualization, pp. 115–123 (2000)
11. Local Government Association: Integrated Public Sector Vocabulary (2006). http://standards.esd.org.uk. Accessed 7 Dec 2017
12. Levin, B.: English Verb Classes and Alternations: A Preliminary Investigation. Conversation Analysis. The University of Chicago Press, Chicago (1993)
13. Olson, M.: The Logic of Collective Action, Public Goods and the Theory of Groups, p. 7. Harvard University Press, Harvard (2002)
14. Perry, R.: What is a Disaster? New Answers to Old Questions, p. 161. Xlibris Corporation, Bloomington (2005)
15. Purohit, H., Hampton, A., Bhatt, S., et al.: Identifying seekers and suppliers in social media communities to support crisis coordination. Comput. Support. Coop. Work (CSCW) **23**, 513–545 (2014)
16. Sandoval-Almazan, R., Gil-Garcia, J.R.: Cyberactivism through social media: Twitter, YouTube, and the Mexican political movement "I'm Number 132". In: Hawaii International Conference on System Sciences, pp. 1704–1713 (2013)
17. Sha, Y., Jinsong, Y., Guoray, C.: Detecting public sentiment over PM2.5 pollution hazards through analysis of Chinese microblog. In: International Conference on Information Systems for Crisis Response and Management, University Park, Pennsylvania, USA, pp. 722–726 (2014)
18. Socher, R., Perelygin, A., Wu, J.Y., Chuang, J., Manning, C.D., Ng, A.Y., Potts, C.: Recursive deep models for semantic compositionality over a sentiment treebank. In: Conference on Empirical Methods in Natural Language Processing (2013)
19. Soltani, R., Abhari, A.: Identity matching in social media platforms. In: International Symposium on Performance Evaluation of Computer and Telecommunication Systems (SPECTS), pp. 64–70 (2013)
20. Stallings, R.A.: Methods of Disaster Research, pp. 49–55. Xlibris Publishing, Bloomington (2003)
21. Cosby, S.L.: Human security concept: the root of U.S. national security and foreign policy. United States Marine Corps, Command and Staff College, Marine Corps Combat Dev, Marine Corps University, South Street, Quantico, VA, p. 9 (2009)
22. Storck, M.: The role of social media in political mobilisation: a case study of the January 2011 Egyptian uprising. University of St Andrews, Scotland, p. 3, December 2011
23. Sutton, J.N., Spiro, E., Johnson, B., Fitzhugh, S., Greczek, M., Butts, C.: Connected communications: network structures of official communications in a technological disaster. In: International Conference on Information Systems for Crisis Response and Management, pp. 1–10 (2012)
24. Twitter: Number of monthly active international Twitter users from 2nd quarter 2010 to 3rd quarter 2017 (in millions). https://www.statista.com/statistics/274565/monthly-active-international-twitter-users/. Accessed 14 Jan 2018
25. United Nations Development Program: Human Development Report, pp. 22–33. Oxford University Press, New York/Oxford (1994)
26. Whiting, A., Williams, D.: Why people use social media: a uses and gratifications approach. Qual. Market Res. Int. J. **16**(4), 362–369 (2013)

Retweet Prediction Using Social-Aware Probabilistic Matrix Factorization

Bo Jiang, Zhigang Lu$^{(\boxtimes)}$, Ning Li, Jianjun Wu, and Zhengwei Jiang

Institute of Information Engineering, Chinese Academy of Sciences, Beijing, China
{jiangbo,luzhigang,lining6,wujianjun,jiangzhengwei}@iie.ac.cn

Abstract. Retweet prediction is a fundamental and crucial task in social networking websites as it may influence the process of information diffusion. Existing prediction approaches simply ignore social contextual information or don't take full advantage of these potential factors, damaging the performance of prediction. Besides, the sparsity of retweet data also severely disturb the performance of these models. In this paper, we propose a novel retweet prediction model based on probabilistic matrix factorization method by integrating the observed retweet data, social influence and message semantic to improve the accuracy of prediction. Finally, we incorporate these social contextual regularization terms into the objective function. Comprehensive experiments on the real-world dataset clearly validate both the effectiveness and efficiency of our model compared with several state-of the-art baselines.

Keywords: Social network · Retweet prediction
Matrix factorization · Social influence · Message semantic

1 Introduction

Online social networks such as Twitter and Facebook have become tremendously popular in recent years. These services are a network structure system formed by interaction among users. The dissemination of information in social networks has brought unprecedented improvement under the structure and has accelerated interpersonal communication and information flow. The retweet mechanism provides a way to allow social users to hold the latest news and help enterprises to carry out marketing on social networking platform. Thus, it is of great practical significance to analyze and explore the retweet behaviors for improving the information propagation and user experience in social networks.

Many approaches has been proposed to model the retweet behaviors based on different social information, such as textual feature [13], social feature [7], social influence [18], visual feature [2], emotion feature [3], or a combination of these various features [13]. Although these methods have made some progress to some extent, the results are unsatisfactory, and can still be improved in a certain space. To improve the performance of prediction, recent works incorporate the observed explicit social information (e.g., social ties) into matrix factorization frameworks

© Springer International Publishing AG, part of Springer Nature 2018
Y. Shi et al. (Eds.): ICCS 2018, LNCS 10860, pp. 316–327, 2018.
https://doi.org/10.1007/978-3-319-93698-7_24

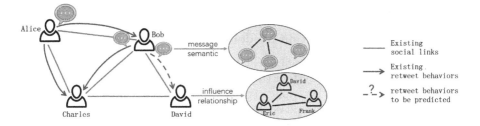

Fig. 1. Illustration of retweet behaviors on online social network.

to design novel models [15,16]. In fact, it is naturally that the retweet prediction can be viewed as the problem of matrix completion by incorporating additional sources of information about social influence between users and message semantic between short texts. As shown in the example of Fig. 1, when users decide to retweet message, they are interested in the content of message and more likely to retweet messages posted by his close friends due to social relationships. We call this phenomenon for social context. These knowledge can be learnt from social influence and message semantic information. Both of these aspects are important for retweet prediction. However, most existing methods simply ignore contextual information, or don't take full advantage of these potential features.

In this paper, we propose a novel retweet prediction model based on probabilistic matrix factorization by integrating the observed retweet data, social influence and message semantic to improve the accuracy of prediction. Specifically, we first introduce social influence matrix based on network structure and interaction history and message similarity matrix based on document semantic. We then utilize user and message latent feature spaces to learn social influence and message semantic respectively. We incorporate these regularization terms into the objective function. Finally, we conduct several experiments to validate the effectiveness of our model with the state-of-the-art approaches. Experimental results show our model performs better than the baseline models.

The main contributions of this paper are the followings:

- We propose a novel retweet prediction model based on probabilistic matrix factorization by incorporating social influence and message semantic information to improve the performance of prediction.
- We utilize low-rank user latent feature space and message latent feature space to learn social influence and message semantic. The predicted social influence and message semantic can assist the applications such as influencer ranking and information recommendation.
- Various experiments are conducted on real-world social network dataset, and the results demonstrate that our proposed model can achieve better prediction performance than the state-of-the-art methods.

Our paper is organized as follows. Section 2 reviews the related work. Section 3 presents the preliminaries. Our model is proposed in Sect. 4. The experiments are presented in Sect. 5, followed by the conclusion in Sect. 6.

2   Related Work

2.1   Social Recommendation Modeling

Matrix factorization (MF) as well as the variants are widely used in ratings prediction in recommendation system [12]. To enhance the prediction performance of recommender systems with explicit social information, considerable social recommendation models are proposed based on matrix factorization [4,8,17,20]. For example, Ma et al. [9] extend the probabilistic matrix factorization model by additionally incorporating user's social network information to eliminate the data sparsity and improve poor prediction accuracy problems. Hereafter, Ma et al. [8] also propose a social trust ensemble analysis framework by combining users' personal preference and their trusted friends' favors together. Guo et al. [4] design a trust-based MF technique by considering both the explicit and implicit influences of the neighborhood structure of trust information when predicting unknown ratings. Yang et al. [17] design a TrustMF model by integrating sparse rating data given by users and sparse social trust network among these same users. Zhao et al. [20] extend BPR by introducing social positive feedbacks and proposed the SBPR algorithm which achieves better performance in items ranking than BPR. Tang et al. [14] give a recommendation framework SoDim-Rec which incorporates heterogeneity of social relations and weak dependency connections based on social dimensions.

In a word, social context-aware model can take various types of contextual information (e.g., time, location) into account when making recommendations. It also provides a way for the prediction tasks based on context dependent.

2.2   Retweet Behavior Modeling

Many studies have been conducted to identify the influence factors of retweet behavior from different perspectives, including user survey [1,10], data statistics [13]. In summary, these studies have identified that user's topic interests and social influence are two important aspects for retweet prediction. Meanwhile, research on user's retweet behavior prediction is more attractive to lots of researchers. Representative works include topic-level probabilistic graph model [6], conditional random field [11], social influence factor graph model [18], non-parametric Bayesian model [19], matrix factorization [15,16]. The above approaches mainly use content and/or structure features to predict retweet behavior. Besides, some works associate with multiple features to predict retweet behavior [7]. However, these studies focus on exploring user-based and message-based features to predict retweet behavior based on the assumption that users and messages are independent and identically distributed. They ignore implicit side information such as social influence among users and semantic structure information among messages.

In summary, research on retweet prediction is still room for improvement. Inspired by social contextual information, we introduce social influence among users and message semantic among messages to devise our retweet prediction method.

3   Preliminaries

Given a message m and a user u, the task of the retweet prediction is to discover whether u retweet m or not. In this work, we use an $M \times N$ user-message retweet matrix $R = \{0, 1\} \in \mathbb{R}^{M \times N}$ to represent the behaviors of users retweet messages, in which user u_i retweet message m_j, R_{ij} is 1, otherwise R_{ij} is 0. Notice that 0s might either be "true" 0s or missing values.

We utilize Probabilistic Matrix Factorization (PMF) [12] to factorize R into user latent feature matrix $U \in \mathbb{R}^{K \times M}$ and message latent feature matrix $V \in \mathbb{R}^{K \times N}$. K is the number of latent features. Also, the retweet matrix R can be approximated by $R' \approx U^T V$. The likelihood function of the observed retweetings is factorised across M users and N messages with each factor as

$$P(R|U,V,\sigma_R^2) = \prod_{i=1}^{M}\prod_{j=1}^{N}[\mathcal{N}(R_{ij}|U_i^T V_j, \sigma_R^2)]^{I_{ij}^{(R)}} \tag{1}$$

where $\mathcal{N}(\cdot|\mu, \sigma^2)$ is the probability density function of the normal distribution with mean μ and variance σ^2. The indicator function $I_{ij}^{(R)}$ is equal to 1 when user u_i retweet message v_j and 0 otherwise. The prior distributions over U and V are defined as

$$P(U|\sigma_U^2) = \prod_{i=1}^{M}\mathcal{N}(U_i|0, \sigma_U^2 \mathbf{I}), \quad P(V|\sigma_V^2) = \prod_{j=1}^{N}\mathcal{N}(V_j|0, \sigma_V^2 \mathbf{I}) \tag{2}$$

We then have the posterior probability by the Bayesian inference as

$$\begin{aligned}
&P(U,V|R,\sigma_R^2,\sigma_U^2,\sigma_V^2) \propto P(R|U,V,\sigma_R^2)P(U|\sigma_U^2)P(V|\sigma_V^2) \\
&= \prod_{i=1}^{M}\prod_{j=1}^{N}[\mathcal{N}(R_{ij}|g(U_i^T V_j), \sigma_R^2)]^{I_{ij}^{(R)}} \times \prod_{i=1}^{M}\mathcal{N}(U_i|0, \sigma_U^2 \mathbf{I}) \times \prod_{j=1}^{N}\mathcal{N}(V_j|0, \sigma_V^2 \mathbf{I})
\end{aligned} \tag{3}$$

This model is learned by maximizing posterior probability, which is equivalent to minimizing sum-of-squares of factorization error with regularization terms

$$\mathcal{L} = \frac{1}{2}\sum_{i=1}^{M}\sum_{j=1}^{N}I_{ij}^{(R)}(R_{ij} - g(U_i^T V_j))^2 + \frac{\eta}{2}\|U\|_F^2 + \frac{\lambda}{2}\|V\|_F^2 \tag{4}$$

where the logistic function $g(x) = 1/(1 + exp(-x))$ maps the value of $U_i^T V_j$ to the range $(0, 1)$, $\eta = \frac{\sigma_R^2}{\sigma_U^2}$, $\lambda = \frac{\sigma_R^2}{\sigma_V^2}$ and $\|\cdot\|_F$ denotes the Frobenius norm.

As we have described above, the retweet prediction can be considered as a matrix completion task, where the unobserved retweetings in matrix R can be predicted based on the observed retweet behaviors. However, R is highly sparse, it is extremely difficult to directly learn the optimal latent spaces for users and messages only by the observed retweeting entries. We argue that social contextual information can assist in prediction. For example, people with social relations are more likely to share same preferences, and users pay close attention to their interested topics. By this idea, we incorporate these social contextual information into our prediction method.

4   Social-Aware Prediction Model

4.1   Modeling Social Influence

User's action can be affected with others in the process of information spread. For example, whether user like message or not will be affected by the publisher to some extent. Here, we argue that the user's retweet behaviors are affected by his direct neighbors due to social influence in social networks. Thus, we employ social influence to improve the prediction performance.

We denote the social influence matrix $F \in \mathbb{R}^{M \times M}$, in which each entry F_{ij} represent the strength of social influence user u_i has on user u_j based on network structure and interaction behaviors. Similarly, we factorize F into user latent feature matrix $U \in \mathbb{R}^{K \times M}$ and factor latent feature matrix $Z \in \mathbb{R}^{K \times M}$. We define the conditional distribution over the observed social influence as

$$P(F|U, Z, \sigma_F^2) = \prod_{i=1}^{M} \prod_{f=1}^{M} [\mathcal{N}(F_{if}|g(U_i^T Z_f), \sigma_F^2)] \tag{5}$$

We also place prior distributions on U and F as

$$P(U|\sigma_U^2) = \prod_{i=1}^{M} \mathcal{N}(U_i|0, \sigma_U^2 \mathbf{I}), \quad P(Z|\sigma_Z^2) = \prod_{f=1}^{M} \mathcal{N}(Z_f|0, \sigma_Z^2 \mathbf{I}) \tag{6}$$

We quantify the strength of influence based on network structure and interaction behaviors. Specifically, we first explore the utilization of network structure to quantify influence. For example, in social network, a user is a high influencer if he is followed by many users. Based on the idea, we denote the network structure influence matrix F_{ij}^S with its (i, j)-th entry as

$$F_{ij}^S = \frac{n_{u_i}^{in}}{n_{u_i}^{in} + n_{u_i}^{out}} \times I_{ij}^{(S)} \tag{7}$$

where $n_{u_i}^{in}$ is the follower number of u_i and $n_{u_i}^{out}$ is the following number of u_i. The indicator function $I_{ij}^{(S)}$ is equal to 1 if u_j is a follower of u_i and 0 otherwise.

We also measure interaction influence from the user interaction history in social networks. Similarly, we compute the (i, j)-th entry for the interaction behavior influence matrix F_{ij}^B as

$$F_{ij}^B = \frac{\sum_{y \in Y(i,j)} (A_{iy} - \overline{A}_i) \cdot (A_{jy} - \overline{A}_j)}{\sqrt{\sum_{y \in Y(i,j)} (A_{iy} - \overline{A}_i)^2} \cdot \sqrt{\sum_{y \in Y(i,j)} (A_{jy} - \overline{A}_j)^2}} \tag{8}$$

where $Y(i, j)$ represents the set of messages accepted by both users u_i and u_j, $\overline{A}_i$ represents the average acceptance of user u_i. To guarantee non negativity, we use the sigmod function to map F_{ij} into $(0, 1)$.

Finally, social influence from user u_i to user u_j is calculated as

$$F_{ij} = g(\rho F_{ij}^S + (1 - \rho) F_{ij}^B) \tag{9}$$

where $\rho \in (0, 1)$ controls the effects of network topology structure and history of interaction.

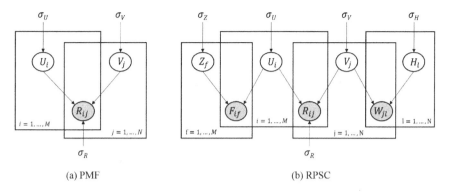

(a) PMF   (b) RPSC

Fig. 2. The graphical representation of (a) PMF and (b) our proposed method.

4.2 Modeling Message Semantic

The findings have been indicated that the content of message is an important factor when users retweet message [1,10]. We argue that the topic distribution of messages can reflect user's personal topic interests. Therefore, we also explore the utilization of message semantic to improve the retweet prediction.

We introduce the content similarity matrix $W \in \mathbb{R}^{N \times N}$ to represent message similarity information. Each entry W_{ij} denotes the similarity score between messages m_i and m_j. Similarly, we factorize W into message latent feature matrix $V \in \mathbb{R}^{K \times N}$ and factor latent feature matrix $H \in \mathbb{R}^{K \times N}$. We then define the conditional distribution over the observed message semantic as

$$P(W|V, H, \sigma_W^2) = \prod_{j=1}^{N} \prod_{l=1}^{N} [\mathcal{N}(W_{jl}|g(V_j^T H_l), \sigma_W^2)] \tag{10}$$

We also place zero-mean Gaussian priors on W and H as

$$P(V|\sigma_V^2) = \prod_{j=1}^{N} \mathcal{N}(V_j|0, \sigma_V^2 \mathbf{I}), \quad P(H|\sigma_H^2) = \prod_{l=1}^{N} \mathcal{N}(H_l|0, \sigma_H^2 \mathbf{I}) \tag{11}$$

In this paper, we employ GPU-DMM [5] method to infer latent topic structure of short texts. After performing GPU-DMM, we can represent each document with its topic distribution $p(z|d)$. Hence, we can compute content similarity matrix W based on cosine similarity method between messages m_i and m_j as

$$W_{ij} = p(z|d_i)p(z|d_j) \tag{12}$$

where $p(z|d_i)$ denotes the topic distribution of message m_i.

4.3 Learning and Prediction

Next, we incorporate social influence and message semantic similarity information into the framework of probabilistic matrix factorization and solve the optimization. The corresponding graphical model is presented in Fig. 2.

Based on Bayesian inference, we model the conditional distribution of U, V, Z and H over social influence and message semantic similarity as

$$P(Z,H,U,V|R,F,W,\sigma_R^2,\sigma_Z^2,\sigma_H^2,\sigma_U^2,\sigma_V^2) \propto P(R|U,V,\sigma_R^2)$$

$$P(F|U,Z,\sigma_F^2)P(W|V,H,\sigma_W^2)P(U|\sigma_U^2)P(V|\sigma_V^2)P(Z|\sigma_Z^2)P(H|\sigma_H^2)$$

$$= \prod_{i=1}^{M}\prod_{j=1}^{N}[\mathcal{N}(R_{ij}|g(U_i^T V_j),\sigma_R^2)]^{I_{ij}^{(R)}} \times \prod_{i=1}^{M}\prod_{f=1}^{M}[\mathcal{N}(F_{if}|g(U_i^T Z_f),\sigma_F^2)]$$

$$\times \prod_{j=1}^{N}\prod_{l=1}^{N}[\mathcal{N}(W_{jl}|g(V_j^T H_l),\sigma_W^2)] \times \prod_{i=1}^{M}\mathcal{N}(U_i|0,\sigma_U^2\mathbf{I}) \times \prod_{j=1}^{N}\mathcal{N}(V_j|0,\sigma_V^2\mathbf{I})$$

$$\times \prod_{f=1}^{M}\mathcal{N}(Z_f|0,\sigma_Z^2\mathbf{I}) \times \prod_{l=1}^{N}\mathcal{N}(H_l|0,\sigma_H^2\mathbf{I}) \tag{13}$$

Maximizing log-posterior distribution on U, V, Z and H is equivalent to minimizing sum-of-of-squared errors function with quadratic regularization terms as

$$\min_{U,V} \mathcal{L} = \frac{1}{2}\sum_{i=1}^{M}\sum_{j=1}^{N} I_{ij}^{(R)}(R_{ij} - g(U_i^T V_j))^2$$

$$+ \frac{\alpha}{2}\sum_{i=1}^{M}\sum_{f=1}^{M}\|F_{ij} - g(U_i^T Z_f)\|_F^2 + \frac{\beta}{2}\sum_{j=1}^{N}\sum_{l=1}^{N}\|W_{ij} - g(V_j^T H_l)\|_F^2 \tag{14}$$

$$+ \frac{\gamma}{2}\|U\|_F^2 + \frac{\eta}{2}\|V\|_F^2 + \frac{\varphi}{2}\|Z\|_F^2 + \frac{\rho}{2}\|H\|_F^2$$

where $\alpha = \frac{\sigma_R^2}{\sigma_F^2}$, $\beta = \frac{\sigma_R^2}{\sigma_W^2}$, $\gamma = \frac{\sigma_R^2}{\sigma_U^2}$, $\eta = \frac{\sigma_R^2}{\sigma_V^2}$, $\varphi = \frac{\sigma_R^2}{\sigma_Z^2}$, $\rho = \frac{\sigma_R^2}{\sigma_H^2}$. In order to reduce the model complexity, we set $\gamma = \eta = \varphi = \rho$ in all of the experiments.

The local minimum of the objective function given by Eq.(14) can be found by using stochastic gradient descent on feature vectors U_i, V_j, Z_f and H_l as

$$\frac{\partial \mathcal{L}}{\partial Z_f} = \sum_{f=1}^{M} g'(U_i^T Z_f)(g(U_i^T Z_f) - F_{if})U_i + \varphi Z_f \tag{15}$$

$$\frac{\partial \mathcal{L}}{\partial H_l} = \sum_{l=1}^{N} g'(V_j^T H_l)(g(V_j^T H_l) - W_{jl})V_j + \rho H_l \tag{16}$$

$$\frac{\partial \mathcal{L}}{\partial U_i} = \sum_{j=1}^{N} I_{ij}^{(R)} g'(U_i^T V_j)(g(U_i^T V_j) - R_{ij})V_j + \alpha \sum_{f=1}^{M} g'(U_i^T Z_f)(g(U_i^T Z_f) - F_{if})Z_f + \gamma U_i \tag{17}$$

$$\frac{\partial \mathcal{L}}{\partial V_j} = \sum_{i=1}^{M} I_{ij}^{(R)} g'(U_i^T V_j)(g(U_i^T V_j) - R_{ij})U_i + \beta \sum_{l=1}^{N} g'(V_j^T H_l)(g(V_j^T H_l) - W_{jl})H_l + \eta V_j \tag{18}$$

where $g'(\mathrm{x})$ is the derivative of logistic function $g'(\mathrm{x}) = \exp(\mathrm{x})/(1 + \exp(\mathrm{x}))^2$. After learning U and V, an unknown retweet entry can be estimated as $U_i^T V_j$.

5 Experimental Analysis

5.1 Dataset Description

We use a real-world dataset collected from Weibo which is a social network in China like Twitter. Weibo allows user to generate following and follower relationships, and retweet the interested message posted by other people. In this paper, we use publicly available Weibo dataset to evaluate the validity of our proposed method [18]. The dataset contains the content of message, the relationships of user's following and follower, and the information of retweet behaviors. The data statistics are illustrated in Table 1. It can be seen from the statistical results that user behaviors data are very sparse on social networks.

Table 1. Retweet data statistics

Dataset	#Users	#Tweets	#Retweets	#Relations	Density
Weibo	1,787,443	300,000	23,755,810	308,489,739	0.005%

5.2 Comparative Algorithms

We compare our method (RPSC) with the following baseline algorithms.

- **PMF**: This method doesn't take into account social contextual information and only uses user-message matrix for the retweet prediction [12].
- **LRC-BQ**: The method designs social influence locality based on pairwise influence and structural diversity, and adds the basic features and influence locality features into the logistic regression to predict retweet behavior [18].
- **MNMFRP**: This method measures the social relationship strength based on network structure and interaction history, and introduces social relationship regularizer under non-negative matrix factorization to predict retweets [16].
- **HCFMF**: The model provides a co-factor matrix factorization by modeling message co-occurrence similarity based on microblog content, word semantic similarity based on word embeddings, and user social similarity based on author information into collaborative filtering when predicting retweets [15].

We also consider the variants of the proposed model to verify the effectiveness. Let $\mathcal{L}_o = \frac{1}{2}\sum_{i=1}^{M}\sum_{j=1}^{N} I_{ij}^{(R)}(R_{ij} - g(U_i^T V_j))^2 + \frac{\gamma}{2}\|U\|_F^2 + \frac{\eta}{2}\|V\|_F^2$, then we have

- **RPSC-U**: This method only considers user's social influence information in our proposed model. The adjusted function is

$$\mathcal{L}(R,U,V,Z) = \mathcal{L}_o + \frac{\alpha}{2}\sum_{i=1}^{M}\sum_{f=1}^{M}\|F_{if} - g(U_i^T Z_f)\|_F^2 + \frac{\varphi}{2}\|Z\|_F^2 \qquad (19)$$

- **RPSC-M**: This method only utilizes message semantic information for the proposed model. The degenerated function is

$$\mathcal{L}(R,U,V,H) = \mathcal{L}_o + \frac{\beta}{2}\sum_{j=1}^{N}\sum_{l=1}^{N}\|W_{jl} - g(V_j^T H_l)\|_F^2 + \frac{\rho}{2}\|H\|_F^2 \qquad (20)$$

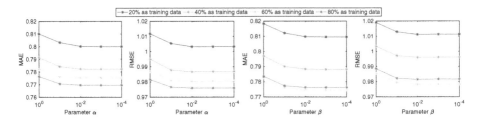

Fig. 3. MAE and RMSE vs. α, β on the different training data settings.

5.3   Evaluation Measures

For the evaluation metrics, we use the Mean Absolute Error (MAE) and the Root Mean Square Error (RMSE) to measure the model accuracy, defined as

$$MAE = \frac{\sum_{R_{ij} \in \mathcal{R}} |R_{ij} - U_i^T V_j|}{|\mathcal{R}|}, \quad RMSE = \sqrt{\frac{\sum_{R_{ij} \in \mathcal{R}} (R_{ij} - U_i^T V_j)^2}{|\mathcal{R}|}} \quad (21)$$

where R_{ij} denotes the retweet value given message m_j by user u_i. $|\mathcal{R}|$ denotes the number of tested entries. A smaller MAE or RMSE means a better performance.

We also employ Precision, Recall, and F_1-score to evaluate whether user retweets or not when receiving message. A simple strategy is that hide some observed entries as unobserved entries for evaluation, and perform classification after training. We perform 5-fold cross validation and report their average values.

5.4   Parameter Settings

Tradeoff Parameters. In our proposed model, the parameters α and β are used to control the strength of social influence and the weight of message semantic respectively, and the rest parameters γ, η, φ and ρ is used to prevent overfitting. In this paper, we use different amounts of training data (20%, 40%, 60%, 80%) to find the optimal values of parameters. From the results shown in Fig. 3, we can see that MAE and RMSE gradually decrease and achieve the best performance when α is around 10^{-2}. Hence, we set $\alpha = 10^{-2}$ for the following experiments. Meanwhile, the impact of β shares the same trends as α. We thus set $\beta = 10^{-2}$. We also conduct the extensive experiments and observe similar results with γ, η, φ and ρ. We directly give $\gamma = \eta = \varphi = \rho = 10^{-2}$ due to the space limitation.

Number of Latent Features. The dimensionality of latent factor indicates the power of feature representation, and the proper dimensionality can be more effective to predict the retweet behaviors. Thus, we train latent feature matrices U, V, Z and H to find the optimal latent space to represent users and messages. In this paper, we use different training datasets to discover the appropriate K. From the results shown in Fig. 4, we can observe that MAE and RMSE decreases gradually when the latent feature K increase. Finally, we choose $K = 100$ as the feature dimension in our experiments due to computational cost.

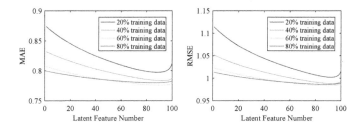

Fig. 4. MAE and RMSE vs. Latent Feature on the different training data settings.

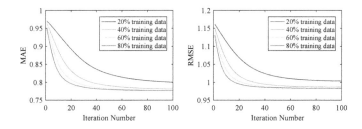

Fig. 5. MAE and RMSE vs. Iteration on the different training data settings.

Number of Iterations. Minimizing the objective function of our proposed method need to seek a proper number of iterations so that the algorithm has a better convergence performance while avoid overfitting. In this paper we try to the different number of iterations with various proportions of training data. The MAE and RMSE values are recorded in each iteration, shown in Fig. 5. From the results, we can conclude that MAE and RMSE values decrease gradually when increasing the number of iterations. Finally, we choose a limited number of iterations (i.e., 100) as the stop condition of our method.

5.5   Performance and Analysis

The underlying intuition that whether user retweet message or not is a binary value. Thus, in this section, we are consider the problem of retweet prediction as the task of classification. Specifically, we use the learned approximate entries as feature for Naïve Bayes classifier, and then evaluate the performance of our model and other baselines on the different training data settings. The experiment results on social network data are shown in Table 2. From the results, we can draw the following observations: (1) our proposed method outperforms all the other baseline methods on the different training datasets and improves the user's retweet prediction to some extent; (2) HCFMF, MNMFRP and RPSC outperforms PMF, which demonstrates that utilizing social contextual information is more effective than simply ignore such social context; (3) the relative improvement of HCFMF, MNMFRP and RPSC over LRC-BQ shows that the matrix factorization method is more suited to the retweet prediction task; (4)

among the RPSC variants, RPSC-U performs better in improving prediction performance in terms of F_1-score, indicating that social influence contributes more than message semantic. The possible explanation is that social influence comprehensively reflects user behavior patterns. In summary, these results suggest that our proposed model can achieve the better performance by casting the prediction problem into the solution of probabilistic matrix factorization with combining social contextual information.

Table 2. Performance of retweet prediction with different training data settings.

Method	60% as training data			100% as training data		
	Precision	Recall	F_1-score	Precision	Recall	F_1-score
PMF	0.484	0.434	0.458	0.584	0.534	0.558
LRC-BQ	0.518	0.677	0.587	0.698	0.770	0.733
MNMFRP	0.674	0.715	0.694	0.796	0.791	0.793
HCFMF	0.787	0.805	0.796	0.802	0.834	0.818
RPSC-U	0.791	0.811	0.801	0.804	0.847	0.825
RPSC-M	0.785	0.815	0.799	0.799	0.829	0.814
RPSC	0.801	0.827	0.814	0.806	0.853	0.829

6 Conclusion

In this paper, we propose a novel model to predict user's retweet behaviors based on probabilistic matrix factorization method, in which incorporates social influence learned from network structure and user's interaction behavior and message semantic obtained by modeling the topic distribution of the message. Then we combine user-user social influence and message-message semantic similarity regularization terms to constrain objective function under probabilistic matrix factorization. To validate the effectiveness and efficient of our model, we construct extensive experiments. The experimental results reveal that the proposed method can effectively improve the accuracy of retweet prediction compare with the state-of-the-art baseline methods. As future work, we plan to extend this work incorporating time delay factor between the posted message and the received user and explore how the deep learning model can be employed so that the feature vectors of users and messages can be further learned efficiently.

Acknowledgement. This work is supported by Natural Science Foundation of China (No. 61702508), and National Key Research and Development Program of China (No. 2016YFB0801004, 2016QY04w0905). This work is also partially supported by Key Laboratory of Network Assessment Technology, Chinese Academy of Sciences and Beijing Key Laboratory of Network security and Protection Technology.

References

1. Abdullah, N.A., Nishioka, D., Tanaka, Y., Murayama, Y.: User's action and decision making of retweet messages towards reducing misinformation spread during disaster. J. Inf. Process. **23**(1), 31–40 (2015)
2. Can, E.F., Oktay, H., Manmatha, R.: Predicting retweet count using visual cues. In: CIKM, pp. 1481–1484. ACM (2013)
3. Chen, J., Liu, Y., Zou, M.: User emotion for modeling retweeting behaviors. Neural Netw. **96**, 11–21 (2017)
4. Guo, G., Zhang, J., Yorke-Smith, N.: TrustSVD: collaborative filtering with both the explicit and implicit influence of user trust and of item ratings. In: AAAI, pp. 123–129 (2015)
5. Li, C., Wang, H., Zhang, Z., Sun, A., Ma, Z.: Topic modeling for short texts with auxiliary word embeddings. In: SIGIR, pp. 165–174. ACM (2016)
6. Liu, L., Tang, J., Han, J., Jiang, M., Yang, S.: Mining topic-level influence in heterogeneous networks. In: CIKM, pp. 199–208. ACM (2010)
7. Luo, Z., Osborne, M., Tang, J., Wang, T.: Who will retweet me?: finding retweeters in twitter. In: SIGIR, pp. 869–872. ACM (2013)
8. Ma, H., King, I., Lyu, M.R.: Learning to recommend with social trust ensemble. In: SIGIR, pp. 203–210 (2009)
9. Ma, H., Yang, H., Lyu, M.R., King, I.: SoRec: social recommendation using probabilistic matrix factorization. In: CIKM, pp. 931–940 (2008)
10. Metaxas, P.T., Mustafaraj, E., Wong, K., Zeng, L., O'Keefe, M., Finn, S.: What do retweets indicate? Results from user survey and meta-review of research. In: ICWSM, pp. 658–661 (2015)
11. Peng, H.-K., Zhu, J., Piao, D., Yan, R., Zhang, Y.: Retweet modeling using conditional random fields. In: ICDM, pp. 336–343. IEEE (2011)
12. Salakhutdinov, R., Mnih, A.: Probabilistic matrix factorization. In: NIPS, pp. 1257–1264 (2007)
13. Suh, B., Hong, L., Pirolli, P., Chi, E.H.: Want to be retweeted? Large scale analytics on factors impacting retweet in twitter network. In: SocialCom, pp. 177–184. IEEE (2010)
14. Tang, J., Wang, S., Hu, X., Yin, D., Bi, Y., Chang, Y., Liu, H.: Recommendation with social dimensions. In: AAAI, pp. 251–257 (2016)
15. Wang, C., Li, Q., Wang, L., Zeng, D.D.: Incorporating message embedding into co-factor matrix factorization for retweeting prediction. In: IJCNN, pp. 1265–1272. IEEE (2017)
16. Wang, M., Zuo, W., Wang, Y.: A multidimensional nonnegative matrix factorization model for retweeting behavior prediction. Math. Probl. Eng. **2015**, 1–10 (2015)
17. Yang, B., Lei, Y., Liu, J., Li, W.: Social collaborative filtering by trust. In: IJCAI, pp. 2747–2753 (2013)
18. Zhang, J., Tang, J., Li, J., Liu, Y., Xing, C.: Who influenced you? Predicting retweet via social influence locality. ACM TKDD **9**(3), 25 (2015)
19. Zhang, Q., Gong, Y., Guo, Y., Huang, X.: Retweet behavior prediction using hierarchical dirichlet process. In: AAAI, pp. 403–409 (2015)
20. Zhao, T., McAuley, J., King, I.: Leveraging social connections to improve personalized ranking for collaborative filtering. In: CIKM, pp. 261–270. ACM (2014)

Cascading Failure Based on Load Redistribution of a Smart Grid with Different Coupling Modes

WenJie Kang[1], PeiDong Zhu[2(✉)], and Gang Hu[1]

[1] College of Computer, National University of Defense Technology,
Changsha 410073, China
{kangwenjie,pdzhu,hugang}@nudt.edu.cn
[2] Department of Electronic Information and Electrical Engineering,
Changsha University, Changsha 410022, China

Abstract. As one of the most important properties of the power grid, the voltage load plays an important role in the cascading failure of the smart grid and load redistribution can accelerate the speed of the failure by triggering more nodes to overload and fail. The subnet structure and different coupling modes also affect the robustness of the smart grid. However, the research on the effect of load, subnet structure and coupling mode on the cascading failure of the smart grid is still rare. In this paper, the smart grid with two-way coupling link consists of a power grid with small world topology and a communication network with scale-free topology. An improved load-capacity model is applied to overload-induced failure in the power grid and node importance (NI) is used as an evaluation index to assess the effect of nodes on the power grid and communication network. We propose three kinds of coupling modes based on NI of nodes between the cyber and physical subnets, i.e., Random Coupling in Subnets (RCIS), Assortative Coupling in Subnets (ACIS) and Disassortative Coupling in Subnets (DCIS). In order to improve the robustness of the smart grid, a cascading failure model based on load redistribution is proposed to analyze the influence of different coupling modes on the cascading failure of the smart grid under both a targeted attack and random attack. Some findings are summarized as: (I) The robustness of the smart grid is improved by increasing the tolerance α. (II) ACIS applied to the bottom-up coupling link is more beneficial in enhancing the robustness of the smart grid than DCIS and RCIS, regardless of a targeted attack or random attack.

Keywords: Cascading failure · Load redistribution algorithm
Node importance · Two-way coupling relationship

Supported by National Natural Science Foundation of China (Grants 61572514 and 61501482) and Changsha Science and Technology Program (Grant K1705007).

© Springer International Publishing AG, part of Springer Nature 2018
Y. Shi et al. (Eds.): ICCS 2018, LNCS 10860, pp. 328–340, 2018.
https://doi.org/10.1007/978-3-319-93698-7_25

1   Introduction

As a kind of critical infrastructure, the smart grid is considered as an interdependent network with two-way coupling links [1]. Most recently, Parshani et al. [2] utilized the idea of complex networks to establish a mathematical model in order to explain the principle of cascading failure. However, many complex network models did not consider functional features, which do not reflect the real situation of the smart grid [3]. For instance, the characteristics of power flow can trigger load redistribution when some nodes fail. In addition, interdependence between cyber and physical networks may cause the cascading failure of interdependent networks. When a cyber node fails, it can cause its coupled physical node to fail and may lead to the failure of more physical nodes due to overload; in turn, those failed physical nodes will result in the failure of more coupled cyber nodes.

Buldyrev et al. [4] used "giant component" to represent the functional integrity of the composite network when a network is divided into multiple small components, and they establish a framework to analyze the mechanism of catastrophic failures in interdependent networks [5]. This framework breaks through the frontier of complex networks theory that still focuses on a single, non-interacting network [6]. Based on this theoretical model, many works used the giant component as a functional component to study the effect of partial support-dependence relationship [7] and coupling strength [2] on the robustness of interdependent networks.

The load has been used to study the cascading failure of interdependent networks in recent works [7–9]. Han and Yang [10] proposed a load-capacity model to analyze cascading failure over networks in both interdependent and isolated statuses, and simulation results prove that network robustness is positively related to capacity and negatively related to the load. When a node is removed by a random attack or targeted attack, the load of the node is distributed to its neighbors, when the load of those nodes exceeds their capacity, they will fail. Recently, more and more details were considered to enhance the robustness of interdependent networks, such as the coupling strength, support-dependence relations, coupling preferences, spatial effect, clustered structures [11], and community structure [12], etc. Cheng and Cao [13] studied in detail the robustness of interdependent networks coupled with different types of networks under both targeted and random attack. Babaei et al. [14] found that the robustness of modular small-world networks is improved by increasing inter-community links against both random and targeted attacks. Tian et al. [12] found that the number of inter-community connection is positively related to the robustness of interdependent modular scale-free (SF) networks.

However, the giant component used as the largest connected set of nodes does not apply to the smart grid, because the smaller components are still functional as long as the generation nodes and load nodes coexist in these components. Similarly, degree [12], betweenness [15,16], the degree of degree [17] considered as the node load also does not satisfy the reality, because they are still the properties of network structure and cannot be used to represent network function.

In most cases, many interdependent networks have multiple dependency links, local dependency links, and two-way dependence links. Coupling relationship between the physical and cyber network is not one-on-one correspondence [18] but two-way dependency [19].

In order to effectively enhance the robustness, China state power corporation has established a strategy that allows the physical nodes provide power supply to uncoupled cyber nodes. This means that we need to know which coupling mode will be beneficial in enhancing the robustness of the smart grid. As such, we propose three coupling modes between nodes in cyber and physical networks, i.e. Random coupling in subnets (RCIS), Assortative coupling in subnets (ACIS) and Disassortative coupling in subnets (DCIS). Secondly, node importance (NI) is defined to evaluate the influence of nodes on the network. We divided two coupling edges into the top-down coupling link and the bottom-up coupling link. Three coupling modes are established by applying ACIS, DCIS, and RCIS to the bottom-up coupling link when the top-down coupling link remains unchanged. The load redistribution caused by power flow is considered in the cascading failure of interdependent networks.

The rest of this paper is organized as follows. In Sect. 2, we propose the coupling model of the smart grid. In Sect. 3, Experiments and analysis are presented, and Sect. 4 concludes this paper and discusses the future work.

2   Coupling Model of the Smart Grid

The smart grid consists of a power grid and a communication network. The power grid and the communication network can be divided into many subnets in terms of geographical location of substations and each subnet is considered an autonomous system. Figure 1 shows two-layer network structure of a smart grid. The upper network is a communication network and different colored nodes form different subnets. Square nodes represent control centers and circular nodes represent measuring/controlling nodes. The lower network is a power grid that contains generation nodes and load nodes. There are internal edges and coupling edges in the smart grid, the internal edge is the link between nodes in a single network and coupling edge is the link between two-layer networks. Coupling edge has two types: $P \rightarrow C$ and $C \rightarrow P$. P represents the physical layer and C represents the communication layer. $C \rightarrow P$ is named the top-down coupling link and is shown as the red dotted edges in Fig. 1. $P \rightarrow C$ is named the bottom-up coupling link and is shown as the black dotted edges in Fig. 1.

Definition 1: The smart grid can be described by $SG = \{V, E, R\}$, where node set $V = \{V^P, V^C\}$ contains the physical node set V^P and the cyber node set V^C. The coupling relationship is $R = \{r_{ij} | i \in V^P, j \in V^C\}$, and node i belongs to V^P and node j belongs to V^C. The power gird is described by $V^P = \{v_1^G, v_2^G, \ldots, v_m^G, v_1^L, v_2^L, \ldots, v_n^L\}$, where v_i^G represents the generation node i and v_j^L represents the load node j that contains transmission nodes and distribution nodes. The communication network is described by

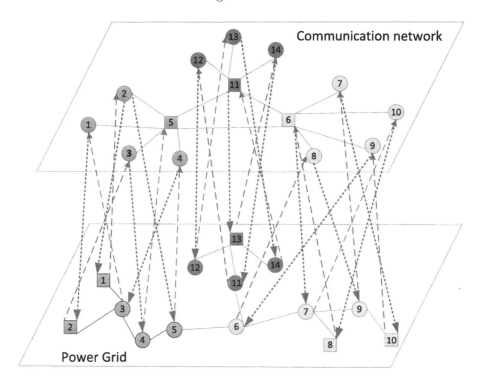

Fig. 1. The framework of the smart grid. Different colored nodes form different subnets and there is coupling relationship between nodes in same colored subnets. The red dotted edges represent the bottom-up coupling links and the black dotted edges represent the top-down coupling links. (Color figure online)

$V^C = \{v_1^C, ..., v_k^C, v_1^M, ..., v_q^M\}$, where v_i^C represents the control center node i and v_j^M represents the measuring/controlling node j.

Coupling relationship matrix R is used to describe dependence between the power grid and communication network. $R_{PC}(i,j) = r_{pi \rightarrow cj} = 1$ indicates that cyber node j depends on the physical node i. $R_{CP}(j,i) = r_{cj \rightarrow pi} = 1$ indicates that the physical node i depends on the cyber node j. $R_{PC}(i,j)$ or $R_{CP}(j,i) = 0$ indicates that there is no dependency relationship between nodes i and j. Here, special explanation $(R_{PC}(i,j) = 1) \neq (R_{CP}(j,i) = 1)$.

2.1 Node Importance Assessment in the Power Grid

The power grid is a special network, which contains the functional characteristic of the power flow. The power flow can cause the load of failed substations to distribute their neighbor nodes. When the load of a substation exceeds its capacity, it will fail. This will result in a new round of load redistribution until there is no overloaded node. Wang et al. [9] used $w_{im} * w_{jn}$ as the initial load of an edge e_{ij} to study the cascading failure of interdependent networks, where $w_{im} = (k_i * k_m)^{\alpha}$ represents the coupled strength between two coupled nodes i and m, and k_i is the degree of node i. Similarly, Han and Yang [10] used λs_i^{α} as the initial load of node i to establish cascading load model, where s_i represents the total weights of all edges connected with node i. Crucitti et al. [20] used the total number of most efficient paths passing through node i as its initial load to study the cascading failure in complex networks. The load of a node is defined as the betweenness centrality in order to study the cascading failure of interdependent networks [12]. Similarly, the initial load of the node i is represented by the betweenness B_i of the node that is defined as the number of the shortest paths between pairs of nodes over the network passing through the node i [21,22].

It is clear that the load mentioned in the above literatures belongs to structural attributes (e.g., betweenness, degree, and coupled strength etc.) rather than functional attributes (e.g., electric current, voltage, frequency, active power, and reactive power etc.). This assumption has certain irrationality. In fact, high voltage or low voltage exceeding a certain threshold may cause substations to fail. In addition, the voltage is associated with active power and reactive power; therefore, the load of substations is defined as its voltage and is written as:

$$L(v_i) = Vol_i \tag{1}$$

where $L(v_i)$ is the load of node i and Vol_i represents the voltage of node i.

Definition 2: The capacity of nodes is defined as tolerance capacity to deal with load changes. The capacity of node i can be described by (2), where α represents a tolerance parameter. $\pm$ represents the range of normal operation of substations, which means that the change of the voltage above α or below α can lead to the failure of node i.

$$C(v_i) = (1 \pm \alpha) * L(v_i) \tag{2}$$

Δf_{ij} represents the proportions of load distribution that the load of the failed node is distributed to the adjacent nodes by computing the impedance of the link between two nodes. $B(i)$ denotes neighbor nodes set of node i. I_{ij} denotes the impedance of a branch between node i and node j. I_{ik} represents the impedance of all branches passing through the node i and I_{Max} is the maximum value of I_{ik}. $\frac{1+(I_{Max}-I_{ij})}{(\sum_{k \in B(i)} I_{ik})}$ indicates that the larger the impedance of the branch is, the smaller the power flow passing through this branch is, which means that the smaller proportion of the load is distributed to the node j. β is a parameter, which determines that the load loss of node i is increased or decreased to its adjacent nodes. $\beta = 1$ denotes that load change $|\Delta f_{ij}| * L(v_i)$ of node i is added to the load of its neighbor node j, $\beta = -1$ denotes that the load of neighbor node j is reduced by $|\Delta f_{ij}| * L(v_i)$.

$$\Delta f_{ij} = \beta * \frac{1 + (I_{Max} - I_{ij})}{(\sum_{k \in B(i)} I_{ik})} \tag{3}$$

Definition 3: Node importance (NI) is used as an evaluation index to assess the influence of a failed node on the power grid, where f_i^P denotes failure node set in which the failure of all nodes is caused by a failed node i due to overload. $n(f_i^P)$ denotes the size of failure node set. NI is described as:

$$NI(v_i^p) = n(f_i^p) \tag{4}$$

The algorithm of load redistribution can be expressed as follows:

Step 1 (Initialization): Get information on the load of each node and the impedance of each branch.

Step 2 (Node Failure): A node is removed from the physical node set V^P. It will lead to the load of the failed node to be distributed to its neighbor nodes by Δf_{ij}.

Step 3 (Load Redistribution): If the removed node is load node, the load is distributed to neighbor nodes by Formula 3 and $\beta = 1$. If the removed node is the generation node, the load of its neighbor nodes changes to zero on the instant, then, the neighbor node's load of their neighbors will be distributed to them by Formula 3 and $\beta = -1$.

Step 4 (Judgment of failure nodes): If the load of a node exceeds the range of its capacity, it will fail. This will break the overall equilibrium of the load and triggers a new round of load redistribution.

Step 5 (Iteration): Repeat step 3 and 4 until the network achieves stabilization state.

Step 6 (Getting NI): Obtain FNS of the failed node until all nodes are handled.

2.2   Node Importance Assessment in the Communication Network

The communication network is an abstract overview of SCADA systems/ Energy Management Systems (EMS) in a smart grid, which is mainly responsible for collecting data and transmitting information. Therefore, the node passed by the bigger information flow has a significant role in transmitting data. Due to the real-time nature of information flow, we have no way to simulate the propagation of data flow in an experimental environment. As such, we assume that the cyber node with a bigger degree has large data transmission because its neighbor nodes must transmit data through it. Therefore, the degree can be used as an evaluation index to assess the importance of cyber nodes. In addition, The NI of cyber nodes also relies on the NI of its coupled physical nodes.

Definition 4: Node importance (NI) in the communication network depends on the degree of nodes and NI of the coupled physical nodes. The bigger degree is, the more important node is. When the degree of two nodes is different, the NI depends on its degree. When two nodes have the same degree, the NI of those cyber nodes depends on the NI of their coupled physical nodes. Where k_i is the degree of the cyber node i, NI_{Max} is the maximum of NI of physical nodes.

$$NI_i^C = k_i + \sum_{R_{CP}(i,j)=1} \frac{NI_j^P}{NI_{Max}^P} \tag{5}$$

2.3   Three Coupling Modes Based on Node Importance

The coupling mode refers to the connection mode of nodes between the cyber and physical networks and has three types: assortative coupling in subnets, disassortative coupling in subnets and random coupling in subnets. The coupling edges contain the top-down coupling link and the bottom-up coupling link. The former indicates that cyber nodes provide the physical nodes with remote monitoring, measurement and controlling. The latter indicates that physical nodes provide power support to the cyber nodes.

The aim of our research is to study which coupling mode applied to the coupling edges can enhance the robustness of interdependent networks. The research object is part of China power grid. Due to the long distance between the two substations, a cyber node coupled with a substation cannot monitor and control another substation. As such, three different coupling modes cannot be applied to the top-down coupling link. However, a substation can provide power-supply to another cyber node by accessing a wire. Similarly, long distances will increase costs, we can divide the cyber and physical network into multiple small subnets and apply ACIS, DCIS, and RCIS to the bottom-up coupling link to study how to improve the robustness of a smart grid when the top-down coupling link remains unchanged. We assume that the communication network A and the power grid B are divided into multiple subnets $A_1, A_2, ..., A_n$ and $B_1, B_2, ..., B_n$, respectively. A_1 and B_1 have the same geographical area, similarly A_2 and $B_2, ..., A_n$ and B_n.

Random coupling in subnets (RCIS): The top-down coupling link between A and B keeps unchanged. A node in B_1 is randomly chosen to connect to a node in A_1 with one-to-one correspondence until all nodes are handled. Repeat this process until all subnets are handled.

Assortative coupling in subnets (ACIS): The top-down coupling link between A and B keeps unchanged. A node with the largest NI in B_1 is connected to a node with the largest NI in A_1, and a node with the second largest NI in B_1 is selected to couple with a node with the second largest NI in A_1 until all nodes are handled. Repeat this process until all subnets are handled.

Disassortative coupling in subnets (DCIS): The top-down coupling link between A and B keeps unchanged. A node with the largest NI in B_1 is connected to a node with the smallest NI in A_1, and a node with the second largest NI in B_1 is selected to couple with a node with the second smallest NI in A_1 until all nodes are handled. Repeat this process until all subnets are handled.

3   Experiments and Analysis

In this section, we first use a small part of the real network, which is used as an example to evaluate our approach. The power grid consists of 154 substations and more than 192 transmission lines. The communication network contains 154 nodes and 175 lines.

Figure 2 shows that the NI in the power grid and the communication network. The NI in the power grid represents the size of failure node set in which the failure of any node is caused by a failed node. A bigger NI indicates that the removed

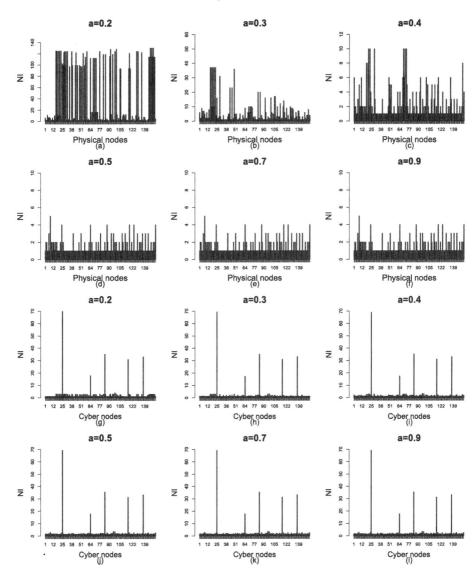

Fig. 2. (a)–(f) The NI of the power grid (g)–(i) The NI of the communication network

node has a more important influence on the smart grid and the NI of each
physical node is displayed with different tolerance parameter in Fig. 2(a)–(f). As
α increases, NI of each node shows a downward trend, but it tends to be stable
when α is greater than 0.5. When α is equal to 0.1, almost every failed node can
lead to the breakdown of the entire power grid except for four nodes. However,
when α is greater than 0.5, any failed node cannot or can only cause very few
node failures. The NI of the communication network is shown in Fig. 2(g)–(i).

Since the NI of the cyber nodes depends on its degree and NI of the coupled physical nodes, in addition, the NI of the physical nodes remains unchanged when $\alpha > 0.5$, the NI of the cyber nodes also has not changed. When the NI of the cyber and physical nodes is obtained, we can apply ACIS, DCIS, and RCIS to the bottom-up coupling link and simulate the cascading failure of the smart grid through removing a fraction $1 - p$ of nodes.

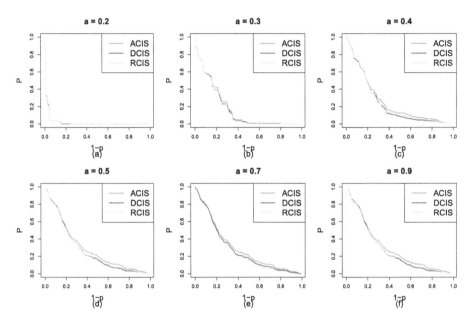

Fig. 3. The cascading failure of the smart grid according to which ACIS, DCIS, and RCIS are applied to the bottom-up coupling link under a targeted attack. (a) $\alpha = 0.2$ (b) $\alpha = 0.3$ (c) $\alpha = 0.4$ (d) $\alpha = 0.5$ (e) $\alpha = 0.7$ (f) $\alpha = 0.9$. It is clear that the ACIS applied to the bottom-up coupling link is more beneficial in enhancing the robustness of the smart grid under a targeted attack than DCIS and RCIS when $\alpha > 0.2$.

Figure 3 shows the robustness curve P of the smart grid with different α, where P represents the node survival rate after a fraction $1 - p$ of nodes is removed. A situation of $\alpha = 0.1$ is not discussed by us, because a failed node may lead to the failure of the entire power grid. When α is greater than 0.5, the curve P has no obvious change, which is because that any failed node cannot cause other nodes to fail or lead to the failure of a few nodes. This means that the robustness of interdependent networks remains unchanged when α exceeds a certain threshold. In Fig. 3(a)–(f), it is easy to find that the ranking of the robustness curve P is $ACIS > DCIS > RCIS$ when a fraction $1 - p$ of nodes is removed. This means that ACIS applied to the bottom-up coupling links is better able to enhance the robustness of the smart grid. That is because any failed physical nodes may cause the physical nodes with the smaller NI to fail, which further leads to the failure of the cyber nodes. If the physical nodes with the smaller NI are coupled with the cyber nodes with the higher NI, those failed physical nodes with the higher NI can lead to the failure of the physical nodes with the smaller NI. Furthermore, it will result in the failure of the more important cyber nodes. Therefore, ACIS applied to the bottom-up coupling link is more beneficial in enhancing the robustness of interdependent networks than DCIS and RCIS. It is clear that the robustness curve of the smart grid does not change because the power grid is sufficient to handle overload and nodes will not fail due to overload when $\alpha > 0.5$.

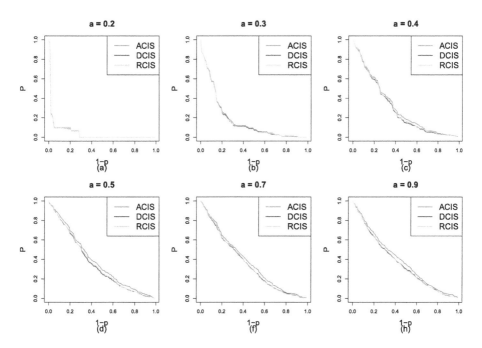

Fig. 4. The cascading failure of the smart grid according to which ACIS, DCIS, and RCIS are applied to the bottom-up coupling link under a random attack. (a) $\alpha = 0.2$ (b) $\alpha = 0.3$ (c) $\alpha = 0.4$ (d) $\alpha = 0.5$ (f) $\alpha = 0.7$ (h) $\alpha = 0.9$. It is clear that the ACIS applied to the bottom-up coupling link is more beneficial in enhancing the robustness of the smart grid under random attack than DCIS and RCIS when $\alpha > 0.2$.

The cascading failure of the smart grid according to which different coupling modes are applied to the bottom-up coupling link under random attack is shown in Fig. 4. It is clear that the ranking of the robustness curve P of the smart grid is $ACIS > RCIS > DCIS$. This means that ACIS applied to the bottom-up coupling link is more beneficial in enhancing the robustness of interdependent networks than DCIS and RCIS against random attack. When α equals 0.2, the robustness curve P suddenly drops to about zero after removing about 30% of the node. When α equals 0.3, the P falls to about 0.1 after removing about 50%

of the node. When α is larger than 0.5, the power grid has enough capacity to handle the overload. Therefore, a failed node is not easy to cause other nodes to fail. At this time, the load redistribution has less impact on the cascading failure of interdependent networks and the robustness curve P is close to the function curve $y + x = 1$ when α is equal to 0.6, 0.7, 0.8, and 0.9.

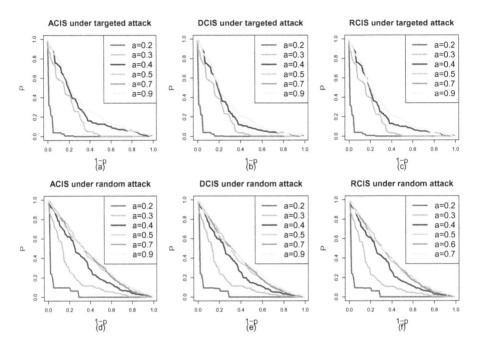

Fig. 5. A comparison of the robustness curves of the smart grid with different α according to which ACIS, DCIS, and RCIS are applied to the bottom-up coupling link. (a) ACIS under targeted attack. (b) DCIS under targeted attack. (c) RCIS under targeted attack. (d) ACIS under random attack. (e) DCIS under random attack. (f) RCIS under random attack. It is clear that α is positively related to the robustness of the smart grid when $\alpha <= 0.5$.

Figure 5(a)–(f) show that the robustness curve P of the smart grid with different α according to which ACIS, DCIS, and RCIS are applied to the bottom-up coupling link. It is clear α is positively related to the robustness of the smart grid regardless of ACIS, DCIS, and RCIS against both targeted attack and random attack when $\alpha <= 0.5$, but it has less impact on the robustness of the smart grid when α is larger than 0.5. This is why the yellow line of $\alpha = 0.9$ covers other lines of $\alpha = 0.5$ and $\alpha = 0.7$ in Fig. 5 (a)–(c). Two interesting conclusions can be drawn as follows: (I) ACIS applied to the bottom-up coupling link is more beneficial in enhancing the robustness of the smart grid than DCIS and RCIS regardless of a targeted attack or random attack when the top-down coupling link remains unchanged. (II) The robustness of interdependence network is improved by increasing the tolerance parameter α. Our research results can provide a meaningful guidance for network architects in order to improve the robustness of interdependent networks.

4 Conclusion

In this paper, we describe a special research scenario that different coupling modes are applied to the bottom-up coupling link when the top-down coupling link remains unchanged. This means that we study which coupling mode applied to the bottom-up link $(P \rightarrow C)$ can enhance the robustness of a smart grid when the top-down coupling link $(C \rightarrow P)$ remains unchanged. The voltage is used as the load of physical nodes to simulate load redistribution of failed nodes caused by power flow. The NI is used as an evaluation index to assess the influence of nodes on the communication network and power grid. Based on the NI, we proposed three coupling modes between the physical and cyber layers, i.e., ACIS, RCIS, and DCIS. Experiment results indicate that the robustness of the smart grid can be improved by increasing tolerance α, and we also find that the ACIS applied to the bottom-up coupling link is more beneficial in enhancing the robustness of the smart grid than RCIS and DCIS, regardless of a targeted attack or random attack.

In the future, we can extend the research scenario to the cyber-physical systems that different coupling modes are applied to both the top-down coupling link and the bottom-up coupling link. In addition, we can study the influence of ACIS, DCIS, and RCIS applied to different network types (e.g., Erdos-Renyi network, Small-World network, Scale-Free network, etc.) on the interdependent networks. The effect of global coupling and local coupling on the interdependent networks is also a very interesting direction. In fact, two coupled networks have different the number of nodes and the coupling relationship between the cyber and physical nodes is multiple-to-multiple correspondence. As such, the more complex coupling models are established in order to study the influence of network type, coupling mode, coupling link, coupling strength, and asymmetric coupling between the cyber and physical layer on the robustness of interdependent networks.

References

1. Rosato, V., Issacharoff, L., Tiriticco, F., et al.: Modelling interdependent infrastructures using interacting dynamical models. Int. J. Crit. Infrastruct. **4**(1/2), 63–79 (2008)
2. Parshani, R., Buldyrev, S.V., Havlin, S.: Interdependent networks: reducing the coupling strength leads to a change from a first to second order percolation transition. Phys. Rev. Lett. **105**(4), 048701 (2010)
3. Gao, J., Buldyrev, S.V., Stanley, H.E., et al.: Percolation of a general network of networks. Phys. Rev. E Stat. Nonlinear Soft Matter Phys. **88**(6), 062816 (2013)
4. Buldyrev, S.V., Parshani, R., Paul, G., Stanley, H.E., Havlin, S.: Catastrophic cascade of failures in interdependent networks. Nature **464**, 1025–1028 (2010)

5. Vespignani, A.: Complex networks: the fragility of interdependency. Nature **464**(7291), 984 (2010)
6. Chakravartula, S.: Complex networks: structure and dynamics. Diss. Theses - Gradworks **424**(4–5), 175308 (2014)
7. Dong, G., Tian, L., Zhou, D., et al.: Robustness of n interdependent networks with partial support-dependence relationship. EPL **102**(102), 68004 (2013)
8. Chen, Z., Du, W.B., Cao, X.B., et al.: Cascading failure of interdependent networks with different coupling preference under targeted attack. Chaos Solitons Fractals Interdisc. J. Nonlinear Sci. Nonequilibrium Complex Phenom. **80**, 7–12 (2015)
9. Wang, J., Li, Y., Zheng, Q.: Cascading load model in interdependent networks with coupled strength. Phys. A Stat. Mech. Appl. **430**, 242–253 (2015)
10. Han, H., Yang, R.: Improvement on load-induced cascading failure in asymmetrical inter-dependent networks: modeling and analysis. Math. Probl. Eng. **2015**(8), 1–10 (2015)
11. Huang, X., Shao, S., Wang, H., et al.: The robustness of interdependent clustered networks. EPL (Europhys. Lett.) **101**(1), 18002–18007 (2012)
12. Tian, M., Wang, X., Dong, Z., et al.: Cascading failures of interdependent modular scale-free networks with different coupling preferences. EPL **111**(1), 18007 (2015)
13. Cheng, Z., Cao, J.: Cascade of failures in interdependent networks coupled by different type networks. Phys. A Stat. Mech. Appl. **430**, 193–200 (2015)
14. Babaei, M., Ghassemieh, H., Jalili, M.: Cascading failure tolerance of modular small-world networks. IEEE Trans. Circ. Syst. II Exp. Briefs **58**(8), 527–531 (2011)
15. Cai, Y., Cao, Y., Li, Y., et al.: Cascading failure analysis considering interaction between power grids and communication networks. IEEE Trans. Smart Grid **7**(1), 530–538 (2016)
16. Zhao, Z., Zhang, P., Yang, H., et al.: Cascading failures in interconnected networks with dynamical redistribution of loads. Physica A-Stat. Mech. Appl. **433**, 204–210 (2015)
17. Yan, J., Zhu, Y., He, H., et al.: Multi-contingency cascading analysis of smart grid based on self-organizing map. IEEE Trans. Inf. Forensics Secur. **8**(4), 646–656 (2013)
18. Havlin, S.: Robustness of a network formed by n interdependent networks with a one-to-one correspondence of dependent nodes. Phys. Rev. E Stat. Nonlinear Soft Matter Phys. **85**(6), 3112–3113 (2012)
19. Habib, M.F.: Cascading-failure-resilient interconnection for interdependent power grid - optical networks. In: Optical Fiber Communications Conference and Exhibition, pp. 1–3. IEEE (2015)
20. Crucitti, P., Latora, V., Marchiori, M.: Model for cascading failures in complex networks. Phys. Rev. E Stat. Nonlinear Soft Matter Phys. **69**(4 Pt 2), 045104 (2004)
21. Zhang, J., Song, B., Zhang, Z., et al.: An approach for modeling vulnerability of the network of networks. Phys. A Stat. Mech. Appl. **412**(10), 127–136 (2014)
22. Hua, Q.: Attack structural vulnerability of power grids: a hybrid approach based on complex networks. Phys. A Stat. Mech. Appl. **389**(3), 595–603 (2010)

Measuring Social Responsiveness for Improved Handling of Extreme Situations

Nikolay Butakov[(✉)], Timur Fatkulin, and Daniil Voloshin

ITMO University, Saint-Petersburg, Russia
alipoov.nb@gmail.com, mellowstripe@gmail.com,
achoched@gmail.com

Abstract. Volunteering and community reaction is known to be an essential part of response to critical events. Rapid evolution and emergence of the new means of communication allowed even further expansion of these practices via the medium of the social networks. A new category of volunteers emerged – those that are not in the proximity to the area of emergency but willing to help the affected. Widely known as digital volunteers, they help aggregate, disseminate and distribute information to increase and maintain the awareness of stakeholders and resourceful individuals about the situation. There has been an upsurge of investigations of roles, timelines and aggregate characteristics of emergent communication. Compared to that, characteristics of crisis-related social media posts that predict wider social response to date have been studied modestly. In this research we are studying the process of reaction of potential digital volunteers to different extreme situations in a social media platform.

1 Introduction

Examples of social media being successfully used to help handle extreme situations are growing in numbers. Platforms can serve as a medium to the self-organization of people during critical events and dissemination of calls for assistance [3, 12, 18]. Though social media on their own provide functionality to improve cooperation, it is the social response of the community that lays at the base of resilience in crisis. However, communicative and cooperative behavior of users is hard to predict, especially if we consider that these are in fact influenced not only by the nature of a critical event, but the way it is reported by emergency managers.

People living in large congregations like cities constantly experience extreme situations at different scales. They react to extreme situations with organizing themselves into communities (or groups) dedicated to the information sharing, situational awareness and volunteering. In social media, the resulting communities become a natural way to interact with users in emergency cases and enact social responses of appropriate scales. Social response, as a component of self-organization effort, is interpreted here as a heterogeneous communicative reaction to critical situation that is discussed through social media. We specify that the distinctive feature of such reaction is its focus on the establishment of cooperation.

One of the most typical examples of such emergency response communities is a group called "ДТП и ЧП" (namely, road accidents and emergency situations, found at https://vk.com/spb_today) from Russian social network "Vkontakte" (https://vk.com). This group serves as a public hub of Saint-Petersburg for situational awareness and information dissemination about extreme situations in the city, a point where volunteers can be found and calls for help may be published. The group has obtained significant influence and attention from the residents of Saint-Petersburg and has been replicated with similar names in other cities of Russia (for example, Moscow and regions).

In this group, social response can be expressed with several main forms: (a) information dissemination via reposting which is the most accessible and the most important way for increasing situation awareness and leveraging social response; (b) help offering (volunteering); (c) discussion and advising which helps to increase attention to the problem and in some cases, may even help to find solution.

However, different resorts to the community via posts receive social response of different scales thus having either limited or amplified attention. Examples of both outcomes include: (a) the event of explosion in Saint-Petersburg on 3 April 2017; (b) frequent requests to help with a broken car.

To obtain a social response of an appropriate scale, it is important to understand what it depends on. Thus, the goal of this research is to address the following questions: (a) which characteristics of the community and messages shared within it predict the social response? (b) how to assess the scale of such response during the extreme situation?

To achieve this goal, we employ a random forest ensemble classifier that allows us to highlight the importance of communication features in social media communities. Some of the features proved to be more significant than others. For instance, the topics of the messages that resemble direct or indirect request for help are shown to be more associated with the social response than other topics and textual features. Answering the abovementioned questions allows us to propose a unified solution that can be effectively used as a basis for decision support in the scope of monitoring of the online social networks. This framework gives decision maker an ability to assess potential social response prior to public interaction with a certain community, depending on the textual representation of the certain event and desired format of the message as a device for effective communication.

The following are the contributions of the research outlined herein:

1. A framework designed as a module for a decision-support system, to estimate social response on message being published
2. Experimental study of the approach and framework.

2   Related Works

At its emergence, the use of social media in critical events has been a bottom-up process [1]. Prior to the first accounts of users engaging into coordination and self-organization via online social networks, new media (discussion, networking and blogging platforms) have been mostly viewed as a means to archive and disseminate the evidence of critical events in parallel with the more traditional centralized sources of information. Slowly, yet steadily, application of social media by emergency management practitioners is becoming more wide-spread [4]. As it is stated in the research literature, social media provides opportunities for decision makers to cope effectively with a number of issues [1] that are characteristic for virtually each step of the disaster management cycle. However, results of a large study of emergency services suggest that practitioners yet see social media as more of a broadcasting tool other than a mean to receive information [5].

Emergent volunteering in critical events is a long-standing research issue in the field of emergency management [6]. Previous research suggests [7] that though spontaneous volunteering is beneficial and in certain circumstances, essential for coping with critical situations, there are apparent issues that may complicate the engagement of so-called "unaffiliated disaster volunteers" [8]. Apart from legal gaps, apparent safety risks, organizational barriers and recognition problems [9], these include difficulties in coordination with official structures and practical absence of control over the activities carried out.

Unaffiliated volunteering can take up different forms. The more traditional ones result from the spatial convergence of people in the relative proximity to the area affected by the critical event. These include on-site transportation, manual labor, situational awareness and other efforts that require physical presence. Newer forms of online voluntarism (often referred to as digital volunteerism [9]) overcome the spatial and temporal limitations of localized ones. Users willing to help can participate in the information aggregation, sharing, manual analysis of data [10], translation [11] and other activities.

There is an increasing body of works that look into the characteristics of the communication of digital volunteers. For instance, in [12] authors analyze the use of ad hoc language and special codes to simplify the online coordination of crowdsourcing activities aimed at providing timely resilience for disaster-struck communities. Reuter et al. [13] analyze the shift in the content of the messages shared on Twitter throughout the lifecycle (i.e. increasing number of external links and decreasing number of reposts) of a particular disaster and the roles that online volunteers undertake in emergencies (including on-site volunteers, information generators and spreaders). More importantly, authors outline the design of the prototype system for bridging and coordinating spontaneous digital volunteers and those who engage in regular volunteering. Ukkusuri et al. [14] in their research carry out the analysis of posts of potential digital volunteers and affected households with a greater emphasis on the topics that are discussed by volunteers and characteristic sentiment of messages. They classify the content of the disaster-related messages spread and track the dynamics of the emergent categories relevant to critical event. Purohit et al. [15] extend the study of social media activities to distinguish between the information posted by users that request and provide help in three major cases spanning from 2010 to 2012.

It is worth to highlight that, in our knowledge, our work constitutes the first attempt for predicting social response by using the analysis of characteristics of the user-generated posts which contain requests for help in critical events. This issue has received attention in other subdomains [16], but has been overlooked in digital volunteering studies, primarily because of the focus of the researchers on detailed study of individual cases. Here we aim at merging these two areas of knowledge – predictive analysis of social response to social media messages and critical informatics. Moreover, we employ a perspective that aims at broader application of analysis than situational awareness or coordination.

3 Approach

To measure the potential scale of social response and turn it into a support tool for decision makers, it is necessary to build a framework which can operate in the environment where communities mentioned above are located. The key component of such framework is a classifier and a machine learning module which is used to train the former. Despite that, it shall contain monitoring and data preprocessing tools.

As it was mentioned above, social response is a collective reaction of community members to a certain event or new bits of information about it. Thus, estimation of social response scale should be based on accounting for individual users' reactions to published posts. The most important reaction is reposting and the rest of paper will be focused on repost count prediction, however it can be extended further to other types of reactions such as help offers.

The task can be formalized as a multi class classification problem where each class corresponds to a certain level of reaction (the classes can be found in Sect. 4). In most situations it is enough to know the scale than exact number of reposts. It should be noted that besides set of classes there is also a small number of posts that reach extremely high levels of reposting and may be seen as anomalies.

The communicative model of post introduced in our framework allows to combine information from structured and unstructured sources. It consists of three groups of features:

- Primary topic – usually there is only one topic that characterizes the type of the event itself such as missing person, fire, car hijack, etc.
- Secondary topics – topics which characterize conditions under which the event is happening. It may include topics about police engagement in the event or presence of casualties. Primary topics are accompanied these secondary topics and the same secondary topic may occur in pairs with different primary topics.
- Presence of special phrases or keywords – it includes explicit calls for help that can be detected by exact matching.
- External attributes – text length, presence of link to coordinator or phone number.

Using this model, the framework is capable of performing required mining and topic modelling to cover requirements for social response measuring. General architecture of the framework is presented on Fig. 1.

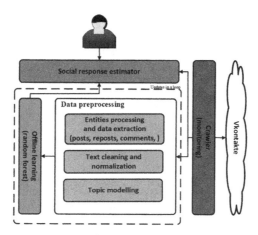

Fig. 1. General framework architecture

The framework consists of the following modules:

Crawler. The crawler module is responsible for collecting data about published messages and social response enacted by these messages. The module performs periodical monitoring of community and send updates to data preprocessing module and estimator module. The estimator module can use these data for assimilation and correcting its own predictions based upon dynamic of reposting for a certain message. The crawler was developed in previous works and its detailed description can be found in [20].

Data Preprocessing Module. The data preprocessing module is responsible for extraction of features from unstructured and half-structured data to be used to train classifier. The important part of this module is topic modelling procedure which uses BigARTM library [17] to mine topics from the text of posts. Topics may represent different aspects of situations such as types of participants, typical actions, locations and implicitly carry information about what part of population may be affected by message and thus who are more likely to repost it.

Offline Learning Module. The offline learning module is responsible for retraining classifier upon arriving data and updating it in estimator. Currently, random forest is used to perform classification. This algorithm has been chosen because of it has lower sensitivity to presence of unbalanced classes in dataset. The module also may perform grid search to ensure that the optimal parameters of the classifier itself have been selected. The need in retraining can be explained by dynamicity of the community. It grows and developing its own standards on message publishing, the users also get used to these standards and develop stable reaction on standard message types.

Social Response Estimator Module. The social response estimator module is responsible for using classifier to answer external requests on response scale estimation. This module serves as an interface to communicate with user or other components of decision support system.

Data assimilation and prediction of the scale on-the-fly can be also used to decide whatever crawler should increase frequency of its monitoring to collect comments as quick as they appear. The latter may be important to detect emerging deviant behaviors of users. Some users can comment using offensive language to deliberately harm others participating in discussion or troll. Such actions may distract community from the problem and reduce social response.

4   Experimental Study

In our experimental study we use the data collected from the public page in Russian social network "Vkontakte" intended for user's reports of road accidents, emergencies, and search for the missing people. The whole dataset for 2017 year amounts to 12457 records.

Our set of classification features consists of topic distribution of post's text across 40 topics extracted with BigARTM [17], and two textual features: text length, and whether text of the post contains phone numbers of possible emergency coordinators.

The number of topics has been established as a result of multiple trials in which we have investigated its impact on the classifier's accuracy, as well as patterns in distributions of main topics for each classification class, which we discuss in more details in the end of the section. In order to obtain more meaningful topics, we use the following set of model regularizers with the following values (Table 1):

Table 1. Values of ARTM model regularizers

Model regularizer	Value
Sparse Phi regularizer tau	−1.5
Sparse Theta regularizer tau	−0.5
Decorrelator Phi regularizer tau	1e+5

These model parameters allow to successfully sharpen important topics and smooth background topics, which yield higher accuracy of classification. To assess the relative importance of classification features we have trained an ensemble of extremely randomized trees [18]. Importance of each feature is shown on Fig. 2:

It is evident that the most important features are text length, topic 23, 20, 14, 2, and topic 36. Importance of other features apart from phone number is distributed more or less uniformly. We can assume that presence of phone number in text doesn't play any vital role in social response prediction. Most important topics are presented in the Table 2:

We treat prediction of social response as a classification problem. To do so, we have distributed posts with different reposts volume into the following categories:

- Reposts volume below 10 (class 0) – 9819 posts
- Reposts volume between 10 & 100 (class 1) – 2257 posts
- Reposts volume higher than 100 (class 2) – 381 posts.

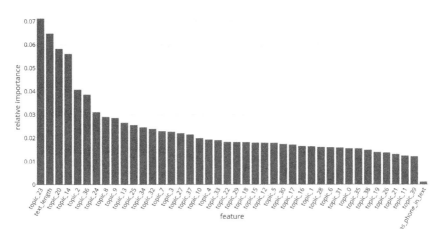

Fig. 2. Feature importance

Table 2. Description of important topics

Topic	Terms
Topic 23	hijack, number, color, year, night, information, plea
Topic 20	number, disappear, wear, black, jacket, call, grandmother
Topic 14	side, road accident, jam, service, avenue, intersection
Topic 2	child, friend, found, dog, owner, call
Topic 36	which, can, police, knew, today, own

These categories were used as labels for the classifier.

In order to test our ability to predict levels of social response, we have trained random forest ensemble [19] using one-vs-rest multiclass strategy. We have employed 5-fold grid-search cross-validation to establish model parameters that correspond to highest classification accuracy. Values of these parameters are shown in the Table 3:

Table 3. Parameters of random forest ensemble

Model parameter	Value
Max tree depth	12
Max features	6
Min samples leaf	1
Min samples split	5
Criterion	Gini
Number of estimators	300

Results of our classification experiment are presented on Fig. 3:

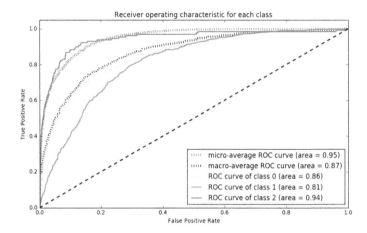

Fig. 3. Receiver operating characteristic for each class of reposting volume (with grid-search)

We further investigate distinctive features of each reposting category by drawing distribution of corresponding main topics (Fig. 4).

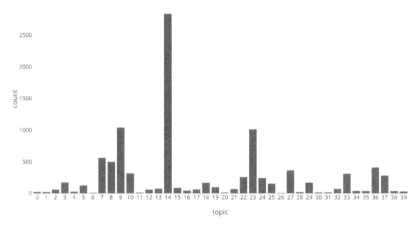

Fig. 4. Distribution of main topics for posts with reposts volume under 10

The most prevailing topic for posts with reposting volume under 10 is topic 14 which corresponds to basic reports of road accidents (Fig. 5).

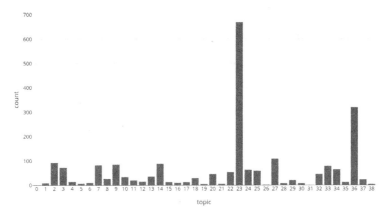

Fig. 5. Distribution of main topics for posts with reposts volume between 10 & 100

In case of reposting volume between 10 & 100 the most dominant topic is topic 23 which corresponds to reports of car theft (Fig. 6).

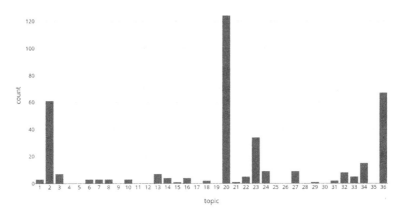

Fig. 6. Distribution of main topics for posts with reposts volume more than 100

Posts with counts for reposts more than 100 are mostly described by topics 20, 36, and 2. These topics correspond to reports of missing people and pets, as well as generic messages involving police notifications.

We see that prevailing topic of the post is indeed a good indicator of potential social response. One of the prominent examples of this is prevailing of topic corresponding to generic road accidents reports across posts with low reposting activity, while posts with reposting volume higher than 10 mostly described by topics related to car high jacking, reports of missing persons, and other important information. However, the most research interest is attracted by the posts with highest reposting activity. Due to their low occurrence (less than 5% of the whole dataset) these posts should be treated as outliers. To investigate which features contribute to such high level of social response, we selected topic 36 that is articulated in both posts with huge amount of reposts and ordinary ones. As a result of side-by-side comparison of posts with the same main topic from both categories, we found out that unlike ordinary posts, posts with high reposting activity often contain explicit or implicit pleas and calls for action that naturally require as wide information spreading as possible. On the other hand, posts with low reposting volume are mostly of informative nature. Such posts are rare among posts with high reposting volume, but if they occur, they often contain information that might be useful for users in the future, like important phone numbers and warnings. We need to take these distinctive features into account, to successfully distinguish posts with very high possible reposting volume on the early stage of their spreading. One of possible ways to do so is to specifically mine such calls for actions or other textual forms that require active participation.

5 Conclusion and Future Work

In this paper we presented a framework for social response estimation, which can be used to predict possible level of reposting activity considering textual features of the post and topics that characterize its semantic. The results of our experimental study show that out framework is able to predict the scale of response with high precision and response is mostly driven by topics. However, while investigating rare posts with very high reposting level it was found out that such level of social response is achieved not only due to the main topics of messages, but rather as interplay between topics and additional features such as pleas, calls for action, and other subtle textual or external attributes. One of the prospect for future work is to use these implicit features to successfully predict which posts are about to obtain wide propagation.

Acknowledgment. This research financially supported by Ministry of Education and Science of the Russian Federation, Agreement #14.578.21.0196 (03.10.2016). Unique Identification RFMEFI57816X0196.

References

1. Simon, T., Goldberg, A., Adini, B.: Socializing in emergencies—a review of the use of social media in emergency situations. Int. J. Inf. Manag. **35**(5), 609–619 (2015)
2. Procopio, C.H., Procopio, S.T.: Do you know what it means to miss New Orleans? Internet communication, geographic community, and social capital in crisis. J. Appl. Commun. Res. **35**(1), 67–87 (2007)
3. Palen, L., Liu, S.B.: Citizen communications in crisis: anticipating a future of ICT-supported public participation. In: Proceedings of the SIGCHI Conference on Human Factors in Computing Systems, pp. 727–736 (2007)
4. Cohen, S.E.: Sandy marked a shift for social media use in disasters. Emerg. Manag. (2013)
5. Reuter, C., Ludwig, T., Kaufhold, M.-A., Spielhofer, T.: Emergency services' attitudes towards social media: a quantitative and qualitative survey across Europe. Int. J. Hum Comput Stud. **95**, 96–111 (2016)

6. Stallings, R.A., Quarantelli, E.L.: Emergent citizen groups and emergency management. Public Adm. Rev. **45**, 93–100 (1985)
7. Fischer, D., Posegga, O., Fischbach, K.: Communication barriers in crisis management: a literature review. In: ECIS, 2016, Research Paper 168 (2016)
8. Sobiegalla, F., Posegga, O., Fischbach, K.: Evaluating a mobile crisis response system for the management of disaster volunteers. In: Designing the Digital Transformation: DESRIST 2017 Research in Progress, Proceedings of the 12th International Conference on Design Science Research in Information Systems and Technology. Karlsruhe, Germany, 30 May–1 June 2017
9. Whittaker, J., McLennan, B., Handmer, J.: A review of informal volunteerism in emergencies and disasters: definition, opportunities and challenges. Int. J. disaster risk Reduct. **13**, 358–368 (2015)
10. Fishwick, C.: Tomnod–the online search party looking for Malaysian Airlines flight MH370. Guard **14**, 37 (2014)
11. Meier, P.: Human computation for disaster response. In: Michelucci, P. (ed.) Handbook of Human Computation, pp. 95–104. Springer, New York (2013). https://doi.org/10.1007/978-1-4614-8806-4_11
12. Starbird, K., Palen, L.: Voluntweeters: self-organizing by digital volunteers in times of crisis. In: Proceedings of the SIGCHI Conference on Human Factors in Computing Systems, pp. 1071–1080 (2011)
13. Reuter, C., Heger, O., Pipek, V.: Combining real and virtual volunteers through social media. In: ISCRAM (2013)
14. Ukkusuri, S., Zhan, X., Sadri, A., Ye, Q.: Use of social media data to explore crisis informatics: study of 2013 Oklahoma Tornado. Transp. Res. Rec. J. Transp. Res. Board **2459**, 110–118 (2014)
15. Purohit, H., Hampton, A., Bhatt, S., Shalin, V.L., Sheth, A.P., Flach, J.M.: Identifying seekers and suppliers in social media communities to support crisis coordination. Comput. Support. Coop. Work **23**(4–6), 513–545 (2014)
16. Bandari, R., Asur, S., Huberman, B.A.: The pulse of news in social media: forecasting popularity. ICWSM **12**, 26–33 (2012)
17. Vorontsov, K., Frei, O., Apishev, M., Romov, P., Dudarenko, M.: BigARTM: open source library for regularized multimodal topic modeling of large collections. In: International Conference on Analysis of Images, Social Networks and Texts, pp. 370–381 (2015)
18. Geurts, P., Ernst, D., Wehenkel, L.: Extremely randomized trees. Mach. Learn. **63**(1), 3–42 (2006)
19. Breiman, L.: Random forest. Mach. Learn. **45**(5), 1–35 (1999)
20. Butakov, N., Petrov, M., Radice, A.: Multitenant approach to crawling of online social networks. Procedia Comput. Sci. **101**, 115–124 (2016)

A Computational Model-Based Framework to Plan Clinical Experiments – An Application to Vascular Adaptation Biology

Stefano Casarin[1,2,3](✉), Scott A. Berceli[4,5], and Marc Garbey[1,2,3]

[1] LASIE UMR 7356 CNRS, University of La Rochelle, La Rochelle, France
[2] Center for Computational Surgery, Houston Methodist Research Institute, Houston, TX, USA
scasarin@houstonmethodist.org
[3] Department of Surgery, Houston Methodist Hospital, Houston, TX, USA
[4] Department of Surgery, University of Florida, Gainesville, FL, USA
[5] Malcom Randall VAMC, Gainesville, FL, USA

Abstract. Several computational models have been developed in order to improve the outcome of Vein Graft Bypasses in response to arterial occlusions and they all share a common property: their accuracy relies on a winning choice of the coefficients' value related to biological functions that drive them. Our goal is to optimize the retrieval of these unknown coefficients on the base of experimental data and accordingly, as biological experiments are noisy in terms of statistical analysis and the models are typically stochastic and complex, this work wants first to elucidate which experimental measurements might be sufficient to retrieve the targeted coefficients and second how many specimens would constitute a good dataset to guarantee a sufficient level of accuracy. Since experiments are often costly and time consuming, the planning stage is critical to the success of the operation and, on the base of this consideration, the present work shows how, thanks to an *ad hoc* use of a computational model of vascular adaptation, it is possible to estimate in advance the entity and the quantity of resources needed in order to efficiently reproduce the experimental reality.

Keywords: Agent based model · Experiment planning · Virtual dataset

1 Introduction

An unfavorable postsurgical vascular adaptation is the main cause of the long-term failure of Vein Graft Bypasses (VGBs), with an incidence rate of 12% after just a month from the original intervention [1].

To improve the current outcome, our group of investigators, in addition to others [2], studied vascular adaptation both on a clinical [3] and a computational base [4–6], from deterministic differential equation models to especially Agent-Based Models (ABMs) that use a so-called bottom up approach depending on the level of spatio-temporal and biological information needed.

Our hypothesis is that the ABM [5] mimics the fundamental biological functions of the vein graft's adaptation (see Fig. 1) with high credibility, being indeed able to

© Springer International Publishing AG, part of Springer Nature 2018
Y. Shi et al. (Eds.): ICCS 2018, LNCS 10860, pp. 352–362, 2018.
https://doi.org/10.1007/978-3-319-93698-7_27

replicate the basic observations driving Intimal Hyperplasia (IH) and Wall Remodeling (WR) that are globally recognized as the leading events for the restenosis [1].

We used standard methods both to restrict the analysis to a minimum set of coefficients and to reach a high level of confidence with our model, respectively by performing a non-linear stability analysis [7], and by cross-validating the ABM on phenomenological models [5, 8].

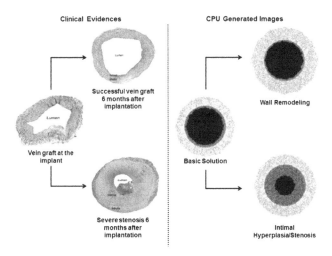

Fig. 1. Agent-Based Model. An ABM (on the right) replicates the clinical evidences (left) of vein bypasses long-term follow-up [5].

The overall goal is to retrieve the fundamental parameters of vascular adaptation on a base of experimental data, a task that implies to perform a large number of experiments. This need is actual both in vascular field as several times demonstrated by different group of investigators [2, 9, 10], but also more in general in the world of computational models developed to replicate pathophysiological phenomena [11].

Before starting the actual experiments, two fundamental questions concern the kind of measurements and the number of subjects needed in order to achieve a realistic outcome.

Considering that the ABM model is stochastic and assuming that it is as noisy as the biological system that replicates, our basic method consists into using the ABM to mimic the experiments by generating a virtual experimental data set.

In this way, we can ask ourselves how large the dataset should be and what kind of measurements will be good enough to recover the unknown biological parameters. This latter is typically a non-trivial exercise, which complexity strongly depends on the kind of the measurements needed.

Finally, the performance of the proposed technique relates on an accurate setup of the ABM's driving coefficients and especially on an effective choice of their range of perturbation, as fluctuations of the ABM can lead to large output variations that would be hard to catch with the proposed inverse problem.

Both the required features are guaranteed by an accurate study of the experimental data preceding the model's implementation [3].

2 Methods

According to the conceptual scheme of Fig. 2, the method is based on a twofold usage of our ABM [5] that acts both as virtual experimental dataset generator (labeled as ABM1) and as a true computational model (ABM2).

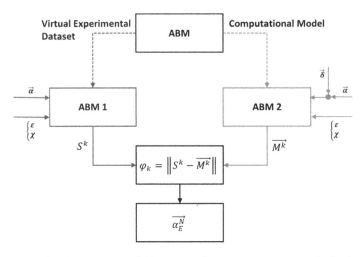

Fig. 2. Conceptual scheme. A twofold usage of an ABM generates both the reference measurements (S^k) intended as experimental data to be replicated, and the perturbed output $(\overrightarrow{M^k})$ to be compared with the reference in order to solve the inverse problem and to plan the experiment.

First, the left part of Fig. 2 refers to the generation of the virtual experimental data. The ABM works as a black box driven in input by hemodynamic perturbations, ε and χ respectively referring to shear stress and wall tension, and by constant coefficients corresponding to the level of activity of the cellular events of interest, i.e. vector $\vec{\alpha}$. ABM1's output is the virtual measurement S^k which relation follows:

$$S^k = \sum_{n=1}^{N} S_n^k, \tag{1}$$

where k is the label identifying the specific measurement (e.g. k = 1 for intimal area, k = 2 for medial area, *et cetera*) and N is the number of ABM1 independent simulations that would be the specimen's size in a true experimental setup.

Second, in the right part of Fig. 2 the ABM is used as a computational model and for the purpose of this work, a browsing of the coefficients' space was performed in order to solve the inverse problem, i.e. starting from the same setup of ABM1, a vector $\vec{\delta} = \{-0.5, -0.375, \ldots, 0, \ldots, 0.5\}$ was applied to the driving coefficients defined with $\vec{\alpha}$. At each element of $\vec{\delta}$ corresponds a new input/output of ABM2. ABM1's output is a constant measurement S^k, while ABM2's output is a vector of measurements $\overrightarrow{M^k}$, where the size of $\overrightarrow{M^k}$ is equal to the size of $\vec{\delta}$, and it corresponds to P = 9.

To solve the inverse problem consists in comparing S^k with $\overrightarrow{M^k}$, i.e. in minimizing the objective function (φ_k) defined as follows:

$$\varphi_k = \sqrt{\frac{1}{P}\sum_{p=1}^{P}(S^k - M_p^k)^2} * 100. \tag{2}$$

If the entity of the measurements (k) is suitable enough, and if the number of samples (N) guarantees a robust analysis, the result of the minimization of φ_k, indicated with $\overrightarrow{\alpha_E^N}$, will correspond to the same values defined with vector $\vec{\alpha}$, i.e. $\vec{\alpha} = \overrightarrow{\alpha_E^N}$.

A counter-proof will be to generate another independent virtual dataset by running the ABM on the base of N simulations and by setting it with $\vec{\alpha} = \overrightarrow{\alpha_E^N}$. In this way the percentile error Ξ_k between S^k, the old reference, and S_N^k, the new reference, is

$$\Xi_k = \frac{\left|s^k - s_N^k\right|}{s^k} * 100. \tag{3}$$

When the Ξ_k vs. N plot goes below an acceptable error threshold, N is suitable to build an experimental setup, and at the same way, k is an effective measurement.

In this work, IH and WR were chosen as case studies and they were addressed both separately and coupled.

2.1 Intimal Hyperplasia

IH is mostly driven by Smooth Muscular Cells (SMCs) division within intima fostered by a decrease in shear stress from the baseline condition, representing the vein at implant. As ABM is stochastic, the related formula corresponds to a probability distribution, true for WR too, which writes:

$$P_{div}^{int} = \alpha_1\left(1 + \alpha_3\left(\frac{\tau(t) - \tau_0(1+\varepsilon)}{\overline{\tau}}\right)\right), \tag{4}$$

where $\alpha_1 = \frac{1}{T_{matrix}} = 0.5$ defines the baseline of cellular division, $\tau(t)$ is the shear stress recorded at t-th time point, τ_0 is the baseline value of the shear stress, $\overline{\tau} = 0.25$ is a normalization constant to maintain the probability discrete value between 0 and 1, $\varepsilon = 0.5$ represents a 50% drop in shear stress to promote SMC division, and finally $\alpha_3 = 0.2$ is the constant coefficient that drives SMC intimal division.

The measurement chosen to test the experimental setup is the intimal area, labeled as $k = 1$, and the accuracy of the inverse problem solution will be tested, in terms of percentile error, with an increasing number of samples starting with N = 10 up to N = 100.

To solve the inverse problem for IH means to be able to retrieve for α_3 the value of 0.2 by minimizing the objective function φ_1 corresponding to the RMS between the output of ABM1, S^1 and ABM2, $\overrightarrow{M^1}$. As last remark, the addressed problem will be one-dimensional as only a single coefficient will be retrieve out of the input vector $\vec{\alpha}$.

2.2   Wall Remodeling

The framework for WR is similar to the one of IH, with the difference that WR is fostered by SMC division within media favored by an increase of wall tension from the baseline condition. The related mathematical formula writes

$$P_{div}^{med} = \alpha_1\left(1 + \alpha_4 \frac{\sigma(t) - \sigma_0(1+\chi)}{\bar{\sigma}}\right), \tag{5}$$

where $\sigma(t)$ is the wall tension recorded at t-th time point, σ_0 is the baseline value of wall tension, $\bar{\sigma} = 40$ is the normalization constant, $\chi = -0.005$ represents a 0.5% increase in wall tension to promote SMC division, and finally $\alpha_4 = 0.3$ is the constant coefficient that drives SMC medial division.

The measurement chosen is the medial area, labeled k = 2, while the number of samples stays between N = 10 and N = 100.

To solve the inverse problem for WR means to be able to retrieve for α_4 the value of 0.3 by minimizing the objective function φ_2 obtained with the RMS between the output of ABM1, S^2 and ABM2, $\overrightarrow{M^2}$. As for IH and for the same reasons, the problem is still one-dimensional.

2.3   Coupled Intimal Hyperplasia and Wall Remodeling

A more realistic implementation considers the simultaneous study of IH and WR which maintains the same setup for both the cellular events, described with Eqs. (4) and (5).

The measurements chosen to solve the inverse problem are still intimal area and medial area respectively, however, if with a single cellular event the inverse problem was one-dimensional (φ_1 and φ_2), with two cellular events acting simultaneously the problem becomes two-dimensional ($\varphi_{1,2}$ and $\varphi_{2,1}$). By maintaining the same vector $\vec{\delta}$ and by applying it both to α_3 and α_4, the output of ABM2 will not be a simple vector of measurements, but a matrix of measurements where the i-th row includes the values for a fixed α_4 at the variation of α_3, while the j-th column includes the values for a fixed α_3 at the variation of α_4. Accordingly, each of the two coefficients will be retrieved by minimizing a 2D-surface instead of a 1D-curve.

In general, by adding more cellular events to the analysis, the complexity and the dimensionality of the inverse problem increase proportionally with the closeness to the physiological reality.

3   Results and Discussions

The virtual experiments performed are described with the density map reported in Fig. 3. In each panel the number of SMCs across the graft wall is represented against the normalized wall thickness, making so both intima (in red) and media (in blue) share the same unitary dimension. The density map is reported as a histogram with 5 steps of discretization for each compartment.

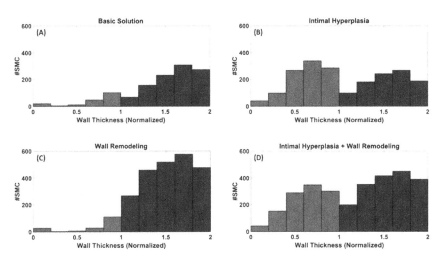

Fig. 3. Virtual Experiments. Starting from a basic solution (A), representing a healthy vein at the implant, ABM1 is setup in order to simulate the hyperplasia of tunica intima (B) and tunica media (C), both acting singularly and coupled (D). (Color figure online)

The analysis of the density map is coherent with the well-known physiological reality: Fig. 3(A) represents the ABM baseline condition that corresponds to a vein at the implant. By fostering intimal SMCs division, a noticeable increase in intimal SMCs number is recorded in Fig. 3(B), well representing IH, while no substantial variation is recorded in the number of medial SMCs. Similar considerations for Fig. 3(C), where SMCs division within tunica media generates an increase in SMCs medial number, while no variation from the baseline is recorded for intimal SMCs, typical of the WR phenomenon. Results appreciated in Fig. 3(B) and (C) are coherent with the single cellular event nature of the experiments performed so far, while a different subject is valid for Fig. 3(D), where SMCs division is active both in intima and in media, doing so both the number of SMCs in intima and in media are prone to increase.

Despite the setups to simulate the WR in Fig. 3(D) and (B) are the same, a lower increase in medial cell numbers is recorded in Fig. 3(D) than in 3(B). This is due to the fact that IH and WR act simultaneously in the last experiment performed, and accordingly, the IH phenomenon accelerates the wall relaxation toward the baseline value and this reduces the SMCs division in media. This is the perfect example of how cellular events can generate noise at experimental level when they act simultaneously, making the identification process way harder, in the specific case by affecting the identification of α_4.

The inverse problem to singularly identify α_3 was successfully solved and the related analysis is reported in Fig. 4.

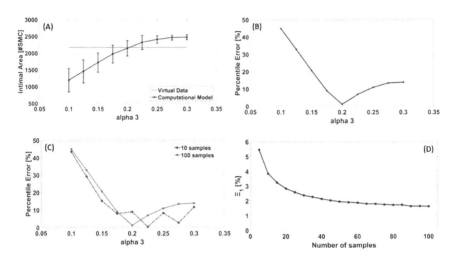

Fig. 4. Intimal Hyperplasia. The interval of confidence (A) and the actual value (B) of α_3 are retrieved on the base of $N = 100$ samples by measuring the intimal area. The accuracy of the retrieval is evaluated by comparing the error using 10 and 100 samples (C). Finally, the accuracy of the fitted model is studied against the number of samples used during the retrieval process (D). (Color figure online)

By monitoring the intimal area as the mean value over 100 samples, a precise identification of $\alpha_3 = 0.2$ was obtained. This is clear from Fig. 4(A) where the intimal area as output of ABM1 (S^1) is plotted in solid red, along with its standard deviation in dashed red, against the intimal area as output of ABM2 ($\overrightarrow{M^1}$) in solid blue, again along with its standard deviation. Fact that the perturbation level-dependent blue curve intersects the constant red curve right in correspondence of $\alpha = 0.2$ is a clear indicator of the goodness of our analysis, also corroborated by Fig. 4(B), where the PRMS function between S^1 and $\overrightarrow{M^1}(\varphi_1)$ is precisely minimized in correspondence of $\alpha_3 = 0.2$. Furthermore, from the comparison between the minimization of φ_1 by using $N = 10$ (blue dashed line) and $N = 100$ (solid red), reported in Fig. 4(C), it is easy to deduce how the number of samples used is pivotal in order to precisely identify the right value of α_3. One can indeed simply appreciate how, by using only 10 samples, φ_1 is not uniquely minimized and not even in correspondence of the right value. Finally, the non-suitability of a low number of samples is further sustained with Fig. 4(D) that shows the trend of Ξ_1 against N. If an error lower than 2% is considered as acceptable, then at least 50 samples are needed to obtain a realistic analysis, a number that increases if a lower error is desired.

Finally, according with the successful minimization result, the intimal area can be considered as a solid biological measurement to prepare the experimental setup, and as its measuring does not pose any significant issue, other potential measurements have not been investigated.

Very similar considerations can be retrieved from the identification of α_4, which is reported in Fig. 5.

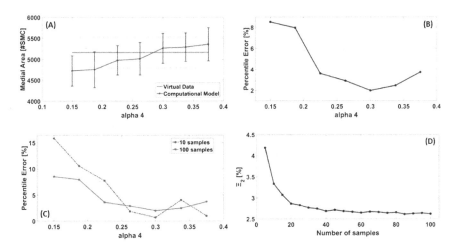

Fig. 5. Wall Remodeling. The interval of confidence (**A**) and the actual value (**B**) of α_4 are retrieved on the base of N = 100 samples by measuring the medial area. The accuracy of the retrieval is evaluated by comparing the error using 10 and 100 samples (**C**). Finally, the accuracy of the temporal simulation is studied against the number of samples used during the retrieval process (**D**). (Color figure online)

The results are here presented with the same fashion of Fig. 4. The accuracy of this identification may be not as high as the one appreciated for α_3, but it is still reasonable enough to be considered as suitable for a modeling purpose. Indeed, if on one side from Fig. 5(A) emerges that the computational model curve (blue) does not perfectly intersect the virtual dataset curve (red) in $\alpha_4 = 0.3$, on the other side it is clear from Fig. 5(B) how φ_2 is still nicely minimized right around 0.3, even though not with the same sharpness of φ_1 in correspondence of $\alpha_3 = 0.2$ (see Fig. 4(B)).

What already appreciated for α_3 about the increased confidence along with an increased number of samples is confirmed for α_4 by observing Fig. 5(C), where φ_2 does not reach a global minimum when minimized on the base of 10 samples. The analysis of Fig. 5(D) not surprisingly confirms the need of a conspicuous sample numbers to ensure the reproduction of the experimental data free from a high error. It is interesting to notice how not even a high number of samples like N = 100 ensures to reach a $\Xi_2 < 2\%$ like instead happened for Ξ_1. However, a sort of plateau is reached with N = 60 that can be considered as a number beyond that the goodness of the analysis does not significantly increase.

Accordingly, if someone assumes a $\Xi_2 \approx 2.6$ as an acceptable error, the medial area can be considered as an appropriate measure to setup the experiment and for the same reason reported for intimal area, other measurements have not been considered in this analysis.

Finally, the inverse problem solution is reported in Fig. 6 for the coupled IH and WR, where a qualitative more than a quantitative analysis is appreciable. It is important to remark how to solve the inverse problem for the coupled IH and WR means to ideally minimize a surface around a straight line instead of a curve around a single point. Also, the number of samples was chosen to be here $N = 60$, which is the highest between $N = 50$ and $N = 60$ to singularly identify α_3 and α_4 respectively.

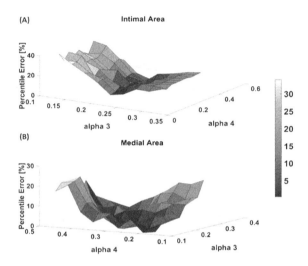

Fig. 6. Intimal Hyperplasia and Wall Remodeling. The value of α_3 (A) by intimal area measurement and α_4 (B) by medial area measurement are retrieved by letting intimal hyperplasia and wall remodeling acting simultaneously.

From Fig. 6(A), the 2D surface corresponding to $\varphi_{1,2}$ is minimized in correspondence of the straight line where $\alpha_3 = 0.2$. This is a remarkable result, indeed even though the level of complexity of the system has increased of one order of magnitude, by maintaining the same experimental setup, a satisfying result is still achievable. However, the same cannot be stated about the minimization of $\varphi_{2,1}$ (see Fig. 2(B)), for which a clear minimization is not visible around the straight line identified by $\alpha_4 = 0.3$. This implies that, in order to setup an experiment able to replicate the coupled IH and WR mechanisms, the number of samples must be incremented to reach a better convergence, or that the medial area is not a suitable measurement to correctly tune α_4, or even both. This was actually to be predicted, indeed, as anticipated while discussing Fig. 3, it was clear how the IH had some kind of noisy influence on the WR, while the *vice versa* was not valid. The resulting limited variation in the number of medial SMCs, at least for the coupled IH and WR respect to the single WR, makes that a different measurement, still representative of WR but not influenced by IH, might be more suitable to setup α_4.

To summarize, the analysis presented showed how, by measuring intimal and medial thickness on the base of 50 and 60 samples, a realistic setup for a model that replicates IH and WR separately is reached and in both cases this task does not pose particular criticalities. However, the same measurements are not suitable enough to inform the model in order to replicate IH and WR when they act simultaneously. Therefore, to design an effective experimental setup cannot exempt itself from an analysis of spatial SMCs density maps across the graft's wall, a procedure undoubtedly more resources-consuming than simply measuring the thickness of the compartments. This necessity becomes even more actual when thinking about cellular motility, not considered for simplicity in this analysis, that also plays a key role in vascular adaptation [2] and that adds to the system an additional level of noise that requires a more complex measurements, and probably also a larger number of samples to be overpassed.

4   Conclusions

This work represents an agile framework to design the experimental setup needed to obtain computational models able to reproduce as accurately as possible the biological reality. With an *ad hoc* use of our ABM [5] the minimum number of samples needed for the analysis can be easily predicted and, not less important, the suitability of the biological measurements verified *a priori*.

This can represent a great turning point in the field of computational models, because it will give the researchers a feeling of the resources needed before conducting the actual experiment, limiting in this way any kind of wastefulness in terms of equipment and of resources more in general, especially animal resources.

The next steps will be (i) to reach a satisfying identification for the coupled cellular events, where the real challenge will be to identify the right biological measurement to rightly tune α_4, and (ii) to improve the framework by getting it even closer to the physiological reality. This will be done by adding more cellular events, like cellular apoptosis, ExtraCellular Matrix (ECM) synthesis, and especially cellular motility.

References

1. Goldman, S., et al.: Long-term patency of saphenous vein and left internal mammary arteries grafts after coronary artery bypass surgery: results from a Department of Veterans Affairs Cooperative Study. J. Am. Coll. Cardiol. **44**, 2149–2156 (2004)
2. Manini, S., Passera, K., Huberts, W., Botti, L., Remuzzi, A.: Computational model for simulation of vascular adaptation following vascular access surgery in haemodialysis patients. Comput. Methods Biomech. Biomed. Eng. **17**, 1358–1367 (2014)
3. Klein, B., et al.: Hemodynamic influence on smooth muscle cell kinetics and phenotype during early vein graft adaptation. Ann. Biomed. Eng. **45**, 644–655 (2017)
4. Garbey, M., et al.: A dynamical system that describes vein graft adaptation and failure. J. Theor. Biol. **336**, 209–220 (2013)

5. Garbey, M., et al.: Vascular adaptation: pattern formation and cross validation between an agent based model and a dynamical system. J. Theor. Biol. **429**, 149–163 (2017)
6. Casarin, S., et al.: Linking gene dynamics to intimal hyperplasia – a predictive model of vein graft adaptation. Procedia Comput. Sci. **108**, 1842–1851 (2017)
7. Marino, S., Hogue, I.B., Ray, C.J., Kirschner, D.E.: A methodology for performing global uncertainty and sensitivity analysis in systems biology. J. Theor. Biol. **254**, 178–196 (2008)
8. Owens, C.D., Gasper, W.J., Rahman, A.S., Conte, M.S.: Vein graft failure. J. Vasc. Surg. **61**, 203–216 (2015)
9. Casarin, S., Berceli, S.A., Garbey, M.: Linking gene dynamics to vascular hyperplasia – toward a predictive model of vein graft adaptation. PLoS One **12**(11), e0187606 (2017)
10. Pries, A.R., Secomb, T.W., Gaehtgens, P.: Structural autoregulation of terminal vascular beds. Hypertension **33**, 153–161 (1999)
11. Poleszczuk, J., Macklin, P., Enderling, H.: Agent-based modeling of cancer stem cell driven solid tumor growth. Methods Mol. Biol. **1516**, 335–346 (2016)

Accelerating Data Analysis in Simulation Neuroscience with Big Data Technologies

Judit Planas$^{(\boxtimes)}$, Fabien Delalondre, and Felix Schürmann

Blue Brain Project, École Polytechnique Fédérale de Lausanne,
Geneva, Switzerland
{judit.planas,fabien.delalondre,felix.schuermann}@epfl.ch

Abstract. Important progress in computational sciences has been made possible recently thanks to the increasing computing power of high performance systems. Following this trend, larger scientific studies, like brain tissue simulations, will continue to grow in the future. In addition to the challenges of conducting these experiments, we foresee an explosion of the amount of data generated and the consequent unfeasibility of analyzing and understanding the results with the current techniques.

This paper proposes Neurolytics, a new data analysis framework, together with a new data layout. The implementation of Neurolytics is mainly focused on simulation neuroscience, although we believe that our design can be applied to other science domains. The framework relies on big data technologies, like Apache Spark, to enable fast, reliable and distributed analyses of brain simulation data in this case. Our experimental evaluation on a cluster of 100 nodes shows that Neurolytics gets up to 374x speed-up compared to a thread-parallel Python implementation and is on par with a highly optimized Spark code. This demonstrates the suitability of our proposal to help scientists structure and understand the results of their experiments in a fast and efficient way.

Keywords: Scientific data analysis · Simulation neuroscience
Big data · Scientific frameworks · Spark · Python

1 Introduction

Since the 1950s, the use of computers has been adopted by many scientific fields to help researchers advance in their areas [1,3,16]. Since then, the evolution of computer technology has helped the progress in computational and simulation science domains. Like many other fields, neuroscience is taking advantage of this growing computational power, but the real progress is yet to come. Neuroscientists collect experimental data at the laboratory which is then used to create models of the brain structure and its behavior. Later, these models are translated into computer programs that can digitally reproduce the neural activity of brain regions. Finally, simulation results are interpreted and sometimes used as an input to refine the computational models. In order to attempt to simulate

© Springer International Publishing AG, part of Springer Nature 2018
Y. Shi et al. (Eds.): ICCS 2018, LNCS 10860, pp. 363–377, 2018.
https://doi.org/10.1007/978-3-319-93698-7_28

the largest possible brain region, the use of high performance computing (HPC) resources is needed. In the past, numerous studies could not have been possible without the aid of computers, and especially HPC, such as [6,13,15,17–19].

The human brain has more than 86 billion neurons and they communicate to each other through a type of connection called *synapse*. Each neuron can have up to 10,000 synapses (in some cases even more) and the brain is able to create, rewire or destroy these connections over time (synaptic plasticity). Many applications simulate the behavior of the brain in different ways. In general, most simulations are divided into *time steps* and the state of neurons is recorded at each step. The final result is that at the end of the simulation we obtain a set of files that describe how the state of neurons evolved over time. The degree of detail, precision and simulated parameters (*e.g.* electrical signals, neuron connectivity, etc.) varies depending on the simulator and the purpose of the study. For example, the degree of detail can vary from modeling neurons as points (point neuron models), to modeling their tree structure (multi-compartment models), to modeling their behavior at a molecular level (subcellular models).

While it is essential to continuously optimize and update simulation science applications to exploit new software and hardware technologies, it is also important to inspect the whole scientific workflow to detect potential bottlenecks. We believe that understanding simulation results is as important as running the simulation itself and, with the growing computational power, there is a growing trend of simulation output data from gigabytes to terabytes (or even more) in the near future. Therefore, we focus our motivation and the work presented in this paper on the post-processing of neural simulation output data. First, we propose a new data layout to structure the information of simulation results that works efficiently with most of the data post-processing tasks done by the scientists. And second, we present Neurolytics, a parallel and distributed framework for data analysis. The particularity of Neurolytics is that it has been designed with domain-specific knowledge of simulation neuroscience. Hence, it is able to better understand and efficiently handle simulation output data. However, we believe that the logical structure of the framework can be easily adapted to other computational science domains. Neurolytics provides two sets of functionalities: one is oriented to users with little programming knowledge, with which they can compute the most common analyses with only a few lines of code, whereas the other one targets users with advanced programming skills and allows them to construct their own analyses with the help of the framework.

The paper is structured as follows: Sect. 2 gives more background information and the related work. Sections 3 and 4 describe our proposal and Sect. 5 contains its experimental evaluation. Finally, Sect. 6 concludes the paper.

2   Background and Related Research

This section gives additional background information related to this paper and explains previous and related work.

2.1   Simulation Neuroscience

An important aspect of simulation neuroscience is to study brain activity by running simulations on a computing system. Scientists often focus only on certain brain regions, therefore it is more precise to refer to those simulations as *brain tissue simulations*. Currently, even the most powerful supercomputers of the world cannot fit certain detailed cellular models representing the full human brain, and it will still take some time until we can fit realistic models.

In order to conduct brain tissue simulations, the first step needed is to create a model from data collected during *in vivo* or *in vitro* experiments. Then, these data are used to drive the *in silico* experiments (brain tissue simulations). Typically, we can divide *in silico* experiments into three phases: first, the user (the scientist) sets up the desired parameters of the simulation, like the neural model (brain region, number of neurons, neuronal connectivity, . . .), the amount of biological time they want to simulate, the simulation time step, etc. Second, the neural simulator starts the simulation and stores the results on persistent storage (commonly hard disk). Usually, simulators alternate between advancing the simulation phase and storing the results to disk in order to improve performance. Thus, the generation of results has a direct impact on simulator execution time. Finally, once the simulation finishes and all the results are generated, they are processed by visualization or analysis tools that neuroscientists use to interpret them. Sometimes, they are also used as an input to refine the computational model. One of the challenges that scientists are currently facing is the complexity of simulation data analysis: as simulation data grows in size, it becomes more difficult for them to manage all the data, and sometimes it is even impossible to analyze the whole dataset due to hardware restrictions (like memory capacity) or programming complexity. In this context, we foresee an emerging need for improving the analysis workflow as more powerful computing systems enable larger or more detailed neural simulations. Consequently, we have detected the need for scalable data analysis solutions applied to neural simulations and also a redesigned data layout that suits the different analysis types.

2.2   Simulation Output Data

Even though different simulators (like NEST [12], NEURON [14] or STEPS [4]) generate different output results, we can find common points between them: first, the identification of different entities, the neurons. Second, the sense of evolution over time: neurons start in a certain state and they evolve to a potentially different state as time advances. And third, simulators record some type of information about neurons. If we look at specific frameworks, we will find many combinations: some have subdivisions of neurons to better represent their state, some will not record data at each time step, but every N time steps, and there is a wide variety of the kind of information (the neuron state) they can collect. But still, we can find the three aforementioned common points in most simulators.

Figure 1 illustrates an example of a simulation data layout and the different access patterns of post-processing tools, that can be divided into two types:

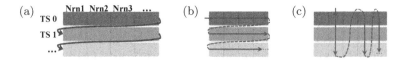

Fig. 1. (a) Example of simulation data layout: organized by time steps (rows), each time step (TS) contains information related to each neuron (Nrn). The contents of each neuron depend on the simulator and its configuration; Different access patterns: (b) sequential access: usually delivers good I/O performance and (c) random access: I/O performance becomes oftentimes the bottleneck

sequential accesses or random accesses. Although Fig. 1 refers to simulation neuroscience data, we can find many other science fields that use the same data structure to organize data in a 2-dimensional way.

2.3   Previous Research

There have been several efforts in the past years to improve the scientist workflow. Eilemann *et al.* [7] and Schürmann *et al.* [20] present a key/value store approach combined with IBM BlueGene Active Storage (BGAS) technology [10]. Later on, this work has been followed by other experiments on database frameworks, like Ceph, Cassandra or LevelDB, and flash-storage caching solutions [9]. What differentiates our proposal from these approaches is: (i) non-specialized hardware: Neurolytics sits on top of a widely adopted software framework that can be deployed on standard systems with no need for specialized hardware and (ii) Neurolytics combines domain-specific knowledge with an efficient data layout specially designed for neuroscience domains.

2.4   Related Work

Dask [5] is a flexible parallel computing library for analytic computing in Python. It has two main components: a dynamic task scheduler optimized for computation and a set of data collections for big data. Dask supports NumPy, Pandas and enables distributed computing by providing parallelized NP arrays and Pandas dataframes. Dask was initially designed for parallel numerical algorithms on a single computer, although nowadays it can run on a distributed cluster as well.

Thunder [11] is a collection of tools to analyze images and time series data in Python. It can run up to large scale clusters, using Spark underneath. Thunder provides the base classes and methods to conduct the analysis of data coming from a variety of fields, like neuroscience, video processing and climate analysis.

Dask and Thunder provide generic tools for data analysis that can be very powerful for scientists with medium to advanced programming skills. The main difference with Neurolytics is that while we also look for generality, we believe that it is still important to provide domain-specific tools, specially designed for those scientists with basic programming skills, or even with limited time, that look for straightforward solutions with low time investment. To the best of our knowledge, such domain-specific tools have not been proposed to date.

BluePy [2] is a scientific library with a pythonic interface. It is developed by the Blue Brain Project (BBP) [8] and provides support for accessing all the entities involved in the ecosystem of BBP simulations. This includes, on the one side, the circuit (neural network) data and, on the other, the simulation data. Scientists use these entities for both circuit and simulation analyses. The main difference between BluePy and our proposal is that BluePy has been designed to run on limited computing resources (single node), like a scientist desktop computer, while Neurolytics is designed to scale on big data computing facilities. Nevertheless, BluePy benefits from the use of several tools underneath, like NumPy, SQLAlchemy or other libraries developed by BBP. In the same way, we believe that libraries like BluePy could be plugged on top of Neurolytics to analyze large sets of data in a fast and easy way from the scientist point of view.

3 Data Organization

Data organization plays an important role at both the computing and post-processing steps. However, sometimes these steps have completely opposite needs. For example, usually, the file structure generated by the simulator is designed to optimize how data is generated and written, but this does not meet the requirements of efficient reading by some post-processing tools, like visualization or data analysis. The latter tend to access data randomly, in small chunks. For example, a typical use case is to access the data belonging to a subset of neurons (whose 3D position in space falls into a certain brain region and is completely unrelated to the order in which the simulator writes the data). This means that only a small, non-contiguous subset of cells in each time step are required, but the reality is that, due to hardware and software design, unneeded adjacent data will also be loaded. In the end, on the one hand, we can find some types of data analysis that are more efficient if data is structured by time step, but on the other, there are other types of analyses that would benefit from a neuron-major structured layout. Consequently, there is no consensus on how simulation output data should be organized. For this reason, we think that there is a need to redesign the data layout.

3.1 Data Layout Proposal

We believe that the best approach to organize data is a key/value layout where the basic structure is a table with the following information: neuron ID (Nrn), time step (TS), data source (Src) and simulation data (Data), that corresponds to the state of each neuron at each time step. This table can be directly instantiated by different types of frameworks, for example as a database table or a dataframe. Figure 2a illustrates this layout. The coloring code matches the one used in Fig. 1a to highlight how information can be redistributed. We leave this design open, as other columns could be added in the future. For example, at the

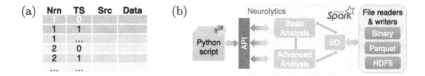

Fig. 2. (a) Proposed data layout, where the (Nrn, TS) key pair is used to access data; (b) Interaction of internal Neurolytics components and scientist's scripts

time of this table creation, certain precomputed analyses could also be added on-the-fly while report data is loaded. This could be interesting if certain operations are commonly computed by a large number of different analyses or users. Similarly, the data field is open to hold any type of information that the simulator generates, from a single value, to a struct, tuple or array of elements.

In addition to the minimum required data (Nrn, TS and Data), we propose to add the data source to have a reference to where data comes from. This may be useful for some types of analyses, but also for troubleshooting or data validation.

In the future, if proved necessary, other information related to simulation parameters or the neural network could be added. In this case, depending on the type of information, instead of creating a single, huge table, it may make more sense to add other tables and create links between them.

4   Neurolytics Framework

In addition to the strictly technical requirements, there are other factors that must be taken into account in our framework proposal.

Scalability. With the growing power of supercomputers, we expect simulations to be either more detailed (finer grain of time steps) or include a wider brain region (larger number of neurons). Therefore, reports will grow in terms of file size as well, most likely exponentially in the near future. In this scenario, it is only feasible to look for parallel, and preferably distributed, software solutions.

Python-Friendly. A large portion of the simulation neuroscience community use Python in their daily work, so proposing a Python-friendly solution would make the transition easier for them. In addition, there is the risk of low adoption, or even rejection by the community, if our framework requires mastering advanced programming skills or non-familiar programming languages.

SQL. Even if it is not a strong requirement, support of SQL-like queries would be preferred, as it would reduce the complexity of some types of analyses.

For all these reasons, and after considering different options, we believe that building Neurolytics on top of Spark is a promising approach for its maturity and the *ecosystem* it provides. Spark is part of the Hadoop BigData suite, the leading open source project in big data. Also, Spark offers interesting features compared to other considered frameworks, i.e., the creation of optimized execution plans.

Neurolytics is a pythonic framework built on top of Spark that offers different types of functionalities classified into two categories: I/O and data analysis.

I/O. This category contains the components that interact with disk files and storage. The loading component includes all the functionalities related to reading simulation output files and loading its data into Spark distributed data structures. The storage component offers different options to store Spark data structures in Spark-supported formats. For example, once simulation data is loaded, we can use this functionality to store it as Parquet files. In addition, any data analysis computed after data loading can also be stored in any file format directly supported by Spark. Alternatively, other file formats could be supported as well, provided that the user implements the appropriate connector (plug-in).

Data Analysis. It consists of all the framework functionalities directly used for data analysis (basic and advanced functions), for example, grouping data with a certain criteria or doing some computation on report data.

Figure 2b shows the main components of Neurolytics and how they interact with each other. On the left side, there is the user (scientist) code, usually a Python script, that interacts with the interface of Neurolytics. Internally, our framework is structured as a set of components that communicate with each other (yellow arrows). Each component groups a different set of functionalities, as mentioned above. And on the right side, there are the *plug-in* agents. We call the plug-in agents all those components that are specific and implementation-dependent on external factors. For example, most of the entities involved in data loading and storage are considered plug-ins, because they need to understand the specific file format they are loading and they completely depend on both the format (binary, HDF5, Parquet, . . .) and the internal layout (data structures, offsets to access certain data, . . .). At this point, we have not identified plug-ins other than file readers and writers for Neurolytics.

We would like to highlight the convenience of Neurolytics design, as the core components are completely independent from file data sources. Therefore, by just adding the appropriate plug-in, the framework can immediately read data coming from any neuroscience simulator. In the same way, our data layout is flexible enough to adapt to many types of information as well. Our implementation targets neural data analysis, so we propose a specialized framework that understands the properties of neural simulation data and the relation between the different entities involved. However, our design can be easily adapted to other areas where data organization includes the sense of time evolution, and with minor changes, the framework could support most of 2-D data organizations.

4.1 User Interaction

As we mentioned before, our user profile are scientists from basic to advanced programming skills, therefore we have divided Neurolytics API into two groups.

Basic Functions. Little programming knowledge is required to interact with these functions. The main features offered by this group are: simulation data loading into Spark distributed structures (RDDs/DataFrames), write simulation data to a Spark-supported file format, aggregate data (by time step or by neuron), compute aggregated average values, generate the corresponding histograms and sample data. We expect advanced users to also use these operations.

Advanced Functions. We expect advanced users to use these functions in order to customize or fine-tune their data analysis. In addition to the basic set, we include here finer grain functions to get meta-information about simulation data, functions to retrieve the internal Spark distributed data structures (to enable custom distributed analysis and data manipulation) and generic functions to operate on the distributed data (for example: filtering, grouping by, element-to-element transformation). The latter accept user-defined functions and can be composed together to form complex analyses.

In order to maximize compatibility with other common Python libraries, we allow the user to choose the data structure returned by each function. In general, we always offer four options: *raw* (the original data structures, usually loaded from simulation output files), Python (basic Python data structures, like lists, tuples, etc.), NumPy N-dimensional arrays and Pandas DataFrames.

Since the amount of simulation output data can be significantly large, it is not uncommon to divide the information into several output files. This division can either be done by the simulator automatically, or manually by the scientist. In any case, grouping back together the information held in the resulting set of files may be a complex task, or even sometimes impossible due to the limited amount of dynamic memory (DRAM). Hence, Neurolytics adds an interesting functionality: the ability to aggregate all these subsequent simulation result files into a single data structure. Thanks to the Spark distributed data structures, we avoid memory problems, and our framework allows scientists to have a broader view of the simulation data at once, without any effort from their side.

4.2   Neurolytics Implementation Details

Spark offers two different distributed data structures: RDDs and DataFrames. Even though DataFrames are recommended over RDDs whenever possible, after a thorough evaluation, we realized that RDDs give several advantages in our context. Most of the data loaded from simulation data can be stored as NumPy arrays and scientists mainly use the NumPy library to do their analyses. Therefore, the main benefit of using RDDs is that they support the storage of NumPy arrays without conversions, as opposed to DataFrames, where NumPy arrays must be converted to a supported data format (like binary data or Python lists). However, the choice of NumPy arrays in the past was motivated for its performance and easiness of use, but this could change in the future, so we do not completely discard using DataFrames at some point.

During the process of loading data, there is a first step where simulation output files are scanned to get their meta-data, like the list of neuron IDs and the time series. Then, this information is used to parallelize the loading of simulation data with Spark. Nevertheless, special care is taken in order to read chunks of data that are large enough to get good file I/O performance. Therefore, several stages are performed until data loading is finished and simulation data is stored following the layout described in Fig. 2a.

In order to proof the suitability of Neurolytics, we have chosen to implement the support for NEURON simulator. NEURON simulates the electrical activity of multi-compartment neurons. It receives different input parameters, like the biological neural model and it generates the desired output data in a single, potentially large file. We think that this use case is interesting and versatile because even though NEURON generates the simulation output files in binary format, a large number of scientists convert the result file into an HDF5 file because it is easier for them to read this file format from their Python scripts. In addition, during the conversion process from binary to HDF5, they also transpose data to organize results by neuron instead of by time step. Consequently, we have developed two different plug-ins to read both file formats with their different internal organizations to demonstrate the flexibility of Neurolytics to adapt to different formats and completely opposed data organization. Moreover, Neurolytics design is open to accept additional plug-ins to support multiple file formats generated by any simulation neuroscience framework.

Finally, Neurolytics adds the ability to store simulation data or, in general, any DataFrame or RDD generated inside the framework into the Parquet file format. This can be particularly useful to convert data from one format to another, or even to accelerate data loading if the same report files must be analyzed in different occasions. As a proof of concept, we have implemented the Parquet support, but this feature can be easily extended by adding other storage plug-ins.

5 Experimental Evaluation

In this section we evaluate the behavior of Neurolytics and compare its performance to an equivalent thread-parallel Python implementation. In order to conduct the evaluation, we have identified three common data analyses that scientists use, along with the process of loading data. The rest of this section explains these types of data analysis and presents the evaluation results.

5.1 Analysis Description

We identified three common types of data analysis. For simplicity we tag them as *Query 1 (Q1)*, *Query 2 (Q2)* and *Query 3 (Q3)*.

The first analysis (Q1) consists of calculating the mean values of each neuron over time. The following steps must be followed in order to get the result:

1. For each neuron, compute the mean value of its data at each time step.
2. Group the mean values by neuron to obtain its evolution over time.
3. Scientists usually create a Python dictionary with neuron IDs as dictionary's keys and values are arrays with the computed mean values per time step.

In the second analysis (Q2), scientists want to generate a histogram for each simulation time step. The procedure to compute Q2 is described as the following:

1. For each neuron, compute the mean value of its data at each time step.
2. Group the mean values by time step.
3. For each time step, generate a histogram of the mean values of each neuron.
4. Similarly to Q1, structure these data into a dictionary with time steps as keys and values contain the computed histogram for each time step.

The third analysis consists of extracting a sample from the whole dataset. In this case, the scientist wants to get all the data related to randomly chosen neurons. Usually, the final result will include the data from tens to few hundreds of neurons. In our evaluation, we have chosen to sample the data of 250 neurons.

We would like to emphasize the relevance of these three analyses to evaluate our proposal. On the one hand, the first analysis requires data to be grouped by neuron and the second analysis groups data by time step. As explained in Sect. 3, some analysis access data per neuron, and thus, would benefit from a neuron-major data layout; but some others access data per time frame, so there is not a clear consensus on how data should be better structured. On the other hand, Q3 requires to filter a small subset of data, so only small chunks of data need to be read at randomly accessed locations. Thanks to the heterogeneity of the three queries, they represent a large set of analyses. This also exposes a challenge to our proposal, as it has to show its versatility against completely opposite data organizations and access patterns.

5.2 Performance Results

The evaluation was performed on Cooley, an analysis and visualization cluster at Argonne National Laboratory (ANL). The system has a total of 126 compute nodes. Each node has 2x Intel Haswell E5-2620 v3 (12 cores) and 384 GB of RAM. Nodes are connected through FDR Infiniband interconnect. Apache Spark version 2.1.2 with Python 3.6.3 were used to run all benchmarks.

We present the scalability results of Neurolytics, running from 1 node up to full scale (96 nodes). For each execution, we placed the Spark master process on a different node than the ones running the Spark slave processes. In all cases we had exclusive access to the computing nodes. The results shown in this paper were computed as the arithmetic average of multiple runs (at least 10).

We ran the three types of data analyses explained in this section with Neurolytics and we include as well the process of loading data from disk (GPFS). In addition, we provide the results of the same actions performed in: (i) a thread-parallel Python script, run on a single node (using 12 cores) and (ii) a Spark optimized code, executed directly on the same Spark cluster. We refer to these three runtime scenarios as Neurolytics, Python and Spark respectively. The Python code tries to mimic the scientist environment and to show what would be the benefits of using Neurolytics. It uses the NumPy library with NumPy structures for computations and data is loaded in chunks as large as possible to favor file I/O reading performance. The optimized Spark code reproduces how an advanced programmer would write these data analysis with Spark (using Python).

In order to make this evaluation more realistic, we have used real simulation data generated by NEURON simulator. The activity of a somatosensory cortex region with 31000 neurons was simulated for 7 min of biological time. The activity was recorded (written to the simulation output files) every 100 ms (biological), generating a total of 4200 time frames. In order to control file size, the simulation was split into 14 runs, so 14 output files were created of 47 GB each (658 GB in total). Furthermore, we artificially duplicated these data to obtain a larger dataset of 1.3 TB. Both datasets were converted to the Parquet file format using Neurolytics, so we then ran all the experiments with both datasets (650 GB and 1.3 TB) in both file formats (original binary and converted Parquet).

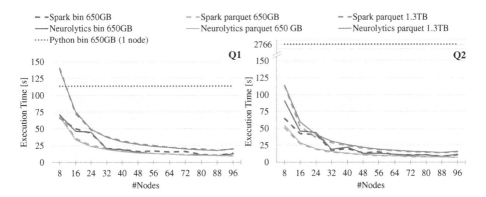

Fig. 3. Wall clock time of Q1 (left) and Q2 (right); note the axis is cut in Q2 (Color figure online)

First, we present the results of executing the three data analysis with the different combinations of runtimes (Python, Spark and Neurolytics), dataset sizes (650 GB and 1.3 TB) and file formats (binary and Parquet), followed by the results of data loading. For simplicity, we do not show all possible combinations, but only the relevant ones. All executions follow a strong scaling evaluation.

All charts presented in this section have the following conventions: (i) colors: **purple** experiments were run with the binary dataset of 650 GB; **orange** refers to the same dataset in Parquet format, and **green** refers to the duplicated dataset of 1.3 TB in Parquet format; (ii) line shape: **small dotted lines** refer to the thread-parallel Python executions; **large dashed lines** refer to the Spark experiments and **solid lines** refer to the Neurolytics executions. Finally, we would like to highlight that the Python data points (purple dotted lines) show the Python execution on a single node, but, for readability, this line has been extended along the charts.

Figure 3 (left) shows the time needed to perform the data analysis presented as *Query 1*. Python's dotted purple line, run on single node, has been extended for readability. We can see that the lines corresponding to Spark and Neurolytics executions overlap almost perfectly, meaning that Neurolytics reaches an optimal performance in this type of analysis. The executions scale properly according to the number of nodes, and Neurolytics is always between 1.6–12x faster than the Python version. We cannot expect perfect scaling because this type of query requires data exchange between Spark slaves in both Spark and Neurolytics versions. There is also a perfect scaling between the 650 GB and the 1.3 TB datasets, as the latter takes at most twice the time (or sometimes even a bit less). As we increase the number of nodes, there is less work to do per Spark slave, reaching up to a point where the gain is minimal. However, these results are encouraging, specially when, in the near future, simulation output data grows even more in size. Finally, we would like to remark that thanks to the big DRAM capacity of the system, the whole dataset can be loaded in memory to perform the Python analysis. However, this is not the usual case, and it would lead to longer execution times on clusters with less DRAM. In such situation, Spark and Neurolytics would not be impacted, as data are stored in a distributed fashion.

Figure 3 (right) shows the time needed to perform the data analysis presented as *Q2*. Note that the vertical axis has been split to better show the results. Spark and Neurolytics present similar scalability compared to *Q1*. However, in this case, the benefit of computing this analysis with Neurolytics is evident. The reason is that the original data organization and the intrinsic operations of this query work in opposite directions, making the Python analysis very inefficient. On the contrary, thanks to our proposed layout, Neurolytics is not affected by these issues and offers good performance, reaching a maximum speed-up of 374x with respect the Python code. Spark executions use the same data layout as Neurolytics, so they also adapt well to different data organizations and operations. Similarly to *Q1*, we would like to remark that the Python analysis was done with all data loaded in memory, but this is only possible thanks to the hardware properties. Otherwise, this analysis would have been more complex to program and slower to execute. In addition, we observe different behavior depending on the file format: when data comes from Parquet files, which are part of the Spark ecosystem, the behavior of both Spark and Neurolytics is more regular, as opposed to the case when data comes from the original binary format, where we can see that in some cases performance scales irregularly.

These two types of analyses clearly show that Neurolytics can perform analyses requiring data in completely opposite formats. Moreover, performance is not impacted by the data layout, as the execution time is very similar in both cases.

Figure 4 (left) shows the time needed to perform the data sampling presented as *Q3*. Like in previous charts, the Python dotted line, run on single node, has been extended for readability. This type of analysis done in Python is quite slow due to the inefficiency of accessing simulation output files in random patterns that hinder I/O performance. In the case of Spark and Neurolytics, our proposed finer grain data layout favors a fastest execution. However, since the amount of data sampled is relatively small, the scaling performance saturates when we use a large amount of nodes. In this query, Neurolytics reaches up to 18x speed-up with respect to the Python execution.

Figure 4 (right) shows the time needed to load the simulation data with the Python script and with Neurolytics (Spark RDD underneath). As in the other cases, the Python dotted line has been extended for readability. Neurolytics shows extremely good performance when loading Parquet data, as this file format has been designed to work with Spark. However, if we load from binary data, good performance is only achieved when using a few compute nodes; as we scale to a larger number of nodes, performance degrades. This is because the original simulation data files are not prepared nor structured to be read from massively parallel processes and, therefore, the data reading collapses when all Spark slaves are simultaneously accessing the same files through GPFS file system.

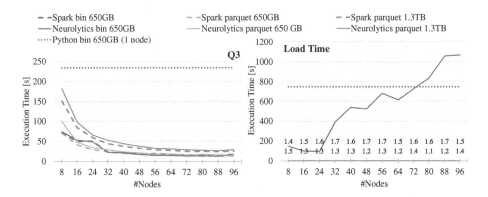

Fig. 4. Wall clock time of Q3 data analysis (left) and data loading (right)

6   Conclusions

With the increasing power of supercomputers, scientists can run larger simulations of their studies, but they also produce larger amounts of data that bring new challenges at the time of analyzing the results. From our point of view, such data analysis is as important as the simulation itself, and in some cases it is even used to refine the computational model to make it more accurate. We present in this paper Neurolytics, a Spark-based data analysis framework, together with a data layout with domain-specific knowledge. The implementation is focused on the field of simulation neuroscience and proves its suitability to process the results of such simulations. However, the design is general enough to be applied to other computational science areas.

In our evaluation, we used a real set of simulation output files (up to a few terabytes) to compute several data analyses and compared the performance of Neurolytics to a Spark optimized implementation (reference of maximum performance) and to a thread-parallel Python implementation (similar to real neuroscientist scripts). We can then extract the following conclusions: first, the suitability of Neurolytics for large data analysis in computational science, specially in simulation neuroscience. Depending on the analysis, Neurolytics can get up to 374x speed-up at full scale compared to the Python parallel code. Our framework scales well up to full-scale executions (100 nodes) and is always on par with the performance of the reference Spark code. Second, the suitability of a new data layout with domain-specific knowledge for neural simulation data analysis. Our proposal adapts well to the most common types of analysis patterns (i.e. by neuron and by time step), one being completely opposite to the other. Finally, the current simulation output file is not the optimal approach for big data frameworks, like Neurolytics. However, low-impact changes, like a file converter, would address this problem and significantly improve the overall performance.

As future work, we would like to evaluate the viability of integrating our proposal into the workflow of scientists, so that the most common data analyses are automatically computed in-place (where the simulator runs) and the results are immediately available to the scientist.

Acknowledgment. We would like to thank the BBP HPC and In Silico teams for their support. This work is funded by EPFL Blue Brain Project (funded by Swiss ETH board). An award of computer time was provided by the INCITE program and the ALCF Data Science Program. This research used resources of ALCF, which is a DOE Office of Science User Facility supported under Contract DE-AC02-06CH11357.

References

1. Baillargeon, B., et al.: The living heart project: a robust and integrative simulator for human heart function. Eur. J. Mech. A/Solids **48**(Suppl. C), 38–47 (2014)
2. BluePy. https://developer.humanbrainproject.eu/docs/projects/bluepy/0.5.9
3. Charney, J.G., Fjörtoft, R., Von Neumann, J.: Numerical integration of the barotropic vorticity equation. Tellus **2**(4), 237–254 (1950)
4. Chen, W., et al.: Parallel STEPS: large scale stochastic spatial reaction-diffusion simulation with high performance computers. Front. Neuroinform. **11**, 13 (2017)
5. Dask: Library for dynamic task scheduling (2016). http://dask.pydata.org
6. Diesmann, M.: Brain-scale neuronal network simulations on K. In: Proceedings of 4th Biosupercomputing Symposium: Next-Generation ISLiM Program of MEXT (2012)
7. Eilemann, S., et al.: Key/value-enabled flash memory for complex scientific workflows with on-line analysis and visualization. In: 2016 IEEE IPDPS, pp. 608–617 (2016)
8. EPFL: Blue Brain Project. http://bluebrain.epfl.ch
9. Ewart, T., Planas, J., Cremonesi, F., Langen, K., Schürmann, F., Delalondre, F.: Neuromapp: a mini-application framework to improve neural simulators. In: Kunkel, J.M., Yokota, R., Balaji, P., Keyes, D. (eds.) ISC 2017. LNCS, vol. 10266, pp. 181–198. Springer, Cham (2017). https://doi.org/10.1007/978-3-319-58667-0_10
10. Fitch, B.: Exploring the capabilities of a massively scalable, compute-in-storage architecture. www.hpdc.org/2013/site/files/HPDC13_Fitch_BlueGene ActiveStorage.pdf

11. Freeman, J., et al.: Mapping brain activity at scale with cluster computing. Nat. Meth. **11**(9), 941–950 (2014)
12. Gewaltig, M.O., et al.: NEST (NEural Simulation Tool). Scholarpedia **2**(4), 1430 (2007)
13. Hereld, M., et al.: Large neural simulations on large parallel computers. Int. J. Bioelectromagn. **7**(1), 44–46 (2005)
14. Hines, M.: NEURON — a program for simulation of nerve equations. In: Eeckman, F.H. (ed.) Neural Systems: Analysis and Modeling, pp. 127–136. Springer, Boston (1993). https://doi.org/10.1007/978-1-4615-3560-7_11
15. Hines, M., et al.: Comparison of neuronal spike exchange methods on a Blue Gene/P supercomputer. Front. Comput. Neurosci. **5**, 49 (2011)
16. Lapostolle, P., Bail, R.L.: Two-dimensional computer simulation of high intensity proton beams. Comput. Phys. Commun. **4**(3), 333–338 (1972)
17. Markram, H., et al.: Reconstruction and simulation of neocortical microcircuitry. Cell **163**(2), 456–492 (2015)
18. Plesser, H.E., Eppler, J.M., Morrison, A., Diesmann, M., Gewaltig, M.-O.: Efficient parallel simulation of large-scale neuronal networks on clusters of multiprocessor computers. In: Kermarrec, A.-M., Bougé, L., Priol, T. (eds.) Euro-Par 2007. LNCS, vol. 4641, pp. 672–681. Springer, Heidelberg (2007). https://doi.org/10.1007/978-3-540-74466-5_71
19. Reimann, M.W., et al.: Cliques of neurons bound into cavities provide a missing link between structure and function. Front. Comput. Neurosci. **11**, 48 (2017)
20. Schürmann, F., et al.: Rebasing I/O for scientific computing: leveraging storage class memory in an IBM BlueGene/Q supercomputer. In: Kunkel, J.M., Ludwig, T., Meuer, H.W. (eds.) ISC 2014. LNCS, vol. 8488, pp. 331–347. Springer, Cham (2014). https://doi.org/10.1007/978-3-319-07518-1_21

Spiral Wave Drift Induced by High-Frequency Forcing. Parallel Simulation in the Luo–Rudy Anisotropic Model of Cardiac Tissue

Timofei Epanchintsev[1,2]([✉]), Sergei Pravdin[1,2], and Alexander Panfilov[3]

[1] Krasovskii Institute of Mathematics and Mechanics, Ekaterinburg, Russia
eti@imm.uran.ru
[2] Ural Federal University, Ekaterinburg, Russia
[3] Ghent University, Ghent, Belgium

Abstract. Non-linear waves occur in various physical, chemical and biological media. One of the most important examples is electrical excitation waves in the myocardium, which initiate contraction of the heart. Abnormal wave propagation in the heart, such as the formation of spiral waves, causes dangerous arrhythmias, and thus methods of elimination of such waves are of great interest. One of the most promising methods is so-called low-voltage cardioversion and defibrillation, which is believed to be achieved by inducing the drift and disappearance of spiral waves using external high-frequency electrical stimulation of the heart. In this paper, we perform a computational analysis of the interaction of spiral waves and trains of high-frequency plane waves in 2D models of cardiac tissue. We investigate the effectiveness and safety of the treatment. We also identify the dependency of drift velocity on the period of plane waves. The simulations were carried out using a parallel computing system with OpenMP technology.

Keywords: Anisotropy · Spiral wave · Overdrive pacing
Heart model · Low-voltage cardioversion · Wave drift

1 Introduction

Mechanical contraction of the heart is caused by electrical excitation of myocardial cells. The electrical waves propagate through the entire myocardium and initiate coordinated cardiac contraction. In normal conditions, such waves originate at the natural pacemaker of the heart, the sinus node, located in the right atrium, and propagate through all cardiac tissue. However, in some cases abnormal cardiac excitation sources can occur. One source is rotating spiral waves, which can appear in the myocardium as a result of special conditions, such as the formation of a regional block for the propagating excitation wave. A spiral

Our work is supported by RSF grant 17-71-20024.

wave is a vortex that rotates at abnormally high frequency. It causes dangerous cardiac arrhythmias, such as paroxysmal tachycardia or fibrillation. In some cases, spiral waves can disappear spontaneously, and arrhythmia stops by itself. However, if this does not occur, an urgent medical intervention is necessary. In this regard, it is very important to develop effective ways to control the dynamics and position of the spiral waves in the heart, as it will result in the development of better ways of managing these diseases.

There are three classical methods of treatment of such rhythm disturbances: anti-arrhythmic drugs, surgery and electrical therapy. Electrotherapy is called 'defibrillation' or 'cardioversion'. There are three kinds of electrotherapy devices: external (electrodes are applied on the skin of the chest or the back of the patient), surgical (the paddles placed directly on the heart; it is mostly used in the operating room) and implantable (small devices under the skin whose electrodes are inserted into myocardium). These methods have serious disadvantages, as defibrillation and cardioversion require huge voltages (up to several kilovolts), which can damage the heart. Therefore, there is a long-standing interest in development of low-voltage cardioversion-defibrillation (LVCD). The idea of LVCD is to overdrive spiral waves using trains of plane waves induced by external stimulation from one or multiple electrodes. This method uses low voltage (≈ 10 V) and does not damage the heart and is much more tolerable by the patients. The LVCD methods were proposed on the basis of theoretical studies of waves in active media. Previously, the theory of LVCD has been developed for the case of isotropic 2D medium [4,6]. The LVCD method also has been tested in clinical settings [21,24].

A spiral wave can rotate around an unexcitable obstacle, for example, around a scar after myocardial infarction. There are theoretical results in 2D and 1D models of the anchored spirals [20]. Stimulation from a point electrode is one method of LVCD. Another method is based on the effect of application of an external electric field to the entire myocardium [2,7,8]. In such case, spiral waves unpin from unexcitable obstacles and start moving toward the boundary. It is known that the stimulation is more effective if the electrode is placed near the spiral wave core. This phenomenon was numerically studied in [6,27].

Spiral waves can appear not only in the myocardium but also in chemical media. For example, the stabilization and destabilization of spiral waves in the Belousov–Zhabotinsky reaction has been studied [9]. Control of spiral waves in confined media was investigated in [28].

However, the aforementioned works considered control processes with simplified models of excitable media and neglected some specific features of the myocardium. In particular, there are no studies about the effects of anisotropy, no research in realistic 3D heart models and no studies using biophysical models of cardiac cells, which should include a description of ionic currents and intercellular interaction. Moreover, electromechanical feedback was not studied, though it strongly affects the spontaneous drift of spiral waves. These limitations can explain the discrepancy between the theory and experimental studies [11,25].

Previously, we studied the induced drift of spiral waves in the isotropic myocardium using simple phenomenological Aliev–Panfilov models [18]. The next step was to check how a simple anisotropic structure based on parallel fibres influences the drift [3].

The speed of electrical excitation is 2–4 times larger along than across the fibres, so the myocardium is highly anisotropic. Moreover, myocardial fibres in the heart are not parallel and have different patterns. The present work is devoted to studying LVCD in anisotropic myocardium models with curved fibres. We used a biophysical ionic Luo–Rudy cell model [12]. After measuring the time of the beginning and end of the spiral drift and determining the type of overall reaction of the spiral on the stimulation, we compare our findings with the results for the isotropic and parallel fibres-based anisotropic cases [3,18].

The implemented program was parallelised using OpenMP technology. Since the heart simulation task is computationally intensive, we used a high-performance computing system for simulations.

2   Materials and Methods

2.1   Electrophysiological Model

We used a well-known biophysical model of the cardiomyocyte 'Luo–Rudy I' LR-I [12]. Propagation of wave excitation in the tissue was modelled using monodomain reaction–diffusion equations:

$$\frac{\partial u}{\partial t} = \mathrm{div}(D \ \mathrm{grad} \ u) - \frac{I_\mathrm{ion} + I_\mathrm{stim}(\boldsymbol{r}, t)}{C_m}, \tag{1}$$

$$I_\mathrm{ion} = I_K + I_{Kp} + I_{K1} + I_{Na} + I_b + I_{si}, \tag{2}$$

where $u = u(\boldsymbol{r}, t)$ is the transmembrane potential at the point $\boldsymbol{r} = (x, y)$ at the time t, I_ion is the sum of ionic currents, C_m is membrane capacitance and $I_\mathrm{stim}(\boldsymbol{r}, t)$ is the external stimulation current.

The original LR-I model was modified as proposed in [22]. We used $g_K = 0.705$ instead of $g_K = 0.282$ and $g_{si} = 0.045$ instead of $g_{si} = 0.09$. This made it easier to make a spiral wave in the 2D domain in comparison with the original parameter set, which provided a spiral wave with a very irregular trajectory.

To model anisotropic conduction along cardiac myofibres, we used a uniaxially anisotropic diffusion tensor D with Cartesian components $D^{ij} = D_a \delta_{ij} + (D_f - D_a) w^i w^j$, $i, j = 1, 2$, where δ_{ij} is the Kronecker symbol and $\boldsymbol{w} = \boldsymbol{w}(\phi) = (\cos \phi, \sin \phi)$ is the unit vector of the myofibre direction. Consequently, the diffusion coefficient is maximal and equal to D_f along $\boldsymbol{w}$, and it is minimal and equal to D_a in the transverse direction. For the anisotropy, $D_f > D_a$, and for the isotropy, $D_f = D_a$. Fibres were arcs of circles with the centre at $(0, 0)$, so the fibre direction angle was $\phi(x, y) = \mathrm{atan2}(y, x) + \pi/2$.

At the medium boundaries, no-flux conditions $\boldsymbol{n} \cdot D \ \mathrm{grad} \ u = 0$ were imposed with the local normal vector $\boldsymbol{n}$.

The stimulation current $I_{st} = 90\,\mu A/cm^2$ was applied on region Ω_{stim} with period T_{stim} by impulses with a duration $t_{stim} = 1.5\,ms$ starting from the moment $\tau_0 = 600\,ms$ when the spiral captured the entire computational space:

$$I_{stim}(x, y, t) = \begin{cases} I_{st}, \text{ if } (x,y) \in \Omega_{stim}, \ t \geqslant \tau_0, \ \left\{\frac{t-\tau_0}{T_{stim}}\right\} \leqslant \frac{t_{stim}}{T_{stim}}; \\ 0, \text{ otherwise.} \end{cases}$$

We found the minimal value $I_{min} = 20\,\mu A/cm^2$ of the current which caused action potential. Then, we set $I_{st} := 4.5I_{min}$. The stimulation was started when the spiral wave 'controlled' the entire computational domain.

It is known that any spiral wave has a tip where the wavefront and waveback meet. The spiral tip rotates around an area called the 'core'. A spiral wave is considered drifting if its core moves. Studying the dynamics of spiral waves is usually simplified by exploring the trajectory of the tip. To find it, we specified a certain level $u^* = -40\,mV$ of the transmembrane potential, then the tip position r_{tip} was approximated by the following equations [5]:

$$u(r_{tip}, t) = u^*, \qquad u(r_{tip}, t + \Delta t) = u^*,$$

where $\Delta t = 2\,ms$. The trajectory of the tip motion helps to determine the average drift velocity of the spiral wave and the type of its dynamics.

2.2 Computational Experiments

As electrical signals in the heart propagate faster along myofibres than across them, our model 2D square was anisotropic. The diffusion coefficients were $D_f = 0.16\,mm^2/ms$ and $D_a = 0.04\,mm^2/ms$. The reaction–diffusion system was integrated using the finite difference and the explicit Euler methods with time step $dt = 0.005\,ms$, space step $dr = 0.25\,mm$ and a mesh size $100 \times 100\,mm$.

The S1S2 protocol [15] was used to make spiral waves. First, the S1 stimulus induces a plane wave, which propagates from one side of a square to another. Then, S2 is given so that it crosses the back-front of the first plane wave. A spiral wave appears near the intersection. Stimulus S1 was applied to the left part of the square $x < 50\,mm$. Stimulus S2 was applied to the bottom half of the square $y < 50\,mm$ at the time $158\,ms$.

The LR-I model is one of the most widely used models in large-scale computational cardiology and reproduces cardiomyocyte excitation in various conditions.

In Table 1, we specify action potential durations APD-90, speeds of 1D waves, temporal periods of spiral waves and filament tensions for LR and Ten Tusscher–Panfilov (TP06) [23] biophysical models of the myocardium. The data on the TP06 model are taken from [18]. The APD-90 is the duration of time of one action potential when the cell potential $u(t)$ relative to its resting state value u_{min} is higher than 10% of its range $u_{max} - u_{min}$:

$$u(t) - u_{min} > 0.1(u_{max} - u_{min}).$$

Table 1. Parameters and characteristics of the isotropic myocardial models

Model	APD-90, ms	1D wave speed V_1, mm/ms	Spiral wave period T_{sw}, ms	Tension, mm^2/ms
LR-I	148	0.74	61	0.55
TP06	296	0.68	240	0.6

We see that the APD-90 and T_{sw} values in LR-I are smaller than in TP06, but the spatial and 3D stability characteristics, V_1 and tension, are the same.

An important characteristic of a spiral wave is its temporal period T_{sw}. It is known that the period of a non-drifting wave is equal to the period of oscillations of the model phase variables outside the core of the spiral. We calculated the period of spiral waves as the time between the maxima of the transmembrane potential averaged by ten periods, at a point outside the stimulation region and outside the core of the wave. We set the period of external stimulation relatively to T_{sw}: $T_{stim} = p \cdot T_{sw}$, where $0.85 \leq p \leq 1.04$. Also, we measured the spiral wave period in two anisotropic models, one with the straight fibres and one with the curved fibres, and obtained the same values as in the isotropic model.

An example of a spiral wave for an arc-like fibre pattern is shown in Fig. 1. Fibres are highlighted by black lines. We see that the spiral wave front does not look like an Archimedean spiral but follows the fibre pattern to an extent. A fragment of the spiral wave tip trajectory is presented in Fig. 2. We see no distinct core shape, but the spiral seems to drift slowly enough to induce its drift with a greater speed.

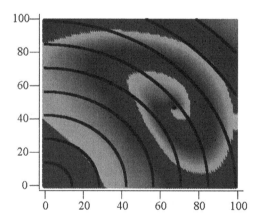

Fig. 1. Spiral wave and fibre directions (black curves) before the overdrive pacing began. The black dot shows the position of the tip. X- and Y-axes are in mm.

We wrote our program in the C language (C99 version) and compiled it using the Intel compiler icc. The most overloaded code sections were determined and

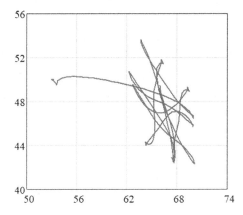

Fig. 2. Spiral wave tip trajectory in the anisotropic myocardial model with curved fibres. 0.25 s were simulated. X- and Y-axes are in mm.

accelerated using OpenMP, which decreased the simulation time significantly. We used a computational node whose configuration is presented in Table 2. The program has a nearly linear scalability (tested by simulation of 5000 ms and one stimulation electrode at the left bottom square corner). Table 3 shows simulation times with different numbers of cores. We achieved ≈21x time speedup on 32 cores. Such scalability is explained by the computational intensiveness of the task and by the independence of each subtask delegated to the computing nodes. The acceleration ratio is similar to the ratio for the Aliev–Panfilov (AP) model because we used the same size of mesh (400 × 400 nodes), thus, each computing node had a subtask of the same size. However, the overall calculation time in the LR-I model is significantly greater than that in AP model since it is more sophisticated.

All simulations were carried out on a single node of the *Uran* supercomputer of the Krasovskii Institute of Mathematics and Mechanics.

Table 2. Configuration of the computational node

CPU	6 x Intel(R) Xeon(R) CPU E5-2697 v4 @ 2.30 GHz
RAM	252 GB
Operating system	CentOS 7.3

Table 3. The simulation time and achieved speedup using OpenMP

Number of cores	1	2	4	8	16	32
Simulation time, s	42215	21716	10992	6155	3542	1973
Acceleration ratio	1	1.9	3.8	6.9	11.9	21.4

3   Results

The anisotropic structure with curved fibres can cause spontaneous drift of spiral waves. We simulated spiral wave dynamics for 60 s without the external stimulation and plotted a spontaneous drift trajectory. The results are shown in Fig. 3. The spiral wave was drifting along the fibres until it reached the boundary.

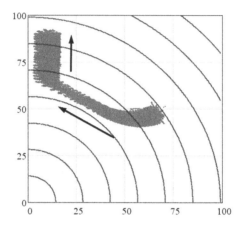

Fig. 3. Spontaneous drift of a spiral wave. No external stimulation. Fibres are shown as blue curves. Arrows show drift directions. X- and Y-axes are in mm. (Color figure online)

In our experiments, we used two electrode locations:

1. One point electrode at the left bottom square corner (Fig. 4, left).
2. One line electrode located at the left edge of the square (Fig. 4, right).

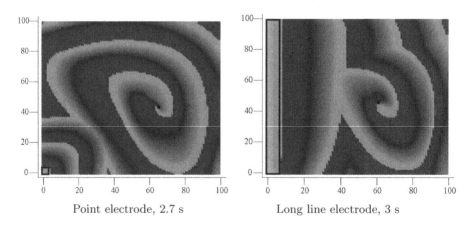

Point electrode, 2.7 s   Long line electrode, 3 s

Fig. 4. Interaction of spiral waves with the trains of plane waves. Electrodes are shown in black rectangles. X- and Y-axes are in mm.

We use the following notations for response types of spiral waves.

A: spiral drifted from the electrode and disappeared at the boundary;
B: a drift to the boundary of the square, then along the boundary;
D: no effect;
E: a spiral wave breakup;
An: n new spirals arose and vanished whereas the main spiral response was A.

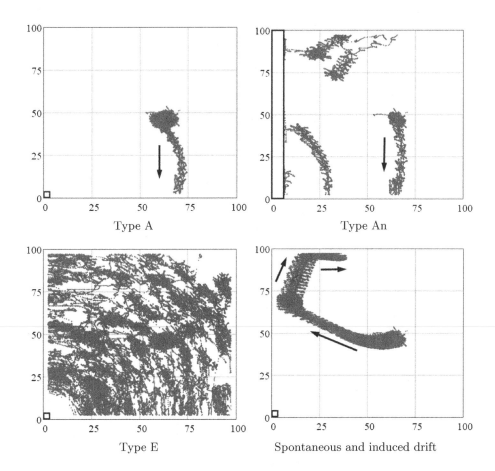

Fig. 5. Spiral wave response types. Red points show tip trajectories. Rectangles display positions of the electrodes. The electrodes were point (type A, type E, and spontaneous and induced drift) and long line (type An). Relative stimulation periods are: 0.96 (type A), 0.93 (type An), 0.85 (type E; multiple red regions represent cores of multiple spiral waves which occur as a result of the spontaneous breakup) and 1.01 (spontaneous and induced drift). Arrows show drift directions. X- and Y-axes are in mm. (Color figure online)

In our previous work [18], we also observed a drift to the boundary and stop (type C). However, we did not observe this type of dynamics in the current work. Figure 5 illustrates the wave types A, An and E. The fourth picture shows spontaneous drift toward the left boundary and the drift induced by the point electrode.

Results of the computational experiments are shown in Tables 4, 5 and 6. For both electrode configurations, the relative period 0.85 caused spiral wave breakup. When the periods exceeded 1.04, no effect was observed for the point electrode, and breakup occured for the linear electrode.

Table 4. Response types of spiral wave

Relative stimulation period	Electrode configuration	
	Point electrode	Long line electrode
0.85	E	E
0.88	E	An
0.905	A7	A2
0.93	A	A3
0.96	A	A1
0.985	A or B?	A1
1.01	B	B
1.04	D	E

Table 5. Time when the spiral began and ended its drift, seconds

Relative stimulation period	Electrode configuration			
	Point electrode		Long line electrode	
	Start	End	Start	End
0.85	—	—	—	—
0.88	—	—	2.1	3.2
0.905	4.8	5.7	2.6	4.2
0.93	6.4	8.4	3.2	5.6
0.96	10	13.3	4.9	7.5
0.985	27	>60	10.4	17.8
1.01	40	46	40.7	45.9
1.04	—	—	—	—

The segment of effective relative periods for the point electrode was 0.905–0.96. However, in case of $T_{stim} = 0.905 \cdot T_{sw}$, seven spiral waves appeared near the NW and SE corners (the electrode was at the SW corner), although they disappeared before the end of the simulation. For the relative period $T_{stim} = 1.04 \cdot T_{sw}$ and the point electrode, there was a spontaneous spiral wave drift toward the boundary, but no induced drift was observed. Hence, this case was

Table 6. Spiral wave's absolute and relative drift velocity components for the case of one line electrode

Relative stimulation period	Total V_x, mm/ms	Net V_x, mm/ms	Net V_x^{rel}	Total V_y, mm/ms	Net V_y, mm/ms	Net V_y^{rel}
0.85	—	—	—	—	—	—
0.88	0.007	0.0087	0.013	−0.045	−0.0455	−0.067
0.905	0.001	0.0027	0.004	−0.025	−0.0255	−0.038
0.93	−0.001	0.0007	0.001	−0.017	−0.0175	−0.026
0.96	−0.001	0.0007	0.001	−0.016	−0.0165	−0.024
0.985	−0.0016	0.0001	0.0001	−0.006	−0.0065	−0.010
1.01	0.0017	0.0034	0.005	0.0047	0.0042	0.006
1.04	—	—	—	—	—	—

defined as D type. Stimulation with $T_{stim} = 0.985 \cdot T_{sw}$ induced a very slow drift, and the spiral still did not reach the boundary after 60 s, so we marked this case as 'A or B?'.

In the case of the long line electrode, we did not achieve pure A type. All spiral wave drifts were followed by additional spiral waves, which also disappeared. The segment of effective relative periods was 0.88–0.985. Type An for $T_{stim} = 0.88 \cdot T_{sw}$ means that multiple spiral waves arose, which shows a high chance of breakup. In A cases, new spiral waves emerged near the long line electrode and far from it.

We checked that the effective stimulation with the minimal relative period, which was 0.88, worked without the Wenckebach/Mobitz pattern [26]. A plot of transmembrane potential is shown in Fig. 6. We considered a point that was initially controlled by the spiral wave and after 2.5 s started being influenced by the external stimulation. The plot shows a period of 53.6 ms, which is equal to the stimulation period. This precludes the possibility of the Wenckebach/Mobitz pattern.

We also measured moments of time when the spiral started to drift, T_1, and when it approached the square boundary, T_2 (Table 5). For both electrode locations, we see that the higher the stimulation period was, the later the spiral wave answered to the external stimulation and came to the boundary. In addition, an increase of the period led to a growth in the drift duration (which equals $T_2 - T_1$) in most of the cases. The only exception was the case $T_{stim} = 0.985 \cdot T_{sw}$ with the point electrode, where the spontaneous drift lasted for a very short time and the spiral was far from the boundaries when its induced drift began. The long line electrode demonstrated better results in comparison with the point electrode – the spiral wave began its drift earlier and approached the boundary faster.

The x- and y-components of spiral wave drift velocity were calculated for the case of one line electrode. Total velocity included the spontaneous drift while net velocity did not. We also computed net relative velocity components by dividing the absolute net values by the 1D wave speed V_1: $V_x^{rel} = V_x/V_1$, $V_y^{rel} = V_y/V_1$.

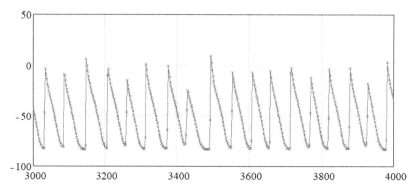

Fig. 6. Transmembrane potential u at the point $x = 25\,\text{mm}$, $y = 40\,\text{mm}$. The stimulation current was applied with $0.88 \cdot T_{\text{sw}}$ period from the long line electrode. Horizontal axis is t, ms; vertical axis is u, mV.

This enabled us to assess dimensionless drift velocity. The results are displayed in Table 6. Both velocities V_x and V_y decreased with an increase of stimulation period. Moreover, spiral waves drifted faster in the y-direction than in the x-direction. An increase in the stimulation period caused a change of the V_x sign from positive to negative and, therefore, a turn of the drift direction toward the electrode.

4   Related Work

Simulations of spiral wave dynamics require integration of the differential equations in time, which can be done using explicit or implicit numerical methods. Explicit methods require very small timesteps, each of which is a computationally easy task, and implicit methods are costly in one step. The drift of spiral waves in 2D and 3D media can be a slow process, so it should be studied during about one minute of model time or more. In any case, the total computational cost of one program run is usually big enough to force researchers to utilise parallel computers, libraries and software. The problem of parallel computation of spiral wave dynamics and cardiac electrophysiology has been addressed in several works (see, for example, [14,15,19]). Vectorisation can provide an x18 increase in the computation speed, and CPU-based parallelisation can afford an x7 increase [15]. Results on 3D heart modelling obtained by our group previously show that a GPU provided essential acceleration. One model minute of simulations required one day if a GPU-based system was used [16] (TP06 model) and about nine days if a CPU-based system was used [17] (EO model [13] without mechanics; its computational cost is comparable to that of the TP06 model).

5   Discussion and Conclusions

Previously published results on the induced drift of spiral waves in isotropic myocardial models [18] showed the following results. Effective drift occurred for relative stimulation periods between 0.8 and 0.97 if one point electrode or one line electrode is used. The time when the induced drift begins and ends increases with an increase in the period. The drift velocity component orthogonal to the line electrode decreases linearly with an increase in the period. Our results from the present study show a slightly narrower segment of the effective periods (0.88–1.01) and the same dependence between the period and the velocity component.

The case of an anisotropic tissue model where fibres are straight and parallel was also studied [3] for a simple phenomenological model AP [1] of the cardiac muscle. Results of those simulations are close to the results with the isotropic medium and those of the present work. It was shown that the segment of effective periods was the same; however, new spiral waves emerged in many cases depending on the fibre direction and electrode configuration. Mathematically, introducing anisotropy with parallel fibre directions, if wave speed is less across fibres, is similar to a compression of the isotropic medium in the direction orthogonal to the fibres. Therefore, studying heart-specific anisotropy requires research on media with curved fibres.

The present work investigates circular-shaped fibres. This pattern is similar to that observed in the atria of the heart around the pulmonary vein region. There are several such regions in the atria: four pulmonary veins (in the left atrium) and two vena-cava regions (in the right atrium). Therefore, the atrial wall has many regions that are topologically equivalent to obstacles (holes) in the tissue. They can anchor spiral waves and result in arrhythmias, such as atrial tachycardia and flutter. We think that the LVCD methodology, which we study in this paper, could be a potential treatment approach for the re-entry arrhythmias.

A theoretical investigation of the overdrive pacing was done in [10]. A formula linking the relative stimulation period $p = T_{\text{stim}}/T_{\text{sw}}$ and the relative drift velocity component $V_x^{rel} = V_x/V_1$ was proposed for the case of a sole line electrode in isotropic medium: $V_x^{rel} = 1 - p$. Here, the electrode is located at the left border $x = 0$ of the squared medium. We computed the velocity component and compared our results with the theory. We see that theoretical V_x^{rel} decreases from 0.12 ($p = 0.88$) to 0.015 ($p = 0.985$), but simulated V_x^{rel} is about 10–20 times less. This shows that the curved fibre-based anisotropy plays an important role in the overdrive pacing. Generalising the theory of overdrive pacing in anisotropic media would be an interesting topic for future research.

Another theory of overdrive pacing was proposed in [6] for waves with a circular core and for an isotropic medium. Unfortunately, it is not applicable in our case because the wave tip followed a complex trajectory even in isotropy, and our medium is essentially anisotropic.

Recently, we performed studies on spiral wave drift in an isotropic square (non-published). Those simulations used the same Luo–Rudy I model and one long line electrode. The results show that limits of the effective relative stimulation period are 0.87–0.97. We see that our limit of 0.88–1.01 is comparable with that segment, which means that anisotropy with curved fibres almost does not affect the effectiveness of the low-voltage cardioversion.

Limitations of this research are connected with the fact that we did not consider thickness, heterogeneity and curvature of the heart wall. Also, we neglect mechano-electrical feedback, which can play a significant role in spiral wave drift and therefore in overdrive pacing. Our future work will be devoted to overcoming these limitations and to using a more detailed ionic myocardial model, such as TP06, which describes more ionic currents.

Our mesh was large, and the main calculation task involved computation of the right-hand parts of the reaction-diffusion system. An increase of task complexity amplifies the amount of calculations per computing node. We believe that the use of MPI technology will speed up our simulations significantly.

References

1. Aliev, R.R., Panfilov, A.V.: A simple two-variable model of cardiac excitation. Chaos, Solitons Fractals **7**(3), 293–301 (1996)
2. Caldwell, B.J., Trew, M.L., Pertsov, A.M.: Cardiac response to low-energy field pacing challenges the standard theory of defibrillation. Circ. Arrhythm. Electrophysiol. **8**(3), 685–693 (2004)
3. Epanchintsev, T., Pravdin, S., Sozykin, A., Panfilov, A.: Simulation of overdrive pacing in 2D phenomenological models of anisotropic myocardium. Procedia Comput. Sci. **119**, 245–254 (2017). Proceedings of the 6th International Young Scientists Conference in HPC and Simulation YSC 2017. Elsevier B.V., Kotka
4. Ermakova, E.A., Krinsky, V.I., Panfilov, A.V., Pertsov, A.M.: Interaction between spiral and flat periodic autowaves in an active medium. Biofizika **31**(2), 318–323 (1986). (in Russian)
5. Fenton, F., Karma, A.: Vortex dynamics in three-dimensional continuous myocardium with fiber rotation: Filament instability and fibrillation. Chaos: Interdisc. J. Nonlinear Sci. **8**(1), 20–47 (1998)
6. Gottwald, G., Pumir, A., Krinsky, V.: Spiral wave drift induced by stimulating wave trains. Chaos: Interdisc. J. Nonlinear Sci. **11**(3), 487–494 (2001)
7. Hornung, D., Biktashev, V.N., Otani, N.F., Shajahan, T.K., Baig, T., Berg, S., Han, S., Krinsky, V.I., Luther, S.: Mechanisms of vortices termination in the cardiac muscle. R. Soc. Open Sci. **4**(3), 170024 (2017)
8. Keener, J.P., Panfilov, A.V.: A biophysical model for defibrillation of cardiac tissue. Biophys. J. **71**(3), 1335–45 (1996)
9. Kheowan, O.-U., Chan, C.-K., Zykov, V.S., Rangsiman, O., Müller, S.C.: Spiral wave dynamics under feedback derived from a confined circular domain. Phys. Rev. E **64**, 035201 (2001)
10. Krinsky, V.I., Agladze, K.I.: Interaction of rotating waves in an active chemical medium. Phys. D **8**(1), 50–56 (1983)
11. Li, W., Ripplinger, C.M., Lou, Q., Efimov, I.R.: Multiple monophasic shocks improve electrotherapy of ventricular tachycardia in a rabbit model of chronic infarction. Heart Rhythm **6**(7), 1020–1027 (2009)
12. Luo, C.H., Rudy, Y.: A model of the ventricular cardiac action potential. Depolarization, repolarization, and their interaction. Circ. Res. **68**(6), 1501–1526 (1991)
13. Markhasin, V.S., Solovyova, O., Katsnelson, L.B., Protsenko, Y., Kohl, P., Noble, D.: Mechano-electric interactions in heterogeneous myocardium: development of fundamental experimental and theoretical models. Prog. Biophys. Mol. Biol. **82**(1), 207–220 (2003)

14. Mena, A., Ferrero, J.M., Rodriguez, J.F.: Computer simulation of the electric activity of the heart using GPU. A multi-scale approach. In: Proceedings of the 41st International Congress on Electrophysiology ICE 2014, Bratislava, Slovakia (2014)
15. Nakazawa, K., Suzuki, T., Ashihara, T., Inagaki, M., Namba, T., Ikeda, T., Suzuki, R.: Computational analysis and visualization of spiral wave reentry in a virtual heart model. In: Yamaguchi, T. (ed.) Clinical Application of Computational Mechanics to the Cardiovascular System, pp. 217–241. Springer, Tokyo (2000). https://doi.org/10.1007/978-4-431-67921-9_21
16. Pravdin, S.F., Dierckx, H., Panfilov, A.V.: Effect of the form and anisotropy of the left ventricle on the drift of spiral waves. Biophysics **62**(2), 309–311 (2017)
17. Pravdin, S., Ushenin, K., Sozykin, A., Solovyova, O.: Human heart simulation software for parallel computing systems. Procedia Comput. Sci. **66**(Suppl. C), 402–411 (2015). 4th International Young Scientist Conference on Computational Science
18. Pravdin, S.F., Nezlobinsky, T.V., Panfilov, A.V.: Modelling of low-voltage cardioversion using 2D isotropic models of the cardiac tissue. In: Proceedings of the International Conference Days on Diffraction 2017, Saint-Petersburg, Russia, pp. 276–281 (2017)
19. Sato, D., Xie, Y., Weiss, J.N., Zhilin, Q., Garfinkel, A., Sanderson, A.R.: Acceleration of cardiac tissue simulation with graphic processing units. Med. Biol. Eng. Comput. **47**(9), 1011–1015 (2009)
20. Sinha, S., Sridhar, S.: Patterns in Excitable Media: Genesis, Dynamics, and Control. Taylor & Francis, London (2014)
21. Sweeney, M.O.: Antitachycardia pacing for ventricular tachycardia using implantable cardioverter defibrillators. Pacing Clin. Electrophysiol. **27**(9), 1292–1305 (2004)
22. Ten Tusscher, K.H.W.J., Panfilov, A.V.: Reentry in heterogeneous cardiac tissue described by the Luo-Rudy ventricular action potential model. Am. J. Physiol. Heart Circ. Physiol. **284**(2), H542–H548 (2003)
23. Ten Tusscher, K.H.W.J., Panfilov, A.V.: Alternans and spiral breakup in a human ventricular tissue model. Am. J. Physiol. Heart Circ. Physiol. **291**(3), 1088–1100 (2006)
24. Wathen, M.S., et al.: Prospective randomized multicenter trial of empirical antitachycardia pacing versus shocks for spontaneous rapid ventricular tachycardia in patients with implantable cardioverter-defibrillators. Circulation **110**(17), 2591–2596 (2004)
25. Weinberg, S.H., Chang, K.C., Zhu, R., Tandri, H., Berger, R.D., Trayanova, N.A., Tung, L.: Defibrillation success with high frequency electric fields is related to degree and location of conduction block. Heart Rhythm **10**(5), 740–748 (2013)
26. Wenckebach, K.F.: De analyse van den onregelmatigen Pols. III. Over eenige Vormen van Allorythmie en Bradykardie. Nederlandsch Tijdschrift voor Geneeskunde, Amsterdam, vol. 2 (1898). (in Dutch)
27. Zhang, H., Bambi, H., Gang, H.: Suppression of spiral waves and spatiotemporal chaos by generating target waves in excitable media. Phys. Rev. E **68**, 026134 (2003)
28. Zykov, V.S., Mikhailov, A.S., Müller, S.C.: Controlling spiral waves in confined geometries by global feedback. Phys. Rev. Lett. **78**, 3398–3401 (1997)

Understanding Malaria Induced Red Blood Cell Deformation Using Data-Driven Lattice Boltzmann Simulations

Joey Sing Yee Tan[1], Gábor Závodszky[2], and Peter M. A. Sloot[1,3,4(✉)]

[1] Complexity Institute, Nanyang Technological University,
50 Nanyang Avenue, 639798 Singapore, Singapore
[2] Computational Science Laboratory, Faculty of Science,
Institute for Informatics, University of Amsterdam, Amsterdam, Netherlands
[3] Computational Science, University of Amsterdam,
Science Park 904, 1098 XH Amsterdam, Netherlands
p.m.a.sloot@uva.nl
[4] National Research University ITMO, St. Petersburg, Russia

Abstract. Malaria remains a deadly disease that affected millions of people in 2016. Among the five Plasmodium (P.) parasites which contribute to malaria diseases in humans. P. falciparum is a lethal one which is responsible for the majority of the world-wide-malaria-related deaths. Since the banana-shaped stage V gametocytes play a crucial role in disease transmission, understanding the deformation of single stage V gametocytes may offer deeper insights into the development of the disease and provide possible targets for new treatment methods. In this study we used lattice Boltzmann-based simulations to investigate the effects of the stretching forces acting on infected red blood cells inside a slit-flow cytometer. The parameters that represent the cellular deformability of healthy and malaria infected red blood cells are chosen such that they mimic the deformability of these cells in a slit-flow cytometer. The simulation results show good agreement with experimental data and allow for studying the transportation of malaria infected red blood cell in blood circulation.

Keywords: Malaria-infected red blood cells · Lattice Boltzmann
Stage V gametocyte

1 Introduction

In spite of treatment with new antimalarial combinations and enhanced vector control, malaria remains as a deadly disease in Africa, South-East Asia and Eastern Mediterranean. Malaria affected more than 200 million people in 2016 and caused about 445000 deaths based on recent WHO World Malaria 2017 report [33]. Among the five Plasmodium (P.) parasite species which contribute to malaria disease in humans, P. falciparum is a lethal one which is responsible for the majority of the world-wide-malaria-related deaths [1, 8]. In an effort to disrupt parasite transmission, the WHO has developed a global technical strategy for malaria (2016–2030), which shifts their focus from disease control to elimination. These parasites are transmitted

© Springer International Publishing AG, part of Springer Nature 2018
Y. Shi et al. (Eds.): ICCS 2018, LNCS 10860, pp. 392–403, 2018.
https://doi.org/10.1007/978-3-319-93698-7_30

among humans by the female Anopheles mosquito vector. The complex life cycle of P. falciparum is associated with a 44–48 h of asexual replication which takes place in the human host. The parasite in the form of merozoite invades healthy red blood cells (hRBC) and matures through the ring, trophozoite and schizont stages. After the first asexual cycle, a subset of these asexual parasites ($\sim 0.1\%–5\%$) develop into male and female gametocytes, known as gametocytogenesis cycle which takes about 10–14 days to mature [13, 27]. Although these gametocytes do not directly contribute to malaria pathology, they play vital role in completing its life cycle by transmitting parasites to mosquito vector.

Gametocytogenesis consists of five distinct stages where the mid-stage (II–IV) gametocytes show low deformability and are sequestered into deep tissues such as bone marrow and spleen cords to avoid clearance by the spleen [8, 22]. Several studies have shown that only the mature banana-shaped stage V gametocytes (vRBC) are able to move freely in the peripheral blood circulation [13, 22, 27, 28]. In 1880, Laveran first found this banana-shaped stage V gametocyte in the blood smear of an Algerian malaria patient through microscopic technique [21]. The cellular deformability switching of the mature gametocytes is correlated to the morphological alterations, where a protein resident tends to modify the arrangement of inner membrane complex after invasion [1, 7, 8, 28]. Experimental studies have suggested that the SubTelomEric Variable Open Reading frame (STEVOR) proteins contribute to the overall stiffness tuning [28]. The underlying mechanisms of shape shifting and increment of cellular deformability is due to the linkage disassociation of STEVORs from the RBC membrane with mature stage V gametocytes. Since the banana-shaped stage V gametocyte is the only reproduction factor, studies of the deformation characteristics of single stage V gametocyte can offer insights into the connections among mechanical state, especially how well it deforms to sequester in the subdermal micro capillaries of skin where they are easily accessible to mosquito during blood meals.

Due to the significant improvement in developing high fidelity patient specific models for blood flow simulation, several macroscopic open-source software has been developed and available freely for researchers. For instance, CVSim (CardioVascular Simulator), SimVascular, and HemoCell (High pErformance MicrOscopic CELlular Library). CVSim models the human cardiovascular system as a lumped-parameter model and it has been used for research and teaching quantitative physiology courses at MIT and Harvard Medical School [14]. CVSim focuses on the normal physiology and pathology of the cardiovascular system. Similarly, SimVascular is another open source software which serves as a platform for cardiovascular simulation [10]. Both CVSim and SimVascular are good for cardiovascular simulation, but they are not useful for application on cellular level and multi-scale modelling. HemoCell, on the other hand, implements multi-scale in-silico modelling for arterial health and diseases [15]. The design of HemoCell allows the user to extend in-silico studies for cellular level of blood suspension with various types of cells and transport mechanisms of single cells in micro-fluidic setting [34]. In addition, the high computational performance enables applications up to macroscopic scales.

In this paper, HemoCell serves as the framework to replicate the stretching forces acting on a cell inside a slit-flow cytometer where the parameters used in representing the cellular deformability of hRBC and vRBC are being tuned in order to obtain the respective optimal parameters values which best fit to mimic the deformability of the cell. The tuned parameters include membrane viscosity (η_m) and elasticity (κ_L) which characterize the cellular deformability and viscoelasticity in shear flow, with a shear stress of 3 Pa. Apart from that, we adopted the exact dimensional measurement from previous research [1] to represent a reliable three-dimensional object for vRBC.

2   Methodology

2.1   Computational Methods

Computational fluid dynamics (CFD) will be used to obtain a more detailed understanding on the biomolecular interactions in blood fluid. Especially in the complex system which involves microscopic interaction of healthy, and malaria-infected red blood cells in blood plasma; such as stretching of the red blood cells due to high shear stress or compression arising from differential pressure. The full simulation of the microscopic interaction between blood plasma and red blood cells is challenging as it does not only involve complex geometries but also highly complex multi-scale physics. For this purpose, we chose a powerful approach known as the lattice Boltzmann method (LBM). In the last two decades, LBM has been widely implemented in several applications, including flow through porous medium [24], wind-driven ocean circulation [26, 35], discontinuous flows with shocks [36, 37], tidal flows on complex geometries with irregular bathymetry [29], microscopic interactions in capillary flow [11, 18–20], blood flow simulations involving time harmonic and pulsatile flows [3–5], and also corals studies [16].

LBM is well-known among scientific computing as the method itself is based on statistical physics and discretized particle velocities in accordance to restricted physical spaces. For instance, in the three-dimensional Lattice BGK model, a particle can only move along 19 directions, including the one staying at rest. Excellent parallelisations of the LBM methods do exist, especially the simulation of flows in complicated geometries [6, 17, 31, 32]. We employed HemoCell [38], where the blood plasma is modelled as an incompressible Newtonian fluid and where the lattice Boltzmann method is used to solve the fluid flows. For this purpose, a fully parallelized LBM-based fluid solver library known as Palabos is utilized to produce accurate flow results in microvascular settings. Both the surfaces of hRBC and vRBC are modelled using the discrete element method, where the boundary layers are immersed into the plasma via Immersed Boundary method (IBM) [34]. These membranes are modelled using discrete element methods where edges, N_e connecting the vertices N_v yielding surface triangles N_{tri}. In our simulations, the membranes of hRBC and vRBC consists of $N_v = 642$; 260 vertices, $N_e = 1920$; 778 edges, and $N_{tri} = 1280$; 516 faces, respectively.

The computational efficiency of HemoCell has been demonstrated recently [2] where comprehensive studies has been done to investigate the fractional load imbalance overhead in a high-performance biofluid simulation. The authors found that in the three-dimensional domain decomposition, the fractional load imbalance overhead was smaller than the fractional communication overhead. Results showed good agreement between the measurements and their load imbalance model.

2.2 Modelling Set-Up and Assumptions

The ability of a red blood cell (RBC) to deform is a significant indicator of its viability since optimal cellular deformability is essential for both micro- and macro circulation. In order to survive in high shear stress while being forced to pass through capillaries, high deformability is a must. The deformability of RBC is primarily determined via three factors: surface area-to-volume ratio of the biconcave disc, membrane viscosity, and viscoelasticity [25, 28, 30]. In HemoCell, the RBC is represented by a discrete element model in which the material model consists of five major parameters in defining the deformability of a RBC as follows [34]:

$$Parameters = \{\kappa_V, \kappa_A, \kappa_L, \kappa_B, \eta_m, \eta\}$$

where κ_V, κ_A, κ_L, and κ_B denote volume conservation coefficient, local area conservation coefficient, link force coefficient, and a combined bending force modulus for membrane and cytoskeleton. For the ease of implementation of these coefficients in the lattice Boltzman environment, the value of these four coefficients are translated into a dimensionless value via numerical computation. The remaining two parameters η_m and η denote the membrane viscosity and dynamic viscosity, respectively.

Surface Area-to-Volume. Healthy red blood cells have a volume of approximately 90 μm3 with a surface area of approximately 136 μm^2 [9]. The shape of a healthy red blood cell as shown in Fig. 1(a) is known to be a biconcave which gives a large surface-area-to-volume ratio. This has been proven via equilibrium of forces in strong-deformation experiments which shown that the surface area-to-volume ratio of the hRBC is 40% greater than a sphere with the same volume [9]. Experimental data from detailed analysis on the cell geometry of the malaria-infected red blood cells during gametocytogenesis have revealed that the surface area-to-volume ratio for each stage was nearly constant [1]. Although significant morphology changes are observed through the maturation of gametocytes, data suggested that any changes in deformability during sexual development cannot be thought as a direct influencer in the changes of surface area-to-volume ratio for the host cell. This is because approximately 70% of the RBC hemoglobin is digested during maturation [8]. Similar results were found via cryopreserved parasites measurement in which the authors claimed that the surface area-to-volume ratio is not a key determinant in the overall deformability changes [12]. Hence, in this paper, we assume that the local area conservation of malaria-infected red blood cell with stage V gametocyte has a similar local area conservation constraint as the hRBC. Meanwhile, in HemoCell, the local area conservation is constrained via a constant dimensionless area conservation coefficient, denoted as κ_A (it is set as 5.0 during simulations).

Membrane Viscosity η_m**.** The RBC membrane is considered as an ultrathin two-dimensional fluid layer endowed with surface viscosity. The thickness of a hRBC is approximately 80 nm [1], while the vRBC has a thickness of approximately 70 nm

[8] which are observed via transmission electron microscope. The membrane viscosity is determined as follows where d and η denote the thickness and the fluid bilayer viscosity, respectively.

$$\eta_m = d \times \eta$$

Note that in the experimental setup using a slit-flow cytometer, the RBC has a dynamic fluid viscosity of 0.025 Pa s. Here, we assume that both the fluid bilayer viscosity and dynamic fluid viscosity are the same. Hence, the membrane viscosity for hRBC and vRBC are 5.0×10^{-10} Ns m^{-1} and 2×10^{-9} Ns m^{-1}, respectively.

Elasticity. This is one of the crucial mechanical properties of a RBC in which the lipid bilayer membranes of RBC are linked to the cytoskeleton for cellular deformability, shape recovery, flexibility, and durability. The shear modulus is one of the parameters used in determining the viscoelasticity of a cell. Data obtained via micropipette aspiration revealed that from stage II to IV, the shear moduli of each stage increase significantly, while there is a sharp drop in shear modulus during the transition of stage IV to stage V [1]. In order to implement shear modulus in HemoCell, the parameter κ_L is used. It is defined as a link force which acts along links of the numerical surface elements to model the response from stretching and shearing caused by external and internal forces [34]. Due to the complex geometry of the surface discretization, recovering the value of the Young and shear moduli corresponding to a given set of parameters is not trivial. In HemoCell, we apply an additional numerical simulation where we stretch and shear a patch of the membrane in order to obtain the module emerging from a given dimensionless κ_L value.

Force-Fitting. In a slit-flow cytometer, the vacuum-generating mechanism is connected to the slit element, where the fluid is allowed to flow through the slit and to be collected in the other end as driven by the differential pressure [23]. As the differential pressure reaches equilibrium state, the fluid stops flowing. During the changes of differential pressure, the RBC morphology changes accordingly from prolate ellipsoid to biconcave. Hence, in order to replicate the stretching forces acting on a cell inside a slit-flow cytometer, we tuned the force of cell stretching simulation and compared the results with experimental data from previous research [8].

Stage V Gametocyte Three-Dimensional (3D) Model. The *in-silico* studies allow us to further understand the mechanical properties of certain living cells in a much convenient way where we can tune the parameters and test the corresponding hypothesis observed from experiments. In this paper, the geometry of vRBC is modelled with the respective dimension measurement obtained from epifluorescence microscopy and 3D imaging as shown in Table 1.

Table 1. Dimension measurement, surface area and volume of infected red blood cells at different gametocytogenesis stages (obtained from [1])

Stage	Length	Width	Thickness	Surface area	Volume	Surface area/ volume ratio
I	6.95 ± 0.66	6.51 ± 0.79	3.34 ± 0.6	102.92 ± 10.39	71.6 ± 11.88	0.81 ± 0.08
II	8.10 ± 1.13	6.58 ± 0.54	3.02 ± 0.52	115.97 ± 14.3	76.41 ± 12.45	0.75 ± 0.05
III	9.92 ± 1.15	5.39 ± 0.86	2.99 ± 0.51	117.71 ± 17.61	78.55 ± 13.58	0.76 ± 0.03
IV	12.09 ± 1.37	4.62 ± 0.69	3.12 ± 0.58	118.71 ± 7.57	73.01 ± 6.84	0.71 ± 0.04
V	10.72 ± 1.32	4.88 ± 0.76	2.94 ± 0.38	122.92 ± 9.92	82.88 ± 10.06	0.75 ± 0.06

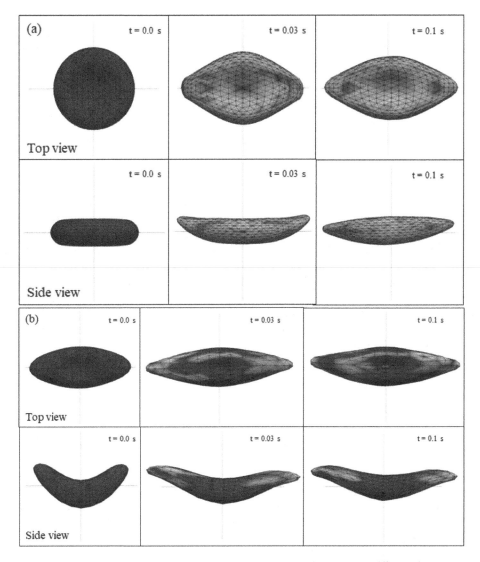

Fig. 1. Screenshots of the deformation for (a) hRBC, and (b) vRBC at different timestep.

Elongation Index. The cellular deformability for hRBC and vRBC are determined by the elongation index (EI) such that

$$EI = \frac{L - W}{L + W} \tag{1}$$

where L and W denote the length (axial) and width (transverse) diameter of the respective cell.

In the case of vRBC, as illustrated in Fig. 1(b), due to the already elongated morphology, the EI is determined as follows

$$EI = EI_t - EI_0 \tag{2}$$

Where EI_t and EI_0 denote the elongation index at time t and the initial elongation index, respectively.

3   Results and Discussion

In this study, we aim to replicate the stretching forces acting on a cell inside a slit-flow cytometer using the HemoCell framework. The parameters used in representing the cellular deformability of hRBC and vRBC are being tuned to respective optimal values that would mimic the deformability of the cell in a slit-flow cytometer. In the experiments performed by Dearnley et al. [8] where the elongation index of hRBC and vRBC are measured via slit-flow cytometer at shear stress of 3 Pa, results showed that hRBC has an elongation index of 0.34 while the vRBC has an elongation index of 0.18. In HemoCell, the parameters in defining the deformability of hRBC as shown in Table 3 has been validated in a previous study [34]. Taking the model of hRBC as a benchmark model, we tuned the respective stretching force to obtain an adequate stretching force value which gives similar elongation index for the hRBC at shear stress of 3 Pa inside a slit-flow cytometer. In the simulation, we stretched the cell with various of stretching force values for 10 ms where the elongation index is measured by using Eq. (1). As illustrated in Fig. 2, the optimal stretch force values fall in the range of 90 pN to 110 pN where the elongation index of hRBC is in the range of 0.3 to 0.35. Therefore, we selected a stretching force of 110 pN for the rest of the simulations in tuning κ_L value for the vRBC model.

As compared to Stage I to IV gametocytes, only the mature banana-shaped stage V gametocytes (vRBC) are able to move freely in the peripheral blood circulation to be uptake by the Anopheles mosquitoes [22]. Although they do not cause pathological effects on patients, they play a crucial role in disease transmission. Hence, Aingaran et al. [1] evaluated the shear modulus of different stages gametocyte using micropipette aspiration. Experiment results indicated that the shear modulus of vRBC is in the range of approximately 20 pN μm^{-1} to 120 pN μm^{-1}. The shear modulus emerging from the model using the given parameters is inferred from a numerical simulation in which a patch of the membrane is being sheared to obtain the corresponding resulting shear

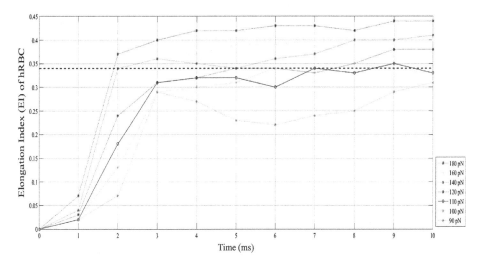

Fig. 2. Elongation index (EI) values for hRBC due to different stretching forces in the simulation, where the dotted forest-green line indicates the observed experimental data for hRBC. (Color figure online)

modulus values. Hence, secondly, in accordance to the given range of shear modulus from experimental data, we generated a set of κ_L values as shown in Table 2.

Table 2. Parameters used in the simulations.

kLink, κ_L	Shear modulus (μN m^{-1})
28	20.3
70	50.7
84	60.9
97	70.3
111	80.5
125	90.6
138	100.1
152	110.2
166	120.3

We investigated which of these κ_L values give an elongation index of 0.18 for the vRBC at a stretching force of 110 pN for 10 ms. In Fig. 3., various elongation index values are obtained via the stretching test. Note that the vRBC model with κ_L value of 28 has an elongation index of 0.18 which is in good agreement with the experimental results. Thus, the best fit κ_L parameter which define the elasticity of vRBC is 28. Figure 4 shows the final simulation results obtained from the parameters values given in Table 3.

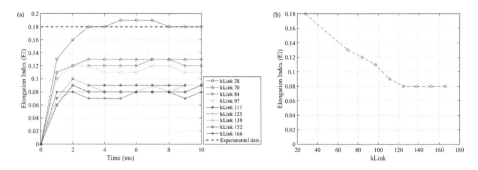

Fig. 3. The variation of the elongation index for stage V gametocyte (vRBC) at a stretching force of 110 pN for 10 ms with (a) time and (b) dimensionless κ_L values. The purple dotted-line indicates the observed experimental data for vRBC. (Color figure online)

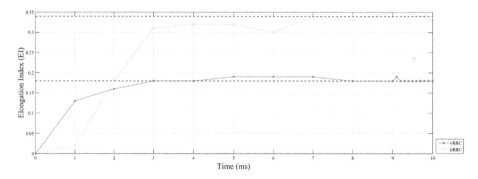

Fig. 4. The estimated elongation index values for healthy RBC and stage V gametocyte at a stretching force of 110 pN. The forest-green and purple dotted-lines indicate the observed elongation index for hRBC and vRBC, respectively. (Color figure online)

Table 3. Parameters used in simulations.

Parameters	Healthy RBC (hRBC)	Stage V gametocyte (vRBC)
kVolume	20	20
kArea	5	5
kLink	15	28
kBend	80	200
Force	110 pN	110 pN

4   Conclusion

In this study, we used Lattice Boltzmann simulations to study the stretching forces acting on a red blood cell inside a slit-flow cytometer. The parameters that represent the cellular deformability of healthy and malaria infected red blood cells are chosen such that they mimic the deformability of the cell in a slit-flow cytometer. The simulation results show excellent agreement with the experimental data and allow for studying the transportation of malaria infected red blood cell in blood circulation. This in turn will provide a better understanding and new insights of the in-host disease development.

References

1. Aingaran, M., Zhang, R., Law, S.K., Peng, Z., Undisz, A., Meyer, E., Diez-Silva, M., Burke, T.A., Spielmann, T., Lim, C.T., Suresh, S., Dao, M., Marti, M.: Host cell deformability is linked to transmission in the human malaria parasite P. falciparum. Cell. Microbiol. **14**(7), 983–993 (2012)
2. Alowayyed, S., Závodszky, G., Azizi, V., Hoekstra, A.G.: Load balancing of parallel cell-based blood flow simulations. J. Comput. Sci. **24**, 1–7 (2018)
3. Artoli, A.M.M., Hoekstra, A.G., Sloot, P.M.A.: 3D pulsatile flow with the lattice Boltzmann BGK method. Int. J. Mod. Phys. C **13**(8), 1119–1134 (2002)
4. Artoli, A.M.M., Hoekstra, A.G., Sloot, P.M.A.: Simulation of a systolic cycle in a realistic artery with the lattice Boltzmann BGK method. Int. J. Mod. Phys. C **17**(1 en 2), 95–98 (2003)
5. Axner, L., Hoekstra, A.G., Sloot, P.M.A.: Simulating time harmonic flows with the lattice Boltzmann method. Phys. Rev. E **75**, 036709 (2007)
6. Bernaschi, M., Fatica, M., Melchionna, S., Succi, S., Kaxiras, E.: A flexible high-performance lattice Boltzmann GPU code for the simulations of fluid flows in complex geometries. Concurr. Comput.: Pract. Exp. **22**(1), 1–14 (2010)
7. Dixon, M.W., Dearnley, M.K., Hanssen, E., Gilberger, T., Tilley, L.: Shape-shifting gametocytes: how and why does P. falciparum go banana-shaped? Trends Parasitol. **28**(11), 471–478 (2012)
8. Dearnley, M.K., Yeoman, J.A., Hanssen, E., Kenny, S., Turnbull, L., Whitchurch, C.B., Tilley, L., Dixon, M.W.: Origin, composition, organization and function of the inner membrane complex of P. falciparum gametocytes. J. Cell Sci. **125**(Pt 8), 2053–2063 (2012)
9. Eggleton, C.D., Popel, A.S.: Large deformation of red blood cell ghosts in a simple shear flow. Phys. Fluids **10**(8), 1834–1845 (1998)
10. Goergen, C.J., Shadden, S.C., Marsden, A.L.: SimVascular as an instructional tool in the classroom. In: 2017 IEEE Frontiers in Education Conference (FIE), Indianapolis, IN, pp. 1–4 (2017)
11. Gross, M., Krüger, T., Varnik, F.: Rheology of dense suspensions of elastic capsules: normal stresses, yield stress, jamming and confinement effects. Soft Matter **10**, 4360–4372 (2014)
12. Hanssen, E., Knoechel, C., Dearnley, M., Dixon, M.W., Le Gros, M., Larabell, C., Tilley, L.: Soft X-ray microscopy analysis of cell volume and hemoglobin content in erythrocytes infected with asexual and sexual stages of Plasmodium falciparum. J. Struct. Biol. **177**(2), 224–232 (2011)
13. Hawking, F., Gammage, K., Worms, M.J.: Evidence for cyclic development and short-lived maturity in the gametocytes of Plasmodium falciparum. Trans. R. Soc. Trop. Med. Hyg. **65**(5), 549–559 (1971)
14. Heldt, T., Mukkamala, R., Moody, G.B., Mark, R.G.: CVSim: an open-source cardiovascular simulator for teaching and research. Open Pacing Electrophysiol. Ther. J. **3**, 45–54 (2011)
15. Hoekstra, A.G., Alowayyed, S., Lorenz, E., Melnikova, N., Mountrakis, L., van Booij, B., et al.: Towards the virtual artery: a multiscale model for vascular physiology at the physics-chemistry-biology interface. Philos. Trans. R. Soc. A **374**, 20160146 (2016)

16. Kaandorp, J.A., Lowe, C.P., Frenkel, D., Sloot, P.M.A.: The effect of nutrient diffusion and flow on coral morphology. Phys. Rev. Lett. **77**(11), 2328–2331 (1996)
17. Kandhai, D., Koponen, A., Hoekstra, A.G., Kataja, M., Timonen, J., Sloot, P.M.A.: Lattice-Boltzmann hydrodynamics on parallel systems. Comput. Phys. Commun. **111**(1–3), 14–26 (1998)
18. Krüger, T., Varnik, F., Raabe, D.: Efficient and accurate simulations of deformable particles immersed in a fluid using a combined immersed boundary lattice Boltzmann finite element method. Comput. Math. Appl. **61**, 3485–3505 (2011)
19. Krüger, T., Gross, M., Raabe, D., Varnik, F.: Crossover from tumbling to tank-threading-like motion in dense simulated suspensions of red blood cells. Soft Matter **9**, 9008–9015 (2013)
20. Krüger, T.: Effect of tube diameter and capillary number on platelet margination and near-wall dynamics. Rheol. Acta **55**, 511–526 (2016)
21. Laveran, A.: A new parasite found in the blood of malarial patients. Parasitic origin of malarial attacks. Bull. Mem. Soc. Med. Hop. Paris **17**, 158–164 (1880)
22. Lavazec, C., Alano, P.: Uncovering the hideout of malaria sexual parasites. Blood **123**(7), 954–955 (2014)
23. Moon, D., Bur, A.J., Migler, K.B.: Multi-sample micro-slit rheometry. J. Rheol. **52**(2), 1131–1142 (2008)
24. Pan, C., Prins, J.F., Miller, C.T.: A high-performance lattice Boltzmann implementation to model flow in porous media. Comput. Phys. Commun. **158**(2), 89–105 (2004)
25. Radosinska, J., Vrbjar, N.: The role of red blood cell deformability and Na, K-ATPase function in selected risk factors of cardiovascular disease in humans: focus on hypertension, diabetes mellitus and hypercholesterolemia. Physiol. Res. **65**(Suppl. 1), 43–54 (2016)
26. Salmon, R.: The lattice Boltzmann method as a basis for ocean circulation modeling. J. Mar. Res. **57**, 503–535 (1999)
27. Sinden, R.E.: Sexual development of malarial parasites. Adv. Parasitol. **22**, 153–216 (1983)
28. Tiburcio, M., Niang, M., Deplaine, G., Perrot, S., Bischoff, E., Ndour, P.A., Silvestrini, F., Khattab, A., Milon, G., David, P.H., Harderman, M., Vernick, K.D., Sauerwein, R.W., Preiser, P.R., Mercereau-Puijalon, O., Buffet, P., Alano, P., Lavazec, C.: A switch in infected erythrocyte deformability at the maturation and blood circulation of P. falciparum transmission stages. Blood **119**(24), e172–e180 (2012)
29. Thommes, G., Sea, M., Banda, M.K.: Lattice Boltzmann methods for shallow water flow applications. Int. J. Numer. Methods Fluids **55**(7), 673–692 (2007)
30. Tomaiuolo, G.: Biomechanical properties of red blood cells in health and disease towards microfluidics. Biomicrofluidics **8**(5), 051501 (2014)
31. Tran, N.-P., Lee, M., Hong, S.: Performance optimization of 3D lattice Boltzmann flow solver on a GPU. Sci. Program. **2017**, 1–16 (2017)
32. Tubbs, K.R., Tsai, F.T.C.: Multilayer shallow water flow using lattice Boltzmann method with high performance computing. Adv. Water Resour. **32**(12), 1767–1776 (2009)
33. WHO World Malaria Report (2017). http://apps.who.int/iris/bitstream/10665/259492/1/9789241565523-eng.pdf
34. Závodszky, G., van Rooij, B., Azizi, V., Hoekstra, A.: Cellular level in-silico modeling of blood rheology with an improved material model for red blood cells. Front. Physiol. **8**, 563 (2017)
35. Zhong, L., Feng, S., Lou, D., Gao, S.: Wind-driven, double-gyre, ocean circulation in a reduced-gravity, 2.5-layer, lattice Boltzmann model. Adv. Atmos. Sci. **23**(4), 561–578 (2006)

36. Zhou, J.G., Causon, D.M., Mingham, C.G., Ingram, D.M.: Numerical prediction of dam-break flows in general geometries with complex bed topography. J. Hydraul. Eng. **130** (4), 332–340 (2004)
37. Zhou, J.G.: Lattice Boltzmann simulations of discontinuous flows. Int. J. Mod. Phys. C: Comput. Phys. Phys. Comput. **18**(1), 1–14 (2007)
38. https://www.hemocell.eu

Towards Model-Based Policy Elaboration on City Scale Using Game Theory: Application to Ambulance Dispatching

Sergey V. Kovalchuk[1(✉)], Mariia A. Moskalenko[1], and Alexey N. Yakovlev[1,2]

[1] ITMO University, Saint Petersburg, Russia
[2] Almazov National Medical Research Centre, Saint Petersburg, Russia
{kovalchuk,mamoskalenko}@corp.ifmo.ru,
yakovlev_an@almazovcentre.ru

Abstract. The paper presents early results on the development of a generalized approach for modeling and analysis of the interaction of multiple stakeholders in city environment while providing services to citizens under the regulation of city authorities. The approach considers the interaction between main stakeholders (organizations of various kind, citizens, and city authorities) including information and finances exchange, activities taken and services or goods provided. The developed approach is based on a combination of game-theoretic modeling and simulation of service providers interaction. Such combination enables consideration of confronting stakeholders as well as determined (e.g., scheduled) and stochastic variation in characteristics of system's elements. The goal of this approach development is supporting of analysis and optimization of city-level regulation through legislative, financial, and informational interaction with organizations and environment of a city. An example of ambulance dispatching during providing emergent care for acute coronary syndrome (ACS) patients is considered. The example is analyzed in a simplified linear case and in practical application to dispatching ambulances providing service for ACS patients in Saint Petersburg.

Keywords: Game theory · Queueing theory · Discrete-event simulation
Policy making · Ambulance dispatching · Acute coronary syndrome

1 Introduction

Currently, complexity city structure is rapidly growing. An idea of a smart city [1] is developed as a way to increase a city performance and human life quality. Still, there are multiple situations where the roots of a problem come from confronting interests of citizens, organizations or global goals (like improving life quality). One of the ways to understand and manage such situation is the application of game theory (GT) to understand optimal behavioral patterns of multiple stakeholders. Nevertheless, the complexity of modern cities leads to the need of considering various temporal and spatial factors regarding citizens' life, existing city environment, and key stakeholders activities. Having this in mind, a mixture of GT-model with models of city environment and various

© Springer International Publishing AG, part of Springer Nature 2018
Y. Shi et al. (Eds.): ICCS 2018, LNCS 10860, pp. 404–417, 2018.
https://doi.org/10.1007/978-3-319-93698-7_31

services in it may be applied. An important goal of this direction of research and development is supporting of city regulation through centralized and decentralized decisions, rules, and policies. In this paper, we present early results in the development of a generalized approach which combine GT modeling with modeling and simulation of city services to manage complex a city and uncertainty in structures and processes in it.

One of the important cases which may be considered in this way is providing healthcare in large cities. The high uncertainty of medical processes [2] is enforced in complex city health care structure with the diverse population being processed in the irregular environment. Moreover, the activity of hospitals, ambulances, drug stores, health insurance companies while providing health care is under the influence of personal interests and limitations (organizational, legislative, financial, policy-based, resource-based, etc.). Although the main goal of health care system is improving life quality, activity in a complex environment with limited resources may lead to cooperation or in contrast concurrency or/and confront between main actors. Additionally, diversity in patients and hospitals, as well as the complexity of healthcare environment (as a part of city environment) lead to growing importance of value-based healthcare [3] as a tool for assessing the impact from healthcare service.

For example, one of the crucial problems is overcrowding and queueing in hospitals. In this case, GT approach may provide certain insights on strategies for improvement, e.g., through collaboration between patients [4], between hospitals [5], between patients and doctors or nurses [6], etc. In the same time, diversity, temporal and spatial variation, the uncertainty of processes make the system more complex and leads to the application of modeling and simulation to the proper estimation of possible scenarios (see, e.g., [7]). On the other hand, city and country government may influence this process significantly through the introduction of regulation through organizational, financial support or defining policies for stakeholders. Still, to assess the possible scenarios a solution should be developed which considers all important aspects of complex city and healthcare environment. In this paper, we discuss the development of model-based solution based on the proposed approach for assessing and elaboration of possible policies in acute coronary syndrome (ACS) patients delivered by ambulances in Saint-Petersburg.

2   Conceptual Basis

2.1   Key Players in City Environment

Complex city environment includes multiple stakeholders involved in providing services, delivering goods, and supporting various city-scale activities. In many cases these stakeholders follow own interests in addition to support achieving the main (usually global) goal. These interests lead to complex patterns of interaction aimed at fulfilling personal tasks. In many cases, the relationship between external and personal goals as well as weights of these goals varies. E.g., in health care, global goal (improvement of population life quality) is of very high importance. Nevertheless, considering activity in circumstances of limited resources personal goals cannot be eliminated. In this section, a brief systematization of main stakeholders is provided to distinguish the main roles of actors and interaction channels (see Fig. 1).

Key considered in the approach include the following roles:

- *Service providers* acting in a city environment and delivering specific services for citizens. A specific type of service providers is transportation service providers, related to mobility of citizens and goods. Service providers may interact within a particular scenario involving several roles and procedures of interaction.
- *Citizens* are the main target consumer of the provided services. Usually, the goal of service providing is considered in a tight relationship with citizens' quality of life support. In addition to services, citizens use personal transportation.
- *City authorities* or other centralized controlling actors are intended to support high-level regulation of activities where it is required to support the development of city, systematic improvement of citizens' life quality and following higher goals (political, economic, etc.).

An essential part of the considered problem is limited resources (public or private) which are accessed by service providers or/and by citizens. The mentioned stakeholders may interact through the various channels or a combination of these channels:

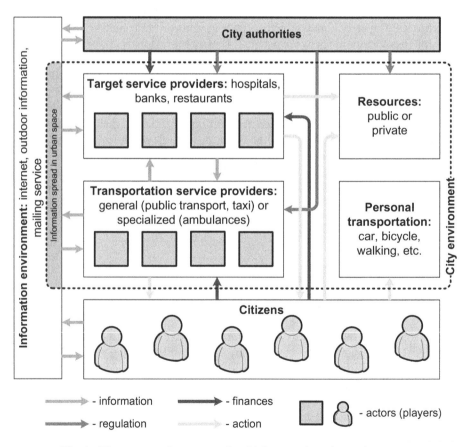

Fig. 1. The conceptual structure of multiple actors in a city environment.

- *Information* transfer may be performed in direct communication between actors or within the information environment. The information environment in general case includes various ways of delivering information through a media in public (broadcast) or private (directed) way.
- *Financial* interaction includes various payments between actors.
- *Regulation* is usually applied by city authorities to control service providers and available resources in a city environment.
- *Action* denote direct interaction between stakeholders: providing services, accessing resources, the mobility of citizens, etc.

The topology of stakeholders' interaction and mutual influence via various channels depending on a particular application. The only one element in this structure is usually presented in any application developed within the proposed approach. City authorities influence is considered as persistent centralized control, delivered by policies and laws, financial support (especially important for state organizations), and public information delivering.

One of the main goals of the developed approach in investigation and elaboration of possible ways of centralized regulation which may be applied in a multi-agent environment with personal interests of the stakeholders. For example, it could be applied to balance the automatically regulated behavior of the stakeholders towards global goals.

2.2 Patterns of Hybrid Modeling

Personalized, cooperative and collective decision making with multiple roles of stakeholders is considered in a framework of GT to identify self-adjustment of the system. In the same time, modeling and simulation of city environment enable deeper analysis of diverse temporal and spatial structures and processes, variation in behavior of the stakeholders, explicit and implicit relationship between them, etc. In this section, various patterns for a combination of GT approaches and city-scale models are considered. The patterns involve (a) GT models describing the interaction between stakeholders; (b) models of the city as a complex system (CS); (c) simulation models (SM) to assess selected scenarios application.

1. *CS-GT.* CS model may be used to assess topology of interaction between stakeholders, possible cooperation, available resources and typical behavior of stakeholders. GT provide additional structuring of the CS models with predicted strategies including cooperation, selected behavior. GT-based structuring becomes especially important in cases where CS model is difficult to identify directly, or in case of changing state and structure of a system (here GT-approaches may be applied within data assimilation algorithms).
2. *SM-GT.* SM enables complex estimation of game parameters, including stochastic parameters (e.g., with non-trivial distribution) of a system, assessment of utility function in various conditions, scenarios and system's structure, etc. GT provides rules identified according to strategies to describe the behavior of simulated entities.

3. *The explorative analysis* includes cyclic interaction within patterns 1 or/and 2 to elaborate and analysis of various hypotheses (also, includes what-if analysis), understand detailed structure of the system.

4. *Optimization, policy and decision making* also include the cyclic application of patterns 1 or/and 2 but for strictly defined goal (e.g., elaboration of best policy for stakeholders' regulation).

Patterns #1 and #2 are more structural and general. To consider integration with SM and CS it is important to consider game type in relation to (a) problem, being analyzed, (b) data structures available for exchange in these mixtures. Patterns #3 and #4 are mainly aimed at application development. Here the most important issue is automatization of uncertainty control to provide most valid and credible modeling and simulation results to support gaining new knowledge (pattern #3) or elaboration of result solution (pattern #4).

3   Case Study: ACS Patients Delivering

This section presents early results on the analysis of a selected case study with application of the developing approach for mixing GT models with models of complex city environment for analysis and optimization of processes within the city environment.

3.1   Problem Definition

World Health Organization reports [8] cardiovascular diseases as a major cause of death the world. Many of them, such as acute coronary syndrome (ACS) or stroke, require urgent and specialized care to be applied within several hours, whereas delays lead to significant increase in risks of complications and even death of a patient [9]. Usually, patient in such condition is delivered with an ambulance to a hospital for coronary angiography with possible percutaneous coronary intervention (PCI, i.e., angioplasty, stent placement which are considered as a major and preferable therapy in these cases). As a result, the goal of the healthcare system is lowering of delays from the appearance of acute state to surgery. This delay is mainly related to dispatching and routing of ambulances to deliver the patient to the selected hospital. Most of the works in the area are focused on delivering process [10, 11]. Still, the important part is a selection of the best hospital which available for processing of such patient. The hospital may be not available due to the overcrowding and queues for limited surgery facilities (which may be occupied either by acute or by the planned patient). Modeling of hospital's surgery facilities may help to assess hospital readiness to accept patient [7]. On the other hand, hospitals are often stimulated by the government, city, or local authorities towards processing as many patients as it is possible. In such condition, it is possible to consider the acceptance of the patient by a hospital as a personal decision taken by a hospital (as a service provider) considering existing queue to available surgery facilities and risks for a particular patient (assessed remotely). This leads to possible consideration of such situation within a framework of the proposed approach. Here hospital and ambulances are service providers, regulated by global authorities with financial support and policies and aimed towards achieving the global goal at the same time keeping own interests.

In Saint Petersburg, the death rate from cardiovascular diseases is about 10% higher than Russia's national average. This is typical for large cities [12] mainly due to the higher average age of the population. In 2015 there were 7913 ambulance calls were related to ACS, 46.7% of patients with ACS were treated with PCI, and 8.6% of patients with ACS died (8.2% within 24 h). Also, the expert analysis shows that the treatment can be improved in 20.1% cases of early deaths among patients. One of the known ways for improvement is reducing transportation delays. The hospital network in Saint Petersburg includes 16 hospitals with ACS facilities (13 of them are working 24/7). Still, this set of hospitals is significantly heterogeneous. Hospitals have own schedule of facilities and doctors, specialization. Also, the spatial distribution of hospitals increases the diversity of patient flow density due to calls placement and availability of current traffic load.

In this research, a model of ACS patients delivering with a special focus on dispatching (selection of target hospital) is developed to analyze the decision made collectively by ambulance service and hospitals.

3.2   ACS Patients in Simplified Case

We started with a simplified case to elaborate detailed solution furtherly applied to an actual network of hospitals and flow of ACS calls in Saint Petersburg. A simplified case (Fig. 2a) include two hospitals H_1 and H_2. Hospitals are placed in opposite ends of a line. Patients P_i appear uniformly in between these hospitals within Poisson process with rate λ. The patient is delivered to the selected hospital in a time $T_{transp.} \sim |P_i - H_i|$, where $H_i \in \{H_1, H_2\}$.

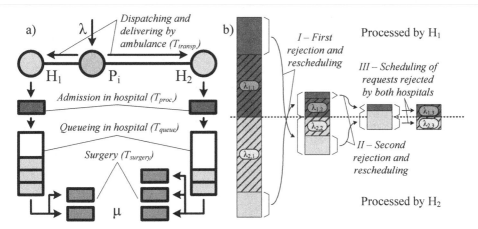

Fig. 2. Simplified case (a) dispatching and queueing; (b) three-stage rescheduling.

Each hospital has a queue to the surgery facilities that produce a delay of T_{queue}. Additionally, time $T_{proc.}$ is spent for various supplementary processes (interaction with admission department, registration of patient, etc.). Finally, patient goes to the surgery and it takes $T_{surgery}$ to complete it (with processing rate $\mu = 1/T_{surgery}$). As a result, total time is calculated as follows:

$$T = T_{transp.} + T_{proc.} + T_{queue} + T_{surgery}. \tag{1}$$

Considering the process with a queueing theory we can conclude that for each hospital, having request rate of λ_i, processing rate μ_i, and number of parallel surgery facilities n_i the probability of empty queue, the probability of k patients in a queue, the average length of a queue, and average processing time are respectively

$$p_i^{(0)} = \left(1 + \sum_{j=1}^{n-1} \frac{\rho_i^j}{j!} + \frac{\rho_i^{n_i}}{(n_i - 1)!} \frac{1}{n_i - \rho_i}\right)^{-1}, \tag{2}$$

$$p_i^{(k)} = \frac{\rho_i^k}{k!} p_i^{(0)}, \tag{3}$$

$$L_i = \frac{\rho_i^{n_i+1}}{n_i!} \frac{n_i}{(n_i - \rho_i)^2} p_i^{(0)}, \tag{4}$$

$$\tilde{t}_i = \frac{L_i}{\lambda_i} + \frac{1}{\mu_i}. \tag{5}$$

Here $\rho_i = \lambda_i/\mu_i$. Within the simplified example we suppose that $\tilde{t}_i$ is estimation of a sum $T_{queue} + T_{surgery}, T_{proc.} = 0$. As calls are distributed uniformly over the range between hospitals $T_{transp.}$ is estimated as average time of delivering patients from source part of the range. E.g. for basic delivering to the nearest hospital the range is divided into equal parts and $T_{transp.} = 0.25t_c$, where t_c is time of transportation along the whole range. As a result, $T_i = T_{transp.} + \tilde{t}_i$.

In this simplified case we consider two main strategies for hospitals:

- Strategy A. Accept all incoming requests.
- Strategy R. Partly reject requests in case number of patients in queue exceed predefined N_{lim}.

In the later strategy R, the probability of rejecting is

$$p_{reject}(\lambda_i) = 1 - p_i^{(0)} - \sum_{k=1}^{N_{lim}} p_i^{(k)}. \tag{6}$$

Normally, all the requests must be processed. In case of hospitals takes different strategies (AR or RA) rejected requests are processed by the hospital with strategy A. As a result, request flow is changed:

$$\lambda_1^* = \lambda_1 \left(1 - p_{reject} \left(\lambda_1 \right) \right), \lambda_2^* = \lambda_2 + \lambda_1 p_{reject} \left(\lambda_1 \right). \tag{7}$$

Here is the case where the first and second hospital has R and A strategies respectively. The opposite situation (AR) leads to exchanging of indices in Eq. (7).

In case of both hospitals with strategy R, we consider the application of recursive processing of requests in three stages (Fig. 2b). Firstly, the request scheduled to hospitals are rejected with probability $p_{reject} \left(\lambda_i \right)$ and flow $\lambda_i^{R1} = \lambda_i p_{reject} \left(\lambda_i \right)$ is redirected to another hospital. In the second round of rejection, redirected patients are rejected with probability $p_{reject} \left(\lambda_i + \lambda_{1-i}^{R1} \right)$. Finally, flow $\lambda_i^{R2} = \lambda_{1-i}^{R1} p_{reject} \left(\lambda_i + \lambda_{1-i}^{R1} \right)$ is redirected for uniformly rescheduling between hospitals (without more rejections). Thus, result inflow of each hospital is composed of three parts:

$$\lambda_i^* = \sum_{j=1}^{3} \lambda_{i,j}, \tag{8}$$

where

$$\lambda_{i,1} = \lambda_i \left(1 - p_{reject} \left(\lambda_i \right) \right) = \lambda_i - \lambda_i^{R1},$$

$$\lambda_{i,2} = \lambda_{i-1}^{R1} \left(1 - p_{reject} \left(\lambda_i + \lambda_{1-i}^{R1} \right) \right) = \lambda_{i-1}^{R1} - \lambda_i^{R2}, \tag{9}$$

$$\lambda_{i,3} = 0.5 \left(\lambda_i^{R2} + \lambda_{i-1}^{R2} \right).$$

Considering rescheduling the transportation time is also changed according to the following rules:

$$T_{transp.}^{AA} = T_{transp.}^{RA} = 0.25 t_c, \tag{10}$$

$$T_{transp.}^{AR} = \frac{0.25 + 0.75 p_{reject} \left(\lambda_R \right)}{1 + p_{reject} \left(\lambda_R \right)} t_c = \left(1 - \frac{1}{2 \left(1 + p_{reject} \left(\lambda_R \right) \right)} \right) t_c, \tag{11}$$

$$T_{transp.}^{RR} = \frac{0.25 \lambda_{i,1} + 0.75 \lambda_{i,2} + 0.5 \lambda_{i,3}}{\lambda_i^*} t_c. \tag{12}$$

To assess utility and global solution quality in GT-models we introduce score function $u_i = \lambda_i / T_i$ and global average time $g = \left(\lambda_1 T_1 + \lambda_2 T_2 \right) / \left(\lambda_1 + \lambda_2 \right)$. The utility function is constructed to maximize flow of processed patients and minimize processing time. Whereas g is constructed to minimize the processing time in the whole system. As a result, game matrix will be the following

$$M = \begin{bmatrix} \left(u_1^{AA}, u_2^{AA} \right) & \left(u_1^{AR}, u_2^{AR} \right) \\ \left(u_1^{RA}, u_2^{RA} \right) & \left(u_1^{RR}, u_2^{RR} \right) \end{bmatrix}, \tag{13}$$

while the global quality of the solution could be assessed through the searching of the minimum in the matrix

$$G = \begin{bmatrix} g^{AA} & g^{AR} \\ g^{RA} & g^{RR} \end{bmatrix}. \tag{14}$$

The described solution was evaluated for searching of Nash equilibrium (at this stage pure strategies were considered). The search was performed at various rates $\lambda \in [0.5;3]$ and $\mu \in [0.5;3]$ and configurations of available facilities $n_i \in \{1, 2, 3\}$. Results are presented in Figs. 3 and 4.

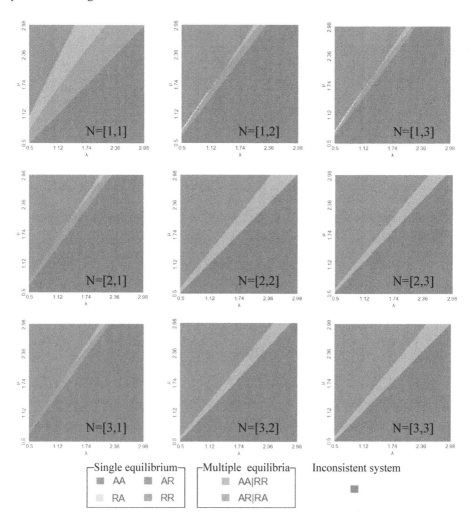

Fig. 3. Nash equilibria for various request rate (λ), processing rate (μ), and number of available parallel surgery facilities (N), colors depict combination(s) of strategies identified as equilibrium. (Color figure online)

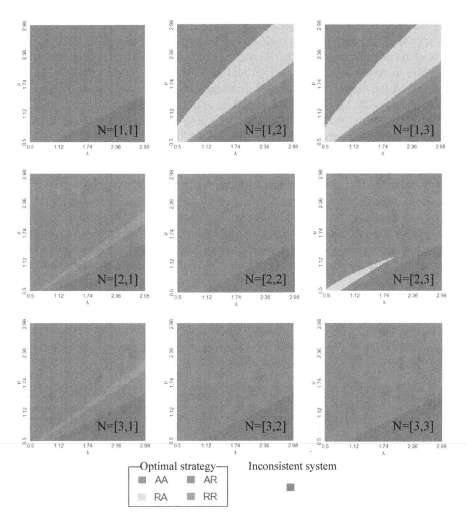

Fig. 4. Globally best solution for various request rate (λ), processing rate (μ), and number of available parallel surgery facilities (N), colors depict combination of strategies with lowest average time. (Color figure online)

Considering Nash equilibria with matrices (13) for various request and processing rates (Fig. 3), the simplest situation where λ and μ allows processing request with low probability of queuing is usually characterized by A strategy taken by both hospitals (AA, here and further a combination of two letters denote strategies taken by first and second hospital respectively). The opposite situation is when the configuration and strategies of two hospitals are insufficient for processing of given incoming request flow. This situation mainly comes to constantly growing queue ($\rho_i = \dfrac{\lambda_i}{\mu_i} > 1$) and is considered as inconsistent (during the automatic processing we interpret it as $u_i = -\infty$). We consider a whole system as inconsistent when a situation exists where one player cannot avoid inconsistency (both available strategies lead to $u_i = -\infty$). More interesting situations appear where queueing is possible, but the system can manage it. The situation may lead to either situation where RR strategies are considered as equilibrium or situation where there are two equilibria (AA and RR) depending on the ration of λ and μ. Moreover, on the border of the areas of such situation more complicated combinations of strategies appear: AR, RA or both equilibria at the same time.

Figure 4 shows globally best solutions according to the criteria (14) characterized by smallest average processing time for total request flow (Fig. 4). Here, the inconsistent situation leads to $g_i = +\infty$. A system considered as inconsistent when $\min(G) = +\infty$ (which is weaker criteria comparing to one described earlier for M matrix and therefore the area of inconsistency is smaller in Fig. 4 comparing to Fig. 3).

An important observation from a comparison of the results presented in Figs. 3 and 4 is various situations where the globally optimal solution (a combination of strategies for two hospitals) differs from the one selected with equilibrium state. Still, the deterministic inference available with queueing theory is not enough in the case where high uncertainty (like in case of healthcare) appears. To analyze the situation in more details a discrete-event simulation model was developed representing the same simplified case. Figure 5a shows simple run of this model with two hospitals in RA situation. The simulation may show situations where overcrowding events appear in hospitals with unlimited A strategy. This results in the multi-modal distribution of total time (Fig. 5b) in such hospitals. Using A strategy leads to higher mortality and complication risks, but also it comes with a higher throughput of the hospital.

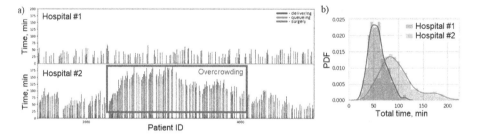

Fig. 5. Discrete-event simulation with queueing for a simplified case in RA situation (a) timelines for sequential patients; (b) total time distribution.

3.3 ACS Patients Delivering in Saint Petersburg

Multiple equilibria appearing depending on flow parameters even in the simplified case along with the high uncertainty of the processes leads to complex strategies which may vary over time (considering scheduling of real hospital facilities, temporal and spatial variation of patient flow, etc.). Figure 6 shows ACS calls in Saint Petersburg during 2015 (circles). The hospitals are denoted with stars of the same color as calls processed in it. Size of a star depicts a number of processed calls. It could be clearly seen that most of the calls are served by the nearest hospital and the city could be divided into several "areas of responsibility" of hospitals (green dividing lines are identified with SVN

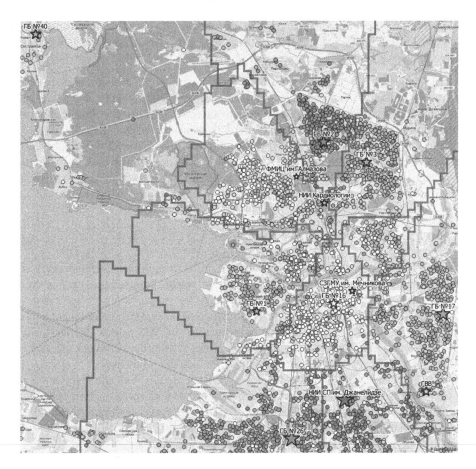

Fig. 6. ACS calls (circles) and target hospitals (stars of corresponding colors, size is proportional to number of processed calls) in Saint Petersburg. (Color figure online)

classifier which predicts target hospital for each point on the map). Still, several features bring complication into the task:

- For most hospitals, there are calls from the areas of neighbor hospitals (usually, near the border) which appears when the traffic or hospitals' load shift the dispatcher's decision towards the other hospital. These calls form blending areas between hospitals which are rather wide in many cases.
- There are cases where the patient is delivered to rather a far hospital. In some cases, it is caused by patient own request (which of cause is checked for not violating requirements of the ambulance service). Still, in many cases, this was an objective decision taken by the dispatcher in a situation of overcrowded nearest hospitals.
- Also, there are several areas with a high mixture of target hospitals (see, e.g., the area to the north from the map center).

- Finally, it worth to mention that the flow of patients varies significantly during 24 h in its level and in the spatial pattern of usual appearance (e.g., by switching working/touristic areas with sleeping areas).

The mentioned observations lead to the conclusion that the decision of dispatcher often has significant uncertainty and depends on multiple factors. To work with the uncertainty and apply the developed solution to the real world case the SM-GT mixture of models will be extended (a) with enhanced delivering simulation delivered within the previous research of authors' [13]; (b) with additional analysis in GT model where the solution becomes multi-dimensional having many stakeholders (besides 16 hospitals, city authorities, and patient being delivered may be considered as stakeholders); (c) with optimization of policies for potential improvement of ambulance dispatching system.

4   Conclusion and Future Works

The developed approach is designed for investigation of multiple stakeholders' interaction during a service providing in the city environment. For example, the approach may be applied to the task of policy optimization or investigation of various scenarios in a city environment. To support this, a combination of GT and city environment model is hired. A working example is devoted to the analysis of ACS patients' delivery with ambulances and possible optimization of this process. Still, the presented research is still ongoing. Further directions of the research include the following.

The general approach will be developed in more details with the elaboration of typical patterns of modeling and simulation with an especial focus on GT application for support of modeling collective decision making and uncertainty management. E.g. consider a mixture of GT and SM a sensitivity and stochastic assessment could be used to analyze possible switching from one equilibrium to another.

The considered GT solution will be extended with more flexible approaches than Nash equilibrium searching in pure strategies. This includes: mixed strategies for probabilistically assessment of strategies, evolutionary strategies for adaptation of the model to the changed environment, quantal response equilibrium (QRE) for dealing with bounded rationality in decision making and working with multiple equilibria with switching between them, consideration of cooperative games for more complex stakeholders' interaction, etc.

Within the considered case study, the further development of the solution includes the detailed elaboration of the of the implemented GT and SM solution and its application to the actual structure of hospitals in Saint Petersburg. The goal is to access a design policy of patient delivery process regulation through introduced policy, financial support, and information exchange.

Finally, the developed solution is aimed to be enriched with the previous experience of authors. Namely, the solution may be used to extend the experimental solution for decision making in ambulance dispatching and routing, developed previously by the authors [7]; implementation of collaborative decision making support tool [14] as a way of cooperative decision making; including of data-driven predictive models of ACS cases [15] for enhanced prediction of episodes and more precise assessment of risks and length of stay for a patient.

Acknowledgements. This research is financially supported by The Russian Scientific Foundation, Agreement #14-11-00823 (15.07.2014).

References

1. Dameri, R.P., Rosenthal-Sabroux, C.: Smart city and value creation. In: Dameri, R.P., Rosenthal-Sabroux, C. (eds.) Smart City. PI, pp. 1–12. Springer, Cham (2014). https://doi.org/10.1007/978-3-319-06160-3_1
2. Mandrola, J.: Doctor Doesn't Always Know Best. http://www.medscape.com/viewarticle/849689
3. Brown, M.M., Brown, G.C.: Update on value-based medicine. Curr. Opin. Ophthalmol. **24**, 183–189 (2013)
4. McCain, R.A., Hamilton, R., Linnehan, F.: The problem of emergency department overcrowding: agent-based simulation and test by questionnaire. In: Osinga, S., Hofstede, G., Verwaart, T. (eds.) Emergent Results of Artificial Economics. LNE, vol. 652, pp. 91–102. Springer, Heidelberg (2011). https://doi.org/10.1007/978-3-642-21108-9_8
5. Deo, S., Gurvich, I.: Centralized vs. decentralized ambulance diversion: a network perspective. Manag. Sci. **57**, 1300–1319 (2011)
6. Wu, C.-K., Chen, Y.-M., Wu, D.: A game theory approach for deploying medical resources in emergency department. In: Li, D.-F., Yang, X.-G., Uetz, M., Xu, G.-J. (eds.) China-Dutch GTA/China GTA -2016. CCIS, vol. 758, pp. 18–30. Springer, Singapore (2017). https://doi.org/10.1007/978-981-10-6753-2_2
7. Kovalchuk, S.V., Krotov, E., Smirnov, P.A., Nasonov, D.A., Yakovlev, A.N.: Distributed data-driven platform for urgent decision making in cardiological ambulance control. Futur. Gener. Comput. Syst. **79**, 144–154 (2018)
8. Health in 2015: from MDGs, Millennium Development Goals to SDGs, Sustainable Development Goals (2015)
9. Moser, D.K., Kimble, L.P., Alberts, M.J., Alonzo, A., Croft, J.B., Dracup, K., Evenson, K.R., Go, A.S., Hand, M.M., Kothari, R.U., Mensah, G.A., Morris, D.L., Pancioli, A.M., Riegel, B., Zerwic, J.J.: Reducing delay in seeking treatment by patients with acute coronary syndrome and stroke: a scientific statement from the American Heart Association Council on cardiovascular nursing and stroke council. Circulation **114**, 168–182 (2006)
10. Andersson, T., Värbrand, P.: Decision support tools for ambulance dispatch and relocation. J. Oper. Res. Soc. **58**, 195–201 (2006)
11. Repede, J.F., Bernardo, J.J.: Developing and validating a decision support system for locating emergency medical vehicles in Louisville, Kentucky. Eur. J. Oper. Res. **75**, 567–581 (1994)
12. Urbanization and cardiovascular disease—World Heart Federation. http://www.world-heart-federation.org/heart-facts/fact-sheets/urbanization-and-cardiovascular-disease/
13. Derevitskiy, I., Krotov, E., Voloshin, D., Yakovlev, A., Kovalchuk, S.V., Karbovskii, V.: Simulation of emergency care for patients with ACS in Saint Petersburg for ambulance decision making. Procedia Comput. Sci. **108**, 2210–2219 (2017)
14. Ivanov, S.V., Kovalchuk, S.V., Boukhanovsky, A.V.: Workflow-based collaborative decision support for flood management systems. Procedia Comput. Sci. **18**, 2213–2222 (2013)
15. Krikunov, A.V., Bolgova, E.V., Krotov, E., Abuhay, T.M., Yakovlev, A.N., Kovalchuk, S.V.: Complex data-driven predictive modeling in personalized clinical decision support for acute coronary syndrome episodes. Procedia Comput. Sci. **80**, 518–529 (2016)

Elucidation of Mechanism for Reducing Porosity in Electric Arc Spraying Through CFD

Ryoji Tamaki[1]([✉]) and Masashi Yamakawa[2]

[1] Daihen Co., Ltd., Koyocho-nishi, Higashinada-ku, Kobe, Hyogo, Japan
tamaki@daihen.co.jp
[2] Kyoto Institute of Technology, Matsugasaki, Sakyo-ku, Kyoto, Japan

Abstract. We elucidated the mechanism for reducing the porosity (a means for achieving smaller globules) through Computational Fluid Dynamics while focusing on the flow of compressed air. A simulation study revealed that a spray gun nozzle comprising a flow splitting plate located upstream of the arc point in the nozzle produces compression waves whereby the flow field made in the nozzle differs substantially from that made in a conventional, plate-less nozzle. Observation using a high-speed camera showed that smaller particles of the molten metal (globules) were made due to the plate, which means that the compression waves generated upstream of the arc point affect the formation of globules at the arc point.

Keywords: Electric arc spraying · Compression wave · Compression
Expansion

1 Introduction

In a wide range of industries, coating processes called thermal spraying are widely used to repair surfaces of mechanical components, increase hardness, and protect outdoor structural materials such as steel bridges against rust and corrosion (see Table 1). Thermal spray coating is a process in which a melted metallic material is sprayed onto a surface.

Table 1. Purposes of thermal spraying.

Function improvement	Used to improve wear resistance
	Used to give electrical characteristics
Rust and corrosion prevention	Used to prevent outdoor structures from getting rusted and corroded (to protect base materials)
	Used to prevent combustion chambers from getting corroded due to high temperature

Various thermal spray coating methods exist, and they are classified into two types by the method employed to heat coating materials to molten or semi-molten state, as

© Springer International Publishing AG, part of Springer Nature 2018
Y. Shi et al. (Eds.): ICCS 2018, LNCS 10860, pp. 418–428, 2018.
https://doi.org/10.1007/978-3-319-93698-7_32

shown in Fig. 1. Oxy-fuel spraying is subdivided into flame spraying and high-velocity flame spraying. The former utilizes a gas mixture of oxygen and acetylene as a heat source to produce combustion flame together with compressed air to accelerate material globules of micro particles toward the workpiece. High-velocity oxy-fuel (HVOF) coating, another type of flame spraying, utilizes high-pressure oxygen to produce confined combustion at high pressures, and hot gas flame jet that accelerates globules toward the workpiece at extreme velocities.

Electric spraying includes plasma spraying, and electric arc spraying which is the subject of this study. In a plasma-arc gun, an inert gas, typically argon, is charged by electrodes whereby it ionizes to generate hot, high-velocity plasma. Plasma spraying uses this plasma as the heat source. Usually, a water-cooled copper nozzle works as the anode, and the cathode is made of tungsten. For plasma spraying, plasma is generated by electric arc burning within the nozzle of the plasma gun and the arc gas is formed into a plasma jet as it emerges from the nozzle. Powder particles injected into this jet strike the workpiece at high velocity to produce a strongly adherent coating.

Electric arc spraying is a form of thermal spraying where two metal wires which ultimately form the coating are fed independently into the spray gun as shown in Fig. 2. Typical wire materials are aluminum/zinc, copper/copper, and steel/steel for example. These wires are fed into a wire feeding unit and electrically charged via electrodes to generate an arc. The wires placed as they face together produce an electric arc to melt the wires. Compressed air or other gas, passing through a nozzle, atomizes the molten metal and sprays it onto the workpiece (substrate surface).

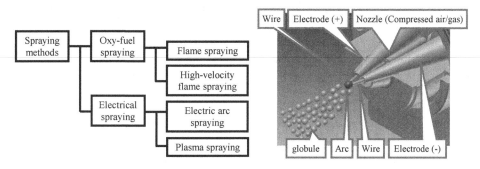

Fig. 1. Spraying methods   **Fig. 2.** Arc spraying system

Among the methods described above, the electric arc spraying delivers a high feed rate of spraying in a short period of time and comparatively high spraying quality at low cost. Thanks to these features, it has been commonly used in a wide variety of industries. However, the method suffers from some disadvantages including a large production of fume (atomized particles) worsening the working environment, larger porosity (voids) in the coating compared to other arc spraying methods, and production of oxides during transportation of globules in air leading to entrainment of the oxides in the coating. Especially, the larger porosity is serious as it is detrimental to the coating strength i.e. corrosion resistance. Therefore, we studied how the porosity could be reduced.

Important parameters that affect the formation of coating film in electric arc spraying are arc voltage, wire feed, and compressed air (or gas) flow (i.e. air pressure and nozzle shape). Many of existing studies [1–5] focused on the arc voltage and wire feed only, considering the compressed air flow (air pressure and nozzle shape) less important except the study [6] focused on the compressible flows. This study is to find a mechanism effective for reducing the porosity. To this end, the compressed flow was examined in detail by means of CFD analysis. The computations were carried out in an OpenMP Parallel environment for the unstructured mesh system [7]. As a visualizing aid, a high-speed camera was used for complementing the CFD result.

2 Numerical Simulation

2.1 Computation Method

The methods used for the computation are given in Table 2. As governing equation, following three-dimensional Navier-Stokes equation written in conservation low form is adopted.

$$\frac{\partial U}{\partial t} + \frac{\partial (E - E_v)}{\partial x} + \frac{\partial (F - F_v)}{\partial y} + \frac{\partial (G - G_v)}{\partial z} = 0 \tag{1}$$

Where, U is a conserved quantity vector. E, F, G and E_v, F_v, G_v are advection-flux and viscous-flux vectors for x, y, z direction respectively.

For advective term data calculation, Rotated-RHLL method [8] was used. The Rotated-RHLL solver, a method that combines the HLL and Roe solvers, is capable of capturing shock waves, expansion waves and contact surfaces at high resolution while not producing Carbuncle phenomena in which impact wave surfaces tend to be unstable. The representative equations of this method are shown below.

$$\varphi_{RHLL} = \frac{S_R^+ H_n(U_L) - S_L^- H_n(U_R)}{S_R^+ - S_L^-} - \frac{1}{2} \sum_{k=1}^{4} \left| \widehat{S}_{RHLL}^k \right| \widehat{w}_{n_2}^k \, \widehat{r}_{n_2}^k \tag{2}$$

where

$$\left| \widehat{S}_{RHLL}^k \right| = \alpha_2 \left| \widehat{\lambda}_{n_2}^k \right|^* - \frac{1}{S_R^+ - S_L^-} \left[\alpha_2 \left(S_R^+ + S_L^- \right) \widehat{\lambda}_{n_2}^k + \alpha_1 S_R^+ S_L^- \right]. \tag{3}$$

H is combined E, F and G. φ_{RHLL} is combined the Roe flux function and the Rusanov flux function.

For diffusion term calculation and time integration, Alpha-damping scheme [9–11] and Defect Correction method were used respectively, and SST k-ω was used for the turbulence model. The SST k-ω turbulence model behaves well in analyses of flows that involve separation, and therefore can simulate separated flows at higher accuracy than typical turbulence models including k-ω. These calculations used a general purpose thermo-fluid simulation software SC/Tetra [12].

2.2 Computational Model and Boundary Conditions

Figure 3 shows the computational model. The total pressure was given together with temperatures as the inflow condition. A cylindrical open space was provided around the nozzle. Assuming that the entire wall surface of the cylindrical open space served as air outlets, the surface pressure (i.e., atmospheric pressure) was given together with environmental temperature. For detailed condition, refer to Table 3.

Table 2. Computation Methods

Governing equation	Three-dimensional Navier-Stokes equation
Advective term	Rotated-RHLL method [8]
Diffusion term	Alpha-damping scheme [9–11]
Time integration	Defect correction method
Steady/Unsteady flow	Steady
Turbulence model	SST k-ω

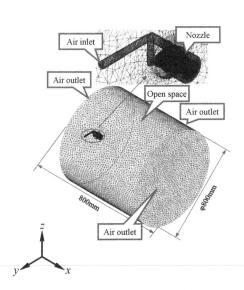

Fig. 3. Computational model

Table 3. Boundary conditions

Inflow condition	Total pressure regulation (0.4 MPa at 39 °C)
Outflow condition	Surface pressure regulation (0.0 MPa at 29 °C)
Wall surface	Stationary wall

As shown in Fig. 4, computations were performed for a total of four different types of nozzle, which included one nozzle of 6 mm in aperture diameter (normal nozzle) and three nozzle that sprayed no jet flow directly to the arc point by mounting a plate on the upstream side from the arc point (i.e., three types of splitter nozzle of 6 mm in aperture nozzle). The plate of 1 mm in width and 6 mm in length was located in the nozzle at L = 0.5 mm, 1.0 mm and 2.0 mm in the distance from the nozzle tip (see Table 4).

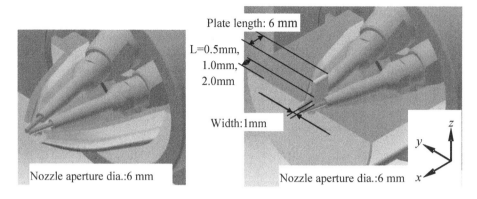

Fig. 4. Nozzle

Table 4. Splitter nozzles

Name	Distance between nozzle tip and plate	Plate size
Splitter nozzle 1	0.5 mm	1 mm in width × 6 mm in length
Splitter nozzle 2	1.0 mm	
Splitter nozzle 3	2.0 mm	

3 Simulation Result

Figure 5 shows the Mach numbers measured in the xy and yz planes for the normal nozzle. The distance from the nozzle tip to the workpiece is normally 100 to 200 mm. Seeing the enlarged view of the xy plane, it was found that the jet flow compresses after leaving the nozzle. Then it undergoes a cycle of expansion and compression while reducing its width. In the yz plane, the jet flow first compresses on the top and bottom surface of the wire at the nozzle aperture and then repeats a cycle of expansion and compression while reducing its width. Seeing the enlarged view to look deep into the jet flow behavior in and around the nozzle tip, larger Mach numbers are measured at closer to the nozzle tip with a Mach number of higher than 2 measured at the arc point. However, in reality, the behavior in this region cannot be simulated accurately since plasma can occur near the arc point due to the heat produced by arc discharge between the wires.

As mentioned above, for the normal nozzle, larger Mach numbers are measured at closer to the nozzle tip; and then the jet flow undergoes a cycle of expansion and compression while reducing its width. The expansion and compression process pulverizes the molten metal into micro globules. Of these, those flowing at high speed at around the center of the nozzle will collide with the workpiece leading to the formation of a film of coating.

For a configuration with a plate located 0.5 mm upstream of the nozzle aperture (splitter nozzle 1), Mach number measurements in the xy and yz planes are shown in

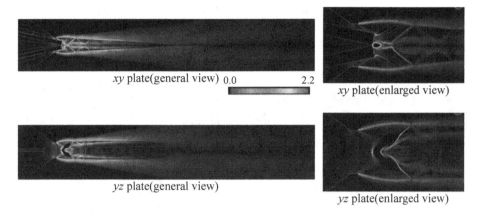

Fig. 5. Mach number contour for the normal nozzle

Fig. 6. In the *xy* plane, compression waves are generated on both sides of the plate. The flow pattern after the nozzle is different from that of the normal nozzle. This is attributed to the plate that changes the flow field in the nozzle.

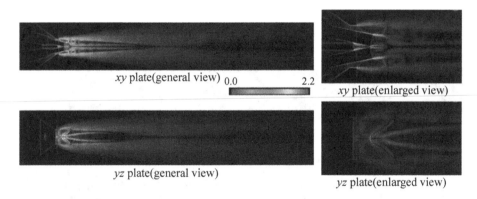

Fig. 6. Mach number contour for the splitter nozzle 1

The configuration with a plate located 1.0 mm upstream of the nozzle aperture (splitter nozzle 2) produces larger compression waves than the configuration with a plate located 0.5 mm upstream of the nozzle aperture. Since this calculation assumes a constant inflow pressure of 0.4 MPa, the plate located closer to the nozzle aperture produces a larger pressure drop at the nozzle aperture. This is probably the reason for the smaller compression waves produced by the plate located 0.5 mm upstream of the nozzle aperture compared to the configuration with the plate located 1.0 mm upstream.

The configuration with a plate located 2.0 mm upstream of the nozzle aperture (splitter nozzle 3) also causes compression waves to be generated on both sides of the plate. However, these compression waves are smaller than those generated by other configurations with a plate located 1.0 mm or 0.5 mm upstream of the nozzle aperture. This is probably because the larger distance between the plate and nozzle aperture may lead to a smaller compression (reduction) of the flow sectional area (Fig. 7).

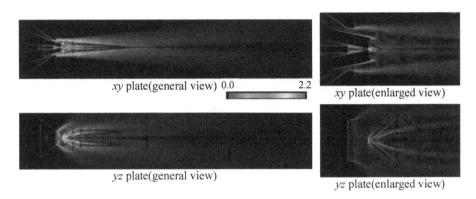

Fig. 7. Mach number contour for the splitter nozzle 2

As mentioned above, with a plate located in the nozzle, compression waves occur in the nozzle, which changes the flow field greatly from that can occur in a conventional, plate-less nozzle (Fig. 8).

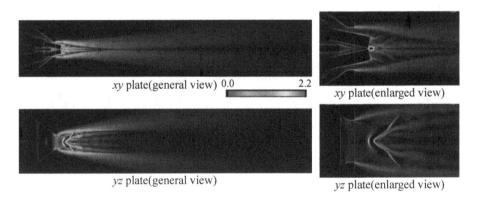

Fig. 8. Mach number contour for the splitter nozzle 3

4   Experimental Method

4.1   Experimental System

To visualize the results of the simulation i.e. the effect of the change in flow field on arc spraying, an experiment was performed using a high-speed camera. The experiment used the equipment shown in Fig. 9, φ1.6 iron-based solid wires (ISO common id:

G49A2UM15) showing a relatively better feedability, thermal spray gun ASTS-2501 manufactured by Daihen, the normal nozzle and splitter nozzle 2 as mentioned above, and power supply unit AS-400 manufactured by Daihen with a reactor inserted between the power unit and the gun. The reactor complemented the power unit AS-400 to supply the power required for melting the iron wires.

A high-speed camera HX-3 of NAC make was used with a shutter speed of $1/10^9$ s and 30000 frames per second. Details of thermal spraying conditions are as shown in Table 5.

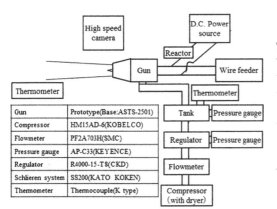

Table 5. Thermal spraying conditions

Tank pressure	0.4 MPa
Wire feeding speed	7.0 m/min
Average arc voltage	26.5 V
Type of wire	φ1.6 iron-based solid wires

Fig. 9. Experiment schematic

5   Result of Experiment

Figure 10 shows a visualization (8 frames, 1/30000 s/frame) of the region around the arc point for the normal nozzle. In the images ([1] through [8]), areas in white represent arcs. They are shown in white because backlighting to extinguish arc lights is not used. These pictures show that the wire is melted by arc heat, and elongated and torn by the flow of compressed air to small globules (areas circled in red in Fig. 10).

Figure 11 shows the same visualization for the splitter nozzle 2. As is the case with the normal nozzle, areas in white represent arcs. Compared to the case with the normal nozzle, the globules made by tearing the arc-heated molten wire are smaller (areas circled in blue in Fig. 11). The simulation mentioned above indicated that the splitter nozzle causes compression waves to be generated on the plate located upstream of the arc point. These compression waves affect the production of globules (pulverization of molten metal) at the arc point.

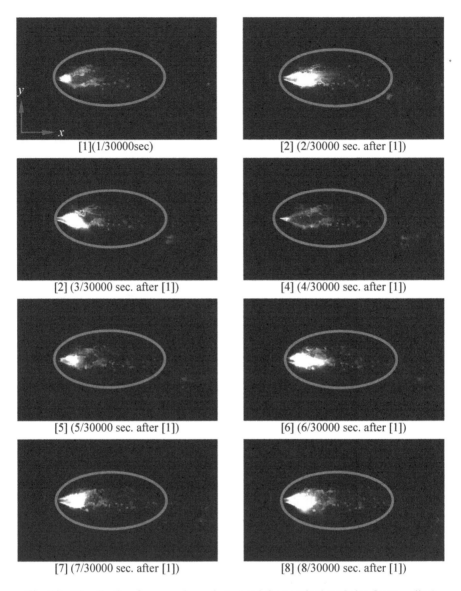

[1](1/30000sec)   [2] (2/30000 sec. after [1])

[2] (3/30000 sec. after [1])   [4] (4/30000 sec. after [1])

[5] (5/30000 sec. after [1])   [6] (6/30000 sec. after [1])

[7] (7/30000 sec. after [1])   [8] (8/30000 sec. after [1])

Fig. 10. Visualization for normal nozzle (around the nozzle tip) (Color figure online)

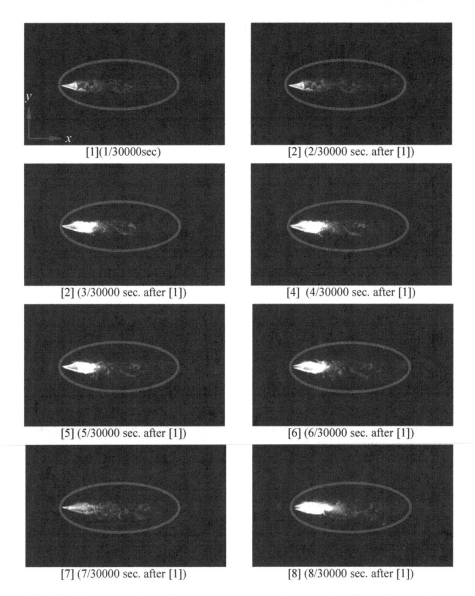

Fig. 11. Visualization for splitter nozzle 2 (around the nozzle tip) (Color figure online)

6 Conclusions

In this study, we aimed to elucidate the properties of a jet flow spurting from the arc spray gun nozzle, and the data presented here supports the following:

1. CFD analyses indicated that, in the normal nozzle, the flow from the nozzle aperture undergoes a cycle of expansion and compression leading to damping. This

expansion and compression process can be considered a cause of molten metal pulverization.

2. CFD analysis indicated that the splitter nozzle, that is, a nozzle with a plate located upstream of the arc point, produces compression waves on the plate, so that the flow field is greatly different from that observed in the normal nozzle.

3. Visualization using a high-speed camera revealed that the splitter nozzle produces molten metal globules of smaller size, which means that the compression waves generated before the arc point affect the process of molten metal pulverization into micro globules.

References

1. Watanabe, T., Usui, M.: Effect of atomizing gas on oxidation of droplets in wire arc spraying. J. Jpn. Inst. Met. **63**, 98–102 (1999)
2. Kawase, R., Kureishi, M., Minehisa, S.: Relation between arc spraying condition and adhesion strength of sprayed coatings. J. JWS 17–22 (1983)
3. Kawase, R., Kureishi, M., Maehara, K.: Arc phenomenon and wire fusion in arc spraying. J. JWS, 82–87 (1984)
4. Kawase, R., Kureishi, M.: Fused metal temperature in arc spraying. J. JWS, 52–58 (1984)
5. Kawase, R., Kureishi, M.: Relation between adhesion strength of sprayed coating and fused metal temperature. J. JWS, 21–260 (1985)
6. Tamaki, R., Yamakawa, M.: Study on the nozzle jet in arc spraying. Appl. Math. Mech. **37** (12), 1394–1402 (2016)
7. Yamakawa, M., Kita, Y., Matsuno, K.: Domain decomposition method for unstructured meshes in an OpenMP computing environment. Comput. Fluids **45**, 168–171 (2011)
8. Nishikawa, H., Kitamura, K.: Very simple, carbuncle-free, boundary-layer-resolving, rotated-hybrid Riemann solvers. J. Comput. Phys. **227**, 2560–2581 (2008)
9. Nishikawa, H.: Beyond interface gradient: a general principle for constructing diffusion schemes. In: AIAA Paper, pp. 2010–5093 (2010)
10. Nishikawa, H.: Robust and accurate viscous discretization via upwind scheme-I: basic principle. Comput. Fluids **49**, 62–86 (2011)
11. Nishikawa, H.: Two ways to extend diffusion schemes to Navier-Stokes schemes: gradient formula or upwind flux. In: AIAA Paper, pp. 2011–3044 (2011)
12. http://www.cradle-cfd.com/

nSharma: Numerical Simulation Heterogeneity Aware Runtime Manager for OpenFOAM

Roberto Ribeiro[1]([⊠])[iD], Luís Paulo Santos[2][iD], and João Miguel Nóbrega[3][iD]

[1] Department of Informatics, Algoritmi Research Center,
University of Minho, Braga, Portugal
rribeiro@di.uminho.pt
[2] Department of Informatics, INESC-TEC, University of Minho, Braga, Portugal
psantos@di.uminho.pt
[3] Institute for Polymers and Composites/I3N,
University of Minho, Guimarães, Portugal
mnobrega@dep.uminho.pt

Abstract. CFD simulations are a fundamental engineering application, implying huge workloads, often with dynamic behaviour due to runtime mesh refinement. Parallel processing over heterogeneous distributed memory clusters is often used to process such workloads. The execution of dynamic workloads over a set of heterogeneous resources leads to load imbalances that severely impacts execution time, when static uniform load distribution is used. This paper proposes applying dynamic, heterogeneity aware, load balancing techniques within CFD simulations. nSharma, a software package that fully integrates with OpenFOAM, is presented and assessed. Performance gains are demonstrated, achieved by reducing busy times standard deviation among resources, i.e., heterogeneous computing resources are kept busy with useful work due to an effective workload distribution. To best of authors' knowledge, nSharma is the first implementation and integration of heterogeneity aware load balancing in OpenFOAM and will be made publicly available in order to foster its adoption by the large community of OpenFOAM users.

Keywords: Computational Fluid Dynamics · OpenFOAM
Heterogeneous systems · Dynamic Load Balancing

1 Introduction

Computational Fluid Dynamics (CFD) simulations have become a fundamental engineering tool, witnessing an increasing demand for added accuracy and larger problem sizes, being one of the most compute intensive engineering workloads. The most common approaches to CFD, such as Finite Elements (FEs) and Finite Volumes (FVs), entail discretizing the problem domain into cells (or elements) and then solving relevant governing equations for the quantities of interest for

© Springer International Publishing AG, part of Springer Nature 2018
Y. Shi et al. (Eds.): ICCS 2018, LNCS 10860, pp. 429–443, 2018.
https://doi.org/10.1007/978-3-319-93698-7_33

each cell. Since each cell's state depends on its neighbours, solvers employ some form of nearest neighbour communication among cells and iterate until some convergence criteria are met. Typically, CFD problems are unsteady, requiring an outer loop which progresses through simulation time in discrete steps. Such very compute intensive type of workloads are obvious candidates to exploit the multitude of resources available on parallel processing systems. Domain decomposition is used to make available a suitable degree of parallelism, i.e., the set of discrete cells is partitioned into subsets which can then be distributed among the computational resources.

Currently, the most widely available parallel systems are distributed memory clusters, which provide a cost-effective, extensible and powerful computing resource. A cluster can be fairly easily extended by adding more nodes with identical architectures, but often from newer generations offering more computing capabilities. This extensibility renders the system heterogeneous in the sense that different generations of hardware, with diverse configurations, coexist in the same system. An additional source of heterogeneity is the integration on current supercomputing clusters [16] of devices with alternative architectures, programming and execution models, such as the new highly parallel Intel KNLs and the massively parallel GPUs [5].

However, this heterogeneity results in different performances across nodes, potentially leading to severe load imbalances. Static and uniform workload distribution strategies, as typically used by CFD software, will result on the computational units waiting on each other and resources underutilization. Properly distributing the workload and leveraging all the available computing power is thus a crucial feature, which has been revisited in the latest years due to increasing systems' heterogeneity [10].

The load distribution problem is further aggravated in the presence of dynamic workloads. CFD solvers often refine the problem domain discretisation as the simulation progresses through time, allowing for higher accuracy in regions where the quantities of interest exhibit higher gradients. In the scope of this work, these applications will be referred to as *adaptive applications*. This refinement entails splitting and merging cells, resulting on a new domain discretisation. Given that the computational effort is in general proportional to the number of cells, its distribution across the problem domain also changes. Not accounting for this refinement and maintaining the initial mapping throughout the whole simulation would lead to load imbalances and huge performance losses.

The combination of the differences in computing power provided by the heterogeneous Computing Units (CUs) with the differences in computing requirements from dynamic workloads, results in a *two-fold computing imbalance*. The adoption of Dynamic Load Balancing (DLB) addresses this computing imbalance as a whole and allow for fully leveraging all the available computing power and improve execution time. This work will thus focus in combining DLB with Heterogeneous Systems (HS) in the context of CFD simulations by integrating DLB mechanisms in a widely used application: Open Source Field Operation and Manipulation (OpenFOAM).

OpenFOAM is a free and publicly available open-source software package, specifically targeting CFD applications [14]. It is an highly extensible package, allowing applied science experts to develop scientific and engineering numerical simulations in an expedite manner. OpenFOAM includes a wide range of functionalities such as simulation refinement, dynamic meshes, particle simulations, among others. OpenFOAM large set of features and extensibility has made it one of the most used and leading open-source software packages across the CFD community. It has also been made available in multiple supercomputers and computing centres, along with technical support. OpenFOAM parallel distributed memory model is based on a domain decomposition approach, however, there is little to no support for either HS or DLB, which is addressed by this work by integrating and evaluating all proposed mechanisms into this package.

Providing such support is of crucial importance, however, this task is too complex to be handled by the CFD application developer. This complexity has two different causes: (i) efficient mapping of the dynamic workload onto a vast set of heterogeneous resources is a research level issue, far from the typical concerns of a CFD expert, and (ii) execution time migration of cells (particularly dynamically refined meshes of cells) across memory spaces requires a deep understanding of OpenFOAM's internal data structures and control flow among lower level code functions and methods. Integration of these facilities with OpenFOAM by computer science experts is proposed as the best solution to provide efficiency and robustness, while simultaneously promoting reuse by the CFD community.

This paper proposes nSharma – Numerical Simulation Heterogeneity Aware Runtime Manager – a runtime manager that provides OpenFOAM with heterogeneity aware DLB features. nSharma monitors the heterogeneous resources performance under the current load, combines this data and past history using a performance model to predict the resources behaviour under new workload resulting from the refinement process and makes informed decisions on how to re-distribute the workload. The aim is to minimize performance losses due to workload imbalances over HS, therefore contributing to minimize the simulation's execution time. DLB minimizes idle times across nodes by progressively and in an educated way assigning workload, which can be itself dynamic, to the available resources. nSharma package integrates in a straightforward manner with current OpenFOAM distributions, enabling the adoption of heterogeneity aware DLB. To best of authors' knowledge, this is the first implementation and integration of heterogeneous-aware DLB mechanism in OpenFOAM.

2   Related Work

Libraries supporting the development of CFD simulations, include OpenFOAM [14], ANSYS Fluent [2], ANSYS CFX [1], STAR-CCM+ [6], among others. OpenFOAM is distributed under the General Public Licence (GPL), allowing modification and redistribution while guaranteeing continued free use. This motivated the selection of OpenFOAM for the developments envisaged in this work. The authors see no reason why this document's higher level assessments and results can not be applied to other similar CFD libraries. This generalization should, however, be empirically verified on a per case basis.

Domain decomposition requires that the mesh discretization is partitioned into sub-domains. This is a challenging task impacting directly on the workload associated with each sub-domain and on the volume of data that has to be exchanged among sub-domains in order to achieve global convergence. Frameworks that support mesh-based simulations most often delegate mesh partitioning to a third-party software. ParMETIS [15] and PTSCOTCH [7] are two widely used mesh partitioners, which interoperate with OpenFOAM. ParMETIS has been used within this work's context because it provides a more straightforward support for Adaptive Mesh Refinement (AMR).

ParMETIS includes methods to both partition an initial mesh and re-partition a mesh that is scattered across CUs disjoint memory address spaces, avoiding a potential full re-location of the mesh in runtime. The (re)partitioning algorithms optimize for two criteria: minimizing edge-cut and minimizing element migration. These criteria have been merged into a single user-supplied parameter (ITR), describing the intended ratio of inter-process communication cost over the data-redistribution cost. ParMETIS also provides an interface to describe the relative processing capabilities of the CUs, allowing more work units to be assigned to faster processors. nSharma calculates these parameters in order to control ParMETIS' repartitioning and thus achieve efficient DLB.

Some frameworks providing DLB to iterative applications have been proposed. DRAMA [4] provides a collection of balancing algorithms that are guided by a cost model which aims to reduce the imbalance costs. It is strictly targeted for finite element applications. PREMA [3] is designed to explore an over-decomposition approach to minimize the overhead of stop-and-repartition approaches. This approach is not feasible in some mesh-based numerical simulations (due to, for instance, data dependencies) and no mention to HS support could be found. Zoltan [11] uses callbacks to interface with the application and integrates with DRUM [12], a resource monitoring system based on static benchmark measured in MFLOPS and averaged per node. The resource monitoring capabilities of nSharma are much more suitable to account for heterogeneous computing devices – see next section. Zoltan is not tied to any particular CFD framework. It does not enforce any particular cost functions and uses abstractions to maintain data structure neutrality. This however comes at the cost of requiring the CFD application developer to provide all data definitions and pack/unpack routines, which in a complex application like OpenFOAM is an programming intensive and error prone task.

nSharma integrates with OpenFOAM, accessing its data structures and migration routines. Although this option implies some code portability loss, it avoids the multiple costs of data (and even conceptual) transformations together with overheads of code binding between different software packages. This allows direct exploitation, assessment and validation of DLB techniques for OpenFOAM applications on HS. The results on conceptually more abstract design options, such as the performance model and the decision making mechanism, should still generalise to alternative software implementations, although empirical verification is required.

Some of the above cited works can handle HS. They do so by using high-level generic metrics, such as vendor announced theoretical peak performances or raw counters associated to generic events such as CPU and memory usage [12,13]. The associated performance models are however generic, ignoring both the characteristics of CFD workloads and emerging devices particular execution models and computing paradigms, and thus tend to be inaccurate [8]. This paper proposes a performance model which explicitly combines the workload particularities with the heterogeneous devices capabilities. The design of this performance model is strictly coupled with the requirements of the proposed DLB mechanisms.

FuPerMod [9] explores Functional Performance Models, extending traditional performance models to consider performance differences between devices and between problem sizes. It is based on speed functions built based on observed performances with multiple sizes, allowing the evaluation of a workload distribution [8]. Zhong applied these concepts to OpenFOAM [17] and validated it in multi-core and multi-GPU systems. This paper introduces a similar performance model tightly integrated with the remaining DLB mechanisms.

3   nSharma's Architecture

OpenFOAM simulations are organized as *solvers*, which are iterative processes evaluating, at each iteration, the quantities of interest across the problem domain. Each iteration includes multiple inner loops, solving a number of systems of equations by using iterative linear solvers. Within this work, *solver* refers to OpenFOAM general solvers, rather than the linear solvers. Since OpenFOAM parallel implementation is based on a zero layer domain decomposition over a distributed memory model, the solver's multiple processes synchronize often during each iteration, using both nearest neighbour and global communications.

nSharma is fully integrated into OpenFOAM and organized as a set of components, referred to as modules or models. The *Online Profiling Module (OPM)* acquires information w.r.t. raw system behaviour. The *Performance Model (PM)* uses this data to build an approximation of each CU performance and to generate estimates of near future behaviour, in particular for different workload distributions. The *Decision Model (DM)* decides whether workload redistribution shall happen, based on this higher level information and estimates. The *Repartitioning Module (RM)* handles the details of (re)partitioning subdomains for (re)distribution across multiple processors, while finally load redistribution mechanisms carry on the cells migration among computing resources, therefore enforcing the decisions made by nSharma.

The whole DLB mechanism is tightly coupled with OpenFOAM iterative execution model. This allows nSharma to learn about system behaviour and also allows for progressive convergence towards a globally balanced state - rather than trying to jump to such a state at each balancing episode. Dynamic workloads are also handled by OpenFOAM and nSharma iterative model, with impact on the whole system balanced state and simulation execution time being handled progressively.

3.1   Online Profiling Module

The *OPM* instruments OpenFOAM routines to measure execution times, crucial to estimate the CUs relative performance differences. This has been achieved by thoroughly analysing OpenFOAM workflow and operations, and identifying a set of low-level routines that fundamentally contribute to the application execution time. It has been empirically verified that these times correlate well, enabling nSharma to monitor only the parts of the simulation that are relevant to the associated performance modelling, while simultaneously implying a low instrumentation overhead without any additional analytical models or benchmarking.

The *OPM* API allows for the registration of which routines to measure, and internally refers to these as Operations. Operations are classified as either *IDLE*, representing a synchronization or memory transfer, or *BUSY*, representing a computational task without any synchronizations or memory transfers. This categorization allows to measure performance individually, otherwise execution time would be cluttered by dependencies and communications.

3.2   Performance Model

The *PM* characterizes the system's – and its individual components, such as each CU – performance and provides estimates of future performances under different workload distributions. Workload and performance characterization requires the definition of a work unit, upon which problem size can be quantified. OpenFOAM uses Finite Volumes, with the problem domain discretisation being based on cells that are combined to define the computational domain. With this approach problem size is often characterized by the number of cells, which is, therefore, the work unit used by nSharma.

Each CU performance is characterized by the average time required to process one work unit, denoted by $TperCell_p$ (where p indexes the CUs). For each iteration i and CU p, the respective performance index $(TperCell_p^i)$ is given by the ratio of the iteration's total busy time over the number of cells assigned to p, N_p^i: $TperCell_p^i = Tbusy_p^i / N_p^i$. The actual metric used for balancing decisions, $TperCell_p$, is a weighted average over a window of previous iterations, which smooths out outliers and, for dynamic workloads, takes into account different problem sizes (different numbers of cells assigned to each CU at each iteration).

Execution time estimates for arbitrary workload distributions, T_p, use the above described metric multiplied by the number of work units to assign to each CU, N_p, as given by Eq. 1 – with P being the number of CUs.

$$T_p = TperCell_p \times N_p, \quad \forall p \in 0, 1, \dots, P - 1 \tag{1}$$

3.3   Decision Module

It is the *DM* role to assess the system balancing state and decide whether a
load redistribution step should take place. It is also the *DM* who decides what
load to redistribute. Assessing and making such decision is referred to as a
balancing episode. Since these episodes represent an overhead, it is crucial to
decide when should they occur. nSharma allows them only at the beginning of a
solver iteration, and defines a period, expressed in number of iterations, for their
frequency. The unpredictability of dynamic workloads makes it unpractical to
define an optimal balancing period, therefore it is auto-tuned in execution time,
as described below.

At the beginning of a new solver's iteration i, the Relative Standard Deviation
(RSD), among the CUs busy times for the previous iteration $i - 1$ is calculated
$\text{RSD}^{i-1} = \sigma^{i-1}/|\overline{T_{busy}}^{i-1}| * 100$; standard deviation, σ, is well known as a good,
light-weight, indicator of a system's balancing state. A linear regression is then
computed over the last few iterations RSD in order to estimate its rate of change,
which is used to update the period. Also, a normalization of the magnitude of
the RSD is added to the contribution to update the period. Therefore, the load
balancing period is adjusted based on how fast the system's balancing state
changes and how much it changes.

When a load balancing episode is triggered the *DM* will compute, for each
CU p, how many cells, N_p^*, to assign to it. It will devise a new load distribution,
where all CUs will take, the same amount of time to process the assigned work
units, according to each CU execution rate, $TperCell_p$. Since the total number
of cells N is known, a well-determined system of P linear equations can be
formulated (see Eq. 2) and solved to find $N_0^*, \ldots, N_{P-1}^*$ – the number of cells to
assign to each CU.

$$
\begin{cases}
TperCell_0 \times N_0^* = TperCell_1 \times N_1^* \\
TperCell_1 \times N_1^* = TperCell_2 \times N_2^* \\
\quad \ldots \\
TperCell_{P-2} \times N_{P-2}^* = TperCell_{P-1} \times N_{P-1}^* \\
N_0^* + N_1^* + \ldots + N_{P-1}^* = N
\end{cases}
\tag{2}
$$

After computing this new distribution, a decision has to be made as to
whether it will be applied or not, by taking into account the cells migration cost,
m. The goal is that the remaining simulation execution time after the load redistribution must be smaller than not migrating. The next iteration i expected execution time without load redistribution is given by $t_i = \max_p(TperCell_p \times N_p)$,
whereas with the new load distribution it is $t_i^* = TperCell_p \times N_p^*, \forall p$ (no need
for max because t_i^* is the same for all p, according to Eq. 2). Let n be
the number of remaining iterations and δ represent some additional execution overheads independent on workload redistribution. Then the condition
$n \times t_i + \delta > m + n \times t_i^* + \delta$ expresses that migration will only take place if it is
expected to reduce the total remaining execution time, while taking into account
the cost of actually enforcing the migration m. This cost is estimated by keeping

track of the costs of previous migrations and using a linear regression to estimate the cost of any arbitrary decomposition.

$$t_i > \frac{m}{n} + t_i^* \tag{3}$$

Equation 3 (a simplification of the condition equation above) makes it clear that a load redistribution should only be enforced if the cost of migrating cells can be properly amortized across the remaining n iterations. Consequently, towards the end of the simulation, as n gets smaller, the cells migration impact on execution times is progressively higher and load redistribution will become proportionally less likely.

3.4 Repartitioning Module

nSharma repartitioning module interfaces with ParMETIS (see Sect. 2), by carefully parametrising the relevant methods and by extending some functionality. ParMETIS' repartitioning method is used, which takes into account the current mesh distribution among CUs and balances cells' redistribution cost with the new cells' partition communication costs during the parallel execution of the next iterations. The relationship between these two costs is captured by the ITR parameter. nSharma learns this parameter by requesting multiple decompositions with different ITR values in initial iterations, assessing the most effective ones and converging to a single one. Besides ITR, this method also receives a list of each CU relative computing power, given by $\omega_p = N_p^*/N$, as evaluated by the Decision module (Sect. 3.3).

OpenFOAM does not natively support migration of refined meshes, which required integrating such support (based on Kyle Mooney's approach, see Acknowledgements). Since each refined cell is always a child of a single original (non-refined) cell and since the refined hierarchy is explicitly maintained, partitioning is applied to the original (non-refined) coarse mesh; after partitioning, the refined mesh is considered to perform migration. To ensure that the original non-refined coarse mesh reflects the correct workload, weights for each coarse cell are provided to ParMETIS based on the number of child cells, which will be used by ParMETIS in devising new partitions.

Table 1. Computing systems and system configurations used in evaluation

System	SeARCH			Stampede2
Nodes	Tag **641** - Ivy Bridge E5-2650v2 @ 2.60GHz, **16** cores p/node			Tag **KNL7250** - Intel Xeon Phi 7250 @ 1.4GHz ("Knights Landing"), **68** cores p/ node
	Tag **662** - Ivy Bridge E5-2695v2@ 2.40GHz, **24** cores p/node			
	Tag **421** - Nehalem E5520 @ 2.27GHz, **8** cores p/node			
	Tag **KNL7210** - Intel Xeon Phi 7210 @ 1.3GHz, **64** cores p/ node			
Multi-node configurations	Homogeneous	Heterogeneous I	Heterogeneous II	Homogeneous
	Multiple 641's	Pair(s) of 641+421	Pair 662+KNL7210	Multiple KNL7250's
Network	Myrinet (**myri**)	Myrinet (**myri**)	Ethernet(**eth**)	Intel Omni-Path (**OPA**)

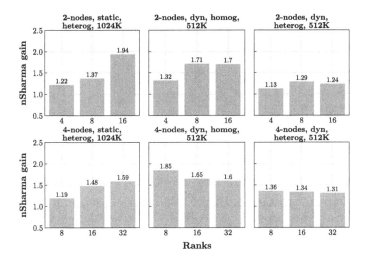

Fig. 1. nSharma gain with SeARCH Homogeneous and Heterogeneous I

4   Results Analysis

For experimental validation, the *damBreak* simulation was selected among those distributed with OpenFOAM tutorials. It uses the *interDyMFoam* solver to simulate the multiphase flow of two incompressible fluids – air and water – after the break of a dam. Adjustable time step was disabled and the nSharma configuration dictionary was introduced – all other parameters are the same as distributed in the package. For dynamic workloads, AMR subdivides a cell into 8 new cells according to the interface between the water and air; cells will thus be refined (and unrefined) following the evolution of the two phases' interface.

This solver requires frequent local and global communications. As the degree of parallelism is increased, more sub-domains are created, increasing the number of cells in sub-domains boundaries and, consequently, increasing communications among sub-domains, with network bandwidth and latency impacting significantly in the simulation's performance.

Four hardware configurations were used from two different clusters – SeARCH cluster (Universidade do Minho, Portugal) and Stampede2 (Texas Advanced Computing Center, USA). Configurations are described in Table 1. OpenFOAM 2.4.0 was used, compiled with GNU C Compiler in SeARCH and with Intel C Compiler in Stampede2. Each MPI process is associated to one CU or processing core: the number of used cores is equivalent to the number of processes. MPI terminology refers to processes as ranks, and this terminology is maintained throughout this section.

4.1   Performance Gain

Performance gain is hereby defined as the reduction in execution time achieved by using nSharma and quantified as the ratio between the execution times without

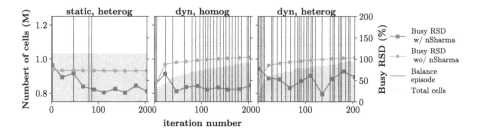

Fig. 2. Busy RSD with and without nSharma for 4 nodes and 32 ranks.

and with nSharma, respectively. Figure 1 illustrates such gain for 200 iterations of the damBreak simulation in SeARCH. The first row depicts results obtained with 2 nodes, the second row results obtained with 4 nodes. Results in the first column were obtained with a static workload and problem size of 1024K cells (Heterogeneous I configuration), whereas in the second and third columns dynamic workloads were used with 512K cells (Homogeneous and Heterogeneous I configurations, respectively).

nSharma achieves a significant performance gain for all experimental conditions. For static workloads, the gain increases with the number of ranks, with a maximum gain of 1.94 gain with 2 nodes and 16 ranks and 1.59 with 4 nodes and 32 ranks. This gain is basically a consequence of nSharma's heterogeneous awareness, which allows remapping more cells to the 641 more powerful cores, which would otherwise be waiting for the 421 processing cores to finish execution.

For homogeneous hardware and dynamic workloads (second column), performance gain is due to moving cells from overloaded cores to underloaded ones, with such fluctuations due to AMR. Significant gains are still observed for all experimental conditions, but this gain suffers a slight decreases as the number of ranks increases for 4 nodes. This is due to an increase in migration and repartitioning costs (see Fig. 3), proportional to the increased number of balance episodes required in a dynamic workload scenario (see Fig. 2). The communication overheads also increase from 2 to 4 nodes sustaining more sub-domains and more communications over a limited bandwidth network.

The last column illustrates the combination of dynamic workload with HS. The gain is mostly constant with the number of ranks. It is lower than with static workloads or homogeneous hardware, because the decision making process is much more complex requiring a much higher level of adaptability, i.e. more frequent balancing episodes and larger volumes of data migration (see Figs. 3 and 2).

Figure 2 illustrates the accumulated busy RSD (as described in Sect. 3.3) with and without nSharma for the same experimental conditions, 4 nodes and 32 ranks. The grey area represents the total number of cells and the vertical lines are balance episodes. Clearly nSharma results in a large RSD reduction, i.e. reduced busy times variation across ranks, thus enabling significant performance

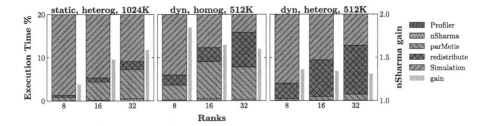

Fig. 3. Execution time percentage breakdown for 4 nodes

gains. This can be clearly seen around iteration number 50 for the static case, where a large RSD reduction occurs.

Figure 3 illustrates, for the 4 nodes cases of Fig. 1, the percentage of execution time spent in different algorithmic segments: *Profiler* represents time used by the OPM, *nSharma* time for decision making, *parMetis* represents repartitioning, *redistribute* is cells migration cost and *simulation* represents the time dedicated to the actual simulation. The side slim bars represent the performance gain, which is the same as in Fig. 1. The vertical axis goes up to only 20%, the remaining 80% are simulation time and add-up to the illustrated.

The overheads associated with profiling and decision making are negligible in all experimental conditions. Repartitioning (ParMETIS) and redistribution costs increase with the number of ranks. The former is negligible as a percentage for the dynamic plus heterogeneous case, but the latter represents an increasing overhead in all cases. This is tightly related to the fact that the numbers of migrated cells and balancing episodes (see Fig. 2) increase with the hardware configuration and the workload complexities (homogeneous versus heterogeneous and static versus dynamic, respectively). Nevertheless the overheads associated with DLB are below 15%, allowing for very significant performance gains.

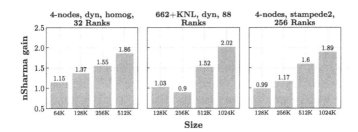

Fig. 4. Increasing problem size for four 641 SeARCH nodes, 662+KNL and four Stampede2 nodes

Figure 4 presents nSharma performance gain for dynamic workload, 4 nodes, fixed number of ranks and increasing problem size for 3 alternative hardware configurations: SeARCH homogeneous, SeARCH Heterogeneous II and Stampede2

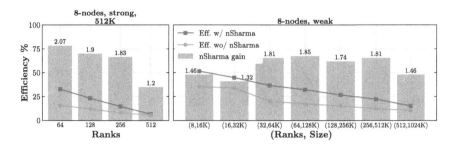

Fig. 5. Efficiency (w/ and wo/ nSharma) with dynamic loads for Stampede2 nodes (Color figure online)

homogeneous (see Table 1). The x-axis shows the rank count (particularly, for 662+KNL configuration, 64 plus 24 ranks are used from KNL and 662 respectively), which corresponds to the use of all available CUs. The performance gain associated with the introduction of DLB increases consistently with the problem size. Larger problems have the potential to exhibit more significant imbalance penalties with dynamic workloads, due to larger local fluctuations in the number of cells. nSharma is capable to effectively handle this increased penalty, becoming more efficient as the problem size increases. Based on the observed data, this trend is expected to continue. No inflection point should be reached and nSharma performance gain will keep increasing with the workload, i.e. exactly when the potential for load imbalances becomes higher.

4.2   Efficiency Gain

Strong and weak scalability based on parallel efficiency are evaluated in this section. Parallel efficiency is evaluated with respect to the timing results achieved with only 1 rank and without nSharma (DLB is senseless for a single rank).

Figure 5 presents performance gain with nSharma (grey bars) and parallel efficiency with and without nSharma (blue and orange lines), using 8 KNL nodes of Stampede2 (up to 512 ranks). For the strong scaling case – left plot – nSharma performance gain is around 2, except for 512 ranks. In this latter case, the workload per rank is so low (the number of cells ranges from 1000 to 2000 per rank) that incurred overheads (partitioning and cells migration) significantly impact on the load redistribution benefits. For the weak scaling case – right plot – problem size increases at the same rate as number of ranks, thus the workload per rank is kept constant; performance gain is quite consistent, since increasing DLB costs are compensated by the added workload.

The scalability curves in Fig. 5 illustrate that OpenFOAM without DLB exhibits very low efficiency even for increasing problem size. Two major penalties contribute to this: aforementioned parallel communications costs and load imbalance due to dynamic workloads. nSharma addresses the load imbalance penalty in a very effective manner, roughly doubling efficiency for most configurations – the (512, 512K) case of strong scalability can not be taken into account due

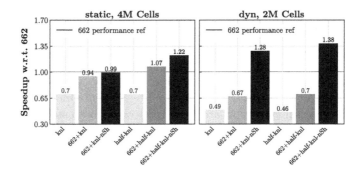

Fig. 6. Speedup in combining a 662 node and a KNL by using nSharma

to the very scarce load per rank. This clearly illustrates that introducing DLB mechanisms results in a very significant reduction of execution time, sustained by an increase in efficiency, i.e. a better utilization of the parallel computing resources.

4.3 Heterogeneity and Dynamic Load Balancing

Effective exploitation of the raw computing capabilities available on heterogeneous systems is hard, with load balancing being one of the main challenges, specially for dynamic workloads.

Figure 6 details the performance speedup when combining a KNL node – with two different core configurations, one with the full 64 cores (*knl*) and another with only 32 cores (*half-knl*) – with a 24-core 662 node. Speedup is illustrated w.r.t to the execution time obtained with the node 662 for static (left) and dynamic (right) workloads. By adding a KNL node to a 662 node (*662+knl* and *662+half-knl*) yields no significant performance gain, with a severe deterioration for the dynamic workloads. This is due the imbalance introduced by the large computing power differences between the nodes (as illustrated by the white bars). By enabling nSharma, the whole system capabilities will be assessed and more load is assigned to 662 node, reducing its idle time and increasing resource utilization. Performance gains between 22% to 38% are observed (**-nSh* bars). The gain is more substantial with dynamic workloads where the potential for load imbalances is larger: heterogeneous resources plus execution time locally varying number of cells. nSharma works at its best under these more challenging conditions, effectively rebalancing the workload and efficiently exploiting the available resources.

5   Conclusions and Future Work

This paper proposes and assesses the integration of heterogeneity aware DLB techniques on CFD simulations running on distributed memory heterogeneous parallel clusters. Such simulations most often imply dynamic workloads due to execution time mesh refinement. Combined with the hardware heterogeneity such dynamics cause a two-fold load imbalance, which impacts severely on system utilization, and consequently on execution time, if not appropriately catered for. The proposed approach has been implemented as a software package, designated nSharma, which fully integrates with the latest version of OpenFOAM.

Substantial performance gains are demonstrated for both static and dynamic workloads. These gains are shown to be caused by reduced busy times RSD among ranks, i.e. computing resources are kept busy with useful work due to a more effective workload distribution. Strong and weak scalability results further support this conclusion, with nSharma enabled executions exhibiting significantly larger efficiencies for a range of experimental conditions. Performance gains increase with problem size, which is a very desirable feature since the potential to load imbalances under dynamic loads grows with the number of cells.

Experimental results show that performance gains associated with nSharma are affected by increasing the number of ranks for larger node counts. This is due to inherent increase of load migration costs associated with a growing number of balancing episodes. Future work will necessarily imply addressing this issue, to allow for increased number of parallel resources by further mitigating load migration overheads. Additionally, nSharma will be validated against a more extensive set of case studies and heterogeneous devices; upon successful validation it will be made publicly available in order to foster its adoption by the large community of OpenFOAM users.

Acknowledgements. The authors would like to thank the financial funding by FEDER through the COMPETE 2020 Program, the National Funds through FCT under the projects UID/CTM/50025/2013. The first author was partially funded by the PT-FLAD Chair on Smart Cities & Smart Governance and also by the School of Engineering, University of Minho within project *Performance Portability on Scalable Heterogeneous Computing Systems*. The authors also wish to thank Kyle Mooney for making available his code supporting migration of dynamically refined meshes, as well as acknowledge the Texas Advanced Computing Center (TACC) at The University of Texas at Austin for providing HPC resources.

References

1. ANSYS: ANSYS CFX Users' Guide (2017)
2. ANSYS: ANSYS Fluent User's Guide (2017)
3. Barker, K., et al.: A load balancing framework for adaptive and asynchronous applications. IEEE Trans. Parallel Distrib. Syst. **15**, 183–192 (2004)
4. Basermann, A., et al.: Dynamic load-balancing of finite element applications with the DRAMA library. Appl. Math. Model. **25**, 83–98 (2000)
5. Brodtkorb, A.R., et al.: State-of-the-art in heterogeneous computing. Sci. Program. **18**, 1–33 (2010)
6. CD-adapco: STAR-CCM+ (2017)

7. Chevalier, C., Pellegrini, F.: PT-Scotch: a tool for efficient parallel graph ordering. Parallel Comput. **34**, 318–331 (2008)

8. Clarke, D., Lastovetsky, A., Rychkov, V.: Dynamic load balancing of parallel computational iterative routines on highly heterogeneous HPC platforms. Parallel Process. Lett. **21**, 195–217 (2011)

9. Clarke, D., et al.: FuPerMod: a software tool for the optimization of data-parallel applications on heterogeneous platforms. J. Supercomput. **69**, 61–69 (2014)

10. Da Costa, G., et al.: Exascale machines require new programming paradigms and runtimes. Supercomput. Front. Innov. **2**, 6–27 (2015)

11. Devine, K., et al.: Design of dynamic load-balancing tools for parallel applications. In: Proceedings of the 14th International Conference on Supercomputing - ICS 2000 (2000)

12. Faik, J., Teresco, J.D., Devine, K.D., Flaherty, J.E., Gervasio, L.G.: A model for resource-aware load balancing on heterogeneous clusters. CS-05-01. Williams College Department of Computer Science (2005)

13. Martínez, J.A., Garzón, E.M., Plaza, A., García, I.: Automatic tuning of iterative computation on heterogeneous multiprocessors with ADITHE. J. Supercomput. **58**, 151–159 (2011)

14. OpenFOAM Foundation: OpenFOAM Users' Guide. Technical report (2018)

15. Schloegel, K., Karypis, G., Kumar, V.: Multilevel diffusion schemes for repartitioning of adaptive meshes. J. Parallel Distrib. Comput. **47**, 109–124 (1997)

16. Top500: TOP500 Supercomputer Site (2017)

17. Zhong, Z.: Optimization of data-parallel scientific applications on highly heterogeneous modern HPC platforms. Ph.D. thesis (2014)

High Performance Computational Hydrodynamic Simulations: UPC Parallel Architecture as a Future Alternative

Alvin Wei Ze Chew[1(✉)], Tung Thanh Vu[2],
and Adrian Wing-Keung Law[1,2(✉)]

[1] School of Civil and Environmental Engineering, Nanyang Technological
University, N1-01c-98, 50 Nanyang Avenue, Singapore 639798, Singapore
wzchew1@e.ntu.edu.sg, cwklaw@ntu.edu.sg
[2] Environmental Process Modelling Centre (EPMC), Nanyang Environment
and Water Research Institute (NEWRI),
1 Cleantech Loop, CleanTech One #06-08, Singapore 637141, Singapore

Abstract. Developments in high performance computing (HPC) has today transformed the manner of how computational hydrodynamic (CHD) simulations are performed. Till now, the message passing interface (MPI) remains the common parallelism architecture and has been adopted widely in CHD simulations. However, its bottleneck problem remains for some large-scale simulation cases due to delays during message passing whereby the total communication time may exceed the total simulation runtime with an increasing number of computer processors. In this study, we utilise an alternative parallelism architecture, known as PGAS-UPC, to develop our own UPC-CHD model with a 2-step explicit scheme from the Lax-Wendroff family of predictors-correctors. The model is evaluated on three incompressible, adiabatic viscous 2D flow cases having moderate flow velocities. Model validation is achieved by the reasonably good agreement between the predicted and respective analytical values. We then compare the computational performance between UPC-CHD and that of MPI in its base design in a SGI UV-2000 server till 100 processers maximum in this study. The former achieves a near 1:1 speedup which demonstrates its efficiency potential for very large-scale CHD simulations, while the later experiences slowdown at some point. Extension of UPC-CHD remains our main objective which can be achieved by the following additions: (a) inclusions of other numerical schemes to accommodate for other types of fluid simulations, and (b) coupling UPC-CHD with Amazon Web Service (AWS) to further exploit its parallelism efficiency as a viable alternative.

Keywords: Parallel computing · Viscous incompressible laminar flow
MPI · UPC · Computational hydrodynamic (CHD) simulations

1 Introduction

Computational hydrodynamic (CHD) simulations has become a useful tool for engineers and scientists to accelerate their quantitative understandings of physical, chemical and even biological processes. For example, CHD has been coupled with the multiscale

© Springer International Publishing AG, part of Springer Nature 2018
Y. Shi et al. (Eds.): ICCS 2018, LNCS 10860, pp. 444–455, 2018.
https://doi.org/10.1007/978-3-319-93698-7_34

perturbation analysis to numerically resolve for various properties at the varying scales which can be difficult to compute analytically (Dalwadi et al. 2015, 2016; Chang et al. 2017). Other CHD works include flow simulations in tight membrane spacers to better understand the physics of membrane fouling and flow short-circuiting (Jajcevic et al. 2013; Bucs. et al. 2014; Sousa et al. 2014). Typically, a large-scale CHD simulation run with high performance computing (HPC) inclusion requires proper management of the parallelization algorithm to achieve optimization. For example, a 100 million two-dimensional (2D) mesh involving three important equations (continuity and momentum equations only) result in an approximate 600 million cell information to be managed during each iterative step. Data sharing among computer processers, i.e. threads, is unavoidable in CHD mesh-bounded numerical domains which underlines the difficulty to achieve optimization.

At present, the message passing interface (MPI) architecture remains the most popular parallelism option. Examples include the utilisation of MPI with a million cores by Balaji et al. (2009) to thoroughly examine its scalability, and many others. At the same time, difficulties have also been reported when designing MPI applications for considerable number of threads with escalated levels of memory hierarchy (Gourdain et al. 2009; Jamshed 2015). Thus, the question remains if MPI can effectively accelerate CHD simulations with the availability of computer threads. The answer is complex as it depends on a multitude of factors which include: (a) type of numerical scheme implemented, (b) size of computational domain, (c) type of flow problem analysed, and most importantly (d) the domain decomposition algorithm which determines the distribution of the threads within the numerical domain, i.e. how many sub-domains are assigned to each thread after decomposition. We underline that pointer (d) is most significant in affecting the speedup of CHD simulation runs.

In this study, we adopt an alternative parallelism architecture for CHD simulations by coupling the Partitioned Global Address Space (PGAS) computing concept with Berkeley's Unified Parallel C (UPC) compiler (Chen et al. 2003) as the programming language. Two key advantages are expected with PGAS: (a) locality in the shared memory structure which facilitates the ease of use, and (b) data layout control of MPI's which enables performance scalability. We note that the PGAS architecture has been utilised before (Johnson 2006 and Simmendinger et al. 2011). However, to the best of our knowledge, coupling CHD simulations with the PGAS architecture has been limited by far. It is also worth noting that no porting of the various computer algorithms/architectures is carried out in this study. Rather, the above-mentioned advantages are already inherent in the adopted parallelism architecture of PGAS-UPC. The key objective is to evaluate the viability of harnessing PGAS-UPC as an alternative to accelerate large-scale CHD simulations, at least by achieving the same parallelism performance as that of MPI's in its base design.

We first develop UPC-CHD by coupling the PGAS-UPC architecture with the 2-step explicit numerical scheme from the Lax-Wendroff family of predictors and correctors. UPC-CHD is then examined on three incompressible, viscous and adiabatic two-dimensional (2D) flow cases having moderate velocities under laminar conditions. Validation of UPC-CHD is achieved by the good agreement between the respective analytical and predicted values. We then demonstrate how UPC-CHD provides early indication of its parallelism efficiency with 100 computer threads maximum in this study as our first initiation. Finally, this paper is structured as follows. In Sect. 2, we describe the numerical scheme implemented in UPC CHD. This is followed by describing UPC-CHD development with the adopted PGAS computing concept in Sect. 3. The parallelism performance of UPC-CHD is then examined in Sect. 4. Finally, Sect. 5 describes the salient pointers as obtained from this study.

2   Governing Equations

To fully describe the unsteady 2D behaviour of an incompressible viscous fluid under laminar adiabatic flow conditions, we adhere to (1) which compactly conserves the mass continuity, momentum flow and energy equations (Anderson 2009).

$$\frac{\partial Q}{\partial t} + \frac{\partial F}{\partial x} + \frac{\partial G}{\partial y} = \frac{\partial G_{Vx}}{\partial x} + \frac{\partial G_{Vy}}{\partial y} \tag{1}$$

where Q is the conservative temporal term, F and G are the convective flux vectors in the x and y directions respectively, G_{Vx} and G_{Vy} are the viscous flux vectors in the x and y directions respectively, and t is time.

The exact forms of Q, F, G, G_{Vx} and G_{Vy} are described in (2) as shown.

$$Q = \begin{bmatrix} 0 \\ u \\ v \\ E_t \end{bmatrix}, F = \begin{bmatrix} u \\ \frac{p}{\rho} + u^2 \\ uv \\ (E_t u) + \frac{p}{\rho} u \end{bmatrix}, G = \begin{bmatrix} v \\ uv \\ \frac{p}{\rho} + v^2 \\ (E_t v) + \frac{p}{\rho} v \end{bmatrix},$$

$$G_{Vx} = \upsilon \begin{bmatrix} 0 \\ u_x \\ v_x \\ \frac{u\tau_{xx} + v\tau_{xy}}{\mu} \end{bmatrix}, \quad G_{Vy} = \upsilon \begin{bmatrix} 0 \\ u_y \\ v_y \\ \frac{u\tau_{yx} + v\tau_{yy}}{\mu} \end{bmatrix} \tag{2}$$

where u is the horizontal velocity $[LT^{-1}]$, v the vertical velocity $[LT^{-1}]$, $\frac{p}{\rho}$ the pressure divided by the fluid density $[L^2T^{-2}]$, E_t the total energy per unit mass $[L^2T^{-2}]$, υ the kinematic viscosity $[L^2T^{-1}]$, μ the dynamic viscosity $[ML^{-1}T^{-1}]$, τ_{xx} and τ_{yy} the normal stresses $[ML^{-1}T^{-2}]$, and τ_{xy} and τ_{yx} the shear stresses $[ML^{-1}T^{-2}]$.

3   Numerical Discretization

To resolve (1) over a 2D numerical domain of regular grids, we adhere to the following numerical schemes (Kermani and Plett 2001a, b) for the respective terms in their discretized forms: (a) two-step explicit approximation from the Lax-Wendroff family of predictors-correctors for Q, (b) Roe linear approximation with the 3rd-order upwind biased algorithm for F and G, and (c) 2nd-order central differencing for G_{Vx} and G_{Vy}.

The implemented numerical schemes are then examined for the following CHD cases, namely (a) Blasius boundary layer, (b) Poiseuille's flow, and (c) Couette's flow. In UPC-CHD, there are four boundaries of concern for a simplified 2D numerical domain as illustrated in Fig. 1. The exact conditions (BCs) adopted for these boundaries in each CHD case are then described in Table 1.

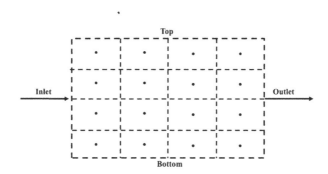

Fig. 1. Boundaries of concern for a simplified 2D numerical domain adopted in UPC-CHD

Table 1. Exact boundary conditions (BCs) implemented in UPC-CHD for respective CHD cases with reference to Fig. 1.

BCs	Blasius boundary layer (CHD case A)	Poiseuille's flow (CHD case B)	Couette's flow (CHD case C)
Inlet	$u = freestream\ velocity$ $v = 0$ $\frac{p}{\rho} \approx 98.1\ \mathrm{m^2\,s^{-2}}$	$u = freestream\ velocity$ $v = 0$ $\frac{p}{\rho} = fixed\ value$	$u = freestream\ velocity$ $v = 0$ $\frac{p}{\rho} = fixed\ value$
Outlet	$\frac{du}{dx} = 0$ $\frac{p}{\rho} \approx 98.1\ \mathrm{m^2\,s^{-2}}$	$\frac{du}{dx} = 0$ $\frac{p}{\rho} \approx 98.1\ \mathrm{m^2\,s^{-2}}$	$\frac{du}{dx} = 0$ $\frac{p}{\rho} \approx 98.1\ \mathrm{m^2\,s^{-2}}$
Top	$u = freestream\ velocity$	$u = 0$ $v = 0$	$u = freestream\ velocity$ $v = 0$
Bottom	$u = 0;\ v = 0$	$u = 0;\ v = 0$	$u = 0;\ v = 0$

4   UPC-CHD Model Development

Within UPC-CHD, we introduce the following procedures to achieve our parallelization objective. Firstly, we identify the time-consuming computational functions and data dependences involved. We then implement appropriate algorithms for data divisions and storage as based on the required data dependences and model workflow. There are three components to fully describe UPC-CHD, namely (a) implemented computational structure, (b) domain decomposition and data storage algorithms, and (c) unique work-sharing function.

(a) Computational Structure

For each node within the numerical domain (Fig. 1.), the flux predictor at the $(n + 1/2)$ time level is first computed followed by the flux correction at the $(n + 1)$ time level. Both the flux predictor and corrector are defined within a nested loop and the complexity of the nested loop algorithm is defined as $O(N^2)$, where N is the number of nodes in a singular direction. The original nested loop is divided into multi sub-loops to prevent data conflicts. After every new nested loop, a synchronization point is inserted using an UPC function, termed as upc_barrier, to synchronize all threads before proceeding to the next function. We note that the fluxes predictions and correctors at the respective time steps contribute to the most time-consuming functions in the algorithm which will be addressed in the following sub-section.

(b) Domain Decomposition and Data Storage Algorithms

The 2D numerical domain of N by N size (Fig. 1) is first divided into a distinct number of computational rows. A defined group of rows then constitutes to a sub-domain having affinity to a computer thread. With T number of threads, we consider the following protocol for domain decomposition: (i) if N is divisible by T, then there will be $\frac{N}{T}$ sub-domains and each contains the same number of rows, or (ii) if N is not divisible by T, then the first $int(\frac{N}{T})$ sub-domains contain the same number of rows, the last sub-domain contains the remaining rows. For example, if $N = 8$ and $T = 3$ then the first 2 threads handle the first two sub-domains with three rows each whereas the last thread contains the third sub-domain with two rows. At this moment, UPC-CHD is only considering an ideal square-shaped numerical domain as our first approach. The above-discussed details is most critical to manage the time-consuming functions in the algorithm in terms of the data distribution in the sub-domains which directly affect the total communication time. The following questions remain to be further investigated: (i) ideal number of sub-domains to be deployed with respect to the number of computer threads available, and (ii) the ideal number of cores to be used.

Finally, the respective threads assigned to the first and last sub-domain are termed as *thread_{start}* and *thread_{end}*, and we note that the domain decomposition is first performed on thread 0. The last thread is termed as $(T - 1)$. The required fluxes $(Q, F, G, G_{Vx}, G_{Vy})$ for each computational node within the domain are computed via a row-by-row method by utilising the respective data values from the two upper and two lower rows. To minimize the communication time involved, each sub-domain is directly affiliated with thread T_i by using the blocked-cyclic technique as illustrated in Fig. 2. We should note that the only exceptions for T_i to access data outside of its assigned sub-domain are restricted to the latter's respective first and last rows.

(c) UPC's Work-Sharing Function

In Berkeley's UPC compiler, the computations within the nested loops, as discussed previously in sub-section (a), are distributed using a work-sharing function, termed as upc_forall. In UPC, the total number of threads is determined with a UPC identifier, THREADS. Each thread is identified by using another identifier, MYTHREAD. With upc_forall, all threads with MYTHREAD from 0 to THREADS-1 undergo the same

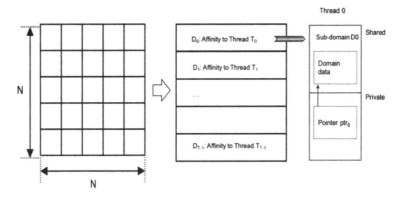

Fig. 2. Simplified illustration of domain decomposition and data storage methodology introduced for a 2D numerical domain of N by N size; D_i represents sub-domain i having affinity to a unique CPU thread

computational steps for the fluxes involved. Each unique thread is designed to compute the fluxes on the different sub-domain which is identified by using different $thread_{start}$ and $thread_{end}$.

5   Results and Discussions

5.1   Numerical Validations

To validate the selected numerical schemes in UPC-CHD, the numerical predictions derived for the three CHD cases are compared with the respective analytical solution: (case A) with analytical solution of White's (White 1991), (case B) with (3) in the following (Munson et al. 2006), and (case C) with (4) in the following (Munson et al. 2006).

$$\frac{u}{U} = \frac{(y^2 - h^2)}{2U\upsilon} \left(\frac{\partial \left(\frac{p}{\rho} \right)}{\partial x} \right) \tag{3}$$

$$\frac{u}{U} = \frac{y}{h} - \frac{h^2}{2U\upsilon} \left(\frac{\partial \left(\frac{p}{\rho} \right)}{\partial x} \right) \left(1 - \frac{y}{h} \right) \left(\frac{y}{h} \right) \tag{4}$$

where U is the freestream velocity $[LT^{-1}]$, h is the total vertical height of the domain $[L]$.

The physical dimensions of the deployed numerical domains and the initial flow conditions adopted for the respective CHD cases are summarized in Table 2. Figure 3 indicates reasonably good agreement between the predicted and analytical values which validates the implemented numerical scheme in UPC-CHD. We note that the maximum error quantification in Table 2, particularly for CHD case A, can generally be attributed to the following reasons: (i) use of regular meshes for sensitive flow regions whereby further refinements are required, and (ii) possible inaccuracies in the imposed boundary conditions at the top and outlet boundaries for Case A.

5.2   Parallelism Performance

We adhere to the speedup (S) parameter in (5) to compare the parallelism performance of UPC-CHD with that of MPI at their basic designs in a SGI UV-2000 server for all CHD cases of very large numerical domains. Technical specifications of the server used are described in Table 3. All other conditions from Table 2 are unchanged with the exception for the N by N parameter for the respective cases: (A) 5000 x 5000, (B) 10000 x 10000, (C) 10000 x 10000.

$$S(c) = \frac{T_1}{T(c)} \tag{5}$$

where $T(c)$ is the run time of the parallel algorithm, T_1 is the run time of the model which employs a singular thread and c is the number of computer threads. We first note that the parallelism evaluation between UPC-CHD and MPI is confined till 100 computer threads maximum in this study due to resources limitations. The key objective is to evaluate the adopted parallelism architecture of UPC-CHD as a viable alternative to that of MPI's in its base design.

Table 2. Dimensions and initial conditions of deployed numerical domains to validate the numerical values obtained for CHD cases A to C

Parameter	Case A	Case B	Case C
$x(L)$	0.3	0.5	0.5
$h(L)$	0.02	0.00016	0.00016
NxN (number of nodes)	65 x 65	300 x 45	300 x 45
$U(m/s)$	0.05	10	10
Re	15000	1600	1600
$\frac{\partial\left(\frac{p}{\rho}\right)}{\partial x}(ms^{-2})$	0	4700	4700
$\Delta t\ (s)$	10^{-6}	10^{-6}	10^{-6}
Total runtime (s)	0.01	0.01	0.01
Temperature (K)	293.15	293.15	293.15
$\upsilon(m^2s^{-1})$	10^{-6}	10^{-6}	10^{-6}
Maximum error percentage $(\%)$	~ 25	~ 1.7	~ 0.5

Generally, both UPC-CHD and MPI achieve a near identical S values up to c = 16 in Fig. 4. However, beyond 16 and up to c = 100 maximum in this study, UPC's speedup is most significant by having a close ratio of 1:1 and reaches nearly 90 times speedup for CHD cases A and B (Fig. 4).

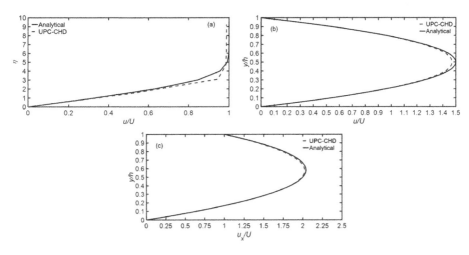

Fig. 3. Comparison between analytical and predicted values for respective CHD cases in UPC-CHD: (a) Blasius boundary layer, (b) Poiseuille's flow, and (c) Couette's flow.

Table 3. Technical specifications SGI-UV 2000

Cluster	Node CPUs	CPU speeds (GHz)	Cores per node	Node RAM (TB)	Available cores	Communication switch
SGI UV-2000	Intel Xeon E5-4657LV & E5-2670	2.4	16	2	up to 100 cores	InfiniBand Shared-memory

MPI achieves relatively significant S values for Cases A and B in Fig. 4 for c beyond 16. The difference in the $S(c)$ between Cases A and B is likely ascribed to the difference in the number of computational nodes deployed (25 million nodes for Case A and 100 million nodes for Case B) which affect the number of messages being transmitted within each assigned sub-domain. For instance, when running with $c = 32$, MPI achieves S values of 26.7 and 22.5 for Case A and B respectively (Fig. 4.). With MPI, thread T_i transmits multiple messages to the neighboring threads at every time-step which include: (a) velocity and convective fluxes data values in x- and y-directions corresponding to thread T_{i-1} and T_{i+1}, and (b) updated data to the main thread. At the maximum $c = 100$, over 900 messages must be processed in the system at each iterative step, despite having only 100 rows of data to be computed for each thread. The respective differences in the number of messages to be transmitted in Cases A and B result in different processing time for each message. As c increases beyond 32 with the MPI architecture, the idling time among the threads takes effect whereby each thread must wait for the other threads to complete their respective computations at each time step which thus explains the gradual stagnation in the parallelism performance after 64 cores and thereafter. Consequently, the total message processing time outweighs the total computational time in each thread, which restricts

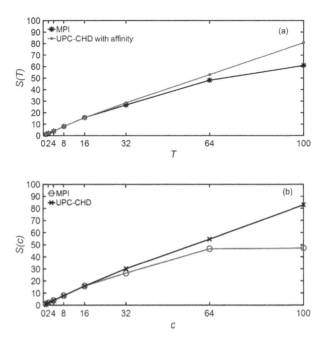

Fig. 4. Comparison of parallelism performance between MPI and UPC-CHD: (a) Blasius boundary layer – CHD Case A, and (b) Poiseuille's flow – CHD Case B.

the continual speedup with an increasing number of threads with MPI. On the contrary, Fig. 4 indicates that UPC-CHD better manages the total message processing time beyond $c = 64$ due to its inherent shared memory component which enables the threads to access the data within the shared memory via a global address.

The advantage of embedded locality consciousness in UPC-CHD is further investigated in Case C by further examining the impact of thread affinity on its parallelism performance. The computational data of each sub-domain are first stored in-block to gain memory locality properties, while the global memory accessing activities are overlapped with remote control technique using the split-phase barrier to conceal the synchronization cost. To further illustrate this advantage, we evaluate the performance for Case C under two scenarios: (a) UPC-A, i.e. UPC with optimizations, and (b) UPC-NA, i.e. UPC without optimizations and employs the defaults setting of the GPAS compilers.

As expected, UPC-NA's speedup performance is vividly inferior to that of UPC-A's as shown in Fig. 5. For instance, at $c = 16$, the respective S values attained are 15.8 and 4.3 for UPC-A and UPC-NA, respectively.

The difference in the attained speedup between UPC-A and UPC-NA can be further described from Fig. 6 by using a 3×3 numerical domain example having an affinity block of 3. In UPC-NA, thread 0 contains the fluxes data of element a, d and g in its local memory section whereby d and g belongs to the other threads, whereas in UPC-A, thread 0 contains the fluxes data of element a, b and c in its local memory (Fig. 6) whereby all three elements belong to the common thread. The observed inferior

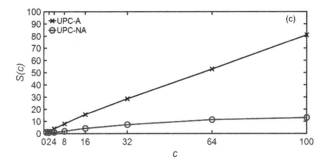

Fig. 5. Comparison of parallelism performance between UPC-A and UPC-NA for CHD case C (Couette's flow)

performance of UPC-NA (Fig. 5) is caused by the need for thread 0 to function with non-affinity data, i.e. element b in thread 1 and element c in thread 2, which results in longer computational run time for UPC-NA. With $c = 1$, there is only a singular thread which computes the fluxes in the entire numerical domain, and functions only with data having affinity with. With an increasing number of threads, the latency issue arises which results in less than ideal computational performance. For instance, at $c = 2$ and 4 respectively, 50% and 25% of the total runtime are attributed to the need to access non-affinity data by the respective threads. While the addition of c would reduce the amount of global accessing activity in UPC-NA, optimization is still unlikely as observed in Fig. 5. This observed behavior for S needs to be further investigated.

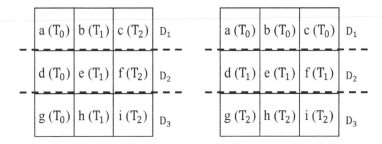

Fig. 6. Schematic representation of UPC-NA (left) and UPC-A (right) concepts

In summary, we recommend distributing the array of data in contiguous blocks as demonstrated in UPC-A, which enables each thread to attend to a system of elements as dependent on the number of threads available. We hypothesize that the proposed UPC-PGAS architecture without any affinity optimization is likely unsuitable in accelerating the speedup performance when compared with to that of MPI's.

6   Conclusion

An alternative parallelism architecture, which couples the PGAS computing concept with Berkeley's UPC compiler, is developed for large-scale computational hydrodynamic (CHD) simulations. The parallelism model developed is termed as UPC-CHD. As our first initiation, UPC-CHD is examined on three incompressible, adiabatic and viscous 2D flow cases having moderate flow velocities. Varying numerical schemes are adopted to resolve the discretized forms for the respective temporal, viscous and convective fluxes within each computational node in UPC-CHD. The selected schemes are then verified by the reasonably good agreement obtained between the predicted and analytical values for all CHD flow cases. Subsequently, the parallelism performance is compared between UPC-CHD and MPI in its base design till 100 computer threads maximum in this study as our first approach. The obtained speedup results provide an early indication of the parallelism capability of UPC-CHD for large-scale numerical domains which can be further exploited by performing the following.

- Introduction of other numerical schemes to examine a wider range of CHD flow cases which include turbulent incompressible flow, heat transfer, porous media flow etc.
- Coupling of UPC-CHD with AWS cloud computing to exploit a greater number of cores to further evaluate the parallelism capability of the former for large-scale simulation domains.

Acknowledgements. This research study is funded by the internal core funding from the Nanyang Environment and Water Research Institute (NEWRI), Nanyang Technological University (NTU), Singapore. The first author is grateful to NTU for the 4-year Nanyang President Graduate Scholarship (NPGS) for his PhD study.

References

Anderson, J.D.: Governing equations of fluid dynamics. In: Wendt, J.F. (ed.) Computational Fluid Dynamics, pp. 15–51. Springer, Heidelberg (2009). https://doi.org/10.1007/978-3-662-11350-9_2

Balaji, P., Buntinas, D., Goodell, D., Gropp, W., Kumar, S., Lusk, E., Thakur, R., Träff, J.L.: MPI on a million processors. In: Ropo, M., Westerholm, J., Dongarra, J. (eds.) EuroPVM/MPI 2009. LNCS, vol. 5759, pp. 20–30. Springer, Heidelberg (2009). https://doi.org/10.1007/978-3-642-03770-2_9

Bucs, S.S., Radu, A.I., Lavric, V., Vrouwenvelder, J.S., Picioreanu, C.: Effect of different commercial feed spacers on biofouling of reverse osmosis membrane systems: a numerical study. Desalination **343**, 26–37 (2014)

Chang, C.-W., Liu, P.L.F., Mei, C.C., Maza, M.: Modeling transient long waves propagating through a heterogeneous coastal forest of arbitrary shape. Coast. Eng. **122**(Supplement C), 124–140 (2017)

Chen, W.Y., Bonachea, D., Duell, J., Husbands, P., Iancu, C., Yelick, K.: A Performance Analysis of the Berkeley UPC Compiler. Lawrence Berkeley National Laboratory (2003). https://escholarship.org/uc/item/91v1j2jw

Dalwadi, M.P., Griffiths, I.M., Bruna, M.: Understanding how porosity gradients can make a better filter using homogenization theory. Proc. R. Soc. A: Math. Phys. Eng. Sci. **471**(2182), 20150464 (2015)

Dalwadi, M., Bruna, M., Griffiths, I.: A multiscale method to calculate filter blockage. J. Fluid Mech. **809**, 264–289 (2016)

Gourdain, N., Gicquel, L., Montagnac, M., Vermorel, O., Gazaix, M., Staffelbach, G.: High performance parallel computing of flows in complex geometries: I. methods. Comput. Sci. Discov. **2**(1), 015003 (2009)

Jajcevic, D., Siegmann, E., Radeke, C., Khinast, J.G.: Large-scale CFD–DEM simulations of fluidized granular systems. Chem. Eng. Sci. **98**, 298–310 (2013)

Jamshed, S.: Chapter 3 - The way the HPC works in CFD. In: Using HPC for Computational Fluid Dynamics, pp. 41–79. Academic Press, Oxford (2015)

Johnson, A.A.: Using unified parallel C to enable new types of CFD applications on the cray X1/E. In: Cray User Group Conference (2006)

Kermani, M., Plett, E.: Roe scheme in generalized coordinates. I – Formulations. In: 39th Aerospace Sciences Meeting and Exhibit. American Institute of Aeronautics and Astronautics (2001a)

Kermani, M., Plett, E.: Roe scheme in generalized coordinates. II - Application to inviscid and viscous flows. In: 39th Aerospace Sciences Meeting and Exhibit. American Institute of Aeronautics and Astronautics (2001b)

Munson, B.R., Young, D.F., Okiishi, T.H.: Fundamentals of Fluid Mechanics. 6th Ed., pp. 263–331. Wiley, Hoboken (2006). (Chapter 6)

Simmendinger, C., Jägersküpper, J., Machado, R., Lojewski, C.: A PGAS-based implementation for the unstructured CFD solver TAU. Partitioned Global Address Space Programming Models, Galveston Island (2011)

Sousa, P., Soares, A., Monteiro, E., Rouboa, A.: A CFD study of the hydrodynamics in a desalination membrane filled with spacers. Desalination **349**, 22–30 (2014)

White, F.M.: Viscous Fluid Flow. 2nd Ed, pp. 457–528. McGraw-Hill (1991). (Chapter 7)

Classifying Aircraft Approach Type in the National General Aviation Flight Information Database

Kelton Karboviak[1], Sophine Clachar[1], Travis Desell[1(✉)], Mark Dusenbury[2], Wyatt Hedrick[1], James Higgins[2], John Walberg[2], and Brandon Wild[2]

[1] Department of Computer Science, University of North Dakota,
Grand Forks, ND 58202, USA
{kelton.karboviak,sophine.clachar,wyatt.j.hedrick}@und.edu,
travis.desell@engr.und.edu
[2] Department of Aviation, University of North Dakota, Grand Forks, ND 58202, USA
{dusenbur,jhiggins,walberg,bwild}@aero.und.edu

Abstract. This work details the development of the "Go-Around Detection Tool", a tool for classification of aircraft approach types for the National General Aviation Flight Information Database (NGAFID). The NGAFID currently houses over 700,000 h of per-second time series flight data recorder readings generated by over 400,000 flights from 8 fleet of aircraft and over 190 participating private individuals. The approach phase of flight is one of the most dangerous, and classifying types of approaches as stable or unstable, and if they were a *go-around, touch-and-go,* or *stop-and-go* is an especially important issue for flight safety monitoring programs. As General Aviation typically lacks the Weight on Wheels (WoW) technology and many others that exist within Commercial Aviation, there is difficulty in detecting landings and go-arounds as these need to be inferred somehow from the raw flight data. The developed application uses several airplane parameters reported by a flight data recorder and successfully detects go-arounds, touch-and-go landings, and stop-and-go landings as either stable or unstable with an accuracy of 98.14%. The application was tested using 100 student flights from the NGAFID, which generated 377 total approaches. Out of those approaches, 25.73% were classified as unstable. It was found that only 20.62% of all unstable approaches resulted with a go-around, which is far from the ideal 100% goal. Lastly, the application was parallelized and found to have a 9.75x speedup in doing so. The Go-Around Detection Tool can be used to provide post-flight statistics and user-friendly graphs on both an organizational- and individual-level for educational purposes. It is capable of assisting both new and experienced pilots for the safety of themselves, their organization, and General Aviation as a whole.

1 Introduction

The National General Aviation Flight Information Database (NGAFID) has been developed at the University of North Dakota as a joint university-industry-

© Springer International Publishing AG, part of Springer Nature 2018
Y. Shi et al. (Eds.): ICCS 2018, LNCS 10860, pp. 456–469, 2018.
https://doi.org/10.1007/978-3-319-93698-7_35

FAA initiative that is responsible for the curation, dissemination, and analysis of flight data for the General Aviation (GA) sector of Civil Aviation [1,2]. The objective of the NGAFID is to proactively identify accident precursors and mitigate risks associated with unsafe flight practices and aircraft maintenance issues within the GA community. This is achieved via non-punitive information sharing so as to educate operators on risks associated with their flights to encourage safer practices [1]. The analytical tools provided by the NGAFID are free and available to GA pilots who participate by uploading their flight data through the NGAFID web application [2] or the GAARD mobile application [3]. Subsequently, their flight data is preprocessed and analyzed using various queries. Many queries are based on threshold criteria called *exceedances*, which are predefined using known limitations of the make/model aircraft or the phase of flight. However, recent work has focused on developing more advanced analytics through machine learning and other holistic techniques [4–9]. Upon logging into the web portal, the user is provided with summaries of any unsafe events and is able to reanimate their flight(s) using X-Plane [10] or Cesium [11]. The intent is to educate participating pilots on any unsafe practices in their flight and maintenance issues with the aircraft which may contribute to an accident/incident. The overall goal of this initiative is to reduce the accident and fatality rates within the GA community.

GA is one of two branches of Civil Aviation, which pertains to the operation of all non-scheduled and non-military aircraft [12–15]. GA includes fixed-wing airplanes, helicopters (rotorcraft), balloons, dirigibles, gliders, etc.; and comprises 63% of all Civil Aviation activity within the U.S. [12,14,16]. Performing GA flight analysis is essential for making the GA community safer, as currently GA has the highest accident rates in Civil Aviation [15,17]. As of 2013, the total accident and fatality rates for GA were 5.77 and 0.99 per 100,000 flight hours, respectively; and 74.0% of GA accidents were caused by pilot actions [15].

Commercial Aviation aircraft have weight on wheels (WoW) sensors that are utilized for detecting when an aircraft is on the ground. For analyzing approaches for Commercial Aviation flights, all that needs to be done is detect when the WoW sensors are reporting the aircraft's approximate weight, which shows that the aircraft has completed a landing. Once a landing has been found, then the corresponding final approach is simply the time leading up to that landing. On the other hand, aircraft in GA typically do not have WoW sensors, which makes the process of detecting approaches and landings much more difficult. Also, as a cheaper alternative to traditional sensors and flight data recorders (FDRs), many GA pilots can now utilize smart phones and tablets (e.g., iPhone, iPad, Android devices, etc.) to record their flight data. Using a smart device severely limits the number of flight parameters that can be recorded as compared to a traditional GA FDR.

The Go-Around Detection Tool was created as an additional tool for the NGAFID to be used for detailed GA flight analysis. The basic question that provided the impetus for this research was, "How many unstable approaches result in a go-around being performed as a result?". The University of North

Dakota *Cessna 172S Standardization Manual* states that a go-around must be conducted if a stable approach is not achieved by 200 ft above ground level (AGL) [18]. The hopeful and theoretical answer to the question should therefore be 100% of unstable approaches result in a go-around, but this is very unlikely due to special circumstances and pilot misjudgment.

To the best of our knowledge, there is currently no existing research that has performed similar unstable approach analysis and landing detection within the scope of General Aviation. The challenge of developing the application lies in the fact that this type of tool does not, and cannot, rely on certain information and technology available to similar projects in Commercial Aviation. Since GA does not typically have this type of information available, a new method was required in order to detect go-arounds. In addition to detection of go-arounds, the application collects and analyzes many other useful statistics about the landing attempt including the landing type, unstableness, and reasons for unstableness (if applicable to the approach). By combining all the aforementioned features together, the tool aims to help pilots fix unsafe habits in their landings, which will reduce the number of pilot-caused landing accidents/fatalities in GA.

2 Related Work

Harris et al. [19] of MITRE Corporation mined accident and incident reports provided by the International Civil Aviation Organization (ICAO) in order to determine the specific attributes that were the cause in each kind of report and also needed to be considered "interesting" (i.e., anything that is an exception to commonly accepted knowledge among aviation experts) by the aviation expert who collaborated with them. They developed a system called Smithers, based on attribute focusing, that uncovered a correlation that having an advanced heads up display (HUD) can help reduce the amount of damage as a result of a runway incursion[1].

Matthews et al. [21] performed similar research in which their goal was to find anomalous data in flights. They differ in the fact that they used algorithms that could analyze at both a fleet-level and flight-level. Doing this allowed them to find anomalies for an entire organization or just a single flight, which makes it very useful in order to find patterns of problems. This idea is similar to the NGAFID project in which flight data can be analyzed on multiple levels while giving statistics for each.

In Dr. Ed Wischmeyer's paper *The Myth of the Unstable Approach* [22], he discusses how the term "unstable approach" is now becoming too vague to be used in accident and incident reports. He argues there are too many factors that play into an approach; therefore, labeling it solely as an "unstable approach" is not sufficient. This aligns with one of the goals of the Go-Around Detection Tool in that it was developed to detect unstable approaches and be able to state what

---

[1] Defined by the Federal Aviation Administration (FAA) as, "any occurrence at an aerodome involving the incorrect presence of an aircraft, vehicle, or person on the protected area of a surface designated for the landing and take off of aircraft" [20].

the specific parameter was that caused the approach to be unstable. In doing this, it allows for further statistics to be generated, which can reveal further patterns to be detected within an organization if it becomes a wide-spread problem.

Nazeri et al. [23] researched accident and incident data from several different commercial flight data sources in order to discover the factors that cause those events. They created eight high-level categories, each with sub-factors, for classification. They used an algorithm to analyze the data for correlations between different attribute-value pairs across the accident and incident data sets. A factor support ratio was calculated for each attribute-value pair and ranked in decreasing order to find the most significant factors. The following high-level factors were the four top ranked in order: company, air traffic control, pilot, and aircraft. They also did a time-series analysis of the data for the ten-year period in which the data was collected (1995–2004). This time-series data showed the pilot and aircraft factors are generally decreasing over time, while the air traffic control factors are generally increasing. By uncovering these patterns and analyzing them over time, they were able to find the factors that are leading causes for accidents/incidents and can address these factors for improvement.

Lastly, CloudAhoy [24] is a commercial product that is very similar to the NGAFID as it has the ability to collect a pilot's flight data then later replay the flight back to the user and analyze it graphically. It serves a similar purpose by giving pilots a fully automated debriefing after each flight. This allows for instant feedback where a pilot can review their flight and detect any issues that may have occurred during flight.

While many of these works give high-level views of how mining flight data could improve safety in the aviation community [25–27], they do not provide specific details on how to apply different mining techniques to the data in order to obtain interesting results. Further, most of these works focus on Commercial Aviation data, instead of General Aviation [21,23]. In addition, the NGAFID project consistently receives data from several organizational fleets such as the University of North Dakota, Ohio State, and Oklahoma State. Some of the related works recognize fleet data [21]; however, there are others that do not such as CloudAhoy [24], which is a considerable disadvantage. Another advantage of the NGAFID is that it is free-to-use and is an open-source project, which is very unique within the flight data monitoring space. Lastly, to our knowledge this project is the first to create an automated analyzer that detects multiple stop-and-goes, touch-and-goes, and go-arounds in a single flight, while being able to categorize each as stable or unstable.

3   Automated Go-Around Detection

The Go-Around Detection Tool provides two main features: approach quality analysis and landing type analysis. The approach quality analysis focuses on the slice of data when the aircraft is between 50 to 150 ft AGL and looks for parameters that have been exceeded, while the landing type analysis focuses on the slice of data when the aircraft is below 50 ft AGL and determines the type of landing that was a result of the approach.

3.1 Approach Quality

The first feature, approach quality analysis, performs several different detections and analyses such as airport detection, runway detection, and unstableness analysis. The algorithm for detecting an aircraft's approach needs to iterate through all of the time values since there can be multiple approaches within a single flight. Once the algorithm detects the aircraft is one mile away from an airport and is less than 500 ft above ground level (AGL), it is determined that the pilot is beginning an approach and a unique approach identifier is generated in order to store meta-data later in the process. Next, the algorithm continues to iterate through time values until either the aircraft goes under 150 ft AGL or it goes back above 500 ft AGL, which is then recorded as a go-around. If the aircraft goes under 150 ft AGL, then it is determined to be on the final approach. At this point, the runway that is being approached can be detected using a combination of the aircraft's current geo-location and heading since the intended runway may not be closest to the aircraft. The aircraft is considered to be on the final approach while it is within one mile away from the airport and it is between 50 and 150 ft AGL inclusive.

The analysis for unstableness is performed during this final approach stage. During this analysis, several flight parameters are checked against predetermined thresholds to see if any were exceeded. The values used for the thresholds can be seen in Table 1, and were obtained from [18,28]. No experimentation was performed on the values for the thresholds since these have been found to be the physical limitations of the aircraft by the manufacturer. Additionally, the FAA Airplane Flying Handbook [29] states that if the procedures and configurations it provides for approaches and landings conflict with those given in the manufacturer's flight manual, the manufacturer's recommendations should take precedence. The logical conditions used to determine if a threshold is exceeded are:

$$F_1 = 180 - |\,|\,\text{runway.hdg} - \text{airplane.hdg}\,| - 180\,| \leq 10° \tag{1}$$
$$F_2 = |\,\text{crossTrackError}\,| \leq 50\,\text{ft} \tag{2}$$
$$A = \text{airplane.IAS} \geq 55\,\text{kts} \wedge \text{airplane.IAS} \leq 75\,\text{kts} \tag{3}$$
$$S = \text{airplane.VSI} \geq -1,000\,\text{ft/min} \tag{4}$$
$$U = \neg(F_1 \wedge F_2 \wedge A \wedge S) \tag{5}$$

A *true* value for a condition means the parameter is stable. Thus if any of the parameters are unstable, U will result to being *true*, meaning the entire aircraft is in an unstable state.

Once the aircraft either goes above 150 ft AGL or goes below 50 ft AGL, then the final approach is marked as finished, and the critical meta-data associated with the approach is stored. The control of the algorithm will then be passed to the landing analysis function, which will detect the type of the resulting landing. The algorithm for this analysis will be discussed further in the next subsection.

Table 1. Exceedance thresholds for Cessna 172S [18,28]

Parameter	Description	Value
F	Flight path correct	Less than 10° off runway heading, less than 50 ft left or right of the runway center line (crosstrack error)
L	Landing configuration correct	N.A.
A	Airspeed proper	Indicated airspeed (IAS) within 55–75 kts
P	Power setting appropriate	N.A.
S	Sink rate appropriate	Vertical speed indicated (VSI) does not exceed -1000 ft/min

3.2 Landing Types

The second feature, landing analysis and type detection, is able to differentiate between a stop-and-go landing, touch-and-go landing, and a go-around. The landing analysis algorithm iterates through time values starting where the final approach analysis finished. It continues to iterate while the aircraft is below 500 ft AGL, or if it is the aircraft's final landing and the time values run out, then it stops analyzing. While the algorithm iterates through the time values, it checks if the aircraft's IAS is less than or equal to 35 knots. If this is true, then it is physically impossible that the aircraft is still flying, thus it is determined to be making a complete stop. In order to detect a touch-and-go landing, the previous five elevation readings are stored and their average is calculated. If it is found the aircraft is not making a stop-and-go landing, then the average elevation for the last five seconds is checked to see if it is less than five feet AGL. This means the aircraft is still at a flying speed (above 35 knots) and is also maintaining a stable elevation of five feet or less for at least five seconds.

Once the aircraft goes above 500 ft AGL or the time values run out, then the landing type is determined from the conditions found during the analysis. If it was found the aircraft was making a complete stop, then a value of 'stop-and-go' is stored. If it was not making a complete stop and had a stable elevation of 5 ft or less, then a value of 'touch-and-go' is stored. The final value type, 'go-around', is used as a fall-through since there are only three classifications. The three landing types and how they are detected are summarized in Table 2.

After the landing is classified, then the critical meta-data found during the analysis is stored. Lastly, the algorithm returns the time value of the landing's ending back to the approach quality analysis algorithm so that it can continue to scan for the aircraft's next approach from that time value. These algorithms will continue to do their respective analysis until the flight has ended and all the time values have been scanned.

Table 2. Landing types and their conditions

Type	Condition
stop-and-go	Aircraft's indicated airspeed speed (IAS) falls below 35 knots
touch-and-go	Aircraft is not making a complete stop and maintains a stable altitude of five feet AGL or less for at least five seconds
go-around	All other cases

4   Implementation

4.1   Programming Language and Libraries Used

The Python programming language was used for implementation due to its ease of use, its reputable scientific and graphing libraries, and the ability to quickly produce a viable application. The libraries utilized are MySQLdb for interacting with the MySQL database, matplotlib for graphing flight parameters in the early stages of the application, NumPy for its scientific functions, and the geodesy scripts created by Chris Veness[2].

4.2   Parallelization

The application was originally created to process the flight data in a linear fashion. This proved to be fairly time consuming when running the application in batch mode with a significant number of flights contained in the NGAFID. In order to improve the performance and efficiency of the application, the built-in multiprocessing module was used. The parallel application uses the Producer-Consumer model in which the parent process acts at the Producer by enqueuing all of the unique flight identifiers onto a queue, and the child subprocesses act as the Consumers by dequeuing a flight identifier and processing it. The multiprocessing module was chosen over the built-in threading module due to the issue with Python's Global Interpreter Lock (GIL) effectively restricting byte-code execution to a single core [30]. This makes the threading module unusable for long-running CPU-bound tasks, which this application heavily relies on.

5   Results

5.1   Experiments

The experiments were run using Cessna 172S flight data produced by students at the University of North Dakota during the month of September 2015. Student flight data is ideal for unstable approach analysis testing as it contains very noisy data, which provides a diverse array of flying patterns. A random sample of 100 flights was chosen for the experiments.

---

[2] http://www.movable-type.co.uk/scripts/latlong.html.

Fig. 1. Example of using a KML file to visualize a flight path in Google Earth. This flight visualization is an example of a student flight that has multiple final approach phases.

First, the application was run against the 100 flights to obtain the automated analysis results. The same 100 flights were then manually analyzed in order to get human results, which could be compared to the automated results then determine the accuracy of the application. The test of the 100 flights was also run ten times each with the single-process version and the multi-process version as described in Sect. 4.2. This was done in order to compare and contrast the performance of the separate versions.

All results were gathered using a 2013 Mac Pro running macOS 10.11.6 with a 3.5 GHz 6 hyper-threaded core Intel Xeon E5 processor (for a total of 12 logical processing cores). The machine also has 32 GBs of 1866 MHz DDR3 ECC RAM.

5.2   Accuracy

The manual validation was performed using a combination of tools available on the NGAFID website: the Cesium flight reanimation tool and the Key-hole Markup Language (KML) generator to visualize the flight path on Google Earth [31] (see Fig. 1).

The Go-Around Detection Tool generated a total of 377 approaches for the 100 flights that were tested. As seen in Fig. 1, student flights typically consist of multiple approaches as this is something that needs to be practiced. Out of the total; there are 370 (98.14%) true positives, five (1.33%) false positives, and two (0.53%) false negatives. These results can also be found in Fig. 2. In the context of this application, a true positive is a case where the tool correctly indicates that an approach is occurring during a specified time frame. A false positive occurs when the tool indicates that an approach is occurring but is not in reality. Typically, a false positive occurs when the flight data has invalid values for about the first ten rows, which then throws off the beginning of the algorithms. This happens infrequently, but could be accounted for in a future work by sanitizing the data before analysis. A false negative is the exact opposite

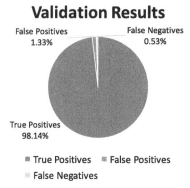

Fig. 2. Pie chart showing the manual validation results including true positives, false positives, and false negatives.

where the tool indicates that an approach is not occurring but it is in reality. Typically, a false negative occurs when the approached airport's geological data is not contained within the database. These types of occurrences should stop once the airports database is expanded with more entries. Lastly, the tool misclassified the approached runway 13 times (3.45%). A runway is misclassified when the difference between the aircraft and runway headings is greater than 20°. This occurs during the runway detection portion of the approach analysis algorithm (Sect. 3.1), and the algorithm either returns a *null* runway or an incorrect runway due to the large heading difference.

In this same context, it is difficult to quantify the number of true negatives since these would be cases where the tool correctly indicates that an approach is not occurring. The difficulty lies in how to define a single occurrence. Should a single true negative be counted for every second the tool indicates that an approach is not occurring? If so, then this would create a numerous amount of true negatives and would dilute the percentages of the other statistics, which are more important in this application.

The validation results demonstrate that the Go-Around Detection Tool is exceptionally accurate in its ability to appropriately detect and classify most approaches in a flight.

5.3   Performance

A secondary aspect of this research was to test how parallelization can help improve the performance of an application in the domain of analyzing flight data. The results of the benchmarking tests showed that the linearly executing application ran for an average of 588.632 s over 100 randomly tested flights. On the other hand, the parallel application ran for an average of 60.402 s over the same flights. This means the average per-flight execution times for the linear and parallel applications were 5.886 and 0.604 s, respectively. As a result, the parallelized application had a 9.75x speedup, which is fairly significant. This shows that the Go-Around Detection Tool can be used practically within the NGAFID as the system itself is currently transitioning into becoming a near real-time system.

As further evidence, the parallel application was tested on a larger subset of flights to see if the average execution time remained stable, in which it was tested on 5,272 flights. For this test, the parallel application was able to analyze the data and insert all the results into the database in 3,007.408 s. This gives a per-flight execution time of 0.570 s, which is slightly less than the average for 100 flights. The reasoning behind this can most likely be attributed to the fact that spinning up the sub-processes creates a substantial overhead. Thus, the longer the application is able to execute, the greater performance gain will be received. This will, of course, start to show diminishing returns as with any other parallel computing application.

5.4   What Did We Find?

The results of the application have provided many possibilities for statistical analysis since numerous statistics can be calculated from the generated approach data. This can be seen in Fig. 3a to d in which a sample of the possible results were calculated for the experiments of the 100 flights performed for this research. With these various results, trends can be found in the data that has been analyzed. For example, we can see in Fig. 3a that out of the 377 approaches in the sample data, 74.27% (280) were stable and 25.73% (97) were unstable. By drilling down into that data, we can see the frequency for each of the landing types for stable and unstable approaches. Figure 3b depicts this more detailed information and shows that stop-and-go landings are the majority for both stable and unstable approaches. This result isn't very surprising for stable approaches; however, it is very undesirable for unstable approaches. If we look even further into the proportions for unstable approaches alone (Fig. 3c), we see that an unstable approach resulted in a go-around only 20.62% of the time. This is far lower than the hopeful 100%, but was expected to be approximately 20% by our aviation safety experts. As mentioned previously, this is largely due to pilot misjudgment since all the analyzed flights were piloted by aviation students; meaning they are still learning and are not professionals.

When looking at the unstable approaches and the parameters that caused them (Fig. 3d), additional interesting results can be found. We found the parameter that was exceeded the most was heading with 52 occurrences. Heading was not predicted to be the leading cause of unstable approaches, but our safety experts believe the 10° threshold (as defined in Table 1) may be too strict. Indicated airspeed was the second highest, but was predicted to be the leading cause since it was stated by our aviation safety experts to be a trend for UND's student pilots to be going too fast on final approaches.

Approach Stableness Results

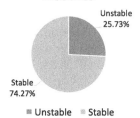

Unstable
25.73%

Stable
74.27%

▪ Unstable ▪ Stable

(a) Pie chart showing the number of stable approaches compared to the number of unstable approaches.

Stable V. Unstable Landing Results

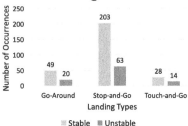

▪ Stable ▪ Unstable

(b) Frequency of the occurrences of each landing type for stable and unstable approaches.

Unstable Approach Results

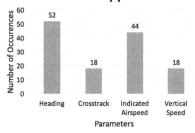

Touch-and-Go
14.43%

Go-Around
20.62%

Stop-and-Go
64.95%

▪ Go-Around ▪ Stop-and-Go
▪ Touch-and-Go

(c) Pie chart comparing the number of occurrences for each landing type after an unstable approach.

Parameters Causing Unstable Approach

(d) Frequency of parameters that caused an aircraft to be unstable during an approach. Note that a single approach can have multiple unstable parameters, which causes the sum of the occurrences to not equal the total number of unstable approaches.

Fig. 3. Sample set of the statistics and trends that can be found from the automated analysis results.

5.5   Website User Interface

A new web page was implemented in the NGAFID for the purpose of dynamically displaying the results produced by the Go-Around Detection Tool to users (Fig. 4). The results are given in four tabs, one for each parameter, as histograms over a specified date range. A user is able to dynamically add additional date ranges, which will create an additional series in the chart for comparison. This feature can be used to detect changes in trends over time. A user is also, optionally, able to filter the results to an airport and further filter to a single runway.

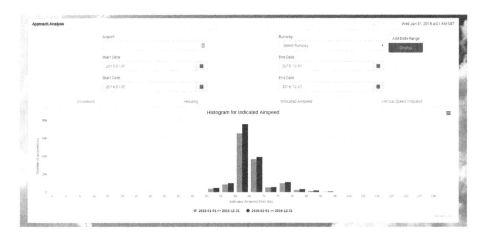

Fig. 4. A screenshot of the newly developed approach analysis tool on the NGAFID. It is showing the histogram for indicated airspeed error with two date range filters: 2015-01-01 to 2015-12-31 and 2016-01-01 to 2016-12-31. The frequency of exceedances can be seen with all values that fall outside of the 55–75 knots range.

This will allow users to identify trends that are potentially occurring at a specific runway but not at any other runways.

6   Conclusion and Future Work

This paper presented the Go-Around Detection Tool, an application designed to augment the existing features of the National General Aviation Flight Information Database (NGAFID). The purpose of creating the application is to help further reduce General Aviation (GA) fatality rates since GA is the most dangerous branch of Civil Aviation. Additionally, the application was geared towards analyzing final approaches and landings because these phases of flight are where a majority of pilot-related accidents occur [15].

This research has provided many avenues for further work and refinement. First, the greatest constraint on the accuracy of the application is the accuracy of the instrument recording the flight data, whether that be a traditional flight data recorder or a smart device. This means that if data is recorded inaccurately, it is useless to the application and cannot be recovered. For example, in several of the 100 tested flights, the first 10 to 20 rows of data can have missing and/or spurious values due to the aircraft's sensors calibrating after first starting the flight data recorder. Thus, further work into filtering or sanitizing faulty data would be very beneficial.

Second, the greatest constraint on the execution time of the application is the algorithm for detecting when an aircraft is about to approach an airport. Currently, the application uses a sequential search algorithm to calculate the closest airport based on the aircraft's geological coordinates every 15 s of flight data.

Since the sequential algorithm has $\mathcal{O}(n)$ run time, and the database of airports that was used in the search contains over 16,000 airports, it quickly became the bottleneck of the application. It isn't immediately clear how traditional path algorithms may be useful in this context since in air transportation all nodes are fully-connected with (relatively) straight paths, and the distance between the aircraft and each of the nodes changes continuously over time. There was no extensive research done to find a more efficient algorithm for this kind of detection, so this is certainly one area that could be researched in the future.

Lastly, future research is planned on combining all the analysis tools currently available on the NGAFID website (high/low fast/slow analysis on final approaches and a self-defined glide path angle calculator) and developing an application which will calculate a "letter grade" based on some predetermined criteria for each approach within a flight. This will provide even more user-friendly methods for users to receive analysis and an overall score for their flights. This will be exceptionally useful for participating aviation universities in which a student pilot could record their flight, have it analyzed by the NGAFID, receive a score, then review the scoring breakdown with their flight instructor.

Once the Go-Around Detection Tool is fully integrated into the NGAFID, it will provide even more possibilities for data visualization and be easily accessible for both novice and experienced pilots. This will allow pilots on an individual or organizational level to become more aware of bad flight habits so they may correct them in future flights and help make General Aviation safer.

References

1. Clachar, S., Higgins, J., Wild, B., Desell, T.: Large-scale data analysis for proactive anomaly detection in heterogeneous aircraft data (Unpublished)
2. National General Aviation Flight Information Database: Welcome to the national general aviation flight information database (ngafid)
3. MITRE: Gaard-general aviation airborne recording device
4. Clachar, S.A.: Identifying and analyzing atypical flights using supervised and unsupervised approaches. J. Transp. Res. Board (2014). (Published as part of an ACRP: Graduate Research Award)
5. Clachar, S.: Novelty detection and cluster analysis in time series data using variational autoencoder feature maps. Ph.D. thesis, University of North Dakota, December 2016
6. Desell, T., Clachar, S., Higgins, J., Wild, B.: Evolving deep recurrent neural networks using ant colony optimization. In: Ochoa, G., Chicano, F. (eds.) EvoCOP 2015. LNCS, vol. 9026, pp. 86–98. Springer, Cham (2015). https://doi.org/10.1007/978-3-319-16468-7_8
7. ElSaid, A., Wild, B., Higgins, J., Desell, T.: Using LSTM recurrent neural networks to predict excess vibration events in aircraft engines. In: The IEEE 12th International Conference on eScience (eScience 2016), Baltimore, Maryland, USA, October 2016
8. ElSaid, A.: Using long-short-term-memory recurrent neural networks to predict aviation engine vibrations. Master's thesis, University of North Dakota, December 2016

9. Desell, T., Clachar, S., Higgins, J., Wild, B.: Evolving neural network weights for time-series prediction of general aviation flight data. In: Bartz-Beielstein, T., Branke, J., Filipič, B., Smith, J. (eds.) PPSN 2014. LNCS, vol. 8672, pp. 771–781. Springer, Cham (2014). https://doi.org/10.1007/978-3-319-10762-2_76

10. X-Plane: X-plane. More powerful. Made usable

11. Analytical Graphics Inc., Bentley Systems: Cesium

12. AOPA: What is general aviation (2009)

13. Allen, W.B., Blond, D.L., Gellman, A.J., General Aviation Manufacturers' Association, National Association of State Aviation Officials, MergeGlobal, Inc.: General aviation's contribution to the U.S. economy, General Aviation Manufacturers' Association, May 2006

14. Federal Aviation Administration: The economic impact of civil aviation on the U.S. economy, November 2016

15. Kenny, D.J.: 25th Joseph T. Nall Report: general aviation accidents in 2013. Technical report, AOPA Air Safety Institute, Frederick (2016)

16. Shetty, K.I., Hansman, R.J.: Current and historical trends in general aviation in the united states. Master's thesis, Massachusetts Institute of Technology, August 2012

17. AOPA Air Safety Institute: 2014–2015 GA accident scorecard. Technical report, AOPA Air Safety Institute, Frederick (2016)

18. UND Aerospace Foundation: Cessna 172S Standardization Manual, August 2015

19. Harris Jr., E., Bloedorn, E., Rothleder, N.J.: Recent experiences with data mining in aviation safety. In: SIGMOD Record, Seattle, WA, June 1998

20. Federal Aviation Administration: Runway safety: Runway incursions

21. Matthews, B., Das, S., Bhaduri, K., Das, K., Martin, R., Oza, N.: Discovering anomalous aviation safety events using scalable data mining algorithms. J. Aerosp. Inf. Syst. **10**(10), 467–475 (2013)

22. Wischmeyer, E.: The myth of the unstable approach. Int. Soc. Air Saf. Investig. (2004)

23. Nazeri, Z., Donohue, G., Sherry, L.: Analyzing relationships between aircraft accidents and incidents. In: International Conference on Research in Air Transportation, February 2008

24. CloudAhoy: Cloudahoy: debriefing for pilots

25. Nazeri, Z., Bloedorn, E., Ostwald, P.: Experiences in mining aviation safety data. In: Proceedings of the 2001 ACM SIGMOD International Conference on Management of Data, SIGMOD 2001, New York, pp. 562–566. ACM (2001)

26. Gallo, D.E.: Data mining applied to aviation data. Ph.D. thesis, Universidad Politécnica de Madrid, June 2012

27. Pagels, D.A.: Aviation data mining. Sch. Horiz.: Univ. Minn. Morris Undergrad. J. **2**(1), 3 (2015)

28. Cessna Aircraft Company: Pilot's Operating Handbook and FAA Approved Airplane Flight Manual: Cessna Model 172S. 2nd edn, November 2010

29. Federal Aviation Administration: Airplane Flying Handbook 2nd edn: FAA-H-8083-3A. Skyhorse Publishing Inc. (2011)

30. Beazley, D.: Understanding the python gil. In: PyCON Python Conference, Atlanta, Georgia (2010)

31. Nolan, D., Lang, D.T.: Keyhole markup language. In: Nolan, D., Lang, D.T. (eds.) XML and Web Technologies for Data Sciences with R. Use R!, pp. 581–618. Springer, New York (2014). https://doi.org/10.1007/978-1-4614-7900-0_17

On Parametric Excitation for Exploration of Lava Tubes and Caves

Victor Parque[✉], Masato Kumai, Satoshi Miura, and Tomoyuki Miyashita

Waseda University, 3-4-1 Okubo, Shinjuku-ku, Tokyo 169-8555, Japan
parque@aoni.waseda.jp

Abstract. Huge lava tubes with an approximate diameter of 65–225 m were found on the surfaces of Moon and Mars in the late 2000's. It has been argued that the interiors of the caves are spacious, and are suitable to build artificial bases with habitable features such as constant temperature, as well as protection from both meteorites and harmful radiation. In line of the above, a number of studies which regard the soft landing mechanisms on the bottom of the lava tubes have been proposed. In this paper, aiming to extend the ability to explore arbitrary surface caves, we propose a mechanism which is able to reach the ceiling of lava tubes. The basic concept of our proposed mechanism consists of a rover connected to an oscillating sample-gatherer, wherein the rover is able to adjust the length of the rope parametrically to increase the deflection angle by considering periodic changes in the pivot, and thus to ease the collection of samples by hitting against the ceiling of the cave. Relevant simulations confirmed our theoretical observations which predict the increase of deflection angle by periodically winding and rewinding the rope according to pivotal variations. We believe the our proposed approach brings the building blocks to enable finer control of exploration mechanisms of lava tubes and narrow environments.

Keywords: Variable-length pendulum · Variable-pivot pendulum
Cave exploration · Lava tubes

1 Introduction

A number of lava tubes with diameter of 65–140 m were found on the Moon [1], and with diameter 100–225 m, were found on Mars [2,3]. It has been argued that the interior section of such caves spreads the vertical and the horizontal directions, possibly bringing appealing features [4,5] such as (1) suitability for artificial bases in the moon, (2) suitability to build environments with constant temperature, and (3) protection from meteorites and radiation.

Generally speaking, exploration of lava tubes imply key tasks such as surface exploration, shape acquisition and surface sampling. A number of previous studies have regarded the exploration using rovers with active suspension [6], rovers with inflatable wheel which functions as outer wheels [7], the wired casting manipulator [8], and the wire-enable vertical hole exploration of caves [9].

© Springer International Publishing AG, part of Springer Nature 2018
Y. Shi et al. (Eds.): ICCS 2018, LNCS 10860, pp. 470–482, 2018.
https://doi.org/10.1007/978-3-319-93698-7_36

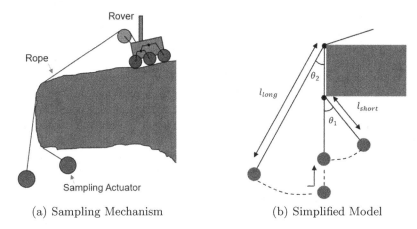

(a) Sampling Mechanism   (b) Simplified Model

Fig. 1. Basic concept of our proposed mechanism. (a) Rover attached to a sampling actuator over a cave, (b) Basic model of parametric excitation in a pendulum with variable pivot.

Also, scientific explorations are being planned by the UZUME (Unprecedented Zipangu (Japan) Underworld of the Moon Exploration) Project.

In this paper, we propose a mechanism to enable the wire-based sampling of the ceiling of lava tubes and underground cave-like channels. Our mechanism consists of a variable-length rope connecting a rover to an oscillating mass under periodically varying length and pivot. The basic concept of our mechanism is depicted by Fig. 1, in which it becomes possible to increase the deflection angle by adjusting the length of the rope parametrically, extending the concept of variable-length pendulum to consider periodically changing pivots. Whereas variable-length pendulum [10–15] and vertically oscillating supports [15–24] have been studied widely, the study of periodic change of the pivot in the pendulum, and its application to space exploration mechanisms, has received little attention. Simulation results confirmed that the angular displacement increases by using the parametric excitation under pivotal changes. Our contributions are as follows:

– the framework which enables the modeling of parametric excitation with periodically varying length and pivot, and
– simulations to show the performance in terms of increase of angular displacement in the order of seconds.

Our proposed approach offers building blocks to realize a versatile class of exploration mechanisms which are not only able to gather samples from the ceilings of cave-like channels, but also able to reach the ceilings efficiently and flexibly. Our method also has the potential to be used in the narrow and harsh environments, to allow studies in space volcanism. Finally, by considering the periodic change of pivot and length explicitly, it becomes possible to model complex structures enabling finer control of oscillating behaviours.

2   Proposed Mechanism

2.1   Basic Concept

Parametric excitation implies the periodic explicit variation of a parameter in a dynamical system. For instance, in the context of a spring-mass system, the parametric excitation occurs when parameters such as mass, spring constant, or damping coefficient vary periodically. In this section, we describe the theoretical framework to allow parametric excitation of our proposed mechanism.

In the context of a swing oscillation, the equation of motion of a general pendulum that consists of a lumped mass suspended by a rigid massless rod from a pivot is derived from the angular momentum as follows:

$$\frac{d}{dt}(ml^2\dot{\theta}) = -mgl\sin(\theta) \tag{1}$$

where:

g is the constant due to gravity,
l is the length of the rigid massless rope, and
m is the lumped mass,
θ is the angular displacement with respect to the pivot and the vertical axis.

The above definition can be simplified as follows:

$$F(\theta, l) = \ddot{\theta}(t) + \frac{2\dot{l}}{l}\dot{\theta}(t) + \frac{g}{l}\sin\theta(t) = 0 \tag{2}$$

In order to enable the angular displacement under conditions of change in the pivot, we allow the pendulum to have variable length according to the position of the pivot. This scheme is applicable to model mechanisms able to sample the ceiling of convex caves, as shown by Fig. 1.

For simplicity and without loss of generality, we assume the simplified model as shown by Fig. 1(b), which represents the main key features of mechanisms able to sample convex caves. Further extensions are possible by considering polygonal shapes with more than four vertices. The study of such environments are expected to be realized in a future work.

2.2   Piecewise Pendulum Mechanism

The key idea of our approach is to model a pendulum with *variable length* and *pivotal variations* by periodically and conditionally winding and rewinding the rope, in the presence of the ceiling of a vertical hole, which results in the excitation of the deflection angle θ, and the modeling through *piecewise* pendular governing equations.

In order to exemplify the above described mechanism,

– Figure. 2(a) shows examples of the phases of the Winding behaviour of a pendulum in a simplified cave model,

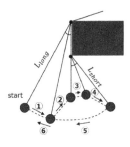

(a) Winding behaviour

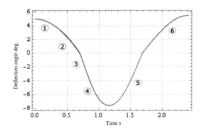

(b) Angular displacement

Fig. 2. Angular displacement as a result of winding the rope. (a) Winding behaviour, and (b) Angular displacement according to the winding phase.

- Figure. 2(b) shows the angular displacement corresponding to the phases of the Winding behaviour of Fig. 2(a)

By observing Fig. 2(a) and (b) one can note the following facts:

- the lower and upper bound of the length of the rope is $[L_{short}, L_{long}]$,
- starting with phase 1, from the left, there exists 6 *piecewise phases* in the pendulum motion, in which each phase is associated with the angular displacement curves depicted by Fig. 2(b).

Along with the above observations, it is important to note that the angular displacement is a *piecewise function* of time resulting from the numerical solutions of the governing equations for each phase i, for $i = \{1, 2, 3, ...6\}$; and each solution of displacement curve of the phase i is subject to angular and velocity constraints with respect to the previous phase $i - 1$.

Concretely speaking, to give a clear description of the above remarks, the angular displacement of the i-th phase can be computed by solving the governing equations of the following classes:

(1) Governing equations along the downward,

$$\theta_i \leftarrow \underset{\theta_i}{\textbf{\textit{Solve}}}\ F(\theta_i, l_i) = 0 \ \Big|\ l_i = f(l_{i-1}, \epsilon, H) \tag{3}$$

subject to

$$t \geq \tau_{i-1}$$
$$\theta_i(\tau_{i-1}) = \theta_{i-1}(\tau_{i-1})$$
$$\dot{\theta}_i(\tau_{i-1})l_i = \dot{\theta}_{i-1}(\tau_{i-1})l_{i-1}$$

(2) Governing equations along the trajectory,

$$\theta_i \leftarrow \underset{\theta_i}{\textbf{Solve}} \; F(\theta_i, l_i) = 0 \; \Big| \; l_i = f(l_{i-1}, \epsilon, H) \tag{4}$$

subject to

$$t \geq \tau_{i-1}$$
$$\theta_i(\tau_{i-1}) = \theta_{i-1}(\tau_{i-1})$$
$$\dot{\theta}_i(\tau_{i-1}) = \dot{\theta}_{i-1}(\tau_{i-1})$$

, where the above subscripts are defined as follows:

- θ_i is the angular displacement of the i-th phase with respect to the pivot and the vertical axis,
- $\dot{\theta}_i$ is the angular velocity of the i-th phase with respect to the pivot and the vertical axis,
- $\dot{\theta}_i(\tau_{i-1})$ is the angular velocity of the i-th phase at time τ_{i-1} with respect to the $(i-1)$-th phase,
- l_i is the length of the rope during the i-th phase of the pendulum,
- ϵ is the amount for winding and rewinding,
- H is the height of the vertical hole (assuming a rectangular shape of the ceiling cave),
- $f : (l_{i-1}, \epsilon, H) \rightarrow l_i$ is a function mapping from the length of the rope of the previous phase $(i-1)$ to that of the current phase i, and considering the winding/rewinding ϵ as well as the height H of the vertical hole,
- τ_i is the time a constraint on angular displacement θ_i or angular velocity $\dot{\theta}_i$ holds true.

The key difference between Eqs. 3 and 4 is the location of the ball. Whereas Eq. 3 is used to constrain the pendular motion along the downward direction, Eq. 4 is used to constrain the motion in arbitrary points along the trajectory. In line of the above, two relevant instances to compute τ_i are as follows:

$$\tau_i = \{t | \theta_i = 0\} \tag{5}$$

, where τ_i is the time at which the pendulum reaches the downward vertical, and

$$\tau_i = \{t | \dot{\theta}_i = 0\} \tag{6}$$

where τ_i is the time at which the pendulum reaches a point closest to the upward vertical.

Thus, by the descriptions of Eqs. 3 and 6, it is possible to allow modeling piecewise pendular displacement curves considering the continuity in time, angular displacement and angular velocity. Furthermore, by introducing the function $f(.)$, it is possible to allow variable-length pendulums under pivotal changes.

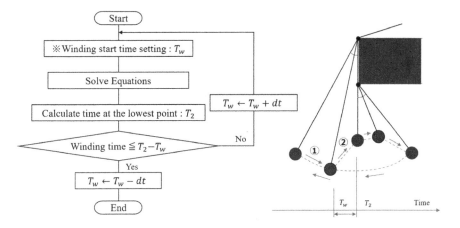

Fig. 3. Basic concept to compute winding time

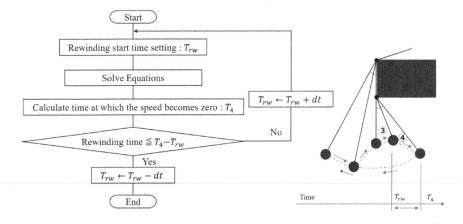

Fig. 4. Basic concept to compute rewinding time

2.3 Winding and Rewinding

Winding (rewinding) aims at shortening (lengthening) the length of the rope by a small constant. Because winding and rewinding are unrealizable instantaneously, we modeled the operation of the pendulum to consider the winding and rewinding time into account. Thus, in line of the above descriptions, computing the timing for winding and rewinding is computed by difference and comparison to a threshold as shown by Figs. 3 and 4, in which:

- The initial value of T_w is the difference between the time to reach the downward position and the rewinding time.
- The initial value of T_{rw} is the difference between the time to reach zero speed and the winding time.

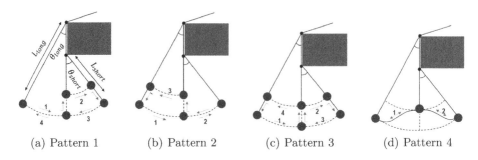

(a) Pattern 1   (b) Pattern 2   (c) Pattern 3   (d) Pattern 4

Fig. 5. Patterns of parametric excitation in our proposed mechanism.

2.4   Parametric Excitation Patterns

Since the basic pendulum model is unable to handle cases in which the pivot is variable, and in order to study the angular displacement under diverse winding and rewinding scenarios, we present four patterns as depicted by Fig. 5 to enable the excitatory oscillation through a variable length pendulum with pivotal changes, as follows:

Pattern 1. The first pattern in Fig. 5(a) implies the periodic winding and rewinding of the rope within the region corresponding to the *shortest* length of the rope. The solutions of the displacement curves are obtained by Algorithm 1, in which four piecewise displacement curves are obtained by regulating the length l_i for each phase, for $i = \{1, 2, 3, 4\}$. Note that winding occurs just after phase 1, and rewinding occurs just after phase 2.

Pattern 2. The second pattern in Fig. 5(b) implies the periodic winding and rewinding of the rope within the region corresponding to the *longest* length of the rope. Here, the solutions of the displacement curves are obtained by Algorithm 2, where three piecewise displacement curves are obtained by regulating the length l_i for each phase, for $i = \{1, 2, 3\}$. Note that winding occurs just after phase 2, and rewinding occurs just after phase 3. Also, note that phase 2 is composed of the motion from the position in the downward vertical to the position where the angular speed is zero, and viceversa.

Pattern 3. The third pattern in Fig. 5(c) implies the periodic winding and rewinding of the rope within the region corresponding to *both the shortest and the longest* length of the rope. The solutions of the displacement curves are obtained by Algorithm 3, in which four piecewise displacement curves are obtained by regulating the length l_i for each phase, for $i = \{1, 2, 3, 4\}$. Note that winding occurs just after either phase 1 or phase 3, and rewinding occurs just after either phase 2 or phase 4.

Pattern 4. The fourth pattern in Fig. 5(d) implies the periodic winding and rewinding of the rope within the region corresponding to *both the shortest and the longest* length of the rope under sinusoidal stimuli. The solutions of the displacement curves are obtained by Algorithm 4, in which two piecewise displacement curves are obtained by regulating the length l_i for each phase, for $i = \{1, 2\}$. Note that winding occurs as a consequence of periodic stimuli of the cosine function.

Algorithm 1. Pattern 1

1: **procedure**
2:     $\tau_4 \leftarrow 0, \ \theta_4(\tau_4) \leftarrow \theta_o, \ \dot{\theta}_4(\tau_4) \leftarrow 0$
3:     **for** $m \leftarrow 1$ **to** M **do**
4:         $\theta_1, \tau_1 \leftarrow \underset{\theta_1}{\textbf{Solve}} \ F(\theta_1, l_1) = 0 \ \Big| \ l_1 \leftarrow L_{long} + \epsilon/2$

   s.t. $t \geq \tau_4 \wedge \theta_1(\tau_4) = \theta_4(\tau_4) \wedge \dot{\theta}_1(\tau_4) = \dot{\theta}_4(\tau_4)$

   $\tau_1 = \{t|\theta_1 = 0\}$

5:         $\theta_2, \tau_2 \leftarrow \underset{\theta_2}{\textbf{Solve}} \ F(\theta_2, l_2) = 0 \ \Big| \ l_2 = l_1 - \epsilon - H$

   s.t. $t \geq \tau_1 \wedge \theta_2(\tau_1) = \theta_1(\tau_1) \wedge \dot{\theta}_2(\tau_1)l_2 = \dot{\theta}_1(\tau_1)l_1$

   $\tau_2 = \{t|\dot{\theta}_2 = 0\}$

6:         $\theta_3, \tau_3 \leftarrow \underset{\theta_3}{\textbf{Solve}} \ F(\theta_3, l_3) = 0 \ \Big| \ l_3 = l_2 + \epsilon$

   s.t. $t \geq \tau_2 \wedge \theta_3(\tau_2) = \theta_2(\tau_2) \wedge \dot{\theta}_3(\tau_2) = \dot{\theta}_2(\tau_2)$

   $\tau_3 = \{t|\theta_3 = 0\}$

7:         $\theta_4, \tau_4 \leftarrow \underset{\theta_4}{\textbf{Solve}} \ F(\theta_4, l_4) = 0 \ \Big| \ l_4 = l_1$

   s.t. $t \geq \tau_3 \wedge \theta_4(\tau_3) = \theta_3(\tau_3) \wedge \dot{\theta}_4(\tau_3)l_4 = \dot{\theta}_3(\tau_3)l_3$

   $\tau_4 = \{t|\dot{\theta}_4 = 0\}$

8:     **end for**
9: **end procedure**

---

3   Results and Discussion

To evaluate the evolution of the deflection angle and the behavioural repertoire of the parametric excitation in the previously introduced winding and rewinding patterns, Fig. 6 shows the oscillation patterns of mass m assuming the longest length of the rope $L_{long} = 2\,\text{m}$, the shortest length of the rope $l_{short} = 1$, the

---

Algorithm 2. Pattern 2

1: **procedure**
2:     $\tau_3 \leftarrow 0$, $\theta_3(\tau_3) \leftarrow \theta_o$, $\dot\theta_3(\tau_3) \leftarrow 0$, $l_3 \leftarrow L_{long}$
3:     **for** $m \leftarrow 1$ **to** M **do**
4:         $\theta_1, \tau_1 \leftarrow \underset{\theta_1}{\textbf{Solve}}\ F(\theta_1, l_1) = 0 \;\Big|\; l_1 \leftarrow l_3 + \epsilon$

            s.t. $t \geq \tau_3 \wedge \theta_1(\tau_3) = \theta_3(\tau_3) \wedge \dot\theta_1(\tau_3) = \dot\theta_3(\tau_3)$

            $\tau_1 = \{t|\theta_1 = 0\}$

5:         $\theta_2, \tau_2 \leftarrow \underset{\theta_2}{\textbf{Solve}}\ F(\theta_2, l_2) = 0 \;\Big|\; l_2 = l_1 - H$

            s.t. $t \geq \tau_1 \wedge \theta_2(\tau_1) = \theta_1(\tau_1) \wedge \dot\theta_2(\tau_1)l_2 = \dot\theta_1(\tau_1)l_1$

            $\tau_2 = \{t|\theta_2 = 0\}$

6:         $\theta_3, \tau_3 \leftarrow \underset{\theta_3}{\textbf{Solve}}\ F(\theta_3, l_3) = 0 \;\Big|\; l_3 = l_2 - \epsilon + H$

            s.t. $t \geq \tau_2 \wedge \theta_3(\tau_2) = \theta_2(\tau_2) \wedge \dot\theta_3(\tau_2) = \dot\theta_2(\tau_2)$

            $\tau_3 = \{t|\dot\theta_3 = 0\}$

7:     **end for**
8: **end procedure**

---

initial displacement $\theta_o = 5$, the gravity constant $g = 9.8066$, the length of wind-rewind $\epsilon = 0.2\,\text{m}$. Fine tuning the above parameters is out of the scope of this paper, and is left in our future agenda.

In Fig. 6, the following can be observed:

- The x-axis denotes the time (in seconds), and
- The y-axis denotes the angular displacement (in degrees)
- The red marks at the top of Fig. 6(a)–(c) denote the oscillations which occur when the *longest* part of the rope achieves the maximal deflection angle.
- Conversely, the blue marks at the bottom of Fig. 6(a)–(c) denote the oscillations which occur when the *shortest* part of the rope achieves the minimal deflection angle.
- Thus, in line of the above observations, red (blue) marks indicate positive (negative) maximal (minimal) angular displacement of $90°$ $(-90°)$

In the context of exploration of lava tubes and caves, minimal negative angular displacements are desirable since they imply the ability to reach the ceiling of the cave. Thus, for practical realizations, reaching $-90°$ with minimal time and effort is highly desirable. In line of the above requirements, by observing Fig. 6, we note the following facts:

Algorithm 3. Pattern 3

1: **procedure**

2: $\quad \tau_4 \leftarrow 0,\ \theta_4(\tau_4) \leftarrow \theta_o,\ \dot{\theta}_4(\tau_4) \leftarrow 0,\ l_4 \leftarrow L_{long}$

3: $\quad$ **for** $m \leftarrow 1$ **to** M **do**

4: $\qquad \theta_1, \tau_1 \leftarrow \underset{\theta_1}{\boldsymbol{Solve}}\ F(\theta_1, l_1) = 0 \ \Big|\ l_1 \leftarrow l_4 + \epsilon$

$\qquad\qquad$ s.t. $t \geq \tau_4 \wedge \theta_1(\tau_4) = \theta_4(\tau_4) \wedge \dot{\theta}_1(\tau_4) = \dot{\theta}_4(\tau_4)$

$\qquad\qquad \tau_1 = \{t | \theta_1 = 0\}$

5: $\qquad \theta_2, \tau_2 \leftarrow \underset{\theta_2}{\boldsymbol{Solve}}\ F(\theta_2, l_2) = 0 \ \Big|\ l_2 = l_1 - \epsilon - H$

$\qquad\qquad$ s.t. $t \geq \tau_1 \wedge \theta_2(\tau_1) = \theta_1(\tau_1) \wedge \dot{\theta}_2(\tau_1) l_2 = \dot{\theta}_1(\tau_1) l_1$

$\qquad\qquad \tau_2 = \{t | \dot{\theta}_2 = 0\}$

6: $\qquad \theta_3, \tau_3 \leftarrow \underset{\theta_3}{\boldsymbol{Solve}}\ F(\theta_3, l_3) = 0 \ \Big|\ l_3 = l_2 + \epsilon$

$\qquad\qquad$ s.t. $t \geq \tau_2 \wedge \theta_3(\tau_2) = \theta_2(\tau_2) \wedge \dot{\theta}_3(\tau_2) = \dot{\theta}_2(\tau_2)$

$\qquad\qquad \tau_3 = \{t | \theta_3 = 0\}$

7: $\qquad \theta_4, \tau_4 \leftarrow \underset{\theta_4}{\boldsymbol{Solve}}\ F(\theta_4, l_4) = 0 \ \Big|\ l_4 = l_3 - \epsilon + H$

$\qquad\qquad$ s.t. $t \geq \tau_3 \wedge \theta_4(\tau_3) = \theta_3(\tau_3) \wedge \dot{\theta}_4(\tau_3) l_4 = \dot{\theta}_3(\tau_3) l_3$

$\qquad\qquad \tau_4 = \{t | \dot{\theta}_4 = 0\}$

8: $\quad$ **end for**

9: **end procedure**

- In all figures, the deflection angle increases as a function of time,
- Pattern 1 and Pattern 3 require less time to achieve a deflection angle equivalent to $-90°$ or more.
- Among the four described patterns in Fig. 6, Pattern 4 requires more time to achieve a deflection angle equivalent to $-60°$, in which achieving minimal angular displacements depends on the amount of rewinding.
- Among the four described patterns in Fig. 6, Pattern 1 shows the simplest operability and the ability to achieve $-90°$ in less than 60 s.

The above observations confirm that the deflection angle is increased by the parametric excitation, and that the deflection angle reaches $-90°$ when the rope becomes shortest. These results offer the possibility to control the impact to the ceiling of convex caves with finer accuracy, which is in line of our future agenda. Also, the above settings are representative to construct sampling mechanisms in small-scale caves, and in our future work, we aim at evaluating the above winding strategies in an experimental scenario.

Algorithm 4. Pattern 4

1: **procedure**
2:    $\tau_2 \leftarrow 0,\ \theta_2(\tau_2) \leftarrow \theta_o,\ \dot{\theta}_2(\tau_2) \leftarrow 0$
3:    **for** $m \leftarrow 1$ **to** M **do**
4:        $\theta_1, \tau_1 \leftarrow \underset{\theta_1}{\textbf{Solve}}\ F(\theta_1, l_1) = 0 \ \Big|\ l_1 \leftarrow L_{long} - \dfrac{\epsilon}{2}cos\Big(2\sqrt{\dfrac{g}{L_{long}}}(t - \tau_2)\Big)$

   s.t. $t \geq \tau_2 \wedge \theta_1(\tau_2) = \theta_2(\tau_2) \wedge$

   $\dot{\theta}_1(\tau_2)\Big(L_{long} - \dfrac{\epsilon}{2}\Big) = \dot{\theta}_2(\tau_2)\Big(L_{short} - \dfrac{\epsilon}{2}\Big)$

   $\tau_1 = \{t | \theta_1 = 0\}$

5:        $\theta_2, \tau_2 \leftarrow \underset{\theta_2}{\textbf{Solve}}\ F(\theta_2, l_2) = 0 \ \Big|\ l_2 \leftarrow L_{short} - \dfrac{\epsilon}{2}cos\Big(2\sqrt{\dfrac{g}{L_{short}}}(t - \tau_1)\Big)$

   s.t. $t \geq \tau_1 \wedge \theta_2(\tau_1) = \theta_1(\tau_1) \wedge$

   $\dot{\theta}_2(\tau_1)\Big(L_{short} - \dfrac{\epsilon}{2}\Big) = \dot{\theta}_1(\tau_1)\Big(L_{long} - \dfrac{\epsilon}{2}\Big)$

   $\tau_2 = \{t | \theta_2 = 0\}$

6:    **end for**
7: **end procedure**

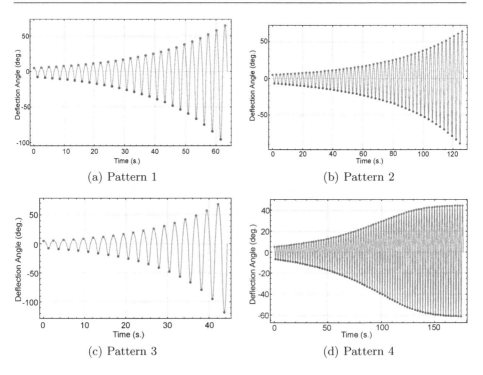

(a) Pattern 1   (b) Pattern 2

(c) Pattern 3   (d) Pattern 4

Fig. 6. Patterns of parametric excitation in our proposed mechanism. (Color figure online)

4 Concluding Remarks

We have proposed a mechanism to reach the ceiling of lava tubes by connecting a rover to an oscillating sample-gatherer, in which the rover is able to adjust the length of the rope parametrically to increase the deflection angle by considering periodic changes in the pivot, and thus to enable the collection of samples by hitting against the ceiling of the cave. Relevant simulations have shown that the deflection angle increases with time, and that there exists oscillating patterns archiving a deflection of $-90°$ in the order of seconds when the rope becomes shortest. Our proposed mechanism enables the building blocks to model versatile sample-gatherers of cave surfaces which perform efficiently. In our future agenda we aim to study the finer control of exploration mechanisms of lava tubes and narrow environments.

References

1. Haruyama, J., Hioki, K., Shirao, M., Morota, T., Hiesinger, H., van der Bogert, C.H., Miyamoto, H., Iwasaki, A., Yokota, Y., Ohtake, M., Matsunaga, T., Hara, S., Nakanotani, S., Pieters, C.M.: Possible lunar lava tube skylight observed by SELENE cameras. Geophys. Res. Lett. **36**(21), 1–5 (2009)
2. Cushing, G.E., Titus, T.N., Wynne, J.J., Christensen, P.R.: Themis observes possible cave skylights on mars. Geophys. Res. Lett. **34**(17), L17201 (2007)
3. Lveill, R.J., Datta, S.: Lava tubes and basaltic caves as astrobiological targets on earth and mars: a review. Planet. Space Sci. **58**, 592–598 (2010). (Exploring other worlds by exploring our own: the role of terrestrial analogue studies in planetary exploration)
4. Robinson, M., Ashley, J., Boyd, A., Wagner, R., Speyerer, E., Hawke, B.R., Hiesinger, H., van der Bogert, C.: Confirmation of sublunarean voids and thin layering in mare deposits. Planet. Space Sci. **69**, 18–27 (2012)
5. Blamont, J.: A roadmap to cave dwelling on the moon and mars. Adv. Space Res. **54**, 2140–2149 (2014). (Lunar Science and Exploration)
6. Naiki, T., Kubota, T.: Study on rough terrain traversability of rover mobility system with active suspension. JSME (2010). (in Japanese)
7. Furutani, K.: Concept of inflatable outer wheel rover for exploration of lunar and planetary holes and subsurface caverns (special issue on innovative actuators). Int. J. Autom. Technol. **10**, 584–590 (2016)
8. Otsuki, S., Arisumi, J.: Exploration of lunar and planetary holes and subsurface caverns: elemental technology of wired casting manipulator system for exploring planetary hole. In: Proceedings of the Space Sciences and Technology Conference (2013). (in Japanese)
9. Moriwa, S.: Research on lunar planet vertical hole exploration robot with wire. Research Summary, JAXA (2014)
10. Akulenko, L., Nesterov, S.: The stability of the equilibrium of a pendulum of variable length. J. Appl. Math. Mech. **73**, 642–647 (2009)
11. Bartuccelli, M., Christiansen, P.L., Muto, V., Soerensen, M.P., Pedersen, N.F.: Chaotic behaviour of a pendulum with variable length. Il Nuovo Cimento B (1971–1996) **100**, 229–249 (1987)
12. Seyranian, A.P.: Swing problem. Dokl. Phys. **49**, 64–68 (2004)

13. Belyakov, A.O., Seyranian, A.P., Luongo, A.: Dynamics of the pendulum with periodically varying length. Phys. D **238**, 1589–1597 (2009)
14. Pinsky, M., Zevin, A.: Oscillations of a pendulum with a periodically varying length and a model of swing. Int. J. Non-linear Mech. **34**, 105–109 (1999)
15. Wright, J.A., Bartuccelli, M., Gentile, G.: The effects of time-dependent dissipation on the basins of attraction for the pendulum with oscillating support. Nonlinear Dyn. **77**, 1377–1409 (2014)
16. Bardin, B., Markeyev, A.: The stability of the equilibrium of a pendulum for vertical oscillations of the point of suspension. J. Appl. Math. Mech. **59**, 879–886 (1995)
17. Bartuccelli, M.V., Gentile, G., Georgiou, K.V.: On the dynamics of a vertically driven damped planar pendulum. Proc. R. Soc. Lond. A: Math. Phys. Eng. Sci. **457**, 3007–3022 (2001)
18. Bartuccelli, M.V., Gentile, G., Georgiou, K.V.: On the stability of the upside-down pendulum with damping. Proc.: Math. Phys. Eng. Sci. **458**(2018), 255–269 (2002)
19. Clifford, M.J., Bishop, S.R.: Locating oscillatory orbits of the parametrically-excited pendulum. J. Aust. Math. Soc. Ser. B Appl. Math. **37**, 309–319 (1996)
20. Bishop, S.R., Xu, D.L., Clifford, M.J.: Flexible control of the parametrically excited pendulum. Proc. R. Soc. Lond. A: Math. Phys. Eng. Sci. **452**, 1789–1806 (1996)
21. Capecchi, D., Bishop, S.R.: Periodic oscillations and attracting basins for a parametrically excited pendulum. Dyn. Stab. Syst. **9**, 123–143 (1994)
22. Kim, S.Y., Hu, B.: Bifurcations and transitions to chaos in an inverted pendulum. Phys. Rev. E **58**, 3028–3035 (1998)
23. Lenci, S., Pavlovskaia, E., Rega, G., Wiercigroch, M.: Rotating solutions and stability of parametric pendulum by perturbation method. J. Sound Vib. **310**, 243–259 (2008)
24. Xu, X., Wiercigroch, M., Cartmell, M.: Rotating orbits of a parametrically-excited pendulum. Chaos Solitons Fract. **23**, 1537–1548 (2005)

Global Simulation of Planetary Rings on Sunway TaihuLight

Masaki Iwasawa[1(✉)], Long Wang[1,2], Keigo Nitadori[1], Daisuke Namekata[1],
Takayuki Muranushi[1], Miyuki Tsubouchi[1], Junichiro Makino[1,3,4], Zhao Liu[5],
Haohuan Fu[5,6], and Guangwen Yang[5,6,7]

[1] RIKEN Advanced Institute for Computational Science, Chuo-ku, Kobe, Japan
cc67803@gmail.com
[2] Helmholtz Institut für Strahlen und Kernphysik, Bonn, Germany
[3] Department of Planetology, Graduate School of Science,
Kobe University, Kobe, Japan
[4] Earth–Life Science Institute, Tokyo Institute of Technology, Tokyo, Japan
[5] National Supercomputing Center in Wuxi, Wuxi, China
[6] Ministry of Education Key Laboratory for Earth System Modeling,
Department of Earth System Science, Tsinghua University, Beijing, China
[7] Department of Computer Science and Technology,
Tsinghua University, Beijing, China

Abstract. In this paper, we report the implementation and measured performance of a global simulation of planetary rings on Sunway Taihu-Light. The basic algorithm is the Barnes-Hut tree, but we have made a number of changes to achieve good performance for extremely large simulations on machines with an extremely large number of cores. The measured performance is around 35% of the theoretical peak. The main limitation comes from the performance of the interaction calculation kernel itself, which is currently around 50%.

1 Introduction

Our understanding of the structure of planetary rings has been advanced greatly, mainly through interplanetary missions such as Voyager 1 and 2, and most recently Cassini. They have made a number of findings, including the dynamic change of small-scale structures of the rings, possibly through complex interactions with satellites. The primary theoretical tool for the understanding of these findings is fluid models, but many features require more detailed modeling, and direct simulation of ring particles is necessary.

Most simulations of ring structures have been based on local approximation, in which we apply the (pseudo-)periodic boundary conditions for both the radial and angular directions [13].

Rein and Latter used up to 200k particles to model the viscous overstability in Saturn's rings using this local assumption [10]. Because very long simulations are necessary, the number of particles has been small. They used REBOUND [11],

© Springer International Publishing AG, part of Springer Nature 2018
Y. Shi et al. (Eds.): ICCS 2018, LNCS 10860, pp. 483–495, 2018.
https://doi.org/10.1007/978-3-319-93698-7_37

an MPI-parallel N-body simulation code. More recently, Ballouz et al. [1] used `pkdgrav` [12] for simulations with up to 500k particles.

Michikoshi and Kokubo [9] performed global simulations of rings around the asteroid Chariklo, using 300M particles. This is to our knowledge the largest simulation of rings around planets (or asteroids). They have used FDPS (Framework for Developing Particle Simulator) [6], to parallelize their calculation code.

Their calculation is probably the first global simulation of rings with the physical size of the ring particles comparable to that of real ones. They could do that with still a relatively small number of particles (300M), since the asteroid and thus rings themselves are small. If we want to model Saturn's rings, the necessary number of particles would be much larger. The radius of the A ring of Saturn is around 1.3×10^5 km. The typical radius of ring particles is 6 m [14], and the optical depth of the ring is around unity. Thus, we need 10^4 particles per km^2 or around 10^{12} particles for the radial range of 100 km. With this radial range, we can model many of the fine features observed by Cassini directly.

In this paper, we describe the result of our effort to perform such extreme-scale simulations of planetary rings on Sunway TaihuLight, the fastest machine as of Nov. 2016. Our implementation is also based on FDPS, but we need to make a number of changes to the code and algorithms to achieve reasonable performance. As a result, the measured performance of our code, on 1/10 of TaihuLight (4096 nodes, 16384 processes) is around 31% of the theoretical peak.

The rest of the paper is organized as follows. In Sect. 2, we summarize the architecture of the Sunway TaihuLight system and its SW26010 processor. In Sect. 3, we discuss the usual implementation of N-body code on accelerator-based systems, and problems of such an implementation on TaihuLight. In Sect. 4, we describe the algorithms we used on TaihuLight. In Sect. 5, we present the measured performance on TaihuLight. In Sect. 6, we summarize the results.

2   Sunway TaihuLight

Sunway TaihuLight consists of 40960 nodes, connected by a network with injection bandwidth of 8 GB/s per node. Each node has one Sunway SW26010 processor. The processor consists of four "core groups" (CGs). One CG has one management processing element (MPE) and 64 computing processing elements (CPEs). MPE and CPEs are both 64-bit RISC processors and have almost the same architecture. Both MPE and CPEs have instruction caches. MPE has L1 and L2 data caches, while each CPE only has local data memory (LDM, 64 KB) and no cache memory. Each CPE can still perform load/store operations to the main memory, and they can also issue DMA transfers between LDM and the main memory. The need for explicit control of data movement between LDM and main memory makes the porting of the existing codes rather complicated. On the other hand, the possibility of explicit control makes performance tuning relatively straightforward.

The 64 CPEs in one CG is organized as an 8×8 array. The communication within the array is not mesh but point-to-point or broadcast within the rows or columns. Thus, extremely low-latency communication can be done within a CG, and barrier synchronization is also extremely fast.

Operating system runs on the MPE, and the user program also runs on the MPE. In order to use CPEs, the user either uses OpenACC or the Athread library, which is a lightweight thread library designed for the SW26010 processor.

The processor runs with a clock speed of 1.45 GHz. Each CPE (and MPE) can perform four double-precision multiply-and-add operations, in the form of a 256-bit wide SIMD operation, in every clock cycle. Thus, the theoretical peak performance of one processor is 3.016 Tflops, and that of the entire machine with 40960 processors is 123.5 Pflops. Each CG has 8 GB of DDR3 memory with theoretical peak transfer rate of 34 GB/s. The B/F ratio is 0.045, much lower than that of most modern processors (both CPUs and GPUs), which is in the range of 0.15 to 0.25. Thus, it is critical to minimize the main memory access to achieve good performance.

3   N-body Algorithms for Accelerator-Based Systems

As we have seen in the previous section, the SW26010 processor has a "heterogeneous many-core" architecture. Technically speaking, the instruction-set architecture itself of MPE and CPE is almost the same, but the absence of the data cache on the side of CPE makes the programming mode completely different.

For accelerator-based machines, there have been a number of research investigations of optimized algorithms for gravitational N-body simulations. Makino [7] applied the vectorizeation algorithm of Barnes [2] to utilize the GRAPE hardware in combination with the Barnes-Hut tree algorithm. Makino [8] describes efficient parallel implementation of the Barnes-Hut tree algorithm on GRAPE cluster systems. This algorithm is then ported to GPGPUs [4] and has been used on many different systems.

In our FDPS system, the methods to use an accelerator is essentially the same as those used for GRAPE or GPGPUs in the works described above. In the original algorithm of Barnes and Hut, the tree structure is used to approximate the forces from distant particles by the force from their center of mass (or multipole expansion if higher accuracy is necessary). To calculate the force on one particle in the original algorithm, the tree structure is traversed to find the required level of approximation.

In Barnes' modified algorithm, the tree is traversed not for each particles but for groups of (nearby) particles, and a so-called "interaction list" is constructed. Then the calculation of forces on particles in that group is done using this interaction list. In this algorithm, tree traversal can be done on a slow general-purpose processor, while the interaction calculation itself is done on a fast accelerator.

For MPI-based parallelization, we need to distribute particles to MPI processes. ORB (Orthogonal Recursive Bisection) has been used on many parallel implementation of tree algorithms, but we used "Multisection" algorithm, in which the division of the domain in one dimension is not limited to bisection but any positive integer. This algorithm has the advantage that it can utilize non-powers-of-two processors.

The following gives the overview of the steps of the parallel tree algorithm on accelerator-based systems:

1. Perform the domain decomposition.
2. Exchange particles between processes so that particles belong to appropriate processes
3. Construct the local tree structure on each process.
4. Exchange the information of the tree structure necessary to construct a "global tree" on each process (so called local essential tree).
5. Construct the "global" tree from the collected information.
6. For each group of particles, construct the interaction list and perform the force calculation.
7. Integrate the orbits of particles.
8. Go back to step 1.

Note that the construction of the interaction list and the force calculation can be overlapped on accelerator-based systems. Thus, if the general-purpose CPU side is not too slow, this algorithm works extremely well, and can achieve very high efficiency.

However, in the case of TaihuLight, MPE is too slow, and the construction of the interaction list cannot be hidden. Moreover, relatively inexpensive calculations such as the construction of the tree also become a large performance bottleneck. Thus, we need new methods to reduce the calculation cost on the side of MPE.

On NVIDIA Tesla systems, Bédorf et al. [3] solved this problem by moving all calculations to the GPU side. However, in the case of the TaihuLight system, we estimated that because of the very limited main memory bandwidth, just moving all calculations to CPEs is still not enough. The expected performance was below 10%.

In the next section, we describe the new algorithms we implemented to achieve good performance on TaihuLight.

4   New Algorithms

In this section, we describe algorithms we modified for simulating a self-gravitating planetary ring on TaihuLight. What we have implemented are:

1. The re-use of the interaction list over multiple timesteps to reduce the cost of both tree construction and tree traversal
2. The construction of the tree in cylindrical coordinates to optimize domain geometry
3. Coordinate rotation to reduce the migration of particles between processors
4. Eliminate the global all-to-all communication for the local essential tree exchange

5. "semi-dynamic" load balance between CPEs
6. manual tuning of the interaction kernel

In the following, we briefly describe these new methods.

4.1   The Re-use of the Interaction List

In the simulation of rings around planets, the timestep is chosen to be small enough to resolve physical collisions between particles, and thus relative positions of particles do not change so much in one timestep. This is quite different from other gravitational many-body simulations such as cosmological simulations, in which single particle can move a distance comparable to the typical interparticle distance. Thus, for ring simulations, it is possible to use the same interaction list for a number of timesteps. This is essentially the same as the "bookkeeping" method used in molecular dynamics simulations, but we construct not just the list of particles but the list of particles and tree nodes.

One issue when reusing the same interaction list over multiple timesteps is that the calculated force can be inaccurate. This can happen when the distance between a tree node in an interaction list and a particle in the group of particles corresponding to the list becomes smaller than the distances at which physical collision occurs or the center-of-mass approximation breaks down for a given opening criterion of the tree θ while reusing the list.

We avoid this problem by constructing an interaction list so that it stores all the particles whose distances from any of the particles in the group are smaller than a pre-specified search radius as particles, not as tree nodes. By taking a sufficiently large search radius, we can calculate all the interactions correctly during the reuse steps. An appropriate value of it depends on the dynamical properties of a physical system simulated as well as the number of the reuse steps. In this study, we determine it by performing simulations repeatedly.

This functionality is now provided as an optional feature in our FDPS distribution.

4.2   Tree and Domain Structures on Cylindrical Coordinate

One problem with handling a narrow ring with a general-purpose domain decomposition algorithm is that the shape of some of the domains can become highly irregular, resulting in an increase in communication between processes. Figure 1 shows an example. We can see the domains near the y axis are very elongated.

The reason why the shapes of domains become irregular is that we are trying to fit a circle to squares and rectangles. A natural way to apply domain decomposition is to use polar coordinates and apply divisions in radial and angular directions.

Conceptually the simplest approach is thus to use polar coordinate (cylindrical in this case) for positions and velocities of particles, and also for coordinates for constructing the tree structure. Since the ring is narrow, the local distance s

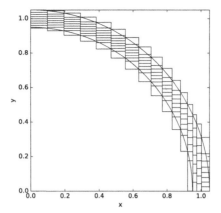

Fig. 1. Schematic figure of domain decomposition by the multisection method in x-y coordinate. Domains are divided by 16×8.

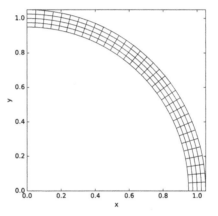

Fig. 2. Schematic figure of domain decomposition by the multisection method in cylindrical coordinate. Domains are divided by 4×32.

in the Cartesian coordinate (x, y, z) can be approximated by that in cylindrical coordinate (r, ϕ, z).

$$ds^2 = dx^2 + dy^2 + dz^2 \sim d\phi^2 + dr^2 + dz^2, \tag{1}$$

when $r \sim 1$. This means that, for domain decomposition and tree construction and even for tree traversal, we can just use polar coordinates, without any modification of the algorithm or program itself. The interaction calculation is faster in Cartesian coordinates and thus Cartesian coordinates should be used.

Figure 2 shows the domain decomposition in cylindrical coordinates. We can see that all the domains have similar, near-square shapes.

4.3   Coordinate Rotation

In any parallel tree algorithm, domain decomposition is done in fixed coordinates, while particles move around. If the distribution of particles is not changing rapidly, even if particles move, the domain structure does not change much.

Usually, the fraction of particle that move from one domain to another is relatively small, and the cost of this part is not dominant, since LET exchange is more costly. However, when we use an extremely large number of processes, and when the simulated system is a narrow ring, at one timestep many (or all) particles can move from one domain to another. Consider the case of using 100k processes for a ring with the aspect ratio of 1:1000. We use a process grid of $10 \times 10,000$. Thus, if the timestep per one Kepler period is smaller than 10,000, all particles in each domain moves to other domain in every timestep, resulting in very high communication cost.

An obvious solution for this problem is to let the coordinates and domain structure rotate, so that particles do not move much. If we rotate the coordinates at the speed of Kepler rotation at the center of the ring, particles at the center of the ring do not move much. Particles at other radial positions do move, but at speed much smaller than that of the Kepler rotation. Thus, communication due to Kepler rotation can be almost eliminated.

Note that we need to (and can) apply this coordinate rotation only at the steps in which the tree is reconstructed. Thus, the additional calculation cost is negligible.

4.4   Elimination of All-to-All Communication

In FDPS, the exchange of LET (local essential tree) data is done as follows. All processes have the information of the domain geometry of all other processes, and thus can determine what information should be sent. Thus, each process first constructs the necessary data for all other processes, and then all processes send and receive information through a single call to the MPI_Alltoallv function.

This implementation works fine even for 10k or more processes, but becomes problematic on large systems like TaihuLight. Even when the implementation of MPI_Alltoallv is ideal, each process receives at least one particle (the center of mass of all particles in one process) from each other process. Thus the total amount of LET data proportional to the number of processes, and thus for a large enough number of processes this part dominates.

Conceptually, we can eliminate this global communication, by constructing the "tree of domains" locally and let only higher-level information be sent to distant processes.

In the current implementation specialized to narrow rings, we implemented a very simple two-level tree, in which the second-level tree nodes have all processes in the radial direction. For example, if we have a process grid of (1000, 10), where 1000 in angular and 10 in radial direction, 10 domains in the radial direction are combined to one tree node, resulting in 1000 second-level nodes. Only these 1000 nodes exchange their center-of-mass information. All LET information other than these center-of-mass data of second-level nodes are sent either to other second-level nodes (and then broadcast to lower-level nodes) or sent directly to lower-level nodes.

In this implementation, there is still one global communication in the angular direction, but we can use MPI_Allgather since only the top-level data are sent. Thus the reduction in the communication is quite significant.

4.5   Load Balance Between CPEs

In the force calculation part, in our current implementation, each CPE handles one interaction list at a time. MPE first prepares a large number of interaction lists, and then CPEs process them one-by-one. Since both the length of the interaction list and the number of particles which share one interaction list varies by a fairly large factor, if CPEs process the interaction lists in a fixed order, a large load imbalance appears. In order to achieve a better load balance between CPEs, we applied the following simple algorithm.

1. Sort the interaction lists by their length.
2. Assign the longest 64 lists on 64 CPEs.
3. For each remaining list, assign it to the the CPE with the shortest total calculation cost.

Since the calculation time of a CPE is quite predictable, this algorithm works very well.

We could further improve the load balance by multiple CPEs handle one interaction list, either by dividing the list or the particles which share the list.

4.6   Interaction Kernel

On CPEs, we found the compiler-generated code for the interaction kernel, even when SIMD operations are used, does not give very good performance. We rewrite the interaction kernel fully in assembly language, with hand-unroll and careful manual scheduling. As a result, we achieved more than 50% of the theoretical peak performance for the kernel.

5   Measured Performance

We have measured the performance of our code on TaihuLight with up to 4096 nodes (16384 MPI processes). In this section we present the results.

5.1   Initial Condition

The ring has central radius of unity in our simulation units and its width is 0.01. These corresponds to 10^5 km and 10^3 km, when we regard this ring as Saturn's A ring. In the weak-scaling test, the number of particles per process is 1M, and in the strong-scaling test the total number of particles is 2G. The mass m and radius r of particles are given by:

$$r \sim 3.1 \times 10^{-5} \left(2G/N\right)^{1/2}, \tag{2}$$

$$m \sim 8.5 \times 10^{-14} \left(2G/N\right)^{3/2}, \tag{3}$$

where N is the total number of particles. The mass of Saturn and gravitational constant are both unity. Thus, the orbital period of ring particles is 2π.

5.2 Interaction Model

Ring particles interact through mutual gravity and physical inelastic collisions. We model inelastic collisions by soft spheres with spring and dashpot. Equation 4 gives the definition of the particle-particle interaction.

$$\boldsymbol{F}_{ij} = \begin{cases} G\frac{m_i m_j}{r_{ij}^3}\boldsymbol{r}_{ij} & (r_{ij} > r_{\text{coll}}) \\ \left[G\frac{m_i m_j}{r_{\text{coll}}^3} + \frac{m_j}{m_i+m_j}\left(\kappa\frac{r_{ij}-r_{\text{coll}}}{r_{ij}} + \eta\frac{\boldsymbol{r}_{ij}\cdot\boldsymbol{v}_{ij}}{r_{ij}^2}\right)\right]\boldsymbol{r}_{ij} & (r_{ij} \le r_{\text{coll}}) \end{cases}, \tag{4}$$

with $\boldsymbol{r}_{ij} = \boldsymbol{r}_j - \boldsymbol{r}_i$, $\boldsymbol{v}_{ij} = \boldsymbol{v}_j - \boldsymbol{v}_i$, $r_{ij} = \|\boldsymbol{r}_{ij}\|$. Here, $\boldsymbol{F}_{ij}$ is the acceleration of particle i due to particle j, $\boldsymbol{r}_{ij}$ and $\boldsymbol{v}_{ij}$ are the relative position and velocity vectors, G is the gravitational constant (taken to be unity in this paper), m_i is the mass of particle i, r_{coll} is the distance at which two particles collide, and η and κ are parameters which determine the coefficient of restitution. We chose these parameters so that the coefficient of restitution in the radial direction is 0.5, which is close to the experimental values (e.g. Hatzes et al. [5]).

Particle-particle interaction consists of 9 multiplications, 8 additions, and one square root and one division operation. The instruction set of Sunway 26010 processor does not include fast approximation for either square root or reciprocal square root. So we implemented fast initial guess and high-order convergence iteration in software. The number of operations in this part is 7 multiplications, 5 additions and two integer operations. Therefore, for particle-cell interactions the number of floating-point operations is 31, and for particle-particle interactions, which include the repulsive force during physical collisions, is 47. The total number of floating-point operations is obtained by counting the number of interactions calculated and multiplying them with these number of floating-point operations per interaction. We ignore all operations other than the interaction calculation, since as far as the number of floating-point operations is concerned, the operation count for interaction calculation is more than 99% of the total operation count.

5.3 Performance

We used the opening criterion of the tree θ of 0.5. The leap frog integrator with a timestep of $1/128$ is used. We use the same interaction list for 64 steps.

To measure the performance, we measure the time for 64 timesteps, including the time for diagnostics. The execution time is measured by the MPI wallclock timer, and the operation count is from the counted number of interactions calculated.

Figures 3 and 4 show the speed in Tflops for weak- and strong-scaling runs. Weak-scaling result is almost ideal. Our code runs at around 35% of the theoretical peak performance of TaihuLight.

Figures 5 and 6 show the breakdown of the time per timestep. We can see that even for 16K processes the time for communication is less than 10% of the total time.

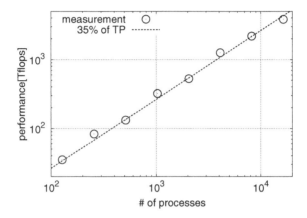

Fig. 3. Performance in Tflops for weak-scaling test. The number of particles per process is 1M. Solid line indicates 35% of the theoretical peak performance of TaihuLight. Open circles indicate measured performance.

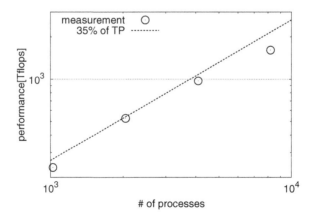

Fig. 4. Performance in teraflops for strong-scaling test. The number of particles per process is 2048M. Solid line indicates 35% of the theoretical peak performance of TaihuLight. Open circles indicate measured performance.

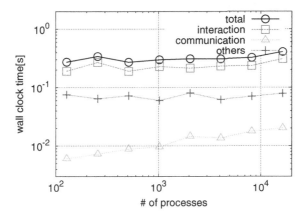

Fig. 5. Time per timestep for weak-scaling test.

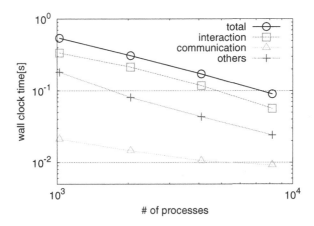

Fig. 6. Time per timestep for strong-scaling test.

Table 1 shows the detailed breakdown of the calculation time for the case of a weak-scaling run with 8192 processes. The terms for which the speedup factor is 64 are performed only once per 64 steps. We can see that the dominant terms apart from the interaction calculation are "Local Tree update", "Global Tree construction", "Global Tree update" and "Interaction list construction". The two "update" terms come from the update of physical quantities of tree nodes, and the two "construction" terms comes essentially from data copying. All are of $O(N)$ calculation cost. Due to the rather limited main memory bandwidth of TaihuLight, it is difficult to further reduce these terms, and therefore we believe our implementation is close to optimal.

Table 1. Break down

Operation	First step	64 averaged	Speedup
Exchange particles	0.308	0.00481	64.0
Local tree construction	0.0568	0.000888	64.0
Local tree update	0.0195	0.0130	1.5
LET construction	0.00416	6.50×10^{-5}	64.0
LET communication	0.0238	0.0128	1.86
Global tree construction	0.178	0.0141	12.6
Global tree update	0.0273	0.0165	1.65
Interaction list construction	0.657	0.0103	64.0
Interaction calculation	0.285	0.235	1.21
Others	0.150	0.0156	9.62
Total	1.71	0.323	5.29

6   Summary and Discussion

In this paper, we report on the implementation and performance of the large-scale realistic simulation of planetary rings on TaihuLight. We need to apply a number of changes to the basic algorithms, but except for the manual rewrite of the interaction kernel in assembly language, all modification of the algorithm is not specific to the architecture or characteristics of TaihuLight and can be used on any other machine. The achieved performance is quite satisfactory, more than 1/3 of the theoretical peak performance or more than 60% of the hand-tuned performance of the kernel itself.

Some of the algorithm developed for this calculation are now available in our standard distribution of FDPS.

References

1. Ballouz, R.-L., Richardson, D.C., Morishima, R.: Numerical simulations of Saturn's B ring: granular friction as a mediator between self-gravity wakes and viscous overstability. Astron. J. **153**, 146 (2017)
2. Barnes, J.E.: A modified tree code: don't laugh it runs. J. Comput. Phys. **87**, 161–170 (1990)
3. Bédorf, J., Gaburov, E., Fujii, M.S., Nitadori, K., Ishiyama, T., Zwart, S.P.: 24.77 Pflops on a gravitational tree-code to simulate the milky way galaxy with 18600 GPUs. In: Proceedings of the International Conference for High Performance Computing, Networking, Storage and Analysis, pp. 54–65, November 2014
4. Hamada, T., Narumi, T., Yokota, R., Yasuoka, K., Nitadori, K., Taiji, M.: 42 TFlops hierarchical N-body simulations on GPUs with applications in both astrophysics and turbulence (2009)
5. Hatzes, A.P., Bridges, F.G., Lin, D.N.C.: Collisional properties of ice spheres at low impact velocities. Mon. Not. R. Astron. Soc. **231**, 1091–1115 (1988)

6. Iwasawa, M., Tanikawa, A., Hosono, N., Nitadori, K., Muranushi, T., Makino, J.: Implementation and performance of FDPS: a framework for developing parallel particle simulation codes. Publ. Astron. Soc. Jpn. **68**, 54 (2016)
7. Makino, J.: Treecode with a special-purpose processor. Publ. Astron. Soc. Jpn. **43**, 621–638 (1991)
8. Makino, J.: A fast parallel treecode with GRAPE. Publ. Astron. Soc. Jpn. **56**, 521–531 (2004)
9. Michikoshi, S., Kokubo, E.: Simulating the smallest ring world of Chariklo. Astrophys. J. Lett. **837**, L13 (2017)
10. Rein, H., Latter, H.N.: Large-scale N-body simulations of the viscous overstability in Saturn's rings. Mon. Not. R. Astron. Soc. **431**, 145–158 (2013)
11. Rein, H., Liu, S.-F.: REBOUND: an open-source multi-purpose N-body code for collisional dynamics. Astron. Astrophys. **537**, A128 (2012)
12. Stadel, J.G.: Cosmological N-body simulations and their analysis. Ph.D. thesis, University of Washington (2001)
13. Wisdom, J., Tremaine, S.: Local simulations of planetary rings. Astron. J. **95**, 925–940 (1988)
14. Zebker, H.A., Marouf, E.A., Tyler, G.L.: Saturn's rings - particle size distributions for thin layer model. Icarus **64**, 531–548 (1985)

Parallel Performance Analysis of Bacterial Biofilm Simulation Models

M. V. Sheraton[1,2] and Peter M. A. Sloot[2,3,4(✉)]

[1] Interdisciplinary Graduate School,
HealthTech NTU, Nanyang Technological University, Singapore, Singapore
[2] Complexity Institute, Nanyang Technological University,
50 Nanyang Avenue, Singapore 639798, Singapore
p.m.a.sloot@uva.nl
[3] Institute for Advanced Studies, University of Amsterdam,
Amsterdam, Netherlands
[4] National Research University ITMO, St. Petersburg, Russia

Abstract. Modelling and simulation of bacterial biofilms is a computationally expensive process necessitating use of parallel computing. Fluid dynamics and advection-consumption models can be decoupled and solved to handle the fluid-solute-bacterial interactions. Data exchange between the two processes add up to the communication overheads. The heterogenous distribution of bacteria within the simulation domain further leads to non-uniform load distribution in the parallel system. We study the effect of load imbalance and communication overheads on the overall performance of simulation at different stages of biofilm growth. We develop a model to optimize the parallelization procedure for computing the growth dynamics of bacterial biofilms.

Keywords: Load imbalance · Communication overhead · Biofilm

1 Introduction

Computational models involving grid based or lattice-based systems are solved in parallel to reduce the overall computation time. In cases of uneven spatial distribution of grids or non-homogenous presence of model objects such as cells, catalysts or solid structures in the domain, the allocation of computational load to the processors may not be uniform. Such discrepancies will result in decrease of parallel computing efficiency. In multiphysics systems comprising of fluid flow, solute diffusion, reaction (or consumption) and cell growth, multiple methods of solving the models need to be implemented. For instance, Finite Element based Method (FEM) [1] or Lattice Boltzmann Method (LBM) [2] can be used to solve fluid dynamic equations, FEM or Finite Volume Method (FVM) [3] to solve the Fick's Equation of diffusion and solute consumption and Agent Based Method (ABM) [4] to handle the cell behavior. When combining these methods, there always exists a communication channel between them. This contributes to communication overhead in parallel computations. In addition, there will be fractional communication overhead [5] within a method resulting from memory access (gathering and scattering) between each processor. Therefore, it is

© Springer International Publishing AG, part of Springer Nature 2018
Y. Shi et al. (Eds.): ICCS 2018, LNCS 10860, pp. 496–505, 2018.
https://doi.org/10.1007/978-3-319-93698-7_38

necessary to estimate the communication overhead between the methods, fractional overhead, and the parallel execution durations to optimize the parallel computation process.

In nature, bacteria exhibit two modes of growth, planktonic and biofilm. During their planktonic form of growth, bacteria exist as individual cells that float around in a fluid medium. Due to their direct exposure to ambient environmental conditions, planktonic bacteria are susceptible to antibiotics, bacteriophages, and other chemicals. In contrast, during the biofilm mode of growth, the bacteria adhere to a solid surface and to other bacteria near them, forming a large colony of bacteria confined within a structure known as biofilm. By shielding the bacteria from harsh environmental conditions, biofilms protect them from detrimental external factors and act as a platform for developing antibiotic drug resistance. Therefore, to tackle the health hazards and environmental issues arising from detrimental bacterial biofilms it is necessary to understand the dynamics of biofilm formation. Bacterial biofilm modelling has become an important tool in analyzing and predicting the quorum sensing [6] within the bacterial community, detachment of biofilms [7, 8], and phage-bacteria interactions [9]. Bacterial biofilms are complex systems that require multiphysics based models to effectively describe their evolution process. In most studies [10–12], proliferation of bacteria is modelled by considering the diffusion of essential nutrients such as oxygen or glucose around them. The individual bacterial cells are commonly represented as 'point sinks' or reaction zones within the diffusion domain. Thus, bacteria consume diffusing nutrients and proliferate based on the rate of consumption governed by Monod kinetics [13], Tessier kinetics [14] or other rate equations. The diffusion process is usually solved using grid-based methods, which can also be parallelized. Bacterial distribution on the grids is non-homogenous and localized to regions where biofilms are present. This leads to variable load allocation on the processors, with maximum load on the processor solving the grid points comprising most bacteria. In addition, bacterial biofilms in experiments are grown in flow cells [15], which have fluid flowing within the chambers growing biofilm. Here, computational fluid dynamics (CFD) needs to be implemented to model the effect of fluid on the mass transfer of nutrients. Such complex model system with CFD and solute mass transfer necessitates parallelization and optimization of the solving process. However, there are only a few studies that address the concerns of parallel computation of biological models [16, 17]. These studies are restricted to analysis of parallel efficiency in a single method (either CFD or solute mass transfer) and ignore the communication overhead arising from coupling multiple methods.

We develop a model to analyze and optimize parallel computations in biofilm growth simulations. In the model, we extend the load balancing model proposed by Alowayyed et al. [16] to include the communication overhead between the methods. The effects of domain size, bacterial cell distribution and mesh element size on the parallelization efficiency are analyzed. Also, we develop a simplified function based on the above parameters to obtain the optimal number of processors required to simulate different stages of biofilm growth.

2 Methodology

2.1 Computational Methods

We have two processes involved in the biofilm model, (m1) fluid dynamics simulation and (m2) solute simulation. To model the fluid dynamics of the growth medium in the simulation domain, we solve the incompressible Navier-Stokes (NS) equation and continuity equation listed in Eqs. 1 and 2 respectively. In Eq. 1 u is the velocity vector, p is the fluid pressure, v is the kinematic viscosity and g is the external force (gravity) acting on the fluid. In cases of biofilm growth, the knowledge of steady-state nutrient concentration is required to model the cell proliferation. There are two ways to predict the steady state velocity profiles, solve the NS and continuity equations assuming no change of velocity with time, i.e., $\frac{\partial u}{\partial t} = 0$, or solve the equations taking small time steps 'dt' until the spatial velocity values converge. In our study, for numerical stability and accuracy we use the latter method of solving the transient state flow to arrive at steady state velocity. For simulating the flow, we use FENICS [18, 19], an open source finite element based partial differential equation solver. NS and continuity equations in FENICS were implemented using Incremental Pressure Correction Scheme (IPCS) [20]. The meshing for the fluid flow domain was done using GMSH [21]. GMSH is an open source mesh generation tool. We generate adaptive meshes to simulate the flow, that is, the mesh elements get finer as they approach the surface of biofilm.

$$\frac{\partial u}{\partial t} = v\nabla^2 u - \nabla \mathbf{p} + g \tag{1}$$

$$\nabla . u = 0 \tag{2}$$

The second simulation (m2) is the solute convection-diffusion-consumption (CDC) simulation, modelled using Eqs. 3 and 4. The solute concentration evolution is defined by Eq. 3 where, C is the concentration of glucose, D is the diffusivity of glucose, r is the rate of consumption of glucose by the cells. The steady state velocity for estimating the convection-diffusion is obtained from the FENICS solution. This solution is coupled with the Finite Volume (FV) mesh generated in FiPy [22]. FiPy is a partial differential solver based on (FV). To solve the equations in parallel we use the solver module, PyTrilinos, a python wrapper for open source Trilinos modules [23].

$$\frac{\partial C}{\partial t} = D\nabla^2 C - u.\nabla C - r \tag{3}$$

$$r = \left(\frac{\mu_m}{Y} + m\right) B \frac{C}{K + C} \tag{4}$$

2.2 Modelling Set-Up and Assumptions

The bacteria in the biofilm are modelled to occupy a set of connected grid points with the simulation domain. In this study, we analyze three different biofilm settings, (i) The initial adhesion stage where only a few cells are present, (ii) Intermediate growth stage with a hemispherical structure and (iii) A final mushroom shaped structure as shown in Fig. 1. For the boundary conditions in FENICS, we assume a constant velocity inlet, atmospheric pressure boundary condition at the outlet and no slip boundary conditions near the bacterial cells in the domain as mentioned in Eqs. 5, 6 and 7 respectively. The mesh is refined near the bacterial cells to improve numerical accuracy. All the simulations are carried out for a Reynold's number, Re, of 100. A fixed number of iterations is carried out such that the solution converges to a steady state.

$$u = u_o, \text{at } x = 0 \tag{5}$$

$$p = 0, \text{at } x = nx \tag{6}$$

$$u = 0, \text{along biofilm surface} \tag{7}$$

(a)   (b)   (c)

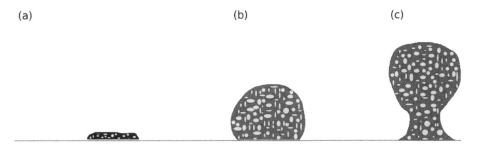

Fig. 1. Schematic of various stages of bacterial biofilm growth, (a) Stage 1: The initial adhesion stage, (b) Stage 2: Intermediate growth stage and (c) Stage 3: Mature mushroom shaped biofilm structure. Yellow color indicates the bacterial cells and dark green color indicates the extracellular polymeric substances (Color figure online).

We model growth dynamics of the bacteria using single substrate Monod kinetics given by Eq. 4 Here, μ_m, is the maximum specific growth rate, Y is the mass yield coefficient, m is the metabolic maintenance coefficient, B is the biomass present at the grid and K is the saturation coefficient. Multiple studies involving the bacteria, *Pseudomonas aeruginosa*, have used Monod kinetics due to its simplicity and the availability of literature data [11, 24]. Here, Glucose (C) is assumed to be the critical nutrient for the bacterial growth and survival. The convection-diffusion-consumption is solved for steady state by assuming $\frac{\partial C}{\partial t} = 0$. A fixed concentration inlet 'G_{ini}' is used at the inlet boundary, x = 0 and at all other boundaries no-flux boundary condition is used. We use a fixed number of iterations, large enough to let the solutions converge. The values used in the simulation are listed in Table 1.

To estimate the parallel performance, we adapt the models developed by Axner et al. [25] and Fox [5]. We use Eq. 8 to estimate the time taken to complete the computation through parallel execution, T_{mi}, from number of processors (P), the time

Table 1. Parameter values used in the biofilm simulations. (g_b is the quantity of biomass, expressed in grams)

Parameter	Value
Length of domain [11]	750×10^{-6} m
Height of domain [11]	450×10^{-6} m
Number of grids in FiPy simulation	1250×750
Initial glucose concentration, G^{ini} [11]	3 g m^{-3}
Initial mass of bacteria, B_C [11]	1.315×10^{-13} g_b
Half-saturation coefficient, K_s [11]	2.55 g m^{-3}
Diffusion coefficient, D$_s$	2.52×10^{-6} m^{2}h^{-1}
Specific growth rate, μ_m [11]	0.3125 h^{-1}
Mass yield coefficient, Y [11]	0.45 $g_B g^{-1}$
Metabolic maintenance coefficient, m [11]	0.036 g g_b^{-1}h^{-1}
Reynold's Number, Re	100

for sequential computation ($T_{i,s}$), and the overheads arising within the individual process ($T_{overheads}$). The term $T_{overheads}$ does not include the communication overhead between the processes m1 and m2. We introduce an additive term T_{comm} which considers the overhead from communication between the two processes m1 and m2. Thus, Eq. 8 is now modified as Eq. 9 which estimates the total time 'T' taken for the computation of both the processes, where the i in T_{mi} indicates the process number.

$$T_{mi} = \frac{T_{i,s}}{P} + T_{overheads} \tag{8}$$

$$T = T_{comm} + \sum_{1,2} T_{mi} \tag{9}$$

Now we estimate the fractional load imbalance on each processor using the model developed by Alowayyed et al. [16]. Consider $t_{j,i}$ the time taken by processor j working on process i to complete the computation. When the load is distributed properly, that is when the domain decomposition and cell data allocation to processors is done evenly, we have $t_{1,i} = t_{2,i} = t_{3,i} = ... = t_{P,i}$. However, due to heterogenous cell distribution in the domain and differences in spatial grid smoothness such a scenario is not possible. Thus, the fractional load imbalance $f_{l,i}$ is calculated depending on the average execution time, $< t_i >$ and maximum processor execution time t_i^m using Eq. 10. The speed up and parallel efficiency are quantified using Eqs. 11 and 12 respectively.

$$f_{l,i} = \left(\frac{\left(t_i^m - \left(\frac{T_{i,s}}{P} \right) \right)}{\frac{T_{i,s}}{P}} \right) = \frac{t_i^m}{< t_i >} - 1 \tag{10}$$

$$S_p = \frac{T_{i,s}}{T_p} \tag{11}$$

$$E_p = \frac{S_p}{P} \tag{12}$$

3   Results and Discussion

Initially, we fix the domain size, the mesh smoothness and run the simulations on a single processor (sequentially) to analyze the velocity patterns and concentration contours developed in the domain containing a mature biofilm structure shown in Fig. 1c. As shown in Fig. 2, the simulations can predict the changes in velocity and glucose concentration in the vicinity of the cells.

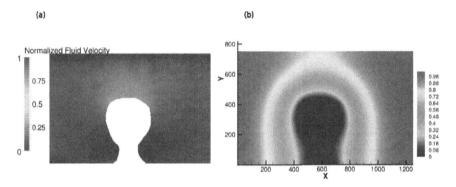

Fig. 2. Simulations on mature biofilm structure, (a) fluid dynamics simulation result showing the normalized velocity within the domain and (b) CDC simulations showing the normalized glucose concentration distribution in the domain.

All the simulations in the study were carried out on 3.20 GHz Intel® Core™ i7-6900 K CPU running Ubuntu Linux 14.04. The parameters shown in Table 1 were used for all the simulations, hence, the effects of change in domain size or change in fluid flow characteristics were not analyzed in the study. The total time taken for the simulations to converge to steady state were 845 s and 145 s for the fluid dynamics and CDC simulations respectively. There will be a communication overhead between the processes even when running sequentially, as indicated by the additive term in Eq. 9. In the next step, we simulated the fluid flow and nutrient diffusion patterns for the various stages of biofilm developments shown in Fig. 1. We restrict ourselves to these three stages of growth since after stage 3, due to nutrient depletion, there is a possibility of bacterial dispersion from the biofilm. In this study, parallel performance analysis during the biofilm dispersion process is not included due to the possibility of multiple structural configurations during the dispersion process. We varied the number of processors P from 1 to 16. The results of the simulations are shown in Fig. 3. We observed a plateauing of the computation time as the number of processors increased. This is due to the increase in overhead between the individual processors with increase in parallelization. Also, an interesting observation is that the stage 2 biofilms required longer processing time than stage 3 due to the larger number of mesh elements required to simulate stage 2 as shown in Fig. 3c. The effect arises solely from the quantity of the mesh elements and not from the quality of the elements, since all the meshes had the same minimal element radius of 0.18. The increase in number of mesh elements could be due to the meshing algorithm being dependent on the geometry of the biofilm area. However, the communication time between the processes did not follow an established trend. Since there is always a load imbalance when using parallel processors as shown in Fig. 4a, the heterogenous distribution of mesh elements would result in variable response duration for each processor to the communication signal, thereby causing inefficient inter-process communication. This inefficient communication is evident in the mesh-dense stage 2 biofilm simulations, where the mesh decomposition is much more heterogeneous.

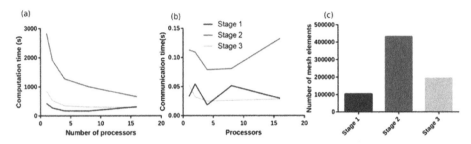

Fig. 3. Parallel performance at different stages of biofilm growth (a) change in computational time with increase in parallel processors, (b) change in communication time between processes m1 and m2 with increase in parallel processors and (c) number of mesh elements (*Ne*) used in the fluid dynamics simulation.

The estimated fractional load imbalance from the simulations is shown in Fig. 4(a). In general, the load imbalance increased with increasing number of processors, and followed a sigmoidal curve pattern indicating the asymptotic nature of the load imbalance. The asymptotic behavior can be explained from the fact that, as the number of processors increase, the heterogeneity between the meshes allotted to the individual process decreases, resulting in an equilibrium value for fractional load imbalance. Figure 4(b) shows a decrease in efficiency of parallel computation at higher processor counts. This trend is expected since there is always an efficiency loss from intra-communication overheads between the processors. We also infer that, efficiency is a function of mesh elements and number of parallel processors. The geometry of the stage 2 biofilm necessitates use of large number of mesh elements to have a refined mesh boundary. Therefore, stage 2 biofilm with large number of mesh elements operates at a higher efficiency with large number of processors (>8) and underperforms with lesser number of processors than its counterparts. Although the fractional load imbalance for stage 1 biofilms is significantly higher than stage 2 and 3 biofilms using 4 processors, the efficiency for stage 1 biofilms is marginally higher than stage 2 and 3 biofilms due to the presence of fewer meshing elements and homogenous element

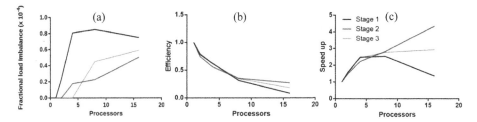

Fig. 4. Parallel efficiency test results, (a) estimate of fractional load imbalance on the processors, (b) change in parallel processing efficiency with increase in parallel processors and (c) Speed up resulting from change in number of processors.

distribution. Thus, the average number of mesh elements per processor (N_p) determines rate of decrease in parallel efficiency. We could therefore write a simplified function,

$$E_p = E_p(P, N_e, N_P) \tag{13}$$

Increase in N_p while using large number of processors will therefore result in increased processor efficiency. Practically, this could be done by refining the fluid dynamics mesh. However, the mesh refinement should be optimized such that the trade-off between parallel efficiency and total computation time 'T' stays optimal. A similar trend is observed with the speed up values since it is indirectly proportional to the parallel computation time as shown in Eq. 12.

4   Conclusion

We modeled the parallel computation efficiency at different stages of a multi-physics implementation of biofilm growth. It was found that high parallelization, at initial stages of biofilm growth simulations is not needed, since the computational efficiency from parallelization is offset by the intra-process overheads. The intermediate stage requires more parallel processors to decrease the overall computation time. This is due to the presence of large number of mesh elements at this stage. Therefore, as a rule of thumb, the number of processors needed to optimize the speed of execution of the entire biofilm growth simulation is, $(N_p)_{stage1} < (N_p)_{stage2} > (N_p)_{stage3}$. We have developed a simplified function (E_P) dependent on the number of processors, total number of mesh elements and the mesh elements per processor for optimizing the parallel efficiency in simulating bacterial biofilm growth.

Acknowledgment. P.S. acknowledges the Russian Science Foundation for support under RSCF #14-21-00137.

References

1. Dhatt, G., Lefrançois, E., Touzot, G.: Finite Element Method. Wiley, Hoboken (2012)
2. Chen, S., Doolen, G.D.: Lattice Boltzmann method for fluid flows. Ann. Rev. Fluid Mech. **30**, 329–364 (1998)
3. Versteeg, H.K., Malalasekera, W.: An Introduction to Computational Fluid Dynamics: The Finite Method. Pearson Education, New York City (2007)
4. Zhang, L., Wang, Z., Sagotsky, J.A., Deisboeck, T.S.: Multiscale agent-based cancer modeling. J. Math. Biol. **58**, 545–559 (2009)
5. Fox, G.C., Johnson, M.A., Lyzenga, G.A., Otto, S.W., Salmon, J.K., Walker, D.W.: Solving Problems on Concurrent Processors: General Techniques and Regular Problems, vol. 1. Prentice-Hall, Inc., Upper Saddle River (1988)
6. Fozard, J.A., Lees, M., King, J.R., Logan, B.S.: Inhibition of quorum sensing in a computational biofilm simulation. Biosystems **109**, 105–114 (2012)
7. Morgenroth, E., Wilderer, P.A.: Influence of detachment mechanisms on competition in biofilms. Water Res. **34**, 417–426 (2000)
8. Picioreanu, C., Van Loosdrecht, M.C., Heijnen, J.J.: Two-dimensional model of biofilm detachment caused by internal stress from liquid flow. Biotech. Bioeng. **72**, 205–218 (2001)
9. Weitz, J.S., Hartman, H., Levin, S.A.: Coevolutionary arms races between bacteria and bacteriophage. Proc. Natl. Acad. Sci. U.S.A. **102**, 9535–9540 (2005)
10. Picioreanu, C., Vrouwenvelder, J., Van Loosdrecht, M.: Three-dimensional modeling of biofouling and fluid dynamics in feed spacer channels of membrane devices. J. Membr. Sci. **345**, 340–354 (2009)
11. Fagerlind, M.G., Webb, J.S., Barraud, N., McDougald, D., Jansson, A., Nilsson, P., Harlén, M., Kjelleberg, S., Rice, S.A.: Dynamic modelling of cell death during biofilm development. J. Theor. Biol. **295**, 23–36 (2012)
12. Popławski, N.J., Shirinifard, A., Swat, M., Glazier, J.A.: Simulation of single-species bacterial-biofilm growth using the Glazier-Graner-Hogeweg model and the CompuCell 3D modeling environment. Math. Biosci. Eng.: MBE **5**, 355 (2008)
13. Han, K., Levenspiel, O.: Extended monod kinetics for substrate, product, and cell inhibition. Biotech. Bioeng. **32**, 430–447 (1988)
14. Beyenal, H., Chen, S.N., Lewandowski, Z.: The double substrate growth kinetics of pseudomonas aeruginosa. Enzyme Microb. Technol. **32**, 92–98 (2003)
15. Sternberg, C., Tolker-Nielsen, T.: Growing and analyzing biofilms in flow cells. Curr. Protoc. Microbiol. (1), 1B.2.1–1B.2.15 (2006)
16. Alowayyed, S., Závodszky, G., Azizi, V., Hoekstra, A.: Load balancing of parallel cell-based blood flow simulations. J. Comput. Sci. **24**, 1–7 (2018)
17. Cytowski, M., Szymanska, Z.: Large-scale parallel simulations of 3d cell colony dynamics. Comput. Sci. Eng. **16**, 86–95 (2014)
18. Logg, A., Mardal, K.-A., Wells, G.: Automated Solution of Differential Equations by The Finite Element Method: The FEniCS Book. Springer, Heidelberg (2012). https://doi.org/10.1007/978-3-642-23099-8
19. Alnæs, M., Blechta, J., Hake, J., Johansson, A., Kehlet, B., Logg, A., Richardson, C., Ring, J., Rognes, M.E., Wells, G.N.: The FEniCS project version 1.5. Arch. Numer. Softw. **3**, 9–23 (2015)
20. Guermond, J.-L., Minev, P., Shen, J.: An overview of projection methods for incompressible flows. Comput. Methods Appl. Mech. Eng. **195**, 6011–6045 (2006)
21. Geuzaine, C., Remacle, J.F.: Gmsh: A 3-D finite element mesh generator with built-in pre-and post-processing facilities. Int. Journal Numer. Methods Eng. **79**, 1309–1331 (2009)

22. Guyer, J.E., Wheeler, D., Warren, J.A.: FiPy: partial differential equations with python. Comput. Sci. Eng. **11**, 6–15 (2009)
23. Heroux, M.A., Bartlett, R.A., Howle, V.E., Hoekstra, R.J., Hu, J.J., Kolda, T.G., Lehoucq, R.B., Long, K.R., Pawlowski, R.P., Phipps, E.T.: An overview of the trilinos project. ACM Trans. Math. Softw. (TOMS) **31**, 397–423 (2005)
24. Picioreanu, C., Kreft, J.-U., Klausen, M., Haagensen, J.A.J., Tolker-Nielsen, T., Molin, S.: Microbial motility involvement in biofilm structure formation–a 3D modelling study. Water Sci. Technol. **55**, 337–343 (2007)
25. Axner, L., Bernsdorf, J., Zeiser, T., Lammers, P., Linxweiler, J., Hoekstra, A.G.: Performance evaluation of a parallel sparse lattice Boltzmann solver. J. Comput. Phys. **227**, 4895–4911 (2008)

Parallel Solutions to the k-difference Primer Problem

Leandro Feuser and Nahri Moreano$^{(\boxtimes)}$

School of Computing, Federal University of Mato Grosso do Sul,
Campo Grande, Brazil
leandrofeuser@gmail.com, nahri@facom.ufms.br

Abstract. This paper presents parallel solutions to the k-difference primer problem, targeting multicore processors and GPUs. This problem consists of finding the shortest substrings of one sequence with at least k differences from another sequence. The sequences found in the solution are candidate regions to contain primers used by biologists to amplify a DNA sequence in laboratory. To the authors' knowledge, these are the first parallel solutions proposed for the k-difference primer problem. We identified two forms, coarse- and fine-grained, of exploiting parallelism while solving the problem. Several optimizations were applied to the solutions, such as synchronization overhead reduction, tiling, and speculative prefetch, allowing the analysis of very long sequences in a reduced execution time. In an experimental performance evaluation using real DNA sequences, the best OpenMP (in a quad-core processor) and CUDA solutions produced speedups up to 5.6 and 72.8, respectively, when compared to the best sequential solution. Even when the sequences length and the number of differences k increase, the performance is not affected. The best sequential, OpenMP, and CUDA solutions achieved the throughput of 0.16, 0.94, and 11.85 billions symbol comparisons per second, respectively, emphasizing the performance gain of the CUDA solution, which reached 100% of GPU occupancy.

Keywords: Inexact matching · High performance computing
Parallelism · Multicore processor · GPU

1 Introduction

Advances in DNA sequencing technologies have been causing biological databases to grow almost exponentially. Given this huge amount of data and the long length of biological sequences, high performance solutions to sequence analysis problems have been proposed in order to allow biologists to extract useful information from these data. Approximate string comparison is an essential operation in biological sequence analysis and serves as basis for several more complex manipulations. It properly models changes that happen in DNA sequences through the evolution process, such as insertions, deletions, and substitutions of nitrogenous bases [1].

© Springer International Publishing AG, part of Springer Nature 2018
Y. Shi et al. (Eds.): ICCS 2018, LNCS 10860, pp. 506–523, 2018.
https://doi.org/10.1007/978-3-319-93698-7_39

The k-difference primer problem is one of such manipulations and consists of, given two sequences α and β and an integer k, find for each position j in α, the shortest substring of α that begins at j and has at least k differences from any substring of β [2]. For instance, assume $\alpha = ACTG$, $\beta = AGCAAG$, and $k = 2$. The substrings $\alpha_{1..3} = ACT$ and $\alpha_{2..4} = CTG$ form the solution, since they have at least two differences from any segment of β. The sequences found in the solution of the k-difference primer problem are candidate regions to contain primers [2]. Primers are short strands of DNA that bind (hybridize) to a DNA sequence and are used by biologists to amplify that sequence in laboratory, through the Polymerase Chain Reaction technique [7]. For instance, in order to identify the causative agent of a disease, it is necessary to select a primer that hybridizes to the DNA sequence of the causative agent and that does not hybridize to the DNA sequence of the infected organism or other pathogens.

This paper presents parallel solutions to the k-difference primer problem, targeting multicore processors and GPUs. The solutions are able to analyze very long sequences in a short execution time. The multicore and GPU solutions achieve speedups up to 5.6 and 72.8, respectively, when compared to the best sequential solution.

The paper is organized in six sections. Section 2 describes two sequential algorithms to the k-difference primer problem and identifies forms to exploit parallelism in it. In Sects. 3 and 4 we present our parallel solutions targeting multicore processors and GPUs, respectively. We also describe the optimizations applied to them and analyze their performance. Section 5 reviews previous works in parallel solutions to the approximate string matching problem, which is closely related to the problem studied here. Finally, Sect. 6 summarizes the results.

2 Solutions to the k-difference Primer Problem

The solution to the k-difference primer problem described in [2] is based on the resolution of several instances of the approximate string matching problem. The latter problem consists in, given two sequences and an integer k, find all occurrences of one sequence in the other with at most k differences. The differences can correspond to insertions, deletions, or substitutions of symbols in the strings. The idea is that, in order to solve the k-difference primer problem, i.e., to find the shortest substrings of α that have at least k differences from any substring of β, we can find the longest substrings of α with $k - 1$ differences from β and add one symbol to these substrings [3]. Two solutions to the approximate string matching problem, presented in [4,5], are adapted and used here as substeps, producing two solutions to the k-difference primer problem, referred as *conventional* and *alternative* solutions.

Figure 1 shows the main function of both sequential k-difference primer solutions. For each position r of sequence α of length m, we solve an instance of the approximate string matching problem, invoking a subroutine which finds the longest prefix of $\alpha_{r..m}$ with $k - 1$ differences from all substrings of sequence β, of length n, and add one symbol to the prefix found. At each iteration r, a shorter suffix of α is processed by the subroutine, which returns the length of the prefix found. If no solution is found at a certain iteration, we can stop the execution because the next iterations will not produce solutions either. The conventional and alternative solutions differ only in the algorithm used for the subroutine.

> *Initializations*
> **while** $r \leq m - k + 1$ **and not** *stop* **do**
> $\quad$ $c := $ *longest prefix with differences*$(\alpha_{r..m}, \beta, k)$
> $\quad$ **if** $c \neq 0$ **and** $r + c < m$ **then** Solution $\alpha_{r..r+c+1}$ found
> $\quad$ **else** *stop* := 1
> $\quad$ $r := r + 1$

Fig. 1. k-difference primer sequential solution, for sequences α and β: $m = |\alpha|$ and $n = |\beta|$

Figure 2(a) and (b) shows the subroutines *longest prefix with differences* used in the conventional and alternative solutions, respectively. The first subroutine computes a dynamic programming matrix D with dimensions $(m + 1) \times (n + 1)$. The rows and columns of D correspond to symbols of α and β, respectively. The cell $D[i, j]$ represents the number of differences between $\alpha_{1..i}$ and any substring of β ending at β_j. The algorithm searches the highest row i with a cell that satisfies $D[i, j] = k-1$. Using this subroutine, the conventional solution to the k-difference primer problem has time complexity $O(m^2 \times n)$. The space complexity is $O(n)$, since the same matrix D is reused in all invocations of the subroutine, which is optimized in order to reduce the amount of memory needed, by allocating only one row for D, and reusing it for all iterations of the outer loop.

Initializations
for $i := 1$ **to** m **do**
$\quad$ **for** $j := 1$ **to** n **do**
$\quad\quad$ **if** $\alpha_i \neq \beta_j$ **then**
$\quad\quad\quad$ $t := 1$
$\quad\quad$ **else**
$\quad\quad\quad$ $t := 0$
$\quad\quad$ $D[i, j] := \min \begin{cases} D[i, j-1] + 1 \\ D[i-1, j] + 1 \\ D[i-1, j-1] + t \end{cases}$
$\quad\quad$ **if** $D[i, j] = k - 1$ **then**
$\quad\quad\quad$ $c := i$
return c
$\qquad\qquad$ (a)

Initializations
for $e := 0$ **to** $k - 1$ **do**
$\quad$ **for** $d := -e$ **to** $n - 1$ **do**
$\quad\quad$ $row := \max \begin{cases} L[d-1, e-1] \\ L[d+1, e-1] + 1 \\ L[d, e-1] + 1 \end{cases}$
$\quad\quad$ $row := \min(row, m)$
$\quad\quad$ **while** $row < m$ **and** $row + d < n$
$\quad\quad\quad$ **and** $\alpha_{row+1} = \beta_{row+1+d}$ **do**
$\quad\quad\quad$ $row := row + 1$
$\quad\quad$ $L[d, e] := row$
$\quad\quad$ **if** $e = k - 1$ **and** $L[d, e] > c$ **then**
$\quad\quad\quad$ $c := L[d, e]$
return c
$\qquad\qquad$ (b)

Fig. 2. Subroutine *longest prefix with differences*, used in the (a) conventional and (b) alternative solutions, computes dynamic programming matrix D and L, respectively, in order to find the longest prefix of α with $k - 1$ differences from all substrings of β

The subroutine *longest prefix with differences* used in the alternative solution (Fig. 2(b)) computes a dynamic programming matrix L with dimensions $(n + k + 2) \times (k + 2)$. The rows and columns of L correspond to diagonals of matrix D and number of differences, respectively. A diagonal d of D is formed by cells $D[i, j]$ such that $j - i = d$. The cell $L[d, e]$ represents the highest row i of D such that $D[i, j] = e$ and $D[i, j]$ belongs to diagonal d. Then, e is the number of differences between the prefix $\alpha_{1..L[d,e]}$ and any substring of β that ends at $\beta_{L[d,e]+d}$. The algorithm searches the maximum value in column $k - 1$ of matrix L, which represents the highest row i of D with a cell that satisfies $D[i, j] = k - 1$. Using this subroutine, the alternative solution to the k-difference primer problem has time complexity $O(m^2 \times n \times k)$. The space complexity is $O(n + k)$, since the same matrix L is reused in all invocations of the subroutine, which is also optimized in order to reduce the amount of memory needed, by allocating only one column for L, and reusing it for all iterations of the outer loop.

2.1 Optimizations and Preliminary Results

We developed two optimizations that can reduce the number of cells of matrices D and L that need to be computed in the conventional and alternative solutions. In the first optimization, referred as *optimization 1* and applied only to the conventional solution, when executing the subroutine *longest prefix with differences* (Fig. 2(a)), if we find a row i of matrix D, such that $D[i, j] \geq k$, for all j, we conclude we have already found the solution and there is no point in computing the remaining cells of D. This optimization is implicit in the alternative solution, since matrix L is computed only up to column $k - 1$. The second optimization, referred as *optimization 2*, is applied only to the alternative solution. When executing the subroutine *longest prefix with differences* (Fig. 2(b)), if we find an occurrence of α in β with less than k differences, we conclude no solution will be found and we do not compute the remaining cells of L.

We evaluated the sequential solutions and the proposed optimizations on a computer with an Intel Xeon quad-core processor and 32 GB RAM, using GCC with $-O3$ optimization option. In all experiments, our biological input data set consists of DNA sequences homologous to the IL1RAPL1 gene, from *Homo sapiens* chromosome X, and obtained from the HomoloGene database, available at NCBI (National Center for Biotechnology Information) [9]. In a final experiment in Sect. 4.3, huge sequences are used.

Table 1 compares the conventional and alternative sequential solutions and the optimizations applied. The execution times correspond to the arithmetic mean of several executions, which produced a standard deviation of only 1.04. The table also shows the number of comparisons of symbols from α and β performed by each solution. The conventional non-optimized solution computes the matrix D entirely in every call to the subroutine *longest prefix with differences*, leading to approximately 230 trillions comparisons, which make its execution impracticable. Optimization 1 applied to this solution enables an almost 100-fold reduction in the number of comparisons. Despite having a higher worst-case time complexity than the conventional solution, the alternative solution produced smaller execution times, since the computation based on diagonals produces less comparisons than the conventional solution. Optimization 2 applied to the alternative solution produces a small reduction in the comparisons, since it allows us not to compute completely only the last matrix L. Therefore, it results in a slightly shorter execution time.

Table 1. Evaluation of sequential solutions and optimizations: execution time and number of comparisons of α and β symbols, for $|\alpha| = 43,606$, $|\beta| = 241,494$, and $k = 100$

Solution+optimization	Execution time (s)	# of symbol comparisons ($\times 10^{10}$)
Conventional	*	$\sim$22960
Conventional+1	12216.1	$\sim$243
Alternative	8376.7	$\sim$137
Alternative+2	8230.9	$\sim$137

*Not measured due to extremely long execution time.

2.2 Exploiting Parallelism

Although they have polynomial time complexity, both conventional and alternative solutions can be very computationally demanding, due to the long length of biological sequences. Therefore, we seek high performance solutions that compute cells of the dynamic programming matrices in parallel, in order to reduce the execution time. Analyzing the data dependences for computing these cells, we identify two forms to exploit parallelism in the k-difference primer problem.

We can execute in parallel different calls of the subroutine *longest prefix with differences* (for both conventional and alternative solutions), since the computation of each matrix is independent from the others. This way, several matrices (D or L) are computed in parallel, which we call *coarse-grained parallelism*. We can also exploit *fine-grained parallelism* by computing different cells in a same matrix (D or L) in parallel. Figure 3(a) and (b) illustrates the computation of matrices D and L, respectively, in conventional and alternative solutions. The arrows represents data dependences. We can compute in parallel all cells in a same anti-diagonal of D (or column of L), since they are independent from each other, while different anti-diagonals of D (or columns of L) are computed sequentially. Both forms of parallelism can be exploited in conjunction.

3   OpenMP Solutions to the k-difference Primer Problem

Based on the two forms of parallelism identified, we developed parallel solutions to the k-difference primer problem, targeting multicore processors and using the OpenMP parallel programming model [11]. Figure 4(a) shows how to exploit coarse-grained parallelism in the conventional and alternative solutions, using OpenMP. The while loop of Fig. 1 must be transformed into a for loop, so we can use the directive *omp parallel for*, which creates a parallel region and distributes the loop iterations among the threads. Each thread calls different instances of subroutine *longest prefix with differences*, computes different matrices D or L and produces its results separately from other threads. The flag *stop* is shared among the threads, in order to stop the execution of subsequent loop iterations when, at a certain iteration, no solution is found.

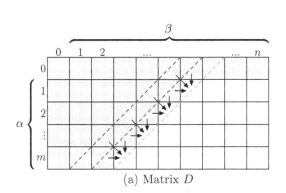

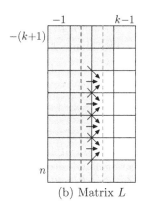

(a) Matrix D (b) Matrix L

Fig. 3. Data dependences and fine-grained parallelism: (a) cells in the same anti-diagonal of matrix D computed in parallel in conventional solution; (b) cells in the same column of matrix L computed in parallel in alternative solution

Figure 4(b) shows how to use OpenMP to exploit fine-grained parallelism in subroutine *longest prefix with differences* of the alternative solution. The directive *omp parallel for* is used around the inner loop, creating a parallel region and distributing the iterations among the threads. Each thread computes different cells in a column of matrix L. At the end of this region, an implicit barrier synchronization guarantees that successive columns are computed sequentially. The directive *omp critical* creates a critical section and ensures the shared variable c (which holds the result) is updated with mutual exclusion by the threads.

In order to exploit fine-grained parallelism in the conventional solution, using OpenMP, the subroutine *longest prefix with differences* in Fig. 2(a) must be adapted in order to compute matrix D by anti-diagonals. An outer loop computes successive anti-diagonals sequentially, while an inner loop computes the cells in a same anti-diagonal. The directive *omp parallel for* is used around this inner loop, creating a parallel region and distributing the iterations among the threads, so that each thread computes different cells in an anti-diagonal of D. An implicit barrier synchronization at the end of this parallel region guarantees that the next anti-diagonal is not computed before the current one is completed.

The optimization that reduces the amount of memory needed to compute matrix D (or L), used in the sequential solutions, is also applied to the OpenMP solutions (for simplicity, it is not shown in Fig. 4). If we exploit only coarse-grained parallelism, one row of D (or column of L) is needed. Exploiting fine-grained parallelism, we need three anti-diagonals of D (or two columns of L).

```
#pragma omp parallel for \
schedule(static,1) \
shared(result,stop) private(c) \
firstprivate(alpha,beta,m,n,k)
for(r = 0; r <= m−k; r++)
  if(r < stop){
    c = longest_prefix_w_differences(
        alpha,beta,k);
    if((c != 0) && (r+c < m))
      result[r] = r+c;
    else stop = r;
  }
```
(a)

```
for(e = 1; e <= k; e++)
  #pragma omp parallel for shared(L,c) \
  schedule(static) private(row)\
  firstprivate(alpha,beta,k,m,n,e)
  for(d = k−e+1; d < n+k; d++){
    row = max(L[d−1][e−1],
        L[d+1][e−1]+1, L[d][e−1]+1);
    if(row > m) row = m;
    while((row<m)&&(row+d−k<n)&&
        (alpha[row]==beta[row+d−k]))
      row = row+1;
    L[d][e] = row;
    if(e == k)
      #pragma omp critical
      if(row > c) c = row;
  }
```
(b)

Fig. 4. OpenMP implementations exploiting: (a) coarse-grained parallelism for the conventional and alternative solutions; and (b) fine-grained parallelism in the subroutine *longest prefix with differences* of the alternative solution

3.1 Optimizations and Preliminary Results

Optimization 1 (from Sect. 2.1) can also be applied to the conventional coarse-grained OpenMP solution. Nevertheless, it cannot be applied to the conventional fine-grained OpenMP solution because the solution scans matrix D by antidiagonals and the optimization needs to check D by rows. Since this optimization produced a huge reduction in the symbol comparisons, the execution of this solution, even in parallel, was impracticable. Optimization 2 (from Sect. 2.1) can be applied to both alternative coarse- and fine-grained OpenMP solutions.

In order to reduce the synchronization overhead, another optimization, referred as *optimization 3*, is applied to OpenMP fine-grained conventional and alternative solutions. It eliminates the critical section that guards the shared variable c update shown in Fig. 4(b). A vector with one position for each thread is used, so that each thread stores its result in a different position of the vector, instead of sharing the variable c. Therefore, the critical section is no longer needed. After finishing the execution of the nested loops, a small loop finds the maximum value of the vector, which is then assigned to variable c.

Table 2 compares the parallel OpenMP conventional and alternative solutions, exploiting coarse- and fine-grained parallelism, and the optimizations applied. We used the same biological input data employed for the sequential solutions, as well as the same platform (a quad-core processor now running 8 threads). The speedups compare the parallel solutions to the best sequential one (alternative+optimization 2). The alternative coarse-grained solutions achieved better performance than the conventional coarse-grained solution with optimization 1 because it performs less symbol comparisons, as we have seen in Table 1. Optimization 2 applied to the alternative solution produces a very small reduction in the execution time. Comparing coarse- and fine-grained approaches used in alternative solution+optimization 2, the latter produces worse results, because it is not suitable to the processor reduced number of cores. Nevertheless, when optimization 3 is applied to the alternative fine-grained solution, it produces a significant improvement in performance, almost doubling the speedup and showing the impact of the synchronization overhead reduction. Given the limited parallel processing capability of the quad-core processor, the combination of coarse- and fine-grained parallelism produces worse results.

Table 2. Evaluation of OpenMP parallel solutions and optimizations, using 4 cores and 8 threads: execution time and speedup wrt. best sequential solution, for $|\alpha| = 43,606$, $|\beta| = 241,494$, and $k = 100$

Parallel solution+optimizations	Execution time (s)	Speedup
Conventional coarse-grained+1	2067.2	4.0
Alternative coarse-grained	1509.8	5.4
Alternative coarse-grained+2	1481.1	5.6
Alternative fine-grained+2	3091.2	2.7
Alternative fine-grained+2+3	1544.1	5.3
Alternative coarse/fine-grained+2+3	2114.8	3.9

Figure 5 shows how the performance of the best OpenMP solution (alternative coarse-grained+optimization 2) scales as the number of threads increases, from 1 (sequencial solution) to 8, using the quad-core processor. The speedups compare the parallel solution to the best sequential one (alternative+optimization 2). The speedup grows linearly with the number of threads,

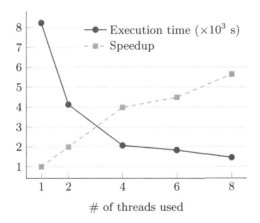

Fig. 5. Performance of best OpenMP solution (speedup wrt. best sequential one), using 4 cores and varying the number of threads, for $|\alpha| = 43,606$, $|\beta| = 241,494$, and $k = 100$

up to four threads, matching the number of cores available. For 6 or 8 threads, the speedup grows more slowly, since the threads have to share the cores.

4 CUDA Solutions to the k-difference Primer Problem

We also developed parallel solutions to the k-difference primer problem, targeting GPUs and using the CUDA programming model [10]. Since GPUs have a large number of cores, they are suitable for exploiting both forms of parallelism identified. Each matrix D or L is computed by a block, in parallel to the other matrices, exploiting coarse-grained parallelism. The threads in a block compute the cells in an anti-diagonal of D (or a column of L) in parallel, exploiting fine-grained parallelism. If the number of matrices that have to be computed is larger than the maximum number of blocks which can be created in a kernel invocation, we compute these matrices in batches. We have one kernel invocation for each batch, where the matrices in the same batch are computed in parallel and successive batches are executed sequentially.

We started with two base CUDA solutions, derived from the conventional and alternative approaches. In both solutions, the data structures used for sequences α and β and matrix D or L are allocated in GPU global memory, since the sequences are extremely long and GPU shared memory has limited capacity. Optimization 1, presented in Sect. 2.1, cannot be applied to the conventional CUDA base solution because this solution computes matrix D by anti-diagonals and the optimization needs to check D by rows. When optimization 2, presented in Sect. 2.1, is applied to the alternative CUDA solution, it worsens the execution time, therefore we discarded it. Since it provides only a small reduction in the symbol comparisons and the GPU computes many more comparisons in parallel than the sequential and OpenMP solutions, the intrinsic optimization overhead surpassed the performance gain.

Optimization 3, presented in Sect. 3.1, is applied to both conventional and alternative CUDA solutions. For each block computing a different matrix, we keep a vector in GPU shared memory with one position for each thread to store its result in a different position. Therefore, no synchronizations are needed. Before finishing the kernel execution, a reduction operation is performed in parallel by the block threads, in order to find the maximum value of the vector, which is the result for this matrix.

4.1 Tiling Optimization

In order to take advantage of GPU memory hierarchy, the tiling technique, referred as *optimization 4*, is applied to both conventional and alternative CUDA solutions. Matrix D (or L) is divided into tiles, so that, inside a tile, we compute in parallel the cells in an anti-diagonal of D (or column of L), however successive tiles are computed sequentially. Therefore, we no longer have to allocate an entire anti-diagonal of D (or column of L), in order to compute the tile cells. The data structure used to keep this cells is reduced and can be allocated in GPU shared memory, avoiding access to global memory which is much more slower.

Figure 6(a) and (b) shows matrix D and L, respectively, split into tiles, where the tile size is determined by the number of threads per block used. The thick lines in the figure represent the tiles separation. A tile in matrix D has a rectangular shape, while in matrix L it has a parallelogram shape, due to the different data dependences pattern in this matrix. The shaded areas in the figure represent the cells that must be saved after finishing to compute a tile, and that are used for computing the next tile. For the conventional solution and matrix D, this structure has size $O(n)$, which is the length of input sequence $|\beta|$. Consequently, this structure must be allocated in GPU global memory. However, for the alternative solution and matrix L, this structure has size $O(k)$ (the minimum number of differences) and can be allocated in shared memory.

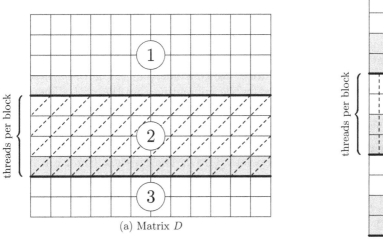

(a) Matrix D

(b) Matrix L

Fig. 6. Tiling technique: (a) matrix D split into rectangular tiles for conventional CUDA solution; (b) matrix L split into parallelogram-shaped tiles for alternative CUDA solution. Tile size determined by the number of threads per block and successive tiles computed sequentially

Another advantage of optimization 4 is that it enables us to apply optimization 1 on the conventional CUDA solution. Inside a tile, matrix D is computed by anti-diagonals and optimization 1 needs to check D by rows. However, we can check the cells saved after computing a tile (shaded cells) and, depending on the result, we do not compute the remaining tiles.

4.2   Prefetch and Speculation Optimizations

Sequences α and β are allocated in GPU global memory because they are too long to fit on shared memory. However, before computing each tile, we can prefetch to shared memory segments of theses sequences that will be used during the tile calculation, in order to avoid access to global memory and to improve performance. We refer to the prefetch of segments of α and β from global memory to shared memory as *optimizations 5* and *6*, respectively.

In the conventional CUDA solution, the division of matrix D into tiles allows us to know exactly which segment of α is used for computing a tile, then we prefetch this segment to shared memory before computing the tile and no access to α in global memory is done while computing it. However, the entire sequence β is used while computing a tile of D, which prevents us from using prefetch on it, which remains being accessed from global memory. In the alternative CUDA solution, we cannot predict which symbols of α and β will be used while computing a tile of matrix L, therefore we developed a speculative mechanism, which prefetchs to shared memory segments of α and β that are likely to be used. During the tile calculation, when a thread accesses a symbol of α or β which is present on shared memory, we have a hit. Otherwise, we have a misprediction in our speculation mechanism and the global memory must be accessed.

Analyzing the alternative solution, we conclude that the initial symbols of α are the most likely to be used, while computing any tile of L. Therefore, we prefetch the initial segment of α from global to shared memory only once and use it for all tiles. We estimate the length *prefetch*$_\alpha$ of this segment as $\left\lceil \frac{c \times k}{threads\ per\ block} \right\rceil \times threads\ per\ block$, since the minimum number of differences k affects the number of symbols of α and β used. The constant factor c is determined through an experiment in Sect. 4.3 and we round the value to be multiple of the number of threads per block. We allocate on shared memory a segment of β of length *prefetch*$_\beta$, estimated as $prefetch_\alpha + threads\ per\ block$. However, before computing each tile, a new segment with only *threads per block* symbols is prefetched. During the tile calculation, this segment and previously prefetched ones are used.

4.3   Results

The execution platform used for the CUDA solutions consists of a GPU NVIDIA GeForce Quadro M4000 with 8 GB RAM and 1664 cores, connected to the same computer (which acts as a host) used for the sequential and OpenMP solutions. The same biological input data set is used. The *nvprof* profiler tool was used to extract performance metrics used in the experimental evaluation. In all CUDA solutions, the time spent transferring data between host memory and GPU global memory is insignificant, when compared to the time spent executing the kernel invocations.

Figure 7 shows the performance of all conventional and alternative CUDA solutions, applying optimizations incrementally. The execution times were obtained through the arithmetic mean of several executions, which produced

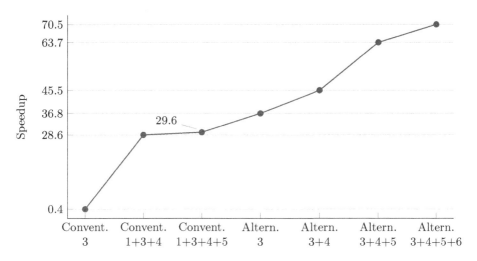

Fig. 7. Speedups of conventional and alternative CUDA solutions and optimizations, wrt. to the best sequential solution, for $|\alpha| = 43,606$, $|\beta| = 241,494$, and $k = 100$

a standard deviation of only 0.02. The speedups compare the parallel solutions to the best sequential one (alternative+optimization 2).

The tiling technique (optimization 4) has a great impact improving the performance of the conventional solution, while its impact on the alternative solution seems to be lower. The difference is that the tiling technique enables the application of optimization 1 on the conventional solution, reducing the number of matrix D cells computed. This optimization is implicit in the alternative base solution. Sequence α prefetch (optimization 5) has a great impact improving the performance of the alternative solution, however its impact on the conservative solution is small. The reason is that, in conventional solution, we prefetch a segment of α from global to shared memory before computing each tile, while in alternative solution, we prefetch a segment of α only once and use it for all tiles.

Table 3 compares the best conventional and all alternative CUDA solutions with respect to several performance metrics. The throughput measure *comparisons per second* indicates how many comparisons of α and β symbols are performed by the solution in one second. Figure 8 shows the number of load and store operations performed in GPU global and shared memory by these solutions. Analyzing these results in conjunction enables us to evaluate the effect of the optimizations on the metrics and their impact on the solutions performance.

All alternative solutions have better performance than all conventional ones. Even though the best conventional solution achieves good instructions per cycle rate and issue slot utilization, it performs nearly twice as many symbol comparisons as the alternative solutions. The best conventional solution has its memory access optimized, but even so it performs many more memory operations than the best alternative solution. The conventional solution keeps on global memory the cells that are saved, after computing a tile, and used for computing the

Table 3. Comparison of best conventional and all alternative CUDA solutions, for $|\alpha| = 43,606$, $|\beta| = 241,494$, and $k = 100$

Performance metrics	Convent. 1+3+4+5	Altern. 3	Altern. 3+4	Altern. 3+4+5	Altern. 3+4+5+6
# of symbol comparisons ($\times 10^{10}$)	~274	~137	~137	~137	~137
Comparisons per second ($\times 10^8$)	~98.5	~61.5	~76.0	~106.5	~118.0
# of instructions executed ($\times 10^{10}$)	~910	~402	~432	~366	~352
Instructions per cycle	3.3	1.8	2.4	2.9	3.1
Issue slots utilization*	76%	43%	54%	63%	65%

*Percentage of issue slots that issued at least one instruction.

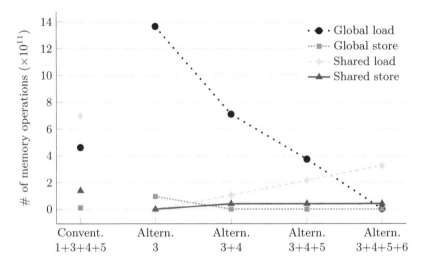

Fig. 8. GPU global and shared memory load and store operations of best conventional and all alternative CUDA solutions, for $|\alpha| = 43,606$, $|\beta| = 241,494$, and $k = 100$

next one, while the alternative solution uses shared memory for this. Besides, sequence β prefetch (optimization 6) is not applied to the conventional solution.

Each alternative solution achieves a better performance than the previous one, although they compute the same number of symbol comparisons. It produces a higher comparisons per second rate, executes more instructions per cycle, and increases the issue slots utilization. As more optimizations are applied, the number of access to global memory decreases a lot, while the access to shared memory increase more slowly. Using the tiling technique (optimization 4), the data structure used for computing matrix L is kept in shared memory, reducing drastically the access to global memory. The load and store operations in global memory become almost restricted, respectively, to access to α and β symbols and to saving the results produced. Prefetching α and β segments from global to shared memory (optimizations 5 and 6, respectively) exchanges many global memory load operations for less load operations in shared memory. Optimization 5 is more effective in improving performance than optimization 6 because we prefetch a segment of α only once and use it for computing all tiles, while a segment of β is prefetched for each tile computed.

The performance gain produced by the speculative prefetch mechanism depends on the accuracy of the prediction. We prefetch to shared memory segments of α and β, of lengths $prefetch_\alpha$ and $prefetch_\beta$ respectively, that are likely to be used. However, if a thread accesses a symbol of α or β that is not present on shared memory, we have a misprediction and an access to global memory is done. We measure the miss rates, which indicate the percentage of access that generate misses with respect to the total number of access to α or β, for different lengths $prefetch_\alpha$ and $prefetch_\beta$, defined using the constant factor c. Table 4 shows the results obtained using the best alternative solution and varying c from 1 to 3. For $c = 1$, the miss rate for α is very high, reflecting on the worst execution time. For $c = 3$, there are no more mispredictions in both α and β access, even though the prefetched segments are not very long, and we have the best execution time.

Table 4. Speculative prefetch of α e β symbols, using best alternative CUDA solution, for $|\alpha| = 107,280$, $|\beta| = 2,220,391$, $k = 256$, and 256 threads per block: constant factor c defines length $prefetch_\alpha$ and $prefetch_\beta$ of prefetched segments; miss rates correspond to symbols not found in shared memory and accessed in global memory

c	Execution time (s)	Prefetch$_\alpha$	Prefetch$_\beta$	Miss rate for α	Miss rate for β
1	8193.3	256	512	49.0%	0.1%
2	7453.7	512	768	1.5%	0.0%
3	7401.4	768	1024	0.0%	0.0%

Figure 9 shows the results obtained using the best alternative solution and varying the number of threads per block used for executing the GPU kernels. The number of threads per block defines the tile size and represents a compromise between exploiting fine- and coarse-grained parallelism. Using more threads per block, we compute in parallel more cells in a same matrix, however, the number of active blocks per GPU multiprocessor is reduced, so we compute fewer matrices in parallel. We reach the best trade-off for 256 threads per block, which produced the best execution times, for both $k = 50$ and 100.

Figure 10 compares the performance of the best sequential, OpenMP and CUDA solutions, for five test cases with huge sequences from our biological input data set. We generated synthetic sequences only for the last test case, with $|\alpha| = 10 \times 10^5$ and $|\beta| = 40 \times 10^5$. Due to the long execution time, the sequential solution was not executed for last two test cases. These execution times were estimated based on the speedups obtained for the other test cases. The CUDA solution reaches speedups that go from 70.0 to 72.8 as the lengths of α and β and the number of differences k increase, while the OpenMP solution speedups

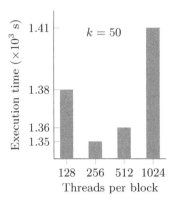
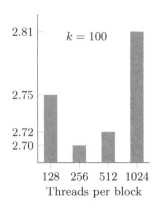

Fig. 9. Execution time of best alternative CUDA solution, for $|\alpha| = 107,280$, $|\beta| = 2,220,391$, and $k = 50$ and 100, varying the number of threads per block: best trade-off between fine- and coarse-grained parallelism achieved for 256 threads per block

remain constant at approximately 5.6. The CUDA solution achieved a 100% GPU occupancy, indicating that the hardware resources were used properly.

Table 5 shows the throughput measure comparisons per second produced by the best alternative sequential, OpenMP and CUDA solutions, stressing the performance gain achieved by the parallel solutions.

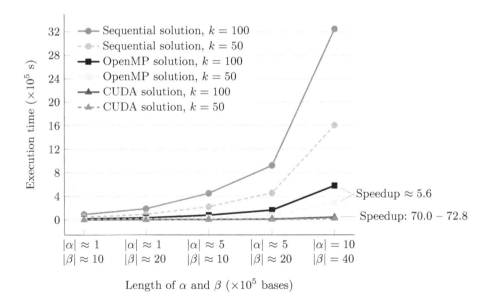

Fig. 10. Performance of best sequential, OpenMP and CUDA solutions, for sequences α e β of different lengths: speedups wrt. sequential solution

Table 5. Comparisons per second of best sequential, OpenMP and CUDA solutions, for $|\alpha| = 107{,}280$, $|\beta| = 1{,}088{,}386$, and $k = 100$

Best alternative solution	Sequential	OpenMP	CUDA
Comparisons per second ($\times 10^8$)	~ 1.6	~ 9.4	~ 118.5

5 Related Work

We have not found in the literature works with parallel solutions to the k-difference primer problem. Nevertheless, there are parallel solutions to the approximate string matching problem, which is a substep in our problem.

Landau and Vishkin [4,5] present a parallel algorithm to approximate string matching based on suffix trees, with a theoretical time complexity of $O(\log m + k)$ using n processors. Nakano [8] proposes solutions to the problem of finding substring of β with the minimum number of differences from α. Two theoretical parallel computing models are used to reflect GPU memory hierarchy features, and the solutions have time complexity of $O(\frac{n \times m}{w} + n \times l)$ using m threads and w memory banks with memory latency l.

In [13] the authors present GPU and FPGA solutions to approximate string matching based on regular expression operators. The dynamic programming matrix is split into regions which are computed in parallel. Using a GPU NVIDIA Tesla C2070 and a FPGA Xilinx Virtex-4, they achieved speedups of 8,3 and 2,9, respectively, with respect to the sequential implementation, for a pattern of length 320. For a pattern of length 3200, the speedup was 18, using the GPU, while the FPGA solution could not be executed due to hardware limitations.

Rastogi and Guddeti [12] describe a GPU solution to approximate string matching of several short patterns to a long sequence with at most two differences, using the Burrows-Wheeler transform (BWT). Using a GPU NVIDIA NVS 300, they achieved speedups up to 8, compared to the sequential implementation, without taking into account the time spent with the BWT. In [6] the authors present GPU solutions to approximate string matching, using the Hamming distance, instead of the edit distance, to compute the number of differences. Therefore, insertions and deletions in the sequences are not allowed, resulting in a simpler algorithm where only symbol substitutions are allowed. Using a GPU NVIDIA GeForce GTX 260, the best solution reached speedups between 40 and 80, with respect to the sequential implementation, while the other solutions achieved speedups of nearly 10.

6 Conclusion and Future Works

This paper presented parallel solutions to the k-difference primer problem, targeting multicore processors and GPUs. For both platforms, we developed several optimizations that allowed the analysis of very long sequences consuming a reduced execution time. To the authors' knowledge, these are the first parallel solutions proposed for the k-difference primer problem.

Starting with two different algorithms, we identified two forms of exploiting parallelism in the k-difference primer solutions, coarse- and fine-grained parallelism. Among the OpenMP solutions, the alternative coarse-grained solution was the one that produced the best performance results, reaching speedups up to 5.6, when compared to the best sequential solution and using a quad-core processor. Given the reduced number of cores, the fine-grained parallelism is not adequate for this platform.

Several optimizations were applied to the CUDA solutions in order to improve performance. The synchronization overhead is reduced by allowing each thread to produce its result separately and using a parallel reduction operation to find the final result. The tiling technique enabled the solutions to handle input data sets with very long sequences and reduced drastically the global memory access. A speculative prefetch mechanism improved even more the use of the GPU memory hierarchy and reached an accuracy of 100%.

The best CUDA solution produced impressive speedups up to 72.8, with respect to the best sequential solution, and this performance is not affected when the sequences length and the number of differences k increase. The best sequential, OpenMP, and CUDA solutions reached the throughput of 0.16, 0.94, and 11.85 billions comparisons per second, respectively, emphasizing the performance gain of the CUDA solution. Since this solution reached 100% of GPU occupancy, if executed on a more powerful GPU, it would achieve an even better performance, because more matrices and cells would be computed in parallel.

Despite the significant results achieved with our parallel solutions, an interesting research subject is to investigate other sequential algorithms for the k-difference primer problem and how to map them to a parallel platform.

References

1. Baxevanis, A., Ouellette, B.: Bioinformatics - A Practical Guide to the Analysis of Genes and Proteins, 3rd edn. Wiley, Hoboken (2005)
2. Gusfield, D.: Algorithms on Strings, Trees and Sequences: Computer Science and Computational Biology. Cambridge University Press, Cambridge (1997)
3. Ito, M., et al.: A polynomial-time algorithm for computing characteristic strings under a set of strings. Syst. Comput. Jpn **26**(3), 30–38 (1995)
4. Landau, G., Vishkin, U.: Introducing efficient parallelism into approximate string matching and a new serial algorithm. In: Proceedings of the Annual ACM Symposium on Theory of Computing, pp. 220–230 (1986)
5. Landau, G., Vishkin, U.: Fast parallel and serial approximate string matching. J. Algorithms **10**(2), 157–169 (1989)
6. Liu, Y., et al.: Parallel algorithms for approximate string matching with k mismatches on CUDA. In: Proceedings of the IEEE International Parallel and Distributed Processing Symposium Workshops & PhD Forum, pp. 2414–2422 (2012)
7. Mandoiu, I., Zelikovsky, A.: Bioinformatics Algorithms: Techniques and Applications. Wiley, Hoboken (2008)
8. Nakano, K.: Efficient implementations of the approximate string matching on the memory machine models. In: Proceedings of the International Conference on Networking and Computing, pp. 233–239 (2012)

 9. NCBI: National Center for Biotechnology Information. https://www.ncbi.nlm.nih.gov
10. NVIDIA Corporation: CUDA Parallel Computing Platform. http://www.nvidia.com.br/object/cuda_home_new_br.html
11. OpenMP Architecture Review Board: OpenMP Application Programming Interface Version 4.5. http://www.openmp.org/mp-documents/openmp-4.5.pdf
12. Rastogi, P., Guddeti, R.: GPU accelerated inexact matching for multiple patterns in DNA sequences. In: Proceedings of the International Conference on Advances in Computing, Communications and Informatics, pp. 163–167 (2014)
13. Utan, Y., et al.: A GPGPU implementation of approximate string matching with regular expression operators and comparison with its FPGA implementation. In: Proceedings of the International Conference on Parallel and Distributed Processing Techniques and Applications, pp. 1–7 (2012)

RT-DBSCAN: Real-Time Parallel Clustering of Spatio-Temporal Data Using Spark-Streaming

Yikai Gong[1(✉)], Richard O. Sinnott[1], and Paul Rimba[2]

[1] University of Melbourne, Melbourne, VIC, Australia
yikaig@student.unimelb.edu.au
[2] Data61, CSIRO, Sydney, NSW, Australia

Abstract. Clustering algorithms are essential for many big data applications involving point-based data, e.g. user generated social media data from platforms such as Twitter. One of the most common approaches for clustering is DBSCAN. However, DBSCAN has numerous limitations. The algorithm itself is based on traversing the whole dataset and identifying the neighbours around each point. This approach is not suitable when data is created and streamed in real-time however. Instead a more dynamic approach is required. This paper presents a new approach, RT-DBSCAN, that supports real-time clustering of data based on continuous cluster checkpointing. This approach overcomes many of the issues of existing clustering algorithms such as DBSCAN. The platform is realised using Apache Spark running over large-scale Cloud resources and container based technologies to support scaling. We benchmark the work using streamed social media content (Twitter) and show the advantages in performance and flexibility of RT-DBSCAN over other clustering approaches.

Keywords: DBSCAN · Clustering · Real-time systems

1 Introduction

Clustering is one of the major data mining methods used for knowledge discovery [11] on big data. Density-based clustering algorithms like DBSCAN [8] are in widespread use and numerous extensions are now available for discovering patterns and clusters in large data sets [2,12,15]. However, neither DBSCAN nor its extensions support real-time processing or allow to tackle streamed (high velocity) data [16]. Rather, DBSCAN operates in a batch mode where all the data is acquired and then processed. This feature makes it unsuitable for supporting the ever growing data from real-time data streams.

There is a strong need for real-time cluster discovery in many diverse application domains such as urban traffic monitoring, emergency response, network accessing analysis. The demands for real-time clustering of big data raise several needs and requirements for improvements and refinements of the DBSCAN

© Springer International Publishing AG, part of Springer Nature 2018
Y. Shi et al. (Eds.): ICCS 2018, LNCS 10860, pp. 524–539, 2018.
https://doi.org/10.1007/978-3-319-93698-7_40

algorithm, including the ability to: (1) generate a series of up-to-date intermediate result checkpoints when processing real-time (incoming) data; (2) support scalable parallel execution capabilities to reduce the response time for generating checkpoints; and (3) offer consistent performance in tackling ever growing amounts of data.

Existing extensions of DBSCAN offer no solution to the combination of these requirements. In this paper, we present a real-time parallel version of DBSCAN (RT-DBSCAN) to address the above requirements. Compared to the original version of DBSCAN, optional parameters are added to the algorithm for controlling the efficiency and granularity of parallel-workload division. For clustering spatio-temporal data in time and space, a spatio-temporal distance is applied, noting that the definition of distance in this algorithm can be adapted to other kinds of higher dimensional data. We have implemented RT-DBSCAN using Apache Spark Streaming. We benchmark the system using large-scale streamed social media data (tweets) on the National Research Cloud (NeCTAR) in Australia.

2 Related Clustering Algorithms

Extensions of DBSCAN can be classified into two types: performance optimized DBSCAN and application optimized DBSCAN. The former aims at reducing the execution time for data clustering [12,18], whilst the latter focuses on adapting DBSCAN to different high-dimensional data structures required for specific application scenarios [6,17,19].

There are many good ideas in performance-oriented extensions of DBSCAN. *l*-DBSCAN [18] proposes a method to reduce the size of datasets before running DBSCAN. It employs a graph-based hybrid clustering algorithm [3] to pre-generate a few candidate (approximate) clusters. Only the points in those clusters are then input into DBSCAN for final clustering. However, this two-phased clustering method has several major limitations. Firstly, two critical parameters are added for hybrid clustering. As the authors point out, unsuitable selection of these parameters can lead to inconsistent clustering results. Secondly, the pre-clustering phase is used for filtering out noise data, e.g. data outliers. If a highly skewed dataset is input, this phase can become useless and consume unnecessary computing resources. This extension also does not meet any of the real-time clustering requirements, but the idea of reducing or sampling all of the data in DBSCAN is meaningful and been incorporated into RT-DBSCAN.

MR-DBSCAN [12] proposes a parallel version of DBSCAN in a MapReduce manner [5]. The major contribution of this extension is that it provides a method to divide a large dataset into several partitions based on the data dimensions. Localized DBSCANs can be applied to each partition in parallel during a map phase. The results of each partition are then merged during a final reduce phase. For the overall cost, a partition-division phase is added into DBSCAN. A division method called *Cost Balanced Partition* is used to generate partitions with equal workloads. This parallel extension meets the requirements of scalable execution for handling large scale data sets and the MapReduce approach makes it suitable for many popular big data analytic platforms like Hadoop MapReduce and

Apache Spark [10]. However, this extension does not meet all the requirements of real-time clustering. It needs to traverse the whole dataset for parallel clustering which means that its execution time is still dependent on the size of the dataset. Thus, whilst MR-DBSCAN has good performance for batch-oriented data scenarios, it is not suitable for high velocity datasets.

For those application-oriented extensions to DBSCAN, we consider two of them which are most closely related to our approach.

Stream data is often spatio-temporal in nature and comprised of time-stamped, geographic location information [6]. This can be, for instance, social media data, trajectory data, Internet of Things data. This raises a requirement for clustering those data in time and space according to their spatio-temporal characteristics. [2] presents a method for handling this requirement. It provides an example for clustering spatio-temporal data according to its non-spatial, spatial and associated temporal values. In addition, they propose a notion of density factor for each cluster which is helpful to identify the density of clusters.

Incremental DBSCAN [7] is another extension of DBSCAN suitable for mining in data warehouses. It supports incremental updates when clustering by inserting new data and deleting old data. It provides controls over the size of the involved data. Old data are excluded from clustering processes based on a time-based threshold which can be specified by the user. This method meets the real-time requirements of tackling ever increasing volumes of data. However, it only works for time-based clusters. The definition of old data is a critical factor in this algorithm. Essential information can be lost by dropping data if inappropriate thresholds are set. Although this method is designed for daily batch-oriented tasks, the idea of dropping old irrelevant data and inserting new data into existing clusters is essential when designing real-time, high velocty clustering solutions.

Apart from DBSCAN, there are many other density-based clustering algorithms such as OPTICS [1], DENCLUE [13] and CURD [14]. D-Stream [4] is a density based clustering approach for handling real-time streams, but it cannot handle data arriving in arbitrary time-stamped orders. In this paper, we present a new DBSCAN-based clustering approach that overcomes many of the issues and limitations related to both DBSCAN and the above mentioned systems when dealing with high velocity, streamed data.

3   Real-Time Parallel DBSCAN Clustering

Clustering algorithms like DBSCAN normally need to input the whole dataset into a clustering process (all-in with single-out). The complexity of DBSCAN is $O(n^2)$. A typical DBSCAN traverses the whole dataset, and identifies the neighbors of each point. Each data element can be used/processed multiple times (e.g. as candidates to different clusters). Although incremental-DBSCAN supports updating of clusters by inserting new input data into existing clusters, this algorithm does not cope with ever growing sizes of historical data due to the data traversal demands of DBSCAN. To deal with this, incremental-DBSCAN drops outdated data to keep a fit size of dataset.

A key challenge of real-time DBSCAN is in controlling the size of traversal data needed to cluster ever growing data volumes. In the DBSCAN algorithm, for each new input data, a group of potential near-by points needs to be identified for cluster detection. For each new input point, if there is an efficient way to identify a full set of near-by context points in the historical dataset, only this subset of data is needed for clustering against any new input. Therefore, we can input the data point-by-point into the cluster process and get a series of up-to-date cluster checkpoints. If the performance of this pre-filtering method is not sensitive to the size of dataset, then we can cluster real-time stream data on-the-fly without being challenged by the ever growing volume of data streamed over potentially extended time periods.

This idea forms the basis for the definition of our real-time clustering (RT-DBSCAN) method. Specifically, *for a new input point p and a group of historical clustered points cPoints, nearbyCtx(p, cPoints) is used to obtain a subset of cPoints which contains essential information of nearby inputs. Checkpoints produced by* RT-DBSCAN *on this subset must be identical to the result of applying normal* DBSCAN *on the whole dataset for each input.*

3.1   Identify a Full Set of Nearby Context Points for Each Input

DBSCAN involves two key parameters: ε and *minPts*. The distance parameter ε defines how close two points need to be to be considered in the same neighbourhood. The border parameter *minPts* defines how many neighbourhoods related to a single point there should be for this to be considered as a cluster. In the following examples, we consider a scenario where $\varepsilon = 1$ unit and *minPts* $= 3$ points. In Fig. 1, we highlight three scenarios related to putting a new point P_i into a set of historical clustered points. In scenario A, we consider firstly retrieving all the historical data within 1-ε distance to P_i, to get 3 non-clustered (noise) points. Since their distances to P_i are smaller than ε, P_i now have 3 neighbours and thus these four points form a new cluster. This seems sensible, but it can be wrong. If there is a point P_b that is less than 1-ε away from point P_a but more than 1-ε away from P_i, as shown in scenario A of the Fig. 1, P_b will be ignored by this procedure. Although a new cluster is identified, P_b is not marked as a member of this cluster which it should be. This result disobeys the assertion made in the previous definition. If we consider extending the range of near-by-context from 1-ε to 2-ε in scenario B, 4 points are discovered including P_b. These 5 points are grouped into the same cluster. A similar question naturally arises. What if there is a point P_c which is less than 1-ε away from P_b and is more than 2-ε away from P_i as shown in scenario C? This sounds like an endless issue but it is not. Since P_a, P_b and P_c are historical processed points and *minPts* $= 3$, a cluster must have already been identified when the last of these three points was input in a previous iteration. In scenario C, although P_c is ignored as a nearby context point, its cluster information is carried by P_a and P_b and subsequently passed to P_i. With this information, P_i and two other noise points can be absorbed into the existing cluster. This result meets the requirements of the previous definition. In this case where *minPts* $= 3$, we find that historical points within

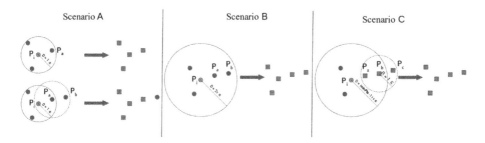

Fig. 1. Illustration of getting nearby points context

distance 2-ε away from the input data contain enough information to establish connections between the input point and the existing historical noise points and existing clusters. The minimum distance ($minDis$) of nearby-contexts, which is 2ε in this case, is related to the parameter ε and $minPts$. $minDis$ is given as: $minDis = (minPts - 1) \times \varepsilon$. In the following section, we mark this procedure as $nearbyCtx(p, cPoints)$ where p is the input and $cPoints$ is the historical dataset. If $cPoints$ are indexed in a database, the response time of this procedure needs to be fast and non-sensitive to the growing size of $cPoints$. An incremental-DBSCAN is then applied on $nearbyCtx$.

3.2   Convert Point-by-Point Clustering to Tick-by-Tick Clustering

Executing a single process for RT-DBSCAN by tackling the incoming data stream point-by-point is not an efficient approach and would not meet the requirements of real-time data intensive applications. The next challenge is to process the incoming data in parallel. However, considering the nature of DBSCAN, it is hard to process data streams in a fully parallel manner. The reason is that DBSCAN and RT-DBSCAN are based on a sequential processing model, e.g. using data in batches or micro-batches. For each input data, a group of nearby data will be queried and involved in the calculation. It is very likely that one input point can be used within the context of another input point. Therefore, these input data cannot be processed without impacting one another when used in a fully parallel manner. In addition, writing the historical datasets simultaneously can lead to consistency issue. From this we can conclude that: (1) each input point should know the other input data that is being processed in parallel; (2) conflicts between the results of each parallel processor need to be solved before clusters are used/persisted, and previous results need to be persisted into historical datasets before tackling new (incoming) data.

To tackle these challenges for parallel processing, we convert the point-by-point RT-DBSCAN to a (temporal) tick-by-tick RT-DBSCAN where data points from incoming data-streams are divided into separate ticks based on their arriving times; within each tick, data are processed and clustered in parallel; the results of each parallel processing step (within one tick) need to be merged before being persisted to solve any/all conflicts in data consistency, and at the end of each tick, the result must be persisted into the historical dataset before a new tick is started. The updated dataset at the end of each tick is a checkpoint for the clusters. A series of checkpoints forms the growth history of clusters.

Parallel processing is applied on data of each tick. To get nearby context points for a group of inputs in a given tick, the first task of each tick is to get the nearby points context for input point-set (iPs) $\{P_1, P_2, \ldots, P_j\}$. Depending on how the historical data (cPoints) is persisted, there are different ways to achieve this. The first option is to execute *nearbyCtx* multiple times for each point and merge the returned sets. The second option is to get the nearby context at one spot by generating a bounding box for iPs. If cPoints are stored in a database, the second option is normally preferred since it reduces the number of queries to the database. Firstly, a minimum bounding box is calculated to cover every point in the iPs. Then a new bounding box is generated by extending the previous rectangle with minDis for each border. The new bounding box is used for establishing the nearby points context from cPoints. Compared to option 1, the drawback of this method is that it can add unnecessary historical data into the nearby context. These noise points are filtered out by a partitioning method before applying Incremental-DBSCAN. The nearby context aggregates historical points together with the iPs passed into parallel processing.

The next task is to support location-based data partitioning and parallelisation of RT-DBSCAN. Inspired by MR-DBSCAN [12], each tick of our parallel RT-DBSCAN is designed in a MapReduce manner. In step 1, the data space is geographically divided into many cells. Each cell contains localised input points. In step 2, multiple local DBSCANs are executed on each cell in parallel. In step 3, the results from each cell are merged to recover the border information broken by the space division. For example, single clusters appearing in multiple cells need to be identified for merging. This is achieved in several steps. Firstly, a fast data division for parallel RT-DBSCAN is required. MR-DBSCAN uses cost-balanced (CB) partitioning to divide the data points in space into cells. It first divides the data space into equal sized small unit cells. Then, a balanced tree is calculated for merging these unit cells into many CB cells where each CB cell contains nearly the same number of points. This method is good at generating balanced workloads for parallel DBSCAN, but generating a balanced tree is computationally expensive. MR-DBSCAN is designed for processing a large amount of data in a single batch task and its CB partition is only applied once at the beginning of the clustering procedure. However in our RT-DBSCAN realisation, partitions are calculated at the beginning of each tick. This approach makes it is impossible to reuse the partitions in previous ticks since point-sets within different ticks have different nearby point contexts. To address this, a new partition method, Fast Clustering (FC) partitioning, is designed which is more suited to RT-DBSCAN. As illustrated in Fig. 2, the idea of this partitioning method is to iteratively divide a 2D space into four sub-cells until a threshold is reached (i.e. a threshold on the number of points in a cell). Then, we drop the cells where the number of contained points is less than *minPts*. Finally we extend each quad-cell by 1-ε distance on each border. One benefit of this extension is to find overlapping areas between cells so that a merge phase can be applied at the end of each tick. Another purpose is to get the nearby points context for each cell since some essential contexts can be carried in dropped cells that need to be re-used.

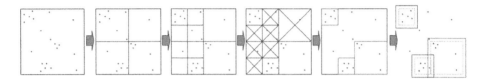

Fig. 2. Illustration of the fast clustering partition method for RT-DBSCAN (Color figure online)

As shown in Fig. 2, there are two kinds of thresholds used for dividing the space. The space is iteratively divided into 4 cells until either the number of points within the current cell is less than 6 or the minimum border of current cell is less than 2ε.

The first condition, called $maxPts$, is to prevent a single cell from having too many points to process. The value 6 for $maxPts$ in Fig. 2 is only used for demonstration purpose. In real-case, $maxPts$ must be greater or equal to $minPts \times 2^n$, where n is the number of dimensions in FC partitioning. This is to avoid over-partitioning a potential cluster. The second condition, called $minSize$, is to prevent the partitioned cells from having very small sizes. If the cell size is less than 1-ε, points that are potentially in the same cluster will likely be divided into separate cells. Although they will be merged and sorted out in the final merging task, this can lead to a large amount of work for merging and thus be very inefficient. These thresholds are free to be customized depending on the specific cases. After the space is divided into a quad-tree, certain cells are dropped if either the number of points within the cell is less than $minPts$ or no new input points fall inside this cell. The propose of this dropping is to reduce the number of parallel tasks/partitions. The first condition helps to drop blank cells and/or cells with very limited numbers of points. It is predetermined that points inside this cell cannot form a cluster. Hence these cells can be dropped. Some of the dropped cells may contain points that belong to clusters in other cells. Those points will be re-selected when other valid cells are extended by 1-ε distance. The second condition is to overcome the flaw of $nearbyCtx(iPs, cPoints)$ mentioned in the previous section, where cells with only historical data can be dropped. Similarly, those dropped essential-nearby-context to other cells with new data will be re-selected when those cells are extended. If the input spatio-temporal data arrives in arbitrary order, the single bounding box for nearby context could be huge in size. Although dropping 'blank' cells can filter out non-necessary historical data before starting DBSCAN, it can still generate many workload to I/O and FC partitioning. Using multiple discrete bounding boxes can be a solution for that case. In this paper, we only use single bounding box which is more suitable for data that arrives in (time) sequence. After dropping 'blank' cells, all remaining cells (the red rectangle in Fig. 2) now meet both of the following conditions: they have more than one new input data and they have more than one core point of a cluster (regardless of whether they are historical or new points).

Finally, those cells are extended by 1-ε distance (the green rectangle in Fig. 2). As mentioned above, the purpose of this extension is to identify overlapping areas when merging cells and pick up lost contexts during the cell dropping process. Figure 3 illustrates some of these scenarios. If data are in a high-dimensional space, this method can be adjusted by dividing the space based on multiple dimensions.

Iteratively divding a space into 4 cells is a naive version of FC partitioning in 2D space. This version suffers from dividing flat rectangle shaped cells, *i.e.*, partitioning can stop in the first iteration due to the smallest border of a flat rectangle reaches the threshold. This problem is solved by dividing each cell into $2^{(n-m)}$ sub-cells. n is the number of total dimensions and m is the number of dimensions which their corresponding borders reach the size threshold. After this improvement, the partitioning is driven by each dimension and its corresponding border of the target cell.

After this FC partition method, those points in $iPs \cup nearbyCtx(iPs, cPoints)$ are divided into two groups: $aPts$ where each point belongs to one or multiple cells and group $dPts$ where each point does not belong to any cell. Only $aPts$ will be applied parallel and DBSCAN for each cell. This procedure is marked as $PCluster(aPts)$. The result of $PCluster(aPts)$ may contain duplicated points (i.e. points belonging to duplicate cells). This result will be union-ed with $dPts$ before being merged/cleaned. All points in $aPts$ and $dPts$ will be persisted at the end of this tick.

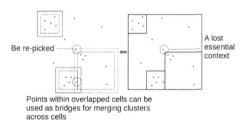

Points within overlapped cells can be used as bridges for merging clusters across cells

Fig. 3. Illustration of cell extensions

Points inside each partition contain both new input and historical clustered data. An incremental-DBSCAN approach is applied to those points for each partition. It can generate duplicated data belonging to different clusters. Since the final merging procedure handles this problem, duplicated points are not fixed in the local partition. The implementation supports a customizable function for calculating the distance between two data points in multi-dimensional spaces.

A spatio-temporal distance function is created for clustering social-media data. This spatio-temporal distance is given in Eq. 1, where P_i and P_j are vectors representing two spatio-temporal data (*e.g.*, Tweets). x and y in vector are values of GPS information (*e.g.*, longitude/latitude) and t is the time-stamp value. This equation is based on Euclidean distance. A customized spatio-temporal ratio s is used to convert the temporal value t into a spatio-value, so that all spatio-temporal values (*i.e.*, x, y, t) can have the same unit in the distance calculation.

$$P_i = (x_i, y_i, t_i), P_j = (x_j, y_j, t_j), D_g = \sqrt{(x_i - x_j)^2 + (y_i - y_j)^2}, \triangle t = |t_i - t_j|$$
$$Distance = \sqrt{D_g^2 + (\triangle t \times s)^2}$$

$$(1)$$

After the parallel local DBSCAN finishes, the result sets (U_r) are union-ed with $dPts$, i.e. $U_r = PCluster(aPts) \cup dPts$.

Duplicated points can appear in U_r. For example, in Fig. 3 point P is on the overlapped area thus it exists in two partitions. After applying local DBSCAN on each partition, one instance of P is a 'NOISE' point and another instance belongs to a cluster. In this final procedure, these kinds of inconsistencies are handled by a merge function: $U_q = merge(U_r)$. Points inside U_q are ensured to be unique. The merging solutions are described in the following paragraphs.

If a point belongs to multiple clusters, the use of this point is key. When a point P has duplicates: if all instances of P are 'NOISE' then we keep one of them and drop the others. If all non-noise instances of P belong to the same cluster A, then we create a singleton of P, mark it as a member of cluster A and merge its roles in cluster A using the priority order: CORE > BORDER > NOISE. If non-noise instances belong to multiple clusters then we create a singleton of P and merge its roles among multiple clusters using the priority order: CORE > BORDER. If the merged role is 'BORDER', where a border point can belong to multiple clusters we add $clusterIds$ into a list and attach it to the new singleton. If the merged role is 'CORE' then the point is a solid joining point for multiple clusters. All such clusters must be merged into one cluster. To do this we create a singleton of P and mark it as 'CORE'. We then randomly pick a cluster A from the non-noise instances and attach it to the singleton and then identify members in other clusters which are to be merged. Finally we change their $clusterId$ to cluster A. However, what if some to-be-merged cluster points are not in U_r? Data in U_r come from $iPs \cup nearbyCtx(iPs, cPoints)$. There is no guaranteed that all the cluster member are covered by this set. Figure 4 illustrates this issue.

In Fig. 4, two triangle-shaped points are not merged because they are absent in U_r. Since the clusterIds of those potential absent points are known, according to the cluster conversion table, all points in the to-be-merged clusters can be retrieved from cPoints. This procedure is given as: $U_c = getClusterPoints(ConvTbl)$. A union operation is then applied on U_r and U_c. Cluster merging is finally applied on this combined set.

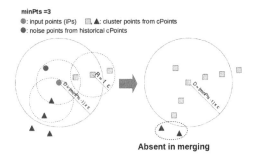

Fig. 4. Illustration of the pitfall in merging clusters

Almost all the merging code can be executed in parallel except the procedure for building a global cluster conversion table. Each computation node needs to report their discoveries to a centralised node for generating the global conversion table. After the above procedures (*i.e.*, partitioning; clustering; merging), the output set U_q contains unique points with their up-to-date cluster information. Finally U_q should be persisted before a next tick starts.

4   Implementation of RT-DBSCAN

The RT-DBSCAN algorithm proposed above has been implemented using Apache Spark Streaming leveraging a platform called SMASH [9]. SMASH is a platform for hosting and processing historical data and Spark applications. It provides a Cloud based software infrastructure utilizing HDFS, Accumulo, GeoMesa, Spark, Kafka and GeoServer integrated together as a platform service for analysing spatial-temporal data. This platform was originally used for traffic data analysis. In deploying the RT-DBSCAN on SMASH, Kafka is used as the streaming source for feeding new data. GeoMesa over Accumulo provides a distributed geo-spatial database. It is used for storing and querying historical data. Spark Streaming is a framework for building streaming applications on Apache Spark. This framework treats data streams as ticks of chunks and executes micro-batch tasks for each tick of data. Spark itself has many other interfaces for running MapReduce functions. These functions suit the needs of RT-DBSCAN and save a lot of work in implementing the clustering algorithm. Twitter data (tweets) are used for the case studies and benchmarking of the platform.

Figure 5 illustrates the procedure of realizing RT-DBSCAN using Spark nodes and Spark Streams as the framework for tackling data stream as a series of data chunks in ticks. At the beginning of each tick, a FC partition is applied against incoming data chunks on a single master node. Data shuffling (*i.e.*, sending data to the node which holds the cell it belongs to) and local DBSCAN are then executed in parallel on each worker node. A cluster merging table is generated on the master node after all local DBSCANs stop. Finally result merging and data persistence are handled in parallel on worker nodes. A new tick procedure starts after the results of the previous tick have been persisted.

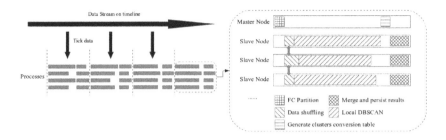

Fig. 5. Illustration of RT-DBSCAN procedure using spark streaming.

5   Benchmarking of RT-DBSCAN on Spark Stream

Our case studies and benchmarking works were realised on the federally funded Australia-wide National eResearch Collaboration Tools and Resources (NeC-TAR) Research Cloud (https://nectar.org.au/research-cloud/). The NeCTAR Research Cloud is based on OpenStack. NeCTAR provides almost 30,000 servers across multiple availability zones across Australia including Melbourne, Monash, Brisbane, Canberra, Adelaide and Tasmania. Fifteen computation nodes (Virtual Machines) from the Melbourne zone were used to form the core infrastructure for the case studies on RT-DBSCAN. The specification of each node was as follows: one master node: VCPUs @2.60 GHz × 4; 12 GB RAM; 120 GB HDD; 13 slave nodes: VCPUs @2.60 GHz × 2; 8 GB RAM; 70 GB HDD and one interface node: VCPUs @2.60 GHz × 4; 16 GB RAM; 130 GB HDD. The results of I/O benchmarking on the computational resources was: bi-directional network bandwidth: 7.88 ± 1.03 Gbits/s; cached reads rate: 3036.1 ± 67.1 MB/s; buffered disk reads rate: 134.6 ± 18.1 MB/s, and disk write rate: 599.7 ± 39.1 MB/s.

Figure 6 illustrates the architecture of the software-stack (SMASH) used on the Cloud nodes for implementing RT-DBSCAN. The software components were packaged into Docker images for scaling of the platform. Instead of using scaling tools like Kubernetes (https://kubernetes.io) or Docker Swarm (https://docs.docker.com/engine/swarm/), a bespoke tool (https://github.com/project-rhd/grunt-clouddity) was developed and used for auto deployment and scaling the SMASH platform, *e.g.,* creating/terminating VMs, managing security groups/rules and scaling Docker containers. This is a command line interface tool that relies on http clients interfacing to OpenStack and Docker.

In Fig. 6, the software containers are divided into three layers: an *Application layer* comprising GeoServer (v2.9.4) and Apache Kafka (v0.11.0.0). These two applications/containers are deployed on interface nodes for data visualization and stream pipelines. A *Computation layer* including Apache Spark (v2.1.1) with a master node and thirteen slave nodes, and a *Data Storage* layer deployed across the master node and slave nodes. The Hadoop Distributed File System (HDFS) (v2.7.4) is installed as the file system of the SMASH platform (block replication 2 and *sync.behind.writes* and *syncconclose* are enabled to ensure data is written immediately into disk; Hadoop data directories are mounted to the local file system of the nodes; Default values are used for other configurations). Apache Accumulo (v1.8.1) is deployed over HDFS as a key/value data store which is similar to Google's BigTable storage. GeoMesa (v1.3.2) is a distributed, spatio-temporal database which is deployed on top of the Accumulo cloud data storage. In RT-DBSCAN, historical/checkpoint data created is persisted and indexed in GeoMesa/Accumulo.

Master Node	Slave Nodes		Interface Node	Docker Images
			GeoServer & Kafka	Application Image
Apache Spark	Apache Spark	...		Computation Image
GeoMesa/Accumulo	GeoMesa/Accumulo	...		Data Storage & File System Image
HDFS	HDFS	...		

Fig. 6. Illustration of dockerized SMASH platform

Tweets are used as the data source for our benchmarking cases studies. We collected a fixed size of tweets data which were post in Melbourne within 6 months in 2015. This dataset contains 604,529 tweets ($\approx$220 MB) with GPS and time-stamps. An application was built for reading this dataset and generating the actual data stream. This generator controls the output rate of the stream and pushes it into the Kafka service on the SMASH platform. Our stream application running on Spark gets continuous data streams from Kafka, applies the RT-DBSCAN algorithm on this stream and persists/updates the results on GeoMesa/Accumulo clusters.

Figure 7 illustrates a series of checkpoints generated by RT-DBSCAN (on-the-fly). The results are visualized by GeoServer on SMASH. Each red point on the maps of Fig. 7 represents a noise point which does not belong to any clusters. Each larger green point represents a in-cluster point. RT-DBSCAN is able to start either from a blank or using existing clusters result as the initial starting point (checkpoint). Incremental update is then conducted at each tick (corresponding to micro-batches in Spark Stream) which handles new inputs and generates up-to-date checkpoints based on previous checkpoint.

Fig. 7. Cluster checkpoints generated by RT-DBSCAN (Color figure online)

RT-DBSCAN on Spark Streaming is naturally a "micro-batching" based architecture. A streaming engine is built on the underlying batch engine, where the streaming engine continuously creates jobs for the batch engine from a continuous data stream. There are two important concepts in this architecture. One is the "Batch Interval Time" (BIT) which is a fixed interval value decided by the user of Spark Streaming. This value controls the interval used for generating micro-batch tasks for the underlying batch engine, *i.e.*, the tick interval. Another concept is the "Batch Processing Time" (BPT) which is the exact execution time for each batch task. Ideally, Spark Stream needs to ensure a batch task is completed before the next batch is queued. If the processing times of arriving batches continuously takes longer than the batch interval time, a "snowball effect" can take place. This effect can eventually exhaust Spark resources. Depending on the setting, Spark may discharge this pressure by killing the application or by pushing this pressure back to the broker of data source, *e.g.*, Apache Kafka. Therefore it is important to ensure that for most of the batches that the BPT < BIT. The scheduling delay τ_i for each batch i in sequence is defined as: $\delta_i = BPT_i - BIT$ where

$$\tau_i = \begin{cases} 0, & \text{if } i = 0 \\ \tau_{i-1} + \delta_i, & \text{else if } \tau_{i-1} + \delta_i > 0 \\ 0, & \text{else} \end{cases} \qquad (2)$$

The total delay T_i for each batch i in sequence is defined as: $T_i = \tau_i + BPT_i$. The average processing delay ν_i for each arriving input data involved in batch i can be estimated by: $\nu_i = T_i + \frac{BIT}{2}$, where BIT is a fixed configurable parameter on Spark Streaming. When $\tau_i = 0$, the system achieves its optimal performance. If the value of τ_i and T_i keep increasing, a "snowball effect" occurs and the system is considered unstable against the input stream. On the other hand, if the value of τ_i and T_i are stable under a red line, this system is considered stable. In the following case studies, we benchmark the RT-DBSCAN on Spark Streaming by using different numbers of Spark executors and different input rates of data streams. τ_i and BPT_i are monitored for evaluating the stability and performance of RT-DBSCAN. The default parameters used in our following RT-DBSCAN benchmarking included DBSCAN parameters: spatio-temporal ϵ calculated by Eq. 1, where inputs are: $D_g = 100\,\text{m}$; $\triangle t = 600\,\text{s}$; $s = 1.667\,\text{m/s}$ and $minPts = 3$. As well as non-DBSCAN parameters: FC partition config: $maxPts = 100$; $minSize = 2 \times \epsilon$. Time $(BIT) = 30\,\text{s}$.

The selected value for the spatial-temporal ratio s reflects walking speed. The source code of RT-DBSCAN implementation using Spark Streaming is available at our GitHub repository (https://github.com/project-rhd/smash-app/tree/master/smash-stream).

Figure 8 presents the results of benchmarking the scalability of RT-DBSCAN. The data input rate here is set to $1,000$ points per second. Performance on different numbers (scales) of Spark executors are benchmarked under the same data stream. The two charts in Fig. 8 show the timeline on the x axis and τ_i, BPT_i on the y axis. According to the charts, the first batch usually takes a

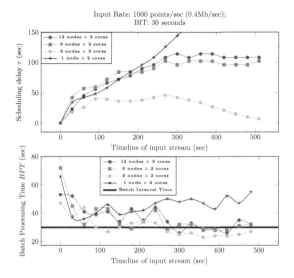

Input Rate: 1000 points/sec (0.4Mb/sec);
BIT: 30 seconds

Fig. 8. Benchmarking scalability under input rates = 1,000 points/s

longer time to process. This is because several initiations are conducted at the beginning of the first tick, *e.g.*, database connections. Almost all the BPT_i of 1 *node* × 2 *cores* are larger then BIT and thus τ_i keeps growing. This pattern means 1 *node* × 2 *cores* is not stable with the default parameters in tackling this rate of input data stream. Following this rule, 3 *nodes* × 2 *cores* is the most stable and efficient scale among the candidates in Fig. 8 since its τ_i reaches zero after several batches from the initiation. The delay of 6 *nodes* × 2 *cores* and 12 *nodes* × 2 *cores* are even larger than 1 *node* × 2 *cores* at the beginning of processing. However the trends of their τ_i stablilises and their BPT_i wavers near the BIT line. These two scales are considered stable under this data rate but

Input Rate: 600 points/sec (0.24Mb/sec);
BIT: 30 seconds; Scale: 1node × 2cores

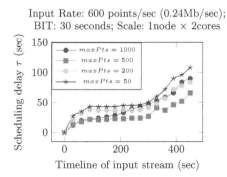

Input Rate: 600 points/sec (0.24Mb/sec);
maxPts: 100; Scale: 1node × 2cores

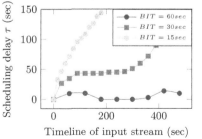

Fig. 9. Performance benchmarking using different maxPts settings

Fig. 10. Performance benchmarking using different BIT values

they are not the optimal options. The overhead of network I/O among multiple nodes is the major bottleneck with these numbers of nodes. To conclude, scaling the number of executors of RT-DBSCAN has a positive effect on its performance but having too many nodes can impact the efficiency due to the data transmissions required over the network. In addition to the number of Spark executors, there are several non-DBSCAN parameters that can impact on the efficiency and stability of RT-DBSCAN under high data velocity situations, *e.g.,* FC partition parameters and the BIT (tick time). Figure 9 benchmarks the performance of RT-DBSCAN according to $maxPts$ which is a parameter/threshold used in the FC partition method. A 1 *node* × 2 *cores* Spark cluster is used and the input rate is 600 points/s. $maxPts$ has a direct impact on the number of points in each cell and the number of data partitions needed for parallel computing, *i.e.,* it impacts on the granularity of parallelization. As seen, $maxPts = 200$ is the optimal setting for the cluster among all other candidates. We also find that the value of $maxPts$ does not have a significant impact on the performance (delay). Figure 10 benchmarks the performances on BIT *i.e.,* the tick time. A 1 *node* × 2 *cores* Spark cluster is used and the input rate is 600 *points/s*. As seen, BIT has a significant impact on the stability of RT-DBSCAN. A larger value of BIT can make the system more stable under higher input rates. However increasing BIT will improve the average delay for processing each input data. Therefore, an elastic BIT is a good strategy to balance the stability and output delay for RT-DBSCAN.

6   Conclusions

In this paper, we propose a new extension of the DBSCAN algorithm for clustering spatio-temporal data targeted specifically to real-time data streams. The novelties of this algorithm are that it tackles ever-growing high velocity data streams and utilizes density based clustering. Furthermore, the spatio-temporal data does not need to arrive in time based sequence.

In the benchmarking, we identify and discuss several configurations that were explored for the performance of RT-DBSCAN over Spark Stream. For future works we shall consider auto-scaling at both the platform level and Spark workers level. We shall also consider In-memory indexing/caching for recent data, *e.g.,* if streamed data arrives in a particular sequence. Data label sensitive clustering *e.g.,* identifying social media data created by the same user in a cluster can also be considered. The FC partition can also be applied to other algorithms for real-time parallel processing. Finally we are considering variability in the tick times and use of other stream processing engine such as Apache Storm.

References

1. Ankerst, M., Breunig, M.M., Kriegel, H.-P., Sander, J.: Optics: ordering points to identify the clustering structure. In: ACM Sigmod Record, vol. 28, pp. 49–60. ACM (1999)
2. Birant, D., Kut, A.: ST-DBSCAN: an algorithm for clustering spatial-temporal data. Data Knowl. Eng. **60**(1), 208–221 (2007)
3. Chandra, B.: Hybrid clustering algorithm. In: Proceedings of the IEEE International Conference on Systems, Man and Cybernetics, pp. 1345–1348. IEEE (2009)
4. Chen, Y., Tu, L.: Density-based clustering for real-time stream data. In: Proceedings of the 13th ACM SIGKDD International Conference on Knowledge Discovery and Data Mining, pp. 133–142. ACM (2007)
5. Dean, J., Ghemawat, S.: MapReduce: simplified data processing on large clusters. Commun. ACM **51**(1), 107–113 (2008)
6. Erwig, M., Gu, R.H., Schneider, M., Vazirgiannis, M., et al.: Spatio-temporal data types: an approach to modeling and querying moving objects in databases. GeoInformatica **3**(3), 269–296 (1999)
7. Ester, M., Kriegel, H.-P., Sander, J., Wimmer, M., Xu, X.: Incremental clustering for mining in a data warehousing environment. In: VLDB, vol. 98, pp. 323–333 (1998)
8. Ester, M., Kriegel, H.-P., Sander, J., , Xu, X., et al.: A density-based algorithm for discovering clusters in large spatial databases with noise. In: KDD, vol. 96, pp. 226–231 (1996)
9. Gong, Y., Morandini, L., Sinnott, R.O.: The design and benchmarking of a cloud-based platform for processing and visualization of traffic data. In: IEEE International Conference on Big Data and Smart Computing (BigComp), pp. 13–20. IEEE (2017)
10. Hagedorn, S., Götze, P., Sattler, K.-U.: The STARK framework for spatio-temporal data analytics on spark. In: BTW, pp. 123–142 (2017)
11. Halkidi, M., Batistakis, Y., Vazirgiannis, M.: On clustering validation techniques. J. Intell. Inf. Syst. **17**(2), 107–145 (2001)
12. He, Y., Tan, H., Luo, W., Feng, S., Fan, J.: MR-DBSCAN: a scalable MapReduce-based DBSCAN algorithm for heavily skewed data. Front. Comput. Sci. **8**(1), 83–99 (2014)
13. Hinneburg, A., Keim, D.A., et al.: An efficient approach to clustering in large multimedia databases with noise. In: KDD, vol. 98, pp. 58–65 (1998)
14. Ma, S., Wang, T.J., Tang, S.W., Yang, D.Q., Gao, J.: A new fast clustering algorithm based on reference and density. In: Dong, G., Tang, C., Wang, W. (eds.) WAIM 2003. LNCS, vol. 2762, pp. 214–225. Springer, Heidelberg (2003). https://doi.org/10.1007/978-3-540-45160-0_21
15. Sander, J., Ester, M., Kriegel, H.-P., Xiaowei, X.: Density-based clustering in spatial databases: the algorithm gdbscan and its applications. Data Min. Knowl. Disc. **2**(2), 169–194 (1998)
16. Sayad, S.: Real Time Data Mining (2017)
17. Spieth, C., Streichert, F., Speer, N., Zell, A.: Clustering-based approach to identify solutions for the inference of regulatory networks. In: The 2005 IEEE Congress on Evolutionary Computation, vol. 1, pp. 660–667. IEEE (2005)
18. Viswanath, P., Pinkesh, R.: L-DBSCAN: a fast hybrid density based clustering method. In: 18th International Conference on Pattern Recognition, ICPR 2006, vol. 1, pp. 912–915. IEEE (2006)
19. Wen, J.-R., Nie, J.-Y., Zhang, H.-J.: Query clustering using user logs. ACM Trans. Inf. Syst. **20**(1), 59–81 (2002)

GPU-Based Implementation of Ptycho-ADMM for High Performance X-Ray Imaging

Pablo Enfedaque[1(✉)], Huibin Chang[1,2], Hari Krishnan[1],
and Stefano Marchesini[1]

[1] Computational Research Division, Lawrence Berkeley National Laboratory,
Berkeley, USA
pablo.enfedaque@gmail.com

[2] School of Mathematical Sciences, Tianjin Normal University, Tianjin, China

Abstract. X-ray imaging allows biologists to retrieve the atomic arrangement of proteins and doctors the capability to view broken bones in full detail. In this context, ptychography has risen as a reference imaging technique. It provides resolutions of one billionth of a meter, macroscopic field of view, or the capability to retrieve chemical or magnetic contrast, among other features. The goal is to reconstruct a 2D visualization of a sample from a collection of diffraction patterns generated from the interaction of a light source with the sample. The data collected is typically two orders of magnitude bigger than the final image reconstructed, so high performance solutions are normally desired. One of the latest advances in ptychography imaging is the development of Ptycho-ADMM, a new ptychography reconstruction algorithm based on the Alternating Direction Method of Multipliers (ADMM). Ptycho-ADMM provides faster convergence speed and better quality reconstructions, all while being more resilient to noise in comparison with state-of-the-art methods. The downside of Ptycho-ADMM is that it requires additional computation and a larger memory footprint compared to simpler solutions. In this paper we tackle the computational requirements of Ptycho-ADMM, and design the first high performance multi-GPU solution of the method. We analyze and exploit the parallelism of Ptycho-ADMM to make use of multiple GPU devices. The proposed implementation achieves reconstruction times comparable to other GPU-accelerated high performance solutions, while providing the enhanced reconstruction quality of the Ptycho-ADMM method.

1 Introduction

Ptychography provides the unprecedented capability of imaging macroscopic specimens at nanometer wavelength resolutions while retrieving chemical, magnetic or atomic information. It was proposed in 1969 with the aim of improving

Y. Shi et al. (Eds.): ICCS 2018, LNCS 10860, pp. 540–553, 2018.
https://doi.org/10.1007/978-3-319-93698-7_41

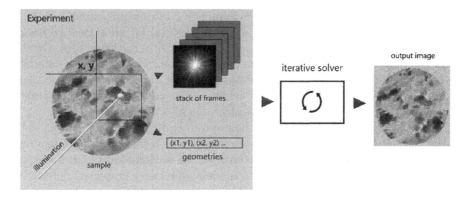

Fig. 1. Overview of a ptychography experiment. An illumination source consecutively scans regions of the sample to produce a stack of phase-less intensities. The stack and the geometry of the measurements are fed to an iterative solver that retrieves the phases and reconstructs an image of the original sample.

the resolution of x-ray and electron microscopy. Since then, it has been successfully employed in a large array of applications, and shown to be a remarkably robust technique for the characterization of nano materials. For this reason, it is currently used in scientific fields as diverse as condensed matter physics [1], cell biology [2], materials science [3] and electronics [4], among others. Ptychography is based on recording the distribution of the scattering pattern produced by the interaction of an illumination with a sample. In a ptychographic experiment, only the signal intensities are measured, so one has to retrieve the corresponding phases to be able to reconstruct an image of the sample. It falls under the category of phase retrieval problems [5]. In the case of ptychography, the phases can usually be recovered by exploiting the redundancy inherent in obtaining diffraction patterns from overlapping regions of the sample.

From an algorithmic point of view, ptychography reconstruction can be briefly explained as follows (Fig. 1). The input is a stack of multiple frames containing phase-less measured intensities. Each frame corresponds to a snapshot of the light source through a specific region of the sample. These regions are known for each frame, and they are referred to as the geometry of the measurements. Using the stack of frames and their geometries, a non-linear iterative solver repeatedly approximates the phases of the measurements using two constraints: (1) the match between overlapping regions of the frames and (2) the match with a given model for the data. After the solver reaches an exit condition, the output is the overlap of the stack of frames (now with phases) in their corresponding geometries. This overlap corresponds to the 2D reconstructed image of the sample.

Computationally, ptychography poses multiple challenges. The primary challenge is that the stack of measured frames is typically two orders of magnitude bigger than the final reconstructed image. A real case example: a 700×700 pixels image of a cluster of iron particles is recovered from a stack of 900 frames, each one containing 256×256 samples (1:125 output/input ratio). It is also common that the reconstruction algorithms employ additional copies of the measured frames (or additional auxiliary structures of the same size). On the bright side, the algorithms employed in ptychography reconstruction commonly use highly fine-grained parallel operations with few dependencies. This inherent parallelism is usually exploited to achieve reasonable reconstruction times, frequently employing many-core accelerators, such as GPUs [6].

An essential consideration in ptychography algorithms resides in the data models and solver employed. Choosing the proper ones is far from trivial. In a real scenario, models for the illumination source or the background of the measurements are also usually considered. The models and solver employed determine the robustness of the reconstruction (regarding noise or experimental uncertainties), the convergence speed, and the image quality. One of the latest advances in ptychography reconstruction has been recently developed by the CAMERA team at the Lawrence Berkeley National Laboratory (LBNL). The research proposes a new model for data fitting and a new algorithm based on the Alternating Direction Method of Multipliers (ADMM) [7]. The proposed method, referred to from now on as Ptycho-ADMM [8], has been mathematically proven to converge faster than state-of-the-art algorithms, while producing better quality images, and to be more resilient to noise. Ptycho-ADMM benefits come at the expense of increased computational requirements. Besides the input stack, Ptycho-ADMM needs to keep in memory the solution stack and an additional multiplier of the same size, thus handling three times the amount of measured data. The multiplier needs to be updated in each solver step, and it is employed in the optimization of all models, so additional computation is also required.

In this paper we tackle the computational constraints of Pytcho-ADMM and design the first high performance implementation of the method. Pytcho-ADMM parallelism is analyzed to develop a CUDA-based multi-GPU solution that can efficiently make use of multiple GPU devices to achieve state-of-the-art reconstruction times. The performance of the proposed implementation is compared with SHARP [6], a high performance GPU-based ptychography solution. Although the number of arithmetic operations and memory footprint of Ptycho-ADMM is higher than that of solvers employed in SHARP, our implementation is able to achieve comparable reconstruction times, in addition to providing the robustness inherent to the Pytcho-ADMM models. The proposed Pytcho-ADMM implementation is already being used in the microscopes installed in the Advanced Light Source in the LBNL, and the code will be soon available in the Department of Energy online repository system [9].

This paper is structured as follows. Section 2 first overviews the Pytcho-ADMM method and its models, and later reviews the CUDA programming model and the basics of GPU computing. Section 3 presents the proposed solution with a detailed description of the techniques employed, and Sect. 4 assesses its performance through experimental tests. The last section summarizes this work.

2 Background

2.1 Ptycho-ADMM Overview

A ptychography experiment is usually defined as follows. A localized X-ray illumination ω scans through a specimen u, while a detector collects a sequence J of phase-less intensities a. The goal is to obtain a high resolution reconstruction of the specimen u from the sequence of intensity measurements. In a discrete setting, $u \in \mathbb{C}^n$ is a 2D image with $\sqrt{n} \times \sqrt{n}$ pixels, $\omega \in \mathbb{C}^{\bar{m}}$ is a localized 2D illumination with $\sqrt{\bar{m}} \times \sqrt{\bar{m}}$ pixels, and $a_j^2 = |\mathcal{F}(\omega \circ \mathcal{S}_j u)|^2$ is a stack of phase-less measurements $a_j \in \mathbb{R}_+^{\bar{m}} \; \forall 0 \le j \le J-1$. The operator $|\cdot|$ represents the element-wise absolute value of a vector, $\circ$ denotes the element-wise multiplication, and $\mathcal{F}$ denotes the normalized 2-dimensional discrete Fourier transform. Each $\mathcal{S}_j \in \mathbb{R}^{\bar{m} \times n}$ is a binary matrix that crops a region j of size $\bar{m}$ from the image u.

In practice, as the illumination is almost never completely known, one has to solve a blind ptychographic phase retrieval problem [10], as follows:

$$\text{To find } \omega \in \mathbb{C}^{\bar{m}} \text{ and } u \in \mathbb{C}^n, \; s.t. \; |\mathcal{A}(\omega, u)|^2 = a^2, \tag{1}$$

where bilinear operators $\mathcal{A} : \mathbb{C}^{\bar{m}} \times \mathbb{C}^n \to \mathbb{C}^m$ and $\mathcal{A}_j : \mathbb{C}^{\bar{m}} \times \mathbb{C}^n \to \mathbb{C}^{\bar{m}} \; \forall 0 \le j \le J-1$, are denoted as follows:

$$\mathcal{A}(\omega, u) := (\mathcal{A}_0^T(\omega, u), \mathcal{A}_1^T(\omega, u), \cdots, \mathcal{A}_{J-1}^T(\omega, u))^T,$$
$$\mathcal{A}_j(\omega, u) := \mathcal{F}(\omega \circ \mathcal{S}_j u),$$

and $a := (a_0^T, a_1^T, \cdots, a_{J-1}^T)^T \in \mathbb{R}_+^m$.

Instead of directly solving the quadratic multidimensional systems in (1), Ptycho-ADMM is based on the following nonlinear least squares model:

$$\min_{\omega \in \mathbb{C}^{\bar{m}}, u \in \mathbb{C}^n} \tfrac{1}{2} \big\| |\mathcal{A}(\omega, u)| - a \big\|^2. \tag{2}$$

A mapping $\mathcal{B}(\cdot, \cdot) : \mathbb{R}_+^m \times \mathbb{R}_+^m \to \mathbb{R}_+$ is used to measure the distance between the recovered intensity $g \in \mathbb{R}_+^m$ and the collected intensity $f \in \mathbb{R}_+^m$ as

$$\mathcal{B}(g, f) = \tfrac{1}{2} \| \sqrt{g} - \sqrt{f} \|^2. \tag{3}$$

Based on the above mapping $\mathcal{B}(\cdot, \cdot)$, a general nonlinear optimization model for blind ptychography similar to (2) can be rewritten as follows:

$$\text{Model:} \quad \min_{\omega \in \mathbb{C}^{\bar{m}}, u \in \mathbb{C}^n} \mathcal{G}(\mathcal{A}(\omega, u)), \tag{4}$$

with $\mathcal{G}(z) := \mathcal{B}(|z|^2, |a|^2)$. The support or amplitude constraints of the illumination and image [6,11] can also be incorporated into (4).

To solve (4), Ptycho-ADMM employs an auxiliary variable $z = \mathcal{A}(\omega, u) \in \mathbb{C}^m$, such that an equivalent form of (4) is formulated as below:

$$\min_{\omega, u, z} \mathcal{G}(z), \quad s.t. \quad z - \mathcal{A}(\omega, u) = 0. \tag{5}$$

The corresponding augmented Lagrangian reads:

$$\Upsilon_\beta(\omega, u, z, \Lambda) := \mathcal{G}(z) + \Re(\langle z - \mathcal{A}(\omega, u), \Lambda \rangle) + \frac{\beta}{2}\|z - \mathcal{A}(\omega, u)\|^2, \qquad (6)$$

with multiplier $\Lambda \in \mathbb{C}^m$, a positive parameter β, $\langle \cdot, \cdot \rangle$ representing the L^2 inner product in complex Euclidean space, and $\Re(\cdot)$ denoting the real part of a complex number. Consequently, instead of minimizing (4) directly, one seeks a saddle point of the following problem:

$$\max_{\Lambda} \min_{\omega, u, z} \Upsilon_\beta(\omega, u, z, \Lambda). \qquad (7)$$

Ptycho-ADMM proposes the following update steps to solve the problem in (7), which summarize the method:

$$u^{k+1} = \frac{\sum_j \left(\mathcal{S}_j^T((\omega^{k+1})^* \circ \mathcal{F}^* \hat{z}_j^k)\right)(t)}{\sum_j (\mathcal{S}_j^T |\omega^{k+1}|^2)(t)}, \qquad (8)$$

$$\omega^{k+1} = \frac{\sum_j (\mathcal{S}_j(u^k)^*)(t) \times (\mathcal{F}^* \hat{z}_j^k)(t)}{\sum_j |(\mathcal{S}_j u^k)(t)|^2}, \qquad (9)$$

$$z^{k+1} = \frac{a(t) + \beta|z(t)|}{1 + \beta} \times \text{sign}(z(t)), \qquad (10)$$

$$\Lambda^{k+1} = \Lambda^k + \beta(z^{k+1} - \mathcal{A}(\omega^{k+1}, u^{k+1})), \qquad (11)$$

given an iteration k and with $\hat{z}^k := z^k + \frac{\Lambda^k}{\beta}$.

2.2   CUDA and GPU Computing

GPUs are massive parallel devices composed by multiple SIMD units called streaming multiprocessors (SM). Modern GPUs have up to several dozens of SMs, and each SM can execute multiple 32-wide SIMD instructions simultaneously. The CUDA programming model defines a computation hierarchy formed by threads, warps, and thread blocks. A CUDA thread represents a single lane of a SIMD instruction. Warps are sets of 32 threads that advance their execution in a lockstep synchronous way. Commonly, all threads in a warp are executed simultaneously as a single SIMD operation. Control flow divergence among the threads of the same warp results in the sequential execution of the divergent paths, so it is commonly avoided. Thread blocks group several warps that are executed independently but that can cooperate using synchronization operations to share data. The unit of work sent from the CPU (host) to the GPU (device) is called kernel. The host can launch multiple kernels for parallel execution in one or multiple GPUs, where each kernel is composed of tens to millions of thread blocks.

The GPU memory is organized in three logical spaces: global, shared, and registers. The global memory is typically allocated in the device main memory, and it is visible to all threads in a kernel. The shared memory is only accessible by warps in the same thread block, while the registers are local to each thread. The communication between the threads in a thread block is commonly carried out via the shared memory. The occupancy of the GPU (or of a SM) is the percentage of allocated threads relative to the theoretical maximum. It is constrained by the amount of shared memory and registers assigned per thread. The registers have the highest bandwidth and lowest latency, whereas the shared memory bandwidth is lower than that of the registers. The shared memory provides flexible accesses, while the accesses to the global memory must be coalesced to achieve higher efficiency. A coalesced access occurs when consecutive threads of a warp access consecutive memory positions.

3   Proposed Implementation

The main operations involved in the models of Ptycho-ADMM are point-wise parallel, either across the stack of frames, the reconstructed image or a single frame. In this section we will present and discuss a GPU-based implementation of Ptycho-ADMM that exploits such parallelism.

The overview of the proposed solution is presented in Algorithm 1. The inputs are the measured frames ($frames_m[x, y, z]$), the coordinates of the measurements ($coord[z]$), the solver maximum iterations ($iter_{max}$) and a given tolerance. The outputs are the final $image[i, j]$ and $illumination[x, y]$ after the solver reaches an exit condition. The $frames_s[x, y, z]$ stores the partial-solution frames, whereas the $multiplier[x, y, z]$ corresponds to the additional variable required in ADMM. The $image, illumination, frames_s$ and $multiplier$ store complex numbers that represent pairs of intensity and phase values (stored as $float2$). The input $frames_m$ store the original phase-less values ($float$), whereas $coord$ stores pairs of x, y coordinates ($int2$).

The main operations of the proposed solution are highlighted in bold. **Split** corresponds to the operator $\mathcal{S}_j$, which defines a j subsection of a 2D image, whereas **Overlap** is the transposed operator $\mathcal{S}_j^T$, which merges all subsections back into an image. **SumAll** performs an addition across the third dimension of a 3D volume, as follows:

$$forall(x) \{ \quad forall(y) \{ \quad forall(z) \{$$
$$output[x, y] = output[x, y] + input[x, y, z] \quad \} \} \}$$

ForwardFT and **InverseFT** perform z 2D Fast Fourier Transforms (FFT) over a 3D input, where z is the third dimension of the input. **UpdateFrames** computes the update step in Eq. (10), and **ComputeResidual** calculates the residual between the measured and solution frames. Operators $+, -, ^*$ and $| \cdot |^2$ correspond to point-wise addition, subtraction, complex conjugate and complex norm, respectively. The operator $\times$ denotes a point-wise multiplication when both operands are of the same size, or multiple 2D point-wise multiplications when a 2D plane is multiplied with a 3D volume, as follows:

Algorithm 1.   Ptycho-ADMM

Parameters: $frames_m[x, y, z]$, $coord[z]$, $iter_{max}$, *tolerance*

1: **allocate** $image[i, j]$, $illumination[x, y]$,
                  $frames_s[x, y, z]$, $multiplier[x, y, z]$
2: $frames_s = frames_m$
3: $multiplier = 0$
4: **for** $k = 0$ **to** $iter_{max} - 1$ **do**
5:     $frames_s = \boldsymbol{ForwardFT}(frames_s)$
6:     $frames_s = \boldsymbol{UpdateFrames}(frames_s, frames_m)$
7:     $frames_s = \boldsymbol{InverseFT}(frames_s)$
8:     $frames_s = frames_s + multiplier$
9:     $illumination = \dfrac{\boldsymbol{SumAll}(frames_s \times \boldsymbol{Split}(image)^*)}{\boldsymbol{SumAll}(\boldsymbol{Split}(|image|^2))}$
10:    $image = \dfrac{\boldsymbol{Overlap}(frames_s \times illumination^*)}{\boldsymbol{Overlap}(|illumination|^2, coord)}$
11:    $residual = \boldsymbol{ComputeResidual}(frames_s, frames_m)$
12:    **if** $residual < tolerance$ **then break**
13:    $multiplier = multiplier - (illumination \times \boldsymbol{Split}(image, coord)) + frames_s$
14:    $frames_s = (illumination \times \boldsymbol{Split}(image, coord)) - multiplier$
15: **end for**
16: **return** $image$, $illumination$

$$forall(x) \{ \quad forall(y) \{ \quad forall(z) \{$$
$$output[x, y, z] = input1[x, y] \times input2[x, y, z] \quad \} \} \}$$

The most computational demanding operations correspond to **Overlap**, **Split** and **UpdateFrames**. In all three functions, the arithmetic intensity[1] is low, so the key performance considerations are the thread-to-data mapping, the device occupancy and the GPU main memory transfers. The ultimate goal is to maximize main memory bandwidth while re-using as much local data as possible. To this end, improving the device occupancy leads to more active threads, while an optimal thread-to-data mapping allows for higher data locality and coalesced accesses, both strategies leading to (potentially) higher main memory bandwidth utilization.

The proposed **Split** kernel implementation maps all CUDA threads over the output stack of frames. A single thread block is mapped to a frame so that memory is always read and written in a coalesced way. Contrary to **Split**, the **Overlap** function presents inherent data dependencies: values from different frames can overlap on the same image position. To handle such dependencies, threads are mapped over the input stack and written into the image via atomic additions over main memory. Atomic operations risk serializing multiple high latency operations when concurrency is high, penalizing performance even in latest CUDA architectures. In our scenario, atomic operations provide the best performance compared to more elaborated solutions. This is because the arith-

---

[1] Ratio of number of arithmetic operations computed per memory access.

metic load of the **Overlap** kernel is low, and the latency of the atomic operations can be easily hidden by the main memory transfers.

Data sharing is not required across the solution's main operations. This permits avoiding shared memory to use only register allocation instead, improving in this way the latency of local accesses and the overall occupancy [12]. The thread block size employed is typically 128, which permits optimal theoretical occupancy in current GPU architectures. The mapping of CUDA threads to data employed always guarantees coalesced main memory access, normally using strides of wide equal to the thread block size. To further reduce GPU main memory transfers, some lesser operations are fused into the main CUDA kernels. For instance, basic point-wise arithmetic operations, the illumination multiply or residual computations are usually computed with the nearest **Overlap** or **Split** kernel calls. Several kernel fusions implemented in the code are not reflected in Algorithm 1 for illustrative purposes.

Forward and Inverse 2D FFTs represent a significant amount of the pipeline arithmetic computation. FFT GPU implementations have been extensively studied, being the cufft library one of the most competitive solutions performance-wise. In the proposed implementation, we employ the cufft library to compute **ForwardFT** and **InverseFT**. To further maximize performance, multiple 2D FFTs are batched together, which permits the library to fusion kernel calls and maximize data re-using.

The above explanation omits multiple minor steps across the whole solving process. Different stabilizers, regularizers, penalization factors, etc. are introduced in some of the models to maximize converge speed and stability. Many of the minor computation steps are implemented using the Thrust library in order to maintain pipeline flexibility and clean interfaces. This necessary trade-off slightly hinders performance, considering that the ideal case is to fuse all minor computation steps with surrounding kernel calls.

3.1 Multi-GPU Solution

The above algorithm and discussion focus on a single GPU implementation. We extend the Algorithm 1 to support multi-GPU execution. The proposed solution employs the NVIDIA Collective Communications Library (NCCL) to implement inter-GPU communication. The partition scheme employed breaks down the workload by means of dividing the different copies of the stack of frames. This way, the $frames_m[x, y, z]$, $frames_s[x, y, z]$ and $multiplier[x, y, z]$ are divided across the z dimension based on the number of GPUs employed.

Almost all operations computed in Algorithm 1 present no dependencies across different frames when processing the 3D stacks. The exceptions are the operations carried out in lines 9, 10 and 11 of Algorithm 1. **SumAll** performs an addition over the z dimension of a 3D volume, whereas **Overlap** requires all frames to add their values into the result image. **ComputeResidual** also have to consider the residuals generated from all independent executions. All three dependencies can be solved in the following way: (1) compute the local partial result, (2) reduce across all partial results (3) broadcast the reduced output to

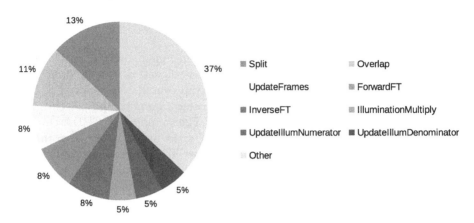

Fig. 2. Percentage of computational time of the main Ptycho-ADMM CUDA kernels when executed on a single GK210B GPU. The input data is a stack of 1600 256×256 frames. Similar results hold for other input sizes.

all independent processes. The reduce operation is an addition in all three cases. Step (2) and (3) are implemented using the directive $ncclAllReduce()$, which performs both the reduced addition and the broadcast. Step (1) is implemented in the same way as in the single-GPU execution, but taking sub-sets of frames instead of the whole stacks.

The proposed partition scheme permits a very efficient handling of the data dependencies. Communication is limited to 2D reductions when computing **Overlap** and **SumAll**, and it is only a scalar reduction when calculating **ComputeResidual**. The amount of communication is in this way comparatively small, with respect to the 3D volumes processed locally. To further reduce communication, we propose an additional optimization: communication can be configured to occur every solver iteration (default) or every n iterations. When $n > 1$, the iterations with no communication employ previous iteration results as non-local data. This can slightly reduce convergence speed, in exchange of increased performance (see next section). During iterations with no communication, the solver can be executed entirely in parallel across all GPUs. The option to enable periodic communication is provided via a command line parameter.

4   Experimental Results

The results presented in this section are executed in a dual socket workstation with two Intel Xeon E5-2683 v4, with a clock frequency of 2.10 GHz and 16 cores each. The workstation is equipped with 4 dual-slot Tesla K80 GPUs, for a total of 8 GK210B devices. Each device has 2496 CUDA cores. The implementations are compiled with gcc 5.4.0 and nvcc 8.0. The profiling results have been obtained with both Nvidia visual and inline profilers, nvvp and nvprof, respectively. All performance results consider the full pipeline execution time, including

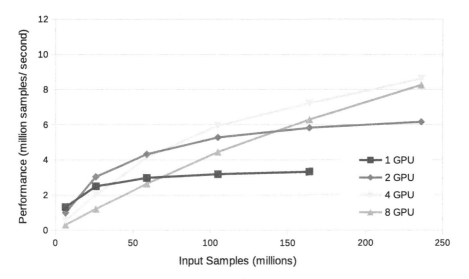

Fig. 3. Performance of the proposed Ptycho-ADMM implementation when executed using 1, 2, 4 and 8 GPUs. Multi-GPU executions communicate every single iteration.

loading the experimental data, GPU runtime initialization, memory allocation and transfers, and writing back the reconstructed image. The dataset employed corresponds to an experiment performed in the ALS during 2015 that measured a cluster of iron catalyst particles. We have selected different size slices of said experiment to analyze the performance of the proposed implementation with different input sizes. Experimental results presented below hold for other datasets and simulations tested. To simplify the computational analysis, all experiments presented in this section always run 100 solver iterations.

The proposed Ptycho-ADMM implementation achieves a GPU compute utilization of 88%, on average, when executed with significant input sizes (around 100 million input samples). Figure 2 reports the percentage of computational time of the main Ptycho-ADMM CUDA kernels. *UpdateIllumNumerator* and *UpdateIllumDenominator* compute the numerator and denominator of line 9 Algorithm 1, whereas *IlluminationMultiply* computes the multiplication of an illumination with a stack of frames. *Other* refers to the rest of kernel calls, which have a computational share of less than 5%. A single solver iteration executes a total of 64 CUDA kernels, 42 of which employ less than 0.5% of the total computational time. Out of the kernels with more than 4% of computational time, the theoretical occupancy is 100%, whereas the achieved experimental occupancy is 96%, on average.

The following experiment assesses the performance and scalability of the proposed Ptycho-ADMM solution for both single- and multi-GPU execution. Figure 3 shows the performance of the proposed implementation when executed

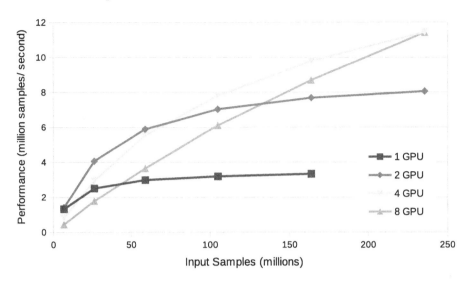

Fig. 4. Performance of the proposed Ptycho-ADMM implementation when executed using 1, 2, 4 and 8 GPUs. Multi-GPU executions communicate every 8 iterations.

using 1, 2, 4 and 8 GPU nodes[2]. This experiment employs 6 different input sizes. The vertical axis measures performance in millions of input samples divided by total execution time (the higher the better). The horizontal axis corresponds to millions of input samples. The multi-GPU executions presented in Fig. 3 perform communication every iteration.

A horizontal performance line in Fig. 3 represents linear scaling, meaning that the execution time increases proportionally to the input size. Each one of the experiments reported in Fig. 3 presents better-than-linear scaling. This is because the data sizes employed are not big enough to saturate multiple high-end GPU devices, specially with the smaller input sizes. The proposed implementation begins to saturate a single GPU at around 60 millions input samples, although the performance keeps slightly increasing for larger experiments. This proportion holds when executing the solution on 2 GPUs, with a close-to-saturation point at about 200 million input samples. With 4 and 8 GPUs, we can extrapolate the saturation point to be around 400 and 800 million samples. This suggests that, when executed on similar size GPUs, bigger data sets could still benefit from additional multi-GPU performance.

With significant input sizes, multi-GPU executions are 1.7, 2.1 and 1.8 times faster than a single GPU, using 2, 4 and 8 GPUs, respectively. A significant consideration in multi-GPU performance resides on the communication frequency employed. The above results can be improved up to a 55% by means of reducing the communication frequency. The tradeoff between communication frequency and solution convergence is maximized when communicating every 8 iterations,

---

[2] The experiment with a single GPU and more than 200 million input samples is not reported because it does not fit into the device main memory.

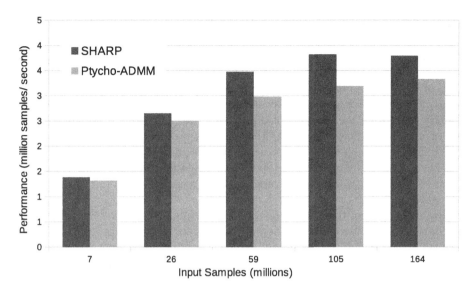

Fig. 5. Performance of the proposed Ptycho-ADMM implementation compared to that of SHARP, both executed on a single GK210B GPU. Different input sizes are employed, ranging from 100 256×256 frames to 2500 256×256 frames. Similar results are obtained with other datasets.

on average. When enough iterations are executed, this communication frequency has close-to-no impact on the convergence speed, and significantly accelerates the multi-GPU performance. Figure 4 presents the same experiment as before, but communicating every 8 iterations. In this experiment the performance of multi-GPU implementations is increased on a 40%, on average, achieving speedups of 2.3, 2.9 and 2.6 respect single GPU, for execution with 2, 4 and 8 GPUs, respectively.

The last test compares the performance of the proposed Ptycho-ADMM implementation with that of SHARP, a GPU-accelerated ptychography solution. SHARP employs the RAAR algorithm [13], a less computational intensive algorithm than Ptycho-ADMM, finely tuned for ptychography reconstruction. The results of the experiment are depicted in Fig. 5, using the same datasets as previous experiments, and executed on a single GPU. The vertical axis represents performance, in millions of input samples divided by execution time (seconds), and the horizontal axis are input samples (in millions). On average, RAAR is 10% faster than the proposed Ptycho-ADMM solution. Besides being extensively optimized for GPU computing, RAAR employs one less additional variable (of the same size of the input stack) and requires one less update step compared to Ptycho-ADMM. On the other hand, the RAAR algorithm does not provide any mathematical convergence guarantee and does not expose the robustness to noise and features proposed by Ptycho-ADMM.

5   Conclusions

This paper presents the first high performance multi-GPU implementation of Ptycho-ADMM. The solution is designed to efficiently exploit the inherent parallelism of the ptychography basic operations. The experimental results show how the implementation is able to saturate multiple high-end GPU devices and to properly scale with the increase of input data size. The ever improving brightness of accelerator based x-ray sources enables novel discoveries by means of providing faster frame rates, larger fields of view and higher resolutions. In this context of continuous increase of input data, scalable reconstruction times and robust solvers that guarantee convergence on a reasonable amount of iterations are highly valuable.

The main future work lines are related to implement a dynamic data feed system that does not require all the data to be allocated (and processed) at the same time. Employing CUDA unified memory could help achieving this goal by means of oversubscribing the GPU main memory. Additional tests with larger datasets (synthetic or real) will also be considered, together with execution on larger scale distributed memory systems using MPI.

Acknowledgment. This work was partially funded by the Center for Applied Mathematics for Energy Research Applications, a joint ASCR- BES funded project within the Office of Science, US Department of Energy, under contract number DOE-DE-AC03-76SF00098, and by the Advanced Light Source, which is a DOE Office of Science User Facility under contract no. DE-AC02-05CH11231.

References

1. Shi, X., Fischer, P., Neu, V., Elefant, D., Lee, J., Shapiro, D., Farmand, M., Tyliszczak, T., Shiu, H.-W., Marchesini, S., et al.: Soft x-ray ptychography studies of nanoscale magnetic and structural correlations in thin $SmCo_5$ films. Appl. Phys. Lett. **108**(9), 094103 (2016)
2. Giewekemeyer, K., Thibault, P., Kalbfleisch, S., Beerlink, A., Kewish, C.M., Dierolf, M., Pfeiffer, F., Salditt, T.: Quantitative biological imaging by ptychographic x-ray diffraction microscopy. Proc. Natl. Acad. Sci. **107**(2), 529–534 (2010)
3. Shapiro, D.A., Yu, Y.-S., Tyliszczak, T., Cabana, J., Celestre, R., Chao, W., Kaznatcheev, K., Kilcoyne, A.D., Maia, F., Marchesini, S., et al.: Chemical composition mapping with nanometre resolution by soft x-ray microscopy. Nat. Photonics **8**(10), 765–769 (2014)
4. Holler, M., Guizar-Sicairos, M., Tsai, E.H., Dinapoli, R., Müller, E., Bunk, O., Raabe, J., Aeppli, G.: High-resolution non-destructive three-dimensional imaging of integrated circuits. Nature **543**(7645), 402–406 (2017)
5. Marchesini, S.: Invited article: a unified evaluation of iterative projection algorithms for phase retrieval. Rev. Sci. Instr. **78**(1), 011301 (2007)
6. Marchesini, S., Krishnan, H., Daurer, B.J., Shapiro, D.A., Perciano, T., Sethian, J.A., Maia, F.R.: Sharp: a distributed GPU-based ptychographic solver. J. Appl. Crystallogr. **49**(4), 1245–1252 (2016)

7. Glowinski, R., Tallec, P.L.: Augmented Lagrangian and Operator-Splitting Methods in Nonlinear Mechanics. SIAM Studies in Applied Mathematics, Society for Industrial and Applied Mathematics, Philadelphia (1989)
8. Chang, H., Enfedaque, P., Marchesini, S.: Blind Ptychographic Phase Retrieval via Convergent Alternating Direction Method of Multipliers (2018, submitted)
9. Department of energy online repository system, January 2018. https://github.com/doecode/
10. Thibault, P., Dierolf, M., Bunk, O., Menzel, A., Pfeiffer, F.: Probe retrieval in ptychographic coherent diffractive imaging. Ultramicroscopy $\mathbf{109}(4)$, 338–343 (2009)
11. Hesse, R., Luke, D.R., Sabach, S., Tam, M.K.: Proximal heterogeneous block implicit-explicit method and application to blind ptychographic diffraction imaging. SIAM J. Imaging Sci. $\mathbf{8}(1)$, 426–457 (2015)
12. Enfedaque, P., Auli-Llinas, F., Moure, J.C.: Implementation of the DWT in a GPU through a register-based strategy. IEEE Trans. Parallel Distrib. Syst. $\mathbf{26}(12)$, 3394–3406 (2015)
13. Luke, D.R.: Relaxed averaged alternating reflections for diffraction imaging. Inverse Probl. $\mathbf{21}(1)$, 37–50 (2005)

Elastic CPU Cap Mechanism for Timely Dataflow Applications

M. Reza Hoseinyfarahabady[1][(✉)], Nazanin Farhangsadr[1], Albert Y. Zomaya[1], Zahir Tari[2], and Samee U. Khan[3]

[1] School of IT, Center for Distributed and High Performance Computing,
The University of Sydney, Sydney, Australia
{reza.hoseiny,albert.zomaya}@sydney.edu.au
[2] School of Science, RMIT University, Melbourne, Australia
zahir.tari@rmit.edu.au
[3] Department of Electrical and Computer Engineering, North Dakota State
University, Fargo, USA
samee.khan@ndsu.edu

Abstract. Sudden surges in the incoming workload can cause adverse consequences on the run-time performance of data-flow applications. Our work addresses the problem of limiting CPU associated with the elastic scaling of timely data-flow (TDF) applications running in a shared computing environment while each application can possess a different quality of service (QoS) requirement. The key argument here is that an unwise consolidation decision to dynamically scale up/out the computing resources for responding to unexpected workload changes can degrade the performance of some (if not all) collocated applications due to their fierce competition getting the shared resources (such as the last level cache). The proposed solution uses a queue-based model to predict the performance degradation of running data-flow applications together. The problem of CPU cap adjustment is addressed as an optimization problem, where the aim is to reduce the quality of service violation incidents among applications while raising the CPU utilization level of server nodes as well as preventing the formation of bottlenecks due to the fierce competition among collocated applications. The controller uses and efficient dynamic method to find a solution at each round of the controlling epoch. The performance evaluation is carried out by comparing the proposed controller against an enhanced QoS-aware version of round robin strategy which is deployed in many commercial packages. Experimental results confirmed that the proposed solution improves QoS satisfaction by near to 148% on average while it can reduce the latency of processing data records for applications in the highest QoS classes by near to 19% during workload surges.

Keywords: Shared resource interference
Distributed stream processing
Scheduling and resource allocation algorithms

1   Introduction

Timely data-flow is a recent powerful general-purpose low-level abstraction layer to be used in developing scientific/enterprise programs that consist of large-scale *iterative* computations over batch- or streaming- based data records [22]. The growing demand for fast analysis over a high volume of unstructured data records [3,16] has led to the development of several *acyclic* batch processing or streaming data processing such as MapReduce [11], CStream [26], and Microsoft Sonora [31]. However, an important feature of emerging applications in several domains, such as deep learning algorithms, is their need to *iteratively* execute certain modules with many parallel tasks over a large amount of data elements (either in batch or in streaming mode) until a termination condition is matched [13].

The goal of the timely data-flow model is to bring together all *three key advantages* of the previous computational models, namely (i) batch computational model, (ii) the streaming computational model, and (iii) the graph computational model, into a common paradigm, while retaining the performance of each system. To this end, the timely data-flow model supports both *stateful iterative* and *incremental computations* to coordinate the fine-grained synchronous and asynchronous execution of parallel tasks. The model involves a directed *cyclic* graph where its vertex set represents the computational tasks, each can send and receive logically timestamped *stateful* data elements along the directed edges of the graph. Nevertheless, the new model satisfies the three main requirements: (i) low-latency, (ii) synchronous/asynchronous iteration, and (iii) strict consistency of the intermediate sub-computational results, alongside each other [12].

On the other hand, handling the fast processing requirement over a large volume of data in a scalable manner, taking advantage of a server farm of tens or even hundreds of server nodes seems inevitable [14]. Two important design objectives of such large-scale systems are to employ parallelism techniques to attain a high scalable solution by avoiding single-node bottlenecks while the hardware resource usage needs to be utilized in a cost effective way. To enable better scaling at a lower cost, a service provider (SP) of such frameworks often chooses hosting tens of thousands of users applications on the available computing resources at the same time. While the main objective of the service provider is to maximize her revenue, an end-user (*e.g.*, an application owner) may demand fast execution time. However, Satisfying such incompatible objectives can disappointingly lead to under/over-utilization of precious cycles of computing resources in many practical cases.

Another critical requirement for a data-flow processing system is fulfilling the **quality of service** (QoS) requested by the application owners as specified in the **service level agreement** (SLA). While a dynamic resource allocation strategy can provision a new server once the capacity of the available resources is not enough to cope with the incoming load, there exists several practical scenarios in which it is almost impossible to avoid QoS violations for executing all applications over the course of their execution, particularly if there are unexpected spikes in the incoming traffic. In case of such scenarios, a QoS-aware resource manager needs to carefully comply with the service-level objectives while maximizing the overall system performance.

This paper proposes a low-overhead feedback controller for elastic adjustment of CPU resources in a timely data-flow platform running on a shared distributed environment. The key features of our solution is taking QoS enforcements and shared-resource interference among collocated threads into account when making resource allocation decisions. Our solution uses a prediction module to estimate the latency of each computational module by employing a queue-based model and estimating of the future rates for incoming data records. We benchmarked the proposed solution against the enhanced round robin policy with respect to two major performance metrics of response time of data records processing (18.8% improvement), and QoS violation rates (77% overall improvement) for the workloads that either resemble Poisson distribution for arrival or heavy-tailed patterns (Weibull distribution).

The remainder of this paper is organized as follows. Section 3 concisely introduces the background knowledge to help the reader appreciate the corresponding concepts of the new paradigm. Section 4 gives insights into the proposed controller. Section 5 summarizes the results on the experimental evaluations, followed by some comparison to related work presented in Sect. 2. Finally, Sect. 6 draws some final conclusions.

2   Related Work

Parallel data-flow platforms have been effectively employed in the field of big data mining where algorithms show an iterative nature. Naiad [22] has been designed as the first distributed system for running parallel and iterative operations over either batch or streaming data-flows. In Naiad, each message has a logical time-stamp as well as some location-generation meta-data that allows the underlying system to figure out the right order and the associated priority of each message. However, the thread-level elasticity is not supported by the system.

Apache Spark [33] is a fast, in-memory data processing engine to execute iterative algorithms over the streaming data-sets. It probably has the most similarity with timely data-flow paradigm when compared to other existing frameworks. However, the big difference between the two paradigms is that while the timely data-flow engine maintains a set of persistent tasks that repeatedly send and receive the data records, the Apache Spark engine starts and stops worker tasks (by breaking the computation into lots of independent tasks) similar to most batch processing engines do. This allows the TDF engine to support very fast scheduling of operators in microsecond scales, as shown by [19].

Many existing resource allocation strategies, *e.g.*, [15,17] manage resources based on OS level metrics, such as per core utilization, I/O capacities, and energy usage of resources while ignore the negative performance caused by interference at the shared resources (LLC or memory bandwidth). However, a careful study by [30] confirmed that any resource management scheme that is unaware about the interference of shared resources is entirely a failure. Such a mechanism is necessary to avoid the performance degradation problem caused by consolidation decision among collocated workloads.

The work in [32] attempted to anticipate the micro-architecture-level interference by using an *offline* profiling phase. Rao *et al.* proposed an effective metric to predict the performance of applications running in a NUMA system [24]. Such a metric can be leveraged to design a resource allocation that is aware of contention among shared resources. However, obtaining such an interference signature through profiling might not be feasible in every practical cases, as the interference attributes of applications could change over the run-time. Authors in [7,8] proposed a method to reduce the negative impact of architecture-level shared resource contention on a hyper-visor-based cloud platform. However, it seems that these projects concern mainly with tuning resources on one server node, while our focus is to devise a resource allocation mechanism in a cluster of server nodes where *parallelization* of each data-flow application is of great importance to the overall performance of the system.

Using a predictive-based model is not new in computing systems [20,21]. [2,20,21,23]. Most of these works proposed a multi-input, multi-output (MIMO) resource controller that automatically adapts to dynamic changes in a shared infrastructure. Such models try to estimate the complex relationship between the application performance and the resource allocation, and adjusts the embedded model by measuring the clients' response time. While there are similarities between the proposed solution with previous MPC-based controllers, our solution responds to the degraded performance level by measuring the number of waiting messages and then applying a more accurate queuing based formula to estimate the response time of each application.

3   Background

Designing a scalable and fault-tolerant distributed system for running parallel programs for processing streaming data (or data-flow) has been recently receiving a lot of attention. This includes dealing with the upcoming issues in the processing of data-flow in near real-time fashion. This section provides brief background information about the core concepts used in this area, called *timely dataflow*, which is first introduced by Microsoft researchers in 2013 [22].

3.1   Cyclic Data-Flow Model

Timely data-flow proposes a new concept to embrace the three advantages of prevalent giant models for processing large amount of data. It offers (1) *high throughput* (for batch processing systems), (2) *low latency* (for stream processing engines), and (3) the ability to perform *iterative*, *stateful*, and *incremental* computations over incoming data-flow. This new model resolves the complexities of combining such features under one umbrella, *e.g.*, nesting loops inside streaming contexts that keeps state of the computations [22].

The model supports a new form of logical timestamps attached to each data-flow computation as an efficient, lightweight coordination mechanism for supporting iterative and incremental processing. At any given time, the platform maintains a set of point-stamps of those message which are still in progress. This is done to track the progress of messages processing. So, each parallel worker knows the number of outstanding data-flow messages that are still live and needs to be delivered for further processing. The directed data-flow graph allows the platform to efficiently track the set of data records that might possibly flow throughout the computational graph. Such information can be used to quickly coordinate among all working threads to detect the possibility of additional data records to arrive at future epochs or iterations [6].

3.2 Shared Resource Interference

To enhance the utilization of the computational resources, a service provider can employ the "consolidation" method to host multiple data-flow applications submitted by different end-users into one (or more) physical node(s). Nevertheless, one cannot ignore the performance degradation experienced by consolidated applications due to the fact that one application may evict the data of other collocated applications whenever it is context switched to a CPU core. The consequence is an undesirable increase in the latency of other applications to access their own data in the main memory in the next CPU cycles.

It is well known that finding an effective consolidation solution in a shared-memory platform is challenging [27, 29, 30], mainly because each application has its unique resource consumption attributes while at the same time it requires a certain amount of quality of service level to be guaranteed by the underlying platform. Furthermore, applications can compete with each other to access the shared micro-architecture level resources such as last level cache and/or memory bandwidth, while the incoming traffic of data-flow to each application can vary temporally. To the best of our knowledge, no empirical research study exists to address the problem of the negative performance impact of shared resource contention among collocated timely data-flow applications.

4 QoS-Aware CPU Cap Adjustment

To achieve the required performance level enforced by QoS rules, e.g., end-to-end response time, we use a model based on queuing theory to adjust CPU caps of each sub-component. We also employ "control theory" principles to design a robust strategy that dynamically regulates the performance parameters of each sub-component in response to the continuous feedback from the state of the underlying platform. The key idea is to leave the resource allocation decision to run-time, in which the resource controller can measure the following performance metrics: (1) the incoming rate of each application, (2) the available capacity of CPU capacity per host, (3) the QoS violation rate per each application, and (4) the contention on shared resources per host.

To resist against the temporal changes in the arrival rate of each module, we adjust the percentage of the CPU core to allocate to each working thread according to the number of outstanding messages in the main buffer of each computational module which is a good approximation of the end-to-end delays that each data-flow message may experience. We use a model predictive control (MPC) as a mathematically well-defined mechanism (1) to predict the future average arrival rate of messages to each data-flow, and (2) to dynamically make CPU cap decision based on the current and the predicated future states. At each controlling epoch the controller measures a set of performance metrics and compares them with their desired value reflected in SLA contract. MPC-based controller can provide a robust performance despite the modelling errors [25] is to keep the tracking error within an acceptable range.

The proposed mechanism consists of four components of system model, estimator, optimizer, and anti-saturation. The system model uses a formula for $G/G/M$ queues to abstract the complex running time behaviour of each thread. A $G/G/M$ queue represents a system with M servers where both the interarrival times of customers and the relevant service times have a general distribution.

The estimator uses a simple formula based on auto regressive integrated moving average (ARIMA) model to predict the input traffic rate of each application. The optimizer module uses a dynamic programming method to iteratively adjust CPU cap of each thread by considering the performance values obtained from the other two modules. Lastly, the anti-saturation component is used to prevent over-utilization of CPU in each host, particularly in cases when the CPU demand is higher than the available capacity.

4.1   QoS Guarantee Semantic

We assume that there are exactly Q different classes of QoS contracts that an end-user can choose from. Each QoS class $1 \leq q \leq Q$ is indicated using a predefined pair of values, denoted by $\langle w_q^*, V_q \rangle$, each reflects a fixed service parameter. The w_q^* value defines the maximum acceptable average processing delay of messages belonging to an application of class q.

$V_q(\Delta T)$ reflects an acceptable upper bound for the percentage of QoS violation incidents for all applications in class q during an arbitrary interval of size ΔT. A good candidate for V is a linear rule like $V_q = 1 - \frac{q}{Q+C}$, where C is a constant. As a concrete example, assume a scenario that $|Q| = 3$, and the associated upper bounds of each QoS class is taken from are $V_{q=1..3} \in \{0.99, 0.90, 0.70\}$, where the first class ($q = 1$) has the highest priority. So, the delay of processing data-flows belonging to q_1 can be higher than w_1^* only for 1% of the entire messages entered to the system during any arbitrary interval.

4.2   System Model

We use Allen-Cunneen approximation of $G/G/M$ queue [4] to estimate an upper-bound of the *average* end-to-end response time experienced by each message in the main buffer of each computational vertex. Based on this formula, the average waiting time of customers (denoted as W_M) in any general $G/G/M$ queue can be approximated by the following equation:

$$W_M = \frac{P_{cb,M}}{\mu M(1-\rho)} \left(\frac{C_S^2 + C_D^2}{2} \right), \tag{1}$$

where $C_D = \sigma_D/E_D$ and $C_S = \sigma_S/E_S$ are the coefficients of variation for inter-arrival time and service time, respectively. Sometimes, the term $\frac{C_S^2 + C_D^2}{2}$ is referred to the *stochastic variability* of the queue. The term $P_{cb,M}$ is the probability that all servers are busy; hence, the waiting time of a recently arrived customer is above zero. For a queuing system with only one server ($M = 1$) this parameter can be calculated as $P_{cb,M} = \rho_{C_i}$, where $\rho_{C_i} = \frac{\lambda_{C_i}}{\bar{\mu}_{C_i}}$ is the service traffic intensity of component C_i (*i.e.*, its utilization). Here, λ_{C_i} is the average number of messages arriving to the main buffer of component C_i per unit of time, and $\bar{\mu}_{C_i}$ is the average number of messages to be served per unit of time by each working thread associated with component C_i. Otherwise, *i.e.*, $M \geq 2$, one can use the following formula as suggested by [5].

$$P_{cb,M} \approx \begin{cases} (\rho^M + \rho)/2 & \text{if } \rho \geq 0.7 \\ \rho^{\frac{M+1}{2}} & \text{otherwise} \end{cases}, \tag{2}$$

where $\rho_{C_i} = \frac{\lambda_{C_i}}{M\bar{\mu}_{C_i}}$. It is worth noting that while the A-C formula was developed using some computational-based estimation techniques without a formal proof, it gives a very good approximation to the average waiting time of customers in a $G/G/M$ queuing system. As reported by Tanner in [28], the value obtained by the A-C formula were within 10% of their actual values in most scenarios.

At any given time, each computational module needs to identify the right number of concurrent working threads, *i.e.*, the parallel degree, shown by M in (1) and (2). To make the problem tractable, we allow each computational module to increase or decrease its parallel degree at most by *one* during every controlling interval. Let $M^o_{(\tau,C_i)}$ denote the parallel degree of a computational module C_i during a given interval τ. The controller just needs to recompute (1) and (2) for the subsequent intervals by replacing the parallel degree with $M^o_{(\tau,C_i)}$, $M^+_{(\tau,C_i)} = M^o_{(\tau,C_i)} + 1$ and $M^-_{(\tau,C_i)} = M^o_{(\tau,C_i)} - 1$, respectively, and then choose the best result among them.

If a computational module resides within a loop context, the average waiting time obtained by (1) needs to be multiplied by the average number of times that the loop context is run over its input messages. Let $\bar{v}_{C_i}$ denote the average value of the loop variable for C_i as a computational module within a loop context. Finding the exact value of $\bar{v}_{C_i}$ is computationally expensive, as one needs to keep track of all messages processed by each computational module. A good estimation of the loop variable for each module perfectly works in most practical scenarios, as the MPC-based scheme is not too sensitive to the correctness of its input values.

To this end, we employ an estimation procedure based on a well-known Monte Carlo sampling method, called the *AA Algorithm* [10]. This algorithm is a fully-polynomial randomized approximation scheme (FPRAS) that uses the *minimum possible number of measurement* to estimate the value of $\bar{v}$.

Using the *AA Algorithm*, we can drive a good estimation of the total average processing time of messages that belong to an application by summing up the response time of a vertex (multiplied by $\bar{v}_{C_i}$ if C_i resides in a loop context).

We use ARIMA model to estimate the average arrival rate of messages to the first computational component of each data-flow application for the next controlling intervals. Based on this model, the future value of a random variable, such as $\lambda_{\kappa}^{C_1}$, can be estimated using a series of previous observations [9]. The controller then can calculate the desirable amount of CPU capacity to be assigned to each thread such that the application meets its QoS requirements.

4.3   Resource Allocation Parameters

The optimization module operates in periodic control intervals to adjust the CPU cap for each data-flow application. The optimization goal is accomplished through a two-phase process. First, it determines the desirable demand of each application for the CPU credit. Then, it computes the resource share that can be allocated to each application based on available resource capacity, a cost-benefit analysis, and the server nodes' status. Upon receiving of initial desirable CPU demands from all applications, the optimization module determines the possibility of satisfying all demands by considering the fact that there might not be enough resource capacities available within the entire cluster. This enables all applications to meet their performance targets as specified by the QoS requirements.

In case of *resource scarcity*, however, the optimization module tries to maximize the contribution (or the reward) that the system provider receives from a resource allocation decision by applying a cost-benefit analysis. Each working process has been assigned a quantum-based *cap*. A non-zero cap means that the amount of CPU time to be assigned to the thread process cannot run above the certain cap amount (even if the other processes are idle). So, a cap value of 200 means two CPU cores and 50 means half a core [1].

4.4   Optimization Module

We define a contribution function to reflect that quantifies the value of the gains (and losses) for all applications affected by a CPU adjustment decision. Let $D_{a_i,\tau}^*$ denote the CPU cap demanded by a particular application a_i at any given time τ. Let R_τ^o denote the total amount of CPU cap that the available switched-on server nodes can provide. Further, let R_τ^+, and R_τ^- denote the provided CPU cap if one server is added or removed from the current set of switched-on server nodes, respectively.

To mitigate the negative effect of poor RA decisions on the overall revenue, we only calculate the R^+ and R^- at any controlling epoch. We will allow the controller to add or remove at most one server node from the available server nodes at any decision interval; hence, the feedback loop can detect the negative effect of any poor decision and let the controller stop such results.

Let us define a *contribution* function for each application a_i, denoted by $\mathcal{C}_{a_i}(r_{a_i})$, that determines the reward that is received by the service provider if r_{a_i} CPU cap is allocated to this application as follows.

$$\mathcal{C}_{a_i}(r_{a_i}) = \mathcal{I}(q_{a_i}) \times (r_{a_i} - D^*_{a_i}), \tag{3}$$

where q_{a_i} is the QoS class that the application belongs to, and $\mathcal{I}(q_{a_i})$ represents the importance weight associated with each QoS class. At any given controlling interval τ, we would like to maximize the total contribution of the service provider as $\max_r \sum_{a_i \in \mathcal{A}} \mathcal{C}_{a_i}(r_{a_i})$, where $\mathcal{A}$ denotes the set of available applications. We solve the aforementioned optimization problem with subject to the obvious constraint of $r_{a_i} \geq 0$ and another constraint on the available resource cap on three different cases (*i.e.*, R^o, R^+ and R^-).

$$\sum_{a_i \in \mathcal{A}} r_{a_i} = R^*_\tau \text{ where } R^*_\tau \in \{R^o_\tau, R^+_\tau, R^-_\tau\}. \tag{4}$$

We then pick the best solution among the three cases. If we assume that r_{a_i} can be only taken from discrete values, *e.g.*, $r_{a_i} \in \{10, 20, \cdots\}$, then solving this problem can be done using a standard dynamic programming strategy as follows. Let $V_i(R_i)$ denote the value of having R_i resource cap remaining to allocate to any application a_j where $j \geq i$. So, we only need to recursively solve the following Bellman's equation:

$$V_i(R_i) = \max_{0 \leq r_i \leq R_i} \left(\mathcal{C}_{a_i}(r_{a_i}) + V_{i+1}(R_i - r_{a_i}) \right). \tag{5}$$

Let $n = |\mathcal{A}|$ denote the total number of applications. The initial step is to solve the problem of $V_n(R) = \max_{0 \leq r_{a_n} \leq R^*} \mathcal{C}_{a_n}(r_{a_n})$, for all possible values of $0 \leq R \leq R^*_\tau$.

To quantify the slowdown rate caused by a consolidation action, we pursue an effective method based on the solution initially introduced in [27,30]. So, the impact of workloads' contention on both LLC and memory bandwidth can be computed as a sudden rise in the *memory bandwidth utilization*, denoted by MBW_{util}. By measuring the two standard hardware events as an indicator of memory reads and writes, one can compute the utilization level of memory bandwidth [27,30] (using *perf* in Linux).

5   Experimental Evaluation

We built a proof-of-concept prototype using a modular open-source implementation of timely data-flow in Rust (the source code is obtainable from [18]). We performed a set of experiments using synthetic applications to validate the versatility of the proposed solution under sudden changes in the arrival rate of data-flow applications. We measure the effectiveness of the proposed solution with respect to the following metrics: (1) the average latency experienced by each data-flow application, and (2) the amount of QoS violations experienced by each data-flow application.

We compare our solution against an enhanced round robin method (ERR) which assigns a fixed value for the number of working threads determined by the QoS class that the application belongs to. We fixed the number of QoS classes to three and the parallel degree values to $\{8, 4, 2\}$ to be used by ERR heuristic. The enhanced interference-aware version of this strategy averts sending extra load to a physical machine that is marked as over-utilized.

All of the experiments reported in the following sections have been performed in a local cluster consisting of 4 nodes (from Amazon EC2) with total 16 logical cores. Each machine is installed with 8 GB of main memory and equipped with a 3.40 GHz Intel i3 CPU. The controller developed in C++ uses a dedicated node equipped with 2.3 GHz CPU with 16 GB of RAM.

5.1   Attributes of Synthetic Applications

We created $|\mathcal{A}| = \{50, 100, 200\}$ different data-flow applications where each application has four computational modules. Each computational module runs a CPU-intensive script (taken from RUBiS benchmark, a well-known cloud web application that emulates the core functionality of an auction site) that its running time varies based on the type of the incoming message ranging from 100 ms to 3400 ms with an average of 900 ms. We select three different QoS classes in our experiments and randomly assign each application to one of the QoS classes, where the associated upper bound of each class is $\mathcal{V}_{q=1..3} \in \{0.99, 0.90, 0.50\}$.

We bind the first computational module of each application to an external message emitter where its generation rate is a *varied* value taken from either a Poisson or a Weibull distribution. The corresponding parameter in Poisson case varies in range of $\lambda_P \in [0.2, 1]$, where λ_P represents the average number of messages generated per hundred milliseconds. The Weibull distribution occurs often in applications with heavy-tailed patterns. We allow the two corresponding parameters in Weibull case, *i.e.*, α_W as the scale and β_W as the shape parameter, to vary as $\alpha_W \in [1.1, 4]$ and $\beta_W \in [2, 6]$. The average number of incoming data elements per hundred milliseconds in the Weibull case can be derived by $\alpha_W \Gamma(1 + 1/\beta_W)$ (Γ: Gamma function). The controller also uses a history window of 3 past intervals prior to the current epoch.

Figure 1(a) represents the 99th percentile average response time of applications belong to the highest priority class (q_1) as a function of time (controlling epochs) when the QoS target sets to 620 ms to achieve. Initially all applications have the same CPU cap allocations. Compared to the static allocation strategy, the proposed scheme can co-ordinate CPU cap adjustment based on the QoS requirements in the run-time. It automatically adjusts the CPU cap of q_1 applications to reduce their response time from 1500 ms close to the target value (by augments their initial CPU cap by a factor of 3.4×).

In fact, we dynamically modify the workload stress of some applications in a way that there are not enough CPU shares to comply with the performance targets of all applications as follows. During the first 40 control epochs (*Phase I*), there are enough CPU caps so that all applications belonging to different QoS classes can meet the requested performance target. But at this time (and continuously toward the last epoch) (*Phase II*), we intentionally allow applications from different QoS classes increase their message generation rates by a factor of $1.8\times$, $2.7\times$, and $3.6\times$ for q_1, q_3, and q_3 classes, respectively, in a linear fashion from 40th epoch till 51th epoch. The generation rates remain still toward the end of the experiment for all QoS classes.

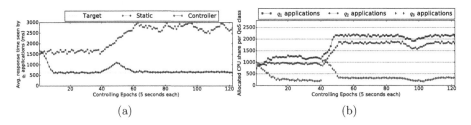

Fig. 1. (a) Improvement in average response time compared to the static allocation scheme, and (b) CPU allocation share for applications in different quality of service classes. An unexpected burst of messages arrives to the system at 40-th epoch (a majority of the burst messages ($>75\%$) belongs to the lowest QoS class, q_3).

In the second phase, the controller cannot fully satisfy all incoming demands; hence, it runs the cost/benefit of compromising among the performance level of different applications. So, it decides to assign more CPU shares to q_1 applications; hence, force their response time converge to the target faster than the q_2 and q_3 applications. As a result, it refrains from satisfying almost all (87%) and some (33%) of the demands from q_3 and q_2 applications, respectively, to meet the requested target value during the burst period, when the target is set to be 1400 ms and 1100 ms, respectively.

The static scheme tends to equally (or based on the incoming workload of applications) distribute CPU shares among applications which in most scenarios can cause a performance degradation (*i.e.*, QoS violations) for both q_1 and q_2 applications ($> 91\%$ and $> 74\%$ during the run-time when the target is set to be 900 ms and 1200 ms, respectively). Nevertheless, the issue can be amplified (by a factor of up to $3\times$) due to the resource scarcity during the burst periods.

Figure 1(b) depicts the amount of CPU caps assigned by our solution to different applications belonging different QoS classes. It confirms that the controller exhibits a fast convergence for adjusting CPU caps for applications of highest QoS classes to satisfy their demands. During Phase II the controller decides to add a new server node to the existing cluster as it recognizes that the current computing capacity is not enough to satisfy all demands from q_1 applications.

On the other hand, the static ERR scheme over-provisions CPU cap for q_3 applications severely diminishes achieving the performance target for both q_1 and q_2 applications ($> 91\%$ and $> 77\%$ on average, respectively).

Table 1. Improvement in (a) average latency [%] of processing of data records, and (b) average reduction in QoS violation incidents [%] (during Phase II) achieved by the proposed solution compared to ERR in different scenarios.

Application's QoS class	Poisson (θ)		Weibull (α, β)		Avg.	Application's QoS class	Poisson (θ)		Weibull (α, β)		Avg.
	1	0.2	(1.1, 4)	(4, 6)			1	0.2	(1.1, 4)	(4, 6)	
q_1	14.2	18.1	13.6	29.3	18.8	q_1	89	96	178	227	147.5
q_2	6.8	12.3	9.0	21.7	12.45	q_2	75	80	103	98	89
q_3	1.1	-1.9	1.2	-6.5	-1.5	q_3	14	3	-7	-28	-4.5
Average	7.3	9.5	8.0	14.8	9.9	Average	59	60	91	99	77

(a)   (b)

Table 1(a) lists the improvement in average processing time per data records experienced by each application grouped by the corresponding QoS class. The total number of data-flow applications in this scenario is fixed to 200. Modifying the arrival distribution of data records affects the performance of the proposed approach in reducing the overall average processing time of applications with highest QoS requirements (*i.e.*, q_1 and q_2). Particularly, such an improvement is more significant in the Weibull distribution of incoming traffic (which can be considered as a heavy-tailed workload) by an average of 21.5% (max 29.3%).

Table 1(b) lists the amount of reduction in the QoS violation incidents experienced by applications in different QoS classes that is achieved by applying our solution compared to the outcome of the enhanced round robin scheme in different scenarios. Our solution can reduce the QoS violation incidents on average by near 78% (maximum 227%) compared to the ERR heuristic that uses all available computing resources. Particularly, the improvement in reducing QoS violation of applications in highest QoS classes is more significant when the incoming traffic follows a heavy-tailed (Weibull) pattern. The average of such improvement in such cases is 203%.

6   Conclusions

Designing a well-utilized CPU cap adjustment strategy for timely data-flow platform requires understanding the dynamic functioning of computational modules in a shared platform. Timely data-flow is a powerful and general-purpose programming abstraction for creating iterative and streaming computational components that no other existing system (such as streaming/batch processing engines) supports. While the timely data-flow programming model supports thread-level parallelism as form of thread communication via ordered messages at scale, it is an absolute requirement to design an elastic CPU cap adjustment algorithm that continually monitors the related performance metrics of the underlying system to assign the right amount of CPU capacity to applications that might request different QoS level. In a shared distributed environment, such non-cooperative applications fiercely compete for obtaining shared resources (such as last level cache) at the cost of performance degradation of each other.

An uncontrolled resource allocation discipline along with the uncoordinated execution of each computational component can severely damage the overall QoS fulfillment, by not hitting the performance target. In this paper, we presented a low-overhead feedback-driven resource allocation mechanism that dynamically adapts computational resources for co-running timely data-flow applications in a shared cluster. It consists of a model predictive based controller that adjust the resource share of each application by solving an optimization problem using a dynamic programming method to fulfil application's SLO. The effectiveness of the proposed solution has demonstrated an average improvement of performance in terms of latency of processing data records for applications in high QoS classes by 21% in average compared to the enhanced round robin policy.

Future Work. We realized that the proposed controller has a certain upper bound on achieving its performance when running on a local cluster, particularly when a majority of computing modules suddenly receives a huge traffic. In such cases, the proposed controller needs to be equipped with a migration technique to launch more threads to stop further QoS violation. The next step can be a comprehensive study for comparing the effectiveness of the proposed method with some advanced sophisticated scheduling algorithms.

Acknowledgement. We would like to acknowledge the support by Australian Research Council (ARC) for the work carried out in this paper, under Linkage project scheme (LP160100406). Samee U. Khan's work is supported by (while serving at) the National Science Foundation. Any opinion, findings, and conclusions or recommendations expressed in this material are those of the authors and do not necessarily reflect the views of the National Science Foundation.

References

1. Xen credit scheduler. wiki.xen.org/wiki/Credit_Scheduler. Accessed 1 Nov 2017
2. Abdelwahed, S., et al.: On the application of MPC techniques for adaptive performance management of computing systems. IEEE Trans. Netw. Serv. Manag. **6**(4), 212–225 (2009)
3. Akidau, T., Balikov, A., et al.: Millwheel: fault-tolerant stream processing at internet scale. Proc. VLDB Endow. **6**(11), 1033–1044 (2013)
4. Allen, A.O.: Probability, Statistics, and Queueing Theory. Academic Press, Cambridge (2014)
5. Bolch, G., Greiner, S., de Meer, H., Trivedi, K.S.: Queueing Networks and Markov Chains. Wiley, Hoboken (2006)
6. Thekkath, C.: Naiad project (2017). https://www.microsoft.com/en-us/research/project/naiad

7. Chen, L., Shen, H.: Considering resource demand misalignments to reduce resource over-provisioning in cloud. In: IEEE Conference on Computer Communications (2017)
8. Chen, L., Shen, H., Platt, S.: Cache contention aware VM placement & migration in cloud. In: International Conference on Network Protocols, pp. 1–10. IEEE (2016)
9. Croarkin, C., Tobias, P., Filliben, J.J., Hembree, B., Guthrie, W.: NIST/SEMATECH e-Handbook of Statistical Methods. NIST, U.S. Department of Commerce, NY, USA (2006). http://www.itl.nist.gov/div898/handbook
10. Dagum, P., Karp, R., Luby, M., Ross, S.: An optimal algorithm for Monte Carlo estimation. SIAM J. Comput. **29**(5), 1484–1496 (2000)
11. Dean, J., Ghemawat, S.: Mapreduce: simplified data processing on large clusters. Commun. ACM **51**(1), 107–113 (2008)
12. Murray, D.: An introduction to timely dataflow (2017). bigdataatsvc.wordpress.com/2013/09/18/an-introduction-to-timely-dataflow/
13. Dudoladov, S., Xu, C., et al.: Optimistic recovery for iterative dataflows in action. In: ACM SIGMOD International Conference on Management of Data, pp. 1439–1443 (2015)
14. Hirzel, M., Soulé, R., Schneider, S., Gedik, B., Grimm, R.: A catalog of stream processing optimizations. ACM Comput. Surv. (CSUR) **46**(4), 46 (2014)
15. Huang, X., Xue, G., Yu, R., Leng, S.: Joint scheduling and beamforming coordination in cloud radio access networks with qos guarantees. IEEE Trans. Veh. Technol. **65**(7), 5449–5460 (2016)
16. Li, B., Diao, Y., Shenoy, P.: Supporting scalable analytics with latency constraints. Proc. VLDB Endow. **8**(11), 1166–1177 (2015)
17. Li, K., Liu, C., Li, K.: An approximation algorithm based on game theory for scheduling simple linear deteriorating jobs. Theor. Comput. Sci. **543**, 46–51 (2014)
18. McSherry, F.: A modular implementation of timely dataflow in rust. https://github.com/frankmcsherry/timely-dataflow. Accessed 1 Nov 2017
19. McSherry, F., Isard, M., et al.: Scalability! but at what cost? In: HotOS (2015)
20. Mencagli, G.: Adaptive model predictive control of autonomic distributed parallel computations with variable horizons and switching costs. Concurrency Comput.: Pract. Exp. **28**(7), 2187–2212 (2016)
21. Mencagli, G., Vanneschi, M., Vespa, E.: A cooperative predictive control approach to improve the reconfiguration stability of adaptive distributed parallel applications. ACM Trans. Auton. Adapt. Syst. **9**(1), 2 (2014)
22. Murray, D.G., McSherry, F., et al.: Naiad: a timely dataflow system. In: ACM Symposium on Operating Systems Principles, pp. 439–455 (2013)
23. Padala, P., et al.: Automated control of multiple virtualized resources. In: European Conference on Computer Systems (EuroSys), pp. 13–26. ACM (2009)
24. Rao, J., Zhou, X.: Towards fair and efficient SMP VM scheduling. In: SIGPLAN Symposium on Principles & Practice of Parallel Programming, pp. 273–286. ACM (2014)
25. Rawlings, J.B., Mayne, D.Q.: Model Predictive Control: Theory and Design. Nob Hill Publishing, LLC, Madison (2009)
26. Şahin, S.: C-stream: a coroutune-based elastic stream processing engine. Ph.D. thesis, Bilkent University (2015)
27. Subramanian, L., Seshadri, V., Ghosh, A., Khan, S., Mutlu, O.: The application slowdown model. In: Microarchitecture (MICRO), pp. 62–75. IEEE (2015)
28. Tanner, M.: Practical Queueing Analysis. McGraw-Hill, New York City (1995)
29. Tembey, P., Gavrilovska, A., et al.: Application & platform-aware RA in consolidated systems. In: Symposium on Cloud Computing, pp. 1–14. ACM (2014)

30. Wang, H., Isci, C., Subramanian, L., Choi, J., Qian, D., Mutlu, O.: A-DRM: architecture-aware distributed resource management of virtualized clusters. ACM SIGPLAN Not. **50**(7), 93–106 (2015)
31. Yang, F., Qian, Z., Chen, X., Beschastnikh, I., Zhuang, L., Zhou, L., Shen, J.: Sonora: a platform for continuous mobile-cloud computing. Technical report, Microsoft Research Asia (2012)
32. Ye, K., et al.: Profiling-based workload consolidation & migration in VDCs. IEEE Trans. Parallel Distrib. Syst. **26**(3), 878–890 (2015)
33. Zaharia, M., Chowdhury, M., Franklin, M.J., Shenker, S., Stoica, I.: Spark: cluster computing with working sets. HotCloud **10**(10–10), 95 (2010)

Blockchain-Based Transaction Integrity in Distributed Big Data Marketplace

Denis Nasonov[(✉)], Alexander A. Visheratin, and Alexander Boukhanovsky

ITMO University, Saint Petersburg, Russia
denis.nasonov@gmail.com

Abstract. Today Big Data occupies a crucial part of scientific research areas as well as in the business analysis of large companies. Each company tries to find the best way to make generated Big Data sets valuable and profitable. However, in most cases, companies have not enough opportunities and budget to solve this complex problem. On the other hand, there are companies (i.e., in insurance or banking) that can significantly improve their business organization by applying hidden knowledge extracted from such massive data. This situation leads to the necessity of building a platform for exchange, processing, and sale of collected Big Data sets. In this paper, we propose a distributed big data platform that implements digital data marketplace based on the blockchain mechanism for data transaction integrity.

Keywords: Data marketplace · Distributed systems · Security · Blockchain

1 Introduction

Today, it is impossible to imagine any area in business and no one branch of science, where large data could not be used to gain additional benefits or new knowledge. [10] However, for effective use of large volumes, it is not enough just to have them, it is necessary to understand how data can be used and how the results will give the desired benefit. Moreover, in many cases, large data has a higher value to related spheres of business rather its owner, where the obtained knowledge after processing the data can significantly affect the company's profit (for example, in the area of banking or insurance). This situation leads to the necessity of building a platform for the exchange, processing, and sale of collected big data. In this paper, we propose a distributed big data platform that implements digital data market, based on the blockchain mechanism for data transaction integrity. For the last nine years, blockchain-based technologies have attracted a lot of attention. Since the publication of Nakamoto's paper application areas of blockchain has expanded from cryptocurrencies to many other fields - databases, legal activities, medicine, etc. [1]. Researchers try to find novel ways to provide robust and scalable consensus [11] and to protect the data that

© Springer International Publishing AG, part of Springer Nature 2018
Y. Shi et al. (Eds.): ICCS 2018, LNCS 10860, pp. 569–577, 2018.
https://doi.org/10.1007/978-3-319-93698-7_43

is stored in blockchain [13]. Authors of [12] propose a second-layer, off-chain network Enigma that enables secure, decentralized data computation and exchange. One of the possible applications of Enigma is a data marketplace, but the idea behind the proposed concept is closer to standard blockchain-based markets, where people sell their data, e.g., Datum platform (https://datum.org) [9]. In [4] authors provide a substantial investigation of existing projects related to data marketplaces and state that blockchain paradigm can be successfully applied to the development of data marketplace solutions. In another work, [7] authors proposed a market model for Big Data selling. However, they are concentrated near pricing optimization ideas without discussions on transaction integrity.

2   Data Marketplace Concept

2.1   Problem Statement

As big data marketplace is a new research area a lot of different questions appear in the field of interacting organization between customers and providers within dataset offerings in distributed data market platform. The main issues divide into four categories:

1. data processing integrity organization - formalized schema of used decentralized algorithms in cooperation between providers and platform, other providers and customers;
2. data processing limitations - discuss how Big Data should be processed in different interaction schema and which methods are allowed during processing (transfer, analysis, filtering, anonymization, simplification);
3. data validation procedure - specifies main principles of data checking that gives customer insurance in data veracity and truthfulness as well as checking for duplication offering;
4. data consolidation - defines methods how data from different resources can enrich processed data analysis and what can be done with anonymization.

All of this issues are crucial and should be investigated carefully in details. However, this paper is more concentrated on proposed data integrity approach and how it influences on other points.

2.2   Platform Architecture

Basic platform architecture is presented in Fig. 1. It consists of three main parts: DMP portal, DMP server and provider's infrastructure. Further, all the modules of the platform are briefly described for DMP processes understanding in the following section.

    DMP portal includes digital data marketplace with showrooms and specific work environments. Environments are divided into three types: customer workspace, data holder workspace, and Administrative Tools. When new data holder joins the market, he registers and verifies his organization as well as create his data description, providing all necessary information. Data holder can

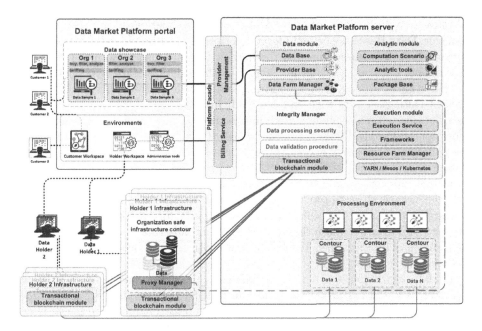

Fig. 1. Data marketplace platform concept

also change already existed offers, including used policy, prices, and other conditions. Customer workspace allows the user to manage already bought data and provides access to remote data that can be only processed by selected methods in the data owner infrastructure. The user also may create different processing scenarios on workflow DSL using platform integrated analytic packages as well as other embedded tools. Administrative module hides all configurable system parameters, like user management, access policy, and showcase demonstration.

DMP server offers public functional API through the Platform Facade service, which extends CLAVIRE Facade Service [2] and manages user session activity. User session communicates with Billing service for financial requests and checks user rights for requested methods. However, the principle Platform Facade goal is to provide access to Data, Analytic and Execution modules.

The execution module is based on the CLAVIRE Execution Service [3] and combines several types of task execution on computational resources. The first type takes integrated frameworks (configured on Docker containers or VM), like Apache Spark or Apache Hadoop and processes data using provided users scenarios (in the form of workflow). The second type executes packages that were embedded in PackageBase (another CLAVIRE service) and were deployed on the available resources controlled by Resource Farm Manager.

An analytic module as Execution module is a part of CLAVIRE platform and contains services for packages and analytic tools management. Computational Scenario block interprets computational user requests extracting task parameters, which are described in Package Base and Analytic tools.

Data module has three blocks: Data Base, Provider Base, and Data Farm Manager. Data Base service includes a description of all providers' data sets that currently are distributed through the market. It contains a description of meta information, such as data format, anonymization details, showcase conditions, etc. Data Farm Manager, in its turn, operates with all controllers of all registered in Data Base sets with enabled configurations and their locations. While Provider Base stores provider's meta information as well as offered datasets with limitation and applied policy. In other words, Provider Base defines all the rules upon methods and data access through the Analytic module and traditional selling.

In this paper, we concentrate our research studies on Integrity Manager module. It manages all essential transactions with data through its all life cycle, that guarantees data truthfulness and invariability for customers. The core of Integrity Manager is transactional blockchain module that is deployed on every registered provider and uses blockchain paradigm to make available trusted the decentralized system.

In data marketplace, there is a different option for data holders in data placement and data access. Data holder may decide to provide data access only within own private infrastructure contour that is remotely integrated with Data Farm Manager and Resource Farm Manager. Moreover, it can set strict access to specific analytical tools or even methods from Package Base. On the other hand, the provider may place his data in DMP infrastructure and provide user widespread access to the data processing tools. Finally, the provider can sell his data directly to the customer.

3   Data Processing Integrity

3.1   Data Processing Scenarios

In the data marketplace platform described in the previous section, one of the most crucial blocks is the Integrity manager, which is responsible for tracking internal operations over data, such as uploading of datasets by providers. The primary aim of this block is to make sure that the data used in processing operations is always the very same data, which was initially uploaded into the system. But since the marketplace itself has no direct access to the data, standard verification techniques are not applicable for this case, and there is a need for the development of the procedure, which would allow to control data integrity and prevent possible frauds by data providers.

There are two basic scenarios for data processing in the marketplace platform - data collecting and data analysis. The first scenario is quite simple - client searches for the data on the platform portal, orders the data and after successful payment, the data passes from the provider to the client. In the second scenario, the data is processed by platform's processing environment or provider's infrastructure depending on where the data locates. In both scenarios, it is essential to make sure that the data, on which the operations are performed, does not change over time and from client to client. A data processing security and validation procedure are used to improve confidence and security between data marketplace participants. More detailed information about Integrity Manager and its components is presented it the following sections.

3.2 Blockchain-Based Solution

In this section, we describe the solution, which can provide integrity of the data in the distributed data marketplace platform. Because data providers do not have full trust to other providers and the platform, and to overcome the case of single point of failure, the integrity manager is decentralized by design and based on blockchain concept [6].

Integrity manager has two main components - data validation component and data blockchain instance. Data blockchain consists of blocks, each of which holds information about one dataset that was added to the platform. New blocks are generated when a provider adds new dataset in the system. Data can be added by uploading the data to the platform or by registering the data located in the provider's infrastructure. The process of block generation is depicted in Fig. 2. Dataset is composed of a set of data slices, which are internally represented as byte arrays. Blockchain builds a Merkle tree [5] using data slices of the dataset. In this structure, the root node contains a hashed representation of all data slices, which cannot be decoded to obtain the initial data. After that, the root hash, the hash of the previous block, the unique ID of the provider and the list of key-value pairs $< ID, H >$ (where ID is a data slice identifier, and H is the hash of that data slice) are written to the data block, which is then added to the data blockchain.

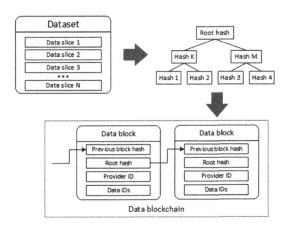

Fig. 2. Schema of blocks generation and chain structure.

Every provider, as well as the marketplace platform, holds its own instance of data blockchain. When provider adds a new dataset, the block is added first into its blockchain instance and after that is replicated to other instances in a P2P manner. To prevent situations when two or more providers add their data at the same time, we apply simple consensus algorithm - if a collision of blocks is detected, the block, which was already synchronized across the largest part of the network, is held, other blocks are replaced by it. In this case, the data related to this block is discarded from the system and provider has to add the data again. This approach allows keeping the consistency between all instances of the blockchain. Although the described algorithm works good, there is a room for its improvement, e.g., usage of different consensus algorithms, such as Raft [8].

When a client tries to perform some operation on the data (collecting or analysis), this data is validated by all instances of the data blockchain in the following way:

1. Client requests an operation over some data slices to the marketplace.
2. Marketplace gets data slices from corresponding providers.
3. Data blockchain instance of the marketplace calculates hashes of data slices and validates them.
4. Data blockchain instance of the marketplace sends a validation request to all blockchain instances across the network.
5. Data blockchain instance of the marketplace collects responses from other instances until all responses come or more than 50% of all instances confirm that data slices are correct.
6. Operation requested by the client is performed over data slices, which were successfully verified.

As we can see, described method of data verification excludes a single control authority from the network, making possible reliable data verification without full trust between parties. The only considerable threat to this mechanism is collusion between data providers to change the data in the major part of the network. But since providers in the marketplace platform are usually big companies who take care of their reputation, such scenario is quite unlikely. Nevertheless, currently, we are working on a developed mechanism for elimination any possibility for blockchain interference. This mechanism is based on having a backup copy of the data blockchain, which has no collisions and is encrypted by every provider in the marketplace. Whenever any conflict in the network occurs, the marketplace would always be able to force the replacement of the current state of the blockchain by the backed up one.

3.3 Experimental Study

To conduct an experimental investigation of the proposed blockchain-based approach, we have developed a simulator of the data marketplace platform, which implements logic described in the previous section. Source code for the simulator is available on Github - https://github.com/visheratin/market-sim. The simulator can perform following operations:

1. Create a specified set of data providers.
2. Initialize data blockchain for the marketplace and all providers.
3. Add data for a specific provider and add a corresponding block into the blockchain. There is 0.001% probability that the uploaded data will be corrupted after uploading.
4. Search for the data according to user-specified criteria.
5. Collect data slices from providers and validate them through blockchain.

We conducted an experimental investigation of influence of data providers number and providers' reaction latency, which represents network latency and other overheads, to the speed of data verification. Providers number varied between 10, 100 and 1000; maximal latency was in range 10, 100, 1000, 5000 and 10000 ms. Search, and extraction was performed for correctly uploaded data slice and the corrupted one. Results of experiments are presented in Fig. 3. We can see that with an increase in providers number the difference between validation time for correct and corrupted data equals up and goes closer to the average latency time. In the case of 10 providers, average validation time is much smaller than for other cases because in this scenario it is much easier to reach the consensus in data blockchain.

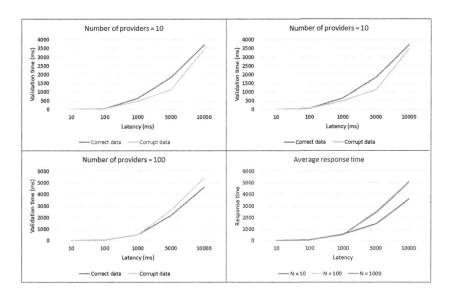

Fig. 3. Results of experimental evaluation of blockchain validation procedure.

4   Other Features

To provide efficient data processing integrity between customers and provider we need: to guarantee that the data corresponds to the declared description and the data could not be used in offering the second time on the DMP by another provider. To meet these issues, data validation, unification, and duplicates detection mechanisms are discussed below.

4.1 Data Validation

Data validation helps the customer to be insured in data veracity and truthfulness. *Data prying* allows the user to check any shot part of the data in a randomized way for the limited amount of times. It helps the customer to make sure that showcase reflects the quality and characteristics of all data. For instance, customer intends to buy some measurement sensor data of level water in Baltic Sea; he can check the correctness and credibility of data in control points (some critical values on select dates).

4.2 Data Consolidation Procedure

Marketplace admits performing analysis on the enriched data from the aggregation of multiple sources (providers), including anonymous data. The algorithm is presented below:

1. Customer selects all dataset that should be merged;
2. Unique identification field is selected within all datasets (same UID in all data structures);
3. Upon each dataset, a hash function is applied to UID;
4. Data anonymization for all other field is performed;
5. All anonymized data sets are merged on platform infrastructure side using Data Consolidation Procedure;
6. UIDs of merged data sets are hashed one more time (in a case if some provider plays role of the customer);
7. Data is given to the customer.

This algorithm makes possible to combine open data (for instance, collected from social networks) with private data from financial or retail companies and conduct analysis over enriched data.

4.3 Duplicates, Financial Transactions

Duplicates can appear in two cases: provider tries to sell the same sets, or someone proposes already offered data. To avoid duplicates, the platform calculates statistical parameters as well as takes some randomized data markers. This information can be used by the customer to understand the difference between data sets and by providers to interpret the data originality. Integrated blockchain approach can also be used for financial interactions within the platform.

5 Conclusion

In this paper blockchain transaction integrity within distributed Big Data marketplace concept was proposed. Experimental studies on developed simulator show appropriate results which inspire us to repeat them on a real system in the nearest future. Also different aspects of the platform, such as security, data truthfulness and union were discussed and proposed in present section above. However, we are looking forward to implementing all of them in a real system.

Acknowledgments. This work financially supported by Ministry of Education and Science of the Russian Federation, Agreement #14.575.21.0165 (26/09/2017). Unique Identification RFMEFI57517X0165.

References

1. Crosby, M., Nachiappan, Pattanayak, P., Verma, S., Kalyanaraman, V.: Blockchain Technology - Beyond Bitcoin. Berkley Engineering, p. 35 (2016)
2. Knyazkov, K.V., Kovalchuk, S.V., Tchurov, T.N., Maryin, S.V., Boukhanovsky, A.V.: CLAVIRE: e-Science infrastructure for data-driven computing. J. Comput. Sci. **3**(6), 504–510 (2012)
3. Knyazkov, K.V., Nasonov, D.A., Tchurov, T.N., Boukhanovsky, A.V.: Interactive workflow-based infrastructure for urgent computing. Procedia Comput. Sci. **18**, 2223–2232 (2013)
4. Koutroumpis, P., Leiponen, A., Thomas, L.: The (Unfulfilled) Potential of Data Marketplaces. Working Paper 2420(53) (2017)
5. Merkle, R.C.: A digital signature based on a conventional encryption function. In: Pomerance, C. (ed.) CRYPTO 1987. LNCS, vol. 293, pp. 369–378. Springer, Heidelberg (1988). https://doi.org/10.1007/3-540-48184-2_32
6. Nakamoto, S.: Bitcoin: A Peer-to-Peer Electronic Cash System, p. 9 (2008). www.Bitcoin.Org
7. Niyato, D., Alsheikh, M.A., Wang, P., Kim, D.I., Han, Z.: Market model and optimal pricing scheme of big data and internet of things (IoT) (2016)
8. Ongaro, D., Ousterhout, J.: In search of an understandable consensus algorithm. In: Proceedings of 2014 USENIX Annual Technical Conference, USENIX ATC 2014, vol. 22, no. 2, pp. 305–320 (2014)
9. Ren, X., London, P., Ziani, J., Wierman, A.: Joint data purchasing and data placement in a geo-distributed data market (2016)
10. Wang, H., Xu, Z., Fujita, H., Liu, S.: Towards felicitous decision making: an overview on challenges and trends of big data. Inf. Sci. **367**, 747–765 (2016)
11. Watanabe, H., Fujimura, S., Nakadaira, A., Miyazaki, Y., Akutsu, A., Kishigami, J.J.: Blockchain contract: a complete consensus using blockchain. In: 2015 IEEE 4th Global Conference on Consumer Electronics, GCCE 2015, pp. 577–578 (2015)
12. Zyskind, G., Nathan, O., Pentland, A.: Enigma: decentralized computation platform with guaranteed privacy, pp. 1–14 (2015)
13. Zyskind, G., Nathan, O., Pentland, A.S.: Decentralizing privacy: using blockchain to protect personal data. In: Proceedings of 2015 IEEE Security and Privacy Workshops, SPW 2015, pp. 180–184 (2015)

Workload Characterization and Evolutionary Analyses of Tianhe-1A Supercomputer

Jinghua Feng[1,2(✉)], Guangming Liu[1,2], Jian Zhang[2], Zhiwei Zhang[2], Jie Yu[1], and Zhaoning Zhang[1]

[1] College of Computer, National University of Defense Technology,
Changsha, China
yujie@nscc-tj.gov.cn
[2] National Supercomputer Center in Tianjin, Tianjin, China
{fengjh,liugm,zhangjian,zhangzw}@nscc-tj.gov.cn

Abstract. Currently, supercomputer systems face a variety of application challenges, including high-throughput, data-intensive, and stream-processing applications. At the same time, there is more challenge to improve user satisfaction at the supercomputers such as Tianhe-1A, Tianhe-2 and TaihuLight, because of the commercial service model. It is important to understand HPC workloads and their evolution to facilitate informed future research and improve user satisfaction.

In this paper, we present a methodology to characterize workloads on the commercial supercomputer (users need to pay), at a particular period and its evolution over time. We apply this method to the workloads of Tianhe-1A at the National Supercomputer Center in Tianjin. This paper presents the concept of quota-constrained waiting time for the first time, which has significance for optimizing scheduling and enhancing user satisfaction on the commercial supercomputer.

Keywords: HPC · Workload · Quota-constrained · Scheduling

1 Introduction

High Performance Computing (HPC) is a mainstream for performing large-scale scientific computing [1, 2]. Currently, large scientific computations that include high-throughput, data-intensive jobs, and stream-processing are increasingly becoming more common in HPC centers. It is important to understand HPC workloads and the first step in understanding workload is to understand the evolution of workload on the current systems. Previous works have been on workloads on various grids [3] and cloud [4] systems. However, these studies were earlier and not the same as the current workloads. The research on Carvers and Hopper at the National Energy Research Institute (NERSC) [5], and Mira at the Argonne Leadership Computing Facility (ALCF) [6], none of these supercomputers are representative of commercial supercomputers.

In this paper, we first give the details about the methodology for characterizing workloads, including the process for submitting jobs on the commercial supercomputer, system description, data source, definition and calculation of various variables, especially the quota-constrained waiting time.

© Springer International Publishing AG, part of Springer Nature 2018
Y. Shi et al. (Eds.): ICCS 2018, LNCS 10860, pp. 578–585, 2018.
https://doi.org/10.1007/978-3-319-93698-7_44

Because there are more than 70% jobs are single node jobs, and they only occupy about 10% of the CPU Hours. We divided the jobs into two kinds, single and multi.

In this paper, we provide an evolutionary analysis of the Tianhe-1A supercomputer. We study the trend of runtime, waiting time, core time from 2011 to 2017 about the two kinds of jobs. Especially for the waiting time, this paper analyzed the relationship between the quota-constrained waiting time and the waiting time, runtime, and job size, which is instructive for the future optimizing scheduling and enhancing user satisfaction on the commercial supercomputer.

2   Background and Related Work

HPC schedulers use the FCFS (First-Come, First-Served) [9] and backfilling [10] techniques to achieve the highest system utilization possible with a reasonable turn-around. On commercial supercomputer, FCFS is more often chosen for business fairness reasons.

Currently, there are some researches focus on workload characterizations, [14] presented the history of HPC system development and applications in China, HPC centers and facilities, major research institutions, but it's before 2010. [5] investigate the evolution trend of Hopper and Carver. [15] analyzed the characterization of the workload on google compute clusters using the k-means algorithm. [7, 8] analyzed the system features of three supercomputers (Hopper, Edison, and Carver). [11] analyzed the I/O features of 6 years of applications on three supercomputers, Intrepid, Mira, and Edison.

In fact, the characteristics of job scheduling and system workload have changed a lot on commercial supercomputer, which are the focuses of this paper.

3   Methodology

In this section, we present the system and workloads in focus for our investigation and elaborate on the key parameters studied.

3.1   Data Source

All workload analysis is performed on the job summary entries from the SLURM [13] workload manager logs. The data includes seven years and 10735864 jobs. The data after filtering and parsing is reduced to 3 GB. Because there are more than 70% jobs are single node jobs, and they only occupy about 10% of the CPU Hours. In the paper, we divided the jobs into two datasets, single-node jobs and multi-nodes jobs.

The data fields consist of Jobid, Submit time, Start time, End time, Alloccpus, State and so on. And we complement existing scientific workload characterizations work [12] by adding the quota-constrained waiting time. Especially, we used 2016–2017 data to fully analyze the relationship between the quota-constrained waiting time and the waiting time, runtime, job size (Table 1).

Table 1. Workload of Tianhe-1A from 2011 to 2017

No. of jobs	2011	2012	2013	2014	2015	2016	2017	Total
Single node	21205	561954	640614	899509	1610001	2488108	1769195	7990586
Multi nodes	86784	231600	326046	397861	472651	597243	633093	2745278
Sum	107989	793554	966660	1297370	2082652	3085351	2402288	10735864

3.2   Systems Description

Tianhe-1A is the world's top supercomputer in 2010 at the National Supercomputer Center in Tianjin. It has been in service since 2011 and has been in operation for more than seven years. It is a typical representative of commercial supercomputer.

Tianhe-1A supercomputer consists of 7168 computing nodes (12 cores, 24 GB of memory per node) with a peak performance 4.7PFlops. The workload is composed of applications that belong to a wide range of scientific fields including Chemistry, Material Science, Climate Research, Astrophysics, Life Sciences, and Basic Science.

3.3   Analysis Variables

When using the commercial supercomputer, users need to pay for the computing, and they usually use resources in accordance with the contract, the contract mainly limits the size of the total resources that users submit jobs, which is the quota constraint.

For example, if the user can submit k jobs, each job occupies the resource N_j, and the user's quota constraint is M, thus $\sum_{j=1}^{k} N_j \leq M$.

Figure 1 describes the process of submitting a job under the quota restraint environment. After the user submits the job, the workload manager first performs quota check, if including the job, the sum of user's resource has not exceeded the quota. Then, proceeds to the next step for resource check, On the contrary, the job needs to wait.

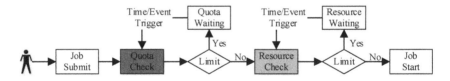

Fig. 1. The step from job submit to job start on a quota-constrained supercomputer

The job has Submit time (t_{sub}), Start time (t_{str}) and End time (t_{end}). The runtime of job j is the timespan between End time and Start time (t_{end} - t_{str}); the waiting time of job j (W_j) is the timespan between Start time and Submit time (t_{str} - t_{sub}); the response time of job j (R_j) is the timespan between End time and Submit time (t_{end} - t_{sub}). And the core time is defined as the total CPU time of the job.

If a user has a quota constraint (size of cpus), the waiting time consists of two parts: waiting time caused by quota-constrained and resource-constrained

$$W_j = Wq_j + Wr_j. \tag{1}$$

4 Trend Analysis

Figure 2 shows the percentages of job count and core time for each year, taking the total number of jobs and the core time respectively from 2011 to 2017. According to Fig. 2 we can see that from 2012, the number of single node jobs is much bigger than multi- node jobs (basically keeping the ratio of 7:3), but the actual core time multi-nodes jobs is much larger than single node jobs (basically keeping the ratio of 9:1). We can also see that from 2011 to 2016, the number of jobs and the core time used are all increasing (the average utilization rate of resources in 2016 is over 85%), a slight decrease from 2017 in 2016.

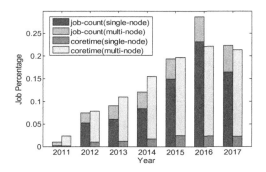

Fig. 2. The percentage of job count and core time from 2011 to 2017

4.1 Trend Analysis

Figure 3 shows the box plot (the vertical axis is logarithmic) for job runtime from 2011 to 2017. The runtime time of single node jobs is significantly lower than that of multi-nodes jobs from 2013 to 2017, and median of single node jobs is 88,118,26,19,52 s. Because 2016 submitted the largest number of single node jobs (2488108), and the operation of the lower runtime, so the median in 2016 is the lowest.

Figure 4 The core time shows a similar trend with runtime in both job types.

Figure 5 shows the box plot (the vertical axis is logarithmic) for job waiting time from 2011 to 2017. There are several phenomena that deserve our attention. The first point is the higher waiting time value of single node jobs in 2012, median reached 2490 s, because some users submitted a large number of consecutive single node jobs, making these jobs increase the quota waiting time, so the overall waiting time increases; Second, from 2013 to 2016, the number of jobs and the core time are increasing. However, the waiting time value changes are not very obvious. Even the

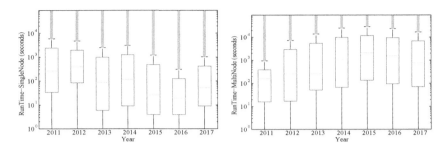

Fig. 3. The runtime of the two kinds of jobs from 2011 to 2017. Left (a), Right (b)

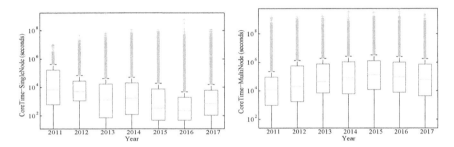

Fig. 4. The core time of the two kinds of jobs from 2011 to 2017. Left (a), Right (b)

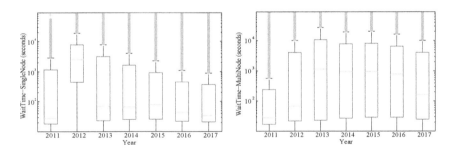

Fig. 5. The waiting time of two kinds of jobs from 2011 to 2017. Left (a), Right (b)

waiting time of the multi nodes jobs, the median value is decreasing. The median value gradually drops from 1156 s to 788 s. This point is different from [5], the waiting time of Hopper supercomputer gradually increased, because of the number of jobs increasing. Third, in 2017, the waiting time for multi-node jobs has dropped because users can use more clustered systems, resulting in an increase of the inter-arrival of jobs.

4.2   Analyze the Characteristics of Waiting Time Caused by Quota-constrained

Figure 5 (b) shows that the waiting time tends to decrease as the number of jobs increases. In order to figure out the reason, we used 2016-2017 data to fully analyze the relationship between the quota-constrained waiting time and the runtime, waiting time, job size. Figure 6 shows the changing trends of Average waiting times influenced waiting time, runtime, and job size, respectively.

Figure 6(a), (b) the trend is similar. With the increase of waiting time, quota-constrained waiting time increases rapidly and near linearly, and takes up the main proportion of waiting time. However, the increase of resource-constrained waiting time is not obvious, and the proportion is smaller. Note that in commercial supercomputer,

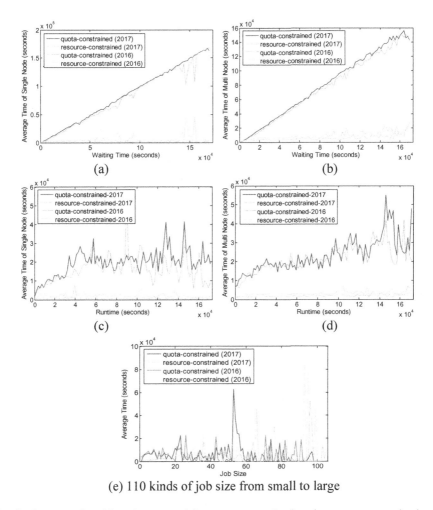

(e) 110 kinds of job size from small to large

Fig. 6. Average of waiting time caused by quota-constrained and resource-constrained as a function of (a) (b) Waiting time, (c) (d) Runtime, (e) Job Size

the waiting time is mainly due to the quota constraint, it is difficult to effectively reduce the waiting time of the job without changing the business restriction of the quota constraint. The quota-constrained waiting time is mainly affected by the job submission behavior of users. If users submit jobs frequently, many jobs wait for quota constraints, which increases the quota-constrained waiting time. The phenomenon in Fig. 5(b) is also caused by a change in the user's submission behavior and a decrease in the quota-constrained waiting time. In the future, we will do the research to understanding the user behavior, in order to effectively reduce the waiting time.

Figure 6(c) and (d) show a similar trend. As the runtime increases, the quota-constrained waiting time increases obviously and dominates.

Figure 6(e) shows that the two-part waiting time is not very affected by the job size when the job size is small, but when the job size is larger, the resource-constrained waiting time rapidly increases to the dominant factor.

5   Conclusions

In this paper, we present a methodology to characterize workloads on the commercial supercomputer, at a particular period and its evolution over time. We apply this methodology to the workloads of Tianhe-1A at the National Supercomputer Center in Tianjin. This paper presents the concept of quota-constrained waiting time for the first time, which has significance for optimizing scheduling and enhancing user satisfaction on the commercial supercomputer. In the future, we will do the research to understanding the user behavior, in order to effectively reduce the waiting time.

References

1. Geist, A., et al.: A survey of high-performance computing scaling challenges. Int. J. High Perform. Comput. Appl. **33**(1), 104–113 (2017)
2. Reed, D.A., Dongarra, J.: Exascale computing and big data. Commun. ACM **58**(7), 56–58 (2015)
3. Iosup, A., et al.: The Grid workloads archive. Future Gener. Comput. Syst. **24**(7), 672–686 (2008)
4. Di, S., et al.: Characterization and comparison of cloud versus grid workloads. In: IEEE International Conference on CLUSTER Computing (CLUSTER) (2012)
5. Rodrigo, G.P., et al.: HPC system lifetime story: workload characterization and evolutionary analyses on NERSC systems. In: International Symposium on High-Performance Parallel and Distributed Computing (HPDC) (2015)
6. Schlagkamp, S., et al.: Consecutive job submission behavior at mira supercomputer. In: International Symposium on High-Performance Parallel and Distributed Computing (HPDC) (2016)
7. Rodrigo, G.P., et al.: Towards understanding job heterogeneity in HPC: a NERSC case study. In: IEEE/ACM International Symposium on Cluster, Cloud and Grid Computing (2016)
8. Rodrigo, G.P., et al.: Towards understanding HPC users and systems: a NERSC case study. J. Parallel Distrib. Comput. **111**, 206–221 (2017)

9. Feitelson, D.G., Rudolph, L., Schwiegelshohn, U.: Parallel job scheduling—A status report. In: Feitelson, D.G., Rudolph, L., Schwiegelshohn, U. (eds.) JSSPP 2004. LNCS, vol. 3277, pp. 1–16. Springer, Heidelberg (2005). https://doi.org/10.1007/11407522_1

10. Lifka, D.A.: The ANL/IBM SP scheduling system. In: Feitelson, D.G., Rudolph, L. (eds.) JSSPP 1995. LNCS, vol. 949, pp. 295–303. Springer, Heidelberg (1995). https://doi.org/10.1007/3-540-60153-8_35

11. Luu, H., et al.: A multiplatform study of I/O behavior on petascale supercomputers. In: International Symposium on High-Performance Parallel and Distributed Computing (HPDC) (2015)

12. Feitelson, D.: Parallel workloads archive http://www.cs.huji.ac.il/labs/parallel/workload. Accessed 11 Feb 2018

13. Yoo, A.B., Jette, M.A., Grondona, M.: SLURM: simple linux utility for resource management. In: Feitelson, D., Rudolph, L., Schwiegelshohn, U. (eds.) JSSPP 2003. LNCS, vol. 2862, pp. 44–60. Springer, Heidelberg (2003). https://doi.org/10.1007/10968987_3

14. Sun, N., et al.: High-performance computing in China: research and applications. Int. J. High Perform. Comput. Appl. **24**, 363–409 (2010)

15. Mishra, A.K., et al.: Towards characterizing cloud backend workloads: insights from google compute clusters. ACM Sigmetrics Perform. Eval. Rev. **37**(4), 34–41 (2010)

The Design of Fast and Energy-Efficient Linear Solvers: On the Potential of Half-Precision Arithmetic and Iterative Refinement Techniques

Azzam Haidar[1]([✉]), Ahmad Abdelfattah[1], Mawussi Zounon[4], Panruo Wu[2],
Srikara Pranesh[4], Stanimire Tomov[1], and Jack Dongarra[1,3,4]

[1] Innovative Computing Laboratory, University of Tennessee, Knoxville, USA
{haidar,ahmad,pwu11,tomov,dongarra}@icl.utk.edu
[2] University of Houston, Houston, TX, USA
[3] Oak Ridge National Laboratory, Oak Ridge, USA
[4] University of Manchester, Manchester, UK
{mawussi.zounon,srikara.pranesh}@manchester.ac.uk

Abstract. As parallel computers approach exascale, power efficiency in high-performance computing (HPC) systems is of increasing concern. Exploiting both the hardware features and algorithms is an effective solution to achieve power efficiency, and to address the energy constraints in modern and future HPC systems. In this work, we present a novel design and implementation of an energy-efficient solution for dense linear systems of equations, which are at the heart of large-scale HPC applications. The proposed energy-efficient linear system solvers are based on two main components: (1) iterative refinement techniques, and (2) reduced-precision computing features in modern accelerators and coprocessors. While most of the energy efficiency approaches aim to reduce the consumption with a minimal performance penalty, our method improves both the performance and the energy efficiency. Compared to highly-optimized linear system solvers, our kernels deliver the same accuracy solution up to 2× faster and reduce the energy consumption up to half on Intel Knights Landing (KNL) architectures. By efficiently using the Tensor Cores available in the NVIDIA V100 PCIe GPUs, the speedups can be up to 4×, with more than 80% reduction in the energy consumption.

Keywords: FP16 · Tensor cores · Mixed-precision · HPC · Solvers

1 Introduction

As parallel computers approach exascale, power efficiency in high-performance computing (HPC) systems is of increasing concern. Over the last few decades, many challenges in science and engineering have been successfully addressed

© Springer International Publishing AG, part of Springer Nature 2018
Y. Shi et al. (Eds.): ICCS 2018, LNCS 10860, pp. 586–600, 2018.
https://doi.org/10.1007/978-3-319-93698-7_45

thanks to the improving performance of HPC systems. However, it comes at a cost: electrical power consumption. This leads to two main concerns—increase of the power bills beyond affordable budgets, and increasing impact on the environment.

To help mitigate the power constraints in modern and future HPC systems, different approaches have been investigated to assess and reduce the energy consumption of scientific applications. So far, the most promising solution is the intensive use of field-programmable gate arrays (FPGA) and graphics processing unit (GPU) technologies in HPC applications [2]. To reduce the power consumption of HPC applications that still require CPU processors, dynamic voltage and frequency scaling (DVFS) strategies are commonly used [6]. In fact, the two most influential factors on the power consumption of CPU cores are the clock frequencies and the voltages. As a result, most of the energy-efficient strategies focus on DVFS methods with low performance overhead. In this work we propose a new approach to energy efficiency, which, in addition to significantly decreasing the power consumption, radically improves the performance.

Another approach to energy efficiency is to redesign the most time-consuming kernels in HPC applications and provide energy efficient alternatives. In this work we use this approach. Solving linear systems of equations is at the heart of numerical simulations used in HPC application, and is one of the most time-consuming steps. In this work we design a novel energy-efficient algorithm for the solutions of linear system of equations. To that end, we exploit both hardware solutions, such as energy efficient NVIDIA GPUs and Intel Xeon Phis, and algorithmic techniques such as iterative refinement (IR) techniques.

The problem of interest in this work is the solution of linear systems of equations $Ax = b$, where A is a general nonsingular $n \times n$ dense matrix, and b is a general $n \times 1$ vector. In most HPC applications, the input data A and b are stored in double precision, and the solution x is expected in the same precision. The standard method for solving these linear system of equations is via Gaussian elimination. However, the accuracy of the obtained solution using this method is often unsatisfactory because of the round-off errors it generates. The iterative refinement technique, first introduced by Wilkinson [21], aims to improve the accuracy of the computed solution.

The iterative refinement algorithm for solving linear systems consists of the following three steps. First, the computation of the initial solution $\bar{x}$. This step is the most expensive because it consumes $O(n^3)$ floating-point operations (FLOPs). Second, computation of the residual $r = b - Ax$. This step consumes $O(n^2)$ FLOPs, and checks the accuracy of the computed solution. Finally, the correction d is computed by solving $Ad = r$, and next $\bar{x}$ is updated by $\bar{x} \leftarrow \bar{x} + d$, which also requires $O(n^2)$ FLOPs. The last two steps are iterated until a satisfactory accuracy is achieved. The original iterative refinement algorithm used double precision for the three steps. However, the emergence of multiple-precision floating-point arithmetic units in modern architectures motivated the design of mixed-precision variants.

On modern architectures, single-precision floating-point arithmetic (FP32) is twice as fast as double-precision floating-point arithmetic (FP64). For example, the Intel Knights Landing (KNL) can deliver 3 teraFLOP/s of FP64 performance, but in FP32, it can achieve more than 6 teraFLOP/s. In addition, the latest version of NVIDIA accelerators—the V100 PCIe GPU—provides hardware support for half-precision floating-point arithmetic (FP16). This new V100 PCIe GPU has a peak performance of 7 teraFLOP/s in FP64, 14 teraFLOP/s in FP32, and 112 teraFLOP/s in FP16 using the Tensor Cores. It is then possible to compute the most expensive operation (which is the matrix factorization) in FP32 or FP16, and use FP64 in accuracy refinement iterations. The different implementations of the resulting mixed iterative refinements are summarized in Table 1.

Table 1. Variants of iterative refinement implemented in this work. From left to right, the first column lists the different kernels where the first entry dgesv is the standard method without iterative refinement process. The second and the third columns specify, respectively, the precision used for the factorization and refinement, where TC stands for Tensor Core. In the last two columns, ✓indicates we have implemented for the corresponding architecture, ✗indicates "arithmetic not supported."

Kernel	Factorization	Refinement	KNL	V100
dgesv	FP64	–	✓	✓
dsgesv	FP32	FP64	✓	✓
dhgesv	FP16	FP64	✗	✓
dhgesv-TC	FP16-TC	FP64	✗	✓

2   Contributions

This work aims to respond to the power constraints in modern and future HPC systems through the design and implementation of fast and energy-efficient solvers for linear systems of equations. To this end, our main contributions are:

– The design and implementation of a highly-optimized iterative refinement kernel for Intel KNL architectures. Compared to the standard algorithm (dgesv), our kernel (dsgesv) is up to 2× faster in delivering the same accuracy solution, and reduces the power consumption by half.
– Analysis of the energy efficiency of the high-bandwidth memory (HBM) multichannel dynamic random-access memory (MCDRAM) technology in Intel KNL architectures.
– The design and implementation of very efficient iterative refinement kernels for the NVIDIA V100 PCIe GPUs. Compared to the highly-optimized dgesv GPU kernel, our solution dhgesv-TC, exploiting the Tensor Cores, achieves the same accuracy of the solution up to 4× faster, and with up to 80% reduction in power consumption.

– Performance analysis of the NVIDIA V100 PCIe GPU, and insight into the possible energy efficiency opportunities.

The rest of the paper is organized as follows. We discuss related work in Sect. 3, and present the design and implementation details of our algorithm in Sect. 4. The experimental configurations and results are discussed in Sect. 5, followed by concluding remarks in Sect. 6

3   Related Works

Energy-Aware Algorithms for Scientific Computing: The first step toward the design of an energy-efficient system is an understanding of the power consumption of its components. The PowerPack project [7] serves this objective by providing detailed power-monitoring information on the disks, memories, NICs, processors, and even applications of HPC systems. Such power-monitoring details assist in identifying the most energy-consuming components, and working out energy reduction plans. For example, Global Extensible Open Power Manager (GEOPM) [5] provides a power management framework that enables an automatic online rebalancing of power among nodes. It also helps minimize the time-to-solution of applications while remaining within a target power budget. Another class of energy-efficient algorithms consists of designing energy-aware schedulers. The key idea is to divide an application into a set of tasks, and estimate the optimal power budget of each task. Then the energy-aware scheduler dynamically changes the frequency and voltage of CPU cores depending on the task to execute. This strategy is implemented by Adagio in a runtime system that makes dynamic voltage scaling (DVS) practical for complex scientific applications [17]. A variant has also been proposed by Kimura et al. [14], which uses DVFS to adapt the execution speed of each task to reduce the power consumption without increasing the overall execution time. Similar to DVFS, power-capping mechanisms, for example, to directly set power limits were introduced and accessed by tools like the Intel Running Average Power Limit (RAPL). Haidar et al. [8] studied these power-capping mechanisms and their effect in saving energy for various algorithms on Intel Xeon Phi architectures, specifically KNL.

Accurate power management for NVIDIA GPUs can be done using NVIDIA's Management Library (NVML) [16]. Work on validating it on dense linear algebra algorithms has shown that results are within 10% accurate [13]. Algorithmic work on making numerical libraries energy efficient for embedded systems with GPUs can be found in [9].

The History of Iterative Refinement: In the first version of iterative refinement introduced by Wilkinson, the factorization and the refinement process used the same precision [21]. The rounding errors analysis by Skeel [18] for LU solver, and extended by Higham [11] for a general solver, helped in gaining a deep understanding of iterative refinement. Other than the accuracy improvement, there has been a renewed interest in iterative refinement to improve the execution time of linear systems solvers in the 2000 s. With FP32 twice as fast as FP64 on modern processors, Langou et al. [15], [1] proposed a mixed-precision iterative refinement where the matrix factorization step is in FP32 and everything else in FP64. More advanced versions of mixed-precision iterative refinement using FP16 have been recently studied by Carson and Higham [3,4] with the corresponding parallel implementations by Haidar et al. in [10].

4   Algorithmic Techniques Toward Energy Efficiency

4.1   Motivation

The main motivation for using lower-precision arithmetic is the speedup that can be achieved compared to the classical higher precision. We illustrate in Fig. 1 the performance that can be achieved by LU factorization using different precisions and on two different machines. In Fig. 1a, we show the obtained performance of the LU factorization (Xgetrf routine) on an NVIDIA V100 GPU for the four available precisions (FP64, FP32, FP16, and FP16-TC). We consider the FP16-TC as a precision since it consists of a mixed-precision Xgemm, where the multiplication is performed in FP16 while the accumulation is in FP32. Thus, FP16-TC is more accurate than the classical FP16 computation. We also note that, in addition to being more accurate, the FP16-TC is faster due to the use of Tensor Cores. As shown in Fig. 1a, the FP16-TC hgetrf-TC reaches about 4× speedup over its FP64 dgetrf counterpart. Furthermore, as expected, the FP16 hgetrf and the FP32 sgetrf are about 3× and 2× faster than the FP64 dgetrf. Similar behavior was observed on the Intel KNL 7250 system, reported in Fig. 1b. The LU factorization using FP32 achieves 2× speedup over the FP64 dgetrf. Such attractive performance results of the lower-precision LU guided our attention to the possibility of solving the linear system $Ax = b$ using a lower-precision LU factorization combined with an IR process to bring the solution to the FP64 arithmetic.

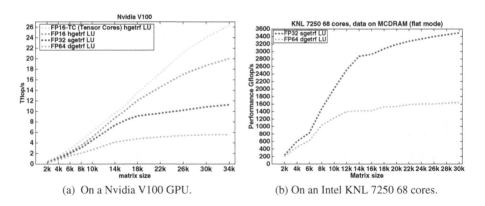

(a) On a Nvidia V100 GPU.   (b) On an Intel KNL 7250 68 cores.

Fig. 1. Performance of the Xgetrf routine with different arithmetic precisions.

4.2   Iterative Refinement Techniques

IR is one of the most promising techniques used to obtain a high-precision solution to a linear equation using low-precision arithmetic for most of its computations. Specifically, we use FP16 for the LU factorization, which consumes $2n^3$ FLOPs and FP64 for everything else. The idea of (mixed precision) iterative refinement is to solve a linear system using low precision for its speed, and then refine the solution by solving the correction equation using high-precision arithmetic as shown in Algorithm 1. However, traditional convergence analysis of IR depends on the assumption that the matrix A is safely bounded away from singularity—meaning that its condition number $(\kappa(A))$ should be much less than u^{-1}, the inverse of the computing precision. Put differently, the condition $\kappa(A)u < 1$ should be satisfied. This condition seriously limits the applicability of FP16 since the unit roundoff error is around $u \approx 5 \times 10^{-4}$, in which case the condition number of A should be much less than $u^{-1} \approx 2000$. Many well-conditioned matrices in FP32 or FP64 will become ill-conditioned in FP16.

Data: An $n \times n$ matrix A, and size n vector b
Result: A solution vector x_i approximating x in $Ax = b$, and a LU factorization of $A = LU$.
(FP16) Solve $Ax_0 = b$ using FP16 LU factorization and triangular solve;
$i \leftarrow 0$;
repeat
  (FP64) Compute residual $r_i \leftarrow Ax_i - b$;
  (FP64) Solve $Ad_i = r_i$ using   IR: triangular solve using the LU factors, or
                                       IRGM: GMRES preconditioned by $M = LU$;
  (FP64) Update $x_{i+1} = x_i + d_i$;
  $i \leftarrow i + 1$;
until $x^{(i)}$ *is accurate enough*;

Algorithm 1. IR: classic mixed-precision iterative refinement using triangular solve. IRGM: iterative refinement with GMRES to solve correction equation.

A recent study [4] relaxed this restrictive condition, and extended the application of IR for matrices where $\kappa(A) > u^{-1}$. They provided the following two new conditions to guarantee the convergence of IR:

- The correction equation $(Ad_i = r_i)$ is solved relatively accurately: $\|d_i - \hat{d}_i\|_\infty / \|d_i\|_\infty = u\theta_i < 1$. Where θ_i is a constant depending on A, b, n, and u.
- The residual r_i contains a significant amount of components in every direction of the left singular vectors of A, such that we have $\mu_i \leq 1$ where μ_i defined as $\|r_i\| = \mu_i \|A\| \|x - \hat{x}_i\|$.

The first condition can be satisfied by replacing the typical LU-based solver for the correction equation with a variant of the generalized minimal residual method (GMRES), preconditioned by the low-precision LU factors. This is made possible by two observations: (1) even for an ill-conditioned matrix, the partial pivoting LU still contains useful information. That is, using LU factors as preconditioner improves condition number: $\kappa(\hat{U}^{-1}\hat{L}^{-1}A) \approx 1 + \kappa(A)u$ even for $\kappa(A) \gg u^{-1}$; (2) GMRES is backward stable. The second condition is empirically observed in numerical experiments.

The convergence rate of IRGM depends on the convergence behavior of GMRES, which is complicated to predict. A preconditioner that is FP16 accurate $M = LU \approx A$ further complicates the convergence rate picture. In general, for normal matrix A the GMRES converges faster as the condition number of A decreases, thus the low-precision LU would be of help because the preconditioning decreases condition number by a factor of $u = 5 \times 10^{-4}$; for a non-normal matrix the convergence rate cannot be entirely predicted by condition number. Thus, the convergence rate of IRGM depends on the matrix type, spectral properties, and matrix size. Therefore, we take a primarily empirical approach in the next sections.

We note that our iterative refinement process uses formula 1 as stopping criteria. The purpose of this paper is not the numerical study of the convergence of the IR methods, but rather to demonstrate how we can use techniques such as the IR methods to speed up the solution and obtain large energy gains. We note that, as described above, there is some limitation on where IR methods can work based on the matrices' condition number.

$$\frac{\| b - Ax \|_\infty}{\| x \|_\infty \cdot \| A \|_\infty} \le \epsilon\sqrt{n} \tag{1}$$

To make the paper self-contained and to highlight matrices' practical use of the IR methods, we show how the different IR methods discussed in this paper converge toward an FP64 solution. For that we illustrate in Fig. 2 the convergence history of the three IR methods on an NVIDIA Volta GPU for a practical problem where the condition number of the matrix is about 10^4. The hardware detail is the same as the one described in the next section. This study aims to provide an analysis of each arithmetic as well as to provide insight into the expected performance from the iterative refinement methods.

We observe that the FP32 technique requires 3 iterations, while the FP16 slightly increases to about 7–8 iterations. Interestingly, the FP16–TC converges faster (4 iterations) than the FP16 and slightly slower than the FP32. This is because the accumulation in the FP16–TC happens in FP32 arithmetic and thus produces a better result than the FP16. We believe that the FP32 routine will achieve a 2× speedup and that both of the FP16 routines will achieve about 3×–4× speedup while delivering a solution at the FP64 accuracy. More details about the performance are provided in the next section.

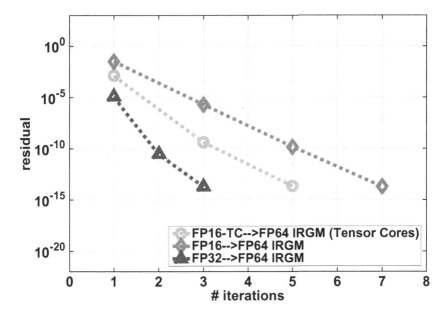

Fig. 2. Convergence history for the iterative refinement with GMRES using the three proposed low arithmetic for a matrix of size $n = 10000$, $\kappa_\infty(A) = 10^4$.

5   Experimental Results

This section presents the performance results and the power measurements of our iterative refinement methods—dhgesv-TC, dhgesv, and dsgesv—on either an NVIDIA V100 GPU or an Intel KNL 7250. The performances are computed by dividing the same FLOP count: $\frac{2}{3}n^3$ by the time to solution. As a result, a high performance reflects a fast time to solution. We used the KNL in self-hosted mode, i.e., without connection to CPU. This is not the case for the V100 GPU, which is used as an accelerator. We use LU factorization kernels from the Matrix Algebra on GPU and Multicore Architectures (MAGMA) library [19,20] in order to exploit both the CPU cores and the V100 GPU efficiently. Consequently, the V100 GPU performance results reported include both the CPU and GPU execution times. In the same way, the V100 energy efficiency results include both the power consumption on CPU and GPU. For the power measurement, we used the Performance Application Programming Interface (PAPI) [12], a performance-monitoring library recently updated for an efficient and accurate power measurement on both CPU and GPU.

5.1   Study of the Power Efficiency on KNL

The Intel KNL 7250 has two types of memory. A large 96 GB DDR4 memory providing up to 90 GB/s of bandwidth (e.g., the conventional DRAM memory) and a 16 GB MCDRAM high-bandwidth memory that delivers up to 425 GB/s.

The MCDRAM can be configured into three modes: flat mode, cache mode and hybrid mode. In this experiment, the KNL has been configured in flat mode—that is, the entirety of the MCDRAM is used as an addressable memory. We mention that if the matrix size requires less than 16 GB, all these modes will behave the same.

Figures 3a and 4a, show the performance obtained by our proposed FP32 IR solver dsgesv, and the reference FP64 dgesv solver for a matrices with $\kappa_\infty(A) \leq 10^4$. The number of iterations that the IR dsgesv required was not varying with the matrix size and took about 3 or 4 iterations to achieve the FP64 solution. In the first experiments displayed in Fig. 3a, the data are allocated on the DDR4 memory. The direct solver dgesv reaches an asymptotic performance of 1600 gigaFLOP/s, while the IR solver dsgesv provides up to 2800 gigaFLOP/s; that represents 1.75× speedup over dgesv. That's the main motivation behind proposing IR methods to achieve higher performance and thus better energy efficiency.

The speedup of the IR method is directly translated into energy savings. The corresponding power consumption details are depicted in Fig. 3b. In total, dgesv (orange curve) consumed about 2610 Joules to compute the solution. The IR solver dsgesv (purple curve) helps, achieving 43% of energy reduction by using only 1488 Joules to deliver a similar accuracy solution. We have also displayed the gigaFLOP/s per Watt—the higher the better—which is the common energy efficiency metric used in the HPC community. The IR solver has an energy efficiency of 12.7 gigaFLOP/s per Watt, as opposed to 7 gigaFLOP/s per Watt for the standard solver dgesv; this demonstrates the energy efficiency of the IR solver. The power consumption of the sgesv function (green curve) is illustrated only for sake of completeness and to determine—when compared to the purple curve—the portion of the IR loop. In contrast to the compute intensive portion (e.g., the LU factorization), we can see that the power of the IR loop drops to about 160 W. This is normal because memory-bound routines do not drain high power since the CPU activity will be limited by the bandwidth and, thus, does not run at full speed in order to drain the maximal power.

We have repeated the same experiments, but this time, the data are allocated in the high-bandwidth memory MCDRAM. Since the MCDRAM has about 4× higher bandwidth, one can expect that memory-bound operations will be around 3–4 times faster. Note that, as described in Sect. 4.2, the IR method consists of the LU factorization and the iterative loop. The LU factorization is known to be a compute-intensive algorithm while the IR loop consists of a sequence of matrix-vector products (e.g., dgemv) and a linear solution (e.g., using Xtrsv), thus the memory-bound portion. This means that one can expect that the IR loop will be faster when the data are allocated in the MCDRAM rather than the DDR4, while the LU portion will achieve roughly same the performance wherever the data are allocated. One can expect the dsgesv routine to provide slightly higher performance than when the data are allocated on DDR4 because the IR iterations (usually 3 or 4 iterations) are faster. The performance and the energy efficiency results are displayed in Fig. 4a and b, respectively. As expected, one can observe that the MCDRAM provides no performance gain for the standard solver dgesv,

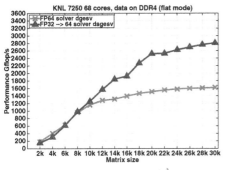

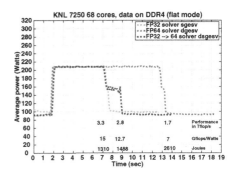

(a) Achieved Performance, $P = \frac{2n^3}{3}$ meaning higher is faster.

(b) Power and joules Consumption. Also shown is the Performance per Watt.

Fig. 3. Performance and power measurement of the linear solvers $Ax = b$ for the `IR` method compared with the `FP64` solver on KNL 7250 68 cores when data is on DDR4. (Color figure online)

this because `dgesv` is compute-bound and does not benefit from the high bandwidth. However, the IR solver `dsgesv` has shown a performance improvement of 14%, reaching 3200 gigaFLOP/s. As indicated above, this is due to the fact that the iterations of the IR consist of memory-bound kernels, which are sensitive to the bandwidth.

Regarding the energy efficiency, the IR technique revealed success. First, it brings an outstanding energy gain of 45% while providing a solution to the `FP64` accuracy. This is mainly due to the fact that (1) the LU factorization using the lower `FP32` precision is about $2\times$ faster than its `FP64` counterparts, meaning it consumes about half the energy of the `FP64` and (2) the IR required less than 5 iterations. Further, we remark that both `sgesv` and `dgesv` consumed about 5% less energy. This energy reduction is due to the DDR4 being idle, which dropped its power consumption to 7 W, compared to 25 W in Fig. 3b where the DDR4 was used. `dsgesv` will also benefit from data on MCDRAM and will bring 5% energy economy compared to the one of Fig. 3b. In addition, since the MCDRAM provides higher bandwidth, the IR portion will be faster, as shown in Fig. 4b and thus will also offer further energy gains. Finally, the `dsgesv` showed an energy improvement of 10% thanks the MCDRAM.

5.2 Study of the Power Efficiency on GPU V100

NVIDIA's V100 PCIe GPU is the latest version of accelerator from NVIDIA with the Volta architecture. It has 5120 CUDA cores, along with the new 640 Tensor Cores. This new Tensor Core architecture is exclusively to accelerate GEMM-update operation in mixed precision. V100 has a peak performance of 7 teraFLOP/s in double precision, 14 teraFLOP/s in single precision, and 112 teraFLOP/s on Tensor Cores. It has 16 GB high-bandwidth memory, with a bandwidth of 900 GB/s. The interconnect bandwidth is 32 GB/s, and maximum energy consumption of the V100 is 250 W.

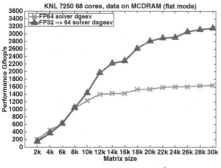 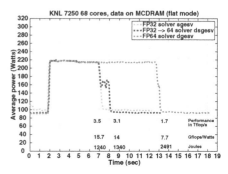

(a) Achieved performance, $P = \frac{2n^3}{3}$ meaning higher is faster.

(b) Power and joules consumption. Also shown is the performance per Watt.

Fig. 4. Performance and power measurement of the linear solvers $Ax = b$ for the IR method compared with the FP64 solver on KNL 7250 68 cores when data is on MCDRAM.

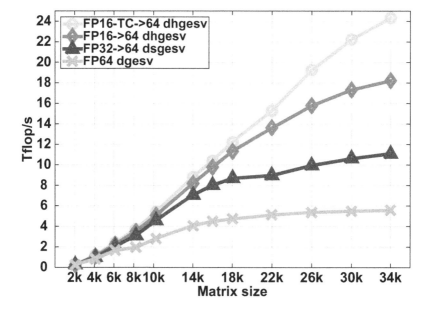

Fig. 5. Performance comparison of the linear solvers $Ax = b$ for the IR method using three different arithmetic and compared with the FP64 solver on NVIDIA V100 GPU.

Figure 5 shows the performance obtained by the different IR solvers, as well as the reference FP64 dgesv solver for matrices with $\kappa_\infty(A) \le 10^4$. All the IR variants' iterations ranged from 3 to 10 to converge for all matrix sizes. For example, the FP32 algorithm converged with about 3 or 4 iterations while the FP16 required between 7 and 10 iterations and the FP16-TC about 5 to 7 iterations. Thus, one can expect that the low-precision iterative refinement algorithms will bring a large speedup compared to dgesv. Since the number of iterations is small, we envision that the speedup ratio will be similar to the one observed in Fig. 1a for the LU factorization. The FP16-TC dhgesv-TC solver is up to 4× faster than its FP64 dgesv counterpart. Similarly, the FP16 dhgesv and the FP32 dsgesv variants showed around 3× and 1.8× speedup over the dgesv, respectively. These observations endorse our findings that low-precision techniques can be used to speed up linear solvers by a large factor, and, as a consequence, one can expect similar improvements in terms of energy consumption.

The energy efficiency results are displayed in Fig. 6. We note that, here, since the GPU implementation is hybrid (meaning it uses the CPU and the GPU), we reported in Fig. 6 the sum of the CPU, DRAM, and GPU power measurement. The standard dgesv solver provides an energy efficiency of 14 gigaFLOP/s per Watt. Using the FP32 IR dsgesv solver helps in doubling the energy efficiency, which increased up to 27 gigaFLOP/s per Watt. This follows our performance analysis described above, since the dsgesv is about twice as fast and thus we can observe twice the energy efficiency using the dsgesv routine. The results become more impressive with the FP16 dhgesv, which showed more than 3× the energy efficiency of dgesv. Finally, the most pronounced result is shown by the FP16-TC dhgesv-TC solver. It achieved an unprecedented energy efficiency of 74 gigaFLOP/s per Watt—that is a more than 5× improvement over the standard dgesv solver. These results demonstrate that the IR methods and half-precision arithmetic will be decisive in helping mitigate the power constraints in large-scale

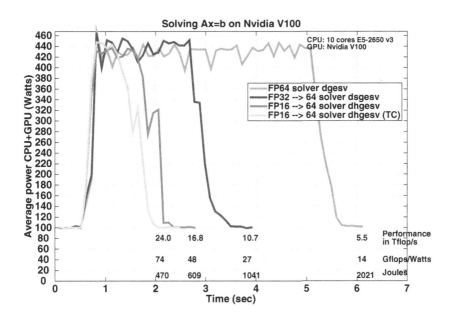

Fig. 6. Power consumption of the linear solvers $Ax = b$ for the IR method using three different arithmetic and compared with the FP64 solver on NVIDIA V100 GPU. Also shown is the performance per Watt.

HPC systems. To make this description self-contained, we would also mention that similarly to the KNL observation, we can easily determine the portion of the IR loop in these graphs. It is the portion with the lower power consumption (e.g., the portion draining 300 W). We can also see that the IR portion for dsgesv is short compared to the one for either the dhgesv and the dhgesv-TC. This is normal since, as mentioned above, the dsgesv required about 3 or 4 iterations while both dhgesv and dhgesv-TC required 7–10 and 5–7 iterations respectively.

6   Conclusion

This work is a direct response to increasing concerns about power efficiency in the HPC community. Existing works focus on dynamically tuning hardware voltage and frequency to save energy at the cost of performance. In this work, we propose a new approach to power efficiency and demonstrate that it is possible to increase both performance and power efficiency by leveraging the knowledge of applications. For the solution to linear systems of equations, a novel algorithm is designed and implemented. The initial approximation of the solution is computed using power efficient and fast reduced-precision arithmetic. This is followed by accuracy iterations to improve the accuracy in a higher precision. We have shown that, by combining FP32 and FP64, we can accelerate the execution time on Intel KNL architectures up to 2×—and reduce their power consumption by up to half. The results on the new NVIDIA V100 PCIe GPUs are even more promising. We have achieved 4× speedup, and more than 80% reduction in power consumption, by exploiting the FP16 features of the V100 GPU Tensor Cores.

In the 2000s, the potential of mixed-precision iterative refinement has been investigated for performance reasons. To the best of our knowledge, this work is the first study that demonstrates the immense potential of mixed-precision iterative refinement for large-scale computation. In future work, we aim to extend this work to ARM and IBM POWER architectures, and build a framework that will automatically identify the operations to be executed in reduced precision in applications without compromising the final accuracy.

Acknowledgments. This research was supported by the Exascale Computing Project (17-SC-20-SC), a collaborative effort of the U.S. Department of Energy Office of Science and the National Nuclear Security Administration. The work was also partially supported by NVIDIA and NSF grant No. OAC-1740250.

References

1. Baboulin, M., Buttari, A., Dongarra, J., Kurzak, J., Langou, J., Langou, J., Luszczek, P., Tomov, S.: Accelerating scientific computations with mixed precision algorithms. Comput. Phys. Commun. **180**(12), 2526–2533 (2009)
2. Betkaoui, B., Thomas, D.B., Luk, W.: Comparing performance and energy efficiency of FPGAs and GPUs for high productivity computing. In: 2010 International Conference on Field-Programmable Technology, pp. 94–101, December 2010

3. Carson, E., Higham, N.J.: Accelerating the solution of linear systems by iterative refinement in three precisions. MIMS EPrint 2017.24, University of Manchester (2017)
4. Carson, E., Higham, N.J.: A new analysis of iterative refinement and its application to accurate solution of ill-conditioned sparse linear systems. SIAM J. Sci. Comput. **39**(6), A2834–A2856 (2017). https://doi.org/10.1137/17M1122918
5. Eastep, J., Sylvester, S., Cantalupo, C., Geltz, B., Ardanaz, F., Al-Rawi, A., Livingston, K., Keceli, F., Maiterth, M., Jana, S.: Global extensible open power manager: a vehicle for HPC community collaboration on co-designed energy management solutions. In: Kunkel, J.M., Yokota, R., Balaji, P., Keyes, D. (eds.) ISC 2017. LNCS, vol. 10266, pp. 394–412. Springer, Cham (2017). https://doi.org/10.1007/978-3-319-58667-0_21
6. Etinski, M., Corbalán, J., Labarta, J., Valero, M.: Understanding the future of energy-performance trade-off via DVFS in HPC environments. J. Parallel Distrib. Comput. **72**(4), 579–590 (2012)
7. Ge, R., Feng, X., Song, S., Chang, H.C., Li, D., Cameron, K.W.: Powerpack: energy profiling and analysis of high-performance systems and applications. IEEE Trans. Parallel Distrib. Syst. **21**(5), 658–671 (2010)
8. Haidar, A., Jagode, H., YarKhan, A., Vaccaro, P., Tomov, S., Dongarra, J.: Power-aware computing: Measurement, control, and performance analysis for Intel Xeon Phi. In: 2017 IEEE High Performance Extreme Computing Conference (HPEC), pp. 1–7, September 2017
9. Haidar, A., Tomov, S., Luszczek, P., Dongarra, J.: Magma embedded: towards a dense linear algebra library for energy efficient extreme computing. In: 2015 IEEE High Performance Extreme Computing Conference (HPEC 2015), (Best Paper Award). IEEE, Waltham, September 2015
10. Haidar, A., Wu, P., Tomov, S., Dongarra, J.: Investigating half precision arithmetic to accelerate dense linear system solvers. In: SC16 Scal A17: 8th Workshop on Latest Advances in Scalable Algorithms for Large-Scale Systems. ACM, Denver, November 2017
11. Higham, N.J.: Iterative refinement enhances the stability of QR factorization methods for solving linear equations. BIT Numer. Math. **31**(3), 447–468 (1991). https://doi.org/10.1007/BF01933262
12. Jagode, H., YarKhan, A., Danalis, A., Dongarra, J.: Power management and event verification in PAPI. In: Knüpfer, A., Hilbrich, T., Niethammer, C., Gracia, J., Nagel, W.E., Resch, M.M. (eds.) Tools for High Performance Computing 2015, pp. 41–51. Springer, Cham (2016). https://doi.org/10.1007/978-3-319-39589-0_4
13. Kasichayanula, K., Terpstra, D., Luszczek, P., Tomov, S., Moore, S., Peterson, G.: Power aware computing on GPUs. In: SAAHPC 2012 (Best Paper Award), Argonne, IL, July 2012
14. Kimura, H., Sato, M., Hotta, Y., Boku, T., Takahashi, D.: Empirical study on reducing energy of parallel programs using slack reclamation by DVFS in a power-scalable high performance cluster. In: 2006 IEEE International Conference on Cluster Computing, pp. 1–10, September 2006
15. Langou, J., Luszczek, P., Kurzak, J., Buttari, A., Dongarra, J.: Exploiting the performance of 32 bit floating point arithmetic in obtaining 64 bit accuracy (revisiting iterative refinement for linear systems). In: SC 2006 Conference, Proceedings of the ACM/IEEE, p. 50, November 2006
16. NVIDIA Management Library (NVML), NVIDIA (2018). https://developer.nvidia.com/nvidia-management-library-nvml

17. Rountree, B., Lownenthal, D.K., de Supinski, B.R., Schulz, M., Freeh, V.W., Bletsch, T.: Adagio: making DVS practical for complex HPC applications. In: Proceedings of the 23rd International Conference on Supercomputing, ICS 2009, pp. 460–469. ACM, New York (2009). https://doi.org/10.1145/1542275.1542340
18. Skeel, R.D.: Iterative refinement implies numerical stability for Gaussian elimination. Math. Comput. **35**(151), 817–832 (1980)
19. Tomov, S., Dongarra, J., Baboulin, M.: Towards dense linear algebra for hybrid GPU accelerated manycore systems. Parallel Comput. Syst. Appl. **36**(5–6), 232–240 (2010). https://doi.org/10.1016/j.parco.2009.12.005
20. Tomov, S., Nath, R., Ltaief, H., Dongarra, J.: Dense linear algebra solvers for multicore with GPU accelerators. In: Proceedings of the IEEE IPDPS 2010, Atlanta, GA, pp. 1–8, 19–23 April 2010
21. Wilkinson, J.H.: Rounding Errors in Algebraic Processes. Prentice-Hall, Upper Saddle River (1963)

Design of Parallel BEM Analyses Framework for SIMD Processors

Tetsuya Hoshino$^{(\boxtimes)}$, Akihiro Ida, Toshihiro Hanawa, and Kengo Nakajima

Information Technology Center, The University of Tokyo, Tokyo, Japan
{hoshino,ida,hanawa,nakajima}@cc.u-tokyo.ac.jp

Abstract. Parallel Boundary Element Method (BEM) analyses are typically conducted using a purpose-built software framework called BEM-BB. This framework requires a user-defined function program that calculates the i-th row and the j-th column of the coefficient matrix arising from the convolution integral term in the fundamental BEM equation. Owing to this feature, the framework can encapsulate MPI and OpenMP hybrid parallelization with $\mathcal{H}$-matrix approximation. Therefore, users can focus on implementing a fundamental solution or a Green's function, which is the most important element in BEM and depends on the targeted physical phenomenon, as a user-defined function. However, the framework does not consider single instruction multiple data (SIMD) vectorization, which is important for high-performance computing and is supported by the majority of existing processors. Performing SIMD vectorization of a user-defined function is difficult because SIMD exploits instruction-level parallelization and is closely associated with the user-defined function. In this paper, a conceptual framework for enhancing SIMD vectorization is proposed. The proposed framework is evaluated using two BEM problems, namely, static electric field analysis with a perfect conductor and static electric field analysis with a dielectric, on Intel Broadwell (BDW) processor and Intel Xeon Phi Knights Landing (KNL) processor. It offers good vectorization performance with limited SIMD knowledge, as can be verified from the numerical results obtained herein. Specifically, in perfect conductor analyses conducted using the $\mathcal{H}$-matrix, the framework achieved performance improvements of 2.22x and 4.34x compared to the original BEM-BB framework for the BDW processor and KNL, respectively.

1 Introduction

The boundary element method (BEM) has several scientific applications. This method requires fewer unknowns and has a lower meshing cost compared to other volume discretization methods because it requires only the surface of the target objects for analysis. However, the computational cost and memory footprint of BEM analysis are significantly high because a dense coefficient matrix is generated during the analysis. To overcome these problems, parallel computing and approximation techniques, such as hierarchical matrices ($\mathcal{H}$-matrices) [1–3], $\mathcal{H}^2$-matrices [4], and the fast multipole method (FMM) [5] are often used for

© Springer International Publishing AG, part of Springer Nature 2018
Y. Shi et al. (Eds.): ICCS 2018, LNCS 10860, pp. 601–613, 2018.
https://doi.org/10.1007/978-3-319-93698-7_46

BEM analysis. Although these techniques have huge programming costs, BEM-BB [6], an open-source software framework for parallel BEM analysis, is useful to for reducing these costs. The framework employs $\mathcal{H}$-matrices to approximate the dense coefficient matrix, and it is parallelized using the MPI and OpenMP models. The BEM-BB framework allows for faster BEM analysis on parallel computers by simply preparing programs to calculate the integrals of boundary elements, settings of boundary conditions, and analysis output. In addition, the parallelization and the approximation programs are encapsulated in the framework. Thus, users can concentrate on developing the most important aspects of BEM analysis, namely, a user-defined function for calculating the i-th row and the j-th column of the coefficient matrix. Furthermore, the user-defined function may vary depending on the targeted physical phenomena.

However, this framework does not consider single instruction multiple data (SIMD) vectorization, which is important for achieving high-performance computing on existing processors. For example, the most recent Intel processors, such as Skylake EP/EX and Xeon Phi Knights Landing (KNL), support AVX-512, that is, a 512-bit SIMD instruction set. SIMD vectorization cannot be separated from user-defined functions, unlike in MPI and OpenMP parallelization, because SIMD vectorization is instruction-level parallelization and because user-defined functions can vary. However, SIMD vectorization is difficult for application programmers because it requires knowledge of the compiler and the target processor architecture.

In this paper, we present a framework design based on BEM-BB for SIMD vectorization. A design to encapsulate SIMD-related aspects is proposed. In addition, we evaluate the performance of the proposed framework by solving two problems, namely, static electric field analysis with a perfect conductor and static electric field analysis with a dielectric, which contain different user-defined functions, on Intel Broadwell processor (BDW) and Intel Xeon Phi Knights Landing (KNL). We compare the performance of the proposed framework with the original framework and that of hand-tuned user functions. The results show that the proposed framework offers performance improvements of 2.22x and 4.34x compared to the original framework for the BDW processor and the KNL processor, respectively. Furthermore, the experimental results demonstrate that the performance of the framework is comparable to that achieved using the hand-tuned programs

The remainder of this paper is organized as follows. In Sect. 2, we provide an overview of the BEM-BB framework. The proposed framework is described in Sect. 3. Numerical experiments involving electric field analysis are described in Sect. 4, and a few conclusions and suggestions for future work are presented in Sect. 6.

2   BEM-BB Framework

In this section, the BEM-BB framework, which is the baseline implementation in this study, is introduced. The BEM-BB software framework is used for parallel

BEM analysis. It is implemented in the Fortran90 programming environment and parallelized using the OpenMP + MPI hybrid programming model. To reduce the computational cost of parallel programming, the framework supports model data input, assembly of the coefficient matrix, and solution of linear systems, steps that are generally required in BEM analysis. When employing this framework, users are required to generate user-defined functions that calculate each element of the coefficient matrix. In other words, users are required to implement a program to calculate the integrals of boundary elements, which depend on the governing target of BEM analysis. The target integral equation of the BEM-BB framework is described as follows. For $f \in H'$, $u \in H$ and a kernel function of a convolution operator $g : \mathbb{R}^d \times \Omega \to \mathbb{R}$,

$$\int_\Omega g(x,y)u(y)\mathrm{d}y = f \tag{1}$$

where $\Omega \subset \mathbb{R}^d$ denotes a $(d-1)$-dimensional domain, H the Hilbert space of functions on a Ω, and H' dual space of H. To numerically calculate Eq. (1), we divide the domain, Ω, into the elements $\Omega_h = \{\omega_j : j \in J\}$, where J is an index set. In weighted residual methods, such as the Ritz-Galerkin method and the collocation method, the function u is approximated from a n-dimensional subspace $H^h \subset H$. Given a basis $(\varphi_i)_{i \in \beth}$ of H^h for an index set $\beth := \{1, \ldots, N\}$, the approximant $u^h \in H^h$-u can be expressed using a coefficient vector $\phi = (\phi_i)_{i \in \beth}$ that satisfies $u^h = \sum_{i \in \beth} \phi_i \varphi_i$. Note that the supports of the basis $\Omega^h_{\varphi_i} :=$ supp φ are assembled from the sets ω_j. Equation (1) is then reduced to the following system of linear equations.

$$A\phi = b \tag{2}$$

$$A_{ij} = \int_\Omega \varphi_i(x) \int_\Omega g(x,y)\varphi(y)\mathrm{d}y\mathrm{d}x \tag{3}$$

$$b_i = \int_\Omega \varphi_i(x)f\mathrm{d}x \tag{4}$$

Here, $i, j \in \beth$. The user-defined function required to calculate the elements of the i-th row and the j-th column of the coefficient matrix is expressed as Eq. (3).

There are two versions of the implementation: one based on dense matrix computations and the other based on $\mathcal{H}$-matrix computations. Although the $\mathcal{H}$-matrix version depends on the distributed parallel $\mathcal{H}$-matrix library $\mathcal{H}$ACApK [7], the problems of vectorization are similar. As shown in Fig. 1, the proposed framework consists of three components: model data input, coefficient matrix generation, and linear solver. In this study, the objective is to interface coefficient matrix generation with user-defined function. Therefore, we focus on the coefficient matrix generation component.

Figure 2 shows the coefficient matrix generation part. The target coefficient matrix is distributed to multiple thread and each thread sequentially calculates the i-th row and the j-th column element by using user-defined function. The coefficient matrices generated using the dense matrix version and the $\mathcal{H}$-matrix version are a dense matrix and an $\mathcal{H}$-matrix, respectively. A $\mathcal{H}$-matrix

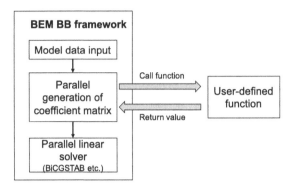

Fig. 1. The design of BEM-BB framework

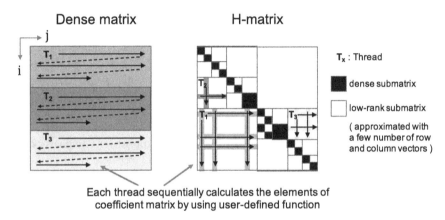

Each thread sequentially calculates the elements of
coefficient matrix by using user-defined function

Fig. 2. Parallel generation of coefficient dense matrix and $\mathcal{H}$-matrix.

is also called a hierarchical matrix. $\mathcal{H}$-matrices are among the techniques used to approximate dense matrices. An $\mathcal{H}$-matrix is a set of low-rank approximated sub-matrices and small dense sub-matrices as shown in Fig. 2. $\mathcal{H}$ACApK generates the coefficient $\mathcal{H}$-matrix by exploiting the user-defined function according to the Adaptive Cross Approximation (ACA) algorithm [9]. The ACA algorithm is an approximation technique used to generate a low-rank approximated matrix of a dense matrix without generating the target dense matrix.

The interface of the user-defined function is shown in Fig. 3. In both versions, the function is called from each thread concurrently. To vectorize the user-defined function, the caller of the function, too, is important. Figures 4 and 5 show the callers of the user-defined functions of the dense matrix version and the $\mathcal{H}$-matrix version, respectively. Both programs call the user-defined function in loop structures. These loops are the target of SIMD vectorization. In the following sections, we treat the implementation shown in Fig. 4 as the baseline.

```
1   real(8) function ppohBEM_matrix_element_ij(i,j,nond,nofc,nond_on_fc,np,
          intpara_fc,nint_para_fc,dble_para_fc,ndble_para_fc,face2node)
2     !$omp declare simd
3     type :: coordinate
4       real(8) :: x,y,z
5     end type coordinate
6     integer ,intent(in) :: i,j,nond,nofc,nond_on_fc,nint_para_fc,
          ndble_para_fc
7     type(coordinate),intent(in) :: np(*)
8     integer, intent(in) :: face2node(3,*),int_para_fc(nint_para_fc,*)
9     real(8), intent(in) :: dble_para_fc(ndble_para_fc,*)
10
11    ! User defined calculations for the i-th row and the j-th column
          element
12
13  end function ppohBEM_matrix_element_ij
```

Fig. 3. An interface of a user-defined function to calculate the i-th row and the j-th column element of the coefficient matrix. The function arguments after i and j are used as input variable of the calculation.

```
1   do i=lhp, ltp
2     !$omp simd
3     do j=j_st, j_en
4       a(j,i) = ppohBEM_matrix_element_ij( i, j, nond, nofc, &
5                                nond_on_fc, np, intpara_fc, &
6                                nint_para_fc, dble_para_fc, &
7                                ndble_para_fc, face2node )
8     enddo
9   enddo
```

Fig. 4. User-defined function caller for dense matrix. Here, a(j,i) is a coefficient dense matrix. The ranges of i and j are assigned to each thread adequately.

3   Framework Design for SIMD Vectorization with OpenMP SIMD Directives

In general, three methods are used to perform SIMD vectorization: (1) relying on compiler auto-vectorization, (2) using compiler directives, and (3) using intrinsic functions. However, vectorization using intrinsic functions is cumbersome job, and the required intrinsic functions depend completely on the user-defined function. In this study, we employ compiler auto-vectorization and the directive method. To use SIMD instructions efficiently, there are two constraints on the SIMD target vectors.

- There should be no data dependency among the elements of the target vector.
- Vector elements should be stored contiguously.

In addition, to generate efficient code by using compiler vectorizations, the code should be obviously vectorizable from the compiler's view point. Any new framework design should consider the above points. Furthermore, the design should be user-friendly. Efficiently vectorized SIMD code should be generated if users are unaware of compiler requirements.

```
1  if( column vector calculation )
2    i = ip + nstrtl-1
3    !$omp simd private(j)
4    do ii=1,s_m
5      if(colmsk(ii)==0) then
6        j = ii + nstrtt-1
7        colvec(ii)=HACApK_entry_ij(i,j,st_bemv)
8      endif
9    enddo
10 else if( row vector calculation )
11   j = ip + nstrtt-1
12   !$omp simd private(i)
13   do ii=1,t_m
14     if(rowmsk(ii)==0) then
15       i = ii + nstrtl-1
16       rowvec(ii)=HACApK_entry_ij(i,j,st_bemv)
17     endif
18   enddo
19 endif
```

Fig. 5. User-defined function caller for sub-matrix of $\mathcal{H}$-matrix. Here, HACApK_entry_ij is a wrapper function of ppohBEM_matrix_element_ij. The structure st_bemv contains the variables required as arguments of the user-defined function.

3.1 New Interface Definition for Compiler Vectorization

According to the two compiler requirements, the main problem associated with vectorization pertains to data access. Even though the computations associated with a user-defined function can be executed independently, if a compiler detects possibilities of data dependency, it conservatively generates instructions that are not fully vectorized. Therefore, we propose to handle data access and computation separately in the proposed framework design. We introduce two new interfaces set_args (Fig. 6) and vectorize_func (Fig. 7) for data access and computation, respectively. Figure 8 shows the function caller based on Fig. 4. The variables SIMDLENGTH, which appear in Figs. 7 and 8 and are defined by users, represent the SIMD length of the target processor. For example, the recommended SIMDLENGTH for KNL, which has a 512-bit (= sizeof(double) ×8) wide SIMD unit, is 8. From the compiler's viewpoint, the !$omp simd loop (Fig. 8 line 14) has no data dependency because the arguments and the return values of vector_func have no alias and are accessed independently for each iteration of the loop. In addition, the arguments and return values are stored contiguously. At this point, if the SIMD interface of the vectorize_func corresponds to the SIMD length, the loop (Fig. 8 lines 13–17) is vectorized similarly to a vector function.

To safely vectorize vectorize_func, we constrain the function such that it cannot contain globally accessible variables, allocatable arrays, or save variables. In addition, the SIMD interfaces of all functions or subroutines called from vectorize_func should correspond to the SIMD length. This parallelization method is similar to the Single Program Multiple Data (SPMD) programming model because each SIMD element executes a single program simultaneously.

```
1   subroutine set_args(i,j,nond,nofc,nond_on_fc,np,intpara_fc,nint_para_fc,
        dble_para_fc,ndble_para_fc,face2node,darg1,darg2,...,dargN,iarg1,
        iarg2,...,iargM)
2     real(8), intent(out) :: darg1,darg2,...,dargN
3     integer, intent(out) :: iarg1,iarg2,...,iargM
4
5     ! User defined data access for calculating an element of the i-th row
        and the j-th column from arrays to scalar args
6
7   end subroutine set_args
```

Fig. 6. New interface for data access. The former arguments are the same as ppo-hBEM_matrix_element_ij. The latter arguments are the scalar variables used in vectorize_func. The number of arguments depends on the target application.

To reduce the data access cost, we introduce a pair of interfaces set_args_i and set_args_j. In BEM analysis, the required data such as coordinate of the i-th element and the j-th element usually depends only on the variables i and j, respectively. Therefore, the subroutines set_args_i and set_args_j are used to set arguments depending only on i and j, respectively. The pair of interfaces work effectively in the $\mathcal{H}$-matrix version. As shown in Fig. 5, i and j are constants in the lines 4–9 loop and lines 13–18 loop, respectively.

3.2 Using the Framework

The new interfaces are easy to vectorize for compilers, but they are not user-friendly. Specifically, the numbers of arguments of the set_args subroutine and the vectorize_func function depend on the target application, which means users are required to modify the framework program in order to add variable declarations and correspond to the interface. In addition, users must vectorize the user-defined functions by using !$omp declare simd pragma. Furthermore, if users insert a wrong directive, the compiler generates a correct but unvectorized slow executable, which is often more cumbersome compared to a bug.

To minimize these difficulties, we require users to prepare the followings.

- Implement include files.
- Implement the set_args, set_args_i, set_args_j and the vectorize_func without the SIMD directives in the file "user_func.f90".
- Correctly implement the dummy function ppohBEM_matrix_element_ij_dummy (Fig. 9) without modifying the dummy function itself.
- Provide SIMDLENGTH of the target processor by using the -D compiler flag.

The include files that appear in the dummy function are used in the subroutine call interface. First, users of the framework must implement the include files as a fill-in-the-blank puzzle to correct the dummy function. In other words, the return value of the dummy function should be equal to ppohBEM_matrix_ele-ment_ij. At this point, users need not consider SIMD vectorization. Notably, users cannot modify the dummy function itself. If users do not need the set_args function, they must create an empty

```
1   real(8) function vectorize_func(darg1,darg2,...,dargN,iarg1,iarg2,...,
        iargM)
2     !$omp declare simd simdlen(SIMDLENGTH)
3     real(8), intent(in) :: darg1,darg2,...,dargN
4     integer, intent(in) :: iarg1,iarg2,...,iargM
5
6     ! User defined calculations for an element of the i-th row and j-th
          column
7
8   end function vectorize_func
```

Fig. 7. New calculation interface. This function should be called after the set_args subroutine and vectorized. All arguments of this function should have intent(in) attribute.

"call_set_args.inc" file. Second, the users must implement the user-defined functions in "user_func.f90." Notably, users need not consider SIMD vectorization as well. Finally, users must define the variable SIMDLENGTH by using a compiler option. During compiling, the compile script automatically inserts SIMD directives into the user-defined functions implemented in user_func.f90 and automatically transforms the include files to adjust the framework, as shown in Fig. 10. Based on the results of the auto-transformation, we succeeded in separating almost all aspects related to SIMD vectorization from the user-defined function. Therefore, users are required to set only the SIMDLENGTH of the target processor.

4   Numerical Evaluations

4.1   Test Model and Processors

In this section, we evaluated the proposed framework by performing BEM analysis of two electrostatic field problems. We assumed a perfectly conductive sphere and a dielectric sphere. The electric potentials of the perfect conductor and the dielectric are given by the following functionals $\mathcal{P}$ and $\mathcal{D}$, respectively:

$$\mathcal{P}[u](x) := \int_{\Omega} \frac{1}{4\pi||x - y||} u(y)\mathrm{d}y, x \in \Omega \tag{5}$$

$$\mathcal{D}[u](x) := \int_{\Omega} \frac{\langle x - y, n(y)\rangle}{4\pi||x - y||^3} u(y)\mathrm{d}y, x \in \Omega \tag{6}$$

where Ω is the domain surface. Equations (5) and (6) correspond to Eq. (1) and the details of them are described in [3]. The spheres were set at a distance of 0.25 m from the ground with zero electric potential. The radius of the spheres was 0.25 m, and the electric potential of the spheres was 1 V.

For the numerical evaluations, we used the BDW and the KNL processors, which have a 256-bit SIMD unit and a 512-bit SIMD unit, respectively. The processor specifications are summarized in Table 1. For both processors, Intel Fortran compiler ver. 18.0.1 was used. The compiler options for BDW were -align array64byte -xAVX2 -qopenmp -O3 -fpp -ipo -lm -qopt-report=5 -DSIMDLENGTH=4, and those for KNL were -align array64byte -xMIC-AVX512 -qopenmp -O3 -fpp -ipo -lm -qopt-report=5 -DSIMDLENGTH=8.

```
1    real(8),dimension(SIMDLENGTH) :: ans
2    real(8),dimension(SIMDLENGTH) :: darg1,darg2,...,dargN
3    integer,dimension(SIMDLENGTH) :: iarg1,iarg2,...,iargM
4      ...
5    do i=lhp, ltp
6      do jj=j_st, j_en, SIMDLENGTH
7        ii = 1
8        do j=jj,min(jj+SIMDLENGTH-1,j_en)
9          call set_args(i,j,...,darg1(ii),darg2(ii),...,dargN(ii) &
10                       ,iarg1(ii),iarg2(ii),...,iargM(ii))
11          ii = ii+1
12        end do
13        !$omp simd
14        do ii = 1, SIMDLENGTH
15          ans(ii) = vectorize_func(darg1(ii),darg2(ii),...,dargN(ii) &
16                       ,iarg1(ii),iarg2(ii),...,iargM(ii))
17        end do
18        ii = 1
19        do j=jj,min(jj+SIMDLENGTH-1,j_en)
20          a(j,i) = ans(ii)
21          ii = ii+1
22        end do
23      enddo
24    enddo
```

Fig. 8. User-defined function using new interface caller for dense matrix.

4.2   Hand Tuning Using OpenMP SIMD Directives

To test the compiler vectorizations, we refactored and evaluated two user-defined functions. Vectorization with compiler directives often requires users to converse with the compiler. We tried to vectorize the user-defined functions by preparing the following series of implementations.

H1:   Original implementation without compiler directives.

H2:   !$omp simd directives are inserted above the SIMD target loops of H1.

H3:   !$omp declare simd directives are inserted in the function shown in Fig. 3 and all user-defined functions called from the function of H2 shown in Fig. 3.

H4:   A simdlen(SIMDLENGTH) clause is attached to each !$omp simd and !$omp declare simd directive of H3.

H5:   Replace the user-defined functions of H4 with the set_args and vectorize_func interfaces.

H6:   The interfaces set_args_i and set_args_j are used as alternatives to set_args of H5.

H7:   linear clauses are attached to a !$omp declare simd directive of vectorize_func of H6.

H8:   uniform clauses are used as constant variables instead of linear clauses of H7.

Implementations H1-H4 are based on the original framework. The differences among these implementations are only in terms of the OpenMP directives. Therefore, users familiar with SIMD can implement H1-H4 with relative ease. Implementations H5-H8 are based on the proposed framework. Specifically, implementation H7 corresponds to the automatically generated program. Note

```
1   real(8) function ppohBEM_matrix_element_ij_dummy(i,j,nond,nofc,nond_on_fc
        ,np,intpara_fc,nint_para_fc,dble_para_fc,ndble_para_fc,face2node)
2     implicit none
3     type :: coordinate
4       real(8) :: x,y,z
5     end type coordinate
6     integer ,intent(in) :: i,j,nond,nofc,nond_on_fc,nint_para_fc,
          ndble_para_fc
7     type(coordinate),intent(in) :: np(*)
8     integer, intent(in) :: face2node(3,*),int_para_fc(nint_para_fc,*)
9     real(8), intent(in) :: dble_para_fc(ndble_para_fc,*)
10    integer :: ii,jj,j_st,j_en,lhp,ltp
11    real(8) :: ans
12  #include "declaration.inc"
13  #include "call_set_args_i.inc"
14  #include "call_set_args_j.inc"
15  #include "call_set_args.inc"
16  #include "vectorize_func.inc"
17    ppohBEM_matrix_element_ij_dummy = ans
18
19  end function ppohBEM_matrix_element_ij_dummy
```

Fig. 9. Dummy function of user-defined function. Although the function is not used in the framework, users are required to implement this function correctly.

Table 1. Processor specifications

	Processor name	Number of cores	Peak performance	Length of SIMD unit
BDW	Intel Xeon E5-2695 v4	18	605 GFlops	256 bit
KNL	Intel Xeon Phi 7250	68	3,046 GFlops	512 bit

that implementation H8 is more optimized than implementation H7. However, to automatically generate implementation H8, syntactic analysis is required. This will be realized in the future.

Figures 11, 12, 13 and 14 show the increase in speed compared to the speed of implementation H1, and Table 2 summarizes the elapsed times of implementations H1 and H7. The results discussed in this section are the averages of 10 measurements. As summarized in Table 2, although we recommend the BEM-BB H-matrix version, we evaluated the dense matrix version, the performance of which depends to a greater extent on the user-defined function. The main difference between the two functions from the viewpoint of SIMD vectorization is whether the function has a branch. Although the increase in speed in case of the dielectric problem shows a trend similar to that in case of the perfect conductor problem, it is slightly worse owing to the branch divergence caused by the dielectric function. The results obtained by solving the perfect conductor problem on a machine with the KNL processor (Fig. 11) show that the proposed implementation (H7) achieved performance improvements of 4.34x and 6.62x compared to implementation H0 for the $\mathcal{H}$-matrix and the dense matrix versions, respectively. The theoretical speedup with SIMD vectorization equals SIMDLENGTH,

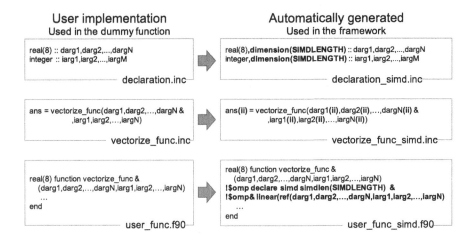

Fig. 10. The users program automatically transformed at the compile time.

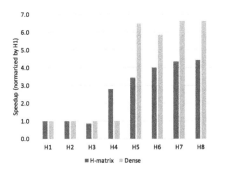

Fig. 11. Solving perfect conductor problem using KNL processor

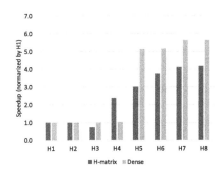

Fig. 12. Solving dielectric problem using KNL proccesor

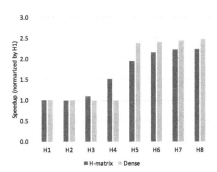

Fig. 13. Solving perfect conductor problem using BDW processor

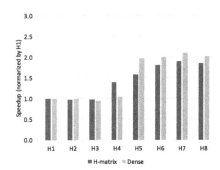

Fig. 14. Solving dielectric problem using BDW processor

and the results of the dense matrix version demonstrate that the framework improves SIMD vectorization performance considerably. In the results obtained on a machine with the BDW processor (Fig. 13), implementation H7 achieved performance improvements of 2.22x and 2.44x compared to implementation H0 for the $\mathcal{H}$- matrix and the dense matrix versions, respectively.

5   Related Work

The literature contains many studies about software frameworks for parallel PDE solvers of the finite element method, such as GeoFEM [10] and Free FEM++ [11]. Moreover, $\mathcal{H}$-matrices have been used in a few BEM applications [8,9,12], and parallelized in their application. Although many frameworks allow for MPI + OpenMP hybrid parallelization, few frameworks support SIMD vectorization, which highly depends on user-defined functions. The main contribution of this study is a SPMD-like SIMD vectorization method that handles data access and computation separately, and hides SIMD-related aspects in the framework. The method uses the characteristics of BEM analysis: the kernel function is relatively computationally intensive, and there exists no data dependency among the calculations of elements of coefficient matrix.

Table 2. The elapsed times of coefficient generation component of original implementation (H1) and implementation of proposed framework (H7)

	Perfect conductor				Dielectric			
	KNL		BDW		KNL		BDW	
	H-matrix	Dense	H-matrix	Dense	H-matrix	Dense	H-matrix	Dense
H1	10.00	215.0	10.51	233.2	13.07	249.5	13.53	265.5
H7	2.307	32.47	4.728	95.61	3.167	44.11	7.140	126.10

6   Conclusion

We refined the open-source framework for parallel BEM analysis to enhance SIMD vectorizations, which is important for realizing high-performance computing. By using the refined framework design, we could successfully separate SIMD-related aspects from the user-defined function, which depends on target applications. We evaluated the proposed framework by solving two static electric field analysis problems containing different user-defined functions on a BDW processor and a KNL processor. The numerical results demonstrated the improved performance of the framework. Specifically, in solving the perfect conductor problem by using the KNL processor, we achieved performance improvements of 4.34x and 6.62x in the $\mathcal{H}$-matrix case and the dense matrix cases, respectively.

The main contribution of this paper is separating the SIMD-related aspects from the user-defined function and hiding them to minimize the difficulties associated with SIMD. This SPMD-like SIMD vectorization technique can be used for other applications. In the proposed framework, the arguments of the `vectorize_func` must be scalar variable. This specification is not user-friendly but compiler-friendly. For example, to adjust the user-defined functions in the proposed framework, we separated the vector argument `coordinate(3)` to scalars x, y, and z. This type of transformation is a typical Array of Structure (AoS) to Structure of Array (SoA) transformation. To improve the not user-friendly specification, we will challenge to support the AoS to SoA transformation in future.

Acknowledgment. This work was supported by JSPS KAKENHI Grant Number 16H06679 and 17H01749.

References

1. Hackbusch, W.: A sparse matrix arithmetic based on H-matrices. Part I: introduction to H-matrices. Computing **62**(2), 89–108 (1999)
2. Hackbusch, W., Khoromskij, B.N.: A sparse H-matrix arithmetic. Part II: application to multi-dimensional problems. Computing **64**(1), 21–47 (2000)
3. Börm, S., Grasedyck, L., Hackbusch, W.: Hierarchical matrices. Technical report, Max Planck Institute for Mathematics in the Sciences (2003)
4. Börm, S., Bendoraityte, J.: Distributed h^2-matrices for non-local operators. Comput. Vis. Sci. **11**(4), 237–249 (2008)
5. Yokota, R., Barba, L.A., Narumi, T., Yasuoka, K.: Petascale turbulence simulation using a highly parallel fast multipole method on GPUs. Comput. Phys. Commun. **184**(3), 445–455 (2013)
6. ppOpen-HPC: Open Source Infrastructure for Development and Execution of Large-Scale Scientific Applications on Post-Peta-Scale Supercomputers with Automatic Tuning (AT). http://ppopenhpc.cc.u-tokyo.ac.jp/ppopenhpc/
7. Ida, A., Iwashita, T., Mifune, T., Takahashi, Y.: Parallel hierarchical matrices with adaptive cross approximation on symmetric multiprocessing clusters. J. Inf. Process. **22**(4), 642–650 (2014)
8. Iwashita, T., Ida, A., Mifune, T., Takahashi, Y.: Software framework for parallel BEM analyses with H-matrices using MPI and OpenMP. Procedia Comput. Sci. **108**, 2200–2209 (2017)
9. Kurz, S., Rain, O., Rjasanow, S.: The adaptive cross-approximation technique for the 3D boundary-element method. IEEE Trans. Magn. **38**(2), 421–424 (2002)
10. Okuda, H., Nakajima, K., Iizuka, M., Chen, L., Nakamura, H.: Parallel finite element analysis platform for the earth simulator: GeoFEM. In: Sloot, P.M.A., Abramson, D., Bogdanov, A.V., Gorbachev, Y.E., Dongarra, J.J., Zomaya, A.Y. (eds.) ICCS 2003. LNCS, vol. 2659, pp. 773–780. Springer, Heidelberg (2003). https://doi.org/10.1007/3-540-44863-2_75
11. Hecht, F.: New development in freefem++. J. Numer. Math. **20**(3–4), 251–265 (2012)
12. Ohtani, M., Hirahara, K., Takahashi, Y., Hori, T., Hyodo, M., Nakashima, H., Iwashita, T.: Fast computation of quasi-dynamic earthquake cycle simulation with hierarchical matrices. Procedia Comput. Sci. **4**, 1456–1465 (2011)

An Experimental Assessment of Three Point-Insertion Sequences for 3-D Incremental Delaunay Tessellations

Sanderson L. Gonzaga de Oliveira[1(✉)], Diogo T. Robaina[2], Diego N. Brandão[3], Mauricio Kischinhevsky[2], and Gabriel Oliveira[1]

[1] Universidade Federal de Lavras, Lavras, Minas Gerais, Brazil
sanderson@dcc.ufla.br, g.oliveira@computacao.ufla.br
[2] Universidade Federal Fluminense, Niterói, Rio de Janeiro, Brazil
{drobaina,kisch}@ic.uff.br
[3] CEFET-RJ, Nova Iguaçu, Rio de Janeiro, Brazil
diego.brandao@eic.cefet-rj.br

Abstract. Currently, state-of-the-art algorithms for building 3-D Delaunay tessellations are incremental. Thus, their execution costs depend on the order of point insertion. This work evaluates three point-insertion sequences in incremental algorithms for building 3-D Delaunay tessellations. An incremental algorithm with point-insertion sequence provided by the cut-longest-edge kd–tree is evaluated against the BRIO–Hilbert order in conjunction with spatial middle and median policies employed in the 4.11 version of the Computational Geometry Algorithms Library. The results of computational costs (time and space) of these three algorithms are evaluated experimentally. Extensive results show that the incremental algorithm with a point-insertion sequence provided by the BRIO–Hilbert order with spatial middle policy employed in the latest version of the Computational Geometry Algorithms Library shows lower execution and storage costs than the two other algorithms evaluated.

1   Introduction

Delaunay tessellations have been employed in various scientific and engineering applications, including FEM analysis, computer graphics, medical applications, the modeling of deformable objects, and terrain modeling [8]. In present day, incremental algorithms are considered as state-of-the-art methods to build Delaunay tessellations in various point distributions [7].

The efficiency of an incremental algorithm for generating Delaunay tessellations is profoundly influenced by the point-insertion sequence, as both the numbers of orientation operations and conflicting polytopes depend on the insertion order (e.g. see [9] and references therein). In addition, paging policies and modern hierarchical memory architecture benefit programs that consider locality of reference. In particular, spatial locality is achieved when a sequence of recent memory references is grouped locally rather than randomly in the memory address space. Therefore, spatial locality should be considered highly significant in the design of algorithms. Thus, an efficient incremental algorithm for Delaunay tessellations uses properly the cache hierarchy to obtain high cache hit rates.

In an important paper in this field, Amenta *et al.* [1] evaluated the sequence in which the points are added to the mesh with the Biased Randomized Insertion Order (BRIO) technique. In this approach, an adequate spatial location of points is assumed to produce a large amount of cache hits.

Liu and Snoeyink [10] presented an incremental algorithm for building Delaunay tessellations in which points are added to the mesh in the sequence provided by the Hilbert curve. Liu and Snoeyink [10] and Schrijvers *et al.* [11] provide a complete description about the influence of selecting the sequential order and the proper quantity of randomness. Zhou and Jones [14], Buchin [5,6], and Boissonnat *et al.* [4] also evaluated methods that integrate randomness with deterministic orders. Thus, currently, the incremental algorithm for Delaunay tessellations implemented in the latest version of the Computational Geometry Algorithms Library (CGAL) [12] employs the Hilbert space-filling curve order combined with the BRIO scheme [1]. Specifically, the incremental algorithm that uses the BRIO–Hilbert strategy with *spatial middle* policy employed in CGAL [12] splits each partition exactly at its center [12] (https://doc.cgal.org/latest/ Spatial_sorting/index.html). Instead of subdividing each partition in a rigid way at its center, the incremental algorithm that uses the BRIO–Hilbert strategy with *spatial median* policy employed in CGAL [12] subdivides each partition considering the median point alternately in each coordinate. To be more specific, these incremental algorithms implemented in CGAL [12] organize the point set in random buckets of increasing sizes, and the Hilbert order is used only inside a bucket [12]. Thus, these geometric algorithms available in CGAL [12] combine randomness and spatial locality [1]. A number of works [1,4–6,14] have demonstrated that this approach yields sufficient randomness to incorporate the gains of both random and locality provided by a space-filling curve order when generating Delaunay tessellations.

Liu *et al.* [9] presented an incremental method for generating 3-D Delaunay tessellations in which points are added to the mesh conforming to a level-order traversal of the cut-longest-edge kd–tree. Liu *et al.* [9] exhibited extensive experiments in which this incremental algorithm with point-insertion sequence provided by the cut-longest-edge kd–tree order outpaced the preceding possible state-of-the-art method (an incremental algorithm with point-insertion sequence provided by the Hilbert curve [10]) in various 3-D point distributions. Recently [7], this incremental algorithm with point-insertion sequence provided by the cut-longest-edge kd–tree surpassed incremental algorithms with several point-insertion sequences. In this publication [7], the experiments focused on implementation characteristics of incremental algorithms employing deterministic orders (i.e. without the use of randomness) to build Delaunay tessellations in seven 3-D point distributions (i.e. the same 3-D point distributions used by Liu *et al.* [9]).

Liu *et al.* [9] compared their algorithm with the incremental algorithm implemented in the 4.0 version of CGAL (in 2013), which did not use the middle and median policies. In particular, the median policy employed in the incremental algorithm for Delaunay tessellations implemented in the latest version of CGAL [12] is similar to the idea of the kd–tree order introduced by Liu *et al.* [9] in their algorithm. A difference in these schemes is that Liu *et al.* [9] used a cut-longest-edge strategy instead of splitting the partition alternately in each coordinate, which is the original approach of the kd–tree order [3].

The purpose of this present paper is to conduct a comparison of three state-of-the-art incremental algorithms for generating 3-D Delaunay tessellations. Specifically, this work evaluates the algorithm with point-insertion sequence provided by the cut-longest-edge kd–tree against the BRIO–Hilbert order (i.e. with the use of randomness) using spatial middle and median policies in inexact predicates employed in the 4.11 version of CGAL, which was released in September of 2017 [12].

To evaluate the three incremental algorithms for 3-D Delaunay tessellations, this present computational experiment uses eight 3-D point distributions, with sets ranging from 1 to 40 million points. Specifically, the unit interval is used as domain in our experiments. In addition, four 3-D test models are used in the experiments.

The remainder of this paper is structured as follows. Section 2 presents and analyzes the results. Finally, Sect. 3 addresses the conclusions.

2   Results and Analysis

The three incremental algorithms evaluated here were implemented in the C++ programming language. The g++ 4.6.3-1 compiler was used. The experiments were performed on an Intel® Xeon® E5620 CPU 2.40 GHz (12 MB cache, 24GB of main memory 1067MHz) (Intel; Santa Clara, CA, USA) workstation. The Ubuntu 16.04.3 64-bits operating system was used in this machine, with kernel 4.4.0-98-generic.

Table 1 and Figs. 1, 2, 3 and 4 show the results of execution times in eight point distributions in the 3-D unit cube when using three point-insertion sequences in incremental algorithms for building Delaunay tessellations: random points, points on a cylinder, points around a disk, points around three planes, points along three axes, points around a paraboloid, points around a spiral, and points on a saddle. Three executions were carried out for each point set, ranging from 1 to 40 million points. Numbers in bold face in Table 1 are the best results.

Although the BRIO–Hilbert strategy together with the middle policy has obtained higher execution costs than the other two incremental algorithms evaluated here when applied to instances composed of 30 and 35 million points around a spiral, the BRIO–Hilbert order with middle policy obtained lower execution costs when applied to instances comprised of 40 million points in this 3-D point distribution. Thus, the trends remained consistent over the eight 3-D point distributions used. Although Table 1 shows that the execution times of the algorithm with point-insertion sequence provided by the BRIO–Hilbert order along

Table 1. Execution times (in seconds) of incremental algorithms with point-insertion sequence provided by three orders [CGAL BRIO–Hilbert order with spatial middle (SMi) and median (SMe) policies, and cut-longest-edge kd–tree (KDt)] in eight 3-D point distributions ($N * 10^6$).

N	Axes			Cylinder			Disk			Paraboloid		
	SMi	KDt	SMe	SMi	KDt	SMe	SMi	KDt	SMe	SMi	KDt	SMe
1	10	10	12	10	10	10	10	10	10	10	10	10
10	**97**	101	119	**97**	100	98	100	100	101	**97**	99	99
20	**196**	201	233	**195**	200	198	199	199	202	**194**	199	198
30	**292**	301	354	**291**	301	297	**299**	300	304	**291**	297	297
35	**339**	350	412	**341**	352	347	353	353	357	**343**	349	349
40	**387**	399	471	**390**	402	397	397	397	404	**392**	402	401
N	Planes			Random points			Saddle			Spiral		
	SMi	KDt	SMe	SMi	KDt	SMe	SMi	KDt	SMe	SMi	KDt	SMe
1	**9**	10	10	10	10	10	10	**9**	10	9	9	10
10	**96**	99	102	**97**	99	99	**97**	98	99	**96**	98	98
20	**194**	199	207	**195**	198	197	**193**	197	197	**194**	199	197
30	**290**	295	311	**293**	297	299	**290**	294	298	305	271	**269**
35	344	344	367	**341**	347	346	**338**	342	348	361	315	**314**
40	**388**	395	425	**388**	397	395	**386**	392	396	**390**	393	395

with the spatial middle policy employed in the latest version of CGAL [12] are lower than the two other algorithms evaluated in the eight 3-D point distributions used, Figs. 1, 2, 3 and 4 indicate that in most of the cases the differences between the algorithms are rather small.

Figures 5, 6, 7 and 8 show that the memory requirements of the three point-insertion sequences in incremental algorithms for building 3-D Delaunay tessellations analyzed in this computational experiment are very similar when applied to instances arising from eight point distributions in the 3-D unit cube. In particular, we used the sysconf function to record the memory consumption. This computational experiment shows that the execution times and memory usage of the algorithm with point-insertion sequence provided by the BRIO–Hilbert order along with the spatial middle policy used in the latest version of Computational Geometry Algorithms Library [12] are slightly lower than the two other algorithms evaluated in the eight 3-D point distributions used.

Exploratory investigations with both schemes employed in CGAL [12] using exact predicates showed that the spatial median policy dominated the spatial middle policy in seven 3-D point distributions. Specifically, the incremental algorithm with point-insertion sequence provided by the BRIO–Hilbert order with spatial middle policy achieved lower execution times than the spatial median policy only when applied to instances from points along three axes.

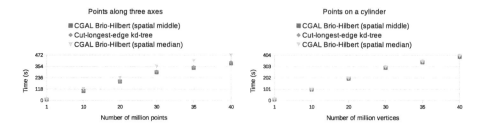

Fig. 1. Execution times (in seconds) of incremental algorithms with three point-insertion sequences evaluated in two point distributions (points along three axes and points on a cylinder) on the 3-D unit cube.

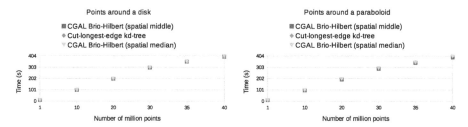

Fig. 2. Execution times (in seconds) of incremental algorithms with three point-insertion sequences evaluated in two point distributions (points around a disk and points around a paraboloid) on the 3-D unit cube.

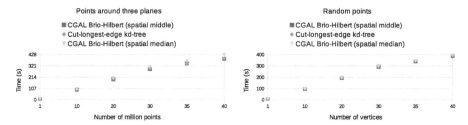

Fig. 3. Execution times (in seconds) of incremental algorithms with three point-insertion sequences evaluated in two point distributions (points around three planes and random points) on the 3-D unit cube.

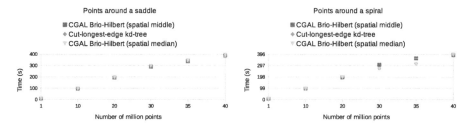

Fig. 4. Execution times (in seconds) of incremental algorithms with three point-insertion sequences evaluated in two point distributions (points around a saddle and points around a spiral) on the 3-D unit cube.

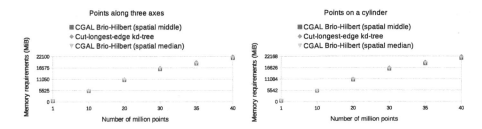

Fig. 5. Memory requirements (MiB) of incremental algorithms with three point-insertion sequences evaluated in two point distributions (points along three axes and points on a cylinder) on the 3-D unit cube.

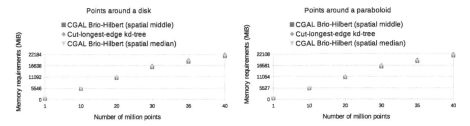

Fig. 6. Memory requirements (MiB) of incremental algorithms with three point-insertion sequences evaluated in two point distributions (points around a disk and points around a paraboloid) on the 3-D unit cube.

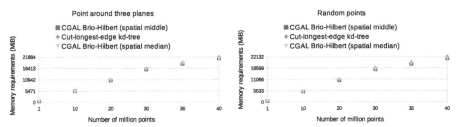

Fig. 7. Memory requirements (MiB) of incremental algorithms with three point-insertion sequences evaluated in two point distributions (points around three planes and random points) on the 3-D unit cube.

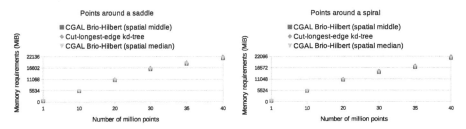

Fig. 8. Memory requirements (MiB) of incremental algorithms with three point-insertion sequences evaluated in two point distributions (points around a saddle and points around a spiral) on the 3-D unit cube.

Table 2. Execution times (in seconds) of incremental algorithms with point-insertion sequence provided by three orders [CGAL BRIO–Hilbert order with spatial middle (SMi) and median (SMe) policies, and cut-longest-edge kd–tree (KDt)] applied to four 3-D test models (Vellum manuscript, Asian Dragon, Thai Statue [13], and Napoleon [2]).

3-D test model	No. of points	KDt	SMi	SMe
Vellum manuscript	2155617	19.1	19.8	20.4
Napoleon	3396797	19.9	23.4	24.0
Asian Dragon	3609600	32.8	34.6	34.3
Thai Statue	4999996	38.2	37.5	39.5

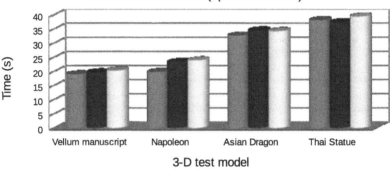

Fig. 9. Execution times (in seconds) of incremental algorithms with three point-insertion sequences evaluated for four 3-D test models (see Fig. 10).

Four 3-D test models available on two different repositories [2,13] were used in this computational experiment. Table 2 and Fig. 9 show that the execution times of the incremental algorithm with point-insertion sequence provided by the cut-longest-edge kd–tree order were lower than the two other incremental algorithms evaluated in this computational experiment when applied to three (Vellum manuscript, Asian Dragon [13], and Napoleon [2]) 3-D test models used here. On the other hand, the incremental algorithm with point-insertion sequence provided by the BRIO–Hilbert order alongside spatial middle policy obtained lower execution times than the two other incremental algorithms evaluated in our experiments when applied to the Thai Statue 3-D test model [13] (see Fig. 10). In addition, Fig. 11 shows that the memory requirements of the incremental algorithm with point-insertion sequence provided by the cut-longest-edge kd–tree were slightly larger than the two other incremental algorithms evaluated here when applied to these four standard 3-D test models.

Fig. 10. Four 3-D test models: Vellum manuscript, Asian Dragon, Thai Statue [13], and Napoleon [2]).

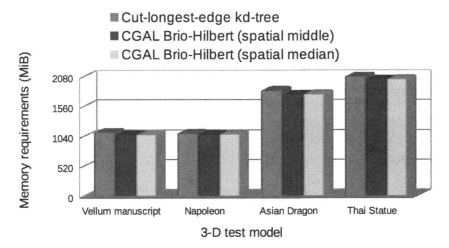

Fig. 11. Memory requirements (MiB) of incremental algorithms with three point-insertion sequences evaluated for four 3-D test models (see Fig. 10).

3   Conclusions

This work evaluated three point-insertion sequences in incremental algorithms for 3-D Delaunay tessellations. Experiments were performed in instances ranging from 1 to 40 million points.

The median policy implemented in the latest version of CGAL [12] is similar to the sequence provided by the kd–tree order. Despite this fact, the incremental algorithm with point-insertion sequence provided by the cut-longest-edge kd–tree order obtained, in a larger number of runs, lower execution costs than the BRIO–Hilbert order along with the median policy implemented in this version of CGAL [12]. Moreover, the incremental algorithm with point-insertion sequence provided by the cut-longest-edge kd–tree obtained overall lower execution costs than the two other incremental algorithms included in our experiments when applied to small 3-D test models (see Table 2). In spite of this and also despite the fact that the CGAL default constructor applies the median policy, the incremental algorithm with point-insertion sequence provided by the BRIO–Hilbert order combined with spatial middle policy employed in the latest version of CGAL [12] obtained slightly lower execution times and slightly smaller memory requirements than the two other algorithms evaluated in the eight 3-D point distributions and in the largest 3-D test model used. These results are consistent with the findings presented in the literature. Therefore, the incremental algorithm with point-insertion sequence provided by the BRIO–Hilbert order combined with spatial middle policy in inexact predicates employed in the latest version of CGAL [12] can be considered as the current state-of-the-art method for the building of Delaunay tessellations in the eight 3-D point distributions that were included in our experiments.

We plan to evaluate an incremental algorithm with point-insertion sequence provided by the cut-longest-edge kd–tree in tandem with the BRIO scheme against the other strategies analyzed in this appraisal. In addition, we intend to implement parallel versions of these methods.

Acknowledgements. We are grateful to Prof. Dr. Jianfei Liu, from the Department of Mechanics and Engineering Science, College of Engineering, Peking University, for sharing his program code and for his helpful comments.

References

1. Amenta, N., Choi, S., Rote, G.: Incremental constructions con BRIO. In: Proceedings of the Nineteenth Annual Symposium on Computational Geometry, SCG 2003, pp. 211–219. ACM, San Diego, June 2003
2. Artec3D. Artec3D (2018). https://www.artec3d.com/3d-models
3. Bentley, J.L.: Multidimensional binary search trees used for associative searching. Commun. ACM **18**(9), 509–517 (1975)
4. Boissonnat, J.D., Devillers, O., Samuel, H.: Incremental construction of the Delaunay graph in medium dimension. In: Proceedings of the Twenty-Fifth Annual Symposium on Computational Geometry, SCG 2009, Aarhus, Denmark, pp. 208–216. ACM, June 2009
5. Buchin, K.: Constructing Delaunay triangulations along space-filling curves. In: Proceedings of the 2nd International Symposium Voronoi Diagrams (ISVD) in Science and Engineering, Seoul, Korea, pp. 184–195 (2005)
6. Buchin, K.: Organizing point sets: Space-filling curves, Delaunay tessellations of random point sets, and flow complexes. Ph.D. thesis, Free University, Berlin (2007)
7. Gonzaga de Oliveira, S.L., Nogueira, J.R.: An evaluation of point-insertion sequences for incremental Delaunay tessellations. Comput. Appl. Math. **37**(1), 641–674 (2018)
8. Gonzaga de Oliveira, S.L., Nogueira, J.R., Tavares, J.M.R.S.: A systematic review of algorithms with linear-time behaviour to generate Delaunay and Voronoi tessellations. CMES - Comput. Model. Eng. Sci. **100**(1), 31–57 (2014)
9. Liu, J.-F., Yan, J.-H., Lo, S.H.: A new insertion sequence for incremental Delaunay triangulation. Acta Mechanica Sinica **29**(1), 99–109 (2013)
10. Liu, Y., Snoeyink, J.: A comparison of five implementations of 3D Delaunay tessellation. In: Goodman, J.E., Pach, J., Welzl, E. (eds.) Combinatorial and Computational Geometry, vol. 52, pp. 439–458. MSRI Publications, Cambridge (2005)

11. Schrijvers, O., van Bommel, F., Buchin, K.: Delaunay triangulations on the word RAM: towards a practical worst-case optimal algorithm. In: Proceedings of the 10th International Symposium on Voronoi Diagrams in Science and Engineering (ISVD), Saint Petersburg, Russia, pp. 7–15 (2013)
12. The CGAL Project. CGAL User and Reference Manual. CGAL Editorial Board, 4.11 edition (2017). http://doc.cgal.org/4.11/Manual/packages.html
13. The Stanford Models. The Stanford 3D Scanning Repository (2014). http://graphics.stanford.edu/data/3Dscanrep
14. Zhou, S., Jones, C.B.: HCPO: an efficient insertion order for incremental Delaunay triangulation. Inf. Process. Lett. **93**, 37–42 (2005)

Learning Knowledge Graph Embeddings via Generalized Hyperplanes

Qiannan Zhu[1,2], Xiaofei Zhou[1,2(✉)], JianLong Tan[1,2], Ping Liu[1,2], and Li Guo[1,2]

[1] Institute of Information Engineering, Chinese Academy of Sciences, Beijing, China
{zhuqiannan,zhouxiaofei}@iie.ac.cn
[2] School of Cyber Security, University of Chinese Academy of Sciences, Beijing, China

Abstract. For knowledge graph completion, translation-based methods such as Trans(E and H) are promising, which embed knowledge graphs into continuous vector spaces and construct translation operation between head and tail entities. However, TransE and TransH still have limitations in preserving mapping properties of complex relation facts for knowledge graphs. In this paper, we propose a novel translation-based method called translation on generalized hyperplanes (TransGH), which extends TransH by defining a generalized hyperplane for entities projection. TransGH projects head and tail embeddings from a triplet into a generalized relation-specific hyperplane determined by a set of basis vectors, and then fulfills translation operation on the hyperplane. Compared with TransH, TransGH can capture more fertile interactions between entities and relations, and simultaneously has strong expression in mapping properties for knowledge graphs. Experimental results on two tasks, link prediction and triplet classification, show that TransGH can significantly outperform the state-of-the-art embedding methods.

Keywords: Knowledge representation · Knowledge embedding
Knowledge graph completion

1 Introduction

Knowledge graphs like Freebase [1], WordNet [14] and Google Knowledge Graph play extremely practical roles in numerous AI applications, such as Question Answering System [6] and Information Extraction [8]. A typical knowledge graph (KG) is a multi-relational directed graph, in which nodes represent entities and edges represent different types of relations. That is, a basic triplet fact (h, r, t) in KG represents that the relationship r links the head entity h and tail entity t. e.g., (Barack_Obama, Place_of_Birth, Hawai). Although there are huge amounts of structured data, a knowledge graph is factually far from completeness. Knowledge graph completion aims to predict new relational facts under supervision of the existing knowledge graph.

In the past decade, massive traditional approaches based on logic and symbol [15,16] have been done for knowledge graph completion, but they are intractable and not enough convergence for large scale knowledge graphs. Recently an emerging approach called knowledge graph embedding, which embeds all objects (entities and relations) of a KG into a low-dimensional space, have highly attracted attention. Following this approach, many models described in Section "Related Work" have been presented. Among these models, Trans(E, H, R and D) [4,10,11,18] are fundamental and efficient while achieving state-of-the-art predictive performance. TransE [4] simply and directly build entity and relation embeddings by regarding a relation as translation from head entity to tail entity, but there are flaws in dealing with complex relations, such as reflexive, one-to-many, many-to-one, and many-to-many relations. To address these issues of TransE, TransH [18] considers some mapping properties of complex relations in embedding, and projects entity embeddings into relation-specific hyperplanes. But for TransH, there is only one normal vector used for modeling relation-specific hyperplane, which leads that entities and relations are still in the same space and a limit representation for mapping properties. TransR [11] regards to map entity embeddings into r-relation space with a transfer matrix, and TransD [10] uses the product of two projection vectors of an entity-relation pair to construct the transfer matrix. Such transfer matrix can build entity and relation embeddings in separate spaces and has more general representation for mapping properties, however, it will cost much more computations and memories on the mappings.

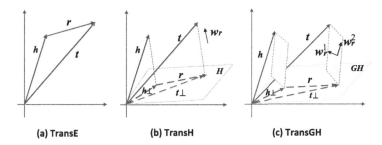

Fig. 1. Simple visualization of TransE, TransH and TransGH.

In this paper, we propose an expressive model named translation on generalized hyperplanes (TransGH) to promote TransH. Instead of the only one normal vector, TransGH uses a set of basis vectors to determine a generalized hyperplane. Figure 1 simply shows the differences of TransE, TransH and TransGH.

- TransE builds the translation from head embedding to tail embedding as $\mathbf{h} + \mathbf{r} \approx \mathbf{t}$ when the triplet (h, r, t) holds.
- TransH projects entity embeddings into relation-specific hyperplanes characterized by one normal vector $\mathbf{w}_r$, and builds translation between the projected entities on the hyperplane as $\mathbf{h}_\perp + \mathbf{r} \approx \mathbf{t}_\perp$, where $\mathbf{h}_\perp = \mathbf{h} - \mathbf{w}_r^T \mathbf{h} \mathbf{w}_r$ and $\mathbf{t}_\perp = \mathbf{t} - \mathbf{w}_r^T \mathbf{t} \mathbf{w}_r$.

– Different from TransH, TransGH uses a set of basis vectors $\{\mathbf{w}_r^1, \mathbf{w}_r^2, ..., \mathbf{w}_r^v\}$, $(v \ll |\mathbf{h}|)$ to determine a generalized relation-specific hyperplane, and the mappings of the entity embeddings on the hyperplane are $\mathbf{h}_\perp = \mathbf{h} - \sum_i {\mathbf{w}_r^i}^T \mathbf{h} \mathbf{w}_r^i$ and $\mathbf{t}_\perp = \mathbf{t} - \sum_i {\mathbf{w}_r^i}^T \mathbf{h} \mathbf{w}_r^i (i \in [1, v])$.

The basic idea of TransGH illustrated in Fig. 1(c) is that for a given triplet (h, r, t), firstly the entity embeddings $\mathbf{h}$ and $\mathbf{t}$ are projected on the generalized hyperplane as $\mathbf{h}_\perp$ and $\mathbf{t}_\perp$ with a set of basis vectors respectively, where the embedding $\mathbf{h}_\perp$ is expected to be close to the embedding $\mathbf{t}_\perp$ by adding the relation embedding $\mathbf{r}$.

Our contributions in this paper are: (1) We propose a novel model TransGH, which models each relation as a vector on the generalized hyperplane determined by a set of basis vectors. (2) TransGH has the similar parameters to TransH as it only extends one normal vector to a set of basis vectors, indicating that TranGH is applicable to large scale KGs. (3) In the two tasks of link prediction and triplet classification, TransGH has significant improvements comparing with previous Trans(E, H, R and D).

2   Related Work

2.1   Translation-Based Models

Translation-based models usually embed entities and relations into a low-dimensional vector space, and enforce vector embeddings compatible under a score function $f(h, r, t)$. Different models have the different definitions of score functions. Below we briefly summarize some baseline translation-based models and give the corresponding score functions.

TransE [4] embeds entities and relations into the same space R^m, and interprets each relation as a translation vector from the head entity embedding to tail entity embedding. Hence the score function is defined as $f(h, r, t) = \parallel \mathbf{h} + \mathbf{r} - \mathbf{t} \parallel_2^2$ for a triplet (h, r, t). TransE is effective for one-to-one relations but has flaws in dealing with one-to-many, many-to-one and many-to-many relations.

To overcome the issues of TransE, TransH [18] projects entity embeddings into relation-specific hyperplanes to enable an entity has distinct representations when involved in different relations. It models each relation r as a vector $\mathbf{r}$ on the hyperplane with a normal vector $\mathbf{w}_r$, therefore the scoring function is defined as $f(h, r, t) = \parallel \mathbf{h}_\perp + \mathbf{r} - \mathbf{t}_\perp \parallel_2^2$. With $\parallel \mathbf{w}_r \parallel_2 = 1$, it is easily to get $\mathbf{h}_\perp = \mathbf{h} - \mathbf{w}_r^T \mathbf{h} \mathbf{w}_r$, $\mathbf{t}_\perp = \mathbf{t} - \mathbf{w}_r^T \mathbf{t} \mathbf{w}_r$, and $\mathbf{h}, \mathbf{t}, \mathbf{r}, \mathbf{w}_r \in R^m$.

Both TransE and TransH embed entities and relations into the same vector space without considering that entities and relations are different types of objects. TransR/CtransR [11] regards entities and relations as completely different objects via embedding entities and relations into entity space R^m and relation spaces R^n, respectively. It maps entity embeddings from entity space to r-relation space with a mapping matrix $\mathbf{M}_r$. Then the score function is defined as $f(h, r, t) = \parallel \mathbf{h}_r + \mathbf{r} - \mathbf{t}_r \parallel_2^2$, where $\mathbf{h}_r = \mathbf{h}\mathbf{M}_r$, $\mathbf{t}_r = \mathbf{t}\mathbf{M}_r$ and $\mathbf{h}, \mathbf{t} \in R^m, \mathbf{r} \in R^n, \mathbf{M}_r \in R^{m \times n}$. CtransR is an extension of TransR, which divides all the entity pair(h, t) in the training data into multiple groups(clusters) and learns independent relation vector for each group.

TransD [10] is an improvement of TransR/CtransR, which considers the multiple types of entities and relations simultaneously. It replaces the transfer matrix by the product of two projection vectors of an entity-relation pair. Therefore score function is denoted as $f(h, r, t) = \| \mathbf{M}_{rh}\mathbf{h} + \mathbf{r} - \mathbf{M}_{rt}\mathbf{t} \|_2^2$, where $\mathbf{M}_{rh} = \mathbf{r}_p\mathbf{h}_p{}^T + \mathbf{I}^{n \times m}$, $\mathbf{M}_{rt} = \mathbf{r}_p\mathbf{t}_p{}^T + \mathbf{I}^{n \times m}$, and $\mathbf{h}, \mathbf{h}_p, \mathbf{t}, \mathbf{t}_p \in R^m, \mathbf{r}, \mathbf{r}_p \in R^n$.

Recently TransE-RS and TransH-RS [19] combine a limit-based scoring loss for learning knowledge embeddings, which have significant improvements compared to state-of-the-art baselines.

2.2 Other Models

Unstructured Molel (UM) [3] is a simplified version of TransE with considering the knowledge graph as none-relation and setting all relation vectors as $\mathbf{r} = 0$, which leads to the score function $f_r(h, r, t) = \| \mathbf{h} - \mathbf{t} \|$. Obviously, this model can not deal with the different relations.

Structured Embedding (SE) [5] interprets entities as vectors and each relation as two independent matrices $\mathbf{M}_r^h$ and $\mathbf{M}_r^t$ for projecting the head entity embedding and tail entity embedding. Then score function is $f_r(h, r, t) = -\|\mathbf{M}_r^h\mathbf{h} - \mathbf{M}_r^t\mathbf{t}\|$. SE can not capture the information between entities and relations since it uses the two separate matrices.

Latent Factor Model (LFM) [9,17] encodes entities as vectors and sets each relation as a matrix. Each r-specific matrix is asymmetric and directly operates between two entity embeddings. The score function is $f(h, r, t) = \mathbf{h}^T\mathbf{M}_r\mathbf{t}$.

Semantic Matching Energy (SME) [2,3] introduces two definitions of semantic matching energy functions for optimization, a linear form $f(h, r, t) = (\mathbf{M}_1\mathbf{h} + \mathbf{M}_2\mathbf{r} + \mathbf{b}_1)^T(\mathbf{M}_3\mathbf{t} + \mathbf{M}_4\mathbf{r} + \mathbf{b}_2)$, and a bilinear form $f(h, r, t) = (\mathbf{M}_1\mathbf{h} \otimes \mathbf{M}_2\mathbf{r} + \mathbf{b}_1)^T(\mathbf{M}_3\mathbf{t} \otimes \mathbf{M}_4\mathbf{r} + \mathbf{b}_2)$, where $\mathbf{M}_1, \mathbf{M}_2, \mathbf{M}_3, \mathbf{M}_4$ are weight matrices, $\mathbf{b}_1$ and $\mathbf{b}_2$ are bias vectors and $\otimes$ is Hadamard product.

Single Layer Model (SLM) [16] is designed as a plain baseline of NTN. It introduces nonlinear transformations by neural networks. The score function is $f(h, r, t) = \mathbf{u}_r{}^T g(\mathbf{M}_{rh}\mathbf{h} + \mathbf{M}_{rt}\mathbf{t} + \mathbf{b}_r)$, where $\mathbf{M}_{rh}$ and $\mathbf{M}_{rt}$ are weight matrices, and $g(\cdot)$ is the function $\tanh(\cdot)$.

The Neural Tensor Network (NTN) [16] uses a bilinear tensor layer related two entity vectors to replace a standard linear neural network layer. It computes a score to measure the plausibility of a triplet (h, r, t) by the function $f(h, r, t) = \mathbf{u}_r{}^T g(\mathbf{h}^T\mathbf{M}_r\mathbf{t} + \mathbf{V}_r[\mathbf{h}; \mathbf{t}] + \mathbf{b}_r)$ where $g(\cdot) = \tanh(\cdot)$; $[\mathbf{h}; \mathbf{t}]$ denotes the vertical stacking of vectors $\mathbf{h}$ and $\mathbf{t}$, $\mathbf{V}_r$ is weight matrix and $\mathbf{M}_r$ is a 3-way tensor.

3 Our Model

TransGH considers the translation operation on a generalized hyperplane determined by a set of basis vectors, to achieve the generalized ability for preserving mapping properties of complex relation facts, and also avoid much more computations on entity mappings.

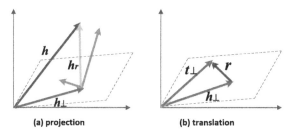

(a) projection   **(b) translation**

Fig. 2. The two phases of TransGH. The red bold arrows represent $\mathbf{w}_r^{i^T}\mathbf{hw}_r^i$. (Color figure online)

3.1   Generalized Hyperplane

We extend the hyperplane of TransH to the generalized hperplane by a set of basis vectors $\{\mathbf{w}_r^1, \mathbf{w}_r^2, ..., \mathbf{w}_r^v\}$, $(\mathbf{w}_r^i \in R^m, i \in [1, v])$, the basis vectors are orthogonal to each other. With the same setting of TransH, we also restrict $\|\mathbf{w}_r^i\|_2 = 1$ for each set of r-relation vectors. For an entity embedding $\mathbf{e}$, a transfer vector $\mathbf{e}_r$ on the set of basis vectors can be written as:

$$\mathbf{e}_r = \mathbf{w}_r^{1^T}\mathbf{ew}_r^1 + ... + \mathbf{w}_r^{v^T}\mathbf{ew}_r^v = \sum_i \mathbf{w}_r^{i^T}\mathbf{ew}_r^i$$

where v is the number of vectors and m is the dimension of entity (relation) vector space. Based on the transfer vector $\mathbf{e}_r$, we can obtain the projection $\mathbf{e}_\perp$ of entity embedding $\mathbf{e}$ on the generalized hyperplane as $\mathbf{e}_\perp = \mathbf{e} - \mathbf{e}_r$. Thus the generalized hyperplane determined by the set of basis vectors $\{\mathbf{w}_r^1, \mathbf{w}_r^2, ..., \mathbf{w}_r^v\}$, can be described as

$$\{\mathbf{e}_\perp | \mathbf{e}_\perp = \mathbf{e} - \sum_i \mathbf{w}_r^{i^T}\mathbf{ew}_r^i\}$$

where $\mathbf{w}_r^i \in R^m$ and $\|\mathbf{w}_r^i\|_2 = 1$. The proposed hyperplane is a generalisation of that in TransH.

3.2   TransGH

As shown in Fig. 2, the basic idea of TransGH can be summed up in two steps: (1) *projection*: projecting entity embeddings on the generalized hyperplane. (2) *translation*: connecting projected entities with the relation-specific translation vector. Specifically, for a triplet (h, r, t):

- In the *projection* phase, with the restriction $\|\mathbf{w}_r^i\|_2 = 1$, it is easily to get the projections of head and tail embedding on the generalized hyperplane, that is

$$\mathbf{h}_\perp = \mathbf{h} - \sum_i \mathbf{w}_r^{i^T}\mathbf{hw}_r^i, \quad \mathbf{t}_\perp = \mathbf{t} - \sum_i \mathbf{w}_r^{i^T}\mathbf{tw}_r^i$$

- In the *translation* phase, the relation r is interpreted as the translation vector $\mathbf{r}$ from the head projections $\mathbf{h}_\perp$ to the tail projection $\mathbf{t}_\perp$. Therefore, the score function is denoted as:

$$f(h, r, t) = \|(\mathbf{h} - \sum_i \mathbf{w}_r^{i\,T} \mathbf{h} \mathbf{w}_r^i) + \mathbf{r} - (\mathbf{t} - \sum_i \mathbf{w}_r^{i\,T} \mathbf{t} \mathbf{w}_r^i)\|_2^2$$

The score function is to measure the compatible of a positive triplet, and also is expected to be low for a positive triplet, otherwise high for a negative triplet.

3.3 Training Method and Implementation Details

We use the following margin-based loss function to encourage discrimination between positive triplets and negative triplets:

$$L = \sum_{(h,r,t) \in P} \sum_{(h',r,t') \in N} [0, f(h, r, t) + \gamma - f(h', r, t')]_+$$

Here, $[x]_+ = max(0, x)$ means to get the maximum number between 0 and x, P is the set of positive triplets; N is the set of negative triplets, that is $N = \{(h', r, t) \mid (h' \in E \wedge h' \neq h) \cup (h, r, t') \mid (t' \in E \wedge t' \neq t)\}$. E is the entities set. $\gamma > 0$ is the margin hyper-parameter with expectation of dividing the positive triplets and negative triplets. Then we minimize the loss function with considering the following constraints:

$$\forall e \in E, \|\mathbf{e}\|_2 \leq 1, \forall r \in R, \|\mathbf{r}\|_2 \leq 1 \qquad (1)$$

$$\forall r \in R, i \in [1, v], \|\mathbf{w}_r^i\|_2 = 1 \qquad (2)$$

$$\forall r \in R, i \in [1, v], \frac{|\sum_i \mathbf{w}_r^{i\,T} \mathbf{r}|}{\|\mathbf{r}\|_2} \leq \epsilon \qquad (3)$$

$$\forall r \in R, i, j \in [1, v](i \neq j), \frac{|\sum_{(i,j)} \mathbf{w}_r^{i\,T} \mathbf{w}_r^j|}{\|\mathbf{w}_r^j\|_2} \leq \epsilon \qquad (4)$$

where ϵ is a small scalar, R is the relations set, constraint (3) assures the translation vector $\mathbf{r}$ is on the generalized hyperplane and constraint (4) guarantees each two basis vectors are orthogonal. Afterwards we directly optimize the following loss function with soft constraints:

$$L = \sum_{(h,r,t) \in P} \sum_{(h',r,t') \in N} [0, f(h, r, t) + \gamma - f(h', r, t')]_+ \\ + C(A_1 + A_2) \qquad (5)$$

where we set

$$A_1 = \sum_{e \in E} [\|\mathbf{e}\|_2^2 - 1]_+ + \sum_{r \in R} [\|\mathbf{r}\|_2^2 - 1]_+$$

$$A_2 = \sum_{r \in R} \{[(\frac{\sum_i \mathbf{w}_r^{i\,T} \mathbf{r}}{\|\mathbf{r}\|_2})^2 - \epsilon^2]_+ + [(\frac{\sum_{(i,j)} \mathbf{w}_r^{i\,T} \mathbf{w}_r^j}{\|\mathbf{w}_r^j\|_2})^2 - \epsilon^2]_+\} \qquad (6)$$

and C is a hyper-parameter used to measure the importance of soft constrains.

Table 1. Complexity (the number of parameters and the number of multiplication operations).

Model	# Parameters	# Operations (time complexity)
UM [3]	$O(N_e m)$	$O(N_t)$
SE [5]	$O(N_e m + 2N_r n^2)(m = n)$	$O(2m^2 N_t)$
LFM [9]	$O(N_e m + N_r n^2)(m = n)$	$O((m^2 + m)N_t)$
SME (BILIN) [2]	$O(N_e m + N_r n + 4mks + 4k)(m = n)$	$O(4mksN_t)$
SLM [16]	$O(N_e m + N_r(2k + 2nk))(m = n)$	$O((2mk + k)N_t)$
NTN [16]	$O(N_e m + N_r(n^2 s + 2ns + 2s))(m = n)$	$O(((m^2 + m)s + 2mk + k)N_t)$
TransE [4]	$O(N_e m + N_r n)(m = n)$	$O(N_t)$
TransH [18]	$O(N_e m + 2N_r n)(m = n)$	$O(2mN_t)$
TransR [11]	$O(N_e m + N_r(m + 1)n)$	$O(2mnN_t)$
TransD [10]	$O(2N_e m + 2N_r n)$	$O(2nN_t)$
TransE-RS [19]	$O(N_e m + N_r n)(m = n)$	$O(N_t)$
TransH-RS [19]	$O(N_e m + 2N_r n)(m = n)$	$O(2mN_t)$
TransGH (this paper)	$O(N_e m + N_r(1 + v)n)(m = n), v \ll m$	$O(2vmN_t)$

The loss function favors the lower scores for positive triplets than that for negative triplets. We adopt stochastic gradient descent (SGD) [7] to minimize the above loss function. Notice that the constrain (2) is missed in Eq. 5. To satisfy it, we set each vector $\mathbf{w}_r^i$ to unit l_2-ball before traversing each mini-batch. Moreover, negative triplets are generated via replacing either the head or tail of original triplets exited in KGs by a random entity, but not both at the same time. For reducing the false negative triplets, here we follow [18] and set different probabilities for the replacement. In experiment, the traditional sampling method is denoted as "unif" and the new method [18] as "bern".

Generally, all embeddings of entities $\{\mathbf{e}_i\}_{i=1}^{|E|}$, relations $\{\mathbf{r}_k\}_{k=1}^{|R|}$ and relation-specific vectors $\{\mathbf{w}_r^1, \mathbf{w}_r^2, ..., \mathbf{w}_r^v\}_{r=1}^{|R|}$ are learned by TransGH. Hence parameters of this model is $N_e m + N_r(1 + v)n$ and the time complexity is $2vmN_t$, which is similar to TransH as we usually set $v \ll m$, e.g., $v = 2, 3, 4$. We compare the parameters and time complexities with several baselines in Table 1. We denote N_e as the number of entities, N_r as the number of relations and N_t as the number of triplets in a knowledge graph respectively. m and n separately represent the dimension of entity space and relation space. d denotes the average number of clusters of a relation. k is the number of hidden nodes of a neural network, s is the number of slice of a tensor. v is the number of vectors for a relation.

4   Experiments and Analysis

We study and evaluate our model on two tasks: link prediction [4,18] and triplet classification [16]. In our experiments, two datasets including FreeBase [1] and WordNet [14] are used. Then we show the experimental results and some analysis of them.

4.1 Datasets

WordNet is designed to build an usable dictionary and support automatic text analysis. In WordNet, each entity represents a *synset* containing several words, which are corresponding to a distinct word sense. Relationships indicate the lexical relations between synsets, such as *hypernym, hyponym, meronym* and *holonym*. An example of triplets is (__*warship_NN_1*, _*hyponym*, __*torpedo_boat_NN_1*). The two data sets from WordNet, WN18 and WN11, are used in our experiments. WN18 contains 18 relations and WN11 contains 11 relations. The number of entities involved in the two data sets is close.

FreeBase is a large and rising knowledge graph of general facts. An example of FreeBase is (*nietzchka_keene, place_of_death, madison*), it builds a relation *place_of_death* between a name entity *nietzchka_keene* and a place entity *madison*. We use two data sets with FreeBase in this paper, FB15k and FB13. FB15k consists of 592,213 triplets with 14,951 entities and 1,345 relations. FB13 is a more dense subgraph including 75,043 entities and 13 relations. The statistics of these data sets are listed in Table 2.

Table 2. Data sets used in the experiments.

DataSet	#Relation	#Entity	#Train	#Valid	#Test
FB15k	1,345	14,951	483,142	50,000	59,071
WN18	18	40,943	141,442	5,000	5,000
FB13	13	75,043	316,232	5,908	23,733
WN11	11	38,696	112,581	2,609	10,544

4.2 Link Prediction

Link prediction is to predict the missing h or t for a positive triplet (h, r, t), used in [4,10,11,18]. In this task, it focuses more on ranking a set of candidate entities from the knowledge graph rather than obtaining the best one for each position of missing entity. The data sets used in this task are WN18 and FB15k, which are same settings to [4,10,11,18].

Evaluation Rules. We adopt the same protocols used in [4,10,11,18] to evaluate this task. Specifically, in testing phase, for each test triplet (h, r, t), we replace the head(tail) entity by every entity e from the set of entities for a KG and calculate the scores of these corrupted triplets by using the score function $f(h, r, t)$, then we get the rank of the original triplet after ranking these scores in ascending order. Following [4,10,11,18], two metrics are used to evaluation: the average rank(Mean Rank) and the proportion of ranks not larger than 10 (Hit@10). This is called "raw" setting. Notice that the corrupted triplets may exit in the KG, they can be regarded as correct triplets, hence it is not wrong to rank them before the original triplet. To eliminate this case, we filter out corrupted triplets existing in a KG before ranking. This is called "filt" setting. In both settings, lower Mean and higher Hit@10 are excepted.

Table 3. Link prediction results.

Dataset	WN18				FB15k			
Metric	Mean		Hits@10		Mean		Hits@10	
	Raw	Filt	Raw	Filt	Raw	Filt	Raw	Filt
RESCAL [15]	1,180	1,163	37.2	52.8	828	683	28.4	44.1
UM [3]	315	304	35.3	38.2	1074	979	4.5	6.3
SE [5]	1011	985	68.5	80.5	273	162	28.8	39.8
SME(LIN) [3]	545	533	65.1	74.1	274	154	30.7	40.8
SME(BILIN) [2]	526	509	54.7	61.3	284	158	31.3	41.3
BILINEAR [9]	469	456	71.4	81.6	283	164	26.0	33.1
TransE [4]	263	251	75.4	89.2	243	125	34.9	47.1
TransH(unif) [18]	318	303	75.4	86.7	211	84	42.5	58.5
TransH(bern) [18]	400.8	388	73.0	82.3	212	87	45.7	64.4
TransR(unif) [11]	232	219	78.3	91.7	226	78	43.8	65.5
TransR(bern) [11]	238	225	79.8	92.0	198	77	48.2	68.7
CTransR(unif) [11]	243	230	78.9	92.3	233	82	44	66.3
CTransR(bern) [11]	231	218	79.4	92.3	199	75	48.4	70.2
TransD(unif) [10]	242	229	79.2	92.5	211	67	49.4	74.2
TransD(bern) [10]	224	212	79.6	92.2	194	91	53.4	77.3
TransE-RS(unif) [19]	362	348	80.3	93.7	**161**	**62**	53.1	72.3
TransE-RS (bern) [19]	385	371	80.4	93.7	**161**	**63**	53.2	72.1
TransH-RS(unif) [19]	401	389	81.2	94.7	163	64	53.4	72.6
TransH-RS(bern) [19]	371	357	80.3	94.5	178	77	53.6	75.0
TransGH(unif)	**191**	**179**	**81.4**	**94.8**	186	66	**54.0**	**79.8**
TransGH(bern)	**210**	**197**	**81.6**	**95.3**	186	64	**54.1**	**80.1**

Implementation. In training phase, we select the learning rate η for SGD from $\{0.001, 0.01, 0.1\}$, the γ from $\{1, 2, 3, 4, 5, 6, 7, 8\}$, the entity(relation) embedding dimension m from $\{50, 100, 150\}$, the number of vectors v from $\{0.25, 0.5, 1, 2, 3, 4, 5, 6, 7, 8, 9, 10\}$, the batch size b from $\{480, 960, 1200, 4800\}$, the hyperparameter C from $\{0.005, 0.0625, 0.25, 0.5\}$. The best parameters are determined by validation set. Under *unif* setting, the best optimal configures are $\eta = 0.01$, $\gamma = 7$, $m = 100$, $v = 2$, $b = 1200$, $C = 0.0625$ on WN18; $\eta = 0.01$, $\gamma = 2$, $m = 100$, $v = 6$, $b = 1200$, $C = 0.0625$ on FB15k. Under *bern* setting, the best optimal configures are $\eta = 0.01$, $\gamma = 7$, $m = 100$, $v = 2$, $b = 1200$, $C = 0.005$ on WN18; $\eta = 0.01$, $\gamma = 1$, $m = 100$, $v = 4$, $b = 480$, $C = 0.0625$ on FB15k. We traverse all the training triplets for 5000 rounds and take *L1* as dissimilarity on both datasets.

Table 4. Results on FB15k by relation category.

Dataset	Predicting left (Hit@10)				Predicting right (Hit@10)			
Relation category	1-to-1	1-to-n	n-to-1	n-to-n	1-to-1	1-to-n	n-to-1	n-to-n
UM [5]	34.5	2.5	6.1	6.6	34.3	4.2	1.9	6.6
SE [5]	35.6	62.6	17.2	37.5	34.9	14.6	68.3	41.3
SME(LIN) [3]	35.1	53.7	19.0	40.3	32.7	14.9	61.6	43.3
SME(BILIN) [2]	30.9	69.6	19.9	38.6	28.2	13.1	76.0	41.8
TransE [4]	43.7	65.7	18.2	47.2	43.7	19.7	66.7	50.0
TransH(unif) [18]	66.7	81.7	30.2	57.4	63.7	30.1	83.2	60.8
TransH(bern) [18]	66.8	87.6	28.7	64.5	65.5	39.8	83.3	67.2
TransR(unif) [11]	76.9	77.9	38.1	66.9	76.2	38.4	76.2	69.1
TransR(bern) [11]	78.8	89.2	34.1	69.2	79.2	37.4	90.4	72.1
CTransR(unif) [11]	78.6	77.8	36.4	68.0	77.4	37.8	78.0	70.3
CTransR(bern) [11]	81.5	89.0	34.7	71.2	80.8	38.6	90.1	73.8
TransD(unif) [10]	80.7	85.8	47.1	75.6	80.0	54.5	80.7	77.9
TransD(bern) [10]	86.1	95.5	39.8	78.5	85.4	50.6	94.4	81.2
TransE-RS(unif) [19]	87.2	**96.2**	35.9	71.8	**87.0**	45.0	**95.5**	75.4
TransE-RS(bern) [19]	87.4	**96.3**	35.3	71.7	86.5	44.2	95.4	75.2
TransH-RS(unif) [19]	87.6	95.9	35.6	72.5	86.3	44.9	**95.5**	75.8
TransH-RS(bern) [19]	85.6	95.5	37.4	75.5	85.7	47.4	94.9	78.7
TransGH(unif)	**86.4**	95.6	**47.6**	**80.6**	85.8	55.8	94.8	83.4
TransGH(bern)	**87.0**	95.8	**47.9**	**80.8**	86.8	55.7	94.8	**84.3**

Results. The results on both WN18 and FB15k are shown in Table 3. The results of previous studies are referred from their report, since the same datasets are used. Our model consistently and significantly outperforms previous models on both the metrics of WN18 and FB15k, where the results of our Mean(raw) is 191, Mean(filt) is 179, Hit@10(raw) is 94.8%, Hit@10(filt) is 95.0% on WN18, and that of Mean(raw) is 186, Mean(filt) is 64, Hit@10(raw) is 54.1% and Hit@10(filt) is 80.1% on FB15k. Moreover, our model has respectively remarkable improvements on metrics of Mean(raw), Mean(filt), Hit@10(raw) and Hit@10(filt) comparing with TransH, which are 172, 124, 6.2% and 8.3% on WN18, and 25, 23, 8.4% and 15.7% on FB15k higher than those of TransH. We believe the improved performance of our model is due to its use of the set of basis vectors.

Table 4 analyzes Hits@10 results on FB15k with respect to the relation categories. Following the same rules in [4] on FB15k, we separate the 1345 relations into four categories, including one-to-one, one-to-many, many-to-one and many-to-many relations. From Table 4 we can observe that TransGH significantly performs better results than all baselines on both *unif* and *bern* settings. Our method has highest accuracies on predicting head (one-to-one 87.0%, one-to-

Table 5. Hits@10(filt)*bern* of TransGH and TransH on some examples of one-to-many*, many-to-one†, many-to-many‡ and symmetric§ relations.

Relations	Hit@10(TransH/TranGH) on FB15k	
	Predict head	Predict tail
/football_position/players*	100/100	22.2/**88.9**
/production_company/films*	85.6/**96.8**	16.0/**52.4**
/director/film*	89.6/**96.2**	80.2/**94.3**
/disease/treatments†	66.6/66.6	100/100
/person/place_of_birth†	37.5/**77.9**	87.6/**92.0**
/film/production_companies†	21.0/**47.5**	87.8/**96.7**
/field_of_study/students_majoring‡	66.0/**92.2**	62.3/**70.5**
/award_winner/awards_won‡	87.5/**99.0**	86.6/**99.5**
/sports_position/players‡	100/100	86.2/**99.6**
/person/sibling_s§	63.2/**68.4**	36.8/**68.4**
/person/spouse_s§	35.2/**70.4**	42.6/**59.3**

many 95.8%, many-to-one 47.9% and many-to-many 80.8%) and predicting tail (one-to-one 86.8%, one-to-many 55.8%, many-to-one 94.8% and many-to-many 84.3%). Additionally, comparing with TransH, we also give the result on Hit@10 metric of some typical complex relations in Table 5. In this experiment, we directly copy the results reported in [18] shows TransGH has remarkable improvement on Hit@10 metric of some typical complex relations compared with TransH. It indicates TransGH can capture more fertile information between entities and relations, and achieve the better ability for modeling mapping properties of complex relation facts. As Tables 6 and 7 shown, TransGH rationality enables the same category objects (entities and relations) to have similar vector embeddings.

4.3   Triplet Classification

Triplet classification is to decide whether a given triplet (h, r, t) is correct or not. This is a binary classification task, which has been presented by [16]. In this task, three data sets WN11, FB13 and FB15k are used, and negative triplets are needed to the evaluation of binary classification. The first two sets appeared in [16] already have negative triplets, but the third one including negative triplets has not been published recently. For FB15k, we construct it by following the same principles used for FB13 in [16].

Evaluation Rules. There exists a simple decision rule for triplet classification: we first get a relation-specific threshold δ_r determined by maximizing the classification accuracy on the validation set. For a triplet (h, r, t), if the dissimilarity

Table 6. The top-3 similarity entities with regard to some examples on WN18. The similarity scores are computed with *cosine* function.

Dataset	WN18	
Entity and definitions	_mountain_sheep_NN_1	Any wild sheep inhabiting mountainous regions
Similar entities and definitions	_white_sheep_NN_1	Large white wild sheep of northwestern Canada and Alaska
	_rocky_mountain_sheep_NN_1	Wild sheep of mountainous regions of western North America having massive curled horns
	_wild_sheep_NN_1	Undomesticated sheep
Entity and definitions	_sharpen_VB_8	Make (one's senses) more acute
Similar entities and definitions	_screw_up_VB_1	Make more intense
	_raise_VB_13	Increase
	_intensify_VB_2	Make more intense, stronger, or more marked

Table 7. The top-3 similarity relations with regard to some examples on FB15k. The similarity scores are computed with *cosine* function.

Dataset	FB15k
Relation	/location/statistical_region/rent50_3./measurement_unit/dated_money_value/currency
Similar relations	/location/statistical_region/rent50_0./measurement_unit/dated_money_value/currency
	/location/statistical_region/rent50_1./measurement_unit/dated_money_value/currency
	/location/statistical_region/rent50_2./measurement_unit/dated_money_value/currency
Relation ·	/people/person/nationality
Similar relations	/people/person/places_lived./people/place_lived/location
	/people/person/place_of_birth
	/people/deceased_person/place_of_death

score gained by the score function $f(h, r, t)$ is below δ_r, then predict positive. Otherwise predict negative.

Implementation. We compare our model with several baseline methods mentioned in [10]. For the sake of fairness, word embedding [13] is not used in our experiments. In training stage, we select the same configuration with link prediction. The best parameters are also determined by validation set. On *unif* setting, the best optimal configures are $\eta = 0.01$, $\gamma = 11$, $m = 100$, $v = 3$, $b = 480$, $C = 0.25$ on WN11; $\eta = 0.01$, $\gamma = 0.25$, $m = 100$, $v = 2$, $b = 1200$, $C = 0.0625$ on FB13; $\eta = 0.01$, $\gamma = 1$, $m = 100$, $v = 6$, $b = 480$, $C = 0.0625$ on FB15k. On *bern* setting, the best optimal configures are $\eta = 0.01$, $\gamma = 11$, $m = 100$, $v = 3$,

Table 8. Triplet classification accuracies.

Dataset	WN11	FB13	FB15k
SLM	69.9	85.3	-
NTN	70.4	87.1	-
SE	53.0	75.2	72.2
SME	70.0	63.7	71.6
TransE(unif)	75.9	70.9	79.5
TransE(bern)	75.9	81.5	80.4
TransH(unif)	77.7	76.5	79.9
TransH(bern)	78.8	83.3	80.0
TransR(unif)	85.5	74.7	81.2
TransR(bern)	85.9	82.5	82.5
TransD(unif)	85.6	85.9	86.0
TransD(bern)	86.4	89.1	88.2
TransE-RS	85.3	83.0	81.9
TransH-RS	86.4	81.6	83.2
TransGH(unif)	**87.2**	84.7	**91.4**
TransGH(bern)	**87.3**	85.2	**91.2**

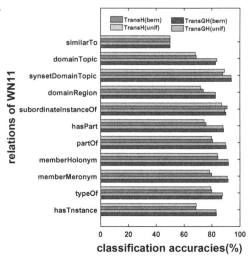

Fig. 3. Classification accuracies of on WN11.

$b = 480$, $C = 0.0625$ on WN11; $\eta = 0.01$, $\gamma = 0.25$, $m = 100$, $v = 2$, $b = 1200$, $C = 0.005$ on FB13; $\eta = 0.01$, $\gamma = 1$, $m = 100$, $v = 10$, $b = 480$, $C = 0.0625$ on FB15k. We set the number of epochs to 5000 for three data sets. Meanwhile we also take *L1* as dissimilarity on WN11, FB15k and *L2* on FB13.

Results. Evaluation results of triplet classification are shown in Table 8. TransGH consistently scores better accuracy on WN11 and FB15k than the current state-of-the-art model, where accuracies are 87.3% and 91.2% on WN11 and FB15k respectively. TransGH has slightly worse accuracy on FB13. This is mainly because that FB13 has the most entities and therefore good representations of rarely occurring entities are difficult for learning. Additionally TransGH achieves at least 8.5%, 1.9%, 11.4% higher than TransH on the three datasets. Therefore we believe the set of basis vectors is beneficial to model the complex relations and learn the embeddings of entities and relations of a knowledge graph. We also compare the classification accuracies of different relations by TransH and TransGH on WN11. In this experiment, we rerun TransH with the parameters reported in [18], and obtain slightly different accuracies 76.5%(*unif*) and 77.6%(*bern*) with the reported results in Table 8. We ignore the differences derived from randomly experiments. The accuracies of eleven relations on WN11 are given separately in Fig. 3. From results of Fig. 3, TransGH significantly improve TransH in each relation classification expect for the relation _similar_to. As reported in [10], the prediction accuracy needs more information while the number of entity pairs linked by relation _similar_to only accounts for

1.5% in all train data, therefore the inadequate entity pairs linked by relation
_similar_to is the main cause.

5   Conclusion and Future Work

In this paper, we have proposed a new knowledge graph embedding method
TransGH. The key idea of TransGH is to learn embeddings via modeling each
relation as the translation vector between projected entities on the generalized
hyperplane, which is characterized by a set of basis vectors. In addition, TrasGH
is efficient for preserving mapping properties of complex relation facts while
keeping low complexity of parameters. We empirically conduct experiments on
triplet classification and link prediction with two knowledge graphs FreeBase
and WordNet. The experimental results show that TransGH significantly and
consistently has considerable improvement over baselines, and achieve state-of-
the-art performance, which demonstrates the superiority and generality of our
model.

In the future, we will explore the following directions: (1) We will utilize the
word embeddings obtained from *word2vec* [12] in our experiments for improving
the performance of our model TransGH. (2) We will train our model TransGH
using the promising limit-based scoring loss function introduced by [19] for future
improvement. (3) We will devise and exploit a question answering system based
on TransGH.

Acknowledgment. This work is supported by National Key R&D Program No.
2017YFB0803003, and the National Natural Science Foundation of China (No.
61202226), We thank all anonymous reviewers for their constructive comments.

References

1. Bollacker, K., Evans, C., Paritosh, P., Sturge, T., Taylor, J.: Freebase: a collaboratively created graph database for structuring human knowledge. In: ACM SIGMOD
   International Conference on Management of Data, SIGMOD 2008, Vancouver, BC,
   Canada, June, pp. 1247–1250 (2008)
2. Bordes, A., Weston, X.G.J., Bengio, Y.: A semantic matching energy function for
   learning with multi-relational data. CoRR abs/1301.3485 (2013)
3. Bordes, A., Glorot, X., Weston, J.: Joint learning of words and meaning representations for open-text semantic parsing. In: International Conference on Artificial
   Intelligence and Statistics (2012)
4. Bordes, A., Usunier, N., García-Durán, A., Weston, J., Yakhnenko, O.: Translating
   embeddings for modeling multi-relational data. In: Advances in Neural Information
   Processing Systems 26: 27th Annual Conference on Neural Information Processing
   Systems 2013. Proceedings of a Meeting Held, Lake Tahoe, Nevada, United States,
   5–8 December 2013, pp. 2787–2795 (2013)
5. Bordes, A., Weston, J., Collobert, R., Bengio, Y.: Learning structured embeddings
   of knowledge bases. In: AAAI Conference on Artificial Intelligence, AAAI 2011,
   San Francisco, California, USA, August 2011

6. Bordes, A., Weston, J., Usunier, N.: Open question answering with weakly supervised embedding models. In: Calders, T., Esposito, F., Hüllermeier, E., Meo, R. (eds.) ECML PKDD 2014. LNCS (LNAI), vol. 8724, pp. 165–180. Springer, Heidelberg (2014). https://doi.org/10.1007/978-3-662-44848-9_11

7. Bottou, L.: Large-scale machine learning with stochastic gradient descent. In: Lechevallier, Y., Saporta, G. (eds.) Proceedings of COMPSTAT 2010, pp. 177–186. Springer, Heidelberg (2010). https://doi.org/10.1007/978-3-7908-2604-3_16

8. Hoffmann, R., Zhang, C., Ling, X., Zettlemoyer, L., Weld, D.S.: Knowledge-based weak supervision for information extraction of overlapping relations. In: Meeting of the Association for Computational Linguistics: Human Language Technologies, pp. 541–550 (2011)

9. Jenatton, R., Roux, N.L., Bordes, A., Obozinski, G.: A latent factor model for highly multi-relational data. In: International Conference on Neural Information Processing Systems, pp. 3167–3175 (2012)

10. Ji, G., He, S., Xu, L., Liu, K., Zhao, J.: Knowledge graph embedding via dynamic mapping matrix. In: Proceedings of the 53rd Annual Meeting of the Association for Computational Linguistics and the 7th International Joint Conference on Natural Language Processing of the Asian Federation of Natural Language Processing, ACL 2015, Beijing, China, 26–31 July 2015, vol. 1: Long Papers, pp. 687–696 (2015)

11. Lin, Y., Liu, Z., Sun, M., Liu, Y., Zhu, X.: Learning entity and relation embeddings for knowledge graph completion. In: Proceedings of the Twenty-Ninth AAAI Conference on Artificial Intelligence, Austin, Texas, USA, 25–30 January 2015, pp. 2181–2187 (2015)

12. Mikolov, T., Chen, K., Corrado, G., Dean, J.: Efficient estimation of word representations in vector space (2013)

13. Mikolov, T., Sutskever, I., Chen, K., Corrado, G.S., Dean, J.: Distributed representations of words and phrases and their compositionality. In: Advances in Neural Information Processing Systems 26: 27th Annual Conference on Neural Information Processing Systems 2013. Proceedings of a Meeting Held, Lake Tahoe, Nevada, United States, 5–8 December 2013, pp. 3111–3119 (2013)

14. Miller, G.A.: WordNet: a lexical database for English. Commun. ACM **38**(11), 39–41 (1995)

15. Nickel, M., Tresp, V., Kriegel, H.: A three-way model for collective learning on multi-relational data. In: Proceedings of the 28th International Conference on Machine Learning, ICML 2011, Bellevue, Washington, USA, 28 June–2 July 2011, pp. 809–816 (2011)

16. Socher, R., Chen, D., Manning, C.D., Ng, A.Y.: Reasoning with neural tensor networks for knowledge base completion. In: Advances in Neural Information Processing Systems 26: 27th Annual Conference on Neural Information Processing Systems 2013. Proceedings of a Meeting Held, Lake Tahoe, Nevada, United States, 5–8 December 2013, pp. 926–934 (2013)

17. Sutskever, I., Salakhutdinov, R., Tenenbaum, J.B.: Modelling relational data using Bayesian clustered tensor factorization. In: Advances in Neural Information Processing Systems 22: Conference on Neural Information Processing Systems 2009. Proceedings of A Meeting Held, Vancouver, British Columbia, Canada, 7–10 December 2009, pp. 1821–1828 (2009)

18. Wang, Z., Zhang, J., Feng, J., Chen, Z.: Knowledge graph embedding by translating on hyperplanes. In: Proceedings of the Twenty-Eighth AAAI Conference on Artificial Intelligence, Québec City, Québec, Canada, 27–31 July 2014, pp. 1112–1119 (2014)

19. Zhou, X., Zhu, Q., Liu, P., Guo, L.: Learning knowledge embeddings by combining limit-based scoring loss. In: CIKM 2017, pp. 1009–1018 (2017)

Fast Higher-Order Functions for Tensor Calculus with Tensors and Subtensors

Cem Bassoy$^{(\boxtimes)}$ and Volker Schatz

Fraunhofer IOSB, 76275 Ettlingen, Germany
`cem.bassoy@iosb.fraunhofer.de`

Abstract. Tensors analysis has become a popular tool for solving problems in computational neuroscience, pattern recognition and signal processing. Similar to the two-dimensional case, algorithms for multidimensional data consist of basic operations accessing only a subset of tensor data. With multiple offsets and step sizes, basic operations for subtensors require sophisticated implementations even for entrywise operations.

In this work, we discuss the design and implementation of optimized higher-order functions that operate entrywise on tensors and subtensors with any non-hierarchical storage format and arbitrary number of dimensions. We propose recursive multi-index algorithms with reduced index computations and additional optimization techniques such as function inlining with partial template specialization. We show that single-index implementations of higher-order functions with subtensors introduce a runtime penalty of an order of magnitude than the recursive and iterative multi-index versions. Including data- and thread-level parallelization, our optimized implementations reach 68% of the maximum throughput of an Intel Core i9-7900X. In comparison with other libraries, the average speedup of our optimized implementations is up to 5x for map-like and more than 9x for reduce-like operations. For symmetric tensors we measured an average speedup of up to 4x.

1 Introduction

Many problems in computational neuroscience, pattern recognition, signal processing and data mining generate massive amounts of multidimensional data with high dimensionality [9,12,13]. Tensors provide a natural representation for massive multidimensional data [7,10]. Similar to matrix analysis algorithms, many recently developed iterative tensor algorithms apply basic tensor operations within subdomains of tensors, i.e. subtensors where their sizes usually depend on induction variables. For instance, the higher-order Jacobi method described in [3] accesses different subtensors of the same tensor in each iteration. In [5], subtensors are used to perform a histogram-based tensor analysis.

While basic tensor operations for multidimensional data have been implemented and discussed in the literature, the design and runtime analysis of algorithms with subtensors have only been sparsely considered. The implementation of entrywise operations for contiguously stored tensors can be efficiently and

© Springer International Publishing AG, part of Springer Nature 2018
Y. Shi et al. (Eds.): ICCS 2018, LNCS 10860, pp. 639–652, 2018.
https://doi.org/10.1007/978-3-319-93698-7_49

conveniently implemented with a single loop where the storage format does not influence the runtime. In case of contiguously stored tensors, template functions of the C++ standard algorithm library can be applied. Operating on subtensors is more subtle and requires either index transformations for single loops or algorithms with a complex control-flow for multi-indexed access. Moreover, we have observed that single-index implementations are slower than recursive multi-index approaches in case of subtensors even if the spatial data locality is preserved.

In this work, we discuss optimized implementations of entrywise operations for tensors and subtensors in terms of their runtime behavior. We provide a set of optimized C++ higher-order template functions that implement a variety of map- and reduce-like tensor operations supporting tensors and subtensors with any non-hierarchical storage and arbitrary number of dimensions. The storage format, number of dimensions and the dimensions are latter can be specified at runtime. Our base implementations are based on a single-index approach with a single loop and multi-index approaches using recursion and iteration. We additionally present optimization techniques to minimize the performance penalties caused by recursion including data streaming, parallelization, loop unrolling and parametrized function inling with template meta-programming techniques. Each optimization is separately implemented in order to quantify its effects. Our proposed optimizations can also be applied for more complicated tensor operations such as tensor multiplications or transposition in order to efficiently support subtensors. In summary, the main contributions and findings of our work are:

- Multi-index higher-order functions with subtensors outperform single-index ones on a single core by one order of magnitude and perform equally well for any non-hierarchical storage format using permuted layout tuples.
- Dimension extents corresponding to the loop counts of the inner-most loops can reduce the throughput of recursively implemented higher-order functions by 37%. The runtime can be speed up by a factor of 1.6 using templated-based function inlining.
- Applying data- and thread-level parallelization, our implementations reach 68% of the maximum CPU throughput. Compared to competing implementations described in [1,6,14] the functions yield a speedup of up to 5x for map-like and more than 9x for reduce-like operations.

The remainder of the paper is organized as follows. Section 2 discusses existing libraries that are related to our work. Section 3 introduces the notation and states the problem based on the preliminary. Section 4 provides the research methodology and experimental setup used in this work. The following Sect. 5 introduces the single- and multi-index implementation. Section 6 describes optimized multi-index versions of the multi-index implementation. Section 7 discusses and analyzes benchmark results with other libraries. The last Sect. 8 contains the conclusions.

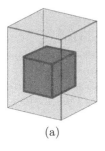
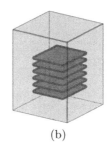
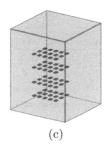

(a)   (b)   (c)

Fig. 1. Subtensors with an index offset $f_r > 1$ where (a) is generated with $t_r = 1$ for all $r \in \{1, 2, 3\}$, (b) with $t_1 > 1$ and $t_2 = t_3 = 1$ and (c) with $t_r > 1$ for all $r \in \{1, 2, 3\}$.

2   Related Work

Due to the wide range of applications using tensor calculus, there is a large number of libraries implementing it. In this section we will restrict ourselves to implementations that, like ours, support dense tensor operations. Blitz, described in [14], is one of the first C++ frameworks. It supports tensors up to 11 dimensions including tensor and stencil operations. Multidimensional arrays are generic data types where the number of dimensions are compile-time parameters. The framework supports high-level expressions for entrywise tensor operations and also allows to manipulate subtensors for single core execution. The authors of [6] describe Boost's MultiArray. They discuss the design of generic data types for tensors, including the addressing elements and subtensors with first- and last-order storage formats. Users of the library must implement their own higher-order tensor operations using the provided tensor data structures. In [2], the library MArray and its implementations are presented. The order and dimensions of the tensor templates are runtime parameters similar to our work. The paper also discusses addressing functions, but only for the first- and last-order storage format. The entrywise tensor operations can also process subtensors. The Cyclops-Tensor-Framework (CT) offers a library primarily targeted at quantum chemistry applications. The order and the dimensions of their tensor data structures are dynamically configurable. LibNT, discussed in [8], serves a similar purpose. Both frameworks, however, do not allow manipulation of subtensors with entrywise tensor operations. Eigen's tensor library is included in the Tensorflow framework [1]. The runtime of the latter contains over 200 standard operations, including mathematical, array manipulation, control flow, and state management operation. Among other features, the C++ library framework also provides entrywise tensor operations with tensors and subtensors.

3   Notation

A tensor of order p shall be denoted by $\underline{\mathbf{A}}$ where p is the number of dimensions. Dimension extents are given by a shape tuple $\mathbf{n} = (n_1, \ldots, n_p)$ where $n_r > 1$ for

Table 1. Implemented higher-order template functions.

Abbreviation	Function	Description	Example (MATLAB)
scal	for_each()	$c_{ij\ldots k} \leftarrow \alpha \odot c_{ij\ldots k}$	C(1:4,:,2:6) = C(1:4,:,2:6)+3
copy	copy()	$c_{ij\ldots k} \leftarrow a_{ij\ldots k}$	C(1:4,:,end) = A(2:5,:,end)
add	transform()	$c_{ij\ldots k} \leftarrow \alpha \odot a_{ij\ldots k}$	C(1:4,:,2:6) = A(2:5,:,3:7)+3
addc	transform()	$c_{ij\ldots k} \leftarrow a_{ij\ldots k} \odot b_{ij\ldots k}$	C(1:4,:,:) = A(2:5,:,:)+B(3:6,:,:)
min	min_element()	$\min_{ij\ldots k}(a_{ij\ldots k})$	min(A(2:5,:,3:7)(:))
equal	equal()	$c_{ij\ldots k} \overset{!}{=} a_{ij\ldots k}$	all(C(1:4,:,:)(:)==A(2:5,:,:)(:))
all	all_of()	$a_{ij\ldots k} \overset{!}{=} \alpha$	all(C(1:4,:,:)(:)==3)
acc	accumulate()	$\sum_{ij\ldots k} a_{ij\ldots k}$	sum(C(1:4,:,:)(:))
inner	inner_product()	$\sum_{ij\ldots k} a_{ij\ldots k} \cdot c_{ij\ldots k}$	dot(C(1:4,:,:)(:),C(2:6:,:)(:))

$1 \leq r \leq p$. Elements of $\underline{\mathbf{A}}$ are denoted by $a_{i_1,i_2,\ldots,i_p}$, $\underline{\mathbf{A}}(i_1, i_2, \ldots, i_p)$ or $\underline{\mathbf{A}}(\mathbf{i})$ with $i_r \in I_r$ and $I_r = \{1, \ldots, n_r\}$ for all p dimensions. The set of all multi-indices is given by $\mathcal{I} = I_1 \times \cdots \times I_p$.

A subtensor denotes a selection of a multidimensional array $\underline{\mathbf{A}}$ that is defined in terms of p tuples such that $\underline{\mathbf{A}}' = \underline{\mathbf{A}}(\mathbf{s}_1, \ldots, \mathbf{s}_p)$. The r-th tuple $\mathbf{s}_r$ has n'_r elements with $n'_r \leq n_r$ and $s_k \in I_r$ for $1 \leq k \leq n'_r$. Most tensor algorithms use index triplets (f_r, t_r, l_r), where f_r, l_r define the first and last index satisfying $1 \leq f_r \leq l_r \leq n_r$. The parameter t_r with $t_r > 0$ is the step size or increment for the r-th dimension such that $n'_r = \lfloor (l_r - f_r)/t_r \rfloor + 1$. The index sets I'_r and the multi-index set $\mathcal{I}'$ of a subtensor $\underline{\mathbf{A}}'$ are defined in analogy to the index and multi-index set of tensor $\underline{\mathbf{A}}$. Figure 1 illustrates three types of subtensors with different index triplet configurations.

4   Methodology and Experimental Setup

Table 1 lists some of the implemented and optimized higher-order functions. The offsets, increments, the number of dimensions and layout of the tensor can be dynamically set. The first four functions read from and write to memory regions. The following three functions read from memory regions and perform a reduce operation returning a scalar result. The last two functions are commonly used in numerical algorithms and also perform a reduce operation. Our implementation of higher-order functions support subtensors and tensors with any non-hierarchical storage format equally well. They can be thought as an extension of higher-order functions that are described by the C++ standard. Being applicable to contiguously stored tensors, they cannot be used to iterate over a multidimensional index set of a subtensor. We have applied multiple approaches and optimizations for all higher-order functions listed in Table 1 each of which is separately implemented. The implementations are as follows:

- *single-index* implementation uses a single loop.
- *multi-index-rec* implementation contains recursive functions calls.
- *multi-index-iter* is an iterative version using multi-indices.

The following optimizations are based *multi-index* and are denoted as follows:

- *{minindex}* contains less index computations.
- *{inline}* avoids recursive function calls for a given compile-time order.
- *{parallel}* applies implicit data- and explicit thread-level parallelism.
- *{stream}* applies explicit data-parallelism and uses stream instrinsics.

We first quantify the runtime penalties that arise from index transformation within a single loop comparing *single-index* and *multi-index* implementations with subtensors. Based on the unoptimized *multi-index* implementation, we measure combinations of optimizations, such as *{minindex,inline}*. We have defined multiple setups for measuring the runtime and throughput of the higher-order functions.

- *Setup 1* contains four two-dimensional arrays N_k of shape tuples for subtensors with 10 rows and 32 columns where each shape tuple $n_{r,c}$ is of length $r + 1$. The initial shape tuples $n_{1,1}$ for all arrays are $(2^{15}, 2^8)$, $(2^8, 2^{15})$, $(2^8, 2, 2^{14})$ and $(2^8, 2^{15})$, respectively. The value of the k-th element is given by $n_{r,c}(k) = n_{1,1}(k) \cdot c/2^{r-1}$. If $k = 4$, the last element of all shape tuples instead of the fourth is adjusted. The remaining elements are set to 2 such that all shape tuples of one column exhibit the same number of subtensor elements. The subtensor sizes range from 32 to 1024 MB for single-precision floating-point numbers.
- *Setup 2* contains two-dimensional arrays N_k of shape tuples with 10 rows and 64 columns. The shape tuples are similarly created starting with the same initial shape tuple $(2^4, 2^{19})$. The first shape tuple elements are given by $n_{r,c}(1) = n_{1,1}(1) \cdot c$. The second and last dimension are adjusted according to $n_{r,c}(2) = n_{1,1}(2) / 2^{r-1}$ and $n_{r,c}(r + 1) = n_{1,1}(r + 1) / 2^{r-1}$, respectively. The remaining shape tuple elements are set to 2. The subtensor sizes range from 32 to 2048 MB for single-precision floating-point numbers.
- *Setup 3* contains shape tuples that yield symmetric subtensors. The setup provides a two-dimensional array N of shape tuples with 6 rows and 8 columns where each shape tuple $n_{r,c}$ is of length $r + 1$. Elements of the shape tuples $n_{r,1}$ for $r = 1, \ldots, 6$ are each 2^{12}, 2^8, 2^6, 2^5, 2^4 and 2^3. The remaining shape tuples for $c > 1$ are then given by $n_{r,c} = n_{r,c} + k \cdot (c-1)$ where k is respectively equal to 2^9, 2^5, 2^3, 2^2, 2, 1 for $r = 1, \ldots, 6$. In this setup, shape tuples of a column do not yield the same number of subtensor elements. The subtensor sizes range from 8 to 4096 MB for single-precision floating-point numbers.

The first two configurations with 4×320 and 2×640 shape tuples exhibit an orthogonal design in terms of tensor size and order, where the algorithms are run for fixed tensor sizes with increasing tensor order and vice versa. Varying only one dimension extent for a given order helped us to quantify its influence on the runtime. The last setup contains 48 tuples for symmetric tensors.

$$\mathcal{J}' \xrightarrow{\lambda_{\mathbf{w'}}^{-1}} \mathcal{I}' \xrightarrow{\gamma} \mathcal{I} \xrightarrow{\lambda_{\mathbf{w}}} \boxed{\mathcal{J}}$$

Fig. 2. Accessing contiguously stored elements requires the computation of scalar indices in $\mathcal{J}$. Function $\lambda_{\mathbf{w}}$ is applied if tensors are accessed with multi-indices in $\mathcal{I}$. Function $\lambda_{\mathbf{w}} \circ \gamma$ is applied if subtensor are accessed with multi-indices in $\mathcal{I}'$. Accessing elements subtensors with scalar indices in $\mathcal{J}'$ requires the application $\lambda_{\mathbf{w}} \circ \gamma \circ \lambda_{\mathbf{w'}}^{-1}$.

Subtensors are created with increments equal to one for all dimensions in order to analyze runtime penalties introduced by index computations and recursive function calls. Each subtensor is selected from a tensor that has a shape tuple of the last row of the corresponding two-dimensional array $\mathbf{N}_k$. One extent n_k of the subtensor is chosen smaller than the dimension extents of the referenced tensor. The sizes of the subtensors were chosen greater than the last-level cache to avoid caching effects. Spatial data locality is always preserved meaning that relative memory indices are generated according to storage format. Tensor elements are stored according to the first-order storage format for all setups. All of the following findings are valid for any other non-hierarchical storage format if the optimization in Sect. 6.2 is applied.

The experiments were carried out on an Core i9-7900X Intel Xeon processor with 10 cores and 20 hardware threads running at a base frequency of 3.3 GHz. It has a theoretical peak memory bandwidth of 85.312 GB/s resulting from four 64-bit wide channels with a data rate of 2666 MT/s. The examples and tests were compiled with GCC 7.2 using the highest optimization level including the -march=native and -pthread options. The benchmark results presented below are the average of 10 runs. The throughput is given as number of operations times element size in bytes divided by the runtime in seconds. The comparison were performed with Eigen's tensor library (3.3.4), Boost's multiarray library (1.62.0) and Blitz's library (0.9) that were described in the Sect. 2.

5 Baseline Algorithms

If tensors are allocated contiguously in memory, a single index suffices to access all elements. The set of scalar indices is denoted by $\mathcal{J}$ with $\mathcal{J} = \{0, \ldots, \bar{n} - 1\}$ where $\bar{n} = \prod_{r=1}^{p} n_r$ with $|\mathcal{I}| = |\mathcal{J}|$. The mapping of multi-indices in $\mathcal{I}$ onto scalar indices in $\mathcal{J}$ depends on the layout of a tensor. The following mappings include any non-hierarchical layouts that can be specified by a layout tuple $\boldsymbol{\pi}$. The most common layouts are the first- and last-order storage formats with their respective layout tuples $\boldsymbol{\pi}_F = (1, 2, \ldots, p)$ and $\boldsymbol{\pi}_L = (p, p\text{-}1, \ldots, 1)$. The layout function $\lambda_{\mathbf{w}}$ with

$$\lambda_{\mathbf{w}}(\mathbf{i}) = \sum_{r=1}^{p} w_r(i_r - 1). \tag{1}$$

Algorithm 1. Recursive algorithm.	**Algorithm 2.** Iterative version.
Input: $\underline{\mathbf{A}} \in T^{\mathbf{n}}$, $\underline{\mathbf{B}} \in T^{\mathbf{n}}$, $\mathbf{n} \in \mathbb{N}^p$, $\quad \mathbf{i} \in \mathbb{N}^P$, $r = p$ **Result:** $\underline{\mathbf{C}} \in T^{\mathbf{n}}$	**Input:** $\underline{\mathbf{A}} \in T^{\mathbf{n}}$, $\underline{\mathbf{B}} \in T^{\mathbf{n}}$ with $\mathbf{n} \in \mathbb{N}^p$, $\quad \mathbf{i} \in \mathbb{N}^P$ **Result:** $\underline{\mathbf{C}} \in T^{\mathbf{n}}$

1 transform($\underline{\mathbf{A}}, \underline{\mathbf{B}}, \underline{\mathbf{C}}$, w, n, i, r)	1 transform($\underline{\mathbf{A}}, \underline{\mathbf{B}}, \underline{\mathbf{C}}$, w, n, i)
2 if $r > 1$ then	2 $r \leftarrow 1$
3 for $i_r \leftarrow 1$ to n_r do	3 while $r \leq p$ do
4 transform($\underline{\mathbf{A}}, \underline{\mathbf{B}}, \underline{\mathbf{C}}$, w, n, i, $r{-}1$)	4 for $k \leftarrow 2$ to r do
	5 $i_k \leftarrow 1$
5 else	6 for $i_1 \leftarrow 1$ to n_1 do
6 for $i_1 \leftarrow 1$ to n_1 do	7 $j \leftarrow \lambda_{\mathbf{w}}(\mathbf{i})$
7 $j \leftarrow \lambda_{\mathbf{w}}(\mathbf{i})$	8 $\underline{\mathbf{C}}[j] \leftarrow \underline{\mathbf{A}}[j] \odot \underline{\mathbf{B}}[j]$
8 $\underline{\mathbf{C}}[j] \leftarrow \underline{\mathbf{A}}[j] \odot \underline{\mathbf{B}}[j]$	9 for $r \leftarrow 2$ to p do
	10 if $i_r < n_r$ then
	11 break;
	12 $i_r \leftarrow i_r + 1$

maps multi-indices in $\mathcal{I}$ to scalar indices in $\mathcal{J}$ for a fixed stride tuple $\mathbf{w}$ whose elements are given by $w_{\pi_1} = 1$ and

$$w_{\pi_r} = w_{\pi_{r-1}} \cdot n_{\pi_{r-1}} \quad \text{for } 1 < r \leq p. \tag{2}$$

The inverse layout function $\lambda_{\mathbf{w}}^{-1} : \mathcal{J} \to \mathcal{I}$ of $\lambda_{\mathbf{w}}$ is given by

$$\lambda_{\mathbf{w}}^{-1}(j) = \mathbf{i}, \quad \text{and} \quad i_r = \left\lfloor \frac{k_r}{w_r} \right\rfloor + 1, \tag{3}$$

with $k_{\pi_r} = k_{\pi_{r+1}} - w_{\pi_{r+1}} \cdot i_{\pi_{r+1}}$ for $r < p$ and $i_{\pi_p} = \lfloor j/w_{\pi_p} \rfloor + 1$. We can analogously define a scalar index set $\mathcal{J}'$ for a subtensor with $\bar{n}'$ elements where $\bar{n}' = \prod_{r=1}^p n'_r$. Note that λ can only be applied if $1 = f_r$, $l_r = n_r$ and $1 = t_r$ such that $n'_r = n_r$. In any other case, each multi-index in $\mathcal{I}'$ needs be mapped onto an multi-index in $\mathcal{I}$. The mapping $\gamma : \mathcal{I}' \to \mathcal{I}$ with $\gamma(\mathbf{i}') = \mathbf{i}$ is given by

$$\gamma_r(i'_r) = f_r + (i'_r - 1) \cdot t_r = i_r, \tag{4}$$

for $1 \leq r \leq p$. Subtensor elements can be accessed with single indices in $\mathcal{J}'$ by applying the function $\lambda_{\mathbf{w}} \circ \gamma \circ \gamma_{\mathbf{w}'}$ such that

$$j = \lambda_{\mathbf{w}} \left(\gamma \left(\lambda_{\mathbf{w}'}^{-1}(j') \right) \right), \tag{5}$$

where $\mathbf{w}'$ and $\mathbf{w}$ are stride tuples of a subtensor and tensor. Figure 2 illustrates how a single-loop approach for subtensors requires scalar indices to be transformed according to Eq. (5).

5.1 Recursive Multi-index Algorithm *multi-index-rec*

The baseline algorithm `transform` in Algorithm 1 exemplifies an implementation of entrywise operation for tensors and subtensors where $\odot$ is be a binary operation. It is a nonlinear recursive algorithm and has variable number of recursive function calls in each recursion level. The first input arguments denote a tensor or subtensor of order p all exhibiting the same shape tuple $\mathbf{n}$. Before each recursive function call, an element of the multi-index is incremented and passed to the following function instance for $r > 1$. The inner-most recursion level for $r = 1$ computes the first element i_1 of the multi-index and applies the layout function defined in Eq. (1). Once the memory indices for all data structures are computed, the binary operation in line 7 is applied. Using Eqs. (1) and (4), the layout function of subtensor is given by $\lambda' = \lambda_{\mathbf{w}'} \circ \gamma$ such that $\lambda'_{\mathbf{w}'}(\mathbf{i}') = \lambda_{\mathbf{w}}(\mathbf{f}) + \lambda_{\mathbf{w}''}(\mathbf{i}')$ where $\mathbf{f}$ is the tuple of the first indices of the subtensor and $\mathbf{w}''$ is a modified stride tuple with $w''_r = w'_r t_r$. The first summand $\lambda_{\mathbf{w}}(\mathbf{f})$ is an offset with which the pointer to the tensor data is shifted to set the position of the first subtensor element. In this way, the algorithm is able to process tensors and subtensors equally well.

5.2   Iterative Multi-index Algorithm *multi-index-iter*

The basline algorithm provides an elegant solution for traversing the multi-index space and generating unique multi-indices with no redundant computation. However, recursion may introduce runtime overhead due to stack operations for saving the callers state [4]. In our case, $p - 1$ stack frames are repeatedly created before the inner-most loop is executed.

Nonlinear recursive algorithms can be transformed into an iteration using a software stack [11,15]. With no processing in between the recursive calls except the adjustment of the multi-index, we applied the method described in [15] and eliminated function calls which resulted in a much simpler control flow. We further simplified the algorithm, by only storing multi-index elements and to use a single array, where the r-th entry stores the r-th multi-index element.

The resulting iterative version of the recursive baseline algorithm is given in Algorithm 2. The multi-indices are modified in lines 3 to 5 and 8 to 11 just as it is done in line 2 to 4 in Algorithm 1. A multi-index element i_r is reset in lines 3 to 5 if any i_k with $k > r$ has reached the loop count n_k.

5.3   Single-Index Algorithm *single-index*

Higher-order functions for tensors can be implemented with one loop where tensor elements are accessed with a single index j. The memory address of the j-th element is given by the addition $k + \delta \cdot j$ where δ is the size of an element and k the memory location of the first element. We have used higher-order functions of the C++ standard library to perform elementwise operations for tensors. However, they cannot be used in case of subtensors where the values of the induction variable are in $\mathcal{J}'$. Each memory access with a scalar index needs a transformation according to Eq. (5). The loop body for first-order storage format first increments the scalar j with $w_r \cdot i$ and updates k and i with $k \leftarrow \bar{k} - w'_r \cdot \bar{i}$ and $i \leftarrow k/w'_{r-1}$ where $\bar{k}$ and $\bar{i}$ are previously computed values.

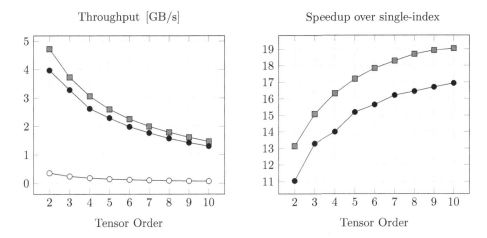

Throughput [GB/s]   Speedup over single-index

Fig. 3. Comparison of —○— *single-index*, —■— *multi-index-rec* and —●— *multi-index-iter* implementations of the entrywise addition of two subtensors. Data is stored in single precision. Tests are run on a single core with shape tuples of *Setup 1*. *Left*: Mean throughput. *Right*: Mean speedup of *multi-index-rec* and *multi-index-iter* over *single-index*.

6 Optimizing the Multi-index Algorithm

In this section we will turn to algorithms optimized for accessing subtensors. The first subsection will present an iterative algorithm for higher-order functions. The following sections describe successive optimizations of the multi-index recursive algorithm from Sect. 5.1. Three of those subsections explain methods that can be applied in order to reduce the runtime penalties caused by the recursive approach. The last subsection discusses data- and thread-level parallelization with which bandwidth utilization can be maximized.

6.1 Reducing Index Computation {minindex}

The baseline algorithm for higher-order functions computes relative memory indices in the inner-most loop. We can further reduce the number of index computations by hoisting some of the summands to the previously executed loops. In each recursion level r, line 3 and 6 only modify the r-th element i_r of the multi-index **i**. Moreover, the k-th function call at the r-th level adds k to i_r, i.e. increments the previously calculated index. We can therefore move the r-th summand $w_r \cdot i_r$ of Eq. (1) to the r-th recursion level. In this way, unnecessary index computations in the inner-most loop can be eliminated allowing to pass a single index j that is incremented by w_r. Algorithm 1 therefore needs to be modified in line 3, 6 and 7 to substitute j. At the recursion level r, the single index j is incremented n_r times with w_r until the stride $(r+1)$-th element of the stride tuple **w** is reached. The last element of the stride tuple **w** is given by $w_p \cdot n_p$. As j denotes a memory index, we can manipulate pointers to the data structures

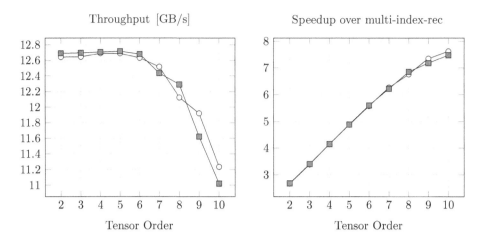

Fig. 4. Comparison of the *multi-index-rec{minindex}* ―■― and *multi-index-iter {minindex}* ―○― implementations of the entrywise addition of two subtensors. Data is stored in single precision. Tests are executed on a single core with shape tuples of *Setup 1*. *Left*: Mean throughput. *Right*: mean speedup over *multi-index-rec* implementation.

in the same manner. In this way only a dereferencing in the inner-most loop is necessary. The same holds for subtensors.

6.2 Preserving Data Locality

The spatial data locality of Algorithm 1 is always preserved for the first-order storage as the inner-most loop increments the first multi-index by $w_1 = 1$. For any other layout tuple, the elements are accessed with a stride greater than one. This can have a greatly influence the runtime of the higher-order function. In order to access successive element, we can reorder the loops or stride tuple according to the layout tuple. However, the modification of a stride tuple can be performed before the initial function call. Using the property $1 \leq w_{\pi_q} \leq w_{\pi_r}$ for $1 \leq q \leq r \leq p$, a new stride tuple $\mathbf{v}$ with $v_r = w_{\pi_r}$ for $1 \leq r \leq p$ can be computed. The runtime penalty for the permutation of the stride tuple becomes then negligible.

6.3 Reducing Recursive Function Calls *{inline}*

The recursion for the multi-index approach consists of multiple cases where each function call contains multiple recursive function calls, see [11]. Function inlining is more likely to be achieved if calls to the next recursion level is performed with a different function type. This can be accomplished with class templates and partial specialization with a static member function containing a loop in order to reduce the number of function implementations. The order of the tensor and subtensor is a template parameter that allows the compiler to generate jump

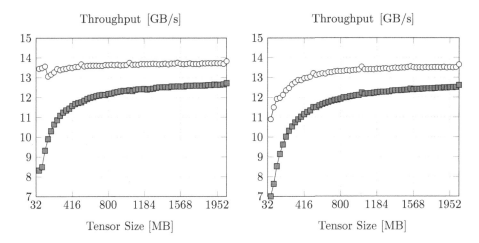

Fig. 5. Comparison of the recursive multi-index implementations of the entrywise sub-tensor addition with *{minindex,inline}* —o— and *{minindex}* —■— optimizations. Data is stored in single precision. Tests are executed on a single core with shape tuples of *Setup 2*. Left and right plots contain mean throughputs of the implementations executed with the first N_1 and second shape tuple array N_2, respectively.

instructions for the specified order and to avoid recursive function calls. In order to leave the order runtime flexible, the static function is called from a switch statement. If the runtime-variable order is larger than the specified template parameter, the standard recursive implementation is called. In order to prevent a code bloat of multiple implementations for different orders, we chose the order to 20.

6.4 Data- and Thread-Parallelization *{parallel,stream}*

By data-level parallelization we refer to the process of generating a single instruction for multiple data. The inner-most loop of the higher-order function is an auto-vectorizable loop if the stride of a tensor or subtensor is equal to one. In such a case, the compiler generates vector instructions with unaligned loads and regular store operations. In order to yield a better memory bandwidth utilization, we have explicitly placed Intel's aligned load and streaming intrinsics with the corresponding vector operation in the most inner loop. Note that pointers to the data structures must be aligned and the loop count must be set to a multiple of the vector size.

By thread-level parallelization we refer to the process of finding independent instruction streams of a program or function. Thread-level parallel exuction is accomplished with C++ threads executing the higher-order function in parallel where the outer-most loop is divided into equally sized chunks. Each thread executes its own instruction stream using distinct memory addresses of the tensor or subtensor. In case of reduction operations such the inner product with greater data dependencies, threads perform their own reduction operation in parallel and

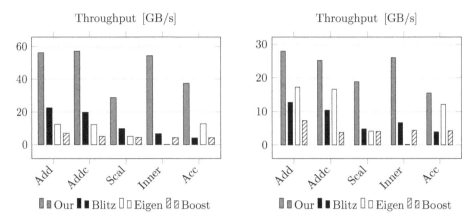

Fig. 6. Comparison of our implementation ▌▯ to Blitz ▐▌ , Eigen ▯▯ and Boost ▨▨ . Entrywise operations are executed with subtensors in single precision on all available cores. Function descriptions are found in Table 1. *Left:* Setup 1 was used for this benchmark. Our refers to *multi-index-rec {minindex,inline,parallel,stream}* reaching 68% of the theoretical peak memory bandwidth. *Right:* Setup 3 was used for this benchmark. Our refers to *multi-index-rec {minindex,inline,parallel}*.

provide their results to the parent thread. The latter performs the remaining reduction operation.

7   Results and Discussion

A comparison of the *single-index, multi-index-rec* and *multi-index-iter* implementations of the entrywise addition for subtensors is provided in Fig. 3. The throughput for a given order is constant over all subtensor sizes and only varies between two different orders. The throughput of the *multi-index-rec* and *multi-index-iter* implementations speed up with increasing order and run up to 20 times faster than the *single-index* version. Note that both multi-index implementations perform equally well. We observed similar speedups for all other implemented higher-order functions.

Hoisting the index computation of the recursive *multi-index* approach with the *{minindex}* optimization significantly reduces the number of index computations, as shown in Fig. 4. The recursive and iterative *multi-index {minindex}* linearly speed up with increasing order outperforming the unoptimized versions by almost a factor of 8. We measured a slowdown of at most 10% for any tuple shape of *Setup 1.*

Without the *{inline}* optimization, the recursive multi-index implementation runs slower for tensors and subtensors with a small extent of the first dimension. We did not observe similar behavior for shape tuples belonging to *Setup 1* where the extents of the first dimension is kept always greater than 256. Figure 5 illustrates the impact of the first dimension where only the first dimension is increased from 16 to 1024. Decreasing the first dimension causes a slow down almost up to a factor of 2. The positioning of the large dimension has a minor impact on the throughput. The *{inline}* optimization reduces the runtime up to a factor of 1.6.

Comparing the throughput of the recursive implementations in Figs. 4 and 6 using *{minindex,inline}* and *{minindex,inline,parallel,stream}* reveals that data- and thread-parallel execution with stream operations almost quadruples the sustained throughput from almost 14 GB/s on a single-core to almost 58 GB/s reaching about 68% of the theoretical peak performance. In comparison to other C++ libraries our fastest implementation performs up to 5x faster for map-like operations and 9x for reduce operations with unsymmetric subtensors. Using implicit vectorization with unaligned access and store instructions reduces the throughput by 37%. With shape tuples of *Setup 3*, we did not use explicit vectorization and vector streaming instructions. In this case, higher-order functions utilized at most 34% of the theoretical peak memory bandwidth. Despite the lower throughput, all our functions yield speedups between 2x and 4x compared to the competing implementations as shown in Fig. 6. While higher-order functions had almost a constant throughput with *Setup 1*, we measured a linear decrease of the throughput with increasing order for all implementations with *Setup 3*. This observation coincides with measurements based on the previous description shown in Fig. 5.

Although *Blitz* does not support parallel execution, some of its entrywise operations perform almost as fast as our implementations on a single core. A parallelized version could also compete with our functions in terms of runtime. However, the implementation only supports a fixed number of dimensions which allows to provide an optimized implementation for each version. We implemented all entrywise operations for subtensors using *Boost*'s data structures and executed them on a single core. *Eigen*'s implementation executes entrywise operations in parallel. We observed a decrease of the throughput with increasing order as well. The performance of the reduce-like operations provided by the libraries is lower compared to the map-like operations.

8   Conclusion and Future Work

We have investigated the runtime behavior of higher-order functions for subtensors and showed that the recursive multi-index implementation linearly speeds up with increasing order over the single-index approach. Experimenting with a large amount of shape tuples we have shown that the dimension extents corresponding to the loop counts of the inner-most loops can reduce the throughput by 37%. Hoisting index computation and inlining function calls, the multi-index approach can be optimized, minimizing the performance penalties introduced by the recursion.

Applying explicit data-level parallelism with stream instructions and thread-level parallelism, we were able to speed up higher-order functions reaching 68% of the theoretical peak performance. In comparison to other C++ libraries our fastest implementation performs up to 5x faster for map-like and 9x for reduce-like operations with unsymmetric subtensors. For symmetric subtensors we measured an average speedup of up to 4x. The findings of our work are valid for any type of tensor operation that includes recursive implementations.

In future work, we intend to create fast implementations of other tensor operations such as the tensor transposition and contractions and analyze the impact of the recursion.

References

1. Abadi, M., Barham, P., Chen, J., Chen, Z., Davis, A., Dean, J., Devin, M., Ghemawat, S., Irving, G., Isard, M., Kudlur, M., Levenberg, J., Monga, R., Moore, S., Murray, D.G., Steiner, B., Tucker, P., Vasudevan, V., Warden, P., Wicke, M., Yu, Y., Zheng, X.: TensorFlow: a system for large-scale machine learning. In: Proceedings of the 12th USENIX Conference on Operating Systems Design and Implementation, OSDI 2016, pp. 265–283. USENIX Association, Berkeley (2016)
2. Andres, B., Köthe, U., Kröger, T., Hamprecht, F.A.: Runtime-flexible multidimensional arrays and views for C++98 and C++0x. CoRR abs/1008.2909 (2010)
3. Brazell, M., Li, N., Navasca, C., Tamon, C.: Solving multilinear systems via tensor inversion. SIAM J. Matrix Anal. Appl. **34**, 542–570 (2013)
4. Cohen, N.H.: Eliminating redundant recursive calls. ACM Trans. Program. Lang. Syst. (TOPLAS) **5**(3), 265–299 (1983)
5. Fanaee-T, H., Gama, J.: Multi-aspect-streaming tensor analysis. Knowl.-Based Syst. **89**, 332–345 (2015)
6. Garcia, R., Lumsdaine, A.: MultiArray: a C++ library for generic programming with arrays. Softw. Pract. Exper. **35**(2), 159–188 (2005)
7. Hackbusch, W.: Numerical tensor calculus. Acta Numer. **23**, 651–742 (2014)
8. Harrison, A.P., Joseph, D.: Numeric tensor framework: exploiting and extending einstein notation. J. Comput. Sci. **16**, 128–139 (2016)
9. Kolda, T.G., Sun, J.: Scalable tensor decompositions for multi-aspect data mining. In: Proceedings of the 8th IEEE International Conference on Data Mining, pp. 363–372. IEEE, Washington (2008)
10. Lim, L.H.: Tensors and hypermatrices. In: Hogben, L. (ed.) Handbook of Linear Algebra, 2nd edn. Chapman and Hall, New York (2017)
11. Liu, Y.A., Stoller, S.D.: From recursion to iteration: what are the optimizations? ACM SIGPLAN Not. **34**(11), 73–82 (1999)
12. Savas, B., Eldén, L.: Handwritten digit classification using higher order singular value decomposition. Pattern Recogn. **40**(3), 993–1003 (2007)
13. Suter, S.K., Makhynia, M., Pajarola, R.: Tamresh - tensor approximation multiresolution hierarchy for interactive volume visualization. In: Proceedings of the 15th Eurographics Conference on Visualization, EuroVis 2013, pp. 151–160. Eurographics Association (2013)
14. Veldhuizen, T.L.: Arrays in blitz++. In: Caromel, D., Oldehoeft, R.R., Tholburn, M. (eds.) ISCOPE 1998. LNCS, vol. 1505, pp. 223–230. Springer, Heidelberg (1998). https://doi.org/10.1007/3-540-49372-7_24
15. Ward, M.P., Bennett, K.H.: Recursion removal/introduction by formal transformation: an aid to program development and program comprehension. Comput. J. **42**(8), 650–650 (1999)

The t-Modified Self-Shrinking Generator

Sara D. Cardell[1(✉)] and Amparo Fúster-Sabater[2]

[1] Instituto de Matemática, Estatística e Computação Científica, UNICAMP,
R. Sérgio Buarque de Holanda, 651, Campinas, SP 13083-859, Brazil
`sdcardell@ime.unicamp.br`
[2] Instituto de Tecnologías Físicas y de la Información, C.S.I.C.,
Serrano 144, 28006 Madrid, Spain
`amparo@iec.csic.es`

Abstract. Pseudo-random sequences exhibit interesting properties with applications in many and distinct areas ranging from reliable communications to number generation or cryptography. Inside the family of decimation-based sequence generators, the modified self-shrinking generator (an improved version of the self-shrinking generator) is one of its best-known elements. In fact, such a generator divides the PN-sequence produced by a maximum-length LFSR into groups of three bits. When the sum of the first two bits in a group is one, then the generator returns the third bit, otherwise the bit is discarded. In this work, we introduce a generalization of this generator, where the PN-sequence is divided into groups of t bits, $t \geq 2$. It is possible to check that the properties of the output sequences produced by this family of generators have the same or better properties than those of the classic modified self-shrunken sequences. Moreover, the number of sequences generated by this new family with application in stream cipher cryptography increases dramatically.

Keywords: Decimation · Modified self-shrinking generator
Linear complexity · Characteristic polynomial

1 Introduction

Many of the pseudo-random sequence generators are based on maximum-length Linear Feedback Shift Registers (LFSRs) [1,2] whose output sequences, known

The first author was supported by FAPESP with number of process 2015/07246-0 and CAPES. This research has been partially supported by Ministerio de Economía, Industria y Competitividad (MINECO), Agencia Estatal de Investigación (AEI), and Fondo Europeo de Desarrollo Regional (FEDER, UE) under project COPCIS, reference TIN2017-84844-C2-1-R, and by Comunidad de Madrid (Spain) under project reference S2013/ICE-3095-CIBERDINE-CM, also co-funded by European Union FEDER funds.

The title of the originally published version was erroneously "The Modified Self-Shrinking Generator?". This has now been corrected. The erratum to this chapter is available at https://doi.org/10.1007/978-3-319-93698-7_55

© Springer International Publishing AG, part of Springer Nature 2018
Y. Shi et al. (Eds.): ICCS 2018, LNCS 10860, pp. 653–663, 2018.
https://doi.org/10.1007/978-3-319-93698-7_50

as PN-sequences, are combined via a non-linear Boolean function in order to produce pseudo-random sequences. Traditionally, LFSRs have been designed to operate over the binary field of two elements, which is an appropriate approach for hardware implementations. One of the best-known and more promising families of pseudo-random sequence generators is the family of decimation-based generators. The underlying idea of this kind of generators is the irregular decimation of a PN-sequence according to the bits of another one. The result of this decimation is a binary sequence that will be used as keystream sequence for encryption/decryption in stream cipher cryptography [3].

The first generator based on irregular decimation was introduced in 1993 by Coppersmith *et al.* [4] and deeply studied in [5,6]. Such a generator, called the shrinking generator, uses two maximum-length LFSRs; one generates output bits while the other controls (accepts/rejects) such bits. Later, Meier and Sttafelbach introduced the self-shrinking generator [7], a more simple version of the shrinking generator, where a single PN-sequence decimates itself. Both generators are attractive since they are fast, simple to be implemented and their output sequences exhibit good cryptographic properties. In [8], Kanso introduced the modified self-shrinking generator, a new variant of the self-shrinking generator that used an extended selection rule based on the XORed value of a pair of bits.

In this work, we introduce a new family of keystream generators called the t-modified self-shrinking generators, which is a generalization of the modified self-shrinking generator introduced in [8]. For a given value of t, the PN-sequence is divided into groups of t bits. When the XOR of the first $t - 1$ bits of each group is one, then we keep the last bit of the group, otherwise, it is discarded. If the length of the PN-sequence and the parameter t satisfy certain conditions, then the t-modified sequences have similar properties to those of the modified self-shrunken sequence [8] as well as we dramatically increase the number of generated sequences with application in cryptography.

The work is organized as follows: in Sect. 2, the family of self-shrinking generators are introduced as well as their formation rules and main characteristics. In Sect. 3, we introduce the novel definition of t-modified self-shrinking generator and some illustrative examples. The properties of the sequences produced by this generator and its relationship with the generalized self-shrinking generator are described in Sect. 4. Finally, conclusions in Sect. 5 end the paper.

2   The Self-shrinking Generators

The **self-shrinking generator** was introduced by Meier and Sttafelbach in [7]. This generator is a more simple version of the shrinking generator [4], where the PN-sequence $\{a_i\} = \{a_0, a_1, \ldots\}$ generated by a maximum-length LFSR is self-decimated. In this case, consecutive pairs of bits are considered. If a pair happens to take the value 10 or 11, then it produces the bit 0 or 1, respectively. On the other hand, if a pair happens to be 01 or 00, then this pair is discarded. More formally speaking, the decimation rule can be described as follows: given two consecutive bits $\{a_{2i}, a_{2i+1}\}$, $i = 0, 1, 2, \ldots$, the output sequence $\{s_j\} =$

$\{s_0, s_1, \ldots\}$ is computed as:

$$\begin{cases} \text{If } a_{2i} = 1 \text{ then } s_j = a_{2i+1}, \\ \text{If } a_{2i} = 0 \text{ then } a_{2i+1} \text{ is discarded.} \end{cases}$$

The sequence $\{s_j\}$ is called the **self-shrunken sequence**. If L is the number of stages of the maximum-length LFSR, then the linear complexity of $\{s_j\}$, denoted by LC, meets the condition $2^{L-2} < LC \le 2^{L-1} - (L-2)$ [9]. In addition, the characteristic polynomial of this sequence has the form $p_{LC} = (x+1)^{LC}$ [7].

Example 1. Consider the LFSR of $L = 3$ stages with characteristic polynomial $p_1(x) = x^3 + x^2 + 1$ and initial state $\{100\}$. The PN-sequence generated is $\{1001110\ldots\}$. Now the self-shrunken sequence can be computed in the following way:

$$R : \underbrace{1 \quad 0}_{0} \quad 0 \quad 1 \quad \underbrace{1 \quad 1}_{1} \quad 0 \quad 1 \quad 0 \quad 0 \quad \underbrace{1 \quad 1}_{1} \quad \underbrace{1 \quad 0}_{0} \quad \cdots$$

The self-shrunken sequence $\{0110\ldots\}$ has period $T = 4$ and it is possible to check that its characteristic polynomial is $p_3(x) = (x+1)^3$, then $LC = 3$. ∎

The **modified self-shrinking generator** was introduced by Kanso in [8]. The PN-sequence $\{a_i\}$ generated by a maximum-length LFSR is self-decimated as follows: given three consecutive bits $\{a_{3i}, a_{3i+1}, a_{3i+2}\}_{i \ge 0}$, the output sequence $\{s_j\} = \{s_0, s_1, \ldots\}$ is computed as:

$$\begin{cases} \text{If } a_{3i} + a_{3i+1} = 1 \text{ then } s_j = a_{3i+2}, \\ \text{If } a_{3i} + a_{3i+1} = 0 \text{ then } a_{3i+2} \text{ is discarded.} \end{cases}$$

The output sequence $\{s_j\}$ is known as the **modified self-shrunken sequence**.
According to [8], if L is the number of stages of the LFSR, then the linear complexity LC of the modified self-shrunken sequence satisfies:

$$2^{\lfloor \frac{L}{3} \rfloor - 1} \le LC \le 2^{L-1} - (L-2),$$

and the period T, when L is odd, is given by

$$2^{\lfloor \frac{L}{3} \rfloor} \le T \le 2^{L-1}.$$

Furthermore, the characteristic polynomial of the modified self-shrinking sequences is of the form $p_{LC} = (x+1)^{LC}$ [10].

Example 2. Consider the LFSR with $L = 5$ stages with characteristic polynomial $p(x) = x^5 + x^2 + 1$ and initial state $\{11111\}$. The PN-sequence generated by this register is the following: $\{1111100011011101010000100101100\ldots\}$. Then, the corresponding modified self-shrunken sequence is given by $\{1100100101110010\}$. The obtained sequence has period $T = 16$ and it can be checked that its characteristic polynomial is $p_4(x) = (x+1)^4$, then $LC = 4$. ∎

The key of both generators is the initial state of the LFSR. Additionally, the characteristic polynomial of the register is also recommended to be part of the key.

Algorithm: Generating the t-modified self-shrunken sequence

Input: $p(x)$, $\boldsymbol{a}$, t
01:    Compute $T = 2^L - 1$.
02:    Compute $d = \gcd\{T, t\}$.
03:    Compute $t \cdot T/d$ bits of $\{a_i\}$ using the polynomial $p(x)$ and the initial state $\boldsymbol{a}$.
04:    Initialize $\boldsymbol{s}$.
05:    for i=1: $t \cdot T/d$
06:       if $\sum_{j=1}^{i+t-2} a_j = 1$
07:          Store a_{i+t-1} in $\boldsymbol{s}$.
08:       endif
09:    endfor
Output:
       The t-modified self shrunken sequence $\{s_j\}$

---

3   The t-modified Self-shrinking Generator

Consider an LFSR with L stages and characteristic polynomial $p(x)$ that generates the PN-sequence $\{a_i\}$. We can construct an **t-modified self-shrinking generator**, with $(t = 2, 3, \ldots, 2^L - 2)$ whose decimation rule is very simple: given t consecutive bits $\{a_{ti}, a_{ti+1}, a_{ti+2}, \ldots, a_{ti+(t-1)}\}$ of the PN-sequence, the t-modified self-shrunken sequence is computed as follows:

$$\begin{cases} \text{If } \sum_{j=0}^{t-2} a_{ti+j} = 1 \text{ then } s_j = a_{ti+(t-1)}, \\ \text{If } \sum_{j=0}^{t-2} a_{ti+j} = 0 \text{ then } a_{ti+(t-1)} \text{ is discarded.} \end{cases} \tag{1}$$

Notice that the value $t = 2$ gives rise the self-shrunken sequence while the value $t = 3$ produces the modified self-shrunken sequence.

Algorithm 1 shows how to generate the sequence produced by the t-modified self-shrinking generator, given the characteristic polynomial $p(x)$ of the LFSR, an initial state $\boldsymbol{a}$ and the parameter t.

Next, a simple example of t-modified self-shrinking generator is presented.

Example 3. Consider the PN-sequence sequence generated by the primitive polynomial $p(x) = x^7 + x + 1$ and the initial state $\{1111111\}$:

$\{1111111000000100000110000101000111100100010110011101010011111101000011$
$1000100100110110101101111011000110100101110111001100101010\}$.

The 5-modified self-shrunken sequence is given by:

$\{0010101000110110011010010000000111010101101111100101110010111100\}$.

This sequence has period $T = 64$ and linear complexity $LC = 57$. If we consider the classic modified self-shrunken sequence from the same PN-sequence, then the resultant sequence is given by:

$\{0010010111100011010100100110010000111111101010001101000111101010\}$.

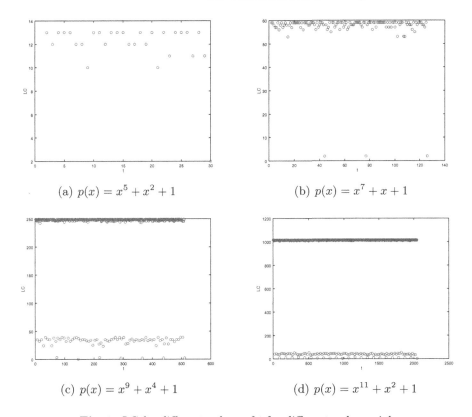

(a) $p(x) = x^5 + x^2 + 1$

(b) $p(x) = x^7 + x + 1$

(c) $p(x) = x^9 + x^4 + 1$

(d) $p(x) = x^{11} + x^2 + 1$

Fig. 1. LC for different values of t for different polynomials

This sequence has period $T = 64$ and linear complexity $LC = 59$. This means that the sequence generated by our 5-modified self-shrinking generator is comparable to the classic modified self-shrunken sequence in terms of period and linear complexity. ∎

In [8], the author considered exclusively modified self-shrinking generators where the LFSR characteristic polynomial had odd degree. In Fig. 1, it is possible to check the values of the linear complexity for several t-modified self-shrunken sequences with different values of t and different polynomial degrees.

In Fig. 1(a), we consider the LFSR with primitive polynomial $p(x) = 1 + x^2 + x^5$ and initial state $\{11111\}$. It is possible to check that the linear complexity of the sequences generated by different $t = 2, 3, \ldots, 30$ flutuates between 10 and 13.

In Fig. 1(b), we consider the LFSR with primitive polynomial $p(x) = 1 + x + x^7$ and initial state $\{1111111\}$. In this case, we consider $t = 2, 3, \ldots, 126$ and in most cases LC oscillates between the values 53 and 59. Nevertheless, there are also a few cases where the linear complexity is 2.

In Fig. 1(c), we consider the LFSR with a primitive polynomial $p(x) = 1 + x^4 + x^9$ (with degree different from a prime number) and initial state $\{111111111\}$.

In this case, it is possible to check that the range of values of LC is much wider than that of the previous examples. In most cases the LC is between 242 and 249. Nevertheless, there are other cases where the LC ranges in the interval between 20 and 40 as well as there are also a few cases with complexity 2, 3 or 0.

In Fig. 1(d), we consider the LFSR with primitive polynomial $p(x) = 1 + x^2 + x^{11}$ and initial state $\{11111111111\}$. In this case, 11 is prime but $2^{11} - 1$ is not prime and it happens the same fact as that of the previous case. In general, the LC is between 1000 and 1015. However, there are several cases where the LC is much smaller.

The previous numerical results for the LC of the t-modified self-shrunken sequences will be justified in next section.

4   Analysis of the Sequences

In order to analyse the characteristics of the t-modified self-shrunken sequences, two fundamental concepts, the generalized self-shrinking generator and the cyclotomic cosets, are introduced.

The generalized self-shrinking generator:

Let $\{a_i\}$ be a PN-sequence generated by a maximum-length LFSR of L stages. Let G be an L-dimensional binary vector $G = (g_0, g_1, g_2, ..., g_{L-1}) \in \mathbb{F}_{2^L}$ and $\{v_i\}$ a sequence defined as: $v_i = g_0 a_i \oplus g_1 a_{i-1} \oplus g_2 a_{i-2} \oplus \cdots \oplus g_{L-1} a_{i-L+1}$, where the symbol $\oplus$ represents the XOR logic operation. For $i \geq 0$, let us define the following decimation rule:

$$\begin{cases} \text{If } a_i = 1 \text{ then } s_j = v_i, \\ \text{If } a_i = 0 \text{ then } v_i \text{ is discarded.} \end{cases}$$

The sequence generator with the previous decimation rule is known as the **generalized self-shrinking generator** [11]. Its output sequence $\{s_j\}$, denoted by $s(G)$, is called the **generalized self-shrunken sequence** associated with the vector G.

When G ranges over $\mathbb{F}_{2^L}$, $\{v_i\}$ corresponds to the $2^L - 1$ possible shifts of $\{a_i\}$. Furthermore, the set of sequences denoted by $S(a) = \{s(G) \mid G \in \mathbb{F}_{2^L}\}$ is the **family of generalized self-shrunken sequences** based on the PN-sequence $\{a_i\}$.

It is worth noticing that the sequence $\{v_i\}$ is a shifted version of the sequence $\{a_i\}$. When the sequence $\{v_i\}$ is shifted 2^{L-1} bits regarding the sequence $\{a_i\}$ [12], then the generated sequence $\{s_j\}$ is the self-shrunken sequence introduced in Sect. 2. The family of generalized self-shrunken sequences includes the identically null sequence $\{0000...\}$, the identically 1 sequence $\{1111...\}$ and the sequences $\{1010...\}$ and $\{0101...\}$ with $T = 2$ and $LC = 2$. The remaining elements of this family are balanced and have period $T = 2^{L-1}$ and LC satisfies

$$2^{L-2} < LC \leq 2^{L-1} - (L - 2). \tag{2}$$

Table 1. Family $S(a)$ of GSS-sequences generated by $p(x) = x^3 + x + 1$

	G	$\{v_i\}$	s(G)
0	0 0 0	0 0 0 0 0 0 0	0 0 0 0
1	0 0 1	1 0 1 1 1 0 0	1 0 1 0
2	0 1 0	0 1 1 1 0 0 1	0 1 1 0
3	0 1 1	1 1 0 0 1 0 1	1 1 0 0
4	1 0 0	1 1 1 0 0 1 0	1 1 1 1
5	1 0 1	0 1 0 1 1 1 0	0 1 0 1
6	1 1 0	1 0 0 1 0 1 1	1 0 0 1
7	1 1 1	0 0 1 0 1 1 1	0 0 1 1
$\{a_i\}$		1 1 1 0 0 1 0	

Example 4. Consider the LFSR with characteristic polynomial $p(x) = x^3 + x + 1$ and output PN-sequence $\{1\ 1\ 1\ 0\ 0\ 1\ 0\}$. For this parameters, we can compute the generalized self-shrinking sequences shown in Table 1. The underlined bits in the different sequences $\{v_i\}$ are the digits of the corresponding $s(G)$ sequences. The PN-sequence $\{a_i\}$ is written at the bottom of the table. Note that in this example there are exactly 4 different sequences. The remaining sequences are just shifted versiones of these four sequences. Furthermore, the self-shrunken sequence computed in Example 1 corresponds to the GSS-sequence number 2.■

Now, let us consider the concept of cyclotomic coset $\mathrm{mod}(2^L - 1)$ given in [1].

Cyclotomic cosets $\mathrm{mod}(2^L - 1)$: Let $\mathbb{Z}_{2^L}$ denote the set of integers with 2^L elements. An equivalence relation R is defined on its elements $k_1, k_2 \in \mathbb{Z}_{2^L}$ such as follows: $k_1\ R\ k_2$ if there exists an integer j, $0 \leq j \leq L - 1$, such that

$$2^j \cdot k_1 = k_2\ \mathrm{mod}\ (2^L - 1).$$

The resultant equivalence classes into which $\mathbb{Z}_{2^L}^*$ is partitioned are called the **cyclotomic cosets** $\mathrm{mod}\ (2^L - 1)$. The leader element of every coset is the smallest integer in such an equivalence class. The cardinal of a coset (the number of elements in such a coset) is L or a proper divisor of L. The characteristic polynomial of a cyclotomic coset E is a polynomial $P_E(x) = (x + \alpha^E)(x + \alpha^{2E})...(x + \alpha^{2^{r-1}E})$, where the degree r ($r \leq L$) of $P_E(x)$ equals the cardinal of the coset E and α is a root of the LFSR characteristic polynomial.

Example 5. Consider the set $\mathbb{Z}_{2^5}^*$. There are six cyclotomic cosets given by:

$C_1 = \{1, 2, 4, 8, 16\}$ $C_5 = \{5, 10, 20, 9, 18\}$ $C_{15} = \{15, 30, 29, 27, 23\}$
$C_3 = \{3, 6, 12, 24, 17\}$ $C_7 = \{7, 14, 28, 25, 19\}$ $C_{11} = \{11, 22, 13, 26, 21\}$

In this case, all cosets are *proper* cosets in Golomb's terminology [1, Chap. 4] and have cardinal 5. ■

Notice that when $2^L - 1$ is prime, known as *Mersenne prime*, then the number of primitive polynomials of degree L coincides with the number of cyclotomic cosets of cardinal L in $\mathbb{Z}_{2^L}^*$. Furthermore, each coset has L elements and an associated primitive polynomial of degree L (see [1]).

Notice that when $2^L - 1$ is not prime, then different types of cyclotomic cosets can appear:

1. Cyclotomic cosets with cardinal L whose associated polynomial is primitive.
2. Cyclotomic cosets with cardinal L whose associated polynomial is irreducible but not primitive.
3. Cyclotomic cosets with cardinal r, where r is a proper divisor of L, whose associated polynomial is primitive or irreducible of degree r.

In fact, if $\gcd(2^L - 1, t) = 1$, then the PN-sequence $\{a_i\}$ decimated by distance t gives rise to a new PN-sequence $\{b_i\}$ and the sum $\sum_{j=0}^{t-2} a_{ti+j}$ of $t - 1$ bits in Eq. (1) is just a bit of $\{b_i\}$. Thus, in this case the decimation rule of the t-modified self shrinking generator coincides with that of the generalized self-shrinking generator [13].

Depending on the type of coset in which t takes values, the corresponding t-modified self-shrunken sequences will have different values for the linear complexity. Observing the previous examples, we can draw the following conclusions:

- When $2^L - 1$ is prime, all the t-modified sequences generated with $t = 2, 3, \ldots, 2^L - 2$ are generalized sequences obtained from different primitive polynomials of degree L. Thus, the LC of such sequences satisfies the Eq. (2). It is the case of Fig. 1(a) and (b) whose LC satisfies the Eq. (2) for $L = 5$ and $L = 7$, respectively. In particular, in Fig. 1(b) we can find some values of $LC = 2$ when the corresponding t-modified sequence is the sequence $\{1010\ldots\}$ or $\{0101\ldots\}$.
- When $2^L - 1$ is not prime we have observed different cases:
  - For t in cosets of cardinal L whose associated polynomial is primitive (that is when $\gcd(2^L - 1, t) = 1$), all the t-modified sequences generated are generalized sequences obtained from different primitive polynomials of degree L. Indeed, the greatest values of LC in Fig. 1(c) and (d) correspond to the upper bound of Eq. (2) for $L = 9$ and $L = 11$, respectively.
  - For t in cosets of cardinal L whose associated polynomial is irreducible (not primitive), the t-modified sequences generated are not generalized sequences nor necessarily balanced. This case corresponds to the intermediated values of Fig. 1(c). However, the balanced ones have relatively high LC compared with their periods. These sequences are cryptographically interesting.
  - For t in cosets where the cardinal is a proper divisor of L, the produced sequences are generalized sequences with low LC as long as the associated polynomials are primitive. This case corresponds to the lowest values of Fig. 1(c).

Table 2. t-modified sequences for $p(x) = x^5 + x^3 + x^2 + x + 1$

t	t-modified sequence	LC
2	1 1 0 1 0 1 1 1 1 0 0 0 0 0 1 0	10
3	0 1 0 1 1 0 1 0 0 1 1 0 0 1 1 0	13
4	1 1 1 1 1 0 1 0 0 0 0 1 0 1 0 0	12
5	0 1 1 1 1 0 0 1 1 0 0 1 1 0 0 0	13
6	0 0 1 1 1 0 1 1 0 0 1 1 0 1 0 0	13
7	0 0 0 1 1 1 1 1 0 1 0 0 1 0 1 0	10
8	1 1 0 0 1 1 0 1 0 0 1 0 1 1 0 0	13
9	0 1 0 0 1 1 0 0 1 1 0 0 1 0 1 1	13
10	1 0 0 1 0 0 1 0 0 1 0 1 1 1 1 0	11
11	1 0 1 1 1 1 0 1 0 0 1 0 0 1 0 0	11
12	1 1 1 1 0 1 0 0 1 0 0 0 1 1 0 0	13
13	0 0 1 0 1 1 0 0 0 1 1 1 0 1 1 0	13
14	1 1 1 1 0 0 0 1 0 0 0 0 1 1 1 0	9
15	1 0 1 1 0 1 0 0 0 0 0 1 1 1 1 0	10
16	1 0 1 1 1 0 0 1 0 0 0 0 1 1 0 1	13
17	1 1 0 0 0 0 1 0 0 0 1 1 1 1 0 1	9
18	0 1 0 1 1 1 1 0 0 0 1 1 1 0 0 0	11
19	1 0 0 1 0 0 1 1 0 0 1 0 0 1 1 1	13
20	0 0 0 0 1 0 1 1 1 1 0 1 0 1 1 0	12
21	0 1 1 1 1 1 0 1 0 0 0 0 1 0 1 0	12
22	1 1 0 1 1 0 0 0 1 1 1 0 0 1 0 0	13
23	0 1 0 1 0 1 0 1 0 1 0 1 0 1 0 1	2
24	1 0 1 0 0 1 0 1 1 1 1 1 0 0 0 0	10
25	0 0 1 1 0 1 1 0 0 1 1 0 1 1 0 0	13
26	0 0 1 0 1 0 0 1 1 1 1 1 0 1 0 0	12
27	0 0 1 1 0 0 0 0 1 0 1 1 0 1 1 1	13
28	1 0 1 0 1 0 1 0 1 0 1 0 1 0 1 0	2
29	0 0 0 0 0 1 1 1 1 0 1 0 1 1 0 1	10
30	1 0 1 0 1 0 1 0 1 0 1 0 1 0 1 0	2

Example 6. Let us consider the primitive polynomial $p(x) = x^5+x^3+x^2+x+1$. In Table 2 one can find the different t-modified sequences generated by $p(x)$ for different values of t. Since 2^5-1 is prime, all the sequences are generalized sequences produced by other primitive polynomials of degree 5. Indeed, in Example 5, we checked that all the cosets have length 5 and that the associated polynomial to each one is a primitive polynomial of degree 5. ∎

Let us consider a more complex example.

Table 3. Cosets for $L = 6$

Coset	Associated polynomial
$C_1 = \{1, 2, 4, 8, 16, 32\}$	$x^6 + x^5 + x^2 + x + 1$
$C_3 = \{3, 6, 12, 24, 48, 33\}$	$x^6 + x^5 + x^4 + x^2 + 1$
$C_5 = \{5, 10, 20, 40, 17, 34\}$	$x^6 + x^5 + x^3 + x^2 + 1$
$C_9 = \{9, 18, 36\}$	$x^3 + x + 1$
$C_7 = \{7, 14, 28, 56, 49, 35\}$	$x^6 + x^3 + 1$
$C_{11} = \{11, 22, 44, 25, 50, 37\}$	$x^6 + x^5 + 1$
$C_{13} = \{13, 26, 52, 41, 19, 38\}$	$x^6 + x + 1$
$C_{21} = \{21, 42\}$	$x^2 + x + 1$
$C_{15} = \{15, 30, 60, 57, 51, 39\}$	$x^6 + x^4 + x^2 + x + 1$
$C_{23} = \{23, 46, 29, 58, 53, 43\}$	$x^6 + x^4 + x^3 + x + 1$
$C_{27} = \{27, 54, 45\}$	$x^3 + x^2 + 1$
$C_{31} = \{31, 62, 61, 59, 55, 47\}$	$x^6 + x^5 + x^4 + x + 1$

Example 7. For $L = 6$ the distribution of cosets can be found in Table 3. Since $2^6 - 1$ is not prime, we have to analyse different cases :

- When t is such that $\gcd(2^6 - 1, t) = 1$, the corresponding cosets have primitive associated polynomials. In this case these cosets are: $C_1, C_5, C_{11}, C_{13}, C_{23}$ and C_{31}, each one associated to a primitive polynomial of degree 6. When $t \in C_i$ with $i = 1, 5, 11, 13, 23$, the t-modified sequences generated are generalized sequences. For example, for $p(x) = x^6 + x + 1$ and $t = 5 \in C_5$, we can generate the sequence $\{0010010111101010110110100100001\}$ which is a generalized sequence obtained with polynomial $1 + x + x^2 + x^5 + x^6$.
- For t such that $\gcd(2^6 - 1, t) \neq 1$, we observe two different cases:
  - C_3, C_7, C_{15} have cardinal equal to six and their associated polynomials are irreducible. In this case, the sequences produced are not generalized nor necessarily balanced. For example, for $t = 14 \in C_7$ and the same $p(x)$ considered before, we can generate $\{01000\}$, which is not a generalized sequence neither balanced.
  - C_9, C_{21}, C_{27} have cardinal less than 6 and their associated polynomials are primitive with degree less than 6. In this case, the elements t contained in these cosets produce generalized sequences with low LC. For instance, using $t = 21 \in C_{21}$ we generate the zero sequence and for $t = 27 \in C_{27}$ we can generate the sequence $\{1100\}$. ∎

5 Conclusions

In this work, we have proposed a generalized version of the modified self-shrinking generator by using and extended selection rule based on the XORred value of t bits of a PN-sequence. Via the concept of cyclotomic coset, we have classified the generated sequences and analysed their characteristics. Emphasis is on the linear complexity of such sequences. For some values of t, the t-modified sequences coincide with the sequences produced by the generalized self-shrinking generator. Thus, the t-modified self-shrinking generator here proposed provides a large class of sequences most of them with a clear application to stream cipher cryptography.

References

1. Golomb, S.W.: Shift Register-Sequences. Aegean Park Press, Laguna Hill (1982)
2. Delgado-Mohatar, O., Fúster-Sabater, A.: Software implementation of cryptographic sequence generators over extended fields. Logic J. IGPL **23**(1), 73–87 (2015)
3. Paar, C., Pelzl, J.: Understanding Cryptography. Springer, Berlin (2010). https://doi.org/10.1007/978-3-642-04101-3
4. Coppersmith, D., Krawczyk, H., Mansour, Y.: The Shrinking Generator. In: Stinson, D.R. (ed.) CRYPTO 1993. LNCS, vol. 773, pp. 22–39. Springer, Heidelberg (1994). https://doi.org/10.1007/3-540-48329-2_3
5. Cardell, S.D., Fúster-Sabater, A.: Modelling the shrinking generator in terms of linear CA. Adv. Math. Commun. **10**(4), 797–809 (2016)
6. Cardell, S.D., Fúster-Sabater, A., Ranea, A.: Linearity in decimation-based generators: an improved cryptanalysis on the shrinking generator. Open Math. **16**(1), April 2018
7. Meier, W., Staffelbach, O.: The self-shrinking generator. In: De Santis, A. (ed.) EUROCRYPT 1994. LNCS, vol. 950, pp. 205–214. Springer, Heidelberg (1995). https://doi.org/10.1007/BFb0053436
8. Kanso, A.: Modified self-shrinking generator. Comput. Electr. Eng. **36**(5), 993–1001 (2010)
9. Blackburn, S.R., Galbraith, S.: Cryptanalysis of two cryptosystems based on group actions. In: Lam, K.-Y., Okamoto, E., Xing, C. (eds.) ASIACRYPT 1999. LNCS, vol. 1716, pp. 52–61. Springer, Heidelberg (1999). https://doi.org/10.1007/978-3-540-48000-6_6
10. Cardell, S.D., Fúster-Sabater, A.: Recovering the MSS-sequence via CA. Proc. Comput. Sci. **80**, 599–606 (2016)
11. Hu, Y., Xiao, G.: Generalized self-shrinking generator. IEEE Trans. Inf. Theory **50**(4), 714–719 (2004)
12. Zhang, Y., Lei, J.G., Zhang, S.P.: A new family of almost difference sets and some necessary conditions. IEEE Trans. Inf. Theory **52**(5), 2052–2061 (2006)
13. Cardell, S.D., Fúster-Sabater, A.: Discrete linear models for the generalized self-shrunken sequences. Finite Fields Appl. **47**, 222–241 (2017)

Simulating Negotiation-Based Cloud Markets

Benedikt Pittl$^{(\boxtimes)}$, Werner Mach, and Erich Schikuta

Faculty of Computer Science, University of Vienna, Vienna, Austria
{benedikt.pittl,werner.mach,erich.schikuta}@univie.ac.at

Abstract. Today, the so called supermarket approach is used for trading Cloud services on Cloud markets. Thereby, consumers purchase Cloud services at fixed prices without negotiation. More dynamic Cloud markets are emerging as e.g. the recent development of the Amazon EC2 spot market shows - with spot blocks and spot fleet management. Hence, autonomous Bazaar-based negotiations are a promising approach for trading Cloud services on future Cloud markets. Thereby, market participants negotiate the characteristics of Cloud services which are described in Service Level Agreements (SLAs). Specifications such as the WS-Agreement Negotiation standard foster the development of such Bazaar-based Cloud markets.

In this paper we present a scientific simulation environment for the simulation of Bazaar-based Cloud markets which conforms to the WS-Agreement Negotiation standard. A two-stepped process is required for using the simulation environment: first consumers, intermediaries and providers have to be created, then strategies have to be assigned to them before the result of the simulation can be analyzed. The aim of the simulation environment is to support market participants during the evaluation of their negotiation strategies.

Keywords: Cloud simulation · Cloud market · Cloud SLAs

1 Introduction

A Cloud market is the culmination point of stakeholders providing and requiring services. Recently, Gartner predicted a growth of 38.6% for the Infrastructure as a Service (IaaS) market in 2017 [12]. Infrastructure services such as virtual machines (VMs) are mainly traded on provider platforms whereby Amazon Web Services (AWS) with the EC2 platform is market leader [9]. Amazon EC2 supports four different marketspaces for trading virtual machines: (i) On the reservation marketspace consumers and providers have a long-term relationship with a fixed, predefined price. (ii) A marketspace exists where consumers can resell virtual machines with a long-term contract - which were purchased on the reservation market - to other consumers. (iii) Consumers on the on-demand marketspace pay per hour for a virtual machine whereby the prices are higher than the prices on the reservation marketspace. (iv) The spot marketspace is more dynamic: here consumers can bid for virtual machines. The higher the bid, the higher is the chance of getting the virtual machine. The recent development of Amazons spot marketspace - with spot blocks and spot fleet management - shows that dynamic Cloud markets are gaining popularity. The notion of such a dynamic Cloud market is not a simple buyer-seller relationship, there are numerous other intermediaries involved in it. Papers of e.g. Weinmann [31,32] consider intermediaries as important players on future Cloud markets - see also [3,8,20]. Strategies as well as a detailed analysis of the impact of such intermediaries are missing. We envision a whole network of market participants which negotiate autonomously with each other against end-user requirements resulting into binding SLAs and consequently to a temporary value network. During negotiation the participants exchange offers and counteroffers - such negotiations are called Bazaar-based negotiations - see e.g. [17,24] for our previous work on this topic. Specifications such as the Web Service Agreement Negotiation specification (WS-Agreement) [30] support the development of such Bazaar-based Cloud markets. Due to the high number of different market participants as well as the infinite number of possible negotiation strategies, simulation environments are an eligible approach to assess the success of negotiation strategies under changing market conditions. For simulating such markets no appropriate frameworks exist: (i) The framework wsag4j [33] allows to create WS-Agreement documents in Java but has no simulation capabilities. (ii) The simulation environment greenCloud [14] was developed by the University of Luxembourg. It focuses on the simulation of energy consumption of Cloud infrastructures only. (iii) iCanCloud [21] is a Cloud simulation framework for analyzing trade-offs between costs and performance of a given set of applications executed on a certain hardware. (iv) Genius is a generic simulation environment focusing on negotiations without any Cloud specific simulation capabilities. (v) The CloudSim framework [5] was developed at the University of Melbourne and is widely used in the scientific community. It is able to simulate Cloud datacenters but no Cloud markets.

The previous ICCS conferences underpin a trend towards domain-specific simulation environments in the scientific community - see [1] for a detailed analaysis. So e.g. in [7] the authors present a simulation approach for search engine services with the special aim on measuring the impact of different configurations on the performance. In [11] the authors focused on simulating financial portfolios for stress testing scenarios with Suppes-Bayes Causal Networks while in [19] the authors developed a simulation environment for evacuation scenarios at the Gdansk University of Technology. Unlike generic simulation environments such as e.g. Genius[1] domain-specific simulation environments are designed for simulating a narrow domain comprehensively[2].

Due to the lack of a simulation environment which is able to simulate the envisioned Bazaar-based Cloud market we developed our own simulation envi-

---

[1] Genius is a negotiation simulation tool - see http://ii.tudelft.nl/genius/.

[2] The distinction between domain specific and generic simulation environment is fuzzy and a discussion about this is out of the scope of this paper.

ronment based on CloudSim. This framework (i) is well known by the community and, (ii) offers Cloud specific simulation capabilities. The subject of negotiation of our simulation environment is a virtual machine as an example of a Cloud service.

The remainder of the paper is structured as follows: In the following section we present foundations of Cloud markets. The architecture of the simulation environment is summarized in Sect. 3 while an overview of the implemented simulation environment is given in Sect. 4. Section 5 contains a summary of a use case which we executed with the simulation environment. The paper closes with the conclusion in Sect. 6.

2   Background

Amazon's EC2 on-demand marketspace[3] is an example of a platform which applies the supermarket approach. Here, consumers and providers trade services without negotiating price and service characteristics. More dynamic market mechanisms are currently emerging - see e.g. Amazon's EC2 spot marketspace [4]. The scientific community suggests e.g. auction-based approaches [4,28] or bilateral negotiation-based approaches [10,23] for future Cloud markets. Latter are based on the alternating exchange of offers which leads to negotiation trees - hence they are called Bazaar-based negotiations. The WS-Agreement Negotiation standard [30] is maintained by the Open Grid Forum and aims on specifying such negotiations. It is an extension to the WS-Agreement standard [2] and describes a XML based structure of offers as well as their possible states. In total the WS-Agreement Negotiation standard defines four states of offers. These four states and their transitions are illustrated in Fig. 1a.

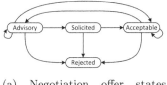

(a) Negotiation offer states (message types) of the WS-Agreement Negotiation standard

(b) High level architecture of the main components

Fig. 1. Offer states and architecture of the simulation environment

An offer in the advisory state requires further negotiation as it is e.g. not completely specified. The solicited state is used for offers which are completely

---

[3] https://aws.amazon.com/de/en/ec2/pricing/on-demand/.

[4] https://aws.amazon.com/en/ec2/spot/.

specified. The negotiation party which receives such an offer has to either accept the offer so that the state of the offer becomes acceptable or reject it which leads to the state rejected. Acceptable offers might result into agreements. Agreements are offers to which consumers and providers agree. Offers in the acceptable state of the WS-Agreement Negotiation standard are not binding: *The ACCEPT-ABLE state indicates that a negotiation participant is willing to accept a negotiation offer as it is.* But it is also described that *there is no guarantee that a subsequent agreement is created.* So in [16] we extended the specification by introducing a binding state. The rejected state is used for offers which are rejected. To improve the readability of the paper we call offers in the acceptable state acceptable messages, offers which are in the rejected state are termed reject messages and offers which are in the solicited state are called solicited messages. We use the term offers to either refer to all offers or to refer to offers in the advisory state - it should be clear from the context.

While the WS-Agreement Negotiation standard describes XML based offers and different states of offers, a concrete negotiation strategy is not specified. We surveyed existing bilateral service negotiation strategies in [25] but we have not found any WS-Agreement Negotiation compliant negotiation strategy. However, the need for WS-Agreement Negotiation compliant strategies was emphasized in [22,27]. Descriptions of negotiation frameworks such as in [13,18] elaborate on the importance of the WS-Agreement Negotiation standard without introducing compliant strategies. The negotiation strategy introduced in [34] mentions the WS-Agreement standard but does not use the WS-Agreement Negotiation standard. Instead, the strategy was developed to comply with the FIPA standard. In [29] a bilateral negotiation strategy was introduced. Thereby, the WS-Agreement Negotiation standard is mentioned but not considered for the introduced negotiation strategy. In [26] foundations of the simulation environment were introduced without a concrete negotiation strategy and use case.

Our analysis shows that the scientific community introduced bilateral SLA negotiation strategies. However, a systematic analysis of these strategies under changing market conditions is missing as well as a simulation environment which allows to asses and compare them.

3 Architecture Overview

Our simulation environment implements the concepts of the WS-Agreement standard described in Sect. 2. A high level architecture of the simulation environment is depicted in Fig. 1b. The simulation environment is based on CloudSim and uses fxyz for the creation of the 3D-View. There are three different types of participants: datacenter (representing providers), intermediary and broker (representing consumers). They inherit the structure and behavior of the CloudSim entity. Each entity has a negotiation manager which acts as a gateway: it forwards received messages to the corresponding negotiations. The negotiation component is a container which stores the negotiation history. Further, it has a reference to the used negotiation strategy. The components are detailed in the following paragraphs.

Negotiation Messages. Bazaar-based negotiations are characterized by the alternating exchange of offers between market participants. These offers are stored in messages - also termed events. In CloudSim, a event has three important fields which are summarized in Fig. 2a:

- The content of a message is stored in the field MsgContent which is of type *Object*.
- The type of a message is represented by the field MsgType. It is an integer and also termed tag. For example, the integer 2 represents the type of message *Register_Resource*. It is used by datacenters to register at the CIS[5].
- Each entity has an id which is used by CloudSim to deliver messages. This id is stored in the *To* field.

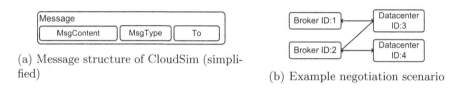

(a) Message structure of CloudSim (simplified)

(b) Example negotiation scenario

Fig. 2. Message structure and negotiation example

For the simulation environment we created tags representing the offer states defined in the WS-Agreement Negotiation specification.

Precondition for running negotiations on CloudSim is the exchange of offers. Therefore, the message content field cloud be used. A sender has to add its offer to the field *MsgContent*, set the type of message and set the destination using the *to* field. As CloudSim adds the entity id of the sender to CloudSim messages, the receiver is able to identify the sending entity - also termed source. Hence, entities could negotiate in parallel as Fig. 2b shows. Here, broker 2 negotiates with two datacenters in parallel. Entity 3 uses the added source field to distinguish between the two brokers. However, if an entity requires virtual machines e.g. for two different systems then it has two negotiations in parallel with another entity such as a datacenter. In such a case e.g. broker 3 is able to distinguish between the different entities using the source field. However, it is unable to distinguish between different negotiations with the same entity. This issue underpins the need of a negotiation id. Instead of adding offers directly to the message content field we suggest to use an intermediary object of type *NegotiationMessage* which is added to the field *MsgContent*. The most important fields are shown in Fig. 3a.

- Each negotiation message has an unique id (UDDI).
- Each negotiation message stores a reference to the preceding negotiation message (if existing).

---

[5] Cloud Information System - an internal CloudSim component.

– The source field represent the id of the entity which created the negotiation message. It is part of the negotiation message to simplify it's processing.
– In the field VM the offered virtual machine is stored.

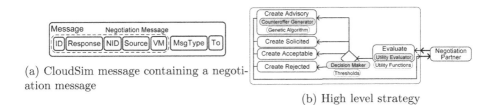

(a) CloudSim message containing a negotiation message

(b) High level strategy

Fig. 3. Negotiation message and summary of the high level strategy

Negotiation Manager. The negotiation manager is responsible for two tasks: forwarding negotiation messages and creating new negotiations. An example is depicted in Fig. 4. The CloudSim framework uses the entity id of the destination (field to) for forwarding messages. In the illustrated example, CloudSim forwards the message to the entity with the id 1. A negotiation entity - an entity which we introduced with our simulation environment - passes received messages to its negotiation manager. The negotiation manager checks, if the received message is a negotiation message (as described before). In such a case, the negotiation manager accesses the negotiation message stored in the received message and forwards it to the corresponding negotiation. If the negotiation does not exist, then the negotiation manager has to create one. In cases in which the received message is not a negotiation message the negotiation manager ignores it.

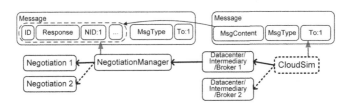

Fig. 4. Forwarding negotiation messages to the corresponding negotiation

Negotiation. The negotiation component acts as a container which stores the negotiation id as well as the negotiation history. Further, it has a reference to the used negotiation strategy - see next paragraph. The negotiation strategy creates offers which it forwards to the negotiation component, which forwards the offers to the negotiation manager. The negotiation manager adds the source to the negotiation message and forwards the message to the CloudSim framework which delivers the offer.

Strategy. The simulation environment simulates Cloud markets. Each market participant uses a negotiation strategy. The strategy is responsible for deciding how to repose to received offers. The user of the introduced simulation environment is responsible for creating them and assigning the strategies to the market participants. For test purposes, we implemented initial negotiation strategies which follow the high-level strategy process illustrated in Fig. 3b. The figure contains dark boxes as well as dashed boxes. Former are components of the strategy which are shown in Fig. 1b. Latter will be discussed in the following use case section. The process starts with the collection of received offers. Then, these offers are ranked. Thereby, utility functions such as described in [23] are used[6]. The ranking of the offers is the precondition for making decisions - in Fig. 3b the *decision maker* decides if an offer is rejected or if a counteroffer (an advisory message) is created. In all the other cases offers in the states *acceptable* and *solicited* will be created.

4   Simulation Environment

CloudSim supports the simulation of technical algorithms such as allocation algorithms which map physical resources to virtual resources (time-shared, space-shared) and VM placement algorithms (which determine which host runs which virtual machine). The negotiation process is usually executed before VMs are placed on datacenters. Free capacities - which is determined by the used technical algorithms - might be considered by negotiations strategies during negotiations. For our simulation environment we created a result view. Figure 5a depicts the structure of it. The numbers in the figure represent three sections. The main section is Sect. 3 which composes the menu bar as well as the other two sections. Section 1 shows the participants of the simulated market. By selecting a negotiation of a market participant its negotiation details are loaded into Sect. 2 which consists of two visualizations:

- The exchanged offers of a negotiation are visualized in a tree list. Each offer contains a description of a virtual machine - it's characteristics are shown in in the rows of the tree list.
- The utility-utility plot visualizes the tree list. As Fig. 7a shows, the ordinate shows the utility of the offers for the selected market participant (from Sect. 1) while the abscissa shows the utility of the offers of the negotiation partner. The points in the plot represent the exchanged messages which contain the offered VMs. The utility evaluator is responsible for assigning utility values to offers. The different colors indicate in which iteration an offer was exchanged. So e.g. the negotiation starts with an initial offer represented by a red point. The negotiation partner responds to this offer with counteroffers which are visualized by the green points. It is possible to calculate the Pareto-border which visualizes the efficiency of the exchanged offers.

---

[6] Utility values represent the satisfaction experienced by an individual from a good - for more information see [23].

The messages exchanged during negotiation can be further visualized using a 3D-Plot which is shown in Fig. 5b. Thereby, the white dots represent the offers while the axis represent the characteristics of the VMs contained in the offers. So the red axis represents the RAM, the blue axis represents the storage while the green axis represents the processing power.

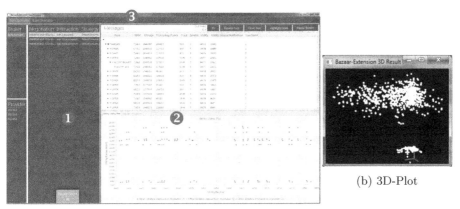

(b) 3D-Plot

(a) Screenshot of the GUI of the simulation environment based on JavaFX

Fig. 5. Screenshots of the simulation environment

Evaluations such as scalability test are out of the scope of this paper. Scalability tests for CloudSim are published in [6].

5   Use Case

In this section we summarize a consumer-provider negotiation scenario. Following the high level strategy depicted in Fig. 3b three components are necessary for a negotiation strategy. The dashed boxes show how we implemented these components for the use case. For the use case we reverted to utility functions developed in [23]. They are depicted in Table 1. The min/max values are part of the utility functions introduced in [23]. Usually, neither consumers nor providers will publish these values and so in our simulation environment market participants can not see these values of other market participants. U is a typical example of a utility function used by a consumer where the utility value increases with additional VM resources. For the decision maker predefined utility values were used as threshold. A genetic algorithm is used for creating counteroffers and considers the valuation of negotiation partners in the fitness function as suggested in [15]. By assuming that the utility functions of the negotiation partners are unknown the creator of a counteroffer has to estimate the utility functions used by the negotiation partners. This assumption is typical for bilateral negotiations

- see e.g. [10]. The utility function $\hat{U}$ in Table 1 represents an estimation of a typical utility function which is used by a provider and which represents the profit contribution. For example 0.001 are the estimated costs for 1 MB RAM. The most important parameters are summarized in Table 1. With a focus on demonstrating the described genetic algorithm we assumed these parameters. In the paper at hand we focus on the genetic algorithm only.

In the following we use the vector (x_1, x_2, x_3, x_4) for describing the characteristics of a virtual machine. The first element of the vector, x_1 represents the storage (GB), x_2 represents the processing power (MIPS), x_3 represents the RAM (GB) and x_4 represents the price ($). In the following, we describe the main components of the used genetic algorithm. The individuals generated using the genetic algorithm represent counteroffers.

Population. The population consists of the virtual machines which can be represented using the vectors introduced before. They are the individuals. We identified two options for generating the initial population.

1. The initial population is generated randomly without considering received offers.
2. The initial population is generated based on the received offer.

By using option 1 individuals will be created randomly so that they may not have a utility for the sender as well as for the receiver - more details are described in the following paragraph. Therefore, we used option 2. Here the initial population is created by modifying the received offer. For example, an individual is created by changing one of the before-mentioned characteristics of a virtual machine. So an individual could be created by modifying the RAM of the received virtual machine. Due to the following mutation and crossover operations the generated individuals will have less similarity with the received offers. However, they are more similar to the received offer than offers which are generated from a random initial population which is implied by option 1.

Fitness Function. The introduced fitness function aims on representing the utility of an offer for the sender as well as for the receiver. This results into a fitness function which has two components. The first component reflects the utility of an offer for the sender while the second component reflects the utility of an offer the receiver. As the sender does not know the utility function of the receiver it uses an estimated utility function $\hat{U}$ for the second component while it uses its own utility function for the first component. For generating estimated utility functions techniques such as genetic programming could be used. They are part of our further research and so they are not described in this paper. A high fitness value of an individual is an indicator that it has utility for the sender as well as for the receiver of the offer. Consequently, the probability that the offer is accepted is high.

However, the used estimated utility function could be imprecise so that an individual with a high fitness value might not have value for the receiver of the offer. In other words, the high fitness value could be result of a wrong estimated utility function. To avoid such errors we decided to use option 2 for creating the initial population in order to keep the counteroffer similar to the received offer - the received offer is generated by the receiver and so it usually has utility for the receiver. By using option 2 the received offer is used as guideline for the creation of counteroffers. This reduces the risk of creating offers with high fitness values and low utility for the receiver. The structure of the used fitness functions are shown in Eq. 1. The fitness function $F_{consumer}$ is used by consumers. It considers its utility function as well as an estimated utility function of the provider $\hat{U}_{provider}$. Similarly, the fitness function used by the provider considers its utility function and an estimated utility function of the consumer $\hat{U}_{consumer}$. The estimated utility functions have to be weighted with weight w for an adequate share. The higher the weight, the stronger is the consideration of the negotiation partner. Therefore, w is called *consideration factor*. For the scenarios we have pre-defined the size of w. In our simulation environment w could also be calculated dynamically.

$$F_{consumer} = U_{consumer} + \hat{U}_{provider} \cdot w, F_{provider} = U_{provider} + \hat{U}_{consumer} \cdot w \quad (1)$$

Crossover and Mutation. New generations are created using elitism, mutation and crossover operations as described in the following. (i) In our genetic algorithm we used elitism for creating a new generation. This implies that the fittest individuals become part of the next generation. (ii) While the fittest individuals of the previous generation become part of the next generation, the remaining individuals are generated using mutation and crossover. For the selection of the parents of new individuals a Roulette Wheel Selection is used during the crossover operation. Thus, the parent selection probability is proportional to the fitness of an individual:

$$P_i = \frac{F_i}{\sum_{n=0}^{p} F_n} \quad (2)$$

P_i represents the selection probability of an individual i, F_i is the fitness of the individual i while p is the size of the population. After the two parents are determined a new individual is generated by taking two characteristics of the virtual machine of the first parent while the other characteristics are taken from the second parent. (iii) The so generated new individuals are mutated with a certain probability. This means that one of their characteristics is randomly modified.

The fittest offers which result from the algorithm become counteroffers. Figure 6 depicts negotiation examples where different consideration factors were used. In all graphs the ordinate represents the utility of the provider and the abscissa represents the utility of the consumer. The initial offer is represented by a white point with a black border and the message exchanged between consumer and provider are visualized by grey points. In all figures the black points forming a border represent an approximation of the Pareto-border. Messages on that border are Pareto-optimal. In Fig. 6c the consumer uses a high consideration factor while in Fig. 6b the provider uses a high consideration factor. In the negotiations 6a and 6d consumer as well as provider use a moderate consideration factor. Consumer and provider use real utility functions ($\hat{U} = U$) in the negotiation depicted in Fig. 6a. So almost all points are on the Pareto-border.

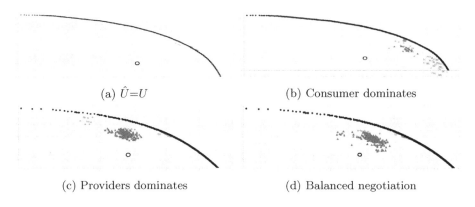

(a) $\hat{U}{=}U$ (b) Consumer dominates

(c) Providers dominates   (d) Balanced negotiation

Fig. 6. Screenshot of the result view of the simulation environment

The simulation environment supports two utility-utility plots. In the one depicted in Fig. 7a the ordinate represents the utility of the consumer while the abscissa represents the utility of the provider. The red dot represents the first offer with which the negotiation started. As already described, the colors of the other dots represent the negotiation round in which they were sent to the negotiation partner. The consumer created counteroffers in response to the first offer to which the provider responded with messages represented by green points. After the counteroffers were received, the provider responded to them with counteroffers visualized as blue triangles. A lot of offers have a great distance to the Pareto-border. The distance occurs because (i) the genetic algorithm calculates approximations and (ii) the estimated utility function $\hat{U}$ is imprecise.

(a) Utility-utility plot - ordinate represents $U_{consumer}$
(b) Utility-utility plot - ordinate represents $\hat{U}_{consumer}$

Fig. 7. Two utility-utility plots

Figure 7b visualizes the perspective of the provider where the ordinate represents the estimated utility ($\hat{U}_{consumer}$) of the consumer. The offers created

Table 1. Genetic algorithm setup summary

Parameters	Values	Parameters	Values
Population Size	96	Mutation Probability	5%
Received VM	(200,10000,7,30)	Elitism	best 5%

Fitness Function

$$U_x = \begin{cases} log(x) & x \geq Min_x \\ -\infty, & x < Min_x \end{cases} \quad x \in \{RAM, Storage, Proc.Power\}$$

$$U_{Price} = \begin{cases} log(Max_{Price} - Price + 1) & Price \leq Max_{Price} \\ -\infty, & Price > Max_{Price} \end{cases}$$

$$U = 1 \cdot U_{Price} + 1 \cdot U_{RAM} + 1 \cdot U_{Storage} + 1 \cdot U_{Proc.Power} + 100000$$

$$\hat{U} = Price - RAM \cdot 0.001 - Storage \cdot 0.0005 - Proc.Power \cdot 0.001$$

$$w = 25$$

by the provider are approximately Pareto-optimal - from the perspective of the provider (with the estimated utility function).

With a focus on the architecture as well as on the functional capabilities of the simulation environment we neglected non-functional characteristics such as performance which we see as part of our further research. An analysis of other possible negotiation strategies was done in [25]. This survey shows that Bayess theory is heavily used for negotiation strategies. We plan to implement and compare them with the introduced strategy.

6   Conclusion and Further Research

In this paper we presented a simulation environment based on CloudSim for the simulation of Bazaar-based Cloud markets. The simulation environment is compliant to the WS-Agreement negotiation specification. In the paper we describe its architecture as well as a negotiation strategy based on a genetic algorithm. Using the simulation environment brokers, intermediaries and datacenters are created, then negotiation strategies are assigned to them before the negotiation results can be analyzed.

In our future research we will develop further components based on the simulation environment: For example taxes on Cloud Markets have not been considered yet by the scientific community as well as smart contract technology which can be used for the created SLAs. Further, novel negotiation strategies based on deep learning techniques are part of our future research.

References

1. Abuhay, T.M., Kovalchuk, S.V., Bochenina, K.O., Kampis, G., Krzhizhanovskaya, V.V., Lees, M.H.: Analysis of computational science papers from ICCS 2001–2016 using topic modeling and graph theory. In: International Conference on Computational Science ICCS 2017, pp. 7–17, Zurich, Switzerland, 12–14 June 2017
2. Andrieux, A., Czajkowski, K., Dan, A., Keahey, K., Ludwig, H., Nakata, T., Pruyne, J., Rofrano, J., Tuecke, S., Xu, M.: Web services agreement specification (WS-Agreement). In: Open Grid Forum, vol. 128 (2007)

3. Böhm, M., Koleva, G., Leimeister, S., Riedl, C., Krcmar, H.: Towards a generic value network for cloud computing. In: Altmann, J., Rana, O.F. (eds.) GECON 2010. LNCS, vol. 6296, pp. 129–140. Springer, Heidelberg (2010). https://doi.org/10.1007/978-3-642-15681-6_10

4. Bonacquisto, P., Modica, G.D., Petralia, G., Tomarchio, O.: A strategy to optimize resource allocation in auction-based cloud markets. In: 2014 IEEE International Conference on Services Computing (SCC). IEEE, pp. 339–346 (2014)

5. Buyya, R., Ranjan, R., Calheiros, R.N.: Modeling and simulation of scalable cloud computing environments and the CloudSim toolkit: challenges and opportunities. In: 2009 International Conference on High Performance Computing & Simulation HPCS, pp. 1–11. IEEE (2009)

6. Calheiros, R.N., Ranjan, R., Beloglazov, A., Rose, C.A.F.D., Buyya, R.: Cloudsim: a toolkit for modeling and simulation of cloud computing environments and evaluation of resource provisioning algorithms. Softw. Pract. Exper. **41**(1), 23–50 (2011)

7. Carrión, J., Puntes, D.F., Luque, E.: Simulating a search engine service focusing on network performance. In: International Conference on Computational Science ICCS 2017, Zurich, Switzerland, pp. 79–88, 12–14 June 2017

8. Chhabra, S., Dixit, V.S.: Cloud computing: state of the art and security issues. ACM SIGSOFT Softw. Eng. Notes **40**(2), 1–11 (2015)

9. Coles, C.: Overview of cloud market in 2017 and beyond (2017). https://www.skyhighnetworks.com/cloud-security-blog/microsoft-azure-closes-iaas-adoption-gap. Accessed 14 Oct 2017

10. Dastjerdi, A.V., Buyya, R.: An autonomous reliability-aware negotiation strategy for cloud computing environments. In: 2012 12th IEEE/ACM International Symposium on Cluster, Cloud and Grid Computing (CCGrid), pp. 284–291. IEEE (2012)

11. Gao, G., Mishra, B., Ramazzotti, D.: Efficient simulation of financial stress testing scenarios with suppes-bayes causal networks. In: International Conference on Computational Science ICCS 2017, Zurich, Switzerland, pp. 272–284, 12–14 June 2017

12. Gartner: Gartner says worldwide public cloud services market to grow 18 percent in 2017. In: Gartner (2017). https://www.gartner.com/newsroom/id/3616417. Accessed 14 Oct 2017

13. Hudert, S., Ludwig, H., Wirtz, G.: Negotiating SLAs-an approach for a generic negotiation framework for WS-Agreement. J. Grid Comput. **7**(2), 225–246 (2009)

14. Kliazovich, D., Bouvry, P., Khan, S.U.: Greencloud: a packet-level simulator of energy-aware cloud computing data centers. J. Supercomput. **62**(3), 1263–1283 (2012)

15. Ludwig, S.A., Schoene, T.: Matchmaking in multi-attribute auctions using a genetic algorithm and a particle swarm approach. In: Ito, T., Zhang, M., Robu, V., Fatima, S., Matsuo, T. (eds.) New Trends in Agent-Based Complex Automated Negotiations. Studies in Computational Intelligence, vol. 383, pp. 81–98. Springer, Heidelberg (2012). https://doi.org/10.1007/978-3-642-24696-8_5

16. Mach, W.: A simulation environment for ws-agreement negotiation compliant strategies. In: Proceedings of the 18th International Conference on Information Integration and Web-based Applications and Services iiWAS 2017, Salzburg (2017)

17. Mach, W., Pittl, B., Schikuta, E.: A forecasting and decision model for successful service negotiation. In: 2014 IEEE International Conference on Services Computing (SCC), pp. 733–740. IEEE (2014)

18. Mach, W., Schikuta, E.: A generic negotiation and re-negotiation framework for consumer-provider contracting of web services. In: Proceedings of the 14th International Conference on Information Integration and Web-based Applications & Services, pp. 348–351. ACM (2012)
19. Malinowski, A., Czarnul, P., Czurylo, K., Maciejewski, M., Skowron, P.: Multi-agent large-scale parallel crowd simulation. In: International Conference on Computational Science ICCS 2017, Zurich, Switzerland, pp. 917–926, 12–14 June 2017
20. Mitchell, J.: What's the best way to purchase cloud services? IEEE Cloud Comput. **2**(3), 12–15 (2015)
21. Núñez, A., Vázquez-Poletti, J.L., Caminero, A.C., Castañé, G.G., Carretero, J., Llorente, I.M.: icancloud: a flexible and scalable cloud infrastructure simulator. J. Grid Comput. **10**(1), 185–209 (2012)
22. Pichot, A., Waeldrich, O., Ziegler, W., Wieder, P.: Dynamic SLA Negotiation Based on WS-Agreement. In: WEBIST (1), pp. 38–45 (2008)
23. Pittl, B., Mach, W., Schikuta, E.: A negotiation-based resource allocation model in IaaS-Markets. In: 2015 IEEE/ACM 8th International Conference on Utility and Cloud Computing (UCC), pp. 55–64. IEEE (2015)
24. Pittl, B., Mach, W., Schikuta, E.: Bazaar-extension: a cloudsim extension for simulating negotiation based resource allocations. In: IEEE International Conference on Services Computing SCC 2016, San Francisco, CA, USA, pp. 427–434, 27 June - 2 July 2016
25. Pittl, B., Mach, W., Schikuta, E.: A classification of autonomous bilateral cloud SLA negotiation strategies. In: Proceedings of the 18th International Conference on Information Integration and Web-based Applications and Services iiWAS 2016, Singapore, pp. 379–388, 28–30 November 2016
26. Pittl, B., Mach, W., Schikuta, E.: An implementation of the WS-agreement negotiation standard in Cloudsim. In: 20th IEEE International Enterprise Distributed Object Computing Workshop, EDOC Workshops 2016, Vienna, Austria, pp. 1–4, 5–9 September 2016
27. Rumpl, A., Waeldrich, O., Ziegler, W.: Extending WS-agreement with multi-round negotiation capability. In: Wieder, P., Yahyapour, R., Ziegler, W. (eds.) Grids and Service-Oriented Architectures for Service Level Agreements, pp. 89–103. Springer, Boston (2010). https://doi.org/10.1007/978-1-4419-7320-7_9
28. Samimi, P., Teimouri, Y., Mukhtar, M.: A combinatorial double auction resource allocation model in cloud computing. Inf. Sci. **357**, 201–216 (2014)
29. Silaghi, G.C., Erban, L.D., Litan, C.M.: A time-constrained SLA negotiation strategy in competitive computational grids. Future Gener. Comput. Syst. **28**(8), 1303–1315 (2012)
30. Waeldrich, O., Battr, D., Brazier, F., Clark, K., Oey, M., Papaspyrou, A., Wieder, P., Ziegler, W.: Ws-agreement negotiation version 1.0. In: Open Grid Forum (2011)
31. Weinman, J.: Cloud pricing and markets. IEEE Cloud Comput. **2**(1), 10–13 (2015)
32. Weinman, J.: Migrating to-or away from-the public cloud. IEEE Cloud Comput. **3**(2), 6–10 (2016). https://doi.org/10.1109/MCC.2016.45
33. WSAG4J: Wsag4j. http://wsag4j.sourceforge.net/site/index.html
34. Yan, J., Kowalczyk, R., Lin, J., Chhetri, M.B., Goh, S.K., Zhang, J.: Autonomous service level agreement negotiation for service composition provision. Future Gener. Comput. Syst. **23**(6), 748–759 (2007)

Structural Learning of Probabilistic Graphical Models of Cumulative Phenomena

Daniele Ramazzotti[1], Marco S. Nobile[2], Marco Antoniotti[2],
and Alex Graudenzi[2(✉)]

[1] Department of Pathology, Stanford University, Stanford, CA, USA
daniele.ramazzotti@stanford.edu
[2] Department of Informatics, Systems and Communication,
Università degli Studi di Milano-Bicocca, Milan, MI, Italy
{marco.nobile,marco.antoniotti,alex.graudenzi}@unimib.it

Abstract. One of the critical issues when adopting Bayesian networks (BNs) to model dependencies among random variables is to "learn" their structure. This is a well-known *NP*-hard problem in its most general and classical formulation, which is furthermore complicated by known pitfalls such as the issue of *I*-equivalence among different structures. In this work we restrict the investigation to a specific class of networks, i.e., those representing the dynamics of phenomena characterized by the *monotonic accumulation* of events. Such phenomena allow to set specific structural constraints based on Suppes' theory of probabilistic causation and, accordingly, to define constrained BNs, named *Suppes-Bayes Causal Networks* (SBCNs). Within this framework, we study the structure learning of SBCNs via extensive simulations with various state-of-the-art search strategies, such as canonical local search techniques and Genetic Algorithms. This investigation is intended to be an extension and an in-depth clarification of our previous works on SBCN structure learning. Among the main results, we show that Suppes' constraints do simplify the learning task, by reducing the solution search space and providing a temporal ordering on the variables, which simplifies the complications derived by *I*-equivalent structures. Finally, we report on tradeoffs among different optimization techniques that can be used to learn SBCNs.

1   Introduction

Bayesian Networks (BNs) are probabilistic graphical models representing the relations of *conditional dependence* among random variables, encoded in *directed acyclic graphs* (DAGs) [21]. In the last decades, BNs have been effectively applied in several different fields and disciplines, such as (but not limited to) diagnostics and predictive analytics [21].

One of the most challenging task with BNs is that of *learning* their structure from data. Two main approaches are commonly used to tackle this problem.

© Springer International Publishing AG, part of Springer Nature 2018
Y. Shi et al. (Eds.): ICCS 2018, LNCS 10860, pp. 678–693, 2018.
https://doi.org/10.1007/978-3-319-93698-7_52

1. *Constraint-based* techniques: mainly due to the works by Judea Pearl [26] and others, these approaches aim at discovering the relations of conditional independence from the data, using them as constraints to learn the network.
2. *Score-based* techniques: in this case the problem of learning the structure of a BN is defined as an *optimization* task (specifically, *maximization*) where the search space of the valid solutions (i.e., all the possible DAGs) is evaluated via *scores* based on a *likelihood function* [21].

Regardless of the approach, the main difficulty in this optimization problem is the huge number of valid solutions in the search space, namely, all the possible DAGs, which makes this task a known *NP*-hard one in its most general instance, and even when constraining each node to have at most two parents [9,10]. Therefore, all state-of-the-art techniques solve this task by means of meta-heuristics [21,23,35].

Moreover, the inference is further complicated by the well-known issue of *I-equivalence*: BNs with even very different structures can encode the same set of conditional independence properties [21]. Thus, any algorithm for structural learning can converge to a set of equivalent structures rather than to the correct one, given that the inference itself is performed by learning the statistical relations among the variables emerging from their induced distributions rather than the structure itself [21].

In this paper, we investigate the application of BNs for the characterization of a specific class of dynamical phenomena, i.e., those driven by the *monotonic accumulation of events*. In particular, the process being modeled/observed must imply:

1. a *temporal ordering* among its events (i.e., the nodes in the BN), and
2. a monotonic accumulation over time, which probabilistically entails that the occurrence of an earlier event must be *positively correlated* to the subsequent occurrence of its successors, leading to a *significant temporal pattern* [29].

An example can be found in the dynamics of *cascading failures*, that is a failure in a system of interconnected parts where the failure of a part can trigger the failure of successive parts. These phenomenon can happen in different contexts, such as power transmission, computer networking, finance and biological systems. In these scenarios, different configurations may lead to failure, but some of them are more likely than others and, hence, can be modeled probabilistically [5].

The two particular conditions mentioned above can be very well modelled by the notion of *probabilistic causation* by Patrick Suppes [19,34], and allow us to define a set of *structural constraints* to the BNs to be inferred, which, accordingly, have been dubbed as *Suppes-Bayes Causal Networks* (SBCNs) in previous works [4,29]. SBCNs have been already applied in a number of different fields, ranging from cancer progression inference [7,24,28] to social discrimination discovery [4] and stress testing [15].

We specifically position our work within the aforementioned optimization-based framework for BN structure learning. The goal of this paper is to investigate how structure learning is influenced by different algorithmic choices, when representing cumulative dynamical phenomena. In particular, it is known that given a *temporal ordering* on the variables (i.e., a partially ordered set among the events, *poset* in the terminology of Bayesian networks) of a BN, finding the optimal solution that is consistent with the ordering can be accomplished in time $O(n^k)$, where n is the number of variables and k the bounded in-degree of a node [6,12]. Thus, the search in the *space of orderings* can be performed way more efficiently than the search in the *space of structures*, as the search space is much smaller, the branching factor is lower and acyclicity checks are not necessary [30,35].

The determination of the right ordering ordering. in complex dynamical phenomena is generally a difficult task, which often requires considerable domain knowledge. However, the representation of cumulative phenomena via SBCNs allows to soften this hurdle, as Suppes' constraints dramatically reduce the search space of valid solutions, also providing a temporal ordering on the variables. This represents a serious theoretical advancement in structure learning of BNs for the modeling of cumulative phenomena, which we investigate in this work with a series of synthetic experiments.

In particular, in this paper we quantitatively assess the performance of learning the structure of a BN when:

- the temporal ordering among variables is given/not given, i.e., when Suppes' constraints are imposed/not imposed (in the former case we deal with SBCNs);
- different heuristic search strategies are adopted, i.e., *Hill Climbing* (HC), *Tabu Search* (TS), and *Genetic Algorithms* (GA);
- different regularization terms are used, i.e., *Bayesian Information Criterion* (BIC) and *Akaike information criterion* (AIC).

2   Methods

In this Section we present the foundations of our framework and, specifically, we define the main characteristics of the SBCNs and of some heuristic strategies for the likelihood fit. Without losing in generality, from now on, we consider a simplified formulation of the problem of learning the structure of BNs where all the variables depicted in the graph are Bernoulli random variables, i.e., their support is $(0, 1)$. All the conclusions derived in these settings can be also directly applied to the general case where the nodes in the BN describe geneal random variables [21].

More precisely, we consider as an input for our learning task a dataset D of n Bernoulli variables and m cross-sectional samples. We assume the value 1 to indicate that a given variable has been observed in the sample and 0 that the variable had not been observed.

2.1   Suppes-Bayes Causal Networks

In [34], Suppes introduced the notion of *prima facie causation*. A prima facie relation between a cause u and its effect v is verified when the following two conditions are true.

1. *Temporal Priority* (TP): any cause happens before its effect.
2. *Probability Raising* (PR): the presence of the cause raises the probability of observing its effect.

Definition 1 (Probabilistic Causation, [34]). *For any two events u and v, occurring respectively at times t_u and t_v, under the mild assumptions that $0 < \Pr(u), \Pr(v) < 1$, the event u is called a* prima facie cause *of v if it occurs before and raises the probability of u, i.e.,*

$$\begin{cases} \text{(TP)} & t_u < t_v \\ \text{(PR)} & \Pr(v \mid u) > \Pr(v \mid \neg u) \end{cases} \tag{1}$$

The notion of prima facie causality has known limitations in the context of the general theories of causality [19], however, this characterization seems to appropriate to model the dynamics of phenomena driven by the monotonic accumulation of events where a temporal order among them is implied and, thus, the occurrence of an early event positively correlates to the subsequent occurrence in time of a later one. Let us now refer again to systems where cascading failure may occur: some configurations of events, in a specific order, may be more likely to cause a failure than others. This condition leads to the emergence of an observable *temporal pattern* among the events captured by Suppes' definition of causality in terms of statistical relevance, i.e., statistical dependency.

Let us now consider a graphical representation of the aforementioned dynamics in terms of a BN $G = (V, E)$. Furthermore, let us consider a given node $v_i \in V$ and let us name $\pi(v_i)$ the set of all the nodes in V pointing to (and yet temporally preceding) v_i. Then, the joint probability distribution of the $n = |V|$ variables induced by the BN can be written as:

$$\Pr(v_1, \dots, v_n) = \prod_{v_i \in V} \Pr(v_i | \pi(v_i)) \tag{2}$$

When building our model, we need to constrain the characteristics of the considered relations as depicted in the network (i.e., the arcs in the graph), in order to account for the cumulative process above mentioned, which, in turns, needs to be reflected in its induced probability distribution [29]. To this extent, we can define a class of BNs over Bernoulli random variables named *Monotonic Progression Networks* (MPNs) [14,22,29]. Intuitively, MPNs represent the progression of events monotonically[1] accumulating over time, where the conditions for any event to happen is described by a probabilistic version of the canonical

---

[1] The events accumulate over time and when later events occur, earlier events are observed as well.

boolean operators, i.e., conjunction ($\wedge$), inclusive disjunction ($\vee$), and exclusive disjunction ($\oplus$).

MPNs can model accumulative phenomena in a probabilistic fashion, i.e., they are also modeling irregularities (noise) in the data as a small probability ε of not observing later events given their predecessors.

Given these premises, in [28] the authors describe an efficient algorithm (named CAPRI, see [28] for details) to learn the structure of constrained Bayesian networks which account for Suppes' criteria and which later on are dubbed *Suppes-Bayes Causal Networks* (SBCNs) in [4]. SBCNs are well suited to model cumulative phenomena as they may encode irregularities in a similar way to MPNs [29]. The efficient inference schema of [29] relies on the observation (see [35]) that a way for circumventing the intrinsic computational complexity of the task of learning the structure of a Bayesian Network is to postulate a pre-determined ordering among the nodes. Intuitively, CAPRI exploits Suppes' theory to first mine an ordering among the nodes, reducing the complexity of the problem, and then fits the network by means of likelihood maximization. In [29] it is also shown that a SBCN, learned using CAPRI, can also embed the notion of accumulation through time as defined in a MPN, and, specifically, conjunctive parent sets; nevertheless SBCNs can easily be generalized to represent all the canonical boolean operators (*Extended Suppes-Bayes Causal Networks*), notwithstanding an increase of the algorithmic complexity [29]. We refer the reader to [29] for further details and, following [4], we now formally define a SBCN.

Definition 2 (Suppes-Bayes Causal Network)
Given an input cross-sectional dataset D of n Bernoulli variables and m samples, the Suppes-Bayes Causal Network $SBCN = (V, E)$ subsumed by D is a directed acyclic graph such that the following requirements hold:

1. [**Suppes' constraints**] for each arc $(u \rightarrow v) \in E$ involving the selective advantage relation between nodes $u, v \in V$, under the mild assumptions that $0 < \Pr(u), \Pr(v) < 1$:

$$\Pr(u) > \Pr(v) \quad and \quad \Pr(v \mid u) > \Pr(v \mid \neg u). \tag{3}$$

2. [**Simplification**] let E' be the set of arcs satisfying the Suppes' constraints as before; among all the subsets of E', the set of arcs E is the one whose corresponding graph maximizes the log-likelihood $\mathcal{LL}$ of the data and the adopted regularization function $R(f)$:

$$E = \underset{E \subseteq E', G=(V,E)}{\arg\max} \; \mathcal{LL}(G, D) - R(f). \tag{4}$$

Before moving on, we once again notice that the efficient implementation of Suppes' constraints of CAPRI does not, in general, guarantee to converge to the monotonic progression networks as depicted before. To overcome this limitation, one could extend the Algorithm in order to learn, in addition to the network structure, also the logical relations involving any parent set, increasing the overall computational complexity. Once again, we refer the interested reader to the discussions provided in [28,29] and, without losing in generality, for the purpose of this work, we consider the efficient implementation of CAPRI presented in [28].

It is important to remark that the evaluation of Suppes' constraints might be extended to longer serial dependence relations, by assessing, for instance, the statistical dependency involving more than two events. We here decide to evaluate pairwise conditions to keep the overall computational complexity at a minimum. However, we leave the investigation of this issue to further development of the framework.

2.2 Optimization and Evolutionary Computation

The problem of the inference of SBCNs can be re-stated as an optimization problem, in which the goal is the maximization of a likelihood score. Regardless of the strategy used in the inference process, the huge size of the search space of valid solutions makes this problem very hard to solve. Moreover, as stated above, the *general* problem of learning the structure of a BN is *NP*-hard [10][2]. Because of that, state-of-the-art techniques largely rely on heuristics [21], often based on stochastic global optimization methods like Genetic Algorithms (GAs) [23,29]. Methods for BN learning can roughly be subdivided into two categories: single individual or population-based meta-heuristics.

Hill Climbing (HC) and Tabu Search (TS) both belong to the first category. The former is a greedy approach for the structural learning of BNs, in which new edges are attached to the current putative solution as long as they increase the likelihood score and they do not introduce any cycles in the network. TS is a stochastic variant of HC able to escape local minima, in which solutions visited in the past are not repeated by means of a tabu list.

GAs [20], a global search methodology inspired by the mechanisms of natural selection, belong to the second category. GAs were shown to be effective for BN learning, both in the case of available and not available *a priori* knowledge about nodes' ordering [23,29]. In a GA, a population $\mathfrak{P}$ of candidate solutions (named individuals) iteratively evolves, converging towards the global optimum of a given fitness function f that, in this context, corresponds to the score to be maximized. The population $\mathfrak{P}$ is composed of Q randomly created individuals, usually represented as fixed-length strings over a finite alphabet. These strings encode putative solutions of the problem under investigation; in the case of BN learning, individuals represent linearized adjacency matrices of candidate BNs with K nodes, encoded as string of binary values whose length[3] is $O(K^2)$.

---

[2] We are aware of *special* formulations of the problem that are solvable in polynomial time. Their existence points to interesting questions regarding the "barrier" between *NP* problems and polynomial ones; however, these are questions beyond the scope of the present paper.

[3] Since BNs are DAGs, the representation can be reduced by not encoding the elements on the diagonal, which are always equal to zero. In such case, the strings representing the individual have length $K \times K - K$.

The individuals in $\mathfrak{P}$ undergo an iterative process whereby three genetic operators—selection, crossover and mutation—are applied in sequence to simulate the evolutionary recombination process, which results in a new population of possibly improved solutions. During the selection process, individuals from $\mathfrak{P}$ are chosen, using a fitness-dependent sampling procedure [3], and are inserted into a new temporary population $\mathfrak{P}'$. The crossover operator is then used to recombine the structures of two promising selected parents. Finally, the mutation operator replaces an arbitrary symbol of an offspring, with a probability $\mathcal{P}_m$, using a random symbol taken from the alphabet. In the case of BNs, the mutation consists in flipping a single bit of the individual with a certain probability. It is worth noting that in the case of ordered nodes both crossover and mutation are *closed* operators, because the resulting offsprings always encode valid DAGs. To the aim of ensuring a consistent population of individuals throughout the generations, in the case of unordered nodes the two operators are followed by a correction procedure, in which the candidate BN is analyzed to identify the presence of invalid cycles. For further information about our implementation of GAs for the inference of BNs, including the correction phase, we refer the interested reader to [29].

3   Results

We now discuss the results of a large number of experiments we conducted on simulated data, with the aim of assessing the performance of the state-of-the-art score-based techniques for the BN structure inference, and comparing the performance of these methods with the learning scheme defined in CAPRI.

Our main objective is to investigate how the performance is affected by different algorithmic choices at the different steps of the learning process.

Data Generation. All simulations are performed with the following generative models. We consider 6 different topological structures.

1. *Trees*: one predecessor at most for any node, one unique root (i.e., a node with no parents).
2. *Forests*: likewise, more than one possible root.
3. *Conjunctive DAGs with single root*: 3 predecessors at most for each node, all the confluences are ruled by logical conjunctions, one unique root.
4. *Conjunctive DAGs with multiple roots*: likewise, possible multiple roots.
5. *Disjunctive DAGs with single root*: 3 predecessors at most for each node, all the confluences are ruled by logical disjunctions, one unique root.
6. *Disjunctive DAGs with multiple roots*: likewise, possible multiple roots.

We constrain the induced distribution of each generative structure by implying a cumulative model for either conjunctions or disjunctions, i.e., any child node cannot occur if its parent set is not activated as described for the MPN in the Method Sect. 2. For each of these configurations, we generate 100 random structures. Furthermore, we simulate a model of noise in terms of random observations (i.e., false positives and false negatives) included in the generated datasets with different rates.

These data generation configurations are chosen to reflect: (a) different structural complexities of the models in terms of number of parameters, i.e., arcs, to be learned, (b) different types of induced distributions suitable to model cumulative phenomena as defined by the MPNs (see Sect. 2.1), i.e., conjunction ($\wedge$) or inclusive disjunction ($\vee$)[4] and, (c) situations of reduced sample sizes and noisy data.

We here provide an example of data generation. Let now n be the number of nodes we want to include in the network and let us set $p_{\min} = 0.05$ and $p_{\max} = 0.95$ as the minimum and maximum probabilities of any node. A *directed acyclic graph without disconnected components* (i.e., an instance of types (3) and (5) topologies) with maximum depth $\log n$ and where each node has at most $w^* = 3$ parents is generated.

Algorithm 1. Data generation: single source directed acyclic graphs

---

Input: n, the number of nodes of the graph, $p_{\min} = 0.05$ and $p_{\max} = 0.95$ be the minimum and maximum probabilities of any node and $w^* = 3$ the maximum incoming edges per node.

Result: a randomly generated single source directed acyclic graph.

1 Pick an event $r \in G$ as the root of the directed acyclic graph;
2 Assign to each node $u \neq r$ an integer in the interval $[2, \lceil \log n \rceil]$ representing its depth in the graph (1 is reserved for r), ensuring that each level has at least one node;
3 **forall the** *nodes* $u \neq r$ **do**
4   Let l be the level assigned to the node;
5   Pick $|\Pr(u)|$ uniformly over $(0, w^*]$, and accordingly define the parents of u with events selected among those at which level $l - 1$ was assigned;
6 **end**
7 Assign $\Pr(r)$, a random value in the interval $[p_{\min}, p_{\max}]$;
8 **forall the** *events* $u \neq r$ **do**
9   Let α be a random value in the interval $[p_{\min}, p_{\max}]$;
10   Let $\pi(u)$ be the direct predecessor of u;
11   Then assign:
$$\Pr(u) = \alpha \Pr(x \in \pi(u));$$
12 **end**
13 **return** *The generated single source directed acyclic graph.*

Performance Assessment. In all these configurations, the performance is assessed in terms of:

– accuracy $= \dfrac{(TP+TN)}{(TP+TN+FP+FN)}$;

---

[4] Here we stick with the efficient search scheme of CAPRI and, for this reason, we do not consider exclusive disjunction ($\oplus$) parent sets.

- sensitivity $= \frac{TP}{(TP+FN)}$;
- specificity $= \frac{TN}{(FP+TN)}$;

with TP and FP being the true and false positives (we mark as positive any arc that is present in the network) and TN and FN being the true and false negatives (we mark negative any arc that is not present in the network) with respect to the generative model. All these measures are values in $[0,1]$ with results close to 1 indicators of good performance.

Implementation. In all the following experiments, the adopted likelihood functions (i.e., the fitness evaluations) are implemented using the *bnlearn* package [33] written in the R language, while GA [20] the *inspyred* [16], *networkx* [31] and *numpy* [25] packages.

The framework for the inference of SBCNs is implemented in R and is available in the TRONCO suite for TRanslational ONCOlogy [2,13]. TRONCO is available under a GPL3 license at its webpage: https://sites.google.com/site/troncopackage or on Bioconductor.

Algorithm Settings. We test the performance of classical search strategies, such as Hill Climbing (HC) and Tabu Search (TS), and of more sophisticated algorithms such Genetic Algorithms (GA)[5].

For HC and TS, we generate data as described above with networks of 10 and 15 nodes (i.e., 0/1 Bernoulli random variables). We generated 10 independent datasets for each combination of the 4 sample levels (i.e., 50, 100, 150 and 200 samples) and the 9 noise levels (i.e., from 0% to 20% with step 2.5%) for a total of $4,320,000$ independent datasets. The experiments were repeated either (*i*) including or (*ii*) not including the Suppes' constraints described in CAPRI [28], and independently using 5 distinct optimization scores and regularizators, namely standard (*i*) log-likelihood [21], (*ii*) AIC [1], (*iii*) BIC [32], (*iv*) BDE [18] and (*v*) K2 [11], leading to a final number of $86,400,000$ different configurations.

Being more precise, given an input dataset of observations D and a graphical model G, we can define a function to evaluate the goodness of this structure given the data:

$$f(G,D) = \mathcal{LL}(D|G) - \mathcal{R}(G),$$

where $\mathcal{LL}(\cdot)$ is the log-likelihood, while $\mathcal{R}(\cdot)$ is a regularization term with the aim of limiting the complexity of G. The DAG induced by G in fact defines a probability distribution over its nodes, namely $\{x_1, \ldots, x_n\}$:

$$\Pr(x_1, \ldots, x_n) = \prod_{x_i=1}^{n} \Pr(x_i \mid \pi_i), \qquad \Pr(x_i \mid \pi_i) = \boldsymbol{\theta}_{x_i|\pi_i},$$

---

[5] Further experiments on multi-objective optimization techniques, such as *Nondominated Sorting Genetic Algorithm* (NSGA- II), were performed, but are not shown here because of the worse overall performance, and of the higher computational cost, with respect to canonical GA.

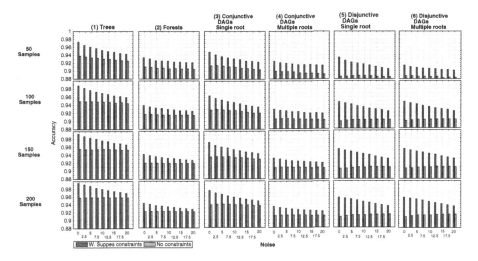

Fig. 1. Performance in terms of accuracy for the 6 considered structures with 15 nodes, noise levels from 0% to 20% with step 2.5% and sample sizes of 50, 100, 150 and 200 samples. Here we use BIC as a regularization scheme and we consider HC as a search strategy both for the classical case and when Suppes' priors are applied.

where $\pi_i = \{x_j \mid x_j \rightarrow x_i \in G\}$ are x_i's parents in the DAG, and $\theta_{x_i \mid \pi(x_i)}$ is a density function. Then, the log-likelihood of the graph can be defined as:

$$\mathcal{LL}(D|G) = log\Pr(D \mid G, \boldsymbol{\theta})\,.$$

Then, the regularization term $\mathcal{R}(G)$ introduces a penalty for the number of parameters in the model G also considering the size of the data. The above mentioned scores that we considered differ in this penalty, with AIC and BIC being Information-theoretic score and BDE and K2, Bayesian scores [8].

While a detailed description of these regularizators is beyond the scope of this paper, we critically discuss the different performances granted by each strategy for the inference of BNs.

With respect to GA we used a restricted data generation settings, using networks of 15 nodes, datasets of 100 samples and 5 noise levels (from 0% to 20% with step 5%) for a total of 3,000 independent datasets. We tested the GA either (*i*) with or (*ii*) without Suppes' constraints, using BIC regularization term, leading to the final total of 6,000 different configurations. Finally, the GA was launched with a population size of 32 individuals, a mutation rate of $p_m = 0.01$ and 100 generations.

We summarize the performance evaluation of the distinct techniques and settings in the next Subsections and in Figs. 1, 2, 3 and 4.

Performance Assessment

By looking at Fig. 1, one can first appreciate the variation of accuracy with respect to a specific search strategy, i.e., HC with BIC, which is taken as an

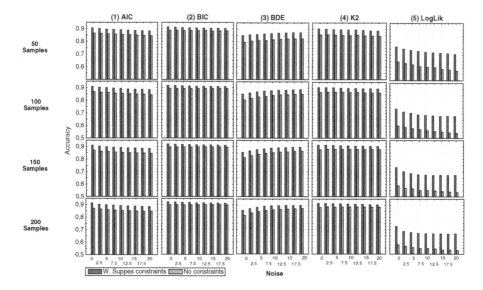

Fig. 2. Performance in terms of accuracy for directed acyclic graphs with multiple sources and disjunctive parents (structure vi) of 15 nodes, noise levels from 0% to 20% with step 2.5% and sample sizes of 50, 100, 150 and 200 samples. Here we consider HC as a search strategy both for the classical case and when Suppes' priors are applied and we show the results for all five regularizators introduced in the text.

example of typical behavior. In brief, the overall performance worsens with respect to: (i) a larger number of nodes in the network, (i) more complex generative structures, and (iii) smaller samples sizes/higher noise rates. Although such a trend is intuitively expected, given the larger number of parameters to be learned for more complex models, we here underline the role of statistical complications, such as the presence of *spurious correlations* [27] and the occurrence of *Simpson's paradox* [17].

For instance, it is interesting to observe a typical decrease of the accuracy when we compare topologies with the same properties, but different number of roots (i.e., 1 root vs. multiple roots). In the former case, we expect, in fact, a lower number of arcs (i.e., dependencies) to be learned (on average) and, hence, we may attribute the decrease of the performance to the emergence of spurious correlations among independent nodes, such as the children of the different sources of the DAG. This is due to the fact that, when sample sizes are not infinite, it is very unlikely to observe perfect independence and, accordingly, the likelihood scores may lead to overfitting. The trends displayed in Fig. 1 are shared by most of the analyzed search strategies.

Role of the Regularization Term. By looking at Fig. 2 one can first notice that the accuracy with no regularization is dramatically lower than the other cases, as a consequence of the expected overfitting (in this case we compare the performance of HC on disjunctive DAGs with multiple roots, but the trend is maintained in

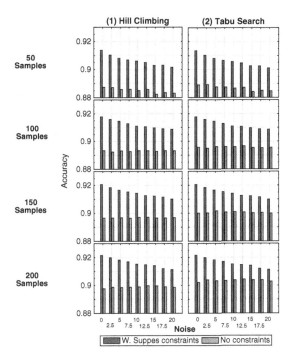

Fig. 3. Performance in terms of accuracy for directed acyclic graphs with multiple sources and disjunctive parents (structure vi) of 15 nodes, noise levels from 0% to 20% with step 2.5% and sample sizes of 50, 100, 150 and 200 samples. Here we use BIC as a regularization scheme and we consider both HC and TB as search strategies for the classical case and when Suppes' priors are applied.

the other cases). Conversely, all regularization terms ensure the inference of sparser models, by penalizing the number of retrieved arcs. BDE regularization term seems to be the only exception (see Fig. 2), leading to unintuitive behaviors: in fact, while for all the other methods the performance decreases when higher level of noise are applied, for BDE the accuracy seems to improve with higher noise rates. This result might be explained by observing that given a topological structure, structural spurious correlations may arise between a given node and any of its undirected predecessors (i.e., one of the predecessors of its direct parents): with higher error rates, and, accordingly, more random samples in the datasets, all the correlations are reduced, hence leading to a lower impact of the regularization term. Given these considerations, one can hypothesize that the overall trend of BDE is due to a scarce penalization to the likelihood fit, favoring dense networks rather than sparse ones.

Search Strategies. No significant differences in the performance between the accuracy of HC, TS and GA are observed. However, one can observe a consistent improvement in sensitivity when using GA (see Figs. 3 and 4). This suggests different inherent properties of the search schemes: while with HC and TB the

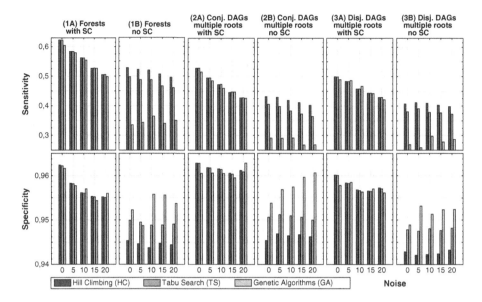

Fig. 4. Performance of HC, TB and GA, in terms of sensitivity and specificity for forests (panels 1A, 1B), directed acyclic graphs with multiple sources and conjunctive parents (panels 2A, 2B) and directed acyclic graphs with multiple sources and disjunctive parents (panels 3A, 3B) (configurations (*ii*), (*iv*) and (*vi*)) of 15 nodes, noise levels from 0% to 20% with step 5% and sample sizes of 100 samples. Here we use BIC as a regularization scheme for HC and TB, and for all the algorithms we either consider (panels A) or not consider (panels B) Suppes' constraints (SC).

regularization terms, rather than the search strategy, account for most of the inference performance, GAs are capable of returning denser networks with better hit rates. This is probably due to GA's random mutations, which allow jumps into areas of the search space characterized by excellent fitness, which could not be reached by means of greedy approaches like HC.

Suppes' Structural Constraints. Finally, the most important result, which can be observed across all the different experiments, is that the overall performance of all the considered search strategies is dramatically enhanced by the introduction of Suppes' structural constraints. In particular, as one can see, e.g., in Fig. 1, there is a constant improvement in the inference, up to 10%, when Suppes' priors are used. Even though the accuracy of the inference is affected by the noise in the observations, in fact, the results with Suppes' priors are consistently better than the inference with no constraints, with respect to all the considered inference settings and to all the performance measures. This is an extremely important result as it proves that the introduction of structural constraints based on Suppes' probabilistic causation indeed simplify the optimization task, by reducing the huge search space, when dealing with BNs describing cumulative phenomena.

4   Conclusion

In this paper we investigated the structure learning of Bayesian Networks aimed at modeling phenomena driven by the monotonic accumulation of events over time. To this end, we made use of a subclass of constrained Bayesian networks named Suppes-Bayes Causal Networks, which include structural constraints grounded in Suppes' theory of probabilistic causation.

While the problem of learning the structure of a Bayesian Network is known to be intractable, such constraints allow to prune the search space of the possible solutions, leading to a tremendous reduction of the number of valid networks to be considered, hence taming the complexity of the problem in a remarkable way.

We here discussed the theoretical implications of the inference process at the different steps, also by comparing various state-of-the-art algorithmic approaches and regularization methods. We finally provided an in-depth study on realistically simulated data of the effect of each inference choice, thus providing some sound guidelines for the design of efficient algorithms for the inference of models of cumulative phenomena.

According to our results, none of the tested search strategies significantly outperforms the others in all the experimental settings, in terms of both sensitivity and specificity.

Yet, we could prove that Suppes' constraints consistently improve the inference accuracy, in all the considered scenarios and with all the inference schemes, hence positioning SBCNs as the new benchmark in the the efficient inference and representation of cumulative phenomena.

Acknowledgments. This work was supported in part by the ASTIL Program of Regione Lombardia, by the ELIXIR-ITA network, and by the SysBioNet project, a MIUR initiative for the Italian Roadmap of European Strategy Forum on Research Infrastructures (ESFRI). We would like to thank for the useful discussions our colleagues Giulio Caravagna of ICR, London, UK, Giancarlo Mauri of DISCo, Università degli Studi di Milano-Bicocca, Milan, Italy, and Bud Mishra of Courant Institute of Mathematical Sciences, New York University, NY, USA.

References

1. Akaike, H.: Information theory and an extension of the maximum likelihood principle. In: Parzen, E., Tanabe, K., Kitagawa, G. (eds.) Selected Papers of Hirotugu Akaike, pp. 199–213. Springer, New York (1998). https://doi.org/10.1007/978-1-4612-1694-0_15
2. Antoniotti, M., Caravagna, G., De Sano, L., Graudenzi, A., Mauri, G., Mishra, B., Ramazzotti, D.: Design of the TRONCO bioconductor package for translational oncology. R J. **8**(2), 39–59 (2016)
3. Back, T.: Selective pressure in evolutionary algorithms: a characterization of selection mechanisms. In: Proceedings of the First IEEE Conference on Evolutionary Computation, 1994. IEEE World Congress on Computational Intelligence, pp. 57–62. IEEE (1994)

4. Bonchi, F., Hajian, S., Mishra, B., Ramazzotti, D.: Exposing the probabilistic causal structure of discrimination. Int. J. Data Sci. Anal. **3**(1), 1–21 (2017)
5. Buldyrev, S.V., Parshani, R., Paul, G., Stanley, H.E., Havlin, S.: Catastrophic cascade of failures in interdependent networks. Nature **464**(7291), 1025–1028 (2010)
6. Buntine, W.: Theory refinement on Bayesian networks. In: Proceedings of the Seventh Conference on Uncertainty in Artificial Intelligence, pp. 52–60. Morgan Kaufmann Publishers Inc. (1991)
7. Caravagna, G., Graudenzi, A., Ramazzotti, D., Sanz-Pamplona, R., De Sano, L., Mauri, G., Moreno, V., Antoniotti, M., Mishra, B.: Algorithmic methods to infer the evolutionary trajectories in cancer progression. Proc. Natl. Acad. Sci. **113**(28), E4025–E4034 (2016)
8. Carvalho, A.M.: Scoring functions for learning Bayesian networks. Inesc-id Technical report (2009)
9. Chickering, D.M.: Learning bayesian networks is NP-complete. In: Fisher, D., Lenz, H.J. (eds.) Learning from Data, pp. 121–130. Springer, New York (1996). https://doi.org/10.1007/978-1-4612-2404-4_12
10. Chickering, D.M., Heckerman, D., Meek, C.: Large-sample learning of Bayesian networks is NP-hard. J. Mach. Learn. Res. **5**(Oct), 1287–1330 (2004)
11. Cooper, G.F., Herskovits, E.: A Bayesian method for constructing Bayesian belief networks from databases. In: Proceedings of the Seventh Conference on Uncertainty in Artificial Intelligence, pp. 86–94. Morgan Kaufmann Publishers Inc. (1991)
12. Cooper, G.F., Herskovits, E.: A Bayesian method for the induction of probabilistic networks from data. Mach. Learn. **9**(4), 309–347 (1992)
13. De Sano, L., Caravagna, G., Ramazzotti, D., Graudenzi, A., Mauri, G., Mishra, B., Antoniotti, M.: TRONCO: an R package for the inference of cancer progression models from heterogeneous genomic data. Bioinformatics **32**(12), 1911–1913 (2016)
14. Farahani, H.S., Lagergren, J.: Learning oncogenetic networks by reducing to mixed integer linear programming. PloS One **8**(6), e65773 (2013)
15. Gao, G., Mishra, B., Ramazzotti, D.: Efficient simulation of financial stress testing scenarios with Suppes-Bayes causal networks. Procedia Comput. Sci. **108**, 272–284 (2017)
16. Garrett, A.: Inspyred: bio-inspired algorithms in Python (2012). https://pypi.python.org/pypi/inspyred
17. Good, I.J., Mittal, Y., et al.: The amalgamation and geometry of two-by-two contingency tables. Ann. Stat. **15**(2), 694–711 (1987)
18. Heckerman, D., Geiger, D., Chickering, D.M.: Learning bayesian networks: the combination of knowledge and statistical data. Mach. Learn. **20**(3), 197–243 (1995)
19. Hitchcock, C.: Probabilistic causation. Stanford encyclopedia of philosophy (2010)
20. Holland, J.H.: Adaptation in Natural and Artificial Systems: An Introductory Analysis with Applications to Biology, Control, and Artificial Intelligence. U Michigan Press (1975)
21. Koller, D., Friedman, N.: Probabilistic Graphical Models: Principles and Techniques. MIT Press, Cambridge (2009)
22. Korsunsky, I., Ramazzotti, D., Caravagna, G., Mishra, B.: Inference of cancer progression models with biological noise. arXiv preprint arXiv:1408.6032 (2014)
23. Larranaga, P., Poza, M., Yurramendi, Y., Murga, R.H., Kuijpers, C.M.: Structure learning of Bayesian networks by genetic algorithms. IEEE Trans. Pattern Anal. Mach. Intell. **18**(9), 912–926 (1996)
24. Loohuis, L.O., Caravagna, G., Graudenzi, A., Ramazzotti, D., Mauri, G., Antoniotti, M., Mishra, B.: Inferring tree causal models of cancer progression with probability raising. PloS One **9**(10), e108358 (2014)

25. Oliphant, T.: A Guide to Numpy, vol. 1. Trelgol Publishing, Spanish Fork (2006)
26. Pearl, J.: Causality. Cambridge University Press, Cambridge (2009)
27. Pearson, K.: Mathematical contributions to the theory of evolution on a form of spurious correlation which may arise when indices are used in the measurement of organs. Proc. R. Soc. Lond. **60**(359–367), 489–498 (1896)
28. Ramazzotti, D., Caravagna, G., Olde Loohuis, L., Graudenzi, A., Korsunsky, I., Mauri, G., Antoniotti, M., Mishra, B.: CAPRI: efficient inference of cancer progression models from cross-sectional data. Bioinformatics **31**(18), 3016–3026 (2015)
29. Ramazzotti, D., Graudenzi, A., Caravagna, G., Antoniotti, M.: Modeling cumulative biological phenomena with Suppes-Bayes causal networks. arXiv preprint arXiv:1602.07857 (2016)
30. Ramazzotti, D., Nobile, M.S., Cazzaniga, P., Mauri, G., Antoniotti, M.: Parallel implementation of efficient search schemes for the inference of cancer progression models. In: IEEE International Conference on Computational Intelligence in Bioinformatics and Computational Biology. IEEE (2016)
31. Hagberg, A., Swart, P., Chult D.S.: Exploring network structure, dynamics, and function using NetworkX. In: Proceedings of the 7th Python in Science Conferences (SciPy 2008), vol. 2008, pp. 11–16 (2008)
32. Schwarz, G., et al.: Estimating the dimension of a model. Ann. Stat. **6**(2), 461–464 (1978)
33. Scutari, M.: Learning Bayesian networks with the bnlearn R package. arXiv preprint arXiv:0908.3817 (2009)
34. Suppes, P.: A Probabilistic Theory of Causality. North-Holland Publishing Company, Amsterdam (1970)
35. Teyssier, M., Koller, D.: Ordering-based search: a simple and effective algorithm for learning Bayesian networks. arXiv preprint arXiv:1207.1429 (2012)

Sparse Surface Speed Evaluation on a Dynamic Three-Dimensional Surface Using an Iterative Partitioning Scheme

Paul Manstetten[1]([✉]), Lukas Gnam[1], Andreas Hössinger[2], Siegfried Selberherr[3], and Josef Weinbub[1]

[1] Christian Doppler Laboratory for High Performance TCAD,
Institute for Microelectronics, TU Wien, Vienna, Austria
{manstetten,gnam,weinbub}@iue.tuwien.ac.at
[2] Silvaco Europe Ltd., St Ives, UK
andreas.hoessinger@silvaco.com
[3] Institute for Microelectronics, TU Wien, Vienna, Austria
selberherr@iue.tuwien.ac.at

Abstract. We focus on a surface evolution problem where the local surface speed depends on a computationally expensive scalar function with non-local properties. The local surface speed must be re-evaluated in each time step, even for non-moving parts of the surface, due to possibly changed properties in remote regions of the simulation domain. We present a method to evaluate the surface speed only on a sparse set of points to reduce the computational effort. This sparse set of points is generated according to application-specific requirements using an iterative partitioning scheme. We diffuse the result of a constant extrapolation in the neighborhood of the sparse points to obtain an approximation to a linear interpolation between the sparse points.

We demonstrate the method for a surface evolving with a local surface speed depending on the incident flux from a source plane above the surface. The obtained speedups range from 2 to 8 and the surface deviation is less than 3 grid-cells for all evaluated test cases.

Keywords: Surface mesh · Surface evolution · Interpolation
Robust · Scalar · Sparse evaluation

1 Introduction

The simulation of dynamic surfaces is an integral part of a large number of areas including fluid simulations [5], computer graphics [4], and semiconductor fabrication [9]. The maximum time step for the simulation of the dynamic surface is limited by the underlying discretization, the advection scheme, and the maximum surface speed. If the surface speed depends on global properties of the domain, it must be re-evaluated in each time step, even for non-moving parts of the surface. This full re-evaluation – especially for high resolution simulations – potentially leads to situations where the surface speed model evaluation dominates the overall simulation run time.

© Springer International Publishing AG, part of Springer Nature 2018
Y. Shi et al. (Eds.): ICCS 2018, LNCS 10860, pp. 694–707, 2018.
https://doi.org/10.1007/978-3-319-93698-7_53

The approach presented in the following provides a robust method to reduce the number of necessary evaluations of the surface model. From a dense set of evaluation points given by the resolution of the surface mesh, a subset of points is selected using an iterative partitioning scheme. The scheme is controlled by a freely definable refinement condition, allowing to adopt the method for different application-specific requirements. After evaluating the surface model for this subset of points, the solution for the remaining points in the dense set is obtained by diffusing the result of a constant extrapolation in the neighborhood of the sparse points using the error smoothing properties of the Jacobi method [1, p. 895].

We evaluate our method based on an etching simulation problem, taken from the area of semiconductor fabrication. We use a generic etching simulation test case with a single material region to investigate our method. The refinement condition for the iterative partitioning scheme is modeled using fixed thresholds for local flux differences and surface normal deviations. As illustrating example, a study of an etching process involving high aspect ratio holes can be found in [2]. The etching process selectively removes material from a substrate, representing a surface evolution problem. When modeling etching processes, typically the surface speed evaluation is the dominating part of the overall simulation run time. This, together with the fact that simulations become more and more intricate (i.e., both with respect to geometry and involved physics), leads to unacceptable long simulation run times. The central motivation for this work is to reduce the simulation run time in such scenarios as much as possible to enable more intricate simulation problems.

2   Iterative Partitioning Scheme

We require a triangulated surface mesh – representing the evolving surface – and define the *dense* set of evaluation points as the set of all triangle centroids. Algorithm 1 is used to iteratively select a *sparse* subset of evaluation points depending on (a) the maximal globally allowed edge distance (d_{max_0}) between two points in the subset, (b) an array of maximal allowed edge distances for each point in the dense set where each entry is between 0 and d_{max_0}, and (c) a refinement condition. The refinement condition defines in each iteration and for each point in the sparse set, if additional points in the surrounding should be added to the sparse set. Additionally to the sparse set, Algorithm 1 assigns one of the sparse points to each of the points in the dense set. All points with the same sparse "parent" are referred to as *patch* in the following. The patches are the "spacers" between the points in the sparse set and are used to efficiently identify neighbors in the sparse set and to generate the initial guess for the Jacobi solver discussed in Sect. 3. The refinement condition used in Sect. 4 is based on a fixed threshold for the angular deviation of the surface normal and the deviation of the surface speed between a sparse point and its sparse neighbors (cf. Eq. 2).

Details for the subroutines in Algorithm 1 can be found in Appendix A. Figure 1 illustrates the individual stages of the algorithm using a small, regular triangulated mesh:

(a) In the initial iteration, a triangle is selected as active and a patch (red) is formed out of the surrounding triangles until the maximum allowed distance d_{max_0} is reached. In this example, we use $d_{max_0} = 8$. The first triangle is selected arbitrarily; the simplest choice is the first triangle in the list of triangles of the mesh.

(b) One of the remaining triangles (the simplest choice is again the first unprocessed triangle in the list of triangles) in the unprocessed region of the mesh is selected and a new patch (blue) is formed, which overwrites the red patch where the edge distance is smaller to the blue origin. In the initial iteration, this procedure is repeated until all triangles of the mesh have been processed. The result of (b) is a list of patches covering the whole surface.

(c) The connection between the two points of the sparse set (black line) is detected, when the two corresponding patches share one or more edges of the mesh. The result of step (c) is a set of connections between neighboring sparse points (triangles with label "0").

(d) In the next iteration (first refining iteration), if the refinement condition is evaluated to true for a sparse point, the sub region of the associated patch, where the edge distance to the origin is above $d_{max_0}/4$, is withdrawn from the patch; the threshold for the withdrawal ($d_{max_0}/4$) results in a core patch of "diameter" $d_{max_0}/2$, surrounded by a withdrawn region with a minimum "thickness" of $d_{max_0}/4$.

(e) In the withdrawn region, patches are created (analog to the initial iteration) until all triangles have been processed, but now using $d_{max_1} = d_{max_0}/2$; the division by 2 leads to a bisection of the maximal edge distance between sparse points on the patch. Like before, which of the triangles is selected as origin of a patch is arbitrary as long as it is unprocessed; typically the first triangle in the list of withdrawn triangles is chosen.

(f) The connections between the 6 sparse points, as a result of the refinement of the red patch, are illustrated (black lines).

After the refinement is completed for all patches where the refinement condition evaluates to true, the refinement condition is re-evaluated for all sparse points. Subsequently, the refinement is repeated with $d_{max_2} = d_{max_1}/2$, continuously leading to a bisection of the maximal edge distance between sparse points on the patch. The algorithm is terminated either because the refinement condition evaluates to false for all sparse points or $d_{max_i} = 1$, corresponding to a patch consisting of only one triangle. If the refinement condition depends on the surface velocity at the sparse points, the surface model must be evaluated for the newly added sparse points in each iteration.

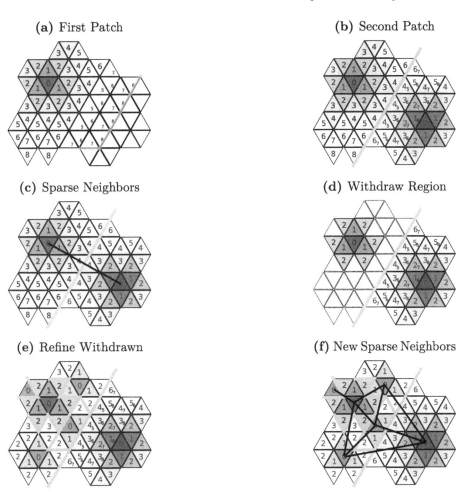

Fig. 1. Schematic depiction of the stages of the iterative partitioning scheme for an exemplary mesh. Yellow lines denote patch boundaries. (a) Initial creation of a patch where the numbers refer to edge distances to the origin; for visualization purposes only, the triangles which will be removed from the patch in the next step use a smaller font size. (b) Creation of a second patch (blue) starting at one of the unprocessed triangles. (c) Sparse neighbor connection between the two origins of the patches. (d) Withdrawal of subregion in red patch. (e) Refinement of the withdrawn region in the red patch with $d_{max_1} = d_{max_0}/2$. (f) Updated sparse neighbor connections after the red patch was refined. (Color figure online)

How well the edge distances between the centroids map to arc length distances on the triangular mesh depends on the uniformity of the mesh with respect to triangle shape and size. Only with a mesh consisting of triangles with comparable size and quality the algorithm will produce "convex" patches (convex with respect to the polygon constructed out of the outermost centroids).

After completion, Algorithm 1 provides a sparse set of points with corresponding sparse neighbors and patch information.

Algorithm 1. Adaptive decimation of evaluation locations on a triangular surface mesh.

Input: d_{max0}, distTarget$[i]$, RefinementCondition(i)
Output: active$[]$, sparseNeighbors$[]$, patches$[]$
Algorithm

> withdrawn$[N_{tri}]$ = true; reflagged$[N_{tri}]$ = false; active$[N_{tri}]$ = false;
> distance$[N_{tri}]$ = d_{max0}; parent$[N_{tri}]$ = -1;
> patches$[]$ = empty map(activeIndex,patchIndices);
> sparseNeighbors$[]$ = empty map(activeIndex,activeNeighbors);
> indices$[N_{tri}]$ = iota(0,N_{tri});
> FlagTriangles(*indices, d_{max}*)
> RebuildPatches();
> EvaluateSurfaceModel(for all active indices)
> **for** $n=1\ldots\log 2(d_{max0})$ **do**
>> reflagged$[N_{tri}]$ = false;
>> withdrawn$[N_{tri}]$ = false;
>> numNewPatches = 0;
>> **foreach** *patch in patches* **do**
>>> i_{active} = *patch.activeIndex*;
>>> **if** *RefinementCondition(i_{active}) == true AND reflagged[i_{active}] == false* **then**
>>>> numNewPatches += RefinePatch(i_{active}, $d_{max0}/2^n$);
>>
>> **if** *numNewPatches == 0* **then**
>>> break;
>>
>> RebuildPatches();
>> EvaluateSurfaceModel(for all newly active indices)

---

3   Interpolation Between Sparse Points

Inherent to its construction method, the sparse set of points and the connections between sparse neighbors do not necessarily allow to construct a sparse mesh covering the complete original surface, which could be used for interpolation. To provide a robust, non-supervised, and computationally efficient interpolation between the sparse points, we start with a constant extrapolation inside the patches using the corresponding values at the origins. We use the properties of Laplace's equation (Eq. 1) and the error diffusion properties of the Jacobi method to smooth the jumps in the constant extrapolation and to approximate a linear interpolation between the sparse points:

(a) In one dimension, the solution of Laplace's equation (Eq. 1) is equivalent to a linear interpolation between a sparse set of points when using the sparse set as Dirichlet boundary conditions and model the boundaries of the domain as zero gradient Neumann boundary conditions.

(b) In one iteration of Jacobi's method, local information travels only across one edge; using this property we can restrict the radius of influence to not exceed the maximal patch radius of $d_{max_0}/2$ by only performing $d_{max_0}/2$ or less iterations.

We approximate a linear interpolation between the sparse points on the surface by using the same boundary conditions (cf. (a)) and starting with the constant extrapolation as an initial guess. We do not solve Eq. 1 until convergence but only perform a fixed number of iterations of Jacobi's method.

$$-\nabla^2 \mathbf{u} = 0 \tag{1}$$

We use a finite volume approximation to discretize Eq. 1 on the triangulated mesh by

integrating over the volume
$$-\int_{V_i} \nabla^2 \mathbf{u}\, dV = 0,$$

applying Green's Theorem
$$-\int_{\delta V_i} \nabla \mathbf{u} \cdot \mathbf{n_i}\, dS = 0,$$

summing over the triangle edges
$$-\sum_{j=1}^{3} \int_{\delta V_{ij}} \nabla \mathbf{u} \cdot \mathbf{n_{ij}} = 0,$$

using the midpoint rule
$$-\sum_{j=1}^{3} L_{E_{ij}} \nabla \mathbf{u} \cdot \mathbf{n_{ij}}\, dS = 0, \quad \text{and}$$

using a central difference between centroids
$$\nabla \mathbf{u} \cdot \mathbf{n_{ij}} \approx \frac{\mathbf{u}(x_{n_{ij}}) - \mathbf{u}(x_i)}{\| x_{n_{ij}} - x_i \|},$$

where $\mathbf{u}$ is the scalar function (in this case the local surface velocity), $L_{E_{ij}}$ is the length of the edge shared by triangle i and j, and x_i is the centroid of triangle i, and $x_{n_{ij}}$ is the centroid of the triangle connected to triangle i across edge j. Using this discretization and the boundary conditions described above results in a system of linear equations. The number of unknowns is the number of all centroids minus the size of the sparse set.

4   Results

We evaluate our method using a generic etching simulation test case with a single material region. The model for the surface speed is a linear relation to the direct incident flux from a remote source plane above the surface. All results were produced using a vertically focused ($n = 100$) power cosine source distribution $\Gamma(\Theta) = cos(\Theta)^n$. We use an integration method based on a 5 times subdivided icosahedron as presented in [6] to calculate the direct flux rates on the surface. The direct flux rates are normalized to the flux rate on a fully exposed horizontal plane. As in [6], we used *Embree* [3,10] as ray tracing engine and *OpenVDB* [7,8] for level-set based surface advection and extraction.

The initial geometry (Fig. 2a) is a cylindrical hole with diameter 1 and depth 6 in a bulk region of thickness 8. Figure 2b–e show the intermediate surface positions using the dense centroid-set for surface model evaluation (dense flux evaluation) from time T = 0 up to T = 8, where the bulk region is completely etched.

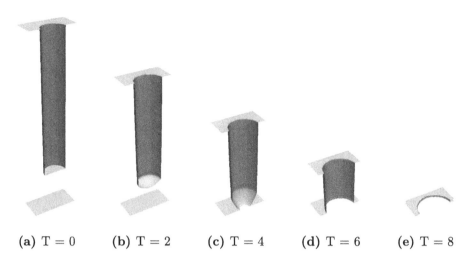

(a) T = 0   **(b)** T = 2   **(c)** T = 4   **(d)** T = 6   **(e)** T = 8

Fig. 2. Cylindrical hole with diameter 1 and depth 6 in a bulk region of thickness 8. Surface evolution during the simulation at times T = [0, 2, 4, 6, 8] (all units are arbitrary). The level-set resolution is 64 cells per unit length.

To model the refinement condition we define for each sparse point i,

the maximal normal deviation $\quad\quad \nu_{max_i} = \max_{\forall k \in N_k} \angle(\mathbf{n}_i, \mathbf{n}_k),$

the average flux difference $\quad\quad du_{avg_i} = \dfrac{1}{n(N_k)} \displaystyle\sum_{\forall k \in N_k} \dfrac{|u_i - u_k|}{|u_{max} - u_{min}|},$

and the maximal flux difference $\quad du_{max_i} = \max_{\forall k \in N_k} \dfrac{|u_i - u_k|}{|u_{max} - u_{min}|},$

where N_k is the set of neighboring sparse point indices, and u_{max} and u_{min} are the global maximum and minimum flux value, respectively. We use a combination of fixed thresholds in all of the following results to model the refinement condition in Algorithm 1:

$$RefinementCondition(i) = \begin{cases} true, & \text{if } \nu_{max_i} > \pi/10 \\ true, & \text{if } \frac{du_{avg_i} + du_{max_i}}{2} > 0.2 \\ false, & \text{otherwise} \end{cases} \quad (2)$$

Furthermore, we use $d_{max_0} = 32$ in all simulations, which gives a total of 6 iterations (1 initial iteration, and $log2(d_{max_0}) = 5$ refinements), whereas the number of Jacobi iterations is fixed to $d_{max_0}/4 = 8$. Figure 3 illustrates the resulting sparse centroid-set at time T = 4.5 for different level-set resolutions.

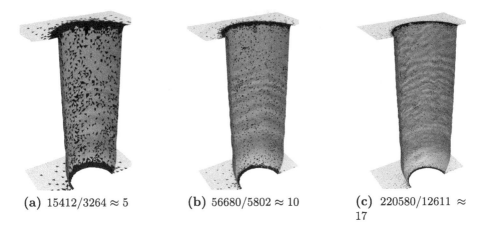

(a) $15412/3264 \approx 5$ (b) $56680/5802 \approx 10$ (c) $220580/12611 \approx$ 17

Fig. 3. Sparse set of triangles (cf. triangles with labeled with "0" in Fig. 1) for level-set resolutions 16 (a), 32 (b), and 64 (c) at time $T = 4.5$. The ratios between the total number of triangles and the sparse set of triangles (black) are denoted.

In Fig. 4, we compare the results between the dense and sparse flux evaluation at times $T = 3$ and $T = 6$. For a level-set resolution 64, this corresponds to time step 800 and 1600, respectively. The two surfaces reveal deviations of up to 3 level-set cells, most prominent in the lower vertical region of the hole. In the upper region of the hole and the top surface, nearly no deviations are present.

Table 1. Level-set resolutions, resulting initial domain resolutions, initial mesh properties, and resulting number of time steps until $T = 8$.

Cells per unit length	Cells vertical	Cells horizontal	Triangles	Time steps
16	128	32×32	17k	540
32	256	64×64	67k	1080
64	512	128×128	262k	2160

We evaluate the performance of our method by tracing the run time per time step from $T = 0$ to $T = 8$ for three different level-set resolutions summarized in Table 1 for the dense and the sparse flux calculation. For each time step, the run time for the flux evaluation and for the remaining parts (velocity extension, advection, normalization, and mesh extraction; referred to as *other tasks* in the following) is tracked (cf. Figs. 5, 6 and 7 green and red areas, respectively). The flux integration method, which is used for a single point, is identical for both cases. The implementation of Algorithm 1 is serial, in contrast to the flux evaluation, which is OpenMP-parallelized in both cases to form a basis for a realistic estimation of the speedups. The serial overhead generated by Algorithm 1 is accounted to the run time of the flux evaluation. All performance benchmarks were conducted on an Intel Devil's Canyon platform (i7-4970K, four physical, eight logical cores) with 32 GB of main memory, using a C++ implementation of the presented algorithm.

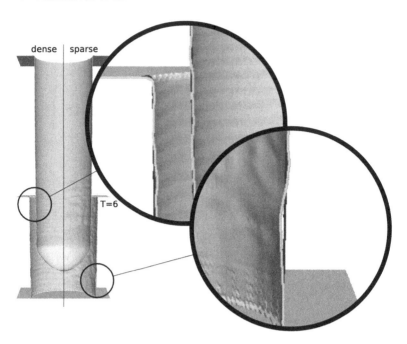

Fig. 4. Comparison of surface positions at times T = [3, 6] for resolution 64. The surface mesh for the dense and sparse flux evaluation is displayed on the left and right half-space, respectively. Two regions are magnified on the right side where the blue and red line correspond to slices of the dense and the sparse evaluation, respectively. (Color figure online)

Figure 5 summarizes the performance differences for resolution 16; the upper plot shows the run time per time step for the dense flux evaluation. The run time at the beginning of the simulation is ≈ 5.5 s per time step. As soon as the hole has reached the bottom of the bulk material, the number of triangles starts to decrease and consequently the run time per time step drops linearly from T = 3.6 to T = 8. The ratio between flux evaluation (green) and other tasks (red) is ≈ 20 for the whole simulation, emphasizing the dominance of the computational cost for the flux evaluation, even for small domain resolutions. The lower plot in Fig. 5 is analog to the upper plot, but for the sparse flux evaluation. A second y-axis on the right is used to plot two additional properties: the ratio of dense to sparse points (dashed line) and the speedup of the flux evaluation (solid line) over the dense flux evaluation. Throughout the simulation, the dense/sparse ratio is between 2.5 and 6 while the speedup is ≈ 2.0.

Figures 6 and 7 compare the performance for resolution 32 and 64, respectively. With increasing resolution, the dominance of the flux evaluation in terms of run time is also increased, leading to a negligible share of run time for the other tasks in the case of dense flux evaluation. For sparse flux evaluation a dense/sparse ratio of 3 to 14 and 4 to 35 is achieved for resolution 32 and 64, respectively. However, different to resolution 16, the obtained speedups (5 and

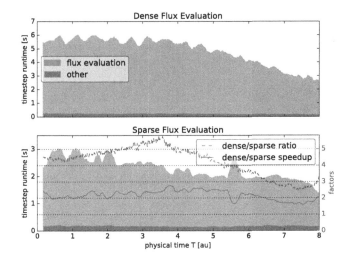

Fig. 5. Performance results for resolution 16. (Color figure online)

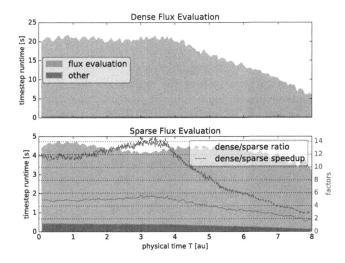

Fig. 6. Performance results for resolution 32. (Color figure online)

8, respectively) are only constant up to T = 3.6, where the hole reaches the bottom of the bulk material. From T = 3.6 to T = 8 the speedups decrease to approximately 2 (following the dense/sparse ratio) keeping the total run time per time step approximately constant up to T = 6.5.

The "gap factor" between achieved and potential speedup (i.e., dense/sparse ratio) is higher for large meshes and ranges from ≈ 2 for resolution 16, to ≈ 4 for resolution 64 before the hole reaches the bottom. When approaching T = 8, all three tested resolutions converge to a speedup of ≈ 2.

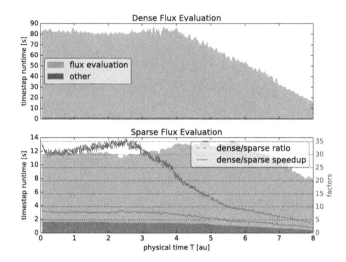

Fig. 7. Performance results for resolution 64. (Color figure online)

5 Summary

We presented a method to reduce the number of necessary evaluations of a surface speed model in each time step of the simulation of a dynamic surface. A sparse point-set and corresponding neighborhoods are constructed using an iterative partitioning scheme. The surface speed model is only evaluated for this sparse point-set. The variable limits for the allowed distance between sparse points enables to balance between computational complexity and accuracy in a robust way. Furthermore, a linear interpolation between the sparse points is approximated by diffusing the result of a constant extrapolation in the neighborhoods using the error smoothing properties of the Jacobi method.

Using a cylindrical hole with a directed vertical source as a generic etching simulation test case, inspired by etching processes arising in semiconductor fabrication, we compare the results against a dense evaluation of the surface speed. Deviations in the surface position are below 3 level-set cells for all tested configurations. The achieved speedups range from 2 for the lowest resolution up to 8 for the highest resolved surface. The speedups are tracked during all time steps of the simulations starting from thick initial geometries to very thin geometries at the end of the simulated physical process.

The method can be adapted to specific application requirements via a freely definable refinement condition for the iterative partitioning scheme. We used a refinement condition based on fixed thresholds of local deviations in surface normal direction and surface speed.

Acknowledgment. The financial support by the *Austrian Federal Ministry of Science, Research and Economy* and the *National Foundation for Research, Technology and Development* is gratefully acknowledged.

A   Algorithm Subroutines

Algorithm 2. Recursive flagging and refinement of patches.

Function FlagNeighborhood(i, i_{parent}, i_{prev}, d_{path}, d_{max})**:**

  $d_{max_{local}} = \text{distTarget}[i]$;

  if *withdrawn[i] AND $d_{max} >= d_{path}$ AND $d_{max_{local}} > d_{path}$ AND distance[i] > d_{path}* **then**

    touched[i] = true;

    parent[i] = i_{parent};

    distance[i] = d_{path};

    foreach i_{ne} *in edgeNeighbors[i]* **do**

      if $i_{ne}! = i_{prev}$ **then**

        FlagNeighborhood(i_{ne}, i_{parent}, i, $d_{path} + 1$, d_{max})

  else

    SetNeighbors(i, i_{parent});

Function FlagTriangles($indices$, d_{max})**:**

  touched[] = false;

  $d_{path} = 0$;

  numNewPatches = 0;

  foreach i *in indices* **do**

    if *!touched[i] and withdrawn[i]* **then**

      ++numNewPatches;

      active[i] = touched[i] = reflagged[i] = true;

      parent[i] = i;

      distance[i] = d_{path};

      foreach i_{ne} *in edgeNeighbors[i]* **do**

        FlagNeighborhood(i_{ne}, i, i, $d_{path} + 1$, d_{max})

  return numNewPatches

Function RefinePatch(i_{active}, d_{max})**:**

  count = Withdraw(i_{active}, $d_{max}/2$)

  if *count == 0* **then**

    return 0

  else

    UnSetAllNeighbors(i_{active})

    numNewPatches = FlagTriangles($patches[i_{active}].patchIndices$, d_{max})

    RebuildNeighbors(i_{active})

    UnWithdraw(i_{active})

  return numNewPatches

Algorithm 3. Helper functions for sparse neighbor handling.

Function SetNeighbors(i, i_{active}):
$\quad$ **if** $parent[i] \mathrel{!=} -1$ and $parent[i] \mathrel{!=} i_{active}$ **then**
$\quad\quad$ sparseNeighbors[parent[i]].insert(i_{active});
$\quad\quad$ sparseNeighbors[i_{active}].insert(parent[i]);

Function UnSetAllNeighbors(i_{active}):
$\quad$ **foreach** i_{ns} in $sparseNeighbors[i_{active}].activeNeighbors$ **do**
$\quad\quad$ sparseNeighbors[i_{ns}].erase(i_{active});
$\quad\quad$ sparseNeighbors[i_{active}].erase(i_{ns});

Function RebuildNeighbors(i_{active}):
$\quad$ **foreach** i in $patches[i_{active}].patchIndices$ **do**
$\quad\quad$ **if** $!withdrawn[i]$ **then**
$\quad\quad\quad$ **foreach** i_{ne} in $edgeNeighbors[i]$ **do**
$\quad\quad\quad\quad$ SetNeighbors(i_{ne}, i_{active});

Algorithm 4. Helper functions for withdrawal and building patch information.

Function Withdraw(i_{active}, d):
$\quad$ count $= 0$;
$\quad$ **foreach** i in $patches[i_{active}].patchIndices$ **do**
$\quad\quad$ **if** $distance[i] > d$ **then**
$\quad\quad\quad$ withdrawn[i] = true;
$\quad\quad\quad$ distance[i] = d_{max_0};
$\quad\quad\quad$ parent[i] = -1;
$\quad\quad\quad$ ++count;
$\quad$ **return** count

Function UnWithdraw(i_{active}):
$\quad$ **foreach** i in $patches[i_{active}].patchIndices$ **do**
$\quad\quad$ withdrawn[i] = false;

Function RebuildPatches():
$\quad$ patches.clear();
$\quad$ **for** $i = 0 \ldots N_{tri} - 1$ **do**
$\quad\quad$ **if** $parent[i] == -1$ **then**
$\quad\quad\quad$ patches[parent[i]].insert(i);

References

1. Bronshtein, I., Semendyayev, K., Musiol, G., Mühlig, H.: Handbook of Mathematics, vol. 5. Springer, Heidelberg (2007). https://doi.org/10.1007/978-3-540-72122-2
2. Cheong, H.W., Lee, W.H., Kim, J.W., Kim, W.S., Whang, K.W.: A study on reactive ion etching lag of a high aspect ratio contact hole in a magnetized inductively coupled plasma. Plasma Sources Sci. Technol. **23**(6), 065051 (2014)
3. Embree. https://embree.github.io/
4. Hoetzlein, R.K.: GVDB: raytracing sparse voxel database structures on the GPU. In: Proceedings of High Performance Graphics, pp. 109–117 (2016)
5. Lee, C., Dolbow, J., Mucha, P.J.: A narrow-band gradient-augmented level set method for multiphase incompressible flow. J. Comput. Phys. **273**, 12–37 (2014)
6. Manstetten, P., Weinbub, J., Hössinger, A., Selberherr, S.: Using temporary explicit meshes for direct flux calculation on implicit surfaces. Procedia Comput. Sci. **108**, 245–254 (2017)
7. Museth, K.: VDB: high-resolution sparse volumes with dynamic topology. ACM Trans. Graph. **32**(3), 27:1–27:22 (2013)
8. OpenVDB. http://www.openvdb.org/
9. Silvaco Inc: Victory Process - 3D Process Simulator. http://www.silvaco.com/products/tcad/process_simulation/victory_process
10. Wald, I., Woop, S., Benthin, C., Johnson, G.S., Ernst, M.: Embree: a kernel framework for efficient CPU ray tracing. ACM Trans. Graph. **33**(4), 143 (2014)

Accurate, Automatic and Compressed Visualization of Radiated Helmholtz Fields from Boundary Element Solutions

Matthieu Maunoury[1]([✉]), Christophe Besse[2], Vincent Mouysset[1], and Sébastien Pernet[1]

[1] ONERA/DTIS, Université de Toulouse, Toulouse, France
matthieu.maunoury@onera.fr
[2] Institut de Mathématiques de Toulouse, UMR 5219, Université de Toulouse, CNRS, UPS IMT, 31062 Toulouse Cedex 9, France

Abstract. We propose a methodology to generate an accurate and efficient reconstruction of radiated fields based on high order interpolation. As the solution is obtained with the convolution by a smooth but potentially high frequency oscillatory kernel, our basis functions therefore incorporate plane waves. Directional interpolation is shown to be efficient for smart directions. An adaptive subdivision of the domain is established to limit the oscillations of the kernel in each element. The new basis functions, combining high order polynomials and plane waves, provide much better accuracy than low order ones. Finally, as standard visualization softwares are generally unable to represent such fields, a method to have a well-suited visualization of high order functions is used. Several numerical results confirm the potential of the method.

Keywords: Boundary equation methods
Integral representation formulas · High order reconstruction
Directional interpolation · Visualization

1 Introduction

The Boundary Element Methods (BEM) are efficient methods to solve partial differential equations. They are based on a boundary integral formulation which allow to reduce the discretization of the problem to the boundary and therefore reduce the costs in comparison with classic methods such as finite differences or finite elements. In this contribution, we will focus on Helmholtz problem [10].

While BEM's unknowns are lying on the surface of the scatterer, using representation formulas [10], it is possible to compute the solution of the problem in any point (even off the boundary). A common way [13] to visualize the scattering in an arbitrary domain is to define an *a priori* Cartesian grid, compute with the representation formula the radiated field in each vertex of the grid and use a linear interpolation to approximate the solution. The problem is that many

© Springer International Publishing AG, part of Springer Nature 2018
Y. Shi et al. (Eds.): ICCS 2018, LNCS 10860, pp. 708–721, 2018.
https://doi.org/10.1007/978-3-319-93698-7_54

information are lost due to linear interpolation. Therefore, to keep a good accuracy of the approximation, a huge number of interpolation points is needed. As a consequence, the costs (CPU time and memory) to evaluate the integral representation explode. High order interpolation allows much better approximation. Furthermore, as an asymptotic behaviour of the kernel is known, the use of a combination of high order and plane waves can be used to improve the approximation of the solution [3,6,9]. Finally, as standard visualization softwares are unable to visualize such high order polynomials nor plane waves functions, we combine this with an algorithm to visualize high order functions in any visualization software [8].

This paper is organized as follows. In Sect. 2, Helmholtz problem and the BEM formulation used to solve it are given. In Sect. 3, we give a method and an algorithm to get a correct visualization of high-order solutions. In Sect. 4, we propose a methodology to adaptively subdivide the domain and reconstruct radiated Helmholtz fields. Section 5 is devoted to numerical examples to show the potential of our method. Finally, conclusions and future works are given in the last section.

2   Formulation of the Scattering Problem

We consider the scattering of an incident wave w (for instance a plane wave) from an object Ω_s. This problem is modeled by Helmholtz equation [10]

$$
\begin{cases}
\Delta u + k^2 u = 0, & \text{in } \mathbb{R}^d \backslash \overline{\Omega}_s, \\
u = 0, & \text{on } \Gamma = \partial \overline{\Omega}_s, \\
\lim_{|x| \to \infty} |x| \left(\partial_{|x|}(u-w)(x) - ik(u-w)(x) \right) = 0,
\end{cases}
\tag{1}
$$

where Δ denotes the laplacian, k is the wave number, d is the dimension of the problem ($d = 2$ or 3), n is the unit outward normal and u is the total acoustic field. The second equation in (1) is the Dirichlet boundary condition. The third equation in (1) is the Sommerfeld radiation condition [10] so (1) is well-posed in the unbounded domain $\mathbb{R}^d \backslash \overline{\Omega}_s$.

An integral formulation is used to solve the well-posed problem (1). First, we parametrize the solution of (1) from the Cauchy data $(q := \frac{\partial u}{\partial n})$ by using the single layer operator $\mathcal{S}$ [10] defined by

$$
\mathcal{S}q(x) = \int_\Gamma G(x,y)q(y)d\gamma_y, \qquad \forall x \notin \Gamma,
$$

where G is the fundamental solution of Helmholtz Eq. (1):

$$
G(x,y) = \begin{cases}
\frac{i}{4} H_0^{(1)}(k\,|x-y|), & \text{if } d = 2, \\
\dfrac{e^{ik|x-y|}}{4\pi\,|x-y|}, & \text{if } d = 3,
\end{cases}
\tag{2}
$$

and $H_0^{(1)}$ is the Hankel function of first kind and order 0 [1]. Then, the solution is given by

$$u(x) = w(x) + \mathcal{S}q(x), \qquad \forall x \notin \Gamma. \tag{3}$$

To determine the solution u over the domain, we need to compute the density q. The boundary condition is therefore used to get the integral formulation. In the case of a homogeneous Dirichlet boundary condition, (3) is reduced to

$$u(x) = w(x) + \int_{\Gamma} G(x, y)q(y)d\gamma_y, \qquad \text{in } \mathbb{R}^d \backslash \overline{\Omega}_s, \tag{4}$$

In the case of Neumann or more general boundary conditions, the densities q and $\varphi := u_{|\Gamma}$ are computed by integral formulations constructed from appropriate trace formulas of (3). For more details, one can refer to [10]. In all cases, the representation formula (3) is obtained by convolution with corresponding kernels.

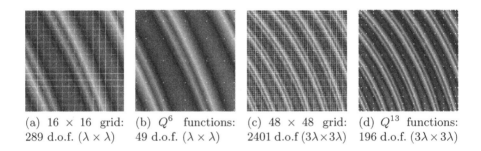

(a) 16×16 grid: 289 d.o.f. $(\lambda \times \lambda)$ (b) Q^6 functions: 49 d.o.f. $(\lambda \times \lambda)$ (c) 48×48 grid: 2401 d.o.f $(3\lambda \times 3\lambda)$ (d) Q^{13} functions: 196 d.o.f. $(3\lambda \times 3\lambda)$

Fig. 1. Representation of several radiated fields with low order functions (a) and (c) and high order functions (b) and (d) (L^∞ interpolation error under 1%).

Figure 1 plots several radiated fields and shows the advantages of high order interpolation. In the first two cases, the lengths of the square to visualize are equal to the wavelength. If a Cartesian grid is defined, 289 d.o.f are needed to interpolate the field with low order functions to get 0.95% interpolation error in L^∞-norm whereas with functions of order 6 and 49 d.o.f. (shown as white points in the figure) the error is 0.23 %. In a larger domain, (the two last cases of Fig. 1), 2401 d.o.f are needed to get 0.95% interpolation error in L^∞-norm whereas with functions of order 13 and 196 d.o.f., the error is 0.45 %. Thus, to get an approximation under 1%, high order interpolation needs much less degrees of freedom. Note that in the case of high order functions, the visualization has been generated following the method described in next section and 504 (resp. 3096) elements composed the representation mesh in figure (b) (resp. (d)).

3   Construction of a Well-Suited Visualization

In this section, we present a method developed by the authors [8] to visualize a hp solution noted f_{num}. Standard visualization softwares are unable to visualize and post-treat such solutions. Indeed, these softwares were originally thought and developed for low order method (finite differences, low order finite elements). Our method is based on a low order remeshing [12] which consists to transform f_{num} into a combination of linear functions defined on simple elements which will be handled by any visualization software. A representation mesh is built by means of a refinement strategy. An approximation of the solution, noted f_{vis}, is constructed. A visualization error is consequently introduced due to the P^1 approximation of high order functions. We define three objectives that f_{vis} has to respect to be "well-suited" in our sense:

1. The representation f_{vis} is defined from affine functions on simplexes.
2. The visualization error between f_{num} and f_{vis} is controlled in L^∞-norm.
3. The representation f_{vis} is (locally) continuous if f_{num} is (locally) continuous.

The first objective comes from the compatibility with visualization softwares. Indeed, only piecewise affine functions on simplexes are represented without loss of accuracy by any visualization software. The second objective is linked to the need to control the error between f_{vis} and f_{num} and to the specific use of data represented. Indeed, under its picture form, the data corresponds to values mapped on elements where anyone can pick up a pointwise information. Hence, the control in L^∞-norm is natural. The third objective ensures that f_{vis} does not introduce gaps when f_{num} is continuous. However, gaps can also coming from the Physics (material change) or discontinuous methods (such as Discontinuous Galerkin) and need to be well-rendered.

The function f_{num} is defined as a mapping from a subset $\mathcal{V}$ of a given space $\mathbb{X}$ (whose norm is noted $\|\cdot\|_{\mathbb{X}}$) into a space $\mathbb{Y}$ equipped with norm $\|\cdot\|_{\mathbb{Y}}$. The mesh of $\mathcal{V}$ is designed by $\mathcal{T}(\mathcal{V})$ and is assumed to be a conformal mesh of $\mathcal{V}$. Each element $K \in \mathcal{T}(\mathcal{V})$ is defined as the image of a given reference cell $\widehat{K}$ by a bijective geometrical transformation g_K. Hence, the numerical solution f_{num} is defined locally on any given cell $K \in \mathcal{T}(\mathcal{V})$, such that

$$\forall x \in K, \ f_{num}^K(x) = \sum_{i=1}^{N_K} f_i^K \varphi_i^K \left(g_K^{-1}(x)\right), \tag{5}$$

where f_{num}^K is the local expression of f_{num}, f_i^K are the degrees of freedom and φ_i^K are basis functions which are assumed to be continuous on the reference cell.

Following (5), the representation f_{vis} is defined by constructing local visualizations noted $(f_{vis}^{\widetilde{K}})_{K \in \mathcal{T}(\mathcal{V})}$. Hence, a meshing of K, noted $\mathcal{T}(K)$, composed of simplexes is performed. The exponent $\widetilde{K}$ recalls that an approximation of the element is therefore introduced $\widetilde{K} := \cup_{S \in \mathcal{T}(K)} S \neq K$. The local representation $f_{vis}^{\widetilde{K}}$ is then constructed from affines functions on these simplexes.

We introduce a quantification of the error between f_{num} and f_{vis}. To this purpose, we introduce Hausdorff distance on $\mathbb{X} \times \mathbb{Y}$ allowing to measure the gap between the graph of two functions [8]. As Hausdorff distance involves two embedded optimizations, it is expensive to employ. Thus, we introduce the following application for any given $K \in \mathcal{T}(\mathcal{V})$ and its associated mesh $\mathcal{T}(K)$

$$\Delta_{\mathcal{T}(K)} : (f, \widetilde{f}) \in C^0(K, \mathbb{Y}) \times C^0(\widetilde{K}, \mathbb{Y}) \mapsto \sup_{\hat{x} \in \widehat{K}} \max \left(\alpha \left\| g_K(\hat{x}) - P^1 g_{\mathcal{T}(K)}(\hat{x}) \right\|_{\mathbb{X}}, \right.$$
$$\left. \beta \left\| (f \circ g_K)(\hat{x}) - \left(\widetilde{f} \circ P^1 g_{\mathcal{T}(K)} \right)(\hat{x}) \right\|_{\mathbb{Y}} \right),$$

where the constants α and β are two scaling parameters which allow pertinent comparisons between values on $\mathbb{X}$ and $\mathbb{Y}$. For any $K \in \mathcal{T}(\mathcal{V})$, Hausdorff distance between f_{num} and f_{vis} is bounded by the *a posteriori* estimate $\Delta_{\mathcal{T}(K)}$. As this estimate is localized, it provides a tool to measure the quality of the representation $f_{vis}^{\widehat{K}}$ at each step of its construction. Then, the convergence of this estimate (under a prescribed tolerance) ensures that the second objective is satisfied. The method is therefore based on the construction of a mesh $\mathcal{T}(\widehat{K})$ of the reference cell guided by the control of the errors made when the geometry is approximated by simplexes and the functions are approximated by affine functions. Then, the $\mathbb{P}^1$ interpolation of g_K, noted $P^1 g_{\mathcal{T}(K)}$, permits to construct $\mathcal{T}(K)$ from $\mathcal{T}(\widehat{K})$. Finally, the values of f_{num}^K are computed at each vertex of $\mathcal{T}(K)$ to construct the representation $f_{vis}^{\widetilde{K}}$.

In order to guarantee the third objective, we propose an approach based on the decomposition of all boundaries elements in lower dimension and a construction of a mesh for each element. To fix a unique mesh at the interface between elements, a representation mesh of each edge is built. The mesh of each 2D element starts with the recovery of all the points on the boundary (from the meshes of the boundary) and then the interior mesh is built. The generation of the representation meshes follows a Bowyer-Watson algorithm [4,11,14]. It is an adaptive remeshing method guided by an *a posteriori* estimate which is evaluated by a global optimization algorithm known as *direct* [7]. The algorithm *direct*, acronym of *di*viding *rect*angles, is an usual branch and bound one.

Thus, all objectives are verified and an accurate visualization is possible.

4 Accurate, Adaptive and Compressed Reconstruction of Radiated Fields

Given a boundary Γ of a scattering object, a solution q has been computed on Γ by a Boundary Element Method (Sect. 2). Then, we want to visualize the radiated solution, noted u, in a domain $\mathcal{V}$. We can approximate u by interpolation

$$u(x) \approx \sum_{j=1}^{N_\mathcal{V}} u(\xi_j) \phi_j(x), \qquad \forall x \in \mathcal{V},$$

where $N_\mathcal{V}$ denotes the number of interpolation points, $(\xi_j)_{j=1,N_\mathcal{V}}$ are interpolation points and $(\phi_j)_{j=1,N_\mathcal{V}}$ are basis functions with collocation types (see hereafter). The degrees of freedom $(u(\xi_j))_{j=1,N_\mathcal{V}}$ are therefore computed by the representation formula (4). Each computation is expensive because of the convolution by the fundamental solution G. The objective is to get a good approximation of u for a reasonable number of degrees of freedom. Then, the choice of smart basis functions (and the interpolation points) is crucial. Note that if we use an interpolation on the kernel G, instead of u, with the same basis functions and interpolation points, we get the same approximation

$$u(x) \approx \int_{\Gamma} \sum_{j=1}^{N_{\mathcal{E}}} G(\xi_j, y)\phi_j(x)q(y)d\gamma_y = \sum_{j=1}^{N_{\mathcal{E}}} \underbrace{\int_{\Gamma} G(\xi_j, y)q(y)d\gamma_y}_{u(\xi_j)} \phi_j(x), \ \forall x \in \mathcal{V}.$$

Thus, to control the approximation of the solution (for any incident wave), the control of the approximation of the kernel is equivalent.

4.1   Formulation of Compressed Reconstruction of Radiated Field

The quality of the reconstructed radiated field depends on the accuracy of the kernel interpolation. For large wave number k, this function is highly oscillating. The use of directional interpolation [3,6,9] permits to get an improvement on this interpolation.

Directional Interpolation with One Direction. For the sake of simplicity, we show the developments with the 3D Green function [3] but the results are similar in 2D. Indeed, the Atkinson expansion [5] shows that the asymptotic behaviour of the kernel is similar in both dimensions. The function G to interpolate is given by (2). Let consider $y \in \Gamma$ given, and $x \in \mathbb{R}^d$ defined such that $x = y + \alpha c + \epsilon$, where $c \in \mathbb{R}^d$, α and ϵ are constants. Then,

$$\|x - y\| = \left\langle x - y, \frac{x - y}{\|x - y\|} \right\rangle = \left\langle x - y, \frac{\alpha c + \epsilon}{\|\alpha c + \epsilon\|} \right\rangle \underset{\frac{\epsilon}{\alpha} \to 0}{\approx} \left\langle x - y, \frac{c}{\|c\|} \right\rangle. \quad (6)$$

We define a modified kernel G_c linked to a direction $c \in \mathbb{R}^d$ with $\|c\| = 1$

$$G_c(x, y) = G(x, y)e^{-ik\langle c, x-y \rangle} = \frac{e^{ik(\|x-y\| - \langle c, x-y \rangle)}}{4\pi \|x - y\|}, \qquad \forall x \in \mathcal{V}, \forall y \in \Gamma. \quad (7)$$

Equation (6) shows the behaviour in the case the direction is chosen such that $x = y + \alpha c + \epsilon$ and $\epsilon/\alpha \to 0$. The choice of the direction is therefore relevant if

$$c \approx (x - y)/\|x - y\|, \qquad \forall x \in \mathcal{V}, \forall y \in \Gamma. \quad (8)$$

In the case this assumption holds, the quantity $(\|x - y\| - \langle c, x - y \rangle)$ is reduced and therefore the oscillations of G_c are limited.

Figure 2 shows the advantage of the plane wave use. Green kernel is plotted with y taken at the origin and $x \in \mathcal{V}$ where $\mathcal{V}$ is a square whose abscissas and ordinates lie between 5λ and 6λ with $\lambda = 2\pi/k$. A direction $c = x_c/\|x_c\|$ is defined where x_c is the center of the square. A plane wave is plotted ($e^{ik\langle c, x \rangle}$)

in the same domain. A function G_c is defined according to (7). This function clearly presents less oscillations than Green function G and hence is easier to interpolate with accuracy. Thus, last figure is obtained from an interpolation of G with Lagrangian polynomials of order 4 in each direction (25 d.o.f.) combined with the directional plane wave (i.e. $G(x,0) \approx \sum_{j=1}^{N_\mathcal{E}} G(\xi_j, 0)\mathcal{L}_j(x)e^{ik\langle c,x-\xi_j\rangle}$) to get an accuracy of 0.24 % L^∞ error on the approximation of G.

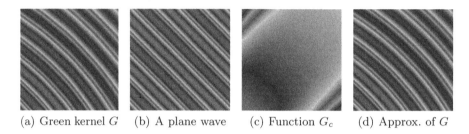

(a) Green kernel G (b) A plane wave   (c) Function G_c (d) Approx. of G

Fig. 2. Visualization of Green kernel G (a), a plane wave (b), the function G_c (c) and an approximation of G using a directional interpolation of G with orders 4 (d). (Color figure online)

Remark 1. The approximation of G used for Fig. 2 (d) is independent of the source term w in (1) so by comparison to Fig. 1 (d), we can extrapolate that for the same accuracy, this strategy will reduce by a factor 8 the number of d.o.f.

An approximation on G_c is introduced with $G_c(x,y) \approx \sum_{j=1}^{N_\mathcal{E}} G_c(\xi_j, y)\mathcal{L}_j(x)$ where $(\mathcal{L}_j)_{j=1,N_\mathcal{V}}$ are the Lagrangian polynomials. Then, for any $x \in \mathcal{V}$,

$$u(x) \approx \int_\Gamma \sum_{j=1}^{N_\mathcal{E}} G(\xi_j, y)e^{-ik\langle c,\xi_j-y\rangle}\mathcal{L}_j(x)e^{ik\langle c,x-y\rangle}q(y)d\gamma_y$$

$$\approx \sum_{j=1}^{N_\mathcal{E}} u(\xi_j)\mathcal{L}_j(x)e^{ik\langle c,x-\xi_j\rangle}.$$

In this case, the basis functions are chosen such that $\phi_j(x) = \mathcal{L}_j(x)e^{ik\langle c,x-\xi_j\rangle}$ where $x \in \mathcal{V}$. In order to verify the assumption (8), the angle between c and $(x-y)/\|x-y\|$ must be small. As previously, the direction c is defined as $c = (x_c - y_c)/\|x_c - y_c\|$ where x_c and y_c are defined as "average" of $\mathcal{V}$ and Γ. If the assumption (8) is not satisfied (i.e. ϵ/α does not tend toward 0 in (6)), a subdivision of the domain $\mathcal{V}$ (and eventually of Γ) is needed and multiple directions are defined.

Directional Interpolation with Multiple Directions. In order to define judicious basis functions, a subdivision of $\mathcal{V}$ can be done. A mesh of $\mathcal{V}$, noted $\mathcal{T}(\mathcal{V})$, will be constructed and composed of elements $\mathcal{E}_\mathcal{V}$ such that $\mathcal{T}(\mathcal{V})$ is a conformal mesh of $\mathcal{V}$, that is $\cup_{\mathcal{E}_\mathcal{V} \in \mathcal{T}(\mathcal{V})} \mathcal{E}_\mathcal{V} = \mathcal{V}$ and without overlapping between elements. In each element $\mathcal{E}_\mathcal{V}$, a local field will be therefore reconstructed with local directions and basis functions. Furthermore, a subdivision of Γ can be established to respect the assumption on the directions (8). The boundary Γ is decomposed in $\Gamma = \cup_{\Gamma_n} \Gamma_n$ such that there is no overlapping between each part Γ_n. For each Γ_n a direction c_n is then defined from two points x_c and y_c where x_c is the center of the element $\mathcal{E}_\mathcal{V}$ and y_c is an "average" of Γ_n. Furthermore, to each portion Γ_n, we introduce a function, noted G_c^n, similar to the case one direction (7)

$$G_c^n(x,y) = \frac{e^{ik(\|x-y\| - \langle c_n, x-y \rangle)}}{4\pi \|x-y\|}, \qquad \forall x \in \mathcal{E}_\mathcal{V}, \forall y \in \Gamma_n. \tag{9}$$

Using all these directions, the approximation of u is for any $x \in \mathcal{E}_\mathcal{V}$,

$$
\begin{aligned}
u(x) &\approx \sum_{n=1}^{N_\Gamma} \int_{\Gamma_n} \sum_{j=1}^{N_\mathcal{E}} G(x,y) q(y) d\gamma_y \mathcal{L}_j(x) e^{ik\langle c_n, x-\xi_j \rangle} \\
&\approx \sum_{n=1}^{N_\Gamma} \sum_{j=1}^{N_\mathcal{E}} u_{|\Gamma_n}(\xi_j) \mathcal{L}_j(x) e^{ik\langle c_n, x-\xi_j \rangle},
\end{aligned}
\tag{10}
$$

where $u_{|\Gamma_n}(\xi_j)$ is the *piece* of radiated field computed at an interpolation point (computed from a portion $\Gamma_n \subset \Gamma$). Note that for a given number of degrees of freedom, the computational cost in the integral equation code is the same with one or more directions. Indeed, at one interpolation point, the sum of all contributions is a constant and corresponds to the discretization of Γ.

4.2   Algorithm

We propose a relevant subdivision of $\mathcal{V}$. We assume that $\mathcal{V}$ is an axis-parallel box (rectangle in 2D or parallelepiped in 3D), or we define an axis-parallel box including the domain to visualize. In the same way, we introduce $\mathcal{G}$, an axis-parallel box including Γ. For each element $\mathcal{E}_\mathcal{V} \in \mathcal{T}(\mathcal{V})$, a subdivision of $\mathcal{G}$ is constructed such that its elements, noted $\mathcal{B}_\mathcal{E}$, verify $\cup_{\mathcal{B}_\mathcal{E} \subset \mathcal{G}} \mathcal{B}_\mathcal{E} = \mathcal{G}$. The subscript on $\mathcal{B}_\mathcal{E}$ shows the dependence on the element $\mathcal{E}_\mathcal{V}$ considered. The boundary Γ can be decomposed, following the subdivision of $\mathcal{G}$, such that $\Gamma = \cup_{\Gamma_n \subset \mathcal{B}_\mathcal{E}} \Gamma_n$ and $\Gamma_n = \Gamma \cap \mathcal{B}_\mathcal{E}$. For each portion Γ_n included in a box $\mathcal{B}_\mathcal{E}$, a direction c_n is defined from the centers x_c and y_c of respectively $\mathcal{E}_\mathcal{V}$ and $\mathcal{B}_\mathcal{E}$.

In Algorithm 1, we propose a methodology to generate the subdivision of $\mathcal{V}$ and for each element $\mathcal{E}_\mathcal{V} \in \mathcal{T}(\mathcal{V})$, the subdivision of $\mathcal{G}$ associated. Therefore, we provide a criterion to decide whether a refinement is needed or not. We fix an arbitrary constant $R > 0$ and ask in each element to limit the oscillations of the kernel by controlling the ratio between the lengths of the element and the wavelength.

Admissibility Criterion. Two cases are considered whether or not there are directions. First, when no direction is used, we define the ratio

---

Algorithm 1: Subdivision of $\mathcal{V}$ and assignation of the orders

Initialize the criterion R, $\mathcal{E}_\mathcal{V} = \mathcal{V}$ and $\mathcal{B}_\mathcal{E} = \mathcal{G}$.
Compute $r_{\max}$ corresponding to the couple $(\mathcal{E}_\mathcal{V}^{\max}, \mathcal{B}_\mathcal{E}^{\max})$.
while $r_{\max} > R$ **do**
 | Subdivide $(\mathcal{E}_\mathcal{V}^{\max}, \mathcal{B}_\mathcal{E}^{\max})$.
 | Compute $r_{\max}$ for a new couple $(\mathcal{E}_\mathcal{V}^{\max}, \mathcal{B}_\mathcal{E}^{\max})$.
end
for *each element $\mathcal{E}_\mathcal{V} \in \mathcal{T}(\mathcal{V})$* **do**
 | Assign the interpolation orders in each direction.
end

$r = \max(L_1, L_2)/\lambda$ where λ is the wavelength and L_1 (resp. L_2) is the length of the element in the first (resp. second) direction. The bigger this ratio is, the more the function is possibly oscillating. An element is said admissible if its ratio is smaller than R. Otherwise, this element needs to be subdivided. However, when directions are used, for a couple $(\mathcal{E}_\mathcal{V}, \mathcal{B}_\mathcal{E})$, a direction c_n is defined and we define the ratio $\widetilde{r} = \max(L_1, L_2)/\widetilde{\lambda}$, where $\widetilde{\lambda} = 2\pi/\widetilde{k}$ and $\widetilde{k}$ is defined by

$$\widetilde{k} = k \max_{(x,y) \in (\mathcal{E}_\mathcal{V}, \mathcal{B}_\mathcal{E})} \left| 1 - \left\langle c_n, \frac{x-y}{\|x-y\|} \right\rangle \right|. \tag{11}$$

This definition of $\widetilde{k}$ is therefore equivalent to a wave number. Indeed, G_c^n (9) is then equivalent to $e^{i\widetilde{k}r}/(4\pi r)$ where r is the distance between two given points. The ratio $\widetilde{r}$ allows to quantify the oscillations after introduction of the direction.

Subdivision of the Domain. The construction of the subdivision of $\mathcal{V}$ is based on a hierarchically partition of this domain. This partitioning is recursive and therefore a tree structure is used. Level 0 corresponds to the whole domain $\mathcal{V}$. Tree level $l+1$ is obtained from level l by subdividing each leaf $\mathcal{L}_\mathcal{V}$ equally into 2 children. The direction of subdivision (in the first or second direction) is chosen such that the maximum of the new ratios $\widetilde{r}$ in the new configuration is the lowest. At the same time, a tree structure is also used to define the subdivision of Γ associated to each leaf $\mathcal{L}_\mathcal{V}$. Let note $\mathcal{A}_\Gamma$ the tree linked to $\mathcal{L}_\mathcal{V}$. The leaf where the ratio is maximal is subdivided into 2 children. The same criterion is used to define in which direction the subdivision is done. When a subdivision is done on a couple, four configurations are tested (two directions possible for each leaf).

When each element respects the admissibility criterion (ratio under R), a mesh of $\mathcal{V}$ is constructed by taking all the leafs (elements without children) of the tree of $\mathcal{V}$. Furthermore, to each element of this mesh, from the leafs of the associated tree $\mathcal{A}_\Gamma$, a subdivision of Γ is constructed such that $\cup_{\mathcal{B}_\mathcal{E}} \mathcal{B}_\mathcal{E} = \mathcal{G}$.

Assignation of the Interpolation Orders. The last step of Algorithm 1 is to assign the interpolation orders and define the associated interpolation points. Let

$\mathcal{E}_\mathcal{V}$ be an arbitrary element whose lengths are L_1 and L_2. The decomposition of Γ is constructed from elements $\mathcal{B}_\mathcal{E} \subset \mathcal{G}$ and we note $\{\mathcal{B}_\mathcal{E}\}$ this set. Then, similarly to the admissibility criterion, we define two ratios $\tilde{r}_1 = L_1/\tilde{\lambda}$ and $\tilde{r}_2 = L_2/\tilde{\lambda}$ for the element $\mathcal{E}_\mathcal{V}$ and $\tilde{\lambda} = 2\pi/\kappa$. However, κ must take into account all the subdivision of $\mathcal{G}$ and is therefore defined as

$$\kappa = k \sup_{\{\mathcal{B}_\mathcal{E}\}} \max_{(x,y)\in(\mathcal{E}_\mathcal{V},\mathcal{B}_\mathcal{E})} \left| 1 - \left\langle c, \frac{x-y}{\|x-y\|} \right\rangle \right| = \sup_{\{\mathcal{B}_\mathcal{E}\}} \tilde{k}. \tag{12}$$

Table 1. Rules to fix the order for a given accuracy ε according to the ratio length/wavelength

Ratio r		1/4	1/3	1/2	3/4	1	3/2	2	3
Order ($\varepsilon = 1\%$)	3	5	6	8		10	13	17	24

Finally, using *a priori* rules [2], according to the two ratios, the interpolation orders in both directions are fixed. The following 1D problem is used to fix these rules (some of them are reported in Table 1): For a given tolerance $\varepsilon > 0$, find the smallest N such that

$$\left\| f - \tilde{f}_N \right\|_{\infty,[0,1]} \leq \varepsilon,$$

where $f(x) = \sin(2\pi r x)$, r is the ratio, $\tilde{f}_N(x) = \sum_{i=1}^{N+1} f(\xi_i^N)L_i^N(x)$. For each order N, the $N+1$ 1D Chebyshev points on $[0,1]$ are noted $(\xi_i^N)_{i=1,N+1}$ and the Lagrangian polynomials associated are noted L_i^N. It ensures the control in L^∞-norm of the interpolation error for a given accuracy (for instance $\varepsilon = 1\%$).

Overall Formulation. Finally, following (10), in an element $\mathcal{E}_\mathcal{V}$, the local reconstructed radiated field $u_{rad}^{\mathcal{E}_\mathcal{V}}$ is

$$u_{rad}^{\mathcal{E}_\mathcal{V}}(x) = \sum_{i=1}^{N_\mathcal{E}.N_r^\mathcal{E}} u_i^{\mathcal{E}_\mathcal{V}} \phi_i^{\mathcal{E}_\mathcal{V}}(x), \qquad \forall x \in \mathcal{E}_\mathcal{V} \subset \mathcal{V}, \tag{13}$$

where $u_i^{\mathcal{E}_\mathcal{V}}$ are the degrees of freedom whose basis functions $\phi_i^{\mathcal{E}_\mathcal{V}}$ are composed of high order polynomials and directional plane waves (10). The method explained in Sect. 3 is therefore used to visualize this field. In comparison with (5), the link between the basis functions $\phi_i^{\mathcal{E}_\mathcal{V}}$, defined on the element $\mathcal{E}_\mathcal{V}$, and the functions φ_i^K defined on the reference cell in the previous section is given by

$$\phi_i^{\mathcal{E}_\mathcal{V}}(x) = (\varphi_i^K \circ g_K^{-1})(x), \qquad \forall x \in \mathcal{E}_\mathcal{V},$$

where g_K is the geometrical transformation between the reference cell and $\mathcal{E}_\mathcal{V}$.

5   Numerical Results

Several numerical examples are presented to demonstrate the potential of the method. The first example illustrates the advantages of our strategy with a one direction interpolation application. In the second case, the domain to visualize is wider and the adaptive method proposed in Sect. 4 is used. The last example is more realistic and shows in particular the benefits of the coupling of the reconstruction with the visualization method proposed in Sect. 3.

5.1   One Directional Interpolation

The first problem is a wave propagation scattered by a disk obstacle. The radius of the obstacle is 0.9 and its center is the origin. The incident plane wave is horizontal and coming from the left. The wave number is $k = 6\pi$ so the wavelength is $\lambda = 1/3$. The abscissas and ordinates of the domain to visualize both lie between 5λ and 8λ such that the lengths of the elements are 3λ. We define only one direction from the center of the element and the origin (corresponding to the center of the boundary). In this case, no subdivision is done and the order prescribed by Table 1 is 5 in each direction. Thus, 36 interpolation points are defined to reconstruct the radiated field. Figure 3 compares the diffracted field obtained with and without a direction. Figure (a) is the *reference* field computed with a very high order to have a good accuracy. Without direction, the radiated field is very far from the reference as shown by the pointwise absolute error

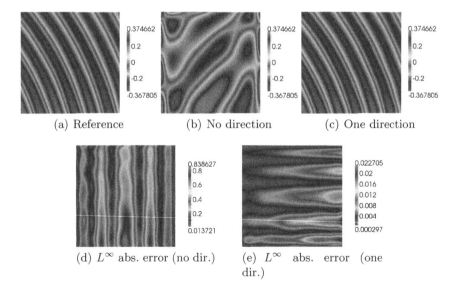

(a) Reference   (b) No direction   (c) One direction

(d) L^∞ abs. error (no dir.)   (e) L^∞ abs. error (one dir.)

Fig. 3. Some scattering of diffracted fields (a, b and c) by a disk. Except the reference, the others figures are obtained with order 5 in each direction. We compare the addition of only one direction (fig. c and e) to the case without direction (b and d).

with more than 111 % relative error at some points. With the same points, the addition of the direction permits to have a very low error (maximum of 3%).

5.2 Adaptive Method

For this second example, the parameters (disk, wave number k) are unchanged. However, the domain where we want to reconstruct the solution is different and larger. The abscissas (resp. ordinates) of this domain lie between 2 and 6 (resp. −4 and 4) such that its lengths are 4. It corresponds therefore to 12 wavelengths in each direction (as $\lambda = 1/3$). We fix $R = 0.1$, then a subdivision of the domain is done and 112 elements are constructed. Figure 4 shows the subdivision of the domain and the orders needed to have the same accuracy whether there are or not directions. Figure 5 compares for the same degrees of freedom (d.o.f.), the solution obtained with or without directions. For this given subdivision, in order to have the same accuracy, the number of degrees of freedom goes from 1120 to 32508 (factor 29).

5.3 A More Realistic Example

The last problem deals with a more realistic wave propagation. The scattering boundary is a L-shape object whose maximal length is 1. The wave number is $k = 6\pi$. The domain we want to visualize the total radiated field is large such that its abscissas and ordinates both lie between −2 and 2. Note that in this case the scattering object is included inside the visualization domain. The adaptive method is use to subdivide this domain such that 360 elements are created and 9219 degrees of freedom (average of 25 d.o.f. by element) are used. The admissibility criterion chosen was $1/2$. Then, the number of d.o.f. is relatively low as in each element and following Table 1, this number is bounded by 6×6. Figure 6 shows the representation obtained. Note that the total field is plotted. Thus, in addition to the scattered field, the incident field is taken into account. The consequence is the addition of only one basis function which is $e^{i\nu x}$ where

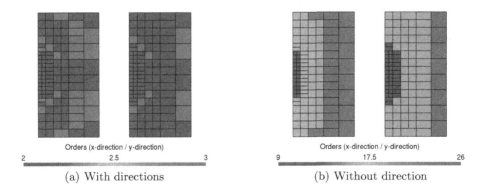

	Orders (x-direction / y-direction)			Orders (x-direction / y-direction)	
2	2.5	3	9	17.5	26

(a) With directions   (b) Without direction

Fig. 4. Subdivision of the domain and comparison of the orders needed

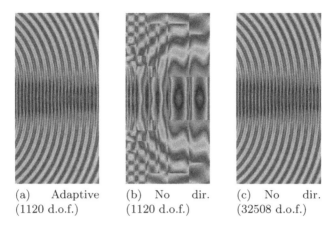

(a)   Adaptive
(1120 d.o.f.)

(b)   No   dir.
(1120 d.o.f.)

(c)   No   dir.
(32508 d.o.f.)

Fig. 5. Visualization of the diffracted field. Comparison of our method and the case without direction for the same number of d.o.f. (a-b) and for a similar accuracy (a-c).

ν is the direction of the plane wave. Figure 6 (b) shows the representation mesh used to represent the solution (accuracy asked is 0.5%). The number of elements in the representation mesh is 51999 (average of 144 triangles in each element). The subdivision of the domain is also shown with ticker lines.

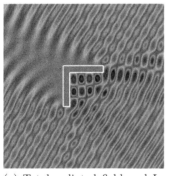

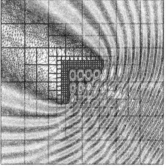

(a) Total radiated field and L-shape object (white)

(b) Domain   subdivision and representation mesh

Fig. 6. Visualization of the total radiated field scattered (real (a) and absolute (b) parts) by a L-shape object

6   Conclusions

An accurate and automatic method is proposed to reconstruct radiated Helmholtz fields from boundary element solutions. An adaptive method for the visualization of such fields, in particular able to handle functions composed of high order polynomials and special functions as plane waves, is presented and used.

References

1. Abramowitz, M., Stegun, I.A.: Handbook of Mathematical Functions: with Formulas, Graphs, and Mathematical Tables, vol. 55. Courier Corporation, Chelmsford (1964)
2. Bériot, H., Prinn, A., Gabard, G.: Efficient implementation of high-order finite elements for helmholtz problems. Int. J. Numer. Meth. Eng. **106**(3), 213–240 (2016)
3. Börm, S., Melenk, J.M.: Approximation of the high-frequency helmholtz kernel by nested directional interpolation: error analysis. Numerische Mathematik **137**, 1–34 (2017)
4. Bowyer, A.: Computing Dirichlet tessellations. Compu. J. **24**(2), 162–166 (1981)
5. Colton, D., Kress, R.: Inverse Acoustic and Electromagnetic Scattering Theory, vol. 93. Springer Science & Business Media, Newyork (2012)
6. Engquist, B., Ying, L.: Fast directional multilevel algorithms for oscillatory kernels. SIAM J. Sci. Compu. **29**(4), 1710–1737 (2007)
7. Jones, D.R., Perttunen, C.D., Stuckman, B.E.: Lipschitzian optimization without the Lipschitz constant. J. Opt. Theory Appl. **79**(1), 157–181 (1993)
8. Maunoury, M., Besse, C., Mouysset, V., Pernet, S., Haas, P.A.: Well-suited and adaptive post-processing for the visualization of hp simulation results (Submitted)
9. Messner, M., Schanz, M., Darve, E.: Fast directional multilevel summation for oscillatory kernels based on chebyshev interpolation. J. Comput. Phys. **231**(4), 1175–1196 (2012)
10. Nédélec, J.C.: Acoustic and Electromagnetic Equations: Integral Representations for Harmonic Problems, vol. 144. Springer Science & Business Media, Newyork (2001)
11. Rebay, S.: Efficient unstructured mesh generation by means of delaunay triangulation and bowyer-watson algorithm. J. Comput. Phys. **106**(1), 125–138 (1993)
12. Remacle, J.F., Chevaugeon, N., Marchandise, E., Geuzaine, C.: Efficient visualization of high-order finite elements. Int. J. Numer. Methods Eng. **69**(4), 750–771 (2007)
13. Tzoulis, A., Eibert, T.: Fast computation of electromagnetic near-fields with the multilevel fast multipole method combining near-field and far-field translations. Adv. Radio Sci. ARS **4**, 111 (2006)
14. Watson, D.F.: Computing the n-dimensional Delaunay tessellation with application to Voronoi polytopes. Comput. J. **24**(2), 167–172 (1981)

Erratum to: The t-Modified Self-Shrinking Generator

Sara D. Cardell and Amparo Fúster-Sabater

Erratum to:
Chapter "The Modified Self-Shrinking Generator?" in:
Y. Shi et al. (Eds.): *Computational Science – ICCS 2018*,
LNCS 10860,
https://doi.org/10.1007/978-3-319-93698-7_50

The original version of this chapter had a typing error in the title. The title has now been corrected from "The Modified Self-Shrinking Generator?" to "The t-Modified Self-Shrinking Generator".

The updated online version of this chapter can be found at
https://doi.org/10.1007/978-3-319-93698-7_50

Author Index

Printed in the United States
By Bookmasters